SHAKESPEARE'S CHARACTERS
for Students

SHAKESPEARE'S
CHARACTERS
for Students

Catherine C. Dominic, Editor

GALE

DETROIT • NEW YORK • TORONTO • LONDON

STAFF

Catherine C. Dominic, *Editor*

Marie Lazzari, James E. Person, Jr. *Contributing Editors*

Aarti D. Stephens, *Managing Editor*

Victoria B. Cariappa, *Research Manager*
Barbara McNeil, *Research Specialist*
Laura Bissey, Julia Daniel, Tamara C. Nott, Michele P. LaMeau,
Tracie A. Richardson, Cheryl Warnock, *Research Associates*
Alfred Gardner, *Research Assistant*

Mary Beth Trimper, *Production Director*
Shanna Heilveil, *Production Assistant*
Sherrell Hobbs, *Macintosh Artist*
Randy Bassett, *Image Database Supervisor*
Mikal Ansari, Robert Duncan, *Imaging Specialists*

Library of Congress Cataloging-in-Publication Data

Shakespeare's characters for students / Catherine C. Dominic, editor.
     p.   cm.
    Includes index.
    ISBN 0-7876-1300-2 (alk. paper)
    1. Shakespeare, William, 1564-1616--Characters--outlines, syllabi, etc. 2. Characters and characteristics in literature--outlines, syllabi, etc. I. Dominic, Catherine C., 1970- .
    PR2989.S53 1997
    822.3'3--dc21
                                             97-8515
                                           CIP.

∞™ This book is printed on acid-free paper that meets the minimum requirements of American National Standard for Information Sciences—Permanence Paper for Printed Library Materials, ANSI Z39.48-1984.

Library of Congress Catalog Card Number 97-8515
ISBN 0-7876-1300-2

Printed in the United States of America
10 9 8 7 6 5 4 3 2 1

Gale Research

Contents

How to Use Shakespeare's Characters for Students

Purpose of the Book

The purpose of *Shakespeare's Characters for Students* (*SCFS*) is primarily to provide students who are studying Shakespeare's plays with easy access to information about characters in the plays. This information includes an explanation of a given character's role in the play, as well as discussion about the character's relationship to other characters in the play--how the character's actions and choices affect the other characters in the play, and the possible motivation for the character's actions. In some cases, students will also be provided with information about the historical figure a character is or may be based on, as many of Shakespeare's plays concern figures from English and ancient Greek and Roman history.

In addition to these character descriptions of every character in every play (from an unnamed porter in *Henry VI, Part One* to Crab the dog in *The Two Gentlemen of Verona* to Juliet in *Romeo and Juliet*), students are also provided with a plot summary of each play. This summary will help students untangle the sometimes confusing plot lines, which often feature cases of mistaken identities and secret conspiracies.

To further aid the student in understanding each play, a "Modern Connections" section explains how themes in a play, and sometimes issues surrounding the play's composition, are relevant today.

Finally, a list of suggested items for additional reading is provided for each play. The books and articles listed offer students additional explication or analysis of the characters, themes, and plots of the plays.

How Each Entry is Organized

Each entry, or chapter, in *SCFS* focuses on one play. Each chapter lists the full name of the play and the probable date of the play's composition. The following elements are contained in each chapter:

- **Plot Summary**: an act by act summary of the play's action.

- **Modern Connections**: a section relating issues and themes in the play to modern times.

- **Characters**: an alphabetical listing of characters in the play. Each character name is followed by a brief to an extensive description of the character's role in the play, as well as discussion of the character's actions, relationships, and possible motivation.

Characters are listed, as mentioned, alphabetically. The alphabetical arrangement typically ignores titles, unless the title is the only name by which the character is known (for example, "queen" in *Cymbeline* or "porter" in *Henry VI, Part One*). Characters are listed by last name or last name "equivalent" (for example George, duke of Clarence from *Richard III* would be listed under "Clarence''), and then by first name, if that is the only name by which the character is known (for example, Ophelia in *Hamlet*).

NOTE: The rendering of the titles of the plays, the spelling of characters' names, as well as line numbers, when cited, vary among the numerous editions of Shakespeare's works. For the sake of consistency, the play titles, spellings of names, and the line numbers found in *SCFS* reflect those in *The Riverside Shakespeare*, edited by G. Blakemore Evans, 1974.

Also, please note that the dates given for the composition of Shakespeare's plays, though based on scholarship, are somewhat conjectural.

Other Features

SCFS includes an **"An Introduction to 'The Bard,'"** an essay which discusses what is known and believed about Shakespeare's life. It also provides the possible dates of composition for, and a brief description of Shakespeare's dramatic works. Additionally, this introduction briefly discusses the early forms of the texts of the plays and the First Folio, the first published collection of Shakespeare's works.

A **Character/Topic Index** provides easy reference for students who prefer fast access to character descriptions to reading through the Plot Summary and Modern Connections sections of an entry before browsing through the character list for a particular play. The index lists character names and cross references, as well as the topics treated in the Modern Connections section of each entry. Page references for characters refer to the page on which the character description begins, and page references for topics refer to the page on which the Modern Connections section begins. Character names under which several play names are listed indicate that characters with the same name appear in more than one play, *or*, more rarely, that the same character appears in several plays. An asterisk (*) appearing directly after the character name indicates that it is the *same character* who appears in all the plays listed below that character name.

A Note on the History Plays

Shakespeare wrote ten plays dealing English history and the nation's monarchy. Eight of these plays follow one another in chronological order of the historical events covered in the plays, although Shakespeare did not write the plays in this order. These eight plays can be further divided into two groups of four plays, or tetralogies. For students studying any one of these history plays, it is helpful to know where it fits in the larger sequence of historical events. (Although it is not always possible in a classroom setting to study a complete tetralogy, it is often suggested that students interested in the history plays read all four plays in a tetralogy, in order. While this is not necessary for the enjoyment of the play, it does provide a more complete experience and understanding.

The first tetralogy deals with the events that divide the world of the nobles, and the line of succession to the throne, into two groups: Lancaster and York. The second tetralogy deals with the conflict between the Lancastrians and the Yorkists; this conflict is known as the Wars of the Roses. What follows is a list of these eight plays, in chronological order, and a brief comment on what occurs in each play:

Richard II: King Richard II gives up his throne to Henry Bolingbrook, who becomes King Henry IV. Henry is supported in his efforts by a group of nobles, the Percys. After Henry is crowned king, Richard is murdered.

Henry IV, Part One: King Henry's former supporters, the Percys, turn against him and prepare for war. Meanwhile, Henry's son, Prince Hal, is busy having fun with friends his father does not approve of, particularly the jolly and usually drunk Sir John Falstaff. Although Henry expresses his doubts about his son's ability to rule, father and son fight side by side and defeat the rebels.

Henry IV, Part Two: Under King Henry's rule, the country continues to be divided by civil discord. Henry dies and his son, Prince Hal, becomes King Henry V.

Henry V: King Henry V wages war against France and wins; he also wins the heart of the French Princess Katherine. The play ends as peace is restored.

Henry VI, Part One: King Henry V dies while his son, Henry VI, is still a child. Henry VI's uncles struggle for power and for control of the young king. The country is troubled by civil disruptions and France is lost in war.

Henry VI, Part Two: Henry VI grows up, and is generally acknowledged to be a weak king, with little power over his nobles. The Wars of the Roses begin, with Henry on the side of the Lancastrians.

Henry VI, Part Three: King Henry VI is defeated by the Yorkists, and Edward IV is crowned king.

Richard III: King Edward IV dies, and his brother, Richard, eliminates everyone who is in line for the throne ahead of him. He is crowned King Richard III, but is killed in battle by Henry, earl of Richmond. Henry is crowned King Henry VII, and establishes the Tudor dynasty.

(The other two history plays are *King John* and *Henry VIII*. For more information of this briefly descriptive nature on these and the rest of Shakespeare's plays, read ''An Introduction to 'The Bard.''')

An Introduction to "The Bard"

Shakespeare in Stratford

William Shakespeare was born in 1564 in Stratford-upon-Avon, Warwickshire, England. His birthday is traditionally given as April 23, because his notice of baptism was entered in the parish register at Holy Trinity Church on April 26, 1564; during that time in England, it was customary to baptize infants three days after birth. Shakespeare's father was a local merchant (a glover) who held several local offices. Shakespeare was the third of eight children, and the oldest son. It is believed that in 1571, Shakespeare entered grammar school, as seven years was the usual age for admission. In 1575 Queen Elizabeth visited Kenilworth Castle, near Stratford. Popular legend has it that the young Shakespeare witnessed the royal procession and later recreated it in his dramatic works. Being the oldest son, Shakespeare would have been apprenticed to take over his father's business; there are several rumors as to why he did not. It has been suggested that he was apprenticed to a butcher, due to a decline in his father's financial situation. According to another rumor, Shakespeare became a schoolmaster. On November 27, 1582, when Shakespeare was eighteen years old, he married twenty-six-year-old Anne Hathaway at Temple Grafton, a village near Stratford. Soon after the wedding (about five months after), the first child of William and Anne Shakespeare was born. They named their daughter Susanna. Records also show that Anne gave birth to twins in 1585. The boy was named Hamnet, the girl, Judith. Hamnet died in 1596, while both daughters outlived their father.

Shakespeare in London

Some time between 1585 and 1592, it is believed that Shakespeare left Stratford for London and joined a company of actors as a performer and a playwright. Legend long held that Shakespeare left Stratford because he was being pursued by the law for poaching deer on private property. By 1592 Shakespeare had received some recognition, though not entirely positive, as an actor and playwright. He was mentioned in a pamphlet (*A Groats-worth of Wit*) written by Robert Greene. Greene refers to Shakespeare as an "upstart crow" in the London theater and charges that Shakespeare was an unschooled player and a writer who used material written by his better educated contemporaries. Also during this year, the theaters in London closed due to the plague. By 1594 Shakespeare had joined a theater troupe known as the Lord Chamberlain's Men. Scholars attribute several of Shakespeare's plays to this time period. Although no one can be certain of the dates of composition for any of the plays, a considerable amount of scholarship has gone into the endeavor of accurately determining an approximate time period during which Shakespeare wrote each play. Some believe that *The Comedy of Errors*, a farcical play centering on the mistaken identities of two sets of twins, may have been Shakespeare's first play. A few counter that *The Two Gentlemen of*

Verona, which focuses on the conflict between romantic love and friendship, may have been Shakespeare's first play. Some scholars suggest that these plays may have been written as early as 1588 or 1589, while many others date both plays several years later, suggesting that they were written between 1592 and 1594. Other plays written during this early period include one of the history tetralogies: *Henry VI, Part One* (1589-90); *Henry VI, Part Two* (1590-91); *Henry VI, Part Three* (1590-91); and *Richard III* (1592-93). Many people believe that *Henry VI, Part One* was Shakespeare's first play. This tetralogy treats the Wars of the Roses, the conflict between two factions of nobles. The last play of the sequence, *Richard III,* ends with the establishment of the Tudor dynasty, to which belonged Queen Elizabeth, who ruled during much of Shakespeare's life. It is also believed that Shakespeare wrote *Titus Andronicus* (1592-94), *The Taming of the Shrew* (1593-94), and *Love's Labor's Lost* (1593-95) during this period of his life. *Titus Andronicus,* Shakespeare's earliest tragedy, deals with the cycle of revenge which destroys the families involved in the play's action. *The Taming of the Shrew* is a lively comedy featuring the willful Kate and her "tamer," Petruchio. Kate's "taming" (her apparent and uncharacteristic submission to her husband) often troubles modern audiences. *Love's Labor's Lost* has been described as a satirization of the courtly and somewhat artificial love of male nobles, and of the academic pursuits, which were often more fashionable than serious in Shakespeare's time, of the nobility. In addition to these dramatic works, it is believed that Shakespeare wrote the poem *Venus and Adonis* and began composing his sonnets in 1592 or 1593. He eventually wrote 154 sonnets. Between 1593 and 1594, he probably wrote the poem *The Rape of Lucrece.*

In 1596 the patron of the Lord Chamberlain's Men (Henry Carey, Lord Hunsdon, the Queen's Chamberlain) died, leaving Shakespeare's company under the patronage of his son, George Carey, second Lord Hunsdon. The next year, Shakespeare bought a spacious Stratford home, known as New Place. Shakespeare continued to be noted as an actor; in 1598 he appeared in a performance of Ben Jonson's *Every Man in His Humor,* and was listed as a principal actor in the London performance of the drama. Soon after, in 1599, Shakespeare and other members of the Lord Chamberlain's Men leased land for the Globe Theater, which opened later that year. Also in 1599, the poet John Weever published a poem ("Ad Guglielmum Shakespeare")

in which he praised Shakespeare as a poet and playwright. During this period of his life, from about 1595 through 1600, Shakespeare wrote a number of plays, including the second historical tetralogy (*Richard II* [1595]; *Henry IV, Part One* [1596-97]; *Henry IV, Part Two* [1598]; and *Henry V* [1599]) . This tetralogy deals with the events leading up to the Wars of the Roses: Richard II is usurped by Henry Bolingbrook and later assassinated. The new king, Henry IV, worries over his role in Richard's death and about the ability of his "madcap" son, Hal, to rule. A subplot focuses on Hal's wild adventures with the comical knight, Sir John Falstaff. Hal becomes King Henry V after his father's death; he conquers France and restores peace. *King John*, a historical drama dealing with the reign of King John and the tragedy of the young Arthur, is estimated to have been written between 1594 and 1596. *A Midsummer Night's Dream* and the famous tragedy *Romeo and Juliet* were probably written in 1595 or 1596. *A Midsummer Night's Dream*, a fantastical comedy complete with fairies and magic, deals with such topics as love, imagination, and art. One of Shakespeare's most popular and well-known plays, *Romeo and Juliet* is the story of ill-fated lovers who attempt to escape the disapproval of their feuding families. The comedies *The Merchant of Venice* and *The Merry Wives of Windsor* are believed to have been written between 1596 and 1597. Identified by critics as a problem play (one that raises moral dilemmas which it does not resolve), *The Merchant of Venice* is like *The Two Gentlemen of Verona* in that it deals with the relationship between romantic love and masculine friendship; the play also focuses on the theme of mercy. *The Merry Wives of Windsor* is a farce dealing with middle class life and values; it features the knight Falstaff, who was introduced in *Henry IV, Part One* as Hal's drunken and wayward companion.

Other plays written during this period of Shakespeare's life include *Much Ado about Nothing* (1598-99); *Julius Caesar* (1599); and *As You Like It* (1599-1600). *Much Ado about Nothing* is the witty comedy featuring Beatrice and Benedick. The play is sometimes considered flawed by critics due to what they and many audiences see as the insensitive treatment of the female characters, particularly the falsely accused Hero. The Roman tragedy *Julius Caesar* dramatizes the downfall of the title character and examines the nature of political rivalry, ambition, and power. *As You Like It* depicts the beautiful Forest of Arden as a haven from the trappings of courtly life.

In 1603 Queen Elizabeth died. The new king, James I, granted a license (or patent) to Shakespeare's acting troupe, the Lord Chamberlain's Men. The group needed the patent to be allowed to perform, and in honor of the new king, they renamed themselves the King's Men. It is also reported during this year that Shakespeare appeared in another Ben Jonson play (*Sejanus*). The plague also struck again, killing at least 33,000 people in London; in 1608 the plague again forced the closure of London theaters. Also in 1608, the King's Men leased the Blackfriars Theater. This was the first permanent enclosed theater in London. From notes in the stage directions, it seems that *The Tempest* was written with the specific features of the new theater in mind. During this period, Shakespeare wrote a number of plays, including what are considered his best tragedies: *Hamlet* (1600-01); *Othello* (1603-04); *King Lear* (1605); and *Macbeth* (1605-06). Probably Shakespeare's best known play, *Hamlet* is like many of Shakespeare's other tragedies in that the theme of revenge takes center stage. But the title character in this drama is paralyzed by indecision and for most of the play he is unable to act on his thoughts of revenge. The play and the issues it raises have been hotly debated by critics for centuries. *Othello* is a tragedy dealing with jealousy and murder. The title character is a Moor in the Venetian army who is driven into a jealous rage against his wife Desdemona by the scheming Iago. *King Lear* dramatizes the tragic effects of the king's and the earl of Gloucester's misjudgement of their children. Like other Shakespearean tragedies, *Macbeth* deals with the theme of ambition. The play also delivers a heavy dose of the supernatural in the form of the witches, or weird sisters, who feed the flame of Macbeth's desire for power. During this period, perhaps between 1600 and 1601, Shakespeare also wrote the narrative poem *The Phoenix and the Turtle*.

Shakespeare also wrote several comedies during these years, including *All's Well That Ends Well* (1601-03); *Twelfth Night* (1601-02); and *Measure for Measure* (1604). *All's Well That Ends Well* and *Measure for Measure* have both been tagged as problem plays. The first comedy ends abruptly with Bertram's sudden acceptance of his wife Helena, whom he had essentially abandoned earlier in the play. In *Measure for Measure,* deception plays a central role in the play's action; this includes the deception perpetuated by a character depicted as a paragon of virtue, Isabella. *Twelfth Night* is typically seen as one of Shakespeare's more mature comedies. Like other comedies, it features some disguise and role-playing, such as that of one of the central figures, Viola, who disguises herself as the page Cesario. The play also concerns gender roles and class differences.

In this period Shakespeare also produced Greek and Roman dramas, including *Troilus and Cressida* (1601-02); *Antony and Cleopatra* (1605-07); *Coriolanus* (1607-08); and *Timon of Athens* (1607-08). *Troilus and Cressida*, a Greek drama, emphasizes the differences between the ideal and the real by portraying legendary Greek figures as people with less-than-admirable qualities. *Antony and Cleopatra* is the story of the love and passion between the famous Roman general and the sensuous, legendary Egyptian queen. *Coriolanus* is a Roman political tragedy dealing with issues of character and pride. Feelings of bitterness and disillusionment permeate the Greek drama, *Timon of Athens*. Shakespeare also wrote *Pericles, Prince of Tyre* probably between 1607 and 1608. *Pericles* is an adventurous tale of a prince who suffers the loss of his wife and daughter, but is, in the end, reunited with his family. *Pericles* is thought by some scholars to have been a collaborative effort.

After 1608 Shakespeare's dramatic production lessened somewhat. The Globe Theater burned down, but was rebuilt a year later on the opposite bank of the Thames River. During these years, Shakespeare wrote romantic tragicomedies (that is, romances featuring elements of both tragedy and comedy). The romantic tragicomedies include *Cymbeline* (1609-10); *The Winter's Tale* (1610-11); and *The Tempest* (1610-11). *Cymbeline* and *The Winter's Tale* are both stories of loss and pain, but, like *Pericles*, they end with a happy reunion. *The Tempest* features the same elements of loss and reunion, but it also emphasizes the balance of wisdom and power that Prospero achieves at the play's end. It has been noted that *The Tempest* was probably the last play Shakespeare wrote on his own, and that the character of Prospero, as one who manipulates events, stages masques, and directs the actions of other characters, represents Shakespeare the playwright and his farewell to the theater.

During this later period, Shakespeare also wrote two plays that most scholars believe were composed in collaboration with the dramatist John Fletcher: *Henry VIII* (1612-13), a historical drama, and *The Two Noble Kinsmen* (1613), the story of the love two men have for the same woman. It is also believed that Shakespeare wrote another play around 1612 or 1613, *Cardenio*, but it has been completely lost.

The First Folio

Shakespeare died on April 23, 1616, the cause of death not reported. The date of his burial is recorded as April 25, 1616 in the register of Stratford's Holy Trinity Church. In 1623 the same year that Shakespeare's widow, Anne Hathaway Shakespeare, died, the first collection of Shakespeare's works was published. Several of Shakespeare's fellow actors compiled thirty-six of Shakespeare's plays; the published collection was known as the First Folio. (The word ''folio'' refers to a book made up of sheets of paper folded once to form two leaves of equal size, or four pages.) The First Folio did not include *Pericles, Prince of Tyre* or *The Two Noble Kinsmen*. Scholars suggest that the reason for this exclusion may have been the likely dual authorship, though it was believed that *Henry VIII* was co-authored by John Fletcher, and yet it appears in the First Folio. The mystery remains unsolved.

The First Folio contained eighteen plays which had never been previously published. These eighteen plays included: *All's Well That Ends Well; Antony and Cleopatra; As You Like It; The Comedy of Errors; Coriolanus; Cymbeline; Henry VI, Part One; Henry VIII; Julius Caesar; King John; Macbeth; Measure for Measure; The Taming of the Shrew; The Tempest; Timon of Athens; Twelfth Night; Two Gentlemen of Verona;* and *The Winter's Tale.* These plays were presumably printed from some type of authoritative manuscript, or unpublished original copy. The other eighteen plays which appeared in the First Folio had been published before, in what is known as a quarto edition. (The word ''quarto'' refers to a book made up of sheets of paper folded twice to form four leaves of equal size, or eight pages.) Scholars have distinguished the

quarto editions of these plays as being either good quartos or bad quartos. A good quarto was one which was printed from an authoritative, reliable manuscript. Bad quartos were those which contained textual inaccuracies, such as unintelligible language, omissions, repeated lines, inaccurate speech headings, and other types of defects. Shakespearean scholars attribute these types of problems to a couple of possible causes. One theory is that the text of bad quartos was based on the memory of an actor or group of actors who had performed in the play. Another theory is that the text was composed by people who wrote down the play, or transcribed it, as it was being performed. When the First Folio was compiled, it is believed that quarto editions of the plays were in some cases reprinted with a few minor modifications. In other cases the quartos were revised using some form of authoritative manuscript, for example, Shakespeare's original manuscript (often referred to as the ''foul papers'') or a prompt book, or version of the play used by the actors. (Prompt books were usually transcribed from a playwright's foul papers.)

The second collected edition of Shakespeare's plays, or the Second Folio, was published in 1632. It is primarily a reprint of the First Folio, but a number of changes were made in order to modernize spelling and correct stage directions and names. The Third Folio was published in 1663 and it contained corrections to the text of the Second Folio but also introduced errors not found in earlier editions. The Third Folio was reprinted in 1664 and included seven new plays. One of these plays, *Pericles*, is generally accepted as Shakespeare's work (though some believe another dramatist may have collaborated). The other six plays were not considered by later editors to be Shakespeare's. A Fourth Folio was published in 1685 and was the last of the folio editions of the plays. This edition introduced new errors as well as some modernization of the text.

Guest Foreword to Shakespeare's Characters for Students

When students ask me why there is so much awe surrounding the name of William Shakespeare, I usually make the All-Time Great Baseball Player analogy. It is not difficult to illicit from the class the names of the men who comprise the handful of baseball's greatest stars. Babe Ruth is usually mentioned first, and discussion of his qualifications ensures: home-run king, .342 lifetime batting average, superb pitcher, 21 years in the game. After everyone had agreed that Ruth was surely one of the All-Time Greats, I offer a nominee. What about Mark ''The Bird'' Fidrych? Most of the young people in the room look puzzled, but there is usually one student who has heard about Mark. Wasn't he a pitcher for the Detroit Tigers in the 1970s? Never a baseball fan but a native Detroiter, I can still picture the curly-haired teenager who talked to the baseball before he threw it and by doing so won an unbelievable 19 games in his rookie season. The students are amused by Mark Fidrych, but they add that it's easy to understand why he is not considered in the same class as Ruth. The Bird lacked the Babe's amazing versatility. More importantly, Fidrych didn't stay in the game long enough to prove that as a pitcher he was not a fluke. And that, I say, is exactly the point I want to make about Shakespeare.

Like Babe Ruth, Shakespeare certainly stayed in the game long enough to prove he was not a fluke. He didn't play just one position, either--he played them all. He was a master storyteller, poet, philosopher, and psychologist. He wrote plays that make us cry with laughter and others that bring the bitter tears of recognition. There are plays that recount history and those that anticipate science fiction. In some the focus is tightly on the individual, while in others the main character is society itself. Youth? Middle age? Advanced age? Those bases are covered, too. All that and over 21 years in the game.

I have often wondered what part of the creative process Shakespeare found the most enjoyable. I have a strong suspicion it was not developing story lines, though he could certainly forge a dramatic tale. If Shakespeare truly enjoyed inventing plots, it seems doubtful that he would have borrowed so many from other writers. Then there is Shakespeare the poet. I have absolutely no doubt that language itself gave Shakespeare extreme pleasure. But there is also the sense that the creation and original use of words came so easily to him that the exercise may not have provided a consistent challenge. When I imagine Shakespeare in deep concentration, working and re-working, and finally feeling the rush of gratification that comes with creating something truly original, I think of him fashioning the characters that populate his worlds: Richard III, gleefully evil; Hamlet's Gravedigger, rough and honest; Hostspur, glory driven; Beatrice, sensible and vulnerable; Mercutio, edgy and brilliant; Macduff, the genuine article; Juliet, demanding truth and brave enough to face it. It has been said that William Shakespeare is the father of the most compelling people who never lived.

This book, *Shakespeare's Characters for Students,* is intended to help you as you make their acquaintances. In it you will find a wealth of material: an act-by-act summary of every play written by Shakespeare, a section called "Modern Connections," in which the issues of each play are discussed in terms of similar issues from our own times, and a list of recommended readings for further study. The centerpiece and most impressive aspect of this book, however, is that for each of Shakespeare's plays there is a thorough description of every one of its characters. Whether you are beginning your study of the play, preparing an analysis for a course assignment, or refreshing your memory for the fifth or twenty-fifth time around, you will find this section invaluable.

For now, your most difficult decision may be choosing which play and which character to explore first. When it comes to discovering the possibilities of Shakespeare's plays, as well as those of life, perhaps the best advice may be from another baseball legend, Yogi Berra: "When you come to a fork in the road, take it."

By Cynthia Burnstein,
Plymouth-Salem High School,
Canton, Michigan

All's Well That Ends Well

1602-03

Act I:

The play opens at the court of Rossillion, a province in southern France. Following the death of the count of Rossillion, his son Bertram is bidding his mother the countess farewell before departing for the court of the king of France in Paris. The lord Lafew is in attendance, along with Helena, a gentlewoman attending on the countess. Helena grieves secretly because she is in love with Bertram, but as the daughter of a physician she is too low-born to marry him. After Bertram departs, his friend Parolles enters, and banters with Helena about her virginity in rather lewd terms. In the next scene, Bertram is welcomed by the king of France, who is incurably ill but nevertheless holds court. Then the action returns to Rossillion, where the countess speaks with her clown, Lavatch, and her steward, Rinaldo. Lavatch jokes with the countess about sex and marriage; then Rinaldo informs her of Helena's love for her son. The countess, who loves Helena dearly herself, responds with sympathy. Helena admits her love, and further reveals that she plans to follow Bertram to Paris. Although she intends to win Bertram there, she tells the countess that her main purpose is to offer a cure to the sick king.

Act II:

The act opens in Paris, where the king's lords are departing for Italy in order to win honor by

fighting in the war between Sienna and Florence. (The king of France is not involved in this war, nor has he even taken a side.) Bertram, following the king's will, reluctantly stays behind. Lafew comes to court and announces the arrival of Helena with her recipe for a cure for the king's disease. In a protracted argument, Helena eventually convinces the king at least to try her medicine, and asks in return that she be allowed to marry one of his lords, of her own choice. The king miraculously recovers from his illness. He calls the lords of his court together, so that Helena can choose her husband. But when she chooses Bertram, the young count disdains her as a poor physician's daughter. The king flies into a rage. Bertram finally acquiesces to the king's will, and the two are married on the spot. After the courtiers leave the stage, Lafew and Parolles have an argument, based on the fact that Lafew, an honorable old lord, finds the young, lewd, and arrogant Parolles offensive. Bertram, with Parolles, resolves to join the Italian wars in order to get away from Helena. He lies to her that he will return in a few days, and commands her to return to the court at Rossillion, which she does obediently.

Act III:

Two French lords, in Florence to aid in the war, travel to Rossillion bearing a letter from Bertram to Helena. Lavatch the clown also arrives in Rossillion, bearing a letter from Bertram to his mother. The letters inform them that he will never sleep with his new wife, and will stay away from France as long as she is there, unless she does the impossible: takes a ring from his finger and bears him a child of his own. Helena, knowing that her presence keeps him away from his home, resolves to leave France on a pilgrimage. The countess is full of grief at her departure. She sends word of it to Bertram in the hopes that he will return and that Helena will follow. Meanwhile, Helena stops in Florence on her pilgrimage, and meets a widow and her daughter, Diana. At first, Helena pretends she doesn't know the count, but eventually she confesses to the widow, who resolves to help her gain his love. Bertram and the two French lords plot to test Parolles by making him cross enemy lines in search of the drum he lost in battle.

Act IV:

The French lords impersonate enemy soldiers and seize Parolles. Bertram meanwhile seduces Diana, who asks for the ring on his finger and says she will let him in her chamber window that night

and give him a ring in exchange. What really happens is that Helena meets him that night and gives him her own ring. But first, still pretending to be enemy soldiers, the lords and Bertram torment the captured Parolles and prompt him to speak ill of all his fellows. When they all reveal themselves, he is shamed and effectively kicked out of their army. After her night of lovemaking with Bertram, Helena leaves, with the widow and Diana, to seek reward from the king of France. Back in Rossillion, the countess hears word that Helena is dead (a false report), and that the king of France is actually on his way to visit Rossillion.

Act V:

Arriving in Paris, Helena finds that the king has left for Rossillion. Exhausted, she sends a gentleman after him with a letter, intending to follow him more slowly with the widow and Diana. In Rossillion, Parolles seeks the protection of Lafew, whom he had so offended earlier in the play. The king and the countess mourn the death of Helena, but the king quickly forgives Bertram for rejecting her. They begin to make arrangements for Bertram to marry Lafew's daughter. When Bertram arrives, however, no sooner has he reconciled with the king than the king spots Helena's ring on Bertram's finger. Bertram insists that a mere flirt gave him the ring, but the king begins to suspect the count of having murdered his wife. He has Bertram seized by his guards. Diana arrives, claiming that Bertram vowed to marry her upon the death of his wife. In the confrontation between Bertram and Diana that follows, she produces the ring he gave away. At first she plays the role of wronged lover, but she becomes increasingly enigmatic in her references to her relations with Bertram, until the king becomes so frustrated he has her seized by his guards. Finally, the widow and Helena appear. Helena has gotten the ring off his finger, and has become pregnant with his child. He quickly vows to love her. The play ends when the king tells Diana she can choose a husband from among his lords.

Modern Connections

All's Well That Ends Well focuses on what makes a marriage work. Helena is in love with Bertram from the very beginning of the play, and although she recognizes that her class status makes her an inappropriate match, she seeks to marry him anyway. In modern day America, marriage across classes is a common enough affair, so that Helena's low-born status may seem a superficial reason for Bertram's refusal of her. Certainly, the play makes Bertram himself into a superficial, vain, and arrogant young nobleman. But the class difference between the two is significant to Bertram, Helena, and the society in which they live. What other barriers, in addition to class distinction, exist in our own society?

When Helena wins Bertram in marriage, it is as though the play reaches a fairy-tale ending too soon. She has her Prince Charming, but he is not charming at all: ''A poor physician's daughter my wife! Disdain / Rather corrupt me ever!'' (II.iii.115-16). What follows is an exploration of the meaning and value of their marriage. Bertram's challenge to her is to get a ring from his finger and bear his child, as though he believes that these are the elements that constitute the true marriage bond. Helena, on the other hand, begs a kiss from him (II.v.86), and later talks about how pleasurable their experience was in bed (IV.iv.21). Physical desire is a vital element of the bond for her. But she also behaves submissively when he tells her to return without him to Rossillion (II.v): to Helena, being a wife means fulfilling the duties of obedience and even servitude. By the end, she apparently wins Bertram's submission as well. When she comes back from the dead, his response is to beg her pardon, and promise to love her ''dearly, ever ever dearly'' (V.iii.316). Different ideas about the meaning of the marriage bond are evident even today. Although the traditional Christian ritual includes a promise to ''honor and obey'' each other, some couples prefer not to promise obedience. Marriage and family mean different things to different people: for instance, the current argument about whether gay people can get married legally in America raises the question of how people define marriage. The issue is no simpler today than it was in Shakespeare's time.

All's Well That Ends Well has been called a ''problem play'' because it fails to fulfill conventions in a number of different ways. Even its title serves as an ironic comment on the play: all may seem to end well, but whether or not all is truly well in the end remains open to question. Although the play has the happy ending of a typical comedy, Bertram's humble acceptance occurs so abruptly and seems so out of character that the happy ending seems, at best, unrealistic. Other comic conventions are changed, reversed, or simply ignored. In comedy, marriages generally occur at the end, and marriages are generally based on mutual love. In *All's Well*, the marriage occurs near the beginning, and is

even consummated in the course of the play, but it is never based on mutual love. In comedy, the older generation typically blocks the happiness of the younger generation by objecting to the younger characters' love affairs. In *All's Well*, the older generation supports Helena's love for Bertram, and it is the younger generation—Parolles and Bertram himself—who block the marriage. The younger generation holds onto the value of class difference much more tightly than the older characters, who value Helena for her noble conduct and do not condemn her for her low-born status. Thus *All's Well That Ends Well* resembles a sitcom that doesn't even try to be funny, or a TV drama that refuses to be a tear-jerker. The genre or category of sitcom makes an audience expect certain conventional material, like jokes; the genre of TV drama makes an audience expect conventional emotional appeals. When these conventions are not fulfilled, the audience's expectations are left hanging awkwardly.

A central element of the unconventional plot of *All's Well That Ends Well* is the female heroine. Seldom does a female character in Shakespeare's plays hold the stage as fully as does Helena; seldom does the will of a female character guide nearly all the action and seldom is that will fulfilled with such drama in the end. Helena behaves with an apparent meekness and propriety throughout the play. She keeps her love secret initially, and is embarrassed when the countess confronts her about it (I.iii). She does not force her cure on the king (II.i.125-28). Once she has married Betram, she behaves meekly. But Helena nevertheless insists on getting what she wants in the end.

Characters

Bertram (Bertram, Count of Rossillion):

Bertram is the hero of the play. Forced to marry Helena against his will, he flees from her, but is tricked into sleeping with her unknowingly, and in the last moments of the play accepts her as his wife.

When the play opens, Bertram is off to join the king's court at Paris, where he will presumably put the finishing touches on his education as a courtly gentleman. Bertram is hardly an ideal gentleman: he is at best, as his mother says, ''an unseason'd courtier'' (I.i.71). The first indication of Bertram's character comes when we encounter the company he keeps: the lewd and parasitic courtier Parolles, who banters with Helena on the topic of her sexual experience (I.i.99). Then, soon after his arrival in France, Bertram grows petulant because the other lords are running off to the Italian war, while the king makes him stay home. Even before he enters the play's central action, then, Bertram emerges as something other than a decorous gentleman—in fact, according to Lafew, he is ''an ass'' (II.iii.100).

Then, when Helena cures the king's illness and he rewards her by allowing her to choose a husband from among his lords, she chooses Bertram. Bertram rejects Helena because she is low-born—and because of the king's high-handedness in giving away his young lord. ''My wife, my liege? I shall beseech your Highness, / In such a business, give me leave to use / The help of mine own eyes. . . . / A poor physician's daughter my wife!'' (II.iii.104-15). Perhaps there is an element of fear in Bertram's protest, for his youth suggests sexual inexperience along with a will to be free of the control of his elders. But sympathetic responses to Bertram's callow character are few and far between. His display of arrogance ignites the wrath of the king, and receives no support from the other noble characters in the play, Lafew and, later, his mother the countess. In fact, when she learns that Bertram has fled from spending even one night with his new wife, the countess disowns him: ''I do wash his name out of my blood'' (III.ii.67).

Bertram's youthful arrogance and inexperience and the influence of his friend Parolles contribute to his rejection of Helena. He launches into an extended rebellion, leaving France, fighting in the Florentine wars, and seducing the daughter of a Florentine widow. He is apparently successful in war, thereby gaining a certain kind of honor as a knight. But the shame of his treatment of both Helena and Diana calls into question the value of such honor. Indeed, Bertram's character calls into question the very notion of noble birth itself.

When Bertram pleads with Diana to satisfy his ''sick desires,'' (IV.ii.35) he shows himself to be not only arrogant but lustful as well. He woos her persistently, even though he clearly never intends to marry her—for he himself is already married, and besides, Diana is at least as low-born as Helena. But Diana, in turn, bargains with him: his ring for her chastity, his honor for hers. Since it is plain that Diana no more intends to sleep with him than he intends to marry her, Bertram's persistent pleadings come to seem trivial and ridiculous. Diana has control of his courtship, and his apparent success in

winning her will later be his downfall. She exposes his honor as a sham.

When, in the last act, Bertram is finally trapped by the net of his own vows and attempts to escape those vows, it becomes clear that he has treated Diana in the way of many well-born men and low-born women. He claims never to have been serious about loving her. As Parolles puts it, ''He did love her, sir, as a gentleman loves a woman. . . . He loved her, sir, and loved her not'' (V.iii.245-48). Bertram cannot disentangle all the strands of his experience—primarily because he does not realize, even after Helena's ring has been identified, that the woman he slept with in Florence was not Diana but Helena. This failure to distinguish between women is further evidence of Bertram's youthful blindness—and, more specifically, of the fact that he has made no attempt to recognize Helena as an individual woman. At the very end, when the dead Helena returns and all is revealed, Bertram speaks only three lines—words of absolute acquiescence. For most audiences, the suddenness and brevity of his consent fail to outweigh his callow behavior through the course of the play.

Citizens of Florence:

These citizens appear in III.v, when Helena meets the widow and Diana on the street, as the soldiers go by in a procession. Helena mingles among the citizens, while Bertram parades past in a parade, accentuating their class difference.

Count of Rossillion:

See Bertram

Countess of Rossillion:

See Rossillion

Diana:

Diana is the Florentine woman who helps Helena fulfill the impossible tasks that Bertram sets for her. She first appears in Act III, as Helena herself arrives in Florence. Diana is a chaste young woman herself, and sympathetic to Helena's cause even before Helena reveals her identity (III.v.63-65). When Bertram tries to seduce her, Diana uses language with enough double meanings so that she seems to encourage him, while at the same time she points out his immoral behavior. She says that his ''oaths / Are words and poor conditions'' (IV.ii.29-30); she doesn't believe him even when he swears to love her. She is aware of the behavior typical of high-born men toward low-born women: she has no reason to trust that he would actually marry well below his station.

Nonetheless, when he gives her his ring, she makes arrangements to meet him that night. Diana and Helena have plotted together, so that it will actually be Helena who sleeps with him. Diana thinks twice about lying at all, but concludes that ''I think't no sin / To cozen him that would unjustly win'' (IV.ii.75-76).

Diana then travels with her mother (the widow) and Helena to the court of Paris, and then to Rossillion, to help Helena win Bertram, but also in the hope that the king will reward her. In the final scene of the play, Diana confronts Bertram with the ring he gave to her and the promises he swore to her: she tells the assembled court that he vowed to marry her when his wife died. Helena is presumed dead at this point. When Bertram tries to escape his vow— along with the consequences of all his actions— Diana begins speaking in riddles. She makes so little sense that the king grows frustrated, and starts to send her to prison. Diana persists: ''He knows I am no maid, and he'll swear to't; / I'll swear I am a maid, and he knows not'' (V.iii.290-91). Finally, at the height of the drama created by her inexplicable riddling, Helena appears. She makes sense of Diana's doublespeak, and prompts Bertram to accept her at last.

The king's final act in the play is to offer Diana a husband of her choice from among his lords. The play thus closes with a repetition of the very action that began its central conflict: at the king's bidding, a woman strong enough to know her own desires chooses her husband regardless of the man's desires.

Duke of Florence:
See Florence

Florence (Duke of Florence):
The duke of Florence makes only brief appearances (III.i, III.iii) to welcome the aid of the French lords and of Bertram and Parolles.

France (King of France):
The king of France is the highest authority in the play. The scenes in which he presides are the most dramatic and ritualistic, as well. In his first appearance, he is ill, old, and fretful. But then Helena arrives with her promise of a cure. At first, the king seems almost to want to stay ill: he says he will not ''prostitute'' his malady to anyone, when

> **Even before he enters the play's central action . . . Bertram emerges as something other than a decorous gentleman—in fact, according to Lafew, he is 'an ass' (II.iii.100).''**

there is no cure (II.i.121). But Helena, in a long, clever, and modest set of speeches, seduces him into trying her cure. Unexpectedly, the cure works, setting in motion the central conflict of the play.

The king has welcomed Bertram to his court nostalgically, praising Bertram's dead father because ''his tongue obey'd his hand'' (I.ii.41)—that is, his words matched his deeds. The king's words should match his deeds as well, as it is his duty to uphold the truth and honor of his court. After his cure, the king upholds his promise to Helena to reward her for her cure: in a pageant-like scene, he allows her to choose a husband from among his lords. When she chooses the reluctant Bertram, the king insists on his own absolute authority. But there is a limit to that authority, of course. Even though Bertram has been sent to his court to become a polished courtier, the king cannot make an ignoble man noble. When he threatens to ''throw [Bertram] from my care forever'' (II.iii.163), the count responds by accepting Helena in marriage, but only superficially. And Bertram soon throws himself free of the care of the king after all.

The limits of the king's authority are revealed in other ways as well. He is not involved in the Italian wars, and in fact he allows his lords to go off and fight for whichever side they want. The lack of political weight to these wars contributes to the play's larger theme of the emptiness of honor. But the king's reticence about the war makes his reign seem strangely divorced from the world of politics. More dramatically, when the king presides over the final scene, he struggles to play his proper role as judge and mediator among conflicting parties. He can forgive Bertram, until he suspects him of murdering Helena; he cannot make sense of Diana's riddling story; his impulse, once again, is to force the concerned parties to behave according to his will, to obey his absolute command—so he has both

Bertram and Diana seized by his guards. When Helena finally appears, his tone changes to one of toleration. He asks to hear the whole story of Helena's travels, "To make the even truth in pleasure flow" (V.iii.326), as though the entire episode has been merely pleasurable. He speaks the epilogue as well, a point at which the players' masks and roles are taken off, and he simply asks for applause.

French Lords:

The two French lords become more active in the play as it progresses. They are two of the king's courtiers who join the Florentine army, and unlike the king they express a genuine support for Florence in the war (II.i). They act as witnesses to Bertram's departure, and later urge Bertram to test Parolles; they are therefore, in a small way, responsible for upholding the moral values of Helena, the countess, and Lafew. They are not named until the scapegoating of Parolles, when they refer to themselves as the Dumaines (IV.iii.248). In that scene, they are the principal interrogators of Parolles.

Gentleman:

A gentleman helps Helena by carrying a letter from her to the king (V.i, V.iii). It is worth noting that he is one of the many bourgeois, non-courtly people whose allegiance Helena wins in the course of the play.

Helena:

Helena is the main character in the play. The daughter of a recently deceased physician and therefore both low-born and poor, she is under the protection of the countess of Rossillion. That is, as a member of the countess's court, she has her material needs taken care of and has probably received some courtly education. Helena's character thus draws much from the countess's courtly values. But Helena also contributes to the play a miraculous cure and demands a fairy-tale marriage as her reward. Moreover, she persists until she is accepted as Bertram's wife: as Helena says of herself from the beginning, "my intents are fix'd, and will not leave me" (I.i.229). This persistence has sometimes been read as controlling and hard-headed. But Helena also represents a stubborn attachment to a set of ideals that no other character in the play exhibits.

Helena makes most of the play's action happen. After Bertram leaves in the first scene, she declares her love for him in a soliloquy (which is accidentally overheard by Rinaldo, the countess's steward),

then holds her own when Parolles baits her about her virginity. She resolves to follow Bertram to the king's court to "show her merit" (I.i.227) by curing the king. When the countess discovers her intentions, Helena expresses proper embarrassment, and says she knows her birth is too lowly for her to expect Bertram for a husband. But though she is quick to be frank with the countess about her intention to go to Paris, she does not reveal the larger plan: her own request to receive, as the reward for curing the king, her choice of his lords in marriage. The fact that Helena carries out this plot completely independent of any other influences, and regardless of anyone else's desires, makes her a highly unconventional comic or romantic heroine.

Helena's character is not only defined by simple persistence, though. She carries out what she intends to do, and what she says she will do, throughout the play. She makes her words match her deeds. When she offers to cure the king, she employs a combination of modesty and insistence similar to that in her interaction with the countess. The king refuses her help almost immediately; she says she will go; but then she says, "What I can do can do no hurt to try. . ." (II.i.134). She swears on her own virginity ("my maiden's name" [II.i.172]) and even her life that her cure will work. The king finally agrees, and agrees further to reward her with a husband.

Helena, of course, chooses Bertram. In the face of Bertram's refusal of her, Helena continues to make words and deeds match—this time, those of her husband. He writes to her that he will never accept her as his wife until she gets the ring off his finger that never will come off, and becomes pregnant with his child after he vows never to sleep with her. She takes his impossible task literally, setting out to get the ring and to sleep with him even though he refuses. She also continues to express a quite openly sexual desire for him. Here again, though, her humble and modest persona mask an ability to ask for—and ultimately, to receive—what she wants. As a bride, she is for the most part submissive, but she asks Bertram directly for a physical token of love, a kiss (II.v.86). And after they have actually made love, she remarks on the strangeness of being embraced as another woman (Diana, who Bertram thinks he's making love to), but also recalls Bertram's "sweet use" and "play" in bed (IV.iv.21-25).

Helena's most elaborate plotting is required for the so-called "bed-trick." When Bertram vows never to return home as long as Helena is there, she decides to leave Rossillion—"I will be gone. / My being here it is that holds thee hence" (III.ii.122-23). Helena goes on pilgrimage, and again the very humility of her pose allows her to take control of her situation. She meets a Florentine widow and her daughter, Diana, and without revealing her identity at first, encourages their sympathy for the plight of the young Bertram's wife, whom he has left behind. Bertram then woos Diana, who gets his ring off his finger, and then arranges to meet him at night. Helena meets him instead. She then promulgates the rumor of her own death, so that Bertram will think it safe to go home. The three women travel to Rossillion, where, in a climactic final scene, they reveal Bertram's broken vows, Diana's "cozening," and Helena's bed-trick. Helena's pretended death is yet another example of her ability to take control by suppressing or humbling herself. Her appearance in the final scene causes great drama. She calls herself "but the shadow of a wife" (V.iii.307), prompting Bertram's plea for her pardon and promise to love her ever dearly.

The character of Helena is at the center of the play. But it is unconventional to have a woman heroine who controls all the action, and Helena does so by contradictory means: she is at once quite deliberate and gentlewomanly and humble as well. Although she gets what she wants in the end, the rapidity with which Bertram has made and broken promises, especially in the last scene, call into question the value of his promises to her. The king barely retains control of the court scene, and Helena herself does not speak much after her appearance. Moreover, the same action that began the central conflict is about to be repeated: the king offers Diana to choose a husband from among his lords as well.

King of France:
See France

Lafew:
Lafew is an old lord in the countess of Rossillion's court. Like the countess herself, Lafew supports Helena in her desire to marry Bertram, in spite of Helena's low birth. Lafew accompanies Bertram to the king's court, as his advisor. He acts as a moral guide, but his judgements go largely unheeded by the callow Bertram.

Lafew's role first comes to the fore when, at the king's court in Paris, he convinces the king to listen

> " . . . Helena says of herself from the beginning, 'my intents are fix'd, and will not leave me' (I.i.229)."

to Helena's offer of a cure. Lafew and the king seem to share a past, or at least a set of social conventions, that enable them to behave familiarly with each other: Lafew even teases the king a bit (II.i.64-65). Furthermore, the old lord's support for Helena becomes clear at this point in the play. He has thus been established as a character whose judgment and integrity can be trusted. He comments on the scene as Helena chooses her husband from among the king's lords (II.iii). The lords respond with apparent acceptance of her, but Lafew seems to think they disdain her, either because, critics explain, he is out of earshot or because the lords are responding ironically. But Lafew is on the side of Helena.

Lafew is also an index to the outrageousness of Parolles's behavior. When Lafew and Parolles discuss the king's recovery, Parolles says nothing of substance while Lafew fills in meaningful and gracious responses (II.iii.1-37). After Bertram has been forced to marry Helena, Lafew refers to Bertram as Parolles's "master" (II.iii.186), to which the young lord takes offense. Parolles then insults Lafew, calling him "too old" (II.iii.196). The two of them then engage in a direct and hostile confrontation, in which Lafew exposes Parolles for what he is: a court hanger-on, a parasite, and a fake, one who claims to be better travelled than he is and more gentlemanly than he is, and who insults his superiors (II.iii.257). Lafew warns Bertram not to trust Parolles (II.v.44), indirectly setting in motion the trick by which Bertram tests Parolles later in the play. At the end, though, when Parolles has been exposed as a liar and begs Lafew for help, the old lord is characteristically generous: in spite of his lack of respect for the man, Lafew tells him, "Though you are a fool and a knave, you shall eat" (V.ii.53-54).

After Bertram runs away from the French court, Lafew returns to Rossillion, where he is when the countess hears the false news of Helena's death. Lafew banters with the clown a bit, though without the relish that the countess has for this activity; he calls the clown "a shrewd knave and an unhappy"

> **The fact that Helena carries out this plot completely independent of any other influences, and regardless of anyone else's desires, makes her a highly unconventional comic or romantic heroine."**

(IV.v.63), suggesting a certain unpleasantness. But his interchange with the countess, like that with the king, is based upon both intimacy and shared standards of polite and gracious behavior, so his criticism of the clown is quickly smoothed over ("'tis not amiss," he says [IV.v.68]). He then asks the countess to arrange for her son to marry his own daughter—even knowing Bertram's faults. There is a kind of idealism to this act, as though Lafew hopes in spite of everything that a marriage bond will cement the court community. Nevertheless, like the countess herself, Lafew acts with undue haste, and when Bertram's misbehavior begins to be fully revealed, Lafew retracts his offer: "Your reputation comes too short for my daughter" (V.iii.176). Still, the old lord retains his idealism at the end. When Bertram finally accepts Helena as his wife, Lafew starts to cry.

Lavatch:

Lavatch, the countess's clown, is a so-called "allowed fool": that is, he can get away with making jokes about all kinds of sensitive topics because he is always only joking. His main function in the play is to entertain and bear messages for the countess, but he also comments indirectly on much of the action—especially the conflicts about sexuality and class that the play struggles to come to terms with.

Lavatch first appears in I.iii, where he makes a mock request to marry one "Isbel." His main reason for marrying is that he is "driven on by the flesh" (I.iii.29). But soon after this request, he goes on to argue that the fear of being cuckolded, or betrayed, makes men reluctant to marry (I.iii.49-51). In raising these issues, the clown highlights the concerns of both Helena and Bertram: desire to marry, and fear of marriage. The clown's image of marriage as sexual play makes Helena's fairy-tale image of marriage look idealistic and even innocent.

Later in the play, Lavatch makes light of the values that define court behavior when he says to the countess, "Ask me if I am a courtier" (II.ii.36). When she does, he answers with complete evasion, parodying a courtier desperate not to offend his lord. The countess is so entertained that she doesn't notice time passing. But Lavatch has highlighted the class conflicts in the play—the degree to which the lower-born characters like Helena are dependent upon the nobility, and also the potential that those protected by the nobility can become empty, parasitical creatures, like Parolles. In fact, he makes fun of Parolles directly: "To say nothing, to do nothing, to know nothing, and to have nothing, is to be a great part of your title" (II.iv.24-27). Parolles gives no indication of being entertained by this, unlike the countess, whose social status makes her safer from mockery.

Lavatch's role as messenger makes him intimately involved in the affairs he comments on, but although he can be blunt he is not ruthless. He bears a letter from the countess to Helena shortly after Helena has married Bertram. When the clown returns to Rossillion, he bears the countess a letter from Bertram; even before she opens it, the clown seeks to warn her of its contents by telling her Bertram seemed "melancholy" (III.ii.4) and talking about his own supposed marriage to Isbel, which he now has lost the stomach for. When he hears that Bertram has run off to Italy, he seems reluctant to hear the bad news and exits (III.ii.44). Lavatch's final appearance is to announce Parolles to Lafew, when he makes fun of the humiliated courtier uncompromisingly, calling him a "poor, decay'd, ingenious, foolish, rascally knave" (V.ii.23-24), but then says he pities him nevertheless. Lavatch is absent from the play's final scene, an occasion full of such disorder that his disorderly voice is not needed.

Lords:

See French Lords

Mariana:

Mariana is a neighbor of the widow in Florence. She appears only once (III.v).

Page:

A page interrupts Parolles's banter with Helena in the first scene to announce that Bertram is waiting for him.

Parolles:

Parolles is Bertram's friend and a hanger-on at court who insults Helena, offends Lafew, encourages the count to flee from his marriage, and is finally tricked into revealing his true colors when Bertram and two French lords capture him and pretend to be enemy soldiers. He is thus a kind of scapegoat, and suffers exclusion from the court, but only temporarily; by the end of the play Lafew has promised not to let him starve.

Even before his downfall, many of the other characters in the play recognize Parolles as a threat to the moral order of society. Helena says she speaks to Parolles only for the sake of Bertram, whose friend he is, and that he is ''a notorious liar, / . . . soly a coward'' (I.i.100-01). The clown Lavatch calls him a fool (II.iv.35). The countess calls him ''A very tainted fellow, and full of wickedness'' (III.ii.87). One of the French lords tells Bertram, ''he's a most notable coward, an infinite and endless liar, an hourly promise-breaker, the owner of no one good quality worthy your lordship's entertainment'' (III.vi.9-12).

In fact, many of the other characters call attention to the influence of Parolles on Bertram. The countess blames Parolles for Bertram's rejection of Helena (III.ii.88). Diana says that Parolles leads him astray—''Yond's that same knave / That leads him to these places'' (III.v.82-83). And the French lords urge Bertram to plot against his friend in order to avert danger to himself: ''It were fit you knew him, lest reposing too far in his virtue, which he hath not, he might at some great and trusty business in a main danger fail you'' (III.vi.13-16). That is, the lords warn Bertram not to put his own life in Parolles's hands during the Italian wars. Yet although Parolles certainly encourages Bertram's flight from his forced marriage, the play does not make clear that Parolles is really to blame for Bertram's actions. Indeed, the plot against Parolles diverts attention away from Bertram; Parolles thus acts as a scapegoat, receiving punishment while his friend goes unpunished.

Parolles does not end up reformed, but he is forced to admit his own folly: he says he is a braggart and an ass (IV.iii.336). In fact, the French lords trick him in the hope of reforming not the

> **Lavatch makes light of the values that define court behavior when he says to the countess, 'Ask me if I am a courtier' (II.ii.36). When she does, he answers with complete evasion, parodying a courtier desperate not to offend his lord.''**

corrupt courtier but the count himself. They want Bertram to understand Parolles's corruption in order to see his own unethical conduct more clearly: ''I would gladly have him see his company anatomiz'd, that he might take a measure of his own judgments'' (IV.iii.31-34), says one of the lords. Bertram does finally recognize Parolles's faults, but never says anything about his own.

Parolles's punishment is that he is blindfolded and questioned about his own fellow soldiers. His interrogators are the French lords and Bertram, who pretend to be enemy soldiers. They essentially force him to betray themselves—especially Bertram. Although Parolles's accounts of the two lords are insulting, his description of Bertram is all the more pointed because it has been shown to be true. The lords read aloud a letter Parolles wrote warning Diana of Bertram's less than trustworthy intentions: ''the Count's a fool, I know it'' (IV.iii.229), he has written. This letter reveals not only that Parolles betrayed the count even before he was ''captured,'' but also that Parolles sees clearly the count's vices and has nonetheless encouraged them. Bertram responds angrily to hearing the letter read aloud, but gives no acknowledgement of his own vice. Although Parolles is looked down upon and condemned by almost everyone else in the play, he at least has the insight to warn Diana about the count. ''Simply the thing I am / Shall make me live'' (IV.iii.333-34), he says—that is, he will continue to survive by being a braggart and an ass. Parolles might not be a virtuous character, but he emerges as somewhat more self-aware than his friend the count. And because he undergoes such elaborate humiliation, it is also possible to treat him—as does Lafew—with a bit of sympathy.

> **Helena says she speaks to Parolles only for the sake of Bertram, whose friend he is, and that he is 'a notorious liar, / . . . soly a coward' (I.i.100-01). The clown Lavatch calls him a fool (II.iv.35). The countess calls him 'A very tainted fellow, and full of wickedness' (III.ii.87)."**

Rinaldo:

Rinaldo is the countess's steward. He overhears Helena declaring her love for Bertram, and reports it to the countess (I.iii). Later, he delivers Helena's announcement of her departure on pilgrimage, but too late for the countess to be able to stop her (III.iv).

Rossillion (Count of Rossillion):

See Bertram

Rossillion (Countess of Rossillion):

The countess of Rossillion is the mother of Bertram, the count of Rossillion. The countess also protects Helena, the daughter of a physician who recently passed away. When Helena marries Bertram, the countess supports her against her son. But when Helena is rumored to be dead, the countess agrees quickly to marry off Bertram to someone else. The countess represents established courtly conventions and morals in the play; she is, like Lafew and the king, of the older, more powerful generation. Yet throughout the play, she watches as events unfold before her, without her control.

As the play opens, the countess bids goodbye to Bertram, who is on his way to the king of France's court. Here she praises her son, but calls him an "unseason'd courtier" (I.i.71). Later, the countess banters with the clown, Lavatch, who makes jokes about marriage and cuckoldry and sings her a song about the end of Troy. Then the countess's steward confirms her suspicion that Helena is in love with Bertram, and the countess confronts Helena with her knowledge. To Helena's surprise, the countess offers her blessing, in spite of the fact that Helena is low-born, and sends her on her way to the king of France's court. The countess's generosity and open-minded acceptance of Helena as her potential daughter-in-law flies in the face of comic conventions. Usually, in comedy, the older generation blocks the love of the younger generation, and the younger characters find ways to trick or play their ways into desirable marriages. The bond between the countess and Helena is also unusual in Shakespearean comedy: although bonds between women certainly occur elsewhere, they rarely take center stage.

Even after Helen has left, the countess sends her letters and looks after her as much as she can from afar. When Helena returns to Rossillion in the hope that Bertram will soon meet her there (II.ii), both the countess and Helena receive letters from the young count saying that he will never accept her as his wife. The two letters work together, like two halves of a whole, to indicate both his whereabouts and the impossible task he sets for Helena. The bond between the two women is cemented at this point, for the countess disowns her son: "I do wash his name out of my blood, / And thou art all my child" (III.ii.67-68). He may be off to the wars, but battleground heroics will, she says, never win him enough honor to make up for what he has done to Helena (III.ii.93-94). Helena herself, however, leaves Rossillion and the countess in the next scene. It rapidly becomes clear that the countess has not in fact disowned her son at all, but holds out hope for him. She bids her steward write to both Helena and Bertram, in the hopes both will come home, for she cannot tell "Which of them both / Is dearest to me" (III.iv.38-39).

When the countess next appears, she believes Helena to be dead, and she speaks of her "rooted love" for the young woman (IV.v.12). Yet she rapidly consents to arrange Bertram's marriage to another woman, the daughter of her lord Lafew. In the final scene, when Bertram returns to Rossillion and the king arrives there as well, the countess begs the king to forgive her son. Yet as soon as Bertram's integrity comes under question again—because of his mysterious ring—the countess recalls having seen the ring on Helena's finger (V.iii.90). She is also ready to believe Diana. Throughout the play, the countess's love for her son is at war with her own set of values and morality. She can thus be read as a somewhat rash and inconstant, but well-meaning mother, or as a standard-bearer for the courtly values of gentility and generosity that characterize her generation.

Soldiers:

Soldiers aid in the humiliation of Parolles in IV.i and IV.iii.

Violenta:

Violenta is a neighbor of the widow in Florence. She appears only once (III.v).

Widow:

The widow is Diana's mother, and one of Helena's principal helpers in the plot to win Bertram's acceptance. She greets Helena (who is disguised as a pilgrim) with friendliness and gossiping, and with ready sympathy for the plight of Bertram's wife, even before she knows that Helena is his wife (III.v.66-68). Helena lodges with her in Florence, and later confides in her. The widow does not want to engage in any "staining act" (III.vii.7), but she willingly consents to help in the "deceit so lawful" (III.vii.38) that will bring Bertram to Helena's bed. The widow then travels with Diana and Helena, first to the king's court at Paris and then, when he is not there, to the court at Rossillion. She describes herself as "well born" (III.vii.4) and respectable even though she has little money and makes her living taking boarders. Therefore the prospect of a dowry and an aristocratic marriage for her daughter is appealing. But the widow is not purely selfish in her motives—she also helps uphold the virtue of Helena's desires.

Further Reading

Anderson, Linda. "Problem Comedies." In *A Kind of Wild Justice*, 126-27, 144-56. Newark: University of Delaware Press, 1987.

> Anderson argues that the conventions of revenge tragedies inform the action of *All's Well That Ends Well*—that Helena almost enacts a brutal revenge plot, against her husband, but instead turns toward love and forgiveness in the end.

Barton, Anne. Introduction to *All's Well That Ends Well,* by William Shakespeare. In *The Riverside Shakespeare,* edited by G. Blakemore Evans, 499-503. Chicago: Houghton Mifflin, 1974.

> Barton discusses the play's relation to its source in Boccaccio's *Decameron,* and analyzes the play's nostalgia for attitudes of the past. She argues that the play is a reminder that the fairy-tales of the past are, ultimately, not true.

Fraser, Russell. Introduction to *All's Well That Ends Well,* by William Shakespeare, 1-37. The New Cambridge Shakespeare. Cambridge: Cambridge University Press, 1985.

> Includes sections on the date, sources, stage history and critical history of *All's Well*, along with an analysis of the play. Argues that the problematic ending of the play both evokes compassionate response and forces interrogation. Asserts that the play is unified in design and intent, that the ending is prepared for from the beginning.

Haley, David. *Shakespeare's Courtly Mirror: Reflexivity and Prudence in* All's Well That Ends Well. Newark: University of Delaware Press, 1993.

> A detailed, book-length study of the play, with chapters on Bertram, Providence, Helena, Shakespeare's biblical sources, justice and revenge, Lavatch the clown, and the courtly values reflected in the play. Haley calls *All's Well That Ends Well* Shakespeare's "most searching exploration of courtly self-knowledge" (p. 12).

Hillman, Richard. Introduction and "*All's Well That Ends Well.*" In *William Shakespeare: The Problem Plays,* 1-16 and 54-91. Twayne's English Authors Series. New York: Twayne Publishers, 1993.

> The introduction discusses the history of the critical term "problem play," the texts of all three so-called "problem plays," and the historical context of the early 17th century, when the plays were probably all written at roughly the same time. The chapter on *All's Well That Ends Well* argues that the play raises even more interpretative problems than its source in Boccaccio, and that the ending does not make things "well" at all.

Hunter, G. K. Introduction to *All's Well That Ends Well,* by William Shakespeare, xi-lix. The Arden Edition of the Works of William Shakespeare. London: Methuen and Co., Ltd., 1959.

> Analyzes text, date, source, criticism, and verse form in *All's Well That Ends Well*. Views the play as disunified and therefore more sophisticated than what it seems at first, an "Elizabethan pot-boiler" (p. li). In an appendix (pp. 145ff), Hunter also prints a version of the story from William Painter's *Palace of Pleasure*, arguing that this is the play's primary source.

McCandless, David. "Helena's Bed-Trick: Gender and Performance in *All's Well That Ends Well.*" *Shakespeare Quarterly* 45 (1995): 449-68.

> Argues that *All's Well That Ends Well* calls traditional gender roles into question by making fairy-tale romance fail. Helena has certian masculine characteristics, especially because she actively expresses desire. But ultimately, McCandless argues, both Helena and Bertram have unstable gender roles, which demands that the audience actively interpret them.

Muir, Kenneth. "Problem Comedies." In *Shakespeare's Comic Sequence,* 103-08, 124-33. Liverpool: Liverpool University Press, 1979.

> Muir argues that *All's Well That Ends Well* is about the necessity for repentance and forgiveness in a world full of human weakness. Although the ending

does not provide a clear and final resolution, Muir maintains, it nevertheless leaves hope for Bertram's reformation and for love in his marriage to Helena.

Parker, Patricia. "*All's Well That Ends Well*: Increase and Multiply." In *Creative Imitation: New Essays on Renaissance Literature In Honor of Thomas M. Greene*, 355-90. Binghamton, NY: Center for Medieval and Early Renaissance Studies, 1992.

Parker argues that Helena's role in *All's Well That Ends Well* is to open up an aristocratic family to a more expansive notion of marriage and of the roles of women. But in the end, Helena's innovation coexists uneasily with her subjection to patriarchal structure.

Price, Joseph G. *The Unfortunate Comedy: A Study of* All's Well That Ends Well *and Its Critics*. Toronto: University of Toronto Press, 1968.

Contains three sections, on the stage history of *All's Well That Ends Well*, the critical history of the play, and an interpretation of the play. Price argues against those who criticize the play on the basis of its disunity by asserting that the play should be exploited for this lack of unity, for the diversity and "humanity" of its issues.

Snyder, Susan. Introduction and Appendices to *All's Well That Ends Well*, by William Shakespeare, 1-67, 217-40. The Oxford Shakespeare. Oxford: Clarendon Press, 1993.

The introduction contains sections on the play and its source, its dating, its status as a "problem play," the unconventionality of its heroine, its genre, its relation to the sonnets, and its textual evolution; the appendices contain notes to several cruxes or problematic lines, notes on speech prefixes and lineation, and related material from Boccaccio and Erasmus. Snyder argues for Helena's central disruptive role as a powerful and desiring woman.

Styan, J. L. *All's Well That Ends Well*. Shakespeare in Performance Series. Manchester: Manchester University Press, 1984.

Approaches the play in terms of its possibilities for performance. Part I takes up interpretative problems: the question of the degree of realism in the play, key topics, and the characters of Helena, Bertram, and Parolles. Part II analyzes the performance demands of the play, act by act. Also includes a bibliography and a list of twentieth-century productions and principal casts.

The Tragedy of Antony and Cleopatra

circa 1606-07

Act I:

The play's setting shifts constantly between Rome and the Egyptian court at Alexandria; some of the action takes place in other parts of the Mediterranean region as well. Historical events that occurred between 41 B.C. and 30 B.C. are compressed into a much shorter span of time. The play depicts the last years of Roman rule by a triumvirate, that is, three men with equal power and authority: Mark Antony, Octavius Caesar, and Aemilius Lepidus. As the play begins, the political situation is in turmoil. Antony is in Egypt with his lover Cleopatra, Egypt's queen. A messenger brings him news that his wife Fulvia and his brother Lucius have raised an army against Caesar. Antony also learns that a Roman general has defected to a foreign enemy, the Parthians, and they have seized significant parts of Roman territory in Asia Minor. Furthermore, Pompey—another rebellious Roman and a sworn enemy of the triumvirs—is marching on Rome and seeks to overthrow the government. Another messenger arrives and informs Antony that Fulvia is dead. Antony decides to return to Rome, and he and Cleopatra part. In Rome, as Caesar and Lepidus discuss the grave political situation, they receive further reports: Pompey is drawing many new followers, including the notorious pirates, Menecrates and Menas. Unaware that Antony is on his way to Rome, Caesar complains of Antony's

absence and makes plans with Lepidus to engage Pompey in battle. At the Egyptian court in Alexandria, Cleopatra cannot be distracted from thoughts of Antony. She sends messengers to him several times a day to remind him of her love.

Act II:

At an unspecified place somewhere in Italy, Pompey boasts that he now has control of the sea, while his enemies sit idle. Menecrates tells him he's heard that Caesar and Lepidus have raised a mighty army and are preparing for battle. A messenger brings them news that Antony has left Egypt and is expected to reach Rome within a few hours. In Rome, Lepidus warmly greets Antony and his aide Enobarbus. Caesar receives Antony more coolly. Antony denies having any part in his wife and brother's rebellion. He explains his lack of response to Caesar's requests for help as neglect or oversight rather than intentional acts of betrayal. Several military officers who are present during this exchange between Caesar and Antony urge them to reconcile for the sake of Rome. One of them, Agrippa—an aide to Caesar—proposes a solution to end their differences: Antony should marry Caesar's sister Octavia. The two leaders agree to the match. Octavia also agrees to the proposal.

Near Naples, Pompey meets with Antony, Caesar, and Lepidus to discuss a peace treaty. Pompey accepts their terms and hosts a banquet for them that night, aboard a ship anchored in the harbor. While everyone else is drinking and carousing, Menas draws Pompey aside. He suggests catching the triumvirs off guard and slitting their throats. Pompey turns down the proposal.

Act III:

Two of Antony's followers, Ventidius and Silius, defeat the Parthians in Asia Minor and regain territory for Rome. Antony and Octavia leave Rome and go to Athens. After some time passes, Antony hears that Caesar has stirred the Roman people against him, has spoken of him as if they were no longer allies, and has made new wars against Pompey. Octavia goes to Rome in an attempt to reconcile Caesar's and Antony's differences, but she is unsuccessful. Antony returns to Egypt and begins to prepare his forces to meet Caesar's. Cleopatra insists on taking part in the battle, and Antony agrees. The rival fleets meet off the eastern coast of Greece, near Actium. The battle ends abruptly when Cleopatra turns her ships away from the action and sails off. Antony and his ships follow hers, and the victory

belongs to Caesar. Antony returns to Alexandria, deeply shamed. He storms at Cleopatra, but when she begs his pardon, he forgives her immediately. Caesar sends one of his followers, Thidias, to Cleopatra, proposing terms of a truce between them. She treats Thidias graciously, and when Antony sees this, he flies into a rage. After he calms down, he resolves on one more battle with Caesar.

Act IV:

Following the humiliating defeat at Actium, many of Antony's supporters have deserted him and joined Caesar's army. Antony gathers his remaining followers together for an evening of feasting. During the night, strange music is heard in the streets, and one soldier interprets this as a sign that Antony's legendary ancestor, the god Hercules, has deserted him too. The following morning, Cleopatra helps Antony put on his armor, and they bid each other farewell. Before the battle begins, Antony learns that Enobarbus has defected. He orders that the "chests and treasure" (IV.v.10) Enobarbus has left behind be sent after him, together with a letter expressing "gentle adieus and greetings" (IV.v.14). When Enobarbus receives these, he is overwhelmed by thoughts of his treachery and Antony's generosity. Heartbroken, he crawls into a ditch and dies.

In the first phase of the battle between Antony and Caesar—fought on land near Alexandria— Antony's forces are triumphant. In the second phase—fought at sea—the Egyptian ships suddenly desert Antony, and Caesar is victorious. Antony directs his fury against Cleopatra. Frightened by his rage, she withdraws to an isolated part of her palace known as the monument. She instructs Mardian, one of her attendants, to go to Antony and tell him she has killed herself. When Mardian brings Antony the message, Antony "falls on his sword" (S.D.IV.xiv.103), but he does not die. Another messenger comes to tell him that Cleopatra is alive, and Antony asks to be taken to her. In the final scene of Act IV, the mortally wounded Antony is lifted to the elevated monument where Cleopatra has sought refuge. He dies in her arms.

Act V:

Caesar receives the news of Antony's death. Fearing that Cleopatra will kill herself and thus foil his plan to exhibit her in Rome as his captive, he sends an aide, Proculeius, to tell her that he means her no harm. As Proculeius is delivering this message, Roman soldiers break in and seize Cleopatra. Dolabella, another aide to Caesar, arrives and takes command. When they are alone, he tells Cleopatra of Caesar's plan to humiliate her. Caesar himself appears at the palace. Cleopatra offers him a list of all her possessions. She calls for her treasurer Seleucus to affirm that the inventory is accurate. Seleucus, however, says that some things are missing from the list. Cleopatra rages at him, then admits to Caesar that she's kept a few things back. Caesar leaves, assuring Cleopatra that he means to treat her kindly. She turns to her attendants and begins to make preparations for her death. A ''rural fellow'' (V.ii.233) enters with a basket containing figs—and several deadly snakes. (Cleopatra has arranged for the delivery of the snakes.) Cleopatra instructs her attendants, Charmian and Iras, to clothe her in her royal robes and crown. Taking two of the snakes to her breast, she encourages their bite and dies. Roman guards intrude and summon Dolabella. He's quickly followed by Caesar and several attendants. At the sight of the dead queen, Caesar remarks that she ''looks like sleep, / As she would catch another Antony'' in her snare of beauty (V.ii.346-47). He orders that she be buried beside Antony, with ''great solemnity'' (V.ii.366).

Modern Connections

Antony and Cleopatra depicts the conflict between Roman and Egyptian values. The play does not present one as superior to the other. It does, however, seem to demonstrate that in order to achieve worldly success, one must be cautious, self-disciplined, and rational. And choosing this course means turning one's back on spontaneity, joy, and laughter. Antony cannot find a way to combine these two ways of living. Is such a compromise possible? Or must each of us choose between professional achievement and personal happiness? Is it possible to ''have it all''?

Commentators repeatedly point out that there are no answers to many of the questions raised by the play. The quality of Antony's love for Cleopatra, the essence of her eternal fascination, and Caesar's motivations remain uncertain and debatable. No single interpretation of *Antony and Cleopatra* is possible. On the one hand, this is frustrating. But on the other, it mirrors the complexity of human experience. Perhaps the play suggests that trying to judge Antony's love or Cleopatra's sincerity is just as risky as attempting to define or categorize human beings.

Similarly, the ambiguous presentation of the central characters in *Antony and Cleopatra* may be a reflection of the contradictions inherent in all of us. The combination of comic and tragic perspectives in the play troubles many readers and commentators. Antony's love for Cleopatra sometimes seems foolish—particularly when one considers that he's a middle-aged man. But it also enriches his life and adds to our appreciation of him as a person who has an all-embracing view of the world and its pleasures. Is Cleopatra as devoted to Antony as her great speeches in the final portion of the play would lead us to believe? Or is she playing a part, trying to convince herself as well as those around her that her love for Antony is beyond the experience of ordinary mortals? Is Caesar a pompous, self-important, and narrow-minded man, or is he the best leader for Rome at this time in history? Maybe the answer to each of these questions is ''yes.'' Perhaps choosing between alternative views of characters—or between contradictory assessments of the people we encounter in our own lives—is a serious error. It might be better, as perhaps the play suggests, to acknowledge conflicting elements and celebrate these contradictions rather than condemn them.

Sometimes we say we ''know'' ourselves or our friends and acquaintances. Is this really possible? We form judgments about people we know only by reputation—people whose actions and personalities are reported to us by intermediaries. Do we ever consider whether these reports are reliable? Are modern intermediaries any more dependable than the various messengers in *Antony and Cleopatra*? Are the reports we receive biased or objective? Are they timely or out-of-date? Do they offer only one perspective or do they provide a fully rounded view? Is an ''eye-witness'' report necessarily accurate or truthful? If one report contradicts another, which one should we believe? Or should we not believe either one?

The central characters in the play are all mindful of how the world perceives them. Each of them tries, consciously or unconsciously, to control his or her own public image. Antony uses inflated language to amplify his achievements and his greatness. Cleopatra is almost always performing for an audience—whether the audience consists of a single person or the population of an entire city. Caesar foreshadows the modern public relations experts who advise politicians and celebrities. But it isn't only the great ones of the world who are concerned with what people think of them. Most of us would prefer to have our strong points noticed and our flaws overlooked. Many people modify their appearances, wear clothes that flatter them, and try to keep the less attractive aspects of their personalities hidden from public view. We may scorn the play's protagonists for their concern with public image and reputation, but perhaps we should ask ourselves whether wanting to influence the way the world sees us isn't a trait shared by all human beings.

Characters

Aemilius Lepidus:

See Lepidus

Agrippa:

A Roman officer, he is Caesar's aide and closest confidante. He is the one who suggests that a marriage between Octavia and Antony would be the most effective way to reconcile the differences between Caesar and Antony. Commentators generally agree that the idea is Caesar's and that he has instructed Agrippa to launch the suggestion.

Agrippa and Maecenas, another aide to Caesar, make up the audience for Enobarbus's speech about Cleopatra and her barge. Maecenas disapproves of what he hears. Agrippa, however, is captivated by the picture conjured up by Enobarbus. ''O rare for Antony!'' and ''Rare Egyptian,'' he blurts out (II.ii.205, 218) during Enobarbus's narrative. Agrippa is a steadfast supporter of Caesar, but he also appears to have at least some measure of sensitivity to the delights of Egypt.

Alexas:

Cleopatra's principal male attendant, he frequently performs services for Antony as well. Alexas appears to enjoy his superior position in Cleopatra's household. He is sometimes pompous or overbearing, and Charmian and Iras delight in making fun of his pretentious ways. After the battle of Actium, Antony sends Alexas to Herod, the king of Judea, seeking his support. However, instead of representing Antony, Alexas tries to persuade Herod to join Caesar's faction. We learn of this from Enobarbus, who comments on Alexas's treacherous behavior—after he himself has betrayed Antony. According to Enobarbus, Alexas's efforts on behalf of Caesar earned him a brutal reward: ''Caesar hath hang'd him'' (IV.vi.15).

Ambassador:

See Schoolmaster

Antony:

Historically, Mark Antony lived from 82-30 B.C. After the assassination of Julius Caesar in 44 B.C., Antony became part of a triumvirate—with Octavius Caesar and Aemilius Lepidus—that governed Rome for more than a dozen years. He met Cleopatra in 41 B.C., and they were lovers until their deaths in 30 B.C.

In *Antony and Cleopatra*, Antony is portrayed as the greatest military hero of his era. He is the last survivor of an age that reserved its highest honors for bravery and heroism on the battlefield. Antony is closely associated with Mars, the Roman god of war. He is also proud of his alleged descent from Hercules, the mythical Greek hero. He is driven to become, like them, a supreme symbol of heroic achievement. But times have changed. Rome's new heroes are those who excel in political maneuvering. Antony doesn't have the capacity to manipulate public opinion, and he doesn't know how to wage a propaganda war against Caesar. He tries to find a way to combine the values of Rome and Egypt—to be both a soldier and a lover—but he is frustrated in his search. He's humiliated by his losses at Actium and Alexandria. On the first occasion, he overcomes his shame, but the second one overwhelms him. He rages helplessly at the disparity between the glorious hero he once was and the defeats handed to him by the ''boy'' Caesar. In his eyes, the shame and disgrace he suffers erase all that he has accomplished up until now.

Unlike Caesar, Antony doesn't seek power for its own sake or pursue the role of supreme ruler. It seems he would be content if he were in charge of a third of the world—sharing power with Caesar and Lepidus. His outbursts of rage and his difficulty in acting on his resolve to leave Egypt and attend to his duties in Rome are signs of an inability to govern himself. Nor does he appear to have the capacity to govern others. Yet he has an instinctive gift for leadership.

Men are drawn to Antony. He has a personal magnetism that attracts soldiers such as Enobarbus and Scarus, and a heroic dimension that elevates him to superhuman stature. He's the kind of leader who inspires love and loyalty in his followers. Ironically, he is plagued by the desertions of his closest aides when his fortunes decline. Those who stand by him appear to do so even though it's clear he's on the losing side in his struggles with Caesar. On the night before the battle of Alexandria, he gathers his remaining followers together for a grand banquet, celebrating their past achievements and, he hopes, their future glory. His generosity of spirit is remarkable. It makes his followers weep and Enobarbus die of shame.

Balanced against these virtues are personal traits that contribute to Antony's downfall. He prolongs his stay in Egypt because he's self-indulgent. He's unwilling to give up the pleasures of Cleopatra's court. He is also inclined to self-pity and blames Cleopatra—with at least some justification—at times when he is clearly at fault too. When he follows her fleeing ships at Actium, the defeat that follows is chiefly his own responsibility. Moreover, he seems unable to resist a dare: when Caesar challenges him to a battle at sea—rather than on land where his forces are superior—Antony foolishly accepts the challenge. His bungled attempt to commit suicide is almost farcical. He "falls on his sword" (S.D.IV.xiv.103) in the manner of legendary heroes, but he fails to kill himself. Instead of a dignified ending, he has to plead with his followers to finish the job he has botched.

For many audiences, Antony's greatest failing is his passion for Cleopatra. It causes him to neglect his duty and his country. It affects his capacity to rule and to be an effective soldier. From time to time, he seems to understand that his obsession for her compromises his stature as one of Rome's most eminent men. But he continues to grant her too much power over him. He allows her whims to influence his decisions about military strategy. Enobarbus, Canidius, and Scarus repeatedly try to show him that his love for Egypt's queen has led to her domination over him. Occasionally he agrees with them, but he seems to lack the resolve to carry through on his intentions to leave her. Even though he returns to Rome in the first half of the play, he knows he can't stay away from her forever. Before his wedding to Octavia, he promises his bride-to-be that from now on he will keep his life on a straight course. Only moments later, however, when he is alone, he declares: "I will to Egypt; / And though I make this marriage for my peace, / I' th' East my pleasure lies" (II.iii.39-41).

There is another way of looking at Antony's love for Cleopatra; perhaps he is made even more noble by his passion for her. It gives him a broader perspective on life. His love it seems is so extraordinary—so beyond the experience of ordinary human

> " For many audiences, Antony's greatest failing is his passion for Cleopatra. . . . There is another way of looking at Antony's love for Cleopatra; perhaps he is made even more noble by his passion for her."

beings—that it lifts him to new heights of experience. Antony's recognition that the kingdoms of the earth are made of clay (I.i.35) stems from his having known more of the richness of human life than Caesar ever will. When Antony embraces Cleopatra, he embraces the creative principal of life itself.

Antony's death is frequently seen as a mixture of triumph and defeat. Caesar's victory at Alexandria humiliates Antony. It is a devastating blow to his identity as a military hero. He seems to have lost his sense of himself, as he explains to Eros in the famous passage (IV.xiv.1-22) in which he compares himself to a cloud that cannot hold its shape. Antony dies in Cleopatra's arms, clinging to thoughts of his "former fortunes" and the time when he was "the greatest prince o' th' world" (IV.xv.53, 54). The world has lost its worthiest man, cries Cleopatra: without Antony "there is nothing left remarkable" on the face of the earth (IV.xv.67). In the opinion of some commentators, Antony is transfigured in death—raised to an exalted level—less by his own actions or character than by Cleopatra's eulogies of him. It's debatable whether Antony achieves a comprehensive understanding of himself before he dies. Readers may ask if his sacrifice was worth it, or whether, given his nature, such an ending was inevitable. Antony attempted to alter reality, to shape the world so that it would allow him to combine the values and principles of opposing views of life. His daring to achieve the impossible may be sufficient in itself to qualify him as a great tragic hero.

Boy:

At II.vii.113-18, during the banquet aboard Pompey's ship, the boy sings a drinking song. The drunken revellers loudly join in singing the refrain.

" Antony dies in Cleopatra's arms, clinging to thoughts of his 'former fortunes' and the time when he was 'the greatest prince o' th' world' (IV.xv.53, 54). The world has lost its worthiest man, cries Cleopatra: without Antony 'there is nothing left remarkable' on the face of the earth (IV.xv.67).**"**

Caesar:

Historically, Octavius Caesar was the first emperor of Rome. He was born in 63 B.C. and died in 14 A.D. He was the nephew of Julius Caesar, who adopted him and treated him as his own son. In 27 B.C., Octavius received the honorary title Caesar Augustus; this is the name modern historians generally use when they refer to him.

In *Antony and Cleopatra*, Caesar is a man of destiny. He will be successful in achieving his goal: the destruction of the republic and the restoration of one-man rule. He accurately predicts the "time of universal peace" (IV.vi.4) when civil wars will come to an end and the Roman empire will flourish as never before. Caesar seems to be fortune's child. He views his consistent good luck as evidence that his cause is divinely ordained. He believes the gods have chosen him as the agent to carry out their plan. He claims that the course of action he is following will ultimately serve the best interests of Rome, and he's determined to achieve his goal.

"Single-minded" is the adjective most often used by commentators when they discuss Caesar. Political success is the only thing he's interested in. Though he's depicted in the play as a relatively young man—somewhere in his twenties—he's already a masterful politician. He shapes events and manipulates them for his own purposes. He takes advantage of other people's weaknesses, seizing on their mistakes and transforming them into opportunities to advance his cause. As a political strategist, Caesar is pragmatic and impersonal. He knows

what he wants, and he carefully assesses the most effective means of getting it.

For many readers and commentators, the attributes which make him politically successful—self-discipline, single-mindedness, pragmatism—also make him personally offensive. He seems incapable of warmth or spontaneity. He shows no signs of affection toward any of his subordinates, nor does he receive any from them. His emotions are always carefully controlled. Control is also the hallmark of his relations with women. We never see his wife Livia, though Cleopatra refers to her at V.ii.169, so we know she exists. He seems to have no difficulty resisting the charms of Cleopatra. And his relationship with Octavia is disturbing.

Most commentators believe that Caesar genuinely loves his sister. They point out, however, that he's willing to sacrifice her for political gain. Despite his apparent affection for his sister, Caesar uses Octavia as he would anyone else. He refers to her in impersonal terms: she is a "piece of virtue" (III.ii.28) and the "cement" that will bind him and Antony together. He is moved by her tears when she leaves Rome with her new husband. Nevertheless, Octavia's happiness seems less important to him than fulfilling the destiny of Rome.

There is general agreement among commentators that Caesar has decided before Antony returns to Rome that a marriage between his sister and Antony will be to his own advantage. They argue that Caesar coaches Agrippa on what to say and tells him to present the suggestion as if it were his own idea. Caesar probably knows the marriage will not last, and he expects to make use of its failure. When Antony deserts Octavia and returns to Egypt, Caesar can treat this as an insult to his family—one more reason for declaring war on Antony. Romans will be scandalized by Antony's treatment of Octavia, and this will provide more material for Caesar's continuing effort to sway public opinion against his rival.

Caesar is a master at controlling public opinion. He sees to it that Antony's failings are widely known among the citizens of Rome, so that his own political image will be enhanced by comparison. After the battle of Alexandria, Caesar invites all of his officers to his tent to show them the written record he has made of his actions. He declares that these papers will show how reluctantly he was "drawn into this war" as well as the "calm and gentle" tone he used in all his letters to Antony (V.i.74, 75). Caesar has carefully prepared a record that will justify his own actions and cast Antony's in an unfavorable light. His intention to humiliate Cleopatra by exhibiting her in the streets of Rome is part of his public relations scheme: the sight of Egypt's queen in chains would delight the crowd and increase the significance of Caesar's triumph.

Cleopatra knows he's lying to her when he swears he means to treat her well, but most of his other victims fail to appreciate Caesar's lack of honor and his willingness to break his word. He signs a treaty with Pompey and then violates it as soon as Pompey is no longer a threat. Having made all the use of Lepidus he can, Caesar invents charges against him and imprisons him for life. Even the lowly servant Alexas doesn't escape Caesar's attention: he has him killed after Alexas betrays Antony and tries to help Caesar. Commentators who emphasize Caesar's viciousness often call attention to an incident before the battle of Alexandria. On that occasion, Caesar orders that the soldiers who deserted Antony should march into battle in front of all the others. This strategy will humiliate Antony and degrade his former followers. Caesar's ruthless treatment of his enemies contributes to his military victories and guarantees his political success.

Canidius:

A lieutenant-general, he is one of Antony's chief military officers. Before the battle of Actium, Canidius and an anonymous soldier discuss the folly of Antony's decision to accept Caesar's challenge and fight by sea. Canidius questions the soldier about Caesar's lieutenant-general (III.vii.77), perhaps because he's curious about his counterpart in the opposing army or perhaps because he's already thinking of leaving Antony and joining Caesar. After Antony's disastrous retreat at Actium, Canidius defects to Caesar, taking with him the foot soldiers and horsemen under his command. He justifies his desertion by remarking that Antony himself "has given example for our flight / Most grossly by his own!" (III.x.27-28).

Captain:

The term "captain" appears throughout the play in association with a variety of characters. At IV.iv.24, an individual designated as the captain enters the room where Cleopatra and Eros have been arming Antony before the battle of Alexandria. Accompanied by soldiers and a flourish of trumpets, the captain greets Antony and tells him they have fair weather for the contest.

> **Despite his apparent affection for his sister, Caesar uses Octavia as he would anyone else. He refers to her in impersonal terms: she is a 'piece of virtue' (III.ii.28) and the 'cement' that will bind him and Antony together."**

Charmian:

She is Cleopatra's most trusted servant. Charmian has a forceful personality and an independent spirit. When she thinks the queen's treatment of Antony is unfair or misguided, she tells her so. Charmian is on familiar terms with her mistress and can tease her about her past life and former lovers. At I.v.66-67, Cleopatra asks Charmian whether, in her judgment, she ever loved Julius Caesar as much as she now loves Antony. Charmian responds with praise of "that brave Caesar" (I.v.67). "Say, 'the brave Antony,'" the queen commands, but Charmian saucily replies, "the valiant Caesar!" (I.v.69). Cleopatra threatens to give her "bloody teeth" (I.v.70) if she says anything flattering about Caesar again. Charmian apologizes—though she notes that she's only repeating what Cleopatra herself used to say.

Charmian's devotion to her mistress seems deep and genuine. On one occasion, however, she unintentionally does her a grave disservice. When Cleopatra runs away from Antony's fury after the battle of Alexandria, it is Charmian who suggests that the queen lock herself in the monument and send word to Antony that she's dead. Cleopatra follows her suggestion, and Antony's suicide is the result—an outcome that apparently neither one of them anticipated.

Cleopatra entrusts Charmian with the task of arranging for delivery of the poisonous snakes, and then she prepares to die royally. Charmian stays by her, though her heart is breaking. The queen dies with a half-spoken sentence on her lips, and Charmian completes it for her. Charmian speaks a brief but now famous epitaph: "Death, in thy pos-

Caesar is a master at controlling public opinion. He sees to it that Antony's failings are widely known among the citizens of Rome, so that his own political image will be enhanced by comparison."

session lies / A lass unparalleled'' (V.ii.315-16). She tenderly straightens her mistress's crown. As she places an asp on her own breast, she reminds her on-stage audience—one Roman guard—and the wider one as well that Cleopatra's ending was ''well done, and fitting for a princess / Descended of so many kings'' (V.ii.326-27).

Cleopatra:

Historically, she became queen of Egypt in 51 B.C., at the age of eighteen. When she was twenty-one, Julius Caesar became her lover. Seven years later she met Antony, and their relationship continued until their deaths by suicide in 30 B.C. Cleopatra was a woman of remarkable poise and unusual intelligence. She was highly educated, spoke several languages, and dealt shrewdly with foreign ambassadors and heads of state. She also had a reputation as an extraordinarily sensuous woman.

In *Antony and Cleopatra*, Egypt's queen is portrayed as eternally fascinating. She is no longer a young woman, but her charm is ageless. Cleopatra's magnetism has little do with physical beauty. She has vitality, grace, intensity, and a radiance that excites awe. She is regal—the descendant of generations of monarchs. She is associated with divinities, particularly Isis, the Egyptian goddess of the sea. She is also the human counterpart of the river Nile, which overflows its banks each year, enriching Egyptian soil and breeding new life. She represents a kind of human richness that dazzles ordinary mortals. The source of her fascination cannot be pinned down. The range of her personality is beyond measurement—though the Romans try to do so. Cleopatra is a paragon of sexuality. Like others before him, Antony finds her irresistible. An experienced lover, she delights in erotic games. Her sexual

appetite is legendary, and her love of pleasure inexhaustible.

But Cleopatra is more than the goddess of love. Generations of commentators have described her as the most complex of Shakespeare's female characters. She is a tangle of contradictions. She is depicted as being alternately splendid, foolish, mean-spirited, and extravagant. One of her principal faults is vanity. She demands attention and frequently acts like a spoiled or selfish child. At least through Act IV, she demonstrates only a small measure of concern for other people. Her treatment of her servant Mardian seems cruel. She is rash and impetuous, and she has a capacity for violence. Several commentators have argued that her abuse of the messenger who brings her the news of Antony's marriage to Octavia shows Cleopatra at her worst. She jokes with her handmaidens on several occasions, yet she can just as easily assume a tyrannical attitude toward them. She is Egypt's queen, and she does not expect them to ever forget that. From time to time she also appears untrustworthy. There are indications—in the scenes with Thidias and Proculeius, for example—that if she could have worked out an arrangement with Caesar that was to her advantage, she might have done so. The play provides no answers as to why she orders her fleet of ships to turn tail and run from the battle of Actium. Is she afraid? Does she think that Caesar is going to win in the end and thus there's no point in continuing the battle? Does she order her ships to desert Antony at the battle of Alexandria—as he believes—or do her captains betray Antony on their own? Concern for her own safety seems uppermost in her mind when the dying Antony is carried to the monument and she refuses to come down to him. So that she may avoid being captured by Caesar's soldiers, Antony must be hauled up to her, in a humiliating and painful maneuver.

Some commentators believe the play demonstrates that her love for Antony destroys him. They point out that in the initial scenes she teases and manipulates him so that he always appears to be in the wrong. They see her as a dangerous spell-binder who enchants Antony and keeps him from fulfilling his potential for greatness. Many think that her love for Antony doesn't match his love for her. Others believe that in the final scenes she achieves an understanding of the importance of love and becomes transformed by it. Some argue that her characterization is inconsistent: that she's a comic figure in Acts I through IV—vain, insensitive, and childish—and a tragic figure in the last, long scene of the play.

One facet of her personality that seems to remain constant is her identity as an actress. Whenever she appears, she commands center stage. She has a strong sense of spectacle or pageantry, whether she is stage-managing the glorious progress of her galley down the river Cydnus or arranging the scenic details of her own death. Readers and commentators alike wonder whether Cleopatra ever stops acting. It has been suggested that for her there is no line distinguishing illusion from reality.

This is one reason why her final hours are so impossible to evaluate. To some, Cleopatra's death is a triumph: it represents both a victory over Caesar and a self-transformation into a noble, tragic figure. For others, her death spells defeat: she has not been able to negotiate terms with Caesar that are favorable to her, so she chooses to die. The prospect of being paraded through the streets of Rome while commoners jeer at her is reason enough for this daughter of kings to kill herself. Some believe that she does so because she realizes she cannot live without Antony. They point to her dream of "an Emperor Antony" (V.ii.76-92.) as evidence that she truly loves him, and they argue that her vision of Antony comes from her heart. To other commentators, it is a work of her imagination, an elaborate fantasy of an Antony that never was or could be. After her death, Charmian calls her a woman with whom no other can be compared. Caesar remarks on the bravery she showed in ending her life and notes that she did it royally, true to her nature. Yet she dies on a bed, not her throne, and her crown slips to one side. Nevertheless, as he orders that Cleopatra be buried next to Antony, Caesar remarks that "No grave upon the earth" will ever enclose "A pair so famous" (V.ii.360).

Clown:

He is the "rural fellow" (V.ii.233) who brings Cleopatra the basket of figs and poisonous snakes. He seems to be simple-minded, yet he understands what use Cleopatra intends to make of "the pretty worm of Nilus" (V.ii.243). Some commentators view the clown as ghoulish. Others see him as presenting a non-threatening, even comic perspective on death. Several of his garbled, self-contradictory remarks have religious or spiritual overtones; he seems to suggest that death is not final. His several references to what people say and what may be believed underscore the motif of unreliable evidence that runs throughout the play. He tells Cleopatra

> **To some, Cleopatra's death is a triumph: it represents both a victory over Caesar and a self-transformation into a noble, tragic figure. For others, her death spells defeat: she has not been able to negotiate terms with Caesar that are favorable to her, so she chooses to die."**

that only yesterday he had a report of the effectiveness of the asp—from the lips of a woman who had died from its bite. The clown loves to talk. He rambles on and on as Cleopatra, with the means of her death now at hand, repeatedly tries to dismiss him. At last he leaves, wishing her "joy o' th' worm" (V.ii.279).

Decretas:

One of Antony's soldiers, he responds with other aides when Antony bungles his suicide and calls for help. Neither he nor any of the others is willing to give Antony the death blow. Decretas sees Antony's fallen sword and picks it up. He thinks that if he carries the sword to Caesar and is the first to tell him of Antony's death, Caesar will look favorably on him. Decretas enters Caesar's presence boldly, the blood-stained sword unsheathed. He describes himself as a loyal follower of the noble Antony and offers his services to Caesar. Decretas's theft of Antony's sword is a dishonorable act, but it may also be seen as shrewd and practical. Devoted to Antony while he was alive, Decretas recognizes that with Antony dead, he will need a new patron.

Demetrius:

He is a Roman soldier who, with his companion Philo, observes and comments on Antony and Cleopatra in the play's opening scene. He is surprised when Antony refuses to listen to a messenger from Caesar; from Demetrius's point of view, this is disrespectful. He remarks that what he has just seen confirms the rumors being spread by "the common liar" (I.i.60)—that is, general gossip, hence usually not to be trusted. Demetrius now agrees with those

> "... as he orders that Cleopatra be buried next to Antony, Caesar remarks that 'No grave upon the earth' will ever enclose 'A pair so famous' (V.ii.360)."

reports about Antony: he is indeed betraying his greatness and failing in his duty to Rome.

Diomedes:

He is one of Cleopatra's attendants. From her refuge in the monument, she sends him to tell Antony that she is still alive. Diomedes arrives after Antony has tried to kill himself. He explains that Cleopatra sent the earlier, false report because Antony was in a towering rage and she feared that he might harm her. Diomedes also swears that Cleopatra had nothing to do with the Egyptian ships deserting Antony during the battle near Alexandria.

Dolabella:

A Roman officer and aide to Caesar, he appears late in the play and becomes the last of Cleopatra's conquests. Caesar sends Dolabella to guard the queen in her monument. She describes for him her glorious vision of Antony—one of the most famous passages in the play (V.ii.76-91). When she asks him if he thinks "there was or might be such a man / As this I dreamt of?" Dolabella replies in the manner of a practical but gracious man: "Gentle madam, no" (V.ii.93-94). Though he is unable to imagine such an Antony, Dolabella is strongly moved. Recognizing this and taking advantage of his sympathy, she asks him what Caesar intends to do with her. Dolabella is caught between his duty to Caesar and his infatuation with Cleopatra. He hesitates for a moment. But when Cleopatra says "He'll lead me then in triumph," Dolabella confirms her worst fears: "Madam, he will, I know' t" (V.ii.109-10).

After Cleopatra's interview with Caesar, Dolabella returns. He appears completely enamored. In the language of courtly love, he declares that he is devoted to serving her. Then he tells her that Caesar has made plans to send her and her children to Rome

within three days. "Make your best use of this," he says (V.ii.203). Dolabella knows full well what Cleopatra will do—and that her suicide will frustrate Caesar's plans. He gently bids her farewell and leaves her so that he may fulfill his other obligation: "I must attend on Caesar" (V.ii.206).

Domitius Enobarbus:

See Enobarbus

Egyptian:

An anonymous messenger from Cleopatra, he goes to Caesar after Antony's death and tells him that Cleopatra has confined herself in the monument. The tone of his message is submissive—she wants to know, he says, what Caesar intends to do with her so she can make preparations to obey his wishes. Caesar assures the Egyptian that he means to treat Cleopatra honorably. The messenger prays that the gods will preserve Caesar, and then he departs.

Enobarbus:

Antony's chief aide, he deserts his leader before the battle of Alexandria and dies of shame. Enobarbus often functions as a commentator on events and on other characters. His judgments are generally detached and objective. Frequently, however, they are ironic or cynical as well. He scoffs at the great ones of the world and makes fun of the poses they assume. He recognizes Antony's weaknesses and tries to point them out. He attempts to show Antony how his love for Cleopatra has affected his reason, but Antony refuses to listen to him. Though Enobarbus is often cynical about the lovers' passion for each other, he's also sympathetic toward them. And the sensuous pleasures of Egypt have a strong pull on him as well as on his master.

This attraction is most apparent at II.ii.200-50, when he describes Cleopatra's first meeting with Antony. His on-stage audience for this piece consists of two Roman officers who have heard rumors about Egypt's queen but have no first-hand knowledge themselves. One of them is enchanted; the other expresses his disapproval of what he's just heard. Interestingly, they represent the divided opinions toward Cleopatra held by generations of readers, audiences, and commentators.

Enobarbus's description of Cleopatra's river barge (II.ii.191-218) is one of the most famous passages in the play. Many critics regard it as among the foremost descriptive passages in all of

Shakespeare's dramatic poetry. Enobarbus paints a breathtaking picture of purple sails "so perfumèd that / The winds were love-sick with them"; of silver oars that beat the water like lovers' strokes; of "pretty dimpled boys, like smiling cupids," whose fans cooled Cleopatra's cheeks even as they made them glow with greater warmth (II.ii.193-94, 202). Enobarbus's description of Cleopatra as a woman of "infinite variety" and fascination (II.ii.235), but also one whose sexual appetite is legendary, conveys her power to bewitch men—even Enobarbus from time to time.

For the most part, Enobarbus is depicted as a man of reason who sizes up a situation rationally and objectively. He undergoes a long struggle with himself before he finally leaves Antony. When Canidius deserts Antony after Actium, Enobarbus says that he'll continue to follow his leader, "though my reason / Sits in the wind against me" (III.x.35-36). As Antony's judgment grows more clouded, Enobarbus wonders if loyalty to fools makes faithfulness absurd. On the eve of the battle of Alexandria, Enobarbus decides that it's irrational to stay with Antony any longer, and he leaves. When he learns that Antony has generously sent all of his belongings after him, Enobarbus is stricken with guilt. "I am alone the villain of the earth," he says (IV.vi.29). Weighed down by shame and dishonor, he vows to "go seek / Some ditch wherein to die" (IV.vi.36-37). With his last words he condemns himself as a "master-leaver and a fugitive" (IV.ix.22). As commentators often point out, Enobarbus does not commit suicide. He simply lies down and dies.

Eros:

A trusted servant of Antony, he has a tender heart and the spirit of a peacemaker. His name signifies love. After the battle of Actium, when Antony is feeling deep shame and frustration, Eros tries to persuade him to speak to Cleopatra. As devoted as he is to Antony, Eros pities Cleopatra. The queen will surely die of grief, he says, unless Antony comforts her.

Before the initial battle of Alexandria, Antony summons Eros to help him put on his armor. Cleopatra insists on helping too, and the scene is charming, filled with tenderness and optimism. The next service Antony asks of Eros is to help him die. Eros is reluctant, but Antony insists. Eros gives in, but he asks Antony to turn his face away so that he doesn't have to see it as he stabs him. "Farewell, great chief," says Eros to his master (IV.xiv.93),

> **Enobarbus's description of Cleopatra's river barge (II.ii.191-218) is one of the most famous passages in the play. . . . Enobarbus paints a breathtaking picture of purple sails 'so perfumèd that / The winds were love-sick with them'; of silver oars that beat the water like lovers' strokes; of 'pretty dimpled boys, like smiling cupids,' whose fans cooled Cleopatra's cheeks even as they made them glow with greater warmth (II.ii.193-94, 202)."**

then he plunges the blade into his own body. Inspired by his servant's courage, Antony "falls on his sword" (S.D.IV.xiv.103).

Gallus:

One of Caesar's aides, he is present in V.i when Caesar learns of Antony's death. He is also in attendance when Caesar visits Cleopatra, in V.ii, to discuss the implications of his conquest of Egypt. Gallus says nothing on either occasion.

Guards:

Antony and Caesar are each attended by a unit of soldiers described as guards or guardsmen. When Antony falls on his sword but fails to kill himself, he cries out for his guards to come and help him. "Let him that loves me strike me dead," pleads Antony (IV.xiv.108). Though the guards are shocked and grief-stricken, none of them will do as he asks. When Antony learns that Cleopatra is still alive, he requests their help in transporting him to the monument. The guards mournfully comply, and, once they are there, they "heave Antony aloft to Cleopatra" (S.D.IV.xv.38).

After Antony's death, Caesar sends guards to Cleopatra's palace. They seize her while she is talking to his agent Proculeius. Dolabella, another of Caesar's aides, arrives and announces that he is taking over responsibility for her. Guardsmen are left in the queen's vicinity, however. One of them escorts the clown with his basket of figs into her presence. Another returns later to bring Cleopatra a message from Caesar; he enters just as Charmian has finished straightening the dead queen's crown and is applying an asp to her own breast.

Iras:

One of Cleopatra's principal attendants, she usually appears in the company of Charmian, the queen's chief handmaiden. By comparison with Charmian, Iras seems young and impressionable. However, her jests in I.ii are as bawdy as her companion's. Iras dies before Cleopatra and Charmian. There is no explanation for her death. The queen bids them both farewell and kisses them. Then Iras simply "falls and dies" (S.D.V.ii.293). Cleopatra marvels at the ease with which the young woman departed from life—then uses the event as the basis for one final jest. If Iras meets Antony in the next world before her mistress does, he'll "spend that kiss / Which is my heaven to have," says Cleopatra (V.ii.302-03). With this, the queen picks up an asp and places it on her breast.

Lamprius:

A Roman soldier and one of Antony's followers, he appears in I.ii. While Cleopatra's attendants make bawdy remarks and playfully joke with a fortune-teller, Lamprius stands aside and says nothing.

Lepidus:

One of the triumvirs, he is known as a valiant soldier. Despite his official standing, Lepidus is essentially a weak and ineffective man. Antony and Caesar have selected him to share the triumvirate because he commands a large army. He becomes a tool in the struggle that develops between them. Commentators generally view Lepidus as a man hopelessly out of his element, trying to fulfill a role that is beyond his abilities.

When Antony returns to Rome in II.ii, Lepidus tries to reconcile the differences between Caesar and Antony. He points out that with the triumvirate under attack by Pompey, this is the time for unity, not dissension. Both in this scene and in II.iv, when the rulers are negotiating with Pompey, Lepidus has a limited part to play. While those with stronger wills dominate the conversation, Lepidus is limited to an occasional interjection. However, he becomes

the focus for a while during the banquet on Pompey's galley, where he becomes drunk and passes out—but not before he becomes the butt of everyone's jokes. Hardly a man of keen intellect to begin with, his mind is now befuddled by the wine. "What manner o'thing is your crocodile?" he asks Antony (II.vii.41). The mockery in Antony's description—that it is "shaped, sir, like itself," that "it is as broad as it hath breadth," and "is just so high as it is" (II.vii.42, 42-43, 43)—passes right over Lepidus's head. Eventually Lepidus has to be carried off the ship by one of Pompey's servants. Enobarbus jokes that the servant must be very strong, for he's bearing the weight of a "third part of the world" (II.vii.90). Lepidus faces an unkind fate. At III.v.7-8, Eros tells Enobarbus that "Caesar, having made use of him in the wars 'gainst Pompey," has ousted Lepidus from the triumvirate now that his usefulness is ended. Furthermore, reports Eros, Caesar accused Lepidus of conspiring with Pompey and ordered him imprisoned for life.

Lucillius:

A Roman soldier and one of Antony's followers, he appears in I.ii. He watches without speaking as Cleopatra's attendants amuse themselves with bawdy jokes and the predictions of a fortune-teller.

Maecenas:

A Roman officer, he is part of Caesar's retinue of attendants on many occasions—though he rarely has anything to say. Maecenas appears to be a rather dull man. Whereas his colleague Agrippa is carried away by Enobarbus's description of Cleopatra and her exotic barge, Maecenas's response is stolid and prudish. His resistance to the sensuous pleasures of Egypt is evident in his expressed preference for the "beauty, wisdom, modesty" (II.ii.240) of the Roman matron Octavia.

Mardian:

One of Cleopatra's attendants, he is a eunuch. The queen likes to jest with Mardian about his inability to please women sexually. When she does so—for example, at I.v.9-12 and II.v.5-6, 8-9—it's uncertain whether her teasing is affectionate or malicious. After Antony has been defeated at Alexandria, Cleopatra flees in alarm from her lover's fury. She instructs Mardian to report to Antony that she has killed herself. Mardian faithfully carries out her instructions. He tells her lover that "the last she spake / Was 'Antony, most noble Antony!'" (IV.xiv.29-30). Half-way through her last utterance, he reports, ''a tearing groan'' escaped from her body (IV.xiv.31), and she died with the ''name of Antony . . . divided between her heart and lips'' (IV.xiv.32-33). Mardian's performance is completely convincing, though his report is false from beginning to end. Antony is stunned, and he immediately resolves to end his own life.

Mark Antony:

See Antony

Menas:

A notorious pirate, he joins forces with Pompey against the triumvirs. Menas is a pragmatic man. Like others in the play, he believes that the gods determine men's fate. Yet he also believes that men must make the most of opportunities that are presented to them. Menas is present when Pompey negotiates a truce with the triumvirs—and gives away more than he gets in return. Afterwards Menas remarks to himself that Pompey's renowned father ''would n'er have made this treaty'' (II.vi.82-83).

During the banquet for the triumvirs and their aides aboard Pompey's galley, Menas draws Pompey aside. He offers to make him ''lord of the whole world'' (II.vii.62) by cutting first the anchor cables and then, when the ship is underway, the throats of the ''three world-sharers'' (II.vii.70). Pompey turns down Menas's proposal. Menas thinks Pompey is a fool to have passed up this chance, and he ends their alliance.

Menecrates:

A friend and supporter of Pompey, Menecrates is a notorious pirate. He appears in II.i. In some editions of the play, he is assigned two brief speeches in that scene; in others, he has no lines.

Messengers:

Anonymous messengers—and ones whose names are known—are crucial to the play. They appear on more than thirty occasions. Their news is often out-of-date, biased, or inaccurate. The unreliability of their reports underscores the notion that it's often impossible to determine the ''truth'' about people.

One messenger is beaten for telling the truth. His message—that Antony has married Octavia—so enrages Cleopatra that she strikes him and draws a knife as if to kill him. ''Should I lie, madam?'' he asks her (II.v.93), and the answer is yes. When she summons him again, he describes Octavia as having a pudgy face, a creeping gait, and a stiff, almost lifeless form. ''The fellow has good judgment,'' Cleopatra remarks (III.iii.25), and she rewards him handsomely for his lies.

In some scenes—for example, I.ii, I.iv, and III.vii—two or more messengers bring reports that either confirm or contradict earlier ones. These quick sequences of messages emphasize how many things are happening in the world of *Antony and Cleopatra* and how quickly the situation can change, as the fortunes of various characters rise and fall. They also illustrate the difficulty of making judgments when the available evidence is conflicting or ambiguous.

Octavia:

Caesar's sister, she marries Antony for the sake of Roman unity. Octavia is selfless and submissive, a pawn in the political battle between her brother and her husband. Her marriage to Antony brings about a temporary settlement of their differences, and she and Antony establish their home in Athens. When the truce appears to be threatened, Octavia takes on the role of peacemaker and travels to Rome to speak with her brother. When she arrives there, however, she finds there is no possibility of reconciliation. She also learns that Antony is no longer in Athens but is back in Egypt with Cleopatra.

Octavia has only a few speeches in the play. What others say about her helps define what we think of her. However, these remarks frequently reveal as much about the characters who make them as they do about Octavia. Caesar's aide Agrippa describes her as full of virtues and graces (II.ii.129). Maecenas, another Roman on Caesar's staff, remarks that she is beautiful, wise, and modest (II.ii.240). Caesar himself refers to her as ''the piece of virtue which is set / Betwixt us as the cement of our love'' (III.ii.28-29). Enobarbus characterizes her as ''holy, cold, and still'' (II.vi.122-23). The messenger who brings Cleopatra word that Antony is married concocts an unflattering portrait of Octavia—in fear of his life if he does not. He describes the Roman matron as shorter than Cleopatra and ''low-voiced''; the jealous queen converts this into ''Dull of tongue and dwarfish'' (III.iii.16). When Cleopatra asks the messenger if there is majesty in the way Octavia walks, he says that ''She creeps'' (III.iii.18). Octavia is, he says, more like a statue than a living, breathing woman. Cleopatra rewards the messenger handsomely for his report.

❝Octavia is selfless and submissive, a pawn in the political battle between her brother and her husband.❞

Octavius:

See Caesar

Philo:

A Roman soldier, he provides a harsh and highly critical perspective on Antony and Cleopatra. Philo and Demetrius, another Roman soldier, frame the first appearance of the lovers in I.i, commenting on them both before they enter with their attendants and after they exit. Philo charges that Antony, once the world's most famous warrior, has lost his zeal for fighting. Instead, says Philo, Antony's passions are now solely focused on Cleopatra, and he has become "a strumpet's fool" (I.i.13). Commentators have remarked on Philo's severity, his disdain for Egyptian ways, and his seeming lack of feelings or emotions. They also point out the sneering tone of his first speech and the racist attitude he displays toward Cleopatra—for example, when he calls her a gipsy and alludes to her skin color (I.i.10, 6).

Pompey:

Sextus Pompeius, as he is formally known, is the son of Pompey the Great, who was, historically, a leading senator and one of Rome's most famous generals. Pompey the Great regarded Julius Caesar as a tyrant; he was killed by members of Caesar's political faction. In *Antony and Cleopatra*, Pompey carries on his father's opposition to the triumvirate. Like his father, he has been proscribed—that is, condemned as outside the law—and his financial estate has been confiscated by the government. His defiance of the triumvirs appears to be motivated by a combination of revenge for his father's death, republican idealism, and personal glory.

In the first part of the play, he represents a real threat to the triumvirs. For example, at I.ii.185, Antony says he's learned that Pompey and his ships dominate "the empire of the sea." Pompey also controls Sicily, an important source of Rome's supply of grain. At I.iv.36-40 and 48-55, messen-gers tell of his increasing popular support and the alliances he has made with pirates such as Menas and Menecrates.

In his initial appearance in the play, Pompey is self-assured and confident: "I shall do well. / The people love me, and the sea is mine" (II.i.8-9). When he's told that "Caesar and Lepidus / Are in the field" with a mighty army (II.i.16-17) and that Antony is returning to Rome, he becomes less boastful. He recognizes that Caesar and Antony may call an end to their quarrel in the face of his continued success. This is indeed what happens, and a direct confrontation between Pompey and the triumvirs seems likely. In II.ii and II.iv, they make plans to attack his stronghold at Mount Misena near Naples. However, in II.vi, Pompey meets with them to discuss the terms of a truce. He agrees to peace terms that are not very favorable to him and invites everyone to a feast on board his ship, lying at anchor in the nearby harbor.

While the triumvirs and their aides are feasting and drinking, Menas draws Pompey aside and makes a daring proposal: "Wilt thou be lord of all the world?" he asks him (II.vii.61). Menas offers to cut the anchor cables and then the throats of the triumvirs. Pompey's response underscores the element of political cynicism in the play. He says that if Menas had done this without consulting him, he would have approved of it as a good deed. However, having been informed in advance of Menas's intention, he "must condemn it now" (II.vii.80). Pompey rejoins the triumvirs and the banquet continues.

Commentators have offered varying perspectives on Pompey's reaction to Menas's proposal. Some believe that he lacks sufficient resolution to carry out his political convictions. Others suggest that he doesn't want to be the sole "lord of all the world." Perhaps he recognizes he doesn't have the capacity to fill that role, or perhaps he isn't personally ambitious. It seems that like many others in the play, he is very concerned with his reputation; he says he doesn't want it tarnished with the stain of villainy. For whatever reason or mixture of reasons, Pompey lets what some would see as a golden opportunity slip away from him. After this scene he disappears from the play. At III.v.18-19, it's reported that one of Antony's officers has murdered Pompey.

Proculeius:

A Roman officer and aide to Caesar, he is sent to talk with Cleopatra after Antony's death. Caesar instructs him to convince the queen that she will be treated well—though he reveals to Proculeius that he means to make her the centerpiece of his triumphant return to Rome by exhibiting her as a captive. Proculeius goes to the queen and introduces himself. In an elegant speech, he describes Caesar as a man of generous spirit, "so full of grace that it flows over / On all that need" it (V.ii.24-25). He assures Cleopatra that Caesar pities her. As he says this, two guards come up behind the queen and seize her. "You see how easily she may be surprised," he remarks (V.ii.35). The queen draws a dagger and appears about to kill herself, but Proculeius disarms her. His parting words to Cleopatra, after Dolabella has arrived to relieve him, are puzzling: "To Caesar I will speak what you shall please, / If you'll employ me to him" (V.ii.69-70). He knows what Caesar's true intentions are. Moreover, he diverted her attention so she could be easily captured by the guards. Now he appears to be offering to serve as an even-handed negotiator between her and Caesar.

Rannius:

A Roman soldier and one of Antony's followers, he appears in I.ii. As Cleopatra's attendants joke and play, Rannius says nothing.

Scarus:

He is one of Antony's officers. Scarus has a passionate temperament. After the disastrous battle of Actium, he is furious: "I never saw an action of such shame," he declares (III.x.21). He directs his rage at the absent Cleopatra, cursing her and referring to her as a cow, a worn-out horse, and a loose woman. Scarus declares that the queen has transformed Antony and made him betray his true nature. When Enobarbus deserts Antony, Scarus takes on some of his functions. He is at Antony's side throughout the battle of Alexandria. After Antony's victory on the first day of fighting, Scarus is exuberant, fierce, and eager to attack Caesar's forces again. He makes light of the wounds he's received and helps restore Antony's confidence. Antony commends him for his outstanding bravery and praises him to Cleopatra; he asks her to give Scarus her hand to kiss. Scarus has fought like a god today, says Antony.

Schoolmaster:

An attendant at the court of Alexandria, he is sent as an ambassador to Caesar after the battle of Actium. He reports that Antony asks to be allowed

> **In his initial appearance in the play, Pompey is self-assured and confident: 'I shall do well. / The people love me, and the sea is mine' (II.i.8-9)."**

"to live in Egypt" (III.xii.12) or, if that's not possible, in Athens. The schoolmaster also carries Cleopatra's request that she be allowed to retain the crown of Egypt "for her heirs" (III.xii.18). Antony uses the schoolmaster as an agent once more, when he sends him to Caesar with a challenge to meet him in single-handed combat. As Dolabella points out (III.xii.2-6), Antony's reliance on a lowly schoolmaster to act as ambassador is an indication of how far his fortunes have fallen.

Seleucus:

As Cleopatra's treasurer he is the focus of an episode that continues to baffle readers and commentators. In her final interview with Caesar, Cleopatra hands her conqueror a scroll that lists, she says, all her possessions. She then summons Seleucus and tells him to confirm that this is a truthful report of her assets. Seleucus says he'd prefer not to speak rather than tell a lie. "What have I kept back?" demands Cleopatra (V.ii.147). A very large amount indeed, replies her treasurer. Cleopatra flies into a rage and threatens to scratch his eyes out. Caesar is amused. He tells her he doesn't want to haggle with her over her personal possessions, and besides, he says, he never meant to include them among the treasure that is due to him as Egypt's conqueror.

It seems impossible to determine exactly what is going on here. Does Seleucus betray Cleopatra, hoping to gain favor with Caesar? Have the queen and her treasurer planned this in advance? Is her rage genuine or feigned? Perhaps Cleopatra drew up this scheme herself beforehand. Perhaps she cleverly figures out, on the spot, how to turn Seleucus's words to her own advantage. Whatever the explanation, the episode benefits Cleopatra. Caesar concludes that she has kept back some of her possessions because she means to go on living. He is put off guard, at least temporarily, and she has time to prepare for her death.

Sentry:

He is in charge of a unit of watchmen. They patrol Caesar's camp during the night that passes between the two phases of the battle of Alexandria. The sentry and his watchmen draw aside when they see Enobarbus, and they listen as he laments his betrayal of Antony. Enobarbus dies just as they decide to ''speak to him'' (IV.ix.23). At first they think he's sleeping or has fainted, and they try to wake him. Then the sentry sees that ''the hand of death'' has touched him (IV.ix.29).

Servants:

There are three sets of characters in the play who are designated as servants. Two or three Roman servants appear in the scene on Pompey's galley, commenting among themselves on Lepidus's drunkenness (II.vii.1-16). The servants mock the triumvir, describing him as a man who thinks he's one of the masters of the world but actually has no influence or power. Later in the scene, the servants carry Lepidus—who is too drunk to walk—off the boat and back to his quarters.

Several Egyptian servants appear in III.xiii. They are summoned by Antony, who orders them to take Caesar's messenger Thidias away and whip him for his insolence. One servant returns with Thidias and reports that Antony's orders have been carried out.

In IV.ii, Antony calls his household servants together and asks them to help him make the last feast for his soldiers a memorable one. He thanks them individually for their past services, shakes their hands, calls them his ''honest friends'' (IV.ii.29), and reduces them to tears.

Sextus Pompeius:

See Pompey

Silius:

An officer in Ventidius's army, he appears with him after the Roman victory over the Parthians (III.i). Silius urges Ventidius to press the advantage he has gained on the battlefield that day and pursue the fleeing enemy. More victories are sure to follow, says Silius. Ventidius declines this advice, pointing out that if he were to be too successful, it would diminish Antony's stature. Silius agrees and applauds Ventidius's discretion.

Soldiers:

Roman soldiers appear throughout the play as followers of one leader or another. Sometimes they display loyalty, sometimes they do not. Caught up in the struggle between the triumvirs, they occasionally express their opinions about strategy and the likely outcome of battles.

One soldier speaks directly to Antony before the battle of Actium; ''do not fight by sea,'' he says (III.vii.61). Echoing the advice of Enobarbus and Canidius, he reminds Antony that their forces are ''used to conquer standing on the earth / And fighting foot to foot'' (III.vii.65-66). In IV.v, the same soldier encounters Antony and Eros as they set out for the battle of Alexandria. Antony says he wishes he'd listened to him on the earlier occasion. The soldier informs Antony that Enobarbus has deserted and gone over to Caesar's side. Antony disbelieves him at first. Eros confirms the soldier's report, and Antony sends Enobarbus's belongings and ''treasures'' after him. Shortly after that, in Caesar's camp, a soldier approaches Enobarbus. He tells him of Antony's generosity, and Enobarbus thinks he's joking. ''I tell you true,'' the soldier says, ''Your emperor / Continues still a Jove'' (IV.vi.25, 27-28).

In IV.iii, on the night before the first battle of Alexandria, four soldiers in Antony's army are patrolling the streets of Alexandria. They take up separate positions, apart from each other. Suddenly, music is heard, as if from oboe-like instruments. To one soldier the music seems to be borne on the air. To another it seems to come from beneath the earth. One asks what it might signify, and another answers '''Tis the god Hercules, whom Antony loved,'' now forsaking him. The four men meet two other soldiers who have also heard the music, and they all marvel at it. This episode heightens the sense of the supernatural that recurs throughout the play.

For more on the Roman soldiers in *Antony and Cleopatra*, see Guards and Sentry.

Soothsayer:

He predicts the future and lends emphasis to supernatural elements in the play. The soothsayer's prophecies are sometimes obscure and sometimes forthright. Charmian and Iras, Cleopatra's attendants, turn his predictions into bawdy jokes or discount them as entertainment, a way to pass the time. He understands the quality of Charmian's devotion to her mistress—''You shall be more beloving than beloved''—and presages the moments after Cleopatra's death when Charmian pauses to straighten the queen's crown—"You shall outlive the lady whom you serve" (I.ii.23, 31). With Antony, the soothsayer is more direct. When Antony asks him "whose fortunes shall rise higher, / Caesar's or mine?" he replies tersely and accurately: "Caesar's" (II.iii.16-17, 18). He then goes on to explain why Antony should stay away from Caesar. He says that Antony's guardian spirit is "Noble, courageous, high unmatchable" (II.iii.21), but whenever it is near Caesar it becomes overpowered. The soothsayer alludes to Caesar's reputation for being fortune's favorite: "If thou dost play him at any game," he tells Antony, "Thou art sure to lose; and of that natural luck / He beats thee 'gainst the odds" (II.iii.26, 27-28). Antony sends the soothsayer away, but admits to himself privately that the man "hath spoken true" (II.iii.34).

Taurus:

A friend and follower of Caesar, he is in charge of Caesar's land forces during the battle of Actium. In III.viii, Caesar instructs Taurus not to confront Antony's army until the naval battle is over.

Thidias:

A follower and aide to Caesar, he is sent as a messenger to Cleopatra after the battle of Actium. Caesar instructs Thidias to try to persuade Cleopatra to desert Antony, promising him that if he's successful, he can name his own reward. When Thidias is admitted into Cleopatra's presence, Antony is absent. Thidias says to the queen that Caesar believes she became Antony's mistress not because she loved him but because she was afraid of him. He goes on to declare that it would please Caesar greatly if she were to place herself under his protection rather than Antony's. Cleopatra's response is extremely gracious—at least on the surface. Thidias leans forward and kisses her hand. As he does so, Antony bursts into the room. He is outraged that a messenger of Caesar should take such a liberty with Egypt's queen. He is also furious with Cleopatra for allowing it. Antony orders that Thidias be whipped, and he is led away.

Thidias himself is of small interest in the play. However, Cleopatra's apparent willingness to have Thidias act as a mediator with Caesar raises questions. Is she deceiving Thidias or actually considering the possibility of deserting her lover? Antony violates a significant standard of diplomacy when he orders Caesar's messenger to be whipped. Some

commentators regard this as the moment when Antony fatally compromises his honor.

Varrius:

A friend and supporter of Pompey, he functions as a messenger in II.i. Just as Pompey is saying he's confident that Antony will remain in Egypt with Cleopatra, Varrius enters and tells him that Antony is on his way to Rome.

Ventidius:

He is a Roman general and supporter of Antony. In the early part of the play, Roman provinces in the Middle East are under assault by the Parthians, led by a Roman general opposed to the triumvirate. Antony sends Ventidius to Parthia—what is now Iran and Iraq—to put down the uprising. Ventidius leads Antony's army to a sweeping victory and slays the son of the Parthian king. Silius, Ventidius's aide, urges him to pursue the remnants of the Parthian army into Media and Mesopotamia and thus gain even greater glory. Ventidius declines to do this, and he teaches his aide a valuable political lesson: subordinates should not outshine their masters. He says that while more victories by Antony's forces might enhance their leader's reputation, Antony would be offended if Ventidius won too many honors. Ventidius's perspective on the great ones of the world provides an interesting way of looking at characters and events in the play. Moreover, his defeat of the Parthians eliminates the last threat facing the triumvirs from a foreign enemy. And the location of his victory, far from Rome, enhances the sense of the vastness of the dramatic world of *Antony and Cleopatra.*

Watch:

See Sentry; *see also* Soldiers *and* Guards

Further Reading

Adelman, Janet. "Infinite Variety: Uncertainty and Judgment in *Antony and Cleopatra.*" In *The Common Liar*, 14-52. New Haven: Yale University Press, 1973.
Adelman declares that *Antony and Cleopatra* is unique among Shakespeare's plays in that it provides a

double perspective, both comic and tragic, on its central characters. She points out that the drama forces us to make judgments, ''even as it frustrates our ability to judge rationally.'' Uncertainty is at the heart of the play, Adelman argues: it constantly raises questions but refuses to supply us with reliable answers, and thus the characters of Cleopatra and Antony remain unknowable.

Bevington, David. Introduction to *Antony and Cleopatra,* by William Shakespeare, 1-70. Cambridge: Cambridge University Press, 1990.

Bevington emphasizes the play's ambiguities and uncertainties, suggesting that it's appropriate for readers to have widely varying responses. He believes that the characterization of Cleopatra and Antony raises numerous questions that cannot be answered. Bevington also reviews twentieth-century critical commentary on Octavius Caesar and discusses his possible motivations. The introduction includes an extended stage history of the play as well as sections devoted to language, imagery, and structure.

Charney, Maurice. ''*Antony and Cleopatra.*'' In *All of Shakespeare*, 289-98. New York: Columbia University Press, 1993.

In this chapter from a book written for students, Charney discusses the play's major characters as well as several minor ones, including Enobarbus. He emphasizes Cleopatra's sexuality and eroticism, and asserts that she is Shakespeare's most complex female character. In Charney's judgment, Antony is both ennobled and weakened by his love for Cleopatra. The critic also discusses the play's language and imagery.

Frye, Northrop. ''*Antony and Cleopatra.*'' In *Northrop Frye on Shakespeare*, 122-39. New Haven: Yale University Press, 1986.

Frye's book is based on a series of informal, classroom lectures. In this chapter, Frye focuses on Cleopatra: her magnetism, her extraordinary range of moods, her vanity, and her role as the goddess of love. Frye also looks closely at Antony, stressing his natural leadership abilities, his extraordinary love for Cleopatra, and his failed attempt to imitate the greatness of his ancestor Hercules. The play should not be treated as either ''a morality play or a sentimental love story,'' Frye declares; ''both views are cop-outs.''

Goldman, Michael. ''*Antony and Cleopatra*: Action as Imaginative Command.'' In *Acting and Action in Shakespearean Tragedy*, 112-39. Princeton: Princeton University Press, 1985.

Goldman emphasizes the physical magnetism of Antony and Cleopatra and the way their love for each other shapes our perception of who they are. He points out that their greatness, their glamour, and their stature are linked to their ability to capture other people's imagination. Goldman contends that the play shows how two people deeply in love ''act upon and change each other.''

Kiernan, Pauline. ''*Antony and Cleopatra* as 'A Defence of Drama.''' In *Shakespeare's Theory of Drama*, 154-90. Cambridge: Cambridge University Press, 1996.

Kiernan argues that the play demonstrates the impossibility of ever knowing the ''truth'' about historical events and characters. As readers, she notes, we are unsure about which view of Antony is accurate— Cleopatra's or Caesar's. Our judgments are based on biased accounts, Kiernan remarks, and we should be cautious about coming to any conclusions.

Leggatt, Alexander. ''*Antony and Cleopatra.*'' In *Shakespeare's Political Drama*, 161-88. London: Routledge, 1988.

Leggatt calls attention to the contrast between heroic and realistic views of the principal characters—views derived from their own speeches as well as from what other characters have to say about them. In his opinion, the play diminishes the significance of worldly achievements: by means of close, realistic observation, it shows Rome's political leaders becoming small-minded, trivial figures. Leggatt also examines ''the mixture of triumph and defeat'' in the deaths of Antony and Cleopatra.

Mack, Maynard. ''The Stillness and the Dance: *Antony and Cleopatra.*'' In *Everybody's Shakespeare*, 197-230. Lincoln: University of Nebraska Press, 1993.

Mack regards Antony as a man out of his time—a refugee from a lost world where personal heroism was a supreme value. In Mack's opinion, the play represents ''a world in motion,'' where nothing is certain and contradiction flourishes. He notes the conflicting roles or attitudes each of the title characters takes on in the course of the play and declares that none of them defines who they really are. Mack's book is addressed to the ''common reader'' rather than to his fellow scholars.

Miles, Geoffrey. '''Infinite Variety': *Antony and Cleopatra.*'' In *Shakespeare and the Constant Romans*, 169-88. Oxford: Clarendon Press, 1996.

Miles focuses on Antony, arguing that he refuses to choose between the values of Rome and Egypt but instead tries to fuse these extremes and live life to the fullest. The critic asserts that in Acts III and IV Antony swings wildly between opposing moods and emotions, unable to define for himself who he truly is. Miles also contrasts Antony's flexibility and adaptability to Caesar's consistency—a Roman ideal that Caesar betrays through unprincipled pursuit of political success.

Neill, Michael. Introduction to *The Tragedy of Antony and Cleopatra,* by William Shakespeare, 1-130. Oxford: Clarendon Press, 1994.

Neill examines the baffling contradictions in the characters of Cleopatra and Antony as well as in the play's multitude of perspectives. He believes that the gap between the soaring language in which the lovers wrap themselves and ''the harsh reality of their decline'' is intentional—that it demonstrates the idea that human personality is a fluid, ever-changing mixture of contradictory truths. Neill provides a lengthy and detailed history of *Antony and Cleopatra* in performance. He calls attention to the difficulty of capturing the range and power of the play in a single production and to the repeated failures of some of this century's most celebrated actors to convey the full complexity of the central characters.

Rose, Mark, ed. *Twentieth Century Interpretations of "Antony and Cleopatra."* Englewood Cliffs, N.J.: Prentice-Hall, 1977.

This is a collection of eleven essays by commentators who are among this century's most prominent Shakespearean critics. The essays cover a wide range of topics. These include the play's language and style, its political elements and its epic stature, thematic issues—for example, the opposition between public and private values, and the contrast between Rome and Egypt—and such dramatic techniques as structure and characterization.

Thomas, Vivian. "Realities and Imaginings in *Antony and Cleopatra.*" In *Shakespeare's Roman Worlds*, 93-153. London: Routledge, 1989.

Thomas provides extensive commentary on Octavius Caesar. He views the Roman leader as a man who has centered his life on politics at the expense of all other human activities and emotions. Thomas also points out significant differences in the portraits of Caesar, Antony, and Cleopatra in the play and in classical historical accounts. According to the critic, Shakespeare's Antony is much more attractive and sympathetic than the Antony described in the dramatist's principal sources.

As You Like It

circa 1599-1600

Plot Summary

Act I:

The play opens in the garden of Orlando's older brother, Oliver. Orlando's comments to the servant Adam and the conversation between Oliver and Orlando reveal the tension that exists between the brothers. Their father, Sir Rowland de Boys, has died and left all to Oliver in accordance with the custom of primogeniture, a custom in which the oldest male child receives the entire family inheritance. Orlando resents being deprived of money and education, and in order to get money he arranges to try his skill in an exhibition against Charles, the wrestler of Duke Frederick. Charles is concerned that he might hurt and disgrace Orlando, so he secretly informs Oliver of his brother's intentions. Oliver encourages Charles not to hold back, determined to see his younger brother disgraced or injured. Rosalind and her cousin, Celia, witness Orlando's victory over Charles in the wrestling match, and Rosalind becomes enamored of Orlando, giving him her necklace. Duke Frederick, Celia's father, decides suddenly to banish Rosalind even though he has taken her in and treated her like a daughter for some period of time. Rosalind decides to join her father Duke Senior, whose dukedom, ironically, has been usurped by Duke Frederick, in the Forest of Arden where it is reported by Charles that ''many young gentlemen flock to him every day, and fleet the time carelessly, as they did in the golden world'' (I.i.117-18). Celia cannot bear parting with Rosalind and she resolves to go with her. The two adopt disguises in order to assure their safety and proceed to the Forest of Arden, taking Touchstone, the clown, with them.

Act II:

Duke Frederick discovers Rosalind, Celia, and Touchstone missing and suspects that their disappearance is somehow connected with Orlando. He sends for Orlando, resolved to have Oliver find him if he is missing. Adam, the faithful, old servant of Orlando's father, warns Orlando against Oliver's malevolent intentions and urges him to get away, offering him the money he has managed to save, and the two make their way to the Forest of Arden where they eventually join the exiled society of Duke Senior. Rosalind, in the guise of Ganymede, and Celia, in the guise of Aliena, meet the shepherds Corin and Silvius, and Celia buys the cottage of Corin's master. Silvius reveals that he is hopelessly in love with the shepherdess Phebe. The pessimistic Jaques meets Touchstone in the woods of Arden and is highly amused by the encounter.

Act III:

Duke Frederick demands that Oliver find and deliver Orlando, or his lands and possessions will be seized. Oliver assures Duke Frederick that he also wants to find and punish Orlando. In the Forest of Arden, Touchstone and Corin debate the respective merits of court and country living, and later Touchstone meets and resolves to marry the goatherd Audrey. Orlando, it seems, has been impressed as much by Rosalind as she has been by him, and he hangs poetic verse on the trees of the forest. The quality of that verse is much debated by Rosalind, Touchstone, and Jaques. Since Orlando does not recognize Rosalind in her disguise, Rosalind decides to have some fun with him and offers to help him woo the object of his amorous interest which she knows to be herself. Silvius's love for Phebe is revealed to be unrequited, and Phebe vehemently berates him and wants nothing to do with him. Rosalind intervenes on his behalf, telling Phebe, ''Sell when you can, you are not for all markets'' (III.v.60). In another ironic twist Phebe falls in love with Rosalind/Ganymede at first sight.

Act IV:

Rosalind, still disguised as Ganymede, continues to counsel Orlando on the proper way to court a woman, and when he must leave to dine with Duke Senior, he promises to return in two hours. Rosalind/ Ganymede informs him that she considers that promise an oath and pledge of fidelity. Orlando does not meet the deadline, but Oliver shows up and explains that Orlando has been delayed while saving Oliver from a hungry lioness. He presents Rosalind and Celia with a bloody handkerchief, evidence of that encounter, and recounts how the two brothers have been reconciled, telling of his own miraculous conversion in the Forest of Arden. Silvius presents Rosalind/Ganymede with a letter from Phebe, ostensibly meant to chastise her for her callous treatment of Phebe, but manifestly proclaiming an intense affection that places Phebe in the same position of unrequited love in which she has placed Silvius.

Act V:

In a comical scene, Touchstone acts superior to William, the simple goatherd suitor to Audrey, and dismisses him as a potential rival. It is revealed, as well, that Oliver and Celia have fallen in love during their brief acquaintance and intend to marry. Rosalind orchestrates the moment when she will reveal her true identity by extracting the following promises: Duke Senior agrees to give his daughter away in marriage; Orlando consents to marry Rosalind; Phebe agrees to marry Ganymede, and if she refuses— which of course she will when she discovers Ganymede's true identity—will marry Silvius; Silvius consents to marry Phebe. A brother to Oliver and Orlando appears briefly and relates how Duke Frederick has been miraculously converted in an encounter with a mysterious hermit. Initially intending to subdue Duke Senior and his followers through force, Duke Frederick instead decides to return, to the rightful owners, the lands of those he has exiled. Rosalind reveals herself, and all that has been problematic in gender confusion and misplaced affection is resolved in the multiple marriages of the ending.

Modern Connections

Like many modern television situation comedies, the humor of *As You Like It* depends upon the audience's suspension of disbelief. We are asked, for example, to believe that Duke Senior does not recognize his own daughter in disguise. Similarly, although Orlando does not know Rosalind all that well, we would still expect that he would be able, eventually, to recognize some quality in Ganymede that would remind him of Rosalind. And also like modern sitcoms, Shakespeare's comedy also resolves all problems neatly and quickly at the end. The conversions of the early villains, Duke Frederick and Oliver, are perhaps too neat and too quick to be believable. Similarly, the marriage combinations—Oliver and Celia; Phebe and Silvius; and Touchstone and Audrey—seem to defy rationality. Beyond the confines of the play, we might imagine that the marriages between these couples might not work since they know each other so shallowly. The coercion and deception upon which the marriage of Phebe and Silvius is based, for example, is hardly an ideal circumstance, and the marriage of Audrey and Touchstone, as Jaques suggests, "Is but for two months victuall'd" (V.iv.192), meaning that as an emotional expedition it is meagerly supplied and cannot last. The real function of neat and quick comic resolutions in this play, as in modern sitcoms, is to suggest and reinforce social values. In the idealized Elizabethan world that *As You Like It* presents, marriage represents an important element in social stability.

The idealized world of the Forest of Arden also functions in another way; it can be seen as a critique of the worlds of Duke Frederick's court and Oliver's hierarchical household. *As You Like It* is a pastoral drama, and the pastoral mode was generally accepted in Shakespeare's day as a technique for thinly veiled criticism of social institutions. Shepherds were presented as living simply in a kind of "Garden of Eden" environment remote from the ambition and deception of the court and the city. The simple basic values these shepherds living close to nature express, then, become implicit condemnations of the artificiality of all that is not natural, all that is competitive, coercive, and hierarchical. In this play, Corin is such a pastoral figure, and the simple philosophy of life he espouses can be compared with the elaborate and systematized philosophies of Jaques and Touchstone, often rendering them ridiculous in contrast. The pastoral Forest of Arden is a place in which the characters can be themselves, unpressured by the hidden desires of others. It is the modern equivalent of what we would call an emotional haven from the "rat race" of daily living, a paradisal vacation spot where a person's essence seems to surface.

The Forest of Arden operates on yet another level. It is a magical place with religious suggestions, some critics have argued. Oliver tells of a struggle in the Forest of Arden involving a serpent, typically representative of evil, and a lioness, per-

haps representative of Christianity. The presence of such animals in what is ostensibly the English countryside is unexpected and certainly allows the possibility that the encounter is meant to be read allegorically. Similarly, Duke Frederick has encountered an "old religious man" (V.iv.160) and has abandoned both worldly pursuits and his plans to subdue the exiles by force. On this level, the Forest of Arden is symbolic of a spiritual realm while Duke Frederick's court and Oliver's household represent an earthly world subject to the whims of human frailty.

As You Like It treats time in a way that is significant to our own modern era. In the Forest of Arden, there exists a timelessness in which the characters are free to pursue possibilities and live unfettered by time's constraints. In our own time, so driven by and dependent on technology, we know what it is like to be harried and constrained by time's fleeting moments. We also know, if only occasionally, the feeling of freedom from time's constant presence, those precious, unpressured moments when we can relax and be ourselves. And like the characters in *As You Like It*, we can decide which condition we prefer.

Characters

Adam:

Adam is the faithful, old servant of Sir Rowland de Boys, father to Oliver and Orlando. When Sir Rowland dies, Adam remains as a servant to the household which is now governed by the elder Oliver. He recognizes a certain inherent nobility in Orlando and sympathizes with the younger brother in his complaints against Oliver for neglecting his education and breeding. Adam is ill-treated by Oliver, and after the two brothers quarrel and physically struggle, he sides with Orlando and casts his fortune with his. He gives Orlando all of the money he has managed to save and travels with him to the Forest of Arden. In a society like Elizabethan England with rigid class distinctions, Adam represents the ideal of service, one who is motivated by loyalty and affection rather than greed and ambition. When Jaques, the pessimistic courtier in attendance upon the exiled Duke Senior, utters his fatalistic "Seven Ages of Man" speech (II.vii.139-66), concluding with a description of old age as isolated dependence, Orlando enters carrying Adam. Orlando defiantly protects the servant who has given everything to him, and the mutual generosity and dependence between Orlando and Adam contradicts the dismal picture drawn by Jaques's speech.

Aliena:

See Celia

Amiens:

Amiens is one of the lords in attendance upon Duke Senior in the Forest of Arden. He is not in servitude to Duke Senior; he has voluntarily joined him in exile. Any distinction in social standing is diminished in the egalitarian environment of Arden. He sings several songs or snatches of songs, mostly at the insistence of Jaques, all of which express the sentiment that, even in its extremities of climate, the forest is a simple and direct place, without the dishonesty that sometimes accompanies the communal associations of humans. He appears in the last scene of the play but does not speak.

Attendants:

They are the servants of Duke Frederick. They appear along with Duke Frederick, his lords, Charles, and Orlando in I.ii, a scene in which all are trying to dissuade Orlando from wrestling Charles. They do not have speaking parts.

Audrey:

Audrey is a goatherd and is even less sophisticated than the shepherds in the play. Even Touchstone impresses her, and she agrees to marry him. That marriage appears to be, as some have argued, more the product of lust and Touchstone's desire for conquest than it is of any deep affection between the two. She abandons another suitor, William, in order to be with Touchstone. In a parody of romantic love, Touchstone so twists the simple logic by which Audrey lives that she says, "I am not a slut, though I thank the gods I am foul" (III.iii.38), uttering this statement in response to the convoluted logic he has offered about court values of beauty and chastity. Audrey and Touchstone get married at the end of the play, but they have attempted to marry earlier than this. They arrange to be married by Sir Oliver Martext, but Jaques interrupts the ceremony and argues that the marriage will not be legitimate if it is performed by Sir Oliver. Jaques's argument does not convince Touchstone, but he delays the wedding anyway. Audrey does not express her feelings

> **" In a parody of romantic love, Touchstone so twists the simple logic by which Audrey lives that she says, 'I am not a slut, though I thank the gods I am foul' (III.iii.38), uttering this statement in response to the convoluted logic he has offered about court values of beauty and chastity."**

about the interrupted wedding either way, and this is typical of her reliance on Touchstone's more worldly knowledge.

Celia:

Celia is the daughter of Duke Frederick and lives at the palace. After her father ousts Duke Senior, Duke Senior's daughter Rosalind, Celia's cousin, comes to live with her, and the two seem to be very close. They are like two schoolgirls exchanging witticisms about all they observe in their somewhat sheltered world. Celia takes an active part in the witty exchanges with Le Beau, in which the two girls and Touchstone engage in endless wordplay. She, along with her cousin, tries to convince Orlando that he will be injured if he wrestles Charles, and during the wrestling match, Celia encourages him. After the match, Celia and Rosalind pun on wrestling terms like "fall" and "throw," using these terms in the language of love to discuss Rosalind's infatuation with Orlando. Celia is excited for her cousin, but much of her energy at Duke Frederick's court is siphoned into distancing herself from her father's actions, most noticeably his banishment of Orlando after the wrestling match.

When Duke Frederick suddenly demands that Rosalind leave his household, Celia does not hesitate; she decides to share Rosalind's fate and travel with her to the Forest of Arden. The two adopt disguises because travelling in the sometimes violent Elizabethan underworld was a dangerous undertaking for two women. Celia assumes the persona of a woman being escorted by "Ganymede," Rosalind's male persona, significant since Celia is the less dominant of the two women. It is also significant that Celia takes the name "Aliena." In an obvious sense, she is alienated from her father and the world of Duke Frederick's court. In another sense, she seems alienated from herself; in the Forest of Arden she seems different from the carefree adolescent she is in earlier scenes. She becomes a woman of means living in the world, buying the cottage of Corin's master and establishing a household. As a character, she recedes into the background of the pastoral world of Arden, becoming merely the go-between for Rosalind and Orlando. Her relationship with Oliver is reported to rather than witnessed by the audience. Of the two female friends in the play, Rosalind is clearly the more dynamic, Celia, perhaps, giving modern audiences the glimpse of another dimension of female identity in Elizabethan England.

Charles:

Charles is the king's wrestler, who travels about the countryside challenging all comers to best him in a match. When Charles finds out Orlando has challenged him, he informs Oliver of the fact and that his reputation as a strongman is at stake, and he is confident that he cannot lose. He asks Oliver to intervene and discourage Orlando from what he considers a foolhardy enterprise, believing that Orlando's defeat will disgrace the de Boys name. Oliver misrepresents Orlando to Charles as a dangerous villain, and the wrestler leaves with a firm resolve to punish and defeat Orlando thoroughly. In the arranged matches, Charles, not surprisingly, convincingly beats the first three challengers, but he mocks Orlando and is greatly surprised when Orlando bests him through a combination of the incentive of revenge for that mockery and Orlando's own ability. Charles informs the audience of several important plot details early in the play: Duke Frederick's banishment of his brother Duke Senior; Duke Senior's residence in Arden; Rosalind's living arrangements; and Celia's great affection for Rosalind.

Corin:

Corin is an old shepherd living in the Forest of Arden. He tends sheep for his master, a man who, according to Corin, is not very generous. The cottage of Corin's master is bought by Celia, and she becomes Corin's new mistress. His lot is improved by this transaction. Corin is first seen in the company of Silvius as the latter bemoans the intensity of his love for Phebe. When Corin cannot identify with

Silvius's hyperbolic protestations of love, Silvius accuses him of never having experienced that emotion. But Corin is old and pragmatic, and his inability to share Silvius's current emotional state suggests either that time dissipates the capacity for feeling or that the emotional states of love and rationality are, perhaps, mutually exclusive. Corin lives by a simple philosophy: He is content with the knowledge that rain makes things wet, that fire burns, and that sheep are fattened by grazing on pasture. He eats what he can get with his own hands, wears the clothes he makes himself, and is not envious of the success of others. He debates the virtues of court and country living with Touchstone, and although Touchstone declares victory in this debate, Corin's simple and direct logic contrasts with Touchstone's witty wordplay, exposing the superficiality of court life and revealing its enslavement to convention. Corin's simple honesty and Silvius's lovelorn agitation are split aspects of the stock pastoral figure employed by elite writers to comment on social and political circumstances at court and in the city.

Dennis:

Dennis is another servant in the de Boys household, which is now in the sole possession of Oliver. He appears briefly in an early scene, performing the task of announcing a guest.

Duke Frederick:

See Frederick

Duke Senior:

See Senior

Foresters:

There are no actual foresters in the play, only Duke Senior's attendant lords dressed as foresters. They are playacting in a way that parallels the pastoral mode itself since the literary pastoral voice of the lowly shepherd was invented by aristocrats as they imagined shepherds would speak. *See* Lords

Frederick (Duke Frederick):

Duke Frederick is the younger brother of Duke Senior and has somehow gained enough power to banish him from the court. He plunders the estates of those lords who have accompanied Duke Senior into exile. Duke Frederick seems to be acting capriciously and arbitrarily when he banishes Rosalind, but her banishment probably stems from the animosity that exists between himself and Duke Senior. She is, after all, Duke Senior's daughter, and

Duke Frederick has only taken her in to appease his own daughter Celia. It may also be conjectured that he has witnessed or heard report of Rosalind's attraction to Orlando and her gift of a necklace to him and is upset with her for befriending the son of Sir Rowland de Boys, his avowed enemy. Again, this probably stems from the quarrel between Duke Frederick and Duke Senior, the latter having had a great affection for Sir Rowland. Duke Frederick has already banished Orlando for his paternity and will eventually banish Oliver for the same reason, after Oliver has failed to produce and punish Orlando in accordance with Duke Frederick's desires. Duke Frederick becomes alarmed at the popularity enjoyed by his older brother in the forest, and he sets out to remove Duke Senior and his followers by force. He is dissuaded from this purpose and is miraculously converted to the contemplative life by a religious man in the Forest of Arden.

The rupture in the relationship between Duke Frederick and Duke Senior parallels that of Oliver and Orlando although the virtuous brother is younger in the latter pair and older in the former. Fraternal envy and disharmony is a common theme in several of Shakespeare's plays (for example, *Hamlet* and *The Tempest*), often recalling the Biblical story of Cain and Abel. For Shakespeare, it is necessary to reconcile these fraternal feuds in order to restore the fabric of social order. It is perhaps this necessity for restoring order that accounts for Duke Frederick's sudden conversion by the religious hermit in Arden, a place where the ill effects of desire and ambition are temporarily suspended.

Ganymede:

See Rosalind

Hymen:

Hymen is the Greek god of marriage. In *As You Like It*, a person representing Hymen officiates at the marriages of the betrothed couples, symbolically blessing those unions.

Jaques:

A lord attending the banished Duke Senior, Jaques seems less enthusiastic about the natural simplicity of Arden as the other characters there, but he does not entirely dampen their enthusiasm. Rather, Duke Senior and his followers are amused by his pessimism about an environment which they celebrate as basic and unflattering, an evironment which allows them to be themselves. For example, they are

> Celia assumes the persona of a woman being escorted by 'Ganymede,' Rosalind's male persona, significant since Celia is the less dominant of the two women."

highly amused when Jaques empathizes with the deer wounded by one of them, moaning and weeping for the pain of the deer, the killing of which is seen by Duke Senior and his followers as sad but necessary for survival and part of the correct order of things. Jaques's identification with the deer is illustrative of the alternative perspective he provides throughout the play.

The alternative perspective Jaques provides allows the audience to see the duplicitousness that invades even the Forest of Arden. He accuses Duke Senior and his followers of having usurped the claim that the deer have to the forest as its natural inhabitants. Although Duke Senior regrets having to gore them, he does not see, as Jaques does, that his dominance over the deer is similar to the law of "right by power" Duke Senior thinks he has escaped by fleeing the court and taking refuge in the forest. Jaques also sees through Touchstone's relationship with Audrey. If Touchstone thinks he can feign affection for Audrey and hide "amongst the rest of the country copulatives," (V.iv.55-6) Jaques sees the relationship for what it is, simple lust and a denigration of the institution of marriage.

In his "Seven Ages of Man Speech" (II.vii.139-66), Jaques says, "All the world's a stage, / And all the men and women merely players" (II.vii.139-40). He seems to see nothing of lasting value in life because these players come and go; it would seem that one player is as good as another. About the stages humans pass through as they mature, he has nothing good to say: infants are "mewling" and "puking"; the schoolboy is "whining"; lovers sigh melodramatically; the soldier fights for as inconsequential a thing as reputation; the judge is corpulent and self-indulgent; the aged man shrinks in his clothes and wheezes; and finally, near death, man becomes a child again with no teeth, failing eyesight, and a loss of appetite. Jaques expresses a

> **The rupture in the relationship between Duke Frederick and Duke Senior parallels that of Oliver and Orlando . . .**"

pessimism here that reins in the optimism expressed by Duke Senior and his followers.

Jaques is not unaffected by the transforming power of the Forest of Arden. He has been a libertine, pursuing his appetites and ambitions. The forest has made him contemplative of life and sorry for his past mistakes. It seems fitting that at the end of the play he announces his intention to go and inquire about the contemplative religious life now embraced by Duke Frederick and forego the group weddings and communal celebrations with which the play concludes.

Jaques (brother of Oliver and Orlando):

This is a son of Sir Rowland de Boys and brother of Oliver and Orlando. He is referred to in the beginning of the play when Orlando remarks that Oliver has done the right thing with Jaques, sending him to school where he is reported to be doing well. He does not appear in the play until the final scene and has only a brief role reporting the sudden conversion of Duke Frederick. He is referred to only as "Second Brother" in this instance. Having two Jaques in the play leads to some confusion, and the question of whether the confusion is the result of revision or Shakespeare's inadvertent mistake has not been resolved.

Le Beau:

Le Beau is a courtier, presumably in the court of Duke Frederick. He reports to Celia and Rosalind the result of Charles's earlier wrestling matches and announces that the two cousins will witness the match between Orlando and Charles if they remain where they are. He serves as the pivot point, the straight man, for the witty vollies of Celia, Rosalind, and Touchstone. He later warns Orlando that Duke Frederick is displeased with Orlando's success and advises him to leave the vicinity, suggesting that not all the courtiers have been compromised by the influence of Duke Frederick's ambition, but suggesting, also, the necessity for masking one's true feelings at court.

Lords:

When Duke Senior seeks refuge in the forest from the persecution of his brother, a number of lords, or wealthy landholders, go along with him. In II.i, two characters designated as "1. Lord" and "2. Lord" inform Duke Senior of Jaques's melancholy weeping for the "sobbing deer" which has been wounded in the hunt. Duke Frederick, too, is surrounded by several lords. We can distinguish Duke Senior's lords and Duke Frederick's lords only by setting and context. Amiens and Jaques are lords as are the foresters.

Martext (Sir Oliver Martext):

Sir Oliver Martext is a country vicar, a parish priest. He is consulted by Audrey and Touchstone concerning their impending marriage. Since the text of the spoken marriage ceremony is what makes the wedding official, his name is appropriate: he will mar the text of that ceremony, which is itself a travesty of what a real marriage should be. His name may also suggest the Martin Marprelate controversy of the late sixteenth century. In 1598, an anonymous pamphleteer, adopting the persona Martin Marprelate (to mar or injure a prelate, namely a Protestant bishop), published a series of attacks vilifying and discrediting the Protestant episcopacy (church government based on the hierarchy of bishops). These pamphlets were a matter of great concern to religious and governmental officials. It is appropriate that a character named Sir Oliver Martext is consulted about a marriage that discredits the very institution with which the vicar is intimately connected.

Oliver:

Oliver is Orlando's older brother and takes over the responsibility of raising him. He so dislikes Orlando that when the brothers quarrel, Oliver strikes Orlando and then orders him out of the house. Oliver even goes so far as to assure Duke Frederick that he hates Orlando as much as the duke does, knowing full well that the duke intends to apprehend him and punish him.

As the eldest son of Sir Rowland de boys, Oliver has inherited the entire estate. The play never explains why he elects to send the second brother, Jaques, off to school but neglects the education of Orlando. Perhaps, as some critics have suggested, he is extremely envious of his younger brother's talent, generosity, and aristocratic impulses and wishes to be rid of Orlando so that he might appear in a better light without competition from his younger sibling. This explanation of Oliver's behavior must remain a matter of conjecture only. It is likely, though, that Shakespeare is using Oliver, as he uses Duke Frederick, to emphasize the social upheaval that results when brothers fight. Like Duke Frederick, Oliver has a sudden, almost unbelievable change of heart toward his brother. Since social order is symbolically restored only when brothers reconcile, it may sometimes be necessary for Shakespeare to effect this reconciliation even if it is sometimes unbelievable within the plot. In *As You Like It*, bringing the feuding brothers together again takes precedence over consistent and plausible characterization.

Like so many of the other characters, Oliver changes when he enters the Forest of Arden. Not only is his attitude toward Orlando changed, but his capacity for feeling emotion seems to increase also. Although his betrothal to Celia is somewhat quick, his feelings for her seem genuine. Just as important is Celia's affection for Oliver. Oliver is from an aristocratic family, but Celia is the daughter of a duke, a member of the nobility. This is yet another example of the transforming power of the forest, in that arbitrary social distinctions are suspended. The forest setting allows Oliver's true nature to reveal itself and shows him fit to marry a noblewoman, just as it does with Orlando.

Orlando:

Orlando is the youngest son of the deceased Sir Rowland de Boys and a brother to Oliver. He resents the harsh treatment he receives at Oliver's hands and complains that Oliver neglects to educate him. Orlando feels that he is being ''kept'' like the livestock. He is fed and he grows physically but not intellectually or socially. Despite this neglect, Orlando's talents and his aristocratic nature reveal themselves. Although there is no mention of Orlando having had formal training in the sport of wrestling, he defeats someone who makes his living wrestling. Having seen the match, Rosalind becomes attracted to Orlando, and gives him her necklace.

After escaping to the Forest of Arden, Orlando encounters Rosalind, who is posing as Ganymede. Again, although he has not been taught to write formal verse, Orlando's instinct is to write poetry to Rosalind and express his feelings for her. According to Rosalind and Touchstone, the verse is stiff

> In his 'Seven Ages of Man Speech' (II.vii.139-66), Jaques says, 'All the world's a stage, / And all the men and women merely players' (II.vii.139-40). He seems to see nothing of lasting value in life because these players come and go; it would seem that one player is as good as another.''

and halting, yet Orlando's inclination to turn to poetry as an emotive outlet attests to his aristocratic nature. Thinking that Ganymede (Rosalind) is a young man knowledgeable about the relationships between men and women, Orlando allows himself to be educated in the finer points of courtship.

In a comical scene, Jaques and Orlando meet as strangers and speak to each other according to polite convention. Each tells the other that he would rather be alone, and they agree that they should meet less often. The polite veneer of their speech does not quite fit with the content of their speeches. We get the sense that Jaques and Orlando are complete opposites, Jaques a pessimistic and brooding character, and Orlando an optimistic fellow intent upon experiencing life to the fullest.

Another indicator of Orlando's virtuous nature is his treatment of Adam. As the two make their way to the Forest of Arden, the trip proves too arduous for the faithful, old servant. When he can no longer go on, Orlando is ready to fight Duke Senior and all of his attendant lords in order to procure food for him. And when Jaques expresses a characteristic pessimism about the value of human life, Orlando carries Adam into the company of exiles, mute testimony for the value of mutual respect and support between human beings.

As a disadvantaged younger brother, Orlando probably would have been received sympathetically by a good portion of Shakespeare's audience. Under the system of primogeniture, the eldest male child inherited the entire estate, leaving younger male children to make their own marks in the world. These younger brothers would often have to learn a

❝ Like Duke Frederick, Oliver has a sudden, almost unbelievable change of heart toward his brother.❞

profession and would apprentice themselves to master craftsmen in London. Shakespeare's professional theater was a major source of diversion and entertairment for these young apprentices, and we should expect that they would have identified, to some degree, with Orlando's situation.

Although Orlando's intelligence may seem to be in question because he fails to recognize Rosalind in her disguise as Ganymede in the Forest of Arden, his failure to recognize Rosalind and his willingness to be manipulated by her are better attributed to his eagerness to compensate for his lack of education and become a student of the formal art of courtship. He proves to be a good student and passes the tests Rosalind presents him as she assesses his faithfulness and devotion. In the last act, Rosalind reveals herself, and she and Orlando are married.

Pages:

In Act V, Touchstone encounters two pages who are probably the servants of Duke Senior or the lords who have joined him in exile. They sing a song and quibble with Touchstone about their execution of that song. Quite fittingly, the song is about love and springtime in nature, the Forest of Arden seeming to promote feelings of love in those who venture into its confines.

Phebe:

Phebe is the proud and disdainful mistress of Silvius. She is callous to his feelings and apparently wants nothing to do with him. Ironically, Phebe finds herself in a situation similar to that of Silvius, who is in love with her, when she falls in love at first sight with Rosalind disguised as Ganymede and is rebuked by him/her. She agrees to marry Silvius if she should decide for any reason that she does not want to marry Ganymede. Of course, she will reject Ganymede when she discovers that he is really Rosalind. We may think that Phebe will be upset with her consolation prize of Silvius, feeling somehow duped into marrying someone for whom she

has no affection. But perhaps her own experience of unrequited love will make her sympathetic to his experience and provide a basis for their relationship.

Phebe is really a character of convention. She is the typical object of poetic and pastoral longing, depicted as unattainable in order to make her worthy of intense pursuit. If she were too easily caught, she would not be worth the chase. For Elizabethans especially, the creation of the idealized woman as distant and disdainful was a reaction to Queen Elizabeth, the Virgin Queen, who became a symbol for unattainable desire. In regard to Phebe's pursuit of Ganymede, it is appropriate here to bring up a convention of Shakespearean theater: young boys played the parts of the female characters. It has not been resolved whether Shakespearean audiences suspended disbelief entirely and accepted fully the characters as female or were constantly amused by the gender confusion. In any event, the prospect of a boy playing Rosalind playing a boy and being pursued by a boy playing Phebe is one that would boggle the imagination of most people.

Rosalind:

Rosalind is Celia's cousin and daughter to Duke Senior. When her father is banished by Celia's father, Duke Frederick, Rosalind lives with Celia until Duke Frederick banishes her too. She adopts a male disguise as a measure of security for her journey with Celia and Touchstone to the Forest of Arden. She adopts the name "Ganymede," a telling name since, in Greek mythology, Ganymede was an androgynous youth raped by Zeus. When she arrives in Arden, Rosalind keeps her male disguise even though she is now safe and has no reason to do so.

When Celia discovers Orlando's poetry to Rosalind marring the tree trunks, she informs Rosalind of the author's identity. Initially, it seems as though Rosalind hangs onto her disguise in order to have some fun with Orlando. As the play progresses, Rosalind realizes that her male disguise gives her a certain power that she does not have as a woman. She is able to manipulate Orlando and extract from him his deepest secrets concerning her. Disguised as a man, she has power over other characters too. She is pursued by Phebe and can intervene in her relationship with Silvius.

Like her father, Duke Senior, Rosalind is a dominant presence in the play. She mediates many of the contradictions posed by the play. For example, Orlando wants to be a student of the formal patterns of courtship, but this desire is out of place in Arden where conventions are unimportant. Rosalind teaches him that, in romantic love, faithfulness and devotion are more important than any prescribed steps in a process of wooing. Orlando passes the test and is rewarded with Rosalind's reciprocal love. Faced with Phebe's ill treatment of Silvius, Rosalind teaches her a lesson about the importance of considering others' pain and suffering.

Rosalind's dual nature serves to mediate between the pastoral world of Arden and the rule-bound world of the court. Nature is often characterized as feminine—''Mother Nature''—nurturing growth and diversity. The masculine world is bound by time and conventions, rules and regulations devised to insure order and conformance. Rosalind/Ganymede knows what it is like to be both a man and a woman, and this knowledge enables her to understand the conflicts between the masculine and feminine worlds, the court and the Forest of Arden respectively, and better equips her to deal with those conflicts. It is the increased power granted by Rosalind's dual gender that differentiates her from Celia, the two characters seeming so much alike in the play's earlier scenes. Celia is in a sense bound by her inflexible identity.

Rosalind, like Phebe, represents an aspect of Queen Elizabeth, who liked to speak of her ''two bodies''—her frail womanly body and her body politic, the masculine identity she derived from being the monarch of England. The Queen dressed in masculine attire at Tilbury in order to rally her English soldiers as they awaited an invasion by the Spanish. It is this kind of gender confusion that Elizabethan audiences would have been aware of, and it is perhaps inevitable that they would have seen Rosalind as an allusion to the Queen, at once feminine and powerful.

Senior (Duke Senior):

Duke Senior is the virtuous elder brother of Duke Frederick and is banished by him from the court. He takes up residence in the Forest of Arden and is joined by his loyal followers there. He attracts followers because it is reported that he is living a life there that is simple and attractive, the life lived in the ''golden age'' when men did not work for other men but lived off the land and took care of themselves. Duke Senior praises the environment of Arden as devoid of flattering ambition. He hears honest counselors in the babbling brooks and whispering winds. He feels uncompromised reality in the biting wind and soaking rain.

> **Thinking that Ganymede (Rosalind) is a young man knowledgeable about the relationships between men and women, Orlando allows himself to be educated in the finer points of courtship.''**

Although he retains the title of ''duke'' in the forest, he does not rule by force or coercion; in fact, he does not seem to rule at all. The society formed in the Forest of Arden is an egalitarian one, a society based on equality. At the end of the play, Duke Senior regains all of his hereditary rights befitting his commendable nature. It is also made clear that Duke Senior and the others will return to the court which they have left behind, and we can only assume that the lessons learned in the Forest of Arden will be applied in social relationships when all return to the society from which they have been temporarily banished. Duke Senior does not have a large part in *As You Like It*, but his presence is felt throughout the play as a cohesive force pulling together both discrete characters and situations.

Silvius:

Silvius is a young shepherd deeply in love with Phebe. She is the sole object of his thoughts; he cannot keep his mind on anything else. He has intended to purchase the cottage owned by Corin's master, but, as Corin tells us, this kind of financial concern is the furthest thing from his mind as he dotes on Phebe. Phebe treats Silvius harshly. In one scene, Corin tells Rosalind and Celia that if they wish to witness how the poor lovelorn shepherd, Silvius, is getting on they should follow him. In the spectacle that follows, Phebe not only rejects Silvius's offers of devotion but tells him that if looks could kill he would be at that moment slain.

Like Phebe, Silvius is a conventional character. He speaks the language of hyperbole, perhaps grossly exaggerating his feelings for Phebe, certainly exaggerating her qualities. She is, after all, a working woman with a working woman's chapped and callous hands. Silvius disparages himself and disallows that anyone else might have experienced love as deeply as he, in an attempt to elevate Phebe. As a conventional pastoral character, it might be said that he is more in love with the idea of being in love than he is truly enamored of Phebe.

Touchstone:

Touchstone is a clown, or fool, in Duke Frederick's household. He may not be a vigorous male character, but he is a man nonetheless, and Celia and Rosalind decide to take him along as an extra measure of security on their journey to the Forest of Arden. When he arrives in the forest he finds that his familiarity with the language and customs of the court impress the simple shepherds and goatherds, so he uses this advantage to further his lustful designs on Audrey and marry her in what is typically described as a travesty of romantic love and marriage.

The Elizabethan term ''clown'' could be applied to any simple yokel. The term ''fool'' referred to a court jester often wearing motley, a kind of multi-colored and outlandish attire. Elizabethan fools were very often ''naturals,'' simple unassuming idiots who amused the courtiers with their naivete or misunderstanding. In Shakespeare's plays, fools arguably function as either the conscience of some basically noble but misled character (for example, in *King Lear*) or as a device to deflate and expose the pomposity of characters who overstep their proper positions (for example, in *Twelfth Night*). Additionally, Shakespeare's fools amuse with their convoluted logic and witty plays on words. In *As You Like It*, Touchstone, although he delights with his wit, serves a somewhat different purpose.

A ''touchstone'' was a stone that was used to determine if metals were precious. Rubbed against a touchstone, gold and silver would leave a distinguishable mark. ''Touchstone'' has come to signify anything that tests and reveals virtue or worth. This is the purpose Touchstone serves in the play. When he is in the company of other characters, he brings out their true virtue. For example, when he debates Corin, the audience sees the true value of Corin's simple philosophy in contrast to Touchstone' argument for argument's sake, and Corin's pastoral life seems to have real substance; it is not a life based solely on witticisms and conventional language. In another example, Touchstone discusses with Jaques the ''lie circumstantial,'' one step in an elaborate form of argumentation that replaces genuine passion with social convention. The fact that Jaques participates in this discussion at all reveals that he values that social convention beyond the simple life he is trying to imitate.

Jaques, who is greatly amused by Touchstone, reports that the clown has produced a timepiece from his pocket during their encounter in the forest. Touchstone has brought the ''dial'' with him from Duke Frederick's court where the timepiece was perhaps essential. In the timelessness of the Forest of Arden, the appearance of the watch draws attention to the conflicting values the two different realms place on the experience of time, and the timepiece is as out of place in the forest as Touchstone himself.

William:

William is a simple goatherd and suitor to Audrey. Like the other unsophisticated pastoral figures, he is impressed by Touchstone, and he allows himself to be intimidated by him. He is thoroughly cowed by Touchstone's threats and relinquishes his claims to Audrey with little or no resistance.

Further Reading

Barber, C. L. *Shakespeare's Festive Comedy: A Study of Dramatic Form and Its Relation to Social Custom*. Princeton: Princeton University Press, 1959. Reprint, 1972.
> Barber discusses *As You Like It* as part of a theme developed to explain several of Shakespeare's comedies. He proposes that the Forest of Arden is a place that temporarily suspends society's rules and regulations and allows the characters to gain an understanding of themselves.

Barton, Anne. Introduction to *As You Like It*, by William Shakespeare. In *The Riverside Shakespeare*, edited by G. Blakemore Evans, 365-68. Boston: Houghton Mifflin, 1974.
> Barton gives a general analysis of the play's plot and structure. She emphasizes Rosalind's role in resolving many of the contradictions presented by the play. She also discusses the characterizations of Celia, Jaques, and Touchstone.

Colie, Rosalie L. ''Perspectives on Pastoral: Romance, Comic and Tragic.'' In *Shakespeare's Living Art*, 243-83. Princeton: Princeton University Press, 1974.
> Colie positions *As You Like It* within the history of pastoral from medieval to Renaissance times. In order to understand what Shakespeare is doing in his pastoral drama, Colie argues, it is important to see how he

uses the genre differently than or similarly to his predecessors and contemporaries.

Doebler, John. ''Orlando: Athlete of Virtue.'' *Shakespeare Survey* 26 (1973): 111-17.

Doebler examines the wrestling match between Orlando and Charles and argues that Orlando is a champion of virtue over vice. He compares the wrestling episode to tales of Herculean exploits and biblical stories of David and Goliath.

Frye, Roland M. *Shakespeare and Christian Doctrine*. Princeton: Princeton University Press, 1963.

Those interested in reading the religious resonances in *As You Like It* might want to consult Frye's analysis of the play in light of contemporary theological arguments. Frye argues that the play embraces the ways in which nature was understood through human wisdom and Christian understanding.

Goldsmith, Robert Hillis. *Wise Fools in Shakespeare*. East Lansing: Michigan State University Press, 1955.

Goldsmith discusses the several types of fools in Shakespeare's plays and suggests that Touchstone changes throughout the course of *As You Like It*. He argues specifically that Shakespeare changes Touchstone's characterization to fit the talents of a specific comic actor in his acting company.

Gurr, Andrew. *Playgoing in Shakespeare's London*. Cambridge: Cambridge University Press, 1987.

Gurr's book is especially useful for understanding the properties and circumstances of the Shakespearean stage. He also discusses the dual nature of Shakespearean audiences, those spectators who might have attended plays for the comical and physically raucous action they presented, and the listening audience which might have been more sensitive to the playwrights' intellectual allusions.

Halio, Jay L. '''No Clock in the Forest': Time in *As You Like It*.'' In *Twentieth Century Interpretations of As You Like It*, edited by Jay L. Halio, 88-97. Englewood Cliffs, N. J.: Prentice-Hall, 1968.

Much is made of the timelessness of the golden age present in the Forest of Arden. Halio discusses this timelessness in comparison to the consciousness of time Touchstone brings with him into the forest from the court and city.

Hole, Christina. *English Sports and Pastimes*. London: B. T. Batsford, 1949.

Hole provides information about wrestling as part of an aristocratic education concerned with a gentleman's need to maintain a certain martial prowess.

McFarland, Thomas. ''For Other Than For Dancing Measures: The Complications of *As You Like It*.'' In *Shakespeare's Pastoral Comedy*, 98-121. Chapel Hill: University of North Carolina Press, 1972.

McFarland discusses the allusion to Cain and Abel in the quarrels between the brothers in *As You Like It*. He also discusses the contrast between the comic Touchstone and the bitter Jaques and makes mention of Hymen's song as inadequate for totally resolving the complications of the play.

Muir, Kenneth. *Shakespeare's Comic Sequence*. Liverpool: Liverpool University Press; New York: Barnes & Noble, 1979.

Muir examines the different kinds of love in the play and discusses its pastoral conventions.

Ridley, M. R. ''*As You Like It*.'' In *Shakespeare's Plays: A Commentary*, 121-24. London: J. M. Dent, 1937.

Ridley proposes that Shakespeare wrote *As You Like It* as a diversion from the arduous task of writing the tragedies that preceded it. He is impressed with the play's overall warmth and its good-natured characters.

Turner, Frederick. ''*As You Like It*: 'Subjective,' 'Objective,' and 'Natural' Time.'' In *Shakespeare and the Nature of Time: Moral and Philosophical Themes in Some Plays and Poems of William Shakespeare*, 23-44. Oxford: Clarendon Press, 1971.

Turner discusses the concepts of time advanced in the play especially in relation to the passing of time framed in Jaques's ''Seven Ages of Man'' speech.

Williamson, Marilyn L. ''The Masque of Hymen in *As You Like It*.'' *Comparative Drama* 2 (1968): 248-58.

Williamson argues that Hymen's function is to bring together the themes of love and time in *As You Like It*. By overseeing the marriages in the play, Hymen unites the past and future of the couples while at the same time providing a fitting outlet for their desire to perpetuate the species.

The Comedy of Errors

circa 1592-94

Plot Summary

Act I:

The play takes place in Ephesus, an ancient Greek city in Asia Minor. Ephesus has cut off all trade with the city of Syracuse because the Syracusan duke has treated Ephesian merchants badly, holding them for ransom. The duke of Ephesus has retaliated in kind, proclaiming that all Syracusan merchants apprehended in Ephesus will be killed if they cannot pay a ransom of one thousand marks. In the opening scene, Egeon, a Syracusan merchant, has been apprehended under Ephesian law and is sentenced to death since he does not have the means to pay his own ransom. When he is asked how he has come to be in Ephesus, Egeon recounts a sad tale: many years before, he had been married and had fathered twin boys, both named Antipholus. At the same moment as his own sons were born, a poor woman nearby had given birth to twin boys, both named Dromio. Since she did not have the means to raise those boys, Egeon bought them as servants for his sons. When he and his wife were separated in a shipwreck, one of the infant Antipholuses and one of the infant Dromios were left in the care of his wife; the other infant Antipholus and infant Dromio were left in the care of Egeon. When Antipholus of Syracuse turned eighteen, Egeon allowed him to go in search of his lost mother and twin brother, taking his servant Dromio with him. The confusion begins when, shortly after, Antipholus of Syracuse arrives

in Ephesus, unaware that both his father and brother are there. He sends the Syracusan Dromio to secure their belongings and a sum of gold at the Centaur Inn. In the absence of the Syracusan Dromio, Dromio of Ephesus enters and mistakes the Syracusan Antipholus for his own master, Antipholus of Ephesus. He tells the mistaken twin that his wife Adriana awaits him at the dinner which is going bad in his long absence. Antipholus of Syracuse is not married and believes that Dromio is fooling with him. When Dromio is ignorant of the gold and the Centaur, Antipholus of Syracuse becomes impatient and strikes him. Dromio of Ephesus runs off.

Act II:

Dromio of Ephesus returns home and reports what has transpired to Adriana and her sister, Luciana. They believe that Dromio has spoken to Antipholus of Ephesus, and they suspect the latter of being unfaithful to Adriana. In the meantime, the Syracusan Dromio has returned from the Centaur, and the Syracusan Antipholus berates him for having casually perpetrated a practical joke in environs in which they need to be cautious. The Syracusan Dromio does not know what he is talking about, and in denying his master's charges, he incurs a beating. Adriana and Luciana enter and mistake Antipholus of Syracuse for his twin brother. They call him home to dinner, and although the Syracusan twin does not know them, he goes along with them to dine.

Act III:

Angelo, a goldsmith, and Balthazar, an Ephesian merchant, accompany Antipholus of Ephesus to his home. On the way there, the latter asks Angelo to cover for his time away from Adriana by telling her that he has been at Angelo's shop, watching the goldsmith make a gold necklace intended for her. He then makes fun of the Ephesian Dromio for having suggested that he was beaten by his master in the marketplace for misappropriating a sum of gold given to him. When they reach Antipholus's Ephesian home, the gates are locked against him, the Syracusan Antipholus is dining within, and the Syracusan Dromio has been stationed as a sentry behind the locked door. Although Antipholus of Ephesus protests loudly, he is not permitted to enter because Adriana and Luciana mistakenly believe they are already dining with him and consider the commotion outside just a prank. Balthazar dissuades the Ephesian twin from physically breaking into the

house by suggesting that it would cause a public scandal. Antipholus of Ephesus is quite upset and vows to give the gold necklace made for Adriana to the courtezan, who is the hostess of an inn called the Porpentine. He arranges to have Angelo deliver the necklace to him there later. Meanwhile, inside the home of Antipholus of Ephesus, the Syracusan Antipholus takes Luciana aside and tells her he is interested in her and not her sister and his supposed wife. The Syracusan Dromio expresses to his master his dismay at being pursued by Luce, the Ephesian Dromio's reportedly overweight and ugly romantic interest. Later, Angelo mistakenly gives the gold necklace to Antipholus of Syracuse, who is amazed when Angelo refuses immediate payment for it. Surprised and confused by all that is happening in Ephesus, the Syracusan twin tells his Dromio to book them for passage on the first ship leaving that city.

Act IV:

Angelo is confronted in the marketplace by a merchant to whom Angelo owes money, a sum very close to what Antipholus of Ephesus owes Angelo for the gold necklace. But, of course, the Ephesian twin has never received the necklace, and he denies having received it when Angelo asks him for payment. Angelo has him arrested. Antipholus of Ephesus has sent his Dromio to buy a rope with which the former, still angry at his wife, entertains hanging her. The Syracusan Dromio now appears, instead, and informs the Ephesian Antipholus that their sea passage has been booked, making the Ephesian twin look even more guilty in front of Angelo and the others. The Ephesian Antipholus sends the Syracusan Dromio to Adriana for bail money. Although he is reluctant to return to that place because of the presence there of Luce, whom he finds so distasteful, he does return and procures the money from Adriana and Luciana. But when he returns, he finds the Syracusan Antipholus instead and is astonished that he has escaped arrest. The Syracusan pair are then confronted by the courtezan from the Porpentine, who requests the gold necklace in payment for a ring she has given Antipholus of Ephesus at dinner. The Syracusan Antipholus and Dromio flee the courtezan. Then, the Ephesian Dromio returns to the Ephesian Antipholus with a rope instead of the money for his bail and is beaten for his efforts. At that moment Adriana, Luciana, and the courtezan enter, and the Ephesian twin accuses his wife of having locked him out of his home while she entertained a less-than-reputable crowd. Because his behavior seems highly erratic to Adriana and Luciana—to everyone, in fact—they think that his madness bespeaks his possession by devils, and they have brought along one Doctor Pinch to exorcise those demons. They want to take Antipholus of Ephesus with them, but the jailer is worried about losing his fee and his prisoner and will not let him go. He leaves with the prisoner, and, shortly after, Adriana and Luciana see the Syracusan Antipholus and Dromio running frightened through the streets with swords drawn and think Antipholus of Ephesus has escaped.

Act V:

Angelo is apologizing to the merchant to whom he owes money and has inconvenienced when Antipholus of Syracuse enters with the Syracusan Dromio and openly admits having received the gold necklace. Angelo challenges him for his brazen behavior and they draw swords. Just then, Adriana, Luciana, and the courtezan enter and beg Angelo not to harm Antipholus of Syracuse, whom they mistake for his twin and consider mad. At this, the Syracusan pair flee and take sanctuary in the religious priory of the abbess. Adriana demands that the abbess relinquish the seemingly mad pair, but the abbess refuses, intending to use her own skill to nurse them back to health. The duke enters with Egeon, whose appointed hour of execution has arrived, and offers Egeon one last chance to procure the money for his ransom. Adriana enters and implores the duke to intervene with the abbess, but, just then, a messenger enters and announces that Antipholus and Dromio of Ephesus have escaped their bonds and have beaten Doctor Pinch. Antipholus of Ephesus enters and begs the duke to redress, on the strength of the Ephesian twin's long allegiance, the wrongs done to him by Adriana and Doctor Pinch. Egeon recognizes Antipholus of Ephesus as his son but thinks he is his Syracusan counterpart. The Ephesian Antipholus denies having ever seen Egeon. In trying to sort things out, the duke hears scattered testimonies, and the situation grows more and more confused until the abbess enters and, in a surprise to both the characters and the audience, recognizes Egeon as her long-lost husband. She is accompanied by Antipholus and Dromio of Syracuse, and when the others see the pairs of twins side by side and learn that the abbess had been separated from her young charge, Antipholus of Ephesus, many years before, the confusion of preceding events dissipates and the family that was fragmented by shipwreck is reunited.

Modern Connections

The Comedy of Errors is believed by many scholars to be Shakespeare's first play. (Some argue it may have been written as early as 1589). Many elements of the play seem unbelievable and are deliberately contrived for their comic effect. The confusions of identity in the play turn on the highly unlikely possibility that each pair of twins, the Antipholuses and the Dromios, would have the same name. It is also highly unlikely that the abbess could have lived so many years in Ephesus unaware of the presence, in that city, of her son, Antipholus of Ephesus. And it is improbable that Egeon and Antipholus of Syracuse would simultaneously end up in Ephesus. More importantly, Antipholus of Syracuse never speculates that people in Ephesus might be mistaking him for his twin brother, a brother for whom he has been diligently searching. As the title of the play suggests, the play is a comedy and, perhaps, is not meant to be taken at all seriously. But Shakespeare's selection of Ephesus for the setting points to a more serious element in the play and underscores a stark contrast between Elizabethan and modern conceptions about the "truth" or "reality" of experience.

Ephesus was a place long associated with witchcraft and sorcery, most notably in St. Paul's Epistle to the Ephesians. Antipholus of Syracuse alludes to that witchcraft and sorcery on several occasions. When Dromio of Ephesus mistakenly calls him home to dinner, unaware that Antipholus of Syracuse has just entrusted Dromio of Syracuse with a fair amount of gold, he says, upon the Ephesian Dromio's exit,

> They say this town is full of cozenage:
> As nimble jugglers that deceive the eye,
> Dark-working sorcerers that change the mind,
> Soul-killing witches that deform the body. . .
> (I.ii.97-100)

He is constantly amazed that the citizens of Ephesus give him gifts, invite him to dinner, and seem to know him through supernatural means. His suspicions about witchcraft culminate in his confrontation with the courtezan, a lewd woman who presumes some intimacy with him. He cries, "Avaunt, thou witch!" (IV.iii.79), and he and Dromio flee in fear.

Antipholus of Ephesus has similar problems. He has lived in that city for many years and has a solid reputation as a businessman. When his friends and colleagues encounter the different demeanor of Antipholus of Syracuse, they conclude that the Ephesian Antipholus is behaving madly. They attribute that madness to possession by evil spirits at the instigation of the witches and sorcerers associated with Ephesus. Adriana believes her husband is possessed and has asked Doctor Pinch, a conjurer, to counteract, with his own kind of sorcery, the demonic spirits troubling her husband. The Ephesian Antipholus vehemently denies that he is possessed and strikes Doctor Pinch. To which the doctor responds,

> I charge thee, Sathan, hous'd within this man,
> To yield possession to my holy prayers,
> And to thy state of darkness hie thee straight:
> I conjure thee by all the saints in heaven!
>
> (IV.iv.54-57)

Adriana and Luciana, according to the best wisdom of the age for dealing with the possessed, intend to establish Antipholus of Ephesus in a dark vault and allow Doctor Pinch to perform a ritualized exorcism. The abbess, having been told that Antipholus of Syracuse is possessed, will bring him to his senses again ''With wholesome syrups, drugs, and holy prayers'' (V.i.104). Although the methods of the abbess and Doctor Pinch differ, they both treat madness and possession as a consequence of external manipulation.

Curiously, neither Antipholus of Syracuse nor his twin ever questions his own sanity. Any modern treatment of characters in a similar situation, if it dealt at all with the characters' reactions, would almost certainly focus on internal doubts about sanity and the characters' grasp of an external reality. For Elizabethans, concerns about witchcraft and possession were very real and served, within a religious framework, to explain anything odd or unusual in human experience. Most modern audiences are perhaps more likely to believe in psychological explanations for insanity rather than in witchcraft or demonic possession as causes. The abbess suggests a modern notion of psychological problems when she concludes that Antipholus of Syracuse, whom she believes is Adriana's husband, is troubled by the sharp and persistent tongue of a shrewish wife. Modern audiences would be apt to agree with her explanation and would be much more likely to expect distortions in human experience to be framed in sociological and psychological terms than framed by witchcraft and demonic possession.

Characters

Abbess:
See Aemilia

Adriana:
Adriana is the wife of Antipholus of Ephesus. Her husband has spent a good deal of time away from home with his business dealings and in overseeing the making of a ring intended for her. It seems that their marriage is relatively new, and she is concerned that her husband already finds her uninteresting or unattractive. Luciana, her sister, advises her to make herself more attractive by being more gentle and tolerant of her husband's behavior. Adriana fears that his affections are being given to someone else. When Luciana confirms those suspicions in Adriana's mind—even though it is Antipholus of Syracuse, her husband's twin, who has made advances toward her sister—she wishes that she could denounce her husband totally and cease caring so much for him.

Adriana really does seem to love Antipholus of Ephesus. She shows deep concern for him when she suspects that he has been possessed and has gone mad. She arranges for Doctor Pinch to exorcise the demons from her husband. Although Doctor Pinch intends to subject Antipholus of Ephesus to what we might consider barbaric treatment, Adriana seems well-intentioned and caring.

Aemilia:
Aemilia is the abbess in charge of a priory, a convent for nuns, in the city of Ephesus. As we learn, somewhat surprisingly, at the end of the play, she is also the wife of Egeon and the mother of Antipholus of Ephesus and Antipholus of Syracuse. In the shipwreck that separated her from Egeon, she had tied herself, one of her twin sons, and one of the twin servants to a spare mast from the sunken ship. Egeon had done likewise, tying himself, the other twin son, and remaining twin servant to another mast. According to Egeon's account at the beginning of the play, she and her burdens were lighter and were born more quickly by the wind than his own group, and Egeon believed they had been rescued by fishermen from Corinth. But, in the last scene of the play, Aemilia reveals that she and her charges had really been rescued by men of Epidamium, and the fishermen from Corinth had stolen away Antipholus and Dromio of Ephesus. She had not seen her son or his servant since, and she has been

living in Ephesus for some time, unaware of her son's residence there. Her appearance in the last scene of the play and her recognition of Egeon are the final pieces of the puzzle in explaining the multiple confusions of the preceding action.

Aemilia has a further significance in the play as well. In the last decades of the sixteenth century, Elizabethan England was still working out answers to questions left in the wake of the Reformation. One of those questions was whether Catholics or Protestants were more effective in exorcising demons from the possessed. When Aemilia proposes to dispossess Antipholus of Syracuse by simply tending to his physical well being and praying for his soul, she represents the limits of what a religious person in Protestant England could do for those who were considered mad. Her treatment is in contrast to the ritualized exorcism proposed by Doctor Pinch, a kind of reverse conjuring and sorcery associated with Catholic exorcism at that time.

Angelo:

Angelo is a goldsmith in Ephesus. He has been commissioned by Antipholus of Ephesus to make a gold necklace for the latter's wife. He mistakenly gives that necklace to Antipholus of Syracuse. Angelo owes money to another Ephesian merchant, intending to pay that debt with the sum owed him by Antipholus of Ephesus. He knows Antipholus of Ephesus to be a reputable man, so he cannot believe it when the Ephesian twin passes by and denies having ever received the necklace. Angelo has him arrested since he has no other recourse. In the last scene of the play, he can only give the duke conflicting testimony about the character of Antipholus of Ephesus. Having earlier accompanied the Ephesian Antipholus to his home and having witnessed the doors barred against the owner, he confirms that the Ephesian Antipholus is telling the truth in that instance. But he must also inform the duke that Antipholus of Ephesus has initially denied receiving the necklace and then later has brazenly displayed the same while freely admitting the source and time of its delivery.

Antipholus of Ephesus:

Antipholus of Ephesus is the twin brother of Antipholus of Syracuse and the son to Egeon and Aemilia. In the shipwreck that separates his family, he is left in the care of his mother, Aemilia. According to her amendment of Egeon's account, she and her infant son and the infant Dromio were picked up by men of Epidamium, and Antipholus and Dromio

of Ephesus were later stolen away from her by fishermen from Corinth. In the last scene of the play, Antipholus of Ephesus reveals that he was brought to Ephesus from Corinth by the renowned uncle of the duke of Ephesus.

Unbeknownst to Antipholus of Ephesus, his twin has arrived in Ephesus. A series of bizarre incidents follows, in which Antipholus of Syracuse is confused with Antipholus of Ephesus by the latter's wife and friends. They think he has gone mad and arrange to have him undergo an exorcism. He thinks that his wife is conspiring against him, even enlisting his business acquaintances as confederates in her plot. He pleads his case before the duke and reminds the latter that he has served him faithfully in the duke's wars. At the play's conclusion, the confusion of identity is resolved, and Antipholus of Ephesus is reunited with his entire family.

Antipholus of Syracuse:

Antipholus of Syracuse is the twin brother of Antipholus of Ephesus and the son of Egeon and Aemilia. In the shipwreck, he is left in the care of his father, Egeon, living with him in Syracuse until his eighteenth birthday when he requests that Egeon allow himself and his servant Dromio to go in quest of his long-lost mother and twin brother. That search eventually brings him to Ephesus, and he arrives ignorant of his father's presence and his brother's and mother's residence there.

When the residents of Ephesus begin to mistake him for his twin, Antipholus of Syracuse never guesses that the cases of mistaken identity might indicate that they are presuming he is his twin. Instead, he is continually amazed that those residents call him by name, invite him to dinner, give him gifts, and, in one instance, call him ''husband.'' He attributes all of this to the witchcraft and sorcery for which the city is famous and becomes frightened. He resolves to leave that city as quickly as possible but is prevented from doing so by a complication of circumstances. When he is invited to dinner with Adriana and Luciana, he finds himself attracted to Luciana and informs her of his interest. At the play's conclusion, the confusion of identity is resolved, and Antipholus of Syracuse is reunited with his entire family.

Attendants:

The attendants wait on the duke of Ephesus. They appear in the first and last scenes of the play, coinciding with the duke's two appearances.

Balthazar:

Balthazar is a merchant in Ephesus. He accompanies Angelo and Antipholus of Ephesus to the latter's house. When Antipholus grows angry at being locked out of his own home and decides to break in with a crowbar, Balthazar convinces him not to do so. He argues that breaking in would surely be noticed and commented upon, and it would bring suspicion on the wife of the Ephesian Antipholus and, in turn, on her husband.

Courtezan:

The courtezan is the hostess of the Porpentine Inn and a prostitute. Antipholus of Ephesus, still angry at being locked out of his house, proclaims his intention to give the gold necklace intended for his wife to the courtezan. He will do this to spite his wife, who has often accused him, without cause, of fraternizing with the courtezan. The courtezan later encounters Antipholus of Syracuse and requests the gold necklace Antipholus of Ephesus has promised her in exchange for a ring during dinner earlier at the Porpentine. Antipholus of Syracuse views her as a lewd and despicable creature driven by the devil himself; he flees the supernatural nightmare he sees her to be.

Doctor Pinch:

See Pinch

Dromio of Ephesus:

Dromio of Ephesus is the twin brother of Dromio of Syracuse. He has shared the same fate in the shipwreck as Antipholus of Ephesus, to whom he is a faithful servant. Dromio of Ephesus and his twin brother were born of a poor woman at the same time that Aemilia gave birth to her twin sons. Since the poor woman was in the same inn, this other birth came to Egeon's attention, and he bought the twin Dromios as servants for his own sons. Throughout the play, Dromio of Ephesus confuses his own master with Antipholus of Syracuse. He is sent on a series of errands, always returning to the wrong master with the wrong item or wrong information and is beaten as a consequence. There is little in the play to differentiate the character of Dromio of Ephesus from that of Dromio of Syracuse; however, we do know that they have different tastes in women. Dromio of Ephesus is romantically involved with Luce, a woman that his twin finds extremely disgusting.

" Aemilia is the abbess in charge of a priory, a convent for nuns, in the city of Ephesus. As we learn, somewhat surprisingly, at the end of the play, she is also the wife of Egeon and the mother of Antipholus of Ephesus and Antipholus of Syracuse."

Dromio of Syracuse:

Dromio of Syracuse is the twin brother of Dromio of Ephesus. He has shared the same fate as Antipholus of Syracuse, to whom he is a faithful servant. Like his twin brother, he serves, throughout the play, to compound the comic effect of mistaken identities and is beaten by the twin Antipholuses when the objects of his errands do not correspond to the desires of the masters. Although Dromio of Syracuse has been a constant presence in the life of Antipholus of Syracuse—possibly a childhood playmate—the difference in their social standing is maintained. Antipholus of Syracuse reminds him of that social difference when he thinks that Dromio of Syracuse has been deliberately fooling with him about the gold he was directed to deposit at the Centaur, presuming that the evasive answers given by Dromio of Ephesus on that point were the fooleries of his own servant. He says to the Syracusan Dromio, "If you will jest with me, know my aspect, / And fashion your demeanor to my looks" (II.ii.32-33). The circumstances of their birth have destined the twin Dromios to a life of servitude. Even the name "Dromio" is suggestive of the twins' occupation as the name derives from the Greek "dromos"—to run.

Duke of Ephesus (Solinus, Duke of Ephesus):

See Solinus

Egeon:

Egeon is the father of Antipholus of Ephesus and Antipholus of Syracuse. He is also the husband of the abbess, Aemilia. He is a Syracusan merchant

> **Unbeknownst to Antipholus of Ephesus, his twin has arrived in Ephesus. A series of bizarre incidents follows, in which Antipholus of Syracuse is confused with Antipholus of Ephesus by the latter's wife and friends. They think he has gone mad and arrange to have him undergo an exorcism."**

who has arrived in Ephesus bound to leave no stone unturned in his search for Antipholus of Syracuse, the son he has raised and regrets having allowed to go in search of his mother and brother. When he arrives in Ephesus, he is immediately attached under the Ephesian law that demands Syracusan merchants pay a ransom or forfeit their lives. Egeon cannot pay that ransom, so he is sentenced to die. But the duke is sympathetic to Egeon when he and the audience are acquainted with the sad tale of the separation of Egeon's family in a shipwreck many years before. The duke grants Egeon the rest of the day to somehow secure the thousand marks necessary to pay his ransom.

Egeon's appearance at the beginning and end of the play serves to mark one day's progress, the elapsed time of the play's action. It is also somewhat ironic that Egeon, once a man of means enough to purchase the twin Dromios as servants, finds himself in a situation in which he does not have means enough to pay the ransom for his own life.

First Merchant of Ephesus:

The first merchant of Ephesus befriends Antipholus of Syracuse when the latter arrives in Ephesus. He warns the Syracusan Antipholus that Syracusan merchants are being held for ransom in Ephesus and advises him to pass himself off as being from Epidamium while he remains in the city. He tells Antipholus of Syracuse that just that morning the duke has sentenced a Syracusan merchant to death for his inability to pay that ransom; however, the first merchant of Ephesus is unaware that the poor

Syracusan merchant is Egeon, father to the Syracusan Antipholus.

Headsman:

The headsman enters with the duke in the last scene of the play. He is the head officer of a type of police force the duke maintains to keep order in the city and enforce the law.

Jailer:

A jailer appears in the first scene of the play maintaining custody of Egeon, who has been arrested as a Syracusan merchant banned from the city of Ephesus.

Luce:

Luce is a servant to Adriana. She helps the Syracusan Dromio bar the door against Antipholus of Ephesus when Adriana and Luciana are entertaining Antipholus of Syracuse within, unaware that it is really the husband of her mistress outside. We discover later that she has presumed a familiarity with the Syracusan Dromio, assuming he was his twin brother with whom she is presumably involved. The Syracusan Dromio finds her extremely unattractive and describes her to Antipholus of Syracuse as "the kitchen wench and all grease" (III.ii.95). He describes her complexion as "Swart, like [his] shoe, but her face nothing like so clean kept" (III.ii.102). And he describes her girth as "No longer from head to foot than from hip to hip: she is spherical, like a globe" (III.ii.113-14). When Dromio of Syracuse is later sent to Adriana's house to procure bail for Antipholus of Ephesus, he shudders at the thought of encountering Luce again.

Luciana:

Luciana is the sister of Adriana and seems inseparable from her throughout the play. Their attitudes toward a "correct" marriage relationship, however, are different. When Adriana complains about her husband's absences from home, intending to chastise Antipholus of Ephesus severely when he returns, Luciana counsels her to be patient and recognize that the husband is lord over his wife. Adriana tells her, "This servitude makes you to keep unwed" (II.i.26), but Luciana replies that she has refrained from marriage because she has seen only troubled marriages as examples around her. She tells Adriana, "Ere I learn love, I'll practice to obey'' (II.i.29). Adriana assures Luciana that she will change her tune once she is married and learns that she holds a certain power over her husband.

When Antipholus of Syracuse is dining at his twin brother's house with Adriana and Luciana, Luciana takes him aside and advises him to be more attentive to her sister, especially as they are but newly married. She tells him that if he has married Adriana for her money, he needs to treat her more kindly. If he is having an affair, she cautions him to be secretive about it. Thinking that Antipholus of Syracuse is his twin and Adriana's husband, Luciana is shocked when he reveals his desire for her. She tells Adriana about his advances and attempts to console her sister by explaining that the loss of any man who would do such a thing is not worth mourning. Luciana supports her sister's efforts to exorcise the demons from Antipholus of Ephesus when they later conclude that his bizarre behavior is the result of madness and possession.

Messenger:

The messenger appears in the last scene of the play. As Adriana is pleading with the duke to intervene on her behalf with the abbess, who will not release Adriana's presumably mad husband, the messenger brings her the news that Antipholus and Dromio of Ephesus have escaped confinement. He tells the assemblage that the Ephesian Antipholus and Dromio ''have beaten the maids'' and ''bound the doctor'' (V.i.170). They have set the conjuring schoolmaster's hair on fire and have doused the fire with buckets of foul waste. As a final insult to Pinch, they have cut his hair in the fashion associated with fools.

Nell:

See Luce

Officers:

These are officers of the Ephesian law. They appear in the first and last scenes of the play, accompanying the duke of Ephesus. An Officer is present to arrest Angelo when the second merchant of Ephesus demands it. At Angelo's insistence, he also arrests Antipholus of Ephesus when the latter refuses to pay Angelo the sum he owes him for the gold necklace. In a later scene, the Officer has Antipholus of Ephesus in his custody and refuses to turn him over to Adriana for fear that he will lose the fee he is to receive for apprehending the prisoner.

> When the residents of Ephesus begin to mistake him for his twin, Antipholus of Syracuse never guesses that the cases of mistaken identity might indicate that they are presuming he is his twin.''

Pinch (Doctor Pinch):

Doctor Pinch is a schoolmaster by profession and a conjurer by virtue of his advanced learning. He attempts to exorcise the demons from Antipholus of Ephesus after he has escorted him home. But the Ephesian Antipholus and Dromio break their bonds and turn the tables on the doctor, beating him and humiliating him by cutting off his hair. Doctor Pinch represents the Catholic practice of exorcism rejected by the Protestant doctrine of the Church of England in the late sixteenth century. We know that the brief exorcism Pinch conducts, after the Ephesian Antipholus strikes him, has Catholic associations because he attempts to drive Satan out by saying, ''I conjure thee by all the saints in heaven!'' (IV.iv.57). The belief in saints was peculiar to Catholicism, and no good Protestant in England would have suggested that the spiritual aid of saints could be enlisted.

Second Merchant of Ephesus:

The second merchant of Ephesus is owed money by Angelo, the goldsmith. When he requests payment, Angelo assures him that he can secure a similar amount from Antipholus of Ephesus in exchange for the gold necklace he has given him. When the Ephesian Antipholus denies owing the money, Angelo cannot pay the second merchant of Ephesus. The latter has no other alternative but to have Angelo arrested for non-payment of debt. Angelo, in turn, has Antipholus of Ephesus arrested on the same grounds. In a later scene, Angelo apologizes to the second merchant of Ephesus, who has been delayed in a business voyage by Angelo's inability to pay his debt. The second Merchant of Ephesus asks Angelo about the Ephesian Antipholus's reputation, and Angelo assures him that, in all but this particular instance, Antipholus of Ephesus has

> **Egeon's appearance at the beginning and end of the play serves to mark one day's progress, the elapsed time of the play's action."**

always conducted himself as a reputable man of business.

Solinus (Solinus, Duke of Ephesus):

The duke appears in the first and last scenes of the play. In the opening scene, he sentences Egeon to death, in accordance with the Ephesian policy of retaliation against the duke of Syracuse, who has held Ephesian merchants in Syracuse for ransom. The duke of Ephesus represents law, but that law is tempered with mercy. When he hears Egeon's sad tale of shipwreck and separated family, the duke wishes that he could suspend Egeon's sentence of death but cannot since that leniency would establish a dangerous precedent in Ephesus. He does, however, allow Egeon until the end of the day to accumulate the thousand marks necessary to pay his ransom. In the last scene, the duke appears to enact the sentence against Egeon but is prevented from immediately doing so by several suits which he must settle. When the abbess appears to say that Antipholus of Syracuse has been wronged in being treated as if he were possessed and recognizes Egeon as her husband, it is the duke who is first to put the pieces of the puzzle together and figure out what has happened.

Further Reading

Arthos, John. "Shakespeare's Transformation of Plautus." *Comparative Drama* 4 (1967-68): 239-53.
> The source for Shakespeare's *The Comedy of Errors* was the play *Menaechmi* by the Roman playwright Plautus. Arthos examines how Shakespeare adds a feeling of humanity and a sense of love to his play that is missing in the source play by Plautus.

Babula, William. "If I Dream Not: Unity in *The Comedy of Errors*." *South Atlantic Bulletin* 38, no. 4 (1973): 26-33.
> Babula discusses the characters' loss of identities and comments on the dreamlike quality of life in the play.

Barber, C. L. "Shakespearian Comedy in *The Comedy of Errors*." *College English* 25, no. 7 (1964): 493-97.
> Barber stresses that the comic resolution of the play implies a new beginning for the separated family and a rebirth for all involved.

Barton, Anne. Introduction to *The Comedy of Errors*, by William Shakespeare. In *The Riverside Shakespeare*, edited by G. Blakemore Evans, 79-82. Boston: Houghton Mifflin, 1974.
> Barton gives a good introduction to the play, discussing the witchcraft and sorcery associated with the city of Ephesus, the conflicting views of Adriana and Luciana on marriage, and the ways in which Shakespeare presents the events differently than his source.

Brooks, Harold. "Themes and Structure in *The Comedy of Errors*." *Stratford-upon-Avon Studies* 3 (1961): 54-71.
> Brooks analyzes the play's several themes and identifies the different dramatic techniques Shakespeare uses in presenting the action of the play.

Clayton, Thomas S. "The Text, Imagery, and Sense of the Abbess's Final Speech in *The Comedy of Errors*." *Anglia* 91, no. 4 (1973): 479-84.
> Clayton examines specifically the speech delivered by the abbess in Act V, noting the imagery of rebirth and the suggestion of maternity in that speech.

Freedman, Barbara. "Egeon's Debt: Self-Division and Self-Redemption in *The Comedy of Errors*." *English Literary Renaissance* 10, no. 3 (1980): 360-83.
> Freedman argues that Antipholus of Ephesus and Antipholus of Syracuse represent a division in Egeon's self. Their reunion at the end of the play signals Egeon's return to a world where the law no longer threatens him, a world in which law and imagination are also reunited.

Henze, Richard. "*Comedy of Errors*: A Freely Binding Chain." *Shakespeare Quarterly* 22, no. 1 (1971): 35-41.
> Henze argues that the golden necklace Antipholus of Ephesus intends to give his wife represents social unity. The gold chain connects freedom and individuality in the play.

MacCary, W. Thomas. "*The Comedy of Errors*: A Different Kind of Comedy." *New Literary History* 9, no. 3 (1978): 525-36.
> MacCary presents a psychological analysis of the play, arguing that the play emphasizes the reunion of family and not just the social importance of marriage.

Parker, Patricia. "Elder and Younger: The Opening Scene of *The Comedy of Errors*." *Shakespeare Quarterly* 34, no. 3 (1983): 325-27.
> Parker points out some of the play's allusions to the biblical Genesis and Ephesians.

Petronella, Vincent F. "Structure and Theme Through Separation and Union in Shakespeare's *The Comedy of Errors*." *Modern Language Review* 69, no. 3 (1974): 481-88.
> Petronella examines how certain patterns of language underscore the themes of separation and union in the play.

The Tragedy of Coriolanus

Plot Summary

circa 1607-08

Act I:

As the play opens, rebellious citizens are rushing through the streets of Rome, brandishing clubs and sticks. A shortage of grain has driven its price out of reach of the common people, or plebeians, and the citizens complain that they are on the verge of starvation. They believe there is a sufficient supply of grain in warehouses but that the government is withholding it from them. Two citizens pause to debate whether Caius Martius (a Roman nobleman who will later be known as Coriolanus) is principally to blame for this policy. Their debate is interrupted by the arrival of a senator, Menenius Agrippa. (The Roman republic was led by two consuls, who held supreme authority in the state and were elected annually. The senate, an advisory body to the consuls, was composed of men—senators— who came from the upper classes or patrician order of society.) Agrippa reminds the citizens that the gods, not legislators, cause famines. He then relates a fable designed to show the proper relation between different parts of society. Caius Martius suddenly appears, hurling taunts and insults at the plebeians. He reports that as a result of civil disturbances in another part of the city, five new tribunes have been appointed. (Historically, the office of tribune was created around 494 B.C., during a period of intense struggle between the patricians and the common citizens. Tribunes were elected

annually by the citizens. As representatives of the plebeians and protectors of their rights, tribunes had the authority to summon citizens together, inform them of political developments, and ask for their opinions.) A messenger arrives with news that the Volscians—dangerous enemies of Rome—are preparing for war. A group of noblemen—including the military leaders Cominius and Titus Lartius and several senators—follows on the heels of the messenger; they are joined by Sicinius Velutus and Junius Brutus, two of the newly appointed tribunes. There is a brief discussion of the impending war, and Martius expresses his eagerness to meet the Volscian leader Tullus Aufidius in combat.

A brief scene follows in which Aufidius and some Volscian senators, meeting in their capital of Corioles, discuss military strategy. Back in Rome, after the army has left for Corioles, Martius's mother Volumnia and his wife Virgilia sit at home sewing and talking. They are joined by their friend Valeria, who urges them to join her in visiting a mutual friend. Having vowed not to leave the house until her husband returns safely from the war, Virgilia refuses.

The setting shifts back to Corioles, where, outside the walls of the city, Martius and Lartius have gathered part of the Roman forces. In the distance can be heard the sounds of battle between opposing troops, the Romans led by Cominius and the Volscians by Aufidius. Volscian soldiers suddenly spill out of the city gates, and, in the ensuing fight, the Romans are driven back. Martius leads a counter-charge back to the city gates, which open to receive the Volscian soldiers. Martius follows them into the city, but his soldiers do not, and the gates close. Lartius and the Roman soldiers are convinced that Martius has been slain; however, as they are talking, Martius appears, bleeding and fighting off several Volscians. Spurred by this sight, Lartius and the Roman soldiers join the fray once more and the city is taken. Inside the walls, Martius tells Lartius to keep guard there while he collects some soldiers to go and relieve Cominius and his troops. When he reaches the battlefield, Martius begs for the chance to engage Aufidius himself, and Cominius agrees. The two warriors meet on the field and fight in single combat, but then, to Aufidius's shame, a group of Volscians comes to his aid and drives Martius off. The Romans win the battle, however, and when the three Roman generals meet after it's over, Cominius credits Martius with their victory. So that his exploits at Corioles will never be forgot-

ten, Martius is given a new name: "Coriolanus." Outside Corioles, the defeated Volscians also gather. Aufidius laments that a treaty has been signed between Rome and Corioles, and he vows that the next time he and Martius meet, there will be a fight to the death.

Act II:

In a public place in Rome, Menenius waits with Sicinius and Brutus to hear news of the battle. Volumnia, Virgilia, and Valeria happen along, and they tell the men that Rome has been victorious. The sound of trumpets heralds the approach of Coriolanus, who is accompanied by Cominius, Lartius, and a group of soldiers. Menenius and Volumnia are overjoyed by the accolades heaped on Coriolanus. The soldiers depart, and the patricians leave for the Capitol. A messenger arrives and tells Brutus and Sicinius that they are to go to the Capitol, for it is expected that Coriolanus will be named consul. He also reports that the plebeians are enthusiastically celebrating Coriolanus's heroic exploits. The scene shifts to the senate chamber, where Coriolanus, Menenius, Cominius, and a group of patricians gather, together with Sicinius and Brutus. The tribunes and Coriolanus exchange veiled insults, and Menenius intercedes, trying to keep peace between them. Coriolanus leaves the room before Cominius delivers a speech in which he reviews Coriolanus's extraordinary military career. Coriolanus returns, and Menenius tells him that the senate has elected him consul. The next step, Menenius reminds him, is to address the people. Coriolanus is appalled by the prospect of carrying out the usual custom followed by those seeking the plebeians' approval: he must put on a robe made of coarse fabric—as a symbol of humility—and expose his battle scars to the people. Menenius reminds him that he has no choice: he must comply with the custom. In the marketplace, a group of plebeians debate among themselves whether to vote for Coriolanus. He enters reluctantly, wearing the robe of humility. In groups of twos and threes, the citizens listen to him as he asks for their votes, and then they give him their approval. When Coriolanus has left the marketplace, Sicinius and Brutus join the plebeians, some of whom seem uncertain about the choice they've made. The tribunes encourage their uneasiness and remind them that Coriolanus has been their enemy in the past. Following the lead of the tribunes, the citizens change their minds. They are now determined to revoke the election of Coriolanus as consul.

Act III:

As Coriolanus, his friends, and a group of patricians walk toward the marketplace, they discuss new reports that Aufidius has raised a fresh force of troops. Sicinius and Brutus confront them and halt their progress, informing them that the people have withdrawn their support for Coriolanus. He becomes furious, raging at the tribunes and expressing his contempt for the citizens they represent. They call him a traitor and prepare to have him arrested. A group of citizens appears, shouting "Down with him! Down with him!" (III.i.183). The tribunes call for Coriolanus's death, and he draws his sword. In the struggle that follows, the people and their tribunes are driven away. After Coriolanus and most of the patricians leave, however, Sicinius and Brutus return with the citizens. Menenius persuades them to allow Coriolanus to defend his actions, promising to bring him back to the marketplace. The scene shifts to Coriolanus's house, where his mother and several noblemen attempt to calm his rage. When Menenius and other senators arrive there, they all advise him to apologize to the people. They plead with him to pretend that he regrets his actions, and they give him explicit instructions about how to convince the people that he's genuinely repentant. Reluctantly, Coriolanus agrees to do what they ask. Brutus and Sicinius are waiting for him when he arrives at the marketplace, and they are quickly joined by a group of plebeians. Despite Menenius's attempts to restrain him, Coriolanus's true feelings surface again, and he shows his contempt for the proceedings. The tribunes declare that Coriolanus must be banished from the city, and the plebeians voice their agreement. Coriolanus curses them all and turns his back on Rome.

Act IV:

Near the city gates, Coriolanus bids farewell to his mother, his wife, and his friends. Some time later, he appears outside Aufidius's house in Antium, a city in Volscian territory. He is dressed as a poor man, and his face is partially obscured by his garments. He gains admittance to the house, where Aufidius at first fails to recognize him. When Coriolanus reveals his identity, Aufidius greets him warmly. Coriolanus says he's been banished from Rome and offers his services to the Volscians against the country which, he says, he now hates. Aufidius tells Coriolanus he's overjoyed to help him gain revenge against Rome; they join some Volscian nobles who are Aufidius's guests that night and plan their strategy for a renewed war.

News reaches Rome about this alliance and the movement of enemy troops. Patricians, tribunes, and plebeians all predict a dire outcome. In the Volscian camp, Aufidius and an aide discuss Coriolanus's enormous popularity with the Volscian soldiers. Aufidius tells his aide that he does not fear Coriolanus as a rival; by one means or another, he means to triumph over him.

Act V:

In Rome, Coriolanus's friends and enemies alike try to determine how to prevent a Volscian attack on the city. Cominius describes his recent, unsuccessful, attempt to convince Coriolanus to drop his pursuit of vengeance. Undeterred by this account, Menenius goes to the Volscian camp outside Rome and makes a personal appeal to Coriolanus, but he is no more successful than Cominius. The final appeal is made by Volumnia, Virgilia, Valeria, and Coriolanus's son, young Martius. Coriolanus struggles to resist their combined pleadings, but eventually he yields and arranges a peace treaty. The women return to Rome, and Coriolanus goes back to the Volscian capital, where the commoners greet him as a hero. Aufidius, however, has prepared a trap for him and enlisted the support of several conspirators. He taunts Coriolanus, calling him a traitor and a tearful child. Stung by these accusations, Coriolanus reminds them of his triumphant defeat of the Volscians at Corioles. Calling out the names of relatives who were slain in that battle, the Volscian people attack Coriolanus, and he is killed by the men who conspired with Aufidius. As Coriolanus's body is borne away, Aufidius eulogizes him and declares that he will be remembered as a man of great courage and nobility.

Modern Connections

Coriolanus has been called Shakespeare's most political play. It depicts a society in the midst of rapid change, struggling to adjust to a new form of government. Until recently, Rome was ruled by a king, and the people had no independent voice. Now, in the early years of the republic, they participate in the election of consuls, and they have tribunes to represent their interests and defend them against abuses of power. Similar situations exist around the world in the late twentieth century. Many nations are presently coping with drastic changes in their governments and dealing with the threat of political instability. After the collapse of

Communism in Eastern Europe in the 1990s, states that were formerly under authoritarian rule began to move toward democracy. In this decade as well, South Africa experienced a dramatic change in the structure of its government; recently, for the first time in its history, the country held an election in which all its citizens were encouraged to vote. In Asia, the pressures of Westernization are affecting political life as well as national economies. In countries without a tradition of self-government, ordinary citizens and their leaders face an almost overwhelming challenge. Those who formerly held political power are reluctant to let go of it. Those who never had it before must learn the responsibilities as well as the benefits of power.

These kinds of adjustments are made more difficult when a society is deeply divided on the basis of economic or social class. In *Coriolanus*, the patricians don't believe ordinary citizens are intelligent enough to make thoughtful political decisions. The plebeians are convinced that the senate is only looking out for the interests of the elite class. Yet virtually everyone in the play claims to have the well-being of Rome—not self-interest—as their guiding principle. Is it possible for people to place the unity of a nation above their own interests? Political parties in modern democracies are frequently seen as representing certain groups or factions rather than "all the people." The issue of national identity or integrity sometimes gets lost in the effort to advance the ideas of one group or another, or to protect partisan interests. Do we trust each other—or our political leaders—to make unselfish choices and impartial decisions?

The ordinary citizens of Rome don't trust Coriolanus. His mother and his friends tell him that in order to be elected by the people, he must hide his true feelings—pretend to be what he is not. In modern democracies, candidates for public office emphasize certain elements in their background and try to downplay others. Pollsters report current public opinion, and advisers suggest campaign strategies that will appeal to a majority of voters. Political pragmatism is not considered dishonorable, at least among politicians: that's how elections are won. In *Coriolanus*, the characters who urge the hero to misrepresent himself to the people appear to be less virtuous than their candidate, who insists on personal integrity. Yet the play seems to suggest that Coriolanus's rigid inflexibility is as wrong as the other people's willingness to compromise their beliefs.

The play also raises non-political issues. One of these relates to the role of violence in Roman culture. Volumnia's bloodthirstiness is shocking—yet, to a degree, her attitude is a reflection of her society. She happily counts the number of Coriolanus's wounds in part because she knows they represent a political asset: the people will want to see each scar for themselves. In a culture whose greatest heroes are the ones who make war and destroy enemies, is it surprising that ordinary citizens take up whatever weapons they have at hand when they set out to defend their rights? Young Martius—shredding the butterfly, then later vowing that no one will ever tread on him—shows how a child becomes familiar with the cult of violence and learns to imitate his elders. What factors in modern society contribute to violent behavior? Are our popular heroes those who try to avoid conflict or those who seem to delight in it?

Finally, many commentators have pointed out that *Coriolanus* is unique in its heavy reliance on what other people say or report about the play's hero. In effect, the tragedy raises an important question: what is "character"? Is it what we do? What we say? What others say about us? The "character" of Coriolanus is elusive and problematic. If we cannot determine, with any degree of certainty, the essence of a dramatic character, is it possible to do so in the case of a real person? Are we the authors of our own "characters," as Coriolanus says he wants to be, or do others—parents, teachers, friends and enemies—create them for us?

Characters

Adrian:

He appears in IV.iii, where the designation for his speeches is the anonymous "Volscian." While traveling from Antium to Rome, Adrian unexpectedly meets Nicanor, a Roman spy. Adrian welcomes the news that Nicanor is bringing to Antium: Coriolanus has been banished, the Roman nobles are irate, and the political situation is unstable.

Aediles:

They are minor public officials who serve as assistants to the tribunes. In III.i, after Brutus and Sicinius declare that Coriolanus is a traitor, the aediles are instructed to seize him. Coriolanus resists arrest and strikes the aediles. In III.iii, following orders from the tribunes, an aedile assembles a crowd of plebeians and tells them what to say and do when Coriolanus returns to the marketplace to answer the charges against him. The aedile helps inflame the mob against Coriolanus. In IV.vi, a report about the Volscian army's renewed attack on Roman territories is relayed to the tribunes by an aedile. The tribunes scoff at the news and dismiss it as a rumor.

Aufidius:

He is the Volsces' preeminent military hero. Like Coriolanus, his identity is closely tied to his fame as a warrior. The two men share a long-standing rivalry; their personal combat in I.viii represents the fifth time they have met on a battle-field. Though their hatred of each other is intense, so is their mutual admiration. As many commentators have pointed out, Aufidius's speech at IV.v.101-35—when he discovers that his uninvited guest is Coriolanus—has strong elements of homoeroticism. ''Let me twine / Mine arms about that body,'' cries Aufidius (IV.v.106-07). The sight of Coriolanus makes him happier, Aufidius says, than he was when he saw his bride crossing the threshold on their wedding day.

Though Aufidius's attitude changes when Coriolanus becomes the popular favorite of the Volscian soldiers, he shows profound insight into Coriolanus's character. In a conversation with his lieutenant in IV.vii, he notes that Coriolanus is uncomfortable when people praise him—that it makes him uneasy. Aufidius suggests several reasons to explain what led to Coriolanus's banishment: his pride, a ''defect of judgment'' (IV.vii.39), or his temperament, that served him supremely well as a warrior but that would be fatal in a political leader. Commentators have suggested that the reason Aufidius understands Coriolanus so well is because they are so much alike.

In many ways, however, Aufidius is very different from his rival. He's a pragmatist and a clever analyzer of circumstances. He's willing to affect an attitude of continued good will toward Coriolanus even while he waits for the right moment to undermine him. And he's prepared to use any means—whether they're honorable or not—to accomplish his goal. Aufidius seems to have no qualms about manipulating Coriolanus or about using the Volscian people to carry out his personal revenge. He knows just which charges will most incite Coriolanus into a rage—''traitor'' and ''boy''—and he employs them brilliantly in the play's final scene. The conspirators who have joined Aufidius in the plot

> **Though their hatred of each other is intense, so is their mutual admiration. . . . The sight of Coriolanus makes him happier, Aufidius says, than he was when he saw his bride crossing the threshold on their wedding day.''**

against Coriolanus kill the Roman, and Aufidius arrogantly plants his foot on the corpse—until one of the Volscian lords orders him to remove it.

Aufidius may be sincere when he begins his eulogy of Coriolanus by saying ''My rage is gone, / And I am struck with sorrow'' (V.vi.146-47). Since he has frequently acknowledged Coriolanus's superiority and found fault only with what Coriolanus did, not what he was, Aufidius's declaration that ''he shall have a noble memory'' (V.vi.153) seems to ring true. There is justice in Aufidius's charge that Coriolanus betrayed his Volscian allies. But his scornful claim that Coriolanus was moved to spare Rome because of ''a few drops of women's'' tears (V.vi.45) reveals more about Aufidius's small-mindedness than it does about Coriolanus's character.

Brutus:
See Tribunes

Caius Martius:
See Coriolanus

Citizens:
See Roman Citizens *and* Volscian Citizens

Cominius:

He is a consul and the commander of the Roman army. A sensible man, he generally speaks in a deliberate, cautious manner, though sometimes he shows a fondness for extravagant language. He is practical rather than idealistic, yet he is devoted to Rome and to his friend Coriolanus. When conflict develops between his country and his friend, Cominius is caught in the middle. His efforts to act as a mediator between them are unsuccessful.

Like the other patricians in the play, Cominius constantly fears that the delicate balance between social classes will collapse and that Rome will be plunged into civil war. When an ugly brawl erupts in the marketplace in III.i, Cominius scolds the tribunes and the plebeians. "That is the way to lay the city flat, / To bring the roof to the foundation," he warns them (III.i.203-04). Cominius recognizes that the senate cannot impose its choice for consul on the common people; they must be wooed and won over. At III.ii.93-95, he tells Coriolanus that unless he's prepared to remain calm when he goes back to the marketplace, he shouldn't go at all. When Coriolanus says that he can't possibly play the part of a humble, contrite man, Cominius responds, "Come, come, we'll prompt you" (III.ii.106). Cominius believes that there are times when a politician must compromise in order to be effective and that given the structure of the Roman republic, the power of the common citizens must be respected.

Cominius's tendency to exaggerate is most apparent in his speeches praising Coriolanus. In his address to the senators before they vote on Coriolanus's election to the consulship, Cominius vividly recreates Coriolanus's brilliant military career. "I shall lack voice" to adequately describe his merits, says Cominius (II.ii.82), but he rises to the occasion. In a lengthy speech filled with vivid descriptions, complex sentences, and images that intensify Coriolanus's valor, he depicts a superhuman hero (II.ii.82-122). Similarly, after Coriolanus has been banished and joined the enemy forces, Cominius reports that the Volscians have made Coriolanus "their god" (IV.vi.90). Once again there is the suggestion that Coriolanus is no mere mortal: "He leads them like a thing / Made by some other deity than nature" (IV.vi.90-91). And when Cominius returns to Rome after trying to persuade Coriolanus not to attack the city, his description of Coriolanus evokes awe: "he does sit in gold, his eye / Red as 'twould burn Rome" (V.i.63-64). The words of Cominius contribute significantly to Coriolanus's image in the play as a superhuman force.

Conspirators:

Allies of Aufidius, they appear in the final scene of the play. The conspirators point out to Aufidius that Coriolanus is more popular with the Volscian army than he is. They complain that the new treaty with Rome has deprived them of glory and the spoils of war, and they declare their willingness to help bring about Coriolanus's downfall. After Aufidius has taunted Coriolanus into an ex-

plosive rage, the conspirators clamor for his death, inciting the people further. A Volscian nobleman tries to calm the crowd, but after a final exchange of insults between Coriolanus and Aufidius, the conspirators rush at Coriolanus. Shouting "Kill, kill, kill, kill, kill" (V.vi.130), they stab him to death.

Coriolanus:

Caius Martius Coriolanus dominates the play. He is loud and boisterous, a man of action. His physical strength and courage are almost superhuman. Coriolanus is the greatest warrior of his age. His personal heroism inspires other soldiers, and the men who willingly follow him into battle worship him almost as a god. But the play does not portray him as a natural leader, at ease with his subordinates or respecting them. When the Romans are beaten back to their trenches outside the walls of Corioles, he turns the situation around by cursing his men. He roars for "boils and plagues" to cover their bodies, calls them "souls of geese, / That bear the shapes of men," and threatens to turn his sword against them if they don't "stand fast" (I.iv.31, 34-35, 41).

The qualities that make him Rome's most celebrated soldier are not the ones necessary for effective political leadership. He seems to understand this himself, though he is not an introspective man. Coriolanus's mother appears to be the impulse behind his decision to seek the office of consul. He himself is not adept at campaigning. He uses language as a blunt instrument, as in the passage cited above, not as a means of persuasion or cajoling. It goes against his nature, he says, to have to ask people for their votes: "It is a part / That I shall blush in acting" (II.ii.144-45). Menenius tries to coach his performance and reminds him that "the worthiest men" in Rome have had to put on the robe of humility and appeal directly to the citizens (II.iii.49). Coriolanus acts as if his extraordinary military service entitles him to the office of consul—he shouldn't have to coax the people into voting for him.

He despises the citizens he would be required to serve if he were elected. "Bid them wash their faces, / And keep their teeth clean," he mockingly says as the first group of citizens he is supposed to talk to approaches him (II.iii.60-61). Coriolanus's contempt for the people is evident throughout the play. He calls them rogues, curs, rats, and foul-smelling cowards. His political beliefs stem from his conviction that only aristocrats are fit to rule. He thinks it was a grave mistake for the senators to distribute corn to the people at no charge: the common soldiers were cowardly in the battle outside the city of Corioles, he says, and they shouldn't be rewarded for "this kind of service" (III.i.123). The distribution of corn will only lead them to expect more hand-outs in the future, he argues. Furthermore, Coriolanus says, they will believe the senators acted out of fear, and this will encourage them to think they can intimidate their rulers. He thinks the citizens have been given too much power. He doesn't believe it's possible to have a stable government if ignorant citizens, as he regards them, have the right to help determine policy and elect officials.

Many commentators focus on Coriolanus's arrogance. They see his enormous pride as the key to his character. Several of them have called attention to what they regard as the hero's egotism or self-centeredness. Virtually everyone remarks on Coriolanus's ungovernable temper. His explosive rages repeatedly lead to disastrous consequences. The tribunes make use of this trait, baiting him until he roars his defiance of them and his contempt for the people. In effect, this guarantees his banishment. Aufidius similarly understands that Coriolanus can be trapped into furious and self-destructive rage, and he goads Coriolanus into an offensive display of wrath in the play's final scene. Like a child who hasn't learned to consider the impact of what he's about to say, Coriolanus expresses his emotions immediately and directly. "His heart's his mouth: / What his breast forges, that his tongue must vent," Menenius points out (III.i.256-57).

Coriolanus strikes many readers as being immature. He seems unusually dependent on his mother for praise and approval. He's willing to take a course of action that he knows is wrong—seeking the consulship—because it's what she wants him to do. In III.ii, he compromises his integrity when he gives in to her and agrees to pretend to the people that he's sorry for what he said. And he betrays his soldier's oath to the Volscians when, in V.iii, Volumnia makes her emotional appeal. Some commentators argue that Coriolanus is subconsciously aware of his immaturity, and thus when Aufidius calls him a "boy of tears" (V.vi.100), the charge strikes home and sends him into uncontrollable rage. Three times Coriolanus hurls the word "boy" back at Aufidius, as if in disbelief. To disprove the charge, he reminds everyone of what he accomplished at Corioles. "Like an eagle in a dove-cote," he scattered all before him and he did it single-handedly: "Alone I did it. Boy!" (V.vi.114, 116).

> Like the other patricians in the play, Cominius constantly fears that the delicate balance between social classes will collapse and that Rome will be plunged into civil war. When an ugly brawl erupts in the marketplace in III.i, Cominius scolds the tribunes and the plebeians. 'That is the way to lay the city flat, / To bring the roof to the foundation,' he warns them (III.i.203-04)."

Coriolanus's stubbornness has sometimes been viewed as a sign of immaturity. But other commentators see it as a token of his unswerving commitment to the principles and ideals that he's been taught by his mother and his society. In Coriolanus's world, honor is an end in itself, and he cannot understand why he should compromise it for the sake of political expediency. "You are too absolute," his mother tells him (III.ii.39). Coriolanus disdains the idea that concessions must be made to the people, that he should betray his nature for the votes of ordinary citizens. He resists giving power to the people and creating the office of tribune because he knows these moves will diminish the authority of the patricians—the group to which he belongs and the only one that he believes has the ability to govern Rome. The ideals he seeks to uphold—telling the truth, keeping one's word, holding firmly to one's position—are virtues in a soldier. Unhappily, Coriolanus finds that they have less value in civil society.

His aliention from that society may be traced to this difference in values. Or it may be a result of arrogance. Whatever the reason, Coriolanus is a solitary man. He confides in no one and seems entirely self-sufficient. He sees no bond of humanity between himself and ordinary people. At I.ix.90-92, after the battle of Corioles, he is unable to remember the name of the Volscian who once treated him with kindness; as a result, the man, now

> "Coriolanus's contempt for the people is evident throughout the play. He calls them rogues, curs, rats, and foul-smelling cowards. His political beliefs stem from his conviction that only aristocrats are fit to rule."

a Roman prisoner, will undoubtedly be killed. Coriolanus's lack of humanity is emphasized by other characters' frequent use of "thing" and inanimate or subhuman images when they talk about him. "When he walks, he moves like an engine," says Menenius (V.iv.18-19). As Coriolanus leaves Rome for the last time, he compares himself to "a lonely dragon" (IV.i.30). And in his only soliloquy (IV.iv.12-26), he purposefully distances himself from such emotions as love and friendship.

Ironically, as many commentators have pointed out, it is precisely at the moment when Coriolanus permits himself (or is persuaded) to show his common humanity with others that he assures his own destruction. When he agrees to spare Rome, he knows it will cost him his life. But for once the fierce warrior demonstrates a sense of compassion. He chooses his fate and accepts it. Indeed, in the play's final scene he almost seems to court death. He recklessly reminds the Volscians that he was responsible for the deaths of many of their countrymen, and they respond by demanding his life in return. "Cut me to pieces," he cries (V.vi.111). Coriolanus's death represents an atonement for the lives of many Volscians as well as a courageous sacrifice on behalf of Rome.

Gentlewoman:

She is a companion or attendant of Volumnia. She appears in I.iii and announces that Valeria has "come to visit" (I.iii.26).

Herald:

He makes a formal speech, at II.i.162-66, saluting Coriolanus as a hero and welcoming him back to Rome after the defeat of the Volscians.

Junius Brutus:

See Tribunes

Lartius:

He is one of Rome's leading generals. Though his fame and accomplishments are overshadowed by Coriolanus's, Lartius doesn't appear to resent this. When he learns that his friend has entered Corioles by himself and is likely dead, Lartius delivers an impromptu, though premature, eulogy (I.iv.52-61). As he evokes an image of a man who was a unique soldier and the terror of Rome's enemies, Coriolanus himself appears, covered in blood but most definitely alive. Inspired by his bravery and determination, Lartius and the Roman soldiers enter Corioles with their hero and seize control of the city. Lartius stays behind in Corioles, while his friend goes off to assist Cominius; he's only able to join the others when the battle is nearly over. In his last appearance in the play, Lartius comes to Rome with news about Aufidius. He tells Cominius and Coriolanus that the Volscian leader is presently living in Antium and that his enmity toward Coriolanus is stronger than ever.

Lictors:

Minor public officials, they serve as ushers for the tribunes. Lictors precede Sicinius and Brutus when they enter the senate chamber at II.ii.37.

Lieutenant:

See Roman Lieutenant *and* Volscian Lieutenant

Martius:

See Coriolanus

Menenius:

A Roman senator, he is a close friend to Coriolanus. He sees himself as Coriolanus's mentor and adviser. Menenius is constantly urging his friend to hold his temper in check, to appear humble in front of the people, and to moderate his harsh language. In part, Menenius does so because he understands the need for tact and the effectiveness of mild words. He also wants desperately to avoid an uprising by the people. He believes that "the violent fit of the time" (III.ii.33) may lead to civil war unless Coriolanus answers the charges against him respectfully. Menenius knows the value of conciliatory language and frequently employs it himself.

His retelling of "the fable of the belly" (I.i.96-163) is intended to calm the angry citizens and persuade them to accept their subordinate role in society. As many commentators have noted, the speech is ambiguous. On the surface, it is an allegory of a well-ordered state, in which each social group carries out its assigned function so that the welfare of the entire body politic is ensured. To some readers it appears patronizing—a trite old tale to which Menenius applies his own, self-interested interpretation. His reading of the allegory seems to suggest that the Roman aristocracy is determined to preserve the present order of society and that the country will go on with or without its common citizens. It also may imply that Menenius sees the body politic only in terms of the satisfaction of physical needs and desires. One citizen in his audience points out to him that his retelling of the tale omits mention of the higher operations of the body: intellect, imagination, and benevolence.

Menenius likes to describe himself as a genial old man who is fond of eating and drinking and telling stories. The tribunes seem to regard him as a charming, harmless fellow with a reputation for good-natured teasing. They fail to see that his insults are genuine; when he calls them asses and hypocrites and makes fun of their official duties, they brush his remarks aside as the usual jokes of a man who doesn't take himself or others too seriously. Other people, including some citizens, sense that his jokes have a darker meaning. In I.i, Menenius tries to downplay the shrewdness of one citizen's commentary on the fable of the belly by mocking the man as "the great toe" of the body politic (I.i.155); his true estimation of the people becomes clear a moment later when he refers to them as the rats of Rome.

Menenius is a pitiful figure by the close of the play. Volscian guardsmen sneer at his claims that he's Coriolanus's dearest friend and mock his repeated attempts to persuade them he's a very important man. Coriolanus sends him away and refuses to listen to any more of his advice. This is the kind of treatment Cominius had warned Menenius to expect if he went to the Volscian camp. Perhaps it is to his credit that he endured this abuse and humiliation for the sake of Rome.

Messengers:

Roman messengers appear in six scenes throughout the play, sometimes bringing news of events and sometimes confirming or contradicting earlier reports by other messengers. The first messenger

> **❝ Like a child who hasn't learned to consider the impact of what he's about to say, Coriolanus expresses his emotions immediately and directly. 'His heart's his mouth: / What his breast forges, that his tongue must vent,' Menenius points out (III.i.256-57)."**

comes into the marketplace as Coriolanus is complaining bitterly about the government having granted the plebeians five tribunes "to defend their vulgar wisdoms" (I.i.215). Coriolanus is pleased to hear the messenger's news that the Volscian army is on the march. In I.iv, another messenger appears as Coriolanus and Lartius are preparing to attack the city of Corioles; he tells them that Cominius and his forces have the enemy in view, but that the battle has not yet begun. In I.vi, a messenger reaches Cominius with incomplete information: he witnessed the Roman troops at Corioles being driven back to their trenches by the Volscians. Because he left immediately after the event, he's unaware that the Romans captured the city.

Brutus and Sicinius receive news from messengers on several occasions. In II.i, a messenger tells them they've been summoned to the Capitol, where the senators are about to meet. The messenger also reports that, as he passed through the streets, he saw people from every rank and station paying tribute to Coriolanus, the hero of the hour. In IV.vi, a messenger brings the tribunes another piece of unwanted news: an earlier report about the Volscian army making inroads into Roman territory has been confirmed. Furthermore, he tells them, there's a rumor that Coriolanus has gone over to the Volscians and now shares leadership of the army with Aufidius. The tribunes scoff at the rumor, but a second messenger arrives a moment later and confirms it. He paints a grim picture: "A fearful army, led by Caius Martius" (IV.vi.75), is laying waste to everything in its path. Two messengers also appear in V.iv. The first one tells Sicinius that the plebeians have seized Brutus and have vowed to kill him "by inches"

> " Coriolanus's lack of humanity is emphasized by other characters' frequent use of 'thing' and inanimate or subhuman images when they talk about him. 'When he walks, he moves like an engine,' says Menenius (V.iv.18-19). As Coriolanus leaves Rome for the last time, he compares himself to 'a lonely dragon' (IV.i.30). And in his only soliloquy (IV.iv.12-26), he purposefully distances himself from such emotions as love and friendship."

(V.iv.39) if Volumnia and Virgilia's appeal to Coriolanus is not successful. Just as the first messenger completes his report, a second one arrives. He brings good news: the women have prevailed, the Volscians have broken camp, and Coriolanus has left.

Nicanor:

He appears in IV.iii, where the designation for his speeches is the anonymous "Roman." Nicanor is a spy. He is on his way to Antium when he meets a Volscian citizen named Adrian. Nicanor tells Adrian about the current struggles between the plebeians on the one hand, and "the senators, patricians and nobles" (IV.iii.14-15) on the other. In Nicanor's opinion, the nobles are so disturbed by Coriolanus's banishment that they are ready to strip the people of all the power that has recently been granted them.

Officers:

Two minor functionaries, they appear at the beginning of II.ii. As they arrange cushions in the senate chamber in preparation for a meeting there, they discuss the consulship election. One officer asserts that Coriolanus is overly proud and "loves not the common people" (II.ii.6). He further declares that Coriolanus actively pursues the people's

hate; in his opinion, this is just as bad as if he were "to flatter them for their love" (II.ii.23). The other officer defends Coriolanus, pointing out that "many great men ... have flattered the people" even though they "ne'er loved them" (II.ii.7-8). He believes that Coriolanus is indifferent to the people's regard and does not care whether they love him or hate him.

Patricians:

Roman noblemen, they appear on at least three occasions. They are on hand to witness Coriolanus's defiance of the tribunes and hear his reckless words in III.i. They are also present in III.ii, when Volumnia and Coriolanus's friends try to persuade him to return to the marketplace and reassure the citizens. And several young patricians accompany Coriolanus to the gates of the city when he goes into exile. Other characters frequently talk about the patricians, offering widely different perspectives on their actions and attitudes. For example, at I.i.65-66, Menenius says they are deeply committed to the welfare of the common citizens. They "care for you like fathers," he tells the plebeians (I.i.77). One citizen forcefully disputes this judgment: "Care for us? . . . They ne'er cared for us yet" (I.i.79-80). He charges that the patricians are willing to let the people starve to death, even though the warehouses are full of grain.

The text of the play does not consistently distinguish between Roman patricians and senators. For more on the Roman nobility, see Roman Senators.

Plebeians:

See Roman Citizens

Roman Citizens:

A number of citizens, also known as commoners or plebeians, appear throughout the play. Some of them, especially in the early scenes, are partially individualized characters, but none of them is given a name. Their speech headings are first citizen, second citizen, and so on. These headings refer to the order in which the citizens speak within a specific scene. Thus the first citizen in I.i is not necessarily the same individual as the first citizen in II.iii, for example.

The Roman citizens have drawn a variety of reactions from readers and commentators. Many believe that they have genuine grievances. The citizens' charge about the shortage of corn—that the government has a sufficient supply in storage but refuses to distribute it at prices ordinary people can afford—is never denied by either Menenius or Coriolanus. The citizens also complain that the senate passes laws that favor the rich rather than the poor and that it holds them in low regard. Though senators in the play acknowledge the right of citizens to participate in elections and sometimes grant them special dispensations, they generally do so only when a citizen uprising looks as if it might erupt into civil war.

Individual citizens frequently demonstrate political insight and understanding of the issues at stake. In I.i, the first citizen sees the flaws in Menenius's interpretation of "the fable of the belly," pointing out that several significant parts of the body are missing in his version of the allegory: the head for judgment, the eye for vision, and the heart for compassion. In II.iii, before Coriolanus's first appearance in the marketplace to solicit their votes, a group of citizens thoughtfully discuss whether they are obligated to support him. In a series of interviews with him, they are honest and direct, and they raise important issues. For example, the third citizen is realistic; he reminds Coriolanus that he should be aware that "if we give you anything, we hope to gain by you" (II.iii.71-72). When Coriolanus asks what is the "price o' th' consulship?", the first citizen replies reasonably: "The price is, to ask it kindly" (II.iii.73-74, 75).

The citizens' hesitations about electing Coriolanus to the consulship are understandable. They know he despises them and has consistently opposed government policies that would benefit them. To their faces he has called them untrustworthy dogs, incapable of appreciating the fine points of political issues. The citizens also recognize that Coriolanus's temperament makes him unsuitable for the role of a national leader who must put aside his biases and govern on behalf of all the people. As soon as they've given him their votes, they begin to express their doubts. Influenced, perhaps, by the effect of this legendary hero appearing before them in the robe of humility and personally appealing for their votes, they do not question his sincerity until afterwards. "He mock'd us," says one citizen (II.iii.159). The tribunes exploit the citizens' uneasiness and turn it to their own advantage.

Some commentators have warned against idealizing the Roman citizens, arguing that the play shows them to be politically unsophisticated. Oth-

> **Menenius likes to describe himself as a genial old man who is fond of eating and drinking and telling stories."**

ers have been harsher in their judgment, describing them as gullible, cowardly, greedy, and ungrateful. The citizens' propensity for violence is evident at the very beginning of the play, when they rush through the streets of Rome carrying sticks and clubs, prepared to force the patricians to come to terms with them. And from Act III onward they are easily led, manipulated by the tribunes and reacting according to the directions given them by the aediles. They appear overjoyed at the downfall of their traditional enemy and celebrate his banishment with great enthusiasm, showing no understanding of what this may mean to Rome. It has been noted that as individuals the Roman citizens are admirable, even sympathetic characters. But when they become part of a mob, they lose any capacity they have to judge wisely and act rationally.

Roman Lieutenant:

When Lartius leaves the captured city of Corioles to join Cominius and Coriolanus on the battlefield, he entrusts the city to one of his lieutenants (I.vii).

Roman Senators:

They serve as advisers to the consuls, whom they have the power to appoint. These appointments, however, must be confirmed by a vote of the citizens. The senators are all wealthy patricians, members of Rome's most prominent families. Their attitude toward the common citizens is ambiguous, yet they generally seem to recognize the limits of their own authority and to acknowledge the rights of the plebeians. One citizen, however, claims that the senators have so little concern for the populace that they will allow them to starve to death rather than reduce the price of grain. Further, he charges that they've passed laws encouraging usury, repealed statutes that placed restraints on wealthy people, and consistently enacted legislation that makes life difficult for the poor. Menenius, on the other hand— who is himself a senator—says that the senate is the source of everything that benefits the common citizens. And Coriolanus declares that if it weren't for the vigilance of ''the noble Senate'' (I.i.186), the plebeians would constantly be at each other's throats.

In II.ii, the senators address the tribunes—the people's representatives—with deference. However, they apparently intend to appoint Coriolanus to the consulship, and they do. In III.i, they escort him to the marketplace. As he becomes increasingly impatient with the tribunes, the senators urge him to moderate his words. When the mob arrives, the senators are caught up in the tumult. They draw their weapons and try to separate Coriolanus from the people. After Coriolanus leaves, they speak to the tribunes respectfully and urge them to allow him another chance to address the populace. In III.ii, some senators join Volumnia and others in trying to persuade Coriolanus to return to the marketplace and pacify the people. As one of them points out (III.ii.26-28), the senators fear there will be a civil war unless Coriolanus retracts his words. The senators are equally fearful of an invasion by the Volscians. When Volumnia and her party return from the Volscian encampment outside Rome— having persuaded Coriolanus not to attack the city— the senators lead a celebration in honor of their success.

Roman Soldiers:

On some occasions they fight bravely and earn their leaders' praise. At other times their actions are less than admirable. In I.iv, the Volscian army launches a surprise attack outside the walls of Corioles and quickly gains the upper hand against the Romans. Coriolanus curses his soldiers and threatens to turn on them himself unless they help him repel the Volscians. They respond well and the enemy is beaten back to the city gates. Coriolanus enters the city after the retreating Volscians, but the Roman soldiers declare this is folly and refuse to follow him. In I.v, after the city has been captured, three Roman soldiers are seen carrying off booty. Coriolanus calls them ''base slaves'' (I.v.7) and sneers at the insignificant items they've taken. In I.vi, the soldiers respond enthusiastically to Coriolanus's stirring challenge to return to the battlefield; indeed, more soldiers volunteer to follow him than are actually needed.

Senators:

See Roman Senators *and* Volscian Senators

Servants:

Members of Aufidius's household, they appear in IV.v. Their attitude toward Coriolanus is as changeable as the Roman citizens'. When Coriolanus first enters Aufidius's house—dressed in rags—the servants treat him with scorn; however, after he has been enthusiastically welcomed by Aufidius and offered the leadership of half the Volscian army, they express a different view of him. ''He is simply the rarest man i' th' world,'' says one servant (IV.v.160-61), and they all agree that he is a more valiant soldier than their master Aufidius. They marvel at his strength. ''He turned me about with his finger and his thumb, as one would set up a top'' (IV.v.152-53), claims a servant who had tried to eject Coriolanus from the house. All the servants are elated by the prospect of renewed war with Rome. Peace is dull and boring, they say, and produces nothing of worth—only rusting iron, an increase in the population, and full employment for tailors and writers of ballads. Peace ''makes men hate one another,'' remarks one servant (IV.v.230), and another agrees.

Sicinius Velutus:

See Tribunes

Soldiers:

See Roman Soldiers *and* Volscian Soldiers

Titus Lartius:

See Lartius

Tribunes:

Junius Brutus and Sicinius Velutus are two of the tribunes chosen near the beginning of the play to act on behalf of the Roman citizens. Their principal function is to protect the people's rights by keeping them informed of what is happening in the senate and summoning them together to solicit their opinions. As the citizens' representatives, they are justified in regarding Coriolanus's hatred of the plebeians as a reason to reject him for the consulship. They may honestly feel, as Brutus says at II.iii.256-57, that the small mutiny they are encouraging will ease political pressures and prevent a more widespread civil war in the future. As politicians, they show a clear understanding of effective electioneering. They have a good sense of organization, and they make sure—through the aediles—that people turn out to vote.

But Sicinius and Brutus far exceed their duties. Most commentators judge that they corrupt the office of tribune. They seem much less concerned about service to the people than with maintaining their own power. Coriolanus is their enemy, as well as the citizen's, and they recognize this. If he were to be elected, their positions would be in peril, and this seems to be their principal motivation. They recognize that Coriolanus's arrogance is a political weakness, and they cleverly trap him into exposing it before the people. They appear jealous of the enthusiastic welcome he receives when he returns from Corioles, and this may contribute to the actions they take to bring him down. They taunt him with words they know will inflame him—for example, ''traitor''—and wait for the reaction they know will come.

They seem not so clever in their conversations with Menenius, who makes fools of them without their realizing it. In the days of peace that follow Coriolanus's banishment, they are complacent, remarking that ''the world goes well'' and commenting on tradesmen contentedly ''singing in their shops and going about their functions friendly'' (IV.vi.5, 8-9). The renewal of hostilities by the Volscians, led by Coriolanus, takes them by surprise, and at first they deny this could possibly happen. But the people have not forgotten who orchestrated the banishment of Coriolanus. In V.iv, Sicinius is informed that the citizens have seized Brutus; further, they're hauling him ''up and down'' and threatening to kill him ''by inches'' (V.iv.37, 39) if the women's appeal to Coriolanus is not successful. Sicinius fervently thanks the messenger who brings him word that Volumnia has persuaded her son not to attack Rome; presumably Brutus's life is spared as well.

Tullus Aufidius:
See Aufidius

Usher:
An attendant to Valeria, he accompanies her when she pays a visit to Virgilia and Volumnia in I.iii.

Valeria:
She is a friend of Volumnia and Virgilia, and in I.ii she pays them a visit. Valeria describes to them a recent occasion when she witnessed young Martius playing with a butterfly. She relates how he repeatedly caught and released the butterfly—and then tore it to shreds. Her story over, she invites Virgilia and Volumnia to go with her to visit a mutual friend. Volumnia is willing, but Virgilia declines. Only then does Valeria tell them the news she's heard about Coriolanus and the Roman army: they are fully prepared to meet the Volscians, and the war will undoubtedly be over quickly.

Valeria appears in three more scenes, but she has little or nothing to say there. She is with the other women when they inform Menenius and the tribunes that the war is over and Coriolanus has performed heroically, and when Coriolanus is welcomed back to Rome (II.i). She accompanies them to the Volscian camp when Volumnia and Virgilia plead with Coriolanus to spare the city. The most lengthy description of Valeria by another character comes at V.iii.65-67, where Coriolanus refers to her in chilling terms: ''The moon of Rome, chaste as the icicle / That's curdied by the frost from purest snow / And hangs on Dian's temple.'' (Diana is the patroness of virgins.)

Virgilia:
The wife of Coriolanus, she embodies virtues that are rarely demonstrated elsewhere in the play: integrity, composure, quiet dignity, and tenderness. She takes no part in the political maneuvering and appears relatively uninterested in honors or appearances. Many commentators note that Coriolanus appears to love Virgilia as much as he can love anyone. Coriolanus refers to Virgilia as ''my sweet wife'' (IV.i.48) and salutes her on his return from the Volscian war as ''my gracious silence'' (II.i.175). In their final meeting, he calls her ''best of my flesh'' (V.iii.42), lingers over a kiss, and swears that he is ever true to her.

Virgilia's view of war and her tenderheartedness place her in sharp contrast with her mother-in-law. Volumnia glories in imagining her son in the heat of battle and pictures him wiping the blood from his forehead as he charges against the enemy. ''His bloody brow? O Jupiter, no blood!'' pleads Virgilia (I.iii.38). Virgilia's frequent tears provoke scorn from her mother-in-law and gentle teasing from her husband. But several commentators have argued that her tears are signs of a sensitive nature rather than an indication of weakness. Virgilia stands fast against the coaxing of Volumnia and Valeria, who want her to accompany them on a social visit. ''I will not out of doors,'' she says, ''till my lord return from the wars'' (I.iii.71, 75). In IV.ii, Virgilia

> **Coriolanus refers to Virgilia as 'my sweet wife' (IV.i.48) and salutes her on his return from the Volscian war as 'my gracious silence' (II.i.175). In their final meeting, he calls her 'best of my flesh' (V.iii.42), lingers over a kiss, and swears that he is ever true to her.** "

speaks sharply to Sicinius, one of the tribunes responsible for her husband's banishment—and he accuses her of being unfeminine. Later in that scene, Volumnia orders her to cease her weeping and "lament as I do, / In anger" (IV.ii.52-53). Virgilia is criticized first for acting like a man and then for being too soft or womanly. Perhaps the only Roman who comes close to appreciating her virtues is her husband.

Volscian Citizens:

One anonymous citizen of Antium appears briefly in IV.iv and directs Coriolanus—disguised as a poor man—to the house of Aufidius. At V.vi.49, the sounds of Volscian citizens welcoming Coriolanus back to Antium reach the ears of Aufidius and the conspirators. One conspirator complains bitterly that whereas Aufidius re-entered Antium with no more notice than if he'd been a block of wood, Coriolanus is being greeted with ear-splitting shouts from the throats of "patient fools, / Whose children he hath slain" (V.vi.51-52). The specter of the Volscian defeat at Corioli is raised by Coriolanus himself, later in that scene. Aufidius and the conspirators seize on this reference and inflame the citizens. The conspirators carry out the people's demand that Coriolanus be killed.

Volscian Lieutenant:

An aide to Aufidius, he appears in IV.vii. The lieutenant resents Coriolanus's popularity with the Volscian soldiers. He suggests to Aufidius that it was a mistake to allow Coriolanus to command one-half of the army. According to the lieutenant,

Coriolanus has taken on an almost godlike stature among the Volscian soldiers and Aufidius's reputation has been dulled by comparison. Aufidius shares the lieutenant's resentment and promises that one day, when the time is ripe, he will destroy Coriolanus.

Volscian Lords:

These noblemen appear in only one scene, V.vi. They greet Aufidius after he has returned to Antium and tell him they've read the letter he's sent to them charging that Coriolanus has betrayed his allies. The first lord declares that there can be "no excuse" (V.vi.68) for breaking off hostilities with Rome just when the Volscians were on the verge of success. However, when the Volscian citizens demand Coriolanus's death, the second lord tries to reason with them. "The man is noble," he reminds them (V.vi.124), and deserves the benefit of a formal trial. But the second lord's voice is drowned out by the shouts of Coriolanus, Aufidius, and the conspirators. The lords are shocked by the vicious stabbing of Coriolanus. When Aufidius places his booted foot on Coriolanus's corpse, the third lord orders him to remove it. The first lord commands that the body be taken away and mourned sincerely for it is "the most noble" corpse (V.vi.143) that ever was interred. The second lord offers a less exalted estimation of Coriolanus, suggesting that the hero's quick temper was a significant factor in his death. "Let's make the best" of the situation, he says pragmatically (V.vi.146).

Volscian Senators:

In I.ii, they meet with Aufidus to discuss a letter he has received from a spy in Rome, reporting that the Romans have learned of Volscian preparations for war. Aufidius is angry, for this means the Volscians have lost the element of surprise, and their intention to capture several Roman towns quickly will now be impossible to carry out. The Volscian senators are more complacent. They doubt whether the Romans are ready for war, and they assure Aufidius that they are capable of defending Corioles. In IV.v, two Volscian senators appear on the city walls to address the Roman soldiers before the battle of Corioles begins. Though the city is under threat, they speak defiantly. On another occasion, several Volscian senators are dining with Aufidius on the evening that Coriolanus arrives in Antium (IV.v). They treat Coriolanus with great respect and offer him the command of half their army; in return, Coriolanus promises to lead the Volscians through the gates of Rome and into the city. This episode occurs off-stage and is described by one of Aufidius's servingmen at IV.v.191-202.

Volscian Soldiers:

They appear or are referred to in several scenes. In I.iv, a force of Volscian soldiers rushes out of Corioles and attacks the Roman army, driving the enemy "back to their trenches" (S.D.I.iv.30). Coriolanus rouses his troops, however, and the Volscians are forced to retreat. In I.viii, a number of Volscian soldiers intervene in the combat between Aufidius and Coriolanus; they rescue their leader, and Aufidius is humiliated by their interference. In I.x, two or three Volscian soldiers acompany the wounded Aufidius as he leaves the battlefield. The Volscian soldiers' loyalty passes to Coriolanus after he is banished from Rome and becomes a leader of their army. According to Aufidius's lieutenant, the soldiers now talk of nothing else but Coriolanus's bravery, and he has replaced Aufidius as their hero (IV.vii.2-6).

Volumnia:

She is Coriolanus's mother and the most complex female character in the play. From one perspective, she may be seen as the ideal Roman matron: a fiercely patriotic woman who has raised her only son to seek honor in the service of his country. Indeed, Volumnia proudly acknowledges that she would be willing to see her son Coriolanus killed in battle, if it would contribute to his glory and Rome's welfare. However, her warlike ferocity and bloodthirstiness make many modern readers uneasy. Her preference for the image of blood spurting from a hero's brow over that of a mother nursing her child seems shocking and unnatural. She repeatedly expresses contempt for her daughter-in-law Virgilia's tenderheartedness. When Virgilia asks her how she would feel if Coriolanus were to die in battle, Volumnia responds that she would regard the noble reputation that lived after him as a substitute for her son.

Volumnia's relationship with Coriolanus has raised many questions among readers and commentators. Some believe that her determination to see him wreathed with military honors reflects her own desire to be a warrior—a role that Roman society would not allow her to assume. She is the first one to suggest, after his glorious victory at Corioles, that now there is only "one thing wanting" (II.i.201), that is, the consulship. Whether this is a suitable position for him is a question that does not arise: it

> " Volumnia proudly acknowledges that she would be willing to see her son Coriolanus killed in battle, if it would contribute to his glory and Rome's welfare."

would be the culmination of her ambitions for him. There are also disturbing elements of incestuousness in Volumnia's references to Coriolanus. "If my son were my husband," she says to Valeria, she would rejoice more "in that absence wherein he won honor, than in the embracements of his bed, where he would show most love" (I.iii.2-3, 3-5).

Her passion is sometimes offset by her practicality. She wants her son to be elected consul, and she carefully calculates how this should be achieved. The number of his wounds is important, and at II.i.146-50, 153-54, she adds them up, pointing out the political importance of scars "to show the people" (II.ii.147) when he seeks political office. She urges her son to compromise his principles—the very ones she instilled in him—in order to win the people's votes. Though she has taught him to disdain the common citizens and to be fiercely proud of his integrity, she pleads with him in III.ii to set those things aside and pretend to be something he isn't. In part because he's been taught to be a submissive son, Coriolanus obeys her.

Once more, near the close of the play, she asks him to compromise his honor. Pleading with him to spare Rome, she wants him to be a peacemaker, apparently unaware of the irony: she has raised him and educated him to be a warrior. She asserts that "no man in the world" has been "More bound to's mother" (V.iii.158-59) for what he has achieved, and yet, she claims, "Thou hast never in thy life / Show'd thy dear mother any courtesy" (V.iii.160-61). She shames him by kneeling to him—a shocking reversal of ancient Roman standards calling for children to show reverence to their parents. And she concludes by picturing him as responsible for her death: "So we will home to Rome / And die among our neighbours. . . . I am hush'd until our city be afire, / And then I'll speak a little" (V.iii.172-73, 181-82). She seems not to understand that if he leads the Volscians away from Rome it will mean his death. After Coriolanus gives in and points out to Volumnia the implications of his concession to her, she is silent. When the women return to Rome, they are greeted by a tumultuous welcome. Volumnia does not respond to the senator who congratulates her on her achievement.

Watch:

Volscian guards or watchmen, they appear in V.ii. When Menenius goes to the Volscian camp to appeal to Coriolanus not to attack Rome, they bar his way. They treat him with contempt, calling him a foolish old man and mocking his claims to be Coriolanus's closest friend and adviser. After Menenius's brief and unsuccessful interview with Coriolanus, the guards deride him again and send him back to Rome thoroughly humiliated.

Young Martius:

He is the son of Coriolanus and Virgilia. In V.iii, he goes to the Volscian camp with his mother and his grandmother to plead with Coriolanus not to attack Rome. On that occasion he shows a bold spirit similar to his father's (V.iii.127-28). Valeria's description of young Martius playing with a butterfly (I.iii.57-65) is much more significant than his single appearance in the play. Most commentators view his reported actions—repeatedly catching a butterfly, then releasing it, and finally tearing it to pieces—as sadistic. He must have been in one of his "father's moods," Volumnia comments (I.iii.67). He's "a noble child," responds Valeria (I.iii.66). He's a lively boy, his mother adds.

Further Reading

Brockbank, Philip. Introduction to *Coriolanus,* by William Shakespeare, 1-89. The Arden Edition. London: Methuen, 1976.

In pp. 35-68, Brockbank discusses at length "the tragedy of Coriolanus," including the hero's self-destructive commitment to valor and his vulnerability to ordinary human emotion. In Brockbank's judgment, Coriolanus's death is "a triumph, not a humiliation": the hero surrenders his life to atone for Rome's distorted system of values and for his own reckless adherence to those values. In other sections of his introduction, Brockbank analyzes the language of the play, comments upon its sources, and provides an overview of its stage history.

Charney, Maurice. "*Coriolanus.*" In *All of Shakespeare,* 299-308. New York: Columbia University Press, 1993.

In this chapter from a book written for students, Charney focuses on the character of Coriolanus and on what the critic describes as "an acute feeling of class hatred" in the play. He argues that Coriolanus's rigid sense of integrity and his outspoken honesty are the bases of the tragedy. Charney also discusses imagery in *Coriolanus*, particularly images related to acting and the theater which emphasize the idea that people in the political arena must play roles and assume false appearances.

Dawson, Anthony B. "*Coriolanus.*" In *Watching Shakespeare: A Playgoers' Guide*, 206-18. New York: St. Martin's, 1988.

Dawson approaches *Coriolanus* from the perspective of the challenges that face actors and directors who stage the play. He contends that the most significant feature of the text is its careful balancing of different political viewpoints. Dawson focuses on the plebeians, who are not, he insists, "a witless mob"; Menenius, whom he characterizes as a charming elitist; Coriolanus and his "splendid isolation" from common humanity; and the tribunes, who accurately perceive Coriolanus's unwillingness to compromise.

Givan, Christopher. "Shakespeare's *Coriolanus*: The Premature Epitaph and the Butterfly." *Shakespeare Studies* XII (1979): 143-58.

Givan examines the impact of the many occasions throughout the play when Coriolanus is referred to by others as a "thing"; he concludes that one important result of this usage is to dehumanize the hero. The critic also contends that the elements Coriolanus most despises in the people are those he is most fearful of finding in himself: childishness, faithlessness, inhumanity, and loss of individuality. Givan concludes that though Coriolanus is a victim of Roman society, his self-destructive tendencies are partly responsible for his tragic end.

Goldman, Michael. "Characterizing Coriolanus." In *Acting and Action in Shakespearean Tragedy*, 140-68. Princeton: Princeton University Press, 1985.

Goldman evaluates "the power and magnetism, . . . the sympathetic appeal of Coriolanus as a dramatic character." He notes that the characterization of the play's hero is achieved through a variety of means: the comments of Coriolanus's friends and enemies, his own attempts to create a self-image, and the readers' and audiences' experience of his words and actions. There is a deep, inner nature within Coriolanus, Goldman declares, but it is complex and elusive.

Leggatt, Alexander. "*Coriolanus.*" In *Shakespeare's Political Drama*, 189-213. London: Routledge, 1988.

Leggatt focuses on the conflict between social classes in *Coriolanus*. He contends that when the plebeians are not being influenced by the tribunes, they show keen insight into political issues and personalities, even though Menenius denies their ability to reason and mocks their attempts to make sense of the situation. Leggatt also closely examines the character of Coriolanus, emphasizing his emotional isolation, his hatred of the common people, and his confused sense of who he is after he's been banished from Rome.

McKenzie, Stanley D. "'Unshout the noise that banish'd Martius': Structural Paradox and Dissembling in *Coriolanus*." *Shakespeare Studies* XVIII (1986): 189-204.

McKenzie declares that the dominant mood in *Coriolanus* is uncertainty, and thus "there are simply no 'right' responses for the audience." He points out that Coriolanus's only act of compassion in the play—sparing Rome and its people—comes at the expense of betraying his heroic nature. McKenzie also devotes considerable attention to Volumnia; he views her as a person willing to compromise her principles if political realities call for such behavior, and he argues that Rome is saved only by her readiness to abandon the ideals she has taught her son.

Miles, Geoffrey. "'I Play the Man I Am': *Coriolanus*." In *Shakespeare and the Constant Romans*, 149-68. Oxford: Clarendon Press, 1996.

Miles views Coriolanus as a tragic victim of his conception of constancy and heroic valor, a man whose only values are warlike courage and military glory. From Miles's perspective, the play is deeply ironic. He contends that while Coriolanus believes he is being true to his own nature by striving to become an almost godlike hero, he is actually playing the role that Roman society and his mother have created and imposed on him.

Poole, Adrian. "*Coriolanus*." Boston: Twayne, 1988.

Poole provides a close, scene-by-scene analysis of the dramatic action, emphasizing the different ways that the play—and Coriolanus himself—may be interpreted. Poole calls attention to the dominating physical presence of the central character. He asserts that Coriolanus illustrates in his own person the noise, violence, and dangerous qualities that are characteristic of the play itself.

Thomas, Vivian. "Sounds, Words, Gestures and Deeds in *Coriolanus*." In *Shakespeare's Roman Worlds*, 154-219. London: Routledge, 1989.

Thomas emphasizes the need to understand the historical and political aspects of *Coriolanus* in order to appreciate its portrayal of a society undergoing profound changes. From this perspective, he argues, its hero is the embodiment of long-held values that are being replaced by newer ones to which he cannot adapt. Thomas also provides an extensive comparison of the way various characters in the play—Menenius, Volumnia, Aufidius, and Coriolanus himself—are treated in classical accounts of the period and in Shakespeare's tragedy.

Cymbeline

circa 1609-10

Plot Summary

Act I:

Cymbeline, the king of Britain, has a daughter Imogen from a former marriage. His new queen wants Imogen to marry her son Cloten, also from a former marriage. But Imogen instead marries Posthumus Leonatus, a man very much admired for his courage and his intelligence. Cymbeline banishes Posthumus and confines Imogen to the management of the queen. Just before Posthumus leaves England for the home of Philarius in Italy, the queen allows the couple a few moments to say goodbye. She then informs Cymbeline of their whereabouts, and the displeased king surprises the couple and chases Posthumus away. Posthumus and Imogen only have time to exchange tokens. He gives her a bracelet, and she gives him a diamond ring. Posthumus leaves his servant Pisanio in England to act as a liaison between himself and Imogen. Pisanio enters and reports that Cloten has assaulted Posthumus as the latter made his way to the departing ship, nothing coming of the engagement because Posthumus did not take Cloten seriously. Meanwhile, Doctor Cornelius gives the queen what she thinks are deadly poisons, the queen offering that she will use the poisons on small animals to study the effects and formulate antidotes. Doctor Cornelius does not trust her and has given her potions that will only incapacitate the taker, leaving him refreshed when the effects wear off. The queen hands the drug to

Pisanio, telling him it is an effective restorative, hoping he will poison himself. She then coaxes him to leave the service of Posthumus and serve her. Pisanio declines the offer.

In Italy, Jachimo, a friend of Philario, bets Posthumus gold against his ring that he can seduce Imogen. Jachimo arrives in England and presents Imogen with a commendatory letter of introduction from Posthumus. He tells Imogen that Posthumus is sleeping with other women in Italy. To be revenged, she should sleep with Jachimo. Imogen is outraged, and Jachimo apologizes, saying he was only testing the virtue Posthumus had so often extolled. He asks Imogen if she will keep a trunk for him. The trunk, he explains, contains valuables about which he is concerned, being that he is a foreigner in a strange place. She readily agrees to keep the trunk for him in her bedchamber.

Act II:

Jachimo has hidden himself in the trunk which is now in Imogen's bedroom. When she falls asleep, he sneaks out and writes down everything he observes in the room, records that there is a strangely shaped mole on her breast, and steals Posthumus's bracelet from her arm. He sneaks back into the trunk to wait for morning. In the morning, Cloten has musicians play outside Imogen's door so that she might awake to sweet music and thank him for the kindness he has done for her. Cymbeline and the queen find him outside of Imogen's chamber and encourage him in his wooing of her. But when he speaks with Imogen, she tries to discourage his suit, telling him she is not attracted to him in the least. When Cloten criticizes Posthumus, Imogen says Cloten is a despicable creature worth less than any one of Posthumus's garments. She discovers her bracelet missing and sends Pisanio to look for it.

In Italy, Philario and Posthumus discuss the mission of Caius Lucius, who is a general of the Roman forces and who is, at that moment, in England to ask Cymbeline to pay tribute to the Roman Emperor Augustus. Posthumus thinks the English king will resist and thinks the English forces will surprise the Romans with their courage and prowess. Jachimo returns to Italy and says that he has seduced Imogen. He describes the bedchamber, but Posthumus objects that such a description could have resulted from hearsay. Jachimo then produces the bracelet. Posthumus is ready to concede the bet, but Philario objects that the bracelet

might have been lost. When Jachimo describes the mole on Imogen's breast, he wins the wager, and Posthumus goes off alone to rage against the weak and false nature of women.

Act III:

Cymbeline meets with Caius Lucius and informs him of his decision not to pay tribute to Rome. Caius Lucius then declares war on Britain. Pisanio receives two letters from Posthumus. The first letter informs Imogen that Posthumus will soon be at Milford-Haven in Wales; she might meet him there if she so desires. The second letter instructs Pisanio to kill Imogen at Milford-Haven because she has proved to be untrue to Posthumus.

Outside of a cave in Wales, we meet Belarius, a lord banished by Cymbeline some twenty years earlier on false report; the lord now uses the name of Morgan. We also meet Guiderius and Arviragus, Cymbeline's two sons abducted by Belarius when they were infants. Guiderius and Arviragus are assumed to be the sons of Belarius/Morgan and are called Polydore and Cadwal respectively. They are off to hunt for their dinner.

Pisanio and Imogen are now in Wales also. Pisanio shows Imogen the letter with Posthumus's instructions for killing her. Imogen wants Pisanio to carry out his instructions on the spot, but Pisanio has a different plan. He has brought men's clothing for Imogen, and he suggests that she disguise herself like a man and secure passage with Caius Lucius when he sails from Britain. He gives her the drug which the queen has given him and passes along the misinformation that it is a medicine for the cure of fatigue and illness. When Imogen is discovered missing at Cymbeline's court, the king rages, and Cloten intercepts the recently returned Pisanio and demands to know where Imogen is. Pisanio gives Cloten the letter which implies that Imogen will meet Posthumus at Milford-Haven. Cloten coaxes Pisanio to serve him. Pisanio agrees only to temporarily appease Cloten. Pisanio's first task is to bring Cloten some of Posthumus's clothes. Meanwhile, in her masculine disguise, Imogen travels for two days until hunger makes her too weak to go on. She enters the cave of Belarius and eats some of the food there. She is discovered in the cave by Belarius and Cymbeline's two sons upon their return from hunting. Imogen is fearful, but Belarius treats her kindly, and Guiderius and Arviragus, ironically, vow to treat her like a brother. In the last scene, two Roman senators appear, briefly discussing preparations for war with England.

Act IV:

Belarius, Guiderius, and Arviragus leave the cave in the morning to hunt. Imogen remains behind because she is ill. As they leave, she takes some of the medicine Pisanio has given her. Outside the cave, Belarius and Cymbeline's sons encounter Cloten, who has arrived near that place following the directions in Posthumus's letter to Imogen. Belarius recognizes Cloten from years before, and he and Arviaragus go off to see whether or not Cloten has come alone, while Guiderius confronts Cloten. Cloten threatens Guiderius, assuming he is a lawless mountaineer. They fight, and Guiderius kills Cloten, cutting off his head. Arviragus returns to the cave and thinks that Imogen is dead. Belarius, Guiderius, and Arviragus place Imogen's body next to the headless corpse of Cloten, intending to return at midnight and strew the bodies with dew-laden flowers. In the meantime, Imogen awakes, sees the headless corpse dressed in Posthumus's clothes, and assumes it is Posthumus. She immediately thinks that Pisanio, in league with Cloten, is responsible for the murder of Posthumus, believing he forged the letters and purposfully misinformed her about the nature of the drug she has ingested. She throws herself upon the corpse crying. She is discovered in this position by Caius Lucius and his military officers as they travel by preparing to receive troops from the continent and wage war with the English. Caius Lucius thinks that Imogen is a loyal page lamenting the death of his master, and Imogen, for her own safety, plays along. She tells the Roman general that her name is Fidele, and her dead master Richard du Champ. Caius Lucius, impressed by her loyalty, requests that she enlist in his service.

At Cymbeline's palace, the queen has become sick worrying about Cloten, and the king, too, misses Cloten's services at a time of impending war. Cymbeline threatens to torture Pisanio, believing he knows where Imogen has gone. Pisanio protests that he knows nothing, intending to make up for his deception with Cymbeline by fighting bravely in the upcoming battles. A lord of Cymbeline's court supports Pisanio; he vows that Pisanio was at court on the day of Imogen's disappearance.

Back in Wales, Guiderius and Arviragus are enthusiastic about enlisting with the English troops and repelling the Romans. Belarius is hesitant, fearing he will be recognized. Eventually, he gives in to the insistent enthusiasm of his two youthful charges.

Act V:

Posthumus receives a bloody cloth and believes that Pisanio has sent it to him as proof that he has killed Imogen as instructed. He now regrets giving Pisanio those instructions and feels he must die to compensate for having been instrumental in Imogen's death. He has come to Britain as part of a contingent of Italian gentry led by Jachimo to fight against the Britains, but he disguises himself as an English peasant and fights against the Romans. At first, the Roman soldiers rout the English forces, and Cymbeline is captured as those English forces flee. But Belarius, Guiderius, and Aviragus rescue Cymbeline and make a brave stand, stemming the retreat of the English soldiers. Posthumus joins them in the rescue and fights recklessly, hoping that he will die in battle. He fights with Jachimo and disarms him. The English win the battle, and Belarius, Guiderius, and Aviragus are honored for their bravery. Cymbeline searchs for the fourth brave soldier—Posthumus in a peasant's garb—but cannot find him to reward him. Posthumus has switched back to the uniform of a Roman soldier. He is arrested and is taken to jail. When he falls asleep, the souls of his deceased father, mother, and brothers appear to him in a dream. These ghostly apparitions implore Jupiter to take pity on Posthumus and reward him for his noble actions. Descending upon an eagle, Jupiter is upset to be so summoned by these ghostly souls, and he commands them back to the nether regions, telling them that the lives of mortals are his concern, not theirs. Before Jupiter departs, he leaves a tablet on which there is a riddling prediction. The ghosts of Posthumus's family place the table on his sleeping form and vanish. When Posthumus wakes, he does not understand what is written there. Moments later, he is taken from jail and led, along with a number of other Roman prisoners, to Cymbeline's tent. Cymbeline has just learned from Cornelius that the queen has died after confessing that she had intended to poison both the king and his daughter Imogen in order to make Cloten king. Cymbeline pronounces that all the Roman prisoners must die. Caius Lucius asks that his boy, really Imogen in disguise, might be spared. Cymbeline grants that request. Imogen, seeing Posthumus's diamond ring on the finger of Jachimo, is allowed to question him. He reveals the extent of his deceptive villainy regarding Posthumus and Imogen. Next, all deceptions and confusions are revealed, with Posthumus, Pisanio, and Cornelius all stepping forward and uncovering their roles in in the preceding action, and Imogen's true identity being revealed. Guiderius then admits that he killed and beheaded Cloten. Cymbeline sentences him to death for treasonously killing a prince, but Belario makes it known that Guiderius and Aviragus are really Cymbeline's sons, stolen from him twenty years before by Belarius himself. Cymbeline is overwhelmed but joyous at the many revelations that have come in such rapid succession. Philarmonus, the Roman soothsayer, interprets Jupiter's tablet, which has predicted the reunion of Cymbeline's family and the improved relations of Rome and England. Cymbeline frees the Roman prisoners and announces that he will pay Rome its tribute, having only refused to do so previously at the insistence of the queen.

Modern Connections

Cymbeline deals with a concept as familiar to modern audiences as it was to Shakespeare's audiences: nationalism. The play is set in the ancient, pre-Christian past, a time when the Roman Empire was flourishing and England, or Britain, was an island country comprised of numerous feudal territories with distinctly tribal loyalties. During the reign of Julius Caesar, Roman soldiers occupied England but eventually withdrew when England's isolation and the constant vigilance necessary to contain Celtic barbarities became too much of a drain on Roman resources. Rome still considered England a colony and demanded tribute, a kind of monetary tax, and King Cymbeline's refusal to pay that tribute is the central issue of Shakespeare's play. Shakespeare, though, wrote *Cymbeline* in the early seventeenth century, a time when England was beginning to emerge as an empire in its own right, an empire rivaling that of Rome. It was an era that saw the beginning of English colonization and the flourishing of English arts and literature; these developments contributed to feelings of pride in the English, pride in their nation (nationalism). Shakespeare's play gives the impression that Cymbeline rules a united nation, a political reality that did not come into existence until the late fifteenth century. In the early seventeenth century, England greatly respected the legacy of Roman civilization and saw itself as the next great empire, an attitude Shakespeare re-

flects in his depiction of not only Cymbeline's refusal to pay tribute but also the superior nobility of the English characters over the Roman ones in the play.

Although Cymbeline says, at the end of the play, that he has earlier been dissuaded from paying tribute to Rome by the influence of the queen, the play seems to indicate that there is widespread support for his refusal to do so. When Philario, Posthumus's Italian host, says that he thinks England will pay the tribute, Posthumus objects that England will fight before it grovels to Rome, a fight in which England will show a military strength and united resolve that has been, so far, underestimated. When Caius Lucius departs from Cymbeline's palace to report Cymbeline's refusal of Augustus's demand, Cymbeline himself says, ''Our subjects, sir, / Will not endure [Augustus's] yoke'' (III.v.4-5). And when the queen remarks that it is too bad Caius Lucius has left frowning, Cloten says, '''Tis all the better, / Your valiant Britains have their wishes in it'' (III.v.19-20). After the English soldiers have defeated the Romans, proving themselves equal or superior, Cymbeline can graciously agree to pay the tribute. It was never a question of money; it was a question of English pride. Even Jupiter, the Romans' supreme god, reluctantly endorses the fact that England is equal to Rome. In the tablet that he leaves with Posthumus, Jupiter reveals that, only when the English royal family is reunited, will ''Britain be fortunate and flourish in peace and plenty'' (V.v.441-42). Philarmonus, the Roman soothsayer, interprets the prediction of England's flourishing as the union of ''Th' imperial Caesar'' and ''the radiant Cymbeline, / Which shines here in the west'' (V.v.474-76). The message is clear: England has proved its worthiness to be Rome's successor.

In comparison to the Roman characters in the play, the English characters are depicted as being more noble. Jachimo is a swaggering braggart, the kind of Italian courtier Shakespeare and his Elizabethan and Jacobean contemporaries so loved to ridicule and stereotype for their decadence and arrogance. He thinks he can get any woman that he wants, even Imogen, who Posthumus describes as unquestionably chaste. But Jachimo cannot assail Imogen's chastity and innocence, because she is, as her name suggests, the ideal ''image'' of womanhood, against which the women of all other nations pale in comparison. Jachimo admits as much when, in his long-winded confession of villainy made to

Cymbeline in the last scene, he refers to Imogen as "That paragon, thy daughter" (V.v.147). Although Jachimo gets the upper hand over Posthumus by tricking him, Posthumus proves superior in the end. In the battle, the disguised Posthumus easily bests Jachimo and disarms him, leaving the Italian courtier to wonder aloud about the strength of England's aristocrats, its peasants proving so strong. In the last scene of the play, Posthumus forgives Jachimo and tells him, "Live, / And deal with others better" (V.v.418-19). Like Cymbeline, Posthumus can be generous and gracious from a position of demonstrated superiority.

The play's best argument for the superior nobility of its English characters comes in the depiction of Cymbeline's two sons, Guiderius and Arviragus. Belarius never ceases to be amazed at the inherent nobility they display, as we discover in our first encounter with him in front of the cave in which he has raised them. He says that the boys have no idea they are the sons of a king

> . . . and though train'd up thus meanly
> I' th' cave [wherein they] bow, their thoughts do hit
> The roofs of palaces, and nature prompts them
> In simple and low things to prince it much
> Beyond the trick of others.

(III.iii.82-86)

Their great eagerness to join the battle and their display of courage in the fighting attest to an inborn virtue. And when Guiderius kills and beheads Cloten, he is performing yet another noble deed by preventing the evil blood of the queen and the ignorant blood of Cloten from polluting the truly royal blood of Cymbeline and his children.

For modern audiences, this idea of nationalism—pride in one's nation—is a familiar one. National pride, for example, fuels the competitive atmosphere of world-wide sporting events, such as the Olympics. Sometimes, however, feelings of nationalism become transformed into a destructive force. Ethnocentrism occurs when feelings of pride become an attitude of cultural or national superiority. When groups of people feel that their nation or their culture is superior to another nation or culture, the result can be violence. We can see this in gang warfare, and in wars between countries, or groups of people within countries. What twentieth century wars may have been fueled by feelings of ethnocentrism? Does nationalism always lead to ethnocentrism? Or can people be proud of their country or culture without feeling that other countries or cultures are inferior? How are nationalism, ethnocentrism, and racism related?

Characters

Apparitions:

These are the ghosts of Posthumus's father, mother, and two brothers. They appear to Posthumus in a dream while he sleeps in jail, desperate to end his own life. Sicilius, Posthumus's father, died fighting bravely in battle, as did Posthumus's two brothers. Posthumus's mother died giving birth to him. The apparitions lament that Posthumus is in such a state of despair, and they implore Jupiter to reward Posthumus for his brave actions in battle and his faithfulness to Imogen. They believe that Posthumus is the victim of Cymbeline's unfair banishment of him.

Arviragus:

Arviragus is the son of Cymbeline and the brother of Guiderius, and Imogen. As an infant, he was abducted by Belarius, who raised him for twenty years in the primitive wilds of Wales and renamed him Cadwal. Even though Arviragus has been raised in a cave, he demonstrates the inborn virtue one would expect in the son of a king. He is eager for experiences beyond the homely life of hunting and gathering which he now lives with Belarius, the man he knows as his father. He envies his older brother, Guiderius, when the latter kills Cloten. He wishes that he might have had the opportunity to display his strength and courage in the face of danger. Arviragus feels an instant love for and kinship with Imogen, whom he thinks is a boy and later calls "brother," when he discovers her in the cave. Later, thinking that Imogen has died, he carries her from the cave and convinces Guiderius that they should conduct for her the same funeral rights they conducted for Euriphile, the woman they believed to be their mother. They sing a beautiful song at Imogen's grave and strew her body with flowers. When his brother, Guiderius announces that he will fight on the side of the English in the battle that looms ahead, Arviragus cannot be restrained from going as well. Alongside Belarius and his brother, he fights bravely in that battle, the three of them rescuing Cymbeline and reversing the Roman surge. He, along with Belarius and Guiderius, is honored by Cymbeline for his bravery. In the last scene of the play, he learns of his true identity and is reunited with his father King Cymbeline.

Attendants:

These attendants appear in several scenes without speaking. They attend Cymbeline and the queen at Cymbeline's palace.

Belarius:

Belarius is an English lord who has been banished by Cymbeline twenty years earlier. He claims to have been a loyal follower of Cymbeline, having nobly fought for his king. Cymbeline, though, believed the false report of another man who was jealous of Belarius. Taking revenge, Belarius kidnapped Cymbeline's two infant sons, Guiderius and Arviragus, and raised them in a cave in Wales. He married Euriphile, the nurse of those two boys, after she helped him with the abduction, and Guiderius and Arviragus grew up believing that Euriphile was their mother and Belarius their father. In Wales, Belarius takes the name of Morgan and renames Cymbeline's two sons Polydore and Cadwal. Belarius entertains his two adopted sons with stories of his exploits in days gone by. He is delighted with the princely grace and strength they exhibit despite being raised in such primitive surroundings. Even though Belarius does not know that the young boy discovered in his cave is Imogen, he is pleased that Guiderius and Arviragus treat that young boy with love and kindness. Even when Arviragus says that he would rather see Belarius than Fidele, the name of Imogen as the young boy, die, Belarius is impressed. He believes that Arviragus knows by instinct that Belarius is not his father. Belarius recognizes Cloten when he shows up at the cave, and he is fearful that others might follow. After Guiderius kills Cloten, Belarius insist that Cloten, no matter how loathsome, is a prince and should be given a decent burial. Worried that he, too, might be recognized, Belarius is reluctant to join the battle. Once he does so, he fights valiantly alongside his two adopted sons and is honored by Cymbeline for his efforts. When Cymbeline condemns Guiderius for killing Cloten, Belarius steps forward and reveals who Guiderius and his brother really are. Cymbeline, in the end, forgives him.

British Captains:

These British captains apprehend Posthumus after the battle. Posthumus has changed into the uniform of a Roman soldier. They turn Posthumus over to Cymbeline, who has two jailers take him away.

Caius Lucius:

See Lucius

Cadwal:

See Arviragus

Cloten:

Cloten is the son of the queen by a former marriage. He wants to marry Imogen and despises Posthumus for depriving him of that opportunity. He is depicted as a quarrelsome and boorish fool. He threatens Posthumus with his sword when Posthumus is leaving to begin his exile in Italy. No one is hurt in that quarrel, only because Posthumus does not take Cloten's threat seriously. No one but the queen seems to like Cloten. He is often in the company of two lords of Cymbeline's court, who ridicule him when he is out of earshot. Cloten lends his voice to the queen's insistence that Cymbeline not pay tribute to Rome, but he only mimics and seconds his mother. Cloten makes a futile effort to impress Imogen by having the musicians wake her with sweet song, an action which initially inspires sympathy in some audiences. That is until he ignores her attempts to reject him gently and viciously derides Posthumus. He is terribly upset when Imogen says that he is not worth Posthumus's "meanest garment" (II.iii.133). He finds it fitting, then, that he wears Posthumus's clothes as he sets off to intercept Imogen and Posthumus at Milford-Haven, where he intends to kill Posthumus and rape Imogen. Instead, he meets Guiderius. Even in this confrontation, Cloten acts in an imperious and obnoxious manner. Guiderius kills Cloten and beheads him. Later, Imogen awakes next to Cloten's headless body and assumes, because Cloten is wearing Posthumus's clothes, that he is Posthumus. This is either proof of the axiom that "the clothes make the man" or proof that Cloten's description of himself is accurate when he says, "I mean, the lines of my body are as well drawn as [Posthumus's]" (IV.i.9-10).

Cornelius:

Cornelius is a physician with an extensive knowledge of herbs and medicines. He has been imparting some of that knowledge to the queen, who is an eager student because she would make her own poisons. Early in the play, Cornelius gives the queen the powerful poison she has requested, osten-

> **Cloten makes a futile effort to impress Imogen by having the musicians wake her with sweet song, an action which initially inspires sympathy in some audiences. That is until he ignores her attempts to reject him gently and viciously derides Posthumus."**

sibly to kill small vermin, but really intended to kill Pisanio, or hopefully, Cymbeline. But Cornelius informs the audience, in an aside, that he does not trust the queen. He has handed over a drug that will make the person drinking it appear temporarily dead but feel wonderfully invigorated when the effects wear off. In the last scene of the play, he again explains the nature of the drug when Imogen accuses Pisanio of poisoning her. He also informs Cymbeline that the queen has died after confessing her evil intentions, explaining that she had intended to poison Imogen and use a slow-working drug on the king himself so that Cloten might gain the crown.

Cymbeline:

Cymbeline is the king of England. Imogen is his daughter by a former marriage, as are his two sons, Guiderius and Arviragus, who were abducted from him by Belarius when the two boys were just infants. His present queen has a son named Cloten, and she convinces Cymbeline that a marriage between Imogen and her son would be an expedient one. Politically, a marriage between Cloten and Imogen would make more sense than her marriage to Posthumus, who is an aristocrat but not a prince, since it would give the impression of a greatly consolidated Britain. But Imogen has, in fact, married Posthumus, and Cymbeline, largely at the insistence of the queen, banishes Posthumus from the kingdom. As an example of how the queen manipulates Cymbeline, we need only observe her first appearance in the play. She allows Imogen and Posthumus a few moments of farewell, but then immediately informs Cymbeline that the couple are together in the garden. An angry Cymbeline surpris-

es them and drives Posthumus off. He places Imogen under a kind of house arrest, putting the queen in charge of her freedom. Cymbeline also encourages Cloten to woo Imogen, thinking her resentment will fade and time will weaken her resistance to Cloten's proposals.

But Cymbeline has a greater problem than his daughter's unfortunate marriage. Caius Lucius, the Roman general, has landed in England to demand that Augustus Caesar be paid the tribute promised many years before, by an agreement between Julius Caesar and Cymbeline's uncle, Cassibelan. Cymbeline refuses to pay the tribute—he knows he has a good deal of support in doing so—and Caius Lucius declares war on Britain. Cymbeline has anticipated this declaration, and he has his defenses ready. During the battle that ensues, Cymbeline is temporarily captured by the Romans, and his English troops flee in retreat. But he is rescued by Belarius, Guiderius, Arviragus, and Posthumus, the latter disguised as an English peasant. The bold actions of these four men stem the retreat, and Cymbeline honors their noble actions. At the end of the play, he has the Roman prisoners brought to his tent and condemns them all to death. Caius Lucius says that if the tables were turned, the Romans would not be executing their English prisoners. They would treat them with more respect.

Cymbeline eventually changes his mind and frees the Roman prisoners. He has, in the meantime, been reunited with his two long-lost sons; he has rediscovered Imogen; he has learned that the queen never loved him and had sought to destroy his royal family; and he has accepted Posthumus as a member of that royal family, as one that the king has raised from youth. Cymbeline can now afford to treat the Romans kindly. The battle has proven that the Britains are strong and equal to the Romans, and Jupiter's prediction that Caesar and Cymbeline would blend, harmoniously, in the rays of the sun is fulfilled. Cymbeline can speak from a position of generosity and strength. He bows to no other nation, but, at the same time, he develops, in friendly relationships with other nations, the allies necessary to account, historically, for England having become the world power it is when Shakespeare imagines its ancient past in *Cymbeline*. Although he is the title character of the play and does not appear in a great many of the scenes, Cymbeline has a large presence in the play. In the final scene, he is the object of everyone's attention. He receives one startling revelation after another until he is overwhelmed, and is pivotal in each character's disclosure of events.

Dutchman:

The Dutchman appears without speaking in I.iv, the scene in which Posthumus arrives at Philario's house in Italy and wagers that Imogen will resist Jachimo's advances.

Fidele:

See Imogen

Frenchman:

The Frenchman is present when Posthumus arrives at Philario's house in Italy. He has met Posthumus before in France, and he agrees with Jachimo that Posthumus is not as perfectly wonderful as he is made out to be. He reminds Posthumus of the duel Posthumus had in France with another man, a duel stemming from a petty dispute in which Posthumus proclaimed his mistress more beautiful than any woman in France.

Gentlemen:

These are two gentlemen of Cymbeline's court. They appear in the first scene of the play and, in their conversation, inform the audience that although Cymbeline is annoyed with Imogen for marrying Posthumus, all of Cymbeline's courtiers believe Imogen has done well to shun the match the queen had hoped she would make with her son, the foolish and ill-mannered Cloten. The courtiers, however, hide their pleasure from the displeased Cymbeline. The two gentlemen praise Posthumus and discuss his commendable heritage. They do not approve of Cymbeline's banishment of him.

Guiderius:

Guiderius is the older son of Cymbeline and the brother of Arviragus and Imogen. As an infant, he was kidnapped from Cymbeline by Belarius, who raised him for twenty years in the wilds of Wales near Milford-Haven and renamed him Polydore. He thinks Belarius is his father. According to Belarius, Guiderius showed early signs of his princely nature. When Belarius would tell his tales of past adventures, Guiderius would listen raptly, his excitement evident, his desire for challenging experiences clearly expressed in his stiff attentiveness. Like Arviragus, he feels an instant bond of kinship with Imogen and mourns her when he thinks she has died. He, too, sings at her grave and strews her body with flowers. When Belarius and Arviragus check to see if Cloten has been followed, Guiderius con-

> ❝ . . . Cymbeline has a greater problem than his daughter's unfortunate marriage. Caius Lucius, the Roman general, has landed in England to demand that Augustus Caesar be paid the tribute promised many years before . . . ❞

fronts Cloten, who abuses him and treats him as inferior. Guiderius's royal blood rebels at that abuse, and he defends himself against Cloten's attack, killing him. Quite pleased with himself, he presents Cloten's severed head to Belarius, almost as if it were a trophy or an emblem of his manhood. Guiderius fights on the side of the English in the battle alongside Belarius and his brother. He fights bravely in that battle and is honored by Cymbeline for his bravery. In the last scene of the play, he steps forward to admit he has killed Cloten, and Cymbeline immediately sentences him to death for killing a prince. Belarius, though, says, "Stay, sir King. / This man is better than the man he slew" (V.v.302-03). Belarius reveals the true identity of Guiderius, who is then reunited with his father the king.

Helen:

Helen is a lady waiting on Imogen. With Jachimo hiding in the trunk that has been placed in Imogen's room, Helen, upon request, informs Imogen that it is midnight and is instructed to leave the taper burning and wake Imogen at four in the morning.

Imogen:

Imogen is the daughter of Cymbeline by a former marriage. She marries Posthumus, but the queen, Cymbeline's present wife, does not approve of the marriage that has left her son, Cloten, out of the picture. She plots to kill Imogen. Meanwhile, Jachimo, who has made a bet with Posthumus regarding Imogen's faithfulness, tells Imogen that Posthumus has been unfaithful to her. After suggesting that as revenge Imogen sleep with him, Jachimo tells Imogen he was only testing the virtue Posthumus has so highly praised. Jachimo then hides in Imogen's room, gathers some incriminating "evidence," and convinces Posthumus that Imogen has been unfaithful. Posthumus then arranges to have Pisanio kill Imogen. To avoid killing her as Posthumus has directed him to do, Pisanio fits Imogen with boy's clothes and sends her to Caius Lucius's departing ship in Milford-Haven. On the way there, however, Imogen is overcome with hunger and fatigue and finds herself in the cave of Belarius, Guiderius, and Arviragus. She does not know that the latter two are actually her brothers, but they share an unspoken bond with her that prompts them to call her "brother." After she appears to die, the result of the drug Pisanio has given her, her two brothers lay her in a grave and conduct funeral rites for her. She awakes in that grave next to the headless corpse of Cloten, which she thinks is the lifeless body of Posthumus. She throws herself on that body, weeping and moaning until Caius Lucius discovers her and makes her his page, thinking all the while that she is a boy. After the battle, she is taken to Cymbeline's tent along with the rest of the Roman prisoners. Caius Lucius begs Cymbeline to spare her, and, instead of pleading for Caius Lucius' life, as he fully expects she will, she takes the opportunity to question Jachimo about the ring he is wearing, her ring. In the process of that questioning, the truth comes out, and all the confusions of the play are clarified in rapid succession.

As Imogen's name suggests, she is the "image" of the ideal woman, the woman of Britain, exceeding the women of all other nations. When she adopts the disguise of a young boy, she takes the name "Fidele," another indication that she is meant to be seen as the model of faithfulness. In Jupiter's revelation, Imogen is the "piece of tender air" (V.v.446) that embraces Posthumus, the "lion's whelp" (V.v.443). At the end of the play, Imogen embraces Posthumus, and he says, "Hang there like fruit, my soul, / Till the tree die!" (V.v.262-63). In the union of Imogen's soul and Posthumus's tree-like physical strength will be born the fruit of Britain, its future princes.

Jachimo:

Jachimo is an Italian lord. He is arrogant and brash, believing that he can have any woman he desires. He is present at Philario's house as Philario awaits the arrival of Posthumus. Jachimo claims to have met Posthumus before, a meeting in which Posthumus did not impress him very much. Jachimo is surprised that Posthumus regularly receives so much praise. When Posthumus enters and the French-

man recalls how Posthumus, in the past, dueled another Frenchman in defense of Imogen's great beauty, Jachimo baits Posthumus. Jachimo wagers gold against the diamond ring Imogen has given Posthumus that he can seduce Imogen. When he arrives in England to attempt that seduction, he decides to be direct. He tells Imogen that Posthumus is sleeping around in Italy; she might avenge Posthumus's infidelity by sleeping with Jachimo. When Imogen is outraged and threatens to tell her father, Jachimo realizes that Imogen is as unimpeachable as Posthumus has claimed. Since directness has not worked, he tries deception. He apologizes for his behavior, which he says was meant to test her, and convinces her to store a trunk containing valuables for him and hides in that trunk as it is placed in her chamber. At midnight, when she has fallen asleep, he sneaks out and takes inventory of the room and records a distinguishing mark on her breast. He also steals her bracelet. He needs to win the wager, or Posthumus has pledged that he will answer with his sword for impugning Imogen's reputation. He returns to Italy and presents Posthumus with the alleged evidence he has garnered. Posthumus acceps Jachimo's claim to have seduced Imogen. Later, during the battle, Jachimo encounters Posthumus, who has disguised himself like an English peasant, and is disarmed by him, both figuratively and literally. He cannot believe that an English peasant could have so bested him. In the last scene of the play, Jachimo is taken as a prisoner to Cymbeline's tent, where he is forced to confess his deception of Posthumus. The confession is full of flowery speech and tedious metaphors, prompting Cymbeline to say, "I stand on fire: / Come to the matter" (V.v.168-69). Jachimo is representative of the declining integrity and concern with fashion that many Elizabethans associated with the Italian gentry.

Jailers:

The jailers take possession of Posthumus from Cymbeline and hold him prisoner after he has been apprehended by the two British captains. They are amazed that Posthumus is so pleased with his imprisonment and the prospect of being hanged. After Posthumus has awakened from his dream, in which he saw the apparitions of his family and a vision of Jupiter, the jailers take him to be hanged. But they are interrupted by a messenger who directs them to take the prisoner to the king. One of the jailers says, "Unless a man would marry a gallows and beget young gibbets, I never saw one so prone" (V.iv.198-99): in all his experience, this jailer has never seen a prisoner so eager to die.

Ladies:

These are the ladies of Cymbeline's court. They are seen attending the queen and Imogen. In V.v, two ladies affirm that what Cornelius has told Cymbeline about the queen's dying confession is true.

Leonatus (Posthumus Leonatus):

Posthumus is the husband of Imogen. His marriage to her displeases Cymbeline, and he is banished from England. He goes to Italy to stay at the home of Philario, a friend of Posthumus's deceased father. While there, he enters into an ill-advised wager with Jachimo, who thinks that he can seduce Imogen despite Posthumus's great confidence in her unfailing virtue. When Jachimo presents him with false proof that he has accomplished what he set out to do, Posthumus rails against Imogen and denounces all women, attributing to them every kind of vice and weakness. He writes Pisanio two letters, one meant to deceive Imogen into thinking that he might be met at Milford-Haven in Wales, the other directing Pisanio to kill Imogen when she travels to the appointed place. Pisanio sends him a bloody cloth meant to mislead Posthumus into thinking that Imogen has been killed and thereby set his mind at rest. The bloody cloth has the opposite effect; it throws Posthumus into a state of despair and bitter self-recrimination. He comes to England as part of an army of Italian gentry intending to fight the Britains, but he disguises himself as an English peasant and fights recklessly against the Romans, seeking death. That desire for death makes him change back to the uniform of a Roman soldier after the English have won the battle, in hopes that he might be captured and executed. He almost gets his wish, but as he is being led to the gallows, a messenger tells his jailers to take him to Cymbeline's tent instead. Once there, he discovers that Imogen is not dead, and he is reunited with her and is accepted by Cymbeline.

Posthumus is a difficult character to understand fully. His name can be roughly translated as "inheriting the qualities of a lion," and at first he does not live up to either the implication of his name or the praise he receives from others. Those praises probably result from the actions of his father, Sicilius, and his two brothers, all three dying bravely in battle. Early in the play, Posthumus is praised before the fact, everyone expecting that he will live up to the reputation of his father and his two brothers. At the beginning of the play, one of the gentlemen of Cymbeline's court says of Posthumus,

> At the end of the play, Imogen embraces Posthumus, and he says, 'Hang there like fruit, my soul, / Till the tree die!' (V.v.262-63)."

"I do not think / So fair an outward and such stuff within / Endows a man but he" (I.i.22-24). This is strong praise, but Jachimo says that he has seen Posthumus in Britain, and "He was then of a crescent note, expected to prove so worthy as since he hath been allow'd the name of" (I.iv.1-3). This is hollow praise, and the Frenchman adds, "I have seen him in France. We had very many there could behold the sun with as firm eyes as he" (I.iv.11-13). Posthumus confirms their skepticism; he does not act very nobly. Although Imogen does not die, Posthumus is guilty of intent to commit murder. When he receives the bloody cloth, he moans, "O Pisanio, / Every good servant does not all commands" (V.i.5-6). He wants to shift part of the blame to Pisanio, a blame that would rest entirely on Posthumus even if Pisanio had done as directed. Posthumus might be commended for fighting so bravely in the battle, but that bravery seems to stem more from Posthumus's despair (he fights fiercely and carelessly in battle because he wants to die) than it does from nobility. Perhaps the truest statement about Posthumus's inner qualities is made by one of the gentlemen at the beginning of the play, who says that Imogen has chosen Posthumus, "and his virtue / By her election may be truly read, / What kind of man he is" (I.i.52-54). That is, Posthumus only has greatness in being the husband of Imogen. When he is reunited with Imogen, she embraces him, and he says, "Hang there like fruit, my soul, / Till the tree die!" (V.v.262-63): she is the soul that completes him.

Lords:

For the most part, these are the lords of Cymbeline's court, who attend the king without speaking. Two of these lords are with Cloten during scenes in which Cloten has just come from a quarrel—with Posthumus in I.ii, and with another bowler in II.i. To his face, the two lords agree with Cloten's boastful rationalizations of his behavior. In

> **Jachimo wagers gold against the diamond ring Imogen has given Posthumus that he can seduce Imogen."**

asides, they make fun of his idiotic behavior and misplaced pride. The effect of their sarcasm is quite comic. For example, Cloten complains that, while bowling, he was scolded for swearing by a man of lesser rank than him. He says, "Whoreson dog! I gave him satisfaction! / Would he had been one of my rank! (II.i.14-15), to which one of the lords responds, "To have smell'd like a fool" (II.i.16). In V.iii, a Britain Lord, who has fled the battle, meets Posthumus and inquires what the outcome of that battle was. Posthumus considers him a pampered coward for having fled the action.

Lucius (Caius Lucius):

Caius Lucius is the general of the Roman forces. He comes to England as an ambassador for Emperor Augustus and requests that Cymbeline pay tribute to Rome under an agreement formed in the bygone days of Julius Caesar. When Cymbeline refuses that request, Caius Lucius declares war on England. Despite his declaration, he is treated graciously as a respected ambassador by Cymbeline and the queen. During his preparations for battle, Cauis Lucius comes upon Fidele/Imogen and impresses her into service. Caius Lucius is portrayed as a noble character, somewhat matter-of-fact but neither corrupt nor greedy. His only fault is that he is on the wrong side of the conflict. When he is taken before Cymbeline as a prisoner at the end of the play, he asks that Cymbeline save the life of his boy Fidele. Cymbeline grants him that request and says that Fidele may save one other person. Caius Lucius then says, "I do not bid thee beg my life, good lad, / And yet I know thou wilt" (V.v.102-03). When Fidele does not immediately name him, Caius Lucius is shocked. The arrogance he shows in this scene is, perhaps, meant to be representative of Rome's arrogance toward England.

Messengers:

There are several messengers in the play. In II.iii, a messenger announces to Cymbeline and the queen that Caius Lucius has arrived as an ambassador from Rome. In III.v, a messenger is sent to fetch Imogen for the queen and Cymbeline. He returns and announces that the doors of Imogen's chamber are all locked and there was no response to his knocking. In IV.iv, a messenger interrupts the jailers as they conduct Posthumus to the gallows. He directs the jailers to take their prisoner to Cymbeline's tent.

Morgan:

See Belarius

Musicians:

The musicians are directed by Cloten to play outside of Imogen's door and wake her with sweet harmonies. They sing a short song with beautiful lyrical imagery. Cloten hopes that providing Imogen this novelty will ingratiate him with her.

Officers:

The officers appear without speaking in the last scene of the play. They are present at Cymbeline's tent in the English camp after the battle.

Philario:

Philario is an Italian who fought with Posthumus's father, Sicilius. When Posthumus is banished by Cymbeline, Philario welcomes him to his home because he feels indebted to the deceased Sicilius for having saved his life. When Jachimo and the Frenchman offer that they were not very impressed with Posthumus when they met him in the past, Philario suggests that they met him in his youth; he has since grown into his praises. Philario discusses with Posthumus the situation between Rome and England, offering his opinion that the English will surely pay the tribute, an opinion with which Posthumus disagrees. As Jachimo presents evidence to Posthumus of his seduction of Imogen, Philario objects that the bracelet is no proof since it could have been found or stolen by Jachimo. He has thought the wager a bad idea from the start, and the tension between his friends seems to make him uneasy.

Philarmonus:

Philarmonus is a Roman soothsayer, one who can interpret mysterious signs in nature and the heavens. In IV.ii, he predicts success for the Roman forces because he has seen a vision of the Roman eagle flying from the south to the west and disappearing in the rays of the sun. He is wrong. At the end of the play he revises his interpretation of that vision, offering that it was really a prediction of Rome's reunion with England, harmony between Caesar and Cymbeline. Philarmonus is called upon to read the revelation from Jupiter that Posthumus could not understand. Philarmonus explains that Posthumus, as his name suggests, is the "lion's whelp" (V.v.443). Imogen is the "piece of tender air" (V.v.446) that embraces Posthumus. Cymbeline is the "lofty cedar" (V.v.453). The "lopp'd branches" (V.v.454), which must be regrafted to that cedar, are Guiderius and Arviragus. The message seems clear: when Cymbeline accepts Posthumus as his son-in-law and is surrounded again by his children, the English royal family will find strength, and England will prosper.

Pisanio:

Pisanio is the servant of Posthumus. When his master goes to Italy in exile, Pisanio stays in England to act as a go-between for Posthumus and Imogen. He resists the queen's request that he switch his allegiance from Posthumus to her, knowing the queen's character. When Posthumus informs him by letter that Imogen has proved false, Pisanio is dismayed and believes, accurately, that his master has been deceived by the Italians. He disobeys Posthumus's command to kill Imogen at Milford-Haven and, instead, outfits her like a young boy and sends her to Caius Lucius, who he believes is about to sail from England. On parting from Imogen, he hands her the drug the queen has earlier handed him. He thinks the drug is a medicinal elixir for curing illness, while the queen thinks it is a deadly poison, which she had hoped Pisanio would ingest. When Pisanio returns to Cymbeline's palace from Milford-Haven, he is confronted by the suspicious and jealous Cloten, who tries to bribe Pisanio into switching his loyalty from Posthumus to him. Pisanio makes Cloten believe that he will serve him. He procures some of Posthumus's clothes for Cloten and gives him the letter with which Posthumus has deceived Imogen into travelling to Milford-Haven, the letter which describes the supposed meeting place of the temporarily alienated couple. Pisanio sees no harm in supplying this information to Cloten since he believes Imogen will be long gone before Cloten arrives in Wales. Pisanio is exceptionally loyal to Posthumus, and he feels terrible, later, when he has to lie to Cymbeline to protect his master. He makes it clear that he will make up for his deception by fighting loyally for the

> "Jachimo is taken as a prisoner to Cymbeline's tent, where he is forced to confess his deception of Posthumus. The confession is full of flowery speech and tedious metaphors, prompting Cymbeline to say, 'I stand on fire: / Come to the matter' (V.v.168-69)."

king in the near future. In the scene of multiple revelations that ends the play, it is Pisanio who first identifies Fidele as Imogen. She accuses him of poisoning her, but Cornelius clears Pisanio of any ill intent.

Polydore:
See Guiderius

Posthumus (Posthumus Leonatus):
See Leonatus

Queen:

The queen is the wife of Cymbeline. Cloten is her son from a former marriage. She has great influence with Cymbeline and uses that influence to effect her own ends. Her greatest desire is to see Cloten crowned king of England. To that end, she convinces Cymbeline that Posthumus should be banished, since his marriage to Imogen prevents Imogen's marriage to Cloten. It would seem that Cymbeline is the only character in the play who cannot see through the queen's deception. The two gentlemen of Cymbeline's court who introduce the narrative see how manipulative she is, and Imogen, too, knows that the queen is not being truthful when she offers to be Imogen's advocate and plead with Cymbeline to soften his sentence of Posthumus. Cornelius, who has been instructing the queen in the manufacture and use of herbs for medicines and poisons, does not trust her. Instead of the deadly poison she has asked for, he passes to her a drug that only appears to act like a poison. Pisanio refuses to

> **Although Imogen does not die, Posthumus is guilty of intent to commit murder. When he receives the bloody cloth, he moans, 'O Pisanio, / Every good servant does not all commands' (V.i.5-6)."**

become her servant as he accepts from her the drug with which she hopes he will poison himself. The queen is instrumental in convincing Cymbeline to refuse Rome the tribute it demands. She also convinces Cloten to persist in his wooing of Imogen. She tells him that Imogen will come around, eventually, and agree to marry him. On her deathbed, the queen confesses, in the hearing of Cornelius and two ladies, that she never loved Cymbeline and had intended to kill him with slow-working drugs. She also confesses her intention to kill Imogen so that Cloten might inherit the crown. Cornelius reports in V.v.27 that the queen died directly after making these confessions.

Roman Captain:

Listed as "Captains" in the stage directions, there seems to be only one Roman captain with a speaking part in the play. He informs Caius Lucius that Jachimo will soon arrive in England leading a group of Italian aristocrats who have been levied for battle in England. This captain is with Caius Lucius when the latter meets Fidele (Imogen).

Roman Senators:

Two Roman senators appear briefly in III.vii. They instruct the tribunes to levy an army of soldiers from amongst the Italian gentry. This army will then fight the Britains since the Roman common soldiers are busy fighting the Pannonians and Dalmatians, and the Roman legion in France are too weak to mount an attack on England.

Soldiers:

Soldiers are listed in the Dramatis Personae but not in the stage directions. Since the play depicts several scenes of battle, it can be assumed that the soldiers are present to represent the battle.

Spaniard:

The Spaniard appears without speaking in I.iv, the scene in which Posthumus arrives at Philario's house in Italy and wagers that Imogen will resist Jachimo's advances.

Tribunes:

Two Roman tribunes appear briefly in III.vii. They are instructed by two Roman senators to raise an army of Italian gentry to fight the Britains. Caius Lucius will be in command of that army.

Further Reading

Bergeron, David M. "*Cymbeline*: Shakespeare's Last Roman Play." *Shakespeare Quarterly* 31, no. 1 (1980): 31-41.
Bergeron examines Shakespeare's understanding of Roman history and discusses Shakespeare's sources for the characters in *Cymbeline*.

———. "Sexuality in *Cymbeline*." *Essays in Literature* 10, no. 2 (1983): 159-68.
Bergeron argues that since sexuality assures regeneration, it is often celebrated in the comic world. Bergeron discusses the implications of Cloten's and Jachimo's failure to find sexual fulfillment.

Bryant, Peter. "The Cave Scenes in *Cymbeline*: A Critical Note." *Standpunte* 23, no. 5 (1970): 14-22.
Bryant discusses how Guiderius and Arviragus demonstrate their true nobility despite their homely surroundings and unsophisticated upbringing.

Colley, John Scott. "Disguise and New Guise in *Cymbeline*." *Shakespeare Studies* 7 (1974): 233-52.
Colley examines how the characters' various disguises reveal their inner qualities. He discusses Cloten, Imogen, and Posthumus.

Hunt Maurice. "Shakespeare's Empirical Romance: *Cymbeline* and Modern Knowledge." *Texas Studies in Literature and Language* 22, no. 3 (1980): 322-42.
Hunt argues that Cymbeline, Imogen, and Posthumus gain knowledge through their suffering.

Kay, Carol McGinnis. "Generic Sleight-of-Hand in *Cymbeline*." *South Atlantic Review* 46, no. 4 (1981): 34-40.
Kay examines the elements of folklore in *Cymbeline*, especially its fairy tale beginning.

Lawry, J. S. "'Perishing Root and Increasing Vine' in *Cymbeline*." *Shakespeare Studies* 12 (1979): 179-93.
Lawry examines how the play compares and contrasts the nations of Rome and England. The harmony of the play's ending anticipates the birth of Christianity.

Leggatt, Alexander. "The Island of Miracles: An Approach to *Cymbeline*." *Shakespeare Studies* 10 (1977): 191-209.
Leggatt argues that *Cymbeline* demonstrates a concern with England's destiny. He sees Jupiter's saving of Posthumus as analogous to Christ's saving of humanity.

Mowat, Barbara. "*Cymbeline*: Crude Dramaturgy and Aesthetic Distance." *Renaissance Papers* (1966): 39-47.
Mowat is chiefly concerned with how Shakespeare employs certain dramatic techniques for his own artistic purposes.

Siemon, James Edward. "Noble Virtue in *Cymbeline*." *Shakespeare Survey* 29 (1976): 51-61.
Siemon argues that Posthumus changes throughout the course of *Cymbeline*. He compares the actions of Posthumus to the praise he receives from other characters early in the play.

Smith, Hallett. Introduction to *Cymbeline*, by William Shakespeare. In *The Riverside Shakespeare*, edited by G. Blakemore Evans, 1517-20. Boston: Houghton Mifflin, 1974.
Smith provides an overview of the sources for *Cymbeline* and its textual history. He analyzes the major characters in *Cymbeline* and compares the play to Shakespeare's other romances.

Swander, Homer. "*Cymbeline* and the 'Blameless Hero.'" *ELH: Journal of English Literary History* 31, no. 3 (1964): 259-70.
Swander argues that Posthumus does not live up to the praises he receives early in the play. He traces the changes in Posthumus, asserting that Posthumus eventually arrives at an unconventional excellence.

Taylor, Michael. "The Pastoral Reckoning in *Cymbeline*." *Shakespeare Survey* 36 (1983): 97-106.
Taylor suggests that the innocence of Imogen's pastoral world is shattered by the actions of Posthumus and the discovery of Cloten's headless corpse.

Thorne, William Barry. "*Cymbeline*: 'Lopp'd Branches' and the Concept of Regeneration." *Shakespeare Quarterly* 20, no. 2 (1969): 143-59.
Thorne discusses the communal harmony and coming together of the young and old as elements of folklore in *Cymbeline*.

The Tragedy of Hamlet, Prince of Denmark

circa 1600-01

Act I:

Guards at Elsinore Castle in Denmark twice have seen a ghostly figure resembling the former king, who is now dead. They discuss it with Horatio, a friend of Denmark's Prince Hamlet, who sees it at its third appearance. They think the ghost's appearance is an omen about strained relations between Denmark and Norway. They resolve to tell the king's son about the apparition. The next day, the dead king's brother, Claudius, who has married the widowed Queen Gertrude and become king himself, sits in state hearing petitions. He sends ambassadors to the old, sick ruler of Norway to try to stop attempts made by the Norwegian Prince Fortinbras to regain Danish land lost in battle to the former king. Claudius grants Laertes's petition to return to school in France. He joins with Gertrude in asking Hamlet, the dead king's son, to stay in Denmark rather than returning to school in Wittenberg. Laertes takes leave of his sister, Ophelia, and his father, the Danish courtier Polonius. Polonius instructs his daughter to stop seeing Hamlet since he is royalty and since he is possibly only toying with Ophelia's affections. That night, Hamlet sees and talks with the ghost. The ghost says he is the spirit of the dead king, Hamlet's father, and charges that he was murdered by Claudius; he commands Hamlet to seek revenge. Hamlet plans to pretend to be insane while pursuing vengeance.

Act II:

Some time later, Polonius sends a servant to convey money to Laertes in Paris and to check on Laertes's behavior there. Ophelia, who has obeyed her father's instructions to avoid Hamlet, reports to her father that Hamlet has come to her room behaving irrationally. Polonius becomes convinced that Hamlet has been driven mad because of unrequited love for Ophelia. The king has sent for Rosencrantz and Guildenstern, old friends of Hamlet, to find out what has caused this change in Hamlet's behavior. The ambassadors return to report that there is no further threat of war with Norway as young, warlike Fortinbras has elected to attack Poland. Polonius expresses his belief to King Claudius that Hamlet is mad from lovesickness. Hamlet realizes that Rosencrantz and Guildenstern were sent for by the king and queen to enquire into his changed behavior. Rosencrantz and Guildenstern mention that a company of actors is on its way to Elsinore. When the players arrive, Hamlet asks them to perform a play that resembles the ghost's account of his murder, to see if Claudius's response indicates that he is truly guilty of the crime.

Act III:

Rosencrantz and Guildenstern report to Claudius that they have been unable to learn the cause of Hamlet's erratic behavior. Because Polonius persists in thinking Hamlet's problem is lovesickness, Claudius and Polonius arrange to witness a conversation between Hamlet and Ophelia, in which Hamlet rages against the inconstancy of women. Claudius concludes Hamlet's problem is not lovesickness and vows to send Hamlet to England for a change of scene. The players perform their play for the court. Claudius leaves abruptly during the scene of murder. Hamlet takes this as evidence of Claudius's guilt. He contemplates killing the king at prayer, but does not. On Polonius's advice, Hamlet's mother sends for him to chastise him for unacceptable behavior. Polonius hides behind a tapestry in her room to eavesdrop. Hamlet detects him and kills Polonius by stabbing him through the tapestry. Hamlet then berates Gertrude for her remarriage and her sexual relationship with Claudius. The ghost enters, seen and heard only by Hamlet, and reminds Hamlet that he has not yet achieved his revenge. As Hamlet talks with the ghost, the uncomprehending Gertrude thinks him mad.

Act IV:

The king learns of Polonius's death and arranges for Rosencrantz and Guildenstern to accompany Hamlet to England. In a sealed document Claudius orders Hamlet's death. Hamlet realizes he has not obtained his revenge yet and resolves to be stronger. He uncovers and foils the plot to have him killed in England and returns to Denmark. Both of Polonius's children have learned of their father's death. Ophelia goes mad. Laertes returns from France and, vowing revenge for the murder of his father, is enlisted by Claudius in a plot to kill Hamlet. The queen reports Ophelia has drowned.

Act V:

Hamlet and Horatio pass through the graveyard where two workmen are digging a grave. When a funeral procession comes, they conceal themselves. When Hamlet realizes it is a funeral for Ophelia and sees Laertes's inordinate grief, he leaps into the grave after the grieving Laertes, and they fight. Attendants separate them. The king uses this incident to further strengthen Laertes's resolve to kill Hamlet, and he directs Horatio to look after Hamlet. The king's plot against Hamlet involves a fencing match between Hamlet and Laertes. Claudius poisons a cup of wine that he plans to offer to Hamlet, and Laertes poisons his rapier. During the fight, Hamlet and Laertes are each mortally wounded by the poisoned sword, exchanged at one point during the scuffling. The queen drinks the poisoned wine, and is able to warn Hamlet before she dies. Hamlet then turns on the king, stabbing him with the poisoned sword and forcing him to drink the tainted wine. Hamlet dies after asking Horatio to explain to the court what has happened and recommending that Fortinbras of Norway become king of Denmark. English ambassadors bring word of the deaths of Rosencrantz and Guildenstern. Hamlet is carried off to lie in state.

Modern Connections

Written at the outset of the seventeenth century and based on accounts of several centuries earlier, *Hamlet* is often regarded as remarkably modern in its treatment of themes concerning mental health, political health, and spiritual health.

Hamlet describes himself as afflicted with a melancholy which he does not completely understand. English Renaissance audiences of *Hamlet* based their ideas about psychological disturbances such as melancholy and madness on medieval theories of body humours, or fluids. The humours correlated with the four basic elements of earth, air, fire, and water. The humours consisted of black bile, yellow bile, blood, and phlegm. A predominance of one of these humours resulted in a personality type. The person with an excess of blood was called sanguine, or cheerful. The excess of phlegm resulted in a phlegmatic, or passive, inert sort of person. An excess of black bile resulted in melancholy, or sadness. An excess of yellow bile resulted in choler, or anger. Treatments for melancholy ranged from advice about types of clothing and colors to wear or avoid to settings for one's house to types of food to eat or avoid. The early seventeenth century work *The Anatomy of Melancholy*, by Robert Burton, contains a special section dealing with two difficult-to-treat types of melancholy, love melancholy and religious melancholy. Polonius is convinced that Hamlet suffers from love melancholy. Although Hamlet says he has lost his ability to enjoy his usual activities, several observers, including the king, express the opinion that Hamlet is not mad but brooding over something and thereby is dangerous.

Ophelia, by contrast, is assumed by all of her observers—the queen, the king, Horatio, her brother—to be truly mad. In medieval times, the mad person was thought to be inhabited by an evil spirit. The treatment was identification of the spirit and exorcism by a cleric. Exorcisms of evil spirits were still conducted in Shakespeare's day. The indigent mad person was allowed to live in an almshouse and go about freely unless dangerous. General medical practice in Shakespeare's day emphasized hygiene, herbal remedies, and dietary recommendations. Even in medieval times, teaching hospitals kept botanical gardens and made herbal medicines, and the discovery of the Americas and also voyages to India led to the introduction of many more plants and herbs to Elizabethan England. Ophelia's songs contain herbal lore linking properties and symbolism of various plants, including rosemary, pansies, fennel, columbines, rue, daisies, and violets.

In modern times, the medical community has a wide range of approaches available for the treatment of mental illness. Many patients of longer term psychotherapy, defined as extending over more than six months, report satisfaction with the improvement of their mental health. Some are as well-pleased with this "talk therapy" alone as with a combination of therapy and prescription medication, which can have such unwanted side effects as drowsiness and disorientation. Available treatments include the following therapies: Freudian, cognitive, interpersonal, behavioral, drug, and shock.

Techniques such as meditation and bio-feedback are also used.

Just as maintaining individual physical health was and is viewed as important, maintaining the political well-being of the state is also considered to be of utmost importance, especially to political leaders to whom a good portion of this responsibility falls. Threats against the state in the form of plots, actual or imagined, intended to overthrow the ruler were concerns of the Elizabethan court. Poisons were a cause of concern. In some political settings, including Italian and French courts and sub-kingdoms, ingenious poisons were sometimes resorted to as a way of eliminating enemies. In *Hamlet*, Hamlet's royal father is killed by a rival claimant to his throne by the method of pouring a poison into his ear while he was sleeping. The poison, distilled henbane, was an extraction made from a Mediterranean plant using the relatively new and popular method of distillation just becoming better known in Elizabethan England. Queen Elizabeth feared plotters, and several sensationalized alleged or actual poison plots were uncovered and tried during or shortly after her reign.

In Elizabethan England, suspicion and intrigue played a role in the defense of the realm against dangers from within. Court spying in England and abroad reached an accomplished level under Queen Elizabeth. Her employee Francis Walsingham has the distinction of being the first master of developing the modern spy state. In *Hamlet*, the intelligence-gathering done or attempted by Rosencrantz and Guildenstern was considered, at least by King Claudius, to be a necessary part of maintaining order. Disorder in a state could also be mirrored by disorder in a family. Hamlet is forced to live in a family scarred by murder and what was considered a form of incest by Elizabethan standards. Hamlet laments the disorder in his family and in the realm and exclaims against it when he says: "The time is out of joint—O cursed spite, / That ever I was born to set it right!" (I.v.188-9).

In twentieth-century society, concerns about sophisticated poisons inherent in chemical and biological hazards extend in a number of directions, from industrial pollutants, to medical/biological hazardous wastes, to biological and chemical warfare, to the potential actions of state-sponsored terrorists, private pathologically-oriented citizens, or cult leaders. Safeguards are present in the form of environmental groups, federal and state legislation, industry watchdogs, and government agencies. Governments worldwide have become more aware of the necessity of guarding against attacks on both political leaders and ordinary citizens by terrorists and anarchists. In addition, people of all views along the political spectrum seem to be acknowledging the need for strong, well-functioning families as a basis for a strong society.

Physical health and political health are related to, to some extent, society's view of the universe and the place of humanity in it. The Elizabethan world view, as it was expressed in a classic phrase by the critic E. M. W. Tillyard, was hierarchical and pyramidal. The structure depicted God at the apex, angels and the spiritual world below God, the king below God and receiving his power from God, followed by nobles, gentry, and ordinary people. Below this was the animal kingdom, then plants, then minerals and stones. Each subdivision had its own order of excellence as well. This view is based on Biblical passages, including verses in Genesis. A brief, lyrical expression of the view is found in Psalm 8. Hamlet's own beliefs may be represented by this view, though when he discusses it with Rosencrantz and Guildenstern, he is in, if not a state of disbelief, then a state of melancholy, disgust, and world-weariness. He says of himself "I have of late—but wherefore I know not—lost all my mirth, forgone all custom of exercises" (II.ii.295-7); he refers to man as "this quintessence of dust" (II.ii.308) and says of the rest, "this goodly frame, the earth, / seems to me a sterile promontory; this most excellent / canopy, the air, look you, this brave o'erhanging / firmament, this majestical roof fretted with golden fire, / why, it appeareth nothing to me but a foul and pestilent / congregation of vapors" (II.ii.298-303).

A related theological view is that each individual is called to an accounting of his actions at the moment of his death. Although in the Christian view atonement was gained for all men through Christ's death, the individual believer must nevertheless maintain himself in a state of grace and be a follower of Christ in his own actions. The individual who dies in a state of sin rather than a state of grace may be judged in need of purging (purgatorial) punishments or even deserving of everlasting torments, depending on the severity of the sin(s) and the disposition of the sinner. Because the fiery torments described by the ghost in Hamlet have a terminal point, the ghost is often thought of as coming from Purgatory rather than Hell. Hamlet decides not to kill Claudius while the king is in a praying, repentant state. Instead, Hamlet says he will wait to catch Claudius when he is drunk or "in

th' incestious pleasure of his bed" (III.iii.90) so that Claudius will die in a state of sin, when his "soul may be as damn'd and black / As Hell, whereto it goes" (III.iii.94-5).

In modern society, a range of views is held by both Christians and non-Christians on the nature and extent of what have been called the "Four Last Things"—Death, Judgment, Hell and Heaven. Some people believe that the list of the elect (those saved) is small and is determined ahead of time, while others doubt the existence of Hell or question whether Hell lasts forever. Some people believe that only the members of their own particular religious sect can be saved, while others believe salvation has been gained for all who have faith, regardless of their adherence to the precepts of an institutional church.

Finally, in today's society, many views are also held about the place of humanity in the universe. Each new scientific discovery brings with it a re-examination, restatement, or reformulation of previous views. For example, the recent (August, 1996) apparent discovery of microscopic life on Mars has caused some people to re-examine the question of whether or not the inhabitants of Earth are the only examples of intelligent life in the universe.

Characters

Attendants:

The king appears in state accompanied by attendants, and attendants wait on various members of Danish court and visitors to the court. Attendants follow the king when he enters or exits a scene. They are sent by the king to look for the body of Polonius. Attendants separate Hamlet and Laertes when they fight at Ophelia's funeral.

Barnardo:

Barnardo, with Francisco and Marcellus, is one of the guards of the Danish ruler's castle, Elsinore. He and Marcellus have seen the ghost twice before the opening of the play, and have chosen to tell Prince Hamlet's scholarly friend Horatio about the occurrence. Barnardo speaks the play's first, ominous words: "Who's there?" (i.i.1).

Claudius (King Claudius of Denmark):

Claudius is the king of Denmark and brother of the dead king, which makes him Hamlet's uncle.

> **Claudius has killed his brother to gain the throne and has married his brother's wife, Gertrude."**

Claudius has killed his brother to gain the throne and has married his brother's wife, Gertrude. Throughout the play, the nature of Claudius's kingship is displayed. Because Claudius is shrewd and able, though not always ethical or moral, Hamlet describes the contest of intelligence and will between them as that of "mighty opposites" (V.ii.62).

Claudius has a number of foreign and domestic problems to contend with. One of the first internal problems is to have the country accept him as king. This is handled by having the Council support his marriage to Gertrude and his kingship, and Claudius refers to their support—that they "have freely gone / With this affair along" (I.ii.15-6)—in his opening remarks as he sits in state.

The Danish kingdom is threatened from without by young Fortinbras, son of the old ruler of Norway, who was killed by Hamlet's father. Old Fortinbras's defeat and death resulted in a forfeiture of lands to Denmark; however, young Fortinbras wants the lands returned and thinks to take advantage of the upheaval in Denmark, occasioned by King Hamlet's death, to mount an attack. Claudius sends ambassadors to young Fortinbras's uncle (the brother of that country's dead king and presumably the current king of Norway), asking him to restrain his nephew and make him abide by the heraldic rules of the conflict between old Fortinbras and old Hamlet.

The king has noticed that Hamlet has been depressed since his father's funeral two months ago, and advises him that it is against heaven, the dead, and nature itself to continue immoderate grieving. Claudius names Hamlet as his immediate heir to the throne of Denmark and urges him to remain in Denmark as the "chiefest courtier" (I.ii.117) rather than returning to school in Wittenberg.

Meanwhile, the ghost appears to Hamlet, who subsequently vows revenge for the death of his father. Hamlet however avoids acting on this promise.

The king sends for Rosencrantz and Guildenstern, friends of Hamlet from his youth, to try to learn what is troubling him. Claudius also listens to Polonius's claim that Hamlet is troubled by love-sickness for Ophelia. He agrees to test this theory by observing Hamlet in conversation with Ophelia. Though Polonius continues to be convinced of his own view, the king alertly dismisses this view after their concealed observation of Hamlet. He says: "Love? his affections do not that way tend" (III.i.162) and realizes "There's something in his soul / O'er which his melancholy sits on brood" (III.i.164-5). Claudius plans to send Hamlet to England for a change of scene. He even agrees to Polonius's suggested intermediate step of having Hamlet talk to the queen about his changed demeanor.

In III.ii, the king witnesses his own crime in a play performed before the royal court. When one of the actors pours poison in another actor's ear, the king rises enraged, calling for lights, and leaves. Alone in his room, Claudius tries to pray for forgiveness for his misdeeds but acknowledges to himself that he is not truly penitent because he still enjoys, "those effects for which I did the murther [murder]: / My crown, my own ambition, and my queen" (III.iii.54-55). Fearing for his own safety, the king commissions Rosencrantz and Guildenstern to take Hamlet to England as soon as possible. However, he does not tell Gertrude that he has given Rosencrantz and Guildenstern sealed letters to the English king calling for Hamlet's execution in England.

Concern about public opinion regarding the quick burial of Polonius, the removal of Hamlet from the Danish realm, Ophelia's madness, and Laertes's return from France, compound the king's problems. However, the king is adept in handling Laertes, who initially suspects the king's involvement in the death of Polonius. Claudius says very majestically that "divinity doth hedge a king" (IV.v.124) and appears unafraid by the menacing manner of Laertes. He directs an angry, amazed, and grieving Laertes to let Laertes's wisest followers judge whether the king was involved directly or indirectly in Polonius's death. In a gesture of bravado, the king says he will give up his kingdom, crown, life, and all to Laertes if the followers implicate him in Polonius's death. He further explains to Laertes that no public inquiry was possible because the queen loves Hamlet and also because the public regards Hamlet so well. When the king and Laertes discover together that Hamlet is returning to Denmark, Claudius announces his plan to have Hamlet killed, and Laertes expresses his desire to be a part of that plan. As the details are discussed, Claudius persuades Laertes to agree to a plan less straightforward than Laertes's desire to ''cut his [Hamlet's] throat i' the' church'' (IV.vii.126). In the end, Claudius is tripped up by his own multiple plots against Hamlet; his queen dies by drinking the poisoned wine, intended to be a back-up plan to kill Hamlet, and Claudius himself is killed when Hamlet wounds him with the poisoned sword.

Clowns:

See Gravediggers

Cornelius:

Cornelius and Voltemand are Danish ambassadors, sent by King Claudius in I.ii.26-38, to the king of Norway, the uncle of young Fortinbras, to urge him to squelch his nephew's threats against Danish land. They return in II.ii.40 to report that their mission was successful.

Council:

The Council is a governing body present with the king at official meetings. The Council is said by the king to have approved of his marriage to Gertrude and his succession to the Danish throne.

Doctor of Divinity:

The doctor of divinity is a clergyman who reluctantly officiates at the funeral and burial of Ophelia. When Laertes calls for more elaborate religious ceremony, the doctor states that it is a profanation to bury a probable suicide in sanctified grounds with holy rites. Laertes replies in anger: ''I tell thee, churlish priest / A minist'ring angel shall my sister be / When thou liest howling'' (V.i.240-42).

English Embassadors:

The embassadors (or ambassadors) enter the Danish court at the end of the play. They report the deaths of Rosencrantz and Guildenstern.

Fortinbras:

Fortinbras is the heir to the throne of Norway. His situation resembles that of Hamlet: his father was king, and his uncle is currently ruling. Prior to the play, the old Norwegian King Fortinbras lost both his life and Norwegian lands in the battle with King Hamlet. Early in the play, young Fortinbras is described as seeking to regain the lost Norwegian

> **Claudius tries to pray for forgiveness for his misdeeds but acknowledges to himself that he is not truly penitent because he still enjoys, 'those effects for which I did the murther [murder]: / My crown, my own ambition, and my queen' (III.iii.54-55).''**

land during the period of uncertainty following King Hamlet's death. Negotiations between King Claudius and the current king of Norway, however, result in Fortinbras agreeing to cease hostilities in Denmark. He petitions for safe passage through Denmark to Poland. Hamlet describes Fortinbras as ''a delicate and tender prince'' (IV.iv.48) who is easily incited to fight in the cause of personal or national pride. He passes through Denmark on his return from his conquest of Poland, and is named by the dying Prince Hamlet as the most likely successor to the throne of Denmark. Fortinbras orders a soldier's funeral for Hamlet, and speaks the last words of the play, commending Hamlet as likely to have been a good ruler.

Francisco:

Francisco is a guard on watch at the opening of the play. He is relieved by Barnardo. Since the night is cold, he is glad to go in. He reports that his watch passed by undisturbed: ''Not a mouse stirring'' (I.i.10).

Gentleman:

An unnamed gentleman announces Ophelia's presence to the queen. When the queen seems disinclined to see Ophelia, he plainly states the case for seeing her, describing her distracted speech. An unnamed gentleman announces to Horatio the sailors who come with Hamlet's letter.

Gertrude (Queen Gertrude of Denmark):

Gertrude, queen of Denmark, is the widow of the late King Hamlet and the mother of Prince Hamlet, who is the title character of the play.

Gertrude has recently married her brother-in-law. Claudius, the new king, is the brother of the late king and thus Prince Hamlet's uncle.

Gertrude is central to the action of the play, despite the fact that she has relatively few lines. Hamlet's disgust with his mother's marrying less than two months after his father's death and marrying Claudius is one of the main subjects of his agonized reflections in the course of the play. Not only does Hamlet consider Claudius inferior to his father in every respect, but in Shakespeare's time, it was considered a form of incest for a widow to marry her brother-in-law.

Gertrude first appears I.ii, where she urges Hamlet not to mourn his father's death excessively. In the soliloquy that follows, Hamlet expresses a general weariness and disgust with life, which he links directly to his feelings about his mother's marriage.

Later in Act I, Hamlet encounters the ghost of his father. The ghost accuses Claudius of murdering him and bitterly denounces his brother for seducing Gertrude. Critics continue to dispute whether the ghost's words mean that Gertrude had an adulterous relationship with Claudius before King Hamlet's death, or whether he is referring to their relationship after his death. While demanding that Hamlet avenge his murder, the ghost orders him not to harm Gertrude.

While Gertrude says relatively little, some of her comments are insightful and to the point. She cuts short a lengthy explanation from the long-winded Polonius by urging him to produce ''more matter with less art'' (II.ii.95). Later, during the performance by the players, the player queen makes a long and passionate declaration of devotion to her husband; Gertrude observes, ''The lady doth protest too much, methinks'' (III.ii.230).

Gertrude's most dramatic moments come in the highly emotional ''closet scene'' (III.iv), which takes place in her private chamber or ''closet.'' Acting on Polonius's advice (''Tell him [Hamlet] his pranks have been tobroad [unrestrained] to bear with'' [III.iv.2]), the queen calls Hamlet to her chamber, where Polonius is listening behind a curtain. The queen begins by scolding Hamlet for offending Claudius. Hamlet responds by accusing her of marrying Claudius out of purely sexual desire. Hearing Polonius behind the curtain, Hamlet stabs him through the curtain and kills him, apparently mistaking him for Claudius. He then reveals to Gertrude his belief that Claudius killed his father.

Hamlet's tirade against the queen is cut short when the ghost (who is invisible to Gertrude) again appears to Hamlet and reminds him of his mission of revenge. Toward the end of the scene, Gertrude expresses remorse for her behavior. Her lines, however, do not make clear whether she already knew or, indeed, believes that Claudius murdered Hamlet's father, and whether she thinks Hamlet is sane or mad. Stage and film productions of the play have interpreted these questions in many different ways.

Although Gertrude does not subsequently abandon Claudius, neither does she reveal to him Hamlet's suspicions. She dies in the final scene of the play, when she drinks from a cup of poisoned wine prepared by Claudius and intended for Hamlet. In her dying words she tells Hamlet that the wine is poisoned.

Critics generally regard Gertrude as weak-willed, highly dependent on Claudius and easily manipulated by him. Some critics, however, take a more positive view of her character, arguing that her pointed remarks reveal a perceptive intelligence.

Ghost:

Before the play begins, King Hamlet of Denmark has been found dead. His brother Claudius has become king and has married the widowed queen, Gertrude. Prince Hamlet, grieving the loss of his father and his mother's hasty and incestuous (by Elizabethan standards) remarriage, has descended into a deep melancholy. Moreover, on two consecutive nights the ghost has appeared in armor to palace guards on the battlements of the castle. The two guards have told no one about the ghost except Hamlet's friend Horatio, who has agreed to stand guard with them to see if the ghost appears again.

In I.i, the ghost appears to the two guards and Horatio. Horatio commands the ghost to speak, but it does not. It then reappears and seems about to speak to Horatio, but when a cock crows, signaling daybreak, the ghost vanishes. Horatio resolves to tell Prince Hamlet about the sighting. Hamlet is startled by Horatio's story and decides to watch for the ghost himself.

In I.iv, the ghost reappears in the presence of Hamlet, Horatio and Marcellus and beckons Hamlet to withdraw privately with it. When they are alone in I.v, the ghost tells Hamlet that it is the spirit of Hamlet's father, murdered by Claudius. The ghost denounces Claudius for seducing Gertrude and calls for Hamlet to avenge his death but not to harm Gertrude. The ghost then vanishes. When Horatio and Marcellus appear, Hamlet repeatedly orders them to swear that they will not reveal what they have seen.

Hamlet vows vengeance, but later expresses doubt about the ghost's identity, speculating that it could be a devil appearing in his father's form to tempt him to sin. This reaction characterizes his attitude toward the ghost until the play scene (III.ii). Hamlet's own uncertainty is mirrored in the critical debate about the nature of the ghost. Most critics agree that Shakespeare intended audiences to accept the apparition as the ghost of Hamlet's father, but some contend that it may be an illusion or a demon. Some critics argue that the ghost is in fact a devil whose object is to lure Hamlet to his own demise by arousing his passion for vengeance. Another interpretation is that the ghost is a hallucination seen by only a few characters.

The ghost makes a final appearance in III.iv, shortly after Hamlet stabs Polonius, who has been secretly listening to a confrontation between Hamlet and Gertrude. The ghost reminds Hamlet that he is sworn to vengeance, and as they talk Hamlet expresses his shameful regret that he has not yet acted against Claudius. The ghost then draws Hamlet's attention to Gertrude's "amazement" and urges him to assist her in her moral struggle. Gertrude claims to neither see nor hear the ghost, and this supports the critical interpretation that the apparition Hamlet describes to her is a symptom of his madness. Gertrude's apparent inability to see the ghost has led some critics to suggest that Shakespeare wanted his audience, too, to interpret the ghost as a hallucination. Most critics, however, agree with the view that prevailed during the first three centuries after the writing of *Hamlet*, that the ghost was meant to be taken literally.

Gravediggers:

The gravediggers (in some editions referred to as "clowns") are two rustic working men. One of them, referred to as Goodman Delver, has been sexton (or church warden) for 30 years—ever since "that very day that young Hamlet was born" (V.i.147), which establishes Hamlet's age at this point in the play. The two appear together at the beginning of Act V, engaged in their task of digging Ophelia's grave. They discuss the questionable circumstances of Ophelia's death, and wonder if Christian burial is warranted for an apparent suicide (Church law forbade burying suicides in consecrated ground). The sexton sends the other gravedigger off to fetch "a sup of liquor" (V.i.60). Hamlet and

" **Gertrude is central to the action of the play, despite the fact that she has relatively few lines. Hamlet's disgust with his mother's marrying less than two months after his father's death and marrying Claudius is one of the main subjects of his agonized reflections in the course of the play."**

Horatio encounter him at his work, singing merrily and unearthing bones and dirt together. Hamlet enters into a jocular, equivocating exchange with the sexton, who matches wits handily with the prince. Hamlet becomes serious and contemplative when the gravedigger reveals the identity of one skull as that of Yorick, old King Hamlet's jester and a companion of Hamlet's childhood.

Guard:

The king's guard carries torches to the play. The king is accompanied by two or three guards after Polonius's death. The king calls for his "Swissers" (IV.v.98), or Swiss guards, when a noise is heard after Ophelia's exit and just before Laertes's bursting into the scene at the head of a mob.

Guildenstern:

Guildenstern and Rosencrantz are friends from Hamlet's youth sent for by the king and queen to learn the cause of Hamlet's change of personality. The two are perfectly willing to supply covert intelligence to the king. While both profess to be concerned about Hamlet's welfare, because it is bound up with the welfare of the Danish state, they are commonly considered by commentators on the play as opportunists who are currying royal favor with Claudius solely to remain in the good graces of the current power structure. Their exchanges with Hamlet generally reveal that he is suspicious of them, mistrustful of their purpose in court, and too wary to reveal anything about himself to them. With

> *When they are alone in I.v, the ghost tells Hamlet that it is the spirit of Hamlet's father, murdered by Claudius. The ghost denounces Claudius for seducing Gertrude and calls for Hamlet to avenge his death but not to harm Gertrude."*

Rosencrantz, Guildenstern is unknowingly sent to his death in England by Hamlet's discovery of Claudius's plot and Hamlet's quick construction of a counter-plot.

Hamlet (Prince Hamlet of Denmark):

Hamlet, prince of Denmark and son of Gertrude and the late King Hamlet of Denmark, is the title character of *Hamlet*. When the play opens, he is distraught over his father's recent death, his mother's remarriage to his father's brother Claudius, and the ascension of Claudius to the throne of Denmark. Hamlet's distress turns to rage when a ghost appears in the shape of his dead father and tells Hamlet that Claudius poisoned him. Hamlet vows to avenge his father's murder. Hamlet's erratic behavior as he contemplates acting against Claudius prompts the king and his councillor, Polonius, to employ devious methods to discover the reason for Hamlet's apparent madness. To this end, Claudius and Gertrude summon to Elsinore two of Hamlet's old friends, Rosencrantz and Guildenstern, and ask them to find out what is troubling the prince. Hamlet sees through this ploy, and throughout the play treats Polonius, Rosencrantz and Guildenstern, and even Claudius with some contempt. Meanwhile, in several melancholy soliloquies which include reflections on mortality, suicide, honor, and the apparent futility of life, Hamlet berates himself for his long delay in taking revenge.

Hamlet's supposed insanity includes bizarre behavior towards Polonius's daughter Ophelia, whom he once courted. This convinces Polonius, who had ordered Ophelia to stop seeing Hamlet, that the prince has gone mad out of unrequited love. Claudius and Polonius spy on a meeting between Hamlet and Ophelia during which Hamlet implies that he never loved Ophelia and makes several derogatory comments about women and the nature of marriage. (This scene is often called the "nunnery" scene because Hamlet repeatedly tells Ophelia to "get thee to a nunnery" [III.i.120]; "nunnery" was often used in Elizabethan slang to mean a house of prostitution.) Unconvinced that love is at the root of Hamlet's disturbing conduct, Claudius decides to send him to England. In the meantime, doubting whether the ghost is truly his father's spirit and can thus be trusted, Hamlet arranges for a troupe of traveling actors to perform a play that closely resembles the circumstances of the murder as recounted by the ghost. Claudius's perturbed reaction to the performance convinces Hamlet that the ghost's allegations are true. During a meeting with his mother during which he violently denounces her relationship with his uncle, Hamlet fatally stabs Polonius, who has been eavesdropping behind a curtain; apparently, the prince has mistaken him for Claudius. (When Gertrude asks Hamlet what he has done, he replies "Nay, I know not, is it the King?" [III.iv.26].) After telling Gertrude his belief that Claudius killed his father, Hamlet is interrupted by the ghost who is invisible to Gertrude and who reminds Hamlet of the need for revenge. Alarmed by Hamlet's behavior, Claudius sends him off to England immediately, accompanied by Rosencrantz and Guildenstern, ostensibly on a diplomatic mission but in reality with the intention of having him killed there.

Hamlet manages to escape this plot and returns to Denmark. He finds that Ophelia has gone mad and drowned, an apparent suicide. Claudius convinces Ophelia's brother, Laertes, that Hamlet is responsible for the deaths of both his father and his sister. Learning that Hamlet has returned to Denmark, Claudius persuades Laertes to take revenge against Hamlet by means of a plot which is a bit more sly than anything Laertes conceived of. (Laertes's vengeance, we learn from his answer to Claudius's question about what Laertes would do to avenge his father, would take the form of slitting Hamlet's throat in a church [IV.vii.125-26]). Claudius's plan involves Laertes killing Hamlet during a fencing match in which Laertes will use a rapier that has been tainted with poison. To make doubly sure of Hamlet's death, Claudius prepares a goblet of poisoned wine, which he plans to offer to Hamlet if the prince appears to be winning. During the match, both Hamlet and Laertes are wounded with the poisoned sword, and the queen drinks from the cup intended for Hamlet. As the queen dies, she warns Hamlet that the wine is poisoned. Laertes then reveals the plot against Hamlet, and Hamlet finally takes his revenge, first stabbing Claudius, then forcing him to drink from the poisoned cup. Hamlet and Laertes exchange forgiveness before both die.

Hamlet is one of the most controversial and most widely discussed characters in English literature. Scores of critics have debated the reasons for his actions, the playwright's view of his character, and the meaning of his tragedy. The primary focus of the debate has been the reason for Hamlet's long delay in carrying out his vow of revenge. An early view which survived into the twentieth century was that Hamlet was a man paralyzed by his own intelligence and introverted nature.

A psychoanalytical approach that became popular in the mid-twentieth century suggested that in creating the character of Hamlet Shakespeare anticipated by some three hundred years Sigmund Freud's concept of the Oedipus complex. In this view, Hamlet has never recovered from his natural childhood jealousy of his father. In support of this position, critics point to the prince's obsession with his mother's sexual relationship with Claudius, which has plunged him into depression even before he learns of his father's murder and which throughout the play distracts him from his task of taking revenge against his uncle. By in effect carrying out Hamlet's repressed childhood wish to kill his father and to possess his mother, the argument goes, Claudius revives Hamlet's repressed memories of forbidden childhood thoughts, thereby combining the thoughts of incest and parricide, a combination so unbearable that Hamlet finds himself incapable of taking action.

Horatio:

Horatio is Hamlet's closest friend, a former fellow-student at Wittenberg. Horatio has come to Elsinore from Wittenberg for the funeral of old King Hamlet. He is described by Marcellus as a "scholar" (I.i.42).

Horatio enjoys the absolute trust of those who know him: it is Horatio whom the guards ask to witness the appearance of the ghost, it is Horatio with whom Hamlet trusts his suspicions regarding Claudius, and even Claudius trusts Horatio to look after and further restrain Hamlet after Hamlet attacks Laertes at Ophelia's funeral. In III.ii.54-87 Hamlet professes his faith in Horatio and praises his qualities of judiciousness, patience, and equanimity.

> **During a meeting with his mother during which he violently denounces her relationship with his uncle, Hamlet fatally stabs Polonius, who has been eavesdropping behind a curtain; apparently, the prince has mistaken him for Claudius. (When Gertrude asks Hamlet what he has done, he replies 'Nay, I know not, is it the King?' [III.iv.26].)"**

Horatio is initially skeptical about the ghost. He believes it is a "fantasy" (I.i.23) of the watch. After seeing and attempting to communicate with the ghost, Horatio speculates that its appearance might be related to possible impending war with Norway. In speaking to the ghost, Horatio implores it to tell him if he can do anything to help it, or to avoid trouble befalling his country. Noting that the ghost looks like the dead King Hamlet and seemed about to speak when it vanished with the dawn, Horatio resolves to tell Hamlet about the apparition.

Horatio worries that the ghost may lead Hamlet to suicide or madness, so he and Marcellus try unsuccessfully to prevent Hamlet from meeting with the ghost. After Hamlet's private conference with the ghost, Horatio tells Hamlet that he is speaking in "wild and whirling words" (I.v.132-33), and even jokes grimly that some of what Hamlet claims the ghost has told him is common knowledge: "There needs no ghost, my lord, come from the grave / To tell us this" (I.v.125).

Hamlet does not reveal the true substance of the ghost's claims— that he is the ghost of Hamlet's father, murdered by Claudius—to Horatio until later in the play. Hamlet asks Horatio to watch King Claudius during the staging of a play that will recreate a similar murder in order to judge, by the king's responses, whether he seems guilty. He and Hamlet compare notes on the king's behavior afterwards. Horatio is one of the few fixed points in the play: he remains from first to last a loyal friend to

> **Hamlet is one of the most controversial and most widely discussed characters in English literature. Scores of critics have debated the reasons for his actions, the playwright's view of his character, and the meaning of his tragedy."**

Hamlet, trusted by all. He attempts suicide when Hamlet is dying, but Hamlet asks him to remain alive to give a full account of the tragic events at the Danish court.

King Claudius of Denmark:

See Claudius

Ladies:

Ladies are present at court scenes. Ophelia wistfully bids ladies good night after her mad appearance just before Laertes's arrival at court at the head of a mob.

Laertes:

Laertes is Polonius's son and Ophelia's brother. He has come to Denmark for King Claudius's coronation. In his first appearance in I.ii, he seeks permission to return to France.

When he appears again in I.iii, Laertes bids his sister Ophelia farewell and warns her about Hamlet. He advises her that Hamlet can't choose a mate for himself alone, but, being the prince, must think of the state. Thus, he cautions Ophelia to protect her virtue. Polonius then enters and advises his son on how to conduct himself while in France. When his father is finished, Laertes leaves for France.

Laertes returns to Denmark after Polonius's death, bursting into the room with a group of followers and addressing Claudius, "O thou vile king" (IV.v.116), and vowing revenge for his father's death. Claudius assures Laertes that he played no role in the death of Polonius and asks him if he is prepared to know the truth, if in his desire for vengeance he will look to both "friend and foe"

(Iv.v.143). Ophelia then enters, and Laertes realizes that his sister has gone mad. The king then tells Laertes that he will give up the kingdom, his crown and his life if Laertes and his followers find that he was involved in Polonius's death. Later, Claudius explains to Laertes that there was no formal inquiry into Polonius's death due to the queen's love for Hamlet and due to the high regard the people have for the prince. During this scene (IV.vii) a messenger arrives bearing a letter from Hamlet; Laertes and Claudius learn that the prince has returned to Denmark. The king speaks of a plot to kill Hamlet, and Laertes expresses his wish to be a part of it. When Claudius asks Laertes "What would you undertake / To show yourself indeed your father's son / More than in words?" Laertes replies that he would cut Hamlet's throat in the church (IV.vii.124-26). After further discussion, a plan evolves in which Laertes will fight Hamlet with a poisoned rapier, and, as an additional measure, Claudius will offer a cup of poisoned wine to Hamlet, if it appears as though Hamlet might be winning the match.

After Ophelia's funeral, during which Laertes and Hamlet leap into Ophelia's grave, Laertes and Hamlet prepare to duel. In the course of the duel, just before Laertes wounds Hamlet with the poisoned rapier, Laertes says in an aside "And yet it is almost against my conscience" (V.ii.296). After a scuffle the two change rapiers. Laertes is then wounded with the poisoned rapier by Hamlet. At the same moment, the queen, who has drunk from the cup of poisoned wine, falls and warns Hamlet that the drink is poisoned. Laertes then tells Hamlet the truth about the king's layered plots. He asks Hamlet for forgiveness and in turn forgives Hamlet for his own and his father's death.

Lord:

An unnamed lord comes as a messenger to Hamlet from the king, announcing that the court is ready for the fencing display.

Lords:

Lords attend the play, the fencing match, and other public occasions in the court.

Marcellus:

Marcellus is one of the night watch at Elsinore. He has seen the ghost two times before the opening of the play and asks Horatio to witness the third appearance.

Messengers:

A messenger brings letters from Hamlet to the king. The messenger is also dismissed from the presence of the king.

Norwegian Captain:

He leads forces for Fortinbras in their passage through Denmark to Poland and identifies the Norwegian army to Hamlet. He also expresses his view that the land to be fought over is worthless.

Officers:

Officers enter before the royal party with cushions, foils, and daggers for the fencing scene.

Ophelia:

Ophelia is the sister of Laertes and the daughter of the king's councillor, Polonius. As I.iii opens, Ophelia has apparently confided to her brother that Prince Hamlet has declared his love for her. Laertes, who is saying goodbye to his sister as he leaves for France, warns Ophelia not to take Hamlet's professions of love seriously. Pointing out that the weddings of princes are usually arranged for reasons of state rather than for love, he cautions her to guard her virginity. Ophelia promises to take his words to heart but also urges her brother to follow his own advice and to avoid "the primrose path of dalliance" (I.iii.50). Polonius enters and adds his warnings to those of Laertes. He orders Ophelia not to spend time with Hamlet or even to talk to him. Ophelia promises to obey.

Ophelia next appears in II.i, when she tells Polonius that Hamlet has frightened her by entering her room and behaving in a bizarre manner. Convinced that Ophelia's refusal to speak to Hamlet has caused the prince to lose his mind, Polonius hurries to Claudius and Gertrude, who have also noted Hamlet's odd behavior and are in the process of instructing Hamlet's old friends Rosencrantz and Guildenstern to find out the reason for it. Polonius and Claudius arrange to spy on a meeting between Hamlet and Ophelia so that they can determine if love for Ophelia is really the cause of his apparent madness. This meeting occurs in III.i, and follows Hamlet's "To be or not to be" soliloquy. Ophelia greets Hamlet and tries to return his gifts to her. Hamlet denies having given her anything and subjects her to several vehement and disjointed statements commenting on the falseness of women and

> **Horatio is one of the few fixed points in the play: he remains from first to last a loyal friend to Hamlet, trusted by all."**

questioning the nature of marriage. Hamlet tells Ophelia that he "did love [her] once" (III.i.114). To her response, "Indeed, my lord, you made me believe so," (III.i.115) he answers: "You should not have believ'd me" (III.i.116). Because Hamlet repeatedly charges Ophelia to "Get thee to a nunnery," (III.i.120) with the possible double meaning of "brothel," this scene is often referred to as the "nunnery scene." Although Polonius continues to believe that unrequited love has caused Hamlet's madness, Claudius is not convinced, and resolves to send Hamlet to England.

During the play "The Mousetrap," Hamlet sits next to Ophelia and responds to her attempts at conversation with angry and sexually suggestive remarks. When Ophelia next appears, in IV.v, Hamlet has killed her father and has himself been sent away to England, and Ophelia has gone mad. She comes before the king and queen singing snatches of songs about death, love, and sexual betrayal. She exits briefly, then returns after the arrival of Laertes and distributes various herbs and wildflowers with symbolic meanings. Two scenes later, Gertrude interrupts a meeting between Claudius and Laertes with the news that Ophelia has drowned, an apparent suicide. Blaming Hamlet for the deaths of both his father and his sister, Laertes plots with Claudius to obtain revenge by killing Hamlet.

At the beginning of Act V, two gravediggers discuss the appropriateness of Ophelia being given "Christian burial" even though her death is believed to have been suicide. Hamlet, who has escaped his uncle's plot to have him killed in England and has returned unexpectedly to Denmark, enters with Horatio. Unaware of Ophelia's death, he engages a gravedigger and Horatio in a discussion of mortality. As the funeral procession approaches, Hamlet and Horatio hide. When Laertes shows his grief by leaping into the grave, Hamlet, realizing that the funeral is Ophelia's, follows suit, claiming that his own love for Ophelia was far greater than

> Laertes returns to Denmark after Polonius's death, bursting into the room with a group of followers and addressing Claudius, 'O thou vile king' (IV.v.16), and vowing revenge for his father's death."

Laertes's. The two men grapple and have to be separated by the other mourners.

Ophelia is sometimes seen as an excessively weak character; first, because she obeys her father so unquestioningly, even to the point of helping him to spy on Hamlet, and second, because she loses her mind. Many critics, however, have defended both Shakespeare's choice of making Ophelia the character that she is, and Ophelia's behavior within the play.

Orsic:

Osric is a courtier, described by Hamlet as being of little significance himself, but important insofar as he owns extensive lands. He delivers the king's challenge of a fencing match between Hamlet and Laertes to Hamlet and Horatio (V.ii), speaking effusively in an affected manner which Hamlet mocks and parodies back to him. Even Horatio makes mild fun at Orsic's expense, after Hamlet's own rhetorical flourishes leave him befuddled.

Players:

A troupe of traveling actors already known to Hamlet. They arrive at Elsinore to perform for the Danish court, and Hamlet employs them to enact a play that mirrors the circumstances of his father's murder.

Polonius:

Polonius, Laertes's and Ophelia's father, is an elderly and long-winded courtier and chief counselor in the Danish court. Polonius demonstrates a propensity for hypocrisy and spying: his first major speech (I.iii), to his departing son Laertes, is a lengthy diatribe on, among other things, the virtue

of being close-mouthed and discreet. In II.i Polonius instructs his servant Reynaldo to spy on Laertes in France and report on his conduct. Ophelia enters, describing Hamlet's strange behavior. This causes Polonius to question whether Hamlet is "mad for thy [Ophelia's] love" (II.i.82). Polonius discusses Hamlet's bizarre behavior concerning Ophelia with Claudius, stating bluntly "Your noble son is mad" (II.ii.92). Polonius then arranges for himself and Claudius to secretly observe an encounter between Hamlet and Ophelia to prove Hamlet's insanity to the king.

Polonius dies in III.iv. He hides behind an arras following a brief conversation with Gertrude. From his hiding place, he overhears Hamlet's confrontation with Gertrude, during the course of which Gertrude asks Hamlet if he is going to murder her. When the queen cries out, Polonius, still behind the curtain, calls out for help. Hamlet then stabs him through the curtain and kills him, apparently thinking he was Claudius.

Prince Hamlet of Denmark:
See Hamlet

Queen Gertrude of England:
See Gertrude

Reynaldo:

Reynaldo is a servant whom Polonius instructs to go to Paris in order to observe and report on Laertes's conduct.

Rosencrantz:

Rosencrantz and Guildenstern are friends from Hamlet's youth sent for by the king and queen to learn the cause of Hamlet's change of personality. The two are perfectly willing to supply covert intelligence to the king. While both profess to be concerned about Hamlet's welfare, because it is bound up with the welfare of the Danish state, they are commonly considered by commentators on the play as opportunists who are currying royal favor with Claudius solely to remain in the good graces of the current power structure. Their exchanges with Hamlet generally reveal that he is suspicious of them, mistrustful of their purpose in court, and too wary to reveal anything about himself to them. With Guildenstern, Rosencrantz is unknowingly sent to his death in England by Hamlet's discovery of Claudius's plot and Hamlet's quick construction of a counter-plot.

Sailors:

The sailors are from the pirate ship that intercepts the ship conveying Hamlet, Rosencrantz, and Guildenstern to England. They carry letters from Hamlet to Horatio and the king, ransoming Hamlet back to Denmark.

Soldiers:

Fortinbras's Norwegian troops, marching dutifully to the fight. Hamlet says they ''go to their graves like beds ...'' (IV.iv.62), and seems to regret his own lack of resolute action.

Voltemand:

Voltemand and Cornelius are Danish ambassadors, sent by King Claudius in I.ii.26-38, to the king of Norway, the uncle of young Fortinbras, to urge him to squelch his nephew's threats against Danish land. They return in II.ii.40 to report that their mission was successful.

Further Reading

Bishop, Morris. *The Middle Ages*. New York: American Heritage Press, 1970.
Social history of the time period before the Renaissance.

Brower, Reuben A. *Hero & Saint*. New York: Oxford, 1971.
Offers a comparison between the Graeco-Roman heroic idea and the Shakespearean heroic idea. One chapter (''Hamlet and Hero,'' pp. 277-316) is an analysis of Hamlet as a hero. Brower sees a conflict in Hamlet between ''the relatively simple ancient hero and the Renaissance ideal.''

Charney, Maurice. *Hamlet's Fictions*. New York: Routledge, 1988.
Chapter 3 (''Ophelia and other madwomen in Elizabethan plays,'' pp. 35-47) contains a character analysis of Ophelia and includes references to other madwomen in Elizabethan drama.

———. *Style In* Hamlet. Princeton: Princeton University Press, 1969.
Discusses imagery patterns and staging in Shakespeare's time, including music, costumes, and stage properties. Separate chapters analyze the characters of Claudius, Polonius, and Hamlet.

Cohen, Michael. Hamlet *in My Mind's Eye*. Athens, Georgia: University of Georgia Press, 1989.
Cohen's work is a scene by scene discussion of the questions, issues, and choices raised by the playscript.

Cosman, Madeline Pelner. *Fabulous Feasts*. New York: Braziller, 1976.
Presents medieval and Renaissance recipes for feasts of the religious calendar, celebrations, and festive occasions.

Farnham, Willard. Introduction to *Hamlet*, by William Shakespeare. In *William Shakespeare The Complete Works*, edited by Alfred Harbage, 930-32. Baltimore: Pelican, 1969.
Surveys previous centuries of *Hamlet* criticism noting that pre-twentieth century critics focused on one recognizable flaw in Hamlet. By contrast, Farnham sees twentieth century criticism as stressing mystery.

Frye, Roland Mushat. *The Renaissance* Hamlet. Princeton: Princeton University Press, 1984.
Frye's book discusses the play in its original political, social, and theological climate. Frye uses references to the play as a point of departure for commentary on the history of the period.

Holdridge, Barbara, ed. *Under the Greenwood Tree*. Owings Mills, Maryland: Stemmer House, 1986.
Holdridge's book contains illustrations of a collection of speeches and poetry from Shakespeare, including a depiction of Hamlet's ''To be, or not to be'' speech and Ophelia's drowning.

Jenkins, Harold. Introduction to *Hamlet*, by William Shakespeare. In *The Arden Edition Of The Works Of William Shakespeare*, 1-159. London: Methuen, 1982.
Critical discussion of the play focussing on characters, themes, and specific scenes in *Hamlet*.

Kermode, Frank. Introduction to *Hamlet*, by William Shakespeare. In *The Riverside Shakespeare*, edited by G. Blakemore Evans, 1135-40. Houghton Mifflin: Chicago, 1974.
Discusses sources and dating the play, and characterization.

Mack, Maynard. '''The Readiness Is All': *Hamlet*.'' In *Everybody's Shakespeare*, 107-27. Lincoln: University of Nebraska Press, 1993.
Mack discusses three aspects of *Hamlet*: the play's mysteriousness, the problem of the relationship between appearance and reality, and the play's imagery. The last two sections of the essay relate the features of Hamlet's world to the significant change in his mood in Act V.

McRae, Lee. *Handbook of the Renaissance*. 2130 Carleton St., Berkeley, CA, 1992.
McRae's book, designed for students, contains information on music and pictures of Renaissance instruments. It includes a record list of Renaissance music. Those interested in Hamlet's comment about Rosencrantz and Guildenstern trying to play him like he was a recorder could follow up their musical interests here.

Mercer, Peter. Hamlet *and the Acting of Revenge*. London: Macmillan, 1987.
Mercer's work connects *Hamlet* with the genre of revenge tragedy.

Newell, Alex. *The Soliloquies in* Hamlet. London: Associated University Presses, 1991.

Newell's book is a study of the soliloquies in the play, how they reflect on the speaker, and how they fit in with the overall structure of the play.

Thirsk, Joan. ''Forest, Field, and Garden: Landscape and Economies in Shakespeare's England.'' In *William Shakespeare His World His Work His Influence*, edited by John F. Andrews, 257-67. Vol. 1. New York: Charles Scribner's Sons, 1985.

Discusses the many plant, herb, and flower references in *Hamlet*.

Watkins, Ronald and Jeremy Lemmon. *In Shakespeare's Playhouse*. Hamlet. Totowa, New Jersey: Rowman and Littlefield, 1974.

Watkins's and Lemmon's book is recommended for students seeking detailed commentary on the play as a whole or on individual scenes or acts as viewed by Shakespeare's own theatre audience.

Wilson, J. Dover. *What Happens in* Hamlet. Cambridge: Cambridge University Press, 1962.

Provides a detailed interpretation of the ''nunnery scene'' (III.i) between Hamlet and Ophelia.

The First Part of Henry the Fourth

1596-97

Plot Summary

Act I:

Henry Bullingbrook is King Henry IV of England, thanks in part to the Percys, a family of noblemen who supported his accession to the throne and were also instrumental in deposing his predecessor, Richard II. (Richard II's fall and Henry Bullingbrook's rise to power are the subject of Shakespeare's *Richard II*.) Having suppressed rebellions against his new government, King Henry is now preparing to embark on his delayed but promised voyage to the Holy Land in penance for the murder of Richard II. But he cancels his plans when he hears of further trouble: Welsh leader Owen Glendower has defeated and captured one of the king's officers, Lord Edmund Mortimer; on the other hand, young Harry Percy (Hotspur) has defeated the invading Scots but refuses to relinquish his prisoners to the king. While the king condemns Hotspur's insolence and sends word that Hotspur must account for his disobedience, he also expresses his admiration of the young man's expertise in battle and laments that his own son and heir, Prince Hal, is dissolute. Meanwhile, Prince Hal is with his drunken friend, Sir John Falstaff, who tries to recruit the prince to rob some travelers. As a joke, the prince and Poins, a companion, plan instead to trick Falstaff and rob him of the loot he steals. In a soliloquy, Prince Hal reveals that he intends eventually to stop being "madcap" and to reform into an

admirable leader. (A soliloquy is a speech delivered by a character when he or she is alone; it is meant to indicate to the audience the character's frame of mind or what action he or she plans to undertake.) At a meeting with the king, Hotspur offers to hand over the Scottish prisoners if Henry will arrange for the release of Hotspur's brother-in-law, Mortimer. Calling Mortimer a traitor, Henry refuses. Alone with his father (Northumberland) and his uncle (Worcester), an enraged Hotspur states his regret that the three of them supported Henry against King Richard, and, counseled by his uncle, plots to join with the Scots and Welsh against the king.

Act II:

Falstaff and his men rob the travelers as planned, then run away—leaving behind their loot—when they are set upon by the disguised Prince Hal and Poins. Meanwhile, Hotspur makes further preparations in his plot against the king, then leaves to meet with the other conspirators, telling his anxious wife only that he will send for her once he has arrived at the meeting's secret location. At the Boar's Head Tavern in Eastcheap, London, Falstaff tells of being ambushed, and grossly exaggerates the number and ferocity of his attackers—much to the amusement of Poins and Prince Hal. A messenger arrives from the king with news of Hotspur's rebellion and with orders that the prince must return to court by morning. Knowing that the king will deliver a stern lecture to Hal about his wildness, Falstaff suggests acting out the meeting before hand to give the prince a chance to "practice an answer" to his father (II.iv.375). When Falstaff plays the part of Hal's father, he takes the opportunity to praise that "goodly portly man" (meaning himself) with whom Hal spends his time (II.iv.421). When they switch roles, Hal, now playing king, condemns Falstaff.

Act III:

At their secret meeting in Wales, Hotspur, Northumberland, Worcester, Mortimer, and Glendower provisionally carve up England into equal portions that will go to each after they have defeated the king. Hotspur complains that his portion is too small. In London, when the king sharply criticizes Hal (negatively contrasting him with Hotspur), the prince apologizes for his former recklessness swearing that he will henceforth make his father proud and bravely defeat Hotspur in battle. Hal goes once more to the Boar's Head to issue orders to his old friends and a military commission to the unwilling Falstaff.

Act IV:

At the rebel camp with his uncle Worcester and the Scots nobleman Douglas, Hotspur is informed that his father, Northumberland, is too ill to fight and, what's more, that Glendower will be delayed for fourteen days. Hotspur decides to go to battle without them. Meanwhile, having no desire at all to fight, Falstaff has misused his commission to gather a bunch of "pitiful rascals" to be his soldiers (IV.ii.64). The king's spokesman, Sir Walter Blunt, goes to the rebels' camp to hear their grievances, hoping to avert war. Hotspur agrees to send his uncle to parley with the king early the next morning. In the city of York, Richard Scroop (the archbishop of York and a supporter of the Percy family) fears that the king's impressive forces will defeat Hotspur's small army and then will move north to attack him, so the archbishop arranges to protect himself against them.

Act V:

Accompanied by Sir Richard Vernon, Hotspur's uncle Worcester goes to Henry IV's camp to parley. Prince Hal praises Worcester's nephew for his courage and suggests that "a single fight" between Hotspur and himself should settle the dispute (V.i.100). But the king decides it would be better to pardon all the rebels if they agree to make peace, and he sends Worcester back to Hotspur with this offer. But convinced that the king will never truly forgive the Percys, Worcester decides not to tell Hotspur of this "liberal and kind offer of the King" (V.ii.2) but announces instead that Henry IV is determined to destroy them. The two sides engage in battle. Prince Hal saves the king from an attack by Douglas. Hal and Hotspur encounter each other and fight, and the prince kills Hotspur. Later Falstaff, who has been playing dead to avoid injury, pretends that he in fact killed Hotspur, and Prince Hal agrees to back him in his story. Worcester and Vernon are captured and sent to be executed; Douglas is captured, pardoned, and released. As the play closes, the king and his sons set off to fight the other rebels: Northumberland, Scroop, Mortimer, and Glendower (these battles occur in Shakespeare's *Henry IV, Part Two*).

Modern Connections

Much of *Henry IV, Part One* has to do with the king's power struggle against the Percys, a noble family who once supported him but who now accuses him of arrogance and ingratitude. Yet that aspect of the play which is perhaps most interesting to modern audiences is the conflict that occurs between a father (King Henry) and his oldest son (Prince Hal).

Henry IV repeatedly expresses his disappointment with his first-born son, who spends his time in "rude society," frequenting taverns and brothels when he should be at court or on the battlefield preparing himself to succeed his father as king (III.ii.14). So dissatisfied is the king with Hal that in I.i.86-90 he openly wishes it might somehow turn out that Hotspur and Hal had been switched at birth, and that the brave and clean-living Hotspur were in fact his son and heir.

It is true that the king needs a reliable successor to help legitimize his own claim to the throne (Henry IV usurped King Richard II), but his impatience with his son appears to be personal as well as political. On the eve of his battle with the Percys, Henry delivers a stern lecture to Hal which—although it occurs between a king and a prince and thus concerns affairs of state—is similar in tone to one that might be given today by a father to a rebellious teenager, for the advice is mixed with anger and hurt feelings (III.ii.4-161). Henry begins his lecture by wondering whether God had sent him a bad child as punishment for his own misdeeds. Next, he complains that Hal does not measure up to his ancestors or even to his younger brother, John. He warns his son that everyone believes he's headed for disaster. He advises Hal to stop cheapening his royal worth by consorting with lowlifes and behaving as though he were a commoner. While his final, grim warning is purely political (mend your ways or your rival Hotspur will someday usurp you as I replaced King Richard), his closing comment in which he suggests that his son is capable of committing treason against his own father is bitterly mixed with hurt feelings:

> Why, Harry, do I tell thee of my foes,
> Which art my nearest and dearest enemy?
> Thou that art like enough, through vassal fear,
> Base inclination, and the start of spleen,
> To fight against me under Percy's pay . . .
>
> (III.ii.122-26)

Two remarks in particular show the extent to which Henry's emotions as a parent are involved. In one instance he angrily accuses Hal of being his "nearest and dearest enemy," and one quite possibly capable of joining the rebels' cause against his own father (III.ii.123-26). In another instance, he reproaches Hal for spending too much time away from court and, close to tears, he observes that:

> Not an eye
> But is a-weary of thy common sight,
> Save mine, which hath desir'd to see thee more,
> Which now doth that I would not have it do,
> Make blind itself with foolish tenderness.
>
> (III.ii.87-91)

Hal's response to this lecture from his father is to admit his "intemperance" or dissolute behavior, to apologize for the "wounds" it has caused to King Henry's feelings, and to swear that he will prove himself to be more honorable than his rival, Hotspur (III.ii.129-59).

Another aspect of *Henry IV, Part One* which appeals to modern audiences is the natural, conversational tone of many of its scenes. Critics have called this play a milestone in Shakespeare's development as a dramatist, noting his skillfulness in bringing together in the same play the formal, weighty concerns of the monarchy and the comic, frequently raunchy goings-on of tavern and street life, using Hal as the link between these two worlds. The resulting connection means that the serious and comic scenes rub off on each other, and we get a more varied, realistic portrayal of life—one that today's audiences can still appreciate. This realism affects the play's language. While modern audiences frequently think of Shakespeare's words as alien and incomprehensible, some of the conversations in *Henry IV, Part One* reveal similarities to the ways in which our own conversations work today. The verbal exchanges which most often come to mind are those which occur at the Boar's Head Tavern as Hal and Falstaff trade good-natured insults, but there are also moments in the play's more serious scenes where the conversations sound—in tone if not in content—as though they could occur today.

One such conversation occurs in I.iii.130-302 between Hotspur, his father (the earl of Northumberland), and his uncle (the earl of Worcester). Here, Hotspur is reacting to the king's absolute refusal to ransom his brother-in-law, Edmund Mortimer. So enraged is Hotspur with the king that he can hardly contain himself: his words rush out as he imagines all sorts of insults that he will use against Henry IV. In response, for example, to the king's injunction against speaking Mortimer's name in his presence, Hotspur decides that he will teach a bird "to speak / Nothing but 'Mortimer,' and give it [to Henry IV] / To keep his anger still in motion"

(I.iii.224-26). He is so completely beside himself that he ignores or misinterprets the comments of his listeners, provoking his uncle at last to exclaim, "Farewell, kinsman! I'll talk to you / When you are better temper'd to attend" (I.iii.234-35).

Even after Worcester's rebuke, Hotspur needs more time to cool off before he can hear what his father and his uncle have to say. He is so enraged that his memory is affected, and he interrupts himself and swears in frustration as he tries to remember the name of a place (Berkeley castle), as well as of a person (the duke of York), until his father finally remembers for him:

> *Hotspur*:In Richard's time—what do you call
>   the place?—
> A plague upon it, it is in Gloucestershire—
> 'Twas where the madcap duke his uncle kept—
> His uncle York—where first I bow'd my knee
> Unto this king of smiles, this Bullingbrook—
> 'Sblood!
> When you and he came back from Ravenspurgh—
>   *Northumberland*:At Berkeley castle.
>   *Hotspur*:You say true.
>
> (I.iii.242-50)

This sort of sputtering, head-on language is not unusual today from people who are very angry, and Shakespeare accomplishes this natural reaction even while writing in verse, as he has done in the above passage.

Characters

Archbishop of York (Richard Scroop, the Archbishop of York):
See Scroop

Archibald (Archibald, Earl of Douglas):
See Douglas

Attendants:
Together with lords, messengers, and officers, these are the play's extras, who have at most very brief speaking parts. They help populate the scenes, contributing when needed to the regal and martial atmosphere of the play.

Bardolph:
He is a frequenter of the Boar's Head Tavern and a companion of Falstaff and Prince Hal. He is one of the four men in II.ii who rob the travelers, only to be robbed soon afterward by the disguised Prince Hal and Poins. At Falstaff's bidding, he and Peto hack their own swords and bloody their noses to make it look as though they had been attacked by dozens of robbers. His face, which is bright red from drink and carbuncles, is the source of continual jokes from Falstaff and Hal. In II.iv.324, Bardolph tells the prince that his red face is a sign of "choler" or a hot temper. Prince Hal's punning reply that a collar or "halter" (a hangman's noose) will be Bardolph's fate is prophetic: In *Henry V* Bardolph is hanged for looting.

Blunt (Sir Walter Blunt):
He is a loyal supporter of King Henry IV but is also deeply admired by the rebel camp. The king describes Blunt as a "dear, a true industrious friend" (I.i.62). Hotspur considers him "a gallant knight" (V.iii.20) and wishes that he were on the rebels' side rather than the king's (IV.iii.32-37). Blunt does his best to prevent bloodshed on either side. During a meeting convened to discover why Hotspur has withheld his Scottish prisoners, Blunt tries to mediate between the king's anger and Hotspur's excuses (I.iii.70-76). On the eve of battle, Blunt goes to the rebels "with gracious offers from the King" promising amnesty and reconciliation in exchange for peace (IV.iii.30, 41-51). After his efforts fail, Blunt disguises himself as one of the king's doubles on the battlefield and is killed by Douglas (V.iii.1-13).

Bullingbrook (King Henry IV of England, formerly known as Bullingbrook):
See Henry

Carriers:
They deliver goods for a living (such as the gammon of bacon and the turkeys mentioned in II.i.24, 26) and are staying at the same inn as the travelers of II.ii. Although they detect Gadshill as a crook in II.i, one of them nevertheless lets slip that they will be accompanied by some wealthy gentlemen wishing to ride with a large group for safety's sake. In II.iv.506-11, one of the carriers arrives with the sheriff to bear witness against Falstaff for highway robbery. Beyond inadvertently supplying Gadshill with details useful in his robbery, the two carriers give us a closer look at the world of the play, providing us with atmosphere and color as they discuss their jobs, complain about fleas and poor service at the inn, and worry about the logistics of their trip.

Chamberlain:

He is a dishonest servant who informs Gadshill in II.i about the traveling plans of wealthy merchants and gentlemen staying at the inn where he works. Gadshill and Falstaff then use this information to rob the travellers on the road in II.ii.

Douglas (Archibald, Earl of Douglas):

Usually referred to in the play as Douglas, he is the leader of the Scottish rebels. In I.i we are told that Douglas has battled with and been defeated by Hotspur, and that Hotspur has taken Scottish prisoners but will not relinquish all of them to the king. This incident acts as a catalyst to the rebellion that is dealt with during the rest of the play: Hotspur's disobedience angers the king, and the king's subsequent refusal to ransom Mortimer from Glendower infuriates Hotspur, who then returns the prisoners to Scotland and allies himself with Douglas against the king. The "brave Archibald, / That ever-valiant and approved Scot," is similar in temperament to Hotspur: both are combative and impetuous (I.i.53-54). In IV.iii, he is as keen as Hotspur is to fight the king's forces at night, and he accuses Vernon of cowardice for recommending that they wait until morning for reinforcements. Douglas fights with and almost kills King Henry in V.iv.25-38, which gives Hal the opportunity to save his father and thus prove his loyalty. At the close of the play Douglas has been captured while retreating, and in V.v.17-31, Prince Hal shows his clemency by recommending that "the noble Scot" be set free without ransom.

Falstaff (Sir John Falstaff):

He is the dishonest but appealing "fat knight" who is Hal's friend and a regular at the Boar's Head Tavern. Given to thievery, drunkenness, and overeating, Falstaff is part of the "rude society" which King Henry accuses of corrupting his son and heir, Prince Hal (III.ii.14); he is also the central focus of most of the comedic scenes in the play and the topic of considerable literary discussion.

Falstaff has been compared to the comic characters which represented vice in the morality plays of the medieval period. (Morality plays taught moral lessons by presenting in human form vices such as gluttony and greed competing for a person's soul against virtues such as temperance and mercy, also represented in human form.) Alternatively, Falstaff has been called a second father to Hal—one who fills in the gaps in experience left by Hal's royal education at Henry IV's court and who helps to

> " Given to thievery, drunkenness, and overeating, Falstaff is part of the 'rude society' which King Henry accuses of corrupting his son and heir, Prince Hal (III.ii.14). . . ."

increase the prince's familiarity with the range of people he will eventually govern.

Critics have remarked that Falstaff's words and actions frequently parody the serious scenes and characters in the play. (To parody something is to imitate it closely for the purposes of comic effect or ridicule.) In II.iv.373-480, for example, Falstaff engages the prince in a "practice" question-and-answer session which mocks the genuine, serious confrontation between Hal and his father in III.ii. Elsewhere, Falstaff's assessment of his ramshackle bunch of soldiers as "the cankers of a calm world and a long peace" and as "food for [gun]powder" (IV.ii.29-30; 65-66) acts as a comical contrast to Vernon's description in the preceding scene of Hal's troops as "glittering in golden coats like images" and "gorgeous as the sun at midsummer" (IV.i.100, 102). Similarly, Falstaff's famous "catechism" on the uselessness of honor (V.i.127-41) parodies Hotspur's preoccupation throughout the play with honor and glory in battle. And in V.iv, Falstaff mocks an honorable death, first by playing dead after being challenged to combat by Douglas, and then by stabbing Hotspur's corpse and taking credit for actually killing him.

As a parodist, critics note, Falstaff serves as a social commentator, amusing and educating his audience by identifying and poking fun at society's flaws or its tendency toward extremes. Critics have also noted that Falstaff's parodies threaten to destroy the system of values according to which society is run, and that is why Prince Hal indicates in II.iv.481 that as king, he will banish Falstaff from his company.

It has been argued that Falstaff's mastery of language and brilliant sense of humor are what make him charming in spite of his dishonesty. As proof, critics point to Falstaff's witty disquisition on honor in V.i.127-141 ("Can honor set to a leg? No. Or an arm? No. Or take away the grief of a wound? No. Honor hath no skill in surgery then? No. What is honor? A word. . . ''), as well as to his cleverly invented excuses at the end of the practical joke in II.iv.267-75 ("I was now a coward on instinct").

The insults traded between Falstaff and the prince are likewise engaging for their virtuosity and humor. In II.iv.240-48, Hal's string of invective against Falstaff's fatness and drunkenness ("this sanguine coward, this bed-presser, this horse-back-breaker, this huge hill of flesh—") is rapidly interrupted and bettered by Falstaff's list detailing Hal's thinness: "'Sblood, you starveling, you eel-skin, you dried neat's tongue, you bull's pizzle, you stock-fish! . . . you tailor's yard, you sheath, you bowcase, you vile standing tuck—"

Falstaff appears again in *Henry IV, Part Two.*

Francis:

He is an apprenticed drawer at the Boar's Head Tavern. It is his job to draw wine from the hogsheads or barrels for the tavern guests. In II.iv.36-86, Prince Hal has fun teasing Francis with the help of Poins. Critics have wondered about the purpose of this scene and the meaning of some of Hal's remarks to Francis. It has been suggested that Hal is simply speaking nonsense in order to confuse and distract the drawer as he is being summoned by Poins. Francis's perpetual response: "Anon, anon, sir" ("I'll be there right away, sir") was apparently typical of servants during the Elizabethan age and thus would be a source of amusement to Shake-speare's audience.

Immediately before this episode, the prince jokes with Poins about the friendly and familiar way he was treated while drinking with a group of drawers (one of whom was Francis), thus leading critics to observe that Hal's encounter with Francis is yet another example of the prince's experience with the various social classes of England and his attempts to understand all of the people he will someday govern. It has also been suggested that just as Francis becomes confused when he is called upon by several people at once, so the prince feels over-whelmed by the calls made upon him by his father, the people, and his own desires.

After he has finished questioning Francis, Hal mocks the ambitious and warlike Hotspur, causing some critics to conclude that as the prince examines and rejects other ways of life (in this case, the two very different lives of Francis and Hotspur), he is learning to accept his own destiny.

Gadshill:

He is a thief who plans the robbery on the London road undertaken in II.ii.78-92 by himself, Falstaff, Peto, and Bardolph. On the night before the robbery, he stays at a roadside inn where he gathers useful information about wealthy travellers from a dishonest inn servant and some imprudent, overtalkative carriers.

Glendower (Owen Glendower):

He is the leader of the Welsh forces against King Henry IV. In I.i.37-46, we are told that he has captured Edmund Mortimer, who then marries Glendower's daughter. By III.i, he has allied him-self with the Percys against the king. Glendower is a fierce opponent who believes in omens and practic-es magic. Henry's ally Westmerland calls him "wild;" Falstaff refers to him as a "devil" (I.i.40; II.iv.369). His new son-in-law Mortimer describes him as "a worthy gentleman, / Exceedingly well read, . . . / . . . valiant as a lion, / And wondrous affable, and as bountiful / As mines of India" (III.i.163-67). The fact that "wild Glendower" keeps his temper in the face of Hotspur's rudeness in III.i demonstrates the admiration which "the gallant Hotspur" (I.i.52) inspires in others.

Hotspur's impatience with Glendower's faith in signs and magic comes full circle when, in IV.i.125-26, Vernon reports that Glendower will not fight for fourteen days because, as the archbish-op of York remarks in IV.iv.16-18, he has been "overrul'd by prophecies"; in spite of this bad news, Hotspur is determined to go to battle.

Hal (Prince Henry of Wales, also known as Hal or Harry Monmouth, later King Henry V of England):

See Henry

Henry (King Henry IV of England, formerly known as Bullingbrook):

He is the king of England, the father of Hal, and the title character of the play. Henry rules as a result of the deposition and murder of his predecessor, Richard II, but seems neither secure nor contented in his role. At the beginning of the play, he describes himself as ''shaken'' and ''wan with care'' (I.i.1): his reign so far has been clouded by illness, apparent guilt over his responsibility for Richard's death, and rebellions against his rule. In I.i, he renews his intention to go on a long-promised pilgrimage to atone for his sins against Richard, but his plans are stopped by news of Glendower's incursion into England and Hotspur's defiance.

Critical assessment of King Henry's role in the play varies. Although he is the title character, much of the play revolves around his son Prince Hal as well as the actions of the rebel Hotspur. Nevertheless, it has been argued that Henry is the play's protagonist, and that his main goal is to preserve the health and stability of England.

The major obstacle to accomplishing this goal is the fact that Henry is a usurper who is plagued not only by claims against his leadership but also by his own conscience. At the start of his lecture to Hal in III.ii.4-11, the king reveals his feelings of guilt in his worried observation that his son may have been sent by God to punish him:

> I know not whether God will have it so
> For some displeasing service I have done,
> That in his secret doom, out of my blood
> He'll breed revengement and a scourge for me;
> But thou dost in thy passages of life
> Make me believe that thou art only mark'd
> For the hot vengeance, and the rod of heaven,
> To punish my mistreadings.

Some critics argue that as a usurper, Henry is in an impossible position no matter how earnestly he tries to rule well. Because he overturned order and the ritual of succession when he deposed Richard, he is finding it difficult to maintain order and the ritual of succession now that he is king. The Percys— the family that helped him to the throne—have begun treating him with disrespect. Young Henry Percy or Hotspur has withheld prisoners from the king, and in I.iii.10-13, Thomas Percy, earl of Worcester, complains that his family is being mistreated and reminds Henry that his ''greatness'' depends upon the Percys. King Henry retorts that he is ''majesty'' or king, and that Worcester should remember that he is merely Henry's ''servant'' or subject:

> Worcester, get thee gone, for I do see
> Danger and disobedience in thine eye.
> O, sir, your presence is too bold and peremptory,
> And majesty might never yet endure
> The moody frontier of a servant brow.

(I.iii.15-19)

> " Henry rules as a result of the deposition and murder of his predecessor, Richard II, but seems neither secure nor contented in his role. At the beginning of the play, he describes himself as 'shaken' and 'wan with care' (I.i.1): his reign so far has been clouded by illness, apparent guilt over his responsibility for Richard's death, and rebellions against his rule."

Meanwhile the king worries that his oldest son and heir, Prince Hal, is not acting as a successor to the throne should, but is instead behaving irresponsibly, much as Richard II had been shortly before he was thrown out of power (III.ii.93-95). In his role as a father, Henry has been described as inflexible and somewhat peevish, and in II.iv.378-481, his son Hal mocks his strictness in his ''practice'' interview with Falstaff. In I.i.78-90, the king longs for a son like Hotspur, ''who is the theme of honor's tongue,'' and deplores the ''riot and dishonor'' which ''stain the brow'' of his own son, and by extension, stain Henry's rule.

In an effort to define Henry's role as king, critics have compared his priorities to those of his son Hal. It has been argued that while Hal (as a result of his association with the common populace of England) stresses justice and mercy, King Henry IV—in his attempt to legitimize his rule—focuses on authority and power. An example of his commanding exercise of power occurs in I.iii.118-22, where he angrily orders Hotspur to obey, then exits without waiting for an answer:

> sirrah, henceforth
> Let me not hear you speak of Mortimer.
> Send me your prisoners with the speediest means,
> Or you shall hear in such a kind from me
> As will displease you.

King Henry's authoritativeness, however, does not prevent rebellion.

Henry (Prince Henry of Wales, also known as Prince Hal or Harry Monmouth, afterwards King Henry V of England):

He is the son and heir of King Henry IV. Much of his time is spent away from his responsibilities at court, plotting pranks and robberies in the company of "rude society" at the Boar's Head Tavern (III.ii.14). Prince Hal is described by his rival, Hotspur, as "the nimble-footed madcap Prince of Wales, / . . . that daff'd the world aside / And bid it pass" (IV.i.95-97). His father accuses him of having "inordinate and low desires" unsuitable for a future king (III.ii.12). Sir John Falstaff calls him "sweet wag" and looks forward to the day when Hal will rule England (I.ii.23).

In his soliloquy in I.ii, Hal asserts that his misconduct is strategic: he is behaving irresponsibly now so that he will seem that much more impressive and honorable when he reforms. What is more, his sudden reformation will catch his detractors off guard:

My reformation, glitt'ring o'er my fault,
Shall show more goodly and attract more eyes
Than that which hath no foil to set it off.
I'll so offend, to make offense a skill,
Redeeming time when men think least I will.
(I.ii.213-17)

There has been much critical discussion regarding Prince Hal's behavior. It has been pointed out that as the son of a usurper, Hal is burdened with the task of legitimizing his family's rule and with uniting the country around that rule—two things that his father has been unable to do. How the prince undertakes this task has been a source of debate. Some critics refer to his soliloquy in I.ii as proof that Hal needs neither education nor reformation to fulfill his duties as prince, but that he is a pragmatist who is simply waiting for the right moment to shine. Others argue that the time Hal spends in "riotous" living is in fact an opportunity for him to learn how to be a more effective ruler than King Henry is. In this case, Falstaff functions as a second father to Hal, educating him in the ways of the world, while King Henry's court can only teach him politics and protocol. Further, Hal's irreverent treatment by such shady characters as Falstaff, Bardolph, and Gadshill teaches him humility.

It has also been observed that Hal learns from Hotspur to appreciate honor. Even though he pokes fun in II.iv.101-12 at Hotspur's thirst for glory, Hal acknowledges his rival's worth. In V.i, he praises Hotspur, calling him "valiant," "daring," and "bold," commending him for his "noble deeds," and criticizing himself for having been "a truant . . . to chivalry" (V.i.90, 91, 92, 94).

Hal's apparent love of acting has also been mentioned with regard to his education. In II.ii.102-111, for instance, he and Poins disguise themselves as robbers in order to set upon Gadshill, Falstaff, Peto, and Bardolph and steal their loot. In II.iv.1-79, Hal enlists Poins's help in arranging a scene where the two of them confuse the drawer Francis with questions and requests. Shortly afterward, the prince suggests acting out Hotspur's enthusiasm for glory, with himself in the role of Hotspur, and Falstaff (whom Hal refers to as "that damn'd brawn" or pig) to portray Hotspur's wife (II.iv.108-12). Finally, Hal and Falstaff rehearse a conversation between Hal and his father by acting out the interview that will occur when Hal returns to court (II.iv.373-481). As mocking and sometimes cruel as these performances are, critics observe that they nevertheless work as learning experiences for the prince—increasing his knowledge of himself or teaching him what it feels like to live or think in a certain way—and thus function as useful background for his actual role as king.

Another observation that has been made about Hal is that despite his wild living, he believes in paying debts. After the robbery and escapade at Gadshill, for example, Hal announces that the money stolen from the travellers will "be paid back again with advantage [interest]" (II.iv.547-48).

Critics have remarked that toward the end of the play, Prince Hal demonstrates his loyalty to his father by saving him from Douglas (V.iv.39-43). Shortly afterward, he reveals his courage by battling with and defeating Hotspur, then shows his sense of honor by covering the dead Hotspur's face (V.iv.59-101). He displays mercy at the close of the play by declaring that the captured Douglas should be set free (V.v.27-31). He has, in other words, begun to combine the best of what he has learned from his father, from Falstaff, and from Hotspur on his way toward becoming king.

Hotspur (Henry Percy, also known as Hotspur):
See Percy

John (Prince John of Lancaster):
He is King Henry's son and Prince Hal's younger brother. His appearance in the play is brief; he initially serves as a contrast to his older brother. In

I.i, for example he is at court, while his brother is at the Boar's Head Tavern. In III.ii.32-33, the king complains that John has had to fill in for his reckless brother in affairs of state. John's first, few words occur in V.iv.1-24, when he is impatient to rejoin the fight against the rebels. Both the king and Prince Hal are inspired by John's courage in this, his first battle; indeed, the prince exclaims of him: "O, this boy / Lends mettle to us all!" (V.iv.23-24). Prince John has a larger role in *Henry IV, Part Two*.

Lords:

Together with attendants, messengers, and officers, these are the play's extras, who have at most very brief speaking parts. They help populate the scenes, contributing when needed to the regal and martial atmosphere of the play.

Messengers:

Together with attendants, lords, and officers, these are the play's extras, who have at most very brief speaking parts. They help populate the scenes, contributing when needed to the regal and martial atmosphere of the play.

Michael (Sir Michael):

He is a member of Archbishop Richard Scroop's household. His first and only appearance in the play occurs in IV.iv, when he is asked to deliver letters to Scroop's allies. His efforts to reassure the archbishop that Hotspur's diminished army is capable of defeating Henry IV results in a list of the supporters on each side of the contention.

Mistress Quickly:

See Quickly

Mortimer (Edmund Mortimer, Earl of March):

Also known as the earl of March, he is Lady (Kate) Percy's brother and therefore Hotspur's brother-in-law. His name is introduced in I.i.38, when Westmerland announces that "the noble Mortimer" has fought against and been captured by the Welsh rebel Owen Glendower. In I.iii.83-85, we are told that Mortimer has married Glendower's daughter.

While the Percys have many grievances against the king, the fate of Edmund Mortimer is a particularly virulent source of conflict between King Henry and Hotspur. When Hotspur agrees to hand over his Scottish prisoners on condition that the king will

> In I.i.78-90, the king longs for a son like Hotspur, 'who is the theme of honor's tongue,' and deplores the 'riot and dishonor' which 'stain the brow' of his own son, and by extension, stain Henry's rule."

ransom his brother-in-law from the Welsh, Henry angrily refuses. He insists that "the foolish Mortimer" is a rebel who "hath willfully betray'd / The lives of those that he did lead to fight" against Glendower, and alludes to Mortimer's marriage as proof of his treachery (I.iii.80, 81-82, 84-85).

Hotspur, in contrast, furiously denies that Mortimer is a traitor and suspects instead that the king is afraid of the earl of March. Hotspur's uncle and father confirm his suspicion when they assert that Henry's deposed predecessor, King Richard II, had designated Mortimer (not Henry) as his rightful successor to the throne.

Mortimer and his father-in-law, Glendower, agree to join the Percys in their rebellion against the king. But when Glendower delays his entry into battle for two weeks, Mortimer does so as well.

Mortimer (Lady Mortimer):

She is the daughter of the Welsh leader Owen Glendower and the wife of Edmund Mortimer, who married her after he was captured in battle by her father. She appears in III.i. at her father's castle in Wales, where her husband, Glendower, Worcester, and Hotspur have provisionally divided up England for themselves. As Mortimer tells us in III.i.190-91, he cannot speak Welsh, and Lady Mortimer cannot speak English, so Glendower must translate for them both. Accompanied by musical spirits summoned by her father, Lady Mortimer sings to her husband while Hotspur and his wife sit listening nearby. The episode provides us with further insight into the character of Hotspur, who ridicules the music and mocks the singer while teasing his wife, Kate: he is a man of practical action who does not hide his contempt for magic or genteel pastimes— even at the risk of offending his hosts.

❝ **Prince Hal is described by his rival, Hotspur, as 'the nimble-footed madcap Prince of Wales, / . . . that daff'd the world aside / And bid it pass' (IV.i.95-97). His father accuses him of having 'inordinate and low desires' unsuitable for a future king (III.ii.12). Sir John Falstaff calls him 'sweet wag' and looks forward to the day when Hal will rule England (I.ii.23).❞**

Northumberland (Henry Percy, Earl of Northumberland):

See Percy

Officers:

Together with attendants, lords, and messengers, these are the play's extras, who have at most very brief speaking parts. They help populate the scenes, contributing when needed to the regal and martial atmosphere of the play.

Ostler:

A caretaker of horses at the inn, he is briefly heard but not seen in II.i.4. Although the carriers call for his service, he never appears, and they curse him in frustration.

Percy (Henry Percy, Earl of Northumberland):

This Percy, who is also referred to as Northumberland, is Hotspur's father, and as such, Northumberland is envied by King Henry. The king admires Hotspur's courage and deplores the "riot and dishonor" which "stain the brow" of his own son and heir, Prince Hal (I.i.85).

In Shakespeare's earlier play *Richard II*, Northumberland functions as a chief supporter of Henry IV (then known as Bullingbrook) against King Richard II, whom he holds in contempt. By contrast, his role in *Henry IV, Part One* is brief, and his attitude toward both Henry and Richard has changed. In I.iii.148-49, he expresses regret for his part in deposing Richard—"the unhappy king /(Whose wrongs in us God pardon!)"—and he appears to consent to his brother Worcester's plot against Henry IV (I.iii.300). However, in IV.i.16, Northumberland sends word to his son that "he is grievous sick" and that neither he nor his army will be able to join Hotspur in his battle against the king. Northumberland appears again in *Henry IV, Part Two*.

Percy (Henry Percy, also known as Hotspur):

Hotspur is the younger Henry Percy, the son of the earl of Northumberland, and a rival and contemporary of Prince Hal. With the encouragement of his uncle, the earl of Worcester, Hotspur organizes a rebel force against King Henry. He is admired by both sides for his courage and strong sense of honor, but criticized for his hotheadedness.

We first hear of "the gallant Hotspur" in I.i.50-95, after he has fought back an attack by Douglas. King Henry praises Hotspur's bravery even as he condemns "young Percy's pride" in refusing to hand over all but one of his Scottish prisoners. By I.iii, the situation has deteriorated. Henry rejects Hotspur's demand that Mortimer be ransomed from Glendower, insists that Hotspur relinquish all his prisoners, then angrily cuts off the meeting and departs. Enraged, Hotspur declares to his father:

> And if the devil come and roar for [the prisoners],
> I will not send them. I will after straight
> And tell him so, for I will ease my heart,
> Albeit I make a hazard of my head.
>
> (I.iii.125-28)

Although Hotspur considers himself a man of action rather than of words, he makes numerous speeches in the play which reveal his impetuosity and lack of patience. He is intolerant of men whom he considers cowardly, and he disparagingly compares them to women. His initial excuse for not relinquishing his prisoners is that he disliked the king's messenger, who had arrived on the scene of Hotspur's battle "trimly dress'd" and "perfumed like a milliner," complaining about the dead bodies on the field, talking like a "waiting-gentlewoman," and using "lady terms" to question Hotspur about his prisoners (I.iii.33, 36, 55, 46).

Similarly, when he receives a letter from a hoped-for ally declining to join the Percys' rebellion, Hotspur calls him a "cowardly hind" and scoffs, "'zounds, and were I now by this rascal, I could brain him with his lady's fan'' (II.iii.15, 22-23).

In III.i Hotspur nearly offends his warlike ally Glendower by responding sarcastically to the Welshman's belief in magic and love of music; later, he complains to Mortimer that Glendower "is as tedious / As a tired horse [and] a railing wife" (III.i.157-58).

His rudeness aside, Hotspur is frequently seen as a charismatic figure, who demonstrates bravery, honesty, and affection for his wife. This last characteristic can be observed in two scenes. In II.iii, after a somewhat playful exchange in which Kate questions her husband about why he must leave so abruptly and about his love for her, Hotspur concludes more seriously "whither I go, thither shall you go too" (II.iii.115). Later, the two tease each other as Lady Mortimer sings.

Hotspur's relationships to King Henry and to Hal are important to the play. As the king observes in III.ii.96-105, he was once himself a well-admired rebel as Hotspur is now. In the same scene, Hal acknowledges that Hotspur's widespread reputation for bravery and honor are more suitable to a prince.

Hotspur's preoccupation with honor reaches its climax in V.iv.77-86, when, upon receiving his death blow from Prince Hal, he is more distressed about surrendering his "proud titles" to the prince than he is about losing his life.

Percy (Lady Percy, also known as Kate):

She is Hotspur's wife. She first appears in II.iii when her husband is preparing to leave for Wales to meet with fellow rebels Glendower and Mortimer. Kate worries about Hotspur's restlessness and inattentiveness, asking, "For what offense have I this fortnight been / A banish'd woman from my Harry's bed?" (II.iii.38-39). In response, Hotspur teases her, claiming he doesn't love her and refusing to tell her where he is going. Her next and last appearance occurs after the meeting at Glendower's castle (III.i), where she submits once more to her husband's teasing and witnesses his impatience as the two of them listen to Lady Mortimer's singing. Kate's presence in both scenes demonstrates that Hotspur can be affectionate and playful; her presence also underlines his preoccupation with action, battle, and honor at the expense of domestic life. As Hotspur tells Kate in II.iii.91-93, "This is no world / To play with mammets and to tilt with lips. / We

must have bloody noses and crack'd crowns." Lady Percy appears again, as a widow, in *Henry IV, Part Two*.

Percy (Thomas Percy, Earl of Worcester):

Known as the earl of Worcester—or, simply, Worcester—he is Hotspur's uncle and Northumberland's brother. King Henry IV's supporter Westmerland describes Worcester as "malevolent to [the king] in all aspects" (I.i.97). Westmerland also asserts that Worcester motivated Hotspur to do such disrespectful things as withholding the Scottish prisoners from Henry. Indeed, it is Hotspur's uncle who, in I.iii.187-93 and 259-76, first suggests to his nephew an organized plan for overthrowing the king. Worcester's argument for his plot against the king is that Henry dislikes and fears being indebted to the Percy family, who placed him on the throne after helping him usurp his predecessor, Richard II. Worcester further contends that the king will find any excuse to rid himself of the Percys, and that the only way "to save our heads [is] by raising of a head [army]" (I.iii.284). Returning from his parley with Henry, Worcester chooses not to tell his nephew of the king's "liberal and kind offer" of reconciliation (V.ii.2), his reason being that while Henry might indeed forgive "a harebrained Hotspur, govern'd by a spleen" (V.ii.19), he will never genuinely pardon the two older men who "did train [Hotspur] on"—namely, Worcester himself and Hotspur's father, Northumberland (V.ii.21).

While he encourages Hotspur's revenge against the king, Worcester also tries to curb his nephew's hot temper and enthusiasm when these feelings are directed at what he considers inappropriate targets. Thus after Hotspur is rude to their ally Gloucester, Worcester counsels him:

> You must needs learn, lord, to amend this fault;
> Though sometimes it show greatness, courage,
>   blood—
> And that's the dearest grace it renders you—
> Yet oftentimes it doth present harsh rage,

" His rudeness aside, Hotspur is frequently seen as a charismatic figure, who demonstrates bravery, honesty, and affection for his wife."

Defect of manners, want of government,
Pride, haughtiness, opinion, and disdain . . .

(III.i.178-83)

And when Hotspur is keen to engage the king's forces in battle at night rather that wait until morning, Worcester exclaims, "the number of the King exceedeth our. / For God's sake, cousin, stay till all come in" (IV.iii.28-29).

Finally, it has been argued that Worcester and King Henry are the play's central antagonists, with Hotspur and Hal functioning as instruments for deciding their conflict. When the two encounter each other at the meeting in I.iii, it is Worcester who blames the king for being unfair to the Percy family, and the king's angry response is to order Worcester out of the room, preferring to meet only with Northumberland and Hotspur, who are not being as "bold and peremptory" toward the king as Worcester is (I.iii.17).

At the close of the play, Worcester is captured by the king's forces and, after condemning him for not delivering to Hotspur his offer of reconciliation, Henry IV sentences Worcester to execution.

Peto:

He is one of Prince Hal's companions at the Boar's Head Tavern. Along with Gadshill, Bardolph, and Falstaff, he robs the travellers and, like them, is later hoodwinked by the prince and Poins into giving up the booty. It has been pointed out that Peto replaces Poins as Hal's gentleman-in-waiting in II.iv.526-549 and in III.iii, when Poins drops out of the play. Peto appears again in *Henry IV, Part Two*.

Poins (Edward Poins, also called Ned Poins):

He is Prince Hal's gentleman-in-waiting and a willing participant in Hal's escapades. In I.ii, it is Poins who devises the practical joke which he and the prince play on Falstaff and his fellow highway-

men in II.ii. At the tavern, he agrees to help the prince tease Francis, in order—as the prince puts it—"to drive away the time till Falstaff come" (II.iv.28-29). When Falstaff does arrive, Ned joins Hal in goading the fat knight as he lies about the details of his being robbed of his loot. Poins drops out of the play near the end of II.iv; he reappears in *Henry IV, Part Two*.

Quickly (Mistress Quickly):

She is the hostess of the Boar's Head Tavern, the meeting place for Prince Hal and his drinking companions Falstaff, Peto, Poins, and Bardolph. She enters twice in II.iv, the first time to inform the prince that a messenger from his father has come to speak with him, and the second time to warn him that the sheriff has come to search for Falstaff. Both the sheriff and the king's man—who has been sent to call Hal back to the king's court—function as insistent reminders of the respectable outside world to which the prince must inevitably return.

Mistress Quickly's longest speeches occur in III.iii, after Falstaff has complained that his pockets were picked in her tavern. (In fact, it was the prince who emptied his pockets as he slept behind the arras in II.iv.) Her response to Falstaff's accusation is one of outrage: "I know you, Sir John," she tells him, "you owe me money, Sir John, and now you pick a quarrel to beguile me of it" (III.iii.66-67). As her angry excitement increases, she becomes the butt of Falstaff's jokes.

Scroop (Richard Scroop, the Archbishop of York):

He is the archbishop of York and a supporter of the Percy family. In IV.iv, he worries that without Northumberland and Glendower, Hotspur will not be able to defeat the king, so Scroop musters forces and allies in preparation against the day when Henry will march north to York to fight him. At the close of the play (V.v.35-38), Henry does indeed send an army north to deal with him. The archbishop appears again as the king's enemy (and with a larger role) in *Henry IV, Part Two*.

Sheriff:

He comes to the Boar's Head Tavern in II.iv to arrest Falstaff for the robbery at Gadshill. Prince Hal sends the sheriff away with a false alibi for Falstaff. When the sheriff bids the prince "good night," Hal points out that it is in fact morning: he and his friends have been up all night (II.iv.523-

25). This incident makes clear how close the "madcap" world of drinking and practical jokes is to the grim realities of life, for the highway robbery committed by Falstaff is, as he himself points out, punishable by hanging.

Travellers:

They are robbed by Gadshill, Falstaff, Bardolph, and Peto on the London road near a hill known as Gadshill which was infamous as a site for robberies. They probably include one or both of the carriers of II.i, as well as the money-ladened franklin and auditor referred to by the chamberlain in II.i.53-60.

Vernon (Sir Richard Vernon):

He is an ally of the Percys. He arrives at Hotspur's camp in IV.i.86 to report on the advancing armies of the king and to convey the bad news that Owen Glendower's army will be delayed for two weeks. In IV.iii he joins with Worcester as the voice of moderation, counseling Hotspur and Douglas against their sudden urgency to battle the king's forces at night. When Worcester goes to parley with the king, Vernon accompanies him and later resignedly consents to Worcester's decision not to tell Hotspur about the king's offer of clemency (V.ii.26-27).

Vernon's admiration for the reformed Prince Hal annoys Hotspur. His description of Hal and his advancing troops as "Glittering in golden coats like images, / As full of spirit as the month of May, / And gorgeous as the sun at midsummer," provokes Hotspur to retort, "No more, no more! worse than the sun in March, / This praise does nourish agues" (IV.i.100-03; 111-12). Likewise in V.ii, Vernon is so full of praise for Hal's gentlemanly offer of single combat in lieu of war that Hotspur sneers, "Cousin, I think thou art enamored / On [Prince Hal's] follies" (V.ii.69-70).

At the close of the play Vernon is captured by the king's forces and sentenced to death (V.v.14).

Vintner:

He works at the Boar's Head Tavern and he is master to the indentured drawer, Francis. He adds to Francis's confusion in II.iv.80-81 by scolding him for his slowness, but the main reason for his appearance is to inform Prince Hal that Falstaff has arrived, thus preparing the way for the comical episode where Falstaff exaggerates the details of his attack.

> ❝❝ **Kate worries about Hotspur's restlessness and inattentiveness, asking, 'For what offense have I this fortnight been / A banished woman from my Harry's bed?' (II.iii.38-39)."**

Westmerland (Earl of Westmerland):

He is one of King Henry's advisors. His function in the play is primarily an informational and supportive one. Most of his lines occur in I.i, where he recounts the battle between Glendower and Mortimer, and reports what he has so far heard about the fighting between Hotspur and Douglas. In IV.ii, he and Prince Hal cast doubtful eyes on Falstaff's "beggarly" bunch of soldiers; in V.iv, he tries, at the king's request, to lead the wounded prince away from battle. He also appears in *Henry IV, Part Two*.

Worcester (Thomas Percy, Earl of Worcester):

See Percy

Further Reading

Aldus, Paul J. "Analogical Probability in Shakespeare's Plays." *Shakespeare Quarterly* 6 (Autumn 1955): 397-414.
 Aldus argues that Shakespeare frequently used analogues (interconnections and comparisons between scenes, characters, and language) to create meaning and unity in his plays. While other plays are discussed, the central focus is on *Henry IV, Part One* and *Two*: how the comic and serious elements in the plays reflect upon each other, and how apparently unimportant scenes or speeches underline significant issues discussed elsewhere in each play.

Baker, Herschel. Introduction to *Henry IV, Parts 1* and *2*, by William Shakespeare. In *The Riverside Shakespeare*, by William Shakespeare, edited by G. Blakemore Evans, 842-46. Boston: Houghton Mifflin, 1974.
 Baker gives an overview of *Henry IV, Part One* and *Two*, examining Shakespeare's sources for plot and character names, discussing the characterization of Hal versus Hotspur, and showing how the comic and serious elements of both plays "bear upon and reinforce each other in many subtle ways."

"Worcester's argument for his plot against the king is that Henry dislikes and fears being indebted to the Percy family, who placed him on the throne after helping him usurp his predecessor, Richard II."

Bowers, Fredson. "Theme and Structure in *King Henry IV, Part I*." In *The Drama of the Renaissance: Essays for Leicester Bradner*, edited by Elmer M. Blistein, 42-68. Providence: Brown University Press, 1970.

Bowers discusses the conflict between the modern state and feudalism as a theme in the play and sees Henry IV and Worcester as the play's principal antagonists, with Hal and Hotspur acting as their intermediaries.

Clark, Axel. "The Battle of Shrewsbury (*Henry IV, Part I*)." *Critical Review* (Australia) 15 (1972): 29-45.

Clark argues that the battle of Shrewsbury in V functions as the play's climax and that even Falstaff grows more serious as he tries to stay alive in a play whose tone becomes more solemn. Clark also looks at the conflict between comic and serious in the character of Prince Hal.

Dickinson, Hugh. "The Reformation of Prince Hal." *Shakespeare Quarterly* 12 (Winter 1961): 33-46.

Dickinson considers Prince Hal as the play's protagonist, "whose deeds most explicitly dramatize the theme of the play, which is: the education of a prince." Dickinson also asserts that Hal's character reveals that kingship should be primarily about self-sacrifice rather than honor.

Humphreys, A. R. Introduction to *King Henry IV, Part I*, by William Shakespeare, edited by A. R. Humphreys, xi-lxxxii. The Arden Edition of the Works of William Shakespeare. London: Methuen and Co. Ltd., 1975.

In this overview, Humphreys gives date and source information. Additionally, in a section entitled "The Spirit of the Play," Humphreys shows that "the greatness of [*1* and *Henry IV, Part Two*] lies in their not taking a disapproving view" of human nature.

Levin, Lawrence L. "Hotspur, Falstaff, and the Emblem of Wrath in *I Henry IV*." *Shakespeare Studies* 10 (1977): 43-65.

Referring to Renaissance emblems (pictures accompanied by mottos, which give moral lessons) Levin argues that the characters of Hotspur and Falstaff are connected because they are both manifestations of the sin of wrath, with Falstaff as a comic representation of an emotion which is taken to tragic extremes by Hotspur.

McNamara, Anne Marie. "*Henry IV*: The King as Protagonist." *Shakespeare Quarterly* 10 (Summer 1959): 423-31.

McNamara provides a close look at *Henry IV, Part One*, calls King Henry IV the protagonist of the play, and asserts that the play's theme is the king's success at preserving the soundness of the nation.

Merrix, Robert P. "Prince Hal's Reformation Soliloquy: A Strategy for Survival." *Selected Papers from the West Virginia Shakespeare and Renaissance Association* 7 (Spring 1982): 71-76.

Merrix examines Hal's soliloquy at the end of I.ii and argues that the prince's decision to behave as a reckless youth for a while before becoming a responsible king is meant, among other things, to protect him from his political foes.

Mitchell, Charles. "The Education of a True Prince." *Tennessee Studies in Literature* 12 (1967): 12-21.

Mitchell asserts that both Falstaff and King Henry function as fathers to Prince Hal—"the one standing for Hal's condition as a man and the other for his status as a prince"—and that Hal needs to combine some of the attributes of each to be a good king.

Pinciss, G. M. "The Old Honor and the New Courtesy: *I Henry IV*." *Shakespeare Survey* 31 (1978): 85-91.

Referring to a pair of handbooks on chivalry and courtesy from the Renaissance period, Pinciss contends that Hotspur represents the old, chivalric view of honor while Hal displays the new courtly manners of the Renaissance noble classes.

Shaw, John. "The Staging of Parody and Parallels in *I Henry IV*." *Shakespeare Survey* 20 (1967): 61-73.

Shaw focuses on stagecraft (voice, gesture, and props) to show how particular scenes in the play are meant to emphasize or comment upon other scenes. Special focus is given to the following pairs: II.iv and III.ii (the Falstaff/Hal and Henry IV/Hal interview scenes); II.iii and II.iv (the Lady Percy/Hotspur and Hal/Francis conversations).

The Second Part of Henry the Fourth

Plot Summary

1598

Act I:

The rebellion that was raised against King Henry IV by Hotspur (Henry Percy) and his uncle (Thomas Percy, earl of Worcester) is nearly over: Hotspur has been killed in the battle of Shrewsbury by the king's newly reformed son, Prince Hal; Worcester has been executed; and the Scots leader, Douglas, has been captured but released for his bravery in combat. (The rebellion of the Percys against King Henry IV, as well as the dissolute life of Prince Hal, is the subject of Shakespeare's *Henry IV, Part One*.) The king is now intent upon defeating those who are left of the rebels' allies, namely: the earl of Northumberland (Hotspur's father), Archbishop Scroop, and the Welsh leader Owen Glendower. Meanwhile Northumberland, who played "crafty-sick" (Ind.37) thereby avoiding the fighting at Shrewsbury, hears rumors that the rebels have won the battle and that his son, Hotspur, is still alive. When these rumors prove false, he considers renewing the battle against the king by joining his ally Scroop, who has taken up the cause in the name of the murdered King Richard II, whom Henry IV had usurped. In London, Sir John Falstaff tangles with the chief justice about his involvement in highway robbery (see *Henry IV, Part One*). Since Falstaff has been drafted into the wars against the rebels, the chief justice lets him off with the admonition that he act his age and stop corrupting Prince Hal. In York

at the archbishop's palace, Scroop and his allies weigh the odds of defeating the king without Northumberland's help, and decide to fight whether or not he joins them.

Act II:

In a London street, Hostess Quickly (of the Boar's Head Tavern in Eastcheap) tries to force Falstaff to pay his debts to her, but winds up agreeing to give him another loan. Meanwhile, ''exceeding weary'' after the battle of Shrewsbury, Prince Hal has returned to his dissolute ways; he and Poins plot to take Falstaff by surprise at their old haunt, the Boar's Head Tavern (II.ii.1). At his castle in Warkworth, Northumberland is persuaded by his wife and his daughter-in-law (Hotspur's widow) to flee to Scotland rather than join with Scroop against the king. At the Boar's Head Tavern, Falstaff bickers affectionately with the prostitute, Doll Tearsheet, until his loud-mouthed ensign, Pistol, arrives and nearly causes a fight. After Pistol is driven out, the prince and Poins appear in disguise to spy upon Falstaff and Doll Tearsheet; they tease the fat knight for some insulting comments he makes to Doll about the prince. Peto arrives with the latest news of the rebellion, and the guilt-stricken Hal returns to court. When Falstaff is summoned to war, Doll and Hostess Quickly tearfully bid him farewell.

Act III:

Sick and disheartened, King Henry spends a sleepless night at his palace in Westminster. The earl of Warwick arrives with news that the war against the rebels is going well and that Glendower has died. Meanwhile, with the help of an old acquaintance named Justice Shallow, Falstaff is recruiting troops for battle. In a soliloquy, Falstaff plans to swindle Justice Shallow after the war. (A soliloquy is a speech made by a character when he or she is alone. It is meant to indicate to the audience the character's frame of mind or what action he or she intends to undertake.)

Act IV:

Near the forest of Gaultree in Yorkshire, Archbishop Scroop and his allies receive the news that Northumberland has fled to Scotland. The earl of Westmerland invites them to parley with the king's son Prince John, who promises to redress their grievances if they send their armies home. Once Scroop and his allies do so, John promptly has them arrested for treason, explaining that while he vowed to correct those faults which the rebels found in the

government, he did *not* promise to grant them amnesty for their treachery. Released from fighting, Falstaff sets off to dupe Shallow. After the dying king receives news that the rebels have been defeated and that his son Hal is still consorting with his disreputable friends in Eastcheap, he collapses and is carried to bed. Prince Hal arrives, and thinking that his father is dead, tries on his crown. When the king awakens, he is distressed at finding both Hal and his crown gone, and is convinced that his son wants him dead. The prince returns, deeply remorseful, and he and his father reconcile at last.

Act V:

Henry IV has died, and his retainers fear the worst for themselves and the commonwealth now that Prince Hal is to become king. But the prince surprises them all by announcing that he has given up his dissolute friends and behavior. Pistol appears at Shallow's house with the news that King Henry IV has died and that Hal is now King Henry V. Elated, Falstaff rushes back to London with his friends, convinced that the new king will give him preferential treatment. Meanwhile, in London, Doll Tearsheet is arrested for prostitution. On his coronation day, King Henry V banishes Falstaff from his company with a modest allowance and the admonition that he reform, observing, ''How ill white hairs becomes a fool and jester!'' (V.v.48). The act closes with Prince John prophesying peace at home and war with France—which form the subject of Shakespeare's *Henry V*.

Modern Connections

One of the most popular characters ever created by Shakespeare is the fat old knight Sir John Falstaff, who was appealing to Elizabethan theatergoers and remains so with audiences today. Critics have observed that his popularity is partly the result of his multifaceted personality. He seems cowardly when he runs from the Gadshill robbery in *Henry IV, Part One*, yet his actions suggest bravery when he appears twice on the battlefield—at Shrewsbury in *Henry IV, Part One* and then again outside the forest of Gaultree in *Henry IV, Part Two*. He is dishonest and insensitive in his dealings with Shallow in *Henry IV, Part Two*, but his affection for both Doll Tearsheet (*Henry IV, Part Two*) and Prince Hal (*Henry IV, Part One* and *Two*) appears to be genuine.

Falstaff is also appealing because he is so outrageous. When caught in a lie or an insult, he usually manages to come up with an unbelievable but witty excuse, as he does after exaggerating the facts of the Gadshill robbery in *Henry IV, Part One* and when he slanders Hal and Poins at the Boar's Head Tavern in *Henry IV, Part Two*. As Poins warns the prince in *Henry IV, Part Two*—"my lord, [Falstaff] will drive you out of your revenge and turn all to a merriment . . ." if he is allowed to get away with it (II.iv.297-98).

According to most accounts, Falstaff was extremely popular in Elizabethan times. In fact he is the star of Shakespeare's *The Merry Wives of Windsor*, which may have been written, as some people suggest, for the same reason some movie sequels or television spin-offs sre produced: to capitalize on the popularity of a character. Modern audiences may be startled when Hal, newly crowned as king, sharply rejects Falstaff at the end of *Henry IV, Part Two*. After all, how can he say such cruel things to an old friend who has been the source of so much amusement? Critics point out, however, that Elizabethan audiences were perhaps less sentimental about this issue than we are today. Ruled by a monarch themselves, the audiences in Shakespeare's time probably understood that with his accession to the throne, Prince Hal did not become "King Hal" (as Falstaff calls him in V.v.41) but is transformed into King Henry, who must make a clean break with his notorious past and turn completely to the business of governing the country.

Characters

Archbishop of York (Scroop, the Archbishop of York):
See Scroop

Attendants:
The attendants and servants have small or no speaking parts. They appear in various scenes of the play, attending to the needs of the nobility.

Bardolph:
Bardolph was Falstaff's friend in *Henry IV, Part One*; in *Henry IV, Part Two*, England is still at war with rebels, and Bardolph has become Falstaff's corporal as well as his friend. In II.i.39, he is described as an "arrant malmsey-nose[d] knave" since his nose is red from too much wine. As

corporal, he spends much of his time running errands for Falstaff. In III.ii, in a satire on the corrupt recruiting practices of Elizabethan England, Bardolph accepts bribes to exempt the able-bodied Bullcalf and Mouldy from military service. Bardolph should not be confused with Lord Bardolph (see entry below), who is a rebel and a supporter of the earl of Northumberland.

Bardolph (Lord Bardolph):
He is an opponent of Henry IV. In I.i, he delivers rumor rather than fact to Northumberland when he tells him that the king's forces have been defeated and that Northumberland's son, Hotspur, is still alive. So certain is Lord Bardolph that his information is accurate that he refuses to believe the bad news delivered by Northumberland's servant Travers. Lord Bardolph must accept the truth of the rebels' defeat when Morton arrives to say that he has actually *seen* Hotspur dead on the battlefield. Later, in a strategy meeting at Scroop's palace in York (I.iii), Lord Bardolph argues against going into battle without the guaranteed backing of Northumberland's forces. Finally, he is listed in the stage directions in IV.i when the rebels debate outside the forest of Gaultree over whether or not to surrender to Prince John (Lord Bardolph does not speak in IV.i, and his listing in this scene is absent from some versions of *Henry IV, Part Two*.). All three of these incidents reveal the confusion and lack of unanimity that characterize the rebel forces. In IV.iv.97-99 Lord Bardolph is mentioned along with Northumberland as having been defeated by the sheriff of Yorkshire.

Beadle:
The beadle appears with several officers in V.iv, where he arrests Doll Tearsheet for prostitution.

Blunt (Sir John Blunt):
He is a supporter of King Henry IV. Although Blunt does not have a speaking role, he appears in the stage directions of IV.iii, and is instructed by Prince John in IV.iii.75 to take custody of the rebel Colevile. Sir John Blunt's father, Sir Walter Blunt, is killed by the earl of Douglas in *Henry IV, Part One*, and "both the Blunts" are rumored to have been killed at the beginning of *Henry IV, Part Two* (I.i.16).

Bullcalf:
Peter Bullcalf is one of the potential soldiers rounded up by Justice Shallow in III.ii for Sir John

Falstaff. Bullcalf resorts to bribery to get out of military service after Falstaff rejects his excuse of being "diseas'd" with a cold. Falstaff's willingness to part with Bullcalf—one of the strongest recruits he has to choose from—satirizes the corrupt recruitment methods complained about during the Elizabethan period.

Chief Justice (Lord Chief Justice):

He is a judicial appointee of the king. The Lord Chief Justice tries to arrest Falstaff for robbery (Falstaff's participation in the robbery at Gadshill is part of the action in *Henry IV, Part One*), and he rebukes Falstaff for cheating Hostess Quickly. The chief justice also (we learn in I.ii.55-56) once threw Hal in jail. Thus Falstaff looks forward to the chief justice's humiliation once Hal is king, and the chief justice himself worries about his treatment once King Henry IV is dead (V.ii.6-8). But as proof that he has sincerely reformed, the new King Henry V commends the chief justice for his impartial dispensing of law and order, and reappoints him to his post.

Clarence (Thomas, Duke of Clarence):

He is one of Henry IV's sons, and, according to the king, he is Prince Hal's favorite brother. His presence in IV.iv provides the king with an opportunity to summarize Hal's faults and virtues as he advises Clarence to make the most of Hal's affection by acting as a steadying influence on the "riotous" prince as well as a mediator between him and his two other brothers after Henry IV has died. Clarence's confession to his father that Hal is dining with the rowdy Poins causes the ailing king to mourn for his younger sons at the prospect of the "headstrong" Hal's accession to the throne (IV.iv.62).

Colevile (Sir John Colevile):

He is a knight and a supporter of Archbishop Scroop's cause against Henry IV. Described by Prince John as "a famous rebel" (IV.iii.63), Colevile appears briefly in IV.iii while retreating from Gaultree with the rest of the rebel army. When he runs into Sir John Falstaff, the fat knight promptly claims credit for taking Colevile prisoner. Critics have noted that in addition to providing comic relief after the grimness of Prince John's Gaultree stratagem in IV.ii, this incident gives Falstaff his only opportunity to display his wit during the play's lengthiest act. (Comic relief is an amusing speech, episode, or scene which lightens the tension that comes before

it in a serious play and emphasizes the somberness that occurs after it.)

Davy:

As a servant to Justice Shallow, Davy manages Shallow's land and oversees his other servants in addition to waiting on Shallow at meals. In V.i.60-85, Falstaff observes that Shallow and Davy treat each other as equals, and he considers this an indication of Shallow's foolishness.

Drawers:

A couple of drawers appear in II.iv, where they speak with Francis the drawer. (A drawer is one who draws and serves wine or drink in a tavern).

Epilogue:

The Epilogue appears at the end of the play and consists of three paragraphs spoken by an unnamed person. In the first paragraph, the Epilogue offers *Henry IV, Part Two* as recompense for a "displeasing play" that had been performed sometime earlier. In the second paragraph, the Epilogue offers to dance for the audience to achieve their goodwill. The third paragraph announces the playwright's intention to write a sequel to *Henry IV, Part Two*, "with Sir John in it" as well as "fair Katherine of France"; this is a reference to Shakespeare's *Henry V*. (Although Sir John Falstaff does not, after all, appear in *Henry V*, he is mentioned in it as having died of grief at being rejected by Hal.)

Epilogues encouraging the audience's tolerance and applause were common in plays during Shakespeare's time. Sometimes—as in this play—they were spoken by an actor no longer in character but who is simply referred to in the stage directions as "Epilogue." At other times they were meant to be spoken by characters in the play, as when Puck delivers his closing appeal to the audience in *A Midsummer Night's Dream*.

Falstaff (Sir John Falstaff):

In *Henry IV, Part One*, Falstaff—the "fat knight"—is a dishonest but charismatic friend and father figure to Prince Hal. In *Henry IV, Part Two*, he has gained enough respectability from his so-called "good service" as an officer at the battle of Shrewsbury and from the commission he now holds from Prince John (I.ii.60-62) that the chief justice refrains from arresting him for a robbery he committed before the wars. (Falstaff's involvement in the Gadshill robbery and the battle of Shrewsbury forms part of the action in *Henry IV, Part One*.) In II.iv, he presides as usual at the Boar's Head Tavern, where he becomes the butt of one of Prince Hal's jokes. In III.ii, he travels to Gloucester to recruit soldiers and, as he did in *Henry IV, Part One*, he collects bribes rather than competent troops.

In spite of these similarities, critics note that there is a change in tone with regard to the Falstaff of *Henry IV, Part Two* which corresponds to the play's more somber theme of aging and disease or decay. Toward the end of a comic scene at the Boar's Head Tavern, for example (II.iv.271, 277), Falstaff admits that he is old and asserts that Doll Tearsheet will forget him when he is gone—not specifying whether he means gone to war or to his grave. Critics have also observed that Falstaff becomes less likeable in *Henry IV, Part Two*—probably to make his rejection by Hal more palatable to the audience. During the Gloucestershire scenes of III.ii, V.i, and V.iii, for example, Falstaff takes advantage of his old acquaintance, Justice Shallow, who has been described as honest and generous although a little foolish.

Scene V.iii ends with the news that Henry IV has died and with Falstaff's delight that his friend Prince Hal will soon be king: ''Boot, boot, Master Shallow! I know the young king is sick for me. . . . the laws of England are at my commandment,'' Falstaff exults as he hurries to leave for London (V.iii.134-37). In V.v, however, the fat knight is rejected by the new king. Shocked, Falstaff tries to convince himself and Shallow that ''King Hal'' will send for him later ''in private'' (V.v.41, 77). Instead, Falstaff is apprehended by the chief justice and, on orders from the new king, he is sent for a short stay in the Fleet prison (V.v.91-92).

It has been argued that as appealing as the character Falstaff might be, he still represents anarchy. As leader of the country, Falstaff's former friend Hal must reject anarchy so that he can embrace order and govern well.

Fang:

A sergeant-at-law, who, with his assistant Snare, is recruited by Hostess Quickly in II.i to arrest Falstaff for failing to repay his debts to her and for reneging on his proposal of marriage. During the attempted arrest, Fang, Snare, and Hostess Quickly are attacked by Falstaff, his young page, and Bardolph. The episode is comedic rather than violent, but it also emphasizes Falstaff's dishonesty

> **Scene V.iii ends with the news that Henry IV has died and with Falstaff's delight that his friend Prince Hal will soon be king: 'Boot, boot, Master Shallow! I know the young king is sick for me. . . . the laws of England are at my commandment,' Falstaff exults as he hurries to leave for London (V.iii.134-37). In V.v, however, the fat knight is rejected by the new king.''**

and impudence—traits which make him a liability to Prince Hal.

Feeble:

Francis Feeble is one of the men chosen by Falstaff in III.ii for military service in the wars against the rebels. His name—''Feeble''—is an indication of the type of soldier he will be, and his occupation as a woman's tailor is the object of many of Falstaff's bawdy jokes.

Francis:

He is a drawer at the Boar's Head Tavern whose job it is to draw wine from casks and serve drinks and food to the tavern customers. In II.iv he and two other drawers prepare to lend jerkins and aprons to Poins and Prince Hal so that they can disguise themselves and play a joke on Falstaff. In II.iv.69-70, Francis announces the arrival of Falstaff's ''swaggering'' ensign Pistol. He also appears in *Henry IV, Part One*, where it is his turn to be the butt of one of the prince's practical jokes.

Gloucester (Humphrey, Duke of Gloucester):

He is a son of King Henry and a brother of Prince Hal. In IV.iv Gloucester and his brother Clarence worry about the health of their father and refer to several uncanny events—children born without fathers, seasons occurring out of order, the river Thames flooding repeatedly—as portents of his death.

Gower:

Master Gower is a minor character who makes a single, brief appearance in II.i.134-95 with a message to the Lord Chief Justice containing information important to furthering the action of the play. First, Gower announces that the king and ''Harry Prince of Wales'' are on their way back to London after fighting rebels in Wales, and in the next scene (II.ii) we see the prince at home in London, weary from battle and ready to engage in his former dissolute life. Similarly, in III.i, we see Henry IV back from the wars and in his London palace, unable to sleep and worried about the condition of his kingdom. Gower also reports that of the king's army, ''fifteen hundred foot, five hundred horse, / Are march'd up to my Lord [Prince John] of Lancaster'' (II.i.173-74), buttressing Prince John's military power and preparing the way for his stratagem against Scroop and the northern rebels at Gaultree in IV.ii.

Harcourt:

He is a supporter of King Henry IV. His one appearance occurs in IV.iv.94-101, when he brings word to the dying king that the earl of Northumberland and Lord Bardolph have fought with and been defeated by the sheriff of Yorkshire and that the rebellion is over. Harcourt's report is the only indication given in the play that Northumberland has at last decided to join the battle against the king.

Hastings (Lord Hastings):

He is an opponent of King Henry and a supporter of Archbishop Scroop. Although it is he who observes in I.iii that the rebels' strength depends upon reinforcements from Northumberland, he is keen to go to battle against the king with or without the earl, arguing that Henry IV is running low on funds and that his army is stretched thin—fighting as it has been against the French and the Welsh as well as the English rebels. (His reference to the French foreshadows the wars waged against France in Shakespeare's *Henry V*.) Hastings is with Scroop and Mowbray outside the forest of Gaultree in IV.i-ii. He approves of the truce, arguing once more that the king is too worn out to retaliate (comparing his present, overstretched power to a ''fangless lion,'' [IV.i.216]). It is Hastings who dismisses the rebel forces once the truce at Gaultree has been made. He

is arrested and sent to his execution along with Mowbray and Scroop.

Henry (King Henry IV of England, formerly known as Bullingbrook):

Formerly known as Henry Bullingbrook, Henry IV is the king of England, the father of Prince Hal, and the title character of the play. He became king after the usurpation and murder of his predecessor, Richard II. (King Richard's fall from power and Henry's accession to the throne is the subject of Shakespeare's *Richard II*; for the beginning of the troubles which plague Henry IV's reign, see *Henry IV, Part One*.)

In *Henry IV, Part Two*, King Henry has long been ill and is now close to death. He first appears in III.i, dressed for sleep but tormented by insomnia. In a famous speech, he envies the poorest of his subjects who can sleep even in squalor while he is kept awake all night by worries, despite his wealth and the physical comforts it affords. ''Uneasy lies the head that wears a crown,'' he concludes (III.i.31).

The king seems haunted by memories of Richard II, who prophesied rebellion and destruction under Henry's rule. Henry's remorse for his predecessor's fate is indicated by his repeated attempts to pay penance by going on crusade to Jerusalem (see IV.iv.1-10 and note to 5-7). Closely connected to this is the king's overwhelming concern for the condition of his kingdom and the behavior of his heir. He is profoundly upset that Hal still wastes his time in ''headstrong riot'' with Falstaff at the Boar's Head Tavern (IV.iv.62). Shortly after hearing that Hal has dispensed with the company of his own brothers to dine instead ''with Poins, and other his continual followers'' (IV.iv.53), the king is told that the rebels have at last been entirely defeated. Hearing such bad and good news so close together about the issues which trouble him most, Henry exclaims, ''Will Fortune never come with both hands full, / But write her fair words still in foulest terms?'' (IV.iv.103-04). Immediately afterward, he collapses.

When Henry IV awakes to find both his crown and Hal gone, he accuses his son of being so impatient to rule England that he looks forward to his father's death. In despair, the dying king predicts that his ''poor kingdom'' will be overrun by ''apes of idleness'' and ''peopled with wolves'' once his ''foolish'' son succeeds him on the throne (IV.v.133, 122, 137, 96).

Critics have noted that Henry IV is determined to insure the legitimacy of his rule, and that all of his worries proceed from that one preoccupation. This line of thinking is reinforced by the king's speech of reconciliation to Hal near the close of Act IV:

> God knows, my son,
> By what by-paths and indirect crook'd ways
> I met this crown, and I myself know well
> How troublesome it sate upon my head.
> To thee it shall descend with better quiet,
> Better opinion, better confirmation,
> For all the soil of the achievement goes
> With me into the earth.
>
> (IV.v.183-90)

Henry (Prince Henry of Wales, also known as Prince Hal or Harry Monmouth, afterwards King Henry V of England):

He is King Henry IV's son and heir. In *Henry IV, Part One*, Hal is criticized for being dissolute and "madcap," but he redeems himself by the end of the play when he defeats the rebel Hotspur.

In his first appearance in *Henry IV, Part Two*, Hal seems to have gone back to his old ways, complaining of boredom to his crony Poins and dreaming up practical jokes to play on his old friend, Falstaff (II.ii). But in II.iv.361-66, when Peto seeks him out at the Boar's Head Tavern with news that rebellion is brewing once more, the prince blames himself for "profan[ing] the precious time" and hurries away to resume his place as Henry's heir. Later, in IV.v, after King Henry rebukes his son for disappearing with his crown, the prince begs his forgiveness, swearing that he did not wish his father dead, and promises to be a good king and an honorable successor to the throne.

Critics have suggested that Hal never really falls back into dissolution, but is instead biding his time, learning from his followers before he casts them off, as the earl of Warwick insists in IV.iv.67-78. It has also been argued that Hal's "hot blood" and "lavish manners" are largely projections of his father's anxious imagination (IV.iv.63, 64).

One of the most famous incidents in *Henry IV, Part Two* occurs when Hal, newly crowned as King Henry V, rejects Falstaff with his devastating remark—"I know thee not, old man, fall to thy prayers. / How ill white hairs becomes a fool and jester!" (V.v.47-48). This moment is foreshadowed in *Henry IV, Part One*, when Hal (pretending to be his father) declares that he will banish Falstaff from his company (*Henry IV, Part One*: II.iv.481). All the same, some critics have condemned the new

> ❝ The king seems haunted by memories of Richard II, who prophesied rebellion and destruction under Henry's rule. ❞

king's sudden cruelty, arguing that we are meant to sympathize with the corrupt but appealing Falstaff. Others assert that in order to rule effectively, the new king must sweep away his "riotous" past, and that Falstaff—who has been proven himself to be a liar, thief, and con artist—has no place in Hal's new life as ruler of England.

Hostess Quickly:
See Quickly

Humphrey (Humphrey, Duke of Gloucester):
See Gloucester

John (Prince John of Lancaster):

He is one of King Henry's sons. John appears briefly in *Henry IV, Part One*, where he is regarded as more reliable and honorable than his older brother, Prince Hal; in *Henry IV, Part Two*, Falstaff complains that he is a "sober-blooded boy" who never laughs (IV.iii.87-88).

Prince John's most striking contribution to the play's action occurs in IV.i-ii, when, using Westmerland as his emissary, he negotiates peace with the rebels at Gaultree, only to have them arrested for treason once they dismiss their forces and can no longer fight back. The rebel Lord Mowbray's reaction to Prince John's trick is to ask, "Is this proceeding just and honorable?" (IV.ii.110); likewise, Archbishop Scroop exclaims, "Will you thus break your faith?" (IV.ii.112). Prince John replies that he has not broken faith for he did not promise to pardon their treachery but only to resolve their list of grievances. Nonetheless, some critics have been appalled at Prince John's trickery, describing it as gratuitous when the rebel forces were clearly outnumbered by those of the king. Others have labeled it a Machiavellian strategy to end the war without bloodshed while punishing the war's instigators (Machiavellianism is a political theory

> ❝ In despair, the dying king predicts that his 'poor kingdom' will be overrun by 'apes of idleness' and 'peopled with wolves' once his 'foolish' son succeeds him on the throne (IV.v.133, 122, 137, 96).❞

which argues that the end justifies the means—in this case, a bloodless end to the rebellion excuses Prince John's underhandedness). Alternatively, some critics have argued that according to the beliefs of their time, Hastings, Mowbray, and Scroop commit sacrilege when they rebel against their king, thereby losing their right to be treated fairly.

Prince John's prediction at the close of the play (V.v.105-09) that England will go to war with France articulates the subject of Shakespeare's *Henry V*.

Lord Chief Justice:
See Chief Justice

Lords:
Lords appear in several scenes and have small or no speaking parts. They populate the scenes of *Henry IV, Part Two* and thereby contribute to the varied atmosphere of this play which encompasses palace business, street life, country life, and battlefield.

Morton:
He is a retainer of the earl of Northumberland. Of the three men who deliver news in I.i concerning the battle of Shrewsbury, Morton is the only one who has actually witnessed the fighting; therefore, only he can deliver an accurate account of Hotspur's death and the rebels' defeat. Morton also brings the news that Archbishop Scroop is mobilizing sympathy for the murdered King Richard II against King Henry.

Mouldy:
Rafe Mouldy is one of "half a dozen sufficient men" presented by Justice Shallow to Falstaff as possible military recruits (III.ii.93). Mouldy bribes Bardolph to exempt him from duty. His name ("Things that are mouldy lack use," III.ii.107-08) provides Falstaff with an opportunity for word play.

Mowbray (Lord Mowbray):
Lord Mowbray is an opponent of Henry IV. He is present at the Archbishop Scroop's strategy meeting in I.iii, where he emphasizes the importance of mustering an army strong enough to threaten the king's forces. More significantly, he is with Scroop at the forest of Gaultree, where he argues forcefully against making peace with Westmerland and Prince John, remarking that "There is a thing within my bosom tells me / That no conditions of our peace can stand" (IV.i.181-82). He is arrested as a traitor and sent to his execution along with Scroop and Lord Hastings in IV.ii.107-23.

Northumberland (Henry Percy, Earl of Northumberland):
See Percy

Northumberland (Lady Northumberland):
She is the earl of Northumberland's wife. Strongly aided by her daughter-in-law (Lady Percy), Lady Northumberland succeeds in persuading her husband to seek refuge in Scotland rather than join Archbishop Scroop in the fight against King Henry (II.iii). The result for the rebels is disastrous: without Northumberland and his army, the rebels cannot hold out against the king's forces and choose instead to surrender.

Officers:
Officers appear in a couple of scenes of the play: in II.i, with Fang and Snare, to arrest Falstaff at Hostess Quickly's request; and in V.iv, with the beadle to arrest Doll Tearsheat for prostitution.

Page (Falstaff's Page):
The page is a young attendant sent by Prince Hal to Falstaff in honor of his supposed service during the wars in *Henry IV, Part One*. He is much smaller than his fat master, leading Falstaff to suspect that the prince's real intention of sending the page was to make his old friend look like a fool (I.ii.12-14).

Percy (Henry Percy, Earl of Northumberland):

Henry Percy, or Northumberland as he is often called, is an opponent of Henry IV and the father of Hotspur. In *Henry IV, Part One*, Hotspur was killed at the Battle of Shrewsbury while Northumberland lay ''crafty-sick'' (Ind.37) and failed to send his son reinforcements. (Northumberland's absence from the Battle of Shrewsbury and Hotspur's defeat are part of the action in *Henry IV, Part One*.)

Northumberland had been one of the king's staunchest allies when Henry IV, then known as Henry Bullingbrook, usurped King Richard II (Richard's usurpation and Henry's rise to power are the subject of Shakespeare's *Richard II*.) But he rebels against King Henry's policies in *Henry IV, Part One*. The earl's distinguishing characteristic in both *Henry IV, Part One* and *Henry IV, Part Two* is that he does not deliver military aid to his fellow rebels when it is needed.

Northumberland's first appearance in *Henry IV, Part Two* occurs in I.i as he tries to sift truth from rumor concerning the fate of his son. Upon hearing that Hotspur is in fact dead, he vows to go to battle, calls himself ''enrag'd Northumberland'' (I.i.152), and considers joining with the Archbishop Scroop against the king. However, his resolution weakens in II.iii as his wife and daughter-in-law convince him to flee to Scotland rather than fight. In IV.i.7-16 the archbishop reads letters from Northumberland which explain that the earl would like to fight but has been unable to raise a suitable army. We are told in IV.iv.97-99 that Northumberland joins the fighting later from his refuge in Scotland and is defeated by the sheriff of Yorkshire.

Percy (Lady Percy):

She is the earl of Northumberland's daughter-in-law and the widow of Hotspur (the young Henry, or Harry, Percy). (Hotspur's rebellion and his death at the hands of Prince Hal during the battle of Shrewsbury are presented in Shakespeare's *Henry IV, Part One*.) In *Henry IV, Part One* she appears as Hotspur's wife; her role as widow in *Henry IV, Part Two* is limited to II.iii, when she and her mother-in-law, Lady Northumberland, convince the earl not to join his army with Scroop's against the king but instead to flee to Scotland. In persuading Northumberland, Lady Percy commemorates her dead husband's bravery and sense of honor, describes the way in which he served as a model for the youth of England, and condemns her father-in-law for leaving her son without reinforcements at the battle

> One of the most famous incidents in *Henry IV, Part Two* occurs when Hal, newly crowned as King Henry V, rejects Falstaff with his devastating remark—'I know thee not, old man, fall to thy prayers. / How ill white hairs becomes a fool and jester!' (V.v.47-48)."

of Shrewsbury. In response to Northumberland's argument that his honor depends on his helping Scroop, she exclaims ''Never, O never, do [Hotspur's] ghost the wrong / To hold your honor more precise and nice / With others than with him!'' (II.iii.39-41).

Peto:

He is one of Prince Hal's cronies. He appears briefly at the Boar's Head Tavern in II.iv with an update from the palace on the conflict in the north and to announce that Falstaff is being sought for military service. His message shames Hal into resuming his responsibilities as prince and adds urgency to the play as it moves toward a confrontation between the rebels and the king's forces.

Pistol:

Pistol is Falstaff's ensign. He is also a ''swaggerer''—a fashionable Elizabethan term for someone who bullies, swears, and brags. It has been pointed out that his name is appropriate, because like the pistols of the Elizabethan period he is louder and more inconsistent than he is dangerous. Pistol is thrown out of the Boar's Head Tavern in II.iv for his swaggering. In V.iii, he appears at Justice Shallow's house to announce that Henry IV is dead. His news delights Falstaff and prepares the way for the fat knight's rejection by the new King Henry V in V.v.47-71.

Poins:

He is one of Prince Hal's companions. In *Henry IV, Part One*, Poins helps the prince carry out his

> **Prince John's most striking contribution to the play's action occurs in IV.i-ii, when, using Westmerland as his emissary, he negotiates peace with the rebels at Gaultree, only to have them arrested for treason once they dismiss their forces and can no longer fight back."**

practical jokes, and he does so again in II.iv of *Henry IV, Part Two*, when he and Hal disguise themselves as drawers to spy on Falstaff and Doll Tearsheet. He is present in II.ii, when Hal, "exceeding weary" from fighting the rebels, appears to be falling back into his dissolute habits. In II.ii.44-55, Poins expresses skepticism when the prince suggests that he is unhappy about his father's illness. Hal's conversation with Poins in II.ii, as well as the letter sent by Falstaff which accuses Poins of hoping for a wedding between his sister and the prince, indicates that the regulars at the Boar's Head Tavern consider Hal their equal rather than their superior.

Porter:

The porter appears in I.i. When Lord Bardolph approaches looking for the earl of Northumberland, the porter tells Lord Bardolph that he will find the earl in his orchard.

Quickly (Hostess Quickly, formerly Mistress Quickly):

She runs the Boar's Head Tavern in Eastcheap, London, where Sir John Falstaff spends much of his time. Falstaff owes Hostess Quickly money, and in II.i she tries to have him arrested for that and for breaking his promise to marry her. Instead, Falstaff convinces her into dropping the suit and lending him yet more money. Although she entertains cheats, prostitutes, and robbers, Hostess Quickly's concern for her reputation makes her reluctant to admit the swaggering Pistol into her tavern (II.iv.73-106). Her generosity, her nervous confusion, and her tendency to speak in malapropisms (she uses the

word "honeysuckle" for "homicidal" in II.i.50, and "confirmities" for "infirmities" in II.iv.58) frequently leave her vulnerable to Falstaff's swindles and jokes; nevertheless, she seems sorry to see him depart for war in II.iv.382-84. The "madcap" Prince Hal spends a lot of time at her tavern in *Henry IV, Part One*. He is there less often in *Henry IV, Part Two*, and as the newly crowned King Henry V at the close of the play, he rejects entirely the life Hostess Quickly represents.

Rumor:

Rumor appears in the play's induction (an induction is a scene or speech that is separate from, but that introduces, the action of the play). At first, Rumor speaks truthfully—announcing the king's victory over the rebels at Shrewsbury in *Henry IV, Part One*. But then Rumor describes how "false reports" have spread as far as the earl of Northumberland's castle, leading him to believe that his son Hotspur is victorious and that the king and Prince Hal are dead. Thus *Henry IV, Part Two* opens with a useful summary of the closing action in the play which preceded it, as well as with a strong sense of the confusion and chaos that occurs during times of war or civil unrest. Rumor plagues not only the rebels but the king as well, for in III.i.95-96 Henry worries that the rebels have fifty thousand troops, to which his supporter Warwick replies: "It cannot be, my lord. / Rumor doth double, like the voice and echo, / The numbers of the feared" (III.i.96-98). Traditionally, Rumor was depicted as a human figure ornamented with tongues, eyes, and ears; today, some productions of *Henry IV, Part Two* simply make use of a voice-over.

Scroop (Scroop, the Archbishop of York):

He is an opponent of Henry IV. In I.i.200-09, Northumberland's servant Morton reports that Scroop has amassed a large and loyal army by "turn[ing] insurrection to religion" and by rebelling in the name of the usurped and murdered King Richard. In IV.i.53-87, the archbishop gives his reasons for rebelling and at the same time he articulates the play's theme of illness and decay. Speaking on behalf of the English people, Scroop asserts that he is not warring against the king but against the diseased condition of the country, which has sickened itself with too much ease and luxury. Scroop declares that each time he has tried to present his grievances to the king, he has been turned away by Henry IV's corrupt courtiers.

Although Prince John acknowledges that Scroop's grievances are justified, he and Westmerland criticize the archbishop for misusing religion by turning his "tongue divine / To a loud trumpet and a point of war" (IV.i.51-52). In IV.ii, Scroop is arrested for treason and sentenced to execution.

Servants:

The servants and attendants have small or no speaking parts. They appear in various scenes of the play, attending to the needs of the nobility.

Shadow:

Simon Shadow is one of the three men whom Falstaff recruits into military service. His name leads Falstaff to remark that "we have a number of shadows fill up the muster-book"—a reference to the practice by corrupt officers of padding a list of recruits with phony names in order to collect the pay of nonexistent soldiers (III.ii.134-35).

Shallow:

Robert Shallow is a rural justice of the peace in the county of Gloucestershire. He is an old acquaintance of Sir John Falstaff, and spends much of his time reminiscing about their days as lusty young men. In III.ii.92-93, he provides Falstaff with recruits for service in the fighting against the rebels, and he is with Falstaff at the close of the play when the knight is rejected by the newly crowned King Henry V.

Falstaff regards Shallow as a bragging, senile fool who is as uncomplicated and as easy to "see [to] the bottom of" as his name suggests (III.ii.302). After the war, Falstaff returns to Gloucestershire and swindles dinner and a thousand pounds from the justice (V.v.72). Critics have argued that in spite of Shallow's gullibility, Shakespeare did not write the Gloucestershire scenes to poke fun at country life but to celebrate its comforts. The affectionate portrayals of farming and hospitality in V.i and V.iii support this view.

Critics have also observed that Shallow's wistful reminiscences of the past ("And to see how many of my old acquaintances are dead!" he exclaims to his friend Silence in III.ii.34) reflect the play's themes of aging and decay.

Silence:

He is a justice of the peace and a colleague of Justice Shallow. In keeping with his name, Silence is a man of few words; during his first appearance in

> **"** Northumberland had been one of the king's staunchest allies when Henry IV, then known as Henry Bullingbrook, usurped King Richard II. . . . But he rebels against King Henry's policies in *Henry IV, Part One.***"**

III.ii, he gives only short responses to Shallow's lengthy reminiscences about his youth. However in V.iii, after a meal and plenty of wine, old Master Silence surprises Falstaff by singing one song after another—all of which are about drinking or lust. Critics have remarked that these youthful songs sung by an old man reflect the play's melancholy emphasis on loss and the passage of time.

Snare:

The assistant to Fang, the sergeant-at-law. Fang and Snare are recruited by Hostess Quickly in II.i to arrest Falstaff for failing to repay his debts to her and for reneging on his proposal of marriage. During the attempted arrest, Fang, Snare, and Hostess Quickly are attacked by Falstaff, his young page, and Bardolph. The episode is comedic rather than violent, but it also emphasizes Falstaff's dishonesty and impudence—traits which make him a liability to Prince Hal.

Strewers:

The strewers appear in V.v where they strew rushes in the street as the king and his train approach.

Surrey (Earl of Surrey):

He is a supporter of King Henry IV. Surrey's only appearance in the play is a nonspeaking one. It occurs in III.i when he is summoned by the sleepless king along with the earl of Warwick.

Tearsheat (Doll Tearsheet):

She is a prostitute and a friend of Hostess Quickly. She is also Sir John Falstaff's lover. Although they trade insults in II.iv.37-54, it is clear from their conversation that they are fond of each other, and Doll weeps in II.iv.379-80 when Falstaff leaves to take up his commission in Prince John's army. In keeping with the play's focus on aging and decay, Falstaff and Doll make frequent references to disease, and in II.iv.271 Falstaff admits to Doll that he is old. In V.iv, Doll is arrested for prostitution—an early sign that the reign of King Henry V will be markedly different from the madcap career of Prince Hal.

Thomas (Thomas, Duke of Clarence):

See Clarence

Travers:

He is a servant of the earl of Northumberland. In I.i.28-29 Northumberland announces that he sent Travers "to listen after news" of the battle between the king and the rebel forces at Shrewsbury. In I.i.36-48, Travers reports that the "rebellion had bad luck," and that Hotspur had been killed. This bad news—which is hearsay—contradicts Lord Bardolph's good news—which is also hearsay—of the rebels' victory. Northumberland must wait until Morton's arrival in I.i.65-67 to receive a firsthand account of the rebels' defeat.

Wart:

Thomas Wart is one of the potential recruits presented in III.ii by Justice Shallow to Sir John Falstaff. At first, Falstaff rejects Wart on grounds that he is too ragged and lice-ridden. Later, however, Falstaff chooses Wart in lieu of Bullcalf and Mouldy, both of whom have paid bribes to be exempted from military service.

Warwick (Earl of Warwick):

He is a supporter of King Henry IV. Most of Warwick's appearances in the play are spent reassuring the ailing king. When, for example, Henry IV worries in III.i.39 that his kingdom has grown "foul" with the "rank diseases" of rebellion, Warwick responds that the country's health can be completely restored "with good advice and little medicine" (III.i.43), and that the king's enemy, Northumberland, will be quickly defeated. In IV.iv.67-78, Warwick reassures the king that his son Prince Hal has not been hopelessly corrupted by his cronies in Eastcheap but that he merely "studies" them so that he can later use their behavior as a yardstick to measure badness against goodness. When the dying king complains that Hal has disappeared with his crown, Warwick reports that the prince is "in the next room," weeping and "in great sorrow" for his father (IV.v.82, 84). All the same, after the king has died, Warwick worries that Prince Hal might not be a good king (V.ii.15-18).

Westmerland (Earl of Westmerland):

He is a supporter of Henry IV. At Gaultree in IV.i-ii, he acts as a mediator between the rebels and Prince John, extending John's offer of peace to Scroop and his allies, and delivering to the prince their list of grievances. He participates in Prince John's strategy against the rebels, placing Hastings, Scroop, and Mowbray under arrest for "high treason" once they have dismissed their armies (IV.ii.106-09).

Further Reading

Bacon, Wallace A. "Margery Bailey Memorial Lectures I: The Diseased State in *Henry IV, Part Two*." *Speech Monographs* 40 (June 1973): 75-87.

> Bacon defends Hal's rejection of Falstaff and argues that *Henry IV, Part Two* is meant to reassure us that the prince is capable of being a good leader. In connection with these issues, Bacon also discusses the disease imagery that occurs in the play, noting that most of it centers around Falstaff.

Barish, Jonas A. "The Turning Away of Prince Hal." *Shakespeare Studies* (U.S.) 1 (1965): 18-28.

> Barish supports the argument that Falstaff remains appealing in *Henry IV, Part Two* despite his deterioration, so that when Hal rejects him at the end of the play, we sympathize with Falstaff and condemn the new king for his loss of compassion.

Henze, Richard. "Odds and Opportunities in *2 Henry IV*." *Southern Quarterly* 15 (July 1977): 403-11.

> Henze asserts that the rejection of Falstaff and the destruction of the rebels occur because neither fully understands the values at work in society: Falstaff lives simply for the moment and forgets to calculate the odds for his success in the future, and the rebels are unaware that the traditional notion of honor has been replaced by opportunism.

Holland, Norman N. Introduction to *Henry IV, Part Two*, by William Shakespeare. In *The Complete Signet Classic Shakespeare*, edited by Sylvan Barnet, 678-85. New York: Harcourt Brace Jovanovich, 1972.

> Holland observes that as a play about betrayals and defeated expectations, *Henry IV, Part Two* is similar in mood to Shakespeare's tragedies and problem plays.

Humphreys, A. R. Introduction and Appendices to *King Henry IV, Part II*, by William Shakespeare, edited by A. R. Humphreys, xi-xci, 189-242. The Arden Edition of the Works of William Shakespeare. London: Methuen and Co. Ltd., 1971.

Humphreys provides an overview of the play, including dating and source material. In particular, Humphreys examines the play's treatment of statecraft versus morality, emphasizes Hal's emergence as a good ruler, analyzes Hal's rejection of Falstaff, and discusses the negative critical reaction to Prince John's trick against the rebels at Gaultree in IV.ii.

Knowles, Richard. "Unquiet and the Double Plot of *2 Henry IV.*" *Shakespeare Studies* (U.S.) 2 (1966): 133-140.

Knowles examines the imagery of sound in the play, remarking that elements such as noise, clamor, riot, deafness, and quiet which are present in the play's serious plot are parodied in the comedic plot, and that both contribute to the play's theme of disorder.

Levin, Harry. "Falstaff's Encore." *Shakespeare Quarterly* 32 (Spring 1981): 5-17.

In his assessment of Falstaff's part in *Henry IV, Part Two*, Levin focuses on the Boar's Head Tavern scene (II.iv) and the aging Falstaff's relationship with Doll Tearsheet and Hostess Quickly.

Levitsky, Ruth M. "Shakespeare's *2 Henry IV*, II.iv." *Explicator* 35 (Summer 1977): 23-24.

Levitsky contends that Hostess Quickly's reluctance to admit swaggerers such as Pistol into her tavern is a response to the Puritan warning against swearing rather than against his bullying and yelling. As it happens, she regularly hosts Falstaff and his friends, who swear far more than Pistol does.

Manley, Frank. "The Unity of Betrayal in *II Henry IV.*" *Studies in the Literary Imagination* 5 (April 1972): 91-110.

Manley examines the theme of betrayal in the play. In his discussion of the effects of King Henry's usurpation of Richard II, Prince John's Gaultree stratagem, Prince Hal's relationship with his father, and the new king's rejection of Falstaff, Manley observes that there are two types of betrayal which occur in the play—true and seeming—and that Hal commits seeming betrayal with regard to his father, the monarchy, and Falstaff.

Pettigrew, John. "The Mood of *Henry IV, Part 2.*" In *Stratford Papers, 1965-67*, edited by B. A. W. Jackson, 145-67. Shannon: Irish University Press, 1969.

Pettigrew argues that *Henry IV, Part Two* is not just a sequel to *Henry IV, Part One*, but that it has its own unity as a separate play. He describes the mood of *Henry IV, Part Two* as grim and low-key, with its focus on aging and decay in contrast to the brighter, youth-oriented mood of *Henry IV, Part One*.

Schell, Edgar T. "Prince Hal's Second 'Reformation.'" *Shakespeare Quarterly* 21 (Winter 1970): 11-16.

Schell contends that Hal's second reformation, which occurs in *Henry IV, Part Two* (the first occurred in *Henry IV, Part One*), is Shakespeare's solution to the technical problems involved in writing *Henry IV, Part Two* as a sequel to *Henry IV, Part One*, and that since the prince has already mended his ways, this second reformation is necessary only from his worried father's point of view.

Seng, Peter J. "Songs, Time, and the Rejection of Falstaff." *Shakespeare Survey* 15 (1962): 31-40.

Seng examines the songs in *Henry IV, Part Two*, observing that Falstaff's song in II.iv reveals the extent of his "degradation," and that Silence's songs in V.iii underscore the inevitability of the rejection of Falstaff.

The Life of Henry the Fifth

1599

Plot Summary

Act I:

Worried that King Henry V will act on a proposal to gut the Church of its possessions in England, the archbishop of Canterbury and the bishop of Ely convince the king to turn his attention instead to reconquering France—a country once controlled by his great-grandfather, King Edward III. French ambassadors arrive with a message from Lewis—the Dolphin (Dauphin), or heir, of the reigning French king, Charles VI. With reference to Henry V's dissolute youth, the Dolphin has sent the king tennis balls, warning him not to ''revel'' into France, but to stay home and play as he used to do (I.ii.249-57). (King Henry V's ''madcap'' life as Prince Hal and his subsequent reformation into a serious ruler upon succeeding his father, King Henry IV, are presented in Shakespeare's *Henry IV, Part One* and *Henry IV, Part Two*.) This insulting message makes Henry V all the more determined to recapture France.

Act II:

As England prepares to go to war, a plot to assassinate Henry V is uncovered. Meanwhile, in a London street, Bardolph stops a fight between Nym and Pistol over Pistol's wife, the former Nell Quickly, hostess of the Boar's Head Tavern. News arrives that their old friend and drinking companion, Sir John Falstaff, is dying of a broken heart after being

rejected by the new king. (Prince Hal's friendship with and subsequent rejection of the dishonest but charismatic Falstaff are presented in *Henry IV, Part One* and *Henry IV, Part Two*.) Before sailing for France, King Henry tricks the French king's hired assassins (namely, the earl of Cambridge, Lord Scroop, and Sir Thomas Grey) into sentencing themselves to death. Back at the Boar's Head Tavern, Hostess Quickly announces Falstaff's death; Nym, Bardolph, and Pistol mourn their old friend before setting off to war. From his palace, the French king orders France to arm itself against a fierce attack by the English forces, despite his son the Dolphin's insistence that Henry V is nothing but a "vain, giddy, shallow, humorous youth" (II.iv.28). Ambassadors from King Henry arrive to offer France peace in return for immediate surrender, and the French king requests a night to consider the proposal.

Act III:

England's fleet lands in France and lays siege to the city of Harflew (Harfleur) after the French and English fail to agree on terms for peace. Henry V encourages his troops, exhorting them with the famous lines, "Once more unto the breach, dear friends, once more; / Or close the wall up with our English dead" (III.i.1-2). The cowardly Nym and Pistol are forced to join the siege by Captain Fluellen. Later, the Welsh Fluellen, Scots Jamy, and Irish Macmorris debate points of military tactics. Henry V negotiates with the governor of Harflew for the peaceful takeover of the city, then retires with his weary troops to spend the winter in Callice (Calais). Meanwhile at the royal palace in Roan (Rouen), the French king's daughter Katherine tries to learn English. The French leaders plan an offensive against the English troops, who are now ill and outnumbered. Bardolph's commanders sentence him to hang for stealing from a French church. Confident of victory against the English, the Dolphin engages in a bragging match with other French noblemen on the eve of the battle of Agincourt.

Act IV:

On the eve of battle, the two enemy forces camp side by side. Henry V disguises himself so that he can walk among his troops undetected and sound out their morale. He gets into a brief argument with one of his men, and the soldier, not recognizing his king, challenges him to a duel if they survive the battle (this incident is resolved at the end of the act through a practical joke of the king's). Alone, the king reflects on the heavy responsibilities of leader-ship. Morning comes, and the French prepare eagerly to fight their outnumbered opponents. When the English noblemen worry about their own chances of survival, King Henry replies with a rousing speech that boosts their morale ("We few, we happy few, we band of brothers . . ." IV.iii.60). The English fight so ferociously that the French retreat, but not before slaughtering the boys who guard the supplies in Henry V's camp. In response to this and to the French army's apparent return to the battle with reinforcements, the king orders that all French prisoners be killed. Admitting defeat, the French ask for permission to bury their dead; among those slain is the Dolphin. King Henry thanks God for defending the English cause.

Act V:

The play's Chorus describes King Henry's joyous reception on his return to London, and introduces his last return to France. During this time in France, the Welsh Captain Fluellen forces the insulting and swaggering Pistol to eat a leek, which is the symbol of Wales. Meanwhile, the French and English meet to settle the terms of peace. King Henry woos Katherine, the French king's daughter, and the two are engaged to be married, thus uniting the kingdoms of France and England. The play closes by looking ahead at King Henry V's short but active life, and the succession of his infant son, Henry VI, whose turbulent reign and loss of France are the subjects of Shakespeare's *1, 2,* and *3 Henry VI*.

Modern Connections

Henry V is the last play in a historical tetralogy which includes *Richard II, Henry IV, Part One,* and *Henry IV, Part Two*. While these three plays provide interesting background information about Henry's predecessors and his former life as prince, *Henry V* can be understood and enjoyed as a separate unit.

A central element in *Henry V* is the issue of King Henry's maturation. Henry becomes king in *Henry IV, Part Two*, after the death of his father in Act V of that play. Throughout *Henry IV, Part One* and *Two*, Henry, as Prince Hal, is perceived by many as a reckless youth who spends much of his time with drunks and criminals. When he is crowned king, he begins to reform his image by turning away from his old friends, but he has yet to prove that he will be a responsible king. Critical opinion is divided over whether Shakespeare's character King Henry V is indeed a just and heroic leader who acts as ''the mirror of all Christian kings'' (Ch.II.6), or is instead a ruthless Machiavellian who manipulates people and events to get what he wants. (A Machiavellian is someone who believes that politics is amoral and that it is therefore acceptable to use underhanded methods to obtain and keep power.) Whether he is viewed as a sincere man and a hero, or a ruthless and ambitious leader, the fact remains that Henry leads his troops to victory and unites the kingdoms of England and France.

Similarly, in modern times many people are put in a position where they must prove that, despite what they may have done in their past, they have matured and are ready for new responsibilities. This happens to most everyone, including teenagers who must demonstrate that they are ready for a car, a job, or later, to move out of the house, and even happens to political leaders, who must prove that despite their own checkered past, they are able and qualified to take on the responsibility of representing and leading the people of their city, state, or country. Like King Henry, today's political figures may be seen positively, as competent leaders, or negatively, as individuals who put their desires for personal power over the needs of their constituencies.

Henry V is a play with an international focus, looking not only at the antagonism between England and France, but also at the interaction between the nationalities that coexist on the British Isles. Act III scene ii, for example, features a discussion between the English Gower, the Welsh Fluellen, the Scots Jamy, and the Irish Macmorris. Critics have remarked that the meeting of these four men as soldiers on the same side reflects the fact that King Henry has been able to unite all of Britain against a common enemy. Nevertheless, of the four, only the Englishman, Gower, speaks without an accent; of the rest, the Scotsman says ''gud'' instead of ''good,'' the Welshman substitutes p's for b's and has a verbal tic (''look you''), and the highly emotional Irishman slurs his s's. Such stereotyping would be considered offensive by many modern readers and could be considered a mocking attack against the three men, if it weren't for the fact that Henry V is himself proud of being Welsh (IV.vii.104-05), or that Gower chastises Pistol for being rude to Captain Fluellen merely because he does not ''speak English in the native garb'' (V.i.75-76). Additionally, there is Katherine's comically garbled English lesson in III.iv and the mess that King Henry makes

of French as he is courting Katherine in V.ii: any student who has tried to learn a foreign language can identify with the missteps taken by both Katherine and Henry as they stumble through the early stages of a language that is not their own.

Characters

Alice:

She is a lady who attends Katherine, the daughter of Queen Isabel and King Charles VI of France. She first appears in III.iv, where she tutors the princess in English. Her next and last appearance occurs during the wooing scene in V.ii, where she acts as chaperone to Katherine, and also functions as translator between the princess and Henry V. Alice's help in either scene is minimal, since her knowledge of English is only slightly better than Katherine's. Thus III.iv and V.ii.98-280 provide gentle comic relief from the war and statesmanship which occupy most of the play. (Comic relief is a humorous or light-hearted scene or episode which temporarily alleviates the tension of the action occurring before it and which is sometimes meant to highlight the solemnity of the action following it.)

Ambassadors (to the King of England):

These ambassadors are sent by Lewis, the Dolphin of France, to deliver tennis balls to King Henry V in I.ii.234-97. This insulting gift alludes to Henry's dissolute younger days as Prince Hal (for more on Prince Hal's escapades, see Shakespeare's *Henry IV, Part One* and *Two*), and is meant to warn the king to stay at home and play rather than to try to invade France. Henry V's calm but threatening response to this insult is in keeping with his new role as king: ''When we have match'd our rackets to these balls, / We will in France, by God's grace, play a set / Shall strike his [the Dolphin's] father's crown into the hazard'' (I.ii.261-63).

Archbishop of Canterbury:

See Canterbury

Attendants:

Minor characters with small or no speaking parts who contribute to the regal and martial atmosphere of the French and English courts and cities as they are represented onstage.

Bardolph:

He is a friend of Pistol, Nym, and Hostess Quickly. Bardolph's face and nose are "all bubukles, and whelks, and knobs, and flames a' fire" (III.vi.102-03). He was one of Prince Hal's (the former title of King Henry V) drinking companions in Shakespeare's *Henry IV, Part One* and *Two*, where he engaged in robbery and was sometimes a recipient of the prince's practical jokes. In II.i of *Henry V*, he acts as mediator between Nym (who has been jilted by Nell Quickly) and Pistol (who has become Quickly's husband), and he goes with them to France to fight in Henry V's wars. Now that King Henry is no longer a "madcap" prince, he has no contact with Bardolph, but in III.iv.98-106, the king is told that his former friend has been caught robbing a church and has been sentenced to death by his superior officer. The king's response to this news reflects his position as ruler of England: "We would have all such offenders so cut off" (III.vi.107-08).

Bates:

John Bates is one of the king's soldiers. On the night before the battle of Agincourt, he and his fellow soldier Williams meet the disguised King Henry, and the three of them debate the moral responsibilities of a monarch in wartime. Bates knows that the English troops are badly outnumbered by the French, and because he does not recognize the king (who has hidden his royal clothing under a cloak), he feels free to say whatever he thinks. At first, Bates wishes that he were in the cold river "Thames up to the neck" rather than here on the battlefield, and supposes that the king must feel the same way (IV.i.115). Then he opens the debate by observing that if the king's "cause be wrong, our obedience to the king wipes the crime of it out of us" (IV.i.132-33). In the end, Bates demonstrates his loyalty to the king by declaring that he will "fight lustily for him" (IV.i.189); nevertheless, Henry V has been left with a vivid picture of what it feels like to be a common soldier, and what those soldiers expect of their king.

Beaumont (Duke of Beaumont):

He is a French nobleman. Although he is mentioned as one of the French king's allies in III.v.44 and referred to in the stage directions in IV.ii, he has no speaking part. He is listed among those dead at Agincourt in IV.viii.100.

Bedford (John, Duke of Bedford):

He is one of Henry V's younger brothers. His role in the play is minor: he appears principally as part of the king's entourage. In II.ii, he refers to the king's courage and cleverness in his dealings with the co-conspirators Cambridge, Scroop, and Grey. Bedford also appears in *Henry IV, Part One* and *Two*, where he is called Prince John of Lancaster.

Berri (Duke of Berri):

He is a member of Charles VI's entourage. Although his name appears in the stage directions of II.iv and in the list of the French king's allies in III.v.41, he does not have a speaking part in the play.

Bishop of Ely:

See Ely

Bourbon (Duke of Bourbon):

He is one of the French king's allies. After the French forces have been routed at Agincourt, Bourbon calls on his fellow nobles to return to battle or to live in shame (IV.v). According to the stage directions, Bourbon is in Henry V's custody in IV.vii. He is formally listed among the French prisoners in IV.viii.77.

Boy:

Formerly Sir John Falstaff's page, the boy becomes a servant to Bardolph, Nym, and Pistol. (Falstaff is the charismatic "fat knight" whose riotous friendship with and final rejection by Prince Hal—now Henry V—are presented in *Henry IV, Part One* and *Two*). The boy first enters the play in II.i.81-85 to call Pistol and Hostess Quickly to Falstaff's bedside. In II.iii, he and the Hostess provide a moving description of Falstaff's death. Although the boy subsequently goes with Pistol, Nym, and Bardolph to serve them in the French wars, he appears to have little respect for the three men.

The boy provides us with useful information about the personalities and fates of Pistol, Nym, and Bardolph. In III.ii.28-53, he delivers a soliloquy in which he describes them as dishonest cowards, and decides that he "must leave them, and seek some better service." (A soliloquy is a speech delivered by a character when he or she alone. It is meant to indicate to the audience the character's mood and plans, or his or her assessment of other characters in the play.) In IV.iv, Pistol uses the boy's superior knowledge of French to extort money from a French prisoner. At the close of IV.iv, the boy tells us that Bardolph and Nym have both been hanged for theft. He then leaves to guard the troops' luggage and is probably killed with the rest of the boys by the retreating French soldiers.

Britain (Duke of Britain [Brittany or Bretagne]):

As an ally of King Charles VI of France, the duke of Britain is listed as a member of his entourage in II.iv. Along with the Constable of France and Lewis the Dolphin, Britain curses the English after their unexpected success at Harfleur, and insists that the French go to battle to regain their honor (III.v).

Burgundy (Duke of Burgundy):

He is an ally of Charles VI of France. His only speaking part occurs near the close of the play in V.ii, when he brings Henry V and Charles VI together for the final negotiations and signing of the Treaty of Troyes. In V.ii.23-67, Bourbon eloquently describes the condition of France before and after the wars. In V.ii.281-315, he engages Henry V in racy banter over the king's courtship of Princess Katherine. Although this exchange is lighthearted, its outcome is meant to be serious: Henry V demands that his marriage to Charles VI's daughter will bring with it the "maiden cities" of France and his inheritance of the French crown (V.ii.316-47).

Cambridge (Earl of Cambridge):

He is one of three conspirators paid by the French to assassinate Henry V. The king learns of the plot and has Cambridge, Grey, and Scroop arrested for treason and sentenced to death at the port of Southampton just before he sails to France. When Cambridge is arrested, he declares that "the gold of France did not seduce" him but simply motivated him to carry out his assassination attempt sooner rather than later (II.ii.155). This is an allusion to Cambridge's desire to place his brother-in-law, Edmund Mortimer, on the throne instead of Henry. The Mortimer family's claim to the throne is referred to in *Henry IV, Part One*, I.iii.155-56; their claim is also a strong motivation for the Wars of the Roses, which are covered in Shakespeare's *Henry VI, Part One, Two,* and *Three.*

Canterbury (Archbishop of Canterbury):

The archbishop of Canterbury's first appearance occurs in I.i, immediately after the Prologue.

He enters the scene in worried conversation with the bishop of Ely about a bill presented to the king that would confiscate property and income held by the Church and deliver it over to the monarchy. Canterbury's solution to this attack upon the Church's holdings is to offer the king instead a substantial sum of money to help him claim the crown of France and "certain dukedoms" as his own. (I.i.87).

Also during the course of this scene, Canterbury and Ely discuss the king's transformation from "wildness" to "consideration" (I.i.26, 28) upon his succession to the throne after the death of his father, King Henry IV. (Henry V's early exploits as the dissolute Prince Hal are the subject of Shakespeare's *Henry IV, Part One* and *Two*.)

Shortly afterward, in I.ii, Canterbury defines for the king the "law Salique [Salic]" which prohibits women from inheriting property or titles and from passing property or titles on to their heirs. Henry V bases his claim to France on the fact that his great-grandfather, King Edward III of England, was the son of Isabella, who was the daughter of King Philip IV of France. The French have invoked Salic law to stop Henry's claim, but Canterbury argues that the law applied only to women in ancient German territory and "was not devised for the realm of France"; therefore, the archbishop concludes, Salic law does not prohibit Henry from claiming French lands (and ultimately the French throne) in the name of his great-great grandmother Isabella (I.ii.55). This argument convinces Henry V that his claim is just. Act I closes with the French Dolphin's mocking gift of tennis balls—an insult that clinches Henry's decision to invade France (I.ii.234-310).

Critics are sharply divided on the motivation behind Canterbury's behavior in I.i-ii. Some have argued that he is a self-interested schemer who cynically suggests war with France in order to shift the king's attention away from an anti-Church bill that is popular with "the commons" (common people) but that will cause the archbishop to "lose the better half of [his] possession" (I.i.71, 8). According to this argument, the "mighty sum" promised by Canterbury to help finance the king's invasion of France is an outright bribe (I.ii.133).

Other critics assert that the king does not need Canterbury's encouragement to preserve ecclesiastical holdings, for as "a true lover of the holy Church" King Henry is already inclined to reject the commons' bill (I.i.23, 72-73). As for Henry V's invasion of France, these critics argue that Canterbury defines the limitations of Salic law not because he is manipulative but because he has been asked to do so by the king.

Whether or not the archbishop of Canterbury is a schemer, he provides us with information that is important to our understanding of what goes on during the rest of the play. His brief but vivid description in I.i.24-59 of the king's reformation from a madcap prince into a serious and effective monarch prepares us for the Dolphin's insult as well as for Henry's determination to prove himself a great king, ''Ruling in large and ample empery / O'er France and all her almost kingly dukedoms'' (I.ii.226-27). Further, Canterbury's remarks in I.ii on Salic law and the soundness of departing from England to secure Henry's claims in France pave the way for the battles on foreign soil that dominate the action of the play. Finally, Canterbury contributes to the epic tone of the play with his stirring description of the battle of Crecy, where the king's great-uncle, the Black Prince, defeated ''the full power of France'' with only half of the English forces ''And let another half stand laughing by, / All out of work and cold for action!'' (I.ii.107, 113-14). (An epic presents a character of legendary stature involved in a series of heroic adventures across nations and continents and often occurring over long stretches of time. *The Iliad* and *The Odyssey* by the Greek poet Homer are epics.)

Charles (King Charles VI of France, referred to as the French King):

Charles VI is king of France, husband of Isabel, and father of Lewis the Dolphin and of Katherine. His role in the play is minor in comparison to that of his counterpart, King Henry V. Throughout the play, his principal task is to assess the strength of the English forces and to decide what strategies to take against them. The fiery verbal confrontations with King Henry are left to Charles's son Lewis the Dolphin. In V.ii the French king gives his daughter Katherine's hand in marriage to Henry as part of the treaty between England and France.

Chorus:

In Elizabethan drama the Chorus is usually a single actor who recites the play's prologue and epilogue, apologizing for any defects the play might have and begging the audience's forbearance; sometimes the Chorus also fills in details that cannot be presented onstage and comments on the action of the play. In *Henry V*, the Chorus presents not only the Prologue and Epilogue, but introduces Acts II,

> **Canterbury and Ely discuss the king's transformation from 'wildness' to 'consideration' (I.i.26, 28) upon his succession to the throne after the death of his father, King Henry IV.''**

III, IV, and V as well, so that he appears six times in the play. During these six appearances the Chorus sets the epic tone of this play about one of England's most popular monarchs. (An epic presents a character of legendary stature involved in a series of heroic adventures across nations and continents and often occurring over long stretches of time. *The Iliad* and *The Odyssey* by the Greek poet Homer are epics.)

In the Prologue, the Chorus works immediately to conjure up the epic grandeur that ''the warlike Harry'' and his military accomplishments require (Pro.5). First, in typical epic fashion, he calls upon inspiration, or ''a Muse of fire,'' to provide a suitably vast setting for his lofty subject (Pro.1). Next, he apologizes to the audience for the ''unworthy scaffold,'' or stage, which will in fact form the setting of the play (Pro.10). Finally, he relies upon us, the audience, to use our own imaginations to picture what his few actors and inadequate props can only hint at, and to fill in gaps of time that cannot be covered during so short a performance. For the rest of the play, the Chorus continues to serve as our guide, letting us know before each act whether the action will shift to another country, and notifying us when the play skips over months or years. He also continues to ask us to forgive, for example, the ''four or five most vile and ragged foils'' that are meant to represent a great battle (Ch.IV.50), and reminds us to keep supplementing all such paltry props with our own imaginations—hearing, for example, the whistles of the shipmasters and seeing the sailors climbing the ships' rigging as Henry V's fleet sails for France (Ch.III.1-17).

It has been pointed out that the focus on setting and epic grandeur which the Chorus provides is particularly important to a play like *Henry V*, where the central character does not enliven the action of the play by wrestling with difficult problems or by

> **Whether or not the archbishop of Canterbury is a schemer, he provides us with information that is important to our understanding of what goes on during the rest of the play."**

undergoing the significant moral changes that tragic characters such as Hamlet or Othello do. In other words, since King Henry is and continues to be brave and good throughout, the action of the play tends toward a series of static episodes or portraits of his greatness. The Chorus is therefore needed to connect these disjointed portraits and to remind us that the subject is grander than the limitations of the stage.

Critics who do not consider Henry V an admirable character argue that the Chorus's idealistic appeals to our patriotism and sense of honor fail when we are confronted with the actual behavior of the king. These critics cite Henry V's decision to invade France, his order to kill the French prisoners, and his manipulation of the soldier Williams as proof of his ruthless cynicism. A slightly different interpretation is that the Chorus intentionally invents a heroic, godlike picture of Henry V so that we can compare it to the grim political reality presented in the play.

Finally, some critics have remarked that the Chorus represents an extreme version of patriotism, just as Pistol represents an extreme form of self-interest, so that we can appreciate the balanced outlook represented by King Henry, himself.

Citizens:

Minor characters with small or no speaking parts who contribute to the regal and martial atmosphere of the French and English courts and cities as they are represented onstage.

Clarence (Duke of Clarence):

He is one of King Henry V's brothers. His only appearance occurs in I.ii, where he has no speaking part but is simply referred to in the opening stage directions for that scene. He has a minor speaking

role in *Henry IV, Part Two* as Prince Hal's favorite brother.

Constable (Constable of France):

He is an ally of Charles VI of France. In II.iv. he warns the overconfident Dolphin not to dismiss Henry V as a weakling even though the English king had seemed to be irresponsible and foolish when he was prince. (Henry V's "madcap" life as Prince Hal is presented in *Henry IV, Part One* and *Two*.) Nevertheless, the Constable shares the Dolphin's amazement when the "cold blood[ed]" Englishmen defeat the "quick blood[ed]" French at Harflew (III.v.15-26). On the eve of the battle of Agincourt, he is as keen as the Dolphin is to fight the outnumbered and weakened English army, and his arrogant remarks about the quality of his armor are meant to be ironic in light of the English victory and the long list of French casualties which includes his own name (IV.viii.92).

Court:

Alexander Court is one of the king's soldiers. He is with Bates and Williams when they meet the disguised king on the night before Agincourt, but after pointing out the unwelcome sunrise to Bates (IV.i.85-86) he has nothing further to say in the scene, and does not participate in the debate concerning the wartime responsibilities of the king.

Dauphin (Lewis, the Dolphin [Dauphin] of France):
See Lewis

Dolphin (Lewis, the Dolphin [Dauphin] of France):
See Lewis

Ely (Bishop of Ely):

He has a brief but significant role in I.i-ii as he listens to the archbishop of Canterbury's concerns over the bill aimed at confiscating Church holdings, and marvels along with Canterbury at Henry V's transformation from an irresponsible prince to a noble king and "a true lover of the holy Church" (I.i.23). Both Ely and Canterbury persuade the king to invade France by reminding him of the spectacular French battles of his great-grandfather, King Edward III, and his great-uncle, Edward, the Black Prince. Ely's use of heightened language contributes to the heroic mood of the play particularly when he refers to the king as "my thrice-puissant liege [who] / Is in the very May-morn of his youth"

(I.ii.119-20). Like Canterbury, Ely has been described as manipulative and cynical for his efforts to divert the king's attention from the Church's possessions.

Erpingham (Sir Thomas Erpingham):

He is a "good old knight" in Henry V's service (IV.i.286). In IV.i.24, Erpingham lends Henry his cloak, which the king uses to disguise himself as he walks among his common soldiers on the night before the battle of Agincourt. Appreciated by the king for his loyalty, Erpingham is also admired by the rank and file soldiers who describe him as "a good old commander and a most kind gentleman" (IV.i.95-96).

Exeter (Duke of Exeter):

He is Henry V's uncle and advisor, and as such, frequently appears onstage with him. Along with the bishops and Westmerland, Exeter encourages the king to invade France (I.ii), and in II.iv he acts as Henry's ambassador to the French king, demanding that Charles relinquish the lands and crown of France to Henry, and pouring scorn on the Dolphin for his insulting gift of tennis balls. On the morning of the battle of Agincourt, he calculates that the fresh French troops outnumber the worn-out English soldiers five to one—a tally which makes the ensuing English victory seem all the more extraordinary (IV.iii.4). Finally, in V.ii, he helps in the negotiations for the Treaty of Troyes.

Fluellen (Captain Fluellen):

Fluellen is a Welsh captain in Henry V's army who appears frequently once the play's action has shifted to France. He is intensely loyal to Henry V, and is proud of the king's Welsh heritage. Besides his Welshness, Fluellen's distinguishing characteristic is a rigid belief in the ancient methods of war. His admiration for the military tactics of ancient Rome results in his argument with Macmorris (III.ii), whose methods are too modern to suit Fluellen.

Fluellen has been described as pedantic but endearing, and some critics have observed that his type of comic character—honest, brave, and successful under King Henry V's rule—replaces the dishonest comic characters who were Prince Hal's cronies in *Henry IV, Part One* and *Two* but who meet with disaster in *Henry V*. One example of this is Bardolph: he lives inoffensively as a barfly and crook in *Henry IV, Part One* and *Two*, but he is hanged in *Henry V* for robbing a French church. And while Pistol swaggers his way relatively un-

> In *Henry V*, the Chorus presents not only the Prologue and Epilogue, but introduces Acts II, III, IV, and V as well, so that he appears six times in the play. During these six appearances the Chorus sets the epic tone of this play about one of England's most popular monarchs."

scathed through *Henry IV, Part Two*, he is beaten and forced to eat a leek after insulting Fluellen in *Henry V*.

Alternatively, other critics have suggested that the character Fluellen is intended to reveal Henry V's cruelty. According to this argument, the Welsh captain's comparison of Henry V to the ruthless Alexander the Great highlights the English king's harshness as a leader, particularly with regard to his rejection of Falstaff (which Fluellen mentions approvingly in IV.vii.42-51), and his order to cut the throats of the French prisoners (IV.vii.55-65).

French King (King Charles the Sixth of France, referred to as the French King):

See Charles

French Soldier:

He is captured by Pistol at Agincourt in IV.iv. Pistol's awkward but successful attempt to extort money from the soldier by using his servant (see Boy) as translator provides a bit of comic relief from the grimness of battle. (Comic relief is a humorous or light-hearted scene or episode which temporarily alleviates the tension of the action occurring before it and is sometimes meant to highlight the solemnity of the action following it.)

Gloucester (Humphrey, Duke of Gloucester):

He is one of the king's brothers, and has only a minor speaking role in the play as part of Henry V's

> **Both Ely and Canterbury persuade the king to invade France by reminding him of the spectacular French battles of his great-grandfather, King Edward III, and his great-uncle, Edward, the Black Prince."**

entourage. His role in *Henry IV, Part Two* is slightly larger.

Governor (Governor of Harflew [Harfleur]):

The governor of Harflew's one appearance in the play (III.iii) occurs in response to Henry V's demand that the besieged town surrender or else face rape and pillage at the hands of Henry's soldiers. The governor accepts the king's terms of surrender, explaining that the town's only hope of rescue—the Dolphin—has sent word that his army is "yet not ready / To raise so great a siege" (III.iii.46-47).

Gower:

He is an English captain in Henry V's army and Fluellen's "dear friend" (IV.vii.166). Indeed, the two captains are virtually inseparable, the one always appearing in the same scene as the other. The straightforward Gower serves as Fluellen's foil, listening to and humoring his strong views on military etiquette and tactics, seconding his admiration for King Henry, acting as a voice of moderation—when for example, Fluellen argues with Macmorris (III.ii.134-35)—and supporting him against Pistol's insults. (A foil is someone or something that highlights or enhances someone else's traits by acting as a contrast to those traits.)

Grandpre (Lord Grandpre):

An ally of King Charles VI of France, Grandpre appears in IV.ii to rouse the French nobles to do battle at Agincourt. Grandpre's graphic description of the outnumbered and weary English army with its ragged banners and starved horses (IV.ii.38-55)

increases the wonder of Henry V's subsequent victory.

Grey (Sir Thomas Grey):

Along with Cambridge and Scroop, Sir Thomas Grey is paid by the French to assassinate King Henry V at Southampton before he sets sail to invade France (II.ii). He and his co-conspirators are arrested and sentenced to death. Like Cambridge and Scroop, he repents his crime and accepts his sentence.

Henry (King Henry V of England, also referred to as King Harry, formerly known as Prince Hal and Harry of Monmouth):

Formerly the "madcap" Prince Hal (see Shakespeare's *Henry IV, Part One* and *Two*), Henry V is king of England and the title character of the play, which deals with Henry's efforts to reclaim France as part of his kingdom—a topic well-known to Elizabethan audiences.

Throughout the play, the Chorus and many of Henry's subjects treat him as an epic hero. (An epic presents a character of legendary stature involved in a series of heroic adventures across nations and continents and often occurring over long stretches of time. *The Iliad* and *The Odyssey* by the Greek poet Homer are epics.) The Chorus compares him to Mars, the Roman god of war (Pro.6), while Fluellen likens him to Alexander the Great, as does the archbishop of Canterbury when he describes the king as able to "unloose" the "Gordian knot" of statecraft, much as Alexander sliced through the original Gordian knot with his sword (IV.vii.11-53; I.i.45-47). Exeter warns Charles VI that Henry is descending on France "In thunder and in earthquake, like a Jove" (II.iv.100).

Henry V is also noted for his Christian piety. The bishop of Ely calls him "a true lover of the holy Church," and Canterbury praises the king for his knowledge of religion (I.i.23, 38-40). The Chorus refers to him as "the mirror of all Christian kings" (Ch.II.6). Henry himself repeatedly invokes God. Referring to the upcoming battle of Agincourt, he tells his brother Gloucester that their fate is in "God's hand" (III.vi.169). And when the French herald Montjoy informs him that the English have won at Agincourt, the king replies, "Praised be God, and not our strength, for it!" (IV.vii.87).

Critics have observed that unlike his father (Henry IV), Henry V is not concerned about the legitimacy of his claim to the English throne, nor is he tortured by guilt or inner turmoil; nevertheless, there are a couple of moments on the eve of Agincourt when Henry V expresses his own cares. In IV.i.230-84, he envies the condition of the private citizen and ''the wretched slave,'' who, unlike the king, are able to sleep through the night, untroubled by the responsibilities of government and the difficulties of maintaining peace. He also worries briefly that God might punish him because his father usurped the English crown from his predecessor, Richard II (IV.i.292-305). (Richard II's deposition and murder, and the accession to the throne by Henry's father, Henry IV, are the subjects of Shakespeare's *Richard II*. Henry IV's troubled reign is covered in Shakespeare's *Henry IV, Part One* and *Two*.)

King Henry's most serious direct conflict with someone else occurs on the night before Agincourt when he puts on a disguise so that he can visit his troops and speak freely with them. He and a soldier named Williams argue over the extent to which a king is responsible for the fate of his men. Williams contends that ''if the cause [of a war] be not good, the King himself hath a heavy reckoning to make''—in other words, that the king is responsible for all of those who suffer damnation for dying in an unjust war without a clean conscience (IV.i.134-35). The king's response to this issue is clear and confident. He tells Williams that ''Every subject's duty is the King's, but every subject's soul is his own. Therefore should every soldier in the wars do as every sick man in his bed, wash every mote [of sin] out of his conscience'' (IV.i.176-80).

Critical assessment of the character Henry V is extremely diverse. Some critics believe that Shakespeare's portrait of the king is sympathetic, and that the references to his piety and to his heroic stature are sincere. Others assert that Shakespeare's characterization of the king is an ironic one, and that the Chorus's glowing description of Henry is undercut by Henry's ruthless behavior in the play.

Those who consider the king a sympathetic character contend that he amply fulfills the requirements of the ideal Renaissance king, that his courage and faith inspire his troops, and that modern criticism mistakenly uses twentieth-century standards to judge Henry negatively.

Those who find fault with Henry V refer directly to his actions and to his treatment of other characters in the play. They describe the king as a Machiavellian whose religious devotion is self-serving rather than sincere, and who takes money

> **Throughout the play, the Chorus and many of Henry's subjects treat him as an epic hero. . . . The Chorus compares him to Mars, the Roman god of war (Pro.6), while Fluellen likens him to Alexander the Great, as does the archbishop of Canterbury . . . (IV.vii.11-53; I.i.45-47). Exeter warns Charles VI that Henry is descending on France 'In thunder and in earthquake, like a Jove' (II.iv.100).''**

from the bishops and starts a war with France, doing so not to serve his people but to further his own ambitions. (A Machiavellian is someone who considers politics to be amoral and that any means, however unscrupulous, are justified in order to obtain and hold onto power.) They point to Henry's rejected friend Falstaff and Hostess Quickly's remark that the ''King has kill'd his heart'' as an indication of Henry V's ruthlessness (II.i.88). They mention the king's order to ''cut the throats'' of the French prisoners as proof of his brutality (IV.vii.63). And they contend that Henry's staging of the argument over the glove between Fluellen and Williams is manipulative (IV.vii and viii).

Critics have also suggested that Henry V is not a hero since he doesn't undergo the suffering that is necessary for an audience to identify with him.

Lastly, there are some critics who insist that Shakespeare's characterization of Henry V is ambiguous, and that the playwright has intentionally left it up to us to determine whether or not the king is sincere.

Herald:

After the battle of Agincourt, the English herald presents Henry V with a list of the French and English who died in the fighting. The two lists contrast strikingly with one another, for the number of French soldiers who died runs to ten thousand while the total number of English casualties is twenty-nine (IV.viii.80-106).

Hostess (Hostess Nell Quickly, formerly Mistress Quickly):

See Quickly

Humphrey (Humphrey, Duke of Gloucester):

See Gloucester

Isabel (Queen Isabel of France):

Queen Isabel is the wife of King Charles VI of France and the mother of Katherine. Her role in the play is minor and primarily diplomatic. She appears with her husband in V.ii to greet King Henry on his arrival in France to sign the Treaty of Troyes (the treaty is the reason for Henry's "back-return" to France, Ch.V.41). In V.ii.92-94, she exits with her husband and King Henry's nobles—ostensibly to help them as they discuss the details of the treaty, remarking that "Happily a woman's voice may do some good, / When articles too nicely urg'd be stood on." In reality, her departure gives Henry the opportunity to court Katherine. Her blessing to the engaged couple at the close of the play includes a prayer that the marriage of Henry and Katherine will at last unite England and France in peace (V.ii.359-68).

Jamy:

He is a Scottish captain who tries to be concilia-tory during the argument over military strategy that occurs between his colleagues Fluellen and Macmorris (III.ii). Like Macmorris, he speaks English with a strong accent; however, critics have suggested that his character is not meant to be an unflattering stereotype, but rather that his presence in an English army along with Welsh and Irish captains reveals Henry V's skill at uniting all of the British Isles against a common enemy.

John (John, Duke of Bedford):

See Bedford

Katherine:

She is the daughter of the French King Charles VI and Queen Isabel. Katherine's first appearance

in the play involves an amusingly inaccurate lesson in English from Alice, her lady-in-waiting (III.iv). Significantly, it occurs immediately after Henry V—her future husband—occupies the French town of Harflew. Katherine's next and last appearance is in V.ii, where she is courted by King Henry in a mixture of English and clumsy French as his advis-ors meet with her father to settle Henry V's claims to France and his inheritance of the French crown. Thus while both scenes provide comic relief from the serious business of war, they also underline Henry V's resolute invasion of France. (Comic relief is a humorous or light-hearted scene or episode which temporarily alleviates the tension of the action occurring before it and which is some-times meant to highlight the solemnity of the action following it.)

Ladies:

Minor characters with small or no speaking parts who contribute to the regal and martial atmos-phere of the French and English courts and cities as they are represented onstage.

Lewis (Lewis, the Dolphin [Dauphin] of France):

The Dolphin is the son and heir of the French king, Charles VI. Recalling the stories of Henry V's "madcap" days as prince, the Dolphin does not consider the English king a threat to France. On the contrary, he describes King Henry as "a vain, giddy, shallow, humorous youth" (II.iv.28) and sends him a gift of tennis balls as a sign of his contempt (I.ii.237-58). Both Charles VI and the Constable of France argue that Henry V has re-formed into a strong king; all the same, the French nobility believe that the "wild and savage" English are inferior soldiers (III.v.7). France's overconfidence in the face of Henry's invasion is a recurrent issue in the play, and the Dolphin's attitude, particularly on the eve of Agincourt, is its clearest expression. On the night before the battle, the Dolphin brags about the courage and agility of his horse, describing it as "the Pegasus," and as "a beast for Perseus," that is made of "pure air and fire" (III.vii.14, 20-21). While his references to the Greek hero Perseus and his winged horse Pegasus are in keeping with the epic mood of the play, they are also examples of dramatic irony, since the Elizabethan audience knew well that the French cavalry were the first to fall victim to the English longbowmen at the battle of Agincourt. (Dramatic irony occurs when the audience understands the real significance of a character's words or actions but the character does not.) The Dolphin is listed among the dead on the field of Agincourt in IV.viii.94-95.

Lords:

Minor characters with small or no speaking parts who contribute to the regal and martial atmosphere of the French and English courts and cities as they are represented onstage.

Macmorris:

Macmorris is an Irish captain who gets into a heated debate with the Welsh captain Fluellen over military strategy (III.ii). His heavily accented English and his fiery temperament turn him into an Irish stereotype; all the same, critics argue that his presence in the play is meant to be a positive indication of Henry V's ability to unite the antagonistic nationalities of the British Isles (English, Scots, Irish, and Welsh) to fight against the French rather than among themselves.

Messengers:

Minor characters with small or no speaking parts who contribute to the regal and martial atmosphere of the French and English courts and cities as they are represented onstage.

Montjoy:

He is a French herald sent by Charles VI on the eve of the battle of Agincourt to demand ransom from Henry V in exchange for clemency (III.vii.118-136). Coming as it does after the French defeat at Harflew, Montjoy's message is both defiant and insulting; King Henry rejects it even though his troops are ill and outnumbered. In IV.iii.79-89, Montjoy renews the request for ransom, although this time it comes from the overconfident Constable rather than from King Charles. Montjoy's last appearance is in IV.vii.70-83, when he humbly asks permission to count and bury the French dead.

Nym:

He is the moody companion of Bardolph and Pistol and the jilted fiance of Hostess Quickly. In II.i, Nym nearly comes to blows with Pistol, the man whom Quickly married instead. Along with Bardolph and Pistol, he is a reluctant soldier in Henry V's French wars. According to the boy who serves them, "Nym and Bardolph are sworn brothers in filching" (III.ii.44-45), and indeed in IV.iv.70-74 we are told that, like Bardolph, Nym has been hanged—probably for stealing. Some critics argue that dishonest characters such as Nym parody the behavior of King Henry V who has robbed his people of peace by starting a war with France. (To parody something is to imitate it closely for the purposes of comic effect or ridicule.) Other critics assert that Nym and his cronies are meant to contrast with and therefore emphasize King Henry's goodness.

Officers:

Minor characters with small or no speaking parts who contribute to the regal and martial atmosphere of the French and English courts and cities as they are represented onstage.

Orleance (Duke of Orleance [Orleans]):

He is an ally of King Charles of France. On the night before the battle of Agincourt, Orleance indulges in a bragging match with the Constable and the Dolphin—singing the praises of his horse and scoffing at the Dolphin's own extravagant claims for his (III.vii). The overconfidence of the French nobility is meant to stand in vivid contrast to their massive defeat at the hands of their outnumbered English opponents. Orleance is listed as a prisoner of war in IV.viii.76.

Pistol:

Ancient (Ensign) Pistol is Hostess Quickly's husband as well as a crony and fellow soldier to Bardolph and Nym, with whom he goes to the French wars. He is what the Elizabethans refer to as a swaggerer—a bully who swears and brags but who runs away at the first sign of danger. The boy acting as Pistol's servant calls him a coward with "a killing tongue and a quiet sword" (III.ii.34). Gower describes him as "a gull, a fool, a rogue, that now and then goes to the wars, to grace himself at his return into London under the form of a soldier" (III.vi.67-69). Near the close of the play in V.i, Pistol is beaten by Fluellen for his insolent attacks on the captain's Welsh heritage, and forced to eat a leek which is the symbol of Wales.

Some critics argue that the comical but cowardly Pistol and his cronies expose the hypocrisy behind Henry V's war with France, appearing as they do immediately after the Chorus and therefore apparently undercutting the Chorus's patriotic descriptions of Henry's troops as enthusiastic, honor-seeking ''English Mercuries'' (Ch.II.7). In contrast, others assert that dishonest characters like Ensign Pistol come to ruin in the play and are replaced by honest characters like Captain Fluellen who prosper under Henry V's rule.

Queen Isabel:

See Isabel

Quickly (Hostess Nell Quickly, formerly Mistress Quickly):

She runs the Boar's Head Tavern in Eastcheap, London, and is married to Pistol. Her presence in the play is principally of interest in connection with the fate of her old friend Sir John Falstaff. Falstaff is a dishonest but appealing ''fat knight'' who frequented the Boar's Head Tavern in *Henry IV, Part One* and *Two*, indulging in jokes and idleness with Prince Hal—who rejects the old knight after he (the prince) becomes King Henry V. In II.i.88 of *Henry V*, the Hostess responds to news of Falstaff's illness by declaring that ''The King has kill'd his heart.'' Shortly afterward in II.iii, she poignantly describes Falstaff's death. Critics have argued that Shakespeare chose to dispense with the charismatic Falstaff offstage because his actual appearance in the play would have shifted the focus away from King Henry V and the patriotic battle of Agincourt.

Rambures (Lord Rambures):

He is an ally of the king of France. Rambures participates briefly in the overconfident bragging match which occurs between the Constable, the Dolphin, and Orleance as they wait impatiently to fight against the English at Agincourt (III.vii, IV.ii). In III.vii.85-86 he suggests betting on the number of English soldiers each of them will capture during the battle. Rambures is listed among the French casualties in IV.viii.94).

Salisbury (Earl of Salisbury):

He is an ally of Henry V and a minor character in the play. As the English noblemen nervously anticipate the battle of Agincourt and worry about the odds they face, Salisbury invokes God's help and prepares to go ''joyfully'' into battle (IV.iii.5-10). His cheerfulness and bravery in spite of ''fearful odds'' heighten the patriotic and epic tone of the play and remind us that Henry V seems convinced that God is on his side.

Scroop (Lord Scroop):

He is a co-conspirator with Cambridge and Grey in a plot to assassinate Henry V at the port of Southampton, where the king is preparing to sail for France. Of the three men, Scroop's betrayal distresses the king most, for he had been Henry's close friend and advisor. The fact that this trusted companion allows himself to be tempted to murder the king merely on the strength of a bribe from France provokes Henry to declare that Scroop's revolt ''is like / Another fall of man'' (II.ii.141-42). When his treachery is discovered, Scroop at first begs for mercy along with his co-conspirators. When the king refuses to pardon him, Scroop accepts his death sentence but entreats the king's forgiveness, saying, ''I repent my fault more than my death'' (II.ii.152).

Soldiers:

Minor characters with small or no speaking parts who contribute to the regal and martial atmosphere of the French and English courts and cities as they are represented onstage.

Warwick (Earl of Warwick):

He is an ally of Henry V. The earl of Warwick appears principally in the stage directions as a member of the king's entourage. His only line occurs in IV.viii.19 when, on orders given him earlier by the king, he interrupts the fight between Williams and Fluellen.

Westmerland (Earl of Westmerland):

In *Henry IV, Part One* and *Two*, Westmerland was a supporter and advisor to King Henry IV; he performs the same role for Henry IV's son, King Henry V. Westmerland is among those in I.ii who encourage Henry V to claim the French throne. In II.ii, he expresses outrage along with Exeter and Bedford at the treachery of Scroop, Cambridge, and

Grey. His fervent wish for more troops at Agincourt moves the king to deliver his patriotic Saint Crispin's day speech (IV.iii.18-67). In V.ii, he acts as one of the king's negotiators for the Treaty of Troyes.

Williams:

Michael Williams is one of the soldiers met by Henry V as he tours his camp on the eve of the battle of Agincourt. Along with Bates, Williams engages in a discussion with the disguised king over the responsibilities of a monarch to his troops. Williams contends that since men must go to war when their king commands them to, the king is responsible for the soul of any man who does not die "well"—that is, any man who does not die with a cleansed conscience and with thoughts of God. Williams argues further that "few die well that die in battle; for how can they charitably dispose of any thing, when blood is their argument?" (IV.i.141-43). The king replies that a monarch is responsible only for the justness of the cause, and not for the souls of his troops, some of whom may be criminals who enlisted in the fighting to escape punishment at home. Williams agrees with this argument, but shortly afterward he and the king (whom Williams does not recognize) exchange bitter words and challenge each other to a duel if they survive Agincourt. Once the battle is won, Henry devises a trick whereby Fluellen and not he is challenged by Williams to the promised duel, and then resolves all confusion and hurt feelings by offering Williams a glove filled with money (IV.viii).

Critics disagree on the significance of these two episodes involving Williams. Some argue that as a king, Henry V shows his compassion for his subjects by meeting them on their level and trying to feel what they feel. Others argue that as a person, Henry continues to enjoy playing roles as he did when he was Prince Hal (see *Henry IV, Part One* and *Two*), and that his trickery is a sign of underhandedness.

York (Duke of York):

An ally and cousin of Henry V, the duke of York's only lines occur at IV.iii.130-31, when he asks permission to lead the vanguard of the king's army at Agincourt. In IV.vi.7-32, a grief-stricken Exeter describes York's valiant death on the battlefield.

Further Reading

Adkins, Camille. "Glendower and Fluellen; or, Where Are the Leeks of Yesterday?" *CCTE. Proceedings* 48 (September 1983): 101-08.
Adkins examines Fluellen's function as a national portrait of Wales according to Shakespeare and to the Elizabethans in general, and also analyzes the ways in which Fluellen reflects King Henry's strengths and weaknesses.

Brennan, Anthony S. "'That Within Which Passes Show': The Function of the Chorus in *Henry V*." *Philological Quarterly* 58 (Winter 1979): 40-52.
Brennan describes the play's Chorus as extreme in its display of patriotism. Further, he asserts that the play's other extreme is Pistol's self-interest, and that King Henry functions as the balance between these two extremes.

Coursen, Herbert R., Jr. "*Henry V* and the Nature of Kingship." *Discourse* 13 (Summer 1970): 279-305.
Coursen observes that while Shakespeare draws no moral judgment on King Henry's behavior, the playwright nonetheless characterizes him as a manipulative and clever politician who has always enjoyed playing roles (see *Henry IV, Part One* and *Two*), but who is ultimately controlled by the role he adopts as king and patriot.

Guerrein, Robert T. "The Historical Background to *Henry V*, I.i." *University of Dayton Review* 10 (Summer 1974): 15-28.
Observing that I.i (the conference between the archbishop of Canterbury and the bishop of Ely) undercuts the grandeur of the play's prologue, Guerrein examines the history behind the scene and concludes that it reveals the hypocrisy and self-interest shared by the king as well as the bishops.

Hibbert, Christopher. *Agincourt*. London: Purnell Book Services Ltd., 1964.
Hibbert's historical account of the battle of Agincourt includes information from medieval sources, illustrations of armor and campaign maps, and genealogical tables for both Henry V and the French King Charles VI.

Levin, Richard. "Clown Subplots: Foil, Parody, Magic—*Henry V, Doctor Faustus*." In *The Multiple Plot in English Renaissance Drama*, 116-23. Chicago: The University of Chicago Press, 1971.
Levin disagrees with the argument that the comic scenes in *Henry V* are meant to mock and ridicule the serious incidents in the play. Instead, he asserts that the high jinks of Nym, Bardolph, and Pistol serve "to contrast with, and so render still more admirable," the achievements of King Henry V.

Lusardi, James P. "The Humorous and the Heroic in Shakespeare's *Henry V*." *Pennsylvania English* 10 (Fall 1983): 15-24.
Focusing in particular on the disguised King Henry's encounter with his soldiers in IV.i, Lusardi asserts that

although the play's attitude to war and patriotism is ambivalent, there is still a positive indication of heroism and the ''mutual dependence of all men in an ordered society.''

Rabkin, Norman. ''Rabbits, Ducks and *Henry V*.'' *Shakespeare Quarterly* 28 (Summer 1977): 279-96.

Rabkin argues that in *Henry V*, Shakespeare wanted to illustrate the ambiguity of the world, and so he purposely made it difficult for us to judge whether King Henry is the perfect Christian monarch or a ruthless Machiavellian.

Smith, Gordon Ross. ''Shakespeare's *Henry V*: Another Part of the Critical Forest.'' *Journal of the History of Ideas* 37 (January-March 1976): 3-26.

Smith contends that the play is a negative representation of a country at war and that the dishonest behavior of Nym and Bardolph is meant to parody the actions of the king.

Soellner, Rolf. ''*Henry V*: Patterning after Perfection.'' In *Shakespeare's Patterns of Self-Knowledge*, 113-28. Columbus: Ohio State University Press, 1972.

Soellner contends that Shakespeare's portrait of Henry V is sympathetic, and that the playwright presents the king as an ideal ruler according to the four cardinal virtues propounded by Renaissance Christian humanists. Soellner argues further that twentieth-century critics' dislike of Henry V is the result of modern values and preconceptions.

Walter, J. H. Introduction and Appendices to *King Henry V*, by William Shakespeare, edited by J. H. Walter, xi-xlii, 159-74. The Arden Edition of the Works of William Shakespeare. London: Methuen and Co. Ltd., 1985.

Walter provides composition, performance, and publication dates for *Henry V*. In addition to essays on various characters, themes, and incidents in the play, Walter presents a character study of the king, in which he describes Henry V as an ideal leader.

Wentersdorf, Karl P. ''The Conspiracy of Silence in *Henry V*.'' *Shakespeare Quarterly* 27 (Summer 1976): 264-87.

Wentersdorf discusses the background of the Southampton conspiracy (II.ii), arguing that Scroop, Cambridge, and Grey ''are challenging Henry's right to the English throne on grounds at least as convincing as those justifying Henry's challenge to the French king.''

Williamson, Marilyn L. ''The Courtship of Katharine and the Second Tetralogy.'' *Criticism* 17 (Fall 1975): 326-34.

Williamson argues that the courtship scene (V.ii) in *Henry V* reflects Henry's evolution from the ''madcap'' Prince Hal (in *Henry IV, Part One* and *Two*) to the kingly Henry V by combining the old, play-acting aspect of Henry's personality with his new understanding that he can no longer behave as though he were merely a man.

The First Part of Henry the Sixth

Plot Summary

circa 1589-90

Tetralogy: Henry VI, Parts 1, 2 and 3 + Richard III [handwritten annotation]

Act I:

This play, the first of a tetralogy which includes the three parts of *Henry the Sixth* and *Richard III*, opens with the funeral of Henry V. The English nobles bemoan the death of the king, squabble among themselves, and discuss the fate of the English cause in France. A series of messengers enter and announce that most of France has been lost and Lord Talbot, England's great champion, has been captured by the French. The English nobles vow to fight and defeat the French in order to regain that country for the young king, Henry VI. The scene switches to the city of Orleance, where the French have been driven back by the English. Joan de Pucelle (Joan of Arc) rallies the dispirited French and promises that she will raise the siege. Back in London, the duke of Gloucester's and the bishop of Winchester's men fight over armaments stored in the Tower of London; their skirmish is broken up by the mayor of London. Back in France at the siege of Orleance, the French kill Sir Thomas Gargrave and the earl of Salisbury. Talbot and Pucelle fight inconclusively, but the French nonetheless take back Orleance through her inspiration.

England [handwritten annotation]

France [handwritten annotation]

London [handwritten annotation]

France [handwritten annotation]

Act II:

The English, led by Talbot and with the aid of Burgundy, manage to recapture Orleance. The countess of Auvergne invites Talbot to visit her at her

France [handwritten annotation]

castle with the intent of taking him prisoner. The attempt fails. Back in England, Richard Plantagenet (representing the Yorkist faction) and the duke of Somerset (representing the Lancastrian faction) fall to quarreling. They pluck different colored roses as emblematic of their cause. Other noblemen take sides. Somerset asserts that Richard Plantagenet's father was executed for treason. Richard visits the dying Edmund Mortimer in prison, and asks him how his father died. Mortimer explains recent English dynastic history (the usurpation of the Yorkist Richard II by the Lancastrian Henry IV).

Act III:

Gloucester and Winchester pick up the quarrel between them that broke out in Act I. The king manages to stop them from fighting (at least for now), and restores to Richard Plantagenet the titles that were taken from him. In France, Pucelle and the French take back Roan by stealth. The English recapture it by force of arms but not before Sir John Falstaff flees. Pucelle wins over the duke of Burgundy to the French side. Henry VI bestows on Talbot the title earl of Shrewsbury. Vernon (a Yorkist) and Basset (a Lancastrian) quarrel.

Act IV:

In Paris, Henry VI is crowned king. Sir John Falstaff, who delivers Burgundy's message announcing he has changed sides, is banished for cowardice. Vernon and Basset ask the king for permission to duel; York and Somerset (their masters) themselves almost fight. The king persuades both sides to stop quarreling, but indicates his loyalty to the Lancastrian side. Talbot besieges Burdeaux, but he and his son die in the battle. The French win, largely because York and Somerset do not trust each other enough to send reinforcements.

Act V:

In letters, the pope and the Holy Roman Emperor urge peace on the English, a peace to be ratified by the marriage of Henry VI to the earl of Arminack's daughter. On its way to liberate Paris, the French army is attacked by the English and Pucelle is taken prisoner. Suffolk captures Margaret, daughter of Reignier, duke of Anjou. He is struck by her beauty and decides to take her as his mistress and persuade Henry VI to marry her. In this way, he intends to control the kingdom. Reignier agrees to the marriage. Pucelle meets her father, a shepherd, but denies any relation to him. She swears she is of noble blood and also pregnant, but she is nonetheless condemned to death by burning. The English and the French make peace; the king is persuaded by Suffolk to marry Margaret even though he is betrothed to the earl of Arminack's daughter.

Modern Connections

Although Shakespeare's *Henry VI, Part One* was written over four hundred years ago and deals with events almost two hundred years before that, it speaks in so many ways to modern audiences. It talks about war, marriage, politics, religion, and family in very contemporary language.

In the last century and more, people have witnessed the extraordinary brutality of armed conflict. The Civil War, World Wars I and II, the Korean War, the Vietnam War, and the war of Yugoslavian disintegration among others have become the stuff of shared cultural experience. So, when Salisbury is wounded at the siege of Orleance by a "piece of ord'nance" (I.iv.15), the reader understands, even expects, the result: one of his eyes and part of his face is blown off. And so, when young Talbot dies in a "sea of blood" that "did drench / His overmounting spirit" (IV.vii.14, 15), readers can imagine what he would have looked like because they have seen the terrible effects of war first hand, or in photographs, on television, or on video.

With regard to marriage, Shakespeare raises the issue of its relation to love in terms that this age of palimony and prenuptial agreements can understand. When Suffolk tries to persuade the king to marry Margaret, daughter of the duke of Anjou, and prove faithless to his betrothed, the daughter of the earl of Arminack, he comments that money and legal agreements don't matter when it comes to love: "Marriage is a matter of more worth / Than to be dealt in by attorneyship" (V.v.55-56), that arranged marriages spell disaster; marriages for love promise happiness:

> For what is wedlock forced, but a hell,
> An age of discord and continual strife?
> Whereas the contrary bringeth bliss,
> And is a pattern of celestial peace.
>
> (V.v.62-65)

Some readers would probably agree with Suffolk's assertion, but there are many religions in which arranged marriages are the norm.

Henry VI, Part One is pre-eminently a play about politics. In the absence of a strong ruler (the king is very young and irresolute in this play), the Yorkists and Lancastrians vie for power. In the famous Temple Garden scene (II.iv), on the one side line up Richard Plantagenet, Warwick, Vernon, and a lawyer; on the other, Somerset, Suffolk, and Basset. For a modern audience, such factionalism is not unusual. One need think only of what happened to Yugoslavia after the death of Tito or Russia after the decline of strong, centralized Communist control to recall the deadly infighting that occurs in a power vacuum. A far less extreme example of the result of factionalism is the gridlock that often paralyzes the United States government due to the differing agendas of Democrats and Republicans. Shakespeare's play ends on a note of foreboding, with Suffolk vowing to continue the political game of manipulation through his love for the king's future wife, Margaret, the duke of Anjou's daughter.

As for religion, *Henry VI, Part One* gives center stage to the conflict between two countries convinced that each has God on its side. At Henry V's funeral, the bishop of Winchester eulogizes:

> He was a king blest of the King of kings.
> Unto the French the dreadful Judgment Day
> So dreadful will not be as was his sight.
> The battles of the Lord of hosts he fought.
> (I.i.28-31)

On the French side, Joan de Pucelle (Joan of Arc) is called the "holy maid" inspired by "Heaven and our Lady" (I.ii.51, 74). The French are convinced that she has been sent by God to rescue France from English domination; Shakespeare, however, in a scene that may suprise American audiences brought up to see Joan of Arc as a liberator, has her conversing with fiends (V.iii). For many English, Joan of Arc has typically been viewed as a despised figure, someone who took away land that many believe was rightfully theirs.

Characters

Alanson (Duke of Alanson):

He is a French nobleman in the entourage of Charles the Dolphin. At the siege of Orleance, he begins by deriding the English as more attracted to eating than fighting. He ends by admiring the "courage and audacity" of such "raw-bon'd rascals" (I.ii.36, 35).

Ambassadors:

They appear before Henry VI in V.i. The ambassadors from the pope and the Holy Roman Emperor have come to encourage the king to make peace with France. The ambassador from the earl of Arminack has come to request that the king and the daughter of his master be betrothed. To this last, the king agrees.

Attendants (English and French):

These unnamed characters appear in the formal scenes (such as the funeral of Henry V and the coronation of Henry VI) to swell the numbers.

Auvergne (Countess of Auvergne):

She plays an important role in II.iii by attempting to capture Lord Talbot, England's greatest fighter, through a subterfuge. She sends him an invitation to visit her at her castle (II.ii.38-43), meaning to imprison him, but he expects trouble and brings soldiers with him. When she tries to imprison him, he calls his soldiers out of hiding. She seems to be motivated by patriotism rather than by deceitfulness.

Basset:

He is a servant of the duke of Somerset and a supporter of the Lancastrian faction. He appears in two scenes: III.iv and IV.i. In the first he quarrels with Vernon (a servant of the duke of York) over some criticism he made of Vernon's master and of the white rose (emblem of the Yorkists). In the second scene (IV.i.78-136), Basset pleads his case before the king and explains in detail (IV.i.89-100) what happened. The king unconvincingly tells the disputants to forget their quarrel. Basset represents the degree to which the enmity between noblemen has tainted relations between their servants.

Bastard (Bastard of Orleance [Orleans]):

He is a relatively minor character, a member of the retinue of Charles the Dolphin. He appears in seven scenes, but only speaks in five of those. In those five, too, his comments are usually short. In one he brings the news to the Dolphin of the arrival of the "holy maid," Joan de Pucelle (I.ii.51). In another, he urges desecration of the corpses of the Talbots, father and son (IV.vii.47).

Beauford (Henry Beauford, Bishop of Winchester, afterwards Cardinal):

He is an ambitious prelate who wishes to control the young king, to "sit at chiefest stern of public weal'' (I.i.177). To this end, he is probably corrupt (I.i.41-43) and definitely self-serving. He sees the Lord Protector, Gloucester, as the major obstacle to his success. So, in I.iii he refuses to allow him access to the Tower of London probably because he doesn't want him to discover all the weapons he has been amassing for himself. And so, in III.i he determines to use the authority of the pope to support his plans (III.i.51). In this he succeeds, for in V.i he is made a cardinal, becoming one through bribery (III.i.51-54). It is he who announces the terms of the proposed peace between England and France (V.iv.123-32). By so doing, he shows he is no longer ''inferior to the proudest peer'' (V.i.57). His ambition is arguably greater than anyone else's in the play. As he ruthlessly comments when he is alone on stage at the end of V.i, he will be more powerful than Gloucester, whatever the cost. Earlier in the same scene, indeed, Exeter had recalled Henry V's prophecy about Winchester becoming ''co-equal with the crown'' (V.i.32-33). If he has to, Winchester will ''sack this country with a mutiny,'' he himself says, to achieve his ends (V.i.62-63).

Beauford (Thomas Beauford, Duke of Exeter):

He is the king's great-uncle and has been ''ordain'd his special governor'' (I.i.171). He is also a soothsayer. In a play of few soliloquies (a soliloquy is a speech containing nothing but truth delivered by a character alone on stage directly to the audience), Exeter has the two longest and most important: III.i.186-200 and IV.i.182-194. In the first, having seen the dissent among the English nobles (especially the duke of Gloucester and the bishop of Winchester) he predicts that the ''fatal prophecy'' made in the time of Henry V will come true: Henry VI will lose all the French lands (III.i.194, 196-97). In the second, he predicts civil war will result from a young king's inability to keep his warring nobles at peace: ''There comes the ruin, there begins confusion'' (IV.i.193-94).

Beauford (John Beauford, Earl, afterwards Duke, of Somerset):

He is the most vocal representative of the Lancastrian group. In the Temple Garden scene (II.iv), he asserts the primacy of the Lancastrian claim to the throne and is supported by Suffolk and opposed by the Yorkists (Richard Plantagenet, Warwick, Vernon, and a lawyer). It is this dispute which flares up in III.i between Somerset and Warwick

and in IV.i between Somerset and York. It is this dispute, too, which causes Talbot's death at Burdeaux because Somerset in a personal snub at York refuses to send him the troops that were destined for Talbot.

Bedford (Duke of Bedford):

He is the king's uncle and the regent of France. He appears in only three scenes in the play (I.i, II.ii, and III.ii). In the first of these, his role is to emphasize the renown of the previous king, Henry V; to attempt to smooth over the wrangling between the bishop of Winchester and the duke of Gloucester; and to predict difficult times ahead for the realm. It's an important role, for he has the most lines (42 out of 177) in the scene. In II.ii, he is briefly shown in action at the siege of Orleance, fulfilling his role as regent of France. In the third (III.ii), he is brought in dying of sickness and old age.

Bishop of Winchester (Henry Beauford, Bishop of Winchester, afterwards Cardinal):

See Beauford

Boy:

See Son

Burgundy (Duke of Burgundy):

He is one of the most powerful nobles in France. He begins the play on England's side as ''redoubted Burgundy'' (II.i.8), and is crucial to the English victories at Orleance and Roan. He goes over to the French side in III.iii after parleying with Pucelle. In IV.i, news of his ''monstrous treachery!'' (IV.i.61) is brought to the English, and in response Talbot moves to besiege Burdeaux, the largest town in Burgundy's dukedom. Burgundy last appears fleeing from the English (see the stage direction at V.iii.29). Burgundy also performs three other minor roles: first, to vilify Pucelle (''vile fiend and shameless courtezan!'' [III.ii.45]); second, to praise young John Talbot as a courageous enemy (IV.vii.44); third, to indicate that the French fear even Lord Talbot's ghost (V.ii.16).

Captains:

One captain receives Talbot's whispered instructions in II.ii. Another appears in III.ii to judge Sir John Falstaff's flight from the fighting before Roan: ''Cowardly knight, ill fortune follow thee!''

(III.ii.109). A third accompanies Sir William Lucy in an effort to get aid from the duke of Somerset for the beset Lord Talbot fighting at Burdeaux (IV.iv).

Cardinal of Winchester (Henry Beauford, Bishop of Winchester, afterwards Cardinal):

See Beauford

Charles (Charles the Dolphin [Dauphin], afterwards King of France):

As the heir to the throne of France, Charles fights in this play at every major engagement with the English: the siege of Orleance, the fight for Roan, and the battle of Burdeaux. He also ratifies the terms of peace with the English at the camp of the duke of York at Anjou (V.iv). His personality is not strongly delineated. Rather, Shakespeare has him utter the expected responses to French or English victory. He is cunning enough to test Pucelle's powers in I.ii.60-63. He is also sufficiently disingenuous to agree to peace with England with no intention of keeping his word (V.iv.155-168). He is not a strong fighter (he is beaten in mock combat by Pucelle [I.ii.93-105]), but he is chivalrous enough to stop the Bastard of Orleance from disfiguring Talbot's body (IV.vii.49-50). The English repeatedly accuse him of sleeping with Pucelle. However, this is perhaps more an indication of Shakespeare's intent to discredit the French (England's traditional enemy) by suggesting that Charles consorts with devils than to indicate immorality as such on his part.

Countess of Auvergne:

See Auvergne

Dolphin (Charles the Dolphin [Dauphin], afterwards King of France):

See Charles

Edmund (Edmund Mortimer, Earl of March):

See Mortimer

Exeter (Thomas Beauford, Duke of Exeter):

See Beauford

Falstaff (Sir John Falstaff):

He is not to be confused with the Sir John Falstaff of *Henry IV, Part One* and *Two*, whose

> " As the heir to the throne of
> France, Charles fights in this play
> at every major engagement with
> the English: the siege of Orleance,
> the fight for Roan, and the battle
> of Burdeaux."

death is reported in *Henry V*, or with the Falstaff of *The Merry Wives of Windsor*. This Falstaff is a thorough coward with none of the other Falstaffs' charm and humor. In I.i.110-34 and I.iv.35-37, it is related how in the retreat from Orleance, his cowardice led to Talbot's capture. In III.ii.104-09, he flees from the fighting around Roan. In IV.i.9-47, he makes the mistake of bearing a letter from the duke of Burgundy to Henry VI. Talbot accuses him of cowardice and strips him of his knighthood. The king then banishes Falstaff "on pain of death" (IV.i.47).

Fiends:

These devils appear to Pucelle before the battle at Angiers in V.iii. She summons them in hopes that they will make her victorious as they have before. This time they cannot help her. Her actions are perhaps intended to leave the audience in no doubt that Pucelle is inspired by the Devil not by God.

Gargrave (Sir Thomas Gargrave):

He appears in I.iv at the siege of Orleance in company with Salisbury, Talbot, and Sir William Glansdale. He is killed by cannon fire.

General:

He appears on the battlements of Burdeaux (in IV.ii) to respond to Talbot's challenge to surrender the city. He refuses to surrender, and instead correctly predicts that Talbot will finally be defeated and killed. Shakespeare also uses him to praise Talbot as a valiant and dangerous enemy of the French (IV.ii.15, 31-32).

Glansdale (Sir William Glansdale):

He appears in I.iv at the siege of Orleance in company with Salisbury, Talbot, and Sir Thomas

Gargrave. He is not injured by the cannon fire that kills Salisbury and Gargrave.

Gloucester (Duke of Gloucester):

He is the Lord Protector of the young Henry VI. As such, it is his task to ''proclaim young Henry king'' (I.i.169), which he does in IV.i. He wrangles constantly with the king's uncle, the bishop (later cardinal) of Winchester. In I.i, he accuses the bishop of Winchester of using his religious office for political ends. In I.iii, he visits the Tower of London to check on the munitions and armaments that the young king will need for the wars in France, but is stopped from entering on orders from Winchester (who may have been taking weapons for his own use or profit). In III.i he takes his quarrel before the king, who manages to reconcile both the duke and the bishop but only temporarily.

In IV.i he performs two functions: getting the governor of Paris to swear loyalty to the king, and interpreting the import of Burgundy's letter in which he announces his switch to the French side. In V.i, he urges the king to make peace with France and to seal the agreement by marrying the earl of Arminack's daughter. In the final scene he argues unsuccessfully against the king's decision to break his betrothal to the daughter of the earl of Arminack and instead marry Margaret, the daughter of the duke of Anjou. He can only helplessly and correctly predict what will follow from the king's decision: ''Ay, grief, I fear me, both at first and last'' (V.v.102).

Although Winchester tries to paint him otherwise, Gloucester is a trusted, honest advisor to the king. As the king himself says, ''When Gloucester says the word, King Henry goes'' (III.i.183). Gloucester's quarrel with Winchester shows that not all enmity in this play is between the Houses of York and Lancaster, for both men are Lancastrians (descended, that is, from John of Gaunt, duke of Lancaster). Rather, this quarrel is between the religious and secular branches of the government.

Governor of Paris:

He appears only in IV.i in a non-speaking role. He kneels before the bishop of Winchester and takes an oath of loyalty to the newly-crowned king, Henry VI.

Henry (King Henry VI of England):

The young King Henry VI is in every way the opposite of Henry V, his well-loved, warlike father.

He is ineffectual, weak, and inconsistent. He is easily led by those around him. Shakespeare underlines this weakness by delaying the king's first entrance until half way through the play (III.i) and by having him appear in a total of only five scenes (this in a play bearing the king's name). It is as if he really doesn't matter in the affairs of his own kingdom.

When the king does appear, his behavior does not bode well for the future of his realm. In III.i, he relies upon what he hopes is the power of prayer (''if prayers might prevail'' [III.i.67]) to make Gloucester and Winchester friends instead of enemies. He manages to get the two nobles to shake hands, but Winchester makes it clear in an aside that the act means nothing to him. (An aside is a statement that a character makes directly to the audience without the other characters overhearing him.) He elevates Richard Plantagenet to the titles of earl of Cambridge and duke of York, both of which are indeed rightfully Plantagenet's, but he does nothing to quell Somerset's anger at the move. Later (in IV.i), he mediates the dispute over power between York and Somerset by eloquently arguing for the importance of domestic harmony; he then rather foolishly sides with the Lancastrians (and Somerset) by pinning a red rose to his clothes even as he denies any favoritism.

At the beginning of the final act, the king sensibly agrees to peace and to a marriage intended to knit together the royal families of England and France. In the final scene, however, the king jeopardizes everything by rapidly agreeing with Suffolk's arguments in favor of breaking his betrothal to the earl of Arminack's daughter and marrying the duke of Anjou's daughter instead. One can feel sympathy for a young king ''perplexed with a thousand cares'' (V.v.95), but in the context of the dramatic action one must note his rashness too.

The young king, observers note, is pious, foolish, and lacking in self-knowledge. He respects his uncle Gloucester but doesn't take his sensible advice regarding his marriage. He is aware of the disputes within his kingdom but fails to do anything substantive about them. He admires Talbot's martial prowess, talks about it movingly, and elevates him to an earldom, that of Shrewsbury (III.iv.16-27). However, he then indirectly causes his death by spurring him on to attack Burdeaux, the principal city of the traitrous duke of Burgundy, without having reconciled the two noblemen (York and Somerset) whose soldiers are essential to victory in any such attack. He considers himself more a scholar than a lover (''And fitter is my study and my books / Than wanton dalliance with a paramour'' [V.i.22-23]), but soon finds himself lusting after Margaret, the duke of Anjou's beautiful daughter, even if costs him his kingdom:

> So am I driven by breath of her renown,
> Either to suffer shipwreck, or arrive
> Where I may have fruition of her love.
>
> (V.v.7-9)

Heralds:

These appear in two formal scenes in this play as special messenger or attendants. The first occasion (I.i) is the funeral of Henry V; the second (IV.vii) is the recovery of the bodies of the Talbots, father and son, from the French. The heralds have non-speaking parts.

Humphrey of Gloucester:

See Gloucester

Jailers (to Mortimer):

These appear in only one scene, II.v, accompanying the dying Mortimer.

Joan de Aire:

See Pucelle

Joan de Pucelle:

See Pucelle

John Talbot (John Talbot, son of Lord Talbot):

See Talbot

Keepers:

See Jailers

Lawyer:

He only appears in one scene (II.iv) and has only four lines. The scene, however, is the crucial one (in the Temple Garden) when supporters of the Yorkist and Lancastrian factions pluck roses (white or red) as emblematic of their particular loyalty. Shakespeare uses the lawyer as an indication that the divisions run deep in the country; they involve not only the nobility and their servants but members

> " The young King Henry VI is in every way the opposite of Henry V, his well-loved, warlike father.''

of the professions, too. The lawyer picks a white rose because, from a legal point of view, he finds the Lancastrian argument weak.

Lord Talbot (Lord Talbot, afterwards Earl of Shrewsbury):

See Talbot

Lords (English and French):

These unnamed characters appear in the formal scenes (such as the funeral of Henry V and the coronation of Henry VI) to swell the numbers.

Lucy (Sir William Lucy):

He is a messenger sent by Talbot, who is faced by superior French forces at Burdeaux. He meets York on the plains of Gascony (in IV.iii) and entreats him to send reinforcements. In the next scene (IV.iv), Lucy meets Somerset, who responds to his request for aid by blaming York and Talbot for the rashness of the military campaign against Burgundy. Finally, Lucy appears in IV.vii to claim the bodies of the Talbots, father and son, from the French.

Margaret (daughter of Reignier):

She is the daughter of Reignier, duke of Anjou, and the future queen of England. She sees herself as possessing ''a pure unspotted heart, / Never yet taint with love'' (V.iii.182-83). She is captured by the earl of Suffolk after the French have been routed at Angiers (V.iii), and is so exquisitely beautiful that he is enraptured by her. Within ninety lines of her first appearance, Margaret has acceded to his wish to have her become queen of England as long as her father agrees.

Master Gunner (of Orleance):

In I.iv, he is indirectly responsible for the deaths of the earl of Salisbury and Sir Thomas

Gargrave at the siege of Orleance through a clever military stratagem.

Mayor of London:

In I.iii, he breaks up the fight between the bishop of Winchester's and the duke of Gloucester's servingmen. The mayor issues an official proclamation (I.iii.74-79) that both sides must disperse to their homes and never use traditional weapons again "upon pain of death" (I.iii.79). He appears for a second time in III.i, this time before the king himself, to complain that Winchester's and Gloucester's men have now taken to attacking each other—in light of his proclamation—with stones. The way in which the mayor's proclamation is evaded is an indication of how deep the resentments run between the two sides.

Messengers:

These appear throughout the play to carry news externally between the French and English forces and internally among the two sides themselves. In I.i, three of them appear in sequence to the English nobles assembled for the funeral of Henry V. For about 100 lines (I.i.57-161), the messengers dominate the discussion as bringers of bad news. The first lets the nobles know that England has lost seven French provinces in quick succession because of their factionalism. The second adds to the misery by announcing that all the land in France has been lost except for a few minor towns, the Dolphin has been crowned at Rheims, and the French nobility has formed an alliance. The third reports that Talbot, England's greatest general and fighter, has been captured at the siege of Orleance through the cowardice of Sir John Falstaff.

Mortimer (Edmund Mortimer, Earl of March):

He appears in only one scene (II.v), but his role is a vital one. Mortimer is the cousin of Henry VI, and the rightful heir to the throne after the death without children of Richard II. His role is to indicate the weakness of Henry VI's claim to the throne and to explain to his nephew, Richard Plantagenet, why his (Plantagenet's) father, the earl of Cambridge, was executed. In lines 61-92, he argues that the claim of the House of York is superior to that of the House of Lancaster because the former derives from a son of Edward III (Lionel, duke of Clarence) who was older than the son of Edward III, John of Gaunt, on whom the Lancastrians base their claim. Mortimer

dies at the end of this scene, but not before he names Richard Plantagenet his heir.

Officer:

Employed by the mayor of London, he delivers the official proclamation (in I.iii.74-79) announcing that the servingmen of the bishop of Winchester and the duke of Gloucester must return to their homes and—on penalty of death—lay down their weapons.

Orleance (Bastard of Orleance [Orleans]):

See Bastard

Papal Legate:

In V.i, he is one of the three ambassadors who appear before Henry VI with several formal requests. The cardinal of Winchester speaks to him when the two are alone on stage and makes it clear that he bribed the pope in order to be promoted from bishop to cardinal.

Plantagenet (Richard Plantagenet, afterwards Duke of York):

He is the Yorkist claimant to the throne after the death of Edmund Mortimer. His first appearance is in II.iv, the scene in the Temple Garden. Somerset asserts the primacy of the Lancastrian claim (and hence the right of Henry VI to reign) in response to Plantagenet's offstage assertion of the legality of the Yorkist claim. In response, Plantagenet demands that, just as he has done, those who agree with his position should pluck a white rose from the nearby bush to demonstrate their agreement with his views. Warwick, Vernon, and a lawyer side with him. The discussion then degenerates into invective and threats, with Plantagenet promising Somerset and Suffolk that he will avenge himself for their denial of the Yorkist claim even though he knows that wholesale death will result: "This quarrel will drink blood another day," he remarks to his friends (II.iv.133).

He next appears in III.i to receive from the king the title taken away from him because his father was considered a traitor. Henry VI also restores to him the title duke of York that became his by right after the death of his brother. York now pledges allegiance to the king. He does not, however, forget his quarrel with Somerset. On the contrary, his servant

(Vernon) wrangles with Somerset's servant (Basset) almost to the point of dueling, and both York and Somerset are ready to fight each other before the king forces them to make a temporary peace. In IV.iii, their quarrel causes York to abandon his promised aid to the beleaguered Talbot at Burdeaux because Somerset fails to send him the men he needs.

In V.iv, he brings forth the captured Pucelle and curses her as "wicked and vile," "vicious," a "strumpet," a "sorceress," and a "foul accursed minister of hell!" (V.iv.16, 35, 84, 1, 93). In this role, York is no longer being used by Shakespeare to illustrate the dangers of civil strife (York vs. Lancaster); rather, he becomes the mouthpiece for the traditional hatred of the French in general and of Pucelle in particular.

Pole:

See Suffolk

Porter:

He is the servant of the countess of Auvergne in II.iii. He carries out the stratagem by means of which Auvergne hopes to capture Talbot.

Pucelle (Joan de Pucelle, also called Joan of Aire):

The audience first hears of Pucelle from the French point of view. To them she is a "divinest creature" (I.vi.4) and "holy maid" ordained by God to rid France of the English (I.ii.51-54). At first to the English she is similarly godlike, a "holy prophetess new risen up" (I.iv.102). Within a very few lines, however, the English opinion changes. Lord Talbot calls her a "high-minded strumpet" and a "witch" (I.v.12, 21). The intensity of the contrast between the French and English views never lessens after Act I. On the contrary, it becomes more obvious. Talbot calls Pucelle a "damned sorceress" (III.ii.38) after her temporary victory at Roan; the French feel she deserves "a coronet of gold" (III.iii.89) after persuading Burgundy to switch to the French side. Young Talbot terms Pucelle a "giglot wench" at the battle of Burdeaux even though she considers herself a "maid" (IV.vii.41, 38).

Shakespeare's portrait of Joan de Pucelle is unflattering, but typical of the English attitude to Joan of Arc at that time. The play portrays her as a

> " Shakespeare's portrait of Joan de Pucelle is unflattering, but typical of the English attitude to Joan of Arc at that time."

perjurer, for she says at I.ii.72 that she is the daughter of a shepherd, but strenuously denies that parentage when she meets her father towards the end of the play (V.iv.8-9). The play also depicts her as promiscuous as well as a liar, for on the one hand she can call herself a "maid" (IV.vii.38) while on the other (and in an effort to avoid being burned at the stake) assert that she is pregnant and offer as possible fathers the Dolphin, the duke of Alanson, or the duke of Anjou (V.iv.60-78). Finally, and most importantly, the play portrays Pucelle as coming not from God but from the Devil, for she consorts with "fiends" in V.iii in a last desperate effort at victory and is even prepared to sell her soul for the same. In Shakespeare's play, Pucelle was what the English chroniclers said she was: a formidable opponent inspired by the Devil.

Reignier (Reignier, Duke of Anjou):

He is a trusted member of the entourage of Charles the Dolphin. He is the father of Margaret, whom Henry VI determines, on the advice of Suffolk, to marry. His reward for agreeing to the match is to be allowed to keep his lands, the provinces of Maine and Anjou, free from English domination.

Richard (Richard Plantagenet, afterwards Duke of York):

See Plantagenet

Salisbury (Earl of Salisbury):

He appears in only one scene (I.iv). In it he is killed by cannon fire from the French lines around Orleance. His death symbolizes the brutality of war. He dies after part of his face is blown away.

Scout:

He brings the news in V.ii to the French that although they have defeated the English at Burdeaux, the enemy has regrouped and is ready to fight again.

Sentinels:

In II.i they are told by a French sergeant to keep watch and let him know if any English soldiers try to sneak into Orleance. Shakespeare uses them to make a biting social comment: that war is always hardest on the common soldier (II.i.5-7).

Sergeant:

A French soldier, he instructs the sentinels in II.i to inform him in the guardhouse if any English soldiers try to recapture Orleance.

Servant:

He supports the dying Lord Talbot in IV.vii and shows him where his dead son lies.

Servingmen:

These belong to two rivals, the duke of Gloucester and the bishop (later cardinal) of Winchester. They clash in I.iii as Gloucester is trying to enter the Tower of London to discover whether the place has been run properly since the death of Henry V. Winchester, who has instructed Woodvile (the keeper of the Tower) to deny Gloucester entrance, turns up with his men at the same time as Gloucester does with his. The mayor of London has to break up the skirmish. The servingmen, now forbidden to carry arms, reappear in III.i hurling stones at each other in a continuation of the feud.

Shepherd:

He is the father of Pucelle. In V.iv he meets her as she is being led to the stake to be burned. She denies that he is her father, and does so in such an offensive way (''Decrepit miser! base ignoble wretch!'' [V.iv.7]) that he responds: ''O, burn her, burn her! hanging is too good'' (V.iv.33).

Soldiers:

Only two soldiers have speaking parts: An English soldier (in II.i) states that he intends to pillage Orleance (II.i.78-81); a French soldier (in III.ii) says the same thing about Roan: ''Our sacks shall be a mean to sack the city'' (III.ii.10).

Somerset (John Beauford, Earl, afterwards Duke, of Somerset):

See Beauford

Son (of the Master Gunner):

He fires the shot in I.iv that kills Sir Thomas Gargrave and the earl of Salisbury.

Suffolk (Earl of Suffolk):

He is a supporter of the Lancastrian claim to the throne and, so, sides with Somerset against Warwick and Richard Plantagenet in the Temple Garden scene (II.iv). His major role occurs towards the end of the play. In V.iii he captures Margaret, the duke of Anjou's daughter, and falls in love with her beauty. He decides to try to have the king marry her even though to do so would break his betrothal to the earl of Arminack's daughter. In V.v he succeeds in persuading the king to marry Margaret, intending to rule the king through his wife.

Talbot (John Talbot, son of Lord Talbot):

He is in every way as brave as his father, with whom he dies in the fighting at Burdeaux. According to Sir William Lucy (IV.iii.37-38), John Talbot sees his father for the first time in seven years as comrades-in-arms at Burdeaux; that fact makes their meeting and their deaths more poignant. John Talbot refuses to fly from the battle despite his father's pleading; rather, he distinguishes himself by feats of arms.

Talbot (Lord Talbot, afterwards Earl of Shrewsbury):

Lord Talbot is the great soldier and general on the English side—the ''Frenchmen's only scourge'' (IV.vii.77), as Sir William Lucy puts it. He is an altruistic, intelligent hero in a play characterized by self-interest and double dealing. In I.iv he describes his imprisonment at the hands of the French in terms that display an unshakeable will. In II.iii he outwits the countess of Auvergne when she deceitfully attempts to capture him. He says (at I.iv.109) that he will make ''a quagmire'' of the ''mingled brains'' of the Dolphin and Pucelle. He does his best to do so throughout the play. It is due to his courage and intelligence that the English recapture Orleance and Roan. It is due to his martial achievements that even the name of Talbot strikes fear into the French. He dies in battle at Burdeaux (IV.vii) as a result of squabbling between the dukes of York and Somerset.

Vernon:

He is a servant of the duke of York and a supporter of the Yorkist faction. He appears in two scenes: III.iv and IV.i. In the first he quarrels with Basset (a servant of the duke of Somerset) over some criticism he made of Basset's master and of the red rose (emblem of the Lancastrians). Vernon strikes Basset, and then promises to seek redress from the king. In the second scene (IV.i.78-136), Vernon asks the king for permission to fight, and explains events from his point of view. The king unconvincingly tells the disputants to forget their quarrel. Vernon represents the degree to which the enmity between noblemen has tainted relations between their servants.

Warders:

These are officials at the Tower of London. In I.iii they refuse entrance to the duke of Gloucester on the orders of the bishop of Winchester.

Warwick (Earl of Warwick):

He appears in all the formal court scenes in the play (the funeral of Henry V [I.i], the elevation of Plantagenet to the dukedom of York [III.i], and the coronation of Henry VI [IV.i]). His major role, however, relates to the rivalry between the Houses of Lancaster and York. In the Temple Garden scene (II.iv), he sides with the Yorkists (Richard Plantagenet, Vernon, and a lawyer) against the Lancastrians (Somerset and Suffolk), but only after he has been called upon by Somerset to act as judge and has rendered his opinion that the arguments on both sides are based on obscure points, "nice sharp quillets of the law" (II.iv.17). He prophesies correctly that the dispute between Yorkists and Lancastrians will lead to bloody civil war. He also renders two other judgments important to the play: he considers the enmity between the bishop of Winchester and the duke of Gloucester dangerous to the stability of the realm (III.i.112-117), and he characterizes the king as a good speaker but a weak ruler (IV.i.174-175). He is the member of the aristocracy to whom the others look for advice. It is he, for example, who assures York that the peace between France and England will be to England's benefit (V.iv.113-115).

Watch:

They are fooled by Pucelle in III.ii into letting an advance party of French soldiers into Roan.

William de la Pole:

See Suffolk

> " Lord Talbot is the great soldier and general on the English side—the 'Frenchmen's only scourge' (IV.vii.77), as Sir William Lucy puts it."

Winchester (Henry Beauford, Bishop of Winchester, afterwards Cardinal):

See Beauford

Woodvile:

He is the lieutenant of the Tower of London. In I.iii, he confirms his warders' refusal (on the orders of the bishop of Winchester) to allow the duke of Gloucester into the Tower to inspect its stores of weapons.

Further Reading

Bevington, David. "The Domineering Female in *1 Henry VI*." *Shakespeare Studies* 2 (1966): 51-58.
> Bevington shows that the motif of the strong woman in *1 Henry VI* intentionally parallels the theme of disagreement and division in the play.

Blanpied, John W. "'Art and Baleful Sorcery': The Counterconsciousness of *Henry VI, Part I*." *Studies in English Literature, 1500-1900* 15, no. 2 (Spring 1975): 213-227.
> Blanpied argues that the play is intentionally ironic and iconoclastic, a deliberate undermining of tradition.

Boas, Frederick S. "Joan of Arc in Shakespeare, Schiller and Shaw." *Shakespeare Quarterly* 2 (1951): 35-45.
> Boas argues that Shakespeare's portrait of Joan of Arc as inconsistent matches the pejorative view in Holinshed, his source.

Brockbank, J. M. "The Frame of Disorder: *Henry VI*." In *Early Shakespeare*, edited by John Russell Brown and Bernard Harris, 73-100. London: Edward Arnold, 1961.
> Brockbank traces the way in which Shakespeare alters his sources in order to stress the importance of pageantry in history.

Burckhardt, Sigurd. "'I Am But Shadow of Myself': Ceremony and Design in *1 Henry VI*." *Modern Language Quarterly* 28, no. 2 (June 1967): 139-158.
> Burckhardt shows how the language in the play consists of a self-assertion destructive to long-term goals and good order.

Candido, Joseph. ''Getting Loose in the *Henry VI* Plays.'' *Shakespeare Quarterly* 35, no. 4 (Winter 1984): 392-406.
Candido demonstrates that the *Henry VI* trilogy is unified by repeated scenes of capture and escape.

Greer, Clayton Alvis. ''The Place of *1 Henry VI* in the York-Lancaster Trilogy.'' *PMLA* 53 (1938): 687-710.
Greer hypothesizes that *Henry VI, Part One* may be based on an earlier version of the play called *Talbot* or *Harry the Sixth*.

Kirschbaum, Leo. ''The Authorship of *1 Henry VI*.'' *PMLA* 67 (1952): 809-822.
Kirschbaum provides evidence for *Henry VI, Part One* being Shakespeare's work and for its being written before *Henry VI, Part Two* and *Three*.

McNeir, Waldo F. ''Comedy in Shakespeare's Yorkist Tetralogy.'' *Pacific Coast Philology* 9 (Apr. 1974): 48-55.
Shows the presence of humor in *Henry VI, Part One, Two,* and *Three,* and *Richard III*. In *Henry VI, Part One*, the cowardice of Falstaff is intended to be funny.

Pratt, Samuel M. ''Shakespeare and Humphrey Duke of Gloucester: A Study in Myth.'' *Shakespeare Quarterly* 16, no. 2 (Spring 1965): 201-216.
Pratt shows how Shakespeare enhances the mythic quality of Humphrey as the ''good duke.''

Riggs, David. ''The Hero in History: A Reading of *Henry VI*.'' In *Shakespeare's Heroical Histories[:]* Henry VI *and Its Literary Tradition*, 93-139. Cambridge: Harvard University Press, 1971.
Argues that *Henry VI, Part One* is meant to enshrine ''exemplary truths'' from fifteenth-century English history.

Sheriff, William E. ''Shakespeare's Use of the Native Comic Tradition in His Early English History Plays.'' *Wisconsin Studies in Literature* 2 (1965): 11-17.
Sheriff traces the way in which Shakespeare uses humor in his history plays (including *Henry VI, Part One*).

Turner, Robert Y. ''Characterization in Shakespeare's Early History Plays.'' *ELH* 31, no. 3 (Sept. 1964): 241-258.
Turner demonstrates how Shakespeare's characters in the *Henry VI* trilogy are static rather than dynamic.

Wineke, Donald R. ''The Relevance of Machiavelli to Shakespeare: A Discussion of *1 Henry VI*.'' *Clio* 13, no. 1 (Fall 1983): 17-36.
Wineke delineates the ways in which Shakespeare's political viewpoint is Machiavellian even if he never read the Italian's works.

The Second Part of
Henry the Sixth

circa 1590-91

Plot Summary

Act I:

At the court, the marriage of King Henry VI and Margaret, daughter of the duke of Anjou, is announced and the terms of the peace agreement with France is read out. Neither pleases the nobles. The nobles squabble among themselves about who will have power in a country ruled by a weak king. In the next scene, the duchess of Gloucester reveals her ambitions for her husband, Lord Protector and heir to the throne. She intends to summon a witch to predict future events. When she does so, Buckingham and York arrest her and plan the downfall of her husband. In a scene involving the common people, a petitioner accuses his master of arguing that the duke of York is the rightful heir to the throne. When the case is brought before the king, he asks for a ruling from Gloucester, who judges that the master and his servant must fight in single combat to decide the truth. Gloucester also decides that Somerset will be regent in France rather than York.

Act II:

This act opens with a falconing scene full of allusions to the high-flying ambitions of the nobility. To the assembled nobles and the king and queen, a commoner named Saunder Simpcox, and his wife enter claiming that his sight has been restored by a miracle worked by Saint Albon. The king believes their story; Gloucester cleverly reveals their decep-

tion and sentences them to be whipped. Buckingham enters and announces the arrest of the duchess of Gloucester for consorting with witches and plotting the downfall of the king. The king banishes her for life, orders the other conspirators to be executed, and strips Gloucester of his role as Lord Protector. The duke of Gloucester speaks with his wife as she goes to her banishment; she predicts his downfall at the hands of his enemies. In a brief scene in between the announcement of the duchess's crime and her punishment, York explains to Salisbury and his son, Warwick, why his claim to the throne is superior to the king's. They swear allegiance to York. Meanwhile Gloucester is summoned to appear at the next session of Parliament.

Act III:

In Parliament, the queen, Suffolk, Winchester, Buckingham, and York outline the supposed faults in Gloucester that should lead the king to arrest him. The queen argues that Gloucester is an ambitious man and therefore dangerous. Suffolk speaks of Gloucester as deceitful and suggests he may have had a role in the duchess of Gloucester's plot against the king. Winchester, York, and Buckingham also make note of Gloucester's alleged offences, but the king defends Gloucester. Somerset, the regent in France, enters to announce that all the English lands in France have been lost. Gloucester enters and is arrested by Suffolk for high treason. The king makes no effort to save Gloucester even though he thinks him loyal, but leaves the stage distracted with grief. The queen, Suffolk, York, and Winchester decide to kill Gloucester before he even comes to trial. A messenger enters to announce that a dangerous rebellion has broken out in Ireland; the nobles decide to send York to quell the uprising. York sees this as an opportunity to win the crown and mentions the workers' uprising led by Jack Cade that will soon occur and which he has incited. Two murderers, on the orders of Suffolk and Winchester, kill Gloucester and try to make it look like a natural death. Warwick examines Gloucester's body, explains why it is clear that he was murdered, and accuses Suffolk and Winchester of the crime. Suffolk and Warwick fight. Salisbury enters to announce that the common people want Suffolk to be banished or put to death for the murder of Gloucester, whom they loved. In response, the king banishes Suffolk from England. Vaux enters to announce that Winchester is near death from a sudden illness. On his deathbed, Winchester admits to the king, Salisbury, and Warwick that he is guilty of Gloucester's murder.

Act IV:

Suffolk is captured by pirates and executed. Cade and his men enter. Before he fights the king's men led by Sir Humphrey Stafford and his brother, Cade awards himself a knighthood and names himself Sir John Mortimer (a legitimate claimant to the throne). The two sides fight; Cade's is victorious. The king and queen accompanied by Buckingham and Lord Say are told of the rebels' progress and demands; the queen bemoans the death of Suffolk, whose head is brought in. The rebels' successes continue so that the king has to retreat to Killingworth. The rebels, led by an increasingly power-mad Cade, capture Lord Say and his son-in-law and execute both. Buckingham and Lord Clifford parley with Cade and his men. Cade's men go over to the king's side, persuaded by the promise of a pardon and patriotic talk of the need to fight in France not in England. Cade flees, goes into hiding, and is killed by a landowner, Alexander Iden, who finds him stealing food from his garden. In the meantime, York has returned from Ireland with an army and demanded that the traitorous Somerset be arrested. The king sends Buckingham to parley with York and orders Somerset to be confined in the Tower of London.

Act V:

Camped at Saint Albons, York is temporarily appeased at Buckingham's news that Somerset has been imprisoned in the Tower. Then the queen enters accompanied by Somerset, who is clearly free. In a rage, York asserts his right to the throne. Somerset arrests him for treason, and the nobles line up in support of one group or the other. The Cliffords side with the king; York's sons, Edward and Richard, support their father as do Warwick and Salisbury. The two sides fight at the battle of Saint Albons. York and his supporters win. Old Clifford is slain by York; young Clifford (who discovers his father's body) swears brutal vengeance on York and his family. Richard, son of York and the future Richard III, kills Somerset. The king and queen flee back to London. York and his allies follow in hot pursuit intent on capturing the king before he can hold a parliament and declare them traitors.

Modern Connections

Although Shakespeare wrote for an earlier time, his concerns are so well staged and so poetically presented that they produce powerful echoes for a late twentieth-century audience whose knowledge of the Wars of the Roses is slight at best. *Henry VI, Part Two* is preoccupied with three issues of contemporary relevance: the definition of legitimate authority; the requirements for good government; and the role of the family.

England under Henry VI is in chaos. In part this chaos is the result of Henry VI's uncertainty about whether his right to the crown is legitimate. The duke of York certainly has a better claim based on blood (he traces his line back to a son of Edward III who was older than the son from whom Henry VI derives his claim), but Henry VI has a better claim based on power (his grandfather, Henry IV, overthrew Richard II).

In democratic countries power is derived from the ballot box, but there have been several occasions in recent times in Europe and elsewhere when charges of voter fraud or tampering with the ballot box have made it uncertain who is the legitimate leader. One need think only of events in the former Yugoslavia as an instance. In 1996, for example, Slobodan Milosevic used the Serbian Supreme Court to validate some election results that were favorable to him but questionable. More subtly, one can speculate on what form of the vote best represents the balance of power in a country. Proportional representation most accurately registers the patchwork of opinion in any given country, but that method has led Italy, for example, to change its government more than once a year since the end of the Second World War. From another perspective, one can ask whether a minority government should be allowed to rule in a democracy. Such a government was in power in Britain, for example, in 1979 and 1996. The question comes down to how one defines legitimate authority. That question applies as much to modern democracies or republics as to fifteenth-century monarchies.

England under Henry VI is in chaos for another reason, however. Henry VI governs poorly. He is unable to exert the authority that he has as king. For example, when Suffolk arrests Gloucester on trumped-up charges (III.i.95-222), the king does nothing to stop the arrest even though he knows that Gloucester is loyal. Instead, he simply leaves the stage in tears, unable to cope. Later, in III.ii.236-41, when Warwick and Winchester duel in his presence, the king merely issues the mildest of rebukes. When it comes to decisions, the king simply agrees to what his influential subjects want (III.i.316-17). As a monarch, Shakespeare's Henry VI fails to make the effective decisions that result in good government.

Modern democracies and republics are faced by the same need for effective decision making, but that need has not always been fulfilled. John Major in Britain has not, many feel, been as effective as Margaret Thatcher in making the sort of consistent decisions that Prime Ministers are expected to make. In the United States, polls have indicated that people feel that the House of Representatives and the Senate sometimes create gridlock rather than pass legislation, and that President Clinton, like other presidents before him, has sometimes failed to steer a clear course for the nation. The same sorts of criticisms were leveled at earlier presidents such as Grant, Wilson, Hoover, and Coolidge.

Besides the question of how power is derived and used, *Henry VI, Part Two* devotes much time to the role of family. On the one hand, the prominence of family causes unflattering comparisons: Henry VI is in no way a match for his father, Henry V (perhaps the most beloved monarch in English history). On the other, it becomes a means to perpetuate revenge. *Henry VI, Part Three* has, as a major theme, the importance of vengeance in a society where the idea of legal justice has yet to be fully developed. The end of *Henry VI, Part Two* foreshadows that theme in the death of old Clifford at York's hands and the bloodthirsty cry of revenge from his son. Young Clifford will be merciless:

> Henceforth I will not have to do with pity.
> Meet I an infant of the house of York,
> Into as many gobbets will I cut it
> As wild Medea young Absyrtus did;
> In cruelty will I seek out my fame.
>
> (V.ii.56-60)

Although such a statement is an extreme one, any audience watching this play can probably think of examples of these two issues: the difficulty of the son living up to the father's expectations, and the families that feud with one another long after the initial cause of conflict has been forgotten.

Characters

Aldermen:

These non-speaking characters appear at II.i.65. They enter carrying the crippled Simpcox, who has supposedly regained his sight through a miracle.

Asmath:

See Spirit

Attendants:

These non-speaking characters appear in a couple of scenes (III.ii and IV.viii) to add to the importance of the nobility.

Beadle:

He appears at II.i.144 to whip Simpcox so as to discover whether he is truly lame.

Beauford (Cardinal Beauford, Bishop of Winchester):

Usually referred to as Winchester in the play, he is mercilessly ambitious and a "proud prelate," as Gloucester terms him (I.i.142). His sole concern is power; this he tries to achieve with the aid of Suffolk. He is the first to urge that Gloucester's Lord Protectorship be taken away from him (I.i.147-64), and he schemes with Suffolk to achieve that end. In I.iii.128-29, he seconds Suffolk's call for Gloucester's resignation, alleging his over-taxation of the laity and the clergy. In II.i.14-52, he continues his battle with Gloucester even to the point of agreeing to a duel. Such a fight, however, never takes place, for when the duchess of Gloucester is banished for witchcraft and treason (II.iii.1-4, 9-13) after falling foul of a trap laid by Winchester and Suffolk (I.ii.93-101), the king strips Gloucester of his Lord Protectorship (II.iii.22-27).

For Winchester and several other nobles, however, to see Gloucester stripped of authority is not enough. They want him tried for treason. In III.i, they try to persuade the king that Gloucester is a traitor. Suffolk arrests him, and without serious protest from the king Winchester's men take him away to prison (188). That is still not enough. Now, they want him dead, and Winchester and Suffolk pledge to do the deed (III.i.267-77). By the beginning of III.ii Gloucester has been murdered, and by the end of III.iii Winchester himself is dead from a "grievous sickness" (III.ii.370). Haunted by the ghost of the murdered Gloucester, Winchester's last words from his deathbed are to ask for poison with which to end the torture of a guilty conscience (III.iii.17-18).

Bevis (George Bevis):

He is the first of Jack Cade's men to make an appearance (IV.ii.1). He humorously points out the problems with the English government and be-

moans the lack of respect shown to workers. He brings in the captured Lord Say at IV.vii.23.

Bolingbrook (Roger Bolingbrook):

He appears in I.iv and with Southwell and Jordan conjures up a spirit who answers the duchess of Gloucester's questions about the fate of the king, Suffolk, and Somerset. He is arrested at I.iv.41, and condemned by the king to death by hanging (II.iii.8).

Buckingham (Duke of Buckingham):

He is one of the nobles whose actions collectively weaken the king's ability to govern. In the first scene of the play he reveals how much he wants to get rid of Gloucester, Lord Protector to the king (169). He next appears in I.iii discussing with the king and his nobles who should be the regent in France. He appears to favor Somerset over York, but his real concern is with the ruin of Gloucester. This he thinks he can achieve through destroying Gloucester's wife, Eleanor (150-51). In I.iv he is on hand to arrest her for witchcraft and treason. In II.i he enters to tell the king of the duchess of Gloucester's arrest. He appears in III.i and adds his voice to the other nobles' who succeed in arresting Gloucester for treason.

He does not appear again until IV.iv when he persuades the king to retreat to safety at Killingworth in face of Cade's advance. He is responsible for persuading Cade's supporters to desert to the king's side (in IV.viii), and follows this by meeting York, newly returned from Ireland and with an army at his back. He tells York, wrongly it turns out, that the king has placed Somerset in the Tower of London (York's stipulation if he is to disband his army). He recommends in V.i that Alexander Iden be knighted for killing Cade, and is last invoked by the king (V.i.192) as one of his few remaining supporters. Overall, Buckingham is ambitious (I.i.202), and is used by Shakespeare to emphasize one of the crucial elements in the early part of the plot: the downfall of Gloucester. After that is accomplished, Buckingham's role decreases in importance.

Cade (Jack Cade, also known as John Cade):

Cade's extraordinary attempt to overthrow the king occupies almost all of the action in Act IV, and he even makes an appearance (at least his head does!) in V.i.63. He is first referred to by York in a soliloquy (III.i.348-81). York has "seduc'd" (that is, incited) John Cade to cause civil unrest while York is away in Ireland. Cade will pretend to be

John Mortimer, a claimant to the throne through Lionel, duke of Clarence (the third son of Edward III). York praises Cade for his physical strength, his courage, and his ability to withstand torture.

Before Cade makes his first appearance, then, he is depicted as tough; York, however, makes it clear that he is also "headstrong" and a "rascal" (III.i.356, 381). Throughout Cade's many appearances in Act IV, Shakespeare develops these two sides of Cade and adds a third: his radical social message. Cade's first entrance (IV.ii.31) is preceded by a discussion between two of his followers that emphasizes Cade's revolutionary ideas (IV.ii.4-6). His concern for creating a system based on strict equality and a fair price for food is, however, expressed in the context of a humorous dialogue about his origins. He insists he is of royal blood (a Mortimer); his followers comment on the humbleness of his background and his conviction for sheep stealing. Worse, his belief in equality is undermined by his insistence on becoming a king. Everyone will be equal except Jack Cade. He even begins his quest for kingship in a comical way, by knighting himself as Sir John Mortimer (IV.ii.119-21) in order to better fight Sir Humphrey Stafford, his brother William, and their forces. Yet, there is no denying how radical Cade's message is: he intends the death of all the educated and the rich (IV.iv.36-37).

Cade is also a murderously violent man. His first goal is to murder all the lawyers (IV.ii.76-78); his first murder is actually of a clerk whose only crime is being able to write. His next victims are the Staffords, whom he drags behind his horse to London. Then he has a soldier killed simply for calling him Jack Cade (IV.vi.8-10). After that, it's the turn of Lord Say and Sir James Cromer. Lord Say is killed for pleading so eloquently for his life. Cromer is killed merely because he is a relative of Say's. Then both victims have their heads mounted on poles so that Cade can have them kiss in a humiliating way.

After Buckingham and old Clifford manage to separate Cade from his followers by promising the latter pardons and by appealing to their patriotic hatred of the French, Cade runs off, and after five days without food is caught stealing vegetables from a garden. The landowner, Alexander Iden, kills him because Cade insists on fighting. Even as he is dying, Cade has delusions of his own importance and prowess, for he asserts that he is Kent's "best man" (IV.x.73) and would not have been defeated had he not been weak from starvation.

> **Haunted by the ghost of the murdered Gloucester, Winchester's last words from his deathbed are to ask for poison with which to end the torture of a guilty conscience (III.iii.17-18)."**

It is important to reflect on what Shakespeare may have intended by his tremendously vivid depiction of Cade and his "rabblement" (IV.viii.1). First, he may have meant to show the social dangers of weak government embodied in a diffident king and fractious nobles. Second, he may have meant the audience to compare Cade's tactics and behavior with those of so many of the nobles (Suffolk, Somerset, York, Buckingham, and others). Third, he may have meant to undermine Cade's radical social message by having ideas of social equality come from the mouth of someone so disturbed.

Cardinal Beauford (Cardinal Beauford, Bishop of Winchester):
See Beauford

Citizens:
Two or three citizens appear in IV.v. One of them provides information to Lord Scales about the progress of Cade and the rebels.

Clerk (of Chartam):
Named Emmanuel, he appears in IV.ii.85-110. He is taken away to be hanged on Cade's orders because he can write his name. Shakespeare uses him to symbolize Cade's hatred of the educated.

Clifford (Lord Clifford):
He accompanies Buckingham in IV.viii when they successfully appeal to Cade's followers to stop their rebellion. He reappears in IV.ix, again in the company of Buckingham, to announce to the king the surrender of Cade's followers. In V.i he is the most obviously loyal of the king's subjects. In V.ii at the battle of Saint Albons he is killed by York but

> **"**Overall, Buckingham is ambitious (I.i.202), and is used by Shakespeare to emphasize one of the crucial elements in the early part of the plot: the downfall of Gloucester.**"**

memorialized by his son, young Clifford, in a powerful speech promising vengeance.

Clifford (Young Clifford):

The son of old Clifford (who is also known as Lord Clifford), young Clifford enters with his father at V.i.122 in support of the king and against York, York's sons (Edward and Richard), Warwick, and Salisbury. At the battle of Saint Albons he delivers a moving lament over his dead father's body (V.ii.40-60) and dedicates himself to avenging him by killing York's children. His final speech in the play (V.ii.84-90) exhorts the king, with the battle lost, to flee to London.

Commons:

Commoners appear in III.ii to protest the murder of Gloucester. Through the earl of Salisbury, they call for the execution or banishment of Suffolk whom they blame for Gloucester's death. Their role is to show the common people's love of Gloucester and concern for the safety of the king.

Dick:

From Ashford and by profession a butcher, he is one of Cade's followers. He first appears in IV.ii and in a series of asides makes fun of Cade's assertion that he is of royal blood. (An aside is a comment made by a character which is meant to be heard only by the audience and not by anyone on stage.) He wants all lawyers killed (IV.ii.76-77). For his prowess in the fight against the Staffords, Cade rewards him with a licence to butcher animals during Lent.

Duchess of Gloucester:

See Eleanor

Edward (son of Richard Plantagenet, the Duke of York):

One of two of the four sons of York mentioned in *Henry VI, Part Two,* he appears in V.i to support his father's claim to the throne.

Eleanor (Eleanor, Duchess of Gloucester):

She is the wife of Humphrey, duke of Gloucester, Lord Protector. She has ambitions for her husband and herself and dreams of being queen (I.ii.35-40). She uses witches (Jordan and Bolingbrook) to try to help her see the future, but her plans are betrayed by Hume, paid by her to organize the event. She is arrested in I.iv by York and Buckingham and banished for life by the king to the Isle of Man (II.iii.9-13). In her final appearance (II.iv.17-110), she says farewell to her husband and sorrowfully goes into exile on the Isle of Man.

Falconers:

These appear in II.i at the king's waterfowl hunt. They have non-speaking roles.

Gentlemen:

In IV.i. two gentlemen are captured by pirates. Both are ransomed for 2000 crowns. One remains on stage at the end of the scene in order to bear Suffolk's body to the king.

Gloucester (Humphrey, Duke of Gloucester):

Lord Protector to the king, he is loved by the common people (III.ii.248). Although he is heir to the throne and has an ambitious wife, he appears to have no desire to be king. Because of his power and position, he is the focus of the schemes of the other nobles. They see him as the main obstacle in the way of fulfilling their own ambitions.

In I.i Gloucester criticizes the peace with France and the king's marriage to a penniless Margaret. He tries in I.ii to dissuade his wife from treacherously seeking to overthrow the king. In I.iii.118-37 he defends himself against the queen's, Suffolk's, Somerset's and Winchester's efforts to strip him of his Lord Protectorship. When Simpcox pretends to have had his sight miraculously restored in II.i, Gloucester exposes him as a fraud even though the king embraces his deception. In II.iii, Gloucester is grief stricken at his wife's treachery towards the king, but makes no effort to intervene on her behalf. The king strips him of his Lord Protectorship, which he accepts willingly. In II.iv he movingly bids farewell to his wife as she goes off to banishment. In III.i Gloucester appears in Parliament and is arrested by Suffolk for treason. This comes after a sustained effort by the queen, Buckingham, Suffolk, Winchester, and York to convince the king that he is guilty of a host of crimes. He is taken away even though the king still believes him to be loyal. Gloucester is murdered in III.ii on the orders of Suffolk and Winchester.

Gloucester is depicted as the ideal courtier: honest; outspoken; loyal; loved by the people. There is no truth to the attacks of his enemies, yet those attacks finally bring him down and cause his death. Through Gloucester, Shakespeare seems to be making the point that the court of Henry VI has become so corrupt that not even loyalty and honesty offer protection for men of power. Additionally, the downfall of Gloucester serves as a means of unifying the action in the first three Acts of the play.

Goffe (Matthew Goffe):

He is sent by Lord Scales in IV.v to Smithfield to try to stop Cade's attack on London. In IV.vii he is slain along with all his men. He has a non-speaking part.

Guards:

Guards accompany Buckingham and York in I.iv as they break in upon the duchess of Gloucester who is practicing witchcraft in an effort to predict future events. They take the duchess and her accomplices prisoner.

Henry (King Henry VI of England):

Henry is depicted as weak, indecisive, and unable to keep his fractious nobles at peace with each other. He is highly religious and rather bookish, and seems ill-suited to a role in which decisions have to be made. Reluctance perhaps best characterizes his role.

He begins the play by welcoming his new bride, Margaret, and by confirming the peace with France. Both acts attest to Henry's foolishness: firstly, his love for Margaret appears to be based only on her beauty; secondly, the peace with France leads to a significant loss of English lands in France. In his next appearance, Henry is unable to decide whether York or Somerset should be his regent in France because he really doesn't care (''all's one to me'' [I.iii.102]). So, he simply stands by while his wife and assembled nobles argue among themselves. In

> **. . . there is no denying how radical Cade's message is: he intends the death of all the educated and the rich (IV.iv.36-37).''**

the end, he has Gloucester decide the matter (I.iii.203-10). Then, in II.i when Winchester and Gloucester wrangle with each other over power the king says that he hopes he can settle their argument, but he does nothing at all to achieve this aim. When Simpcox enters pretending that his blindness has been cured by Saint Albon, the king gullibly believes him (I.iii.82). It is Gloucester again who comes to the king's aid by exposing Simpcox as a fraud. In II.iii the king makes a good judgment by banishing the duchess of Gloucester, who is indeed plotting against him, but a poor one when he strips Gloucester of his Lord Protectorship. It is fairly clear that in doing so he has listened to the false charges against Gloucester raised by several nobles and the queen.

Perhaps the king sinks lowest when in III.i he allows Gloucester to be arrested for treason by Suffolk and taken away to prison even though he himself believes Gloucester to be loyal and his queen and many of the nobles to be seeking Gloucester's life (III.i.207-08). Characteristically, Henry refuses to act, and instead gives authority over to the nobles: ''My lords, what to your wisdoms seemeth best, / Do or undo, as if ourself were here'' (III.i.195-96). He does finally act, it is true, by banishing Suffolk for Gloucester's murder (III.ii.295-97). That, however, comes much too late; the damage has been done. It is this failure to assume his responsibility as monarch that indirectly leads to the Cade rebellion.

It is an indication of the king's failure to assert his authority that he scarcely appears after III.ii. Almost the whole of Act IV belongs to Cade, and the king appears only twice: once in retreat to Killingworth (IV.iv), and once merely acceding to York's demand that Somerset be imprisoned (IV.ix). However, even in this latter act the king fails, for though he does send Somerset to be imprisoned in the Tower of London, Somerset reappears in V.i

❝In III.i Gloucester appears in Parliament and is arrested by Suffolk for treason. This comes after a sustained effort by the queen, Buckingham, Suffolk, Winchester, and York to convince the king that he is guilty of a host of crimes. He is taken away even though the king still believes him to be loyal. Gloucester is murdered in III.ii on the orders of Suffolk and Winchester.❞

accompanied by the queen and very much a free man. The king is unable, also, to stop his nobles from choosing sides in his dispute with York and beginning a civil war. The final image the audience gets of the king (V.ii.72-90) is of someone unable to make a decision even when it comes to saving his own life. His wife and young Clifford have to persuade him to flee back to London from defeat at the battle of Saint Albons.

Yet, paradoxically, there is much to admire in the king. He is a very godly man who is singularly lacking in self-interest. He piously refuses to blame Winchester for his crimes (III.iii.31), is genuinely distraught at Gloucester's death (III.ii.141-45), and properly criticizes Salisbury for changing sides after swearing an oath of loyalty to him (V.i.179, 181). He even has enough self-knowledge to realize that he is an ineffective king (IV.ix.48-49). He is someone who lives in a profoundly evil world but believes passionately in purity of soul (III.ii.232-35). Sadly, he is someone who never wanted to be king though he has known no other life (IV.ix.3-6).

Herald:

He appears at II.iv.70-71 to summon Gloucester to a meeting of Parliament at Bury.

Holland (John Holland):

He is one of Cade's followers who, in conversation with George Bevis, criticizes the aristocracy

(IV.ii.1-30). His next and last appearance is in IV.vii where he makes fun in a couple of asides of Cade's intention to dissolve parliament and run the country.

Horner (Thomas Horner):

He is an armorer who is accused by his apprentice, Peter Thump, of saying that York was the rightful heir to the throne (I.iii.25-36). He and his accuser appear before the king (I.iii.177-220), and Gloucester sentences them to trial by combat. The combat takes place at II.iii.59-105. Horner is killed by his apprentice and confesses his treason with his dying breath (II.iii.94). The dispute between Horner and Peter Thump is meant to parallel the disputes among the nobles over the same issue. It shows how deep is the schism within the kingdom over who is the rightful king.

Hume (Sir John Hume):

A priest, he is paid by the duchess of Gloucester to arrange for Jordan and Bolingbrook to raise a spirit to foretell the future. He has, however, also been paid by Winchester and Suffolk to entrap the duchess (I.ii.68-107). This raising of a spirit takes place in I.iv, and Hume along with the others is arrested. He is brought before the king and sentenced to death by hanging (II.iii.5-8).

Humphrey (Humphrey, Duke of Gloucester):

See Gloucester

Iden (Alexander Iden):

He is the landowner (or esquire) from Kent who, in IV.x, surprises Cade as he is stealing vegetables from his garden. They fight, and Iden kills Cade. He carries Cade's head to the king (V.i.64-82), and is rewarded with a knighthood and 1000 marks.

Jordan (Margery Jordan):

She is described as a ''cunning witch'' (I.ii.75), and is responsible along with Hume, Bolingbrook, and Southwell for raising the spirit in I.iv who answers the duchess of Gloucester's questions about the king, Suffolk, and Somerset. She is arrested by Buckingham and York, and is sentenced by the king to be burned at the stake for witchcraft (II.iii.7).

Ladies:

These appear in the court scenes to increase their regality. They are mentioned in the character list at the beginning of the play but are not specifically referred to in the stage directions.

Lieutenant:

He is the leader of the pirates (in IV.i) who capture Suffolk as he is on his way to exile in France. He orders Suffolk's execution, and in a long speech (IV.i.70-103) criticizes Suffolk for committing adultery with the queen, losing France, causing the other nobles to rebel, reawakening York's claim to the throne, and creating rebellion in Kent.

Lords:

These appear in the court scenes to increase their regality. They are mentioned in the character list at the beginning of the play but are not specifically referred to in the stage directions.

Margaret (Queen Margaret):

Margaret, wife of Henry VI, is remarkable for her beauty and eloquence (I.i.32-33). She is motivated by two impulses: an ambition to work her will through the king, and her love for the duke of Suffolk. Queen Margaret conspires with Suffolk, Winchester, and others to overthrow the duchess of Gloucester (whom she sees as a rival) and Gloucester himself. She is the first (at III.i.223-34) to suggest that Gloucester should be murdered. She is a convincing liar (as at III.ii.56-71 when she pretends to lament Gloucester's death) and an effective manipulator (as when she turns the king's sorrow at Gloucester's death into a lament for the king's lack of love for her [III.ii.73-121]).

With Gloucester dead, she turns to her second impulse (her love of Suffolk) to guide her, for Suffolk is accused by the common people and by Warwick of murdering Gloucester. Here, her efforts fail, for Suffolk is banished by the king despite her eloquence in his defense. Now the queen is at her most sympathetic, for her parting with Suffolk seems heartfelt (III.ii.300-66) as does her grief when the head of Suffolk is brought in in IV.iv.

After the death of Suffolk, the queen virtually disappears from the play. She surfaces to challenge York's claim to the throne by refusing to accede to his demand that Somerset be imprisoned (V.i.85-86) and at the end steels the hesitating king to fly rather than wait to be captured (V.ii.74-77).

" Characteristically, Henry refuses to act, and instead gives authority over to the nobles: 'My lords, what to your wisdoms seemeth best, / Do or undo, as if ourself were here' (III.i.195-96)."

Master's Mate:

In IV.i he intends to ransom one of the gentlemen captured by the pirates for 1000 crowns (IV.i.17).

Mayor (of Saint Albons):

In II.i he brings in Simpcox and his wife to be presented to the king. He also summons the beadle, whose whip shows Simpcox to be a charlatan.

Messengers:

Messengers relay information between the various groups of characters within the play. Also known as "posts," they have most impact in relaying information about the Irish rebellion (III.I; IV.ix) and in showing how rapidly Cade's rebellion develops (IV.iv).

Michael:

One of Cade's men, he enters at IV.ii.110 to announce that Sir Humphrey Stafford and his brother with their forces have arrived to oppose Cade. He advises Cade to flee.

Murderers:

In III.ii, they enter after having murdered Gloucester. They point out how pious Gloucester was and tell Suffolk that they did commit the act in such a way that it could look like a natural death.

Neighbors:

In II.iii.59-65 neighbors appear in support of Thomas Horner, who is defending himself in trial by combat against a charge of treason made by his apprentice, Peter Thump. They are drunk and make Horner drunk, too.

"Queen Margaret conspires with Suffolk, Winchester, and others to overthrow the duchess of Gloucester (whom she sees as a rival) and Gloucester himself. She is the first (at III.i.223-34) to suggest that Gloucester should be murdered."

Officers:

In II.iv, officers accompany the duchess of Gloucester as she does her three days of open penance (II.iii.11) before being banished to the Isle of Man.

Old Clifford:

See Clifford

Petitioners:

In I.iii three or four of these wait to present their petitions to Gloucester as Lord Protector. By mistake, they present their petitions to Suffolk and the queen, who rudely dismiss them. Their petitions seek redress against wrongful acts by one of Winchester's men and by Suffolk. Their treatment contrasts with that they would have received from the Lord Protector. One of the petitioners is Peter Thump, whose petition against Thomas Horner is taken up again in II.iii.

Plantagenet (Richard Plantagenet, Duke of York):

He is a remarkable character in this play for he is the only one to be given soliloquies: two lengthy ones (at I.i.214-59 and III.i.331-383) and one short one (at V.i.1-11). (A soliloquy is a speech given by a character alone on stage directly to the audience in which the character's innermost thoughts are revealed.) York seems to have only one purpose in life: to successfully assert his right to the throne. In the first soliloquy he reveals that he will use the power of Salisbury and Warwick and pretend friendship to Gloucester in order to put himself in a position to gain the crown. In his second soliloquy he reveals his plans: to use his expedition to quell the Irish rebels as a means to wrest the crown from the king. To this end, he has incited Cade to lead a workers' rebellion against the king. In the third, he reveals his intent, having returned from Ireland, to seize the crown from Henry VI. He defeats the king at the battle of Saint Albons (V.ii-iii).

Post:

See Messengers

Prentices:

Named Robin, Will, and Tom, they appear in support of the apprentice Peter Thump in II.iii. They drink to Thump's success in trial by combat against Horner.

Queen Margaret:

See Margaret

Richard (son of Richard Plantagenet, the Duke of York):

The future Richard III, he enters at V.i.121 accompanied by his brother, Edward. They come on stage in support of their father, the duke of York, and his claim to the throne. In the battle of Saint Albons, Richard kills Somerset (V.ii.66-71).

Salisbury (Earl of Salisbury):

He is the father of the earl of Warwick. As the Neviles, they form one of the most powerful families in England (I.iii.72-74). In II.ii, Salisbury and Warwick support York's claim to the throne (9-52, 63). Before that crucial event, Salisbury is intent on trying to save Gloucester from the machinations of the queen, Buckingham, Suffolk, Somerset, and Winchester. After that he makes a very powerful enemy of the king.

Despite his power, Salisbury's role in the play is relatively small. He unsuccessfully supports York for the position of regent of France (I.i.194-98). He acts as the mouthpiece for the common people when they call for the banishment or execution of Suffolk for the murder of Gloucester. He (in company with his son, Warwick) goes over publicly to York's side in V.i. He ends the play victorious at the battle of Saint Albons.

Sawyer:

He is a follower of Cade's mentioned in the stage direction at IV.ii.30. His is a non-speaking role.

Say (Lord Say):

He is accused by Dick and Cade (IV.ii.160-73) of selling the dukedom of Maine and, so, ''geld[ing] the commonwealth'' (IV.ii.165). For this, they intend to execute him. He appears in IV.iv, where the king advises him to retreat with the royal party to Killingworth because of the hatred that the rebels bear towards him (IV.ii.19, 43-44). He, however, decides instead to go into hiding in London. Cade's men capture him in IV.vii, and he is executed along with his son-in-law, Sir James Cromer.

Scales (Lord Scales):

In IV.v he is the defender of the Tower of London against Cade. He sends a force led by Matthew Goffe to Smithfield in order to defend the city against the rebels.

Sheriff:

In II.iv, he commands the officers guarding the duchess of Gloucester as she does her three days of open penance (II.iii.11) before being banished to the Isle of Man.

Shipmaster:

In IV.i he intends to ransom one of the gentlemen captured by the pirates for 1000 crowns (IV.i.16).

Simpcox:

Supposedly unable to walk and blind since birth, he appears in II.i accompanied by his wife, the mayor of Saint Albons, and aldermen. He pretends that Saint Albon has cured his blindness, and is presented to the king. The king believes his pretence, but Gloucester demonstrates that he is a fraud and was never blind. In addition, a beadle with a whip demonstrates that he is not lame either, for he manages to run away (II.i.150).

Smith:

A weaver by trade, he is one of Cade's men. He first appears at IV.ii.30 and on three or four occasions in the next few scenes provides commentary on Cade's absurdities and excesses.

Soldiers:

These appear in numerous scenes beginning with Cade's rebellion, continuing with York's return from Ireland, and climaxing in the battle of Saint Albons with which the play ends. The most memorable soldier is the one who appears at IV.vi.6 and makes the mistake of calling on Cade by his real rather than his assumed name (John Mortimer). For this, Cade has his men kill him.

Somerset (Duke of Somerset):

At the beginning of the play, he sides with Buckingham against Winchester (I.i.172-77). Next, he lines up with several nobles against Gloucester (in I.iii). He, rather than York, is appointed regent of France by Gloucester at I.iii.205-06, and he returns to the action at III.i.82 having lost all the French lands. He is passed over to go to Ireland to quell the rebels there, and instead York is chosen (III.i.309). The king subsequently sentences him to imprisonment at the request of York who has returned from Ireland with an army (IV.ix.38-40). The queen, however, ignores the sentence and is seen by York accompanied by Somerset. Somerset's appearance causes York to assert his claim to the throne, and in retaliation Somerset arrests York for treason. The action degenerates into outright war, and in the battle of Saint Albons that follows Somerset is killed by Richard, son of the duke of York (V.ii.66-69).

Southwell (John Southwell):

He is a priest who, in I.iv, takes part in the duchess of Gloucester's raising of a spirit. York and Buckingham arrest him along with the others at the ritual. In II.iii.5-8, the king sentences him to be hanged.

Spirit:

Named Asmath, at the duchess of Gloucester's behest the spirit is summoned by Hume, Southwell, Bolingbrook, and Jordan in I.iv. It prophesies what will happen to the king, Suffolk, and Somerset (I.iv.24-40). Its prophecies prove true.

Stafford (Sir Humphrey Stafford):

He is the captain of the guard in I.iv that arrest those who summoned up the spirit at the behest of the duchess of Gloucester. He enters again in IV.ii along with his brother to stop Cade's rebellion. The two sides fight in IV.iii at Blackheath, and he and his brother are killed. Cade puts on Stafford's armor, and the brothers' bodies are dragged behind Cade's horse as the rebels march on London.

Stafford (William Stafford):

He is the brother of Sir Humphrey Stafford. Along with his brother, he enters in IV.ii to stop Cade's rebellion. The two sides fight in IV.iii at Blackheath, and he and his brother are killed. Their bodies are dragged behind Cade's horse as the rebels march on London.

Stanley (Sir John Stanley):

In II.iv, he accompanies the sheriff and his officers guarding the duchess of Gloucester as she does her three days of open penance (II.iii.11) before being banished to the Isle of Man. He is appointed by the king (II.iii.12-13) to protect the duchess during her banishment. He treats the duchess with sympathy (II.iv.94-95, 98-99, 105-06).

Suffolk (Duke of Suffolk):

The lover of Margaret, daughter of the duke of Anjou, he brings her back to England to marry King Henry and become queen at the beginning of *Henry VI, Part Two*. He also brings back the peace treaty with France, a treaty which displeases the nobility because it gives away part of France in payment for the king's bride and because Suffolk gets a fifteen percent commission for his efforts (I.i.133-34). As he announced at the end of *Henry VI, Part One* Suffolk's intent is to rule the kingdom through Margaret, and in *Henry VI, Part Two* he does his best to do so. He ensnares the ambitious duchess of York in witchcraft and treason and, so, manages to get her banished and as a result her husband stripped of his Lord Protectorship. He arrests Gloucester for high treason (III.i.97) and then schemes to have him murdered (III.i.257-65; III.ii.6, 8-12). His plan backfires, however, and the king banishes him despite the queen's attempts to intercede in his favor. On the way to banishment in France, he is intercepted by pirates and executed.

Thump (Peter Thump):

He is an apprentice to Thomas Horner, the armorer. He accuses his master of saying that York is the rightful heir to the throne (I.iii.25-36). He and

Horner appear before the king (I.iii.177-220), and Gloucester sentences them to trial by combat. The combat takes place at II.iii.59-105. Thump unexpectedly kills Horner, who is drunk, but not before he confesses his treason with his dying breath (II.iii.94). The dispute between Thump and Horner is meant to parallel the disputes among the nobles over the same issue. It shows how deep is the schism within the kingdom over who is the rightful king.

Vaux:

He enters at III.ii.366 on his way to tell the king that Winchester (Cardinal Beauford) is on his deathbed and that his soul is troubled by Gloucester's ghost.

Warwick (Earl of Warwick):

He is the son of the earl of Salisbury and comes from the powerful Nevile family. He is a more hotheaded version of his father. He bemoans the loss of the French provinces of Maine and Anjou as a result of the king's marriage to Margaret (I.i.116-22, 209-13); he strongly asserts York's claim to be regent in France (I.iii.107-08); and he criticizes Somerset for losing France (I.iii.173-74).

His vital role in the play begins, however, with his acceptance of York's claim to the throne (II.ii). From then on, he is York's staunchest ally. It is he who proves that Suffolk and Winchester plotted Gloucester's death (III.ii.149-241); it is he who castigates Winchester for a ''monstrous life'' (III.iii.30). And when York asserts his claim to the throne in V.i, it is Warwick who is the first not of York's blood to come out in support of him. The play ends after the victorious battle of Saint Albons with Warwick urging on York and Salisbury to get to London before the fleeing king and queen do.

Whitmore (Walter Whitmore):

In IV.i the lieutenant of the pirates gives Suffolk to Whitmore as his prisoner. Whitmore is intent on killing rather than ransoming Suffolk because he lost an eye in capturing Suffolk's ship. He takes him offstage at line 138 to execute him.

Wife (of Simpcox):

In II.i she supports her husband's fraudulent claim that Saint Albon cured him of his blindness.

When he is exposed as a fraud, she explains to Gloucester why they fabricated the deception: ''Alas, sir, we did it for pure need'' (II.i.154).

Winchester (Cardinal Beauford, Bishop of Winchester):
See Beauford

York (Richard Plantagenet, Duke of York):
See Plantagenet

Young Clifford:
See Clifford

Further Reading

Baker, Herschel. Introduction to *Henry VI, Parts 1, 2,* and *3,* by William Shakespeare. In the *Riverside Shakespeare,* edited by G. Blakemore Evans, 587-95. Boston: Houghton Mifflin Co., 1974.

> Baker points out the degree to which events in the first part of the trilogy play themselves out in the next two. He finds *Henry VI, Part Two* ''much more soundly built'' than *Henry VI, Part One.*

Bevington, David. Introduction to *The Second Part of King Henry the Sixth,* by William Shakespeare. In *The Complete Works of Shakespeare,* edited by David Bevington, 538-40. Updated 4th ed. New York: Longman, 1997.

> Bevington focuses on the play's ''integrity of theme and dramatic form.''

Cairncross, Andrew S. Introduction to *The Second Part of King Henry VI,* by William Shakespeare, edited by Andrew S. Cairncross, xi-liv. The Arden Edition of the Works of William Shakespeare. London: Methuen & Co., 1969.

> Cairncross discusses the ways in which Shakespeare brings organization to a complex, rather disorganized

story that he inherited from his chroniclers, Holinshed and Hall.

Calderwood, James L. ''Shakespeare's Evolving Imagery: *2 Henry VI.'' English Studies* 48 (1967): 481-93.

> Calderwood traces an improvement in Shakespeare's imagery in *2 Henry VI* from the rhetorical and static to the revelatory and active. He focuses on four image strands in particular.

Carr, William M. ''Animal Imagery in *2 Henry VI.'' English Studies* 53 (October 1972): 408-12.

> Carr sees animal imagery as reinforcing the play's themes of predator, prey, and protector.

Evans, B. Ifor. ''The Early Histories.'' In *The Language of Shakespeare's Plays,* by B. Ifor Evans, 31-44. London: Methuen, 1952.

> Evans sees Shakespeare's use of language in *Henry VI, Part Two* as stronger than in *Henry VI, Part One.*

Friend, E. M., Jr. '''The First Thing We'll Do, Let's Kill All the Lawyers.''' *Alabama Lawyer* 44 (September 1983): 276-77.

> Friend argues that Dick's comment in IV.ii of *Henry VI, Part Two* is an ironic indication of the centrality of lawyers to the maintenance of order in society.

Manheim, Michael. ''Silence in the *Henry VI* Plays.'' *Educational Theatre Journal* 29 (March 1977): 70-76.

> Manheim analyzes III.ii of *Henry VI, Part Two* to buttress his argument that Henry VI's silence makes him morally superior to the other major characters in the play.

Price, Hereward T. *Construction in Shakespeare.* Ann Arbor: University of Michigan Press, 1951.

> Argues that Shakespeare carefully ties all causes of discord to a weak ruler.

Riggs, David. ''The Hero in History: *2 Henry VI.''* In *Shakespeare's Heroical Histories: Henry VI and Its Literary Tradition,* by David Riggs, 113-27. Cambridge: Harvard University Press, 1971.

> Riggs argues for *Henry VI, Part Two* being the best part of the trilogy because of the variety of its action and because of its consistency.

The Third Part of Henry the Sixth

circa 1590-91

Act I:

York and his followers have won the first battle of Saint Albons, sending King Henry VI and his Lancastrian supporters to London in retreat. But York arrives in London first and, encouraged by his sons Edward and Richard as well as by Warwick, defiantly seats himself in King Henry's throne in Parliament. (York's claim to the throne, and the origins of the civil wars known as the Wars of the Roses, which were fought between the Yorkists—whose symbol is a white rose—and the Lancastrians—whose symbol is a red rose—are covered in Shakespeare's *Henry VI, Part One* and *Two*.) King Henry arrives with his supporters, and after debating with York over whose right it is to rule England, Henry finally promises to resign the crown to York and his heirs, provided that the civil war ends and that Henry is allowed to remain king during his lifetime. York agrees to these conditions and returns home to his castle, but Margaret, Henry's queen, is outraged that their son, Prince Edward, has been disinherited. Backed by Henry's disgruntled supporters, Margaret vows to continue fighting. Meanwhile at home in Yorkshire, York's sons convince him to disregard his oath to Henry, and to insist on being crowned king immediately. Margaret appears outside York's castle with a formidable army. Close by, her Lancastrian supporter Clifford drags York's youngest son, Rutland, away from his tutor and kills him

in revenge for the death of his own father, old Lord Clifford (old Clifford is killed by York in *Henry VI, Part Two*). Later, Margaret and Clifford capture, humiliate, and execute York, then place his head on a spike on his castle gates.

Act II:

York's sons Edward and Richard hear that their father has been killed and that Warwick's troops have retreated before Margaret's army. As the oldest son, Edward inherits his father's claim to the throne, and he, Richard, and Warwick vow to wage a counterattack. The two sides—Yorkist and Lancastrian—meet each other on the field and trade insults. The war rages on, with each side winning and losing battles. King Henry is ordered away from the fighting by Margaret and Clifford, who claim that his passiveness disheartens his army. Seated alone on a molehill, Henry dreams of trading his kingship for the simple life of a shepherd. He witnesses the horrors of civil war: a son grieving over the body of his father whom he has inadvertently killed in battle, and a father grieving over the body of his son whom he has likewise killed. After much fighting the Yorkists claim victory and the Lancastrians retreat. Clifford dies from an arrow in his neck, and York's three remaining sons (Edward, George, and Richard) taunt their enemy's dead body. Warwick arranges for Edward's coronation in London; afterwards, Warwick will go to France to contract a marriage between Edward and Lady Bona, the French king's sister-in-law.

Act III:

Homesick, Henry sneaks back to England from exile in Scotland, but is captured by two gamekeepers who are loyal to Edward because he is now king. Meanwhile, newly crowned King Edward IV lusts after Lady Grey. When she refuses to become his mistress, he decides to marry her—despite his planned engagement to Lady Bona and much to the amazement of his brothers George (who is now duke of Clarence) and Richard (now duke of Gloucester). Left alone, Gloucester (Richard, duke of Gloucester) muses over this imprudent marriage and reveals his own wicked ambitions to be king. In France, Margaret and her son, Edward (the prince of Wales), beg the French king, Lewis XI, for help in their struggle to reinstate Henry VI as king of England. They are interrupted by Warwick, who has arrived with his offer of marriage between Lady Bona and King Edward IV and an alliance between

France and England. This offer appeals to Lewis, and he rejects Margaret's request for aid, until a messenger appears with news of Edward IV's marriage to Lady Grey. Humiliated by King Edward's behavior, Warwick vows to abandon him and join forces with Margaret. Angry at King Edward's slight to his sister-in-law, Lewis agrees to aid Margaret and Warwick.

Act IV:

In England, King Edward and his new wife, Lady Grey (now Queen Elizabeth), meet with disapproval from their supporters. Several of them, including Edward's brother Clarence (George, duke of Clarence), leave to join forces with Margaret and Warwick. When fighting breaks out, Edward is captured by Warwick, who takes his crown and goes to free Henry and recrown him. Hearing of Edward's capture, a pregnant Queen Elizabeth flees to sanctuary. Meanwhile, Gloucester frees his brother Edward, and together they recruit troops from Holland. The recently released King Henry discusses strategy with Warwick and Clarence, to whom he has resigned government control. Shortly afterward, King Edward appears, arrests Henry, and sends him back to prison in the Tower of London.

Act V:

As Warwick awaits reinforcements, King Edward and Gloucester appear with their troops, and the two sides taunt each other. Clarence arrives in support of Warwick but after conferring with Gloucester, rejoins his brother Edward's cause instead. As Warwick's reinforcements arrive, the two sides agree to meet again on the battlefield. The battle rages, and Warwick is mortally wounded by King Edward. In spite of this loss, Margaret's forces begin to regroup, but Margaret and her son, Prince Edward of Wales, are captured. The defiant prince of Wales is stabbed and killed by King Edward and his two brothers. His grieving mother, Margaret, begs to be killed as well, but is led away under guard, eventually to be banished to France where she was born. Gloucester, meanwhile, goes to the Tower to assassinate King Henry. Before he dies, Henry prophesies that many people will ''rue the hour'' that Gloucester was born, and in fact, Gloucester has already begun to plot against his brother, Clarence (Gloucester's infamous rise and fall is presented in Shakespeare's *Richard III*). As the play closes, King Edward celebrates his victory and rejoices in his newborn son.

Modern Connections

Henry VI, Part Three begins with a debate between King Henry and York over which of them is the rightful king of England. The argument has its origins in the reign of Henry's grandfather, King Henry IV, a Lancastrian who came to power by usurping Richard II, grandson and direct heir of King Edward III. (Shakespeare's tetralogy of plays—*Richard II*, *Henry IV, Part One* and *Two*, and *Henry V*—dramatizes the ascendancy of the Lancastrians.) York can prove that his family tree follows a more direct line to King Edward III's throne than Henry's does; consequently, York has the right to rule England, while Henry, whose grandfather became king by force, should simply be the duke of Lancaster. This contention between the supporters of York (Yorkists—whose emblem is the white rose) and the supporters of King Henry (Lancastrians—whose emblem is the red rose) is what the Wars of the Roses are all about. In I.i.134, Henry admits to himself that his title to the throne is weak. So in I.i.194-200, he entails the crown to York and to his heirs "for ever," on condition that he be allowed to remain king during his lifetime, and that the Wars of the Roses be ended. York accepts this deal, declaring, "Now York and Lancaster are reconcil'd" (I.i.204).

Unfortunately, an end to the wars is not as simple as York and King Henry suggest. The contention began in *Henry VI, Part One*. The fighting has been long, bitter, and very bloody. Both Clifford and Northumberland, for example, lost fathers in the fight against the Yorkists in *Henry VI, Part Two*. In *Henry VI, Part Three*, "They seek revenge, and therefore will not yield" even though Henry and York announce that the conflict is over (I.i.190). Later, Clifford gets his revenge by brutally killing first York's young son Rutland and next York himself (I.iii and I.iv). The result is that York's remaining sons vow to avenge themselves on Clifford. When they find him already slain on the battlefield, they feed their rage by jeering at Clifford's dead body, chopping off his head, and putting it in place of their father's head on the gates of the town of York—thereby exacting "measure for measure" (II.vi.46-86).

Thus in *Henry VI, Part Three*, the fighting has gone well past its original purpose until what matters most is retribution (or, as Gloucester puts it after killing King Henry: "may such purple tears [of blood] be alway shed / From those that wish the downfall of our house!'' [V.vi.64-65]). To make matters worse, the two sides are evenly matched so that as Henry observes in II.v.1-13, neither side is "conqueror nor conquered," and the fighting drags on while Yorkists and Lancastrians take turns at winning or losing, and while fathers inadvertently kill their sons, and sons accidentally kill their fathers after they are drafted into the fighting on opposite sides.

This chaotic legacy of civil war is familiar to audiences today in, for example, the aftermath of fighting between the Hutus and Tutsis of east Central Africa and between the Serbs, Croats, and Bosnians of the former Yugoslavia. In both modern conflicts, innocent people have been brutalized, neighbors have betrayed neighbors, and the original political and ethnic reasons for the wars have been overshadowed by mass suffering as well as by the bitter, personal need for retribution and reparation which seems impossible to satisfy.

Another element contributing to the acrimony of the Wars of the Roses is that it is essentially a family feud. King Henry and York are distant relatives, as are many of the noblemen arrayed on either side. Toward the end of the play, as the seemingly endless war turns increasingly chaotic, the feuding also occurs within each camp. In IV.i, for example, George, the duke of Clarence, becomes outraged when his brother, the newly crowned Yorkist King Edward, imprudently marries Lady Grey; Clarence is further incensed when Edward gives special treatment to his new wife's relatives at the expense of his own brothers. In retaliation, Clarence joins the Lancastrians. (His defection is temporary, lasting only until V.i.81, but it comes back to haunt him later when his wicked and ambitious brother Gloucester uses this early disloyalty against him in Shakespeare's sequel, *Richard III*.) Today, most family feuds do not precipitate warfare; however, they can result in violence, and they frequently stretch over generations, engulfing grandparents, cousins, and siblings in resentment long after the original argument is forgotten, making family gatherings impossible or, at best, unpleasant.

Characters

Aldermen:

These characters, many of whom are without speaking parts, contribute to the regal, martial, and bureaucratic atmosphere of the play.

Attendants:

These characters, many of whom are without speaking parts, contribute to the regal, martial, and bureaucratic atmosphere of the play.

Bona (Lady Bona):

She is the sister-in-law to King Lewis XI of France. In III.iii, Warwick tries to arrange a marriage between Lady Bona and the newly crowned King Edward IV, thus hoping to form an alliance between France and England against the Lancastrians. This plan, however, is thwarted by Edward's precipitous marriage to Lady Grey. Stung by this insult, Lady Bona asks King Lewis to ally himself with Margaret against Edward, and, in revenge, hopes for the death of Edward's new wife (III.iii.212-13, 227-28).

Bourbon:

He is the high admiral of King Lewis XI of France. Although he is listed in the stage directions of III.iii, Bourbon has no speaking role. After Edward IV snubs Lady Bona by marrying Lady Grey, Lewis orders Lord Bourbon to ship a contingent of soldiers to England in support of Margaret and Warwick's fight against King Edward (III.iii.252-53).

Clarence (George, Duke of Clarence):

As one of York's four sons, George, duke of Clarence, is younger brother to Edward IV and older brother to Gloucester and Rutland. In *Henry VI, Part Three* he is listed by his first name until II.vi.104, when, in anticipation of his own coronation, Edward grants George the title of the duke of Clarence. As long as his father is alive, Clarence is staunchly loyal to him and thus to the Yorkist cause; however, he is impatient with his brother Edward's unwise marriage to Lady Grey, and is offended when Edward arranges advantageous marriages for Lady Grey's relatives but not for his own brothers (IV.i.47-58). As a result, Clarence breaks with Edward and joins Warwick and Margaret's cause (IV.i.118-23). His reward is Warwick's younger daughter in marriage (IV.ii.12). In V.i.81-102, Clarence switches sides once more, leaving his new father-in-law, Warwick, with the declaration, "I will not ruinate my [own] father's house," and apologizing to his brother King Edward for his temporary disloyalty. Along with his brothers, Clarence stabs and kills King Henry's son, Edward, the

> **Along with his brothers, Clarence stabs and kills King Henry's son, Edward, the prince of Wales (V.v.40). Clarence later appears in Shakespeare's sequel, *Richard III*, where he finally pays for his moment of betrayal when his scheming brother, Richard of Gloucester, uses it to turn King Edward against him."**

prince of Wales (V.v.40). Clarence later appears in Shakespeare's sequel, *Richard III*, where he finally pays for his moment of betrayal when his scheming brother, Richard of Gloucester, uses it to turn King Edward against him.

Clifford (Lord Clifford, formerly known as Young Clifford):

He is a supporter of the Lancastrian King Henry VI. At the close of *Henry VI, Part Two* his father (who is also known as Lord Clifford) is killed in combat by York. Thus in *Henry VI, Part Three*, the younger Clifford is consumed with thoughts of revenge. Vowing to kill York and all his relatives, Clifford begins by murdering York's young son, Rutland (I.iii). In I.iv, he participates with Margaret in the humiliation and execution of York himself. Described by his enemies as a "butcher" who is "unrelenting" and "bloody," Clifford dies from an arrow in his neck in II.vi, but not before prophesying that his death will leave the timid King Henry vulnerable to his enemies. When York's remaining sons discover Clifford's body, they taunt it with insults, hoping that Clifford is in fact still alive and able to hear them. Afterwards, they chop off his head and put it on the gates of York in place of their father's head (which had been set there earlier by Margaret and Clifford), thus answering "measure for measure" and underlining the play's theme of revenge (II.vi.46-86).

Edmund (Edmund, Earl of Rutland):

See Rutland

Edward (Edward, Earl of March, afterwards King Edward IV of England):

He is the oldest son of Richard Plantagenet, duke of York; thus when his father is killed at the close of I.iv, Edward inherits his title, York, as well as his claim to the throne of England. It has been noted that one of the play's themes is the opportunistic making and breaking of oaths, and as early as I.ii, Edward reflects this theme when, along with his brother Richard of Gloucester, he encourages his father to disregard his promise to King Henry by proclaiming himself king immediately rather than allowing Henry to reign until his death. Edward insists that "for a kingdom any oath may be broken: / I would break a thousand oaths to reign one year" (I.ii.16-17). Accordingly, in IV.vii, after he has been ousted by Warwick, Edward breaks his oath to the mayor of York that he will be loyal to Henry and satisfied with the title, duke of York; instead, at the urging of his supporters, he reconfirms his title as King Edward.

Edward's distinguishing trait is lasciviousness. In I.iv.74, Queen Margaret describes him as "wanton," and in II.i.41-42, his brother Richard jokes about his fondness for "breeders" (women). Once he is king, Edward's lust gets the better of him when he marries Lady Grey, thereby snubbing Warwick's efforts to arrange a diplomatic marriage between him and the French king's sister-in-law, Lady Bona, and causing the embarrassed Warwick to rebel against him (III.iii). By the close of the play, Edward has regained his title as king, and celebrates with "stately triumphs, mirthful comic shows, / Such as befits the pleasure of the court" (V.vii.43-44). He appears again as king in *Richard III*.

Edward (Prince Edward of Wales):

He is the young son and heir of King Henry VI and Queen Margaret. Throughout the play, he is more assertive, regal, and warlike than his father is. When Henry entails the throne of England to York and his heirs, Edward protests: "Father, you cannot disinherit me. / If you be king, why should I not succeed?" (I.i.226-27). When Margaret goes to war with York to regain her son's inheritance, the prince of Wales fights alongside her. Lancastrians such as the Earl of Oxford describe Edward as a "brave young prince" and are heartened that he resembles his "famous grandfather," King Henry V, rather than his timid father, Henry VI (V.iv.52-53). Prince Edward does not hesitate to let the Yorkists know what he thinks of them. He calls King Edward a "traitor" and demands that he resign the throne (V.v.18-21). He refers to King Edward's brothers as "perjur'd George" and "misshapen Dick," declaring, "I am your better, traitors as ye are" (V.v.34-36). The Yorkists consider the prince a "malapert" carbon copy of his mother, Margaret (V.v.32, 38). Prince Edward is stabbed to death by King Edward and his brothers in V.v.

Elizabeth (Queen Elizabeth, formerly Lady Grey):

Originally Lady Grey, she is a widow who becomes the wife of King Edward IV. In III.ii, Elizabeth arouses Edward's lust when, as Lady Grey, she comes to the palace asking for the return of her husband's lands which were confiscated upon his death in battle. Edward marries her after trying unsuccessfully to make her his mistress. This impulsive marriage sets off a series of events. It infuriates the king's staunch ally, Warwick, who is in the process of arranging a much more advantageous union between Edward and the French king's sister-in-law, Lady Bona. As a result, Warwick deserts Edward and joins forces with Margaret. The marriage also insults Bona and thus the French king, Lewis, who in retaliation supplies Margaret and Warwick with troops. Edward's favoritism to his new wife's relatives antagonizes his brother, Clarence, causing him to join with Warwick and Margaret in revenge. Finally, King Edward's announcement of his planned marriage to Elizabeth provokes a soliloquy from his brother, Richard, duke of Gloucester, which reveals his scheming nature and his ruthless determination to become king. (A soliloquy is a speech delivered by a character when he or she is alone. It is meant to reveal the character's mood, plans, or private opinions.) In IV.iv we learn that Queen Elizabeth has become pregnant; by the close of the play, she has given birth to King Edward's heir, "young Ned," or Edward (V.vii.16), who will be murdered by his ambitious uncle Gloucester in the last play of the tetralogy, *Richard III*.

Exeter (Duke of Exeter):

He is a supporter of the Lancastrian King Henry VI. In I.i Exeter reproaches York for sitting on King Henry's throne, but shortly afterwards, as York and Henry debate over who should rule England, Exeter realizes that York has the stronger claim. Nevertheless, he remains loyal to Henry, and is with him in IV.viii, when Henry is taken away to prison for the last time.

Father (who has killed his son):

He is a soldier in the Wars of the Roses who appears onstage in II.v.79-93 with the body of an opponent he has killed. When he searches the body for gold, he discovers to his sorrow that the man he has killed is his own son. This episode demonstrates the horror of civil war, where neighbors and relatives often find themselves fighting on opposite sides. It also shows how the common people of England are being sacrificed to the quarrels of the nobility, and that it hardly matters who wins as long as the fighting stops. As King Henry puts it after witnessing the father's grief, ''Wither one rose, and let the other flourish; / If you contend, a thousand lives must wither'' (II.v.101-02).

French King:

See Lewis

George (afterwards George, Duke of Clarence):

See Clarence

Gloucester (Richard, Duke of Gloucester):

Richard of Gloucester is a son of York (Richard Plantagenet); a younger brother to both Edward (afterwards, King Edward IV) and George, duke of Clarence; and an older brother to Edmund, Earl of Rutland. He is also a fierce defender of his father's claim to the throne: in I.i.10-16, after the first battle of Saint Albons, Edward and Montague present their bloodied swords as proof that they have killed Lancastrians; Richard, however, displays his victim's severed head. After York's death, Richard receives the dukedom of Gloucester from his oldest brother in anticipation of Edward's coronation; thenceforth, he is usually referred to as Gloucester. Gloucester has a malformed back and a withered arm; his enemies call him ''crook-back'' (I.iv.75; II.ii.96; V.v.29).

Although he appears as early as *Henry VI, Part Two*, Gloucester's villainy is not described until the middle of *Henry VI, Part Three*, after his father has died and his brother, the newly crowned King Edward IV, has unwisely chosen to marry Lady Grey. The likelihood that Edward will now produce an heir provokes Richard in III.ii.124-95 to soliloquize about his desire to rule England even though his chances of succession are slight. (A soliloquy is

Edward insists that 'for a kingdom any oath may be broken: / I would break a thousand oaths to reign one year' (I.ii.16-17). Accordingly, in IV.vii, after he has been ousted by Warwick, Edward breaks his oath to the mayor of York that he will be loyal to Henry and satisfied with the title, duke of York; instead, at the urging of his supporters, he reconfirms his title as King Edward.''

a speech delivered by a character when he or she is alone. It is meant to reveal the character's mood, plans, or private opinions.) Blaming his ''misshap'd trunk'' for his wicked intentions, Gloucester declares that he will scheme, lie, and murder to become king. By the end of the play, he has already disposed of two people who precede him in the line of succession: Henry VI and his son, Edward, prince of Wales. He disposes of the rest in the play which comes last in the Wars of the Roses tetralogy and which also bears his name, *Richard III*.

Grey (Lady Grey, afterwards Queen Elizabeth):

See Elizabeth

Hastings (Lord Hastings):

Described in IV.iii.11 as ''the King's chiefest friend,'' Lord Hastings supports King Edward IV against Warwick. In IV.i.39-46, he defends Edward's marriage to Elizabeth. As Warwick's brother-in-law, Hastings is asked by Edward to reaffirm his loyalty after Warwick changes sides, and he does so readily (IV.i.144). In IV.iii, Lord Hastings and Gloucester are able to escape when Warwick captures Edward in his tent. In IV.v, Hastings helps Gloucester free King Edward from his imprisonment, and later in IV.vii, he and Gloucester convince Edward to proclaim himself once more as

When Henry entails the throne of England to York and his heirs, Edward [Prince of Wales] protests: 'Father, you cannot disinherit me. / If you be king, why should I not succeed?' (I.i.226-27).''

king, despite Edward's vow to the mayor of York that he is loyal to Henry. Lord Hastings also appears in *Richard III*.

Henry (Henry, Earl of Richmond):
See Richmond

Henry (King Henry VI of England):

He is the Lancastrian King of England, the husband of Margaret, and the father of Edward, prince of Wales. His career as a youthful, reluctant, and ineffectual king unfolds in *Henry VI, Part One* and *Two*. At the beginning of *Henry VI, Part Three*, Henry enters the Parliament House and finds his rival, York, seated on his throne. After a brief debate, during which he acknowledges to himself that his claim to the throne is weak, Henry resigns his kingdom to York and his heirs, but reserves the right to be king as long as he lives. Henry's supporters are incensed at this capitulation. Calling him ''faint-hearted and degenerate,'' they hope that Henry will be ''overcome'' in ''dreadful war,'' or ''live in peace abandon'd and despis'd'' (I.i.183, 187-88).

To a certain extent, both of these curses are fulfilled. When Margaret renews the Lancastrian battle against the Yorkists, her central goals are to ''ruin'' them and to regain her son's inheritance (I.i.247-55). Supporters such as Clifford and, later, Warwick fight the Yorkists for personal revenge. Meanwhile, Henry serves as a figurehead who is otherwise ignored or despised. As Margaret and Clifford prepare in II.ii.67-75 for the battle of Towton, they ask Henry to leave the field. When Henry resolves to stay, his supporter Northumberland retorts, ''Be it with resolution then to fight''

(II.ii.77). Left alone and seated on a molehill as the fighting rages around him, Henry delivers his famous speech in which he reveals his peace-loving simplicity (II.v.1-54). Filled with pity, he deplores the ruinous effect of war on people's lives as he witnesses the agony of the son who has killed his father and the father who has killed his son (II.v.55-124). Henry has been described as saintly, and he can be credited with admitting that his rule has been disastrous to his people (although he blames this more on his fate, or ''thwarting stars,'' than on himself [IV.vi.21-22]). But he can also be self-pitying (II.v.123-24), and as he hands his inheritance to York in I.i, and his governmental powers to Warwick and Clarence in IV.vi, he demonstrates that he prefers the title of king to the authority of kingship. Henry VI is murdered by Gloucester in V.vi.

Huntsman:

He keeps watch over the captured King Edward in IV.v, but in fact functions more as an attendant than as a guard, not resisting when Gloucester frees Edward, and even agreeing to go along with them, lightly observing that it is ''better [to] do so than tarry and be hang'd'' (IV.v.26).

Keepers:

They are two gamekeepers who apprehend the homesick King Henry in a forest in northern England as he sneaks across the border from his exile in Scotland for a glimpse of the country he so recently ruled. Although he is disguised, the keepers recognize Henry because he talks as if he were a king (III.i.59), so they capture him and deliver him to King Edward. Part of their function in the play is to demonstrate the ''lightness,'' or fickleness, of the common people of England, who, according to Henry, willingly swear their allegiance to whomever happens to be in power at the time (III.i.89).

Lady Bona:
See Bona

Lady Grey (Lady Grey, afterwards Queen Elizabeth):
See Elizabeth

Lewis (King Lewis XI of France):

He is the king of France and the brother-in-law of Lady Bona. In III.iii, his promise to help Margaret reinstate the exiled King Henry is broken once Warwick arrives with a more expedient proposal: marriage between Bona and King Edward and thus an alliance between England and France. However, when news arrives of Edward's insult to Bona through his impulsive marriage to Lady Grey, Lewis vows revenge against King Edward and offers aid to Margaret and her new ally, Warwick. The ease with which Lewis forms, dissolves, and renews his promises underlines the play's theme of opportunistic oath-making and breaking.

Lieutenant (of the Tower):

He is a guard at the Tower of London, where King Henry is imprisoned each time he is captured. When Henry is freed from prison by Warwick, the Lieutenant asks to be pardoned for being the king's jailer (IV.vi.6-8). After Henry is jailed once more by Edward, the lieutenant makes another appearance (V.vi), only to be sent away by Gloucester, who is there to assassinate Henry in his prison cell.

Margaret (Queen Margaret):

Daughter of the French duke of Anjou, she is the wife of Lancastrian King Henry VI and the mother of Prince Edward of Wales. Margaret appears in all four plays of Shakespeare's Wars of the Roses tetralogy (*Henry VI, Part One, Two,* and *Three,* and *Richard III*). In *Henry VI, Part Three,* she is disgusted with Henry's passiveness and eager to protect her son's rights. When Henry entails his kingdom to York and his heirs (I.i.194-200), the outraged Margaret declares that he has not only disinherited his son from being king but also signed his own death warrant, arguing that York and his sons are too ambitious simply to wait until Henry dies of natural causes. Calling her husband a "timorous wretch" (I.i.231), Margaret levies an army and goes to fight the Yorkists herself, seeking as well to wreak vengeance on York for taking her son's inheritance. In I.iv, she captures and brutally torments York before killing him. When the Lancastrians suffer defeat and Henry is exiled to Scotland, Margaret seeks help from King Lewis of France and joins forces with Warwick after he is humiliated by King Edward. She is captured on the battlefield by Edward and his brothers, watches in grief as they kill her son, and is finally banished to France.

Margaret's Lancastrian allies depend on her strength of purpose: In I.i.182, after Henry entails

" Gloucester has a malformed back and a withered arm; his enemies call him 'crook-back' (I.iv.75; II.ii.96; V.v.29)."

away his throne, an outraged Clifford leaves to "tell the Queen these news," knowing that she will act. They also admire her courage on the battlefield (V.iv.39, 50). Margaret's Yorkist enemies condemn her ruthlessness, calling her the "She-wolf of France" and "a tiger's heart wrapp'd in a woman's hide," and suggesting that her son, Prince Edward, is illegitimate (I.iv.111, 137; II.ii.133-34).

Marquess of Montague:
See Montague

Mayor (of Coventry):

He accompanies Warwick on the walls of Coventry as Warwick waits for his allies against King Edward (V.i). Unlike the mayor of York, the mayor of Coventry does not speak in the play.

Mayor (of York):

Responding to Henry's brief reinstatement as king, the mayor of York locks the gates of the city against King Edward, explaining that "now we owe allegiance unto Henry" (IV.vii.19). Edward persuades the mayor to open the gates by arguing that he, too, is loyal to King Henry, and is simply returning home to claim his title as duke of York. However once inside the city and at the urging of his followers, Edward declares himself king, and the mayor does not object. Throughout the play, as one side or the other gains the upper hand in the Wars of the Roses, common people such as the mayor are faced with shifting their loyalty to those in power.

Messengers:

Most of the messengers in the play deliver news of the location and number of troops to the Yorkists or Lancastrians; however, the messenger in II.i.50-67 gives York's sons Edward and Richard a vivid description of their father's humiliation and death at the hands of Margaret and Clifford.

" Blaming his 'misshap'd trunk' for his wicked intentions, Gloucester declares that he will scheme, lie, and murder to become king. By the end of the play, he has already disposed of two people who precede him in the line of succession: Henry VI and his son, Edward, prince of Wales."

Montague (Marquess of Montague):

He is a brother of Warwick and a supporter of York. (Montague is referred to as York's brother during Act I of the play, but this is an error; for the rest of the play, he is correctly described as Warwick's brother.) After York's death, Montague remains loyal to the Yorkist cause until King Edward embarrasses Warwick and spoils the chance for an Anglo/French alliance by marrying Lady Grey (Elizabeth) instead of Bona. When questioned by King Edward in IV.i.135-43, Montague swears his continued allegiance; however, by IV.vi, he has joined with his brother, Warwick, to help Margaret reinstate King Henry VI. In V.ii.39-47, Somerset informs the dying Warwick that his brother Montague has been killed in battle.

Montgomery (Sir John Montgomery):

He is a supporter of Edward IV. His first entrance occurs after Edward has been toppled from the throne by Warwick. In IV.vii.40-75, Montgomery arrives in the town of York, ready with soldiers ''to help King Edward in his time of storm, / As every loyal subject ought to do.'' When at first, Edward tells him that he is not prepared to reclaim his title as king, Montgomery replies that he will withdraw his support and warn off anyone else from supporting him as well, arguing that there is no point in defending Edward if he refuses to be king. When Edward relents and announces himself king, Montgomery declares, ''Ay, now my sovereign speaketh like himself, / And now will I be Edward's champion'' (IV.vii.67-68). Among other things, this incident reflects the variety of reactions that the

nobility and the common people have when faced with the shifts in power during the Wars of the Roses.

Mortimer (Sir Hugh Mortimer):

He is an uncle and supporter of Richard, duke of York, as well as the brother of Sir John Mortimer. Although he does not speak in the play, he appears with his brother in I.ii.62, ready to fight Queen Margaret's army. In I.iv.2, we learn that Sir Hugh Mortimer and his brother were killed in battle while rescuing their nephew York—we hear this news from York himself, shortly before he is humiliated and killed by Margaret and Clifford.

Mortimer (Sir John Mortimer):

He is an uncle and supporter of Richard, duke of York, as well as the brother of Sir Hugh Mortimer. He appears with his brother in I.ii.62-65, declaring his readiness to ''meet [Queen Margaret's army] in the field'' rather than submit to a siege. We are told in I.iv.2 that Sir John Mortimer and his brother were killed in battle while rescuing their nephew York— we hear this news from York himself, shortly before he is humiliated and killed by Margaret and Clifford.

Nobleman:

This unnamed nobleman appears briefly in III.ii.118-19 to inform King Edward that King Henry has been captured while trying to reenter England from his exile in Scotland.

Norfolk (Duke of Norfolk):

He is a loyal Yorkist, supporting first York and then York's son Edward in their fight for the crown. Norfolk appears briefly in the play, speaking only a few lines.

Northumberland (Earl of Northumberland):

He is a loyal Lancastrian and a supporter of Henry VI. When Henry entails his crown to York and his heirs, Northumberland angrily leaves the stage along with Clifford and Westmerland, exclaiming ''Be thou a prey unto the house of York, / And die in bands for this unmanly deed!'' (I.i.185-86). All the same, York's humiliation at Margaret's hands and his grief at the death of Rutland move Northumberland to tears, and in contrast with the play's theme of vengeance, Northumberland asserts: "Had [York] been slaughter-man to all my kin, / I should not for my life but weep with him" (I.iv.169-70). At the end of the play he is listed among those who died during the wars (V.vii.8).

Oxford (Earl of Oxford):

He is a Lancastrian supporter of Henry VI, appearing with Margaret when she seeks aid from the French King Lewis in III.iii, and fighting alongside Margaret and Warwick against King Edward. In IV.vi, Oxford and Somerset take custody of young Richmond—"England's hope" and future king—and send him to Brittany where he will be safe from the civil wars with the Yorkists. Oxford is captured by Edward at the battle of Tewkesbury and imprisoned (V.iv-v). He appears in *Richard III* as a supporter of Richmond (Henry VII).

Pembroke (Earl of Pembroke):

He is a supporter of Edward IV. In IV.i.130-31, Pembroke and Lord Stafford are instructed by King Edward to levy troops against the rebellious Warwick. Like Stafford, Pembroke never speaks in the play.

Plantagenet (Richard Plantagenet, Duke of York):

Appearing in all three parts of *Henry VI*, York is a distant relative of King Henry (the two men share the surname, Plantagenet) and a claimant to the English throne. He is also father to the future King Edward IV as well as to George of Clarence, Richard of Gloucester, and Edmund of Rutland. Fresh from victory at the first battle of Saint Albons (which occurred in *Henry VI, Part Two*), York seats himself on Henry's throne in Parliament in I.i of *Henry VI, Part Three* and asserts his right to rule—a claim which even some of Henry's supporters admit is just. Henry's ally Clifford, however, articulates the play's theme of vengeance when he vows that, right or wrong, he will defend Henry's claim rather than "kneel to him [York] that slew my father!" (I.i.162).

York is captured by Margaret and Clifford in I.iv and forced to undergo a humiliating mock coronation, complete with paper crown, before he is executed. Margaret also presents him with a handkerchief soaked in the blood of his youngest son, Rutland. York's ensuing grief-filled speech moves

> **After a brief debate, during which he acknowledges to himself that his claim to the throne is weak, Henry resigns his kingdom to York and his heirs, but reserves the right to be king as long as he lives. Henry's supporters are incensed at this capitulation. Calling him 'faint-hearted and degenerate,' they hope that Henry will be 'overcome' in 'dreadful war,' or 'live in peace abandon'd and despis'd' (I.i.183, 187-88). . . . To a certain extent, both of these curses are fulfilled."**

one Lancastrian adversary—Northumberland—to tears. Clifford and Margaret's vengeful killing of York is answered later by vengeance from York's sons.

Posts:

These are express messengers. In III.iii.163-66, a Post delivers letters to Lewis XI, Warwick, and Margaret informing them of King Edward's marriage to Lady Grey. The result is that an embarrassed Warwick, an insulted Lewis, and a triumphant Margaret join forces against Edward. The same Post returns their angry challenges to Edward in IV.i.86-149, causing Clarence's defection. In IV.vi.78-85, a Post informs Warwick that King Edward has escaped imprisonment, ushering in the play's final defeat of Warwick and the Lancastrians.

Richard (afterwards Richard, Duke of Gloucester):

See Gloucester

Richard (Richard Plantagenet, Duke of York):

See Plantagenet

" The ease with which Lewis forms, dissolves, and renews his promises underlines the play's theme of opportunistic oath-making and breaking.**"**

Richmond (Henry, Earl of Richmond):

He is a child who makes his one and only entrance in IV.vi, under the protection of the duke of Somerset. Although Richmond never speaks, he is noticed by King Henry, who has just been released from prison by his new ally, Warwick. Calling the child "England's hope," King Henry accurately predicts that the Lancastrian Richmond will someday be king (IV.vi.68). In fact, Richmond appears as an adult in Shakespeare's sequel, *Richard III*, where he defeats and kills the corrupt King Richard (formerly Richard, duke of Gloucester) at Bosworth Field—in the final battle of the Wars of the Roses—and unites the country under his leadership as Henry VII.

Rivers (Lord Rivers):

He is Queen Elizabeth's brother. Rivers appears briefly in IV.iv, to be told by Elizabeth that her husband Edward IV has been captured by Warwick, and that she is pregnant with "King Edward's fruit, true heir to th' English crown." Rivers then flees with his sister to sanctuary. He appears again in *Richard III*.

Rutland (Edmund, Earl of Rutland):

He is the youngest son of Richard, duke of York. Rutland becomes a victim of the civil wars' ferocity and vengeance when in I.iii, Clifford takes the child from his tutor and murders him to avenge the death of his father, old Lord Clifford, who was killed by York in *Henry VI, Part Two*. In I.iv.78-90, Margaret taunts York with a handkerchief that has been dipped in Rutland's blood.

Soldiers:

These characters, many of whom are without speaking parts, contribute to the regal, martial, and bureaucratic atmosphere of the play.

Somerset (Duke of Somerset):

He is a follower of Edward IV but, along with Clarence, joins Warwick after Edward IV imprudently marries Lady Grey (Elizabeth). In IV.vi, he has the young Lancastrian, Richmond (future king of England), under his protection, and he enlists the help of Oxford to send the child to Brittany where he will be safe from King Edward IV. Somerset is captured at the battle of Tewkesbury by King Edward and executed for his defection (V.iv-v).

Somervile (Sir John Somervile):

He is one of Warwick's allies in his fight against King Edward IV. In V.i, Somervile informs Warwick of the location and progress of his gathering forces, and he witnesses alongside Warwick the unwelcome arrival of King Edward and his troops.

Son (who has killed his father):

He is a soldier in the Wars of the Roses who appears onstage in II.v.55-78, dragging the body of an opponent he has killed. When he searches the body for money, he discovers to his dismay that the man he has killed is his own father. This episode demonstrates the horror of civil war, where neighbors and relatives often find themselves fighting on opposite sides. It also shows how the common people of England are being sacrificed to the quarrels of the nobility, or as the witnessing King Henry puts it, "Whiles lions war and battle for their dens, / Poor harmless lambs abide their enmity" (II.v.74-75).

Stafford (Lord Stafford):

He is a supporter of King Edward IV. Stafford speaks no lines in the play, but in IV.i.130-31, he and his fellow nobleman the Earl of Pembroke are ordered by King Edward to levy soldiers for battle against Warwick, who has deserted Edward and joined forces with Margaret.

Stanley (Sir William Stanley):

He is a supporter of Edward IV and, along with Hastings and Gloucester, frees Edward from captivity in IV.v.

Tutor:

He is a chaplain as well as the tutor of York's young son Edmund, Earl of Rutland. When Clifford appears in I.iii seeking revenge, the tutor wants to stay and protect his young charge, but Clifford has him dragged away, declaring that his connection with the Church will save him, but not Rutland. The tutor's presence in this scene draws attention to Rutland's youthfulness and thus to Clifford's extreme brutality for killing a child.

Warwick (Earl of Warwick):

He is York's staunchest ally, first appearing as his supporter in *Henry VI, Part Two*. In *Henry VI, Part Three*, Warwick defends and advises York during his bid to replace Henry VI as king. After York is killed by Margaret and Clifford, Warwick encourages York's oldest son, Edward, to declare himself king. With Edward's consent, Warwick arranges a diplomatically astute marriage between Edward and Lady Bona, sister-in-law to French King Lewis XI. However, Warwick is embarrassed in the middle of these negotiations by news of Edward's rash marriage to Lady Grey (III.iii.164-198); outraged at being treated so dishonorably, Warwick joins with Margaret and Lewis to depose Edward and reinstate Henry VI. Warwick is defeated and killed by King Edward in V.ii.

During the time that one or the other has his support, first Edward and later Henry confer significant powers on Warwick: in II.vi.104-05, Edward decrees that "Warwick, as ourself, / Shall do and undo as him pleaseth best," and in IV.vi.41, King Henry makes Warwick co-Protector of the realm, along with Clarence. At one point, Margaret calls Warwick the "proud setter-up and puller-down of kings" (III.iii.157). Warwick himself sums up his career as he is dying: "For who liv'd king, but I could dig his grave? / And who durst smile when Warwick bent his brow?" (V.ii.21-22).

Watchmen:

They guard King Edward IV's tent at night as he waits to do battle with Warwick. The conversation between the three of them provides useful introductory information to IV.iii: namely, that Edward will not go to bed until either he or his enemy Warwick is defeated, and that Warwick is close at hand with his army. The watchmen are comical because shortly after they boast about their duties as guards, Warwick and his men chase them off and capture King Edward in his tent.

Westmerland (Earl of Westmerland):

He is a supporter of Henry VI. When Henry entails his throne to York, Westmerland calls him

> **Margaret's Yorkist enemies condemn her ruthlessness, calling her the 'She-wolf of France' and 'a tiger's heart wrapp'd in a woman's hide,' and suggesting that her son, Prince Edward, is illegitimate (I.iv.111, 137; II.ii.133-34)."**

"base, fearful, and despairing," and leaves the stage in disgust, declaring "I cannot stay to hear these articles" (I.i.178, 180, 183-84).

York (Richard Plantagenet, Duke of York):

See Plantagenet

Further Reading

Baker, Herschel. Introduction to *Henry VI, Parts 1, 2,* and *3,* by William Shakespeare. In the *Riverside Shakespeare*, edited by G. Blakemore Evans, 587-95. Boston: Houghton Mifflin Co., 1974.

> Baker provides a discussion of all three plays, as well as a useful family tree of the descendants of King Edward III. He calls *Henry VI, Part Three* "a play of battles, each more savage than the last," and describes Shakespeare's characterization of Richard of Gloucester as a "new advance" in the playwright's skills.

Bergeron, David M. "The Play-within-the Play in *3 Henry VI.*" *Tennessee Studies in Literature* 22 (1977): 37-45.

> Bergeron demonstrates how the inclusion of theatrical details makes I.iv, II.v, III.i, and III.ii function to a certain extent as plays within *Henry VI, Part Three*.

Bevington, David. Introduction to *The Third Part of King Henry the Sixth*, by William Shakespeare. In *The Complete Works of Shakespeare*, edited by David Bevington, 584-85. Updated 4th ed. New York: Longman, 1997.

> Treating *Henry VI, Part Three* as "a play in its own right," Bevington examines the themes of revenge and oath-breaking, comments on the absence of heroes in the play, and focuses upon the dominance of Richard of Gloucester.

Kelly, Faye L. "Oaths in Shakespeare's *Henry VI* Plays." *Shakespeare Quarterly* 24 (Autumn 1973): 357-71.

> Kelly discusses the frequency with which oaths are made and broken in each of the *Henry VI* plays, and

she points out that in *Henry VI, Part Three*, broken vows are used to highlight the chaos which occurs when lawful succession and group allegiances are cast aside.

Manheim, Michael. "Silence in the *Henry VI* Plays." *Educational Theatre Journal* 29 (March 1977): 70-76.
Manheim views King Henry's silence in a positive light, arguing that it is a sign of his honesty and humanity—traits lacked by other, noisier, characters in the play. Manheim draws on I.i in *Henry VI, Part Three* to support his discussion.

Norvell, Betty G. "The Dramatic Portrait of Margaret in Shakespeare's *Henry VI* Plays." *West Virginia Association of College English Teachers. Bulletin* 8 (Spring 1983): 38-44.
Norvell argues that Margaret is a complex character with a variety of roles, such as lover, Machiavellian, mother, and military leader.

Sanders, Norman. Introduction to *The Third Part of King Henry the Sixth*, by William Shakespeare, edited by Norman Sanders, 7-37. The New Penguin Shakespeare. Harmondsworth: Penguin Books Ltd., 1981.
Sanders discusses the interconnected issues of family vengeance and civil war that occur in the play, and how these issues undermine and alter the system of royal succession. Sanders also examines the dominance of Richard, duke of Gloucester, in the play, glancing ahead to Gloucester's title role in Shakespeare's *Richard III*.

Swayne, Mattie. "Shakespeare's King Henry VI as a Pacifist." *College English* 3 (1941): 143-49.
Swayne contends that we are meant to admire Henry VI for his focus on peaceful, private virtues rather than condemn him for his shortcomings when it comes to government and the battlefield.

Utterback, Raymond V. "Public Men, Private Wills, and Kingship in *Henry VI, Part III*." *Renaissance Papers* (1978): 47-54.
Utterback argues that the debate in I.i reveals the contradictions that the warring sides share when it comes to private attitudes toward and public precepts of kingship.

Watson, Donald G. "The Dark Comedy of the *Henry VI* Plays." *Thalia* 1 (Autumn 1978): 11-21.
Watson looks at the three parts of *Henry VI* and at *Richard III*, and contends that in each of these plays, dark comedy forces us to rethink our own ideas concerning the relationship between politics and morality.

The Famous History of the Life of King Henry the Eighth

Plot Summary

1612-13

Act I:

After the Prologue foretells that mightiness will meet misery, the scene opens in London, 1520, shortly after a sumptuous meeting of state in France. Buckingham asks an account from Norfolk, who describes an incredible display of riches, and credits Cardinal Wolsey for the spectacle. Buckingham expresses vehement dislike of Wolsey. Norfolk warns him against arousing Wolsey's anger. Buckingham continues, and Norfolk tries to calm him. Buckingham is arrested, and realizes he has been framed by Wolsey. At court, King Henry prepares to hear Buckingham's case, but is interrupted by Queen Katherine, who pleads on behalf of the commoners against a new tax. Ignorant of the tax, Henry questions Wolsey, who claims the Council approved it. Henry pardons the commoners. Buckingham's servant testifies against him. Despite Katherine's mistrust of the servant, Henry pronounces Buckingham a traitor. Later, the nobles eagerly anticipate Wolsey's banquet. At the banquet Anne Bullen flirts with the nobles. Henry and his men arrive, disguised, and Henry is struck by Anne's beauty.

Act II:

Outside Westminster, two gentlemen blame Wolsey for Buckingham's condemnation. Buckingham goes calmly to his execution, avowing his inno-

cence and loyalty, and forgiving his accusers. The gentlemen discuss rumors that Henry is divorcing Katherine, and again blame Wolsey. Henry welcomes Cardinal Campeius, who arrives from Rome to examine the divorce. In the women's apartments, Anne pities Katherine and swears she would not be queen. Anne's attendant doubts her sincerity, especially when Anne accepts the title Marchioness of Pembroke, offered by Henry. At the hearing for the divorce, Katherine throws herself at Henry's feet, begging to be remembered as a dutiful and loving wife. She asks that he spare her until she can seek advice from her friends in Spain, but Wolsey and Campeius rebuke her. Katherine names Wolsey her enemy and refuses him as judge. After she leaves, Wolsey asks Henry to clear his name. The king publicly excuses him, explaining that the divorce stems from his own misgivings about the legality of his marriage.

Act III:

Wolsey and Campeius offer Katherine counsel, but she declines, fearing betrayal. She says she has been a good wife, and grows angry as the two men continue to press her. They remind her that such stubbornness and disobedience do not become a queen, and she finally relents. Surrey returns to avenge Buckingham. Norfolk and Suffolk inform him that now is a good time to strike at Wolsey because Henry has accidentally intercepted a secret letter from Wolsey to the pope. Meanwhile, Henry has secretly married Anne. Henry discloses that he has accidentally acquired Wolsey's inventory, which reveals embezzlement. In soliloquy, a distressed Wolsey admits his worldly ambitions. When the nobles return to strip Wolsey of his office, he grows indignant, until they read the charges against him. A humbled Wolsey laments the inevitability of the fall of great men.

Act IV:

Two gentlemen exchange news as they admire Anne's coronation procession: Katherine is divorced and many nobles have been promoted. Another gentleman describes the coronation itself, remarking on Anne's beauty. In Katherine's new apartments, her servant Griffith describes Wolsey's death. Katherine falls asleep and sees a vision. Capuchius (an ambassador from Emperor Charles V) arrives with a message of comfort from Henry. Katherine thanks him, but says the comfort comes too late, as she is near death. She sends a message to Henry,

asking him to care for their daughter Mary and to reward her servants after she is dead.

Act V:

Gardiner (the secretary to the king) and Sir Thomas Lovell exchange news: Anne is in labor. Gardiner says that Cranmer, archbishop of Canterbury, will be called before the Council the next day on charges of heresy. Meanwhile, Henry promises Cranmer royal support and gives him a ring. Anne's attendant announces the birth of a princess. The next morning at the Council, Cranmer is made to wait outside with the commoners. Henry, displeased, eavesdrops on the hearing. Nobody dares accuse the archbishop, a fellow member of the Council, but Gardiner explains it is Henry's wish to imprison Cranmer and afterwards judge him as a private citizen. When guards come for Cranmer, he produces the king's ring. Henry enters the chamber. Gardiner flatters the king, but Henry rebukes him and orders them all to love Cranmer. At the palace, the porter complains about the crowd arriving for the christening. The baby is brought out in a sumptuous procession, and Cranmer predicts that the baby, Princess Elizabeth, will be a model of virtue, bringing blessings and prosperity to her kingdom. The king declares a holiday, and the Epilogue asks for the audience's applause.

Modern Connections

Upon first reading, *Henry VIII* seems obscure and inaccessible to modern readers. Its episodic plot leaps from one group of characters to the next, relying on the audience's background understanding of Tudor history to fill in the gaps. Despite its difficulties, however, the basic format of *Henry VIII* looks more familiar. It can be seen as an Elizabethan version of "Lifestyles of the Rich and Famous," a glimpse, although fictionalized, into the lives of the most famous public figures of the era. It examines the private and the public lives of England's rulers, and looks at what happens when personal likes and dislikes get tangled up with politics. Henry's desire to find a new wife is not just the story of a man having an affair; he is the king, and the woman he chooses will influence a nation and mother the heir to the throne. The squabble between Buckingham and Wolsey is not just the jealousy of two men competing for their boss's attention; the outcome is a matter of life and death and will determine whether nobles and commoners have equal right to rule. The popularity of stories about the personal lives of the powerful is borne out by the large collection of history plays written and performed during Shakespeare's time. Audiences wanted to know about the lives of their public figures, just as modern audiences are fascinated with the personal lives of the Kennedy family, or the British royal family.

For all its familiarity as a peek into the lives of the famous, *Henry VIII* contains qualities that are peculiarly Elizabethan. As much as a modern author or director might fictionalize the lives of modern leaders, for example in Oliver Stone's version of the life of John F. Kennedy, modern stories sometimes lack the moral tone prevalent in *Henry VIII*. Shakespeare's play belongs to a medieval tradition known in Latin as *de casibus illustrorum*, ''concerning the falls of great men.'' The typical *de casibus* story depicts a man rising to greatness and then falling at the whims of fortune. The story moralizes the fall, teaching that no amount of worldly power or wealth can survive the final stroke of fortune which is death, and that wise princes will amass spiritual wealth rather than scrambling after fleeting worldly goods. The falls of Buckingham, Katherine, and Wolsey all occur in the *de casibus* tradition; Wolsey especially seems to undergo a spiritual transformation after being stripped of his earthly power. In this sense, the play is meant to be a meditation for members of the audience to contemplate their own existence in the material world. The idea of renouncing material things can still be found in the major religions, in the Catholic Lent or the Islamic Ramadan, for instance.

But *Henry VIII* is not all serious moralization. It is also a celebration and a spectacle. Just as modern movies are often released in conjunction with holidays like Christmas or Thanksgiving, it is believed that *Henry VIII* was first performed during the wedding festivities of Princess Elizabeth, daughter of King James I. In keeping with the tone of celebration surrounding the wedding, the play is full of pomp and spectacle as it celebrates the glory of Henry's reign and his line of heirs that led to James I. Scenes such as Katherine's trial or Elizabeth's christening, in which troops of actors parade across the stage wearing the gorgeous robes of a noble or the gowns of a bishop, would have been equivalent to modern special effects: something visually exciting and very much out of the ordinary. The long list of characters includes many whose sole function is to add to the visual splendor of the play.

The play is not just about politics, it is itself a political act. Throughout the play, but especially in the final scene, Shakespeare celebrates the monarchy, the Tudor line, and the ascension of James I to the throne. Against the backdrop of others' falls, Henry remains steadfast, regal, and above the effects of fortune; he maintains the dignity of the monarchy. Cranmer praises Elizabeth in the final scene and describes her as a phoenix—a mythical bird that rises again out of its own ashes. He predicts that her virtues will be reborn in her heir, the very King James before whom the play was first performed. Flattering to the monarch, to his Protestant religion and to his triumph over the Catholics, the play is like a modern day campaign speech that extols the virtues of the leader and paints an unflattering portrait of his opponent.

Characters

Aburgavenny (Lord Aburgavenny):

Lord Aburgavenny is Buckingham's son-in-law, and he shares Buckingham's dislike of Wolsey. He corroborates Buckingham's charges against Wolsey, explaining that Wolsey bankrupted some of the nobles when he organized the visit to France (I.i.80-83). He is arrested with Buckingham.

Aldermen:

Not listed in the cast of characters, two aldermen are called for in the stage directions in V.iv. They are part of the spectacular procession at Elizabeth's christening. Middle class officers from the city of London, they and the mayor are the only ones in this scene not associated with Henry's court.

Anne (Anne Bullen, afterwards Queen Anne):

See Bullen

Archbishop of Canterbury (Cranmer, Archbishop of Canterbury):

See Cranmer

Baby (Princess Elizabeth):

See Elizabeth

Bishop of Lincoln:

See Lincoln

Bishop of Winchester (Gardiner, afterwards Bishop of Winchester):

See Gardiner

Bishops:

Several bishops are present to hear the case for Katherine's divorce in II.iv. Although their deliberation would have been important historically, their presence in this scene mostly serves to convey a sense of pomp and pageantry.

Brandon:

Brandon is a noble who arrives with a sergeant to arrest Buckingham and Aburgavenny in the name of the king. He seems to be only discharging an official duty, and expresses sympathy for his prisoners.

Buckingham (Duke of Buckingham):

Buckingham is a noble, afterwards condemned as a traitor. In this play about falling from greatness, Buckingham is the first to fall. Beloved of the commoners and respected by his peers, he is the victim of a plot presumably launched against him by Wolsey, whom Buckingham accuses of having bribed his servants to testify against him. Buckingham's surveyor (a kind of overseer), who has been recently discharged after Buckingham's tenants complained about him, tells Henry that Buckingham has pretensions to the throne and has spoken openly about murdering both Henry and Wolsey. In an off-stage court scene described by two gentlemen, the surveyor's story is corroborated by three other servants, including Buckingham's confessor, who as a priest ought to keep Buckingham's confessions confidential, and a monk who supposedly fed Buckingham with prophecies that he would govern England. Despite the questionable characters of all four witnesses, Buckingham is condemned upon this testimony—his unwavering assertion that he is innocent notwithstanding—and he is marched through the streets of Westminster to his execution.

The cause of Wolsey's enmity towards Buckingham is not entirely clear, but it most likely arises from a dislike and perhaps a fear of the duke who is one of his strongest detractors. Norfolk warns Buckingham not to incur Wolsey's ill favor because "What his high hatred would effect wants not / A minister in his power" (I.i.107-08), in other words, Wolsey has the power to strike at those he hates. However, Buckingham is vehement and unrelenting in his dislike for Wolsey. He accuses him of exploiting others in order to fulfill his own ambitions, in this particular case of forcing the gentry to pay for the sumptuous spectacle in France so that he (Wolsey) could claim all the credit for having arranged such an elaborate affair. Buckingham condemns Wolsey's ambitions all the more for being the attempts of a commoner—Wolsey is an Ipswich butcher's son—to rise above his rank. The degree of Wolsey's power is threatening to the nobles, who inherit their wealth and their titles from a long ancestral line, and who earn their right to govern through this noble bloodline. If Wolsey, who was born without wealth, title, or bloodline, can exercise power as Lord Chancellor (a title that belongs to the office, not the family line), then there is nothing to distinguish those born into the nobility from those born as commoners. This notion has the potential to upset the whole structure of society and is Buckingham's over-riding concern when he says "I'll to the King, / And from a mouth of honor quite cry down / This Ipswich fellow's insolence; or proclaim / There's difference in no persons (I.i.136-39). In addition to his scorn for Wolsey's low birth, Buckingham also believes the cardinal guilty of treason. He accuses him of conspiring with Charles the Holy Roman Emperor and accepting bribes from him to "break the . . . peace" with France (I.i.190). All of Buckingham's suspicions about Wolsey are shared by other characters later in the play; the commoners clamor against his French taxation (I.ii.23-25), and the gentlemen believe Wolsey engineered the divorce of Henry and Katherine to revenge himself on Charles (who is Katherine's newphew) for not rewarding him (II.i.161-64).

Except for his dislike for Henry's favorite minister, Buckingham is, in his speech and behavior, loyal to his king. Although he is hot-tempered and proud while speaking against Wolsey, he accepts his arrest and condemnation with humility and "noble patience" (II.i.36). When he realizes he has been framed, he resigns himself: "It will help me nothing / To plead mine innocence; for that dye is on me / Which makes my whit'st part black. The will of heav'n / Be done in this and all things! I obey" (I.i.207-10). Asserting his innocence to the very end, Buckingham nonetheless bears "no malice for [his] death" (II.i.62), forgives his accusers (II.i.83), and is thankful for his noble trial (II.i.119). Some of his last thoughts are for Henry: "My vows and prayers / Yet are the King's; and till my soul forsake, / Shall cry for blessings on him" (II.i.88-90). In the *de casibus* tradition, which teaches that all great men must fall from worldly power,

Buckingham in his farewell speech makes the transition from worldly ambition to spiritual peace. His fall seems due more to unfortunate circumstances than to any treasonous intentions.

Bullen (Anne Bullen, afterwards Marchioness of Pembroke, afterwards Queen Anne):

Anne Bullen is the second wife to Henry. Although the historical Anne Boleyn was a strong woman who played an active part in shaping this segment of England's history, the Anne Bullen of the play has an insignificant and passive role. Her few appearances on stage, which establish her great physical beauty and virtuous temper, are less important than the effect her mere presence has on the whole plot. Henry is instantly struck by her beauty, and Suffolk attributes the king's fascination with her as the reason for his seeking to divorce Katherine (II.ii.17-18). Henry's secret marriage to Anne leads to Wolsey's downfall, when Henry discovers that Wolsey has sent letters to the pope expressly to prevent his marriage to Anne. "In that one woman I have lost for ever," cries Wolsey when he learns of the king's displeasure (IV.i.409). Wolsey detests Anne as too low-born—"a knight's daughter" (III.ii.94)—and disagrees with her religious views, calling her a "spleeny Lutheran" (III.ii.99). Historically, unable to obtain the pope's approval for his divorce, Henry broke with Rome and established himself as head of the English church in order to marry Anne. The tremendous upheaval of this Reformation is barely mentioned in the play. Anne is the mother of Princess Elizabeth, who eventually became Queen Elizabeth I. The historical Anne Boleyn was beheaded for treasonous adultery only three years into her marriage. Even though the play is about the fall of great men and women, it is not surprising that Anne's fall is not foreshadowed here; Shakespeare ends the play on a note of celebration, and Anne is the mother of the Elizabeth whose majesty will transcend the cycle of falling from greatness as it is presented in the play.

Butts (Doctor Butts):

Doctor Butts is Henry's physician. He notices Cranmer being forced to wait outside the Council chamber with commoners and alerts the king to this indignity.

Campeius (Cardinal Campeius):

Cardinal Campeius is sent from the pope to examine Henry's case for divorce. A sullen Henry

> **In addition to his scorn for Wolsey's low birth, Buckingham also believes the cardinal guilty of treason."**

becomes suddenly cheerful upon his arrival. Campeius, always courteous in his speech, flatters the king. Wolsey confides in Campeius and tells him: "Learn this, brother, / We live not to be grip'd by meaner persons" (II.ii.134-35). From this point on, Campeius becomes Wolsey's dedicated co-partner in bringing about Katherine's downfall. He backs Wolsey up at Katherine's trial, and later seconds him in his attempt to gain a private conference with the queen. It is in the interview with Katherine that Campeius's honeyed words are at their most insidious. Along with Wolsey, he courteously and unrelentingly insists that Katherine accept their counsel. He flatters her, and politely denies all of her well reasoned accusations that they are there to betray her. Even his rebuke to her is a courteous reminder that stubbornness and anger are not becoming in a person of her nobility (III.i.168-74). Under such an unwavering and courteous attack, a tired Katherine finally gives in, knowing she has lost.

Campeius reveals how completely he has become the agent of Wolsey when he sneaks away from court without taking leave of Henry (III.ii.56-60). After all the work he has done to secure Katherine's divorce, he has now gone to Rome to thwart it because Wolsey is afraid a divorced Henry will marry the Protestant Anne. Wolsey, with the help of Campeius, is trying to arrange a marriage with the French king's sister, an alliance which will further Wolsey's ambitions while displeasing his enemy Charles V, the emperor.

Capuchius:

Capuchius is ambassador from the Holy Roman Emperor, Charles V of Spain. Capuchius visits Katherine, aunt to Charles, during her final illness and delivers a message of comfort from Henry.

Cardinal Campeius:

See Campeius

Cardinal Wolsey, Archbishop of York:

See Wolsey

Chamberlain (Lord Chamberlain):

The prime minister of the king's Privy Chamber, the chamberlain would be equivalent to a modern chief of staff. The chamberlain is responsible for maintaining the king's household. In the play the chamberlain is most often seen in his official capacity: worrying about a shipment of horses that did not make it to the royal stables, identifying Henry's ring when Cranmer produces it in the Council, or ordering the porter to keep better control over the palace gate at the christening. The chamberlain is necessarily interested in court politics and often makes up part of the group of nobles exchanging news. He is concerned about Wolsey's influence over the king, saying that "he hath a witchcraft / Over the king in' s tongue" (III.ii.18-19). Although the chamberlain describes Wolsey as "a bold bad man" (II.ii.43) and disapproves of his policy, he does not bear the strong personal dislike for Wolsey that many of the other nobles do. Sent with the others to strip Wolsey of his office, the chamberlain is the only one who does not taunt him and in fact offers sympathy: "Press not a falling man too far! . . . My heart weeps to see him / So little of his great self" (III.ii.333, 335-36).

In his more candid moments, the chamberlain's easy temper erupts into humor. He jokes with Sands about French fashion, and teases Sands and Guilford about their over-fondness for women. At Wolsey's party, he is the one who plays along with the king's disguise and informs Henry of Anne's identity.

Chancellor (Lord Chancellor):

The king's chief minister of state, the chancellor would be equivalent to a modern prime minister or secretary of state. The chancellor is responsible for the king's public affairs. He carries the great seal as a sign of office. In the play, the chancellor functions in an official rather than a personal role. The character referred to as chancellor replaces Wolsey in this office at III.ii.393-4. His primary task is to preside over the Council during Cranmer's trial (V.i.36-215). Although the chancellor is named as Sir Thomas More, historically More was not Lord Chancellor at the time of Cranmer's trial, but this inconsistency does not affect the chancellor's official role in the play.

Cranmer (Cranmer, afterwards Archbishop of Canterbury):

Cramner is Henry's right-hand man after Wolsey's fall. Cranmer has been abroad on business concerning the divorce of Henry and Katherine and returns to court with what Henry needs to proceed with it. Wolsey, and later his disciple Gardiner, despise Cranmer as a Protestant and heretic, but Henry promotes him to archbishop of Canterbury. As archbishop, he crowns Anne and later christens Elizabeth. The gentlemen praise Cranmer as "virtuous" (IV.i.105), but the nobles are deeply troubled by his religious views and his influence over politics. Gardiner calls him "a most arch-heretic, a pestilence / That does infect the land" (V.i.45-46) and heads a movement to "root him out" (V.i.53). Cranmer is poised on the brink of a fall similar to Buckingham's, but is saved through the intervention of the king. Henry allows the Council to try Cranmer, but meets secretly with Cranmer before the trial to prepare him for what is coming and to urge him to bear it with patience. Cranmer asserts his "truth and honesty" (V.i.122), but realizes when Henry describes the "malice / Of . . . great size" (V.i.134-35) with which he is opposed that only the king can protect him from this trap. Henry has absolute faith in Cranmer's "truth and. . . integrity" (V.i.114) and gives him a ring in token of his confidence. At his trial Cranmer is calm and polite to his accusers, despite their discourteous treatment of him. When he produces the ring and the Council realizes he has the king's countenance, they grow alarmed: "Do you think . . . / The King will suffer but the little finger / Of this man to be vex'd?" (V.ii.140-42) asks Norfolk. That royal intervention can disrupt the cycle of falling to defeat that almost claimed Cranmer along with Buckingham, Katherine, and Wolsey is a demonstration of the power of monarchs to transcend the cycle, a power which Cranmer himself predicts for Elizabeth. In the final scene of the play, embraced by Henry to be the godfather to his child, Cranmer foretells of Elizabeth's glorious reign, and so ends the play on a note of hope.

Although the historical Cranmer, a favorite of Anne Boleyn, was instrumental in bringing about the Reformation, this aspect of his character is not directly dealt with in the play.

Crier:

The crier is the official whose job it is to call Henry and Katherine to appear before the court during the divorce proceedings.

Cromwell:

Cromwell is a servant to Wolsey. Cromwell sheds tears at his master's fall, and this loyalty and sympathy redeems Wolsey, who until now has been disliked by everybody save the king. Wolsey tells Cromwell to "Be just, and fear not; / Let all the ends thou aim'st at be thy country's, / Thy God's, and truth's" (III.ii.446-48), advice which Cromwell takes to heart. After Wolsey's fall, Cromwell becomes a trusted servant to Henry and is promoted to secretary. He fulfills this role in the Council, where apart from his official duties, he also reminds Cranmer's accusers that "'Tis a cruelty / To load a falling man" (V.ii.111-12). His sympathy for the unfortunate arises perhaps from his having witnessed the fall of his beloved master Wolsey, but his defense of Cranmer turns out to be justified, in light of Henry's judgment.

Historically, Cromwell had a long career as one of Henry's most trusted advisors.

Denny (Sir Anthony Denny):

Denny brings Cranmer to Henry for their secret midnight meeting before Cranmer's trial (V.i.80-85).

Doorkeeper:

Listed in the stage directions merely as "keeper," the doorkeeper of the Council chamber informs Cranmer that he must wait outside.

Dorset (Marchioness of Dorset):

Not listed in the cast of characters, the marchioness appears twice on stage, once during Anne's coronation procession, and once during Elizabeth's christening ceremony. She is named one of Elizabeth's godmothers.

Elizabeth (Princess Elizabeth, referred to as Baby):

Elizabeth is the future Queen Elizabeth I, daughter of Henry and Anne. Although not listed in the cast of characters, and making only a brief appearance in her christening ceremony, Elizabeth is important to the play insofar as it is the story of events leading up to her birth. Cranmer predicts that Elizabeth will have a glorious reign and that her virtues will return, phoenix-like, in her heir after she is gone (V.iv.39-55). As a phoenix, which rises again from its own ashes, Elizabeth transcends the cycle of falling into defeat which has claimed the other great men and women in this play. Written after

> **In the final scene of the play, embraced by Henry to be the godfather to his child, Cranmer foretells of Elizabeth's glorious reign, and so ends the play on a note of hope."**

Elizabeth's long reign in the time of her heir, James I, the play glorifies the princess, but historically Elizabeth was third in line for the throne, and there is a period, during her sister Mary's reign, when she was actually imprisoned in the Tower. Her path to the throne was not as smooth as Cranmer predicts in the play.

Epilogue:

An unspecified actor who closes the drama, the Epilogue's function is to let the audience know the play is over and to call for their applause.

Gardiner (Gardiner, afterwards Bishop of Winchester):

Gardiner is Henry's secretary, and becomes the bishop of Winchester after Wolsey's fall. Although the king's servant, Gardiner is secretly loyal to Wolsey. Gardiner is a man with strong opinions and his own agenda for the kingdom. A Catholic who disagrees with Queen Anne's religious views, he hopes that she will die during childbirth (V.i.22-23). He boasts that he has "incens'd the lords o' th' Council" against the Protestant Cranmer, whom he calls a "rank weed" that must be rooted out (V.i.43, 52). At the Council meeting, Gardiner forces Cranmer to wait outside, and when the Chancellor suggests that he treat Cranmer with more dignity out of respect for his position, Gardiner urges the Council not to be soft on him. Gardiner is curt and officious when he tells Cranmer he will be committed to prison and stripped of his titles according to the king's wishes. When Cromwell reminds him to show some mercy, Gardiner calls him an unsound Protestant. When Cromwell rebukes him, Gardiner's comment that he will "remember this bold language" (V.ii.119) suggests that he is the kind of man to hold a grudge. Gardiner's hypocrisy is revealed when Henry enters the Council chamber.

Officious and domineering with his fellow Councilors, Gardiner is all charm and affability with his sovereign. Henry sees through Gardiner's flattery, however, and rebukes him before the Council as having a "cruel nature and a bloody" (V.ii.164). At the king's order, a humbled Gardiner promises to embrace and love Cranmer.

Garter King-at-Arms:

An important functionary, he marches in the coronation procession as well as the christening procession, where he blesses the princess.

Guards:

Guards escort Buckingham to and from prison. They are impressively armed as they bring Buckingham from his arraignment in a solemn procession.

Gentlemen:

The two gentlemen who appear at the beginning of Act II and again in Act IV, where they are joined by a third, function as narrators, filling in bits of the story not shown on stage and offering their own commentary. They sympathize with Buckingham and distrust Wolsey, they pity Katherine and admire Anne's beauty. Their sentiments are meant to reflect the prevailing opinion.

Other gentlemen are called for in the stage directions at various points in the play, to convey brief messages and to fill out crowd scenes in the court. Gentlemen are the lowest rank in the upper class.

Griffith:

Katherine's gentleman servant, Griffith cares for her at Kimbolton after the divorce. He tells Katherine of Wolsey's death, and when she lists his faults reminds her also to speak of his virtues, which he enumerates for her. Katherine praises him as "an honest chronicler" (IV.ii.72). Griffith demonstrates his deep loyalty as a servant through his concern for Katherine's health (IV.ii.82), and in his rebuke to a messenger who is rude to her (IV.ii. 103).

Guilford (Sir Henry Guilford):

Guilford welcomes the ladies to Wolsey's banquet and bids them to be merry and carefree. The chamberlain teases him that his youth makes him overly fond of women.

Henry (King Henry VIII of England):

Henry VIII is not so much the story of Henry the man, as it is the story of what happens in the kingdom while Henry is king. It begins with Henry's spectacular visit of state to Francis I of France, and ends thirteen years later with the christening of his daughter Elizabeth. The play is foremost a celebration of the Tudor dynasty, which begins with Henry's father and culminates in Queen Elizabeth I and her heir, James Stuart.

Behind the events of this celebratory play looms Henry: royal, benevolent, and beyond the reach of fortune. In Shakespeare's time, it was believed that kings were God's earthly agents, and as such, higher than ordinary men. In the play, Henry is not subject to the whims of fortune that claim Buckingham, Katherine, and Wolsey; in fact, he demonstrates his almost god-like power through his ability to rescue Cranmer from a similar fate. The king's favor is redemptive, but his frown can bring men down, as it does with Wolsey. Henry's power is absolute, and throughout the play—no matter what he does—he inspires the respect, admiration, loyalty, and love of his subjects. Cranmer, speaking of Princess Elizabeth, describes her as a phoenix, able to rise again from her own ashes (V.iv.40). This extraordinary feat applies to Henry as well, as he reforms and reshapes his England after his own liking, while never suffering the disapprobation of his subjects. As king, he is above the ravages of worldly fortune.

As a character, Henry is difficult to pin down, not so much in that he lacks a personality as that his personality is almost completely tied up in his kingship. He is consistently courteous and fair-minded when hearing official business. When Katherine kneels before him with a suit from the people, Henry treats her with great respect and raises her to his side (I.ii.10-13). Even when he believes that Buckingham is a traitor, he grants that "If he may / Find mercy in the law, 'tis his" (I.ii.211-12). For all his courtesy, Henry is not above an occasional burst of temper. Hearing for the first time of a tax he supposedly imposed, a surprised and indignant Henry cries "Taxation? / Wherein? and what taxation?" (I.ii.37-38). Angered at the discourteous behavior Gardiner has shown to Cranmer, he rebukes him before the entire Council and calls him "spaniel" (V.ii.161). Henry's quirk of speech—to cry "Ha!" when displeased—is familiar to all the nobles. The greatest thing to arouse his displeasure is his inability to obtain a divorce from Katherine. The king has a stricken conscience on the matter of his marriage to Katherine. He believes that his "marriage with the dowager, / Sometimes our brother's wife'' is incestuous, and his stillborn sons proof that he stands ''not in the smile of heaven'' (II.iv.181-82, 188). He swears in court that ''no dislike i' th' world against the person / Of the good Queen, but the sharp thorny points / Of my alleged reasons, drives this [divorce] forward'' (II.iv.224-26). Indeed, all of his interactions with Katherine are courteous and respectful; there is no evidence that he does not still love her. At the same time, however, Henry is deeply attracted to the lovely Anne Bullen, whom he secretly marries before the divorce is finalized. At some point, the nobles's suspicion that Henry's conscience has only ''crept too near another lady'' (II.ii.18) becomes accurate.

When the play opens, Henry appears to be in danger of being overshadowed by Wolsey. In his first entrance he is seen leaning against Wolsey's shoulder. Later he learns that Wolsey has caused a tax to be levied without his knowledge. The nobles fear that Wolsey has ''a witchcraft / Over the King in 's tongue'' (III.ii.18-19) and pray that ''Heaven will one day open / The King's eyes, that so long have slept upon / This bold bad man'' (II.ii.41-43). Although Wolsey has been the king's favorite for so long, in the end it is only a matter of time before Henry re-exerts his power over the ambitious cardinal. Already aware at the end of Katherine's trial that ''These Cardinals trifle with [him]'' (II.iv.237), Henry is ready to cast Wolsey down when his private letters accidentally fall into his hands, almost as if in answer to the nobles's earlier prayer. In the end, the usurping Wolsey becomes merely a scapegoat, on whom the falls of Buckingham and Katherine are blamed, and Henry, who was never in any real danger of being overshadowed, re-emerges like the sun he is described as.

Katherine (Queen Katherine):

Katherine of Aragon is wife to Henry and is afterwards divorced. Much of the central action of the play concerns Henry's attempt to divorce Katherine, his wife of over twenty years. Historically, Katherine, daughter of the Spanish King Ferdinand II, had originally been married to Arthur, Henry's older brother and heir to the English throne. However, when Arthur died a few months afterward, his marriage unconsummated, Katherine was married to Henry, the new heir. At the time, it was considered a form of incest to marry a brother's widow, but the pope determined that since the first marriage had never been consummated, Katherine had not really been Arthur's wife and therefore the marriage

> **" Henry's power is absolute, and throughout the play—no matter what he does—he inspires the respect, admiration, loyalty, and love of his subjects."**

between Katherine and Henry was legitimate. However, when nearly all of their children were either born dead or died shortly after birth, Henry began to believe that God was punishing him for incest. It was the fear that he was endangering his immortal soul by living in sin that prompted him to seek a separation from Katherine. By this time Katherine's nephew, Charles V of Spain, who was also the Holy Roman Emperor, had marched into the Vatican and was holding the pope prisoner. It seemed very unlikely that Charles would allow his aunt to be cast aside by the English king. Unable to obtain a divorce sanctioned by the pope, Henry broke with the Catholic church of Rome and established himself head of the church in England. This Reformation, brought about in order to divorce Katherine, had far-reaching effects on all of English history.

In the play, Katherine first appears in a scene which takes place before the divorce is initiated. Henry treats her with great respect and courtesy when she interrupts Buckingham's trial in order to plea on behalf of the commoners that their tax is too high. Katherine is moved out of compassion for the people, but also out of a sense of honor towards the king and a concern that his dignity will suffer if the people continue to grumble. Her arguments are both compassionate and intelligent, and, unlike the king, she is able to penetrate Wolsey's dissembling and confront him directly. Her compassion and her penetration surface again during Buckingham's trial. When Wolsey emphasizes Buckingham's alleged faults, she reminds him to ''Deliver all with charity'' (I.ii.143). She is the only one to perceive that the man testifying against Buckingham might be doing so out of spite (I.ii.171-76).

After Buckingham's arraignment, both gentlemen and nobles are saddened to hear rumors of a separation between Henry and Katherine. Although Henry testifies that his conscience resolved him on it out of fear of incest (II.iv.170-210), his subjects

> **The king has a stricken conscience on the matter of his marriage to Katherine. He believes that his 'marriage with the dowager, / Sometimes our brother's wife' is incestuous, and his stillborn sons proof that he stands 'not in the smile of heaven' (II.iv.181-82, 188).''**

believe that Wolsey is to blame for the divorce. Whatever the cause, Katherine suddenly finds herself the victim of circumstances beyond her control. She is called to trial with great pomp and ceremony, yet she realizes that the formal justice system will do nothing to defend her innocence; like Buckingham, she is aware that her fate has been decided even before the trial. Instead of playing along with the charade, Katherine throws herself at Henry's feet and begins an eloquent, impassioned plea to his sense of right and justice, daring him to do right by her. She demands to know ''In what have I offended you?'' (II.iv.19), reminds Henry that she has been a ''true and humble wife'' (II.iv.23), and asks only that he spare her until she can seek the advice of her advocates, her ''friends in Spain'' (II.iv.55). Katherine's sorrow turns to anger when Wolsey tries to placate her. With a righteous indignation that makes her one of Shakespeare's strongest heroines, she refuses to be judged by the man who is her enemy. The trial is a travesty, the judge is also the accuser, and Katherine turns her back on the whole corrupt system, saying ''I will not tarry; no, nor ever more / Upon this business my appearance make / In any of their courts'' (II.iv.132-34). Her behavior leads Henry to proclaim her ''The queen of earthly queens. / She's noble born; / And like her true nobility she has / Carried herself towards me'' (II.iv.142-44).

Although she is eventually worn down by continued pressure from Wolsey and Campeius, Katherine maintains her regal dignity until the end. She ceases to argue with the cardinals because, as they maintain, such behavior does not befit a queen. After Wolsey's death, she is able to commend his virtues and forgive him. In her final illness, Katherine sees a vision in which spirits bow before her and crown her with a garland, suggesting that she will be honored in heaven. Her spiritual purity gives Katherine strength even after she has been stripped of her worldly titles, and her fall in the material world is superseded by her victory in the spiritual one. Still a loving wife, even after Henry has cast her aside, Katherine sends a final message to her husband: ''tell him in death I blest him'' (IV.ii.163). Although defeated, Katherine still has a noble bearing, and her final wish is to be buried ''like / A queen, and daughter to a king'' (IV.ii.171-72).

Ladies:

Ladies, or noblewomen (as opposed to commoners or untitled members of the gentry), are present in the background at Wolsey's party, and in the coronation and christening processions, where they would most likely be sumptuously dressed, adding to the spectacle.

Lincoln (Bishop of Lincoln):

Lincoln attends Katherine's trial. He testifies that having examined the question of the divorce, he is the one who counseled Henry to go forward with it. This implies that Lincoln found ecclesiastic reasons to believe that Henry's marriage to Katherine, his brother's widow, was incestuous.

Lords:

Lords, or title-bearing noblemen, are present in the background at Katherine's trial, where they carry in the sword and mace, and at Elizabeth's christening, where they carry a canopy over the princess. In both cases their presence adds to the pageantry of the scene.

Lovell (Sir Thomas Lovell):

Lovell is an important knight in Henry's court. He provides a rare flattering portrait of Wolsey when he praises his generosity before the banquet (I.iii.55-57). Lovell has a strong sense of duty and conscience. Even as he leads Buckingham to his execution, he asks for forgiveness. Later, when he relates the news that Anne is having a difficult labor and Gardiner hopes she might die, although he shares Gardiner's sentiment, his ''conscience says / She's a good creature, and . . . does / Deserve our better wishes'' (V.i.24-26). His accidental meeting with Gardiner at midnight seems a bit conspiratorial as they freely exchange secret news, but in his interactions with Henry there is no evidence that Lovell is anything but a loyal servant to his king.

Man:

A servant to the porter at the palace gate, he and the porter complain about the crowd of people coming to the christening. These two characters are the only commoners to have speaking parts in the play. Unlike the nobles, they speak in prose and use slang.

Marchioness of Dorset:

See Dorset

Mayor of London (Lord Mayor of London):

Although the mayor is not listed in the cast of characters, he is called for in the stage directions at the coronation and the christening. The city of London had an autonomous government from the royal court, and the presence of the mayor in these two scenes, which take place on the streets of London, indicate co-operation between the city and the court.

Norfolk (Duchess of Norfolk):

The duchess of Norfolk is not listed in the cast of characters, but is called for in the stage directions in the coronation procession, and again in the christening procession, where she has the important task of carrying the baby Elizabeth. She is one of Elizabeth's godmothers.

Norfolk (Duke of Norfolk):

Norfolk, a high-ranking nobleman, is well acquainted with political affairs. One of his main functions in the play is to share news with other members of the court. As a duke (the highest rank beneath kings and princes), Norfolk shows little of the pride that Buckingham displays; on the contrary, he is humble, temperate, and eager to think well of everybody. He is impressed by Henry's magnificence in France, which he praises, and troubled by Buckingham's vehement dislike for Wolsey. Although he is grieved that Wolsey may have bought peace with France at too high a price, nevertheless he defends the cardinal against Buckingham's attacks and tries to calm his anger. When Buckingham accuses Wolsey of treason, Norfolk replies ''I am sorry / To hear this of him and could wish he were / Something mistaken in't'' (I.i.193-95). However, Norfolk grows to dislike Wolsey when he believes him responsible for urging the king to divorce. Norfolk is upset about the amount of power Wolsey is gaining, but his primary concern seems to be for Katherine's situation, and

> Katherine throws herself at Henry's feet and begins an eloquent, impassioned plea to his sense of right and justice, daring him to do right by her. She demands to know 'In what have I offended you?' (II.iv.19), reminds Henry that she has been a 'true and humble wife' (II.iv.23), and asks only that he spare her until she can seek the advice of her advocates, her 'friends in Spain' (II.iv.55).''

Henry's happiness. He suggests visiting Henry to ''put the King / From these sad thoughts that work too much upon him'' (II.ii.56-57). It is indicative of the kingdom's general dislike for Wolsey that by the time of his downfall, even the mild Norfolk is eager to see him go. He gives Surrey news that will aid his strike against Wolsey, and cries ''amen!'' to the idea that Henry's displeasure will soon oust Wolsey from power (III.ii.56). When Henry sends him to strip Wolsey of his signs of office, unlike the other nobles Norfolk is polite and gentle with the cardinal. Throughout the play, Norfolk demonstrates his concern for others even as his actions prove the strong loyalty he has to the king.

Officers:

Officers are present in the background at Katherine's trial and Anne's coronation. They include anyone who performs an office, but specific officers such as ''verger'' or ''judge'' are often called for in the stage directions.

Old Lady:

She waits on Anne and teases her about her ambitions to become queen. In the tradition of several of Shakespeare's female attendants (for example, the Nurse in *Romeo and Juliet*, Emilia in *Othello*), she uses bawdy language: ''A threepence bow'd would hire me / . . . to queen it'' (II.iii.36-

> **Although defeated, Katherine still has a noble bearing, and her final wish is to be buried 'like / A queen, and daughter to a king' (IV.ii.171-72)."**

37) (with a pun on ''quean'' i.e. ''prostitute''). The old lady announces the birth of Elizabeth, and then complains that Henry hasn't rewarded her enough for bringing the news (V.i.172-76).

Page:

The page listed in the cast of characters is Gardiner's boy-servant, who holds the torch for him when he walks at midnight and encounters Lovell. Other pages, not listed, mill outside the Council chamber door as Cranmer is forced to wait.

Patience:

She is Katherine's attendant, who cares for her at Kimbolton after the divorce. She grows alarmed at Katherine's paleness after she awakens from her vision.

Porter:

He keeps the palace gate and complains about the crowd arriving for the christening. The porter and his man are the only two commoners with speaking parts in the play. Their lower class is reflected in their speech; unlike the nobles, who speak in verse, they speak in prose and use slang.

Prologue:

The Prologue announces the beginning of the play and sets the tone as he asks the audience to imagine the characters ''As they were living'' (Pro. 27), and informs them that it will be a story of how ''mightiness meets misery'' (Pro.30).

Quiristers:

They are members in a choir. They are not listed in the cast of characters, but are called for in the stage directions to sing during the coronation procession. Their presence contributes to the pomp and spectacle of the scene.

Sands (Lord Sands, also referred to as Sir Walter Sands):

One of the lords at Wolsey's banquet, Sands fancies the ladies and flirts with Anne. In an earlier scene, he complains that an ''honest country lord'' such as himself cannot compete for the ladies' attention against the younger, more fashionable men (I.iii.44). The title ''lord'' means that he is a nobleman, but he is inexplicably demoted to ''knight'' in the stage directions that have him escorting Buckingham from his arraignment (S.D.II.i). Such inconsistencies in the text are not uncommon, and pose challenges for any textual editor of Shakespeare.

Scribes:

They are hired to write out or copy official documents. Scribes record Katherine's trial, and one of them prompts the crier to call Henry and Katherine to the court.

Secretaries:

Secretaries make up part of Wolsey's retinue when he first appears in Act I. The secretaries produce the papers that make it possible for Wolsey to arrest Buckingham.

Sergeant-at-Arms:

He arrests Buckingham for treason, in the name of the king. He also appears as part of the official procession in the background at Katherine's trial.

Spirits:

Spirits appear during Katherine's vision. It is unclear whether the spirits are supernatural entities, or if they merely represent a dream Katherine is having. In either case, their curtsies and their presentation of the garland, a sign of honor, indicate that Katherine's greatness is acknowledged in the spiritual world despite her fall in the material one.

Suffolk (Duke of Suffolk):

A high-ranking noble, Suffolk is often the companion of Norfolk. Suffolk has a slightly cynical sense of humor, which causes him to deliver his news with a sharper edge than Norfolk. Informed that Henry's ''marriage with his brother's wife / Has crept too near his conscience'' (II.ii.16-17), Suffolk rejoins ''No, his conscience / Has crept too near another lady'' (II.ii.17-18). Suffolk dislikes Wolsey, but believes himself beyond his reach. He is eager to tell news relating to Wolsey's downfall, news that as "wasps that buzz about [Henry's] nose / Will make this sting the sooner" (III.ii.55-56). When he is sent to subpoena Wolsey, he does so in an officious and unsympathetic manner.

Surrey (Earl of Surrey):

Buckingham's son-in-law, Surrey was abroad in Ireland by Wolsey's orders when Buckingham was executed, and he returns seeking revenge against the cardinal. Although he is hot-tempered and needs to be filled in on the latest news, his attack on Wolsey, when it comes, is cool and well-studied. He resists using his sword (III.ii.277) and instead begins to recite from memory the articles against Wolsey (III.ii.304). When the chamberlain stops him with "Press not a falling man too far!" (III.ii.333), he forgives Wolsey.

Surveyor:

A servant to Buckingham, the surveyor testifies to Buckingham's treasonous intentions and is believed by Henry, although Buckingham calls him "false" and believes Wolsey has bribed him (I.i.222-23). Katherine suspects he is making the charges out of spite, after losing his position when Buckingham's tenants complained about him (I.ii.171-76). Buckingham is condemned upon his testimony.

Vaux (Sir Nicholas Vaux):

Vaux escorts Buckingham to his execution and orders a barge befitting "The greatness of his person" (II.i.100), but Buckingham rebukes him for mocking his fallen state.

Winchester (Gardiner, Bishop of Winchester):

See Gardiner

Wolsey (Cardinal Wolsey, Archbishop of York; Lord Chancellor until III.ii):

Henry's prime minister until his fall, Wolsey is a butcher's son who has risen to his high position through his own ambition. As cardinal, Wolsey holds power in the Catholic Church; as chancellor, he holds power in affairs of state. He is almost universally disliked throughout the kingdom. In almost the first reference to Wolsey in the play, Buckingham complains "The devil speed him! no man's pie is freed / From his ambitious finger" (I.i.52-53). Norfolk warns that "The Cardinal's malice and his potency" are equal, and that "his

nature" is "revengeful" (I.i.105, 108, 109). It is not just the noblemen who distrust Wolsey, but the commoners, the gentlemen, and even the queen. Before he even becomes Henry's agent against her in the divorce, Katherine suspects Wolsey of framing things "which are not wholesome" against the commoners and the king (I.ii.45). The nobles believe the demise of "This bold bad man" cannot come soon enough (II.ii.43).

The suspicions against Wolsey are not unjustified. He reveals his ambitious nature nearly every time he appears on stage. When Henry revokes the tax levied by Wolsey, the cardinal whispers to his secretary to inform every shire that their relief comes about only through his own intercession (I.ii.102-08). Later, he reveals to Campeius that Gardiner, the king's new secretary, is secretly under his command. When Campeius expresses concern for the demise of the old secretary, who was banished by Wolsey, Wolsey cold-heartedly says "He was a fool—/ For he would needs be virtuous" (II.ii.131-32). Wolsey's work on behalf of the king's divorce has ulterior motives. By deposing Katherine, Wolsey wishes to insult her nephew, Charles V, the Holy Roman Emperor. Charles has failed to aid Wolsey in gaining the popedom, and Wolsey's plan to get rid of Katherine and marry Henry to the sister of the French king, Charles's enemy, is revengeful.

Yet for all his conniving and self-interested plots, Wolsey is never truly disloyal to the king. Wolsey believes it is possible to further himself while still acting in the king's best interest, as he tells Henry "Mine own ends / Have been mine so, that evermore they pointed / To th' good of your most sacred person and / The profit of the state" (III.ii.171-74). His role in bringing Katherine down, cruel as it may seem, is at Henry's request. His attempt to block Henry's marriage to Anne, although partially stemming from his own dislike of the woman, is also based on the conviction that Anne is too low-born for his king and that the duchess of Alancon is a better match in terms of birth and politics. Henry relies on Wolsey, and when they first appear together, the king is leaning on the cardinal's shoulder (S.D.I.ii). Wolsey's assertion to Henry that his "duty" will "stand unshaken yours" no matter what happens is sincere (III.ii.196, 199), and until his fall, Henry trusts his minister.

Wolsey is not a universal villain. He is a kind master who rewards his servants well, as when he promotes both Gardiner and Cromwell. He displays

> As cardinal, Wolsey holds power in the Catholic Church; as chancellor, he holds power in affairs of state. He is almost universally disliked throughout the kingdom. In almost the first reference to Wolsey in the play, Buckingham complains 'The devil speed him! no man's pie is freed / From his ambitious finger' (I.i.52-53)."

his liberality when he hosts a splendid banquet, and inspires Lovell to say of him, ''That churchman bears a bounteous mind indeed, / A hand as fruitful as the land that feeds us; / His dews fall every where'' (I.iii.55-57). Even Katherine, who must blame him for her divorce, acknowledges his generosity and honor after his death.

The ambitious Wolsey finally finds redemption in his fall. Preoccupied by his own schemes to separate Henry from Anne, a distracted Wolsey accidentally sends some of his private letters to the king. The letters reveal not only his dislike of Anne, but also his accumulation of private wealth with which to buy the popedom. One frown from the king tells Wolsey he is undone. Yet unlike the falls of Buckingham and Katherine, Wolsey's seems justified, for he brings it about by his own deeds. This realization humbles Wolsey, and in a stirring soliloquy he throws off ambition and finally gains self-knowledge. For the first time in the play, Wolsey can say ''I know myself now, and I feel within me / A peace above all earthly dignities, / A still and quiet conscience'' (III.ii.378-80). Cromwell weeps at his master's fall, and Wolsey warns him ''Mark but my fall, and that that ruin'd me: / Cromwell, I charge thee, fling away ambition!'' (III.ii.439-40). Wolsey sadly realizes the mistakes he has made and says ''Had I but serv'd my God with half the zeal / I serv'd my king, He would not in mine age / Have left me naked to mine enemies'' (III.ii.455-57). It is not too late for Wolsey to transfer his ''hopes'' to ''heaven'' (III.ii.459), and

like Buckingham and Katherine, achieves spiritual peace through resignation of worldly place.

Women:

They are Katherine's waiting women, who sit with her in her apartment as she does needlework. One of them plays the lute and sings (III.i.3-13). Historically, these would have been gentlewomen and noblewomen living in Katherine's court, not common servants.

Further Reading

Baker, Herschel. Introduction to *Henry VIII*, by William Shakespeare. In *The Riverside Shakespeare*, edited by G. Blakemore Evans, 976-79. Chicago: Houghton Mifflin, 1974.
> This introduction concentrates on the textual problems which have led critics to suspect dual authorship in this play.

Bevington, David. Introduction to *Henry VIII*, by William Shakespeare. In *The Complete Works of William Shakespeare*, edited by David Bevington, 913-16. Glenview, IL: Scott, Foresman and Company, 1980.
> Bevington touches on several areas of interest concerning the play, including the question of authorship, the play's relationship to the earlier histories, theme, and character.

Foakes, R. A. Introduction to *Henry VIII*, by William Shakespeare, xv-lxv. The Arden Shakespeare. London: Methuen, 1957.
> Foakes provides a detailed discussion of authorship, date, and sources before going into great detail about the structure of the play. His character sketches focus mostly on the main characters.

Knight, G. Wilson. ''*Henry VIII* and the Poetry of Conversion.'' In *The Crown of Life*, 256-336. London: Methuen, 1947.
> The chapter on Henry VIII is a rich source for further character study. Wilson examines Buckingham, Wolsey, Katherine, Henry, as well as many of the more minor characters.

Margeson, John. Introduction to *Henry VIII*, by William Shakespeare, 1-59. The New Cambridge Shakespeare. Cambridge and New York: Cambridge University Press, 1990.
> The introduction is divided into sections on date, authorship, sources, critical history, the unity of the play, the verse of the play, and stage history. Margeson includes illustrations of some of the characters and stage configurations.

Morrison, N. Brysson. *The Private Life of Henry VIII*. New York: Vanguard Press, 1964.
> This condensed biography of Henry VIII covers most of the events that occur in the play, offering a quick historical insight into the background story of Shakespeare's *Henry VIII*.

Ridley, Jasper. *Henry VIII*. London: Constable, 1984.
This biography of Henry VIII covers the events of the play in greater detail than Morrison's book, and is a useful source for those who want a deeper historical insight into the play.

Starkey, David. *The Reign of Henry VIII*. New York: Franklin Watts, 1986.
Starkey provides a different approach to the historical Henry VIII, telling the story of the politics over which the king presided. It is useful for studying the historical characters of Wolsey, Cromwell, Gardiner, and others of the Council.

Yates, Frances A. *Shakespeare's Last Plays: A New Approach*. London: Routledge & Kegan Paul, 1975.
In the chapter on *Henry VIII*, Yates examines the play's qualities as Shakespeare's last play at the end of a long series of history plays. She examines *Henry VIII* in the context of the Catholic-Protestant conflict.

The Tragedy of Julius Caesar

1599

Act I:

The play opens in Rome on the Feast of Lupercal, a Roman festival celebrated on February 15. The Feast of Lupercal was a major religious event designed to ensure the fertility of people, as well as that of the fields and animals that were a source of food for the Romans. It was believed that if one of the participants in the ritual race struck a barren woman during the course of the race, the woman would become fertile. In the opening scene, two tribunes (officials elected to protect the rights of the commoners) are scolding tradesmen for taking the day off from work and decorating statues of Caesar. The tribunes recall the honor of Pompey, who began a civil war and was eventually defeated by Caesar. The next scene shows Caesar, Mark Antony and others at games in honor of Lupercal. Caesar asks Mark Antony, who will run in the Lupercalian race, to touch Calphurnia, Caesar's wife, during the ritual. At this time, a soothsayer warns Caesar to ''Beware the ides of March'' (I.ii.18). Caesar dismisses the warning. After the others depart to watch the race, Cassius tries to interest Brutus in joining a conspiracy against Caesar. It is reported that Caesar was offered a crown in the marketplace but refused it. Other conspirators including Casca discuss grievances against Caesar and discuss how to win Brutus to their plot.

Act II:

Early on March 15, the Ides of March, Brutus considers his reasons for joining the plot against Caesar. He claims to have no personal grievances against Caesar; rather, he possesses a general love of liberty for himself and his fellow Romans. The conspirators, their faces heavily covered up in their cloaks to avoid detection, visit Brutus and all take an oath against Caesar. When it is suggested that Mark Antony be slain as well, Brutus argues against it. After the conspirators leave, Portia, Brutus's wife, tries to learn what is taking place, but Brutus evades her questions. Brutus then draws Caius Ligarius, a separate visitor to his home, into the conspiracy. At Caesar's house, Calphurnia tries to persuade Caesar not to go to the Capitol. She tells Caesar of the dreams she has had, which she feels are bad omens. The augurers also advise Caesar not to go. Decius, a conspirator, reinterprets Calphurnia's dream in a positive way which is flattering to Caesar. By this and by other arguments, he changes Caesar's mind. Various Romans accompany Caesar to the Capitol. Artemidorus, a teacher, has written a blunt letter warning Caesar of the plot against him. He plans to hand it to Caesar near the Capitol.

Act III:

Caesar approaches the Capitol followed by friends, conspirators, and senators. Artemidorus tries unsuccessfully to get Caesar to read his warning. Various individuals present requests to Caesar. As Caesar refuses a request in spite of being importuned to accept it, the conspirators slay him, all stabbing him. At Brutus's insistence, the conspirators put Caesar's blood on themselves and plan to go the marketplace proclaiming ''Peace, freedom, and liberty!'' (III.i.110). Antony, who had left after the slaying, returns alone, shakes hands with the conspirators, and asks permission to speak at Caesar's funeral. After the conspirators depart, Antony vows revenge over Caesar's body. He receives word that Octavius is on his way to Rome. At Caesar's funeral, Brutus speaks to the Roman populace and explains that Caesar was killed because of his ambition. Initially, Brutus seems to have won the crowd's approval. Then Antony speaks, inspiring the crowd to believe that Caesar was a virtuous man who has been wrongly slain. The crowd decides to turn on the conspirators, burn their houses, and riot. In the final scene, the rioting crowd comes upon Cinna the poet. At first the mob believes the poet is Cinna the conspirator. Even after the poet repeatedly states that he is not the conspirator, the mob kills him anyway.

Act IV:

The triumvirate of Antony, Octavius, and Lepidus meet at Antony's house and are making a list of Romans who should be killed. Antony also shows his disapproval of Lepidus as a co-ruler of the Roman Empire. The scene changes to a military camp in Sardis, a city in Asia Minor. Brutus and Cassius are quarreling in Brutus's tent. Cassius is angry and hurt that Brutus condemned one of Cassius's men for taking bribes. The argument escalates and Brutus accuses Cassius of taking bribes. When Cassius expresses his fear that Brutus no longer cares for him, he bares his chest and offers Brutus his dagger. After this incident, the two reconcile. Brutus then tells Cassius that he has received word that Portia has killed herself. Messengers bring news of Octavius's and Antony's battle plans. Brutus insists that his and Cassius's forces march to Philippi to confront Octavius and Antony. Cassius argues against this plan, but consents to it. Alone during the night, Brutus sees the ghost of Caesar, who tells Brutus that he will see him again, at Philippi.

Act V:

The opposing armies meet on the plains at Philippi. Cassius has begun to believe in the bad omens he says he has witnessed. Resolved to fight, both he and Brutus are also resolved to take their own lives in the event of defeat rather than be led captive back to Rome. After the battle begins, Cassius mistakenly believes his friend Titinius has been captured. Cassius asks his servant, Pindarus, to help him kill himself. When Titinius returns and sees his friend Cassius dead because of a mistake, he kills himself as well. Antony's troops advance on Brutus's forces. In order to protect Brutus, Lucilius, Brutus's friend, pretends to be Brutus. When Lucilius is captured and Antony learns the truth, he recognizes Lucilius's act as a courageous display of loyalty to Brutus. When Brutus believes that his defeat is inevitable, he asks various servants to help him kill himself. Though they refuse, he finally persuades one, Strato, to hold his sword while he (Brutus) runs upon it. Antony and Octavius learn what has happened. Antony proclaims that Brutus was ''the noblest Roman of them all'' (V.v.68), and Octavius plans a soldier's funeral for him.

Modern Connections

One of the major issues *Julius Caesar* deals with is the overthrow of a ruler. In this play, Shakespeare raises the question of whether this is ever justified, and if so, under what circumstances. At the time Shakespeare was writing, a commonly held view on this topic was that the overthrow of any ruler—good or bad—was morally wrong. This view is prevalent in Dante's *The Inferno* (a part of a longer work completed between 1308 and 1321). In the poem, Dante (an Italian poet) put Brutus and Cassius in the lowest level of Hell as punishment for their rebellion. This concept was well-known in Shakespeare's time through literature such as *The Inferno* and through the views of England's rulers. The two English monarchs during Shakespeare's lifetime, Queen Elizabeth and King James I, shared the view that an attack on the ruler was deeply immoral and dangerous to the kingdom. James I felt that even a bad ruler should not be overthrown, for such a person was sent by God to test and mature the character of the Christian subject of the ruler. Hence, in no situations should the subject turn to rebellion. Both Elizabeth and James were the targets of plots against them, but both survived the plots.

A view opposite to the medieval one of Dante was put forward by some Renaissance thinkers in their writings. Two Renaissance writers who supported the overthrow of a tyrant ruler were the Italian political writer Niccolò Machiavelli (1469-1527) and the French essayist Michel Eyquem Montaigne (1533-92). In their philosophical arguments, they discussed the causes which would lead people to seek to overthrow a ruler. Additionally, some Catholic and Protestant polemicists advocated the overthrow and assassination of an unjust ruler when specific circumstances, such as lack of religious toleration in the kingdom, applied.

In *Julius Caesar,* Brutus argues that Caesar was killed because of his ambition. He worries about the change that Caesar might undergo if he were to acquire more power. The historical Julius Caesar was able to achieve a level of personal power exceeding that which the ancient Roman political system was designed to allow. The main governing body in Rome in Caesar's time was the Senate. In *Julius Caesar*, most of the central characters—Caesar, Brutus, Mark Antony—are members of the Senate. The principal officials of the Senate were known as consuls. Two consuls were elected from the Senate by the general public. These two consuls served alternate months during the same year. The power of a consul was intended to be checked by the presence of the second consul, and by the short term of office. However, in a period of civil wars, many exceptions to these rules were made for the victorious military leader, Caesar. The Senate awarded additional honors and power beyond that of a consul to Caesar due to his successful military exploits. Later, Caesar claimed even more power for himself.

Like the ancient Roman legal system, the modern democratic system is one in which officials are elected by the general public, and in which checks and balances are incorporated into the governing process. In a democracy, people have the power to vote out of office individual leaders who are not representing their views in the passing of laws. A system of checks and balances exists with the division of the U. S. government into three branches: legislative, judicial, and executive. Informal checks are also in place which prevent one person from amassing too much power. Such checks include regularly scheduled elections, campaign laws, independent media, a system of public education, well-trained lawyers and a jury system, separation of church and state, and lobbyists for various constituencies.

Another area of interest for the modern audience is the difference between the historical record, mainly as found in the writings of Greek biographer Plutarch (died c. 120 A.D.), and Shakespeare's use of the record. Much of Shakespeare's story for *Julius Caesar* is found in Plutarch. However, Shakespeare omits a number of things: 1) reference to Portia's first marriage or her offspring from that marriage 2) the fact that Caesar saved Brutus's life after the battle of Pharsalus 3) the comment that Brutus stabbed Caesar in the "privities." Suetonius, a Roman biographer/historian and contemporary of Plutarch, reported on a tradition that Brutus was Caesar's illegitimate son, another aspect of Roman record which is not mentioned in the play. It has been suggested that perhaps Shakespeare omitted such information in order to depict Brutus in a sympathetic manner. Additionally, there are a number of other differences between Plutarch's historical record and Shakespeare's play, including compressions of time. Similarly, modern artists rely on historical or official records for inspiration. The artist—whether he or she is a poet, an author, a playwright, a director—may interpret or embellish aspects of such documents for any number of reasons, including theatrical or political purposes. One modern example of variation between the record of an event and an artists's interpretation of that event is the difference between the Warren Commission Report on the assassination of President John F. Kennedy and the movie version depicted by film director Oliver Stone.

Characters

Another Poet:

An unnamed poet approaches the tent of Brutus to seek out Brutus and Cassius. He is ridiculed by both men for his crude verses and philosophy.

Antony (Mark Antony, also Marcus Antonius):

A professional soldier and public official. He has the third largest speaking role in the play. While his role in the first two acts of the play is minimal, in the third act Mark Antony takes on a dominance maintained through the rest of the play.

Antony's first appearance in the play is as a runner in the games in honor of Lupercal. His athletic nature, as well as other virtues, are noted by Brutus who states that Antony is "given / To sports, to wildness, and much company" (II.i.188-89). Caesar also points out that Antony "revels long a-nights" (II.ii.116). This view of Antony is the factor that spares him from being an additional target of the conspirators' murderous plans. When the conspirators are considering whether to kill Antony along with Caesar, Trebonius agrees with Brutus in the assessment that Antony is somewhat of a playboy, and not a threat to their plans. The two reassure the others that there is nothing to fear in Antony.

Though Antony is not regarded before the conspiracy as a serious threat by Brutus, the conspirators still take the precaution of having Trebonius draw him off from the scene of the assassination, and after the deed Antony flees to his home. He sends word immediately afterward via a servant, asking permission to speak to the conspirators. Antony returns to the Capitol and at the sight of Caesar's body, he voices his grief. When Brutus promises to explain to Antony the reasons why Caesar was killed, Antony shakes hands with the conspirators, stating that he does not doubt their wisdom. As he goes on speaking, however, he

begins praising Caesar and grieving for him again. At this point, Cassius asks Antony what his intentions are: does he stand with them or against them? Antony does not directly answer him, but asks again for their reasons for the assassination of Caesar. Brutus reasserts his promise to reveal their motivation for murdering Caesar and, at Antony's request, Brutus allows Antony to speak at Caesar's funeral.

After the conspirators leave Antony with Caesar's body, Antony delivers his first major speech in the play: a soliloquy in which he vows vengeance against the conspirators. This speech is cited by many scholars as evidence that Antony is motivated by his loyalty to Caesar and his promise of revenge (rather than his own self-interest). It is argued that this speech displays the depth of Antony's grief for Caesar, and that as Antony is alone when he delivers it rather than in front of people he might be trying to influence, the emotions are genuine.

In his oration at Caesar's funeral, Antony demonstrates his rhetorical skill. In order to win back the crowd from Brutus, Antony uses irony, flattery, evidence, and the inclusion of natural pauses which allow the audience time to respond emotionally to what he is saying. He mentions Caesar's military accomplishments and the prosperity such endeavors brought to Rome. He discusses Caesar's repeated refusal of the crown. At various points Antony seems unable to proceed in his speech, overcome by emotion. Likewise, he shows compassion for the crowd's feelings, acknowledging their tears. After viewing Caesar's mutilated body and hearing multiple references to Caesar's will, the crowd is incited to riot.

While Antony's oration has been criticized by some for being manipulative and contrived, many audiences respond to its emotion and to the fact that the sentiments of the speech are in line with what Antony expressed privately over Caesar's body. At any rate, the speech inspires the crowd to turn against the conspirators, who have fled the city.

In Act IV, in what is known as the "proscription scene," Antony, Octavius, and Lepidus—who have formed a political alliance—are compiling a list of Romans who will be killed or executed. At Lepidus's request, Antony agrees to the death of his nephew in exchange for the life of Lepidus's brother. When Lepidus leaves, Antony speaks thus of Lepidus to Octavius: "This is a slight unmeritable man, / Meet to be sent on errands" (IV.i.12-13), dismissing him as a temporarily useful tool.

> In order to win back the crowd from Brutus, Antony uses irony, flattery, evidence, and the inclusion of natural pauses which allow the audience time to respond emotionally to what he is saying. He mentions Caesar's military accomplishments and the prosperity such endeavors brought to Rome. He discusses Caesar's repeated refusal of the crown. At various points Antony seems unable to proceed in his speech, overcome by emotion."

Although the proscription scene may supply evidence that Antony is self-serving and cruel, in the last scenes of the play, he seems to be depicted in a more positive manner. When Lucilius, a member of Brutus's party is taken prisoner, Antony asks that he be treated well. Antony also honors Brutus by stating that Brutus was the only one of the conspirators who acted for the general good, rather than out of envy of Caesar. Antony goes on to say that Brutus was "the noblest Roman of them all" (V.v.68).

Army:

Brutus's and Cassius's army is originally encamped at Sardis. In the final act of the play this army confronts the army led by Mark Antony and Octavius at Philippi.

Artemidorus of Cnidos:

Artemidorus is a teacher of rhetoric. He writes Caesar a blunt letter of warning, naming the men who have plotted against Caesar. He plans to stand along the road and hand his letter to Caesar as he goes to the Capitol. On the Ides of March, Artemidorus urges Caesar to read his letter, as it contains a matter of personal interest to Caesar, but Caesar sees that as the very reason to postpone reading it until last, and dismisses Artemidorus as "mad" (III.i.10).

Attendants:

Attendants, servants, and messengers appear in several scenes in the play. One of Caesar's servants is sent to consult the augurers and to report back to Caesar. Another servant delivers a message from Antony to the conspirators shortly after the assassination. Other characters such as Portia also have unnamed attendants. Portia takes her life in the absence of her attendants. Octavius's servant is the most fully depicted of the unnamed messengers. He comes to Rome bearing a message for Antony from Octavius. The servant is shocked at the sight of Caesar's body and weeps. He helps Antony carry the body to the marketplace for the funeral orations. After the orations, he reports that Octavius has arrived in Rome and that Brutus and Cassius have fled the city.

Brutus (Decius Brutus):

Decius is one of the conspirators against Caesar. When Cassius voices his concern that Caesar might be unwilling to go to the Capitol on the Ides of March, Decius confidently states that he will be able to flatter and persuade Caesar to accompany him to the Capitol. When the morning arrives and Caesar is indeed hesitant about leaving and anxious about the augerer's omens and Calphurnia's dream, Decius reinterprets the dream in a way that highlights Caesar's importance to Rome. When Caesar has heard this interpretation, along with Decius's mentioning that the Senate is thinking of offering Caesar the crown, he announces that he has changed his mind and will go to the Capitol.

Brutus (Marcus Brutus):

Brutus is a Roman nobleman who plays a prominent role in the conspiracy against Caesar. The primary issues surrounding Brutus's character are his idealism and devotion to the principle of republicanism, his political judgement, his motives for joining the conspiracy, and his role as a tragic hero. Brutus is typically viewed as a noble man, although some argue that he is flawed in his philosophical commitment to principle. It has also been suggested that Brutus unwittingly creates the chaos that descends upon Rome after the assassination.

When Brutus first appears at the Lupercal, he is approached by Cassius, who discuss with Brutus the weaknesses of Caesar. Although Cassius presses Brutus to join the plot against Caesar, Brutus indicates that he has already considered some of the points that Cassius is making, and in I.ii.79, Brutus states his fear that Caesar will be chosen king by the people of Rome.

Act II opens with Brutus's famous "It must be by his death" (II.i.10) soliloquy. In this speech, Brutus states that he has no personal objections to Caesar, but is concerned for the public good. Additionally, Brutus questions how Caesar's nature would be changed if he were crowned king. The speech has been viewed as an act of self-deception in which Brutus attempts to justify the assassination. It has also been argued that the speech gives evidence to Brutus's being consumed either by political idealism and sense of duty to Rome or by self-righteousness. Later on in the same scene, when the other conspirators propose that Mark Antony be killed as well, Brutus objects, arguing "Our course will seem too bloody . . . Let us be sacrificers, but not butchers" (II.i.162, 166). This is often viewed as an attempt by Brutus to make the murder seem like an honorable deed, a ritual sacrifice. Brutus reasserts this idea when, after the assassination, he instructs the conspirators to wash their hands in Caesar's blood.

In his oration at Caesar's funeral, Brutus declares, in response to any who question why Brutus killed Caesar, that his actions indicate "Not that I lov'd Caesar less, but that I lov'd Rome more" (III.ii.21-2). He goes on to say that Caesar was slain because of his ambition. Brutus's speech initially seems successful, as the crowd cheers in his favor by the time Brutus finishes. As Antony is preparing to speak, members of the crowd state that "Caesar was a tyrant" (III.ii.69) and that they "are blest that Rome is rid of him" (III.ii.70). Following Mark Antony's speech, however, the mob turns against Brutus and the other conspirators.

At Sardis, Brutus and Cassius quarrel at length. The argument, which begins when Cassius accuses Brutus of wrongfully condemning one of Cassius's men for taking bribes, centers around questions of Brutus's and Cassius's honor and the love they have for one another. Brutus also restates his belief that the assassination was an honorable deed. It has been suggested that this quarrel highlights Brutus's inability to distinguish his own motives from noble principles. When the fight has ceased, Brutus tells Cassius that Portia has committed suicide in her despair over the consequences of the assassination. Cassius and Brutus then discuss their upcoming military conflict with the army of Antony, Lepidus, and Octavius. Brutus insists that the enemy will be

> **In his oration at Caesar's funeral, Brutus declares, in response to any who question why Brutus killed Caesar, that his actions indicate 'Not that I lov'd Caesar less, but that I lov'd Rome more' (III.ii.21-2)."**

engaged at Philippi, despite Cassius's protests. Later, Brutus sees the ghost of Caesar, who identifies himself as an "evil spirit" (IV.iii.282) and promises Brutus that they will meet again.

In the final act of the play, at the battle of Philippi, Brutus prematurely attacks the forces of Octavius. When Brutus is certain that his forces will be defeated, he decides to take his own life rather than be captured and led into Rome as a prisoner. A reluctant Strato agrees to hold steady Brutus's sword—the sword with which Brutus killed Caesar—so that Brutus can run upon it and impale himself. In the final scene of the play, Mark Antony eulogizes that Brutus was "the noblest Roman of them all" (V.v.68), and states that Brutus was the only conspirator who acted for the good of Rome, rather than out of personal envy of Caesar. As a final tribute, Octavius orders a soldier's burial for Brutus.

Caesar (Julius Caesar):

Julius Caesar, a Roman statesman and general, appears in only three scenes and is assassinated halfway through the play. Although he is the title character, he speaks fewer lines in the play than Brutus, Cassius, or Antony.

One of the most controversial issues surrounding the character of Caesar is the question of whether he was a good or bad leader, and whether or not his assassination was justified. There is no clear answer to this question. Caesar has been interpreted in a number of ways: as superstitious and weak, as ambitious and arrogant, as a commanding leader concerned with the well-being of Rome.

Caesar's own words and actions, as well as those of other characters in the play, can provide insight into his character. However, as some schol-

> ❝ **In the final scene of the play, Mark Antony eulogizes that Brutus was 'the noblest Roman of them all' (V.v.68), and states that Brutus was the only conspirator who acted for the good of Rome, rather than out of personal envy of Caesar."**

ars emphasize, most of the characters in the play who discuss Caesar are his enemies, so their views of him should be regarded with this in mind.

In the first scene of Act I, the tribunes Flavius and Murellus subdue commoners who are celebrating one of Caesar's recent military victories. This scene gives the reader an early glimpse of Caesar's character. It has been suggested that since the commoners are celebrating Caesar's victory, perhaps they do not feel as though they are oppressed by a tyrannical leader. What of the tribunes, however? Their actions against the commoners indicate negative feelings toward Caesar.

Caesar appears in the next scene at the games in honor of Lupercal. Caesar publicly directs Mark Antony to touch Calphurnia as Mark Antony runs in the race. It was believed that runners in the Lupercalian race could make barren women fertile by touching them during the course of the race. Caesar then ignores a warning shouted by a soothsayer, dismissing the man as a "dreamer" (I.ii.24). After Caesar exits the scene with his followers, Brutus and Cassius remain. Cassius discusses Caesar's weaknesses, telling Brutus how Caesar was boastful about his swimming prowess and challenged Cassius to join him in a swim across the Tiber on a day when the river was churning and turbulent. Caesar almost drowned and had to be rescued by Cassius. Likewise, Cassius recalled a time during one of Caesar's military campaigns in Spain when Caesar fell victim to a "fit" in which he was shaking and feverish. Cassius sums up Caesar's behavior as that of "a sick girl" (I.ii.128).

In the same scene, after Caesar and his entourage return, Caesar pulls Mark Antony aside and tells him of his mistrust of Cassius. Caesar asserts, however, that he does not fear Cassius. Caesar's group exits the scene again, leaving Casca, Brutus, and Cassius. Casca tells Brutus and Cassius how Mark Antony offered Caesar the crown three times, and how Caesar refused it each time, eventually collapsing from an epileptic attack.

There are differing views on how Caesar is depicted in this scene. While Caesar's superstition and physical weakness are presented here, he also demonstrates that he is to some degree a good judge of character: he is suspicious of Cassius, who indeed poses a threat to him.

Act II, scene ii opens at Caesar's residence, where his wife has just had a dream in which a statue of Caesar spouts blood. When Calphurnia discusses her fears with him, Caesar is dismissive and seems unconcerned with the prospect of death. He comments that "Cowards die many times before their deaths, / The valiant never taste of death but once" (II.ii.32-33). A servant reports that the augurers, whom Caesar had ordered to perform a sacrifice, have witnessed an omen and advise him to remain at home. He hears the report but dismisses it. Yet, at his wife's insistent plea, he agrees to stay. When Decius arrives and hears about the omens and Calphurnia's dream, he provides another interpretation which focuses on Caesar's importance to Rome. Caesar is swayed by Decius and, after the arrival of several other conspirators, the men share wine and then leave together for the Capitol.

Caesar's actions in this scene again seem to emphasize his superstitious nature, although it has been argued that Caesar's beliefs were typical at that time in Rome. Additionally, most audiences note that Caesar continues to be concerned about maintaining his image as a fearless leader.

At the Capitol, in Act III, Caesar speaks in a tone that has been characterized as lofty and overbearing. The soothsayer warns Caesar again about the Ides of March, reminding Caesar that they have not yet passed. Artemidorus urges Caesar to read his letter, which details the plot against Caesar. But Caesar responds that personal matters will be attended to last. He tells Metellus Cimber, who is pleading for the return of his banished brother, that he rejects his fawning, comparing the groveling behavior to that of dogs. When Brutus and Cassius offer their support for Metellus Cimber, Caesar associates himself with the North Star and with Mount Olympus, suggesting his constant and unwavering attitude on this issue. The conspirators then gather around him and stab him repeatedly.

Caesar's actions in this scene have been used to support differing views of his character. Some argue that his refusal to listen to others demonstrate his high-handed, arrogant nature. It has also been suggested that perhaps Caesar recognized the need to act in the interest of Rome, rather than on his personal preferences.

After Caesar's death, his spirit is a dominant presence in the play. Mark Antony cries out to Caesar in front of the conspirators. Later, when Mark Antony is alone with the body, he speaks to Caesar, vowing revenge against the conspirators. Caesar's ghost appears to Brutus at night in the camp at Sardis, promising to meet Brutus at Philippi. Before Brutus's own death, he mentions having seen the ghost another time, the night before the battle at Philippi. Both Brutus and Cassius acknowledge the presence of Caesar's spirit at their deaths. Cassius says "Caesar, / thou art reveng'd, / Even with the sword that kill'd thee" (V.iii.45-46), and Brutus's last words are: "Caesar, now be still, / I kill'd not thee with half so good a will" (V.v.50-51).

Caesar (Octavius Caesar):

Octavius is Julius Caesar's adopted great-nephew and heir. He is also a triumvir with Mark Antony and Lepidus after the death of Caesar.

In the meeting of the triumvirs, Octavius shows himself to be fair-minded and judicious. He challenges Antony's slighting view of Lepidus, questioning how Antony could feel this way and still allow Lepidus to condemn people to death. Arguing against Antony's limited assessment, Octavius states his appreciation of Lepidus as a competent soldier.

At the battle at Philippi, Octavius disagrees with Antony's orders for the conduct of the battle, and instead of following those orders, Octavius states and follows his own military strategy. When Brutus and Cassius approach and engage Octavius in a verbal exchange prior to the battle, Octavius replies: "Defiance, traitors, hurl we in your teeth. / If you dare fight to-day, come to the field; / If not, when you have stomachs" (V.i.64-6). When Brutus's body is discovered, Octavius orders that a soldier's honor and burial be given to Brutus. Speaking the closing words of the play, Octavius calls the armies from the field and directs that the "glories" (V.v.81) of the day be shared. It has been suggested that

> ❝❝ Cassius sums up Caesar's behavior as that of 'a sick girl' (I.ii.128)."

Octavius's commanding presence in the last act of the play indicates the future stability of the Roman Empire.

Caius Ligarius:
See Ligarius

Calphurnia (also Calpurnia):

Calphurnia is Caesar's wife. In II.i, she is concerned about the bad omens, which she frankly admits she has never put much credence in before this time. When Calphurnia gets on her knee to Caesar, she temporarily succeeds in persuading him to remain at home. She offers to let Caesar use her anxiety as an excuse for not going to the Capitol.

Carpenter:
See Commoners

Casca:

Casca is one of the conspirators against Caesar. He provides important accounts of scenes which take place both on and off stage. When Caesar and his train depart after the Lupercal festivities and marketplace orations, Casca tells Brutus and Cassius what took place. He ridicules the mob and Caesar alike and reports on the silencing of the tribunes. Cassius persuades Casca to join the conspiracy, and after he has agreed, he recognizes the importance of having Brutus as a member of their group. He is the first to strike Caesar, though his wound alone is not fatal. As soon as Caesar is dead, he asks Brutus to go to the pulpit and defend the conspirators' cause to the public.

Cassius:

Cassius is the instigator in the conspiracy against Caesar. Statements Cassius makes, particularly during the "seduction scene," suggest that his motivation for initiating such a plot is a combination of

> **When Calphurnia discusses her fears with him, Caesar is dismissive and seems unconcerned with the prospect of death. He comments that 'Cowards die many times before their deaths, / The valiant never taste of death but once' (II.ii.32-33)."**

political ideology and personal envy. Throughout the play Cassius reveals himself to be an accurate judge of other men and their abilities. Against this good judgement, Cassius unfailingly defers to Brutus's decisions in various matters throughout the course of the play.

In I.ii, in what is known as the "seduction scene," Cassius attempts to convince Brutus to join the plot against Caesar. Cassius offers no hard evidence of Caesar's tyrannical or ambitious nature, although he does discuss the stature Caesar has achieved. Rather, he speaks at length about Caesar's physical weakness. Cassius compares himself to Aeneas, the legendary founder of Rome, in his saving of Caesar from drowning in the Tiber. He reveals his personal envy of Caesar in expressing resentment that Caesar has risen to the status of "a god" (I.ii.116) and that he, Cassius, must be subordinate to such a man: "and Cassius is / A wretched creature, and must bend his body / If Caesar carelessly but nod on him" (I.ii.116-118). Cassius incorporates references to honor and equality and republican ideals into the speech as well. After Brutus leaves, Cassius in a soliloquy states his intention to further sway Brutus to his cause. Cassius plans to send Brutus forged letters, ostensibly from Roman citizens, which highlight Caesar's alleged ambitions.

During the course of the play, Cassius proves to be a shrewd and accurate analyst of the men and events surrounding the assassination plot. Despite his good judgement, however, he repeatedly defers to Brutus's wishes. It is generally understood that Cassius, in these instances, acts out of the love and friendship he repeatedly expresses for Brutus. Some, however, suggest that perhaps Cassius's primary

interest, at least initially, is the credibility that the widely-respected Brutus brings to their cause.

The first significant instance of Cassius's deferring to Brutus is during II.ii, when Cassius suggests that Mark Antony be slain along with Caesar. Brutus disagrees, reasoning that Antony is merely a "limb of Caesar" (II.i.165). Cassius tries to protest again, but Brutus interrupts him, dismissing any notion that Antony poses any threat. Cassius says nothing further.

In III.i, following the assassination, Brutus gives his consent to Antony's request to be allowed to speak at Caesar's funeral. Cassius pulls Brutus aside and tries to convince Brutus to reconsider, citing the influence Antony has with the citizens of Rome. Brutus brushes aside this concern, stating that Antony's speech "shall advantage more than do us wrong" (III.i.242). Cassius defers to Brutus's decision, although he comments that he does not like it.

Finally, in Act IV, Cassius concedes to Brutus in an important military matter. In IV.iii, Brutus asks Cassius his opinion about attacking their enemy at Philippi. Cassius reasons that it would be better to remain at Sardis, and allow the enemy to seek them and expend valuable resources and energy in the process. Cassius continues, stating that by the time enemy forces reached their own, they would be well-rested and ready. Brutus dismisses this logic, and argues that his plan is a better one. Cassius then agrees to follow Brutus to Philippi.

Just prior to this strategical discussion, the two men quarreled bitterly. As the argument begins, Cassius accuses Brutus of wronging him repeatedly, and following Brutus's own verbal attack, Cassius states that Brutus no longer loves him. In despair, "Hated by one he loves" (IV.iii.96), Cassius asks Brutus to kill him. After this outburst, the two reconcile.

Just before the battle of Philippi, Cassius undergoes an unexplained change, which is often noted by scholars and audiences: he falls prey to superstition. Cassius was once a rationalist who claimed that "The fault, dear Brutus, is not in our stars, / But in ourselves . . ." (I.ii.140-41), and an Epicurean, who believed that the gods had no interest in the lives of men. Cassius now refers to the presence of omens and asks that the gods "stand friendly" (V.i.93).

As the battle ensues, Cassius instructs his friend Titinius to ride towards the nearby troops to determine if they ''are friend or enemy'' (V.ii.18). After Titinius leaves, Cassius asks his bondman Pindarus to watch Titinius and report to him what he sees. The request is made as Cassius says, because his ''sight was ever thick'' (V.ii.21), meaning short or dim. Pindarus then mistakenly reports that Titinius has been captured by the enemy, a report which leads Cassius to ask Pindarus to help him kill himself. Cassius's bad vision is sometimes viewed as symbolic of the limits of his understanding of the conspiracy, his role in it, and its consequences.

Cato (Young Cato):

Young Cato is a friend to Brutus and Cassius. He is Portia's brother. He is slain in the second battle at Philippi. Though the play makes the two battles appear to take place on the same day, in actuality they occurred twenty days apart.

Cicero:

Cicero is a Roman senator. When discussing with Cassius and Brutus Caesar's refusal of the crown, Casca mentions that Cicero spoke a few words in Greek during the ceremony, and that some people smiled and shook their heads at Cicero's comments. His only speaking part in the play is in I.iii, when he speaks to Casca on the stormy night before the Ides of March. Later, the conspirators discuss whether to have Cicero as one of their number, but Brutus decides against this, arguing that Cicero would never follow another man's lead. Brutus and Cassius receive word at Sardis that Cicero has been executed by the triumvirate, though he had no part in the conspiracy.

Cimber (Metellus Cimber):

Metellus Cimber is one of the conspirators. His personal grievance against Caesar is that Caesar has banished Metellus's brother, Publius Cimber. At the Capitol on the day of the assassination, Metellus approaches Caesar and asks to have the banishment lifted. Caesar refuses the request.

Cinna:

Cinna is a member of the conspiracy. He urges Cassius to enlist Brutus for their cause. Immediately after Caesar's assassination, Cinna yells, ''Liberty! Freedom! Tyranny is dead!'' (III.i.78).

Cinna the poet:

Shortly after the assassination Cinna the poet, on his way to Caesar's funeral, is walking through the streets thinking of a dream he has had of dining

> **After Caesar's death, his spirit is a dominant presence in the play. . . . Both Brutus and Cassius acknowledge the presence of Caesar's spirit at their deaths. Cassius says 'Caesar, / thou art reveng'd, / Even with the sword that kill'd thee' (V.iii.45-46), and Brutus's last words are: 'Caesar, now be still, / I kill'd not thee with half so good a will' (V.v.50-51).''**

with Caesar. Confronted by the conspirator-seeking mob, he states repeatedly that he is Cinna the poet, not the conspirator. He is killed by the mob anyway.

Citizens:

Roman citizens are present in various crowd scenes, such as the holiday of Lupercal and the streets of Rome on the Ides of March. After the assassination, Brutus assures the citizens that they have no need to be afraid. For more information on the common people of Rome, see Plebeians.

Claudio:

Claudio is a servant to Brutus. He appears with Varrus in IV.iii.

Clitus:

Clitus is a servant to Brutus. Though Brutus asks Clitus to help in his suicide, Clitus replies that he would rather kill himself than help Brutus in such an action.

Cobbler:

See Commoners

Commoners:

Two tradesmen, a carpenter and a cobbler, have taken a holiday on the feast of Lupercal to see Caesar and to celebrate him. The cobbler jokes about his trade.

> **During the course of the play, Cassius proves to be a shrewd and accurate analyst of the men and events surrounding the assassination plot. Despite his good judgement, however, he repeatedly defers to Brutus's wishes."**

Dardanius:

Dardanius is a servant to Brutus. Though Brutus asks Dardanius to help in his suicide, Dardanius does not wish to assist.

Decius Brutus:

See Brutus

Flavius:

Flavius is a tribune who scolds two tradesmen for spending their time celebrating Caesar's recent military victory by not working. For their offense, he tells them to cry tears into the Tiber. Flavius and his fellow tribune, Murellus, remove from statues of Caesar decorations intended to honor him. In the next scene Casca reports that the tribunes are "put to silence" (I.ii.286) for removing the decorations from the statues. This expression suggests either that they were removed from office, or that they were executed.

Ghost of Caesar:

The ghost appears to Brutus at Sardis and briefly speaks to him. Brutus says he also appears the night before the battle at Philippi.

Julius Caesar:

See Caesar

Lena (Popilius Lena):

Popilius Lena is a Roman senator. Just prior to the assassination, Popilius says to Cassius, "I wish your enterprise to-day may thrive" (III.i.13). Cassius nervously takes the statement as evidence that the plot has been discovered. After a brief discussion between Brutus and Cassius, Brutus decides that Popilius does not know about the plot.

Lepidus (M. Aemilius Lepidus):

Lepidus is one of the triumvirs after the death of Caesar. Antony sees Lepidus as unworthy to be one of the three rulers of the Roman empire, whereas Octavius is willing to honor him as a tested soldier. Lepidus is not present in the battle at Philippi.

Ligarius (Caius Ligarius):

Caius Ligarius is one of the conspirators against Caesar. According to Metullus Cimber, Caius Ligarius bears a personal grudge towards Caesar, for Caesar upbraided him for speaking well of Pompey. Despite his illness, he is drawn in to the conspiracy by Brutus.

Lucilius:

Lucilius is a friend to Brutus and Cassius. He is not a conspirator but is present at Sardis and Philippi. He impersonates Brutus on the battlefield in order to protect him. When he is captured, his worth is recognized by Antony, who does not have him slain.

Lucius:

Lucius is a servant to Brutus. He finds an anonymous note in Brutus's private quarters and gives it to his master. The note urges Brutus to "Speak, strike, redress!" (II.i.47). In the camp at Sardis, Lucius plays a song for Brutus at Brutus's request.

M. Aemilius Lepidus:

See Lepidus

Marcus Antonius:

See Antony

Marcus Brutus:

See Brutus

Mark Antony:

See Antony

Messala:

Messala is a friend to Brutus and Cassius. He discusses current news from Rome with Brutus at Sardis, including the deaths of Portia and the proscribed senators.

Metellus Cimber:

See Cimber

Murellus (in some editions, Marullus):

Murellus is a tribune. With Flavius, he scolds two tradesmen for honoring Caesar. He orders them to pray for forgiveness. Later Murellus and Flavius are ''put to silence'' (I.ii.286). This expression indicates that they have either been removed from office or executed.

Octavius Caesar:

See Caesar

Pindarus:

Pindarus is a servant to Cassius. He incorrectly reports to Cassius that Titinius has been captured. Cassius then promises to give Pindarus his freedom on the condition that Pindarus will assist Cassius in his suicide. As soon as Cassius's death is accomplished, Pindarus flees from the Romans.

Plebeians:

The plebeians are the common people of Rome. They are also referred to as plebs, or the vulgar. Their main characteristics in the play are their fickleness, or changeability, and their tendency toward mob behavior. These characteristics are evident in their responses to Brutus's and Mark Antony's funeral orations. The plebeians find Brutus's speech so persuasive that they wish to give him a statue, a crown, and an escort to his house and they cry out ''Let him be Caesar'' (III.ii.51). In spite of their response to Brutus's speech, they listen attentively to Antony, becoming more and more emotionally aroused throughout his speech. When Antony first takes the pulpit, the crowd believes the conspirators to be honorable men and Caesar to be justly slain as a tyrant. Yet soon the plebeians are calling the conspirators traitors, exclaiming ''Revenge! About! Seek! Burn! Fire! Kill! Slay! Let not a traitor live!'' (III.ii.204-205). Several times they are ready to rush out and do harm, but they are held back by Antony. When they are finally unleashed, they burn Caesar's body as a kind of holy sacrifice and plan to torch the houses of the conspirators. In their fervor, they encounter Cinna the poet, not Cinna the conspirator, but kill him anyway, simply for his ''bad verses'' (III.iii.30).

Popilius Lena:

See Lena

> ❝ Immediately after Caesar's assassination, Cinna yells, 'Liberty! Freedom! Tyranny is dead!' (III.i.78).''

Portia:

Portia, Brutus's wife, displays her concern for her husband and asks that he share with her his burdens. She wishes to know the source of his abrupt mood changes and why Cassius and the others have visited him, claiming that sharing such confidences with her husband is the ''right and virtue'' (II.i.269) of a wife. In an effort to prove her devotion to him, she wounds herself in the thigh. In IV.iii, Brutus learns that Portia has committed suicide.

Publius:

Publius, a senator, appears in II.ii, with the other senators who have arrived at Caesar's house in order to accompany him to the Capitol. When Brutus notices Publius's absence following the assassination, he seeks out the senator in order to reassure him that he will not be harmed. Brutus then instructs Publius to assure the Roman citizens that no harm is meant to anyone else.

Senators:

In III.i, immediately following the assassination, Brutus directly addresses the senators and the people who have witnessed the murder, telling them not to be frightened.

Soothsayer:

The soothsayer is a sort of fortune teller. On the feast of Lupercal he calls Caesar from the crowd. He tries to warn Caesar about the Ides of March, but is dismissed by Caesar as a ''dreamer'' (I.ii.24). Caesar speaks to him dismissively at the Capitol, yet the soothsayer replies that the Ides of March is not over yet.

Strato:

Strato is a servant to Brutus. He holds the sword for Brutus to run on. Brutus says of Strato that he has had some degree of honor in his own life. Strato repays the compliment to his master by saying to

> **The plebeians find Brutus's speech so persuasive that they wish to give him a statue, a crown, and an escort to his house and they cry out 'Let him be Caesar' (III.ii.51). . . . Yet soon the plebians are calling the conspirators traitors, exclaiming 'Revenge! About! Seek! Burn! Fire! Kill! Slay! Let not a traitor live!' (III.ii.204-205)."**

Messala and the conquerors that no man has honor by Brutus's death but Brutus himself. Strato is recommended by Messala, and agrees to work for Octavius.

Titinius:

Titinius is a close friend to Cassius. At Cassius's request, Titinius approaches nearby troops in order to determine if they are friends or enemies. When he is surrounded on his horse by cheers and cries, the sound is misinterpreted by Cassius's bondsman, Pindarus, as meaning Titinius is captured. Cassius takes his own life on the strength of Pindarus's report. When Titinius returns and sees his friend slain, he mourns the end of Rome as he has known it and crowns the dead Cassius with a wreath. He then takes his own life.

Trebonius:

Trebonius is one of the conspirators against Caesar. He visits the home of Brutus with the others. He agrees with Brutus that the others need not fear Antony as a threat to them. Trebonius's role in the plot is to draw off Antony at the Capitol before the assassination.

Varrus:

Varrus is a servant to Brutus. His duty is to be on call for delivering messages. He carries Brutus's message regarding movement of the troops to Cassius.

Volumnius:

Volumnius is a friend to Brutus and Cassius. He denies that Brutus's time of death has come. He and Brutus went to school together, and he feels that holding a sword for a person bent on suicide is not a fit job for a friend.

Young Cato:

See Cato

Further Reading

Bloom, Harold, ed. *William Shakespeare's* Julius Caesar. New York: Chelsea House, 1988.
> Several essays in Bloom's collection are useful for their analysis of character. Bloom's own brief introduction (pp. 1-4) discusses the two leading conspirators, Brutus and Cassius. Derek Traversi ("*Julius Caesar*: The Roman Tragedy," pp. 5-27) discusses a number of characters within a framework organized by the plot of the play, ending with comments on minor characters. A. D. Nuttall's essay ("Brutus's Nature and Shakespeare's Art," pp. 105-20) discusses Brutus as an example of a follower of the Stoic philosophy.

Dean, Leonard F. *Twentieth Century Interpretations Of* Julius Caesar. Englewood Cliffs: Prentice-Hall, 1968.
> Dean's collection of essays includes separate character studies of Caesar, Brutus, Antony, and Decius.

Field, B. S., Jr. *Shakespeare's* Julius Caesar. *A Production Collection*. Chicago: Nelson-Hall, 1980.
> Field's book is a collection of production photographs from seven different productions of the play from the late 1960's to the mid-1970's. It includes act-by-act comments by performers about the play. Students may find it helpful to learn how characters are portrayed differently in various productions.

Johnson, S. F. Introduction to *Julius Caesar*, by William Shakespeare. In *William Shakespeare: The Complete Works*, edited by Alfred Harbage, 895-98. Baltimore: Pelican, 1969.
> Johnson discusses the opposing attitudes members of Shakespeare's audience may have had toward Caesar, as well as attitudes toward the major characters in the play.

Kermode, Frank. Introduction to *Julius Caesar*, by William Shakespeare. In *The Riverside Shakespeare*, edited by G. Blakemore Evans, 1100-04. Houghton Mifflin: Chicago, 1974.
> Kermode's essay discusses plot and character sources for the play, as well as the alteration the plot and characters have undergone. Kermode identifies Plutarch's *Lives*, as translated by Sir Thomas North, as the primary historical source for the play.

Mack, Maynard. ''The Modernity of *Julius Caesar*.'' In *Everybody's Shakespeare*, 91-106. Lincoln: University of Nebraska Press, 1993.

> Mack discusses reasons why the play remains relevant to our time. He discusses a few early episodes in the play to demonstrate how Shakespeare's dramatic imagination built on the barest hints in Plutarch's account to develop character. Mack also discusses the effect on the audience of the plotting. In his summary, he makes a direct connection between issues in the play to twentieth-century concerns.

Miola, Robert S. *Shakespeare's Rome*. Cambridge: Cambridge University Press, 1983.

> Miola's book discusses what Rome meant to Shakespeare in his plays and how his view of Rome developed. Comments on *Julius Caesar* include remarks on how one aspect of the tragedy of the play is the Roman neglect of what the female characters have to contribute.

Ripley, John. Julius Caesar *on stage in England and America, 1599-1973*. Cambridge: Cambridge University Press, 1980.

> Ripley's book is a detailed history of performances of the play in England and America since its debut in 1599. His opening sentence attempts to account for the play's popularity in schools as owing to its ''sensational action, straightforward characters, and absence of sex . . .''

Simmons, J. L. ''Shakespeare's Treatment of Roman History.'' In *William Shakespeare His World His Work His Influence*, edited by John F. Andrews. Vol. 2. 473-488. New York: Charles Scribner's Sons, 1985.

> Simmons discusses Shakespeare's Roman plays as showing in their overall progression from *Titus Andronicus* to *Cymbeline* Shakespeare's perspective on ''Roman history throughout his intellectual life as clearly that of a Christian humanist.'' In his section on *Julius Caesar*, Simmons discusses the major characters and how they reflect Roman philosophies (Stoicism, Epicureanism) and Roman virtues. Simmons sees both Brutus and Cassius as coming to a ''Senecan illumination'' at the end of the play. That is, they know Caesar's spirit has been avenged on them, but they do not fully understand their own role.

Spevak, Marvin. Introduction to *Julius Caesar*, by William Shakespeare. Cambridge: Cambridge University Press, 1988.

> Spevak's essay demonstrates how the play is organized into two parts, which can be identified as *Caesar's Tragedy* and *Caesar's Revenge*. Spevak also discusses the pairing of parallel scenes and addresses time as a main concern of the play. Additionally, Spevak focuses on the oppos* tional forces at work in the play: change vs. constancy, the rational vs. the irrational. Finally, Spevak summarizes the various interpretations regarding the question of who the play's hero is.

Thomas, Vivian. *Twayne's New Critical Introductions to Shakespeare. Julius Caesar*. New York: Twayne Publishers, 1992.

> In Chapter 3, Thomas discusses the difference between a historical figure, as presented in the record of Plutarch, and a dramatic rendering, as presented in Shakespeare. Caesar, Brutus, Cassius, and Mark Antony are discussed. Thomas also discusses Octavius, arguing that it is not certain that Shakespeare read Plutarch's *The Life of Octavius* during the writing of this play. This section was added to the 1603 edition of the translation of Plutarch.

The Life and Death of King John

circa 1594-96

Act I:

The play opens at the English court of King John. Chatillion, an emissary from King Philip of France, declares that Philip claims the English crown and all its territories in the name of Arthur, King John's nephew. John vows that he will sail to France immediately to wage war against Philip. Robert Faulconbridge and Philip the Bastard enter, and present competing claims to the late Sir Robert's Faulconbridge's land and fortune. Robert argues that his father was overseas on a mission and the late King Richard was staying at the Faulconbridge estate when Philip was conceived; he notes that on his deathbed, Sir Robert denied that Philip was his son. Elinor, King John's mother, asks the Bastard if he will forsake his claim to the Faulconbridge inheritance, and he readily agrees. John officially declares Philip the Bastard to be Richard's son. Left alone, the Bastard soliloquizes about honor, flattery, and his new circumstances. Lady Faulconbridge appears, and when the Bastard asks her to tell him who his father was, she admits that it was King Richard, not Sir Robert Faulconbridge.

Act II:

Outside the French city of Angiers, King Philip has assembled his noblemen and allies. King John arrives with his followers, and the two monarchs formally exchange rival claims about who has the

more valid right to the English throne: John or Arthur. Elinor and Constance, Arthur's mother, hurl insults at each other, while the Bastard vows to give the duke of Austria a thrashing. A citizen of Angiers suddenly appears on the city walls above them. John and Philip each demand to be admitted to the city. The citizen replies that since Angiers is an English possession, its gates will open only to the rightful king of England—whoever that is proven to be. The French and English armies engage in battle, with neither side gaining the upper hand. The two kings and their attendants meet near the city walls, and the Bastard points out that the citizens of Angiers have treated them both with contempt. He suggests that they turn their weapons against the city and destroy it. The citizen suggests another solution: that John's niece Blanch become the wife of Philip's son Lewis. John promises to turn over all his French provinces and a huge sum of money as well if the marriage takes place. Lewis and Philip agree to the match. Blanch says she will do whatever is asked of her. Alone after everyone else leaves, the Bastard expresses his astonishment over the turn of events, marveling that self-interest has led the French to abandon a just and honorable course of action.

Act III:

At the French encampment outside Angiers, Constance rages at the news of the alliance between France and England. When John and Philip appear with their followers, she turns on Philip, accusing him of perjury. Cardinal Pandulph arrives and demands to know why John has blocked the pope's appointment of a new archbishop of Canterbury. John tells him that the king, not the pope, rules England. Pandulph declares that John is a heretic and no longer a member of the church, adding that whoever revolts from John's rule will be blessed and whoever takes his life will be doing a good deed. The cardinal further orders Philip to break off his new alliance with John or be barred from the church. Philip hesitates, but after Pandulph presents a complex argument about Philip's primary role as defender of the church, the French king renounces the alliance. Combat resumes between England and France, and Arthur is taken prisoner. While the battle rages, John approaches Hubert, a follower he has named to look after Arthur. By degrees, he reveals to Hubert that he wants the boy killed, and Hubert agrees to do it. With the English clearly victorious, Pandulph, Lewis, and Philip meet. They are confronted by Constance, grief-stricken over the loss of her son. When she leaves, Philip follows her. The cardinal then points out to Lewis that

because Arthur represents a threat to John's title, it is inevitable that John will have him killed—leaving Lewis a clear way to the English throne, through his marriage to Blanch. Lewis agrees to Pandulph's proposal to invade England.

Act IV:

In an English prison, Hubert shows Arthur a document ordering that the young prince be blinded. Arthur pleads with Hubert not to carry out the order, and at last Hubert relents. The setting shifts to the palace of King John, who has just been crowned a second time. When the assembled nobles request the release of Arthur, the king agrees. Hubert arrives and whispers in John's ear. The king turns to the nobles and tells them that Arthur has died that night. Pembroke and Salisbury declare that there must have been foul play. After they depart, a messenger arrives, announcing that French forces have landed in England. The Bastard enters with a man who has predicted that on the next Ascension Day, John will give up his crown. Dispatching the man to prison and the Bastard to bring back the nobles, John tells Hubert he never meant to have Arthur killed. When Hubert shows him the warrant he had signed, John blames Hubert for carrying out his orders. Hubert then reveals that Arthur is still alive. The scene shifts to the prison walls, where Arthur intends to elude discovery by leaping down and running away. He plummets onto the stones below and dies. Pembroke, Salisbury, and Bigot appear nearby. They are soon joined by the Bastard, who tries to convince them to return to the palace. They discover Arthur's body, and the nobles insist he must have been murdered. When Hubert appears, the nobles accuse him of killing Arthur, but he denies it. After they leave, the Bastard demands to know if Hubert is guilty. He denies it again, and the Bastard tells him to bear away Arthur's body.

Act V:

In a room at the English palace, John hands his crown to Pandulph, who places it on the king's head and declares that John's sovereign authority comes from the pope. The king, in turn, urges the cardinal to keep his part of their bargain and halt the French invasion. When Pandulph remarks that it is Ascension Day, John realizes that the prophecy has come true. The Bastard enters and tells the king that several English cities have welcomed the French invader, that many nobles have gone over to Lewis's side, and that Arthur is dead. Yet he urges John to remain steadfast. The king puts him in charge of marshalling the English forces against the invasion. In the French encampment, Lewis and Count Melune confer with the English noblemen who have become their allies. Pandulph arrives and tells Lewis that hostilities should cease. The Bastard appears, learns that Lewis means to fight on, and then delivers a rousing speech in which he portrays King John as determined to carry on the war and defeat the French. On the field of battle, however, John complains of a fever, and when a messenger comes from the Bastard telling him to retire from the field, he assents. The messenger also brings word that ships sent to re-supply the French troops have run aground. In another part of the field, the fatally wounded Melune tells Salisbury, Pembroke, and Bigot that they have been betrayed: Lewis has sworn to cut off their heads that night. Salisbury proposes to the other English nobles that they return to King John and ask him to pardon them. Subsequently, in an orchard at Swinstead Abbey, Prince Henry, Salisbury, and Bigot wait to hear news of John, who has been poisoned by a monk. The king is carried into the orchard, desperately ill and consumed by fever. The Bastard arrives with Hubert, bringing dire news about the course of the war. The king dies as they are speaking. Salisbury counters the Bastard's account with an entirely different report: Pandulph has come to Swinstead Abbey from Lewis, seeking peace and apparently agreeable to any terms the English set. Everyone kneels in loyalty to Henry, the dead king's heir, and the Bastard closes the play with a stirring appeal to the principles of patriotism.

Modern Connections

Many elements of the struggle for political power in thirteenth-century England are universal. They can be found in the history of every country in the world. Shifting alliances within factions and political backstabbing—as when Philip and Lewis desert Arthur's cause in exchange for Blanch's dowry, or when the English nobles desert John and then rush back to him upon learning that Lewis means to kill them—are not uncommon in many nations, even today. The cynicism about national leaders expressed by the Bastard in his second major soliloquy (II.i.561-98) resembles the alienation from politics felt by many people in modern times. And when the Bastard describes the weakened John as a bold leader, a "gallant monarch," and a fierce warrior (V.ii.127-58 and 173-78), his words recall those of

a political image maker, trying to present a candidate in the most favorable light.

On the international level, the historical enmity between England and France depicted in *King John* has many counterparts in contemporary times: in Central Europe, the Mideast, and Southeast Asia, for example. To outside observers, some nations' justifications for declaring war are no more valid than, for instance, the reasons that Pandulph gives to induce Lewis to invade England. And regardless of changes in battlefield technology—from arrows to anti-ballistic missiles, from horses to tanks—the victims of war have always included foot soldiers, widows, and orphans. This is pointed out by several characters, especially in Act II; see II.i.41-3, 210-21, 258-66, 300-11, and 352-60.

A central issue in *King John* is the importance of values in motivating human action. How does a person with deeply held principles react when an unethical course of action would serve his or her self-interest? To what extent should loyalty—to a principle, an individual, a political faction, or a religious belief—determine one's behavior? In the play, rumors of Arthur's death inflame the people against John. Many ordinary citizens are reported to have put up little resistance to the French invasion; some have even welcomed Lewis and his foreign army (V.i.30-35). Are there circumstances in which rebellion against authority can be justified? The Bastard presents the issue of rebelling against "the system" or accommodating oneself to it in his soliloquy on commodity (II.i.561-98). In the course of the play, he goes through a process of "selling out," relinquishing family honor for personal gain; yet when his country is in extreme danger, he is the champion of national unity and England's most passionate patriot. Can moral or political expediency serve a noble or virtuous cause? In *King John*, the distinction between good and evil is not always clear, and choosing the most ethical course of action is no easy matter.

The question of church-state relations takes a different form today than in the thirteenth century, though it is still a relevant issue. In America, for example, there is no official, established church, as there was in many European countries six or seven centuries ago. Yet today there is active debate about what role, if any, organized religions and members of different religious faiths should have in shaping government policies. Cardinal Pandulph appears to have a mixture of motives for his actions, and he is one of the play's most effective manipulators of words. Are late twentieth-century religious leaders always ethical in their conduct, or are some as manipulative or unethical as Pandulph?

One other contemporary issue presented in the play is the role of women in society. In *King John* the female characters—from Elinor the power broker to Blanch the pawn—disappear after Act III. What does this signify, if anything? From time to time, the female characters use deceit (Lady Faulconbridge), manipulation (Queen Elinor), and emotional appeals (Constance). In the thirteenth century, women were denied the independent exercise of power; they had to resort to indirect means to achieve their goals. To what extent is this different today?

Twentieth-century productions of *King John* have frequently focused on the play's topicality and relevance to modern audiences. It raises issues that are not limited to thirteenth-century England but echo throughout human history, and will likely continue to confront us forever.

Characters

Arthur (Arthur, Duke of Britain):

He is the son of Constance and Geffrey, King John's older brother. According to the law of primogeniture, or birth order, Arthur ought to have become king of England when Richard I died. Arthur is generally presented as a helpless young child, yet sometimes he shows adult-like bravery and composure.

At the opening of II.i, he greets the duke of Austria and graciously thanks him for joining the ranks of his supporters. Later in the scene, however, his poise deserts him in the face of the spiteful wrangling between Constance and Elinor, and he seems overwhelmed by the political turmoil swirling around him. When Constance learns that the marriage of Blanch and Lewis has brought peace between England and France, the depth of her outrage frightens Arthur, and he begs her to accept the situation.

Arthur's childish innocence and sweet temperament are highlighted in IV.ii. When Hubert, King John's aide, shows him a warrant ordering that he be blinded, Arthur reminds him that he has shown him nothing but loving care and obedience since they have been together. He asks Hubert how he can carry out such a dreadful act. Shamed and

> **"Arthur is generally presented as a helpless young child, yet sometimes he shows adult-like bravery and composure."**

moved by Arthur's continuing appeals, Hubert relents.

In disguise, Arthur bravely slips away from the prison and climbs onto the wall surrounding it. Believing that the only way to keep John from having him murdered is to escape, Arthur gathers his courage and leaps from the high wall, falling to his death on the stones below. A helpless victim of political power struggles while he lived, after his death he is a nagging reminder to John's conscience and a symbol around which the English nobles can gather.

Austria (Lymoges, Duke of Austria):

He is usually referred to in the play by his title, duke of Austria. He is a blend of two historical figures: the duke of Austria, who imprisoned Richard Cordelion and held him for ransom, and the Viscount Limoges, who killed Richard in battle. In *King John*, Austria allies himself with King Philip in Arthur's cause. The duke is the butt of many of the Bastard's taunts in II.i and III.i, especially with regard to the lion-skin robe he took from Richard's body and now wears himself. When Philip temporarily deserts Arthur, Austria does too, and Constance calls him a coward and a fool. He is killed in battle, and his head is borne in as a trophy, by the Bastard.

Bastard (Philip the Bastard):
See Philip the Bastard

Bigot (Lord Bigot):

An English nobleman, he appears in four scenes in the company of Pembroke and Salisbury. Bigot is among the nobles who discover Arthur's body; desert John and ally themselves with the French; learn that Lewis has betrayed them; and go to Swinstead Abbey to seek John's pardon.

Blanch of Spain:

Queen Elinor's granddaughter and King John's niece, she becomes a pawn in the struggle for the English throne. Marriages arranged for political and economic purposes have been standard practice throughout human history, particularly in the case of royalty. Blanch's submissive response to the suggestion that she marry Lewis is appropriate to her situation. Given her status as an essentially powerless female, she has little choice in the matter. But she tells Lewis that she doesn't love him. On the other hand, she adds, she sees nothing in him that is objectionable.

After the marriage has taken place and Pandulph has arrived on the scene, Lewis supports the cardinal's demand that King Philip renounce the terms of the marriage bargain. Blanch is appalled that her new husband would blacken their wedding day by going back on his word. She pleads with Lewis, naively asking what motive for action he could possibly have that is stronger than his love for her. Torn between loyalty to her uncle and the wedding vows she has just sworn, Blanch reluctantly chooses to remain with Lewis when the battle between the French and English resumes.

Cardinal Pandulph:

See Pandulph

Chatillion:

A French ambassador, he informs King John of King Philip's claim to the English throne, on behalf of Arthur, in the opening lines of the play. He appears again in II.i, bringing Philip the news that King John and the English forces have landed in France.

Citizen of Angiers:

He represents his city in negotiations with the kings of France and England. He appears on the city walls several times in II.i. In some editions of the play, the citizen who appears the last time is identified as Hubert.

During his first appearance, the citizen listens to lengthy speeches by John and Philip, then responds crisply and to the point. "We are the King of England's subjects," the citizen reminds them (II.i.267), declaring that the city gates will be opened to whoever is proven to be the rightful king. The citizen is a cautious man and cannot be easily fooled. When the French and English heralds take turns declaring that their side is winning the battle,

the citizen replies that, from his vantage point on the walls, it's clear that neither of them has gained the upper hand.

When Philip and John agree to turn their cannons on the city and level it, the citizen craftily suggests an alternative that will spare Angiers. With excessive compliments to Blanch and Lewis, he proposes that the hostilities could be brought to an end if the two young people were married. He goes on to promise that if this union takes place, the gates of the city will open to admit all of them. If not, he adds defiantly, no one will be admitted. His stubbornness sets off a chain of events that affects everyone.

Constance:

She is the widow of Geffrey—King John's older brother—and the mother of Arthur. Constance believes fiercely in her son Arthur's right to the throne. Indeed, she's obsessed by it. Constance is essentially powerless, however, and she must depend on allies such as the king of France, the duke of Austria, and Cardinal Pandulph. When she asserts Arthur's claim to the English crown, she represents the voice of conscience. Yet she is also proud and ambitious. There is strong evidence that she would be the power behind the throne if Arthur were king. Furthermore, Constance is frequently reckless in asserting and defending her son.

When John and his mother Elinor land in France to contest Arthur's claim, Constance and Elinor are at each other's throats almost immediately, tossing insults back and forth, and charging each other with adultery. Though Arthur begs Constance to stop quarreling, she continues. She correctly calls John a usurper, but she goes on at such length and so extravagantly that even Philip asks her to hold her tongue.

Ordinarily in the company of the French court, she is absent when Philip deserts Arthur's cause in favor of peace and a lucrative marriage between his son and John's niece. When she learns of this, Constance is outraged. At first she cannot believe that Philip has betrayed Arthur. She refuses to seek out the king, demanding that he come to her. When Philip and Austria arrive, she lashes out at them, charging them with treachery and cowardice. Pandulph appears, and she turns to him for help. Constance is overjoyed when Philip agrees not to honor his newly made treaty with John.

Her final appearance in the play is in III.iv, after the English have captured Arthur. Constance is almost insane with grief; indeed, Pandulph suggests that she is out of her mind. She gruesomely invokes death as a release from her misery (IV.iii.25-36). She denies that she has lost her wits (IV.iii.45-60). And she vividly imagines the effects of imprisonment on her beloved son (IV.iii.82-89). Philip and Pandulph try to console her, telling her that her grief is excessive. She points out that they cannot possibly understand either the depths of maternal love or the extent of her loss. Tearing at her hair, she rushes from the room. Alternately despondent and defiant in her grief, Constance becomes one more victim of the political power struggle.

de Burgh (Hubert de Burgh):

John's aid and right-hand-man, he is chosen to carry out the king's order to murder Arthur. In III.iii, John slowly reveals to Hubert his malicious intentions. The king flatters Hubert, thanks him for his past services, and gradually takes him into his confidence. With implicit promises of great rewards, John tersely spells out what he wants: Arthur's death. Hubert vows that he shall have it. It is difficult to judge Hubert's behavior in this so-called "temptation scene." John is manipulating him, and as a powerless commoner he seems to have little choice except to carry out the king's wishes. Yet once John has made his intentions clear, Hubert seems ready and willing to murder Arthur.

When they have returned to England, however, Hubert appears prepared to blind the boy rather than kill him. Arthur begs him not to do it and makes an emotional appeal to the man who has become his friend. Hubert grits his teeth and tries to resist the child's pleas, but he relents. Realizing that he has put himself in grave jeopardy with this decision, Hubert tells Arthur he must give the king a false report of his death. When he does so, and the king informs his nobles that Arthur has died, they immediately suspect that Hubert has killed him.

In IV.ii, Hubert keeps up the pretense that Arthur is dead—and John tries to lay all the blame on him. The king lies, saying that Hubert has repeatedly urged that Arthur must be killed. Even when Hubert shows him the signed death warrant, the king continues to say that it's Hubert's fault. Frustrated and under attack, Hubert blurts out the truth that Arthur is still alive. The king commands him to bring the news to the outraged nobles, in hopes they will be pacified.

But by the time Hubert catches up with them, they have already discovered Arthur's lifeless body.

> **Constance believes fiercely in her son Arthur's right to the throne. Indeed, she's obsessed by it."**

Convinced that he murdered the boy, the nobles draw their swords and threaten to kill him. Hubert protests his innocence, yet only the presence of the Bastard prevents them from carrying out their threats. When the nobles leave, the Bastard turns on Hubert, demanding to know if he is guilty of this crime. Hubert assures him he had no part in Arthur's death. The Bastard believes him and asks him to carry out the mournful duty of bearing Arthur's body away.

Some editions of *King John* follow the First Folio, a collection of Shakespeare's plays published in 1623, in which the last set of speeches by the citizen of Angiers is assigned to Hubert. In these editions it is Hubert, not an anonymous citizen, who proposes the match between Blanch and Lewis. If Hubert is indeed the one who effectively made King Philip drop his support of Arthur's cause, this provides one explanation for King John's reference in III.iii to the services that Hubert has rendered him in the past.

Elinor (Queen Elinor):

Historically, Eleanor of Aquitaine was Queen of France from 1137 until her divorce from Louis VII in 1152. That same year, she married Henry Plantagenet, Count of Anjou; when he became Henry II of England two years later, she became Queen of England. A gifted political strategist, Eleanor of Acquitance took part in several military campaigns, sometimes leading her forces into battle.

Eleanor and Henry II had five children. The oldest was Henry, who died before his father and thus never succeeded to the throne. Instead the second son, Richard Coeur-de-lion, became king when Henry II died in 1189. The third son, Geoffrey, married Constance of Brittainy and became the father of Arthur; Geffrey died three years before his father. John was the youngest son of Henry II and Eleanor; he succeeded to the throne upon the death of Richard in 1199. The family also included a daughter; she married Alfonso of Castile and became the mother of Blanche of Castile.

In the first half of *King John*, Elinor is her son John's closest adviser. She disputes the claim that her grandson Arthur is the rightful king of England—though she admits privately that John's possession of the throne is stronger than his right to it. When Philip the Bastard and Robert Faulconbridge present their legal dispute, Elinor is struck by the Bastard's resemblance to her late son, Richard Cordelion. She impulsively asks the young man if he will give up his share in the Faulconbridge estate and join the English expedition to France, and he quickly agrees to the proposal, leading John to pronounce him Richard's son.

Elinor and her daughter-in-law Constance quarrel whenever they meet. Their long-standing feud frequently erupts into nasty remarks and malicious charges. At II.i.122-23, Elinor accuses Constance of infidelity, referring to Arthur as a bastard. Constance hotly denies the charge, reminding Elinor that her first husband divorced her because of her own infidelity. They snipe at each other throughout the scene, trading insults and arguing heatedly about the merits of John's and Arthur's claims to the English throne.

When the battle near Angiers is temporarily halted so that each side can appeal to the citizens of Angiers, Elinor resumes her role as John's adviser. Showing her political skills and her understanding of strategy, Elinor urges John to approve the proposal that Blanch be married to Lewis. She tells John that if he provides ''a dowry large enough'' (II.i.469), the French will desert Arthur's cause and the crown will be safe. She prompts John to make them an offer quickly, and seize opportunity to appeal to their personal ambitions. Drawn by the promise of gaining title to England's French provinces—and a handsome sum of money as well—Philip and Lewis agree to the match.

This is the highest point of Elinor's political influence. When Philip is persuaded by Pandulph to go back on the bargain, her appeal to Philip to keep his word is brief and ineffective. The last service she lends John is in III.iii, when she takes the captured Arthur aside so he won't hear the fateful conversation between John and Hubert. Elinor does not accompany her son back to England, but remains in France so that she may keep him informed about developments there. However, she is not able to warn him about Lewis's plan to invade England, because by then she is dead.

English Herald:

In II.i, he prematurely reports to the citizens of Angiers that English forces will soon achieve total victory on the battlefield nearby, and he asks them to admit John into the city.

English Messenger:

On two occasions, an English messenger brings John important news. In IV.ii, he tells the king of a large invasion force from France, led by Lewis. He further reports that Queen Elinor has died and that Constance is rumored to be dead. In V.iii, the messenger brings word from the Bastard that John should retire from the field of battle; he also tells the king that French supply ships have run aground and been destroyed.

Essex (Earl of Essex):

In the play's first scene, the earl of Essex informs John that two men who are embroiled in a legal dispute want the king to settle the matter for them.

Executioners:

Guards at an English prison, they are instructed by Hubert to assist him in blinding Arthur. In response to Hubert's signal, they come out of hiding, with ropes and hot irons. When Arthur begs that they be sent away, Hubert orders them to leave.

Faulconbridge (Lady Faulconbridge):

She is the widow of Sir Robert Faulconbridge and the mother of two sons: Philip and Robert. She appears near the close of Act I, furious at the slurs that have been cast on her honor by her son Robert. But when Philip urges her to tell him who his father was, Lady Faulconbridge admits her infidelity, telling Philip that his father was not her husband, but Richard Cordelion.

Faulconbridge (Robert Faulconbridge):

The second son of Lady Faulconbridge, Robert joins his half-brother Philip in appealing to King John to decide which one is the legal heir of the late Sir Robert Faulconbridge. Robert asserts that Philip is the son of Richard Cordelion (King Richard I), King John's elder brother. When Philip renounces his claim, Robert becomes his father's sole heir.

French Herald:

In II.i, he addresses the citizens of Angiers, falsely claiming that the French have nearly gained the victory on the nearby battlefield. He demands that they open the city gates and acknowledge Arthur as their king.

French Messenger:

In V.v, he tells Lewis that before Melune died of a mortal wound, he persuaded the English noblemen to leave the French side. The messenger also informs Lewis that his supply ships have run aground in shallow waters.

Gurney (James Gurney):

Lady Faulconbridge's servant, his only appearance is in the first scene of the play. Gurney addresses Lady Faulconbridge's older son by his given name, Philip, and the Bastard pretends to be offended.

Henry (Prince Henry):

A young man who is the son and heir of King John of England, Henry attends his dying father and receives vows of allegiance from the Bastard and the English nobles in V.vii. Historically, Prince Henry was nine years old when he succeeded to the English throne in 1216.

Hubert de Burgh:

See de Burgh

John (King John of England):

The king of England, he is the son of Elinor and uncle to Arthur and Blanch. Historically, he became king in 1199 upon the death of his brother Richard I, who had named him his successor two years earlier. John is reported to have been a wicked, tyrannical monarch. Yet Elizabethan historians praised him for being the only English king before Henry VIII to openly defy the pope. King John's defiance later turned to submissiveness, and he eventually acknowledged Rome's authority in English affairs. His noblemen supported him in his contest with the pope, but when he gave up the fight, they turned on him. They threatened a civil war unless he made many concessions to them; these concessions were formally preserved in the document known as Magna Carta, which John signed in 1215. John reigned until his death in 1216. According to legend, he was fatally poisoned by a monk.

Although he is the title character of the play, John is not a typical hero—even though he often behaves like one in Acts I through III. In this portion of the play, he keeps his passions in check whenever the circumstances call for clear thinking. He is

> **In the first half of *King John*, Elinor is her son John's closest adviser. She disputes the claim that her grandson Arthur is the rightful king of England—though she admits privately that John's possession of the throne is stronger than his right to it."**

willing to go to war to defend his throne, and he reacts to the French challenge with courage and determination. Yet he treats his political enemies and their representatives with respect. He is personally gracious toward Chatillion despite his hostile announcement, and he courteously sees to it that the ambassador is given safe passage out of England.

John demonstrates keen judgment of people—and thorough knowledge of the law—when Robert Faulconbridge and Philip the Bastard appeal to him to settle the issue of their disputed inheritance. He is delighted by the Bastard's quick wit and admires the young man's vigorous spirit. When the Bastard accepts Elinor's suggestion that he give up his claim and go with them to France, King John knights him and formally names him Richard Plantagent.

John's attitude toward the king of France, when they meet outside the walls of Angiers, is direct and to the point. As Philip waxes eloquent on the justness of Arthur's claim, John is a man of few words. But when the two kings take turns addressing the citizens of Angiers, John's speech is as fiery as Philip's. A courageous and energetic leader in the battle near Angiers, John is also a shrewd negotiator. He is convinced that every man has his price, and he accurately calculates what it will cost to make Philip drop his support of Arthur.

John's defiance of Pandulph most likely would have delighted Elizabethan audiences. He disputes the Church's authority in England and defends his country's independence of papal rule. Adding insult to injury, he accuses the Church's priests of corruption. John is generally silent as Pandulph tries to persuade Philip to annul the peace treaty with the English. But when the French king bows to Pandulph's

> *Although he is the title character of the play, John is not a typical hero—even though he often behaves like one in Acts I through III."*

authority, John is enraged. Swearing that nothing but the "dearest-valued blood of France" (III.i.343) will cool his temper, he calls for an immediate resumption of war.

John's political judgment first becomes questionable when he takes Hubert into his confidence about what he intends to do about Arthur. The king knows that as long as the boy lives, he represents a threat to John's possession of the crown. At the beginning of what is sometimes referred to as the "temptation scene" (III.iii), the king flatters Hubert, thanks him for his past services, and promises to reward him richly in the future. John gradually reveals his plan. When Hubert vows that he will do whatever the king wishes, John drops any pretense that he means well toward his nephew. A chilling exchange between John and Hubert leaves no doubt as to Arthur's fate: "Death." / "My lord." / "A grave." / "He shall not live." / "Enough" (III.iii.65-66). John is wickedly manipulative in this scene. Yet Hubert's quick and positive response to his proposal may be taken as a sign that Hubert is as guilty of intended murder as is the king.

John's political and moral downfall is precipitous in Acts IV and V. He offends his nobles by having himself crowned king once again. When Hubert gives him the false report of Arthur's death, John seems shocked and says that he regrets trying to secure his throne at the expense of the boy's life. His emotions in turmoil, John is further horrified by a series of devastating reports: the French invasion force has arrived in England, his mother is dead, and his subjects are listening to rumors that he means to give up his crown. Hubert adds to the king's fears with tales of supernatural omens and reports that the common people are on the verge of rebellion. John lashes out at Hubert, saying that he was the one who first suggested that Arthur's death was politically expedient. If you weren't nearby when I was pondering the deed, John charges, and if you weren't

such a villainous person, this never would have happened. Stung by these remarks, Hubert admits that Arthur is still alive. The king hopes that when the nobles hear the good news they will come to his assistance against the French.

In the meantime, John desperately looks for other ways out of his dire political situation. He makes a bargain with Pandulph. In exchange for John accepting his crown from the hands of the cardinal—thus acknowledging the Church as the supreme authority in England—Pandulph will persuade Lewis to return to France with his army. The Bastard brings John more bad news, but he also urges the king to rise to the occasion—to show boldness and inspire confidence in his subjects. However, John's growing helplessness and dependency on others, and his capitulation to Rome, clearly indicate that he is no longer a competent ruler. Recognizing his inability to act forcefully and effectively, King John puts the Bastard in charge of gathering English forces to meet the enemy. During the battle that follows, John tells Hubert that he is troubled by a fever and sick at heart. Even the news of the French retreat fails to revive his spirits. He departs for Swinstead Abbey, so ill that he cannot ride his horse and must be carried there.

John finds death rather than recovery at Swinstead Abbey. A monk at the abbey puts poison in the king's food. In the abbey's orchard, where Prince Henry and several noblemen have gathered, John is carried in on a stretcher, wracked by fever and shrunken by dehydration. The last news he hears before he dies is the Bastard's inaccurate report that the French army is on its way to Swinstead Abbey. Ridden by guilt, he dies in agony, unaware that his crown and his succession have been preserved.

Lady Faulconbridge:
See Faulconbridge

Lewis (Lewis the Dolphin [Dauphin]):
The son of King Philip of France, Lewis is sometimes referred to as the Dauphin (or Dolphin)—that is, the king's eldest son. An ambitious young man, he is easily manipulated by Pandulph. As leader of the French invasion of England, however, he is a capable strategist. Lewis is dogged by bad luck, and as his fortunes decline, he displays a vicious capacity for double-crossing his allies.

Though he is present throughout the exchanges between Philip and John outside the walls of Angiers, he has nothing to say until it is suggested that the way to settle the dispute between the two countries is for him to marry John's niece Blanch. Lewis is taken by surprise, and his response to the suggestion is awkward, to say the least. When his father asks him how he feels about the scheme, Lewis replies that he finds in Blanch's eyes a mirror of himself. Seeing his image there, he says that he never loved himself until this moment. This tribute to love draws a cutting remark from the Bastard.

After the French are handed a devastating defeat at Angiers, Lewis is humiliated. Pandulph tells him to look on the bright side and view Arthur's capture as a golden opportunity. John will surely see to it that Arthur is killed, the cardinal points out, and this will clear the way for Lewis to claim the English throne in the name of his wife Blanch. Lewis agrees with Pandulph's advice to invade England, and they go off together to get Philip's approval of the idea.

Speedily arriving in England with a large army, Lewis at first encounters little resistance. Indeed, the citizens of several English cities greet him with open arms. He forms an alliance with some English nobles who have rebelled against John, and his fortunes seem on the rise. But French ships bringing supplies to his forces are wrecked off the English coast, and the opposition assembled by the Bastard blocks his further progress.

Lewis appears to have become a confident young man, yet he has learned how to exploit other people's self-interest to his own advantage—and how to betray them when their usefulness is over. When Pandulph tells Lewis that he should withdraw his troops from England, he reminds the cardinal who recommended the invasion in the first place. Lewis refuses to abandon his attempt to conquer England. He orders that his English allies be killed—but they learn about this from Count Melune and leave before the order can be carried out. With the tide of war running against him, Lewis sends Pandulph to John with a proposal for an honorable peace. Even before he knows what John's response will be, Lewis leaves for France, his cause abandoned.

Lymoges (Lymoges, Duke of Austria):
See Austria

Melune (Count Melune):
A French nobleman and a member of Lewis's invasion force, he witnesses the agreement between Lewis and the English nobles in V.ii. Fatally wounded in battle, he survives long enough to ease his conscience by informing Salisbury, Pembroke, and

> **" Recognizing his inability to act forcefully and effectively, King John puts the Bastard in charge of gathering English forces to meet the enemy."**

Bigot that Lewis has ordered their deaths that night. He urges them to seek out John and beg forgiveness.

Pandulph (Cardinal Pandulph):
A cardinal of the Church of Rome, he acts as the pope's ambassador to the courts of France and England. He represents one side of a central issue in the play: the conflict between the Church of Rome and the English monarchy. In a world where virtually everyone is consumed by the struggle for power, Cardinal Pandulph is a master of political manipulation. He uses the weapons at hand—excommunication and the threat of eternal damnation—to bring rebellious kings back into line. Adept at exploiting situations for his own purposes, Pandulph teaches Lewis how to turn Arthur's probable death into an opportunity for advancement.

Pandulph's first appearance is in III.i, when he confronts John near Angiers and demands to know why he has kept the newly appointed archbishop of Canterbury from assuming his post. John is defiant, and Pandulph explodes. He declares that John is henceforth ''cursed and excommunicate'' (III.i.173). For good measure, he adds that every English subject who rebels against John will be blessed, and whoever should kill him will be canonized ''and worshipped as a saint'' (III.i.177).

Pandulph turns next to Philip, threatening him with the curse of the Church unless he releases John's hand and renounces their newly achieved treaty of friendship. At first, the French king wavers, so Pandulph launches into an intricate argument, reminding Philip that his primary responsibility is to defend the church and treat its enemies as his enemies. Since your first vow was to the church, he tells Philip, it takes precedence over any agreements you made after that. The king still seems undecided, but when Pandulph threatens to ''denounce a curse upon his head'' (III.i.139), Philip drops John's hand—symbolizing an end to their

> "Lewis is dogged by bad luck, and as his fortunes decline, he displays a vicious capacity for double-crossing his allies."

agreement. The French and English take up their arms once again, and the battle is renewed.

When the English win a decisive victory, Philip and Lewis are dejected, but Pandulph is undismayed. The cardinal is left alone with Lewis. He points out to the young man that John is likely to have Arthur murdered, and with Arthur dead, Lewis can claim the English throne on behalf of his wife Blanch. Assuring him that the English will rise in revolt when they hear of Arthur's murder, Pandulph proposes that Lewis sail to England with French troops and turn the English rebellion to his own advantage. Lewis agrees to the plan.

Pandulph is usually able to talk people into doing what he wants them to do. Sometimes this requires manipulation, and sometimes it necessitates the exercise of political and spiritual power. In a scene that would have outraged Elizabethan audiences, King John yields his crown to the cardinal. Pandulph places it back on John's head, reminding him that the pope is the source of his "sovereign greatness and authority" (V.i.4). The brief ceremony ended, John reminds Pandulph that since he has formally submitted to Rome, it's now time for the cardinal to carry out his part of the bargain: to halt the French invasion. In good humor, Pandulph declares that he will have no trouble ending the mission that began with his encouragement. But when the cardinal goes to Lewis and tells him to make peace with John, Lewis refuses. By the close of this scene, Lewis has completely disregarded Pandulph, refusing to listen to him any more. However, in the play's final scene, Salisbury reports that Pandulph has come to Swinstead Abbey with an offer of peace from Lewis—and that the cardinal is in charge of working out the terms of an agreement.

Though at times he is prevented from achieving his goals immediately, in the end Pandulph has gotten what he wants most: John's submission to Rome. Ever mindful that he speaks for the pope, who in turn speaks for God, Pandulph is serenely confident that the church will eventually defeat its enemies. But it should be noted that he uses his keen intellect and political skills to bring this about, rather than leaving the outcome in the hands of God.

Pembroke (Earl of Pembroke):

As an earl, Pembroke is one of the foremost noblemen in England. Each time he appears in the play he is in the company of the earl of Salisbury, and their actions always coincide: as one moves from indignation to vengeance or from rebellion to loyalty, so does the other.

Though Pembroke is frequently in attendance on King John in the first half of the play, his first words are in IV.ii, when he protests that John's second coronation was an unnecessary demonstration of his right to the crown. To the king's request that his nobles tell him what reform they want him to undertake, Pembroke replies that he should free Arthur. Pembroke argues that it is disgraceful to keep a young boy imprisoned and that if John is confident of his right to be king, he has no reason to feel threatened by Arthur. When the king reports that Arthur is dead, Pembroke mocks the suggestion that he died of natural causes. Predicting that dire consequences will flow from Arthur's death, Pembroke sets off with Salisbury for the prison where the young boy had been held.

When they come upon Arthur's body, Pembroke bursts into a rage and declares that this is the most evil murder of all time. Refusing the Bastard's plea to suspend judgment and charging Hubert with the crime, Pembroke and the other lords storm off. As they leave, they announce their intention to meet Lewis, who has invaded England and declared himself the rightful king of England.

The meeting takes place in V.ii, where Pembroke and the others seal their bargain with the French. For Elizabethans, the nobles' betrayal of their duty to England would have been treachery of the highest order. The fact that they will personally profit from their rebellion against John makes their crime even more vicious. As with Salisbury, Pembroke's motives are ambiguous. The grief and fury he expresses over Arthur's death seem genuine. But like his friend, he seems to have a gift for rationalizing actions that are based on self-interest and personal gain. He is by turns a passionate defender of youthful innocence and a willing traitor. And when his usefulness to Lewis has ended, Pembroke is at the mercy of a man who, like himself, is prepared to abandon his principles if he believes the situation calls for it.

Peter of Pomfret:

A self-proclaimed prophet, he predicts that King John will give up his crown on the next Ascension Day. Brought to court by the Bastard in IV.ii, Peter is questioned by John and imprisoned. In V.i, after John has yielded his crown to Pandulph, the king realizes that Peter's prediction has come true.

Philip (King Philip of France):

He is King John's principal political foe in the first half of the play. As Arthur and Constance's chief ally, Philip is not always dependable. His decisions to abandon Arthur's claim by making peace with John, and then to revoke the treaty at Pandulph's command, raise several questions. Is personal gain his principal motive? Is he a rationalizer or a hypocrite? Does he finally agree with the cardinal that his first duty is to the Church—or is he terrified by the prospect of eternal damnation? In an amoral world dominated by the struggle for political power, King Philip frequently appears torn between honor and self-interest.

He sends an ambassador to John, boldly proclaiming his support of Arthur's claim to the English throne and threatening to wage war on the young man's behalf. He lays siege to the city of Angiers to force its citizens to accept Arthur as England's king. When John lands in France, Philip calls him a usurper and delivers a stirring defense of Arthur's cause. But his resolution melts at the prospect of a lucrative marriage between his son and John's niece. He agrees to the union—and to the terms of the agreement—though he knows that Constance will be angry when she learns he has abandoned Arthur's claim and made peace with John.

When Pandulph demands that Philip revoke his treaty with John, he refuses at first. He continues to clasp John's hand as a sign of their friendship. He points out to Pandulph that he has given his word to John and that he cannot break that vow. Even after listening to Pandulph's intricate argument about his first loyalty being to the Church—and to the appeals by Lewis, Constance and Austria that he obey the cardinal—Philip continues to waver. However, when Pandulph declares that he is prepared to "denounce a curse upon his head" (III.i.319), Philip drops John's hand and breaks their agreement.

> In a world where virtually everyone is consumed by the struggle for power, Cardinal Pandulph is a master of political manipulation. He uses the weapons at hand—excommunication and the threat of eternal damnation—to bring rebellious kings back into line."

This brings a renewal of hostilities. Philip is plunged into gloom when the French are defeated, and his spirits are not improved by the appearance of Constance. His repeated attempts to console her are futile. When she rushes off, he follows, seeming to fear that she will take her life. Philip has no active role in Lewis's invasion of England, and he disappears from the play after Act III.

Philip the Bastard (also called Richard Plantagenet):

Legally, he is the first son of Lord and Lady Faulconbridge. Actually, he is the son of King Richard I and Lady Faulconbridge. Historically, there is no substantial evidence of such a person, though at least one Elizabethan historian reported that Richard I had a bastard son named Philip. After King John acknowledges Philip as Richard's son in I.i, Philip also becomes known as Richard (after his father) Plantagenet (the family name of the members of the royal family).

In *King John*, the Bastard assumes many forms. He is an ambiguous figure, and his character resists simple definitions or explanations. Sometimes he stands outside the action and comments on it, and sometimes he is in the thick of things. In the first half of the play, he is a soldier of fortune, seizing opportunities as they present themselves. Impudent and frequently disrespectful, he lends an element of comedy to a play that is otherwise grim and relentless in its depiction of the realities of power politics. In the second half of *King John*, he tries to fill the gaping hole in England's leadership created by John's weakness. It's debatable whether the Bastard

> **For Elizabethans, the nobles'
> betrayal of their duty to England
> would have been treachery of the
> highest order. The fact that they
> will personally profit from their
> rebellion against John makes their
> crime even more vicious."**

is motivated by loyalty, patriotism, or some less admirable quality.

Philip the Bastard and his brother Robert present themselves at the English court in the play's first scene, asking the king to settle their dispute. The Bastard shows no hesitation in acknowledging that his mother may have been unfaithful to her husband. When Elinor invites him to desert his claim to the Faulconbridge estate and enlist in the English invasion of France, he quickly agrees. King John knights him and formally gives him the name his father bore: Richard Plantagenet. The others depart, and he is left alone to consider the dramatic change in his fortunes. He imagines what it will be like to spend his time now in the company of people of higher rank, learning to be as deceitful as he believes them to be.

He accompanies John and Elinor to France, and treats the French royalty and courtiers insolently. The duke of Austria is his particular target. The Bastard mocks Austria's vanity in presuming to wear Richard's lion-skin robe. Indeed, he continues to make this joke at Austria's expense throughout Acts II and III, frequently commenting contemptuously on the duke's skinny legs.

The Bastard has a realistic view of life. Hearing John's and Philip's bold and competing addresses to the citizens of Angiers (II.i.206-86), the Bastard remarks to himself that such royal disputes generally mean suffering and death for soldiers and subjects. He suggests to the two kings that they settle the question of Angiers' loyalty by turning their cannons on the city and leveling it. A citizen of Angiers suggests an alternative—the union of France and England through the marriage of Lewis and Blanch. When the proposal is approved by everyone involved, and he is left alone, the Bastard marvels at

the insanity he sees around him: "Mad world, mad kings, mad composition" (II.i.561). In this soliloquy, he considers the role of commodity, or self-interest, in men's lives. He says that he despises it—yet he is honest enough to note that up until now he hasn't really had any self-interest to protect or promote. If the situation changes, he tells himself, he may very well find himself as treacherous as those presently in power.

In the battle that follows King Philip's desertion of the peace treaty, the Bastard slays Austria, cuts off his head, and reclaims Cordelion's lion-skin robe. The victory over France achieved, John sends him back to England to wring money out of the Church's monasteries to meet his expenses. Mocking the symbols used in the ritual of excommunication, the Bastard swears by "Bell, book, and candle" (III.iii.12) to carry out the king's orders.

Indeed, he later reports to John that he has "sped among the clergymen" (IV.ii.141) and forced them to contribute to John's treasury. While carrying out this mission, he has encountered the self-proclaimed prophet Peter of Pomfret, whom he brings to the English court. He also informs John that he has met Bigot and Salisbury, who are outraged by the death of Arthur. John entreats the Bastard to go after them and persuade them to come back. Carrying out the king's orders, the Bastard comes upon several nobles who have discovered Arthur's lifeless body. When they jump to the conclusion that John was responsible, he urges restraint. But when he and Hubert are left alone, he turns on him, genuinely appalled by Arthur's death and demanding to know if Hubert had any part in it. He accepts Hubert's denials as the truth and orders him to bear the body away.

From this point on, the Bastard is John's principal connection to the world outside the court. He is also the king's most reliable ally. He brings the king word that Englishmen are in revolt against him, but he urges John to remain steadfast. Trying to put backbone into the fearful John, the Bastard argues that if John puts up a brave front, people will see him as the same courageous and determined leader he has been in the past. The Bastard angrily disagrees with John's decision to negotiate with the French, but he accepts the king's request that he take charge of assembling a military force to confront the invaders.

Part of his duty to John is to negotiate with the French. He meets with Lewis and is passionately defiant. He threatens that John is prepared to hound Lewis and his army out of England—even though he knows that's hardly an accurate description of the king's present abilities. When Lewis suggests his words are nothing but vain boasting, the Bastard insists that John still represents a power to be reckoned with.

The Bastard arrives at Swinstead Abbey only moments before John dies. He is stunned by John's death. He promises his dead sovereign that he will avenge him and then meet him in heaven. When Salisbury tells him that the French have given up their invasion and are pursuing a peace treaty with England, the Bastard calms down. He offers his allegiance to Prince Henry and, in a passionate speech on behalf of patriotism, concludes the play with an appeal to all Englishmen to set their country's interests above their own.

To some readers, the Bastard appears to be two separate and distinct characters in the first and second halves of the play. To others, he seems to grow and develop during the course of *King John*, shedding his youthful cynicism for a realistic perspective on people and what motivates them. He freely exchanges his birthright for the dubious honor of being called the bastard son of Richard I. He taunts and teases people who outrank him. Quick-witted and intelligent, his great personal charm sometimes comes across as arrogance. In his "commodity" speech (II.i.561-98), he seems shocked at the difference between what men say and what they mean privately. But when he commits himself to John's cause, it's not clear whether he has chosen to act on principle or self-interest.

The Bastard understands as well as everyone else that John has usurped the throne from Arthur. But he remains loyal to the king, representing him to others as a healthy, vigorous ruler. Perhaps he recognizes that at the moment John is the only man around whom loyal Englishmen can gather. Or perhaps he now believes there are no moral absolutes in politics—that sometimes it's necessary to use unethical methods to achieve honorable goals. In the course of the play, he becomes increasingly perceptive about people and what motivates them. It isn't clear, however, whether he develops a similar understanding of himself.

Salisbury (Earl of Salisbury):

One of the highest ranking English noblemen in the play, the Earl of Salisbury often seems to waver between honor and self-interest. His behavior and

> **In an amoral world dominated by the struggle for political power, King Philip frequently appears torn between honor and self-interest."**

his motives are complex. If the king is guilty of an outrageous murder, Salisbury and the others would seem to have a worthy reason to refuse to follow the king any longer. But English nobles joining forces with an invader who threatens English sovereignty and national unity is treachery. And striking a bargain that will yield personal gain makes the justice of the rebels' motives questionable.

Salisbury appears only briefly in the first half of the play, but he is a prominent figure in Acts IV and V. In IV.ii, Salisbury says that he suspects the king means to harm Arthur. When John announces that the young prince is dead, Salisbury seems certain that foul play is involved. The first indication that he and the other nobles mean to desert John comes in IV.iii, where he describes to his friends a conversation he has had with Count Melune. Moments later, Salisbury and the others discover Arthur's body. Salisbury immediately declares that the boy was murdered and, kneeling beside Arthur's body, declares he will no longer serve the king. However, his earlier contact with the leaders of the French invasion raises the question of whether Arthur's alleged murder is really Salisbury's motive for rebellion or merely an excuse to justify a course of action he has already decided to take.

When Salisbury and the other English nobles meet with Lewis and Melune, they sign a document that outlines the terms of their alliance—particularly what share the nobles will have in the spoils of war. In an extended speech, Salisbury lays the blame for his rebellion on "the infection of the time" (V.ii.20), declaring that circumstances have forced him to take this action. Weeping, he laments that he and his friends were "born to see so sad an hour as this" (V.ii.26). His language is so exaggerated that Lewis mocks the sincerity of his emotions.

After Salisbury and his friends learn from Melune that they have been "bought and sold" (V.iv.10), they flee to avoid having their heads chopped off.

> **" The Bastard shows no hesitation in acknowledging that his mother may have been unfaithful to her husband."**

Salisbury vows to become, once again, an obedient follower of the man who embodies true English authority: ''our great King John'' (V.iv.57). He goes to Swinstead Abbey in search of the king, and he is in attendance when John dies. When the Bastard formally vows his allegiance to Prince Henry, Salisbury quickly follows with his own promise of love and faithful service forever.

Further Reading

Beaurline, L. A. Introduction to *King John*, by William Shakespeare, 1-57. Cambridge: Cambridge University Press, 1990.

Beaurline provides extensive discussions of several aspects of the play—including style, themes, and characterization—and a detailed history of stage productions. In his analysis of the game of power politics in *King John*, Beaurline demonstrates numerous similarities and contrasts between characters.

Braunmiller, A. R. Introduction to *The Life and Death of King John,* by William Shakespeare, 1-93. Oxford: Clarendon Press, 1989.

Braunmiller discusses the likely date and probable sources of the play and describes its theatrical reputation and stage history. Additionally, he offers extended remarks on the language of *King John* and on several central thematic issues: the political power struggle, relations between older and younger generations, and legitimate versus unlawful inheritance.

Burgoyne, Sidney C. ''Cardinal Pandulph and the 'Curse of Rome.' '' *College Literature* IV, no. 3 (Fall 1977): 232-40.

Burgoyne traces the cardinal's impact on the play's dramatic action, concluding that Pandulph's principal function is to authorize rebellion and create political chaos.

Calderwood, James L. ''Commodity and Honour in *King John*.'' *University of Toronto Quarterly* XXIX, no. 3 (April 1960): 341-56.

Calderwood deals with the conflict between honor and personal gain in *King John*, and shows how this conflict is personified in both John and the Bastard. The king's tragedy arises from his decision to violate honor and virtue by ordering Arthur's murder, while by contrast the Bastard gradually discards self-interest in favor of principled action.

Dusinberre, Juliet. ''*King John* and Embarrassing Women.'' *Shakespeare Survey* 42 (1990): 37-52.

Dusinberre claims that up to the beginning of Act IV, the dramatic action of *King John* is dominated by its female characters. Each of them in turn—Constance, Queen Elinor, Lady Faulconbridge, and Blanch—repeatedly interrupts official (masculine) conversation and speeches, thus undermining the power and questioning the judgment of various male authority figures.

Kastan, David Scott. ' ''To Set a Form upon that Indiges': Shakespeare's Figures of History.'' *Comparative Drama* 17, no. 1 (Spring 1983): 1-16.

Kastan focuses on the Bastard's skillful manipulation of language and events in Acts IV and V. His verbal dexterity transforms John into a monarch who seems worthy of the loyalty of the English nobles, Kastan declares; it also mirrors Shakespeare's creation of characters and history in *King John*.

Manheim, Michael. ''The Four Voices of the Bastard.'' In *King John: New Perspectives*, edited by Deborah T. Curren-Aquino, 126-35. Newark: University of Delaware Press, 1989.

Manheim traces the Bastard's increasing understanding of political reality and of himself in the course of the play. At each stage in his development, Manheim points out, the Bastard uses distinctive manners of speech that reveal his growing commitment to employ any means available to achieve his goal of political unity.

Price, Jonathan Reeve. ''King John and Problematic Art.'' *Shakespeare Quarterly* XXI, no. 1 (Winter 1970): 25-28.

Price sees deliberate ambiguities in the character of King John, with intentional shifts in the way he is portrayed. Although dramatic events are resolved at the conclusion of Act V, we are not told what to think about John and the series of calamities that befall him; rather we are free to choose a range of interpretations about the meaning of his collapse and ultimate ruin.

Van de Water, Julia C. ''The Bastard in *King John*.'' *Shakespeare Quarterly* XI, no. 2 (Spring 1960): 137-46.

Van de Water describes the Bastard as two separate and distinct characters under one name. She sees no connection at all between the witty, hard-headed realist of Acts I through III and the loyal English patriot of Acts IV and V. The Bastard is clearly the liveliest character in the play, she admits, but he is certainly not its ''hero.''

Wormersley, David. ''The Politics of Shakespeare's *King John*.'' *Review of English Studies* XL, no. 160 (November 1989): 497-515.

A central issue in *King John*, according to Wormersley, is how to live in a world without fundamental values or principles. He focuses his discussion of this question on the Bastard's attempts to find his way in this ''mad world'' of dramatic reversals of fortune and violent political upheavals.

The Tragedy of King Lear

Plot Summary

circa 1605

Act I:

The earls of Kent and Gloucester enlighten the audience regarding King Lear's intention to divide his kingdom equally among his three daughters as he retires from office. Both Kent and Gloucester had previously thought that Lear preferred his son-in-law the duke of Albany, husband of Goneril, over his son-in-law the duke of Cornwall, husband to Regan. In Edmund's hearing, Gloucester admits that Edmund is his bastard son. Even though it has been determined that each of his three daughters will receive an equal share of the kingdom, as a formality, Lear asks each to proclaim her love for him. Goneril, the eldest daughter, waxes eloquent about the love she bears Lear; he gives her a third of the kingdom. Regan, the second eldest daughter, outdoes Goneril's rhetoric; Lear gives her a third of the kingdom. When Cordelia, the youngest daughter is asked what she might say to receive a greater share, she answers, "Nothing, my lord" (I.i.87). Upset, Lear divides her portion of the kingdom between Goneril and Regan and banishes Cordelia. He divides the crown between Albany and Cornwall, maintaining for himself only the name and respect due a king. He stipulates that he might monthly alternate his residence between Goneril and Regan, keeping a retinue of one hundred knights.

Both the king of France and the duke of Burgundy have been competing for Cordelia's hand in

marriage, but when the duke of Burgundy realizes she has lost her inheritance, he wants nothing to do with her. The king of France, however, accepts her as she is and takes her with him back to his own country. Kent, a loyal follower of Lear, advises the king not to be so rash in his judgment of Cordelia; incensed, Lear banishes Kent as well.

Edmund is determined to make his brother Edgar, Gloucester's legitimate heir, look bad in the eyes of his father. He too obviously hides a letter, supposedly written by Edgar, from Gloucester's view. Gloucester demands to read the letter, which details Edgar's alleged plan to kill Gloucester in order to receive his inheritance sooner. Edmund then advises Edgar to hide from Gloucester's wrath.

Meanwhile, Lear has taken up residence at Goneril's home, and his knights have acted somewhat boisterously there. Lear has struck Oswald, Goneril's servant, because he has chastised Lear's Fool. Goneril tells Oswald to neglect Lear that she might bring the matter to a head. When Oswald speaks rudely to Lear, Kent, who has gained service with Lear by disguising himself as Caius, trips Oswald and humiliates him. Goneril confronts her father, complaining that she can no longer tolerate his treatment of her servants. She asks him to eliminate the rowdy knights from his train of followers. Still thinking he is a king and believing that he has another daughter who loves him unconditionally, Lear announces his intention to leave immediately for the home of Regan and Cornwall. Instructing him to go to Gloucester first, Lear sends Kent/Caius with a letter to Regan informing her of his intent. At the same time, Goneril sends a letter to Regan informing her of Lear's insufferable behavior.

Act II:

Edmund learns from a servant that Regan and Cornwall plan to visit his father that evening, a rumor of impending war between Cornwall and Albany circulating. Edmund meets with Edgar and again advises him to flee. When Edgar does so, Edmund cries out in alarm and cuts his own arm. When Gloucester responds to that alarm, Edmund pretends to have fought with Edgar. On the strength of Edmund's lie, Gloucester vows to catch and punish Edgar. Regan and Cornwall arrive at Gloucester's estate, and Regan, having received letters from both her father and her sister, pretends to seek Gloucester's advice. The two letter carriers, Oswald and Kent, meet outside and quarrel. Believing that Lear still holds some sway, Kent is somewhat impudent when he is questioned by Cornwall about the matter of the quarrel. Cornwall has Kent put in the stocks, against the counsel of Gloucester. Meanwhile, Edgar disguises himself as ''Poor Tom,'' an insane beggar. Lear discovers that his messenger Caius (Kent) has been put in the stocks. He grows even more frustrated when Regan does not respond readily to his request to see her. When she does appear before Lear, she is not as warm and welcoming as Lear had believed she would be. Goneril soon arrives, and she and Regan try to convince Lear to give up all of his knights. When Lear realizes that his two daughters are in league against him, he stalks off with the Fool into the stormy night. Gloucester, concerned for Lear's welfare in the storm, goes after him. Regan and Goneril turn their backs on Lear and lock the door against him.

Act III:

Kent meets with a gentleman and reveals that the king of France has landed a force in Dover, either at the insistence of Cordelia in her concern for her father or to take advantage of the division between Albany and Cornwall. Kent requests that this gentleman deliver a letter to Cordelia in Dover, and, since Kent is still disguised as the servant Caius, he gives the gentleman a token by which Cordelia will know that the letter is from Kent. The gentleman has informed Kent of Lear's situation, and Kent now goes in search of the king. He finds him raging against the storm and thoroughly mad, accompanied only by his Fool. He coaxes Lear to take shelter in a nearby hovel. Gloucester has returned home only to find his own doors barred against him by Regan and Cornwall for having attempted to aid Lear. He meets with Edmund and ill-advisedly informs his bastard son of the rancor threatening to divide Albany and Cornwall and then tells him the whereabouts of a letter alluding to the French forces afoot in Dover to avenge the wrongs done King Lear. Gloucester finds Lear in the company of the Fool, Kent, and Poor Tom (Edgar), who has been discovered hiding in the hovel. Gloucester does not recognize his son Edgar in disguise. Edmund is at that very moment showing Cornwall the letter Gloucester has told him about. Cornwall declares Gloucester a traitor and names Edmund the new earl of Gloucester. Gloucester confers briefly with Kent and then returns home, where Oswald has mistakenly reported that Gloucester has directed Lear and thirty-five of his knights toward Dover. In fact, all of Lear's knights have by this time deserted him. Cornwall has Gloucester bound and interrogates him about the French forces. Gloucester objects that he has only heard rumors and guesses about that situation. Cornwall does not believe him and plucks out one of Gloucester's eyes. Gloucester cries out for Edmund, and Regan informs him that it was Edmund who had revealed Gloucester's treason. Gloucester at that moment realizes he has been wrong about Edgar. One of Cornwall's servants is outraged at Cornwall's brutality and opposes him. The two fight, and the servant inflicts a wound that will eventually kill Cornwall. Regan takes a sword and slays the servant. Cornwall plucks out Gloucester's other eye and says, ''Go thrust him out at gates, and let him smell / His way to Dover'' (III.vii.93-94).

Act IV:

Edgar, still in the guise of Poor Tom, discovers his now blind father being guided by an old man. Edgar offers to lead Gloucester to Dover. Both Goneril and Regan have fallen in love with Edmund, and Goneril quarrels with Albany, who has shown some sympathy to Lear and only intends to fight the French in order to preserve his own lands. A messenger enters with the news that Cornwall has died of the wound inflicted by the servant. Kent meets again with the gentleman he has encountered earlier. The gentleman informs Kent that the king of France has been called away on urgent business at home and has left Cordelia with the French troops on English soil. Cordelia has heard news that Lear has been seen bedecked with flowers and murmuring madness. She directs her soldiers to search for Lear and bring him to her. A messenger enters and announces that the English troops have been arrayed for battle, and Cordelia says the French forces are prepared. With Cornwall dead, Regan plans to share her wealth and position with Edmund; she has given him control of her own military forces. She tells Oswald that it has been decided that Gloucester must die since his appearance prompts pity and hardens the populace against Regan and Edmund for their complicity in the cruel outrage done him. Gloucester informs Edgar/Poor Tom that he wishes to be led to the steepest cliff of Dover so that he might end his suffering. Instead, Edgar leads him to a level place, pretending that it is a steep precipice. Gloucester allows himself to fall. All in an effort to alleviate Gloucester's despair, Edgar then adopts a different accent and prods Gloucester, pretending that he has seen Gloucester fall from a dizzying height, a demonic looking man having stood at the top by his side. Gloucester revives with a new resolve to suffer ''Affliction till it do cry out itself'' (IV.vi.76). Lear appears, looking and acting as Cordelia has earlier described him. Gloucester is

incredibly moved by Lear's situation, and the two communicate on a deeply emotional level. One of Cordelia's servants and some of her attendants enter and gently lead Lear back to her. Oswald enters intent upon killing Gloucester, but Edgar first warns and then kills the ambitious courtier. In the care of Cordelia's doctors, Lear is bathed and dressed, soft music playing in the background. The doctor assures Cordelia that Lear will awaken after his rest in a more sound frame of mind. Lear awakens somewhat addled but buoys Cordelia's hopes when he says, ''I think this lady / To be my child Cordelia'' (IV.vii.68-69).

Act V:

Edgar gives Albany a letter taken from the dead Oswald, which details Goneril's plot to kill Albany and wed Edmund. Edgar tells Albany to open the letter before he fights the battle. Albany is further instructed to sound the trumpet if he is victorious, and Edgar will produce a champion to prove the truth of the letter. After the English win the battle, Lear and Cordelia are brought in as prisoners. When Albany requests that Lear and Cordelia be brought to him, Edmund argues that he has had them removed lest they invite the sympathy of a populace which might rise against the forces that hold them captive. Secretly, Edmund has arranged for Lear and Cordelia to be executed quickly. Goneril verbally abuses Albany again, and she and Regan jealously squabble over Edmund. Albany accuses Edmund of treason and sounds the trumpet. Edgar responds to the announced challenge, disguised in armor. He fights with Edmund and mortally wounds him, ultimately revealing his true identity. Albany embraces Edgar and asks after his father. Edgar reports that Gloucester has died when his heart '''Twixt two extremes of passion, joy and grief, / Burst smilingly'' (V.iii.198-99). A gentleman enters with a bloody knife and announces that Goneril has committed suicide after confessing that she had poisoned Regan. A dying Edmund, wanting to do one good deed before he dies, urges that word be sent quickly to countermand his order to execute Lear and Cordelia. But it is too late. Lear enters carrying the dead body of Cordelia in his arms. As he mourns his youngest daughter, Lear distractedly brags of having killed one of her executioners. The announcement of Edmund's death does not receive much attention as everyone is focused on the suffering of King Lear. Albany promises to restore Lear's regal wealth and power, but Lear dies. The Kent says that he must follow soon, and the survivors exit to a death march.

Modern Connections

Modern audiences of *King Lear* often observe the recurrence of images and references not only the eyes but things associated with the eyes, like crying, looking, and seeing. The numerous references to the eyes and their associated functions contribute to a thematic development which is almost certainly more than accidental to Shakespeare's purpose. We can look at several specific references to elaborate further the significance of this theme of "eyelessness" or "blindness" in the play.

First, and most obvious is Gloucester's "I stumbled when I saw" (IV.i.19). He comes to believe that when he had full use of his eyes, he still had not been able to see the truth in the situation between his two sons (Edgar and Edmund) and realizes that there is an internal sense more keen in determining the truth than eyesight, which is considered our primary sense.

While initially Lear fails to recognize the truth about his daughters' love for him, he soon realizes that Goneril and Regan, having subsumed the power that was once his, have turned against him. He asks the gods "If it be you that stirs these daughters' hearts / Against their father" (II.iv.274-75). Lear's primary problem, it might be argued then, is not that he, like Gloucester, fails to see the truth about his offspring. Perhaps Lear's ultimate failure is that he cannot see through his tears. He is often moved to cry but feels that the tears he sheds are not becoming to either his gender or his position.

> Old fond eyes,
> Beweep this cause again, I'll pluck ye out,
> And cast you, with the waters that you loose,
> To temper clay.
>
> (I.iv.301-04)

When he does understand that Goneril and Regan have turned on him, he fights his tears fiercly, beseeching the gods in this manner:

> . . . touch me with noble anger
> And let not women's weapons, water-drops,
> Stain my man's cheeks . . .
> . . . You think I'll weep:
> No, I'll not weep.
> I have full cause of weeping, but this heart
> Shall break into a hundred thousand flaws
> Or ere I'll weep.
>
> (II.iv.276-78; 282-84)

His anger at his tears is indicative of his inability to trust and experience the truth of his feelings.

This inability is what caused him, in the first place, to misjudge the emotional bond that existed between him and Cordelia. He had to test her, and her response was, perhaps, an incredulous reaction to that distrust. The result was a peevish rejection of her that overlay his real feelings, prompting Kent to say, "See better, Lear, and let me still remain / The true blank of thine eye" (I.i.158-59). One might argue that Lear's petulance is an emotional truth that must be followed if the argument is that feelings, rather than sight, are the barometer of truth. But, arguably, Lear's love for Cordelia is primary and his dissatisfaction with her only a temporary perversion of the greater emotional truth.

Lear's failure to trust in this emotional truth— that of Cordelia's love for him—is perhaps one of the most universal and timeless aspects of the play. How often is the love between parents and children tested by one, or by both, parties? Today's parents, like Lear, may often feel compelled to question their children's love, pointing out all they have done for them, especially when the children are about to embark on or have chosen a coarse of action disapproved of by the parents. Similarly, children who are being disciplined by their parents may feel the punishment unjust (as perhaps Cordelia felt her banishment was unjust), and may question their parents' love for them.

In 1681, Nahum Tate adapted Shakespeare's *King Lear*. In Tate's version, which superseded Shakespeare's until well into the nineteenth century, the ending is a happy one. Cordelia lives and Lear's crown is restored by Albany. Additionally, Tate eliminated both Lear's Fool and the blinding of Gloucester and added a love affair between Edgar and Cordelia.

Tate's happy ending, which was endorsed by critics and audiences for nearly 150 years, may make modern readers wonder why Shakespeare chose to end his *King Lear* in such a dismal fashion. In fact the issue of Shakespeare's tragic ending has been the focus of much debate for centuries. A number of explanations have been put forth. Some people believe that the play's ending is simply a natural and inevitable culmination of Lear's suffering. While some people read the ending as evidence that there is no divine existence or divine retribution for evil, others argue that the ending emphasizes the play's Christian focus on the redemptive power of love. Finally, many people maintain that the ending is not pessimistic or optimistic, but that it reflects the mystery of human existence.

Characters

Albany (Duke of Albany):

The duke of Albany is Goneril's husband. He is a nobleman with lands of his own, but he inherits half of Lear's kingdom through Goneril. Because Lear's kingdom is divided, tension exists between Albany and Cornwall, Regan's husband. It is rumored that Cornwall and Albany might war against each other. Instead, they end up combining their efforts against the French contingent which has landed at Dover and is trying to redeem Lear and reinstall him as king at the direction of Cordelia. When Lear goes to live with Goneril and Albany, Albany finds out after the event that Goneril has cast her father out. He sympathizes with Lear, but since Lear is Goneril's father, he does not actively intervene. Later, after Goneril and Regan have forced Lear out into the storm, Albany criticizes Goneril's treatment of her father. He says to her, "You are not worth the dust which the rude wind / Blows in your face" (IV.ii.30-31). He calls Goneril and Regan "Tigers, not daughters" (IV.ii.40) and accuses them of making Lear, "a gracious aged man" (IV.ii.41), mad. Goneril, in turn, calls Albany a "Milk-liver'd man, / That bear'st a cheek for blows" (IV.ii.50-51).

Albany bears it patiently when Goneril flirts with Edmund in front of him. He has received letters from Edgar, taken from the dead Oswald, which reveal that Goneril and Edmund are hatching a plot on his life. Although Albany does not know Edgar's true identity, he agrees to summon him after the battle that Edgar might prove Edmund is a traitor. Albany is depicted as a good-hearted optimist. When he receives word that Cornwall has died of the wound inflicted by his own servant, Albany declares,

> This shows you are above,
> You [justicers], that these our nether crimes
> So speedily can venge!
>
> (IV.ii.78-80)

But Albany's optimism is not born out at the end of the play. The wicked are punished, but so are the good. Albany announces his intention to restore Lear's absolute power, but Lear dies before that noble gesture can be realized.

Attendants:

In the opening scene of the play, attendants appear without speaking in the train of King Lear. In

> **" ... after Goneril and Regan have forced Lear out into the storm, Albany criticizes Goneril's treatment of her father. He says to her, 'You are not worth the dust which the rude wind / Blows in your face' (IV.ii.30-31)."**

the same scene, Burgundy and France have their own attendants. While staying at Goneril's home, attendants appear with Lear after he has been hunting. Regan and Cornwall are attended when they show up at Gloucester's home in anticipation of Lear's arrival. Later in the play, Cordelia's attendants appear with a gentleman to apprehend the mad Lear and escort him to the kind treatment of Cordelia.

Burgundy (Duke of Burgundy):

The duke of Burgundy appears only briefly at the beginning of the play. He is a wealthy, powerful nobleman but his actions do not place him in a favorable light. He has been negotiating against the king of France for Cordelia's hand in marriage, but when he learns that she is not to inherit any of her father's wealth, he quickly expresses his lack of further interest in her.

Captain:

After Lear and Cordelia have been captured by the English forces and Edmund has sent them off to prison, the captain agrees to follow with Edmund's command to execute the former king and his daughter quickly. Edmund has already promoted the captain, and he promises to do so again. The captain says, "I cannot draw a cart, nor eat dried oats, / If it be man's work, I'll do't" (V.iii.37-38), meaning that, for the promise of reward, he will do anything of which he is physically capable. Another captain appears in the scene immediately following this one. He sounds the trumpet that calls Edgar to challenge Edmund.

Cordelia:

Cordelia is Lear's youngest daughter. When her turn comes to outdo her sisters in their protests of great love for Lear, she is strangely silent. Lear reacts with passion and withholds her inheritance, casting her fortune to fate since he will have nothing more to do with her. We might question why Cordelia does not say what Lear wants to hear when to do so would take little effort on her part. She demonstrates her deep love for her father later in the play. Why, then, does she not demonstrate this love at the beginning and save her father the torment that follows? The answer to this question may be that Lear has chosen an awkward and arguably inappropriate moment to ask his only unwed daughter to declare him the sole object of her love. Cordelia has two potential suitors, Burgundy and France, waiting in the wings. Since the transfer of a daughter's dependence from father to husband was a critical moment in her life, it would not do for Cordelia to reveal a willingness to cater to a father's every demand, when those demands might conflict with those of the future husband. Goneril and Regan do not have this particular concern since they are already married. Another explanation might be that Cordelia sees the gross flattery of her sisters as hollow and degrading, true expressions of love best delivered in a private not a public forum. Additionally, perhaps Cordelia feels that her love for her father is an obvious fact of their close relationship (which her sisters discuss later: ''He always lov'd our sister most, and with what poor judgment he hath now cast her off appears too grossly'' [I.i.290-91]), a fact which need not be stated verbally and put up for comparision with her sisters' relationship with their father.

Despite Lear's harsh treatment of her, Cordelia remains a loyal and loving daughter. She convinces her husband the king of France, who has graciously embraced her penniless and untitled condition, to mount an effort to save Lear from the cruelties of Goneril and Regan. When that effort fails and Cordelia and Lear are captured, Cordelia suffers for the love she has extended to her father. Yet she remains somewhat stand-offish, never too openly or too profusely professing that love in words. In this reserve, she remains consistent with the reserve she has demonstrated at the beginning of the play. When Lear expresses his glee at the prospect of their life in prison together, Cordelia again is silent. We might imagine that her loyalties are again divided between husband and father, but Cordelia, perhaps, does not relish the thought of imprisonment as much as Lear. Cordelia says to her father, ''For thee, oppressed king, I am cast down, / Myself could else out-frown false Fortune's frown'' (V.iii.5-6). She

is more concerned for her father than for herself, and, as always, she has expressed her love in actions rather than words.

Moreover, it has been suggested that Cordelia is meant to be seen, partly, as a Christ figure. When a messenger informs her that the English troops have assembled to oppose her own, she says, ''O dear father, / It is thy business that I go about'' (IV.iv.23-24). She is on a spiritual mission to save her father's soul, and her words recall those of Christ in the Temple. And like the love Christ extends to humanity, Cordelia's love to Lear is extended freely; it is never a matter of question and cannot be commanded. It is always there for Lear to accept or reject.

In V.iii.244-48, Edmund renounces his decree to have Cordelia and Lear executed but only a few lines later, Lear enters with Cordelia's body.

Cornwall (Duke of Cornwall):

The duke of Cornwall is Regan's husband. Like Albany, his own wealth has been increased by the inheritance of half Lear's former realm. When Cornwall discovers that the French are afoot in England, he feels that wealth being threatened. He ruthlessly tries to find out all that he can about the French intentions and the English who might be conspiring to aid the French. Gloucester has revealed to Edmund the existence of a letter demonstrating just such a conspiracy, and Edmund finds the letter and shows it to Cornwall. Cornwall brings Gloucester in for questioning, first binding the old man and then cruelly gouging out his eyes. Outraged by his master's horrible treatment of Gloucester, one of Cornwall's own servant challenges him and delivers to him a wound that will eventually kill him.

Curan:

Curan is a courtier. He appears in the first scene of the second act of the play. He informs Edmund that he has told Gloucester to expect a visit from the duke and duchess of Cornwall that evening. Curan discusses with Edmund the rumors of war between Cornwall and Albany.

Doctor:

When Cordelia reports that Lear has been seen wandering about mad, the doctor assures her that rest is a cure for that madness. He tells Cordelia he knows of many medicinal herbs to induce the necessary rest. After Lear has been apprehended by Cordelia's attendants, the doctor ministers to Lear.

He directs Cordelia to waken her father, again assuring her that the prescribed rest will have soothed his madness. He directs the music to be played louder, and when, at first, Lear speaks incoherently to Cordelia, the doctor tells Cordelia that Lear is groggy yet from sleep, but will eventually be alright.

Edgar:

Edgar is Gloucester's legitimate son. His half-brother Edmund frames him, letting on to Gloucester that Edgar is impatient for his inheritance and means to kill his father. Edgar is forced into hiding, and he adopts the disguise of "Poor Tom" a mad Bedlam (from Bethlehem hospital, an asylum for the insane) beggar. During the raging storm into which Goneril and Regan have forced Lear, Edgar finds himself in the same hovel with the mad king and Lear's Fool. Acting mad is perhaps the best disguise for Edgar since the insane were invisible in Elizabethan society, quickly dismissed and rarely scrutinized. Edgar is forced to give up his identity as Gloucester's son and heir just as Lear struggles to come to grips with his own conflicting sense of identity: the feigned madness of Edgar parallels the real madness of Lear. Lear, in his confusion, assumes that Poor Tom's madness must result from the same cause as his own. He asks of Edgar, "Has his daughters brought him to this pass?" (III.iv.63) Lear is wrong about the cause, but his remark heightens the sense that madness is the inevitable cause of identity loss.

After Gloucester's eyes have been plucked out by Cornwall, Edgar appears as Poor Tom and leads his father to the Cliffs of Dover, where Gloucester intends to kill himself. Edgar knows that that is Gloucester's intention, so he deludes his father by telling him the flat space upon which he stands is the dizzying height of Dover. After Gloucester falls, Edgar appears with a different identity, pretending that Gloucester has survived the fall. He says, "Why I do trifle thus with his despair / Is done to cure it" (IV.vi.33-34). Edgar further pretends that he has seen a demonic figure with Gloucester before the latter leaps, hoping that Gloucester will think his urge to suicide was prompted by demonic impulses, hoping that, in thinking so, Gloucester will gain a renewed zeal for life.

At the end of the play, Edgar appears in yet another disguise, a suit of armor. He fights and kills his bastard brother to prove him a traitor, while none of the onlookers realize who he is. It is only after he has demonstrated his nobility that he can reveal his true identity. Like that of Cordelia and Kent, Ed-

> Cordelia says to her father, 'For thee, oppressed king, I am cast down, / Myself could else out-frown false Fortune's frown' (V.iii.5-6)."

gar's nobility must be proved in action and not in words.

Edmund:

Edmund, the bastard son of Gloucester and half-brother to Edgar, commits a number of villainous acts throughout the course of the play: he forces his brother, Edgar, into hiding, telling Gloucester that Edgar means to kill him; he betrays his father and leaves him to the barbarous treatment of Cornwall and Regan; he encourages both Goneril and Regan to believe he loves the one to the exclusion of the other, causing them to quarrel and, ultimately, die as a consequence; and he orders the execution of Lear and Cordelia.

At the beginning of the play, Gloucester acknowledges to Kent that Edmund is his bastard son. Gloucester says, "Though this knave came something saucily to the world before he was sent for, yet was his mother fair, there was good sport at his making, and the whoreson must be acknowledg'd" (I.i.21-24). Edmund's nativity is the subject of good sport and joking. He has probably endured a lifetime of being treated this casually and contemptibly. It is no wonder, then, that such a constantly reinforcing experience might have embittered him not only toward his father and half-brother but also toward the world. Edmund compares himself to Edgar and finds that he is his equal in all but the name and legitimacy that is conferred not on the basis of one's qualities, but only on the basis of social convention. Edmund denies that social convention and abandons the dictates of any higher authority. He says, "Thou, Nature, art my goddess, to thy law / My services are bound" (I.ii.1-2). He will operate only by the laws of nature—the survival of the fittest—without any sense of compassion for the suffering of others. He means to get that which he feels has been denied him by the circumstances of his birth, apparently believing ruthless

> **Cornwall brings Gloucester in for questioning, first binding the old man and then cruelly gouging out his eyes."**

ambition to be a fair compensation for his social exile.

Edmund's attitude toward his father and the society his father represents is best illustrated by his dismissal of his father's belief that the stars influence people's lives. When Gloucester learns of Lear's banishment of Kent and Cordelia, he believes Lear's rash behavior to be a consequence of "These late eclipses in the sun and moon" (I.ii.103). Gloucester also believes that one's nature is determined by the placement of stars and planets at one's birth. The consequence of such reasoning is the belief that people's actions are predetermined. Edmund takes the opposite view. He says, "An admirable evasion of whoremaster man, to lay his goatish disposition on the charge of a star!" (I.ii.126-28). In denying Gloucester's belief, Edmund endorses the opinion that man can make of himself anything he chooses, an endorsement that fits well with his Machiavellian behavior. It is curious, then, that at the end of the play Edmund should desire to save the lives of Cordelia and Lear. When he says, "Some good I mean to do, / Despite of mine own nature" (V.ii.244-45), he contradicts his earlier stated position. Perhaps he has been influenced by the noble behavior of many around him.

Fool:

King Lear's Fool is a licensed one. That is, he could say anything he wanted without fear of punishment. This license was extended to Fools partly for the humor it caused Fools to produce, and partly for the insights it provided the Fool's listeners. Lear's Fool is often funny, but he is more often tragically accurate in his assessment of Lear's situation. He acts as Lear's conscience by constantly reminding him of his mistake in banishing Cordelia from his sight, and by insisting that Lear admit the truly vicious natures of Goneril and Regan. When Lear begins to go mad as the result of his elder daughter's ingratitude, the Fool reminds him that he

has brought his suffering upon himself by not seeing that ingratitude earlier.

When Lear takes refuge in the hovel and finally lies down to rest, the Fool utters his last line in the play: "And I'll go to bed at noon" (III.vi.85). He mysteriously disappears after that point. The Fool has been pining the absence of Cordelia, and his disappearance is often explained as the consequence of that pining. It is usually assumed by the audience that the Fool sickens and dies. A theatrical explanation for the Fool's disappearance is that Cordelia and the Fool, some critics have argued, were perhaps played by the same actor, making the Fool's disappearance necessary to allow time for a costume and makeup change. Whatever the reason, the Fool's disappearance works to good effect dramatically. Once Lear has become fully mad, there simply is no reason to provide him with a dramatic conscience in the character of the Fool, since the conscience is dependent on a reasoning process Lear now lacks.

France (King of France):

The king of France is present at the beginning of the play during the praising contest in which Lear tests the love his daughters have for him. He has been negotiating for Cordelia's hand in marriage, competing with the duke of Burgundy for that privilege. But unlike Burgundy, who loses interest in Cordelia the moment she is disinherited, France says he will take her even though she has no money and no title. He will take Cordelia to his own country and make her a queen there. His is a loving and noble gesture, and, as we learn later, he continues to be loving and generous with Cordelia. Because she is saddened by her father's circumstances, France brings his own forces to England in an attempt to save his wife's father. He is called back to France on urgent business there, but he leaves Cordelia to continue the effort.

Gentleman:

In Elizabethan England, the title of "gentleman" was given to a man belonging to the gentry class, landowners just below the nobility in social rank. Several minor characters designated as "a gentleman" appear in *King Lear*. In I.v, a gentleman informs Lear that the horses have been made ready for Kent to carry Lear's letter to Regan; in II.iv, a gentleman agrees with Lear that Regan's sudden departure from home is strange; in III.i, the same gentleman, perhaps, agrees to take Kent's letter and identifying token to Cordelia in Dover; in

IV.iii, that same gentleman tells Kent that Cordelia has received Kent's letters, and the two discuss the circumstances of the king of France's necessary return home; in IV.vi, a gentleman, acting on Cordelia's behalf, finds the mad Lear and sees that he is escorted to Cordelia; in IV.vii, the same gentleman tells Cordelia that he has helped the doctor minister to Lear by putting fresh clothes on the disturbed king; in V.iii, a gentleman enters with a bloody knife and announces that Goneril has killed herself after admitting to poisoning Regan; and, finally, later in that same scene, a gentleman confirms Lear's story about having killed one of Cordelia's assailants.

Gentlemen:

In V.i, a number of gentlemen appear without speaking in the company of Edmund, Regan, and the English soldiers at the advent of battle between the English and French forces.

Gloucester (Earl of Gloucester):

The earl of Gloucester is the father of Edgar and Edmund. As a character, Gloucester connects the main plot with the subplot of the play. His situation parallels the situation of Lear. He mistakenly believes Edmund when the latter pretends to read a letter that is falsely said to be written by Edgar. In that letter, Edgar supposedly tells Edmund of his impatience to inherit Gloucester's estate. Gloucester, like Lear, responds emotionally, immediately denouncing his legitimate son (Edgar) and trusting in the son who really intends to do him wrong (Edmund). And like Lear, Gloucester is to be punished for his lack of insight or moral vision. That punishment comes in the form of a brutal incident wherein his eyes are ruthlessly plucked out by Cornwall. The physical blinding of Gloucester is symbolic of both his own and Lear's blindness to the truth about their children.

When the old man, a longtime tenant of Gloucester and Gloucester's father, tries to assist Gloucester because he cannot see his way, Gloucester replies, ''I have no way, and therefore want no eyes; / I stumbled when I saw'' (IV.i.18-19). He can see better now that his eyes are gone, and he sees that he has placed his trust in the wrong son. He has reached the depth of despair, feeling there is no way to undo what he has done. It is this despair that compels him to say, ''As flies to wanton boys are we to th' gods, / They kill us for their sport'' (IV.i.36-37). Edgar, in disguise, leads Gloucester to the Cliffs of Dover, from which Gloucester intends to hurl himself and

> " Edgar is forced to give up his identity as Gloucester's son and heir just as Lear struggles to come to grips with his own conflicting sense of identity: the feigned madness of Edgar parallels the real madness of Lear."

commit suicide. Edgar deludes Gloucester, making him think he has, in fact, fallen from a great height. This scene would be comical if not for the serious intention Edgar has in doing what he does. He wants to cure Gloucester of his despair, a despair that still blinds Gloucester even though he thinks he now sees the truth about his life.

Both Gloucester's despair and Lear's madness are conditions which allow the two old men to evade one of the inevitable realities of aging. At some point, parents need to depend on their adult children. Both Gloucester and Lear eventually emerge from those conditions which have blinded them and accept the necessity of that dependence. Edgar is able to report at the end of the play that, when finally revealing himself to his father, Gloucester's heart ''Twixt two extremes of passion, joy and grief, / Burst smilingly'' (V.iii.198-99). Again, like Lear, Gloucester dies in the grip of two emotional extremes, but at least he has learned that joy is possible when one accepts the love and devotion of another human being.

Goneril:

Goneril is Lear's eldest daughter. She seems to understand that her father sometimes acts in a petty manner, and she knows how to please him. If she can inherit a third of Lear's kingdom by simply telling him that she loves him profoundly, she will gladly do it. To do so costs her nothing. Unlike Cordelia, Goneril knows how to cover her true feelings with high-blown rhetoric. Later in the play, Goneril treats Lear severely and appears quite monstrous.

After Lear's angry responses to the behaviors of Cordelia and Kent, Goneril and Regan discuss Lear's state of mind. In an effort to explain that state

> **Edmund, the bastard son of Gloucester and half-brother to Edgar, commits a number of villainous acts throughout the course of the play: he forces his brother, Edgar, into hiding . . .; he betrays his father . . .; he encourages both Goneril and Regan to believe he loves the one to the exclusion of the other . . .; and he orders the execution of Lear and Cordelia."**

of mind, Goneril says, "He always lov'd our sister most, and with what poor judgment he hath now cast her off appears too grossly" (I.i.290-91). Regan replies, " 'Tis the infirmity of his age, yet he hath ever but slenderly known himself" (I.i.293-94). The two have obviously been subjected to Lear's whims before, and they feel what is perhaps an understandable resentment at his previous favoring of their younger sister. At first, Goneril and Regan unite against Lear in self defense. It is only later that their behavior becomes inexcusable.

Goneril's increasingly cruel treatment of Lear is proof of the adage that "power corrupts." Her request of Lear to conduct himself civilly in her home is not an unreasonable one. At first, perhaps, she wants to force a confrontation with Lear in order that he might alter his behavior, but when she sees that she can manipulate her weakened father, the sense of her own power seems to go to her head. She apparently does not feel remorse for causing her father anguish, because, in her mind, he deserves it. Inheriting half of Lear's kingdom has also put her on a different, more equal, footing with her husband, Albany. In opposing the threat posed by the French forces at Dover, Goneril's wealth and influence are needed. She abandons all obedience to her husband, calling him a "Milk-liver'd man" (IV.ii.50-51). She appears to be attracted to Edgar because he represents the raw desire and unapologetic quest for power she seems to now find so thrilling. In her

quest for power, she will stop at nothing, even poisoning her sister Regan. In the end, it is reported that Goneril commits suicide after confessing that she has poisoned Regan.

Herald:

In V.iii, after the captain has sounded the trumpet in a general challenge, an act which Edgar has previously requested of Albany, the herald reads the proclamation: any man who would prove by strength of arms that Edmund is a traitor should appear immediately.

Kent (Earl of Kent):

The earl of Kent is a nobleman and an unselfish, devoted supporter of King Lear. When Lear so harshly denies Cordelia, Kent attempts to intervene. He says, "See better, Lear, and let me still remain / The true blank of thine eye" (I.i.157-58). Lear then rashly banishes Kent. But instead of pouting, going off to lick his wounds, or fostering a hatred of Lear for his actions, Kent adopts the disguise of Caius, a rough character of lower social station than Kent really is, and devotes himself to helping Lear see better, sticking by Lear's side and protecting him until the end.

Like Cordelia and Edgar, Kent represents the love and devotion that persists even through adversity. And, like Edgar, Kent extends that love and devotion in disguise. In one sense, disguise functions in *King Lear* to stress the necessity of seeing beyond outer appearances in a hostile world in which those appearances can be deceiving. In another sense, disguise demonstrates that true nobility results, obviously, not from one's title or social distinction, but from an inner sense of morality. Kent and Edgar demonstrate their nobility in their actions, just as the lowly servant of Cornwall performs a noble act of courage in opposing his master and dying in defense of the helpless Gloucester.

Kent's final words in the play pose a mystery. After Lear dies, Kent says to Albany, "I have a journey, sir shortly to go: / My master calls me, I must not say no" (V.iii.322-23). Is Kent referring to Lear or God, his earthly or spiritual "master"? Perhaps the play means to suggest that the distinction doesn't matter, that in serving one, one serves the other.

King of France:
See France

Knights:

One of the conditions upon which Lear insists when relinquishing the crown is that he be allowed to keep one hundred knights. That number steadily dwindles, and, eventually, all the knights see the handwriting on the wall and desert Lear. In I.iv, the knights return to Goneril's home after hunting with Lear. One of those knights reports that he has been treated rudely by Oswald, Goneril's servant. The Knight observes that Lear is no longer treated with the same respect he once enjoyed. He also remarks that Lear's Fool is pining away in sadness since Cordelia has gone.

Lear (King Lear):

As the play opens we learn that King Lear is getting on in years and has decided to divide his kingdom among his three daughters. Lear is already demonstrating his eccentric nature. Although he has previously determined that the realm will be equally divided, he insists that each of his three daughters try to outdo the others in her proclamation of love for him. When Cordelia fails to satisfy his desire for praise and need for love, he immediately reacts in a purely emotional way, disinheriting her and refusing to listen to the reasonable arguments of Kent, whom Lear also banishes quickly without thinking the matter through.

Lear's expectations about his life in retirement are unrealistic. Lear, who uses the royal "we" to refer to himself, announces that

> . . . 'tis our fast intent
> To shake all cares and business from our age,
> Conferring them on younger strengths, while we
> Unburthen'd crawl toward death.
>
> (I.i.38-41)

Lear wants to regain the untroubled life of a second childhood, yet he does not want to relinquish the authority and respect that he has become accustomed to as king. Lear intends that "Only we shall retain / The name, and all th' addition to a king" (I.i.135-36). He wants the best of both worlds, the perks of kingship without its responsibilities. When Lear resides with Goneril, it quickly becomes apparent to her that Lear cannot have both. Although he has supposedly given up authority, he still acts like he is in charge. Both Goneril and Regan realize that Lear has no real power without his knights, and they quickly strip Lear of those. Regan says quite pointedly, "I pray you, father, being weak, seem so" (II.iv.201). But Lear, long conditioned to think

> **When the old man . . . tries to assist Gloucester because he cannot see his way, Gloucester replies," 'I have no way, and therefore want no eyes; / I stumbled when I saw' (IV.i.18-19)."**

of himself as king, cannot reconcile his current condition with his lifelong self-image.

It is this slippage in Lear's self-image which contributes to Lear's descent into madness. He associates weakness with women and scolds himself for his impotence and crying. He tells Goneril, "I am ashamed / That thou hast power to shake my manhood thus" (I.iv.296-97). When Lear says, "[*Hysterica*] *passio*, down, thou climbing sorrow, / Thy element's below" (II.iv.57-58), he is specifically identifying the feelings that threaten to overwhelm him as feminine, since *hysterica passio*, or "the mother," was an affliction of the womb, obviously affecting only women. For Lear, a masculine response to emotion is to harden oneself against feeling. The ultimate crisis of identity comes when he sees Goneril and Regan allied against him. At that moment he realizes the extent of his reliance on others and begins to feel guilt for having treated Cordelia so unfeelingly. Lear's raging against the storm he cannot control reflects his inner struggle against unfamiliar emotions.

When Lear emerges from his mad state, through the gentle ministrations of Cordelia's doctors, he seems to have a different image of himself. In response to Cordelia's request that Lear bless her, he says, "Pray do not mock me. / I am a very foolish fond old man" (IV.vii.58-59). He has learned to be weak. Admitting that weakness and relinquishing the need to control events, Lear can enjoy that second childhood which he so desires. As he and Cordelia are ushered off to jail after their capture, Lear sees their future imprisonment as a time when he and his daughter can "pray, and sing, and tell old tales, and laugh" (V.iii.12), a carefree time in which the intimate bonds of childhood can be regained. Even in his last moments, at the height

> "When Lear so harshly denies Cordelia, Kent attempts to intervene. He says, 'See better, Lear, and let me still remain / The true blank of thine eye' (I.i.157-58)."

of his sorrow at his youngest daughter's death, Lear acts somewhat childishly, distractedly bragging that he has killed one of Cordelia's hangmen, though he also acknowledges the guilt he feels at her death, saying that he "might have sav'd her" (V.iii.271). Lear dies grieving over his daughter's corpse.

Critical assessment of Lear varies widely. One of the main issues surrounding his character is the question of whether Lear is a victim of others or other forces or is responsible for his own tragic downfall. What elements of his own nature contribute to what happens to him in the play? Some argue that his decision to abdicate his throne and divide his kingdom violates natural order and that this act condemns him. Others fault Lear for his early treatment of Cordelia, for his pride, and for his rash nature. Some people wonder whether or not Lear learns anything about himself during the play. It has been argued that during the scene on the heath, as Lear survives the physical storm, he also transcends his own emotional despair and comes to understand himself and his guilt. Other people are not convinced and allow that Lear has only gained a limited understanding of the consequences of his actions. Lear's ending leaves people with the same uncertainty as do these other issues. A few commentators have asserted that Lear actually dies happy, believing that Cordelia lives. Others believe that while Lear does not actually die happy, he is reconciled with what is ultimately a benevolent universe. Finally, many audiences and critics alike feel that Lear's ending offers a mixed message: while evil does not prevail a the play's end, neither does good.

Messengers:

Several messengers appear throughout the play: in IV.ii, a messenger announces to Albany that Cornwall has died of the wound inflicted by his own servant. The messenger relates the circumstances of the struggle between Cornwall and his servant and explains how Edmund is the cause of the outrage done his father; in IV.iv, a messenger informs Cordelia that the English forces have been assembled against her; and in the last scene of the play, a messenger announces that Edmund has died of the wounds suffered in his engagement with his brother Edgar.

Officers:

In V.iii, Edmund directs some officers to take Cordelia and Lear off to prison after their capture.

Old Man:

The old man pities Gloucester after Gloucester's eyes have been gouged out by Cornwall. The old man has lived on Gloucester's land for quite some time. He offers to guide Gloucester but defers to Edgar when the latter offers to do so.

Oswald:

Oswald is Goneril's steward. He is an ambitious social climber, fulfilling Goneril's requests in the interests of his own advancement. When Goneril charges him to be rude with Lear, in order to force a confrontation between herself and her father, Oswald enthusiastically carries out the task with a flourish. Kent sees Oswald's true nature and regards him with utter contempt, tripping him as Oswald walks by purposefully ignoring Lear's summons. He acts primarily as a go-between, carrying letters from Goneril to Regan and Edmund, and on one occasion is drawn into another quarrel with Kent, who is put in the stocks as a consequence. Oswald justifies Kent's contempt of him when he descends on the blind Gloucester, intending to kill him and recover the reward that has been put on Gloucester's life. Thinking that he is attacking only a blind man and a rustic peasant, Oswald is killed by the much stronger and more noble Edgar occupying that rustic disguise. Indicative of Oswald's total lack of moral scruples, he is found to be carrying letters between Goneril and Edmund that plot the murder of Albany.

Regan:

Regan is King Lear's middle daughter. Like her elder sister, she knows that to gain a third of Lear's kingdom by saying what he wants to hear takes little effort on her part. She outdoes even Goneril in her praise of Lear. Regan's protestations of love are so overly flattering that the audience cannot help but realize that she, and by extension Goneril, is being insincere. Like Goneril, Regan has suffered the whimsical nature of her father. She willingly goes along with Goneril's plan to unite against Lear. And Regan, too, finds Edmund attractive perhaps because of his self-assuredness and unstoppable determination to gain the power society has denied him.

Regan and Goneril are almost indistinguishable in their characteristics. When one tries to find differences between them, it becomes apparent that their varying insensitivities balance out in degree of cruelty. If Regan seems less despicable in that she, at least, does not pursue Edmund until Cornwall is dead, she compensates for this almost acceptable behavior by encouraging Cornwall to gouge out Gloucester's eyes. If Regan seems like a victim in being poisoned to death by Goneril, the audience withholds its sympathy, remembering how Regan has viciously stabbed her husband's noble servant in the back. Goneril and Regan die together, along with Edmund, who says, "all three / Now marry in an instant" (V.iii.228-29).

Servants:

In II.i, servants appear with Gloucester as Edmund frames his brother Edgar by lying to his father about Edgar's designs on Gloucester's life. Later in the play, the servants of Cornwall appear. In III.vii, Cornwall's servants have apprehended Gloucester, and Cornwall directs them to bind the former. In a moving scene, one of the servants objects to Cornwall's brutal treatment of Gloucester and fights with his master, inflicting a wound that will eventually kill Cornwall. This servant is slain by Regan who attacks him from behind. In this scene, two other of Cornwall's servants sympathize with Gloucester and comfort him as best they can.

Soldiers:

These are both the French soldiers Cordelia has gathered to liberate her father and the English soldiers assembled by Albany and Cornwall to oppose Cordelia's efforts.

Further Reading

Danby, John. "The Fool." *Durham University Journal* 38 (1945): 17-24.
  Danby examines the function of the Fool in *King Lear*. The Fool occupies the middle ground between two competing contemporary views of what Elizabe-

> **Lear intends that 'Only we shall retain / The name, and all th' addition to a king' (I.i.135-36). He wants the best of both worlds, the perks of kingship without its responsibilities."**

than society should be, arguing that he sympathizes with neither the view that social relationships should be determined by power and self-interest, nor the view that social relationships should be based on compassion for others.

Harbage, Alfred. "Justice in Tragic Fable." In *As They Liked It: An Essay on Shakespeare and Morality*, 142-51. New York: Macmillan Co., 1947.
  Harbage refutes those readings of *King Lear* which either offer that Cordelia is a flawed character deserving of punishment or argue that the unnecessary death of a divine Cordelia flaws the play. Harbage points out that Shakespeare was interested not in dramatizing divine justice, but the effects of human unkindness.

Hawkes, Terence. " 'Love' in *King Lear*." *Review of English Studies* 10 (1959): 178-81.
  Hawkes points out that in the opening scene of *King Lear* the word "love" could be interpreted as "to praise or estimate" or "to adore and treat kindly." Obviously, Hawkes argues, Lear means the word in the first sense while Cordelia understands the word in the second sense.

Heilman, Robert B. "The Time's Plague: The Sight Pattern in *King Lear*." *Quarterly Review of Literature* 4 (1947-48): 77-91.
  Heilman examines the imagery of "seeing" that pervades the play. He discusses the significance, for both Gloucester and Lear, of losing physical sight. Gloucester can see the truth more clearly with gouged eyes, Heilman maintains, and Lear can only see Cordelia's true nature when she is physically absent.

Kermode, Frank. Introduction to *King Lear*, by William Shakespeare. In *The Riverside Shakespeare*, edited by G. Blakemore Evans, 1249-54. Boston: Houghton Mifflin, 1974.
  Kermode gives a brief general introduction to the play's action, themes, and characters.

Kernan, Alvin. "Formalism and Realism in Elizabethan Drama: The Miracles in *King Lear*." *Renaissance Drama* 9 (1966): 59-66.
  Kernan examines the Dover Cliff scene and the reunion of Lear and Cordelia at the end of the play, arguing that both scenes illustrate the value of life and the presence of a caring God.

Knight, G. Wilson. ''The Tragedies.'' In *The Shakespearian Tempest*. 169-217. London: Oxford University Press, 1932.
> Knight discusses the tempest as not only a real storm that Lear physically endures but also a symbolic storm reflecting the turbulence in Lear's mind.

MacLean, Hugh. ''Disguise in *King Lear*: Kent and Edgar.'' *Shakespeare Quarterly* 11 (1960): 49-54.
> MacLean discusses the significance of both Kent and Edgar adopting disguise, noting that Edgar chooses the correct moment to reveal his identity; Kent does not.

Milward, Peter. ''Shakespeare and Christian Doctrine.'' *Shakespeare Studies* 4 (1966): 36-56.
> Milward explains the apparently pagan, non-religious setting of *King Lear* as either an adherence to the Protestant government's prohibition of the explicit treatment of religion on stage or a disguising of Shakespeare's Catholic sympathies. Milward examines the many allusions to Catholicism in the play.

Novy, Marianne. ''Patriarchy, Mutuality, and Forgiveness in *King Lear*.'' *Southern Humanities Review* 13 (1979): 281-92.
> Novy argues that Lear's attempt to suppress what he sees as womanish in himself is the result of the guilt he feels when he recognizes how he has disrupted the proper relationship that should exist between fathers and daughters.

Reid, Stephen. ''In Defense of Goneril and Regan.'' *American Imago* 27 (1970): 226-44.
> According to Reid, Goneril and Regan do not hate Lear at the beginning of the play. Theirs is an accurate appraisal of Lear's weak and feeble condition and a normal reaction to Lear's favoring of Cordelia. It is only later that they are corrupted by the power Lear has bestowed on them.

Siegel, Paul N. ''Adversity and the Miracle of Love in *King Lear*.'' *Shakespeare Quarterly* 6 (1955): 325-36.
> Siegel claims that there are Christian elements in *King Lear*, maintaining that Gloucester and Lear have committed moral transgressions, and their suffering is purgatorial, leading both to a more Christian compassion and understanding.

Stroup, Thomas B. ''Cordelia and the Fool.'' *Shakespeare Quarterly* 12 (1961): 127-32.
> Stroup addresses the question surrounding the Fool's absence in the last part of the play. Stroup argues that the parts of the Fool and Cordelia were probably played by the same actor, that the two are never on stage at the same time, and that the spacing of each character's appearance on stage allowed time for the necessary costume change.

Wilson, John Dover. ''*King Lear*.'' In *Six Tragedies of Shakespeare: An Introduction for the Plain Man*, 35-46. London: Longmans, Green, 1929. Reprint, Folcroft, Penn. Folcroft Library Editions, 1973.
> Wilson argues that the events in *King Lear* are presented through the eyes of two old men, Lear and Gloucester. The play demonstrates the resilience of the human spirit in the face of the worst life can offer, Wilson maintains.

Love's Labor's Lost

Act I:

When the play opens, the king of Navarre and his lords, Berowne, Dumaine, and Longaville, have just sworn an oath together: they will all live at the court of Navarre, forming a "little academe" together, committed to learning and contemplation. They swear to fast, to sleep minimally, and most important, to avoid the company of women for the next three years. The king has issued a proclamation stating that no woman shall come within a mile of his court. But the princess of France is due to pay a visit to the court; the king resolves to speak with her, going back on his oath for her sake. But the first member of the court to disobey the new rules is Costard the clown, whom the Spanish courtier Armado catches with a country woman, Jaquenetta. Dull, the constable, brings Costard before the king, who sentences Costard to a week's confinement with only bread and water, with Armado as his jailkeeper. In the next scene, it is revealed that Armado himself is in love with Jaquenetta.

Act II:

The princess arrives with her three ladies in waiting—Rosaline, Maria, and Katherine—and her lord Boyet. The king arrives and tells the princess she must be lodged in a field, rather than at court, in order to fulfill his prohibition against women at court. The princess and the king negotiate for the

return of Aquitaine, a province in France, which her father the king of France had lost to Navarre's father. Navarre believes the king of France owes him money before he can give up Aquitaine; the princess holds that the money has already been paid, and Aquitaine belongs to France. The negotiations promise to take several days. Meanwhile, the lords have all fallen in love with the princess's ladies.

Act III:

The act begins with Moth, Armado's page, making fun of his master. Armado has written Jaquenetta a love letter. He sets Costard the clown free from confinement in order to pay him to carry the letter to Jaquenetta. Berowne then appears and pays Costard to carry a love letter to Rosaline.

Act IV:

The princess's party are hunting in the forest when Costard delivers his letter—but it is the wrong letter. Boyet reads aloud Armado's suit to Jaquenetta. In the next scene, Holofernes the schoolteacher and Nathaniel the curate encounter Costard and Jaquenetta. Jaquenetta asks Holofernes to read a letter aloud to her. It was intended for Rosaline, and Holofernes decides to deliver it to the king himself. Meanwhile, Berowne appears in the woods, bemoaning his love for Rosaline. The king appears after him, and Berowne climbs a tree. The king reads aloud a love letter he has written to the princess. Longaville and Dumaine appear in turn, both reading love poems aloud. Then each lord emerges one by one. Longaville emerges to accuse Dumaine of breaking his oath; the king accuses both Dumaine and Longaville; finally, Berowne emerges to "whip hypocrisy" and accuse the king himself along with the others. Costard and Jaquenetta reappear with Berowne's letter to Rosaline. All four lords resolve to remain faithful lovers. Berowne gives a lengthy speech about love's capacity for making men virtuous and charitable.

Act V:

Holofernes, Nathaniel, Dull, Moth, and Armado plan to put on a Pageant of the Nine Worthies, nine famous heroes from classical to Biblical to modern times, before the lords and ladies. Meanwhile, the lords have sent the ladies love-tokens and letters of praise. Boyet warns the ladies that the men are dressing up as Russians in order to woo them in disguise. The ladies put on masks of their own and exchange love tokens, so that in this so-called "Masque of the Muscovites," each lord mistakenly

woos the wrong lady. When they return in their usual clothes, Rosaline tells them that a group of foolish Russians has just appeared; Berowne finally confesses they themselves were the Russians. The princess reveals that the ladies knew all along.

Costard the clown arrives to announce another drama, the Pageant of the Nine Worthies. The king almost puts a stop to it, worried the play will cause even further embarrassment. The actors make many mistakes. The lords (with the help of Boyet) interrupt and mock the play so ruthlessly that they only make it worse. They drive Holofernes to say, "This is not generous, not gentle, not humble" (629). The princess interjects a few notes of sympathy, but the men keep taunting the actors. The play is interrupted by the arrival of Marcade, a messenger, who announces the death of the princess's father, the king of France. She must prepare to leave that night. The lords of Navarre's court, including the king himself, make pleas for their ladies' love. But the ladies tell their lords to spend a year in contemplation first, for they are not trustworthy. As Berowne puts it ruefully, a year's time is "too long for a play": this play will not end with marriages but with a song sung of spring and winter by all the performers.

Modern Connections

Love's Labor's Lost focuses on the problem of telling the truth. The play opens with a solemn vow to study and to avoid the company of women. But the king of Navarre, who as leader ought to be a model of truth and virtue, breaks his own promise in the second scene of the play. After that, all of his followers break their promises as well: instead of avoiding women, they fall in love with and pursue the ladies of France who are visiting the king's court. But because they have already broken their first vow, their promises of love do not ring true. Although all four of them write effective love poems, clever poetry does not necessarily express sincere feeling. Even more telling, in the Masque of the Muscovites when everyone involved is disguised, the men cannot recognize their ladies, though the ladies recognize the men. The love promises that the lords have made seem particularly hollow if they cannot even tell their love objects apart. The ladies question the lords' capacity to speak truly of love at all. In modern times as well, the effort to speak truthfully about one's feelings remains difficult. It is often easier to make promises than it is to keep them—especially when it comes to love relationships. Further, it is often easier to love one's ideal image of someone than to recognize him or her for who he or she is.

Yet the ladies in the play insist that it is in fact possible to speak truly, not only of love but of other things as well. The play is full of banter and wordplay, and the ladies participate in the clever use (and abuse) of words just as much as the lords. But the ladies mock the lords in order to point out their mistakes and offer insight, for example after the Masque of the Muscovites. In addition, the ladies mock themselves and each other without being cruel or destructive, whereas the men make fun of the Nine Worthies actors to the point of injuring them. Rosaline points out that the "prosperity" or usefulness of words does not depend on the experience of the speaker, but upon the effect on the audience—in other words, clever language and wordplay are not "prosperous" if they cause harm to those who hear them. The lords behave like bullies, making fun of less privileged men, much as the school bully might make fun of the weaker kids in class. The meaning of words depends on how the audience understands them, not on how much fun the bully might have in his mockery.

To modern audiences, the idea of establishing an "academy" at court might seem foreign. Nothing like the court system exists in modern life in many countries; the renaissance court was a legal and political hub, but also a social center where young gentlemen and gentlewomen lived lives of leisure supported by royalty. The king of Navarre's court is more like a boarding school or college than like a political or legal center. And the academy of *Love's Labour's Lost* represents a rather extreme version of what happened regularly in Renaissance courts: the education of young men (and to some extent women). Young courtiers were taught to read and write as well as to behave like gentlemen.

The king of Navarre has a particularly idealistic notion of the study involved in courtly life. He thinks that in order to create a court as a center of learning, the members of the court must be extreme in swearing off almost all other activity. He even goes so far as to insist that love and studying are mutually exclusive. Certainly in modern life the same conflict can recur—the conflict between studying and social life, or between work and love. Indeed, there are plenty of parents who require that their children finish their homework before they see their friends, and plenty of college students who,

like the lords of Navarre, confront the difficulties of balancing study with newfound desires. But what makes the court of Navarre particularly unconventional is that in the end, neither study nor love wins out. The "academy" is destroyed, but there is nothing left in its place. The king and all his lords are sent off to different corners of the world to live alone and contemplate their lives. In effect, the court itself is exposed as a superficial and untrustworthy place.

Characters

Armado (Don Andriano de Armado):

Armado is first described by the king, just before he enters the stage in the play's first scene, as "One who the music of his own vain tongue / Doth ravish like an enchanting harmony" (I.i.166-7). Armado is a self-important Spanish courtier—not unlike Don Quixote in character—who is in love with the country wench Jaquenetta. When he comes upon her with Costard the clown (outside the play's action) he sends a letter to the king demanding Costard's punishment. Given the task of keeping the clown under his guard, Armado sends him to deliver a courtly and elaborate love letter to Jaquenetta. Armado's language may be described as pretentious throughout. He condescends to his own page, Moth, who in turn makes fun of his master, usually in asides to the audience. Armado claims to be on intimate terms with the king and the ladies of France, who actually ridicule him—especially when his letter is delivered accidentally into the hands of Rosaline instead of Jaquenetta. Yet Armado is one of the courtiers sworn not to keep company with women; he is a member of the academy. He thus acts as a double of the more aristocratic characters in the play. Like them, he writes an illicit love letter; he even holds court, of a kind, with a rebellious follower, Moth—much as the king holds court with his rebellious follower, Berowne.

Later, Armado's role becomes part of the pathetic final comedy of the play. He plays the Trojan warrior Hector in the Pageant of the Nine Worthies, and nearly enters into a duel with Costard, egged on by the mocking lords of Navarre. Armado combines the stereotype of the passionate Spaniard with the elaborate language of what he imagines to be courtly elocution. At the same time his love for Jaquenetta reveals the degree to which his courtly pretensions are false, for his passion is expended on a distinctly

> **Armado claims to be on intimate terms with the king and the ladies of France, who actually ridicule him—especially when his letter is delivered accidentally into the hands of Rosaline instead of Jaquenetta.**"

non-courtly object. Armado's love highlights the self-indulgence of all the court lords.

But it is Armado who brings the Nine Worthies play to its most violent pitch. It is also he who defends the worth of the dead hero he impersonates, against the mockery of the court: "The sweet war-man is dead and rotten, sweet chucks, beat not the bones of the buried. When he breathed, he was a man" (V.ii.660). Armado's passions, even though they may be expressed in ridiculous ways, nonetheless emerge as more genuine and respectful than those of the other courtiers. The pathos of these lines points out a serious problem with any verbal mockery that knows no limits. And Armado brings the play to its rather serious and almost philosophical, plain-style close by insisting that his fellow performers be allowed to sing their song of the seasons. Armado's role defines the limits of what the play portrays as acceptable courtly behavior.

Berowne:

He is the central figure of the play. One of the king's lords, he is infatuated with language (especially his own), and yet even from the beginning exhibits the most suspicion toward the "academy" of the court. In the opening scene, Berowne protests the stringency of the oath of chastity and study he has sworn, arguing that the oath will be too difficult for the lords to keep. He argues further that "all delights are vain" (I.i.72), even the pleasure of scholarship and books—he protests the oath not only because it is impractical but also because it is selfish and vain. Nevertheless, he signs the vow and claims that he will keep it best of all of them. Then, he points out that the princess will soon arrive, forcing the king to break his oath immediately.

Berowne's speech is full of the puns (or "quibbles" as they were called in Shakespeare's language) that characterize the play as a whole. He takes delight in disrupting whatever scene is at hand, criticizing everyone (including himself), and generally expounding upon every step of the play's action. He utters between a fifth and a quarter of the play's lines, and even at several moments takes over authority from the king himself. When the lords confess their loves in succession in Act IV, it is Berowne who witnesses the king's own confession and exposes his hypocrisy—and finally, it is Berowne who confesses his own love as well. The king's oath had provided a courtly bond among the men, but clearly had not done so effectively. In Act IV, it is Berowne's idea to form a bond of love among them all: "Sweet lords, sweet lovers, O, let us embrace! / As true we are as flesh and blood can be" (IV.iii.210-11). Berowne's more practical and tolerant leadership offsets the king's misguided strictness. In the last scene of the play, Berowne again argues against the king's command. Navarre wants to cancel the Pageant of the Nine Worthies because he is ashamed of its actors, but Berowne insists that the players' lack of skill will be all the more reason for humor.

Rosaline's description of Berowne in II.i praises him for his voluble and clever discourse: "His eye begets occasion for his wit, / For every object that the one doth catch / The other turns to a mirth-moving jest" (II.i.69-71). Indeed, Rosaline's words suggest to the princess that her ladies are all in love, even before the lords begin to woo them. Rosaline is the appropriate match for Berowne partly because her beauty is dark (unconventional by Renaissance standards), but also because she herself engages in the puns and mockery at which Berowne excels. By the end, she beats him at his own game. When the lords impersonate Russian courtiers in the Masque of the Muscovites, Rosaline does not hesitate to tell Berown later that the Russians were fools, a joke that Berowne finds "dry" (V.ii.373). Thoroughly humbled by her mockery of their Russian act, Berowne claims that he will no longer trust his own clever language but will accept her mockery: "Here stand I, lady, dart thy skill at me" (V.ii.396). Yet even in claiming that he will speak plainly from now on, Berowne cannot help interjecting a foreign word, "sans" (V.ii.415), into his discourse.

Still, by the last scene of the play, it seems that Berowne has begun to humble himself. His clever language has turned to the subject of love. He gives a long speech at the end of Act IV on the capacity of love to create virtue and charity. But his mocking temperament does not simply evaporate. During the Pageant of the Nine Worthies, Berowne is one of the most brutal mockers of them all. It is for this reason that Rosaline demands in her parting speech that he spend a year doing charitable deeds, helping the sick. ''A jest's posperity lies in the ear / Of him that hears it, never in the tongue / Of him that makes it'' (V.ii.861-63), she tells him. Jests for their own sake, or for the sake of the speaker's pleasure in his own cleverness, do not do the world much good; they are not funny unless the speaker communicates to his audience in a kind or ''prosperous'' way. We have seen evidence during the last two acts that Berowne may be ready to learn this lesson, but Rosaline consigns him to a whole year helping the sick before she will marry him.

Boyet:

The princess's lord, Boyet acts as an intermediary between the lords and the ladies. Boyet is at least middle-aged, and carries gossip to and fro, both enabling and mocking love throughout the play. Katherine calls him ''Cupid's grandfather'' (II.i.253). Boyet introduces the princess onstage in II.i, where he praises her and urges her to negotiate well to acquire Aquitaine. He then goes to the court to announce his lady's arrival. When the king greets the princess and her train, his lords become smitten with her ladies, and each one approaches Boyet to ask his lady's name. Boyet is thus privy to their feelings from the beginning. He also notices the king's feelings for the princess. Boyet engages in the banter that the ladies share among themselves, but is generally treated fondly by them even as they tease him for his age. It is Boyet who recognizes the missent letter from Armado the Spanish courtier; he seems to know the court scene well. More important, he recognizes that Rosalind may be in love, and teases her about having been ''hit'' with Cupid's arrow (IV.i.118). Then, in the final scene of the play, it is Boyet who warns the ladies that the lords are approaching disguised as Russians for the Masque of the Muscovites. Boyet's mirth when he announces their foolish masquerade suggests that in spite of Katherine's accusation about his matchmaking tendencies, he looks down on the lords, and does not endorse any match-making; indeed, he helps the ladies mock their potential lovers. Yet at the end of the act, when the Pageant of the Nine Worthies begins, Boyet is one of the principal mockers; together with Berowne, Dumaine, Longaville, and even the king, Boyet eggs on the offended actors. By the play's end, when solemnity replaces mirth, Boyet himself effectively disappears. His

> **Rosaline's description of Berowne in II.i praises him for his voluble and clever discourse: 'His eye begets occasion for his wit, / For every object that the one doth catch / The other turns to a mirth-moving jest' (II.i.69-71).''**

role as catalyst for the action and spur to love-games is, by the end, unnecessary. Moreover, his lighthearted and gossiping presence is inappropriate for the rather more solemn modd at the end of the play. Perhaps more effectively than any other character, Boyet makes love seem not only ridiculous and infirm but trivial as well.

Costard:

The play's clown is the first to break the court's rule against consorting with women. Don Armado catches him with Jaquenetta, has him arrested, and writes to the king reporting the clown's infraction. Costard gives his own oral version of his misdemeanor, defending it on the grounds that it was perfectly natural: ''Such is the simplicity of man to hearken after the flesh'' (I.i.217), he says. He thus highlights the ridiculous idealism of the king's academy. In addition, his monosyllabic interruptions during the reading of Armado's elaborate letter make the letter look equally ridiculous. Costard's language contains occasional malapropisms, or misused words, but for the most part he merely insists on a rhetorical simplicity that the other characters do not share. He mispronounces Armado's name as ''Dun Adramadio'' (IV.iii.195) in a kind of unwitting mockery. His puns are so obvious that they make fun of the other characters' quibblings, as when he makes fun of legal language in I.i.205-11.

Everyone else considers Costard an entertaining commoner, and for the most part the other characters condescend to him (even while they engage his services in delivering their letters). Boyet refers to him as ''a member of the common wealth'' (IV.i.41), or a commoner; Berowne calls him and Jaquenetta ''turtles'' (IV.iii.208) when they are slow in leaving the lords' company. In the Pageant

> **❝❝ Boyet is at least middle-aged, and carries gossip to and fro, both enabling and mocking love throughout the play. Katherine calls him 'Cupid's grandfather' (II.i.253)."**

of the Nine Worthies, however, Costard is the only actor to finish his part with comparative grace. Costard also appreciates Moth's wit (V.i.72-3), indicating that he is not as witless as the lords may make him out to be.

Costard is also a go-between, but unlike Boyet he botches his mission. Armado gives him a love letter to deliver to Jaquenetta, and Berowne gives him a love letter to deliver to Rosalind, but Costard switches the two so that Rosalind receives Armado's poem, while Jaquenetta (who cannot read) receives Berowne's highly skilled poem to Rosalind. Costard is thus the unwitting instrument by which Berowne's love is revealed to the other lords, for in IV.iii he brings the misdirected letter to the king. Near the end of the play, Berowne encourages Costard to rile Armado by suggesting that Jaquenetta is pregnant by the Spanish courtier. They threaten to duel, but are interrupted by the solemn entrance of Marcade. In the end, their duel is absorbed into the general solemnity of the Spring-Winter song.

Don Andriano (Don Andriano de Armado):

See Armado

Dull:

The constable first appears with Costard, whom he has arrested for being caught in the company of a woman, Jaquenetta (I.i.180). Dull's name indicates his principal characteristic: he is not bright, and as a result speaks little. He stumbles over Armado's name (I.i.187). He takes the fancy Latinate language of Holofernes and Nathaniel at face value, understanding everything so literally that Holofernes is inspired to call out to "monster Ignorance!" (IV.ii.22). He is present throughout V.i, but never speaks until the end, when he makes clear he does not understand the pedant's discourse and will not act in the Pageant of the Nine Worthies.

Dumaine:

Dumaine is one of the king's lords, along with Berowne and Longaville, and falls in love with Katherine. His oath to the king in the opening scene is elaborately and recklessly self-sacrificial; whereas Longaville speaks of the mind's nourishment while the body pines, Dumaine says he is "mortified"—that is, his flesh is in a sense killed, and the pleasures of the world are dead to him—"To love, to wealth, to pomp, I pine and die" (I.i.28-31). Katherine describes Dumaine, before they meet, as goodlooking, young and a bit reckless with words because he is naive to the consequences of his speech: he has "Most power to do most harm, least knowing ill" (II.i.58). It is as though he swears to the king's academy for the sound of the words as much as for their sense.

When he falls in love, Dumaine (unlike Longaville) is more interested initially in praising his lady's attractions than in worrying about breaking his oath. The breaking of the oath, in fact, becomes the reason for writing her a love poem—again, as if he is more interested in the words themselves than in expressing feeling to his beloved. His language repeats and inverts itself, and is least direct of all the lords' poetry: "Do not call it sin in me, / That I am forsworn for thee" (IV.iii.113-14). Later, during the Pageant of the Nine Worthies, Dumaine distinguishes himself in his cruelty to Holofernes, whom he calls "a Judas!" (IV.iii.596), making a punning joke on his character's name. Judas Iscariot, who identified Jesus to his Roman captors with a kiss, had become the ultimate signifier of betrayal. It is ironic that Dumaine, whose betrayal of his oath and whose betrayal of the significance of words themselves have defined his character throughout the play, should mockingly accuse the vulnerable Holofernes of betrayal.

By the end, Dumaine has become only slightly more self-conscious; after Holofernes leaves the stage, he says, "Though my mocks come home by me, I will now be merry" (IV.iii.635). He doesn't care what the consequences are, he will continue to enjoy himself. So he eggs Armado on to challenge Costard to a duel, and when it becomes clear that the ladies must abruptly leave, he still hopes humorously for Katherine's hand: "But what to me, my love? but what to me? A wife?" (IV.iii.823). His recklessness persists to the last, even in his plea for her hand.

Ferdinand (King Ferdinand of Navarre):

See Navarre

Forester:

The forester appears briefly in IV.i to show the ladies where to hunt most successfully.

France (Princess of France):

The princess of France is the moral center of the play. She arrives at the court of the king of France just after he and his lords have sworn an oath to remain celibate and study together in a courtly academy for three years. Because they also swear to avoid the company of women entirely for those three years, and the king issues a proclamation forbidding women in his court, the princess and her three ladies are forced to camp in a field on the grounds of the court rather than be lodged inside. The princess, who greets most of the play's actions with a practical and straightforward reasonablenes, accepts these terms, but not without protest: "The roof of this court is too high to be yours, and welcome to the wide fields too base to be mine" (II.i.93-94), she tells him. Her mission at his court is to resolve a dispute that arose between their fathers. Apparently they traded Aquataine, a French province, for a loan of money some time ago. Though the king of Navarre no longer wants Aquitaine, he does claim that the king of France owes him money in order to get the province back. The princess, as her father's diplomat, tells the king of Navarre that her father already paid him his money, and therefore Aquitaine should belong to France. The two disagree on the facts; their negotiations promise to take a few days; as a result, the princess and her ladies remain camped in the fields.

During the initial scene of negotiations (which are never resumed during the play's action), the king's three lords fall in love with the princess's three ladies. After each lord has asked Boyet about his respective love-object, Boyet further informs the princess that the king must be in love with her—and indeed, we find out later that Boyet is right. But the princess remains modest and, unlike the ladies, never betrays her feelings for the king. Indeed, even at the play's end her intentions are not clear.

Later in the play, the princess and her ladies go deer hunting. The princess's characteristic mercy and compassion are revealed even here, for she remarks upon the cruelty of killing deer for sport

> Costard gives his own oral version of his misdemeanor, defending it on the grounds that it was perfectly natural: 'Such is the simplicity of man to hearken after the flesh' (I.i.217), he says."

(IV.i.21ff). At the same time, though, she is not without a sense of humor. Costard's accidental delivery of Armado's florid letter inspires her to make several jokes, and after the lords have begun to send them love tokens, she is quite happy to make fun of them: "Sweet hearts, we shall be rich ere we depart, / If fairings come thus plentifully in" (V.ii.1-2), she tells her ladies. It is the princess of France's idea to put on masks when the lords come dressed for the Masque of the Muscovites, as well. Here, as always, there is purpose even in the princess's humor: "The effect of my intent is to cross theirs: / They do it but in mockery merriment" (V.ii.138-39). Convinced that the lords are not serious, she wishes to let them know that the ladies cannot take them seriously either. More than her ladies, in fact, the princess sees the lords' limitations. And whereas Rosaline actually enjoys making a fool of Berowne, the princess expresses a more serious and dignified idea that the lords' love, unless expressed and taken seriously, should be pointed out as a sham.

Indeed, the princess also points out the particular hypocrisy of the king. After his appearance as a Russian, he reappears and invites the ladies to come stay inside at court after all. The princess refuses, on the grounds that he would be "perjur'd," that is, he would break his oath. Essentially, she points out that while he was unwilling to break his oath for the sake of being polite to his visitors, he is now willing to do so for the sake of his own desires. She calls attention to his lack of integrity. And then she opens him up to the mockery of Rosaline, who makes fun of the so-called Russians and then reveals that the dressed-up lords misrecognized the masked ladies. The irony of this situation is that the lords, even dressed as foreigners, were completely recognizable to the ladies, whereas the ladies, hastily disguised, were unrecognizable to the lords. The princess's meas-

> Katherine describes Dumaine, before they meet, as goodlooking, young and a bit reckless with words because he is naive to the consequences of his speech: he has 'Most power to do most harm, least knowing ill' (II.i.58)."

ured and dignified speech points out, even more than Rosaline's banter does, that the men are not ready to be serious about their loves.

During the play of the Nine Worthies, the princess of France is the only one to respond politely to the actors, while everyone else is making fun. The king does not silence his increasingly abusive lords. When Marcade appears in the final action of the play and announces that the princess's father has just died, she retains a dignity even in her comparatively brief and plain language. The king's response to her abrupt departure is to propose; the princess replies simply at first, ''I understand you not, my griefs are double'' (V.ii.752). When she recovers her eloquence, she tells him that she will not trust his oaths of love until he has been a hermit for a year. She thus establishes the terms by which her ladies can all refuse to marry as well. In the end, it is the princess's practical, serious behavior that establishes the play's meaning. Of all the characters, it is she who uses language with the least elaboration and the most integrity. It is the princess, that is, for whom language actually has the most direct effects in the world of practical action.

Holofernes:

The pedantic schoolteacher Holofernes, along with the parson Nathaniel, does not appear until late in the play (IV.ii). He speaks in lists of synonyms, words that have roughly the same meaning; he particularly likes Latin-sounding words and Latin tags. Holofernes is a kind of walking, talking thesaurus. He is usually an object of comedy within the play, although the curate Nathaniel treats him with fawning respect and imitates his language. He goes on at length about the death of one deer when the

princess and her party are hunting (IV.ii). Later, he exhibits profound exasperation with Dull, the constable, who misunderstands most of Holofernes's pretentious language. Holofernes has a certain fawning tendency himself, exhibited in his desire to bring Berowne's misdirected letter straight to the king. He is also a bit hypocritical in his treatment of Armado, whom he mocks when Armado is offstage, but very soon praises in his presence (V.i).

There is a serious side to Holofernes as well, just as there are so often serious sides to Shakespeare's comic characters. With his love for synonyms and Latinisms, he takes his place among the other language-infatuated characters. Whereas Armado's language is elaborately courtly, as if he is trying to prove his aristocratic status, Holofernes's language is elaborately academic. More than Armado's, then, Holofernes's language has only a specialized audience (essentially, Nathanial) and therefore risks a kind of isolated disconnection, a failure to communicate, that represents one of the central threats of the whole play. If Holofernes cannot even have a conversation with the constable Dull about the death of a deer, then what good is his elaborate learning anyway? Yet at the same time, Holofernes expresses eloquently the love for poets of the past that permeates not only *Love's Labor's Lost* but other Shakespeare plays as well. When he praises Ovid, for example, there is a heartfelt and poignant appreciation of another poet's art even as the imagery makes that art seem vaguely degraded: ''for the elegance, facility, and golden cadence of poesy . . . Ovidius Naso was the man. And why indeed 'Naso' but for smelling out the odiferous flowers of fancy, the jerks of invention?'' (IV.ii.121-24).

In the Pageant of the Nine Worthies, Holofernes is director; he also plays Judas Maccabeus. His speech is interrupted by Dumaine, joined by Berowne and Boyet; though at first he is determined not to mind their insults, he grows more and more frustrated. ''I will not be put out of countenance'' (V.ii.607), he says; but later, after insults to his face, he says, ''You have put me out of countenance'' (V.ii.621). Finally, he is unable to finish his speech; they dismiss him, effectively calling him an ass, and he objects in uncharacteristically plain language (though retaining his tendency to synonyms), ''This is not generous, not gentle, not humble'' (V.ii.629). The words are profoundly accusatory, and communicate better than much of his discourse has until now: he prompts the princess's first intervention in the baiting of the players. Indeed, it is at Holofernes's aborted speech where the tone of the actor-audience banter becomes outright insulting, and where the lords' use of language becomes not only careless but outright cruel.

Jaquenetta:

The love object of both Costard the clown and Don Armado, Jaquenetta is a country wench, or a lower-class woman. In I.ii.130-45 she meets Armado briefly and answers his declarations of love with humor; during IV.iii she is with Costard when he delivers Berowne's missent letter to the king.

Katherine:

Along with Maria and Rosaline, Katherine is one of the princess of France's ladies, and Rosaline's principal companion in banter. Though Katherine ends up beloved of Dumaine, at first it is Berowne who approaches her. While the princess and the king discuss their political differences, Berowne asks whether Katherine danced with him once; she quickly rejects his advances, though, saying she hopes he will never be her lover (II.i.126). Katherine also banters with Boyet, who flirts with her, offering in jest to kiss her (II.i.223). Later, Katherine and Rosaline debate about their respective beauty. While Rosaline is dark, Katherine is fair, or blond, and therefore more conventionally beautiful in Renaissance terms. They tease each other, playing on the various meanings of "dark" and "fair," in the beginning of V.ii. Then all four ladies complain about their respective lords; Katherine calls Dumaine's message "A huge tranlation of hypocrisy, / Vildly [vilely] compiled, profound simplicity" (V.ii.51-52). When the lords arrive dressed as Russians for the Masque of the Muscovites, Katherine abruptly insults Longaville (who has mistaken her for Maria), essentially calling him a calf and a cuckold. Finally, when pressed by the impatient Dumaine to answer his proposal of marriage, she straightforwardly demands maturity ("a beard" [V.ii.826]), along with honesty. Katherine is a foil to the lively and more central Rosaline, but she also provides much of the play's clever, blunt humor herself.

King (King Ferdinand of Navarre):

See Navarre

Longaville:

Along with Berowne and Dumaine, Longaville is one of the king's lords, and he is in love with

> **" It is the princess of France's idea to put on masks when the lords come dressed for the Masque of the Muscovites, as well. Here, as always, there is purpose even in the princess's humor: 'The effect of my intent is to cross theirs: / They do it but in mockery merriment' (V.ii.138-39)."**

Maria. Longaville is more moderate than either Berowne or Dumaine, and exhibits the heaviest guilt for breaking his oath to the academy. Longaville initially comes to terms with the stringency of the academy's oath by focusing on the mind's growth: "The mind shall banquet, though the body pine" (I.i.25), he says, accepting the term more willingly than either of the other two lords. It is also Longaville who comes up with the idea of banishing all of womankind from the king's court for the three years they have agreed to work together. Longaville thus emerges as the most eager student of the academy, and perhaps it most willing sufferer. Yet when he falls for Maria, he exhibits impatience—first with Boyet, who banters with him instead of telling him Maria's name (II.i.197-208), and later with his own poetry-writing, of which he says, "I fear these stubborn lines lack power to move" (IV.ii.53). When he mistakes Katherine for his beloved in the Masque of the Muscovites, Katherine teases him about being silent, or slow to speak: "What, was your vizard [mask] made without a tongue?" (V.ii.242). He is also less involved in the abuse of the Nine Worthies actors than the other two lords. In the end, his plea to Maria is brief, and he agrees to wait a year quietly. Longaville may be an eager academician initially, but he also emerges as less clever than Berowne and Dumaine: less an abuser of language, and more ready to admit himself a novice at proper linguistic behavior.

Marcade:

Marcade appears only once in the play. He is the messenger who, in the last scene of the play, brings the princess the news of her father's death

" During the play of the Nine Worthies, the princess of France is the only one to respond politely to the actors, while everyone else is making fun."

(V.ii.715). This is an important moment in the play, when solemnity is suddenly injected into the otherwise light and clever action.

Maria:

One of the princess of France's ladies, along with Rosaline and Katherine, Maria is beloved of Longaville. She is the least active of the three ladies, but makes fun of Boyet with Katherine (II.i.254), and enters into a bit of banter herself with Boyet and Costard (IV.i.129). She does her share in the Masque of the Muscovites, where Dumaine mistakes her for Katherine. In the end, she is perhaps the least resistant of the ladies, for she suggests that at the end of the year she might actually marry Longville— "I'll change my black gown for a faithful friend" (V.ii.834), she tells him. Of course, we do not know (nor does he) who that friend might be; but she leaves him more hope than any of the others, who promise only to reconsider in a year.

Moth:

Armado's page is a young, small person, and many of the jokes about him revolve around his small stature (especially as compared to Armado's tall figure). Moth consistently makes fun of his master's pretensions, often through punning asides to the audience. In a sort of reversal of the lords' academy, Moth frequently plays teacher to Armado. At one point, Armado asks him to give a definition, in grammar-school pedagogical fashion: "Define, define, well-educated infant" (I.11.90); at another point, the boy addresses his master as "Negligent student" (III.i.32). Moth is expert at logical twists and repetitions that invert his master's intended meanings.

Moth first appears in III.i, where he sings a lovesong to his master and then warns Armado about the aristocratic love language that Armado

uses, suggesting that aristocratic embellishment is not the proper method for wooing a "coy wench" like Jaquenetta. In V.i, Moth's mockery of Holofernes entertains Costard so well that the clown gives him money—a particularly strange moment, since money is usually a gift from noble to lower-class characters. Moth teases Holofernes for his pedantry and self-importance by implying that he is a cuckold. The lords employ Moth as their Russian herald; when the ladies turn their backs on him unwelcomingly, he humorously changes the language of his greeting, only to be irritably corrected by Berowne. Later, in the Pageant of the Nine Worthies, Moth plays Hercules—an opportunity for physical hilarity, since Moth is small in stature. Holofernes has said that Moth represents "Hercules in minority" (V.i.134), or Hercules as a child, but the humor persists. Moth's role in the play is frequently one of staging reversals of the characters' expectations— especially those of the self-important Armado and Holofernes—so his paradoxical tiny Hercules is actually an appropriate role.

Nathaniel:

Nathaniel is the local curate, or parish priest, and he is Holofernes's companion and friend. His attitude toward Holofernes is one of extreme respect—to the point that he is something of a flatterer. In response to the constable Dull's failure to understand Holofernes's Latin language, Nathaniel bemoans the constable's ignorance in a set of rhymed couplets (IV.ii.28-33). He calls Holofernes a rare teacher and a "good member of the commonwealth" (IV.ii.76), i.e. a good citizen; and in V.i. he praises Holofernes's rhetorical skills in his own elaborate rhetorical terms. In the Pageant of the Nine Worthies, he plays Alexander the Great, but cannot remember beyond the first line of his speech (V.ii.562).

Navarre (King Ferdinand of Navarre):

The king of Navarre is the leader of the so-called academy of lords, all of whom, at the play's opening, take a vow to be celibate and absorb themselves in scholarship for three years. In the course of the play, however, he falls in love with the princess of France. The king is motivated at first by the desire to transcend the world of mortality: he wants to live forever in men's memories. He refers in his opening speech to "cormorant devouring Time" (I.i.4), as if time itself were a predatory creature. He seems to believe that only scholarship and study will bring time to a halt; that social life as a whole—and love in particular—threatens his own and others' autonomous and youthful existence. Thus not only his lords but he himself appears young, and naively idealistic, especially since the vow is immediately called into question. He has forbidden the academy to experience the company of women for three years. But the king, we are reminded from the beginning, is still a king. That is, he is the leader and ruler of a state. And as part of his political duties, he must receive and negotiate with a woman—the princess of France, who is to arrive immediately.

Even before the princess's arrival breaks the new law, though, Costard the clown is brought before the king for consorting with Jaquenetta. The king immediately punishes Costard—though not as brutally as the law threatens—by confining him to the care of Don Armado (himself, of course, in love with Jaquenetta). The king exerts the power of his office particularly ineffectually here, since Armado frees Costard almost immediately in order to get the clown to deliver a love letter. Not only has the king's law been broken, but the punishment he decrees goes unheeded.

Berowne calls into question the king's authority in yet another way. Even from the beginning, Berowne remarks upon the flexibility of the king's laws and of the language of their shared vow (I.i.59-93). He points out that study itself can apply to the art of love, and in fact that study is itself a form of pleasure—that very same thing which the academy claims to avoid for the next three years. Further, he argues that study is meaningless if it is completely removed from real life. In answer to all this, the king says only, ''How well he's read, to reason against reading!'' (I.i.94). The king does not answer Berowne's primary question: What is the good of studying? How does the king' academy benefit the rest of the world? ''What is the end of study, let me know'' (I.i.55), says Berowne. As the play progresses, the king of Navarre shows little ability to abide by his own commands and vows, let alone defend the effectiveness of those commands and vows in any wider context.

In IV.iii, when all four lords declare their love for their ladies, the king is the only one who exhibits no remorse for the vow he breaks. In one sense, this is a perfectly conventional kingly role: his own will can determine the laws and the rules of his realm. In another sense, however, this is evidence of a weak and self-centered king. His elaborate love poem uses as its central image (or ''conceit,'' as such

> ''. . . Katherine calls Dumaine's message 'A huge tranlation of hypocrisy, / Vildly [vilely] compiled, profound simplicity' (V.ii.51-52).''

images were called in Shakespeare's time) the idea that the king's object of desire appears in the very tears he sheds for her (IV.iii.25-40). Significantly, it is Berowne who witnesses the king's outpouring of love for the princess. In fact, at this point Berowne himself takes over some aspects of the leadership of the lords. It is his idea for the four of them to form a bond of love, rather than a bond based on an academic vow (IV.iii.210). Berowne also gives a long speech in praise of the cosmic power of love (IV.iii.285-362). The king, on the other hand, mocks Berowne for being in love with a dark-haired woman, and then proposes that the lords devise some entertainment for their ladies. It is during this entertainment, especially the Masque of the Muscovites, that the king's role becomes least commanding and most pleading. He asks Rosaline to dance (thinking that she is his beloved princess), and she first says yes, then no. Soon, his mistake is revealed: he tried to woo the wrong woman, as did the other lords during the Masque of the Muscovites, and his efforts to swear oaths of love to the princess therefore seem all the more foolish and untrustworthy.

Finally, during the Pageant of the Nine Worthies, the king does not prevent his lords from mocking the actors mercilessly, but even joins in (V.ii.636). When the princess's father dies, the king tries to persuade her not to leave, and asks her to rejoice at having found new friends even as she is grieving for her father. He misreads her situation: she replies simply, ''I understand you not'' (V.ii.752). She then insists that he stay in a hermitage for a year before she will consider marrying him. At this point in the play, the king's authority—like his academy—has been revealed as superficial. It is the play's lower-class citizens, its ''commons,'' who sing the final song of the seasons.

Princess of France:
See France

> As the play progresses, the king of Navarre shows little ability to abide by his own commands and vows, let alone defend the effectiveness of those commands and vows in any wider context."

Rosaline:

One of the princess's ladies, Rosaline is the unconventionally dark beauty who so appeals to Berowne. She is as full of wit as he is, and engages both Boyet and Berowne on their own terms; she challenges the other ladies in banter as well. Although she recalls having met Berowne from the beginning (II.i.67-76), she withholds any encouragement of his love, just as do the other ladies. Especially in the latter half of the play, Rosaline emerges as the most ruthlessly mocking, and at the same time, with the princess herself, the most overtly concerned with the proper and useful application of langauge. Even when Boyet teases her about being in love with Berowne, Rosaline refuses to admit that she may be, so her feelings for him never fully emerge. "Still you wrangle with her, Boyet," Maria observes, "and she strikes at the brow" (IV.i.117). When the ladies banter among themselves, Rosaline stands out as skillful in her use of language.

When the lords make their appearance in the Masque of the Muscovites, the princess dictates how the ladies will trick them. Rosaline plays the princess in the deception, and quibbles with the enamored king about the distance they have travelled and her own supposedly moon-like countenance, and then refuses to dance with him. Afterwards, Rosaline is more dismissive of the men than ever: "They were all in lamentable cases!" (V.ii.273) she cries. And here, she does take over a bit of the princess's role for real—but in a very different manner than Berowne's "o'erruling" of his king. Rosaline presents her suggestion as advice, not usurpation. She advocates continuing to mock the lords by telling them how foolish the Russian visitors were. And when it comes time to do so, Rosaline is the ringleader: she mocks the supposed Russians so mercilessly that Berowne says her

jesting is "dry to me" (V.ii.373). Love for her, in fact, makes Berowne humble himself immensely, calling himself a fool and even begging for her further verbal violence: "Here stand I, lady, dart thy skill at me, / Bruise me with scorn" (V.ii.396-97). Yet she remains merciless. When he claims to abstain from his own elaborately punning language in favor of plain honesty, she catches him out using the foreign word "sans" (V.ii.415-16).

In the end, though, the reasons behind Rosaline's seemingly cruel and unnecessary wit come to the fore. She tells Berowne that he is well known for his own merciless wit, and that she can be won only if he will "weed this wormwood from your fructful brain" (V.ii.847) by working in a hospital for the next year—and, by implication, accomplishing some good with his linguistic skill. As Rosaline puts it, Berowne must learn that mockery has social effects; it is not mere pleasure for the speaker. "A jest's prosperity lies in the ear / Of him that hears it, never in the tongue / Of him that makes it" (V.ii.861-63), she admonishes him. And indeed, her own jests have had the social effect of humbling her suitor, showing up the limits of elaborate language, and insisting on the social uses of jesting itself.

Further Reading

Barton, Anne. Introduction to *Love's Labor's Lost,* by William Shakespeare. In *The Riverside Shakespeare*, edited G. Blakemore Evans, 174-78. Chicago: Houghton Mifflin, 1974.

Barton explains the history of the play's composition and critical reception, calling the play "relentlessly Elizabethan" in its word games and topical allusions. She examines why it is that the play's comic resolution cannot occur within the confines of its plot.

Breitenberg, Mark. "The Anatomy of Masculine Desire in *Love's Labour's Lost.*" *Shakespeare Quarterly* 43, no. 4 (1992): 430-49.

Breitenberg argues that sexuality and violence are linked in *Love's Labour's Lost*: "even such a light-hearted and playful comedy" participates in the darker side of masculine desires.

Carroll, William C. *The Great Feast of Language in* Love's Labour's Lost. Princeton: Princeton University Press, 1976.

Carroll argues that the play has been oversimplified as an argument for "Life" over "Art," and that instead the play is a rejection of bad art. Includes chapters on prose, theatrical, and poetic style; on the transformations within the play; on the play's structure; and finally, on the two final songs that conclude the work.

Curtis, Harry, Jr. "Four Woodcocks in a Dish: Shakespeare's Humanization of the Comic Perspective in *Love's Labour's Lost*." *Southern Humanities Review* 13 (1979): 155-24.

Curtis maintains that the play violates the comic form and repeatedly draws the audience's attention to this deviation. Shakespeare thereby insists, Curtis argues, that the characters undergo change, not only in their external manner but in their approach to life beyond the fiction of the play.

David, Richard. Introduction to *Love's Labour's Lost*, by William Shakespeare, xiii-li. The Arden Shakespeare. London: Methuen, 1951.

David explores the comedy's dating, sources, and topical references, as well as its content. Writing at the beginning of a critical revival of interest in the play, he compares it to a work of music, specifically opera, in its conventional and stylized presentation.

Erikson, Peter B. "The Failure of Relationship Between Men and Women in *Love's Labour's Lost*." *Women's Studies* 9, no. 1 (1981): 65-81.

Erikson argues that the bonding of male characters in the play promotes a view of women as dangerous outsiders, so that the women become inaccessible, domineering, and punitive. The play does not finally affirm such a structure, Erikson maintains, but ends in "uneasy stasis."

Gilbert, Miriam. *Love's Labour's Lost*. Shakespeare in Performance Series. Manchester: Manchester University Press, 1993.

Contains chapters on the historical performances of the play, from the Elizabethan stage to performances in 1857, 1946, 1968, 1978, and 1984. Discusses the balance between language as the wit of sophisticated people, on the one hand, and on the other hand as the efforts of immature people to impress each other. The play has tended to be staged elaborately, but some of its best stagings have been more homespun, Gilbert argues.

Greene, Thomas. "*Love's Labour's Lost*: The Grace of Society." In *The Vulnerable Text*, 140-59. New York: Columbia University Press, 1986.

Greene makes an argument that a variety of styles of speech emerge in the play, and that the appropriateness of these styles is necessary to the proper functioning of society. Additionally, Greene links language style to social virtue to assert that the play's object is to live with poise, decorum, and charity.

Hassel, R. Chris, Jr. "Love Versus Charity in *Love's Labour's Lost*." *Shakespeare Studies* 10 (1977): 17-41.

Examines the doctrine of charity in the context of its opposition in Protestant and Catholic theologies and discusses Shakespeare's treatment of this doctrine in *Love's Labor's Lost*.

Hibbard, G. R. Introduction and Appendices to *Love's Labour's Lost*, by William Shakespeare, 1-84 and 237-46. The Oxford Shakespeare. Oxford: Clarendon Press, 1990.

Analysis of the play, its performances, its date and sources, and its textual history; appendices on revisions, lineation, music, and the name of Armado's page. Discusses the ways in which the play refuses the conventions of comedy. Hibbard argues that the play is stylized and formal, like a dance, and calls attention to the artificiality of its characters and their setting, though unexpected depths are sounded as well.

Hunt, Maurice. "The Double Figure of Elizabeth in *Love's Labour's Lost*." *Essays in Literature* 19, no. 2 (1992): 173-92.

Argues that the play's princess of France evokes two contrasting images of the historical Queen Elizabeth of England: one powerful and seductive, and the other morbid and violent toward her suitors. Hunt maintains that the play thus attempts to make a difficult historical situation more managable.

Muir, Kenneth. *Shakespeare's Comic Sequence*, 135-40. New York: Barnes and Noble, 1979.

Muir argues that *Love's Labor's Lost* is a didactic comedy that criticizes its characters for their linguistic excess and foolish behavior, but ultimately the play is a plea for good sense and balance, as evidenced in the final songs of Winter and Spring.

Taylor, Rupert. *The Date of* Love's Labour's Lost. New York: Columbia University Press, 1932. Reprint, AMS Press, Inc., 1966.

This book marks a turning point in criticism on the play, establishing its date as later than had previously been thought—in 1596 rather than very early. Chapter VI (pp. 72-90) contains a useful analysis of the significance of this date, which reveals a more definite purpose, thorough-going execution, and unified design than critics had previously granted the play. Also makes a less well-accepted argument for topical references within the play.

The Tragedy of Macbeth

circa 1606

Act I:

The play opens during a lightning storm, in the midst of which are three witches, or weird sisters, who are planning to meet Macbeth, a Scottish general. In a Scottish camp, a sergeant reports to King Duncan of Scotland, the king's son Malcolm, and several nobleman that Macbeth, a nobleman with the title thane of Glamis, has defeated invading Norwegian forces led by rebel Scotsman Macdonwald. Duncan then instructs Rosse and Angus (two noblemen) to find Macbeth and confer on him Macdonwald's title, thane of Cawdor. Meanwhile, as Macbeth and his friend Banquo are returning from battle, they encounter the witches who greet them with several prophesies. The salute Macbeth with three titles: thane of Glamis (his current title), thane of Cawdor, and king hereafter. For Banquo, they predict that he will beget kings, though he will not be a king himself. Rosse and Angus then arrive with news from the king that Macbeth has been given the title thane of Cawdor. Later, Duncan meets with Macbeth and the rest of the nobleman. Duncan praises Macbeth, and even states his wish to stay a night at Macbeth's castle in Inverness. The king then announces his son Malcolm as prince of Cumberland, making Malcolm next in line for the throne. Meanwhile, at Macbeth's castle, Lady Macbeth reads a letter sent by her husband in which he discusses the weird sisters, his new title, and the prophesies. She

resolves to help Macbeth clear the way for the prophesies' fulfillment, and she informs Macbeth of this decision upon his arrival at Inverness. After the king arrives, Macbeth contemplates his reasons for not wanting to kill the king. When Lady Macbeth joins him, she argues against his reluctance, and Macbeth resolves to commit the murder.

Act II:

Late at night, Macbeth and Banquo encounter each other and agree to discuss the weird sisters. After Banquo goes to bed, Macbeth imagines that he sees a dagger leading him to kill Duncan, and offstage he commits regicide. Macbeth returns from the murder, having brought the daggers which he took from Duncan's guards and used to slay Duncan. Since he refuses to return to the king's chamber, Lady Macbeth must take the bloody daggers back. The next morning, after repeated knocking at the castle gate, the porter admits Macduff and Lennox, who have come to awaken the king. When Macduff discovers that the king has been murdered, Macbeth goes to verify the report. He returns from his investigation of the scene and mentions that in his fury at the sight of the murdered king he killed the king's guards. The king's sons, Malcolm and Donalbain, anticipate that they might be suspected of the murder and leave the country. In the final scene, Rosse and an old man discuss unnatural omens. Macduff brings news that Macbeth has been chosen to be king.

Act III:

Alone, Banquo states his suspicions about Macbeth. Macbeth announces a feast, inviting Banquo and others. Recalling the witches prophesies about Banquo and his decedents, however, Macbeth orders the deaths of Banquo and Banquo's son, Fleance. He does not confide his latest plans to Lady Macbeth. At dusk, three murderers attack Banquo and his son. They kill Banquo, but Fleance escapes. That evening, Macbeth entertains the Scottish nobles. One of the murderers brings him news of what has happened. When Macbeth sees and speaks to Banquo's ghost, the assembled company all leave abruptly, Lady Macbeth having attempted to dismiss her husband's bizarre behavior. After the guests leave, Macbeth and his wife discuss Macduff's absence at the banquet. Settling the matter with a decision to send for Macduff and visit the weird sisters, Macbeth and his wife retire for the evening, with Lady Macbeth assuring her husband that sleep will ease his fears.

Act IV:

Macbeth comes upon the witches and demands to know answers about his future. They produce three apparitions from their cauldron. The first is an armed head warning him about Macduff, the thane of Fife. The second is a bloody child, telling him that none of woman born will harm him. The third is a child wearing a crown and carrying a tree in his hand. This one tells him ''Macbeth shall never vanquish'd be until / Great Birnan wood to high Dunsinane hill / Shall come against him'' (IV.i.92-4). Macbeth inquires about Banquo's descendants, and a show of eight kings, the last with a mirror in his hand, is displayed. The witches vanish. Lennox arrives with news of Macduff's departure to England. Macbeth plans to murder Macduff's family, and sends murderers immediately. A messenger tries to warn Lady Macduff, but before she can form any plan, murderers arrive and stab her son and pursue and kill her. In England, Macduff tries to convince Malcolm to return and help Scotland. Malcolm tests Macduff's honorable intentions. Satisfied with Macduff's honesty, they plan to return joined with Siward's forces. Rosse brings news of the assault on Macduff's castle, and Macduff grieves.

Act V:

Lady Macbeth, attended by a gentlewoman and a doctor, sleepwalks, speaking in disordered phrases and sentences, which taken together review the murderous events of the play. In the countryside near Dunsinane, the Scottish forces assemble and plan to meet the English forces led by Malcolm and Macduff near Birnan Wood. Macbeth is in his castle relying on the witches' apparitions, yet he receives reports about the gathering forces. The English and Scottish join forces near Birnan Wood. Malcolm orders every soldier to cut down a branch and put it in front of him to conceal his movements. When a cry of women is heard, an aide announces that Lady Macbeth has killed herself. After Macbeth's soliloquy about the futility of life and the inevitability of death, a messenger brings a report that the woods seem to move. Macbeth vows to fight to the death. In the battle, Macbeth encounters Siward's son and kills him. He still relies on the prophecy that ''none of woman born'' could do him harm. In Macbeth's final battle field encounter, he and Macduff meet. Macduff reveals that he was ''from his mother's womb untimely ripp'd'' (V.viii.15-6), that is, that he was not born naturally, but delivered prematurely through cesarean section. Macbeth despairs of the witches' double meanings, fights to the death, and is slain by Macduff. Malcolm is hailed as the new king of Scotland.

Modern Connections

The witches, or weird sisters, of *Macbeth* have remained one of the most popular aspects of the play. The three witches, the first characters the audience encounters, are mysterious beings who set the tone for the rest of the play, most of which takes place in a similarly dark and stormy atmosphere. When the play was performed during the late English Renaissance, the witches would make their initial appearance coming up and out of the trap door on the stage of the Globe theater. Later productions included singing, dancing, and flying witches, attached to ceiling wires.

The witches also perform a more serious function than that of entertainment: their appearance in the play poses the question of whether Macbeth's actions are governed by fate, or determined by his own free will. Critics have questioned the meaning behind the witches statement ''All hail, Macbeth, that shall be King hereafter!'' (I.iii.50). Is this statement a warning to Macbeth or does it tempt him to consider possibilities he may have thought of before? Or, is it a prophesy of the future? Through the witches, some maintain, Shakespeare questions whether our own lives are governed by fate or free will.

Questions regarding gender roles in *Macbeth* may also strike modern students as particularly compelling, as these roles in contemporary society continue to shift and evolve. Some observers read Lady Macbeth's persuasion of her husband to follow through on the murder of Duncan as being guided by her fascination with male power. She appeals to her husband's sense of manhood, and in effect, some maintain, uses seduction and humiliation to convince him to commit the murder. It has also been argued that Lady Macbeth rejects her own feminine ''sensibilities'' and takes on a more masculine role for herself because of her perception that femininity is equated with weakness. She assumes this masculine role for herself in an effort to act on her own ambition and desire for power.

Masculinity in this play appears to be defined almost exclusively by violent action and Macbeth seems driven to prove his manhood through violent deeds, first in battle, then by murder. Macbeth's brutal slaying of Macdonwald is detailed by a sergeant: ''he unseam'd him from the nave [navel] to the chops [jaws], / And fix'd his head upon our battlements'' (I.ii.22-3). When Macbeth begins to back away from the thought of murdering Duncan, telling his wife ''We will proceed no further in this business'' (I.vii.31), she questions his manhood, stating that when he initially broached the subject with her, then he was a man (I.vii.48-49). By the end of the scene, he has decided that he will kill the king. In addition to murdering Duncan, Macbeth murders the king's guards, and then orders the murders of Banquo, Fleance, and Macduff's family. When Macduff learns of these last killings, Malcolm urges the grieving Macduff to take revenge, to act ''like a man'' (IV.iii.219).

It has been argued that Macbeth himself is distanced somewhat from the violence of the play in that he commits the murders of Duncan off-stage, and he orders other people to commit the murder of Banquo, Fleance, and Macduff's family, rather than committing them himself. The notion that in the society in which Macbeth lived, the stereotypical male was characterized by violence, and that the violence was legitimized through warfare, is agreed upon by many critics, however. Just as Macbeth uses violent means to further his own ambition, the play ends with Macbeth's violent removal from the throne, and with Macduff appearing on stage with Macbeth's severed head.

Finally, the theme of ambition and how it relates to governance is a major issue in the play. Macbeth lets his ambition supersede his own judgement. In I.vii he discusses the reasons why he should not kill Duncan. He states that his loyalty to the king has several layers: he is the king's subject, his kinsmen, and his host. After highlighting the king's virtues Macbeth acknowledges that the only reason to kill Duncan is his own ''vaulting ambition'' (I.vii.27). At this point, his thoughts are interrupted by Lady Macbeth. He seems to have had a change of heart, but after his wife's speech, Macbeth is determined to murder the king. After he himself is crowned, he is driven to protect what he has gained by ordering the deaths of anyone who he considers a threat. While violence is an integral part of this warrior society, Macbeth's use of it off the battlefield to further his personal ambition, while unchecked through most of the play, is in the end, not tolerated by his subjects. The twentieth century provides numerous examples of world leaders who to varying degrees abused power until their actions were checked by the citizens of their own nation, or by the rest of the world. This abuse of power could take the form of one man's effort to improve his own political position, as in the case of Richard M. Nixon; his actions resulted in his resignation from the presidency. A far more extreme example would be that of Adolph Hitler, who used the power he attained to practice genocide until he was stopped through international warfare.

Characters

Angus:

Angus is a Scottish nobleman. He travels with Rosse to bring King Duncan news of the battle and to bestow upon Macbeth the title thane of Cawdor. Angus also accompanies Duncan on the journey to Macbeth's castle. Finally, he appears in Act V with the Scottish rebels.

Apparitions:

In IV.i, three apparitions come from the witches' cauldron after animal and human blood is poured in on top of a variety of other ingredients. The first apparition, described in the stage directions as ''an armed head,'' tells Macbeth to beware the thane of Fife (Macduff). The second apparition is a bloody child who tells Macbeth that ''none of woman born'' (IV.ii.80) can harm Macbeth. The third apparition is a child wearing a crown and carrying a tree in his hand. He tells Macbeth that he will not be vanquished until ''Great Birnan wood to high Dunsinane hill'' rise against him (IV.i.93-4).

Attendants:

The king is surrounded by attendants who can carry out such tasks as helping the bleeding sergeant to find surgeons. They travel with the king. His personal attendants are supposed to guard him in his sleep. Macbeth stabs them in the confused moments following the discovery of the murdered king. Macbeth has his own attendants. They help with Macbeth's banquet and are with him in the castle in the last act of the play.

Banquo:

Banquo is a Scottish general in the king's army and Macbeth's friend. With Macbeth, Banquo helps

Duncan's forces claim victory over the king of Norway and the thane of Cawdor. Following the battle, Banquo and Macbeth encounter the witches, who make several prophesies about Macbeth. They then speak to Banquo about his own future, saying that Banquo's descendants will be kings. Unlike Macbeth, who appears to be fascinated by the weird sisters, Banquo expresses doubts about the witches and their prophesies. He comments to Macbeth, for example, that ''oftentimes, to win us to our harm, / The instruments of darkness tell us truths, / Win us with honest trifles, to betray [us]'' (I.iii.123-25).

This unwillingness to subscribe wholeheartedly to the visions of the witches, in addition to Banquo's demonstrated valor in battle contribute to the view that Banquo is a virtuous man. Yet Banquo's virtue is an area of some controversy. A common view is that Shakespeare intended Banquo to be seen as a virtuous character who was not responsible in any way for Macbeth's murderous actions, despite the fact that the source material from which Shakespeare drew depicts Banquo as a co-conspirator in Duncan's death. This line of thinking is supported by the popular belief that *Macbeth* was performed (perhaps even written) for King James I in 1606. Historically, Banquo was an ancestor of King James, and some critics argue that because of this, Shakespeare would not portray him in an unfavorable way. Other observers argue that Banquo's inaction makes him in part morally responsible for the king's murder. These critics cite Banquo's soliloquy following Duncan's death as evidence of his knowledge of (and therefore at least partial responsibility for) Macbeth's actions. In this speech Banquo acknowledges to himself his suspicions about Macbeth's actions: ''Thou hast it now: King, Cawdor, Glamis, all, / As the weird women promis'd, and I fear / Thou play'dst most foully for't . . .'' (III.i.1-3).

Shortly after Macbeth kills Duncan, he remembers the witches' prophesy regarding Banquo: that Banquo's descendants would be kings. Macbeth then arranges to have Banquo and his son Fleance murdered. Fleance escapes the attack; Banquo does not.

Boy:

Macduff's son is a young boy. When the murderers sent by Macbeth arrive at the Macduff residence, the child tries to defend his father's honor and calls the murderer a name. After he is stabbed, he tells his mother to run away.

> " Unlike Macbeth, who appears to be fascinated by the weird sisters, Banquo expresses doubts about the witches and their prophesies. He comments to Macbeth, for example, that 'oftentimes, to win us to our harm, / The instruments of darkness tell us truths, / Win us with honest trifles, to betray [us]' (I.iii.123-25)."

Cathness (in some editions, Caithness):

Cathness is a Scottish nobleman who is another one of the rebels against Macbeth under Malcolm's leadership.

Donalbain:

Donalbain is the king's son and brother to Malcolm. He is present but silent in the early scenes with the king. When the murder of his father is disclosed, he suggests that he and Malcolm flee the country, and he leaves for Ireland. For a time, he and his brother are under suspicion for the murder. He is not present at the battle at the end of the play.

Duncan (King Duncan of Scotland):

Duncan is said by Macbeth to be virtuous and meek in his conduct in office and in his bearing. He seems to be regarded as a good king and, on the battlefield, he appears to be a competent leader who confronts both a rebellion and an invasion. He announces his son Malcolm as the prince of Cumberland, the next in line to the Scottish throne. Duncan does not seem to be a particularly good judge of character, since he misjudged both the former thane of Cawdor and his designated replacement, Macbeth who murders Duncan in his sleep.

Earl of Northumberland (Siward, Earl of Northumberland):

See Siward

English Doctor:

The English doctor comments to Malcolm on the healing touch of the saintly Edward, the English king. Edward's healing stands in contrast to Macbeth's murderous touch.

Fleance:

Fleance is Banquo's son. He and his father encounter Macbeth just before Macbeth murders Duncan. Prior to the banquet to which Macbeth has invited Fleance and Banquo, father and son are approached by murderers who have been ordered by Macbeth to kill both of them. Fleance escapes the attack.

Gentlemen:

Unnamed gentlemen are addressed by Rosse at Macbeth's banquet.

Gentlewoman:

The gentlewoman is an attendant on Lady Macbeth. She speaks knowledgeably to the Scottish doctor about Lady Macbeth's sleepwalking routine.

Ghost of Banquo:

Banquo's ghost appears at Macbeth's banquet scene and is only seen by Macbeth. It is commonly held that the ghost is a hallucination, conjured from Macbeth's guilt.

Hecat (also Hecate):

Hecat is the goddess of witchcraft. She is described by the weird sisters as looking angry when she first appears on stage. She scolds them for their dealings with Macbeth, who loves the witches not for themselves but for his own purposes. She plans apparitions that will confuse and mislead Macbeth. Accompanied by three other witches, she appears briefly in the cauldron scene, commending the witches and instructing them to dance and sing.

King of Scotland (King Duncan of Scotland):

See Duncan

Lennox:

Lennox is a Scottish nobleman who appears with the king at his camp near the battlefield. He travels with the king to Macbeth's castle. The morning after Duncan's murder, Lennox arrives with Macduff, intending to awaken the king. Based on his initial survey of the evidence Lennox speculates that the king's chamberlains were his killers. Lennox appears again in III.iv at Macbeth's banquet. During the hasty departure of the guests from the banquet, he wishes a better health to the king. In the final scene of Act III, he speaks of recent events in Scotland. In the first scene of Act IV, when he brings Macbeth word of Macduff's departure from England, he does not see the weird sisters vanish past him in the air. He is aligned with the Scottish noblemen rebelling against Macbeth in Act V.

Lords:

Some unnamed lords attend Macbeth's banquet. One lord speaks to Lennox after the banquet about recent events in Scotland, the whereabouts of Malcolm and lately of Macduff, and the anger of Macbeth at Macduff's absence from the banquet. He prays for better times in Scotland.

Macbeth:

Macbeth is nobleman and a Scottish general in the king's army. At the beginning of the play, he has gained recognition for himself through his defeat of the king of Norway and the rebellious Macdonwald. Shortly after the battle, Macbeth and another of the king's general's, Banquo, encounter three witches (or weird sisters), who greet Macbeth as thane of Glamis, thane of Cawdor, and future king. Macbeth, unaware that King Duncan has bestowed upon him the title thane of Cawdor, appears to be startled by these prophesies. As soon as the witches finish addressing Macbeth, Banquo asks him, ''why do you start, and seem to fear / Things that do sound so fair?'' (I.iii.51-52). The witches vanish after telling Banquo that he will father kings. Shortly thereafter, Rosse and Angus arrive to tell Macbeth that the title of thane of Cawdor has been transferred to him. Upon hearing this he says to himself that the greatest title, that of king, is yet to come. When Duncan announces that his son Malcolm will be next in line for the throne, Macbeth acknowledges the prince as an obstacle which will either trip him up, or one which he must overcome.

After Macbeth sends words to his wife about the witches prophesies, Lady Macbeth hears that the

> **After murdering Duncan, then framing and murdering Duncan's attendants, Macbeth, disturbed by the witches' prophesy about Banquo's descendants, orders the murder of Banquo and Banquo's son, Fleance.''**

king will be coming to stay at the castle. She then decides that the king will die there. When Macbeth arrives at Inverness, Lady Macbeth discusses with her husband her intentions. Soon after, he reviews in his own mind the reasons for not killing the king. He has many, including his obligations to the king as a kinsman, a loyal subject, and a host. Other reasons listed by Macbeth include the goodness of the king, and the general lack of any reason other than ambition. However, when his wife argues with him, attacking his manhood, Macbeth resolves to follow through with the murder.

The extent of Lady Macbeth's power over her husband is debated. Some critics blame Lady Macbeth for precipitating Macbeth's moral decline and ultimate downfall. Others argue that while Lady Macbeth appears to be increasingly guilt-ridden as the play progresses, as evidenced by her sleepwalking episodes, Macbeth becomes increasingly murderous.

After murdering Duncan, then framing and murdering Duncan's attendants, Macbeth, disturbed by the witches' prophesy about Banquo's descendants, orders the murder of Banquo and Banquo's son, Fleance. The son escapes, but Banquo is slain, as the murderers report to Macbeth at the banquet in III.iv. Upon hearing this news, Macbeth is haunted throughout the banquet by Banquo's ghost, who no one else can see. As the scene ends, Macbeth vows to visit the weird sisters again, which he does in IV.i. During this visit, Macbeth receives three messages from apparitions conjured by the witches. The first apparition warns Macbeth to beware the thane of Fife; the second tells him that he cannot be harmed by anyone born of a woman; the third states that Macbeth will not be vanquished until ''Great

Birnan wood to high Dunsinane hill'' rise against him (IV.i.93-4). Next, Macbeth asks whether or not Banquo's descendants will ever rule Scotland, and the witches show him a vision of Banquo, followed by eight kings. The vision and the weird sisters disappear as Lennox arrives with the information that Macduff has gone to England, and that Malcolm is there as well. At this point, Macbeth decides to have Macduff's family murdered.

As Act V opens, Lady Macbeth's sleepwalking is revealed, Malcolm and Macduff have gathered an army against Macbeth, and many of Macbeth's own thanes have deserted him. But Macbeth seems to rely on his belief in his interpretation of the witches' prophesies, which he reviews in V.iii. He vows that his heart and mind will not ''shake with fear'' (V.iii.10). After learning of the his wife's death, however, Macbeth in a famous speech (V.v.16-28) expresses his weariness with life.

Clinging to the witches' words about his not being harmed by any one ''of woman born,'' (IV.ii.80) Macbeth tells Macduff that his life is charmed, only to learn that his opponent was delivered via cesarean birth (''from his mother's womb / Untimely ripp'd'' [V.viii.150-16]). Offstage, Macduff kills Macbeth and returns with his severed head.

Overall assessment of Macbeth's character varies. Some view him as a tragic hero, who held every potential for being a good man, but was overcome by the evil forces in his world. Others argue that Macbeth completely lacked any moral integrity. Finally, he is viewed most harshly by some who see him as a Satanic figure, in that he knowingly choose evil and unleashes it upon the world.

Macbeth (Lady Macbeth):

Lady Macbeth is Macbeth's wife. When the audience first sees her in I.v, she is reading a letter from Macbeth about his encounter with the weird sisters and about his new title. Lady Macbeth promises to provide Macbeth with the courage he needs to make the prophecy come true, fearing that his nature is too soft to take the direct route to the throne.

There is some controversy over the role Lady Macbeth plays in the murders that follow. Some critics maintain that responsibility for the deaths of Duncan and Banquo rests solely with Macbeth,

whose own ambition and nature are the cause of his deeds. Others cite Macbeth's reluctance prior to Duncan's murder and argue that Lady Macbeth goads her husband into the action. Lady Macbeth does however set the time and the place of Duncan's murder, claims that she would kill a baby at her breast to honor a vow, and argues that when Macbeth first conceived of killing Duncan, then he was a man.

In contrast to Lady Macbeth's forceful disposition on the first three acts of the play, her actions in the last two acts are much less confident or ambitious. Lady Macbeth in the sleepwalking scene appears to be tormented by her knowledge of Macbeth's actions. In V.i Lady Macbeth reviews the various crimes her husband has committed and appears to be attempting to wash blood from her hands. This scene contains Lady Macbeth's famous ''Out damn'd spot!'' (V.i.35) speech. The doctor diagnoses her mind as ''infected'' (V.i.72) and says she needs spiritual counsel more than she needs a doctor. Later she commits suicide.

Macduff:

Macduff, the thane of Fife, is a Scottish nobleman. He travels with Duncan to Macbeth's castle, and with Lennox, arrives the morning after the king has been murdered to awaken Duncan, but instead finds him dead. Macduff announces to the gathered nobleman, including the king's sons, that Duncan has been killed.

Macduff's words in the next scene are considered significant by some observes who argue that Macduff is the first character to suggest his suspicion regarding Macbeth's ascension to the throne. Macduff tells Rosse that will not be attending Macbeth's coronation, but will instead be returning home to Fife. After Rosse states that he will be going to the coronation, Macduff replies: ''Well, may you see things well done there: adieu, / Lest our old robes dit easier than our new'' (II.iv.37-8). Additionally, Macduff is not present at the banquet during which Macbeth sees Banquo's ghost. This absence is noted by Macbeth directly after the banquet, at which time Macbeth vows to see the weird sisters again. When he does, the apparition they conjure tells him to beware the thane of Fife, and just after the witches vanish, Lennox approaches with the news that Macduff has fled to England. Macbeth then vows to have Macduff's family killed.

Meanwhile, Macduff has met with Malcolm in England. The two return to Scotland, having gathered an army with which to challenge Macbeth. At this time, Macduff learns of his family's death. Although many readers view Macduff, and Malcolm as well, as Scotland's saviors, Macduff is often harshly criticized for deserting his family. At the same time, critics have praised Macduff for not being ashamed to show his emotion when he learns that his family has been murdered.

In V.viii, Macduff and Macbeth confront each other. Macbeth appears to be convinced by the witches' prophesy that "none of woman born" can harm him. When he reveals this to Macduff, Macduff replies that he wasn't *born* of woman; rather, he was "from his mother's womb / Untimely ripp'd" (V.viii.15-16). Macduff then kills and beheads Macbeth, clearing the way for Malcolm's ascension to the throne.

Macduff (Lady Macduff):

Lady Macduff is Macduff's wife. When Macduff leaves for England, she is left unprotected with her son at her castle. She questions her husband's wisdom in leaving his family, and later speaks gently yet seriously to her son of Macduff's absence, saying he is dead. They have a conversation about how they will live without Macduff. She and her son are murdered by those sent by Macbeth.

Malcolm:

Malcolm is one of King Duncan's sons, the other being Donalbain. In the early part of the play he is scarcely present, but overall he has one of the three main speaking parts, the other two being Macbeth and Lady Macbeth. Early in the play Malcolm introduces to King Duncan the sergeant who saved Malcolm from capture. When the king's assassination is discovered, Malcolm agrees with his brother's suggestion to flee for their lives, and he goes to England, where he is later said to be living at the court of King Edward the Confessor, an English king noted for his holiness. The sudden departure of the king's sons casts some suspicion on their complicity in his murder.

In IV.iii, Macduff goes to England to seek Malcolm's help in restoring rightful rule in Scotland. In the interview that then takes place, Malcolm acknowledges his doubts about Macduff's motives

> **Clinging to the witches' words about his not being harmed by any one 'of woman born' (IV.ii.80), Macbeth tells Macduff that his life is charmed, only to learn that his opponent was delivered via cesarean birth ('from his mother's womb / Untimely ripp'd' [V.viii.150-16]). "**

quite directly to Macduff. He wonders whether Macduff is a paid agent of Macbeth, and he also questions why Macduff suddenly left his family unprotected to come to England. In order to test his suspicions about Macduff, Malcolm tells Macduff that he himself loves women, land and jewels, and discord among people. In sum, he accuses himself of lacking all kingly graces. When Macduff responds with a cry of hopelessness and despair for his country, Malcolm reveals that this is the first lie he has ever told. Later, Malcolm encourages Macduff to use the sudden news of his family's slaughter as a motive to fight Macbeth.

In the final scene of the play, Malcolm shows himself assuming the role of kingship with grace and dignity, expressing his concern for the soldiers who are not present, and urging Siward to take time to mourn for his son. In his final speech, he states his plans to inaugurate a new era in Scotland, rewarding the soldiers, calling home exiles, and serving by the grace of God.

Menteth (in some editions, Menteith):

Menteth is a Scottish nobleman who is one of the rebels against Macbeth serving under Malcolm. He seems confident that their cause will succeed and restore peace and order to Scotland.

Messengers:

One messenger brings news to Lady Macbeth that the king is coming to stay at their castle.

> **Lady Macbeth promises to provide Macbeth with the courage he needs to make the prophecy come true, fearing that his nature is too soft to take the direct route to the throne."**

Another messenger tries to warn Lady Macduff that her family is in danger at Macduff's castle. In the last act, as Malcolm's army advances under cover of branches cut from trees, another messenger brings Macbeth word that the woods seem to be moving.

Murderers (Three Murderers, or murtherers):

The murderers are hired by Macbeth to kill Banquo and Fleance. He speaks to two of them, who say they are willing to perform as ordered. At the site of the murder a third appears, apparently unknown to the other two, making the first two murderers think that Macbeth does not trust them. The first one goes with blood on his face to the door of Macbeth's banquet hall to tell him about the deed. Macbeth is happy about Banquo's death but shaken by the news that Fleance escaped. He plans to meet the murderers again. These may be the murderers who kill Lady Macduff also.

Officers:

Nonspeaking parts. These would be appropriate to battle scenes, camp scenes, and Duncan's arrival at Macbeth's castle.

Old Man:

The anonymous old man represents experience and memory, and is at least 70 years old ("Threescore and ten I can remember well" he says in II.iv.1). He comments on the disturbances in nature on the night of Duncan's murder, unprecedented in his recollection. He is referred to by Rosse several times as father. He wishes a blessing on Rosse as he travels to Scone.

Porter:

He is the doorman at Macbeth's castle. He hears knocking but takes his time in answering the knocking, imagining that he is at hell's gate and letting in "some of all professions" into the "everlasting bonfire" (II.iii.18-19). After he opens the gate, admitting Lennox and Macduff, he reveals that he was up until the early hours of the morning, drinking and "carousing" (II.iii.24).

In his drunken rambling, the porter, speaks at length about welcoming "equivocators" to the castle. In Elizabethan England, the word equivocate meant much more than speaking with a double meaning. Shakespeare's audience would most likely have been familiar with the Doctrine of Equivocation, which gave Catholics permission to perjure themselves for morally acceptable reasons. In 1606, two Catholics were interrogated about their role in what became known as the Gunpowder Plot, which was a conspiracy to kill King James I and blow up Parliament in an effort place a Catholic on England's throne. Henry Garnet and Guy Fawkes invoked the Doctrine of Equivocation during their trial. Critics note that in the porter's speech about equivocation, Shakespeare associates the use of equivocation by Elizabethan Catholics like Garnet and Fawkes with the words of the weird sisters. Like Garnet and Fawkes the witches words invariably carry double meanings. Perhaps the most notable instance of this is when the witches tell Macbeth that "none of woman born" (IV.i.80) can harm him. Macbeth finds out just before Macduff kills him the real truth behind the witches' words: that Macduff was taken from his mother's womb through cesarean section.

Rosse (in some editions, Ross):

Rosse is a Scottish nobleman who reports to the king on the Macdonwald's rebellion and on the Norwegian king's desire to have a peace treaty. Rosse and Angus bring the news to Macbeth of his new title. He goes to Macbeth's castle with the king. Rosse comments on unusual things happening in nature after the king's assassination, such as the king's horses eating each other. He plans to travel to Scone to see Macbeth crowned. He attends Macbeth's banquet and notices that the king is unwell. Rosse's appearance at Macduff's castle is unclear in intent, but it seems to be only to check on Lady Macduff. He brings the news to Macduff of her death, but appears to have a difficult time stating clearly what happened, saying initially that Macduff's family is well and at peace. He appears with the rebelling Scottish noblemen in Act V, and he is present in the final scene bringing Siward news of his son's death.

Scots Doctor:

The Scots (or Scottish) doctor attends to Lady Macbeth. He has watched for several nights and not seen the sleepwalking. He questions the gentlewoman about Lady Macbeth's actions during the sleepwalking, and advises that Lady Macbeth needs spiritual rather than physical healing. When he reports to Macbeth, he gives his opinion that she is not sick but troubled by her imagination. He says to himself that if he can get away from the castle, no desire for profit will make him come back.

Sergeant:

This soldier, sometimes identified as a captain, is present only in the second scene in the play, but introduces the image of the spreading bloodshed which stains the land. He begins reporting to Duncan on the battle and on Macbeth's bravery but is too weakened from his wounds to finish his speech.

Servant:

In V.iii, a servant brings Macbeth news of the ten thousand English invaders approaching the castle.

Sewer:

The sewer is a butler who waits on Macbeth and his guests at the castle. A supper goes on in the other room while Macbeth deliberates about Duncan's murder. This is not a speaking part.

Seyton:

Seyton is Macbeth's only trusted subordinate at the end of the play. He brings Macbeth confirmation of battle reports. He also brings news of the death of Lady Macbeth. Although Macbeth calls for him impatiently, he does not scream at him the way he does at other messengers. It has often been noticed that his name resembles Satan.

Siward (Siward, Earl of Northumberland):

Siward's help for the Scottish cause is sought by Malcolm and Macduff at the English court of

> **In V.i Lady Macbeth reviews the various crimes her husband has committed and appears to be attempting to wash blood from her hands. This scene contains Lady Macbeth's famous 'Out damn'd spot!' (V.i.35) speech."**

Edward the Confessor. Siward is described by Malcolm as an experienced and accomplished soldier. Siward and Malcolm enter Macbeth's castle together. Some of Macbeth's own people turn against him and join with the invaders. When Siward learns the news of his son's death in the final scene, he is satisfied that his son received his injuries on the front of his body, facing the battle rather than running away, and declares him now ''God's soldier'' (V.ix.13).

Siward (Young Siward):

Siward's son is a young man. He fights against Macbeth, and dies in the battle at Macbeth's sword.

Soldiers:

The soldiers marching with Malcolm and the rebelling Scottish nobles in Act V suggest the numbers massing against Macbeth. The Scottish have their soldiers, and Siward arrives with ten thousand English soldiers.

Weird Sisters (Three Witches, The Weird Sisters):

See Witches

Witches (Three other Witches):

See Hecat

Witches (Three Witches, The Weird Sisters):

The witches in *Macbeth* are present in only four scenes in the play, but Macbeth's fascination with

"Macduff tells Rosse that will not be attending Macbeth's coronation, but will instead be returning home to Fife. . . . Additionally, Macduff is not present at the banquet during which Macbeth sees Banquo's ghost. This absence is noted by Macbeth . . ."

them motivates much of the play's action. When they meet with Banquo and Macbeth, they address Macbeth with three titles: thane of Glamis, thane of Cawdor, and king hereafter. Next, they predict that Banquo will father kings, though he will not be king himself. Refusing to answer questions, they vanish.

Later in III.v, Hecat lectures the witches for talking to Macbeth without involving her. In IV.i, when Macbeth pays another visit to the witches, Hecat has briefly appeared to the witches, but leaves before Macbeth's arrival. Though the Riverside edition has her accompanied by three other witches, most editions do not. In this scene, the witches make a thick gruel in a cauldron, using animal and human body parts. Many of the animals are reptilian or associated with night. The human body parts come from people who were considered outsiders to the Christian world of the English Renaissance: Jews, Turks, Tartars. The witches refer to their activity as a "deed without a name" (IV.i.49). They sense that Macbeth is coming; one says she can tell "By the pricking of my thumbs, / Something wicked this way comes" (IV.i.44-45). This time, the witches submit to some of Macbeth's questions. They pour in sow's blood and a murderer's blood into the cauldron, and produce apparitions. When Macbeth has seen the apparitions (see Apparitions) and heard their messages, he demands to know about Banquo. The weird sisters then produce a show of eight kings followed by Banquo. As the witches produce this display, they say "Show his eyes, and grieve his heart" (IV.i.110). When Macbeth grows enraged, they dance and depart with great cheer.

There is a frustrating duplicity about the witches' nature as there is about their prophecies and

predictions to Macbeth. They are interpreted variously as custodians of evil, spinners of the future, and as something slightly more neutral, creatures with knowledge of the future but with limited powers.

Further Reading

Brown, John Russell, ed. *Focus on* Macbeth. London: Routledge & Paul, 1982.

    R. A. Foakes ("Images of Death: Ambition in *Macbeth*," pp. 7-29) discusses Macbeth's and Lady Macbeth's characters. Stallybrass's essay ("*Macbeth* and Witchcraft," pp. 189-209) discusses Lady Macbeth and the witches. Derek Russell Davis, a health care professional, discusses the characters of Macbeth and Lady Macbeth as though they were real. His essay ("Hurt Minds," pp. 210-28) uses a psychopathological approach to the two partners in crime and presents the results as a case-report. Students who are interested in specialist topics like "what are thanes?" are directed to the essay by Michael Hawkins on historical context.

Coles, Blanche. *Shakespeare Studies. Macbeth.* 1938. Reprint, New York: AMS Press, 1969.

    Coles paraphrases the play scene by scene.

Harbage, Alfred. Introduction to *Macbeth*, by William Shakespeare. In *William Shakespeare The Complete Works*, edited by Alfred Harbage, 1107-09. Baltimore: Pelican, 1969.

    Harbage's essay discusses source, date, topical references, interpolations, and Macbeth's character.

Holdridge, Barbara, ed. *Under the Greenwood Tree*. Owings Mills, Maryland: Stemmer House, 1986.

    The illustrations in this poetry collection give students one imaginative way of visualizing the witches and the ingredients of their cauldron and also the somberness of Macbeth's "Tomorrow and tomorrow" speech.

Jorgensen, Paul A. *Our Naked Frailties: Sensational Art and Meaning in* Macbeth. Berkeley: University of California Press, 1971.

    Chapter 7 (" 'More Strange Than Such a Murder Is,' " pp. 110-39) discusses the witches and Chapter 10 (" 'Torture of the Mind,' " pp. 185-216) discusses Macbeth's character.

Kermode, Frank. Introduction to *Macbeth*, by William Shakespeare. In *The Riverside Shakespeare*, edited by G. Blakemore Evans, 1306-11. Houghton Mifflin: Chicago, 1974.

    Kermode's introduction discusses themes, printing history, sources, topical matters relating to the meaning of equivocation, the nature of the weird sisters, and the character of Macbeth.

Long, Michael. *Twayne's New Critical Introductions to Shakespeare. Macbeth.* Boston: Twayne, 1989.

> Chapter 4 ("The Developmpent of the Play's Action," pp. 65-112) discusses the plot act by act. Chapter 2 ("Doers of Deeds," pp. 30-53) is a character study of Macbeth. The first part focuses on Macbeth. The remainder of the chapter compares Macbeth with other literary and dramatic figures, especially Romantic figures such as Captain Ahab in *Moby Dick* and characters in medieval Christian works.

Mack, Maynard. "The Many Faces of *Macbeth.*" In *Everybody's Shakespeare*, 183-96. Lincoln: University of Nebraska Press, 1993.

> Mack comments on many thematic, topical, and structural features of the play. His essay includes insightful comments on how the Macbeths complement each other in their outlook, and on the significance of feasting and children in the play.

McDonald, Russ. "Theatre a la Mode: Shakespeare and the Kinds of Drama." In *The Bedford Companion to Shakespeare: An Introduction With Documents*, 151-79. Boston: St. Martin's Press, 1996.

> McDonald's discussion of the genre of tragedy in Chapter 5 helps students to understand the literary concept of tragedy. The discussion draws heavily on Macbeth for illustration of its concepts. It presents a standard description of the tragic action of the play, a sample of the subversive political analysis popular in more recent criticism, and concludes that *Macbeth* is not simply about ambition.

Muir, Kenneth. Introduction to *Macbeth*, by William Shakespeare. In *The Arden Edition Of The Works Of William Shakespeare*, xi-lxv. London: Methuen, 1972.

> In addition to discussion of such matters as the play's date and sources, the last part of Muir's introduction contains insightful character study.

Paul, Henry N. *The Royal Play of* Macbeth. 1948. Reprint, New York: Octagon, 1971.

> Paul's book contains much information on James I and the topical references in *Macbeth*.

Schoenbaum, S. Macbeth *Critical Essays*. New York: Garland, 1991.

> Schoenbaum's book is a collection of classic essays from the past three centuries on many aspects of *Macbeth*. Carolyn Asp, for example, (" 'Be bloody, bold and resolute': Tragic Action and Sexual Stereotyping in *Macbeth*," pp. 377-95) discusses sexual stereotyping in connection with the major characters.

Walker, Roy. *The Time Is Free*. London: Andrew Dakers, 1949.

> Walker's book contains scene–by–scene commentary on *Macbeth*.

Watkins, Ronald and Jeremy Lemmon. *In Shakespeare's Playhouse. Macbeth*. Totowa, New Jersey: Rowman and Littlefield, 1974.

> Watkins and Lemmon attempt to describe what Shakespeare's play would have been like on stage.

Measure for Measure

1604

Plot Summary

Act I:

On his departure from Vienna, Duke Vincentio deputizes Angelo to administer the laws of the city in his place, and appoints the wise "old Escalus" as Angelo's assistant (I.i.45). The duke, who is concerned that he has been too lax in keeping order in the city, in fact has no intention of leaving Vienna. Instead, he plans to disguise himself as Friar Lodowick so that he can monitor the effect that the "precise" Angelo's enforcement of the laws has on the citizens, and to see whether the exercise of power causes any change in Angelo (I.iii.50). The new deputy's first actions are to shut down all the brothels in the suburbs and to arrest and sentence to death young Claudio for impregnating his fiancee, Juliet. On his way to prison, Claudio is met by his friend Lucio, who promises to ask Claudio's sister, Isabella, to beg Angelo for her brother's life. Lucio seeks out Isabella at the convent where she has recently become a novice and tells her of Claudio's plight. Distressed at this news, she agrees to speak to Angelo.

Act II:

When Escalus tries to persuade Angelo to reduce the severity of Claudio's sentence, the deputy refuses and instead instructs the provost to have Claudio executed the next morning. Constable El-bow appears before Angelo and Escalus with the

''bawd'' Pompey and a gentleman named Froth in custody, and Angelo leaves it to Escalus to sort out Elbow's confusing complaint against his two prisoners. Meanwhile, Isabella arrives and pleads with Angelo for her brother's life, all the while being coached by Lucio to be more compelling in her entreaties. Aroused by Isabella's virtue, Angelo instructs her to return the next day for his answer. Meanwhile, the disguised Duke Vincentio visits the prison where Claudio and Juliet are being held and speaks with the loving but repentant Juliet. When Isabella meets with Angelo, he tells her that she must have sex with him if she wants to save her brother. Outraged, Isabella declares that she will ''tell the world aloud'' about Angelo's hypocritical proposition, and he retorts that, thanks to his spotless reputation, no one will believe her accusations (II.iv.153). Distressed and alone, Isabella refuses to submit to Angelo's blackmail. ''More than our brother is our chastity,'' she concludes, and goes to prepare her brother for death (II.iv.185).

Act III:

Disguised as Friar Lodowick, Duke Vincentio visits Claudio in prison and reconciles him to his death sentence, but when Isabella tells her brother of the deputy's proposition, Claudio loses heart and, much to Isabella's disgust, begs her to submit to Angelo. ''O Isabel!. . .'' he exclaims, ''Death is a fearful thing'' (III.i.114, 115). The disguised duke intervenes. He tells Isabella about Mariana, a lady who was once engaged to be married to Angelo but whom he shamefully rejected after her dowry was lost at sea. The duke suggests a plan where Mariana, who still loves Angelo, would secretly sleep with Angelo in Isabella's place, thereby reclaiming her fiance, saving Claudio's life, and preserving Isabella's chastity. Isabella gratefully agrees to the plan. Meanwhile, Pompey is arrested once more and taken to jail, and so is his employer, the brothel-keeper Mistress Overdone. Unaware that the friar is really the duke in disguise, Lucio strikes up a conversation with him and—unwisely pretending to know the duke well—claims that Duke Vincentio is a fool, a drunk, and a libertine. The duke closes Act III with a pronouncement on his deputy: ''Twice treble shame on Angelo, / To weed my vice and let his grow!'' (III.ii.269-70).

Act IV:

The disguised duke, Mariana, and Isabella meet to confirm the details of their plan. But after Angelo sleeps with the woman he thinks is Isabella, he reneges on his promise to spare her brother and instead sends a note to the provost, instructing him to deliver Claudio's head as proof of his execution. The disguised duke plots with the provost to save Claudio by substituting the head of Barnardine, a drunken criminal also condemned to death, for Claudio's head. As it turns out, Barnardine is too drunk to be executed. Fortunately, a pirate who resembles Claudio has died overnight in his sleep, so it is the pirate's head which is finally sent to Angelo. Isabella appears, and the disguised duke tells her that Angelo has broken his promise and that her brother is dead. He then instructs the grieving Isabella to condemn Angelo in public when he goes to meet the returning duke tomorrow at the city gate. Meanwhile, Angelo is feeling guilty about his treachery, and wonders whether Isabella will dare to accuse him the next day in front of the duke. He also regrets having insisted upon Claudio's execution but believes that, if he had been allowed to live, Claudio would have joined with his sister to expose the deputy's crime. ''Alack,'' he cries, ''when once our grace we have forgot, / Nothing goes right—we would, and we would not'' (IV.iv.33-34).

Act V:

At the city gate, Angelo and Escalus welcome Duke Vincentio home. As instructed, Isabella accuses Angelo of being ''a virgin-violator'' (V.i.41) and of murdering her brother—without as yet revealing that it was Mariana with whom he had sex. Calling Isabella insane, Angelo denies any wrongdoing. The duke pretends to believe him and orders Isabella's arrest. Mariana arrives to declare that Angelo is by rights her husband, explaining that he slept with her, not Isabella. The duke departs briefly, to return as Friar Lodowick and support Mariana's and Isabella's claims. Accused of bearing false witness, Friar Lodowick loses his hood as he is being arrested, and is revealed to be Duke Vincentio. The duke orders an immediate marriage between Angelo and Mariana, then afterward sentences his former deputy to death, declaring ''An Angelo for Claudio, death for death!'' (V.i.409). Although both Mariana and Isabella plead for Angelo's life, the duke refuses to remit his sentence. All is at last resolved when Claudio is shown to be alive. The play ends as the duke proposes marriage to Isabella, pardons Angelo, reminds Claudio to marry Juliet, and orders the troublesome Lucio to marry a prostitute ''whom he begot with child'' (V.i.511).

Modern Connections

Measure for Measure is considered one of Shakespeare's "problem plays." Problem plays introduce moral dilemmas without offering clear-cut or comforting solutions to these dilemmas. Since these plays deal with universal topics such as sex, power, and life and death, they are still appreciated and debated over by audiences today.

While the mores and living conditions of Shakespeare's time were significantly different from what they are today, several interesting parallels can still be drawn between our world and the one dramatized in *Measure for Measure*.

If, for example, the play were set in modern Vienna rather than the Renaissance Vienna of nearly 400 years ago, Claudio would not be facing execution for engaging in premarital sex. On the other hand, casual, unprotected sex today carries with it a potential death sentence in the form of AIDS. As he is being led to jail, Claudio tells his friend Lucio that the relationship between himself and Juliet is not casual, but that they were joined by a "true contract" which was sanctioned by common law if not by the church (I.ii.145). Today, unmarried couples often face other obstacles. Depending, for instance, on the state or country in which they live and work, they may find that they are not covered by each other's medical insurance, or that they are treated differently from legally married couples by the tax system or by the laws.

Laws and their enforcement are what motivate Duke Vincentio to leave Vienna in the care of his deputy, Angelo. The duke explains that in Vienna, "We have strict statutes and most biting laws /. . . / Which for this fourteen years we have let slip" (I.iii.19, 21). Vincentio hopes that Angelo—"A man of stricture and firm abstinence"—will be more effective at enforcing the laws than the duke has been or ever could be (I.iii.12). Once deputized, Angelo adheres to the letter of the law by closing down the city's brothels and condemning Claudio to death. In reaction to Angelo's harsh measures, the citizens of Vienna complain that their deputy would have to throw everyone in jail in order to stop some crimes, or, as Isabella observes with regard to Claudio's offense, "There's many have committed it" (II.ii.89). Today, people put forth similar arguments with regard to everything from prostitution, drug use, and tax evasion to parking infringements and speeding: there are some laws, they argue, that no one cares enough to follow or enforce, or

that the crimes are widespread enough to make the laws extremely difficult to enforce.

The duke's rationale for putting a disciplinarian such as Angelo in charge is that Vienna had become a decadent and morally lazy city. Today, people who worry about the lack of politeness in our society, the decay of family values, and the onset of crime and overcrowding wonder whether re-education, stronger laws, and stricter law enforcement would solve some of these problems.

Beyond his desire to see Vienna's laws enforced, Duke Vincentio offers another reason for deputizing Angelo. Angelo, the duke argues, is "precise"—that is, he is a perfectionist when it comes to morals and behavior (I.iii.50). By putting Angelo in charge, the duke hopes to see "if power change [or corrupt] purpose" and whether his deputy is as virtuous as he seems (I.iii.54). As it turns out, Angelo abuses his power by trying to force Isabella to have sex with him. When Isabella threatens to expose Angelo's abuse, he replies that no one will believe her charges when they are weighed against his "unsoil'd name" and "th'austereness" of his life (II.iv.155). This issue remains a compelling one for us today, when some rape cases are decided on the credibility of the accuser versus that of the accused.

It has been argued that Duke Vincentio also misuses power by manipulating people as though they were puppets. Today, people are worried enough about the corrupting effects of power that they have called for and in some instances voted in favor of political term limits.

Ultimately, true to its designation as a problem play, *Measure for Measure* poses difficult questions that we are still trying to answer today: What should we do when the rules and penalties that we apply to our society don't fit every case? When should punishment give way to mercy? How do we stop power from corrupting those who have it? How do we protect ourselves from those in power? And is anyone completely free from hypocrisy?

Characters

Abhorson:

He is the executioner at the prison where Claudio is being held. His role in the play is a minor one. In IV.ii.21-60 when the provost offers him the bawd Pompey as an apprentice, Abhorson initially objects, arguing that Pompey will "discredit" the executioner's profession. In IV.iii.20-65, Abhorson is prevented from executing Barnardine because that prisoner is too drunk to be prepared for death. While Abhorson's encounters with Pompey and Barnardine are comical, his presence in the play also functions as a grim reminder that Claudio has been sentenced to death.

Angelo:

He is one of Duke Vincentio's assistants (the other, more senior, assistant is Escalus). On the pretext that he must leave Vienna for a while, the duke deputizes Angelo, praising his virtues and giving him authority over the administration of the laws in the city. When Angelo protests that he is not yet ready for such responsibility ("Let there be some more test made of my mettle" [I.i.48], he suggests), the duke insists that he accept the commission. Angelo's first actions as deputy are to close down Vienna's brothels and to arrest and sentence to death Claudio for impregnating his fiancee, Juliet. When Claudio's sister, Isabella, begs Angelo to be lenient, the deputy is excited by her purity, and tries to coerce her into having sex with him in exchange for her brother's life.

Angelo has a reputation for rigid self-control and for supporting a strict moral code. Escalus says that Angelo is "most strait in virtue" (II.i.9). The duke describes his deputy as "precise," or puritanical (I.iii.50). Dissolute Lucio complains that Angelo is so cold and prudish that his blood "is very snow-broth" (I.iv.58) and claims that the deputy controls his passions by fasting and studying. Angelo himself argues that people must see others punished before they themselves are willing to behave, and that being lenient with criminals only makes them disrespectful of law and order:

> We must not make a scarecrow of the law,
> Setting it up to fear the birds of prey,
> And let it keep one shape, till custom make it
> Their perch and not their terror.
>
> (II.i.1-4)

Critics have observed that despite these testimonials to his strictness, Angelo's apparent goodness and self-control are subject to doubt early in the play—even *before* he propositions Isabella. In I.iii.50-54, for example, the duke explains that part of his reason for deputizing Angelo with full authority to govern Vienna is to discover whether such power will corrupt this "seemingly" incorruptible man. And well before his sister ever meets Angelo, Claudio casts doubt on the purity of the deputy's

> "Escalus says that Angelo is 'most strait in virtue' (II.i.9). The duke describes his deputy as 'precise,' or puritanical (I.iii.50)."

motives by complaining that Angelo must have resurrected the "neglected" law against fornication simply because he hopes to make a name for himself (I.ii.170-71). Later in the play, the duke reveals that Angelo was once engaged to a gentlewoman named Mariana, but when her brother and her dowry were lost at sea, Angelo abandoned Mariana, "left her in her tears, and dried not one of them with his comfort," and, in order to break his engagement, he accused Mariana of being unchaste (III.i.225-26).

When they try to persuade Angelo to be merciful with Claudio, both Escalus and Isabella reason that if Angelo were ever tempted, he might fall like anyone else. Isabella in fact takes the argument a step further. Referring to her brother, Claudio, who is driven by affection rather than by rules, Isabella asserts that "If he had been as you, and you as he, / You would have slipp'd like him, but he, like you, / Would not have been so stern" (II.ii.64-66). When Angelo finally *does* fall, he compounds his offense with hypocrisy, leading Isabella to exclaim that "This outward-sainted deputy . . . is yet a devil" (III.i.88, 91).

Angelo's own theories concerning his loss of self-control have to do with his absolutism—or his insistence that something is either right or wrong, good or evil, but never in-between. As he puts it, he is tempted to badness by Isabella's goodness: "Most dangerous / Is that temptation that doth goad us on / To sin in loving virtue" (II.ii.180-82). Once he surrenders to temptation—that is, once he propositions Isabella—Angelo decides that there is no going back: if he can't be completely good, then he has to be completely wicked. "I have begun," Angelo declares, "And now I give my sensual race the rein" (II.iv.159-60). At this point, Angelo seems determined to do all he can to abuse his power. He warns Isabella that if she refuses to submit to him, he will make certain that her brother dies a long and painful death (II.iv.163-67). After the bed-trick, when he sleeps with Mariana but thinks he is with Isabella, he breaks his word and

> "... the duke reveals that Angelo was once engaged to a gentlewoman named Mariana, but when her brother and her dowry were lost at sea, Angelo abandoned Mariana, 'left her in her tears, and dried not one of them with his comfort,' and, in order to break his engagement, he accused Mariana of being unchaste (III.i.225-26)."

orders Claudio's execution, worried that Isabella's brother might otherwise try to avenge her rape (IV.iv.28-32).

Critics have observed that *Measure for Measure* is, among other things, a play about self-knowledge. In IV.iv.33-34, Angelo confronts his feelings of remorse for having (so he thinks) sent Claudio to his death after coercing his sister, Isabella: ''Alack, when once our grace we have forgot, / Nothing goes right—we would, and we would not.''

Later, when Isabella accuses him in front of the duke, Angelo feels compelled to continue in his lies, and claims that Isabella is insane (V.i.33). When Mariana calls herself his wife, Angelo renews his accusation that she is promiscuous, and complains that both Isabella and Mariana are ''informal,'' or mentally unbalanced (V.i.236).

Once his abuses are presented in public, Angelo asks the duke to give him the same, absolute penalty that he had intended to impose on Claudio:

> Then, good Prince,
> No longer session hold upon my shame,
> But let my trial be mine own confession.
> Immediate sentence then, and sequent death,
> Is all the grace I beg.
>
> (V.i.370-74)

During his final speech in the play, penitent but still absolute, Angelo continues to ask for death rather than mercy (V.i.475-77), but the duke chooses to let him live, and orders him instead to love his new wife, Mariana.

Attendants:

Anonymous, unnamed characters with small or no speaking parts who nevertheless contribute to the atmosphere of the play with its emphasis on city life and law and order.

Barnardine:

He is a prisoner at the jail where Claudio is being held, and like Claudio, he has been sentenced to death. In contrast to Claudio, however, he is a hardened criminal. The provost describes him as ''A man that apprehends death no more dreadfully but as a drunken sleep, careless, reakless, and fearless of what's past, present, or to come'' (IV.ii.142-44). Barnardine's neutral attitude to death differs markedly from the terror of death which Claudio confesses to his sister in III.i.115-131. In IV.ii, the duke arranges with the provost to have Barnardine executed in place of Claudio, but in IV.iii.43-63, Barnardine insists that he is too drunk to die, and comically refuses to be executed. Duke Vincentio pardons Barnardine at the close of the play (V.i.482-85), hoping that he will take advantage of this merciful treatment to lead a better life.

Boy:

He is a servant to Mariana. The boy appears only once—in IV.i.1-9—when he sings a melancholy song of false love (''Take, O, take those lips away'') at the request of the forsaken Mariana as she sits in seclusion at the moated grange. In IV.i.7, Mariana sends the boy away so that she can talk to the disguised duke without distraction.

Citizens:

Anonymous, unnamed characters with small or no speaking parts who nevertheless contribute to the atmosphere of the play with its emphasis on city life and law and order.

Claudio:

He is Isabella's brother and Juliet's fiance. On orders from the newly deputized Angelo, Claudio is arrested and sentenced to death for having sex with Juliet out of wedlock. As he is being led to prison, Claudio bitterly observes that the law under which he has been arrested has not been enforced for nineteen years, and suggests that Angelo has revived ''the drowsy and neglected'' statute simply to make a name for himself (I.ii.170). In I.ii.176-86,

Claudio asks Lucio to inform Isabella of his plight so that she will persuade Angelo to be lenient with her brother. Claudio thus sets in motion the central conflict in the play, since Isabella's pleas ultimately arouse Angelo's lust.

Claudio has been described as affectionate and dependent upon others for guidance. His graphic speculations in prison about the afterlife reveal an overwhelming terror of death—especially now that he is so close to it:

> Ay, but to die, and go we know not where;
> To lie in cold obstruction, and to rot;
>
> . . .
>
> To bathe in fiery floods, or to reside
> In thrilling region of thick-ribbed ice;
> To be imprison'd in the viewless winds
> And blown with restless violence round about
> The pendant world; or to be worse than worst
> Of those that lawless and incertain thought
> Imagine howling—'tis too horrible!
>
> (III.i.117-18; 121-27)

It has been pointed out that just before Isabella arrives to tell her brother about Angelo's proposition, the duke (in his disguise as Friar Lodowick) successfully reconciles Claudio to the fact that he will be executed. "To sue to live, I find I seek to die, / And seeking death, find life. Let it [death] come on," Claudio declares with resignation (III.i.42-43). However, once his sister informs him of Angelo's demand for sex with her in exchange for her brother's life, Claudio's acceptance of death weakens. The possibility of survival is impossible for Claudio to resist, and he tries to convince himself that Angelo's proposition is not as bad as Isabella thinks it is. "If it were damnable," Claudio argues, why would "wise" Angelo risk being "perdurably fin'd" just for a moment of pleasure? (III.i.112, 114).

When Claudio begs Isabella to save his life by sleeping with Angelo (III.i.132-35), she recoils in disgust. Shortly afterward, he feels sorry for having made the suggestion, and says remorsefully to the disguised duke, "Let me ask my sister pardon. I am so out of love with life that I will sue to be rid of it" (III.i.171-72).

Duke (Duke Vincentio):

See Vincentio

Elbow:

He is a constable, or policeman. In II.i, he arrests the bawd Pompey and the foolish gentleman Froth and brings them to Angelo and Escalus for

> **"Once he surrenders to temptation—that is, once he propositions Isabella—Angelo decides that there is no going back: if he can't be completely good, then he has to be completely wicked. 'I have begun,' Angelo declares, 'And now I give my sensual race the rein' (II.iv.159-60)."**

judgment. Elbow is a comic figure who tends to speak in malapropisms. (A malapropism is an error in speech which occurs when one word is incorrectly and unintentionally used in place of another, often with a comical result. So, for example, when Elbow calls Pompey and Froth "two notorious benefactors" [II.i.50], he actually means "malefactors.") Elbow's explanation of what happened to his pregnant wife when she encountered Pompey and Froth is so confusing, and Pompey's defense is so long-winded, that Angelo leaves in frustration and Escalus finally lets the two offenders go, but not before discovering that the incompetent Elbow owes his continual reappointment as constable to the laziness and corruption of his fellow citizens. This scene occurs just before Isabella's fateful meeting with Angelo in II.ii, and thus serves as comic relief. (Comic relief is a humorous speech, episode, or scene which is meant to alleviate the tension that precedes it or—as it does in this instance—to heighten the seriousness that follows it.) Elbow arrests Pompey once more in III.ii, but this time there is enough evidence to send the bawd to jail.

Escalus:

He is Duke Vincentio's subordinate, and while the duke is away, he acts as Angelo's "secondary," or assistant (I.i.46). Although "Old Escalus" has more seniority in office than Angelo has, the duke passes over Escalus to promote Angelo as deputy— probably to test the younger man's mettle (see the Duke's conversation with Friar Thomas about Angelo in I.iii.50-54). Undisturbed by Angelo's pro-

> **". . . Claudio is arrested and sentenced to death for having sex with Juliet out of wedlock."**

motion, Escalus remarks sincerely to the duke that ''If any in Vienna be of worth / To undergo such ample grace and honor, / It is Lord Angelo'' (I.i.22-24).

Critics have noted that the compassionate and honest Escalus serves as a foil to the absolute and increasingly hypocritical Angelo. (A foil is someone who highlights someone else's traits by providing a contrast to those traits.) Indeed, in II.i.6-16, Escalus urges Angelo to be merciful with Claudio, reminding the deputy that Claudio is a gentleman who ''had a most noble father,'' and prophetically suggesting to him that, had he ever been in Claudio's place, Angelo might have likewise broken the law:

> Let but your honor know
> (Whom I believe to be most strait in virtue)
> That in the working of your own affections,
> Had time coher'd with place, or place with
>   wishing,
> Or that the resolute acting of your blood
> Could have attain'd th' effect of your own
>   purpose,
> Whether you had not sometime in your life
> Err'd in this point which now you censure him,
> And pull'd the law upon you.
>
> (II.i.8-16)

Angelo is unconvinced, and refuses to revoke Claudio's sentence.

Alternatively, some critics focus on the practical aspects of Escalus's governing style, noting that while Angelo is too harsh, his assistant is too lenient. They argue that Escalus's philosophy of law and order—''Let us be keen, and rather cut a little / Than fall, and bruise to death'' (II.i.5-6)—is an ineffective method of dealing with such hardened criminals as Pompey. When, for example, Escalus releases him with simply a warning, Pompey declares in an aside that he will remain a bawd as long as it continues to be a lucrative trade (II.i.253-54). (An aside occurs when a character speaks to the audience without being overheard by the other characters onstage.)

Thus while Escalus is admirable, he is also ineffective. He sets professional criminals free, but

is unable to stop Angelo from condemning young Claudio to death for sleeping with Juliet who is, according to Renaissance common law, ''fast [his] wife'' (I.ii.147).

Francisca:

She is a nun at the convent which has accepted Isabella as a novice. She appears at the beginning of I.iv, instructing Isabella on the convent's rules and privileges. Francisca's role in the play is brief (she is never even referred to by name in the dialogue); nevertheless, her remark in I.iv.9 that Isabella is as ''yet unsworn'' into the sisterhood of nuns makes it clear to the audience later, at the close of the play, that Isabella is free to marry the duke. What is more, Isabella's observation to Francisca that the convent's austere rules are not severe enough tells us much—very early in the play—about the strictness of Isabella's character.

Friar Peter:
See Peter

Friar Thomas:
See Thomas

Froth:

He is a ''foolish gentleman'' who, along with the bawd Pompey, is arrested by Elbow at a brothel run by Mistress Overdone, and brought before Angelo and Escalus for sentencing (II.i.41-212). Froth remains silent during most of Pompey's rambling excuses, yet says enough to indicate that he is a gullible man living on a moderate income and is often cheated by ''tapsters'' (bawds) such as Pompey. Escalus lets him go with a warning to stay away from bawds and brothels.

Gentlemen:

These two gentlemen (1.Gentleman and 2.Gentleman) are friends of Lucio who appear briefly with him in I.ii. The three of them tease each other about their fondness for brothels and the likelihood that one or other of them has by now contracted a venereal disease. They are also present when the brothel-keeper Mistress Overdone announces that Claudio has been arrested and sentenced to death for fornication, and they exit with Lucio to find out whether Overdone's story is true. According to the stage directions, the two gentlemen reappear with Lucio shortly afterward in I.ii when he questions Claudio about his arrest.

These two gentlemen with their nonchalantly lewd conversation and their familiarity with Mistress Overdone represent the moral "liberty" (I.iii.29) that has sprouted in Vienna under Duke Vincentio's rule and which the duke hopes will be weeded out by Angelo. Their presence in I.ii, occurring as it does immediately after Angelo is deputized in I.i, demonstrates both Angelo's swiftness to act and his misguided sense of proportion, for by the end of I.ii, the new deputy has arrested Claudio for impregnating his common-law wife, Juliet, but has not jailed two men who are self-avowedly dissolute.

Isabella:

She is Claudio's sister. She becomes a novice of the order of Saint Clare on the same day that her brother is arrested and condemned to death for fornication. Claudio sends his friend Lucio to seek out Isabella at the convent and ask her to beg the deputy, Angelo, for her brother's life. "In her youth," Claudio explains, "There is a prone and speechless dialect, / Such as move men; beside, she hath prosperous art / When she will play with reason and discourse, / And well she can persuade" (I.ii.182-86). As it turns out, Isabella's youthful beauty and skill at "reason and discourse" do not convince Angelo to release Claudio, but they do arouse his lust. When Angelo suggests that she have sex with him in return for her brother's life, Isabella refuses in disgust, and goes to tell Claudio that he must prepare to die. She is confident that her brother will agree with her rejection of Angelo, because Claudio has "in him such a mind of honor / That had he twenty heads to tender down / On twenty bloody blocks, he'ld yield them up, / Before his sister should her body stoop / To such abhorr'd pollution" (II.iv.179-83). She is horrified when, instead of sharing her outrage, her brother pleads with her to save his life by sleeping with Angelo. Calling him a "beast" and a "faithless coward" for wanting to live at the cost of his "own sister's shame," she concludes that it would be best after all if Claudio died quickly (III.i.135, 136, 139, 150).

Isabella's behavior in the play has been the subject of negative as well as positive assessments. It has been pointed out that she gives up too easily in her efforts to persuade Angelo to spare her brother, and that Lucio has to remind her again and again to argue her case more forcefully (II.ii.29-55). Critics have also asserted that Isabella's ideas about right and wrong are too extreme and that she mistakenly assumes that everyone shares her beliefs—when in fact, the only other character who believes in abso-

> **Claudio sends his friend Lucio to seek out Isabella at the convent and ask her to beg the deputy, Angelo, for her brother's life. 'In her youth,' Claudio explains, 'There is a prone and speechless dialect, / Such as move men; beside, she hath prosperous art / When she will play with reason and discourse, / And well she can persuade' (I.ii.182-86)."**

lutes (absolutists follow the theory that something is either right or wrong, good or evil, but never in-between) is her adversary, Angelo. Critics argue further that Isabella is coldly insensitive in her treatment of the terrified Claudio—angrily rejecting him after he begs her to sleep with Angelo, and even suggesting that her brother is illegitimate since, according to her, he is too dishonorable a person to be her father's son:

> Heaven shield my mother play'd my father fair!
> For such a warped slip of wilderness
> Ne'er issu'd from his blood. Take my defiance!
> . . .
> I'll pray a thousand prayers for thy death,
> No word to save thee.
>
> (III.i.140-42, 145-46)

Finally, the character of Isabella has been criticized for inconsistencies in her behavior. For example, her willingness to participate in the "bed-trick" (when Mariana secretly sleeps with Angelo in place of Isabella) contradicts the young novice's ardent belief in honesty. Another inconsistency occurs at the close of the play when, at Mariana's urging, Isabella speaks in Angelo's defense. Still thinking that her brother has been executed, Isabella argues that Claudio "had but justice, / In that he did the thing for which he died," but that by contrast and thanks to the bed-trick, Angelo's "act did not o'ertake his bad intent"—he did not sleep with Isabella as he had planned—and therefore he does not deserve to die (V.i.448-49, 451). Critics point out that Isabella's defense here is inconsistent because while Angelo did not have sex with Isabella, he *did* have sex with Mariana, and his relationship to her is similar to Claudio's relationship to Juliet.

Those critics who view Isabella in a favorable light argue that she is forced to cope as best she can in a society where she has very little power. They point out that initially, Isabella is tolerant of Claudio and Juliet's predicament, and that her views become inflexible only after she is frightened by Angelo's lust. Before she has spoken with Angelo, and in response to Lucio's news that Juliet is pregnant by Claudio, Isabella declares, "O, let him marry her" (I.iv.49). Later, when she tries to persuade Angelo to be lenient, she tells him that nothing is as admirable as mercy:

> No ceremony that to great ones 'longs,
> Not the king's crown, nor the deputed sword,
> The marshal's truncheon, nor the judge's robe,
> Become them with one half so good a grace
> As mercy does.
>
> (II.ii.59-63)

Left alone with her thoughts after Angelo has made his proposition, Isabella realizes that she is no match for Angelo's authority or his reputation for integrity, and there is nothing she can do but complain to herself about his hypocrisy:

> To whom should I complain? Did I tell this,
> Who would believe me? O perilous mouths,
> That bear in them one and the self-same tongue,
> Either of condemnation or approof,
> Bidding the law make curtsy to their will,
> Hooking both right and wrong to th'appetite,
> To follow as it draws!
>
> (II.iv.171-77)

Critics sympathetic to Isabella also note that although she is ultimately saved from being raped by Angelo, she is nevertheless discouraged by her society from leading the convent life she has chosen: at the end of the play, the powerful Duke Vincentio proposes marriage to her. While Isabella does not respond to his proposal, some audiences and critics assume from Isabella's silence that she will marry him.

Juliet:

She is Claudio's fiancee who was impregnated by him and who, like him, is imprisoned by Angelo for fornication. Unlike Claudio, Juliet is not sentenced to death—probably because she is pregnant. Juliet appears three times during the play: in I.ii she is seen being led to prison with Claudio; in II.iii, during her only speaking part, she expresses her love for Claudio as well as her repentance; finally,

at the close of the play in V.i, she is reunited with Claudio, and the two of them are ordered by the duke to get formally married. Juliet's importance in the play is primarily visual: on their way to prison, Claudio remarks that his and Juliet's "most mutual entertainment / With character too gross is writ on Juliet" (I.ii.154-55)—in other words, Juliet's obvious pregnancy is the proof Angelo uses to imprison her and to sentence Claudio to death.

Justice:

He is a minor character whose sole appearance occurs in II.i, at a court of justice where Angelo and Escalus are presiding over cases. Although he is introduced as early as the stage directions of II.i, he remains silent until II.i.277, when he answers Escalus's question about what time of day it is, and accepts his invitation to dinner. His remark to Escalus that "Lord Angelo is severe" (II.i.282) contributes to our overall impression of the deputy's harshness.

Lords:

Anonymous, unnamed characters with small or no speaking parts who nevertheless contribute to the atmosphere of the play with its emphasis on city life and law and order.

Lucio:

He is a fashionable, dissipated gentleman and a friend of Claudio. During his first appearance in the play, he jokes with two other gentleman about soldiers, prostitutes, and venereal disease. However, once he hears that Claudio has been arrested and condemned to death, Lucio stops his joking and rushes off "to learn the truth of it" (I.ii.81).

Critics have pointed out that Lucio's character is a mixture of widely different traits. He is a go-between, a good friend, a heartless lecher, a comic, a liar, and a gadfly who, unlike the other characters in the play, remains rebellious to the end. At his friend Claudio's request, Lucio convinces Isabella to speak to Angelo on her brother's behalf, then coaches her when he thinks she is not being persuasive enough during her interview with the deputy. He laughs when Pompey is sent to jail, and he is accused by Mistress Overdone of heartlessly abandoning a prostitute whom he promised to marry after getting her pregnant (III.ii.199-203). Escalus complains that Lucio is "a fellow of much license" (III.ii.204). By contrast, after Claudio's apparent execution, Lucio sympathizes with the "pretty Isabella" and mourns her brother's death, declaring, ''By my troth, Isabel, I lov'd thy brother'' (IV.iii.151, 156).

Lucio gets himself into trouble when he slanders Duke Vincentio to his face. The duke is disguised at the time as Friar Lodowick and therefore unrecognizable. Falsely claiming to be his ''inward,'' or close friend, Lucio calls Vincentio ''the old fantastical Duke of dark corners,'' and describes him as a drunk, a lecher, and a coward (III.ii.130; IV.iii.156-57). Lucio himself has been described as a comic foil to the duke and his search for virtue. (A foil highlights another character's traits by acting as a contrast to those traits.)

Some critics assert that Lucio is never fooled by the duke's disguise, and that he is simply taking the opportunity to give Vincentio some healthy criticism. Whether or not Lucio recognizes Vincentio, he winds up being soundly punished by the duke at the close of the play. Knowing that Lucio has impregnated and abandoned a prostitute, Vincentio calls him a ''lewd fellow,'' and sentences him first to marry any woman ''whom he begot with child'' and afterward to be whipped and hanged (V.i.509, 511). When the duke later revokes the whipping and hanging sentences, Lucio protests that forcing someone to marry a prostitute is as bad as ''pressing to death, whipping, and hanging'' (V.i.522-23).

Mariana:

She is Angelo's jilted fiancee. According to the duke (see III.i.209-223), Mariana and Angelo were engaged to be married until Mariana's brother, Frederick, was lost at sea along with his sister's dowry. Unwilling to marry Mariana without her dowry, Angelo nullified their engagement with the false excuse that Mariana was not a virgin. It is revealed that Mariana still loves Angelo in spite of his treachery, and she lives out her days secluded in a ''moated grange'' (III.i.264).

In III.i.243-58, the duke convinces Isabella to participate in a ''bed-trick,'' whereby she and Mariana secretly switch places so that it is Mariana who actually sleeps with Angelo—thus reconfirming her engagement with him as well as saving Isabella's honor, while at the same time setting up Angelo to commit the same act for which he has condemned Claudio to death.

Mariana herself first appears in the play at the moated grange in IV.i, when she is told about and agrees to the duke's plan. She appears for the last time at the close of the play in V.i, when she

> **At his friend Claudio's request, Lucio convinces Isabella to speak to Angelo on her brother's behalf, then coaches her when he thinks she is not being persuasive enough during her interview with the deputy.''**

declares Angelo to be her husband, becomes formally married to him on orders from the duke, and passionately pleads for Angelo's life when the duke orders his execution.

Although her role is brief, Mariana is useful to the action of the play because, thanks to the bed-trick, she provides Isabella with a way out of her difficulties with Angelo. Perhaps more importantly, critics have noted that by convincing Isabella to join her in pleading for Angelo's life (V.i.429-453), Mariana helps to soften the young novice's absolutist personality. Nevertheless, the bed-trick with which Mariana's character is identified increases the play's problematical nature, since this trick requires the strictly honest Isabella to be deceitful.

Mistress Overdone:
See Overdone

Nun:
See Francisca

Officers:
Anonymous, unnamed characters with small or no speaking parts who nevertheless contribute to the atmosphere of the play with its emphasis on city life and law and order.

Overdone (Mistress Overdone):
She runs a house of prostitution which is closed down as a result of the newly deputized Angelo's strict enforcement of Vienna's laws. According to the provost, Mistress Overdone has been a bawd for eleven years (III.ii.196-97). In II.i.63-67 Elbow mentions that she has reopened her brothel under the guise of a bathhouse. She is arrested and sent to prison by Escalus in III.ii.190-206; at the same

> In III.i.243-58, the duke convinces Isabella to participate in a "bed-trick," whereby she and Mariana secretly switch places so that it is Mariana who actually sleeps with Angelo . . ."

time, Escalus informs the provost that Angelo will not revoke Claudio's death sentence (III.ii.207-08).

Mistress Overdone is the first to deliver the news of Claudio's arrest (I.ii.60-73). In comparison to the death sentence placed on him, the punishment meted out to Mistress Overdone is lenient.

Peter (Friar Peter):

He is one of two friars in the play (the other is Friar Thomas—see Thomas). Friar Peter appears briefly in IV.v-vi and V.i. His central function is to help the duke orchestrate the final scene where Angelo's hypocrisy is revealed and Mariana asserts her right to be Angelo's wife. He also performs the offstage marriage ceremony between Mariana and Angelo (V.i.378-79). Some critics have suggested that he and Friar Thomas (see I.iii) were meant to be the same character, but that Shakespeare forgot the name he had given to the friar and consequently renamed him Peter.

Pompey:

Although he claims to be a tapster, or bartender, Pompey Bum is actually a bawd, or pimp, who works for Mistress Overdone; he is thus part of Vienna's illicit underworld. Pompey is arrested by Elbow and brought before Escalus and Angelo in II.i, but he is released for lack of evidence. He is arrested once more in III.ii for pandering and for carrying "a strange picklock"; this time, he is sent to jail. In prison, he takes a job as assistant to the executioner, thereby avoiding a whipping and also reducing his time of imprisonment (IV.ii).

Pompey is an unrepentant career criminal. His arrest is part of the general clean-up of Vienna which is undertaken by Angelo and Escalus. In II.i, he tells Escalus that the authorities would have to "geld and splay all the youth of the city" in order to

stop prostitution (II.i.230-31). In IV.iii, he lists the numerous other criminals who, like him, have recently been rounded up and jailed, and remarks that most of them have at one time or another frequented Mistress Overdone's brothel. "One would think [this prison] were Mistress Overdone's own house, for here be many of her old customers," Pompey observes (IV.iii.2-4). The mild punishment that he receives in prison is in striking contrast to the death sentence that is placed upon Claudio.

Provost:

He is the warden of the prison where Claudio is being held. In I.ii.116-93, he conducts Claudio to jail. In II.i.32-36, he receives instructions from Angelo for Claudio's speedy execution. He spends much of the rest of the play helping the disguised duke with his plan to save Claudio from death; it is the provost, for example, who suggests substituting the dead pirate Ragozine's head for Claudio's after Barnardine proves "unfit" for execution (IV.iii.69-75).

The provost has no illusions with regard to his prisoners: he recognizes Mistress Overdone as a "bawd of eleven years' continuance" (III.ii.196-97), and, although he saves Pompey from a whipping and a long prison sentence by making him the executioner's assistant, he has no time for Pompey's comical "snatches," or quibbles (IV.ii.6). Critics have described the provost as an advocate of equity, and it becomes clear fairly early in the play that he disapproves of Angelo's treatment of Claudio. In II.ii.1-14, for example, he irritates the deputy by double-checking on his verdict that Claudio must be killed. Shortly afterward (II.ii.125), he hopes that Isabella will succeed in persuading Angelo to spare her brother's life. Duke Vincentio describes the provost as "gentle," or kindly, observing that it is not often the case that a "steeled jailer is the friend of men" (IV.ii.86-87).

As kind-hearted as the provost is, he is nevertheless obedient to authority. When the disguised duke initially asks him to save Claudio by substituting heads, he refuses, saying "Pardon me, good father, it is against my oath" (IV.ii.181). It is not until Vincentio reassures him with letters "in the hand and seal of the duke" that the provost is willing to disobey Angelo's orders (IV.ii.192).

Servant:

He is a retainer to Angelo. In II.ii.1-2, the servant receives the provost, who has come to double-check that Angelo indeed wants Claudio put to death. Shortly afterward (II.ii.18-19), the servant introduces a crucial moment in the play when he announces the fateful arrival of Isabella, who has come to plead with Angelo for her brother Claudio's life.

Thomas (Friar Thomas):

He is one of two friars in the play (Friar Peter is the other; Friar Lodowick is merely the duke in disguise). Friar Thomas's only appearance occurs in I.iii, when he and Duke Vincentio are alone in conversation, and the duke reveals to him (and to the audience) his plan to disguise himself as a monk so that he can secretly observe Angelo's enforcement of Vienna's laws. During this brief but important scene, we learn that the duke considers himself immune to love, and that he prefers a ''life removed,'' or secluded, rather than one that is expensive and flamboyantly high-profile (I.iii.1-10). We also learn that the duke believes he has been too lax in fighting crime in Vienna, and that he hopes his new deputy, Angelo, will do a more thorough job of law enforcement than he himself has. Finally, the duke tells Friar Thomas that Angelo seems to be a ''precise,'' or extremely scrupulous person, but that his term as deputy should prove whether he is indeed what he seems or whether he will be corrupted by power (I.iii.50-54). Friar Thomas is never mentioned by name in I.iii itself, but only in the stage directions to the scene; therefore, some critics believe that he is the same character as Friar Peter (see Peter), who appears later in the play, and that Shakespeare simply forgot what name he had given the character first.

Varrius:

He is a follower of Duke Vincentio and appears in only two scenes—IV.v and V.i. Although the duke speaks to him in IV.v.11-13, Varrius himself has no speaking part at all in the play. It has been suggested that as a gentleman of the duke's court, Varrius's function is to provide Vincentio with a fitting escort now that he is appearing in public as himself rather than as Friar Lodowick. It has also been suggested that Varrius might originally have had lines in the play which have since been lost.

Vincentio (Duke Vincentio):

He is the ruler of Vienna. As the play opens, Duke Vincentio is preparing to leave the city for a while, and when he appoints the puritanical Angelo to govern during his absence, he tells him that

''Mortality and mercy in Vienna / Live in thy tongue and heart'' (I.i.44-45). Shortly afterward, he informs Angelo that ''Your scope is as mine own, / So to enforce or qualify the laws / As to your soul seems good'' (I.i.64-66). Thus before he leaves, Duke Vincentio reminds Angelo twice of the need for balance in administering Vienna's laws: ''Mortality'' (the death sentence) should be tempered with mercy, and strict law enforcement should be ''qualified,'' (modified) according to the case at hand.

In I.iii, we discover that the duke has not left Vienna after all, but plans instead to disguise himself as Friar Lodowick so that he can observe undetected the way in which Angelo administers law and order. The duke gives two reasons for setting up this plan. First, he is disappointed with his own lax enforcement of the laws: ''We have strict statutes and most biting laws,'' he explains, ''Which for this fourteen years we have let slip'' (I.iii.19, 21). As a result, the people of Vienna do whatever they feel like, secure in the knowledge that the strict laws won't be enforced against them. Or, as the duke puts it, ''liberty plucks justice by the nose,'' and ''the baby beats the nurse'' (I.iii.29, 30).

When asked why he doesn't simply begin to enforce the city's laws himself, Vincentio explains that since it is his fault that the citizens are ignoring the rules, it would seem tyrannical if he were suddenly to begin punishing people for disobedience. Thus he employs Angelo, who can administer the laws and punishments without hurting the duke's reputation (I.iii.31-43).

Duke Vincentio's second reason for his subterfuge has to do with Angelo himself. He is worried that his scrupulous deputy might not be as honest as he seems, or that he might be corrupted by power:

> Lord Angelo is precise;
> Stands at a guard with envy; scarce confesses
> That his blood flows; or that his appetite
> Is more to bread than stone: hence we shall see
> If power change purpose: what our seemers be.
>
> (I.iii.50-54)

Once the duke is gone, Angelo arrests Claudio and sentences him to death for sleeping with his fiancee, Juliet. The deputy's ''unqualified,'' and unmerciful enforcement of the law against fornication soon backfires on him when he begins to lust after Claudio's sister, Isabella. When he tries to force Isabella to have sex with him, Angelo demonstrates that his strict notion of what is right and wrong for others hypocritically does not apply to

> "... before he leaves, Duke Vincentio reminds Angelo twice of the need for balance in administering Vienna's laws: 'Mortality' (the death sentence) should be tempered with mercy, and strict law enforcement should be 'qualified,' (modified) according to the case at hand."

him. Thus by the end of Act II, Angelo has fulfilled Duke Vincentio's worst suspicions.

Critics note that, at this point, the duke begins to direct the action of the play. Still disguised as Friar Lodowick, he suggests the "bed-trick" (the substitution of Mariana for Isabella in bed with Angelo) to Isabella as a solution to her problem, and concludes: "by this is your brother sav'd, your honor untainted, the poor Mariana advantag'd, and the corrupt deputy scal'd" (III.i.253-55).

Vincentio has been called a godlike figure who solves potentially tragic dilemmas and who turns the play into a Renaissance comedy, complete with multiple marriages and a happy ending. According to this interpretation, the duke is in full control of the close of the play. What's more, he triumphs in his attempt to replace absolutism with moderation when he exposes and then forgives Angelo's crimes, and when he teaches Isabella to be more tolerant and sympathetic of others to the extent that she joins Mariana in pleading for the life of her enemy Angelo.

The duke has also been described as a puppeteer who abuses his power and takes advantage of his anonymity as Friar Lodowick to run people's lives. This interpretation focuses on the problematical aspects of the play. It takes issue, for example, with the duke's orchestration of the bed-trick and of the phony executions, both of which involve honest people such as Isabella, Mariana, and the provost in dishonest acts.

The interpretation of the duke as a manipulator also underlines his blunders. Despite his efforts,

Duke Vincentio's puppets do not always behave according to plan. Lucio, for example, continually ruffles the duke's dignity with his insinuations, and repeatedly interrupts discussions and revelations—even at the close of the play. As for Angelo, after the bed-trick (during which the deputy thinks he has slept with Isabella) he unexpectedly breaks his promise to save Claudio and instead renews his order for Claudio's swift execution (IV.ii.120-26). When Vincentio tries to solve this glitch by substituting the condemned criminal Barnardine's head for that of Claudio, the drunken Barnardine refuses to be executed (IV.iii.53-63). When Angelo's villainy is at last exposed, the deputy begs for death, and continues to do so even after the duke has ordered his marriage to Mariana and has forgiven him for his crimes (V.i.366-74; 474-77). Finally, it has been pointed out that the duke chooses to marry Isabella despite the fact that she has clearly decided to become a nun. In this light, her silence in response to his offer of marriage at the close of the play is not regarded as a tacit acceptance of his proposal, but as unwillingness to conform to this part of Duke Vincentio's plans.

Further Reading

Barton, Anne. Introduction to *Measure for Measure,* by William Shakespeare. In *The Riverside Shakespeare,* edited by G. Blakemore Evans, 545-49. Boston: Houghton Mifflin Co., 1974.
> Barton presents an overview of the play, including date and source material and an analysis of the characters. Barton also compares *Measure for Measure* with Shakespeare's earlier, more optimistic comedies.

Battenhouse, Roy W. "*Measure for Measure* and Christian Doctrine of the Atonement." *PMLA* 61 (1946): 1029-59.
> Battenhouse defines the play as a Christian allegory, with the duke symbolizing Christ and Isabella representing the soul of man.

Cacicedo, Alberto. " 'She Is Fast My Wife': Sex, Marriage, and Ducal Authority in *Measure for Measure.*" *Shakespeare Studies* 23 (1995): 187-209.
> Cacicedo examines the play in light of Renaissance society's ambivalent feelings about women and the Renaissance assessment of marriage as a necessary evil.

Dodge, Dennis. "Life and Death in *Measure for Measure.*" *Recovering Literature* (San Diego) 4 (1975): 43-58.
> Dodge looks at the comic subplot of the play and argues that the comic characters (Lucio, Pompey,

Mistress Overdone, and Barnardine) push the serious upper class characters (the duke, Angelo, and Isabella) into the human and practical world.

Hapgood, Robert. ''The Provost and Equity in *Measure for Measure*.'' *Shakespeare Quarterly* 15 (Winter 1964): 114-15.

Hapgood briefly examines the small but significant role of the provost and describes him as a force for justice and fairness.

Hayne, Victoria. ''Performing Social Practice: The Example of *Measure for Measure*.'' *Shakespeare Quarterly* 44 (Spring 1993): 1-29.

Hayne discusses the ambiguous and contradictory legal and social rules that governed marriage in Renaissance England and how these rules influence the action and characters in *Measure for Measure*.

Lever, J. W. Introduction to *Measure for Measure,* by William Shakespeare, edited by J. W. Lever, xi-xcviii. The Arden Edition of the Works of William Shakespeare. London: Methuen and Co. Ltd., 1965.

Lever provides date and source information for the play and analyzes the play's characters. For example, Lever points out that minor characters such as Pompey and Mistress Overdone are given more freedom than are the major characters.

Lewis, Cynthia. '' 'Dark Deeds Darkly Answered': Duke Vincentio and Judgment in *Measure for Measure*.'' *Shakespeare Quarterly* 34 (Autumn 1983): 271-89.

Lewis examines Duke Vincentio's belief in moderation and his efforts throughout the play to present and achieve a balance between strict justice and mercy. Lewis also discusses the conflict between private and public in the duke's character.

MacFarlane, Linda. ''Heads You Win Tails I Lose.'' *Critical Survey* 5, no. 1 (1993): 77-82.

MacFarlane examines the sexual politics which are present in the play, including the male characters' prejudiced attitudes toward women—particularly toward Isabella.

Marsh, D. R. C. ''The Mood of *Measure for Measure*.'' *Shakespeare Quarterly* 14 (Winter 1963): 31-38.

Marsh argues that Duke Vincentio is the only character in *Measure for Measure* who can maintain a cheerful attitude with regard to the play's outcome, and even then, the play undermines his credibility because it demonstrates that the duke is as much interested in his own reputation as he is with justice for everyone else. Marsh also asserts that the ending of the play is satirical rather than happy.

Rossiter, A. P. ''The Problem Plays'' and *''Measure for Measure*.'' In *Angel with Horns and Other Shakespeare Lectures,* edited by Graham Storey, 108-28, 152-70. New York: Theatre Arts Books, 1961.

Measure for Measure has been called a ''problem play,'' and Rossiter gives a definition for this expression, explaining that Shakespeare's problem plays are in fact tragicomedies. Rossiter also focuses on the ambiguities or double meanings in *Measure for Measure* and shows how they are part of the play's structure.

Schanzer, Ernest. ''The Marriage-Contract in *Measure for Measure*.'' *Shakespeare Survey* 13 (1960): 81-89.

Schanzer looks at different types of Renaissance marriage-contracts to support his comparison of Juliet and Claudio's contract with that of Angelo and Mariana.

Siegel, Paul N. ''*Measure for Measure*: The Significance of the Title.'' *Shakespeare Quarterly* 4 (July 1953): 317-20.

Siegel defines the term ''measure for measure'' as it is used in the play, arguing that since the play is a comedy, punishment is administered with mercy.

Wiles, R. M. ''*Measure for Measure*: Failure in the Study, Triumph on the Stage.'' *Royal Society of Canada. Transactions* 2 (4th Series) (June 1964): 181-93.

Wiles calls *Measure for Measure* a simple comedy instead of a ''problem play.'' He praises the play's final act and argues that the play is best understood and enjoyed when it is seen in performance rather than merely read.

The Merchant of Venice

1596-97

Plot Summary

Act I:

The play opens on a street in Venice with Antonio, a successful merchant in that city, expressing an unexplained sadness. Salerio, a friend of Antonio's, suggests that Antonio is just preoccupied with and concerned about his merchandise, at that very moment oceanbound for different ports. Antonio denies the suggestion, and another friend of his, Solanio, concludes that Antonio's sadness must be a consequence of love. When Antonio denies this, the cause of his melancholy goes unexplained. Bassanio, a young friend to Antonio, enters and reveals to him his passion for Portia, a young woman who stands to inherit a good deal of money. Bassanio admits to having squandered his fortune by being a spendthrift. Bassanio asks Antonio for enough money to make him a suitable suitor to Portia. But since Antonio's assets are tied up at the moment, he tells Bassanio to borrow the money from some merchant in the city who loans money out at interest with Antonio agreeing to secure that loan. Bassanio approaches Shylock the moneylender and asks for three thousand ducats for a period of three months. Shylock does not like Antonio and sees a chance to take advantage of him. He agrees to loan the money to Bassanio if Antonio will agree to forfeit a pound of flesh if the conditions of the loan agreement are not met. Antonio believes that his financial ventures will have been successfully concluded well before the three-month deadline, so he consents to the conditions proposed by Shylock. At Portia's house in Belmont, Portia and her waiting woman Nerissa reveal the conditions of Portia's inheritance. She will inherit her dead father's money only if she marries the suitor who chooses correctly between a gold, silver, and lead casket. Portia and Nerissa catalog the prospective suitors, Nerissa naming and Portia commenting, somewhat cruelly, on each.

Act II:

In a comical exchange, Launcelot Gobbo, the servant of Shylock, encounters his father who does not recognize him. Launcelot quits his service to Shylock and is taken into the service of Bassanio. Shylock lets him go, hoping he will be as big a drain on Bassanio's finances as he has been on Shylock's own. Shylock's daughter Jessica sends Launcelot with a letter to her love interest Lorenzo who is another from Antonio's circle. The letter confirms the arrangements the two have made to elope. When Shylock leaves for dinner later that evening, Lorenzo and friends appear in disguise and take Jessica away from Shylock's home. Jessica, too, is disguised, and she takes her father's jewels when she leaves. It is reported by Solanio that when Shylock discovers his daughter missing he wanders the streets saying, "My daughter! O my ducats! O my daughter!" (II.viii.15). Shylock is ridiculed by Solanio for seeming to value his daughter and his ducats equally. In Belmont, Morocco, the first of Portia's suitors, incorrectly chooses the gold casket. He is followed by Arragon, who unwisely picks the silver casket. Portia expresses relief at being rid of both of them. Portia receives the news that Bassanio has arrived in Belmont, and she reveals that he is her favorite.

Act III:

In Venice, Salerio and Solanio discuss the news that one of Antonio's ships has sunk, all his merchandise lost. Shylock enters and suggests they remind Antonio of his bond. He recounts how Antonio has publicly humiliated and maligned him. In Belmont, Portia advises Bassanio to ponder his choice of caskets before he commits, but Bassanio is too anxious to wait. As he makes his selection, a song in the background gives him hints: the opening lines of the song end in words rhyming with lead; the middles stanza reminds him not to be superficial; and the concluding lines refer to the clapper of a bell, clappers often being made of lead. Bassanio

chooses the lead casket and wins Portia's hand. As Portia and Bassanio exchange vows of love and devotion, Nerissa and Gratiano, a friend who has accompanied Bassanio to Belmont, announce their plans to marry also. Jessica and Lorenzo arrive in Belmont accompanied by a messenger, who delivers to Bassanio a letter informing him that all of Antonio's financial enterprises have failed and Shylock has had Antonio arrested with the intention of exacting payment from him. Out of concern for her new husband's friend, Portia offers to pay the debt and even offers to increase the sum if necessary. Bassanio and Gratiano leave immediately for Venice, and Portia and Nerissa follow after having sent a letter to Portia's cousin Doctor Bellario, who will provide them with disguises and legal credentials. Jessica and Lorenzo are left in charge at Belmont.

Act IV:

In this act, Antonio is brought to trial. The duke of Venice and Antonio's friends plead with Shylock to show mercy to Antonio, and Bassanio offers Shylock six thousand ducats to let Antonio go. Shylock insists on the terms of the bond; he will have his pound of flesh. Nerissa enters the courtroom disguised as a young law clerk and presents a letter from Doctor Bellario, advising the court to hear the counsel of "a young and learneddoctor" (IV.i.142) who is really Portia in disguise. Portia pretends to consider the matter and at first seems to side with Shylock in the advisability of adhering to the letter of the law. But then she too tries to evoke mercy from Shylock. When the pleas for mercy and the offer of nine thousand ducats fail to sway Shylock from his purpose, Portia reveals a loophole in the bond: Shylock may cut off exactly a pound of Antonio's flesh—no more, no less—and he may not take any blood. Shylock realizes that this is an impossible task and opts for the money, but it is too late; his adversaries take their revenge not only by denying him the ducats he has loaned out but by seizing his goods and forcing him to convert to Christianity. To express his gratitude for Antonio's rescue, Bassanio offers compensation to the young doctor (Portia). The only thing she will accept from him is his wedding ring, an object he has sworn never to part with. Bassanio at first denies the request but eventually sends Gratiano to give the ring to the doctor/Portia. Nerissa arranges to have Portia extort the wedding ring from Gratiano, who too has sworn never to part with it. Portia and Nerissa leave immediately so that they arrive in Belmont before their husbands return there.

Act V:

In Belmont, Jessica and Lorenzo compare their love to some of the most well-known loves in history. They are informed by a messenger of the impending return of Portia and Nerissa who arrive in Belmont shortly before the return of Bassanio, Antonio, Gratiano, and others. Portia and Nerissa accuse their husbands of giving away their wedding rings on a whim and accuse them of devaluing the symbolic importance of those rings. The two men protest that they reluctantly gave the rings away to compensate for an invaluable service done their friend Antonio. Portia and Nerissa enjoy making their husbands squirm but eventually admit that Portia was the young doctor and Nerissa the young law clerk. Antonio, whose situation caused Bassanio to place Portia second in his concern temporarily, takes the ring from Portia and gives it to Bassanio, symbolically reuniting the couples at the end of the play.

Modern Connections

The Merchant of Venice is considered one of Shakespeare's problem comedies in part due to its anti-semitism. A problem play introduces moral dilemmas without offering clear-cut or comforting solutions to these dilemmas. In *The Merchant of Venice*, the Christian Antonio and his friends plead with the Jewish Shylock to show mercy towards Antonio, yet when the situation is reversed and Antonio and his friends are in a position to show Shylock mercy, they do not. Instead, they strip him of his worldly possessions and force him to convert to Christianity. Since there were few or no Jews in Shakespeare's England, his depiction of Shylock is probably based on stereotypes rather than the intimate knowledge acquired through contact. Shylock is depicted as a Jewish moneylender who makes his money through "usury," a practice in which exorbitant interest is charged on loans. He hates Antonio because Antonio loans money without interest and cuts into Shylock's business. It is reported by Solanio that when Shylock discovers his daughter and his money missing he wanders the streets crying, "My daughter! O my ducats! O my daughter!" (II.viii.15). Solanio implies that Shylock values his daughter and his money equally, another stereotypical image of Jews in the Elizabethan age.

Shakespeare's audience would have expected this kind of stereotype and probably would have applauded Shylock's harsh treatment at the hands of the Christians in the play. But for modern audiences, this treatment of Shylock is neither funny nor necessary. In fact, we tend to read a certain hypocrisy in the contrast between the Christians' speeches and actions. For all their talk of "mercy," they show Shylock none at all when the tables are turned. We can read, after all, the glimpses of Shylock's humanity Shakespeare gives us beneath the veneer of stereotype. Shylock asks, "Hath not a Jew hands, organs, dimensions, senses, affections, passions?" (III.i.59-60). When his friend Tubal tells him that one of Shylock's stolen jewels has been given in exchange for a monkey, Shylock reveals that the jewel was one he had given his wife, Leah. He says, "I would not have given it for a wilderness of monkeys" (III.i.123). From these references, one can infer that Shylock has loved deeply and experiences pain.

In *The Merchant of Venice*, Shakespeare dramatizes the contrast between "law" and "mercy" in the Judeo-Christian tradition. Shylock represents law as it is stressed in the Old Testament of the Bible, and Portia and the others represent the mercy associated with Christianity and the New Testament. The message of the play seems to be that laws are necessary but must be tempered with mercy and compassion. Shakespeare emphasizes that it is important to observe the "spirit" rather than the "letter" of the law. For example, the spirit of the law or bond negotiated between Shylock and Antonio is the guarantee of restitution—Antonio will see that the ducats loaned by Shylock will be repaid. Shylock should have been satisfied with the offers by Bassanio and Portia to double or even triple the original amount of the loan; instead, he insists on cutting off a pound of Antonio's flesh. Since this surgery would most certainly have killed Antonio, conforming to the letter of the bond would have been an instance of state-licensed murder, disrupting the system of laws instituted for the protection of Venetian society. The play's insistence on conforming to the spirit rather than the letter of the law is evident not only in the main plot but in the two subplots as well.

In the subplot of the caskets, Portia is faced with the law of her deceased father's will. She must marry the suitor who passes the test devised by her father to correctly choose a certain casket. Portia perhaps violates the letter of her father's will by helping Bassanio choose correctly but not the spirit of her father's will. We can only imagine that the test was devised to procure for Portia an intelligent and financially stable husband with certain values. If the test of choosing the right casket is meant to insure Portia's happiness, we can hardly imagine that Portia's father would have been disappointed with the success achieved by Bassanio through her manipulation.

In the subplot of the rings, Bassanio and Gratiano have promised never to give away their wedding rings. Obviously, they have not really given the rings away since it is Portia who receives them after she and Nerissa have tricked them. Even so, the two men are correct to argue that they have not violated the commitment of love and devotion for which the rings are only the outward symbol. Today, we would call what Portia does to Bassanio entrapment—encouraging someone to commit a crime he did not actively seek to commit. Portia and Nerissa forgive their husbands because they realize that Bassanio and Gratiano have not betrayed a trust by giving their wedding rings to the young doctor; their intention was to reward the young doctor for a perceived kindness. This forgiveness is another example in the play of the importance of weighing intention when judging a person's actions.

The concern with the letter and the spirit of the law shown in *The Merchant of Venice* is not peculiar to Shakespeare's time. In our own age, we know that laws are necessary to prevent anarchy and to insure peace and order. But we also know that no law can anticipate every circumstance and intention. At the same time we realize that a proliferation of laws to remedy this situation would compromise our freedom. The alternative to this dilemma is to enforce each law with common sense, always remembering the spirit or intention with which that law was formulated.

Characters

Antonio:

Antonio is a merchant of Venice, perhaps "the" merchant of Venice. When Bassanio asks him for money to impress Portia, Antonio wants to give it to him but cannot because all of his money is tied up in goods that are being transported by ship to ports where they will be sold. Out of kindness to Bassanio he agrees to secure any loan Bassanio might get in the marketplace. Bassanio requests that loan from Shylock, a moneylender with whom Antonio is not on the best of terms. Antonio has criticized Shylock for usury, and Shylock, in turn, resents Antonio's generosity in loaning money out at no interest. To get back at Antonio, Shylock proposes a bond that stipulates Antonio will forfeit "a pound of flesh" if he cannot repay the loan. Again, out of kindness to his friend and a certainty that his ships will have come in by the deadline, Antonio agrees to the terms of the bond. When he loses his fortune through a series of unexpected accidents, Shylock brings him to trial, intending to fulfill the terms of the bond. Antonio's reputation for generosity and kindness is such that when his friends are informed of his predicament they rally around him and appeal to Shylock to show him mercy.

Antonio is a difficult character to interpret. At the beginning of the play he expresses a troubling sadness which is the result of neither a concern for the safety of his merchandise nor a condition of love. Although the play never explains Antonio's sadness, it might, perhaps, result from an uneasiness with the very profession he has chosen. So often praised for his Christian generosity in loaning money and charging no interest, we might wonder how Antonio makes any money. Obviously, his impulse to give freely contradicts the nature of his dealings as a merchant, a profession requiring that profit be made off of others. Although the play is set in Venice, it is likely that Shakespeare communicates the cultural values of Elizabethan England as he depicts the characters and plans the narrative of the play. Shakespeare's Protestant audience may have seen the completely unexpected loss of Antonio's goods as perhaps a providential condemnation of the profit-driven desires of Antonio.

The carving of flesh which Shylock proposes cannot be taken lightly. In the absence of any sophisticated surgical procedures, it would have killed Antonio. Yet Antonio faces the prospect calmly, concerned only with the well-being of his friend. It has been observed that he is Christ-like in his unselfishness, and here, too, Shakespeare's audience would have perhaps responded to anti-semitic attitudes, seeing Shylock's intended killing of Antonio as parallel with the Jews killing of Christ in Biblical accounts of the story. But as we have seen, this reading of Antonio must be weighed against the reading of Antonio's hypocrisy in both his condemnation of Shylock for business practices in which he himself engages and for the revenge he exacts on Shylock instead of showing the mercy he expected in his own situation.

> **Although the play never explains Antonio's sadness, it might, perhaps, result from an uneasiness with the very profession he has chosen. So often praised for his Christian generosity in loaning money and charging no interest, we might wonder how Antonio makes any money.''**

Arragon (The Prince of Arragon):

The prince of Arragon is the second suitor to try for Portia's hand. He reveals the conditions of the trial: all those gambling to win Portia in marriage agree that if they lose they will never reveal their choice, never propose marriage to another maid, and leave immediately upon failing to choose correctly. Arragon rejects the lead casket because it is a base metal not worth hazarding all for. He reads the inscription on the gold casket—''Who chooseth me will gain what many men desire''—and concludes that he is far and above the commonplace multitude represented by the ''many,'' his very name suggesting the arrogance of this supposition. He chooses the silver casket and finds only the picture of a fool's head and a note describing the aptness of this image to his attitude. According to the agreement, he leaves immediately saying, ''With one fool's head I came to woo, / But I go away with two'' (II.ix.75-76).

Attendants:

The princes of Arragon and Morocco are described as having trains of followers amongst whom would have been several attendants. Portia's train of followers is also referred to.

Balthazar:

Balthazar is Portia's servant. When Bassanio leaves Belmont upon learning that Antonio is in trouble, Portia sends Balthazar with a letter acquainting her cousin Doctor Bellario with the present circumstances and urges Balthazar quickly to convey to her whatever disguises or letters of rec-

ommendation Bellario sends. The young doctor that Portia impersonates is named ''Balthazar'' in Bellario's letter to the duke, a letter which praises the intelligence and judicial knowledge of one so young.

Bassanio:

Bassanio is a young and not very frugal friend of Antonio's. He is a spendthrift who has wasted whatever inheritance he might have had. Having heard of the fortune that will belong to the man who marries Portia, he wants to borrow money from Antonio so that he can present himself as a financially suitable suitor to her. He has met Portia before and has read amorous looks in her glances, quite probably presenting himself as having greater means than he actually has, as is his habit. With the money he receives from Antonio, he hopes to recoup his losses with Portia's estate. A good indication of his impulsive character can be found in the description he gives Antonio of a childhood procedure for finding lost arrows. It was his practice, as a child, to shoot a second arrow in the direction of the lost one, paying closer attention to the arrow's flight on this subsequent shooting. This procedure is at best foolhardy and more likely to lose a second arrow than recover the first. Knowing that Bassanio will be taking a similar gamble in the choosing of the correct casket, it is surprising that Antonio agrees to the proposal. The fact that he does agree is another indication of how ill-suited he is to the role of merchant.

Bassanio is what some today would call a gold digger. Although he is helped along in his choice of caskets by the hints provided by Portia, his situation fits the inscription on the lead casket—''Who chooseth me must give and hazard all he hath'' (II.ix..21)—and he might have chosen correctly on his own since he must know he is indeed hazarding all. His fortune-hunting intentions do not seem likely to provide a good foundation for a lasting relationship with Portia. Still, it becomes obvious that the two are genuinely in love with each other. The acute anticipation they experience before Bassanio's trial with the caskets and their impassioned exchanges after he has chosen successfully are reminiscent of the breathless and intense love demonstrated by Romeo and Juliet at their first meeting.

Bassanio, many commentators note, is not the self-indulgent character he at first seems to be in his generosity with Portia's money; he offers to take Antonio's place and forfeit his hands, head, or heart, attesting to the real friendship between the two men. In Elizabethan society the amorous relationships between men and women were considered secondary to the fraternal bonds between men. It is fitting, then, that Antonio appears in the last scene of the play transferring the wedding ring from Portia to Bassanio. In this transfer, Antonio symbolically sanctions the marriage and discharges the debt Bassanio owes Antonio for having endured so much on Bassanio's behalf.

Gobbo (Launcelot Gobbo):

Launcelot is a clown and a servant to Shylock. While in Shylock's employ, he carries a letter from Jessica to Lorenzo. Shylock describes Launcelot as "kind enough, but a huge feeder, / Snail-slow in profit, and he sleeps by day / More than the wildcat" (II.v.46-48). Launcelot is lazy and a huge drain on Shylock's money, and Shylock is glad when Launcelot quits his service and becomes a servant to Bassanio, hoping he will be a similar drain on Bassanio's resources.

Launcelot's name reminds us of Sir Lancelot from Arthurian legend. That knight was reputed for the chivalric code of ideals he embodied. Launcelot in *The Merchant of Venice* seems to embrace no ideals at all. At one point, in a confused struggle with his conscience, he determines to leave Shylock's service because he believes the Jew to be the devil incarnate, but later he confidently offers, to Jessica and Lorenzo, the ridiculous argument that Christians raise the price of pork by converting Jews to Christianity. Lorenzo responds that the financial consequence of those conversions would be easier to justify than the ethically irresponsible act Launcelot has committed by impregnating and abandoning a Moorish woman.

Gobbo (Old Gobbo):

Old Gobbo is Launcelot's father. He is nearly blind and does not recognize his son when he encounters him on the street. Launcelot tries to evoke recognition from his father but is at first unsuccessful. When Old Gobbo finally does recognize Launcelot, he tries to help his son gain employment with Bassanio, adding his own confused appeals to those offered by Launcelot. Both men ramble, offer garbled arguments, and utter comic malapropisms (using a word that sounds similar to the intended one but is incorrect in context).

"Bassanio is what some today would call a gold digger."

Gratiano:

Gratiano talks a great deal but says very little. According to Bassanio, "Gratiano speaks an infinite deal of nothing, more than any man in Venice" (I.i.114-15), and "His reasons are as two grains of wheat hid in two bushels of chaff" (I.i.115-16). He pleads with Bassanio to allow him to go with him to Belmont, and Bassanio consents after cautioning Gratiano to keep quiet once there, lest his enthusiasm and loose tongue reveal Bassanio's real social station and financial circumstances. Gratiano mimics Bassanio. When the latter marries Portia, Gratiano marries Nerissa. Similarly, when Bassanio gives his wedding ring to the young doctor, Gratiano is easily persuaded to do the same.

At Antonio's trial in the Court of Justice, Gratiano is extremely vocal in his criticism of Shylock. He says that Shylock's wolflike behavior might make Gratiano believe in Pythagoras's philosophy of reincarnation. When the tables are turned on Shylock, and Portia inquires what mercy Antonio might extend to the moneylender, Gratiano chimes in with "A halter gratis" (IV.i.379). That is, he will give Shylock a noose to hang himself, perhaps alluding to the halter Judas Iscariot used to hang himself after betraying Christ. But we must question how important and how representative Gratiano's statements are in this instance, when even his friends characterize him as something like an empty-headed loudmouth.

Jailer:

The jailer appears briefly on a street in Venice with Antonio in his custody. Shylock encounters the two and admonishes the jailer for having been persuaded by Antonio to let him out of close confinement. Shylock also admonishes the jailer not to talk of mercy for Antonio; he reminds the jailer that Antonio has lent money out at no interest, a foolish act in Shylock's estimation.

Jessica:

Jessica is Shylock's daughter. She has agreed to run away with the Christian Lorenzo, who comes by

> According to Bassanio, 'Gratiano speaks an infinite deal of nothing, more than any man in Venice' (I.i.114-15) . . ."

her house disguised amongst a group of masquers, when her father is away. Jessica adopts the disguise of a young male torchbearer in order to avoid notice. She steals her father's money and jewels when she elopes with Lorenzo, and the two go on a spending spree of sorts. Tubal reports to Shylock that Jessica has spent eighty ducats in Genoa in one night. Tubal also tells Shylock that his daughter has traded one of her mother's jewels for a monkey. This news infuriates Shylock, and he says that Jessica will be damned for her actions.

Launcelot Gobbo, on the other hand, tells Jessica that she is damned in her very birthright, the unalterable fact that she has Jewish parents. Jessica responds to this by saying, "I shall be sav'd by my husband, he hath made me a Christian!" (III.v.19). Shakespeare's audience would have applauded her conversion to Christianity as the proper course, but her callous treatment of her father and her mother's memory seems to be a rather harsh consequence of that conversion. Even though Jessica has converted to Christianity, there is the sense that she is never fully accepted into the communal atmosphere of Belmont.

Launcelot Gobbo:

See Gobbo

Leonardo:

Leonardo is Bassanio's servant. He is sent by Bassanio to procure a number of items for a dinner to which Bassanio has invited Shylock. The dinner provides Lorenzo and friends the opportunity to abduct Jessica and Shylock's money and jewels while he is away from his house.

Lorenzo:

Lorenzo is part of the circle of friends that includes Antonio, Bassanio, Gratiano, Salerio, and Solanio. In arranging for his elopement with Jessica, Lorenzo takes advantage of the fact that Shylock will be dining with Bassanio. Lorenzo assembles a group of his friends as masquers—like Halloween celebrants, masquers adopted disguises to enact historical episodes or short dramatic pieces written for specific occasions. This group of masquers arrives at Shylock's house, and Lorenzo carries away Jessica and Shylock's money and jewels. After a short but seemingly extravagant stay in Genoa, he and Jessica travel to Belmont. He and Jessica are installed as masters of Portia's Belmont estate when Bassanio and Portia return to Venice to help Antonio.

It is difficult to get beyond the impression that Lorenzo, like Bassanio, marries for money. Everything that Lorenzo gets comes through the efforts of others. Even though he steals Shylock's wealth, at the end of the play he stands to inherit that wealth legally through Antonio's negotiations. He is temporary master at Belmont and seems perfectly comfortable in that role; throughout the play, the only role he plays is that of an impostor. Unlike Bassanio, whose affection for Portia seems genuine, Lorenzo's love for Jessica is suspect. Near the end of the play, Lorenzo and Jessica compare their love to the loves of famous historical figures: Troilus and Cressida; Aeneas and Dido; and Medea and Jason. Each of these famous love affairs involved betrayal and desertion. The allusion to these historical personages is perhaps a foreshadowing of the same kind of fate for Lorenzo and Jessica.

Magnificoes:

The magnificoes are high-ranking noblemen of Venice. They are present at Antonio's trial because they have an interest in its outcome. Like the duke of Venice, they do not want to see Venice's reputation as a center of commerce suffer as a consequence of the government's failure to enforce a mutually agreed upon contract. If it became widely known that Venice did not recognize the contracts into which its merchants entered, the financial interests of Venice would suffer.

Morocco (The Prince of Morocco):

Morocco is the first suitor who tries to choose the correct casket and win Portia in marriage. He reads the inscription on the gold casket—"Who chooseth me shall gain what many men desire" (II.vii.37)—and debates with himself that "what many men desire'' is certainly Portia. He concludes that since she is much desired by men everywhere, the lead and silver caskets are beneath her dignity; he chooses the gold casket. When he opens it he discovers a death's-head and a scroll that reminds him ''All that glisters is not gold . . .'' (II.vii.65). Like Arragon, Morocco has agreed never to reveal his choice, never propose marriage to another maid, and leave immediately upon failing to choose correctly. Unlike Arragon, he seems to value Portia above himself. So, when Portia says ''Let all of his complexion choose me so'' (II.vii.79) her dismissal of him seems exceptionally cruel.

Nerissa:

Nerissa is Portia's waiting woman and confidante. She sympathizes with Portia's frustration at being constrained by her father's will and participates in Portia's expression of dissatisfaction with the list of suitors. When Portia goes to Antonio's trial disguised as a young doctor, Nerissa accompanies her disguised as a young male law clerk. When Portia marries Bassanio, Nerissa marries Gratiano. Almost a mirror image of Portia, Nerissa imitates the actions and embraces the values of her mistress. In the copycat wedding of Nerissa and Gratiano and in the parallels of the ring subplot, *The Merchant of Venice* offers a lesson in Elizabethan social conduct: lower-class persons should mimic their social superiors.

Officers:

These are the officers of the Venetian Court of Justice. We can assume that some of these officers serve as bailiffs, executive officers present to preserve order in the courtroom. Another officer, a clerk, is ordered by Portia/Balthazar (the young but learned doctor) to draw up a deed of gift recording Shylock's agreement to bequeath all his possessions to Jessica and Lorenzo, an agreement insisted upon by Antonio as part of the settlement with Shylock.

Old Gobbo:

See Gobbo

Portia:

When we first hear of Portia, Bassanio is extolling her virtues to Antonio. Chief among these virtues, in Bassanio's estimation, is the money she stands to inherit. When we first meet Portia in

> Near the end of the play, Lorenzo and Jessica compare their love to the loves of famous historical figures: Troilus and Cressida; Aeneas and Dido; and Medea and Jason. Each of these famous love affairs involved betrayal and desertion."

Belmont, she is bemoaning the constraints her deceased father has placed on that inheritance. She must marry the man who correctly identifies one of three caskets, and Portia punningly complains, ''so is the will of a living daughter curb'd by the will of a dead father'' (I.ii.24-25). Portia, however, is not a character who will allow her will to be curbed.

Bassanio may have wanted to marry Portia for her money, but that wedding would never have become a reality if Portia had not wanted him. She guides Bassanio to the correct choice by giving him hints in a song. Later, in the ring subplot, she manipulates Bassanio further. She gets his wedding ring and evokes his jealousy, telling Bassanio she has slept with the young doctor Balthazar to get it. She uses his jealousy and breach of promise to reinforce his fidelity to her. As the young doctor Balthazar in the Venetian Court of Justice, she exhibits a keen and aggressive intelligence that only her femininity prevents her from exhibiting in every aspect of her life.

As with Antonio, Portia's good nature is praised by other characters in the play. Morocco says of her, ''From the four corners of the earth they come / To kiss this shrine, this mortal breathing saint'' (II.vii.39-40). Jessica says that ''the poor rude world / Hath not her fellow'' (III.v.82-83). According to Jessica, no woman on earth can compare with Portia. Yet for all the praise of her virtue, Portia's own speeches and actions embody a contradiction. As Balthazar at the trial of Antonio she delivers a moving speech on the quality of mercy; then, she refuses to extend mercy to Shylock when she gets an advantage over him. She utters a racist slur against Morocco, saying ''good riddance'' to him and all of his dark com-

> **Almost a mirror image of Portia, Nerissa imitates the actions and embraces the values of her mistress."**

plexion. And the ethnic stereotypes she uses to describe her original four suitors are nothing short of malicious. At times, Portia seems to be a model of Christian tolerance. At other times, she seems narrow-minded, malicious, and petty.

Salerio:

Salerio, like Antonio, is a merchant in Venice. He is a friend to Antonio and Bassanio. In the opening scene of the play, he attributes Antonio's sadness to a concern for the merchandise Antonio has shipped to distant ports, admitting that an enterprise like that would cause him a good deal of concern. He is one of the masquers who aids Lorenzo in his abduction of Jessica, and he is present at Antonio's trial. He appears at intervals throughout the play discussing rumors and reports of Antonio's losses. It is Salerio who travels to Belmont with Jessica and Lorenzo as a messenger informing Bassanio of Antonio's situation with Shylock. He engages in harsh exchanges with Shylock on the streets of Venice. In his virulent condemnation of Shylock and his glorification of the qualities of Antonio, Salerio acts as a representative of public opinion.

Servants:

These are the servants of Portia in Belmont. In I.ii, a servingman enters and announces the arrival of Morocco and Arragon in quest of marriage to Portia. Morocco and Arragon are not part of the group of four suitors whose qualities Portia has earlier derided; those four suitors have left, deciding that Portia's fortune was not worth the risk.

Shylock:

A rich Jewish moneylender in Venice, Shylock is the villain of *The Merchant of Venice* in that the problem he initiates causes great concern in the Christian community of that city. He insists that Antonio keep his bond and forfeit a "pound of flesh" since he has failed to make good the three thousand ducats Shylock has loaned to Bassanio on Antonio's guarantee. When the case goes to trial, it presents a problem for the government of Venice. The duke, along with Antonio's friends, asks Shylock to drop the case and demonstrate mercy toward Antonio. Shylock will not do so, and we must ask ourselves why he refuses what seems to be a reasonable request.

Shylock admits that he does not like Antonio, saying at one point, "I hate him for he is a Christian" (I.iii.42). He goes on to offer another reason for disliking Antonio: Antonio lends money out without charging interest and brings down the interest rates on loans in Venice. At Antonio's trial he is asked why he persists in his hatred of Antonio, and he answers that his reason for disliking the man is as inexplicable as the reason some men cannot stand to see cats or gaping pigs or cannot stand the sound of bagpipes. None of these perhaps is the real reason he hates Antonio; it seems more likely that he hates Antonio because Antonio hates him. Antonio has spat upon Shylock and treated him like a dog in the Rialto, a public area of commercial exchange. Salerio asks Shylock what he will do with Antonio's flesh since, unlike the meat of cows or goats, it is useless. Shylock responds, "To bait fish withal" (III.i.53). In the speech which follows this statement—Shylock's famous speech about his humanity—Shylock relates how Antonio has laughed at his losses and mocked his successes. Shylock says that Jews have learned to take revenge from the example set by Christians. He sees himself as the wronged party in the dispute and considers his actions to be justified vengeance rather than malicious instigation.

The sentence pronounced upon Shylock at the end of the civil action may seem merciful at first glance, but when examined, it will most likely sap his will to live. Shylock is commanded to turn over half of his wealth to the government of Venice. The other half he must give to Antonio to loan out at interest. These two actions will strip Shylock of his livelihood, a man's lifeblood. To add insult to injury, he is informed that the principal and the profits on the money given to Antonio, along with any other wealth Shylock might manage to accumulate, will be given to Lorenzo, the man who has robbed him of his daughter and his goods. Finally, he is ordered to convert to Christianity. With this final stroke, Shylock is effectively stripped of all his financial, emotional, and spiritual supports.

Solanio:

Solanio is yet another merchant in Venice and friend to Antonio and Bassanio. In the opening scene of the play, after Antonio has dismissed Salerio's conjecture that Antonio's sadness is caused by a concern for his property, Solanio offers that Antonio's sadness is a consequence of love. It is Solanio who reports Shylock's reaction to Jessica's theft and abandonment of him. He describes how the children follow Shylock and make fun of his agonized losses. Like Salerio, he appears occasionally throughout the play informing the audience of Antonio's misfortunes. He too, in his disgust with Shylock and praise of Antonio is meant to function as a representative attitude of the Venetian populace.

Stephano:

Stephano is another of Portia's servants. He is sent by her to Belmont where he announces to Lorenzo and Jessica that Portia will return the next morning. He inquires if his master—his newly acquired master Bassanio—has yet returned. Lorenzo informs Stephano that Bassanio has not yet returned, and since Lorenzo does not make the obvious connection, we can assume that he and Jessica are ignorant of Portia's disguised presence in Venice.

Tubal:

Tubal is Shylock's friend and a Jewish money-lender in Venice. Shylock does not have the cash at hand to loan to Bassanio, but he knows that he can get the three thousand ducats from his friend Tubal. After Jessica has eloped with Lorenzo, Tubal brings Shylock a mixture of good and bad news. He reports Jessica's spending spree and the news of Antonio's loss at Genoa. Tubal's presence in the play works against the flat portrayal of Shylock as an insensitive and totally alien person. When the two men part, Shylock reminds Tubal to meet him at the synagogue, the audience glimpsing in this reminder a reference to a sense of community and sense of values different from the dominant Christian ones.

Venice (Duke of Venice):

The duke of Venice is placed in a difficult situation by the litigation of the quarrel between

> As with Antonio, Portia's good nature is praised by other characters in the play. Morocco says of her, 'From the four corners of the earth they come / To kiss this shrine, this mortal breathing saint' (II.vii.39-40). Jessica says that 'the poor rude world / Hath not her fellow' (III.v.82-83). According to Jessica, no woman on earth can compare with Portia."

Shylock and Antonio. Although he sympathizes with Antonio and, in fact, appeals to Shylock to show him mercy, he cannot nullify the bond between them. To do so would be to establish a dangerous precedent unscrupulous businessmen might use to wrangle out of their financial obligations. The duke must consider the reputation Venice has as a center of commerce. It is highly likely that other tradespeople would not be inclined to transact their business in a city where the government suspended legal commercial contracts at its whim.

Further Reading

Barber, C. L. "The Merchants and the Jew of Venice: Wealth's Communion and an Intruder." *Shakespeare's Festive Comedy: A Study of Dramatic Form and Its Relation to Social Custom*, 163-91. Princeton: Princeton University Press, 1959.

Barber discusses the different attitudes toward wealth that are evident in the play. He refers to masques in relation to Jessica's elopement.

Barnet, Sylvan. "Prodigality and Time in *The Merchant of Venice*." *Publications of the Modern Language Association* 87 (1972): 26-30.

Barnet argues that Portia and Bassanio are the opposite in their prodigality to Shylock's frugality. Like the true merchant, Antonio, they take risks whereas

Shylock does not; Shylock deals in time—the period of the loan—and not venture capital.

Barton, Anne. Introduction to *The Merchant of Venice*, by William Shakespeare. In *The Riverside Shakespeare,* edited by G. Blakemore Evans, 250-53. Boston: Houghton Mifflin, 1974.

Barton give an overview of the play. She discusses the characterizations of Antonio, Bassanio, Portia, and Shylock. She also discusses the casket and ring subplots.

Harbage, Alfred. *Conceptions of Shakespeare.* Cambridge: Harvard University Press, 1966.

Harbage argues that the play should end with the triumph of love over hate, not the triumph of Christians over Jews. He sees Antonio as an intelligent and sensitive man, but one ignorant of Jewish culture.

Hunter, G. K. *Dramatic Identities and Cultural Tradition: Studies in Shakespeare and His Contemporaries.* New York: Barnes and Noble, 1978.

Hunter's work is interesting because he does not see the values in the play as a projection, by Shakespeare, of Elizabethan values onto Venice, especially in relation to money and theology.

Hurrell, John D. "Love and Friendship in *The Merchant of Venice.*" *Texas Studies in Literature and Language* 3 (1961): 328-41.

Hurrell addresses the cause of Antonio's sadness. He believes that Antonio is aware of the cause but reluctant to discuss it. Hurrell attributes Antonio's sadness to his deep feelings for Bassanio.

Kermode, Frank. "The Mature Comedies." In *Early Shakespeare,* edited by John Russell Brown and Bernard Harris, 210-27. London: Edward Arnold, 1961.

Kermode discusses the play as a "problem" comedy, one that has for its theme the contrast between legal and merciful justice.

Klein, David. "Shakespeare and the Jew." In *The Living Shakespeare*, 108-23. New York: Twayne, 1970.

Klein argues that Shakespeare, a man ahead of his time, admired Shylock but found it necessary to hide that admiration so as not to offend his audience. He

describes the lengths to which Shakespeare goes in order to obscure his real purpose.

Leventen, Carol. "Patrimony and Patriarchy in *The Merchant of Venice.*" In *The Matter of Difference: Materialist Feminist Criticism of Shakespeare,* edited by Valerie Wayne, 59-79. Ithaca: Cornell University Press, 1991.

Leventen examines money's relationship to women's social status in the financial choices Portia and Jessica have. She says that a woman in Venice had much more financial freedom than her counterpart in Elizabethan England.

Lewalski, Barbara. "Biblical Allusion and Allegory in *The Merchant of Venice.*" *Shakespeare Quarterly* 13 (1962): 327-43.

Lewalski suggests that the caskets are allegorical symbols for the choices people make about spiritual life and death. She also points out the Biblical allusions in the characters' names.

Milward, Peter. *Shakespeare's Religious Background.* London: Sidgwick and Jackson, 1973.

Milward identifies the Christianity in the play as specifically Roman Catholic, based on the play's allusions to the plight of Catholic priests in Elizabethan England.

Muir, Kenneth. *Shakespeare's Comic Sequence.* New York: Barnes and Noble, 1979.

Muir maintains that the play is not anti-semitic and suggests that the main plot and casket subplot are not to be taken literally.

Shirley, Frances A. *Swearing and Perjury in Shakespeare's Plays.* London: George Allen and Unwin, 1979.

Oaths were taken quite seriously in Shakespeare's time, and Shirley examines the consequences of the many oaths uttered in the play.

Siegel, Paul N. "Shylock, the Elizabethan Puritan and Our Own World." In *Shakespeare in His Time and Ours*, 237-54. South Bend: University of Notre Dame Press, 1968.

Siegel claims that Shakespeare's audience would have associated the Christians' rejection of Shylock with the contemporary situation of Puritans in England.

The Merry Wives of Windsor

circa 1597*

*There is considerable disagreement about when the play was composed. Many scholars agree with Leslie Hotson that textual evidence links the play with the feast of the Knights of the Garter at Windsor in 1597, before the completion of *Henry IV, Part Two*; others prefer a date closer to the quarto edition of 1602, after the composition of *Henry IV, Part One*, where the figure of Falstaff first appears.

Plot Summary

Act I:

The play is set in Windsor, an English country town; its main characters are the middle class townsfolk who live at the periphery of royal Windsor castle. Falstaff, the play's central figure, is a dissolute courtier from out of town. As the play opens, Justice Robert Shallow, his nephew Abraham Slender, and the parson Hugh Evans seek out Falstaff for robbing Shallow and Slender the night before. Falstaff amiably admits his wrongdoing, and goes in to dine at the home of Mister and Mistress Page. Shallow and Evans convince Slender to woo the Page daughter, Anne, who will inherit her father's wealth. Evans sends his servant to one Mistress Quickly, to ask her to be the go-between for Slender and Anne Page. Mistress Quickly agrees, even though she is also working for her own

master, the French Doctor Caius, and for Fenton, a gentleman. Falstaff, low on cash, has to let his servant Bardolph go to work for the innkeeper, the host of the Garter Inn. He plans to procure money by sleeping with Mistress Page (Anne Page's mother) and Mistress Ford.

Act II:

Mistresses Page and Ford, on receiving love letters from Falstaff, vow to get revenge by leading him on, without telling their husbands. Meanwhile, Falstaff's own disloyal servants have informed the husbands of Falstaff's plans. Ford becomes jealous and, posing as a Mister Brook, finds out the details of Falstaff's trysts with his wife. Meanwhile, Doctor Caius has challenged Evans to a duel over Anne Page. Shallow, Slender, and Mister Page have all congregated to watch the duel, but the host of the Garter deliberately misdirects Caius and Evans, averting the conflict.

Act III:

After some confusion, Caius and Evans meet and the host admits to having misled them. Doctor and parson make peace and vow to be revenged on the host. Page has come to prefer Slender as son-in-law. Ford, meeting the whole group, convinces them to go to his house and catch Falstaff with his wife. Mistresses Page and Ford plot to have Falstaff hidden in the laundry basket, carried out by two servants, and dumped into a muddy ditch near the Thames. When Mistress Page arrives at the Ford home with word that Mister Ford is on his way home, Falstaff falls into the trap and proceeds to climb into the laundry basket. He is on his way to the Thames by the time Mister Ford arrives. Meanwhile, Anne Page and Fenton declare their love for each other. Her parents reject Fenton on the basis of his being too aristocratic and too poor. Back at the Garter Inn, Falstaff rails about having been dumped in the Thames. Mister Ford, as Brook, finds out he has been deceived, igniting his jealousy all over again.

Act IV:

Mistress Page takes her boy William to school, but when she meets the boy's teacher, parson Evans, he sends the boy home to play. Mistresses Page and Ford have invited Falstaff to come again. This time they dress him up in the clothes of an old fortune-teller, the widow of Brainford, to disguise his departure when Mister Ford comes home. Ford doesn't like the fortune-teller either, and beats her/Falstaff

as s/he runs away. The wives disclose their plotting to their husbands, and all four together decide to trick Falstaff one further time. They will arrange a tryst by an old oak, ask Falstaff to disguise himself as Herne the Hunter, and then beset him with ''fairies'' played by their children. Back at the Inn, Falstaff complains of his treatment. Caius and Evans report that ''Germans'' have stolen the host's horses. (Whether Caius and Evans have anything to do with this element of the plot is a point of critical contention.) Fenton offers the host more than he just lost in horseflesh to procure him a priest, so Fenton can marry Anne Page secretly.

Act V:

Falstaff agrees to meet Mistress Ford again. Page tells Slender that Anne will be the fairy dressed in white, and that Slender should take her off and marry her. Mistress Page, at the same time, tells Caius that Anne will be in green and that he should take her off and marry her. That night, everyone converges at the oak. The wives flirt with Falstaff and then run away, and the ''fairies'' find Falstaff face-down on the ground. They pinch and torment him, burning his fingertips with candles. Slender and Caius carry off fairies dressed in white and green; Fenton carries off the real Anne Page. Finally, the Fords and the Pages reveal themselves to Falstaff, who amiably accepts his losses. Caius and Evans return, having abducted boys. Fenton returns and asks the forgiveness of the Pages for having married their daughter. They grant forgiveness and invite everyone to dinner, including Falstaff.

Modern Connections

The Merry Wives of Windsor focuses on how a community establishes and preserves its own standards. Outsiders like Falstaff, Fenton, Caius, and Evans cause a wide range of threats to Windsor's inhabitants. Evans and Caius threaten the conventions of language use that other characters rely on: the Welsh Evans has an accent, and Caius frequently misunderstands English expressions and imports French words into his speech. Even native speakers within the community often lack language skills—Mistress Quickly mistakes Latin for vulgar English, and Slender frequently mistakes the prefixes and suffixes of words. But language is nevertheless used by the characters to define an inside group and an outside group; and foreigners are on the outside.

They are the object of the host's tricks, and remain the subject of humor throughout the play. There are many ways in which modern communities use language to distinguish among groups, and sometimes to exclude certain people or groups of people. For example, slang associated with younger people often receives ridicule and rejection from the adult community.

Falstaff poses a different kind of threat to the community of Windsor: he uses language exceedingly well, and in fact he is fully in control of his own jokes, fully capable of mocking other people (and himself) through language. But his cleverness also works against him. The very ruse he sets up to earn himself money reveals his capacity for using other people for his own ends. Trickster figures often appear as social outsiders, in many other literatures and in social life. Falstaff is not unlike a modern "class clown" who plays clever tricks, shows off, or tells jokes to get attention. As a result, he is punished in an elaborate and ceremonial way that may appear strange to modern audiences. The entire community dresses up as fairies from local folklore in order to torment a stranger. A distant analogy in modern life might be the jokes and disguises designed to frighten people on camping trips or at Halloween. But the punishment Falstaff receives is also quite strange, and it takes on a magical and even solemn quality all its own.

Class anxiety is the source of much of the play's conflict. The Order of the Garter, which provides an underlying context for the whole play, was an order of knights with special privileges and a special relationship to Queen Elizabeth. Much of the play is staged at the Garter Inn, so named because the Order had its annual feast at Windsor. The host and inhabitants of the Inn aspire to be members of the court culture of Windsor—or at least to serve that culture—but none of them actually has any contact with the court. Indeed, the community of the play is actually quite marginal to the court and to the trappings of nobility. Although they may have titles—Falstaff has the title of knight—these do not necessarily give them the cultivated conduct of gentry. Indeed, the play raises the question of what might constitute gentility, especially in relation to Anne Page. Though Caius has money and court connections, he is a blustering foreigner and therefore unfit to marry Anne Page; though Shallow and Slender remind us of their status as landowners, they are (as Anne says) "idiots" and therefore unfit to marry her. Fenton, with his connections to "the wild Prince and Poins," has

no money, but Anne finds him suitable enough to marry.

In *The Merry Wives of Windsor*, nearly everyone claims to be a gentleman on the basis of title, land, court connection, or money. Falstaff is excluded from the community based on his distinctly ungentlemanlike behavior toward the Mistresses Page and Ford; Caius and Evans are mocked because of their indiscretions. Only Fenton and Anne Page show propriety and discretion—to the point of marrying in secret. In contemporary American life, class relationships are similarly ill-defined. Most people would claim to be "middle class," just as most people in *The Merry Wives of Windsor* claim to be gentry. Although wealth—or lack of it—is often accepted as the defining characteristic between classes, behavior and language are also used to distinguish class, just as they are in *The Merry Wives of Windsor*.

Characters

Bardolph:

Bardolf is one of Falstaff's servants. Because Falstaff doesn't have enough money to pay for the needs of his followers as a knight should do, the host of the Garter Inn takes Bardolph on as his tapster, or bartender.

Brook:

See Ford. *(Francis Ford is at times disguised as a Mister Brook).*

Caius (Doctor Caius):

Doctor Caius is a French doctor, and a foreigner. Along with Slender and Fenton, he wants to marry Anne Page. When he finds out that his housekeeper, Mistress Quickly, is at the service of rival suitors, Caius loses his temper in a stereotypically "Latin" outburst. He challenges the Welsh parson, Evans, to a duel. The comedy of this situation lies in the confusion between two foreigners whose mispronunciations only increase their mutual misunderstanding.

Caius's masculine bravado also has an element of foreign stereotype: in Elizabethan England, the French were frequently mocked as fops, full of transparently false masculine behavior. The host, who sends Caius and his rival Evans to two different places, makes fun of Caius's threatened violence. He also teases him about his profession, a less respectable one in Elizabethan times than in today's society. The host mocks the doctor's English as well.

Caius thinks the host is on his side, but when it turns out he's been misled he vows to get revenge. He and Evans witness Ford's jealous searches of his own house. But in between the central action the two play upon their own foreignness to get back at the host: when his horses are mysteriously stolen by the ''Germans'' staying at the inn, it is Caius and Evans who announce the theft. Though some readers believe there is a missing scene in the play, or that the Germans are part of an undeveloped subplot, it is possible that the parson and the doctor set up the theft to trick the host.

In the end Caius is the object of another trick. At Mistress Page's behest, he tries to steal Anne Page out of the fairy scene and ends up with a boy (another jab at his masculinity). ''By gar, I am cozen'd,'' he cries (V.v.203). As a representation of an immigrant outsider in Renaissance English middle classes, Doctor Caius makes light of prejudice, but his character also reveals the ruthless exclusions of an insulated society.

Evans (Sir Hugh Evans):

A Welsh parson, Evans is, like Doctor Caius, a social outsider. But his place in the town's society is more secure: as the parson, he is also the local schoolteacher, and is looked to for conventional wisdom. The fact that he does not measure up to the ideals of a country parson provides the source of much of the humor of his character.

In his speech, Evans frequently omits initial ''w's,'' replaces final ''d's'' with ''t's,'' and replaces ''b's'' with ''p's.'' His speech is also full of malapropisms (a malapropism is the misuse—generally unintentional and ususally funny—of a word or phrase). When he performs a miniature classroom exercise by quizzing young William Ford in his Latin, his questioning is quite elementary and confined to rote learning.

Evans's ethics are questionable, especially given that he is a parson. In the opening scene, as Shallow threatens to take Falstaff to court, Evans distracts the irate justice by mentioning that the young Mistress Anne Page will inherit a large income, and suggests that Slender marry her. Parsons were often portrayed as the advocates of love in

marriage over economic considerations, but Evans advocates Slender's monetary gain over any more noble aspirations. When Caius finds out Evans's role in setting up his rival, the challenge is issued.

Evans, in a state of fear, waits for the upcoming duel with Caius. As he waits, he sings, confessing that he feels like crying (III.ii.22). Although the host had sent Caius and Evans to different locations to await the duel, Caius and Evans finally meet. Evans makes a show of insulting him, while aside he begs Caius to make peace. Eventually they reconcile. In the fairy scene, Evans participates in the final revenge on Falstaff, commanding the others to ''Pinch them, arms, legs, back, shoulders, sides, and shins'' (V.v.54).

Evans is not portrayed as a devoted servant of God. Although he has a clear role in the local community, he becomes both victim and aggressor in the course of the play.

Falstaff (Sir John Falstaff):

Falstaff is the play's central character. Falstaff also appears in *Henry IV*, *Part One* and *Two*, where he is the comic friend and a kind of surrogate father to Prince Hal. When Hal becomes King Henry V, in a famous and poignant moment, he rejects Falstaff in public: ''I know thee not, old man'' (*Henry IV, Part Two,* V.v.47).

Falstaff's role in the *Henry* plays has been the subject of much critical and dramatic debate; he is a complex figure who has immense power over language and whose conduct raises important moral questions not only about himself but about the young Prince as well. In both histories and comedy, Falstaff is a fat, old, dissolute knight who regards nothing with complete seriousness, not even the violent political turmoil of Henry IV's kingship. Theatrical tradition has it (first suggested by John Dennis in 1702) that Queen Elizabeth I was so enamored of the Falstaff character in the *Henry* plays that she asked Shakespeare to write a play about Falstaff in love, whereupon he produced *The Merry Wives of Windsor* in the space of fourteen days. Many scholars argue that there is no factual evidence to support this story and that in *Merry Wives* Falstaff is not in love. Additionally, the Falstaff Shakespeare portrays in the comedy is quite a different character from the comic knight of the history plays. It is tempting to regard him as the product of hurried composition, reluctance, or simply the overworking of an already-finished character—and in fact, critics of the play have largely expressed disappointment at this tamer and humbler Falstaff.

Falstaff's role in the comedy is simply different than that of the history plays. He is a knight who has led a dissolute life, spending all his money on ''sack'' (drink), to the extent that he cannot even support his followers. His response to this situation is to let Bardolph become the host's tapster and send Robin off to Mistress Page as a token of love. But Falstaff greets all of this with humor, not desperation. In the opening scene, when Justice Shallow calls him to account for having robbed him the night before, Falstaff admits that he did, and makes a show of calling his followers to account as well. But he suffers no remorse or consequences for the incident. And even when Pistol and Nym (followers who appear in the *Henry* plays in different form) refuse to deliver Falstaff's messages for him, he greets the fact with relative equanimity. He later uses their refusal as reason to refuse Pistol a loan, but the implication is that Falstaff has no loan money to spare anyway.

Falstaff's central activity, the wooing of the Mistresses Page and Ford in an effort to seduce them and then con them out of money, and the mishaps that befall him as a result, establish the fat knight as a distinct outsider to the Windsor community. The letter he sends to the women is full of offensive remarks that masquerade as compliments: ''You are not young, no more am I; go to then, there's sympathy'' (II.i.6-7). He combines barroom humor with blunt declarations of love, and at the end offers a mock love poem. As an effort to ingratiate himself, the letter fails miserably; he has essentially misjudged his audience. His efforts at wooing in person are no less clumsy: ''Now I shall sin in my wish: I wish your husband were dead'' (III.iii.49-50), he tells Mistress Ford. He does not hear the double-edged nature of Mistress Ford's declarations, and never suspects (even after being tricked twice) that the wives mean him harm. Indeed, throughout the play Falstaff seems to assume, in spite of his own dishonesty, that everyone else is honest to the point of naivete, and that everyone else means well. When Mister Ford comes to him as Mister Brook, Falstaff believes the man's elaborate story immediately, never suspecting that harm might come to himself as a result.

Falstaff's responses to the tricks played on him make light of the troubles he runs into. After Mistress Ford's servants have dumped him in the Thames, he mocks his own size, saying he would hate to die

> **Caius's masculine bravado also has an element of foreign stereotype: in Elizabethan England, the French were frequently mocked as fops, full of transparently false masculine behavior.''**

by drowning because ''water swells a man; and what a thing should I have been when I had been swell'd!'' (III.v.16-7). But he immediately agrees to see Mistress Ford again the next day, and naively tells ''Mr. Brook'' the whole story. After he has been disguised as an old woman and beaten by Mister Ford, he returns to the Garter Inn. This time, his response is somewhat more serious, worrying that, if those at court knew of his treatment here, they would ''melt me out of my fat drop by drop . . .'' (IV.v.97-8). Nevertheless, he still does not repent; and as soon as Mistress Quickly comes to ask him to meet Mistress Ford one last time, Falstaff invites her in.

The brutality of these scenes increases as the play develops. Though Falstaff, of all the characters in the play, takes himself the least seriously, nonetheless he seems to be the one most in danger, both physically and economically. He is also most at risk of being excluded from any social community, whether it be court, Inn, or Windsor community generally. In his final punishment, he dresses as the spirit Herne the Hunter, complete with horns on his head, to disguise himself for a meeting with Mistress Ford. Ironically, he ends up wearing the cuckold's horns that he intended to put on Mister Ford (cuckold's horns were worn by a man whose wife cheated on him, or cuckolded him). When the ''fairies'' descend upon them—Mistress Quickly, Evans, Pistol, and the children in disguise themselves—the Mistresses Ford and Page run away, but Falstaff simply lies down on his face. The fairy torment is designed to be painful: they burn the tips of his fingers, and torment him with pinching, while accusing him of lechery. It is important to recognize that the comedy of these scenes coexists with violence and humiliation. The scene also resembles certain ritual fetility rites, in which a god of fertility is scapegoated and beaten.

> Falstaff's central activity, the wooing of the Mistresses Page and Ford in an effort to seduce them and then con them out of money, and the mishaps that befall him as a result, establish the fat knight as a distinct outsider to the Windsor community."

In the end, Falstaff rises up again, the fairies run off, and the Pages and Fords appear to reveal the whole thing was a trick. Falstaff gives flimsy excuses for having believed they actually were fairies. He then tries to turn the attention against Evans, making fun of the parson's English, but the others are more concerned with mocking Falstaff instead. Finally, he accepts their mockery with his usual lightness of heart. Mister Page, ever the genial gentleman, invites Falstaff and everyone else to dinner. Falstaff does not exactly become a member of the society, but his acquiescence to their aggression allows him to make peace with them. He has provided not a real threat but an inconsequential comic challenge to their society.

In the *Henry* plays, Falstaff offers a humorous, but also serious, commentary on the dearly held values of king and court. He is also a genuine friend to Prince Hal. His rejection by the prince when he becomes King does not offer comfortable or satisfying closure to their relationship. In *The Merry Wives*, Falstaff is a foolish but relatively benign outsider, and relatively less threatening. He poses no real threat to the Windsor community, and indeed he can even begin to be integrated into it at the end. Perhaps Falstaff belongs more to the middle-class citizenry than to the royal court—but his status as a dissolute gentleman places him outside either social arena.

Fenton:

A gentleman who has kept company with the Prince Hal of the *Henry* plays, Fenton is the man Anne Page actually marries. He makes few appearances in the play. The love affair between Fenton and Anne Page takes place at the margins of the slapstick of jealousy, greed, and revenge that forms the main action of the play. Fenton admits to a certain level of involvement in the general climate of concern with money, and to "riots past" and "wild societies" (III.iv.8) of his own. Like Anne's other suitors, Caius and Slender, he says he began wooing Anne because of her father's income. But he assures her he has fallen in love with her, and he wins her in the end in spite of her parents' preferences for Slender and Caius.

Fenton, unlike Slender and Caius, is a gentleman. Though he has a wart above one eye (II.i.144-52) and therefore appears less than perfectly handsome, and though he admits he has no money, nevertheless he speaks in blank verse (often in Shakepeare the mark of aristocratic birth). Apparently, he spent time with "the wild Prince and Poins" (III.ii.73), that is, in the company of Prince Hal as portrayed in the *Henry* plays. This description of him has led to scholarly speculation about when *The Merry Wives* takes place in relation to the *Henry* plays, but such speculation has proven inconclusive.

Though Mistress Quickly, the go-between, cannot decide whose case she will argue with Anne, she is certain Anne does not love Fenton (I.iv.163-4). However, to the degree that Anne expresses an opinion at all, she appears to prefer Fenton. Unlike Caius and Evans, Fenton also receives the help of the host of the Garter, who procures a priest so the couple can secretly be married. to audiences, Fenton may appear to be more socially accepted, and more desirable, than the other suitors—partly perhaps because of his noble birth, but also because of his substantial absence from the play's central comic action.

Ford (Mistress Alice Ford):

Mistress Ford is the wife of the jealous Mister Ford and one of the two women Falstaff woos. Mistresses Ford and Page join forces to trick Falstaff three times in the course of the play in order to teach him a lesson. Mistress Ford also manages to trick her husband twice by sneaking Falstaff out of her house just as Mister Ford arrives. In the opening scene of Act II, when the two women receive their love letters from Falstaff, Mistress Ford is immediately out for revenge against him. She mocks Falstaff's status as a knight, his fatness, and his writing style. Her response makes clear that he is an outsider at Windsor: "What tempest, I trow, threw this whale . . . ashore at Windsor?" (II.i.64-5).

Indeed, throughout the play, Mistresses Ford and Page together define the acceptable social behavior of their society. When Falstaff writes both of them inappropriate love letters, they expose his self-interested and offensive motives. When Mister Ford's jealousy increases and becomes more explicit, Mistress Ford exposes his unfounded distrust. The women know more than their husbands through much of the play, and certainly more than Falstaff. The first time they trick Falstaff, hiding him in the laundry basket because their husbands are arriving, they do not expect Mister Ford and Mister Page actually to arrive; but Mistress Ford quickly figures out that her husband has some outside knowledge of Falstaff's intentions. The women's next plot against Falstaff anticipates Mister Ford's arrival. They dress the knight up as the widow of Brainford, a fortune-teller whom Mister Ford despises, and the jealous husband beats up the supposed lover without even realizing it.

Every time they trick Falstaff, it is Mistress Ford who plays the willing lover, pretends to be jealous of her friend, and asks the knight back again. She thus plays the part of the adulterous woman, even if she doesn't carry it out. Her language comically makes fun of Falstaff even as she flirts with him: "Well, heaven knows how I love you, and you shall one day find it," she tells him (III.iii.80-1). Indeed, nothing she says can be taken as an unambiguous expression of love for him. Even in her act of deception, she remains, in a sense, true to herself.

In the context of a play whose characters have a great deal of trouble speaking the truth, Mistress Ford's fundamental truth has a purpose. The jealousy subplot and the mock-adultery scenes are materials from the French comic tales known as fabliaux. In fabliaux, however, the adultery is usually enacted, not avoided. Here, the subplot of the jealous husband and adulterous wife plays itself out in a context of profound anxieties about inheritance. Whereas the Pages have at least two children, the marriageable Anne and the young William, the Fords have no onstage children—and hence no evidence of a productive marriage resulting in the continuation of family line and wealth. For them, Falstaff's wooing raises a serious problem: the knight wants to make himself the wrong kind of "inheritor" of Mister Ford's wealth. By entertaining Falstaff's efforts and then tossing him out with the laundry and having him beaten by her husband, Mistress Ford diminishes the threat he represents, and keeps both love and money properly inside her

> "The love affair between Fenton and Anne Page takes place at the margins of the slapstick of jealousy, greed, and revenge that forms the main action of the play."

marriage. Her activities, then, preserve conventional middle-class values.

Ford (Francis Ford):

The jealous husband of Mistress Ford, Mister Ford spends most of the play trying to catch Falstaff and his wife together. When Pistol tells him of Falstaff's intention to woo his wife, Ford is immediately on his guard: "A man may be too confident" (II.i.186-7), he says. Thus, while Page goes off blithely to enjoy the non-duel between Caius and Evans, Ford plots to keep watch on his wife. He engages the aid of the host, who agrees to introduce him to Falstaff in the disguise of one Mister Brook. He tells Falstaff an elaborate tale, claiming that he (as Mister Brook) has loved Mistress Ford for years, but that she claims to remain faithful to her husband and so won't have him. He hires Falstaff to seduce Mistress Ford in order to prove her faithlessness and hence win her for himself.

The complex parameters of this trick reveal a great deal about how Mister Ford views his marriage. As Mister Brook, he assumes that if he can prove Mistress Ford unfaithful in general, then she will accept not only Falstaff but also himself. His fear is that a woman does not differentiate among lovers, and that therefore his own wife cannot remain faithful to him in particular. If she is unfaithful at all, she is proven to be incapable of chosing a partner. This view of his wife as potentially incapable of choice is mirrored in his view of himself. For, as Mister Brook, he plays the part of a completely rejected lover. The fact that this is an act of make-believe does not take away the fact that Mister Ford raises the possibility of his own incapacity as a husband/lover to his wife.

The persona of Mister Brook, of course, ends up getting Ford into trouble rather than giving him useful information. It is through this deception that Ford learns of his wife's planned trysts with Fal-

> Indeed, throughout the play, Mistresses Ford and Page together define the acceptable social behavior of their society."

staff. He tries to catch the two together twice, and is tricked twice by his wife. Both times, he has Page, Caius, and Evans in tow: they accomplish a kind of communal validation of the situation, assuring him that there is no one in the house. But they are also the witnesses to his shameful jealousy, for which both Pages and Mistress Ford herself scold him several times. The first time Ford arrives during one of the trysts, Mistress Ford sneaks Falstaff out in the washing. Hence, the second time, Ford searches through the dirty washing.

Perhaps as a result of his vulnerable state, Ford is something of a domestic tyrant. The calmness with which Page accepts Falstaff's advances on his own wife serves to highlight Ford's comparative bitterness and violence toward Mistress Ford. The first words he speaks to her in the play are to deny his melancholy mood and tell her to "Get you home; go" (II.i.52-3). To this and other commands she generally acquiesces, even while protesting that he does her wrong in his jealousy, and even while delighting in the tricks she plays on him. Ford's violence is displayed when Falstaff is dressed as the widow of Brainford, the fortune-teller whom Mister Ford dislikes. He has forbidden the widow his house, and when Falstaff appears in her dress he beats him and calls him witch, "old cozening [tricking] quean" (IV.ii.172), hag, rag, baggage, polecat, and runnion, or scabby woman.

While the Fords and Pages speak in prose throughout most of the play, Ford's use of prose and poetry stands out. When he is at his most jealous, his prose is full of epithets and overstatements: "Fie, fie, fie! Cuckold, cuckold, cuckold!" (II.ii.213-4) he sputters after first meeting Falstaff at the Inn. His longwinded explanations in the person of Mister Brook, like the complexity of the plot to catch out his wife, reflect a lack of control or self-governance. He apologizes to her after his first unsuccessful search of their house, but immediately seeks out Falstaff to check out his wife's story. Yet after his wife reveals the truth of her plotting, he turns (in

IV.iv) to poetry, speaks briefly and humbly, and asks her pardon at last.

Host of the Garter Inn:

The host acts as enabler and judge of a great deal of the activity around him. He also creates a good deal of purposeful disorder; Page suggests that the host is something less than a fine, upstanding member of the community when he says, "Look where my ranting host of the Garter comes. There is either liquor in his pate, or money in his purse, when he looks so merrily" (II.i.89-91). Like the Fords and Pages, the host represents the middle classes, who earn their money rather than inheriting lands and titles. But his role is to play host to the gentry, specifically Fenton and Falstaff, who represent two extremes of gentlemanly conduct. Both gentlemen, it is worth noting, are low on funds. The Garter Inn refers to the knightly Order of the Garter, to which noblemen were named by the Queen and formally dubbed at Windsor Castle. But knighthood itself, and the Order of the Garter in particular, had a great deal more ceremonial meaning than actual courtly function. The host's character, and the events in and around his Garter Inn, make light of the Order of the Garter, the status of knighthood, and the notion of gentle birth itself.

Like the Fords and the Pages, the host sets up an elaborate ruse, sending the duellers Caius and Evans to two separate places, gaining entertainment and power from the mockery of these two social outsiders. He mocks their malapropisms and their misunderstandings. He teases Falstaff as well, but more respectfully, for Falstaff is after all his client. When Mister Ford asks him to keep his identity secret from Falstaff, the host willingly does so; later, when Fenton asks his aid, he procures a priest so that Fenton and Anne Page can be married. These duties reveal that he is dependent upon the money and goodwill of visiting gentlemen from outside the community and the respect of citizens within it. The host does not treat Caius with the respect he offers those with firmer social standing.

The host is not immune from mockery and genuine harm. Even though stealing and procuring money by trickery are suggested throughout the play, the host is the only character from whom goods are actually stolen. When his horses are stolen, the host becomes serious, and even rather desperate, for the first time in the play. That Fenton immediately makes up for the loss by paying the host to get him a priest does not undo this moment: the host's vulnerability has been exposed.

The host, then, has an unstable role in the play. His class consciousness might be seen as a result of this instability. His Inn exists on the periphery of a royal residence without actually having much to do with the court. His aggression toward Caius and Evans can be seen as light and humorous, or as the more sinister expression of his own marginal status. If he excludes others, he can gain a sense of inclusion himself.

Mistress Quickly:

See Quickly

Nym:

Nym is a follower of Falstaff. Nym joins Pistol in rebellion against Falstaff's lordship, and tells Page that Falstaff is in love with his wife.

Page (Mistress Anne Page):

The marriageable daughter of Margaret and George Page, Anne Page has three suitors: the justice's nephew, Abraham Slender; the French Doctor Caius; and Fenton, a court gentleman and an outsider to Windsor society. Mistress Page has very little to say in the course of the play. Mistress Quickly claims that ''Never a woman in Windsor knows more of Anne's mind than I do'' (I.iv.27-8)—which is to say, no one in Windsor knows Anne's mind. Anne appears in the first scene, where she tries politely to get Slender to come in to dinner; she appears more puzzled than flattered at his clumsy efforts to woo her. Anne also rejects Caius as a suitor, saying she would rather be buried alive and pelted to death with turnips than marry him.

That Anne prefers Fenton is implied in one brief scene in which he assures her that he loves her and has lost interest in her money (III.iv.1-21). But the clearest evidence of her preference is that she allows Fenton to carry her off and marry her amid the confusion of the fairy scene. Her mother plots for Doctor Caius to carry her off, while her father plots for Slender to do so; both are foiled. Even then, Anne says at the end only, ''Pardon, good father! good my mother, pardon!'' (V.v.216). When her parents ask her why she didn't go off with their chosen suitors, Fenton answers for her, claiming that her parents ''amaze'' or bewilder her with their questions. Anne's character is essentially a blank on which others play out their desires. Still, in the conventional comic way, she chooses (it seems) to marry for love rather than for money.

> **The jealous husband of Mistress Ford, Mister Ford spends most of the play trying to catch Falstaff and his wife together.''**

Page (George Page):

A citizen of Windsor, George Page is the husband of Mistress Margaret Page and father of Anne. Unlike Ford, Page does not suspect his wife of adultery with Falstaff. He is more interested in other things: inviting his friends to dinner, watching the entertaining comedy of the non-duel between Caius and Evans, and solving the more serious problem of marrying off his daughter. All of these interests give the audience a view of middle-class social values. Page is eager to watch the two duellers ''scold'' each other (II.i.232), but he would rather not see them fight. While the host manages the bulk of the encounter between them, mocking them and lying to them about each other's whereabouts, it is Page who makes sure each man keeps his sword sheathed. The controlled humor of the scene seems to depend upon his intervention.

Page's attitudes also inform the community's final response to Falstaff. He calls the Herne the Hunter trick ''sport'' (IV.iv.13), making clear that the whole thing is all a game. But at the same time, he also emphasizes that Falstaff is to be punished and disgraced in seriousness as well. He even calls Falstaff a devil (V.ii.13). Yet in the end, it is Page who also invites Falstaff to dinner after the fairy scene. This combination of condemnation with geniality pervades Page's character.

The only time Page expresses anger is when he catches Fenton visiting his daughter privately; even then, he simply forbids the gentleman his house. Page's objection is that Fenton is too much a gentleman for Anne, ''too great of birth'' (III.iv.4). Page believes that Fenton wants Anne because he has led a dissolute life, spent all his inherited wealth, and needs her money. Page's anxieties about the match may be founded on a sense of affection for his daughter, but more explicitly, he is worried about where his own earnings will go. He even threatens not to pass along his wealth if she marries Fenton (III.ii.74-8).

> **Anne also rejects Caius as a suitor, saying she would rather be buried alive and pelted to death with turnips than marry him.**"

Page chooses Slender for his daughter, another act that can be seen in the light of his general social values. Slender's character is summed up in his name, and Page's preference for someone of equal or lesser social standing is a safe, conservative choice. What Page fails to see, of course, is that Slender is as much interested in Anne's money as all her other suitors—and ironically, even more so than Fenton. But when Anne marries against his wishes, Page finally accepts the fact with relative equanimity: "Well, what remedy? Fenton, heaven give thee joy!" (V.v.236).

Page (Mistress Margaret Page):

A citizen of Windsor, Margaret Page is the wife of George Page and mother of Anne. Along with Mistress Ford, she tricks Falstaff into believing that Mistress Ford accepts his advances. In contrast to her friend Mistress Ford, Mistress Page is a mother. She never plays the adulterous woman, never flirts with Falstaff, and from the first time she reads his letters she exhibits more serious offense at it than Mistress Ford, who responds with puns and mockery. When the two women trick Falstaff, Mistress Page plays the messenger, bringing Mistress Ford timely warnings of her husband's approach.

Mistress Page is also involved in the search for a husband for her daughter Anne. She exhibits somewhat more concern for her daughter's welfare than does her husband, asserting in an aside that Slender may own land, but "is an idiot" (IV.iv.86). She prefers Doctor Caius because he has money and connections at court. Neither of the Pages asks Anne whom she loves, and love as a condition for marriage remains a secret and subversive sentiment.

Mistress Page, like her husband and Mistress Ford, serves to uphold the middle-class values of monetary security, marriage security, and proper social conduct generally. She appears late in the play taking her son William to school. Because her husband thinks William is not learning enough, she

asks the parson to show evidence of William's studies; when he quizzes the boy in Latin, she is pleased with the small learning he shows. There is no doubt the Pages value education; but Mistress Page is uneducated herself, and ignorant of the kind of education to which she sends her son. Education, like husbands and wives, emerges as an object to buy and to own.

Pistol:

One of Falstaff's disgruntled followers, Pistol refuses to deliver Falstaff's love letters for him and tells Ford that Falstaff loves his wife. He plays the mock gentleman with gusto: he quotes Ovidian myth and scraps of other plays, and often speaks in blustering blank verse, usually used to mark gentry characters in Shakespeare's work. When the "fairies" torment Falstaff, Pistol plays Hobgoblin and urges them to put burning candles to Falstaff's fingers.

Quickly (Mistress Quickly):

Mistress Quickly serves as the go-between for all of Anne Page's suitors—Fenton, Caius, and Slender—as well as the messenger for the Mistresses Page and Ford in their efforts to trick Falstaff. (She bears the same name, but seems to have no other relation, to the hostess of the tavern in *Henry IV, Part One* and *Two*.) Mistress Quickly's name suggests something about her character, not simply that she is a speedy messenger (which she is not, particularly) but that she is light and superficial; that her intelligence is anything but "quick"; and, since "quick" is a word for "pregnant," that she enables couples to come together. When Simple asks her to play the bawd (or go-between) for Slender, she makes it plain she does not even know Slender, but agrees to take money to help him woo Anne.

Mistress Quickly claims to "know Anne's mind as well as another does" (I.iv. 164). That is not saying much, since Anne's mind is never expressed. Mistress Quickly makes no effort to hide the fact that she is wooing Anne for all her suitors. With Falstaff, however, she is quite effective in convincing him that Mistress Ford wants to accept his advances.

Mistress Quickly, like many of the other characters in the play, has trouble with the English language. She makes constant bawdy mistakes, like telling Falstaff that when the servants dumped him in the Thames "they mistook their erection" (III.v.39-40). When she witnesses the scene in which Evans quizzes young William Page on his Latin, she takes the Latin words for offensive English ones. However, at the end of the play, she suddenly becomes capable of lyrical poetic language. In the fairy scene, she commands the fairies in graceful rhymed pentameter, complete with references to the Order of the Garter. In this speech (V.v.55-76), she commands that the fairies bless Windsor Castle and its royal owner, allowing it to uphold the knightly values of the Garter that have been mocked throughout the play.

Robin:

One of Falstaff's servants, Robin is sent by Falstaff to Mistress Page as a sign of his love, whereupon Robin helps Mistresses Page and Ford trick Falstaff.

Rugby (John Rugby):

A servant to Caius and to Mistress Quickly.

Servants:

Servants appear to help the action along in IV.ii, when Mistress Ford commands them to carry out the laundry basket in which Falstaff has hidden; and again in IV.ii.

Shallow (Robert Shallow):

An old country justice, Shallow makes inflated claims to professional and aristocratic status. He opens the play with a blustering scene of fury against Falstaff and his men for having robbed him the night before. In the process he brags that he is a justice and signs all his papers ''Armigero'' (one who bears arms), thereby claiming knightly status. Essentially, he insists that he is as much a knight as the intruder Falstaff, and will prove it in court. He is easily distracted from his anger, though, at the mention of the potential marriage of his nephew Slender. Indeed, for most of the rest of the play Shallow is absorbed in wooing Anne Page for his nephew, to the extent that Anne tells him, ''Good Master Shallow, let him woo for himself'' (III.iv.50-1). But it is at Shallow's rather fawning request that Page comes to watch the duel, and through the course of the play Shallow becomes successful in obtaining the Page's good will toward Slender.

Shallow is also occupied by the duel between Evans and Caius, to which his response mainly consists of bragging to Page about his own past prowess. Along with Page, Slender, Caius and Evans, he also witnesses (silently) Mister Ford's sec-

> **Unlike Ford, Page does not suspect his wife of adultery with Falstaff. He is more interested in . . . solving the more serious problem of marrying off his daughter.''**

ond search for Falstaff at his house. Shallow is an important professional member of the local community, who is included as the audience to most events. But his role is peripheral, and in his concerns about class status, he exhibits little of the agression that drives many of the other characters.

Simple (Peter Simple):

Simple is a servant to Slender. When Caius rails at him (I.iv) and when Falstaff lies to him (IV.v), he plays the part of his name: passive and not very smart.

Slender (Abraham Slender):

A landowner, and a suitor of Anne Page, Slender is obedient, shy, and superficial in his efforts to woo Anne. This pursuit is his main role in the play. Like Evans and Shallow, he has trouble pronouncing and understanding language, and frequently misuses words. When the parson and the justice convince him to woo the young lady, Slender has trouble understanding what they are asking of him, and even then he has trouble expressing his obedience. ''If you say, 'Marry her,' I will marry her; that I am freely dissolv'd, and dissolutely'' (I.i.251-2), he says, mistaking ''dissolved'' for ''resolved'' and ''dissolutely'' for ''resolutely.'' And when the Pages invite him to dinner, he tries to play the coy lover, but fails miserably, seeming instead only shy and unbearably awkward. Most of the rest of his love suit consists of repeating ''O sweet Anne Page'' throughout the scene of the non-duel (in which it is Evans, not he, who fights his rival lover, Caius). He also allows his uncle Shallow to woo her for him in III.iv. His efforts to win her affection do indeed ''dissolve'' in the end, when he elopes with the postmaster's boy by mistake.

Slender is a member of the local gentry, and as such he owns land and a small inherited income.

> "In contrast to her friend Mistress Ford, Mistress Page is a mother. She never plays the adulterous woman, never flirts with Falstaff, and from the first time she reads his letters she exhibits more serious offense at it than Mistress Ford, who responds with puns and mockery."

Unlike Fenton and Falstaff, he seems to have retained his limited wealth and remained a country gentleman rather than travelling to court and around the countryside. But he is provincial and apparently poorly educated; his use of language is no more reliable than that of the Welsh Evans or the French Caius. His uncle, the pretentious Justice Shallow, apparently claims to have enough land to bear heraldic arms (though it may be doubted that he actually does own that much land). As an accepted member of the local society, though, Slender offers a critique of his own milieu. Page prefers him as a suitor to Anne because he is safe and, unlike the outsiders Caius and Fenton, he fits easily into the Windsor society. Love is not relevant to his suit; indeed, he seems uncertain whether Anne herself is relevant, for at one point in his wooing he tells her, "Truly, for my own part, I would little or nothing with you. Your father and my uncle hath made motions" (III.iv.63-4). Slender does whatever the older men tell him to do. As Anne says, Slender is a fool, and he makes the foolishness of Windsor society apparent.

Further Reading

Anderson, Linda M. *A Kind of Wild Justice: Revenge in Shakespeare's Comedies.* Newark: University of Delaware Press, 1987.

Anderson argues that *The Merry Wives of Windsor* is a play "obsessed" with revenge, and offers a detailed and readable analysis of its three separate revenge plots. She also gives an accessible account of other

critical opinion, including the general tendency to ignore the play.

Barton, Anne. Introduction to *The Merry Wives of Windsor,* by William Shakespeare. In *The Riverside Shakespeare,* edited by G. Blakemore Evans, 286-89. Chicago: Houghton Mifflin, 1974.

Barton discusses the play's possible commission by Queen Elizabeth and its performance at the Feast of the Garter in 1597. She also analyzes the play's content, especially Falstaff's relation to the Windsor community and the meaning of the play's many misuses and abuses of English language.

Bradbrook, Muriel C. *Shakespeare the Craftsman.* The Clark Lectures, 1968. Cambridge: Cambridge University Press, 1979.

In a chapter entitled "Royal Command: The Merry Wives of Windsor," Bradbrook offers a discussion of the play in terms of its (possible) intended audience. She elucidates the play's humor by connecting it to the political events of the time, including English relations with German and French politicians, and argues that the play is a marketable and professionally astute accomplishment because of its topical nature.

Bryant, J. A. "Falstaff and the Renewal of Windsor." *Publications of the Modern Language Society* 89 (1974): 296-301.

Bryant sees Falstaff's role as painful and comic; he argues for the productive effect of the Herne the Hunter scene, where Falstaff is scapegoated to renew Windsor society. *The Merry Wives of Windsor* fulfills the expectations of comedy, making us "see the mysterious terms on which we live, accept those terms, and once more concede that the game shall go on".

Craik, T. W. Introduction to *The Merry Wives of Windsor* by William Shakespeare. In *The Oxford Shakespeare,* 1-72, 223-30. Oxford and New York: Oxford University Press, 1989.

Craik reviews the play's occasion, date, and critical and textual histories; he analyzes the substance and dramatic structure of the play in detail. The edition contains illustrations of Windsor, photos of stage performances and manuscripts, and appendices on a textual "crux," Marlowe's song "Come live with me and be my love" (see III.i), and an explanation of Falstaff's disguise.

Erickson, Peter. "The Order of the Garter, the Cult of Elizabeth, and Class-Gender Tension in *The Merry Wives of Windsor*." In *Shakespeare Reproduced: The Text in History and Ideology,* edited by Jean Howard and Marion F. O'Connor, 116-42. New York and London: Methuen, 1987.

Erickson's exploration of the relations between social forces and the play focuses on class and gender tensions. He argues that although the women characters create comic subversions, they return in the end to a bourgeois, patriarchal framework.

Evans, Betrand. *Shakespeare's Comedies.* Oxford: Clarendon Press, 1960.

Evans coined the term "discrepant awareness" to describe the various levels at which characters understand events. His work explains the understanding of events that various characters in the play possess and analyzes the subtle ironies that stem from the exploration of the discrepancies between these understandings.

French, Marilyn. *Shakespeare's Division of Experience.* New York: Summit Books, 1981.

In the context of an early feminist analysis of Shakespeare, French sees the women in *The Merry Wives of Windsor* as a radical threat to male supremacy. The society of Windsor, which she analyzes in one chapter with *The Merchant of Venice*, is "masculine" in its preoccupation with possession of property, money, and women.

Green, William. *Shakespeare's Merry Wives of Windsor.* Princeton: Princeton University Press, 1962.

Green views the play as an outgrowth of the election of Shakespeare patrons to the Order of the Garter in 1597. Green's book provides useful background and explanatory material—along with some fascinating documents.

Kegl, Rosemary. " 'The Adoption of Abominable Terms': The Insults that Shape Windsor's Middle Class." *Journal of English Literary History* 61:2 (1994): 253-78.

Looking at how characters insult each other in *The Merry Wives of Windsor*, Kegl redefines the social and economic context of the play. She views the play's middle class as defined by a set of unstable social ties among people with often contradictory interests.

Leggatt, Alexander. *Citizen Comedy in the Age of Shakespeare.* Toronto: Toronto University Press, 1973.

Leggatt illuminates a genre otherwise lesser known to students; Shakespeare produced only one citizen comedy, *The Merry Wives of Windsor*, while the genre became increasingly popular with other playwrights. The section on *The Merry Wives of Windsor* specifically (146-9) asserts that the play has the distinct moral purpose of preserving chastity, and views the jokes on Falstaff as "appropriate comic punishments."

Oliver, H. J. Introduction to *The Merry Wives of Windsor,* by William Shakespeare. New Arden Edition, i-lxv. London: Methuen, 1971.

Oliver offers extensive discussion of the text; the relation of *The Merry Wives of Windsor* to the histories of *1* and *2 Henry IV* and *Henry V*; the possible occasion and date of its composition; critical sources; and a critical description of the play.

Roberts, Jeanne Addison. *Shakespeare's English Comedy:* The Merry Wives of Windsor *in Context.* Lincoln: The University of Nebraska Press, 1979.

Roberts explores thematic and genre issues such as Falstaff's character and the comedic content of the play. She argues that the play offers a disturbing look at Falstaff's downfall within the Windsor community.

Slights, Camille Wells. *Shakespeare's Comic Commonwealth.* Toronto: Toronto University Press, 1993.

In a chapter entitled "Pastoral and Parody in The Merry Wives of Windsor," Slights explores the threat posed by Falstaff and his men from outside of the Windsor community. She argues that the play's resolution depends on the "cohesion of the local community and its resistance to external pressures," even as the local community shares the characteristics of greed and pride with the threatening outsiders.

White, R. S. *Twayne's New Critical Introductions to Shakespeare:* The Merry Wives of Windsor. Boston: Twayne Publishers, 1991.

This is the most complete critical introduction to the play. It contains material on the history of stage performance and operatic adaptations, as well as chapters on the town of Windsor, women in the play, plot structure, and language.

A Midsummer Night's Dream

circa 1595-96

Act I:

Theseus, the duke of Athens, and Hippolyta, queen of the Amazons, discuss their upcoming wedding. Theseus directs Philostrate to "stir up the Athenian youth to merriments" (I.i.12). Egeus enters with his daughter Hermia and complains to Theseus about Hermia's unwillingness to marry Demetrius. (Hermia is loved by two men, Demetrius and Lysander, but she loves only Lysander.) Accusing Lysander of bewitching his daughter, Egeus asks Theseus for the right to "beg the ancient privilege of Athens" (I.i.41): being Hermia's father, Egeus has the right to "dispose of her" (I.i.42) by having her marry Demetrius or by having her killed. Hermia argues that Lysander is just as worthy of her as Demetrius is and boldly asks Theseus what will happen to her if she refuses to marry Demetrius. Theseus presents her with two choices, both of which would remove her from the "society of men" (I.i.66): death or lifelong confinement to a nunnery. Hermia opts for the second choice, but Theseus advises her to think it over, giving her until his wedding day to come to a decision. Alone with Hermia, Lysander proposes that they run away, where Athenian law can't reach them, and get married. Hermia agrees and they plan to meet in the wood the next night. Helena enters, lamenting the fact that Demetrius, who she loves, is in love with Hermia. Although Hermia assures Helena that she in no way encourages Demetrius's advances, Helena is not consoled. Lysander and Hermia tell Helena of their plan to elope. When Helena is left alone, she announces her plan to tell Demetrius of Hermia's and Lysander's plan, hoping that this will endear her to Demetrius. She plans to follow him into the wood when he pursues Hermia.

In the next scene, a group of working men, or mechanicals, is assembled at Quince's house. The group includes Quince, the carpenter; Snug, the joiner; Bottom, the weaver; Flute, the bellows-maker; Snout, the tinker; and Starveling, the tailor. The men are discussing their plan to put on a play (*"The most lamentable comedy and most cruel death of Pyramus and Thisby"* [I.ii.11-12]) for Theseus and Hippolyta in honor of their wedding. Quince announces which part each man will play, with each announcement giving way to some discussion. The group agrees to meet in the wood to rehearse.

Act II:

A fairy and Puck, a sprite also known as Robin Goodfellow, are discussing the affairs of Oberon and Titania, king and queen of the fairies. As Puck explains, the royal couple is currently arguing over a changeling (a child fairies have exchanged for another) who Titania has as her attendant and who the jealous Oberon wants as his own attendant. The queen refuses to yield the child to the king. Oberon and Titania enter and argue over the matter Puck has just described. When Titania leaves, Oberon calls for Puck. The king instructs Puck to find a certain flower, and Puck leaves on his mission. Oberon describes the purpose of Puck's errand: he (Oberon) plans to use the juice of this flower on Titania. When the flower is squeezed into her eyes as she sleeps, she will fall in love with the very next creature she spies when she awakens. When she is so entranced, Oberon plans to take the changeling from her and then use another plant to remove the spell. At this moment, Demetrius enters, followed by Helena. Demetrius expresses his frustration with his inability to find Hermia and with Helena's continued pursuit of him. He leaves, and Helena follows. Puck returns with the flower, and Oberon gives some of it to Puck and tells him to use it on Demetrius, who Oberon describes as being dressed in Athenian clothes. The king takes the rest of the flower to use on Titania.

In the next scene, Titania asks her fairies to sing her to sleep, which they do. Oberon enters and squeezes the flower on Titania's eyelids. Lysander

and Hermia appear, having lost their way in the wood. They decide to stop and rest. After they have fallen asleep, Puck sees the two of them, and, thinking Lysander to be the Athenian Oberon had spoken of, squeezes the flower onto Lysander's eyes. Helena, who has been chasing Demetrius but can go no further because she is out of breath, sees the sleeping Lysander. Concerned, she wakes him. As Lysander wakes up, he falls immediately in love with Helena and says that he no longer loves Hermia. Thinking he is mocking her, Helena runs off, and Lysander follows. Hermia wakes up, calling out for Lysander. When he does not answer, she goes off to look for him.

Act III:

Quince, Snug, Bottom, Flute, Snout, and Starveling discuss their upcoming performance. There is some concern that some of the violence in the drama—for example, Pyramus drawing his sword to kill himself—might frighten the female audience members. The men decide to write a prologue to explain that none of the dangers in the play, including the appearance of a lion (to be played by Snug), are real. They also decide that two aspects of the play—the moonshine by which Pyramus and Thisby meet, and the wall which separates them—should be played by people, rather than constructed as props. These things decided, the group proceeds with its rehearsal. At this point, Puck enters and watches, commenting on the comical proceedings. He then mischievously transforms Bottom (who has been playing Pyramus and getting his lines wrong) by changing Bottom's head into the head of an ass. Bottom's friends flee in fright. Bottom thinks they are playing a trick on him, and he begins singing to show them that he is not afraid. Titania, who has been sleeping nearby, awakes to the sound of Bottom's singing and falls in love with him. She calls four of her fairies (Peaseblossom, Cobweb, Moth, and Mustardseed), and asks them to attend to Bottom.

Meanwhile, Oberon wonders if Titania has yet awakened. Puck enters and explains that the queen is in love with "a monster" (III.ii.6). Puck tells Oberon of how he came upon the group of players at their rehearsal, how he put an ass's head on Bottom, and how Titania woke up and fell in love with the transformed Bottom. Oberon seems pleased: "This falls out better than I could devise" (III.ii.35). The king then asks Puck about "the Athenian" and Puck assures him that he has taken care of that as well. At this moment, Demetrius and Hermia enter and Oberon points out that this is the Athenian he's been talking about. Puck replies ''This is the woman; but not this the man'' (III.ii.42). Hermia suspects that Demetrius has killed Lysander. Demetrius, although he speaks scornfully of Lysander, says he has not killed him, and as far as he knows, Lysander is not dead. Hermia departs, and Demetrius lays down to sleep. Oberon assesses the situation and instructs Puck to find Helena, while he places the juice of the flower on Demetrius's eyes. Puck returns saying that Helena is near and is with Lysander. Lysander is trying to convince the disbelieving Helena of his love. Demetrius, under the spell of the love juice, awakens and proclaims his love for Helena. ''O spite! O hell!'' (III.ii.145) Helena exclaims in frustration. She is convinced that the two men are playing a cruel joke on her. When Hermia enters to find Lysander espousing his love of Helena and his hatred of her, Helena thinks Hermia is in on the joke. Hurt deeply by what she perceives as a mockery of her love for Demetrius, Helena verbally attacks Hermia, asking if she has forgotten their lifelong friendship. The argument between the four of them quickly accelerates until they are all insulting one another. Lysander and Demetrius leave, planning to fight for Helena. Hermia tells Helena that the whole mess is Helena's fault. Both women run off.

Oberon then blames the situation on Puck, who maintains his innocence in the affair. Puck reminds the king of his instructions to anoint the eyes of an Athenian, and that is exactly what Puck has done. Oberon then instructs Puck to bring a fog down on the forest and to taunt Demetrius and Lysander until both fall asleep. Then, Oberon instructs, Puck is to crush an herb over Lysander's eyes that will undo the magic that made him love Helena. The king intends to find and take Titania's changeling and then release his queen from her love of the ass-headed Bottom. Puck follows Oberon's orders and before long all four lovers are asleep, and the juice from the herb has been applied to Lysander's eyes.

Act IV:

Titania and Bottom are seated together, and she is caressing him lovingly, as Bottom instructs the fairies to scratch his head. After the fairies depart, the two fall asleep. Oberon tells Puck that he has successfully retrieved the changeling. He then releases Titania from her spell and instructs Puck to remove the ass head from Bottom. While Bottom still sleeps and as the morning comes, Puck, Oberon, and Titania depart.

Theseus, Hippolyta, and Egeus, in the woods for a hunt, come upon Lysander, Hermia, Demetrius, and Helena. The four awaken and describe what they recall of how they came to be in the wood. Demetrius reveals his newfound love of Helena. Egeus demands that Lysander be punished for his attempted elopement with Hermia. Hearing all this, Theseus then announces that the two couples shall be wed along with him and Hippolyta. They all exit, with the lovers discussing the night's events. Bottom, too, awakens and goes off to find his friends. Meanwhile, Quince, Flute, Snout, and Starveling wonder where Bottom is. When he appears, the group leaves for the palace where they will soon perform their unrehearsed play.

Act V:

Theseus and Hippolyta discuss what has happened to the four young lovers, with the duke discounting the existence of fairies and attributing such notions to the imagination. The lovers enter and the group contemplates how to occupy the time between supper and bedtime. Philostrate appears with a list of possible entertainments, from which Theseus selects the play about Pyramus and Thisby.

The players perform a somewhat comical and ludicrous rendition of the tragedy, with their audience commenting frequently on the performance. When the play ends and all depart, Puck, Oberon, Titania, and the fairies enter and Oberon bestows a blessing on the three sleeping couples. Puck ends the play with an apologetic speech, asking the theater audience, if they have been offended by the performance, to imagine that they have been asleep and that the play was just a dream.

Modern Connections

While there are many things in *A Midsummer Night's Dream* that modern audiences enjoy about the play, the theme of love is one that many people, from Shakespeare's original audiences to modern audiences, can relate to.

The four young lovers in the play—Hermia, Lysander, Helena, and Demetrius—all seem to feel love very deeply, even before the fairies work their magic. For Lysander's love, Hermia is willing to go against her father's wishes (he wants her to marry Demetrius). Both Hermia and Lysander would rather run away and risk the punishment of Athenian law if they are caught. Helena, in love with Demetrius, betrays her friendship with Hermia with the hope of gaining a little of Demetrius's favor. She hopes that in telling Demetrius of Hermia's plan and her whereabouts, he will thank her, and that perhaps this attention will lead to something more. Demetrius has pursued Hermia into the wood, and is almost insane from not finding her (''And here am I, and wode [mad] within this wood, / Because I cannot meet my Hermia'' [II.i.192-93]).

This love which seems so strong, however, is weak in two ways: for the men, it appears to be fickle; and for the women, it comes between them as lifelong friends. Lysander and Demetrius are both affected by the love potion of Oberon, applied by Puck to their eyelids. Lysander, who so deeply loved Hermia, suddenly loves Helena. Not only is he completely enamored with her, but he now violently despises Hermia. He ''repent[s] / The tedious minutes'' he has spent with her (II.ii.111-12). Similarly, Demetrius, who had also loved Hermia and so venomously despised Helena (''I am sick when I do look on thee'' he told her in II.i.212), suddenly refers to her as ''goddess, nymph, perfect, divine'' (III.ii.137). The thing that transforms the affections of Lysander and Demetrius in the play is a magical potion; in real life, such seemingly deep emotions are also easily transformed, especially among the young. Like the young lovers in the play, young people in love today are still finding their own identities. Lysander, Demetrius, Helena, and Hermia, in fact, do not really seem to have *any* identifying characteristics. As young people are still finding out who *they* are, what appeals to them in a romantic sense is likely to change as they themselves change.

Helena and Hermia, on the other hand, remain constant in the sense that they each love the same person throughout the play. However, they jeopardize their own friendship as they strive to hold on to the young men they love. Helena, as previously mentioned, betrays Hermia when she tells Demetrius of Hermia's planned elopement to Lysander. Later, when Helena becomes convinced that Hermia is in on what she thinks is Lysander's and Demetrius's cruel joke, she accuses Hermia of betraying their friendship. She asks, ''O, is all forgot? / All schooldays friendship, childhood innocence?'' (III.ii.201-02). Hermia denies that she has scorned her friend, but becomes so increasingly dismayed by Lysander's professed love for Helena and hatred for her, and by Helena's accusations, that she finally lashes back at Helena saying ''I am not yet so low / But that my

nails can reach unto thine eyes'' (III.ii.297-98). The bickering ceases when Hermia blames the whole confused mess on Helena, after which Helena runs off. How often is this scene replayed in modern times? Do today's teenagers, and adults, let romantic relationships come between friendships?

There is another example of love in the play: the bewitched love between Titania and the transformed Bottom. Titania falls in love with the ass-headed Bottom. Having fallen in love with and adored this creature, Titania awakens from this love, and from sleep, feeling a little foolish for having been so blinded by love: ''O, how mine eyes do loathe his visage now!'' (IV.i.77). Again, how many times is this scene replayed in modern times? Do people today fall in love with people who aren't what they seem to be? And don't we feel a little like Titania did when we see what they really are?

The other romantic relationship in the play (aside from that of Pyramus and Thisby, portrayed by Bottom and company) is that of Theseus and Hippolyta. While we don't really get to see the two interact very much during the course of the play, there relationship does not change, perhaps attesting to its stability. Critics have also maintained that the relationship between Theseus and Hippolyta represents love balanced by reason, in contrast to the inconstant, passionate love of the four young people.

Shakespeare presents a variety of views about love in *A Midsummer Night's Dream*, and it is not clear which conception of love he supports. Perhaps the point is that love is different things to different people, and may affect us in any number of ways, depending on where we are in our lives.

Characters

Attendants:

Attendants appear in several scenes during the play, and are sometimes mentioned in the stage directions as ''others'' or as Theseus's train. In IV.i, Theseus addresses attendants directly, instructing them to do various tasks. The attendants have no speaking parts.

Bottom:

Nick Bottom, the weaver, first appears in I.ii, with the other mechanicals, or clowns (Quince,

Snug, Flute, Snout, and Starveling), as they are sometimes called. It is often noted that the mechanicals' names reflect their work. ''Bottom,'' critics explain, refers to the bottom, or skein, around which yarn is wound. Bottom directs Quince to tell the group which play they will be performing and to tell everyone which parts they will be playing. Quince assigns the role of Pyramus to Bottom. Bottom seems enthusiastic about playing this part, and he volunteers also to play the role of Thisby, and that of the lion. Quince convinces him, however, that he ''can play no part but Pyramus'' (I.ii.85).

Bottom appears again III.i as the group of mechanicals gathers in the wood to rehearse. He tells Quince that the play needs a prologue to explain that the dangers in the play (Pyramus drawing his sword to kill himself, and the lion) are not real. After the group decides that the moonshine by which Pyramus and Thisby meet, and the wall which separates the lovers must be played by people, the group proceeds with their rehearsal. Bottom bungles his first line, and Quince corrects him. Flute, playing Thisby to Bottom's Pyramus, doesn't do much better, to Quince's dismay. Puck, who has been watching, intervenes to change Bottom's head into the head of an ass. When the others see this, the run off, frightened. Bottom thinks they are playing a trick on him, trying to scare him, so he begins singing to show them he his not afraid. His song is interrupted by Titania, who has just woken up, having been anointed with the love juice by Oberon. Titania swears she is in love with Bottom, a man with the head of an ass, and he replies ''Methinks, mistress, you should have little reason for that'' (III.ii.142-43). When Titania tells Bottom that he is both wise and beautiful, he assures her that he is not. Nevertheless, he seems to accept her affection, and follows her with little objection.

Bottom is next seen seated upon Titania's ''flow'ry bed'' as she caresses him, adorns his head with flowers, and kisses his ''fair large ears'' (IV.i.1-4). Bottom is busy instructing the fairies to fetch him honey and scratch his ears. When Bottom and Titania fall asleep, Oberon reverses the effect of the love juice on Titania. As Titania wakes up saying that she thought she had been in love with an ass, she sees Bottom lying next her and exclaims ''O, how mine eyes do loathe his visage now!'' (IV.i.78). Puck then removes the ass's head from Bottom. When Bottom awakens, he determines that he has had a ''rare vision'' (IV.i.205) and he vows to get Quince to write it down for him. He then finds his

friends and they leave for the palace to perform *Pyramus and Thisby.*

Act V is comprised primarily of the performance of the Pyramus and Thisby play. Bottom, as Pyramus, and the rest of the group frequently misspeak their lines and mispronounce the names of the legendary lovers referred to in the play. Bottom also interacts with his audience (Theseus, Hippolyta, and the four young lovers). For example, when Theseus comments on the speech of the Wall, Bottom responds, telling him what is about to happen and that ''You shall see it / fall pat as I told you'' (V.i.186-87). Although the on-stage audience scoffs a bit at the performance (for example, Hippolyta says ''This is the silliest stuff that ever I heard'' [V.i.210]), as the performance progresses, they make some positive comments as well. Hippolyta, in fact, seems touched by Bottom's performance: ''Beshrew my heart, but I pity the man'' (V.i.290) she says as Pyramus comes to think that his beloved Thisby is dead. As the play ends, with Bottom and Flute lying on the stage representing the dead Pyramus and Thisby, Demetrius comments that the Wall is left to help Moonshine and Lion bury the dead. Bottom then sits up and says, ''No, I assure you, the wall is down that parted their fathers. Will it please you to see the epilogue . . . ?'' (V.i.351-54). Theseus declines the epilogue.

Bottom is considered by many commentators to be the central figure of the play. He is admired for his humor and his imagination. It has been noted that he seems to represent the common experience of humanity. Additionally, Bottom is the only character in the play who can see and interact directly with the fairy world. And when he wakes up and has been returned to his former self, he acknowledges that something has happened to him and it would be foolish to try to explain it: ''I have had a most / rare vision. I have had a dream, past the wit of / man to say what dream it was. Man is but an ass, / if he go about [t'] expound this dream'' (IV.i.204-07). In fact, it is this speech, referred to as the awakening speech or soliloquy, that intrigues many critics. The speech is often argued to be indicative of Shakespeare's acknowledgment of the possibility of spiritual life beyond our everyday existence. The speech is also said to demonstrate both nature's and love's inexplicability. Additionally, Bottom's lively involvement in the Pyramus and Thisby performance has been cited as proof of Bottom's ability to understand the imaginative process of art. This ability, some argue, sets Bottom apart from the other mortals in the play who don't seem to share this understanding.

Cobweb:

Cobweb is one of Titania's fairies. Cobweb is introduced to Bottom in III.i, and in IV.i, Bottom instructs Cobweb to kill a bumble bee and retrieve its "honey-bag" (IV.i.10-13).

Demetrius:

Demetrius first appears in I.i with Egeus, Hermia, and Lysander. Egeus speaks highly of Demetrius, calling him "my noble lord" (I.i.24), and telling Theseus that it is Demetrius who has his consent to marry Hermia, Egeus's daughter. After Hermia has expressed her desire to marry Lysander, and the duke has outlined her choices (death, nunnery, or marriage to Demetrius), Demetrius asks Hermia to "Relent" and Lysander to "yield / Thy crazed title to my certain right" (I.i.91-92). Lysander replies that Demetrius has in fact "Made love to ... Helena, / And won her soul" (I.i.107-08). Theseus admits that he had heard of this, and meant to speak to Demetrius about it. Nevertheless, he holds Hermia to her father's will. It is not clear why Demetrius transferred his affections from Helena to Hermia, but Helena seems obsessed with getting him back.

When Demetrius learns from Helena of Hermia's and Lysander's plans, he pursues his beloved, and Helena pursues him. Oberon overhears the conversation between Helena and Demetrius, in which she repeatedly professes her love for him. After Demetrius ungently discourages her, he runs off. Oberon then reveals his plan to have Puck anoint Demetrius's eyes with the love juice, so that Demetrius will return Helena's love. Puck instead finds Lysander and puts the juice of the flower on his eyes. As it happens, Helena, who has been chasing Demetrius but can pursue no longer, comes upon Lysander and wakes him. Lysander then falls in love with Helena. In an attempt to rectify the situation, Oberon places the love juice on Demetrius's eyes, so that when he wakes he will indeed be in love with Helena. And this is exactly what happens. Demetrius and Lysander are now both in love with Helena; Hermia does not understand why Lysander now hates her; and Helena is convinced the three of them are playing a cruel joke on her. Oberon then arranges, with Puck's assistance, to finally right what has gone wrong by placing an herb on Lysander's eyes which will reverse the effects of the love juice, thus restoring Lysander's love for Hermia. Once this transformation is complete, Theseus approves of both couples

> **Titania swears she is in love with Bottom, a man with the head of an ass, and he replies 'Methinks, mistress, you should have little reason for that' (III.ii.142-43)."**

and announces that they will all be married. In the last act, Demetrius and the others comment on the Pyramus and Thisby play as it is being performed.

Critics generally agree that the four young lovers are practically interchangeable; it is nearly impossible to distinguish one from the other. Some attribute this lack of characterization to Shakespeare's own inexperience as a playwright. Most commentators, however, argue that this lack of individualization is central to the plot, that Shakespeare did this on purpose. The young Athenians may seem indistinguishable to the audience, but as objects of love to one another they are seen as sheer perfection. Arguably, it is the transformative power of love that makes four almost identical people seem so different and so wonderful in each other's eyes. On the other hand, Shakespeare may have painted the young lovers as he did in order highlight the folly, capriciousness, and inconsistency of their love.

Duke of Athens (Theseus, Duke of Athens):

See Theseus

Egeus:

Egeus is Hermia's father. He appears in I.i, complaining to Theseus that his daughter will not marry Demetrius. Egeus explains to the duke that Lysander has "bewitch'd" (I.i.27) Hermia with his poetry and his moonlight serenades, among other things. Finally, Egeus comes to the point and makes his request of Theseus: "As she is mine," Egeus says, "I may dispose of her; / Which shall be either to this gentleman [Demetrius], / Or to her death, according to our law ..." (I.i.42-44). After Theseus gives Hermia another option, to enter a nunnery, he suggests she follow her father's wishes and marry Demetrius. Later, in the company of Theseus and Hippolyta, Egeus finds his daughter sleeping in the

> **Egeus explains to the duke that Lysander has 'bewitch'd' (I.i.27) Hermia with his poetry and his moonlight serenades, among other things."**

wood. Nearby are Lysander, Demetrius, and Helena. When Lysander awakens and confesses that he and Hermia were in the process of fleeing Athens to elope, Egeus demands that Lysander be punished: "I beg the law, the law, upon his head" (IV.i.155). But Theseus does not back him this time; instead, he insists that the two couples be wed alongside him and Hippolyta.

Fairies:

The fairies appear in several scenes, primarily as attendants of Oberon and Titania. Four of the fairies are individually identified as Cobweb, Moth, Peaseblossom, and Mustardseed and they serve Titania, and later, Bottom. In II.i, one unnamed fairy converses with Puck. In II.ii, Oberon and Titania appear each attended by a train of fairies. Later in the same scene, several fairies sing Titania to sleep at her request. In III.i, the four named fairies appear to be introduced to Bottom, and they appear again in IV.i to do Bottom's bidding (scratch his head and fetch honey). At the play's end, the fairies appear, identified as Oberon's and Hippolyta's train, to sing and dance.

Flute:

Francis Flute, a bellows-maker, is one of a group which is often referred to as the clowns, or the mechanicals. This group also includes Bottom, Quince, Snug, Snout, and Starveling. It is frequently noted that the names of these common laborers reflect the work that they do. "Flute," critics explain, suggests the fluted bellows of church organs that Flute would be likely to repair. In I.ii, Flute appears with the rest of the mechanicals, as Quince the carpenter is assigning the roles in the Pyramus and Thisby play. Quince assigns Flute the role of Thisby. Apparently unfamiliar with the play, Flute asks "What is Thisby? A wand'ring knight?" (I.ii.45), to which Quince replies that Thisby is the lady Pyramus is in love with. Flute objects, arguing

that he's got a beard coming in. Quince will have none of it; he tells Flute to play the part wearing a mask, and that he may "speak as small as you will" (I.ii.50). Bottom offers to play the role of Thisby, and offers a sampling of the voice he would use to do so. But Quince insists that Bottom is Pyramus and Flute is Thisby.

Flute appears again in III.i, rehearsing with the rest of the mechanicals, and getting his lines wrong, much to Quince's dismay. He runs off after Puck has given Bottom the ass's head. In IV.ii, Flute seems overjoyed at Bottom's return, and he praises profusely Bottom's acting abilities.

In V.i, Flute appears as Thisby. With the other players, Flute comically blunders his lines, frequently getting wrong the names of the classical references in the play.

Goodfellow (Robin Goodfellow):
See Puck

Helena:

In the first scene of the play, we are introduced to Helena's problem: she desperately loves Demetrius but he is in love with her friend Hermia. Both Lysander and Helena herself reveal that Demetrius was at one time involved with Helena. Lysander tells Theseus that Demetrius "Made love to . . . Helena, / And won her soul" (I.i.107-08). Helena says that before Demetrius looked upon Hermia, "He hail'd down oaths that he was only mine" (I.i.242-43). In an attempt to win back some of Demetrius's affection, Helena tells him of Hermia's plan to meet in the wood and elope with Lysander. According to Helena's plan, Demetrius pursues Hermia, and Helena follows Demetrius. Continuing to scorn her, Demetrius runs off. In the midst of her pursuit, Helena comes upon the sleeping Lysander, who has mistakenly been anointed with the love juice by Puck. When Lysander wakes up and sees Helena, he falls in love with her instantly. Meanwhile, Demetrius has also been affected by the love potion, and also falls in love with Helena. As the two men vie for Helena's attention, Hermia appears and is completely confused by Lysander's sudden scorn of her. Seeing all this, Helena becomes convinced that the others are mocking her. She asks Hermia if she has forgotten their friendship (III.ii.201-02), apparently forgetting that she herself betrayed the friendship by revealing Hermia's plans to Demetrius. Soon, however, Puck and Oberon rectify the situation by reversing the affect of the love juice on Lysander, thereby removing his love of Helena and restoring his love for Hermia. Theseus announces that the couples will be wed. In Act V, Helena watches the Pyramus and Thisby performance and is later blessed, along with the others, by Oberon.

Critics generally agree that the four young lovers are practically interchangeable; it is nearly impossible to distinguish one from the other. Some attribute this lack of characterization to Shakespeare's own inexperience as a playwright. Most commentators, however, argue that this lack of individualization is central to the plot, that Shakespeare did this on purpose. The young Athenians may seem indistinguishable to the audience, but as objects of love to one another they are seen as sheer perfection. Arguably, it is the transformative power of love that makes four almost identical people seem so different and so wonderful in each other's eyes. On the other hand, Shakespeare may have painted the young lovers as he did in order highlight the folly, capriciousness, and inconsistency of their love.

Hermia:

Hermia's dilemma is introduced early in the first scene of the play, as her father Egeus complains to the duke that she refuses to marry Demetrius. She maintains that she is in love with Lysander, who she argues is as worthy as Demetrius. Claiming that she does not know ''by what power I am made bold'' (I.i.59), she asks Theseus what will happen to her if she does not comply with her father's wishes by marrying Demetrius. Theseus gives her two options: death or lifelong imprisonment in a nunnery. Remarking that she would rather live in a convent all her life than be with Demetrius, Hermia remains constant in her love of Lysander, and later quickly agrees to his plan to escape Athens and elope. As they are discussing this plan, Helena appears, lamenting that Demetrius loves Hermia. Hermia tells her friend to ''Take comfort; he no more shall see my face; / Lysander and myself will fly from this place'' (I.i.202-03). Helena uses this information in an attempt to gain favor with Demetrius.

When Lysander and Hermia become lost in the woods, he suggests they stop and rest, and Hermia virtuously insists that they do not lie next to one another. She awakens calling out to Lysander after dreaming that ''a serpent eat [ate] my heart away, / And you sate smiling at his cruel prey'' (III.i.149-

> Quince assigns Flute the role of Thisby. Apparently unfamiliar with the play, Flute asks 'What is Thisby? A wand'ring knight?' (I.ii.45), to which Quince replies that Thisby is the lady Pyramus is in love with. Flute objects, arguing that he's got a beard coming in.''

50). When Lysander does not answer, Hermia fears the worst and sets out to find him. When she does, she is confused to find that he claims love for Helena and hatred of her. She asks:

> What? Can you do me greater harm than hate?
> Hate me, wherefore? O me, what news, my love!
> Am not I Hermia? Are not you Lysander?
> (III.ii.271-73)

After the four lovers insult each other and nearly resort to physical violence against each other, Oberon and Puck resolve everything. Lysander's love for Hermia is restored, and Theseus soon appears to give his blessing to the couple, much to Egeus's dismay. In the last act, Helena watches the play about Pyramus and Thisby and is later blessed, along with the others, by Oberon.

Critics generally agree that the four young lovers are practically interchangeable; it is nearly impossible to distinguish one from the other. Some attribute this lack of characterization to Shakespeare's own inexperience as a playwright. Most commentators, however, argue that this lack of individualization is central to the plot, that Shakespeare did this on purpose. The young Athenians may seem indistinguishable to the audience, but as objects of love to one another they are seen as sheer perfection. Arguably, it is the transformative power of love that makes four almost identical people seem so different and so wonderful in each other's eyes. On the other hand, Shakespeare may have painted the young lovers as he did in order highlight the folly, capriciousness, and inconsistency of their love.

> **Both Lysander and Helena herself reveal that Demetrius was at one time involved with Helena. Lysander tells Theseus that Demetrius 'Made love to . . . Helena, / And won her soul' (I.i.107-08). Helena says that before Demetrius looked upon Hermia, 'He hail'd down oaths that he was only mine' (I.i.242-43).**

Hippolyta:

The play opens as Hippolyta and Theseus are discussing their upcoming marriage. Theseus comments that he

> . . . woo'd thee [Hippolyta] with my sword,
> And won thy love doing thee injuries;
> But I will wed thee in another key,
> With pomp, triumph, and with revelling.
>
> (I.i.16-19)

Theseus is referring to the fact that he conquered Hippolyta in his war with the Amazons. Hippolyta's only lines in this act are in response to Theseus's comment that they will be wed in "Four happy days" (I.i.2). She says simply, in a few lines, that the time will pass quickly. Hippolyta does not appear again until IV.i. She accompanies Theseus and others on a hunt in the wood, and she fondly remembers a moment from her past as queen of the Amazons when she was hunting "with Hercules and Cadmus" (IV.i.112). She comments on the musical quality of the baying of the hounds on that hunt, that she had "never heard / So musical a discord, such sweet thunder" (IV.i.116-17). Theseus then praises his own hounds, when Egeus stumbles upon the four sleeping young lovers.

Hippolyta appears again in Act V, first discussing with Theseus, the story of the young lovers, commenting that it was "strange and admirable" (V.i.27). During the performance of *Pyramus and Thisby*, Hippolyta makes various remarks throughout the play, sometimes scoffing ("This is the silliest stuff that ever I heard" [V.i.210]) and some-times praising ("Well shone, Moon. Truly, the moon shines / with a good grace" [V.i.267-68]). In the end, she and Theseus are blessed, along with the other couples, by Oberon.

Many commentators see Hippolyta's and Theseus's relationship as providing a framework for the dramatic action of the play, given that the couple only appears in the beginning and the end of the play. Additionally, this relationship undergoes no change during the course of the play and argu-ably represents stability and consistency, in direct contrast to the somewhat capricious relationships of the young lovers. Some commentators, however, have observed Hippolyta's relative silence through-out Act I of the play. They believe that this silence does not reflect Hippolyta's happy acceptance of her marriage to Theseus. Rather, her reticence sug-gests that she has been coerced into the marriage (remember, she *has* been taken captive), and that she seems to regard it with resignation and sadness.

King of the Fairies:
See Oberon

Lion:
See Snug

Lysander:

Lysander first appears in I.i with his love Hermia, her father Egeus, and his competitor for Hermia's love, Demetrius. Egeus accuses Lysander of be-witching his daughter, of writing poems for her, exchanging love tokens with her, singing to her by moonlight at her window. After Hermia is given the choice of death or imprisonment in a convent if she refuses to marry Demetrius, Lysander pleads his own worth to Egeus: "I am, my lord, as well deriv'd as he, / As well possess'd; my love is more than his; / My fortunes every way as fairly rank'd" (I.i.99-101). Furthermore, he accuses Demetrius of having an affair with Helena, in order to demonstrate Demetrius's inconsistency. None of this changes Egeus's mind or Theseus's decision. Lysander then proposes to Hermia that they flee Athenian law and secretly elope, and Hermia agrees to the plan.

After losing their way in the wood, Lysander suggests to Hermia that they stop and rest, and tries to convince Hermia to let him lie next to her: "One turf shall serve as pillow for us both, / One heart, one bed, two bosoms, and one troth" (II.ii.41-42). Hermia virtuously denies him this, so they sleep some ways apart from each other. At this point Puck appears, and mistaking Lysander for Demetrius, squeezes the juice of the flower on his eyes. When Helena, pausing in her pursuit of Demetrius, happens upon Lysander, she wakes him and he falls in love with her. Confused, she flees and he follows. Meanwhile, Demetrius has also been affected by the love potion, and has also fallen in love with Helena. When the four Athenians find each other, Demetrius and Lysander are professing love for Helena and hatred for Hermia; Helena thinks they are all cruelly mocking her; and Hermia is confused by Lysander's rejection of her and hurt by Helena's verbal attacks. Before long, Oberon and Puck sort things out, and Lysander's love for Helena is erased, and his love for Hermia restored. To Egeus's dismay, Theseus approves of both couples and announces that they will be married. In Act V, Lysander comments on the performance of *Pyramus and Thisby*, and is later blessed, along with the others, by Oberon.

Critics generally agree that the four young lovers are practically interchangeable; it is nearly impossible to distinguish one from the other. Some attribute this lack of characterization to Shakespeare's own inexperience as a playwright. Most commentators, however, argue that this lack of individualization is central to the plot, that Shakespeare did this on purpose. The young Athenians may seem indistinguishable to the audience, but as objects of love to one another they are seen as sheer perfection. Arguably, it is the transformative power of love that makes four almost identical people seem so different and so wonderful in each other's eyes. On the other hand, Shakespeare may have painted the young lovers as he did in order highlight the folly, capriciousness, and inconsistency of their love.

Moonshine:

See Starveling

Moth:

Moth is one of Titania's fairies. Moth is introduced to Bottom in III.i, and in IV.i, Moth appears with Cobweb, Mustardseed, and Peaseblossom, but unlike these other fairies, Moth is not asked to do Bottom's bidding.

Mustardseed:

Mustardseed is one of Titania's fairies and is introduced to Bottom in III.i. In IV.i, Bottom instructs Mustardseed to help Cobweb in the scratching of Bottom's head. (Cobweb, however, has been sent to fetch some honey for Bottom, and it is

> **During the performance of *Pyramus and Thisby*, Hippolyta makes various remarks throughout the play, sometimes scoffing ('This is the silliest stuff that ever I heard' [V.i.210]) and sometimes praising ('Well shone, Moon. Truly, the moon shines / with a good grace' [V.i.267-68]).''**

Peaseblossom who has initially been asked to scratch Bottom's head.)

Oberon:

Oberon, the king of the fairies, first appears in II.ii. He is arguing with his queen, Titania, over a changeling (a child exchanged by fairies for another) who she possesses and he desires. When she refuses to give up the changeling, Oberon devises a plan to steal it from her. He sends Puck off to find a certain flower, whose juices when squeezed on the eyes of Titania will make her fall in love with the next creature she sees. Oberon plans to take the child when Titnania is so spellbound. After outlining this plan, Oberon observes Helena's pursuit of Demetrius and his scornful dismissal of her. Oberon decides to use the flower to make Demetrius love Helena, and instructs Puck to find a man wearing Athenian garments (Demetrius) and place the flower's juice on his eyes. Meanwhile, Oberon finds the sleeping Titania and squeezes the flower on her eyelids, hoping that she will ''Wake when some vile thing is near'' (II.ii.34).

Oberon next appears in III.ii. He listens to Puck's report: Titania has fallen in love with a ''monster'' (III.ii.6) whom Puck has created. Puck then relates the tale of how he came upon Bottom and the others, and how he transformed Bottom. When asked about the Athenian, Puck replies that he has taken care of him as well. But Puck and Oberon almost immediately learn that Puck has *not* anointed Demetrius. Oberon resolves to fix the situation by placing some of the love juice on Demetrius's eyes. The four lovers together, Oberon

> **After Hermia is given the choice of death or imprisonment in a convent if she refuses to marry Demetrius, Lysander pleads his own worth to Egeus: 'I am, my lord, as well deriv'd as he, / As well possess'd; my love is more than his; / My fortunes every way as fairly rank'd' (I.i.99-101)."**

sees that he must reverse the effect of the love juice on Lysander. Assessing the mess, Oberon accuses Puck, "This is thy negligence. Still thou mistak'st, / Or else commit'st thy knaveries willfully" (III.ii.345-46). Puck denies that he purposefully placed the love juice on Lysander's eyes instead of Demetrius's. The two finally gather the lovers together, and undo what Puck has done to Lysander, so that Lysander's love for Hermia is restored. Soon after, Oberon reveals to Puck how Titania gave up the changeling to him. Instructing Puck to remove the ass's head from Bottom, Oberon first restores Titania. The couple appears once more, with the rest of the fairies and with Puck at the play's end, as Oberon blesses Theseus and Hippolyta, Lysander and Hermia, and Demetrius and Helena.

Oberon is usually seen be audiences to be a benevolent spirit, and critics have noted that he is associated in the play with light and with dawn, even though as Puck reminds him, he is part of the fairy world, and his activity is limited to the night. When Puck says that they must work quickly to complete their plans because morning is approaching, Oberon replies: "But we are spirits of another sort. / I with the Morning's love have oft made sport . . ." (III.ii.388-89), and goes on do affiliate himself with the rising sun. Other critics have cited Oberon's wish that Titania will awaken and fall in love with some "vile thing" (II.ii.34) as evidence that he does have some malevolent tendencies.

Additionally, Oberon is typically associated with order in the play. He resolves the play's disorder, and some critics note that this can only happen after his relationship with Titania is re-

stored. It has also been argued that the reappearance of Oberon and the fairies at the play's end emphasizes their divine power as they bless the mortals, and that this providential order contrasts with the ineffectual nature of the mortals.

Peaseblossom:

Peaseblossom is one of Titania's fairies. Peaseblossom, along with the other named fairies, is introduced to Bottom in III.i. In IV.i, Bottom instructs Peaseblossom to scratch his head.

Philostrate:

Philostrate is identified as Duke Theseus's Master of Revels. In I.i, Theseus instructs Philostrate to "Stir up the Athenian youth to merriments" (I.i.12) and generally to promote a festive atmosphere in Athens, in anticipation of the duke's wedding to Hippolyta. Later, in V.i, Philostrate presents Theseus with a list of possible entertainments for the evening. When Theseus asks about the description listed for the Pyramus and Thisby play (" 'A tedious brief scene of young Pyramus / And his love Thisby; very tragical mirth' " [V.i.56-57]), Philostrate explains the "tedious" and "tragic" nature of the performance. He also tells the duke that the play is to be performed by common working men "Which never labor'd in their minds till now" (V.i.72), and attempts to discourage the duke from seeing the play. Theseus, however, insists, and instructs Philostrate to bring in the players.

Prologue:

See Quince

Puck (also known as Robin Goodfellow):

Puck, a sprite also known as Robin Goodfellow, first appears in II.ii, as he and a fairy discuss the troubles Oberon and Titania are having. The fairy gives us some indication of Puck's character as she describes how Puck "frights the maidens of the villagery" (II.ii.35) among other activities. When Titania refuses to give up the changeling Oberon wants, he comes up with a plan to steal the child, and enlists Puck's aid in doing so. Puck's first task is to retrieve the very special flower, which he does quickly. Meanwhile, Oberon has learned of the trouble between Demetrius and Helena, and he instructs Puck to use some of the flower on Demetrius (described as wearing Athenian clothes) so that he may return Helena's love. But Puck mistakes

Lysander for Demetrius, and puts the juice on his eyes. Soon after, Puck comes upon Bottom, Quince, and the other mechanicals, who are rehearsing their play. He changes Bottom's head into that of an ass, thereby scaring away the other members of the company, who he then proceeds to taunt and chase through the wood. Before long, Bottom and Titania find each other, and Puck reports all of this to Oberon, in III.ii.

At this time, Puck's error (his mistaking Lysander for Demetrius) is revealed and Oberon decides to place the juice of the flower on Demetrius's eyes to rectify the situation. Puck is instructed to lead Helena toward Demetrius, which he does, and Lysander (now in love with Helena) follows. Puck is delighted at the entertainment that is to ensue as the four young lovers with mixed up emotions come together: "Shall we their fond pageant see? / Lord, what fools these mortals be!" (III.ii.114-15). Oberon accuses Puck of deliberately causing all this trouble, an accusation which Puck denies. The two finally successfully resolve this situation the young lovers are in, and the one involving Titania and Bottom. After Oberon has taken the changeling from Titania, she is released from her spell, and Bottom from his.

Puck appears at the end of the play and offers an apology to the theater audience for the performance. "If we shadows have offended," he offers, "Think but this, and all is mended, / that you have but slumb'red here / While these visions did appear. / And this weak and idle theme, / No more yielding but a dream . . ." (V.i.423-28).

Puck is seen by some to be simply mischievous. Others view him as frightening and dangerous, noting that he is associated with darkness, whereas Oberon is associated with light and the dawn. In II.ii.382-87, Puck urges that he and Oberon work quickly, as their activities must take place under the cover of the night. Oberon's reply contrasts with Puck's speech, as he claims that they are "spirits of another sort" and that he (Oberon) "with the Morning's love have oft made sport" (III.ii.388-89). Additionally, it has been noted that Puck can be seen not only as a spectator of the play's dramatic situations, but as a commentator and interpreter of the play's action. Critics often cite Puck's comment: "Shall we their fond pageant see? / Lord, what fools these mortals be!" (III.ii.114-15) as evidence of this.

Pyramus:
See Bottom

> **When Puck says that they must work quickly to complete their plans because morning is approaching, Oberon replies: "But we are spirits of another sort. / I with the Morning's love have oft made sport . . . (III.ii.388-89) . . ."**

Queen of the Fairies:
See Titania

Quince:

Peter Quince is a carpenter and belongs to the group which is often referred to as the clowns, or the mechanicals. This group also includes Bottom, Flute, Snug, Snout, and Starveling. It is frequently noted that the names of these common laborers reflect the work that they do. "Quince," critics explain, probably refers to a wedge-shaped block of wood used in carpentry. In I.ii, the mechanicals are assembled at Quince's house, and, at Bottom's direction Quince is assigning the roles in the Pyramus and Thisby play. Quince assigns himself the role of Thisby's father and answers questions about the play, making suggestions as to how various parts should be played. When Bottom volunteers to play parts other than the one he was assigned (that of Pyramus), Quince flatters Bottom until the latter agrees to play the part of Pyramus. When Bottom wants to play the lion's part, for example, Quince argues that he will play it too well, and frighten all the ladies, and get himself and the rest of them hanged as a result. When all parts have been assigned, Quince arranges to have a rehearsal in the wood.

The rehearsal takes place in III.i. As the men gather, Bottom brings up his concern that the violence in the play might frighten the female audience members. He suggests that a prologue be written explaining that the dangers in the play—Pyramus drawing his sword to kill himself, and the presence of the lion—are not real. Quince and the others agree on this solution, and he then brings up another concern: how will they represent the moonshine by which Pyramus and Thisby meet? It is agreed that

> **Puck is delighted at the entertainment that is to ensue as the four young lovers with mixed up emotions come together: 'Shall we their fond pageant see? / Lord, what fools these mortals be!' (III.ii.114-15)."**

they will use a person to represent the moonshine, and another person to represent the wall which separates the lovers (since they "can never bring in a wall" [III.i.66]). As the group practices, Quince corrects the errors Bottom and Flute make in their lines. They are interrupted when Puck changes Bottom's head into the head of an ass. In IV.ii, Quince seems dismayed at Bottom's disappearance and says that there isn't anyone in Athens who can play Pyramus like Bottom. When Bottom reappears, Quince expresses his relief and gladness: "Bottom! O most courageous day! O most happy hour!" (IV.i.27). In V.i, Quince reads the part of the Prologue.

Robin Goodfellow:
See Puck

Snout:
Tom Snout, the tinker, is a member of a group which is often referred to as the clowns, or the mechanicals. This group also includes Bottom, Flute, Quince, Snug, and Starveling. It is frequently noted that the names of these common laborers reflect the work that they do. "Snout," critics explain, may suggest a spout of a kettle, an item probably mended by the tinker. In I.ii, Snout appears with the rest of the mechanicals, as Quince the carpenter is assigning the roles in the Pyramus and Thisby play. Quince assigns the role of Pyramus's father to Snout. However, it is decided by the group in III.i that a person will have to play the wall, which, in the play separates Pyramus and Thisby. In V.i we learn that Snout plays the role of Wall. Snout also appears in IV.ii, when Bottom returns from his interlude with Titania, but he does not speak.

Snug:
Snug is one member of a group which is often referred to as the clowns, or the mechanicals. This group also includes Bottom, Quince, Flute, Snout, and Starveling. It is frequently noted that the names of these common laborers reflect the work that they do. "Snug," critics explain, suggests his work as a joiner, one who joined pieces of wood together to make furniture. In I.ii, Snug appears with the rest of the mechanicals, as Quince the carpenter is assigning the roles in the Pyramus and Thisby play. Quince assigns Snug the role of the Lion.

Snug appears again in III.i, rehearsing with the rest of the mechanicals, but he does not speak. He runs off after Puck has given Bottom the ass's head. In IV.ii, Snug enters and announces to Quince, Flute, Snout, and Starveling that the duke has just come from the temple and that "there is two or three lords and ladies more married" (IV.ii.15-17).

In V.i, Snout appears as the Lion. When he comes on stage he announces to the ladies that he is Snug the joiner, so that they will not fear him. Of his performance, Demetrius comments "Well roar'd Lion" (V.i.265).

Starveling:
Robin Starveling is one member of a group which is often referred to as the clowns, or the mechanicals. This group also includes Bottom, Quince, Flute, Snug, and Snout. It is frequently noted that the names of these common laborers reflect the work that they do. "Starveling," critics explain, suggests the proverbial skinniness of tailors. In I.ii, Starveling appears with the rest of the mechanicals, as Quince the carpenter is assigning the roles in the Pyramus and Thisby play. Quince assigns Starveling the role of Thisby's mother. However, it is decided by the group in III.i that a person will have to play the moonshine by which Pyramus and Thisby meet, and in V.i we learn that Starveling plays the role of Moonshine. Starveling also appears in IV.ii, when he suggests that Bottom, who still can't be found, has been "transported" (IV.ii.4), or taken by the fairies. In V.i, when Starveling appears as Moonshine, he receives this accolade from Hippolyta: "Well shone, Moon. Truly, the moon shines with a good grace" (V.i.267-68).

Theseus (Theseus, Duke of Athens):
The play opens as Theseus and his bride-to-be, Hippolyta, are discussing their upcoming marriage.

Theseus comments that he "woo'd thee [Hippolyta] with my sword, / And won thy love doing thee injuries" (I.i.16-17) referring to the fact that he conquered Hippolyta in his war with the Amazons. But now they are to be married, and their discussion is interrupted by Egeus, who comes to Theseus for help in sorting out the affairs concerning Egeus's daughter, Hermia. After hearing Egeus present his case he points out to Hermia that she should be obedient to her father and that Demetrius "is a worthy gentleman" (I.i.52). Hermia asks Theseus how the law will affect her is she refuses to marry Demetrius, and Theseus outlines her options: death, or lifelong confinement to a nunnery. He advises her to abide by her father's wishes but gives her several days to make her decision.

Theseus does not appear again until IV.i, when he, Hippolyta, and Egeus find the four young lovers in the wood. When Theseus hears what they have to say, and after Egeus demands that Lysander by punished for his attempted elopement of Hermia, Theseus announces that the couples will be married along side him and Hippolyta. He goes back on his earlier decision to support Egeus in trying to force Hermia to marry Demetrius. As for Egeus's request that Lysander be punished, Theseus simply says, "Egeus, I will overbear your will" (IV.i.179).

As the last act opens, Theseus and Hippolyta discuss what has happened to the four young lovers, with Theseus attributing tales of fairies and the like to the imagination. Hippolyta responds that the lovers' stories support each other, and that this made the combined image they painted "something of great constancy; / But howsoever, strange and admirable" (V.i.26-27). Theseus then requests to see *Pyramus and Thisby*, despite Philostrate's urging to the contrary. Throughout the play, Theseus and the others watching the performance comment on the actors' abilities and interpretation of the tragedy. When everyone has gone off to bed, Theseus and Hippolyta, along with the other couples, are blessed by Oberon.

Although Theseus has relatively few lines in the play, his role is often considered to be fairly major, for several reasons. Firstly, many commentators see Theseus's relationship with Hippolyta as providing a framework for the dramatic action of the play, given that the couple only appears in the beginning and the end of the play. Additionally, this relationship undergoes no change during the course of the play and arguably represents stability and

> As the last act opens, Theseus and Hippolyta discuss what has happened to the four young lovers, with Theseus attributing tales of fairies and the like to the imagination. Hippolyta responds that the lovers' stories support each other, and that this made the combined image they painted 'something of great constancy; / But howsoever, strange and admirable' (V.i.26-27)."

consistency, in direct contrast to the somewhat capricious relationships of the young lovers.

Perhaps more importantly, many critics believe that Shakespeare uses the character of Theseus to discuss the interlocking themes of imagination and art. Often cited in the discussion of this topic are two passages. The first is Theseus's "lunatic, lover, poet" speech (V.i.2-27) in which Theseus says:

> The lunatic, the lover, and the poet
> Are of imagination all compact.
> One sees more devils than vast hell can hold;
> That is the madman. The lover, all as frantic,
> Sees Helen's beauty in a brow of Egypt.
> The poet's eye, in a fine frenzy rolling,
> Doth glance from heaven to earth, from earth to
>   heaven;
> And as imagination bodies forth
> The forms of things unknown, the poet's pen
> Turns them to shapes, and gives to aery nothing
> A local habitation and a name.
> Such tricks hath strong imagination, . . .
>
> (V.i.7-18)

The second is the later exchange with Hippolyta as they watch *Pyramus and Thisby*:

> *Hippolyta*: This is the silliest stuff that ever I
>   heard.
> *Theseus*: The best in this kind are but shadows;
>   and
> the worst are no worse, if imagination amend
>   them.

Hippolyta: It must be your imagination the, and
not theirs.

Theseus: If we imagine no worse of them than
they
of themselves, they may pass for excellent men.

(V.i.210-16)

Some commentators have argued that both of these passages indicate that Theseus has a lack of aesthetic discrimination, that he cannot distinguish between superior or inferior art. And the "lunatic, lover, poet" speech, while seeming to acknowledge the power of the imagination, at the same times appears to discount the importance of imagination. However, others note that Theseus, especially in the second passage quoted above, seems to understand the importance of the audience's imagination in understanding art. As some commentators have summarized, Theseus realizes the importance of imagination to love and life, as long as it does not undermine reason and sanity.

Thisby:

See Flute

Titania:

Titania, queen of the fairies, first appears in II.i when she and Oberon are arguing. Puck has already outlined their disagreement for us: Titania has a changeling (a child exchanged for another by the fairies) whom she adores. Oberon wants the boy for himself. Titania refuses to give the child to him. As part of a plan to steal the child from her, Oberon instructs Puck to fetch a certain flower. The juice of this flower, when squeezed on Titania's eyes, will make her fall in love with whatever creature she first sees.

Titania next appears in II.ii, asking her fairies to sing her to sleep, which they do, to Oberon's advantage. He uses this opportunity to squeeze the juice on her eyes and he hopes that when she wakes "some vile thing is near" (II.ii.34). The "vile thing" happens to be Bottom, who Puck has transformed from an ordinary man into a man with an ass's head. As expected, Titania is in love. She praises Bottom and gives him several of her fairies to attend to him. In IV.i, we see Titania and Bottom seated together on her "flow'ry bed" where she is caressing him and kissing him (IV.i.1-4). They fall asleep together, after which Oberon tells Puck that he has successfully retrieved the child. Oberon then releases Titania from the power of the potion. She awakens, saying she thought she'd been in love with an ass. When Oberon points out Bottom lying next

to her, she asks "How came these things to pass? / O, how mine eyes do loathe his visage now!" (IV.i.78-79). In Act V, Titania appears with Oberon and the rest of the fairies as they bless the sleeping couples.

Some commentators have noted that Titania, like Hippolyta, is ruled by her husband. Her defiance in not yielding the child to him does not get her very far, since Oberon gets what he wants in the end. Additionally, it has been observed that Titania's rebellion against Oberon's authority parallels Hermia's rebellion against her father and Athenian law. Critics have also noted that order in the play is not restored until Oberon regains his relationship with Titania.

Wall:

See Snout

Further Reading

Barton, Anne. Introduction to *A Midsummer Night's Dream*, by William Shakespeare. In *The Riverside Shakespeare*, edited by G. Blakemore Evans, 217-21. Boston: Houghton Mifflin Co., 1974.

Barton offers an overview of the play's likely sources, themes, and characters.

Bevington, David. " 'But We Are Spirits of Another Sort': The Dark Side of Love and Magic in *A Midsummer Night's Dream*." *Medieval and Renaissance Studies: Proceedings of the Southeastern Institute of Medieval and Renaissance Studies* (Summer 1975): 80-92.

Bevington analyzes the dark and comic elements of the play, seeing this distinction in several different relationships, including that between Oberon and Puck (with Oberon as benevolent and Puck as frightening).

Clemen, Wolfgang. Introduction to *A Midsummer Night's Dream*, by William Shakespeare, edited by Wolfgang Clemen, 524-29. *The Complete Signet Classic Shakespeare*, edited by Sylvan Barnet. New York: Harcourt Brace Jovanovich, 1963.

Clemen provides an overview of the various dramatic elements in the play. He discusses the fairies, and Puck in particular, as spectator, commentator, and interpreter of the play's dramatic action.

Doran, Madeleine. "Pyramus and Thisbe Once More." In *Essays on Shakespeare and Elizabethan Drama in Honor of Hardin Craig*, edited by Richard Holsey, 149-61. Columbia: University of Missouri Press, 1962.

Doran examines a twelfth- and a sixteenth-century version of the Pyramus and Thisby story that Bottom and the rest of the mechanicals perform in *A Midsummer Night's Dream*. She points out that the tale, originally told by Ovid, had been retold "countless" times by the time Shakespeare wrote *A Midsummer Night's Dream*, and was "ripe for parody."

Draper, John W. "The Queen Makes a Match and Shakespeare a Comedy." *Yearbook of English Studies* 2 (1972): 61-67.

Draper asserts that numerous allusions in the plot of the play, as well as "parallels of character and plot" suggest that Shakespeare wrote *A Midsummer Night's Dream* for the wedding of Lady Dorothy, the sister of the Earl of Essex, to the duke of Northumberland, which took place on April 30, 1595.

Epstein, Norrie. "*A Midsummer Night's Dream*." In *The Friendly Shakespeare: A Thoroughly Painless Guide to the Best of the Bard*, 110-16. New York: Viking, 1993.

Epstein offers a brief overview of modern reactions to the characters and themes of the play. The chapter also includes quotes from twentieth-century directors of various productions of *A Midsummer Night's Dream*.

Fender, Stephen. *Shakespeare: "A Midsummer Night's Dream."* London: Edward Arnold, 1968.

Fender argues that the dramatic action of the play follows a path of increasing disorder until Oberon restores harmony in IV.i.

Goddard, Harold C. "*A Midsummer-Night's Dream*." In *The Meaning of Shakespeare*, 74-80. Chicago: University of Chicago Press, 1951.

In addition to examining how the discord in the play is harmoniously resolved, Goddard analyzes Shakespeare's view of the importance of imagination as expressed in the speeches of Theseus and Hippolyta.

Granville-Barker, Harley. "Preface to *A Midsummer Night's Dream*." In *More Prefaces to Shakespeare*, by Harley Granville-Barker, edited by Edward M. Moore, 94-134. Princeton, NJ: Princeton University Press, 1974.

Granville-Barker discusses the poetry of *A Midsummer Night's Dream* and asserts that it is the predominant dramatic feature of the play.

Kermode, Frank. "The Mature Comedies." In *Early Shakespeare*, edited by John Russell Brown and Bernard Harris, 221-27. London: Edward Arnold, 1961.

Kermode argues that the principal themes of the play are fantasy and the disorders of fantasy. The critic

contends that Bottom's "dream" offers an interpretation of blind love as a transcendent passion, which contradicts the beliefs of the young lovers that their own adventures have been fantasies.

Marshall, David. "Exchanging Visions: Reading *A Midsummer Night's Dream*." *ELH* 49, no. 3 (Fall 1982): 543-75.

Marshall argues that the play explores the relationship between the theater and its audience and questions traditional views about marriage. Additionally, Marshall interprets Hippolyta's silence as an indication that she has been forced into marrying Theseus.

Olson, Paul A. "*A Midsummer Night's Dream* and the Meaning of Court Marriage." *ELH* 24, no. 2 (June 1957): 95-119.

Olson discuss several themes in the play. He views Theseus as an "icon of reason" and discusses the conflict between passionate love and love ruled by reason.

Phialas, Peter G. "*A Midsummer Night's Dream*." In *Shakespeare's Romantic Comedies: The Development of Their Form and Meaning*, 102-33. Chapel Hill, NC: University of North Carolina Press, 1966.

Phialas examines what he sees as two antithetical expressions of love in the play: the inconstant, capricious love represent by the fairies and by the four young Athenians, and the matter-of-fact, rational mode reflected by Bottom. He sees the relationship between Hippolyta and Theseus as the "middle ground" between these two extremes.

Priestly, J. B. "Bully Bottom." In *The English Comic Characters*, 1-19. New York: Dodd, Mead, and Co., 1925.

Priestly argues that Bottom is the first of Shakespeare's great comic figures.

Van Doren, Mark. "*A Midsummer Night's Dream*." In *Shakespeare*, 76-83. New York: Henry Holt and Co., 1939.

Van Doren discusses the imagery of the play and comments that the performance of the Pyramus and Thisby play is Shakespeare's self-parody of his own play, *Romeo and Juliet*.

Much Ado about Nothing

circa 1598-99

Plot Summary

Act I:

Don Pedro and his soldiers have returned from a successful battle against Don Pedro's bastard brother, Don John, a battle in which Claudio performed bravely. Don Pedro and his soldiers are invited by Leonato, governor of Messina, to stay and visit with him in Messina, and they reply that they will stay for one month. Now that the soldiers are once more in civilized society, the thoughts of one of them—Count Claudio—turn to love. He becomes interested in wooing Hero, Leonato's daughter. In a parallel romantic plot, Hero's witty cousin, Beatrice, and Claudio's friend Benedick seem drawn to each other in "a merry war" (I.i.62), never meeting but to engage in "a skirmish of wit" (I.ii.63). Yet Benedick vows to live and die a bachelor. Don Pedro offers to act as a negotiator on Claudio's behalf to both Leonato and Hero with the goal of gaining approval for a wedding between Claudio and Hero. Leonato's brother Antonio makes an erroneous report of this plan to Leonato based on misinformation supplied by a servant. In a significant subplot, Don John, illegitimate brother of Don Pedro and villain of the play, decides to foil the marriage plans between Claudio and Hero.

Act II:

At a party that night at Leonato's, in a conversation with her uncle, Beatrice echoes Benedick's

vow of determination to remain unmarried. Don Pedro and his group enter wearing masks, and several dance with the women in Leonato's house. When Beatrice and Benedick dance, Beatrice says ridiculing things about Benedick, who is annoyed by her jests and later removes his mask and leaves. While Don Pedro talks to Hero on Claudio's behalf, Don John tells Claudio, masked and supposedly Benedick, that Don Pedro is interested in Hero for himself. Although Claudio readily believes this, Don Pedro comes to him with the news of the agreed-on engagement, and Claudio and Hero are happy for now. Don Pedro seems to propose to Beatrice but is rejected. Then he and Leonato decide to deceive Benedick, making him think Beatrice loves him. Meanwhile, with Borachio, Don John has formulated his plan to stir up trouble between Hero and Claudio. The plan centers around the destruction of Hero's virtuous reputation. The day after Leonato's party, Benedick, concealed in Leonato's orchard, overhears a conversation between Don Pedro, Leonato, and Claudio about Beatrice's unrequited love for him. He falls for the trick primarily because Leonato, the "white-bearded fellow" (II.iii.118-19), is involved. When Beatrice calls him in to eat, he interprets her behavior as showing signs of love.

Act III:

Hero and her two gentlewomen, Margaret and Ursula, use a similar strategy to deceive Beatrice, who is as easily deceived as Benedick. Subsequently, Benedick endures ridicule from his friends for shaving off his beard, a soldier's "ornament" (III.ii.46), and goes off to speak to Leonato. Later, Don John takes aside Claudio and Don Pedro and tells them of Hero's disloyalty, offering to show proof at her chamber window the night before the wedding. In the next scene, Dogberry and his partner Verges, the local law officers, give orders for a special watch to the night watchmen the night before the wedding. The watch, though bumbling, overhear Conrade and Borachio discussing Borachio's successful plot to fool Claudio into thinking that Margaret, seen in a chamber window with Borachio, was Hero. Borachio mentions the fee, a thousand ducats, he has been paid by Don John to accomplish the deception. The watch arrest them. The next morning, Beatrice is gently ridiculed for her changed attitude to Benedick, and Hero prepares for her wedding. Dogberry and Verges try to tell Leonato about the arrest of Conrade and Borachio, and how it pertains to him and his family, but their language

difficulties and Leonato's haste to leave prevent them from saying all they had to say.

Act IV:

In a dramatic church scene the day of the wedding, Claudio publicly shames Hero by expressing his disgust for her and accusing her of not being a virgin. This accusation is made in front of the priest, Friar Francis, and the whole assembly of wedding guests. Although Hero denies any knowledge of what Claudio is talking about, he is seconded by Don Pedro. Hero faints, and Don Pedro, Claudio, and Don John leave. Leonato, convinced by the plot, turns on his daughter and wishes her dead. The friar devises a plan to ease the newly-created tensions. Following the friar's advice, Leonato agrees to make it seem that Hero is dead. The purposes of this scheme are to make Claudio feel penitent and remember why he valued Hero. Also, it will allow gossip about her to die away. The friar advises that if all else fails, Hero should be put in a convent. Throughout the scene, Beatrice and Benedick have been doubters of the otherwise accepted slander of Hero. When everyone else leaves, Beatrice asks Benedick to challenge Claudio to a duel. Benedick reluctantly agrees, for the sake of his love for Beatrice. In the final scene in this act, Dogberry and Verges conduct their investigation of the arrested men in front of the sexton.

Act V:

Leonato expresses his belief to his brother that Hero has been slandered. When Don Pedro and Claudio encounter them in the street, Leonato accuses Claudio of killing Hero with his cruel accusations. Don Pedro persists in his support of Claudio. After Leonato and Antonio leave, Benedick arrives and issues a challenge to Claudio, who at first believes Benedick is joking. The Constables come through leading their prisoners. They tell the story of the prisoners' deception and guilt to a shocked pair, Claudio and Don Pedro. Claudio agrees to tell the people of Messina of Hero's innocence, to sing an epitaph at her tomb and leave it there, and to come to Leonato's the next morning, to marry with a niece of Leonato. Meanwhile, Benedick composes halting love poems for Beatrice. The morning after Claudio sings his epitaph, he goes to wed Leonato's niece, who is revealed to be Hero after all. Beatrice and Benedick's wedding almost does not take place, but their poems and writings about each other are brought fourth, confirming the love between them. The play ends with Benedick's advice that the prince should get married and the news that Don John has been arrested in flight and returned to Messina.

Modern Connections

Three major aspects of *Much Ado About Nothing* can be related to contemporary life. The first is the idea of the innocent being wrongfully accused. Hero is accused of not being a virgin. False and very slight evidence is offered on the night before her wedding. The evidence is taken at face value and believed by a range of significant people in her life, including her fiance, his influential friend, and her own father. These three individuals immediately believe the worst about Hero. They scarcely question what little evidence is offered. In fact, it is almost a case of one person's reputation and social standing weighed against another's. In addition to the swiftness and injustice of the reaction to Claudio's accusation, the reaction is also severe. Claudio and the prince publicly shame Hero on her wedding day at the ceremony itself. Hero's father utters a wish for her death. Modern audiences may recoil at the shaming scene and many find it almost baffling. For an Elizabethan woman, her value to society, to her family and to herself lay in her marriageability. This in turn was dependent on her physical and moral purity. Also, arranged marriages, or at least marriages where a go-between would play a role, were common. The go-between would be concerned about his own honor and public reputation in this dealing as in all his dealings. In spite of changed social attitudes on these particular points, many people experience the feeling of being accused of some deed they did not do or at least some comment they did not make. Hero is utterly unable to defend herself. Her word is not given any credit. Modern audiences of young people may feel that parents and other adults are sometimes too ready to think the worst on slight evidence, rather than pausing to investigate. A related aspect to this feeling of the unjust accusation is the need for solid evidence. The play contains various points where characters suggest something that they use as a basis for truth. For example, Benedick is fooled by the conversation about Beatrice's love for him because an older, respected gentleman is in on the trick. Beatrice is able to convince Benedick to challenge Claudio to a duel because she says she is certain that her cousin Hero has been wronged. She is as sure as she has "a

thought or a soul" (IV.i.330). Her certitude is enough for Benedick.

The romance in the play also serves as a connection between the play and the contemporary audience. Throughout the play, friends serve as "go-betweens" or in some way help potential lovers come together. Don Pedro helps Claudio woo Hero, and, similarly, Don Pedro, Leonato, Claudio, Hero, Margaret, and Ursula all help Beatrice and Benedick get together. Although the tricking ("gulling") is an Elizabethan stage convention, there is still room today for friends to play an agreed upon role to find out someone's attitude to a potential romantic partner and also to generally stir up an interest.

Another aspect of romance—the time frame in which romance develops in Shakespeare's plays—also interests modern audiences. The action of this play is one week and a day. Claudio and Hero's engagement comes early in this time frame. The very compression of their romance and its being in its first rosy bloom seem to intensify the anguish and shock of the shaming scene.

The third point of interest is the unexplained maliciousness of Don John. He fits the part of the Elizabethan comic villain. His actions seem less than comic, but the fact that he appears in a comedy will mean that ultimately his cruel and hurtful actions will be rendered ineffectual. One possible motive for his behavior is the psychological effect of the stigma attached to his illegitimacy. Laws and social attitudes made illegitimacy more problematic and shunned in Shakespeare's time than it is now. Illegitimate male offspring were publicly branded by distinguishing marks on the shields they used in battle and displayed in their homes. Also, illegitimate children were usually prevented from inheriting their families wealth, with common law favoring the oldest legitimate son.

Characters

Antonio:
Antonio is Leonato's brother. Antonio is described in the *Dramatis Personae* as an old man. Ursula mentions that he has a dry hand, a feature associated with old age just as a modern audience would associate wrinkles or liver spots with old age. He is a minor character, but his relationship to Leonato stands as a model of a good fraternal

relationship, in contrast to that between Don Pedro and Don John.

He is an advisor and confidant to his brother. When a servant tells him of an overheard conversation between Don Pedro and Claudio, he relays the information to Leonato. He is present at Leonato's party and dances with one of Hero's gentlewomen.

At the end of the play, he counsels patience to his brother and a moderating of his grief. Also, like a loyal brother and uncle, he utters defiant words to Don Pedro and Claudio. He challenges Claudio to a duel and calls them both a series of insulting names. In fact, in his turn he has to be counseled to patience by Leonato. Finally, he is asked to give Hero away at the wedding as his own daughter, and does so willingly.

Antonio's Son:

He does not have a speaking part. He provides music and perhaps helps in other ways in Leonato's busy household, especially during the soldiers' visit. Leonato addresses him briefly in Act I.

Attendants:

The attendants do not have speaking parts, but various editors mention attendants at the wedding in Act IV and then again at the weddings at the end of the play. By the fact that their greater numbers make more witnesses to the action, the attendants make the drama of the shaming scene more intense, and then by contrast the closing weddings more festive. Three or four attendants carrying candles go with Claudio and Don Pedro to Hero's tomb, contributing to the somber mood.

Balthasar:

Balthasar is an attendant on Don Pedro. He sings a Shakespearean lyric at the beginning of the gulling of Benedick. The song advises women that men are "deceivers" (II.iii.63) and that women should not sigh over them but let them go.

Beatrice:

Beatrice is the play's witty heroine. Much of her memorable character is original with Shakespeare rather than found in plot sources. She is mainly noted for her firm opposition to marriage and for her verbal dueling with Benedick. Her first comment is a question directed to the messenger about Benedick's welfare. Her asking a series of questions about him reveals an interest which she

herself may be unaware of. Also, once Benedick and the other soldiers arrive, Beatrice makes a comment at the end of their first exchange of wit warfare that indicates that perhaps they knew each other before in some romantic way. Benedick's own comment about her appearance suggests that she would be considered very attractive, were she not so sharp-tongued. Beatrice's good spirits are commented on by her uncle, who says that she is "never sad but when she sleeps" (II.i.343). He quotes Hero as saying that when she has had a dream of unhappiness, she "wak'd herself with laughing" (II.i.345-46).

Indeed, her comments at Leonato's party radiate out in many directions. She gives a negative review of Don John's sour looks and personality. She laughs about bearded and beardless husbands. Beatrice dances with Benedick, recognizing him beneath his mask, and ridicules his wit and his personality, commenting that "he is the prince's jester, a very dull fool" (II.i.137-38). She is also aware of practicality and social niceties of behavior, as is shown in her prompting of Claudio to be other than a mute in his engagement to Hero.

She has a keen insight into everyone's character. For example, she correctly identifies Claudio's silent behavior at the party as a signal of his mistaken jealousy of Don Pedro. Even late in the play, she refers to Claudio as Count Comfect, a sweet or sugary count in terms of manners and behavior. Another example of her insight is her certainty regarding her cousin's innocence. She is also aware of Don Pedro's stature and public importance so she tactfully rejects his proposal of marriage.

Despite Beatrice's perceptiveness regarding other people, she appears to either be unaware of or disguising her romantic feelings toward Benedick. Several comments early in the play suggest that Beatrice and Benedick have already been known to each other in an unsuccessful romantic context. Yet, Beatrice shows that she is open to the opinions of others. She hears the criticisms made of her by Hero and her gentlewomen, and she vows in a brief soliloquy to change her behavior. In the next scene in which she appears, in Hero's room on the morning of the wedding, she shows herself vulnerable like all people who have undergone a change and are a little unsure of themselves. She is sensitive to the comments and apparent double meanings of the other women, especially when they say she needs some "distill'd carduus benedictus" (III.iv.73-74) for her case of jumpy nerves.

> "Beatrice dances with Benedick, recognizing him beneath his mask, and ridicules his wit and his personality, commenting that 'he is the prince's jester, a very dull fool' (II.i.137-38)."

She shows her real strength of character in the scene in which Hero is shamed. She is steadfast in her belief in Hero's innocence. She ministers to her fainting cousin. Then, when all except Benedick leave, she and Benedick are able to declare their love for each other. She convinces Benedick, on the basis of his sworn love for her, to kill Claudio. The apparent cruelty of this request is softened by Beatrice's admission of her crying quietly throughout the shaming scene.

In the last act of the play Beatrice and Benedick seem much more at ease with each other, but they are still engaged in mild forms of wit play. Beatrice and Benedick each ask the other what quality made them fall in love with the other. Her caring for her cousin is displayed again in the final act when she says again after banter with Benedick that she and Hero are both not well. Just before the wedding in the last scene, they learn that the other is not about to die for love, though Beatrice still maintains that she marries Benedick partly to save his life.

Benedick:

Benedick is a soldier returning from war. He is from Padua, a city in northern Italy and part of the Republic of Venice during the Italian Renaissance. He is the main male character in the play, even though his marriage is not the initial focus of the plot. Throughout the play, he displays his quick wit, loyalty, honorable nature, and his perioidic lack of self-knowledge.

When the audience first hears a reference to Benedick, it is via Beatrice's scornfully posed question intended to conceal her interest: "I pray you, is Signior Mountanto return'd from the wars or no?" (I.i.30-31). Beatrice does not even say his name, perhaps for fear of giving away too much to a messenger about her interest in Benedick. Yet even

this nickname, taken from fencing, suggests something about Benedick—that he is skilled with a sword. Indeed, the messenger says Benedick "hath done good service . . . in these wars" (I.i.48-49).

When the entire party of returning soldiers arrives at Leonato's and dismounts, Beatrice and Benedick immediately single each other out for an exchange of witty barbs. Just as Beatrice has a name for Benedick ("Signior Mountanto" [I.i.30]), so he has one for her—Lady Disdain (I.i.118) and another later (my Lady Tongue, in II.i.275). Benedick seems to get the best of Beatrice, which leads her to say that she knows him from before, and that he always ends with a trick. This and other comments suggest a prior knowledge and perhaps even a mutual romantic interest.

Nevertheless, Benedick vows in the opening scene to live and die a bachelor, and declares himself a "professed tyrant" (I.i.169) to women. Benedick's comments indicate that the basis for his attitude is a belief that women render men foolish in their behavior, turning them into sighers and ballad-makers, and eventually domesticating them into husbands who are like hired horses with signs around their necks standing and waiting for their lady's bidding.

Benedick's ability to get the best of the situation varies. At Signior Leonato's party, he is chagrined to find himself labeled by Beatrice the "prince's jester, a very dull fool" (II.i.137-38), during a masked dance with Beatrice. During the famous gulling scene, he seems completely taken in, simply because the "white-bearded fellow" (II.iii.118-19), meaning Leonato, is part of the duping.

Benedick shows a strong, vigorous imagination at Leonato's party. After he is angered by Beatrice's comments about him, he asks to be sent on various fantastical missions to get away from Beatrice. He talks of going on services for the prince from one end of the world to the other, from the Antipodes, from the Mongols, from the Pygmies—anywhere Beatrice is not.

Yet when Benedick is alone at the beginning of the gulling scene, he turns his fertile imagination to the qualities in a woman which would please him. First he meditates on the changes in his friend Claudio, who used to like a soldier's music, armor, and plain speech, who is now turned into the lover. He himself would like a woman who is rich, wise, virtuous, fair (meaning attractive), mild-natured, noble, of good discourse (conversation), an excellent musician, and of any color hair that pleases God. Benedick's wit is perhaps at one of its sharpest moments in this scene of concealment. He refers to Claudio as Monsieur Love. When Leonato, the prince, and Claudio enjoy a song, Benedick comments on how a dog howling like the singer would have been hung.

Benedick began the scene by fearing that love would turn him to an oyster—something flaccid, soft, and spineless. By the end of the scene, he is convinced of the truth of what has been said about Beatrice's affection for him by the seriousness of the conversation, by the presence of the respected Leonato, and perhaps by his own interest in Beatrice. When Beatrice calls him in to dinner, he turns her impertinent approach into something laden with positive double meanings flattering to himself. Benedick's self-deception is engaging because it is such a change from his previous adamant stand against love. He disarmingly says that he has changed because he did not realize he would live long enough to be a married man.

He is the object of some jokes by his friends after the gulling scene. They make fun of his newly shaved face, of his use of civet perfume, and of his wearing of various attention-getting clothes which replace his plain soldier's garb. Yet Benedick still has some repartee in his command, allowing him to disengage himself from the others and step aside with Leonato, possibly to begin some discussion of a change in his view of Beatrice.

In other areas of his character, Benedick is constant, sensible, loyal, and sound in his judgment. Benedick is loyal to Claudio through all manly offices and activities. For example, when he is asked by Claudio his opinion of Hero, he is fully ready with a clever retort making Hero seem not so unusual. This is not a reflection on Hero but on Benedick's concept of what love-sickness does to a man's head. When Claudio thinks too quickly that the prince has wooed Hero for himself, Benedick says sharply to him, "But did you think the prince would have serv'd you thus?" (II.i.195-96).

During the shaming scene, Benedick shows compassion for the fainting Hero and tries to calm the outraged Leonato. He asks Beatrice whether she was Hero's bedfellow last night, thus looking for evidence rather than emotion as a basis for response. In an insightful comment, he defends the honor of the prince and Claudio and suspects that they have been misled by Don John, "whose spirits

> **Despite Beatrice's perceptiveness regarding other people, she appears to either be unaware of or disguising her romantic feelings toward Benedick."**

toil in frame of villainies" (IV.i.189). He counsels Leonato to take the friar's advice, and he swears himself to secrecy. When he is alone with Beatrice, he shows care for her sorrow, owns his love for her, and says "Surely I do believe your fair cousin is wronged" (IV.i.259-60). Though he defends Claudio to Beatrice, his love for her and his conviction that Hero has been wronged finally prompt him to agree to challenge Claudio to a duel.

When Benedick challenges Claudio, he shows himself to be focused and set on his purpose. He does not waste words and does not wish to jest with his friends. He has a mission, and he keeps it uppermost in mind.

Benedick's whimsicality, or odd humor, is shown in the garden scene near the end of the play when he has turned into the lover and tries to compose a love song. His love song is a bit pitiful, and so is the whole idea of finding him in the posture of the conventional lover. Yet Benedick has not been rendered a total oyster. He says to Beatrice, "Thou and I are too wise to woo peaceably" (V.ii.72). Even at his wedding, things threaten to dissolve when Benedick asks Beatrice if she loves him. Harmony is restored by the community of friends, and Benedick's summary comment that "man is a giddy thing" (V.iv.108) applies well to the action of the play as a whole.

Borachio:

Borachio is a follower of Don John. He is an experienced spy and villain. When he first appears, he brings news of the impending marriage between Hero and Claudio to Don John. He obtained the news by working as a perfumer of rooms in Leonato's house and hiding behind an arras (a tapestry wall-hanging) to overhear the conversation between Don Pedro and Claudio about the planned wooing.

> "... Benedick vows in the opening scene to live and die a bachelor, and declares himself a 'professed tyrant' (I.i.169) to women."

Borachio is a master at thinking up deceitful and covert activities. He attempts to mislead Claudio at Leonato's party about the wooing done by Don Pedro on Claudio's behalf. He also plants the thought in Claudio's mind that Hero is not his equal in birth. He devises the plan of appearing with Margaret at Hero's chamber window and making it look to those below that Hero is a "common stale" (IV.i.65), meaning a whore. He even thinks of arranging for Hero to be gone from the room that night. Don John offers him a fee of a thousand gold coins for his plan. The plan is foiled because Borachio cannot stop himself from bragging about it to Conrade during the night. They are overheard by the watch and arrested. During the investigation his answers are very brief. When he is brought before the prince, he freely and honestly confesses his crimes and asks for "nothing but the reward of a villain" (V.i.243-44), namely whatever punishment the law requires. He defends Margaret as being always "just and virtuous" (V.i.302) in her dealings. He also taks responsibility for his deeds. Finally, he speaks one of the most insightful lines in the play to the prince and Claudio. "What your wisdoms could not discover, these shallow fools have brought to light . . ." (V.i.232-34).

Boy:

This character fetches a book for Benedick when Benedick is alone in Leonato's orchard just before his friends come to trick him.

Claudio:

Claudio is a young soldier returning from war. He is originally from Florence, a city in northern Italy noted for culture during the Italian Renaissance. His mind has been dominated by thoughts of war. After his return, however, his thoughts have turned in a new direction. He is smitten immediately by Hero, Leonato's daughter. Her looks and gentle behavior have won him over very quickly, almost prior to any conversation or acquaintance with her. He is a conventional lover, and, as most critics agree, without much depth or complexity in his character.

Despite his apparent lack of complexity, Claudio demonstrates his capacity for friendship in that he is well-liked by Benedick, the central male character in the play. Also, he is capable of reciprocating friendship. He enters into the scheme originated by Don Pedro to help convince Benedick that Beatrice is in love with him. This helpful plot allows Benedick to realize, express, and act on his feelings. Claudio even displays a sense of humor and love of play in this scene.

Claudio proves himself to be a somewhat jealous and gullible man. When Don Pedro woos Hero on behalf of Claudio, the latter readily believes Don John's deceitful claim that Don Pedro is wooing Hero for himself. More seriously, Claudio falls for the window trick in which Borachio and Margaret, whom Borachio calls "Hero" in this scene, have an "amiable encounter" (III.iii.151-52).

Claudio's capacity for anger and wounded pride is demonstrated in his shaming of Hero. During the wedding ceremony, Claudio answers the friar's questions with irony and building anger until he then publicly and vehemently denounces and humiliates Hero, calling her a "rotten orange" (IV.i.32), an "approved wanton" (IV.i.44), and "a common stale [whore]" (IV.i.65). He even questions Leonato's friendship for him in offering him damaged goods in the form of an unvirginal daughter.

Finally, Claudio's capacity for repentance is shown by his willingness to perform observances at Hero's tomb. He hangs an epitaph at her tomb, and he also consents to marry, sight unseen, Leonato's niece. Only at the closing wedding ceremony is Hero unveiled to a chastened and subdued Claudio.

Perhaps the summarizing comment about Claudio is the one made by Beatrice early in the play. "The Count is neither sad, nor sick, nor merry, nor well; but civil count, civil as an orange, and something of that jealous complexion" (II.i.293-95). Beatrice's pun on civil/Seville, a Spanish city known for its oranges, points out a central truth about Claudio— he is bland and smooth, lacking depth or multiple dimensions.

Conrade:

Conrade is a follower of Don John. It is noted that Conrade was born under Saturn. The Renaissance interest in horoscopes and planetary influences on personality would suggest that Conrade is sour or gloomy in disposition. He advises Don John not to display the full range of his bad humor until he can do so without consequences. He also suggests that Don John make use of his discontent. He declares his loyalty to Don John to the death. There is some suggestion that Conrade is inexperienced in villainy. Conrade becomes impatient with the pace and logic of the interrogation which takes place in front of the sexton, and he calls Verges a coxcomb (fool) and Dogberry an ass.

Dogberry:

Dogberry is the constable of Messina. This title is a British usage and refers to a police officer or official in charge of keeping the peace. This part was originally written for a famous comic actor in Shakespeare's day, Will Kemp. Kemp's name appears before Dogberry's spoken parts in the Quarto edition printed in 1600. This is one piece of evidence used in establishing the date of composition of this play, because Will Kemp left the Lord Chamberlain's men in 1599.

Dogberry's name refers to an ordinary hedgerow bush or shrubbery, and is perhaps suggestive of the constable's intelligence level. Dogberry's notable characteristics include his flagrant misuse of language, his pride in who he is and his official position in town, his reckless disregard for actually doing his job according to a reasonable standard of performance, and his overly literal insistence on setting the record straight about being called an ass by Conrade.

Examples of Dogberry's misuse of language abound in scenes in which he appears. He inquires of the watchmen who among them is "the most desartless man to be constable" (III.iii.9-10). By "desartless" he means deserving. When George Seacoal is identified as the proper man, Dogberry interrupts Seacoal in midsentence, as befitting a higher authority figure addressing a lower, and gives him a lantern as a symbol of authority. His charge, or set of directions to the watch, show the ineptitude of his peace-keeping mission. He states the watch's charge as follows: "you shall comprehend all vagrom men; you are to bid any man stand, in the prince's name" (III.iii.25-26). When Dogberry is questioned by the watch about how to carry out their duties, he answers each possible situation with his own logic of how to proceed. For example, those who will not stop when told to do so should be

> **During the shaming scene, Benedick shows compassion for the fainting Hero and tries to calm the outraged Leonato."**

let go, for they are knaves. Those who won't leave taverns to go home to bed should be left there until they are sober. Thieves should be allowed to steal away, thereby showing what they really are. After all, if the watchmen try to stop a thief, they will be tainted by the contact. The watchmen are told to be especially careful in keeping an eye on Leonato's door. Dogberry's final instruction to them is to be "vigitant" (III.iii.94), meaning vigilant.

In III.v, Dogberry attempts to tell Leonato about the arrests of Conrade and Borachio, but is unable to get to the point quickly enough for Leonato. Later, when Dogberry and Verges and the criminals are assembled before the sexton for an official writing up of the case against the arrested men, Dogberry again shows his pride and ineptitude. He goes so slowly about the statement of the case and the instructions to the sexton as to what should be written down that even the sexton tells him that he is not doing the examination correctly. He does more name-calling and labelling than stating of the plain facts of the case. When Conrade, in utter exasperation, calls him an ass, Dogberry responds with a full assessment of this evaluation. He insists four times that he be written down as an ass. He also states the basis of his self-satisfaction: he is wise, an officer, a householder, as handsome as any in Messina, knowledgeable in the law, rich, and an owner of two gowns.

In the scene in which he leads the arrested men, he shows his choicest logic by his ability to divide a subject into parts and communicate it to Don Pedro. He jumps from first and second, to sixth and third. When Leonato gives him money for his efforts, he departs from the company of authorities with full, flattering, and garbled phrases. Dogberry is often a favorite among audiences due to his comic ineptitude.

Don John:
See John

> **". . . Benedick's summary comment that 'man is a giddy thing' (V.iv.108) applies well to the action of the play as a whole."**

Don Pedro:

See Pedro

Friar Francis:

See Francis

Francis (Friar Francis):

Friar Francis is the clergyman who is scheduled to perform the wedding ceremony between Hero and Claudio. He begins the ceremony with traditional questions about impediments to the marriage, when Claudio answers at first ironically and then attacks Hero furiously. During the shaming, the friar is at first silent, and then speaks calmly, proposing a plan to diffuse the chaos.

The friar seems confidant, having observed Hero's blushing and modest face, that she is innocent and that some mistake has been made. He refers to the seriousness of his profession as a priest and to his experience as a confessor and asks for Leonato's trust. He speaks with kindness and gentleness to Hero when he asks her who she is accused of spending time with. Then he suggests the plan of a feigned temporary burial, in order to attain a higher good. His says that his plan will achieve various goals: 1) it will change accusations to sorrow; 2) Hero's absence will make Claudio appreciate her more; 3) Claudio will mourn and repent her loss; 4) time will allow the truth to come out; 5) Hero's supposed death will stop the gossip. If his plan does not succeed, the friar suggests that Hero can be quietly put in a convent away from gossip. When Benedick prevails on Leonato to listen to the friar, the friar once again expresses confidence that his plan will work and that the wedding day is only postponed.

The friar ends with the satisfaction of being able to say to Leonato that he was sure Hero was innocent. He also performs the weddings at the end

of the play, and plans to explain about Hero's death to the amazed Claudio after the wedding in the chapel.

Hero:

Hero, depicted as a virtuous and mild young woman, proves to be loving, affectionate, and dutiful to her father, her cousin, and to her fiance. Claudio describes her as a jewel, and in appearance she is fair, young, short, and dark-haired. She is referred to by other characters in the play as being gentle and modest. Her answer to Don Pedro's attempt to get her to join their conspiracy to trick Beatrice shows her goodness and stands in contrast to Don John's villainy. She says that she "will do any modest office . . . to help [Beatrice] to a good husband" (II.i.375-76). During the trick, she does as much to instruct Beatrice in her deficiencies in being so joking and critical as she does to deceive Beatrice about Benedick.

On the morning of her wedding, Hero has an unexplained sadness but shows an interest in her wedding gown, in the perfumed gloves sent her by Claudio, and in her cousin Beatrice. She reproves Margaret for a mild jest about the wedding night. At her wedding, she blushes at the accusations made against her, asks very brief questions, denies her accuser, and finally faints. At this point, she supposedly dies and is entombed. In accordance with Friar Francis's plan, this ruse will allow the rumors about her to die down and Claudio to grow remorseful. She appears in the final scene, masked until Claudio agrees to marry whoever it is behind the mask. True to her character throughout, her words are mild, but they now have a potential, though unrealized tragic dimension. Because the friar's plan worked, she did "die to live" (IV.i.253), rather than suffer the fate of Shakespeare's tragic heroine, Juliet, who actually dies in the last act of *Romeo and Juliet*. Hero has been wrongfully accused, but is utterly powerless to defend herself. Only through the work, however incompetent, of others (such as Dogberry and Verges), the steadfast belief of Beatrice and Benedick, and the plan of Friar Francis, is her name finally cleared.

Audiences may view Hero as shallow and one-dimensional, defined by her relationships to others, especially male figures in the play. However, there is another aspect to her character, which is more hinted at than fully portrayed. Hero has a firm sense of goodness and does not do or say more or other than what is fair and just. For example, about Don John she simply says that he seems to have a melancholy disposition. In the scene in which Beatrice is tricked, she has a definite interest in seeing some curbing of Beatrice's unrestrained wit. She is all maidenly modesty in contrast to Margaret's chatter about wedding gowns and mildly vulgar punning about the wedding night. In the final scene of the play, Hero helps to repair a threatened breech in Benedick's and Beatrice's wedding plans by producing a poem taken from Beatrice's pocket.

John (Don John):

Don John is the play's villain. Sometimes young audiences find his attempted spoiling of the marriage of Claudio and Hero extremely confusing and unaccountable. His choice of this method to attack his brother's credibility and reputation seems quite indirect and ineffectual in conception, if not in execution.

Don John is largely an unmotivated villain. In addition to his attempt to destroy his brother's reputation, he also attacks Hero's honor and happiness. He describes himself as having an anti-social nature that will not try to fit in with others. He won't laugh at someone else's jokes or eat at someone else's meal time, but rather, will do things as he pleases, when he pleases.

Don John operates by will. What he wishes is what he will do, undirected and unrestrained by others. He admits as much to his followers, several disaffected men who attach themselves to this rebellious outsider. Thus, although Hero says he seems to suffer from melancholy, often the melancholic personality is inactive, and this is not an accurate description of Don John. Prior to the action of the play he had revolted against his brother, who forgave him. Ungratefully, he spends his time in this play looking for ways to hurt his brother. Another action that shows he is not the passive melancholic type is that when the news about Hero and the plot against her is announced, at the same time Don John's sudden fleeing of Messina is also discovered. This hasty escape when the plot is discovered is an index to his overall character of cowardice and sneakiness. At the end of the play, he faces the certainty of "brave punishments" (V.iv.128) the day after the concluding weddings.

Leonato:

Leonato is the governor of Messina, a city in northeastern Sicily in Italy. He is the father of Hero,

> **During the wedding ceremony, Claudio answers the friar's questions with irony and building anger until he then publicly and vehemently denounces and humiliates Hero, calling her a 'rotten orange' (IV.i.32), an 'approved wanton' (IV.i.44), and 'a common stale [whore]' (IV.i.65). He even questions Leonato's friendship for him in offering him damaged goods in the form of an unvirginal daughter. "**

a daughter eligible for marriage. He is a genial host who immediately invites the returning soldiers to stay in Messina. He is concerned with making his guests as comfortable as possible and their stay as pleasant as possible. He seeks to provide music for their rest, dinners for their nourishment, and parties for their diversion. He is also an able, though not a superb wit, who jests in turn with Benedick about Hero's parentage and Beatrice about her marriage prospects. Early in the play he does not seem susceptible to gossip, questioning the source of what soon proves to be an erroneous report his brother delivers him from a conversation overheard by a servant. He is gracious to Claudio as his future son-in-law, and tells the impatient youth that a week is needed to prepare adequately for such an event. He shows insight into his niece Beatrice's character, when he says of her that she is not ever really sad, even when asleep. He willingly enters into the scheme to trick Benedick into believing Beatrice is in love with him, though as a basically honest man he is at first a little slow in inventing proofs of Beatrice's affection for Benedick for the sake of the eavesdropping Benedick. However, once he fully enters into the jest, his made-up evidence is exaggerated and absurdly funny. Though his patience can be tried, he is ever courteous, accustomed as he is to his role as governor and head of an important household. When Dogberry and Verges

> **Dogberry's notable characteristics include . . . his overly literal insistence on setting the record straight about being called an ass by Conrade."**

go to see him on the morning of the wedding, he tells them that they are being tedious, but still offers them a glass of wine before their departure from his house. Because he is in a hurry to get to the wedding, he instructs them to take the evidence from the apprehended criminals.

At the wedding, his behavior is partially consistent with the type of person he has been shown to be thus far. He shows the same readiness of wit at first and the same courtesy that goes with a person in a position of authority. When Claudio questions Hero's virtue, Leonato at first seeks a clarification of Claudio's meaning and intent, and then asks Don Pedro to speak. After their full disclosure of the window scene, however, he gives a long, angry speech in which he wishes that the fainted Hero were dead. He finally listens to Friar Francis, who calms him and invents a plot to allow time to do some good.

In the final act of the play, he is a grieving father who suspects that Hero has been wrongly accused, so much so that he baits and tries to challenge Claudio to a duel. Claudio does not take him seriously, and he leaves. When he returns, everyone has just learned of the plot led by Don John. Leonato uses an uncustomary ironic tone in his comments to the captured men, and then demands a show of remorse and submission from Claudio, who willingly yields. He plans to investigate Margaret's role in the plot, and finally seems back to himself. He seems unwilling at the end to blame Claudio and Don Pedro, instead saying that they, too, were victims of a plot initiated by Don John and participated in unwillingly by Margaret.

Lord:

An unnamed lord identifies Leonato's monument for the penitent Claudio. He speaks only four words.

Margaret:

Margaret is a gentlewoman attending on Hero. Hero likes and trusts her and refers to her as "good Meg" (III.iv.8). Margaret helps Hero dress for her wedding. She compliments Hero's wedding gown and calls the Duchess of Milan's wedding gown a "night-gown" (III.iv.18) in comparison to Hero's. She provides an interesting, detailed description of a high society wedding gown of the time period: cloth with gold and silver thread, sleeves trimmed with pearls, multiple sleeves, skirt trimmed with bluish tinsel. In addition to Margaret's interest in female fashions, she also enjoys speaking in puns with hidden sexual meanings. She speaks to both Hero and to Beatrice this way on the morning of Hero's wedding. She also speaks in a franker way along this line with Benedick later in the play. Margaret's behavior in this play is somewhat mysterious. She entertained Borachio at Hero's chamber window the night before the wedding, allowing him to call her Hero. When Hero is accused at her wedding of disloyalty, Margaret is not mentioned in the list of characters present and never says anything. Yet she is present at the play's end among the dancers.

Messenger:

A messenger is mentioned three different times in the play. In the opening scene of Act I, a messenger brings Leonato news that the soldiers are returning from a war. He conveys news of the brave battle performances of Claudio and of Benedick. At the end of Act III, a messenger brings Leonato word that the wedding party is waiting for him. At the end of Act V, a messenger brings word to Don Pedro that his brother has been captured and returned to Messina.

Musicians:

Leonato has musicians to provide entertainment for his visitors. For example, there is dancing at Leonato's party. Balthasar's song is accompanied by musicians. Claudio's song at Hero's tomb is also accompanied by music. The instruments for social occasions include the lute, the tabor, and the pipe.

Pedro (Don Pedro):

Don Pedro, a nobleman and soldier, is the Prince of Arragon (Aragon), a region of eastern

Spain. He is referred to by Leonato as "your Grace" (I.i.100), and indeed his behavior throughout much of the play is gracious and courtly. When the audience first meets Don John, who is Don Pedro's brother, it hears of Don Pedro's gracious behavior to his rebellious brother.

Don Pedro's actions throughout the play display his power and influence as well as his good humor. He has the power to confer honors for valor on the soldiers in his company and has done so to Claudio just before the beginning of the play. He speaks for his company of men to Leonato. He goes back to call the privately conferring Benedick and Claudio to their duties to Leonato, their host. He also agrees in a separate conversation with Claudio to intervene for him in marriage negotiations with Hero. He says he will disguise himself as Claudio, reveal his affections, and then speak of the matter to Leonato.

Don Pedro announces Claudio's and Hero's successfully negotiated wedding, both to Claudio and to their circle of friends. When he proposes on his own behalf to Beatrice and is rejected, he takes Beatrice's reply in good humor, appreciating her merry nature. He proposes the plot of tricking Benedick, both to pass the time until Claudio's wedding and to challenge Cupid at his own love game. He shows his own playful humor during the gulling scene and also reveals again his own interest in Beatrice. Additionally, he shows an interest in conveying to Benedick that some of his behavior needs mending.

When Don Pedro and Claudio are privately confronted by Don John with a false report about Hero, Don Pedro is at first skeptical. However, he agrees with Claudio's desire to publicly disgrace Hero if the evidence works out against her.

Don Pedro's gracious and good-natured behavior is temporarily displaced whn the evidence against Hero is presented. At the wedding, Don Pedro shows concern for his honor and his friend's honor, and none at all for Hero's reputation. He reports the evidence to the assembled company, in temperate but definite terms. In the encounter with Leonato, he seems in a hurry and refers to Leonato as "good old man" (V.i.50) or simply "old man" (V.i.73). He continues in a light jesting vein when Benedick comes to challenge Claudio and only slowly recognizes that Benedick is serious. Once

Borachio's plot is revealed, Don Pedro immediately suspects his brother as being the instigator of the plot. His continuing loyalty to Claudio is shown in his accompaniment of Claudio to Hero's tomb to hang the epitaph and mourn. Don Pedro's graciousness is once more his leading characteristic as he greets the assembled company at the final wedding. He in turn is told by Benedick to get a wife and is described at the end as looking "sad" (V.iv.122), or serious.

Sexton:

The sexton's name is Francis Seacole (he is not the same as the man named George Seacole in the watch), and he is a town clerk. Sometimes the word sexton refers to a church official in charge of a churchyard and a gravedigger.

The sexton writes down the testimony against the defendants. The testimony takes place in a hearing-room in Messina, probably in the same building as the jail. The sexton has been referred to by Dogberry as a "learned writer" (III.v.63). He demonstrates by his short, logical speeches that he is, unlike Dogberry, experienced and knows what he is doing. He asks to see the malefactors, i.e., the offenders, and he knows what his words mean as he uses them. Unlike the prisoner, Conrade, he controls his responses to Dogberry, but does tell Dogberry directly that he is not doing the examination correctly and instructs him to call forth the watch. He skillfully prompts the watch to disclose the information they possess.

Ursula:

Ursula is a gentlewoman waiting on Hero. She is present at Leonato's party and dances with Antonio. She helps Hero in the scene in which Beatrice is fooled into thinking Benedick is in love with her. Ursula follows Hero's lead in the scene, mainly directing questions and follow-up questions to Hero about the truth of the report. She calls Hero to go to the church for her wedding. She also announces to Beatrice and Benedick the revelations about Don John's plot against Hero.

Verges:

Verges is headborough (a petty constable) and assistant to Dogberry. He appears in the four scenes in which Dogberry appears. He also abuses language and shares Dogberry's logic about how the watch should conduct itself. He swears mild old-fashioned oaths such as ''By'r lady'' (III.iii.83), for ''By Our Lady.'' He does not talk nearly as much as Dogberry does. Dogberry suggests that Verges is old and not as witty as he himself is. However, he is Dogberry's sidekick, and takes his cues from his partner. He seems to admire Dogberry and says, ''You have been always called a merciful man, partner'' (III.iii.61-62).

Watch:

This group is composed of the night watchmen. Some editions of the play show two, and some show three watchmen. If a play editor shows three night watchmen, then it is usually because one is specifically identified as George Seacoal. The basis for this is that the first watchman refers to several able watchmen fit to be the head night constable on the basis of their ability to read and write. The two he names are Hugh Oatcake and George Seacoal. Dogberry specifically calls forth George Seacoal in giving the directions for the night watch.

The watchmen were local citizens whose job it was to protect the citizens of the town from fires, robberies, and other crimes. In addition, the watch were to prevent noises at night which would bother residents.

This group of watchmen fit in well with Dogberry and Verges. They say they would ''rather sleep than talk'' (III.iii.37). They intend to stay in one place, sitting on the church bench, until two, and then go home. Fortunately, they overhear Borachio and Conrade and hide to hear the whole story. Although they misunderstand some references to fashion, they do understand the main outlines of the plot against Hero. When it looks as though Dogberry might fail to say anything sensible against Conrade and Borachio, the watch give important testimony before the sexton.

Further Reading

Bennett, Josephine Waters. Introduction to *Much Ado About Nothing*, by William Shakespeare. In *The Complete Works of William Shakespeare*, edited by Alfred Harbage, 274-77. Baltimore: Pelican, 1969.
    Bennett treats the topics of play source, composition date, plot, and characters.

Carroll, Lewis. Letter to Ellen Terry on Problems in the Plot of *Much Ado About Nothing*. Appendix 2 to *Much Ado About Nothing*, by William Shakespeare, edited by F. H. Mares, 157-58. Cambridge: Cambridge University Press, 1988.
    This brief letter from the author of *Alice's Adventures in Wonderland* to a famous nineteenth-century Shakespearean actress points out some plot inconsistencies in the play.

Coursen, H. R. ''Branagh's *Much Ado*: Art and Popular Culture?'' In *Shakespeare in Production: Whose History?*, 90-117. Athens: Ohio University Press, 1996.
    Chapter 5 of Coursen's book discusses the response of critics and reviewers to Branagh's popular film. This article discusses the well-known movie actors in the film. The list includes Kenneth Branagh, Emma Thompson, Michael Keaton, and Keanu Reeves. It mentions well-known movies and television programs for particular points of comparison, and ends by labelling the film ''conventional.''

Humphreys, A. R. Introduction to *Much Ado About Nothing*, by William Shakespeare, 1-84. London: Methuen, 1981.
    In addition to material on the source, dating, stage history and criticism of the play, this introductory essay to the Arden edition of the play contains a section on the world, i.e., the spirit, of Messina, and another on the plotting of the play.

Hunter, Robert Grams. ''Forgiving Claudio.'' In *Twentieth Century Interpretations of* Much Ado About Nothing, edited by Walter R. Davis, 60-66. Englewood Cliffs: Prentice-Hall, 1969.
    This essay discusses the Elizabethan view of human frailty, as exemplified by Claudio, the religious connotations of his penance, and the Elizabethan audience's probable ultimate sympathy with the offender as an erring son of Adam.

Mares, F. H. Introduction to *Much Ado About Nothing*, by William Shakespeare, 1-47. Cambridge: Cambridge University Press, 1988.
    Mares's introduction to the Cambridge edition of the play includes discussion of sources, the date of the composition of the play, its stage history, and criticism of the play, including character discussion of Claudio, Benedick, and Beatrice. It also includes photos of stage performances and illustrations by C. Walter Hodges of several scenes.

McDonald, Russ. ''Theatre a la Mode: Shakespeare and the Kinds of Drama.'' In *The Bedford Companion to Shakespeare: An Introduction with Documents,* 151-79. Boston: St. Martin's Press, 1996.
    A brief discussion of the genre of comedy early in Chapter 5 helps students to understand the literary concept of comedy. His brief section on mixed modes is helpful for *Much Ado*. Documents at the end of the chapter include a paragraph from Sir Philip Sidney on comedy.

Newman, Karen. ''Mistaking in *Much Ado*.'' In *William Shakespeare's* Much Ado About Nothing, edited by Harold Bloom, 123-32. New York: Chelsea House, 1988.
    Newman discusses Claudio as an example of her general point that Shakespeare goes beyond the usual

boundaries of comedy and comic plotting and makes Claudio a more complex character, though not as deep and complicated as Angelo in *Measure for Measure*.

Prouty, Charles T. *The Sources of* Much Ado About Nothing: *A Critical Study*. Yale: New Haven, 1950.
This book studies Shakespeare's literary sources for his play. Additionally, a defense of Claudio and his motives can be found on pp. 39-52, in a section on Claudio and Hero. Likewise, Beatrice and Benedick are analyzed on pp. 52-61.

Salingar, Leo. *Shakespeare and the Traditions of Comedy*. Cambridge: Cambridge University Press, 1974.
A work about comic forms and literary influences; discusses various comedies.

Storey, Graham. "The Success of *Much Ado About Nothing*." In *Twentieth Century Interpretations of* Much Ado About Nothing, edited by Walter R. Davis, 18-32. Englewood Cliffs: Prentice-Hall, 1969.
This essay discusses plot as it contributes the themes of the play, which the author sees as "deception, miscomprehension, man's 'giddiness' at every level."

The Tragedy of Othello, the Moor of Venice

circa 1603-04

Act I:

The play opens in Venice with Iago trying to convince Roderigo that he dislikes Othello, the dark-skinned Moor and Venetian soldier, as much as Roderigo does. Roderigo is a suitor to Desdemona, and he dislikes Othello because Desdemona has chosen Othello over him. As he tells Roderigo, Iago dislikes Othello because Othello has chosen Cassio, a man who has learned warfare "by the book," to be his lieutenant, overlooking Iago's years of dedicated services as Othello's "ancient" (a rank perhaps equivalent to that of a modern sergeant, the highest rank an enlisted man can achieve). Iago proposes that they go to the house of the senator Brabantio, who is Desdemona's father, and inform him that his daughter is, at that very moment, with Othello. They stand outside of Brabantio's house and yell that his daughter has eloped with Othello, a black Moor, shouting racist remarks to incite Brabantio's anger. Iago has concealed himself in darkness and sneaks off because he does not want Othello, the General of the Venetian forces, to know he has sided against him. He goes to Othello and warns him that Brabantio is incensed and is coming after him. Roderigo escorts Brabantio to the place where Othello and Desdemona are, and Brabantio confronts Othello. They draw their swords. Brabantio accuses Othello of stealing his daughter, but Othello cannot immediately answer the charge because he

has been summoned to appear before the duke of Venice on urgent business. Brabantio goes along to plead his case before the duke of Venice and the Venetian senate. In the meantime, the duke and the senators have received conflicting reports on the whereabouts of the Turkish fleet that is threatening Venice. They decide that the Turks are feinting and will concentrate their efforts on the island of Cyprus, agreeing that Othello should conduct the opposition there. In front of the duke and the senators, Brabantio accuses Othello of having used witchcraft to win his daughter's affections. Othello objects by saying that Desdemona fell in love with him when she heard his tales of exotic adventures and heroic encounters. He has Desdemona brought in to confirm his story, and she does, telling her father that she now owes obedience to her husband, just as her mother did to Brabantio. Since the state of Venice needs the services of Othello at the moment, the duke rules against Brabantio. Brabantio virtually disinherits Desdemona, and she decides to accompany Othello to Cyprus. Iago reassures Roderigo that he will continue to woo Desdemona on Roderigo's behalf, claiming that Desdemona will soon tire of Othello and that her interest in Othello is one of physical lust only.

Act II:

The ship carrying Desdemona, Cassio, Iago, and Iago's wife Emilia arrives in Cyprus before Othello's ship, which has last been seen tossing on the waves of a violent storm. That storm has seriously damaged the Turkish fleet, removing the immediate threat of battle. Othello arrives safely on the island of Cyprus and announces that the ''wars are done; the Turks are drown'd'' (II.i.202). Othello sends a herald to proclaim a general celebration for both the defeat of the Turks and his marriage to Desdemona, but he takes Cassio aside and advises him to keep watch and maintain a condition of military alert. Earlier, while waiting for Othello to arrive, Iago has observed Cassio and Desdemona exchanging courtly pleasantries. He hatches a plan to circulate the notion that Cassio and Desdemona are lovers, not only making Othello jealous but punishing Cassio for having been promoted over him. Iago directs Roderigo, who has also traveled to Cyprus, to make trouble for Cassio, assaulting the latter when he is on watch. Cassio confides to Iago that he cannot hold his liquor, and this information only helps Iago's plan. Iago suggests to Montano, the governor of Cyprus, that Cassio is drunk, unstable, and ill suited to keep order. When Roderigo scuffles with Cassio, Montano approaches the latter

and urges him to behave, assuming all that Iago has told him is true. Cassio and Montano, in turn, scuffle, and Iago has Roderigo run and ''cry a mutiny'' (II.iii.157). An angry Othello responds to the general alarm and chastises Cassio for not being vigilant on his watch. When questioned by Othello about what has happened, Iago is just evasive enough to make Cassio seem guilty, and Othello declares that Cassio is no longer his lieutenant. Iago pursues his plan, telling Cassio that the lieutenant might get back into Othello's good graces through the kind intervention of Desdemona.

Act III:

Cassio takes Iago's advice and asks Desdemona to petition her husband to restore Cassio's rank. Desdemona willingly agrees and says she will do so immediately, her husband approaching with Iago at that very moment. Cassio excuses himself because he feels uncomfortable under the circumstances. Iago takes the opportunity of Cassio's quick exit to suggest to Othello that Desdemona and Cassio are intimate. At first Othello objects, claiming that Desdemona has freely chosen him as her husband. But Iago persists, suggesting that if Desdemona could deceive her father so easily, she could do the same with Othello. Moreover, Iago intimates that her doing so is not unthinkable given her great differences from Othello in age, complexion, and social standing. Othello begins to doubt. He approaches Desdemona and says, ''I have a pain upon my forehead, here'' (III.iii.284), meaning the horns of a cuckolded husband (cuckold's horns symbolized a man whose wife has cheated on, or cuckolded, him). Desdemona attempts to bind his head with the handkerchief Othello has earlier given her as a love token, but Othello pushes it away, the handkerchief falling to the floor. Emilia then retrieves the handkerchief and gives it to Iago, who has asked her to procure it for him on several occasions. The handkerchief is special; ''there's magic in the web of it'' (III.iv.69). Othello's father had given it to Othello's mother, who remained faithful to her husband as long as she possessed it. To increase Othello's suspicion, Iago hides the handkerchief in the chamber of Cassio, who discovers it and gives it to Bianca, a courtezan with whom Cassio is intimate, so that she might remove the handkerchief's valuable and intricate stitching.

Act IV:

Iago continues to turn the screw of Othello's jealousy until Othello's inner struggle causes him to faint, Iago informing Cassio that the fainting is a fit of epilepsy Othello has experienced before. Iago arranges that Othello might stand aside and observe Iago questioning Cassio about the latter's relationship with Desdemona. Really he questions Cassio about Bianca, knowing that Othello will not hear but only see a callous, laughing Cassio somewhat amused by Bianca's pursuit of and desire for him. During this exchange, Bianca enters, carrying the handkerchief. After Cassio and Bianco have left, Iago tells Othello that Desdemona gave the handkerchief to Cassio and "he hath giv'n it [to] his whore" (IV.i.177). Othello becomes convinced of Desdemona's adultery and announces his determination to kill Desdemona by hacking her to bits or poisoning her, but Iago convinces Othello to strangle her in the bed she has betrayed. When Desdemona enters and renews her suit on Cassio's behalf, Othello strikes her, much to the shock and dismay of Lodovico, a kinsmen of Brabantio. Desdemona leaves, unaware of the source of Othello's anger but not wanting to displease him further. Later, Othello questions Emilia and Desdemona separately about Desdemona's affair with Cassio, and both deny it. He then brings them together into Desdemona's chamber, calling Desdemona a whore and Emilia her pimp. Othello has received a letter from the duke of Venice ordering him to return there. He decides to murder Desdemona that night, and he sends her home, telling her to ready herself for bed and dismiss the servants while he takes a walk with Lodovico. The letter from the duke has also named Cassio as Othello's successor. Iago, after convincing Roderigo that he is still at work on Roderigo's behalf, persuades him to attack Cassio that evening at Bianca's home, assuring Roderigo that he will back him up.

Act V:

Iago has no intention of helping Roderigo kill Cassio; it is his hope that they will kill each other. When Roderigo attacks Cassio in the dark, Cassio is grievously wounded, but Roderigo receives only a superficial wound. Iago approaches Roderigo in the darkness and mortally stabs him. Iago is not yet suspected, and he sums up the whole business to Emilia: "This is the fruits of whoring" (V.i.116), implying that the fight between Cassio and Roderigo has been precipitated by jealousy over a woman. Othello tells Desdemona he is going to kill her, and, despite her pleas for mercy, he smothers her with a pillow. Emilia arrives desperate to inform Othello of Roderigo's murder and Cassio's serious wounding. Desdemona revives momentarily and forgives

Othello for murdering her. Emilia is now aware of what Othello has done, and he tells her Desdemona's death was necessary because she had been unfaithful to him with Cassio. When Emilia asks how he ever could have arrived at such a suspicion, Othello tells her that Iago has said it was so. The truth of the situation begins to dawn on Emilia, and she confronts her husband. She confesses to Montano, Gratiano (Brabantio's kinsman), and others the circumstances regarding the handkerchief. Iago tells her to hold her tongue, but she continues to inform on him. Othello, finally realizing how Iago has manipulated him, lunges at Iago but is restrained. Iago then stabs and kills Emilia as he runs away. Iago is captured and brought back, but he refuses to offer any further explanation for his actions. Othello has been disarmed, but he produces a knife that has been hidden on his body and kills himself. Cassio, who has survived his wounds, is named successor to Othello as the military ruler in Cyprus.

Modern Connections

While there are a number of issues in *Othello* that twentieth-century audiences can connect with (crimes of passion are not new to today's society; just turn on the evening news), modern audiences often come away from *Othello* feeling uncomfortable with the racism they see in the treatment Othello receives from the other characters in the play. And just as we are well aware of the racism in our own society, it may be that Shakespeare was writing about the racism in his own society, not just the racism in the Venetian society depicted in the play. Shakespeare's *Othello* is set in Venice and Cyprus, but the Venetian society's fear of cultural difference, manifested in its racism, may be viewed as an indicator of Elizabethan England's concern to maintain its cultural identity in the face of extensive exploration and initial colonization of the New World. The Turk and the Moor, two traditional symbols of cultural values different from those of Western culture, threaten Venetian society but may be read as the embodiments of Elizabethan England's fear that its cultural values will be lost through colonization and the intermingling of different cultural values. In the same way, the depiction of Desdemona as the flower of Venetian society, the ideal of virtuous fidelity, is perhaps less a description of Venetian gender expectations than it is a depiction of woman designed to allay English fears that miscegenation (procreation between a man and a woman of different races) would threaten the order and culture of English society.

On one level, adultery in *Othello* can be seen as an individual infidelity that destroys both Iago and Othello as jealousy is incited in Othello by the promptings of his only confidante, "honest Iago." On another level, adultery may be viewed by some as destructive to a whole society. As some people in Shakespeare's time may have felt, and as some people in modern times may feel, the society that fails to limit the sexual activity of women runs the risk of losing a paternal identification—we can never be certain who the father is in cases of infidelity—but also losing cultural identity in miscegenation. Iago claims to hate Othello because Othello has passed him over for promotion and slept with his wife, Emilia, but a third motive for his behavior is, perhaps, one that he does not or cannot explicitly state: the motive to preserve the racial and cultural identity of his society. Or, perhaps, Iago is motivated by his own more personal feelings of racism (rather than his society's) which come to the fore as Iago deals with the fact that his superior is a black man.

When Iago's schemes have been revealed by Emilia, he is encouraged by the others to reveal his motives. This would certainly seem to be the perfect opportunity to reveal his anger at the loss of promotion and his jealous suspicions of Othello. But instead, he says, "Demand me nothing; what you know, you know: / From this time forth I never will speak word" (V.ii.303-04). In one sense, this exclamation continues his power and control to the end. But in another sense, perhaps he cannot articulate his motives because they are the deep and unidentified racist feelings of his society in general. He is a functionary agent of a state that has irreconcilable misgivings about the marriage of a black Moor to a white woman.

Iago is arguably the voice of racial intolerance: he cries out to Brabantio, "your daughter and the Moor are [now] making the beast with two backs" (I.i.116-17) and "Even now, now, very now, an old black ram / Is tupping your white ewe" (I.i.88-89). These are metaphors calculated to alarm Brabantio and arouse his most primal fears. Racism and woman's unchecked sexuality are themes that resonate throughout the play and ignite the most confusion and fear when they are conceptualized as the offspring of a union between Desdemona and Othello. Thus, Iago makes his fiercest appeal when he cries out to Brabantio: "you'll have your daughter covered with a Barbary horse, you'll have your nephews neigh to you; you'll have coursers for cousins, and gennets for germans" (I.i.111-13). Although Iago takes it upon himself to repair the grievous cultural rupture caused by the marriage of Desdemona and Othello, he is not alone. Desdemona's own father cannot believe his daughter would be one

> To fall in love with what she fear'd to look!
> It is a judgment maim'd, and most imperfect,
> That will confess perfection so could err
> Against all rules of nature. . . .
>
> (I.iii.98-101)

Brabantio believes that Othello has caused her to stray from such perfection by using magic potions and witchcraft to sway her affections.

Iago confesses that he, too, loves Desdemona (II.i.291). But it is a love constituted by neither lust nor an attraction to inner beauty. What he loves is the construction of Desdemona as the "perfect" woman, a perfection of sensibilities that must not be allowed to err. The audience knows full well that Desdemona has not been unfaithful to Othello. However, in the eyes of Iago and the others, she is guilty of a greater betrayal: her marriage to Othello.

Othello brings us closer to an understanding of Greek tragedy than any other of Shakespeare's plays. Othello perhaps never fully realizes how he has erred. What he has blundered into in ignorance is swiftly avenged by powerful and unstoppable forces. What excites fear and pity in the modern reader is an identification with Othello's frailty and the suspicion that those unstoppable forces are produced by the fears and ignorance in society.

Characters

Attendants:

Othello and Desdemona are characters of some stature in the communities of both Venice and Cyprus. In their public appearances throughout the play, they are often accompanied by attendants.

Bianca:

Bianca is a courtezan, a prostitute, in Cyprus. She falls in love with Cassio and pursues him, an unexpected turn of events given the callousness and lack of affection usually associated with her profession. Iago is aware that Cassio is not as affectionate toward Bianca as she is toward him, and he takes advantage of the one-sided relationship. On the pretext that he is questioning Cassio about Desdemona,

Iago really questions Cassio about Bianca. He does this in order to increase Othello's jealousy, as the latter stands off to the side unable to hear but able to see Cassio's cavalier and mocking attitude. When Cassio finds the handkerchief belonging to Othello and planted in his quarters by Iago, he gives it to Bianca that she might remove its valuable stitching. This fortunate event lends itself to Iago's plan since it increases Othello's hatred of Cassio, who seemingly equates Desdemona with a common prostitute.

Brabantio:

Brabantio is Desdemona's father. He is a magnifico, a prominent citizen and landowner in Venice. When the play opens, Brabantio's household is being disrupted by Iago and Roderigo, who are crying out to Brabantio that he has been robbed. Brabantio says, "What tell'st thou me of robbing? This is Venice; / My house is not a grange" (I.i.105-06). He believes he is safely within the civilized society of Venice, not on the dangerous and uncivilized fringe of that society. When Iago cries that Brabantio's daughter is at that moment sleeping with the Moor Othello, he appeals to Brabantio's racial prejudices. When Brabantio recognizes Roderigo, he reminds him that he has prohibited Roderigo from pursuing Desdemona as a suitor. Moments later, Brabantio first reveals his racial prejudice when he tells Roderigo, "O would you had had her! / Some one way, some another" (I.i.175-76). He would prefer anyone to Othello as his daughter's husband, even the unsavory Roderigo.

Brabantio cannot believe Desdemona has freely selected Othello. When Roderigo escorts him to the place where Othello is, Brabantio draws his sword and is ready to fight with the Moor. He accuses Othello of having used spells and charms to seduce and steal his daughter. He makes the same claim to the Venetian senate, arguing that Othello has certainly used witchcraft to win his daughter. In Brabantio's eyes, Desdemona is a maiden so modest that it is unthinkable for her "To fall in love with what she fear'd to look on!" (I.iii.98). When Othello explains that Desdemona was initially fascinated by Othello's tales of exotic adventures, eventually falling in love with him, Brabantio misses the irony. He shared that fascination himself, inviting Othello into his home so that Othello might entertain Brabantio and his guests with the tales of his daring exploits. When Brabantio hears Desdemona support Othello's story, he gives up his appeal. He never sanctions the marriage of his daughter to Othello and leaves uttering his total disapproval.

Cassio:

Cassio is chosen over Iago to be Othello's lieutenant. According to Iago, Cassio is "a great arithmetician" (I.i.19), one "That never set a squadron in the field" (I.i.22). Cassio knows battle only from books, unlike Iago who has had a good deal of experience in combat. Cassio is apparently a handsome man, and the ladies are attracted to him. But Cassio also has his weaknesses. When Iago tries to get him to have a drink in celebration of the Turks' defeat and Othello's marriage, Cassio says, "I have very poor and unhappy brains for drinking" (II.iii.33). Cassio is the perfect dupe for Iago. Cassio is attractive, and this fact encourages Othello's belief in Iago's suggestion that Desdemona desires Cassio. Cassio's inability to drink also gives Iago another weapon in his plan to abuse both Cassio and Othello.

Cassio represents the class privilege of which Iago is so envious and resentful. It rankles Iago that Cassio seems to have bought into the idea that he is socially superior. When they are drinking together, Cassio tells Iago that "the lieutenant is to be sav'd before the ancient" (II.iii.109). Cassio is perhaps referring to a commonplace for maintaining military order, but the implication is that Cassio is superior by virtue of his title alone. Again, when Othello disgraces Cassio by scolding him in public and stripping him of his rank for neglecting his watch and brawling with Montano, Cassio laments most the loss of his reputation. In his great desire to regain that reputation, he plays right into the hands of Iago who suggests that Cassio appeal to Desdemona to intervene with Othello for restoring his rank. For Iago, through whose eyes the audience gets its only sense of Cassio's character, Cassio is all reputation and title with no real substance. Iago refers to "One Michael Cassio, a Florentine" (I.i.20) while a gentleman in Cyprus refers to "A Veronesa; Michael Cassio" (II.i.26). Perhaps Cassio has no inner qualities that identify who and what he is, only his titles. Even so, he ends up in charge of the Venetian troops in Cyprus.

Clown:

In a comic interlude that temporarily breaks the building tension, the clown appears and speaks to a group of musicians who have been directed by Cassio to play outside the quarters of Desdemona and Othello. The clown tells the musicians they sound nasal, alluding to the nasal damage done in advanced cases of syphilis. The clown also engages in some low-brow humor involving a "tale" and a "wind instrument" (III.i.10). The clown appears again in III.iv, punning evasively in response to Desdemona's simple inquiry as to whether or not the clown knows where Cassio lives.

Desdemona:

Desdemona is the daughter of Brabantio, a man of some reputation in Venice. As such, she is part of the upper class of Venetian society. Apparently, she has many suitors vying for her hand in marriage, but she freely chooses to marry Othello, a decision which greatly upsets Brabantio, Iago, and Roderigo. She testifies before the Venetian senate that the story Othello has told about their mutual attraction is true. In that story, Othello recounts how he was invited to Brabantio's home to tell of his journeys to foreign places. Being forced to leave the room on frequent errands for her father and his guests, Desdemona was unable to hear the full account of Othello's exploits in those foreign places. But she was intrigued, and on another occasion Othello told her his story in full. Othello tells the duke and the senators, ''She lov'd me for the dangers I had pass'd, / And I lov'd her that she did pity them'' (I.iii.167-68). Despite what her father and Iago might think, Desdemona does seem to love Othello truly, and, despite Othello's jealous suspicions, she is faithful to him until the end.

In one sense, though, Desdemona presents a contradiction, some critics have argued. After Othello accuses her of being unfaithful, she asks Emilia, ''Wouldst thou do such a deed for all the world?'' (IV.iii.63) Emilia responds realistically that she would not be unfaithful for a trifle, but the world is a big place. While Desdemona's question reveals her innocence, her past actions have shown her to be capable of some level of deception: she secretly elopes with a man of whom her father greatly disapproves. She explains to Brabantio that she has only transferred her love and allegiance from father to husband, just as her mother had done. While many audiences do not judge Desdemona too harshly for this, many critics maintain that through these actions, Desdemona demonstrates the capacity to deceive men. It is this perceived capacity that Iago exploits most aggressively. He virtually seals Desdemona's fate when he tells Othello,

> She did deceive her father, marrying you,
> And when she seem'd to shake and fear your
>   looks,
> She lov'd them most.
>
> (III.iii.206-08)

As he contemplates killing Desdemona, Othello echoes Iago's words, ''Yet she must die, else

> ❝❝ Othello tells the duke and the senators, '[Desdemona] lov'd me for the dangers I had pass'd, / And I lov'd her that she did pity them' (I.iii.167-68).''

she'll betray more men'' (V.i.6). For Iago and Othello, Desdemona can only be totally pure when she can no longer experience desire, when men no longer need to fear that that desire will betray them—in death.

Desdemona has been described by some critics as a Christlike figure. Like the love Christ extends to humankind, Desdemona's love for Othello is freely given and need not be defended by reasoned explanations. Othello's great failing is that he does not simply accept Desdemona's love, but finds reasons to think himself unworthy of her. He gives in to Iago's suggestions that Desdemona could not freely love one who was so different from her in ''clime, complexion, and degree'' (III.iii.23). After Othello has killed Desdemona, Emilia asks who has done such a deed. Desdemona revives and says, ''Nobody; I myself. Farewell! / Commend me to my kind lord'' (V.ii.124-25), echoing the unselfishness and forgiveness of Christ's dying words on the cross.

Duke of Venice:
See Venice

Emilia:

Emilia is Iago's wife. She travels to Cyprus with her husband and acts as a waiting woman to Desdemona. When Emilia and Iago arrive in Cyprus, we get some sense of the relationship between Emilia and her husband. Cassio greets Emilia with a kiss, and Iago says,

> Sir, would she give you so much of her lips
> As of her tongue she oft bestows on me,
> You would have enough.
>
> (II.i.100-02)

Emilia is a strong-willed woman who apparently will not suffer her husband to abuse her. She tries to please Iago by recovering for him the handkerchief dropped by Desdemona, unknowing-

> As he contemplates killing Desdemona, Othello [says], 'Yet she must die, else she'll betray more men' (V.i.6)."

ly contributing to Desdemona's death. But when she understands what Iago has done and why he has so often asked her to steal that handkerchief, she exposes him and will not be silenced even when he commands her to "hold [her] peace" (V.ii.218). Emilia is the only character whom Iago cannot totally manipulate.

The play offers other evidence of Emilia's strong-willed and independent nature. After Othello has struck Desdemona and humiliated her in public, Emilia explains to Iago what has happened. She says that, undoubtedly, some knave has slandered Desdemona to make Othello jealous, an absurd accusation similar to Iago's own accusation that Emilia has been unfaithful with the Moor (IV.ii.145-47). Emilia later explains to Desdemona that some women do cheat on their husbands and are justified in doing so if their husbands have cheated on them. She is a woman who believes that men and women experience the same passions and desires. Near the end of the play, Emilia will not be silenced in her efforts to bring Desdemona's killers to justice. She even defies Othello in his efforts to physically intimidate her. She says, "I'll make thee known / Though I lost twenty lives" (V.ii.165-66). In the end, Iago can only silence Emilia by stabbing her to death.

Gentlemen (of Cyprus):

When the play switches location to Cyprus, two gentlemen talk to Montano, the governor there, about the raging storm tossing the Turkish fleet. A third gentleman enters and announces that the storm has scattered the Turkish fleet, causing the Turks to abandon their intended invasion of Cyprus. He also reports that a Venetian ship has been wrecked and that Cassio worries the ship might have been the one carrying Othello. The second of the first two gentlemen identifies Iago when he disembarks. Later, armed gentlemen appear with Othello when he interrupts the fight between Cassio and Montano and chastises those two for brawling.

Gratiano:

Gratiano is a kinsman of Brabantio. In some editions of the play he is listed as Brabantio's brother. Other editions list him and Lodovico as two noble Venetians. Gratiano appears in the dark streets of Cyprus just after Roderigo has stabbed Cassio. He helps minister to Cassio and sort out the identities of others in the confusing darkness. He is also present when Emilia accuses Othello of killing Desdemona and when Othello is apprehended. His chief function in the play seems to be one of eliciting explanations from the other characters, providing them with the opportunity to sort out complex events. Twice near the end of the play he asks, "What is the matter?" (V.ii.170,259).

Herald:

The herald is sent by Othello to make a public proclamation: in celebration of the Turkish fleet's defeat and Othello's marriage, the populace is directed to feast, make bonfires, and dance, each man pursuing his own sport. This celebration is to continue from five to eleven that night.

Iago:

Iago is Othello's ancient, or ensign. He is a soldier with a good deal of experience in battle, having been on the field with Othello at both Rhodes and Cyprus. He is also one of Shakespeare's greatest villains. He is a master manipulator of people and gets the other characters in the play to do just what he wants. He manipulates others through a keen understanding he seems to have of what motivates them. For example, Iago uses the vision Roderigo has of a union with Desdemona to manipulate Roderigo. Cassio is a man driven by the need to maintain outer appearances and he easily accepts Iago's advice that he recover his rank by going through Desdemona. Iago also uses to his advantage the fact that Desdemona is of a kind and generous nature, one who will gladly accept the opportunity to persuade her husband to make amends with his lieutenant. And, finally, Iago uses Othello's jealous nature and his apparent insecurity to convince Othello of Desdemona's infidelity. Emilia is the only one, it seems, that Iago cannot manipulate, perhaps because she knows him so well.

Iago schemes to have Cassio demoted from his post as lieutenant, next suggesting that Cassio ask Desdemona to intercede for him with Othello on his behalf. She does, which contributes to Othello's suspicions. Othello first begins to distrust Desdemona when Iago points out that, as he and Othello approached Desdemona and Cassio, Cassio quickly departed. Iago also reminds Othello that Desdemona, in eloping with Othello deceived her father, which shows her capacity for deception. Additionally, Iago reminds Othello of the differences between Othello and Desdemona in terms of color, age, and social status. The handkerchief that Othello had given to Desdemona as love token is also used to indicate her guilt, a situation also engineered by Iago.

Iago provides the audience with a number of clues to the motives for his actions. First, he feels a certain rancor at not being chosen as Othello's lieutenant. He reassures Roderigo of this:

> Preferment goes by letter and affection,
> And not by old gradation, where each second
> Stood heir to th' first. Now, sir, be judge yourself
> Whether I in any just term am affin'd
> To love the Moor.
>
> (I.i.36-40)

He is disgruntled at having been passed over for promotion, and he sees a chance to get back at both Othello, who has slighted him, and Cassio, the mocking symbol of that slight. Second, he suspects that Othello has engaged in adultery with his wife, Emilia. He mentions this on two occasions: "I hate the Moor, / And it is thought abroad that 'twixt my sheets / [He's] done my office" (I.iii.386-88) and

> . . . I do suspect the lusty Moor
> Hath leap'd into my seat; the thought whereof
> Doth (like a poisonous mineral) gnaw my inwards;
> And nothing can or shall content my soul
> Till I am evened with him, wife for wife.
>
> (II.i.295-99)

Apparently, Iago is so distressed by the thought of Emilia sleeping with Othello that he has accused Emilia of the act. As is typical of her, Emilia characterizes the accusation as absurd (IV.ii.145-47). In their unfounded jealousy, Iago and Othello are very much alike.

Iago and Othello are alike in another way as well. At the end of the play, when Othello is under arrest and Iago has been apprehended and is brought into his presence, Othello says, "I look down towards his feet; but that's a fable" (V.ii.286). He is looking to see if Iago has cloven feet like the devil Othello now thinks him to be. But for all of Iago's hatred of Othello and Othello's newly discovered contempt for Iago, the two are very much alike in their sense of being excluded from upper-class Venetian society. When Othello calls him "honest, honest Iago" (V.ii.154), he speaks of more than

> **Near the end of the play, Emilia will not be silenced in her efforts to bring Desdemona's killers to justice. She even defies Othello in his efforts to physically intimidate her. She says, 'I'll make thee known / Though I lost twenty lives' (V.ii.165-66)."**

verbal truth. Iago is the only character who speaks directly to Othello's sense of his own inadequacy, a sense of inadequacy Iago perhaps shares. At the end of the play, after killing Roderigo and Emilia and revealing all he has done, Iago is taken prisoner.

Lodovico:

Lodovico is Brabantio's kinsman. (Some editions of the play list Gratiano as Brabantio's brother and Lodovico as Brabantio's kinsman. Other editions list them both simply as two noble Venetians.) When Lodovico arrives in Cyprus, he and Othello greet one another with civil courtesy. Lodovico brings a letter from the duke of Venice, in which Othello is commanded to return to Venice immediately, Cassio taking his place of command in Cyprus. As Othello reads the letter, he overhears Lodovico ask Desdemona if the rift between the general and the lieutenant can be repaired. Desdemona is hopeful and says, "I would do much / T'atone them, for the love I bear to Cassio" (IV.i.232-33). Although she means only that she is concerned for Cassio, Othello strikes her. Othello's action astounds Lodovico. When Othello leaves, Lodovico asks, "Is this the noble Moor whom our Senate / Call all in all sufficient?" (IV.i.264-65). He wonders aloud if the letter has caused Othello to experience such a wild mood swing. Lodovico is present later when Othello is apprehended and all finally realize that Othello has killed Desdemona.

Messenger:

Two messengers appear in the play. The first reports to the Venetian senators that a Turkish fleet of approximately thirty ships has threatened Rhodes but has since turned and headed for Cyprus. The

> **Emilia is the only one, it seems, that Iago cannot manipulate."**

second messenger appears as Cassio and Montano express concern for Othello's survival on the torrid sea. He announces that all of the townspeople have gathered on the shore to keep watch of the turbulent ocean and have spotted the sail of a ship.

Montano:

Montano is the governor of Cyprus. He has sent a messenger to the duke of Venice, confirming the presence of the Turkish fleet near Cyprus. He welcomes the Venetian protectors when they arrive on his isle, anxious for Othello's safety and elated when the tempest scatters the Turkish threat. As all celebrate the defeat of the Turks and Othello's marriage, Cassio must leave the celebration to go on watch. Iago slyly tells Montano that Cassio is an excellent man, but not when he has been drinking. He plays on Montano's concern and suggests that Cassio is not one to whom the safety of the isle should be entrusted. Then, when Roderigo attacks Cassio and the latter cries out, Montano goes to investigate the matter. From his very recent conversation with Iago, he is predisposed to see Cassio's actions as irresponsible; he accuses Cassio of being drunk, and the two men fight, the sounding of a general alarm disrupting the peace of the isle and rousing an irate Othello from his nuptial bed. Montano is present in the later scenes in which the former confusion is sorted out.

Musicians:

See Clown

Officers:

Officers appear in the company of both Brabantio and Othello when the two confront each other, Brabantio charging Othello with having abducted his daughter, and Othello maintaining his innocence of that charge. One of the officers confirms that the duke of Venice wants to see Othello immediately. Officers appear in the company of the duke as he

and the Venetian senators try to deduce the intentions of the Turkish fleet. Again, at the end of the play, officers appear with Iago in their custody after having captured the fleeing villain.

Othello:

Othello, a Moor, is a general of the Venetian armed forces. He is a noble and imposing man, well respected in his profession as soldier. At the beginning of the play he enjoys great successes, and everything seems to be going his way. Desdemona has chosen him over all of her other Venetian suitors, and Othello prevails over Brabantio's charges that Othello has coerced and abducted her. The duke of Venice and the Venetian senators place him in charge of the troops sent to defend Cyprus against the Turks. Things continue to go Othello's way when he arrives in Cyprus and discovers that the tempest has entirely eliminated the Turkish threat. He and Desdemona act differently toward each other in Cyprus. They are more openly loving, much less formal than they appeared in Venice. The couple celebrate their marriage, and, even when that celebration is interrupted by the brawling of Cassio and Montano, Othello still appears confident and self-controlled. In the tradition of the best strong-armed heroic types, he says, "He that stirs next to carve for his own rage / Holds his soul light; he dies upon his motion" (II.iii.173-74). He is a man in charge, one that will shoot first and ask questions later. But Othello's confidence starts to slip when Iago begins to work on his psyche, intimating that Desdemona and Cassio are having an affair.

At first, Othello denies that the attractiveness of his wife's grace, charm, and beauty for other men could make him jealous because, as he says ". . . she had eyes and chose me" (III.iii.189). But Iago's "medicine" (IV.i.46) soon begins to work, and Othello begins to question how Desdemona could continue to love him. After Iago has suggested that Desdemona has already deceived her father and Othello, the Moor begins to think Desdemona's betrayal of him is inevitable given his skin color, greater age, and lack of courtly charm (III.iii.263-68). He begins to act as if her unfaithfulness is a certainty, bemoaning that "Othello's occupation is gone" (III.iii.357).

Iago works Othello into a jealous rage through these many insinuations. But it seems to be the handkerchief, the one Othello originally gave to Desdemona as a love token, that puts Othello over the edge. Iago convinces Othello that the innocently dropped handkerchief was actually given to Cassio (who in turn gives the handkerchief to Bianca) by Desdemona. Othello focuses on this piece of cloth as damning physical evidence in his confrontation with his wife. He refers to it repeatedly before he kills Desdemona: ''That handkerchief which I so lov'd, and gave thee, / Thou gav'st to Cassio'' (V.ii.48-9); ''By heaven, I saw my handkerchief in's hand'' (V.ii.62); and again, ''I saw the handkerchief'' (V.ii.65). Desdemona repeatedly denies giving the handkerchief to Cassio, suggesting that perhaps he found it somewhere, but to no avail.

In the end, Othello is so convinced by Iago's manipulation that he murders his wife in their bed. The most apparent reason for this deed is the one Othello gives to Emilia, stated repeatedly in response to her persistent questioning, immediately after he has smothered Desdemona: ''She turn'd to folly, and she was a whore''; ''She was false as water''; ''Cassio did top her'' (V.ii.132; 134; 136). Desdemona, Othello believes, has betrayed him and the sanctity of marriage, and she paid with her life.

Yet some believe that Othello's motives run deeper, that Othello killed Desdemona because she violated the mores of Venetian society by marrying a Moor. Proponents of this view argue that Othello is accepted by Venetian society as long as he is an external element of that society. Barbantio and the Venetian senators are more than willing to accept his strength and military knowledge, but when Othello is internalized into their society by his marriage to Desdemona, his presence becomes disruptive. In his last speech, Othello asks to be remembered as ''one that lov'd not wisely but too well'' (V.ii.344). Is the object of that love Desdemona or Venice? Perhaps Othello never stops seeing himself as a soldier with the primary goal of preserving Venetian society. Perhaps his last act—his own suicide—is performed in the service of Venice, as mirrored in the language he uses to introduce it. He says that those around him should record events exactly as they have happened,

> And say besides, that in Aleppo once,
> Where a malignant and turban'd Turk
> Beat a Venetian and traduced the state
> I took by th' throat the circumcised dog,
> And smote him—thus.
>
> (V.ii.352-56)

The last word of this speech is punctuated by the sound of Othello's knife sinking into his breast and mortally wounding him.

> At the end of the play, after killing Roderigo and Emilia and revealing all he has done, Iago is taken prisoner.''

Roderigo:

Roderigo is a Venetian desperately desiring Desdemona. He is identified in the Dramatis Personae as a gull, a dupe or easy mark. Roderigo is gullible; he believes everything Iago tells him and does everything Iago commands of him. At the beginning of the play, at Iago's instigation, he alarms Brabantio with the news that Desdemona has eloped with the Moor. He sails with Iago to Cyprus and, while there, serves as a pawn in Iago's plan to destroy Othello and Cassio. Upon instruction, he picks a fight with Cassio when the latter keeps watch during the general celebration. Later, he attacks Cassio in the dark and wounds him, suffering a wound himself. Roderigo has given Iago money to negotiate with Desdemona on his behalf and thinks that the tasks Iago assigns him are intended only to remove Cassio from the picture, paving Roderigo's way to possessing Desdemona. Although his actions are despicable, he does evoke a measure of sympathy in the way that he is so utterly manipulated and ultimately betrayed by Iago, who stabs the wounded Roderigo on the dark street in order that he might not reveal Iago's involvement in Cassio's wounding.

Roderigo is continually threatening to quit his pursuit of Desdemona and cease giving Iago money for his intervention in that matter. Each time he does so, Iago assures him that Desdemona's attraction to Othello is only physical and that she will tire of the Moor fairly quickly. Iago suggests that Roderigo's best course of action is to accumulate a solid financial foundation. Iago tells Roderigo over and over to ''Put money in thy purse'' (I.iii.339-58), implying that, when Desdemona has satisfied her sexual lust, she will be attracted to the rich and stable sort of man. At one point, in his frustration at not realizing his goal, Roderigo says, ''It is silliness to live, when to live is torment'' (I.iii.307). He apologizes for being so silly but says he does not have the ''virtue'' to change, to which Iago responds, ''Virtue? a fig! 'tis in ourselves we are thus or thus'' (I.iii.319).

> At first, Othello denies that the attractiveness of his wife's grace, charm, and beauty for other men could make him jealous because, as he says '. . . she had eyes and chose me' (III.iii.189)."

Iago maintains that men make of themselves what they desire to be; men do not follow a course predetermined by any inner qualities. Iago's advice seems to renew Roderigo's resolve even as his threatened suicide gives evidence to the intensity of his longing for Desdemona.

Sailors:

In I.iii, the duke and the Venetian senators have assembled to try and determine Turkish military intentions. A sailor enters and reports that the Turkish fleet is menacing Rhodes.

Senators:

In the republican city-state of Venice, the senators were powerful men, who, along with the duke, made laws and insured public welfare. In I.iii, the senators have come together to plan a way to counter the military intentions of the Turks. They have received conflicting reports of the Turkish fleet's whereabouts, first seen heading towards Rhodes and later towards Cyprus. One of the senators deduces that the Turkish move on Rhodes is just a feinting maneuver, their real target being Cyprus. This conjecture is confirmed by the messenger from Montano. The senators have sent for Othello, whose military expertise they desperately need in countering the impending attack on Cyprus. They are present when Brabantio pleads his case before the duke, arguing that Othello has bewitched and stolen his daughter Desdemona. We might imagine that they, like the duke, are not inclined to support Brabantio's suit since, under the present circumstances, Othello's services are urgently required.

Venice (Duke of Venice):

The duke of Venice is concerned about the safety of Venice and its interests in Cyprus. He and the Venetian senators have assembled to try and figure out where the Turkish fleet intends to attack. After hearing conflicting reports about Turkish intentions, it is determined that the Turks will attack Cyprus. The duke summons Othello in order to place the defense of Cyprus in his hands. But Othello is being accused by Brabantio of using witchcraft to seduce his daughter. When Brabantio and Othello are brought into the duke's presence, the duke agrees to hear Brabantio's case. Othello counters the charge that he has used witchcraft by relating how he enthralled Desdemona with tales of his suffering and his adventures. When he is done, the duke says, "I think this tale would win my daughter too" (I.iii.171). After Desdemona confirms what Othello has said to be true, the duke rules against Brabantio, something he may have been less inclined to do on an occasion when Othello's services were not so desperately needed. The duke then tries to repair the rift between Brabantio and the newly wedded couple. He says, "The robb'd that smiles steals something from the thief; / He robs himself that spends a bootless grief" (I.iii.2008-09). The duke is urging Brabantio to be generous and accept things he cannot change.

Further Reading

Boose, Lynda. "The Father and the Bride in Shakespeare." *PMLA* 97 (1982): 325-47.

> Boose examines the relationship between fathers and daughters in Shakespeare's plays. In marriage, the management of the daughter is transferred from father to husband. She argues that in *Othello* the transfer of power from Brabantio to Othello is not as smooth as it should be. The scene played before the senate, in which both Brabantio and Othello plead for the possession of Desdemona, is a parody of the wedding ritual, argues Boose.

Campbell, Lily B. "*Othello*: A Tragedy of Jealousy." In *Shakespeare's Tragic Heroes: Slaves of Passion*, 148-74. Cambridge: Cambridge University Press, 1930. Reprint, New York: Barnes and Noble, 1952, 1967.

> Campbell sees *Othello* as a study of love and jealousy. Othello is not the only one who is jealous, Campbell argues, for Iago and Roderigo also suffer from that destructive emotion.

Draper, John W. "Shakespeare and the Turk." *Journal of English and Germanic Philology* 55 (1956): 523-32.

> Draper examines Shakespeare's works for their references to Turks, most of which occur in *Othello*. In that

play, Draper maintains, Shakespeare is expressing a sixteenth-century concern over the Turks as they competed with the English for geographic expansion.

Granville-Barker, Harley. "*Othello.*" In *Prefaces to Shakespeare,* Vol. 2, 3-149. Princeton: Princeton University Press, 1947.

Granville-Barker's study is interesting for the way it points out how Shakespeare's *Othello* differs from its sources. He discusses Shakespeare's reasons for inventing the characters of Roderigo and Iago.

Harting, James Edmund. *The Birds of Shakespeare or the Ornithology of Shakespeare Critically Examined, Explained, and Illustrated.* London: John Van Voorst, 1871. Reprint, Chicago: Argonaut, 1965.

An old work, Harting's study is interesting for the way it explains the sixteenth-century significance of references to birds in *Othello.* Terms like "gull," "daw," and "jaggard" are examined.

Heilman, Robert B. *Magic in the Web: Action and Language in "Othello."* Lexington: University of Kentucky Press, 1956.

Heilman examines the patterns of imagery in *Othello.* Especially interesting is his argument that the magic of the handkerchief represents the magic of love, a kind of witchcraft that alters the emotions as it suspends reason.

Hodgson, John A. "Desdemona's Handkerchief as an Emblem of her Reputation." *Texas Studies in Language and Literature* 19 (1977): 313-22.

Hodgson argues that as the handkerchief changes hands from Desdemona to Emilia to Bianca, Desdemona symbolically declines from goddess to prostitute in Othello's estimation. In its progress throughout the play, the handkerchief represents the cheapening of Desdemona's good name, Hodgson maintains.

Honigmann, E. A. J. *Shakespeare: Seven Tragedies; The Dramatist's Manipulation of Response.* New York: Barnes and Noble, 1976.

Honigmann argues that a sadistic and envious Iago enjoys making people uncomfortable with explicit sexual images. Iago, Honigmann argues, is a lowerclass individual who feels excluded from and envious of upper-class privilege. Both Iago and Othello want to be accepted in that privileged sphere of Venetian society, Honigmann maintains.

Hunter, G. K. "*Othello* and Colour Prejudice." *Proceedings of the British Academy* 53 (1967): 139-63.

Hunter argues that Shakespeare deliberately refutes Elizabethan stereotypes of Moors in presenting Othello as tragically human.

Jones, William M. "Michael Cassio: Venetian or Florentine?" In *Studies in English and American Literature*, edited by John L. Cutler and Lawrence S. Thompson, *American Notes and Queries Supplement*, Vol.1, 65-69. Troy, N.Y.: Whitston, 1978.

Jones argues that when Iago identifies Cassio as Florentine, he is trying to further dupe his audience. Cassio is identified by a gentleman in Cyprus as "Veronese" (II.i.26) and, thus, Venetian.

Kaula, David. "Othello Possessed: Notes on Shakespeare's Use of Magic and Witchcraft." *Shakespeare Studies* 2 (1966): 112-32.

In contrast to readings of *Othello* that imply that accusations of witchcraft are only the product of human fear and anger, Kaula suggests that Iago's manipulations are very much like those of witches and sorcerers.

Kermode, Frank. Introduction to *Othello*, by William Shakespeare. In *The Riverside Shakespeare*, edited by G. Blakemore Evans, 1198-1202. Boston: Houghton Mifflin, 1974.

Kermode gives a brief general introduction to the play's themes and characters.

Siegel, Paul N. "The Damnation of Othello." *PLMA* 68 (1953): 1068-78.

Siegel finds a Christian allegory in *Othello*: Desdemona is like Christ in her innocence and willingness to forgive even those who murder her; Iago is like Satan in his envious desire to separate Othello from the love of the Christlike Desdemona; and Othello is like Adam in being deluded by the temptation of the devil Iago.

Traversi, Derek. "The Mature Tragedies: *Othello.*" In *An Approach to Shakespeare*, 3rd ed., 88-112. New York: Doubleday, Anchor Books, 1969.

Traversi demonstrates that Othello achieves tragic stature at the end of the play. Even though Othello reveals his human frailty, Traversi argues, he recovers a certain nobility when he admits to that frailty and the depth of his love for Desdemona.

Pericles, Prince of Tyre

circa 1607-08

Plot Summary

Act I:

Gower, the Chorus, reveals that Antiochus, the king of Antioch, is engaged in an incestuous relationship with his daughter, and that both Antiochus and his daughter have grown accustomed to the situation and cease to consider it abnormal. The daughter of Antiochus is renowned for her great beauty, and princely suitors from around the world flock to Antioch to try and solve the riddle Antiochus insists they must solve if they are to wed his daughter. If they are unsuccessful in solving that riddle, they are put to death. Pericles, the prince of Tyre, arrives to try his luck. He is greatly impressed with the beauty of Antiochus's daughter and decides to risk his life. He solves the riddle but is reluctant to announce the solution because it refers to the incestuous relationship between father and daughter. He tells Antiochus's daughter that he no longer finds her desirable and tells Antiochus that the solution is best left unsaid since it would bring shame to the king. Antiochus knows that Pericles has solved the riddle. Publicly, he claims that Pericles has provided the wrong answer but, because he is so favored, will be given another forty days to figure it out. Secretly, he determines to kill Pericles before the secret of incest is revealed. He enlists Thaliard to kill Pericles, who knows Antiochus will kill him in order to keep his secret. Pericles flees during the night, and Thaliard is ordered to follow, not returning until he has killed Pericles. Back in Tyre, Pericles is very uneasy. He is sure that Antiochus will not rest until he has eliminated the one other person who knows about his dark secret. He is deeply concerned about the welfare of his people, assuming that Antiochus will eventually find some pretext for declaring war on Tyre. Pericles reveals his problem to Helicanus, a lord of Tyre, and Helicanus advises him to travel abroad. Helicanus is given the government of Tyre in Pericles's absence. Thaliard arrives in Tyre and discovers that Pericles is gone from that city. The scene shifts to Tharsus, a city decimated by famine. Pericles arrives in Tharsus, his ships loaded with grain for the relief of the Tharsian people. He and his followers are gratefully embraced by Cleon, the governor of Tharsus.

Act II:

Gower, the Chorus, informs the audience that Helicanus has sent a letter to Pericles in Tharsus, informing him that Thaliard has been in Tyre, bent on killing Pericles. He advises Pericles to move on. Pericles takes that advice and sails from Tharsus where he has been treated as a god. Caught in a violent storm, his ships sink and all of his followers are drowned. Pericles washes up on the shore of Pentapolis in Greece. He is discovered there by three fishermen, who inform him of a knightly tournament which will soon take place at the court of King Simonides. The victor in the tournament will be allowed to marry Thaisa, the daughter of Simonides. The fishermen draw a suit of armor from the depths of the sea in their nets. Pericles recognizes the armor as that given to him by his father. With a jewel taken from the suit of armor, Pericles purchases a charger and proceeds to the tournament. His armor is rusty, and he is ridiculed and not given much chance of winning. But Pericles outperforms all of the other knights on the field. He is given a special place at the subsequent banquet, and he participates in the feasting and dancing. Thaisa is sent by her father to find out who Pericles is, and Pericles reveals his birthright as well as his present misfortune. After the banquet, the knights are excused for the night and are told to rest before continuing their wooing of the Princess Thaisa the next day. At this point, the scene shifts to Tyre, where Helicanus is in conference with Escanes. Helicanus informs Escanes that Antiochus and his daughter have been killed by a bolt of fire from the heavens, their burnt bodies reeking so badly that no one will bury them. Several lords intrude upon the conversation of Helicanus and Escanes and demand

that Helicanus become their new prince, since the whereabouts of Pericles remain unknown. Helicanus refuses the position, advising them to wait a year, during which time they would be well advised to search for Pericles themselves. Back in Pentapolis the next morning, Simonides tells the assembled knights that Thaisa has decided to wait a year before choosing a husband. After the disappointed knights leave, Pericles enters, and Simonides decides to have some fun with him. Simonides has a letter from his daughter, which reveals that she is greatly impressed with Pericles and has chosen to marry him. Thaisa's choice pleases Simonides as well, but he toys with Pericles, telling him that Thaisa wishes him to be her music teacher. He then accuses Pericles of having bewitched his daughter, at which accusation Pericles protests and draws his sword in defiance. When Thaisa enters, Simonides lets Pericles off the hook and blesses their marriage. Thaisa and Pericles express their desire to marry one another.

Act III:

Once again, Gower summarizes ensuing events: Pericles and Thaisa have married, Thaisa becoming pregnant on her wedding night. Somehow, the knowledge of Pericles's presence in Pentapolis has reached those in Tyre, and Pericles receives letters from that city informing him of Helicanus's refusal of the crown and his arrangement for a one-year waiting period. Pericles decides to return to Tyre with Thaisa. Halfway through their voyage, their ship is racked by a storm, during which Thaisa is in the throes of childbirth. Thaisa delivers a baby girl, and Lychordia, Thaisa's attendant, hands Pericles the newborn infant, simultaneously informing him that Thaisa has died in childbirth. The superstitious sailors insist that Thaisa's body be thrown overboard to appease the storm, and Pericles reluctantly agrees. He puts his wife's body into a well-caulked casket along with jewels and a letter requesting that whoever finds the casket should see that Thaisa is properly buried and take the jewels in recompense. He then orders that the ship change course from Tyre and head for the nearby shores of Tharsus. Five hours later, Thaisa's coffin washes onto the shores of Ephesus where it is discovered and taken to the house of Cerimon, a renowned physician. When Cerimon opens the casket, he detects life in Thaisa's body, and using his skill as a physician, he revives her completely.

We next encounter Pericles at the home of Cleon in Tharsus. He announces that he must return to Tyre immediately, the one-year waiting period expiring soon. He leaves his daughter Marina, so named because she was born at sea, in the care of Lychordia, Marina's nurse, at the home of Cleon and his wife Dionyza. Apparently, he intends to be gone a long time, for he swears that he will not cut his hair until Marina is married.

Back in Ephesus, Thaisa gives the jewels that were in her casket to Cerimon and goes off to become a nun at Diana's temple, thinking she will never see Pericles again.

Act IV:

Gower tells of events at Tharsus. Marina has grown up to be a beautiful young lady with all the refinement of a good education provided by Cleon. Unfortunately, Marina's great beauty makes Philoten, the daughter of Cleon and his wife Dionyza, appear unattractive in contrast, much to Dionyza's displeasure. The jealous Dionyza kills Lychordia to get her out of the way, the more easily to have Marina killed. Dionyza has her servant Leonine take Marina for a walk on the beach, but before he can kill her as he intends to do, three pirates abduct Marina and take her to the city of Mytilene where she is sold to three bawds, the keepers of a brothel. The bawds are eager to buy such a virginal commodity as Marina, hoping to make a good deal of money after her innocence has been advertised.

Back in Tharsus, Dionyza tells Cleon what she has done. She believes that Leonine has, in fact, killed Marina, and she has poisoned him to keep him silent. Cleon is shocked to hear of his wife's woeful deeds, asking her what they will tell Pericles, who has trusted them with the care of his child. Dionyza replies that they will simply tell Pericles that Marina died despite their great love and devotion. To be more convincing in this subterfuge, she has already ordered that a statute commemorating Marina be erected in the city. She also tells him that they should appear to still be in mourning if Pericles does arrive to visit his daughter.

Gower appears again, relating how Pericles has set sail from Tyre to Tharsus to do that very thing. Helicanus sails with Pericles, the government of Tyre now left in the hands of Escanes. When he arrives in Tharsus and discovers that Marina is dead, Pericles displays great sorrow, swearing "Never to wash his face, nor cut his hairs" (IV.iv.28). He takes to the seas again, unmindful of the buffeting his ship takes from the winds of ocean storms.

In Mytilene, Marina is ruining the business of the bawds. Instead of willingly prostituting herself, she appeals to the better natures of her customers and convinces them that she is pure and innocent, sometimes singing or preaching to them. Many of the customers leave swearing never to frequent a house of prostitution again. Lysimachus, the governor of Mytilene, comes to the brothel in disguise to protect his reputation. He is pleased with the prospect of an interlude with Marina, but she protests her innocence and misfortune so eloquently that he changes his mind. He gives her ample gold and leaves the house denouncing the bawds on his way out. The keepers of the brothel are upset with their failing business, so Boult, one of the bawds, is given the freedom to rape Marina and make her more manageable. Marina accuses Boult of being the scum of the earth; any profession is better than the one in which he is now engaged. She convinces him that she can make money in ways other than prostitution—singing, dancing, sewing, or especially teaching—and Boult agrees to broach the subject with Bawd and Pander.

Act V:

We learn from Gower how Marina has been moved to a reputable house and has become very successful, dazzling everyone with her skills in dancing and singing, and impressing even the scholarly with her wisdom, the money she earns being turned over to Bawd. The city of Mytilene is celebrating a festival in honor of Neptune, and Lysimachus spies Pericles's ship, which has been blown toward Mytilene by the winds of the storm, anchored off the coast. He takes a barge and approaches the Tyrian ship, his request to board being readily granted by Helicanus. After exchanging pleasantries, Helicanus informs Lysimachus that Pericles, the king of Tyre is on board the ship. Lysimachus wants to see him. Helicanus leads him to Pericles and tells him that the Tyrian king has spoken to no one for some time, the result of the great grief he has suffered. Lysimachus says that there is a young woman in Mytilene so delightful she might make Pericles speak. He is referring to Marina, and he sends for her immediately when Helicanus says he will try any remedy for Pericles's silence. Marina comes aboard accompanied by another young woman from Mytilene and asks that they might be left alone with Pericles. She tells Pericles that her misfortune might equal his. She tells him of her lineage—something she refused to do when questioned in Mytilene—naming him as her father. Pericles is beside himself and asks her to supply proof after proof that she is his daughter. He calls Helicanus and makes Marina tell her story again to him. Exhausted from such a great emotional experience, Pericles falls asleep and dreams of the goddess Diana, who directs him to sail to her temple in Ephesus and publicly recount all the details of his misfortune at her altar there. When he wakes, he announces that he will sail to Ephesus, delaying for the present his intention to visit Tharsus and avenge the villainy of Cleon and Dionyza, of which Marina has informed him. Before sailing, Pericles and his followers celebrate in Mytilene. As they head for shore, Lysimachus says he has something to request of Pericles, who anticipates that it is a request to marry Marina and grants the request on the spot, having heard that Lysimachus has always treated Marina kindly. In Ephesus, Pericles does as Diana has instructed him in his dream; he recounts aloud his tale of woe. Thaisa, who is present as the high priestess, recognizes Pericles, presents herself to him, and then faints. Pericles is overwhelmed to discover that the wife he has presumed dead still lives. Pericles, Thaisa, and Marina share the joy of their reunion, and Cerimon recounts how the casket containing Thaisa was discovered on the beach and Thaisa revived by his own efforts. Pericles announces that he and Thaisa will live the rest of their lives in Pentapolis paying due respect to the memory of Simonides who has died. Marina and Lysimachus, once married, will reign in Tyre. Gower supplies the audience with the news that Cleon and Dionyza have died when their palace was set on fire by the citizens of Tharsus, who were angry with the knowledge that the governor and his wife had betrayed Pericles.

Modern Connections

Pericles is the first in a group of Shakespeare's last plays called romances or tragicomedies. This group of plays, which also includes *Cymbeline*, *The Winter's Tale*, *The Tempest*, and *The Two Noble Kinsmen* is characterized by improbable situations, and often includes the discovery that characters presumed dead are, miraculously, still alive. In *Pericles*, for example, the title character thinks both his wife Thaisa and his daughter Marina are dead and suffers terribly in his grief over their deaths. There is great joy and celebration at the end of the play when he is reunited with first Marina and then Thaisa. The audience, however, knows throughout that Pericles's wife and daughter are still alive. Shakespeare brings characters back from the dead with similar, perhaps greater, dramatic effect in *The Winter's Tale* when a statue of Hermione comes to life and surprises both the audience and her husband Leontes, who has presumed her dead for nearly twenty years. In the romance plays, there is the lamentation of tragedy and the sense that the will of the gods cannot be opposed by human actions. There is also comic resolution, the plays ending in marriage, reaffirmations of love, and social harmony. The romances are a strange blend of completely different genres, yet they most certainly found an interested audience in Shakespeare's day. They are also curiously appropriate to our own age, an age in which many people are too cynical to believe in a seamlessly comic resolution to all of life's problems, yet not so pessimistic as to believe that all events in life are controlled by a destiny beyond human influence. Additionally, the romances are not so different from today's popular romantic comedy films. Characters in these movies often are touched by pain and grief in some way, but, typically, in the end all is resolved with a happy ending. Of all the romances, *Pericles* is, perhaps, the most strange, a hodgepodge of styles and themes.

On stylistic grounds, critics maintain that *Pericles* was not written entirely by Shakespeare. It has been suggested that the first two acts were written by someone else, Shakespeare adding touches to the first two acts, here and there, and writing the last three acts himself. Despite its stylistic inconsistencies, *Pericles* presents an absorbing story which delights the imagination with its depictions of pirates, storm-tossed ships, and knightly tournaments. The story of *Pericles* is an old one, having been in circulation at least since the fifth century. It is based on the story of Appolonius of Tyre and always proved popular in the telling. In the fourteenth century, the poet John Gower, a contemporary of Chaucer's, presented the story in *Confessio Amantis*. Gower has a place in Shakespeare's play as the Chorus, and his presence is one of a conglomeration of elements accounting for the play's oddities of style.

Gower introduces each scene and provides the audience with a kind of pre-packaged moral attitude toward the characters and their actions. For example, he stresses the abhorrent nature of Antiochus's incest, the goodness of Helicanus, and the generosity and patience of Pericles. Since audiences would, undoubtedly, adopt, on their own, the moral attitudes upon which Gower insists, there is no reason for him to be so didactic, or deliberately instructive. In providing a shorthand version of morality, Gower gives *Pericles* the flavor of a medieval morality play, in which there are no gray areas between right and wrong, good and evil. The play also has an element of folklore. When Pericles first arrives in Tharsus, Dionyza is a tearful woman lamenting the ruin of her fair city by famine and grateful to Pericles for bringing that city grain with which to feed itself. Later, she becomes the wicked step-mother of folklore, intent upon killing Marina because her own daughter Philoten appears ugly in that fair girl's presence. Still another element of the play is that of chivalric romance. When Pericles appears at the knightly tournament hosted by King Simonides in Pentapolis as the disheveled knight in rusty armor who vanquishes the field, it is the stuff of Arthurian legend.

Thrown into this mixture which is *Pericles*, is a theme that can be read in different ways. The moral corruption of Antiochus's daughter is clearly opposed to Marina's moral virtue in the play. The contrast is wonderfully expressed in terms of musical discord and harmony. Pericles expresses his disgust with Antiochus's daughter after he discovers her incestuous relationship with her father. He tells her, ''You are a fair viol, and your sense the strings'' (I.i.81), completing the analogy with, ''But being play'd upon before your time, / Hell only danceth at so harsh a chime'' (I.i.84-85). In contrast, when Pericles is reunited with Marina, who has remained chaste despite being deposited in a Mytilene brothel, Pericles hears heavenly harmony, ''The music of the spheres!'' (V.i.229). Between these two polar extremes, though, the behavior of Pericles is ambiguous. He is repulsed by his experience at Antioch, and he returns home to Tyre, where he becomes fearful for his life, or, as he insists, the lives of his subjects. He then goes on the run instead of exposing Antiochus's corruption to the world, a brave act of moral integrity that would have been more commendable than what is arguably an act of cowardice. But whether we view Pericles as a morally virtuous hero, who ultimately is rewarded for his patience and generosity, or as a morally weak man, who brings suffering upon himself through his avoidance of a direct confrontation with Antiochus, depends on whether we wish to stress the comic or tragic aspects of *Pericles*.

It is the variety of *Pericles* that is its chief delight. The play mixes genres and writing styles; it presents elements of morality plays, folklore, and Arthurian romance; and it suggests the ambiguous nature of its protagonist's actions.

Characters

Antiochus:

Antiochus is the king of Antioch. He is guilty of practicing incest with his daughter. To prevent his daughter from marrying anyone else, Antiochus presents all of her suitors with a riddle. If the suitors cannot answer that riddle, they are put to death. The practice is successful for Antiochus until Pericles arrives and figures the riddle out. To keep Pericles quiet, Antiochus publicly promises him another forty days to provide the answer, but secretly orders Thaliard to pursue and kill the prince of Tyre. While traveling in a chariot Antiochus and his daughter are burned to death by a bolt of fire from the avenging gods, their burnt bodies remaining unburied, being too disgusting to approach.

Bawd:

Bawd is the wife of Pander. She and her husband keep a brothel in the city of Mytilene, and they buy Marina from the pirates who have kidnapped her, because they need to replenish their stock of prostitutes. Marina is a virgin, and Bawd and her husband hope to profit considerably from her presence in their house of ill repute. Bawd instructs Marina, unsuccessfully, in the proper attitude a prostitute should have. When Marina begins to turn customers away from the house with her chaste behavior, Bawd is very upset with her. Eventually, she places Marina in a more reputable home and allows her to earn money through singing, dancing, and teaching, money that is paid to Bawd. Her name is synonymous with ''prostitute'' or ''madam of a house of prostitution.''

Boult:

Boult works for Bawd and Pander. He encounters the pirates and brings Marina to the house of Bawd and Pander so that they might purchase the girl. Marina, in her innocence, is a valuable commodity for the three pimps, and Boult is sent to the marketplace to advertise Marina's innocence and availability. When Marina proves contrary and incorrigibly good, Boult is given the task of raping her and breaking her spirit of resistance. Marina calls him a despicable creature, the lowest on earth, but this derision does not seem to affect him. He does, however, take Marina's proposal that she be allowed to make money singing, dancing, and teaching.

Cerimon:

Cerimon is a lord and an extremely competent physician in the city of Ephesus. He has a great reputation for his medical expertise. When the casket containing Thaisa's body washes up on the shores of Ephesus, it is brought to Cerimon. He pries open the cover and detects life still in her. He ministers to her and Thaisa recovers. In the last scene of the play, Cerimon briefly explains to Pericles the circumstances surrounding the recovery of Thaisa's body and her regaining of health. He invites Pericles to his home so that he might explain those events more fully and show Pericles the items discovered along with Thaisa.

Chorus:

See Gower

Cleon:

Cleon is the governor of Tharsus and the husband of Dionyza. He first appears in the play lamenting the ravages of the famine plaguing his city. Pericles, who is traveling to avoid the assassins he fears Antiochus will send after him, has heard of the situation in Tharsus and brings ships loaded with grain for the city's relief. Cleon expresses his eternal gratitude to Pericles and assures him that the citizens of Tharsus will do likewise. When the ship carrying Pericles and Thaisa back to Tyre runs into a storm, Pericles, after being forced to throw the body of his dead wife overboard, heads for the shores of nearby Tharsus where he knows he will be welcomed by Cleon. Continuing his journey to Tharsus, Pericles leaves his infant daughter Marina to be raised by Cleon and his wife. Cleon raises Marina lovingly and sees that she is educated properly, but fourteen years later, his wife tries to kill Marina because Marina's beauty far exceeds that of Philoten, the daughter of Cleon and Dionyza. When Dionyza informs Cleon of her actions and intents, Cleon is greatly sorrowful and ashamed, but he does not expose Dionyza. At the end of the play, Gower, the Chorus, informs the audience that Cleon and Dionyza have been killed by the citizens of Tharsus after those citizens found out about the great disservice done by Cleon and Dionyza to Pericles, a man whom the townspeople much admire.

Daughter of Antiochus:

The daughter of Antiochus is a fair beauty, and many men, hearing of her great beauty and familiar with her father's wealth, come from around the world to attempt the riddle her father insists they must solve to win her hand in marriage. But she has a dark secret; she is involved in an incestuous relationship with her father. When Pericles solves the riddle and becomes aware of the secret she shares with her father, he quickly shuns her, telling her he no longer finds her attractive. Her relationship with her father seems especially disturbing when Gower informs us that ''But custom what they did begin / Was with long use account'd no sin'' (I.i.29-30): she has become accustomed to the situation with her father, and apparently, after so much time, does not feel the relationship to be wrong in any way. She is destroyed along with him by the bolt of fire from heaven.

Diana:

This is the goddess Diana, in mythology worshipped for her chastity. She appears to Pericles in a dream after he has been reunited with Marina. In that dream, Diana instructs him to go to her temple in Ephesus and recount his sorrowful adventures in front of the altar there.

Dionyza:

Dionyza is Cleon's wife. When we first encounter her in the play, she is punctuating the lamentations of her husband with tears as he extols the tribulations caused by the famine in Tharsus. When Pericles leaves Marina in her care, Dionyza promises to treat her like one of her own children. But when Marina is approximately fourteen years old, Dionyza has grown to hate her because Dionyza's daughter Philoten has become the homely foil for Marina's great pearl of beauty. Dionyza kills Lychordia, Marina's nurse since birth, and instructs the servant Leonine to take Marina for a walk on the beach and kill her. Dionyza is especially dangerous because she covers her evil intentions with deception. Even as she is sending Marina off to supposed death, she acts as if she has Marina's health as her main concern, assuring Marina that the salt air will do her good. Sure that Marina is dead, she has a statue dedicated to her memory so that she might appear properly mournful should Pericles return to visit his daughter. Dionyza tells Cleon that she has done what she has done for the love of her daughter, a love she accuses Cleon of not sharing. Along with Cleon, she is killed by the citizens of Tharsus who avenge the wrongs done to Pericles.

Escanes:

Escanes is a lord of Tyre. Apparently, he is the only confidante of Helicanus, whom Pericles has left in charge of the city in his absence. When Pericles sails from Tyre to Tharsus for the second time and takes Helicanus with him, Escanes is put in charge of the city of Tyre.

Fishermen:

These three fishermen discover Pericles washed up on shore after his ship has been sunk off the coast of Pentapolis in Greece. Within Pericles's hearing they discuss politics and religion, prompting Pericles to say,

> These fishers tell the infirmities of men
> And from their wat'ry empire recollect
> All that may men approve or men detect!
>
> (II.i.49-51)

The fishermen have figured life out in terms of that which they best understand—the sea, where the big fish eat the little fish. In the course of their conversations, they mention the tournament to be held at the palace of King Simonides, a tournament in which Pericles hopes to be successful and reverse his late ill fortune. The fishermen pull a suit of armor from the sea in their nets, and Pericles claims it as his own, having inherited it from his father. The fishermen allow Pericles to have the armor on the condition that he pay them something for it when he is able to do so.

Gentlemen:

There are several gentlemen in the play. In III.ii, two gentlemen appear at Cerimon's home in Ephesus in the early morning. They have discovered Thaisa's casket and have brought it to Cerimon because of his great reputation for wisdom. In IV.iv, two gentlemen have come from the brothel in Mytilene where Marina has reformed them with her preaching, the last thing they had expected to hear in a house of prostitution. In V.i, two or three gentlemen are called by Helicanus to greet Lysimachus when he comes on board Pericles's ship as it rides at anchor off the coast of Mytilene.

Gower:

Gower acts as the Chorus in the play, introducing each act and supplying the audience with a number of essential plot details. Gower continually encourages the audience to use its imagination to envision what he describes. Gower puts his own spin on the information he provides, offering his own opinion of the morality or decadence of the characters' behavior.

Helicanus:

Helicanus is a lord of Tyre. When Pericles returns from Antioch, Helicanus reads concern in his face and questions him about what is troubling him. Pericles confides in Helicanus, telling him of his fear that Antiochus will eventually invent some pretext for assaulting Tyre to get at Pericles. Helicanus advises him to travel and avoid the evil intents of the king of Antioch. Pericles takes that advice and leaves Helicanus in charge. After Pericles has been away for some time, several lords of Tyre, thinking Pericles will not return, want to proclaim Helicanus prince. Helicanus protests his loyalty to Pericles and refuses their election, making them agree to wait a full year before electing another. When Pericles leaves Tyre to visit his daughter in Tharsus, he takes Helicanus with him. Helicanus takes care of Pericles after the prince of Tyre is told that his daughter, Marina, is dead. Pericles falls into despair and ceases to speak. Helicanus welcomes Lysimachus onto the ship when the latter asks to board, and he readily agrees to Lysimachus's offer to bring a young girl from Mytilene who might make Pericles speak. Helicanus admits that he will do anything to try and help alleviate his prince's sorrow. At the end of the play, Pericles, who has just been reunited with the wife he had presumed was dead, presents Helicanus to Thaisa as one about whom he has spoken to her often.

Knights:

These are the five knights who compete against Pericles at the tournament at the palace of Simonides in Pentapolis. Before the tournament of arms begins, each passes by the grandstand and has his page present Thaisa with the knight's emblem and motto, which Thaisa and Simonides interpret. The sixth knight is Pericles. After the tournament all of the knights are present at the banquet provided by Simonides, who presents Pericles with the "wreath of victory" (II.iii.10) and voices his hope than none of those assembled there begrudges his honoring of Pericles. The knights affirm that they do not and thank Simonides for his generosity. Later, they drink and dance in celebration. The next morning,

Simonides announces to these knights, who are still hopeful of wedding Thaisa, that Thaisa has decided to wait a year before selecting a husband—really she has selected Pericles—and the knights leave dejectedly.

Ladies:

These are the ladies of Simonides's palace who grace the banquet provided the knights after their tilting contest. They appear without speaking. Also without speaking, a lady appears in the company of Pericles, Lysimachus, Helicanus, and Marina at Diana's temple in the last scene of the play.

Leonine:

Leonine is the servant Dionyza convinces to kill Marina. At Dionyza's direction, he takes Marina for a walk on the seashore, announces that he is going to kill her, and allows her time to say her prayers. But before he can kill her, three pirates drag her away, and Leonine runs away. He does not run too far, though, because he wants to make certain that the pirates do not just rape Marina and turn her loose to accuse him. When they abduct her, he is sure it is safe to report that he has, in fact, killed her. Later, Dionyza kills Leonine so that he might not divulge her involvement in the death of Marina.

Lords:

There are several lords in the play. In I.ii, two lords of Tyre appear with Pericles. When they take their leave of him, one of the lords says, ''And keep your mind, till you return to us, / Peaceful and comfortable!'' (I.ii.35-36). This remark is out of place since Pericles has not yet announced his intention to leave. In I.iii, other lords of Tyre appear without speaking in the company of Helicanus and Escanes. In I.iv, a lord of Tharsus announces to Cleon that a ship has been spotted sailing toward the city. Cleon fears that the ship brings plunderers who have heard of the city's vulnerability, but the lord assures him that the ship is flying the white flag of peace. The lord later brings Pericles to Cleon. In II.ii, a lord of Pentapolis confirms to Simonides that the knights are ready to begin the procession and pass in review. There are lords of Pentapolis present at the banquet held later for those knights, but they have no lines. In II.iv, three lords of Tharsus demand that Helicanus reveal whether Pericles is dead or not. They fear that without their prince, the kingdom is laid vulnerable to attack. They wish to make Helicanus their new sovereign. Helicanus objects and convinces them to wait a year, during

> **While traveling in a chariot Antiochus and his daughter are burned to death by a bolt of fire from the avenging gods, their burnt bodies remaining unburied, being too disgusting to approach.''**

which time they should search for Pericles themselves. In V.i, there are lords on Pericles's ship when Lysimachus boards. It is not clear whether they are from Tyre or Mytilene.

Lychordia:

Lychordia is Thaisa's attendant. She accompanies Pericles and Thaisa on their voyage from Pentapolis to Tyre. In the storm that wracks their ship halfway through that voyage, Lychordia acts as a midwife to Thaisa. She presents Pericles with his newborn infant and tells him to cherish it because it is all that remains of Thaisa, who has died. Lychordia becomes Marina's nurse and is left with her in Tharsus when Pericles returns to Tyre. Since Lychordia loves Marina and is protective of her, Dionyza kills Lychordia so that she will not encounter any difficulties in killing Marina.

Lysimachus:

Lysimachus is the governor of Mytilene. He frequents the house of prostitution run by Bawd and Pander and wears a disguise, so he is not recognized by the good people of his city. He is directed to Marina and assumes she will be intimate with him as befits the profession in which he believes her to be employed. Instead, she protests her virginity and chaste intentions and appeals to the goodness in him. He is surprised that she speaks so well and so convincingly. He abandons his initial intentions in coming to the brothel and gives her gold. On the way out he scolds Boult and refuses to give him gold, saying, ''Your house, but for this virgin that doth prop it, / Would sink and overwhelm you. Away!'' (IV.vi.119-20). Later, out of curiosity, he sails his barge to the ship carrying Pericles and his followers while it is anchored off the Mytilene coast and is allowed aboard. Informed by Helicanus that Pericles has not spoken for quite some time,

Lysimachus proposes that a delightful young woman with the grace and appearance to melt a stone—Marina—be brought from his city to try and loosen Pericles's tongue. After the miraculous reunion of Pericles and Marina, Lysimachus invites Pericles to revel in Mytilene at the feast of Neptune. Lysimachus has grown quite fond of Marina, and says that he needs to ask something of Pericles. Pericles anticipates the request and is pleased to grant that Lysimachus marry Marina. Lysimachus accompanies Pericles, Marina, and Helicanus to Ephesus, where, after being reunited with Thaisa, Pericles announces that Lysimachus and Marina will govern in Tyre, once they are wed. It may be somewhat surprising to many audiences that Marina consents to marry Lysimachus and that Pericles so quickly graces the union. Not only is Lysimachus's first meeting with Marina a less than noble one but there is no evidence in the play to suggest that he has helped her get out of the compromised situation she has found herself in at the brothel, something it seems he would do if he were a truly noble character.

Marina:

Marina is the daughter of Pericles and Thaisa. She is born at sea—thus, the name given her by Pericles—during a wild storm, and her birth allegedly kills her mother. As an infant, she is left by her father in the care of Cleon and Dionyza in Tharsus. Cleon makes sure that she is educated in all of those things that become a young lady of Marina's stature; she receives an education befitting the daughter of a king. Marina grows up to be a gracious and beautiful young woman, so beautiful, in fact, that she far outshines Philoten, the daughter of Cleon and Dionyza, a fact that Dionyza greatly resents. Dionyza, after killing Marina's nurse Lychordia, plots to kill Marina, convincing Leonine to murder Marina as he walks with her on the seashore. Marina is always gracious. Unaware that Dionyza is sending her to her death at the hands of Leonine, Marina, unselfishly, says that she does not want to deprive Dionyza of her servant even for a short time. When Leonine tells Marina that he is about to kill her on behalf of Dionyza, Marina protests that she has never done anything wrong. Before Leonine can murder her, Marina is abducted by pirates, who take her to Mytilene and sell her to the brothel keepers there. Marina maintains her virginity in the brothel. She is a beam of radiance in that house, reforming those who frequent the brothel for illicit purposes and ruining the brothel's business in the process. As a result, Bawd and Pander, the keepers of the brothel, place her in a legitimate house where Mari-

na can make them money by plying her more virtuous skills, the singing, dancing, and teaching in which she is so accomplished. She gains a reputation for her beauty, charm, and intelligence and is summoned by Lysimachus to Pericles's ship in an effort to alleviate Pericles's great grief and make him speak. Pericles notes certain qualities in Marina's voice and posture that remind him of Thaisa, and, after Marina provides further proof of their kinship, the two embrace in joyful reunion. Another joyful moment occurs at the end of the play when Marina and Pericles are reunited with Thaisa. It is somewhat disconcerting to many audiences that Marina, who is held up throughout the play as a model of beauty and innocence, is betrothed to Lysimachus, a man who was neither exceptionally noble in his first meeting with Marina nor especially helpful in freeing her from the slavery in which he found her at the brothel.

Marshal:

This is the marshal of the tilting tournament held by Simonides in Pentapolis. He appears at the subsequent banquet without speaking.

Messengers:

As Antiochus is convincing Thaliard to kill Pericles, a messenger appears and announces that Pericles has fled the city. In II.i and III.i, messengers appear in the dumb shows presented by the Chorus.

Pander:

Pander is Bawd's husband and together they own and operate the brothel in Mytilene. Concerned with his shortage of healthy prostitutes, Pander buys Marina from the pirates and directs his wife to instruct the young maid in the ways of the profession. When Marina begins to reform his customers, Pander regrets that he ever brought her into the house. His name is synonymous with ''pimp.''

Pericles:

Pericles is the prince of Tyre. On occasion, he is referred to as the king of Tyre, the terms ''prince'' and ''king'' here being interchangeable. Hearing of the great beauty attributed to daughter of Antiochus, Pericles travels to Antioch with the intention of winning her for his wife after solving the riddle posed by her father. Pericles solves the riddle but is devastated to learn in its solution that Antiochus and his daughter are having an incestuous affair. Pericles flees Antioch, sure that Antiochus will kill him in order to protect his dark secret. Once home in

Tyre, Pericles worries that Antiochus will pursue him there. He takes the advice of Helicanus and leaves Tyre to travel the world. His first stop is in Tharsus where he brings grain to alleviate the city's famine and incurs the gratitude of the populace and Cleon, the governor there. He remains in Tharsus until he receives a letter from Helicanus acquainting him with the fact that Thaliard, one in the service of Antiochus, has been in Tyre. Pericles sails from Tharsus and is caught in a storm that sinks his ships and drowns his followers. Pericles, himself, is washed onto the shores of Pentapolis where he meets three fishermen, who inform him of a knightly tournament to be held the next day at the palace of Simonides, the king of Pentapolis. At stake in the tournament is the hand of Thaisa, Simonides's daughter. Pericles wins the tournament and marries Thaisa. He remains in Pentapolis for a short time, eventually receiving letters from Tyre revealing that Helicanus, in his firm loyalty to Pericles, has resisted being named the sovereign of Tyre, but only for a one-year period. In response to this news, Pericles sails from Pentapolis and heads for Tyre, taking his new wife and her attendant Lychordia with him. But Thaisa is thought to have died in giving birth to Marina during that voyage, and Pericles is forced by the superstition of the sailors to throw Thaisa's body overboard. A storm forces Pericles's ship to the nearest harbor, which is Tharsus. Pericles leaves Marina and Lychordia there and returns to Tyre on his own. We learn from Gower, the Chorus, that fourteen years later Pericles sails to Tharsus to visit Marina and is grief-stricken when he discovers that she is dead. On his return home, high winds blow his ship to the coast of Mytilene, the city, coincidentally, in which Marina now resides. In a further coincidence, Marina is brought aboard Pericles's ship to try and cure his melancholy speechlessness. By the clues Marina gives him, Pericles learns that she is the daughter he had presumed was dead. In their rapturous reunion, Pericles hears the divinely pleasing music of heavenly harmony. Later, the goddess Diana appears to him in a dream and directs his course to Ephesus where he is reunited with Thaisa, another loved one he had thought was dead.

On two occasions, the outward appearance of Pericles is disguised in ways that are contradictory in what those disguises reveal about the inner man. On the first occasion, Pericles appears at the knightly tournament in the rusty armor of his father, which has been recovered from the shipwreck by the nets of the fishermen. He is wearing a makeshift skirt under that armor and appears somewhat disheveled.

> Marina grows up to be a gracious and beautiful young woman, so beautiful, in fact, that she far outshines Philoten, the daughter of Cleon and Dionyza, a fact that Dionyza greatly resents."

He is derided by the onlookers, one of whom suggests that Pericles will scour the rust from his armor when he is knocked from his horse and rolls in the dirt. Pericles, of course, proves the doubtful wrong by excelling in the tournament. In this instance, the rusty armor masks the true nobility of Pericles, one who has been trained in the martial arts as befits the son of a king. On the second occasion, when he thinks that Thaisa has died in childbirth, Pericles vows to let his hair grow until he sees Marina properly married. Again, when he thinks that Marina is dead, he vows never to cut his hair or wash his face again. In these latter two instances, Pericles's wild and disheveled outward appearance accurately represents the grief and turmoil within. It is only at the end of the play, when he is reunited with both Marina and Thaisa, that he determines to cut his hair and clean himself up, putting his outward appearance into accord with his inner contentment.

Throughout the play, Pericles suffers one disappointment after another. Although we might view Pericles as a patient and virtuous prince being tested by some divine power, he has alternately been seen as a weak and compromised man who brings about his own suffering. This latter view depends upon seeing Pericles as less than responsible in his devotion to Marina (in that he leaves her to be brought up by someone other than himself) and in his reaction to the discovery of Antiochus's incest. We might ask why Pericles waits fourteen years to visit Marina in Tharsus, or why he leaves his daughter there in the first place. He has already made the voyage to Tharsus twice in the play; what pressing business could he have had in Tyre to prevent him from making that voyage once again to be with his daughter? We might also ask why Pericles does not trumpet Antiochus's foul behavior to the heavens. Pericles tells Helicanus that he fears the citizens of Tyre might suffer if he does so, but some critics

> By the clues Marina gives him, Pericles learns that she is the daughter he had presumed was dead. . . . Later, the goddess Diana appears to him in a dream and directs his course to Ephesus where he is reunited with Thaisa, another loved one he had thought was dead."

question this, arguing that the world probably would have united against Antiochus if Pericles had revealed his foul sin.

Philomen:

Philomen is Cerimon's servant. He appears briefly in Cerimon's house just before Thaisa's body is brought there by the two gentlemen. Cerimon instructs Philomen to start a fire and bring food for a servant, who, having just come in cold from the storm, is at Cerimon's house to procure a prescription for his own ailing master. That servant is accompanied by another man.

Pirates:

These three pirates are identified by Leonine as serving "the great pirate Valdes" (IV.i.96). They abduct Marina from Leonine and take her to Mytilene where they sell her into a life of prostitution with Bawd and Pander.

Sailors:

The sailors work industriously to control the ship carrying Pericles and Thaisa form Pentapolis to Tyre, fighting the storm that has caught them halfway through the voyage. Learning that Thaisa has not survived childbirth, one of the sailors tells Pericles, "The sea works high, the wind is loud, and will not lie till the ship be clear'd of the dead" (III.i.47-49). Pericles calls the sailors superstitious, but they insist that Thaisa's body be thrown overboard. They produce a casket for her that has already been caulked. They inform Pericles that

they are off the coast of Tharsus and assure him that they can make that coast by morning if the wind lets up. In IV.i, two sailors, one from Tyre and the other from Mytilene, appear on board Pericles's ship as it rides at anchor off the coast of Mytilene.

Servant:

This servant, along with another man, comes to Cerimon's house to procure a prescription for his master, who is sick. Cerimon orders his own servant, Philomen, to "Get fire and meat for these poor men" (III.ii.3), poor because they are soaking wet from the storm. Cerimon says that the servant's master will die before the servant returns. He gives the servant a prescription to take to the apothecary, and the servant and the other man leave. Moments later, two or three servants to the gentlemen who have discovered Thaisa's body bring in the chest bearing her body.

Simonides:

Simonides is the king of Pentapolis. On the birthday of his daughter Thaisa, he hosts a celebration for her "and there are princes and knights come from all parts of the world to just and tourney for her love" (II.i.109-10). Pericles hears of this tournament from the fishermen, who refer to the king of Pentapolis as "The good Simonides" (II.i.101). Pericles remarks that "[Simonides] is a happy king, since he gains from his subjects the name of good by his government" (II.i.104-05). Pericles travels to Simonides's court, hoping to win the tournament and gain some material favor there, since he has lost everything in the shipwreck that cast him upon the shores of Pentapolis. Pericles performs better than all the other knights in the tournament, and Thaisa selects him to be her husband. Simonides is pleased by his daughter's choice because Pericles has also impressed him. Simonides is probably being kind when he informs the other knights competing for his daughter's hand in marriage that Thaisa has decided to delay her choice for one year. Simonides then jovially plays with Pericles, informing him that Thaisa wants Pericles to be her music teacher, humorous because Pericles has, perhaps, demonstrated greater skill in jousting at the tournament than in dancing and singing at the banquet. Simonides accuses Pericles of having bewitched Thaisa, and when Pericles draws his sword and protests that he has done no such thing, Simonides is delighted that he shows such mettle. Simonides gives up the jest when Thaisa enters and gives his blessing to their marriage. When Thaisa is reunited with Pericles at the end of the play, she informs him that Simonides has died. In judiciously and freely allowing his daughter to marry the man of her choice, Simonides is a stark contrast to Antiochus.

Thaisa:

Thaisa is the daughter of Simonides. Her father hosts a tournament on her birthday with the express purpose of finding her a husband. Although Pericles wins that tournament, Thaisa, apparently, has the freedom to choose any one of the knights for a husband. She selects Pericles. She becomes pregnant on her wedding night and elects to accompany Pericles when he is summoned to Tyre by letters that have reached him in Pentapolis. Halfway through the voyage to Tyre, Thaisa gives birth to a baby girl as a storm rages and threatens the ship. All those aboard the ship believe that Thaisa has died in childbirth, and the superstitious sailors will not be satisfied until her body is thrown overboard. Her waterproof casket washes onto the shores of Ephesus and is discovered by two gentlemen of that town. It is taken to the physician Cerimon, who opens it and revives Thaisa. Cerimon shows Thaisa the letter Pericles has placed in her casket, a letter merely instructing that Thaisa's body should be properly buried upon discovery, in exchange for the jewels in the casket. Yet, Thaisa says that since she will never see her husband again, she will live the life of a nun at Diana's temple. She becomes a high priestess at that temple and is reunited with Pericles at the end of the play after Pericles has been directed there by Diana in a dream. It is odd that Thaisa so quickly places herself in a nunnery without an attempt to find Pericles. After all, if news of her father's death could reach her in Ephesus, it is more than likely that she could have learned of her husband's whereabouts. Her willingness to serve at Diana's temple of chastity is perhaps meant to be further evidence of how different Thaisa is from the daughter of Antiochus.

Thaliard:

Thaliard is a lord of Antioch. Antiochus appeals to his sense of loyalty and convinces him to kill Pericles. Before Thaliard can do so, Pericles flees the city. Thaliard follows Pericles to Tyre, knowing that if he fails to do as he was instructed by Antiochus, he will be hanged on his return to Antioch. He muses that it is best not to share secrets with kings. But, once arriving in Tyre, he discovers that Pericles has gone. Thaliard pursues him no further.

> **Throughout the play, Pericles suffers one disappointment after another. Although we might view Pericles as a patient and virtuous prince being tested by some divine power, he has alternately been seen as a weak and compromised man who brings about his own suffering."**

Further Reading

Barker, Gerard A. "Themes and Variations in Shakespeare's *Pericles*." *English Studies* 44, no. 6 (1963): 401-14.
    Barker argues that Shakespeare deviates from his source in a way that emphasizes religious faith and the great patience of Pericles.

Brockbank, J. P. "*Pericles* and the Dream of Immortality." *Shakespeare Survey* 24 (1971): 105-16.
    Brockbank examines the several deaths and miraculous reappearances of the presumed dead in the play and suggests that *Pericles* dramatizes rebirth.

Cutts, John P. "Pericles's 'Downright Violence'." *Shakespeare Studies* 4 (1968): 275-93.
    Cutts presents Pericles as a seeker of excitement who brings on his own misfortunes.

Felperin, Howard. "Shakespeare's Miracle Play." *Shakespeare Quarterly* 18, no. 4 (1967): 363-74.
    Felperin examines each scene of *Pericles* and, in its allegory and use of a chorus, likens it to a medieval miracle play.

Flower, Annette C. "Disguise and Identity in *Pericles, Prince of Tyre*." *Shakespeare Quarterly* 26, no. 1 (1975): 30-41.
    Flower focuses on Pericles, Thaisa, and Marina, discussing the significance of the different disguises each adopts throughout the play.

Hoeniger, F. David. "Gower and Shakespeare in *Pericles*." *Shakespeare Quarterly* 33, no. 4 (1982): 461-79.
    Hoeniger examines each scene of the play, discussing the ways in which Gower, as the Chorus, manipulates the audience's reactions.

McIntosh, William A. "Musical Design in *Pericles*." *English Language Notes* 11, no. 2 (1973): 100-06.
    McIntosh discusses the references to music in the play, especially the hellish music of Antiochus's

daughter and the music of the spheres Pericles hears after being reunited with Marina.

Pitcher, John. "The Poet and Taboo: The Riddle of Shakespeare's *Pericles*." *Essays and Studies*, 2nd Series, 35 (1982): 14-29.

Pitcher traces the resonances of incest that run throughout the play.

Semon, Kenneth J. "*Pericles*: An Order Beyond Reason." *Essays in Literature* 1, no. 1 (1974): 17-27.

Semon argues that we can only understand *Pericles* if we resist the impulse to reason out what are meant to be unexplainable events.

Smith, Hallett. Introduction to *Pericles*, by William Shakespeare. In *The Riverside Shakespeare*, edited by G. Blakemore Evans, 1479-82. Boston: Houghton Mifflin, 1974.

Smith discusses the textual history of *Pericles*, noting its relationship to a short novel written by Gerald Wilkins, *The Painful Adventures of Pericles, Prince of Tyre*, Sir Philip Sydney's *Arcadia*, and the fourteenth-century writings of John Gower. He also discusses the characterizations of Pericles, Thaisa, and Marina.

Thorne, W. B. "*Pericles* and the 'Incest-Fertility' Opposition." *Shakespeare Quarterly* 22, no. 1 (1971): 43-56.

Thorne compares the life-giving themes of *Pericles* with those in Shakespeare's comedies.

Woods, James O. "The Running Image in *Pericles*." *Shakespeare Studies* 5 (1969): 240-52.

Noting Pericles's description of his political responsibilities as the topmost branches of a tree protecting the trunk, and marking the image of the tree on the crest of the shield he presents to Thaisa at the tournament in Pentapolis, Woods argues that the image of the tree is a theme that runs throughout the play.

The Tragedy of Richard the Second

Plot Summary

circa 1595

Act I:

In this first play of a tetralogy which includes *Henry IV*, *Part One* and *Two*, and *Henry V*, King Richard II holds a hearing for his cousin Henry Bullingbrook against Thomas Mowbray, duke of Norfolk, whom Bullingbrook accuses, among other things, of misusing funds from the king's coffers and of assassinating the king's uncle the duke of Gloucester. Ignoring the commands of both the king and of Bullingbrook's father, John of Gaunt (who is also the king's uncle), the two adversaries insist on trial by combat, and the king sets a date for that combat to occur. In the meantime, the widowed duchess of Gloucester begs Gaunt to avenge the death of her husband, but Gaunt refuses since he believes that the king himself ordered the assassination. The date for combat arrives, but the king abruptly stops the proceedings and instead banishes Mowbray for life and Bullingbrook for ten years which, upon seeing Gaunt's distress, he reduces to six. Later, the king tells his cousin Lord Aumerle that he dislikes Bullingbrook's popularity with "the common people" (I.iv.24). On advice from his courtier Sir Henry Green, the king decides to travel to Ireland to end a rebellion, and, since the money in the royal coffers has been depleted by his own extravagant expenditures, the king plans to raise funds for the expedition by leasing royal lands. The

act closes as he is called to the dying John of Gaunt's bedside.

Act II:

On his deathbed, Gaunt delivers his famous ''sceptred isle'' speech regarding the state of England under his nephew Richard's poor governance, and counsels the unwilling king to change his ways for the sake of the country. Once Gaunt is dead, Richard seizes his late uncle's holdings to finance his war against Ireland, even though his uncle the duke of York points out that Gaunt's possessions are the rightful inheritance of Gaunt's banished son Bullingbrook. Richard departs for Ireland, leaving York in charge while he is gone. Meanwhile, the queen learns that Bullingbrook has returned illegally to England and has won the support of like-minded noblemen and their armies. Torn between sympathy for his nephew Bullingbrook and loyalty to his king—and underfunded as well as outmanned now that Richard has taken the army to Ireland—York decides to send the queen to safety and to fortify himself at Berkeley castle. The king's favorites—Bushy, Bagot, and Green—flee to protect themselves from Bullingbrook. When Bullingbrook arrives at Berkeley castle, he tells the disapproving York that he has returned to England simply to claim his inheritance and not to overthrow the king. Meanwhile Richard's forces in Wales have deserted after hearing false rumors that the king is dead.

Act III:

Bullingbrook captures Bushy and Green and has them executed for corrupting the king. Richard returns, landing in Wales, only to discover that his troops there have deserted him and have joined with Bullingbrook. What is more, the citizens of England have united with Bullingbrook against Richard, and York is with Bullingbrook as well. In despair, the king dismisses his troops and retreats to Flint castle. Accompanied by York, Bullingbrook arrives at Flint to reclaim his inheritance. Convinced—despite Bullingbrook's denials—that he is being usurped, Richard surrenders and is taken back to London. Richard's queen and her attendants are staying at York's estate, and it is there that the famous ''Garden scene'' occurs: the queen listens in distress as two gardeners compare King Richard's England to an unweeded and infested garden, and subsequently predict the king's fall.

Act IV:

Parliament is convened and Bagot, who is brought in and questioned about Gloucester's murder and the king's complicity in it, accuses Lord Aumerle. A battle of words and challenges results. When Bullingbrook suggests that Thomas Mowbray, the duke of Norfolk, should be recalled from banishment to settle the question, he is told that Mowbray is dead. York arrives to announce that King Richard is willing to give up his throne to Bullingbrook, who promptly accepts. When the bishop of Carlisle objects that no one has the right to judge or replace a king, he is arrested for treason and placed in the custody of the abbot of Westminster. Bullingbrook calls for Richard to be brought to parliament. Richard formally abdicates but refuses to read out a list of accusations made against him. When he asks instead to leave, Bullingbrook sends him to the Tower of London. The abbot of Westminster, the bishop of Carlisle, and Lord Aumerle plot to overthrow Bullingbrook and restore Richard to the throne.

Act V:

The queen waits in a London street to meet Richard as he is being led to the Tower. When he tells her he is resigned to his fate and bids her to return to France, she chastises him for surrendering too easily. The earl of Northumberland arrives to tell Richard that he will be sent north to Pomfret castle rather than to the Tower, and the queen and Richard part from each other tenderly. The duke of York discovers that his son, Lord Aumerle, is plotting against Bullingbrook and goes to turn him in. Distressed, the duchess of York tells her son to rush to Bullingbrook and beg for mercy before his father can condemn him. Meanwhile, Bullingbrook—now King Henry IV—is with his noblemen, worrying about the escapades of his son and heir Prince Hal (later, King Henry V). He is interrupted by Aumerle, who pleads for clemency, then by York, who demands severity for his son's treason, and finally by the duchess of York who insists on clemency for her son. The king agrees to pardon his cousin Aumerle but plans to punish the others involved in the plot. Sir Pierce of Exton overhears Henry wishing that Richard were dead, and decides to assassinate Richard himself in order to gain favor with the new king. In prison at Pomfret castle, Richard muses on his fate. Exton rushes in and murders Richard. The play closes as a guilt-stricken King Henry views Richard in his coffin and condemns Exton for the murder, vowing to go on pilgrimage as penance for Richard's death.

Modern Connections

At first glance, the world of *Richard II* appears to have little in common with ours. The play itself is written entirely in formal, often rhyming, lines of poetic verse rather than in the prose which today's audiences are used to hearing. Also unfamiliar to modern audiences is Richard's preoccupation with divine right, a doctrine which holds that a king's fitness to rule is determined by God only and not by the people. As Richard puts it when he feels his authority as ruler is being questioned:

> show us the hand of God
> That hath dismiss'd us from our stewardship,
> For well we know no hand of blood and bone
> Can gripe the sacred handle of our sceptre,
> Unless he do profane, steal, or usurp.
>
> (III.iii.77-81)

(As king—whether divinely appointed or not—Richard speaks for the nation as a whole, and that is why he refers to himself in the first-person plural: ''show *us* the hand of God,'' ''for well *we* know,'' etc.)

There are, however, other issues in *Richard II* which remain relevant today. One example is the conflict that occurs between family members and between generations. Most of the principal characters in the play are related to one another. Richard's grandfather was King Edward III. Richard's father (who died before he could become king) was Edward, prince of Wales (also known as the ''Black Prince''). The prince of Wales was the oldest brother of John of Gaunt (also known as the duke of Lancaster), Edmund of Langley (also known as the duke of York), and Thomas of Woodstock (the murdered duke of Gloucester). Thus Gaunt, York, and Gloucester are King Richard's uncles, and Gaunt's son Henry Bullingbrook, as well as York's son Aumerle, are the king's cousins.

In the play, Richard's grandfather, Edward III; and his father, the Black Prince, are fondly remembered and deeply admired by Richard's uncles, Gaunt and York. In their opinion, Richard never measures up to his grandfather's and father's formidable reputations and is too preoccupied with luxurious living and with the latest fashions to listen to sound advice (II.i.19-26). Further, they are shocked that Richard was capable of having his uncle Gloucester—his own flesh and blood and the son of his royal grandfather—assassinated.

Richard, on the other hand, is tired of listening to the advice and complaints of ''sullen'' old men like his uncles (II.i.139), and wishes that they would respect his own ''royal blood'' and treat him as they should treat a king (II.i.118).

Another timely issue in the play is taxation. Richard admits that he spends lavishly just to maintain his own extravagances and a large court of followers (I.iv.43-44); nevertheless, when his treasury is empty and he wants to finance a war in Ireland, rather than economize he leases portions of his kingdom for ready cash, and imposes open-ended taxes or ''charters'' on the wealthy people of the nation (I.iv.43-52). Neither of these actions makes Richard II a popular king.

Good government is a significant issue in *Richard II*, as it is today. Richard ignores his subjects' discontentment. By contrast, Bullingbrook is well-loved by the people of England and—according to Richard—actively seeks out their affection by ''div[ing] into their hearts / With humble and familiar courtesy'' (I.iv.25-26). Thus when Bullingbrook defies his sentence of exile and returns to England to reclaim his inheritance, he is supported by the populace, and after Richard is deposed, the people rejoice when Bullingbrook becomes King Henry IV.

Today, taxation and the size and quality of government are the source of much debate and can win or lose an election for politicians. In Shakespeare's time, these topics could be dangerous. On February 7, 1601, supporters of the ambitious earl of Essex commissioned the theatrical company to which Shakespeare belonged to give a special performance of *Richard II*, thereby hoping to incite the populace against Queen Elizabeth, who, like Richard, was resented for levying heavy taxes and for indulging favorites at court. The following day, Essex led an unsuccessful rebellion against the queen, and he was later executed for treason. Shakespeare's acting troupe was questioned regarding their part in the rebellion, but was absolved of any wrongdoing.

Characters

Abbot of Westminster:
See Westminster

Attendants:

In this play about kings, noblemen, and battle, there are numerous lords, officers, soldiers, servants, and other unnamed attendants—many without speaking parts—who fill out the scenes and contribute to the play's royal and martial atmosphere.

Aumerle (Duke of Aumerle, afterwards, Earl of Rutland):

He is the duke of York's son as well as a cousin of Bullingbrook and King Richard. He first appears in I.iii to confirm Bullingbrook's entry into the lists (arena) for combat against Thomas Mowbray, and remains cordial to Bullingbrook throughout this scene. However, in I.iv, Aumerle tells Richard that his dislike for his banished cousin is so strong that he had difficulty pretending he was sorry to see him leave England.

Aumerle is staunchly loyal to King Richard, and tries to bolster Richard's spirits after word is sent that Bullingbrook has invaded England with the support of several noblemen and the approval of the people. ''Comfort, my liege, remember who you are,'' he tells the king (III.ii.82). The fact that ultimately, Richard bitterly rejects Aumerle's comfort—''He does me double wrong / That wounds me with the flatteries of his tongue'' (III.ii.215-16)—serves to reveal Richard's weakness in a crisis.

Aumerle runs into trouble in IV.i when he is accused before parliament and a newly ascendant Bullingbrook of conspiring to kill his uncle Thomas of Woodstock, the duke of Gloucester; IV.i is also the scene in which Richard is deposed, and at its close, Aumerle angrily plots with the abbot of Westminster and the bishop of Carlisle to have Bullingbrook assassinated.

Aumerle's plot ends abruptly once it is discovered in V.ii by his outraged father, the duke of York. In this scene, Aumerle is stripped of his status as duke for his alleged involvement in the murder of Gloucester. He retains the title of earl of Rutland, however. What follows in V.iii is a bit of comic relief as Aumerle, his mother, and his father each rush to Windsor Castle and clamor for the attention of the recently crowned King Henry IV—York wanting to unmask his son's treachery; Aumerle and his mother hoping to win the new king's pardon. Comic relief is a humorous speech, episode, or scene which is meant to alleviate the tension that precedes it in a serious play and to heighten the solemnity that follows it. The chaos which occurs as the duchess, Aumerle, and York fall to their knees in front of the bemused king—who is then obliged to pardon Aumerle more than once to reassure the duchess—offers a respite from the earlier scenes of plotting, deposition, and imprisonment even as it intensifies the grimness of Richard's assassination scene which occurs not long afterward.

Bagot (Sir John Bagot):

Like Bushy and Green, Sir John Bagot is another of the king's hangers-on, but unlike them he is not executed by Bullingbrook but is instead taken before parliament where he accuses Lord Aumerle of conspiring to kill Thomas of Woodstock, duke of Gloucester. Bullingbrook describes Bagot and the other favorites as destructive ''caterpillars of the commonwealth'' (II.iii.166).

Berkeley (Lord Berkeley):

He is sent by the duke of York (who is acting as regent while Richard is away in Ireland) to ask Bullingbrook why he has defied banishment and returned to England. Berkeley angers Bullingbrook by calling him by his old title, the duke of Herford, rather than referring to him as the duke of Lancaster—the title Bullingbrook rightfully inherited with the death of his father, John of Gaunt (II.iii.69-80)

Bishop of Carlisle:

See Carlisle

Bullingbrook (Henry Bullingbrook [Bolingbroke], Duke of Herford, afterwards King Henry IV of England):

Bullingbrook is John of Gaunt's son and King Richard's cousin. With the death of his father, Bullingbrook is supposed to inherit Gaunt's title—the duke of Lancaster. By V.iii he has become King Henry IV.

In the play, the defining moments for Bullingbrook are his banishment by the king in I.iii, followed by Richard's expropriation of his inheritance in II.i—for Richard's taking of his property and the revocation of his new title (Duke of Lancaster) provoke Bullingbrook to defy banishment and return to England as an outlaw and possible usurper.

As Richard's opponent, Bullingbrook is frequently compared to the king concerning his temperament and his potential to govern well. While Richard has been described as imaginative and theatrical with a poetic sensitivity to language, Bullingbrook has been called practical and taciturn.

Indeed, after he is banished, Bullingbrook is chided by his father for saying nothing in response to his friends' farewells (I.iii.253-54). And when Gaunt suggests that his son pretend he is on vacation rather than in exile, Bullingbrook replies that imagining things cannot make them real:

> O, who can hold a fire in his hand
> By thinking on the frosty Caucasus?
> Or cloy the hungry edge of appetite
> By bare imagination of a feast?
>
> (I.iii.294-97)

While many critics describe Richard as being more interested in regal ceremony than in political reality, they refer by contrast to Bullingbrook as a political pragmatist who knows how to turn circumstances to his advantage. They note that Bullingbrook waits until Richard is away in Ireland before returning to England to reclaim his father's legacy, and that he has made himself popular with noblemen and commoners alike. King Richard fears his cousin's popularity; he complains that Bullingbrook purposely lowers himself to the people's level, flattering common merchants and "wooing poor craftsmen with the craft of smiles," calling all of them "'my countrymen, my loving friends,'" as though he expects to be the next king of England (I.iv.28, 34).

Whether or not Bullingbrook does in fact plan to be king has been a source of critical debate. Bullingbrook himself insists that he has returned to England simply to reclaim the inheritance and title that are rightfully his. When Lord Berkeley addresses him as Herford and asks him why he has defied banishment, Bullingbrook sternly reminds him that he should now be called Lancaster, and that he has "come to seek that name in England" (II.iii.71). A short time later, he tells his uncle York virtually the same thing, adding only that he also intends to "weed and pluck away" the king's favorites—Bushy, Bagot, and Green—whom he claims are bad influences over the king (II.iii.167). In III.iii, he comes face to face with Richard, who flatly accuses him of wanting to be king. On his knees before his cousin, Bullingbrook insists once more, "My gracious lord, I come but for mine own" (III.iii.196).

Nevertheless, Bullingbrook's return to England is bolstered by an army which outnumbers the king's, and by the close of III.iii, he has taken Richard into custody. Back in London (IV.i), when Richard sends word that he is willing to "yield" his crown to his cousin, Bullingbrook promptly replies: "In God's name I'll ascend the regal throne" (IV.i.113).

> "Aumerle is staunchly loyal to King Richard, and tries to bolster Richard's spirits after word is sent that Bullingbrook has invaded England with the support of several noblemen and the approval of the people. 'Comfort, my liege, remember who you are,' he tells the king (III.ii.82)."

The ensuing "deposition scene" brings up another contentious issue: Does Bullingbrook depose Richard, or does Richard depose himself? As early as III.ii, even before he has directly encountered Bullingbrook and his army, Richard is in despair, calls himself deposed, and discharges his troops. In III.iii.143-45, after speaking to Northumberland and before meeting with his cousin, Richard asserts that he is willing to be deposed, and in IV.i he officially relinquishes his crown. Be that as it may, at the close of IV.i Bullingbrook still feels it necessary to imprison Richard rather than merely send him away.

Act V looks ahead to King Henry IV's troublesome reign and to the next three plays in what is now considered a tetralogy of Shakespearean history plays. The tone in V.iii.1-22 is upbeat as King Henry grumbles about his "unthrifty" and "dissolute" son Prince Hal (who plays a key role in *Henry IV, Part One* and *Two* and the title role in *King Henry V*), but predicts that Hal will improve with age. In the V.vi, the tone turns ominous as Henry, with his new government plagued by rebellions and overshadowed by Richard's murder, vows to make a pilgrimage to the Holy Land.

Bushy (Sir John Bushy):

Along with Sir Henry Green and Sir John Bagot, Bushy is an advisor and favorite of King Richard, and during the play's first two acts, the three of them frequently accompany the king onstage, often bringing out the worst in him as well as giving poor advice. Bushy's announcement in I.iv, for example, that John of Gaunt is seriously ill leads

> **King Richard fears his cousin's popularity; he complains that Bullingbrook purposely lowers himself to the people's level, flattering common merchants and 'wooing poor craftsmen with the craft of smiles,' calling all of them ' "my countrymen, my loving friends," ' as though he expects to be the next king of England (I.iv.28, 34)."**

Richard to hope that his uncle will die soon so that he can use Gaunt's money to finance his war in Ireland. In II.ii, no sooner does Bushy chide the queen for her feelings of foreboding than Green appears with the news that Bullingbrook has invaded England. Realizing that the king is likely to be deposed, Bushy and Green flee to save themselves, but are captured and executed by Bullingbrook. In the garden scene both Bushy and Green are described as parasitical weeds which feed on Richard until they "are pluck'd up root and all by Bullingbrook" (III.iv.52).

Captain:

He is the leader of King Richard's troops in Wales, and Richard depends on his help to defeat Bullingbrook. In II.iv, he tells the earl of Salisbury that with no word from the king and after rumors of the king's death and ill omens occurring around the country he and his men have decided not to stay and fight. His bad news in itself portends Richard's fall.

Carlisle (Bishop of Carlisle):

He is a loyal supporter of Richard II and a firm believer in the divine right of kings. In III.ii, he chastises the king for losing faith and despairing about his chances against Bullingbrook. At the start of the deposition scene, Carlisle objects to Bullingbrook's willingness to replace Richard (IV.i.113-49), arguing that no subject "can give sentence on his king," and accurately predicting that civil war will be part of England's future if

Richard (ancestor of the Yorkists) is deposed by Lancastrian Bullingbrook. (For further discussion on the Yorkist and Lancastrian civil war known as the Wars of the Roses, see the entries for *Richard III* and for *Henry VI, Part One, Two,* and *Three*). For his protestations, Carlisle is arrested by Northumberland. Although afterward he conspires with the abbot of Westminster and the duke of Aumerle to assassinate Henry IV, Carlisle is regarded by the new king as an honorable opponent and thus receives a relatively light sentence (V.vi.24-29).

Duchess of Gloucester:
See Gloucester

Duchess of York:
See York

Exton (Sir Pierce of Exton):

He assassinates Richard, believing that Bullingbrook (now King Henry IV) wishes him to do so, as indicated by his lines in V.iv. In this scene Exton quotes Richard as asking, " 'Have I no friend that will rid me of this living fear?' " (V.iv.2). At the end of the brief scene, Exton concludes "I am the King's friend, and will rid his foe" (V.iv.11). Far from rewarding him, Henry condemns Exton for the "deed of slander" (V.vi.35), and vows to go on pilgrimage to the Holy Land to atone for his part in Richard's death.

Fitzwater (Lord Fitzwater):

He is one of several noblemen in parliament who support Sir John Bagot's accusation that the duke of Aumerle is responsible for the murder of the duke of Gloucester (IV.i.33-40). In V.vi, he is rewarded by Henry IV for his part in rounding up and executing the new king's enemies. King Henry's praise for Fitzwater and others who have eliminated threats to his rule is in marked contrast to his condemnation of Sir Pierce of Exton for murdering the former King Richard II.

Gardeners:

In the famous garden scene (III.iv), a gardener and his assistant are overheard by the queen defining the qualities of good government and discussing the condition of England under Richard II. They describe England as a "sea-walled garden" that is choked by weeds and infested with caterpillars in the form of unscrupulous courtiers such as Bushy, Bagot, and Green who have poorly advised the king. Critics have pointed out that the garden imagery which fills this scene occurs throughout the play, particularly in John of Gaunt's speech in II.i.40-68, and in Bullingbrook's description of the king's favorites as "caterpillars of the commonwealth" (II.iii.166).

Gaunt (John of Gaunt, Duke of Lancaster):

He is the brother of Edmund of Langley (duke of York), uncle to King Richard, and father of Henry Bullingbrook. Like his brother York, Gaunt is fervently loyal to his king and country, but nevertheless critical of Richard's extravagances and misgovernment. Also like York, Gaunt finds that his duty to his king often conflicts with his concerns for his own family. Acting as Richard's advisor in I.iii, Gaunt agrees that his son Bullingbrook should be banished; however as a father, Gaunt expresses his sorrow at the thought of losing his son and heir for even six years. Conflict between familial feeling and duty to his king also occurs in I.ii when Gaunt refuses to avenge the death of his brother Thomas Woodstock (Duke of Gloucester) on grounds that Gloucester had been assassinated on orders from King Richard.

Gaunt dies in II.i, but not before delivering his famous patriotic speech describing England as a "sceptred isle" and "demi-paradise" which has been "leas'd out" and "bound in with shame" as the result of Richard's constant search for money to finance his luxurious habits. Characteristically, Richard ignores Gaunt's dying advice, and confiscates his wealth after he has died (II.i.153-62).

Gloucester (Duchess of Gloucester):

She is the widow of the murdered Thomas of Woodstock, duke of Gloucester, who was uncle to King Richard and brother to both the duke of York and to John of Gaunt. In I.ii, the duchess implores her brother-in-law Gaunt to avenge Woodstock's death. Gaunt refuses, professing knowledge that King Richard ordered Mowbray to assassinate Woodstock, and suggests that instead the duchess turn to God for revenge. Overwhelmed with grief, the duchess bids farewell to Gaunt and prays that Bullingbrook will defeat Mowbray in their trial by combat and thus prove Mowbray (and by extension King Richard) guilty of the murder. She achieves her revenge indirectly in II.ii, when York announces that he will borrow money from her to defend King Richard from Bullingbrook, and is told that she has died. The duchess of Gloucester's interview with Gaunt is significant because it offers insight into

> Back in London (IV.i), when Richard sends word that he is willing to 'yield' his crown to his cousin, Bullingbrook promptly replies: 'In God's name I'll ascend the regal throne' (IV.i.113)."

Richard's behavior in I.i and I.iii. Since Richard is apparently responsible for Gloucester's death, Bullingbrook's accusations and Mowbray's presence seem inconvenient and embarrassing to the king.

Green (Sir Henry Green):

He is an advisor to the king as well as one of his favorites at court. In I.iv, he counsels Richard that quick action must be taken against a rebellion in Ireland. As a result, the king decides to travel to Ireland himself to suppress the insurrection, leaving England unprotected against Bullingbrook's return. In II.ii, Green reverses himself, declaring that it would have been better after all if the king had not departed for Ireland with his army, since Bullingbrook has just invaded England. Green and Sir John Bushy, another of the king's favorites, are executed by Bullingbrook in III.i, who accuses them of corrupting the king and thus causing a rift between him and the queen, of having turned the king against Bullingbrook, and, finally, of having taken and misused Bullingbrook's lands and looted his household while he was in exile.

Groom:

He worked in the royal stables when Richard was king. He visits Richard in prison to pay his respects and recounts how the new king, Henry IV, rode Richard's favorite horse on the day of his coronation (V.v.67-83). His visit emphasizes Richard's isolation in prison and provokes the former king to describe himself as a beast of burden "Spurr'd, gall'd, and tir'd by jauncing Bullingbrook" (V.v.94).

Heralds:

They are minor officials who preside at tournaments of arms. At the trial by combat in I.iii, there

> Gaunt dies in II.i, but not before delivering his famous patriotic speech describing England as a 'sceptred isle' and 'demi-paradise' which has been 'leas'd out' and 'bound in with shame' as the result of Richard's constant search for money to finance his luxurious habits."

are two heralds, one for Bullingbrook and one for Mowbray; they ritualistically identify, and announce the intentions of, the two prospective combatants.

Herford (Henry Bullingbrook, Duke of Herford, afterwards King Henry IV of England):

See Bullingbrook

Hotspur (Henry Percy, also known as Harry Percy):

See Percy

Keeper:

He is the keeper of the prison at Pomfret castle where Richard is sent after being deposed. In V.v he brings the former king food poisoned by Sir Pierce of Exton, and Richard, shouting "The devil take Henry of Lancaster and thee!" (V.v.102), proceeds to beat the Keeper.

Lady:

She is one of the queen's attendants. In the garden scene (III.iv), she helps to set the increasingly somber tone of the play when she suggests various forms of entertainment to the queen, who, missing the king, sorrowfully rejects each one.

Lancaster (John of Gaunt, Duke of Lancaster):

See Gaunt

Langley (Edmund of Langley, Duke of York):

See York

Lords:

In this play about kings, noblemen, and battle, there are numerous lords, officers, soldiers, servants, and other unnamed attendants—many without speaking parts—who fill out the scenes and contribute to the play's royal and martial atmosphere.

Marshal (Lord Marshal):

He administers the highly ritualized trial by combat between Bullingbrook and Mowbray in I.iii. After Richard calls off the trial and banishes the two participants, the marshal declares his wish to ride with Bullingbrook and see him off on his departure from England.

Mowbray (Thomas Mowbray, Duke of Norfolk):

He appears as early as I.i, when Bullingbrook accuses him of embezzlement and of murdering Thomas of Woodstock, duke of Gloucester. Mowbray and Bullingbrook are so incensed with each other that they ignore King Richard's commands to solve their differences peacefully. His next and final appearance is in I.iii when Richard convenes a trial by combat between him and Bullingbrook, only to call it off and banish them both. In IV.i, we are told that Mowbray has died in exile.

Mowbray's presence in the play is brief but revealing with regard to King Richard's personality and motives. When his calls for a peaceful resolution go unheeded by Mowbray and Bullingbrook, Richard asserts that "We were not born to sue, but to command," yet orders the two men to settle their quarrel by combat and, in effect, follow their own wishes rather than his commands (I.i.196-205). When Richard subsequently stops the battle and banishes both men, it is significant that he sends Mowbray away for life: Mowbray has in fact killed Richard's uncle Gloucester on orders from Richard. Dutiful as Mowbray has been, it is therefore embarrassing and undiplomatic for the king to have him close by.

Mowbray's reaction to banishment is bitter. He feels that the king owes him thanks rather than punishment for following orders, and tells him so:

> A heavy sentence, my most sovereign liege,
> And all unlook'd for from your Highness' mouth.
> A dearer merit, not so deep a maim

As to be cast forth in the common air,
Have I deserved at your Highness' hands.

(I.iii.154-58)

Before departing, Mowbray accurately predicts that King Richard will suffer at the hands of Bullingbrook.

Norfolk (Thomas Mowbray, Duke of Norfolk):

See Mowbray

Northumberland (Henry Percy, Earl of Northumberland):

See Percy

Officers:

In this play about kings, noblemen, and battle, there are numerous lords, officers, soldiers, servants, and other unnamed attendants—many without speaking parts—who fill out the scenes and contribute to the play's royal and martial atmosphere.

Percy (Henry Percy, Earl of Northumberland):

Hotspur's father, this Percy is usually referred to as Northumberland. He is a supporter of Bullingbrook, helping him to regain his inheritance and ultimately the crown. In II.i, Northumberland meets with two other of Bullingbrook's sympathizers, Lord Willoughby and Lord Ross, to complain about the banished duke's mistreatment by King Richard and to criticize Richard for relying on his corrupt favorites, for overtaxing both rich and poor, and for misgoverning the country in general. It is from Northumberland that we first learn of Bullingbrook's decision to return and claim his inheritance.

Throughout most of the play, Northumberland is unique in showing open disrespect for King Richard. In III.iii.7-8, the duke of York reproaches him for referring to the king simply as "Richard." In III.iii.72-76, Northumberland fails to kneel before the king as is required by law and custom. During the deposition scene it is Northumberland who repeatedly insists that King Richard read out loud his list of crimes, provoking Richard to call him a "Fiend" and a "haught insulting man" (IV.i.270, 254). Northumberland also rushes Richard through his final meeting with his queen before sending him to his new prison in Pomfret castle. Calling him the "ladder wherewithal / The mounting Bullingbrook ascends my throne" (V.i.55-56), the former king predicts that soon Northumberland

and King Henry IV will become enemies, and that does in fact occur in Shakespeare's *Henry IV, Part One* and *Two*.

Percy (Henry Percy, also known as Harry Percy or Hotspur):

This Percy is usually called Hotspur and is the son of Henry Percy, earl of Northumberland. Hotpur's role in the play is a small one and differs greatly from his appearance in Shakespeare's *Henry IV, Part One*, where he becomes a fierce enemy of the king and his son, Prince Henry.

Queen:

She is the wife of King Richard II. Although her role in the play is peripheral, it serves to foreshadow and convey information about Richard's personality as well as his fate, and contributes to the somber tone of the play. When Richard leaves for Ireland, the queen feels a foreboding that goes beyond simply missing her husband, and worries that "Some unborn sorrow, ripe in fortune's womb / Is coming towards me" (II.i.10-11). Shortly afterward, Green arrives with news that Bullingbrook has invaded England. In III.iv, she overhears a pair of gardeners discuss the king's fall from power, and in the next scene (IV.i) Richard is in fact deposed. In her final appearance, the queen reproaches her husband for surrendering meekly to imprisonment, and argues that Richard should have the self-respect to remain a king in spirit even though he is no longer one in fact. Comparing him to the "king of beasts" she asserts that "The lion dying thrusteth forth his paw, / And wounds the earth, if nothing else, with rage / To be o'erpow'r'd" (V.i.29-31).

Richard (King Richard II of England):

He is the ruler of England and the title character. Early in the play it becomes clear that Richard's view of himself and his office differs markedly from the view held by his subjects. Richard governs according to the divine right of kings—a precept which argues that God determines who should rule. In keeping with this doctrine, a monarch is sprinkled or "anointed" with consecrated oil on the day of his coronation as a symbol of his election by God.

In the play, Richard's government runs into trouble because he passionately believes that his decrees are sacred and that, as he explains it,

Not all the water in the rough rude sea

> **Richard's enemies complain that he has become a 'most degenerate king' and decide to take action to turn the monarchy back into what they think it should be: to 'make high majesty look like itself' and to restore to health the country as well as their own fortunes (II.i.262, 291-95)."**

Can wash the balm off from an anointed king;
The breath of worldly men cannot depose
The deputy elected by the Lord;

(III.ii.54-57)

Thus King Richard rewards his favorites and levies harsh taxes to pay for his expenses, secure in his conviction that he has a divine right to do so.

His subjects on the other hand believe that a divinely appointed king is meant to govern fairly and well. Thus Richard's allies remind him of his responsibility to follow good rather than bad advice and to work conscientiously to succeed as king, while the populace, hoping to see in him a model for their own behavior, lament to find instead a "wasteful King" (III.iv.55). Meanwhile, Richard's enemies complain that he has become a "most degenerate king" and decide to take action to turn the monarchy back into what they think it should be: to "make high majesty look like itself" and to restore to health the country as well as their own fortunes (II.i.262, 291-95).

Critics have remarked that Richard's great failing is his preference for the ceremonies involved in being a king over the day-to-day business of governing the country. Alternatively, it has been noted that the king's sensitivity to language and the eloquent and powerful speeches he makes as a result transform him into a sympathetic character in spite of his poor leadership.

Richard's character has been the focus not only for a discussion of the nature of good government, but also for an examination of personal identity. Richard was born and raised to be king; are he and

the monarchy therefore one and the same, or does Richard have a personality and a life of his own? Questions regarding the king's identity occur repeatedly in the play. In II.ii.241-42 after Richard has disinherited Bullingbrook, Northumberland declares that "The King is not himself, but basely led / By flatterers" who turn him against the country's noblemen. In III.ii.82-83, when Richard begins to despair because Bullingbrook's troops outnumber his, Aumerle counsels him to remember who he is, and Richard replies, "I had forgot myself, am I not king?"

The most dramatic expressions of Richard's dilemma concerning his identity occur during the deposition scene. Once he has relinquished his crown to Bullingbrook, Richard describes himself as "unking'd" and as "nothing," yet considers himself king of his own griefs (IV.i.220, 201, 193). He calls himself a traitor for agreeing "T'undeck the pompous body of a king" (IV.i.250), and when Northumberland refers to him as "lord," Richard cries,

No lord of thine, . . .
Nor no man's lord. I have no name, no title,
No, not that name was given me at the font,
But 'tis usurp'd. Alack the heavy day,
That I have worn so many winters out
And know not now what name to call myself!

(IV.i.254-59)

In a final gesture indicating the connection he has felt between the kingship and himself, the deposed Richard calls for a "glass" or mirror and smashes it after looking at his face (IV.i.276-91).

Alone in his prison cell Richard continues to question his identity. In an elaborate metaphor (a metaphor explains or describes one thing by imaginatively comparing it to another—for example, the lion is the king of beasts), he compares his prison to the world and his thoughts to the people of that world, so that, as he puts it, "Thus play I in one person many people" (V.v.31). During the course of this game, he tries out several different identities—a saint, a beggar, a king—only to conclude that no man is or ever will be contented "till he be eas'd / With being nothing" (V.v.40-41).

A source of critical debate has been whether or not Richard learns from his suffering and becomes a better person by the close of the play. Most critics agree that Richard starts out as self-occupied and theatrical, and that his love for melodrama and ceremony hinders him from dealing sensibly with the practical realities of government. But while some assert that his attitude and level of incompetence remain much the same throughout the play, others refer to the remarks on music and time in his prison soliloquy as proof that he has come to recognize the responsibility he bears for his fall from power: "I wasted time," Richard, now a former king, observes, "and now doth time waste me" (V.v.49).

Lastly, some critics point to Richard's struggle with his murderers (V.v.102-12) as ultimate proof that he has developed through suffering into someone better than he once was.

Ross (Lord Ross):

He is a supporter of Bullingbrook and a co-conspirator with the earl of Northumberland and Lord Willoughby for Bullingbrook's return to England so that he can reclaim his inheritance and reform the king's government. He is also concerned that his lands and wealth are in danger of being taken by the king and his favorites just as Bullingbrook's have been.

Rutland (Duke of Aumerle, afterwards Earl of Rutland):

See Aumerle

Salisbury (Earl of Salisbury):

A supporter of Richard II, he tries unsuccessfully in II.iv to convince the Welsh Captain and his troops not to desert the king, and afterward he predicts Richard's fall. In V.vi.8, Northumberland announces that Salisbury has been killed while rebelling against newly crowned Henry IV.

Scroop (Sir Stephen Scroop):

He is Richard's ally and, in III.ii, the bearer of bad news: he informs the king that the populace has turned against him, that Bushy and Green have been executed, and that York has sided with Bullingbrook. Richard's response is to dismiss his own troops in despair.

Servants:

In this play about kings, noblemen, and battle, there are numerous lords, officers, soldiers, servants, and other unnamed attendants—many without speaking parts—who fill out the scenes and contribute to the play's royal and martial atmosphere.

> **" Once he has relinquished his crown to Bullingbrook, Richard describes himself as 'unking'd' and as 'nothing,' yet considers himself king of his own griefs (IV.i.220, 201, 193)."**

Servingman:

He is a servant to Edmund of Langley, duke of York, and a bearer of bad news. In II.ii, as the duke is trying to muster forces and money to defend King Richard against Bullingbrook, the servingman informs him that his son Aumerle is away in Ireland fighting alongside the king and that the duchess of Gloucester—a possible source of funds—has died.

Soldiers:

In this play about kings, noblemen, and battle, there are numerous lords, officers, soldiers, servants, and other unnamed attendants—many without speaking parts—who fill out the scenes and contribute to the play's royal and martial atmosphere.

Surrey (Duke of Surrey):

In IV.i.60-71, he sides with the duke of Aumerle when Aumerle is accused by Lord Fitzwater of murdering the duke of Gloucester. Gloucester's murder and the identity of his killers is a recurrent source of recrimination and conflict in the play.

Westminster (Abbot of Westminster):

He is present at King Richard's deposition in IV.i.107-334, and is told by the earl of Northumberland to take custody of the bishop of Carlisle after Carlisle challenges Bullingbrook's right to become king. However, at the close of IV.i, he conspires with Carlisle and Aumerle to assassinate Bullingbrook. In V.vi.19-21, Harry Percy (Hotspur) reports that the abbot has died of a guilty conscience.

Willoughby (Lord Willoughby):

Along with Lord Ross and the earl of Northumberland, Willoughby conspires to bring about the

> "
>
> **'I wasted time,' Richard, now**
>
> **a former king, observes, 'and now**
>
> **doth time waste me' (V.v.49)."**

return of Bullingbrook to England and to his inheritance. Like Ross and Northumberland, Willoughby is worried about losing his own properties to pay for the king's excesses.

York (Edmund of Langley, Duke of York):

He is uncle to King Richard and Henry Bullingbrook, brother of John of Gaunt, and father of the duke of Aumerle. During much of the play York is torn between his sense of what is dutiful and what is just as he struggles to maintain fairness and order within his large royal family.

York's first appearance in the play is at the deathbed of his brother John of Gaunt, and his first remarks—which have to do with the king—are not complimentary. He warns Gaunt not to waste his dying breath by giving advice to Richard, "For all in vain comes counsel to his ear" (II.i.4). When Richard confiscates from Gaunt's estate the inheritance that should have gone to Gaunt's banished son, Bullingbrook, York cries out in dismay at such an injustice: "How long shall I be patient? ah, how long / Shall tender duty make me suffer wrong? (II.i.163-64).

Nevertheless, while York condemns Richard for poor government and even for theft, he insists that as king, Richard is entitled to loyalty and respect from all of his subjects. Thus when Bullingbrook defies Richard and returns to England, York—who has been assigned as regent or "lord governor" in Richard's absence—calls him a traitor to his "anointed King" (II.iii.88-96), and declares that he would arrest Bullingbrook if his own forces were not outnumbered by his rebellious nephew's.

After Richard is deposed, York's sense of duty shifts to the newly crowned Henry IV. He weeps as he tells his wife how "rude misgoverned hands from windows' tops / Threw dust and rubbish on King Richard's head" as the humiliated former king followed the triumphant new king into London

(V.ii.5-6). But when he discovers that his own son, Aumerle, is involved in a plot to assassinate Henry, York shouts "Treason, foul treason!" and rushes off in horror to warn his king (V.ii.72).

York (Duchess of York):

She is the wife of Edmund of Langley, duke of York, and the mother of the duke of Aumerle. Her zealous efforts in V.iii to protect her son from punishment for treason result in comic relief. (Comic relief is a humorous speech, episode, or scene which lessens the tension that precedes it in a serious play and heightens the solemnity that follows it.) The arrival of the duchess at King Henry IV's door as he is confronting her son (the potential assassin) and her husband (the accuser) transforms a deadly political crisis into a comical family affair, or as the king puts it: "Our scene is alt'red from a serious thing, / And now chang'd to 'The Beggar and the King' " (V.iii.79-80).

Further Reading

Baines, Barbara J. "Kingship of the Silent King: A Study of Shakespeare's Bolingbroke." *English Studies* 61 (February 1980): 24-36.
> Baines sees Bullingbrook (King Henry IV) as a practical and competent man who deposes the incompetent Richard and who is realistic enough to recognize his own limitations as king.

Carr, Virginia M. "The Power of Grief in *Richard II*." *Études Anglaises* 31 (April-June 1978): 145-51.
> Looking at Richard, the duchess of Gloucester, and the queen, Carr discusses the importance of unconsoled grief in the play.

French, A. L. "Who Deposed Richard the Second?" *Essays in Criticism* 17 (October 1967): 411-33.
> French refutes the traditional argument that Bullingbrook deposed Richard and suggests instead that although Richard blames Bullingbrook, he in fact deposes himself.

Gaudet, Paul. "The 'Parasitical' Counselors in Shakespeare's *Richard II*: A Problem in Dramatic Interpretation." *Shakespeare Quarterly* 33 (Summer 1982): 142-54.
> Gaudet contends that in the play, Bushy, Bagot, and Green do not corrupt Richard, but that they emphasize the faults which the king already possesses.

Hamilton, Donna B. "The State of Law in *Richard II*." *Shakespeare Quarterly* 34 (Spring 1983): 5-17.
> Focusing on Richard's actions in I.i, Gaunt's accusations in II.i, and the garden scene in III.iv, Hamilton

argues that the play demonstrates Elizabethans' objections to the idea of absolute rule.

Kelly, Michael F. "The Function of York in *Richard II*." *Southern Humanities Review* 6 (1972): 257-67.
Kelly emphasizes York's importance in the play, seeing him as pivotal in the shift of power from Richard to Bullingbrook and as a spokesman for English politics.

McNeir, Waldo F. "The Comic Scenes in *Richard II* V.ii and iii." *Neuphilologische Mitteilungen* 73, no. 4 (1972): 815-22.
McNeir observes that the comic elements in V.ii and V.iii are intentional, and that they center on the duchess of York and provide us with necessary comic relief before the play's somber ending. McNeir further suggests that these humorous scenes set the tone for Shakespeare's *Henry IV, Part One* and *Two* and for *Henry V*.

Montgomery, Robert L., Jr. "The Dimensions of Time in *Richard II*." *Shakespeare Studies* 4 (1968): 73-85.
Proceeding act by act, and examining some of the play's central issues and major characters, Montgomery demonstrates how important the idea of time is to an understanding of *Richard II*. Montgomery refers to time in the play as "a felt presence and an almost palpable condition."

Morris, Faith G. "Shakespeare's *Richard II*." *Explicator* 35 (Winter 1976): 19-20.
Morris looks closely at the imagery in the garden scene (III.iv) and also discusses the development of the queen's role in that scene.

Quinn, Michael. " 'The King Is Not Himself': The Personal Tragedy of Richard II." *Studies in Philology* 56 (April 1959): 169-86.
Quinn uses the concepts of divine right and honor to explain Richard's refusal to act during most of the play, and analyzes his dramatic change into a character of action at the play's close.

Reiman, Donald H. "Appearance, Reality, and Moral Order in *Richard II*." *Modern Language Quarterly* 25 (March 1964): 34-45.
Reiman argues that at some point in the play, nearly all of the major characters say one thing and do another, and hypocritically allow their questionable actions or motivations to be hidden by the semblance of goodness.

Traversi, Derek. "*Richard II*." *Stratford Papers on Shakespeare* 5 (1964): 11-29.
Traversi contrasts Richard's traditional idea of kingship with Bullingbrook's new, more effective and political one based upon the desire for power.

Ure, Peter. Introduction to *King Richard II*, by William Shakespeare, edited by Peter Ure, xiii-lxxxiii. The Arden Edition of the Works of William Shakespeare. London: Methuen and Co. Ltd., 1961.
Ure provides a critical overview of the play as well as information on source material and the play's first performance and publication dates.

——. "*Richard II*, or, 'To Find Out Right with Wrong.' " *Essays in Criticism* 18 (April 1968): 225-29.
Part of an ongoing and useful debate, Ure refutes A. L. French's argument that it is Richard who abdicates, not Bullingbrook who deposes him.

Williams, Pieter D. "Music, Time, and Tears in *Richard II*." *American Benedictine Review* 22 (1971): 472-85.
Focusing in particular on Richard's soliloquy in V.v, Williams analyzes the ways in which time and music imagery are used to demonstrate the lack of order in Richard's realm. Williams also observes that these images are presented in such a manner as to inspire sympathy in us for Richard's fate.

The Tragedy of Richard the Third

circa 1592-93

Plot Summary

Act I:

For the moment, the Wars of the Roses—the long struggle for power between the two noble families known as the House of York and the House of Lancaster—is over. The Yorkists have defeated the Lancastrians, and Yorkist Edward IV is now king of England. However, his youngest brother, Richard of Gloucester (self-described as deformed, unfit for peace, ''subtle, false, and treacherous'' [I.i.37]), is determined to cause trouble. He persuades the king that their brother, George, duke of Clarence, represents a threat and should be imprisoned. Richard then tells Clarence that Queen Elizabeth, Edward IV's wife, is responsible for his being jailed. When he hears that the king is seriously ill, Richard plots to have Clarence murdered so that there will be fewer obstacles to his own succession to Edward's throne. Next, he meets Lady Anne (widow of Henry VI's son Prince Edward whom Richard and his brothers killed) mourning over the coffin of her father-in-law, Henry VI (whom Richard murdered). Initially Anne curses Richard, but eventually he charms her into accepting his ring. Later, Richard publicly accuses Queen Elizabeth of having turned the king against not only Clarence but also against himself and Lord Hastings. Margaret (widow of Henry VI) appears and curses Richard. In prison, Clarence is stabbed by Richard's hired assassins and drowned in a cask of malmsey wine.

Act II:

The dying King Edward insists that the queen and her followers make peace with Richard and his followers, and each group at least pretends to do so. When Richard announces that Clarence has been killed in his prison cell in the Tower, the king is appalled, for although he had ordered Clarence to be executed, he later countermanded that instruction. Richard claims that the revocation came too late. Meanwhile, the duchess of York mourns the death of her son Clarence, as do his two young children. The queen enters, in tears because King Edward has just died. Arrangements are made to send for his young heir, Prince Edward, so that he may be crowned king at once. Citizens of the kingdom talk about the king's death and express concern about the fate of the country. News arrives for the queen that her ally Sir Thomas Vaughan, her brother Lord Rivers, and her son Lord Grey have been jailed by Richard and his right-hand man, Buckingham. Fearing for their own lives, the queen and her youngest son, Richard, the duke of York, flee to sanctuary.

Act III:

Young Prince Edward arrives in London, accompanied by Richard of Gloucester and Buckingham. He wants to see his mother, the queen, and his brother, the duke of York, but is told that they ''have taken sanctuary'' (III.i.28). Buckingham summons York to join Edward in London. On the pretext of keeping them safe until Edward's coronation, Richard lodges the two children in the Tower. For the moment, Richard is their Lord Protector, but he intends to usurp Edward and become king himself. With that in mind, he sends his ally Catesby to discover whether Hastings can be relied upon to aid him in his bid for the throne. Hastings, however, remains loyal to Prince Edward. Meanwhile, Rivers, Grey, and Vaughan, the queen's allies, are executed by Richard's supporters. In London, a council including Richard, Buckingham, Hastings, and Stanley meets to set a date for Edward's coronation. Without warning, Richard accuses Hastings of treason and orders his execution. Later, Richard instructs Buckingham to suggest to the Mayor and the citizens of London that the two young princes are illegitimate and thus not fit to rule England and that the former King Edward IV was himself immoral and illegitimate. Buckingham comes back to report that the citizens are unsure about endorsing Richard as their king. With Buckingham's help, Richard stages a scene where he seems virtuous and

unwilling to accept the crown; the citizens are thus duped into begging him to be king.

Act IV:

The duchess of York, Queen Elizabeth, her son the marquess of Dorset, and Anne (who is now Richard's wife) attempt to visit the two young princes in the Tower but are stopped by Brakenbury on orders from Richard. When Anne is called to Westminster to be crowned King Richard's queen, she reluctantly goes. The women are disgusted that Richard has usurped Prince Edward's throne. Elizabeth sends her son Dorset to the earl of Richmond so that he will be safe from Richard's clutches. Now that he is king, Richard wants to get rid of the two young princes, who constitute a threat to his right to rule. But when he asks Buckingham to have them killed, Buckingham hesitates. Instead, Richard enlists Tyrrel to arrange the murder. In an effort to further secure his reign, he instructs Catesby to spread the rumor that Anne is seriously ill: he plans to get rid of her so that he can marry his brother Edward's daughter Elizabeth. Later, when Richard snubs Buckingham, his former right-hand man sees that his life is now in danger, so he flees Richard's court and joins Richmond. Tyrrel brings the news that the princes have been executed. Pleased, Richard goes to court his brother's daughter, Elizabeth. His wife, Anne, has died, so there is no impediment to his marrying Elizabeth. Queen Elizabeth and the duchess of York weep over the death of their loved ones at Richard's hands. Margaret appears, reminding them that her curses have thus proved true. Although Queen Elizabeth is revolted when Richard tells her he wishes to marry her daughter, she consents to speak to her daughter on his behalf. Stanley warns Richard that Richmond—who is a Lancastrian—is on his way to England to claim the throne. Distrusting Stanley, who is Richmond's stepfather, Richard keeps his son George as a hostage. Messengers arrive, telling Richard that rebellions have begun against him all over the country and that Buckingham has been taken captive. Richard prepares to leave for Salisbury to do battle with Richmond.

Act V:

On the way to be executed, Buckingham repents of the evil he has committed on Richard's behalf. Meanwhile, Lancastrian Richmond and

Yorkist Richard both arrive on Bosworth Field and set up camp. Night comes, and Richard is visited in his tent by the ghosts of those he has murdered. They curse him, condemning him to die on the field of battle. The same ghosts visit Richmond and promise him victory. Morning comes, and the two leaders encourage their troops before going into battle. When next we see Richard, he has been unhorsed and, so, has been fighting on foot. Richard and Richmond fight; Richard is killed; and Richmond, as victor, accepts the crown of England. As Henry VII, he pledges to bring peace to the bloodied nation by marrying Edward IV's daughter Elizabeth, in this way combining the House of Lancaster (red rose) with the House of York (white rose).

Modern Connections

While *Richard III* works as a sequel to Shakespeare's trilogy, *Henry VI, Part One, Two,* and *Three*, it can be read and performed as an independent unit, and as such it remains one of Shakespeare's most popular plays. A key to the play's popularity is its title character, Richard, whose particular brand of wickedness has withstood the test of time. Elizabethan audiences went to the theater for the same reason that we attend movies—to be entertained. Unlike most people today, however, Elizabethans were very familiar with the history of the Wars of the Roses and of Richard's rise and fall from power. To keep his audience interested in what was otherwise a well-known and sometimes dry historical account, Shakespeare had to make Richard a fascinating character, one who speaks directly to the spectators and thus involves them in his own plots, and who jokes about both himself and his victims.

Another factor which might have contributed to *Richard III*'s early popularity was that royal succession, or the order according to which a person lawfully and rightfully becomes monarch, was an issue that greatly concerned English citizens during Shakespeare's time because their aging queen—Elizabeth I—was unmarried and had no heirs. Additionally, the fact that Elizabeth was England's lawful queen did not prevent challenges to her power. In 1588 Philip II of Spain sent his Armada in hope of defeating Elizabeth; earlier, in 1587, Elizabeth had found it necessary to execute Mary, queen of Scots, who had also posed a threat to her rule. So a play about an ambitious nobleman plotting to become king was very relevant to Shakespeare's audience.

Today, some producers of *Richard III* try to recapture this relevance by updating the play's setting. Thus the 1995 film version of *Richard III* takes place during the 1930s and features tanks and machine guns rather than body armor and swords; what's more, actor Ian McKellen's portrayal of a sadistic and unpredictable Richard reminds us of such dictators as Hitler, Mussolini, and Stalin.

Because the personality of Richard, rather than the issue of the Wars of the Roses, is of most interest to modern audiences, many productions today attempt to simplify the play's action by entirely deleting Queen Margaret—Richard's most vocal adversary in the dynastic struggle—and instead focus more closely on Richard himself and the motivation for the evil he commits. Both Ian McKellen's *Richard III* and Laurence Olivier's 1955 film version of the play leave Margaret out of the script.

With or without a modern setting or the elimination of Margaret's character, *Richard III* remains a compelling play. Richard is like a soap opera villain: he is spectacularly wicked but pretends to be honest and caring in order to confuse his victims; he betrays his friends and family and shifts the blame for his betrayals onto unsuspecting others. As Richard himself puts it: ''The secret mischiefs that I set abroach / I lay unto the grievous charge of others'' (I.iii.324-25). So, for example, he feigns shock and distress upon seeing his brother George being led off to jail and blames the queen for his brother's misfortune, even though Richard is himself responsible for having gotten George imprisoned and will shortly plot to have George murdered. Likewise, Richard reproaches Queen Elizabeth and her family for turning the king against him, even while he is slandering them behind their backs and plotting their destruction. To attain power, he will go so far as to risk ruining his own mother's reputation by spreading the rumor that her eldest son, King Edward IV, is illegitimate. Finally, with power nearly in his grasp and in true soap opera fashion, Richard pretends that he is not at all ambitious—that he does not want to rule but will do so only if the people insist—which by now of course they do, seduced and confused as they are by his duplicity.

Characters

Aldermen:

The aldermen are London officials ranking below the mayor in authority. Along with the mayor and the citizens of London, the aldermen are fooled in III.vii into asking Richard to become king.

Anne (Lady Anne):

Anne is the widow of Edward, prince of Wales, who was the son and heir of King Henry VI. She hates Richard for murdering her husband and father-in-law, but Richard charms her into marrying him. As Richard's sad queen, she dies after he tires of her. Anne first appears in I.ii, sorrowfully following the coffin of her father-in-law, Henry VI. She laments King Henry's death and curses his murderer, Richard. Lady Anne puts a curse on any woman who would marry Richard, thus—ironically—cursing herself.

When Richard appears and tries to take over the funeral procession, Anne reacts in disgust. She calls him a "foul devil" and begs for lightning to strike him dead (I.ii.49). But Richard is determined: He flatters Anne and makes excuses for his crimes; he claims he loves her and invites her to kill him with his own sword. Eventually, Anne relents. "I would I knew thy heart," she tells him, and agrees to accept his ring (I.ii.192).

When Anne appears for the next and last time (IV.i), she has married Richard and is miserable. She remembers the curse she made on any woman "mad" enough to become his wife and bitterly regrets that "Within so small a time, my woman's heart / Grossly grew captive to his honey words, / And prov'd the subject of mine own soul's curse" (IV.i.78-80). When called away to Westminster to be crowned Richard's queen, she goes reluctantly. In IV.ii, Richard starts the rumor that Anne is seriously ill. In IV.iii, he briefly mentions that she has died.

Traditionally, Anne has been regarded as weak and vain for being taken in by Richard's flattery. More recently, it has been pointed out that Richard approaches her when she is grieving, so she is vulnerable to his persistent demands. It has also been remarked that since Richard is the king's brother, Anne certainly cannot kill him and has little choice but to accept him. Although her appearance in the play is fairly brief, Anne is important for providing us with an early, revealing glimpse of Richard's cunning and persuasiveness.

> " Richard is like a soap opera villain: he is spectacularly wicked but pretends to be honest and caring in order to confuse his victims; he betrays his friends and family and shifts the blame for his betrayals onto unsuspecting others."

Archbishop of Canterbury (Cardinal Bourchier, Archbishop of Canterbury):
See Bourchier

Archbishop of York (Thomas Rotherham, Archbishop of York):
See Rotherham

Attendants:

Because this is a play about war and politics between royal and noble families, many of the scenes are peopled with noble or royal retainers such as attendants, councillors, gentleman, lords, and soldiers, most of whom are without speaking parts or names and many of whom are simply referred to in the stage directions as "others."

Berkeley:

Berekely and Tressel are two gentlemen attending on Lady Anne as she follows Henry VI's coffin in I.ii. Although Anne calls them by name at line 221, neither of them has a speaking part. They are named in the scene perhaps simply to emphasize how meager the funeral services are which have been allowed for the dead king.

Bishop of Ely (John Morton, Bishop of Ely):
See Morton

Bishops:

To fool the people of London into thinking him holy and fit to rule, Richard appears in III.vii carrying a prayer book and walking "between two Bishops," neither of whom has a speaking part.

> **Lady Anne puts a curse on any woman who would marry Richard, thus—ironically—cursing herself."**

Blunt (Sir James Blunt):

He is a nobleman and a supporter of Henry of Richmond. He first appears in V.ii as the two armies are making their way toward the battlefield.

Bourchier (Cardinal Bourchier, Archbishop of Canterbury):

In III.i, Buckingham persuades the unwilling cardinal to use force if necessary to remove the young duke of York from the safety of sanctuary and bring him to London, ostensibly to provide company for his brother, the prince of Wales, but in reality to be imprisoned by Richard.

Boy (Edward Plantagenet, Earl of Warwick, referred to as "Boy"):

See Plantagenet

Brakenbury (Sir Robert Brakenbury):

As lieutenant of the Tower of London, Brakenbury is in charge of the Tower prison, where first the duke of Clarence and later King Edward's two young sons are imprisoned. He rigidly follows the orders he has been given, requesting, per instructions from King Edward, that Richard not speak to the prisoner Clarence as he is being taken to jail (I.i.84-87), and later, on orders from Richard, preventing Queen Elizabeth from visiting her two young sons in the Tower (IV.i.15-17). In the first instance, he innocently provides Richard with the opportunity to slander the queen and to appear sympathetic to his brother Clarence; in the second instance, he makes it known that Richard now considers himself king. He is listed among the dead at Bosworth Field (V.v.14).

Brandon (Sir William Brandon):

He is a supporter of Henry of Richmond. His first appearance is at Richmond's camp on Bosworth Field (V.iii). He is listed among the dead at Bosworth Field (V.v.14).

Buckingham (Duke of Buckingham):

Buckingham is Richard's co-conspirator. He helps Richard become king, but falls from favor when he hesitates at murdering Edward IV's two young heirs. He then goes over to the earl of Richmond's side against Richard, but is subsequently captured by Richard's forces and executed.

As Richard's co-conspirator, Buckingham's role in the play is important. Richard terms him "My other self" (II.ii.151), and uses him as an advisor and a spy.

Buckingham's first appearances in the play (I.iii and II.i) do not indicate that he is anything more than a minor character; at this point, Richard refers to him merely as one of several "simple gulls" or fools whom he is deceiving (I.iii.327). However, once King Edward dies, Buckingham becomes more prominent. In II.ii, he plots to put the king's heir (Edward, prince of Wales) in Richard's grasp by bringing the child to London without the protection of his mother or her followers. When Elizabeth flees to sanctuary with her youngest son (the duke of York), Buckingham takes it upon himself to order the child back to London (III.i).

In III.v, Buckingham reveals that he is almost as good an actor as Richard is. "I can counterfeit the deep tragedian" (III.v.5), he says, as he and Richard are about to fool the mayor of London into thinking that Richard is a good man who has been cruelly betrayed. "Ghastly looks / Are at my service, like enforced smiles," he insists, "And both are ready in their offices / At any time to grace my stratagems" (III.v.8-11). He proves his point well in III.vii when he helps Richard stage so convincing a performance of humility and royal worth that the citizens of London implore Richard to take the kingship.

Buckingham, however, fails as Richard's "other self" when it comes to murdering the two young princes. In IV.ii, Richard, newly crowned, first hints then baldly states that he wants Edward's heirs killed. Buckingham's reply—"Your Grace may do your pleasure" (IV.ii.21)—fails to satisfy Richard, who wants a confederate in a crime so heinous. Buckingham's next attempt to postpone making a decision only infuriates Richard, who mutters "High-reaching Buckingham grows circumspect" (IV.ii.31). Later, when Buckingham attempts to bargain with Richard over the princes' murder, the king rejects him.

Buckingham's hesitation costs him his life. Although, like Richard, he has been called a

Machiavel (one who views politics as amoral and that any means, however unscrupulous, can justifiably be used to achieve political power), ultimately he is not in the same league as his deceitful king.

Cardinal Bourchier (Cardinal Bourchier, Archbishop of Canterbury):
See Bourchier

Catesby (Sir William Catesby):
He is one of Richard's most loyal supporters and as such, he is sent in III.ii to find out whether Lord Hastings will support Richard's coronation. In III.vii, he helps Richard and Buckingham to fool the Lord Mayor, aldermen, and citizens into asking Richard to be king. On the battlefield in V.iv, he entreats King Richard to withdraw from the fighting until a horse can be found to replace the one he has lost in battle, but Richard angrily rejects this request and continues to fight without one.

Citizens:
In II.iii, three unnamed citizens meet and worry over what will become of England now that King Edward IV is dead and his heir, Edward, prince of Wales, is still a child. Later, in III.vii, a group of citizens joins the aldermen and the mayor of London in entreating Richard to be their king.

Clarence (George, Duke of Clarence):
Brother of King Edward IV and Richard. He is imprisoned in the Tower of London after Richard turns the king against him, and even though the king decides to pardon him, Clarence is assassinated by two murderers sent by Richard. Clarence's death is brutal and humiliating: he is stabbed and his body is thrown into a cask of wine.

Although Clarence's part in the play is brief, what happens to him gives us early insight into Richard's deceitfulness and powers of persuasion. In I.i, Richard commiserates with his brother as Clarence is being taken to prison, when only a few lines earlier, Richard has told the audience that he is responsible for having Clarence jailed. His false sympathy is so convincing that in I.iv, Clarence refuses to believe it when the murderers claim that Richard is their employer. "O, do not slander him," Clarence says—innocently defending his untrustworthy brother—"for he is kind" (I.iv.241).

Clarence is filled with guilt for having switched sides more than once during the Wars of the Roses, and the night before his murder, his past haunts him

> **In III.v, Buckingham reveals that he is almost as good an actor as Richard is. 'I can counterfeit the deep tragedian' (III.v.5), he says, as he and Richard are about to fool the Mayor of London into thinking that Richard is a good man who has been cruelly betrayed."**

in the form of an undersea dream—a dream which is famous for its vivid images of shipwrecks and drowning, and which, it has been argued, also foreshadows the perilous condition of England under Richard's ruthless leadership.

Councillors:
Because this is a play about war and politics between royal and noble families, many of the scenes are peopled with noble or royal retainers such as attendants, councillors, gentleman, lords, and soldiers, most of whom are without speaking parts or names and many of whom are simply referred to in the stage directions as "others."

Derby (Lord Stanley, Earl of Derby):
See Stanley

Dorset (Marquess of Dorset):
He is Queen Elizabeth's son from a former marriage. He escapes Richard's treachery and joins the earl of Richmond's side after Richard is crowned king.

Duchess of York:
See York

Edward (Prince Edward of Wales, afterwards, King Edward V):
He is the young son and heir of King Edward IV. He is imprisoned in the Tower of London by his ambitious uncle Richard of Gloucester, along with his younger brother, the duke of York. Later both children are murdered on Richard's orders.

Edward (King Edward IV of England):

He is the ruler of England and brother of George, duke of Clarence, and Richard, duke of Gloucester. Although he appears in only one scene, he is frequently mentioned by the other characters, and reflects the instability of England's government.

King Edward bears a reputation for promiscuity. In I.i.73, Richard refers to the king's mistress Jane Shore, and in III.vii.179-91, Buckingham describes the king's early entanglements with several women. Richard uses this information to make the king and his heirs appear unfit to rule and to make himself look virtuous by contrast.

As early as I.i.136, we are told that King Edward has become "sickly, weak, and melancholy," and that he is not likely to live much longer. Meanwhile, Richard has convinced him to imprison their brother, George, for treason, and when King Edward makes his first and only appearance (II.i), to order Queen Elizabeth and her followers to reconcile with Richard and his followers in an attempt to bring peace to his court, Richard takes the opportunity to announce that George, the duke of Clarence, has been executed. The king is overwhelmed with guilt at this news, and soon afterward (II.ii) Queen Elizabeth sorrowfully announces that he has died, leaving an underage son—Edward, the prince of Wales—to succeed him as king and providing Richard with the opportunity he has been waiting for to seize power.

Elizabeth (Queen Elizabeth):

Formerly Lady Grey, she is the wife of King Edward IV and mother of Edward, prince of Wales, and Richard, duke of York, the king's two young heirs. She hates Richard for murdering her brother, Earl Rivers, and her sons; nevertheless, he persuades her to think of him as a suitor in marriage to her daughter Elizabeth. Queen Elizabeth's appearance in three out of the play's five acts spotlights Richard's ruthless quest for the throne, for as the king's wife and the mother of the king's heir, she has a direct interest in whether or not Richard will succeed. As early as I.i, he is spreading lies about her influence over the king, and it is evident that there are two factions at court—Elizabeth with her relatives and supporters, and Richard with his henchman Buckingham. The queen first enters in I.iii, expressing her concerns about the king's illness to her brother, Lord Rivers, and her two older sons from a previous marriage, Lord Grey and the marquess of Dorset. She knows that if the king dies, her young son Edward, prince of Wales and heir to the throne, could be put under Richard's protection, "a man," she tells her sons and brother, "that loves not me, nor none of you" (I.iii.13); indeed, Richard appears shortly afterward and insults her.

In II.i, Elizabeth and her followers make peace with Richard at the king's request. By II.ii, the king has died, and the distraught queen agrees with Richard that Prince Edward of Wales—the king's chosen successor—should be brought to court. By II.iv, the queen's situation has become worse, for Richard has jailed Rivers and Grey, and keeps the Prince Edward in his custody. Elizabeth realizes that Richard now has control of the government: "Ay me! . . ." she cries, "Insulting tyranny begins to jut / Upon the innocent and aweless throne" (II.iv.49, 51-52). She flees with her youngest son, York, into sanctuary, but Richard and Buckingham order York to be brought back to London to "lodge" in the Tower with the Prince Edward (III.i), and in IV.i, Elizabeth is barred from visiting them.

Elizabeth's final and most famous meeting with Richard occurs in IV.iv, when she appears to agree to convince her daughter to marry him. This scene has been described as a battle of wits between Richard and Elizabeth, and it is not clear who wins. It has been pointed out that Elizabeth never explicitly says that she will tell her daughter to marry Richard. Instead she asks a question, "Shall I go win my daughter to thy will?" and ends by telling Richard, "I go. Write to me very shortly, / And you shall understand from me her mind" (IV.iv.426, 428-29). Later in IV. v, we are told that she has promised her daughter to the earl of Richmond. It is left for the audience to determine whether Elizabeth has been weak-willed and inconsistent, or, instead, has finally outwitted Richard.

Ely (John Morton, Bishop of Ely):
See Morton

Gentlemen:

Because this is a play about war and politics between royal and noble families, many of the scenes are peopled with noble or royal retainers such as attendants, councillors, gentleman, lords, and soldiers, most of whom are without speaking parts or names and many of whom are simply referred to in the stage directions as "others."

George (George, Duke of Clarence):
See Clarence

Ghosts:

On the night before his battle with Richmond, King Richard is haunted by the ghosts of his victims, including King Henry VI (the Lancastrian king defeated by Richard's family, succeeded by Richard's brother King Edward IV, and murdered by Richard) and Edward, prince of Wales, son of Henry VI. Each ghost curses Richard with death and despair. The same ghosts visit Richmond to bestow him with blessings.

Girl (Margaret Plantagenet, Countess of Salisbury, referred to as "Girl"):

See Plantagenet

Gloucester (Richard, Duke of Gloucester, afterwards King Richard III):

See Richard

Grey (Lord Grey):

He is Queen Elizabeth's son from a previous marriage and he supports the succession of Edward, prince of Wales, to the throne. Since he is therefore a threat to Richard's ambitions, Richard has him imprisoned and then murdered—along with Earl Rivers and Sir Thomas Vaughan—in III.iii.

Hastings (Lord Hastings):

He is Lord Chamberlain to King Edward IV. When he first appears in I.i, Lord Hastings has recently been released from prison, and Richard has convinced him that Queen Elizabeth was responsible for having sent him there. Nevertheless, he remains loyal to King Edward and, and after the king's death, he is staunchly loyal to Edward, the prince of Wales. Lord Hastings does not realize that Richard has ambitions to be king, nor does he know that Richard is a potential enemy. In III.ii, he imprudently tells Richard's ally Catesby that he would never support Richard as king instead of the prince of Wales. Consequently, Richard trumps up a charge of treason against Hastings and has him assassinated (III.iv).

Hastings (a pursuivant):

A government official empowered to serve warrants. Coincidentally, he has the same name as Lord Hastings, to whom he speaks in his one and only scene, III.ii. His function is to emphasize Lord Hastings' blindness to his own danger, for when chatting with the pursuivant, Lord Hastings is optimistic about his future, unaware that Richard has

> " Elizabeth's final and most famous meeting with Richard occurs in IV.iv, when she appears to agree to convince her daughter to marry him. This scene has been described as a battle of wits between Richard and Elizabeth, and it is not clear who wins."

marked him for execution, and in such good spirits that he gives Hastings the pursuivant a purseful of money.

Henry (Henry, Earl of Richmond, afterwards King Henry VII of England):

See Richmond

Herbert (Sir Walter Herbert):

Herbert is a supporter of Henry of Richmond. He first appears in V.ii as the two armies are making their way toward Bosworth Field.

Keeper in the Tower:

He is a warden at the Tower of London prison. His function in the play is to listen to and sympathize with the imprisoned George, duke of Clarence, as he describes his undersea nightmare.

Lords:

Because this is a play about war and politics between royal and noble families, many of the scenes are peopled with noble or royal retainers such as attendants, councillors, gentleman, lords, and soldiers, most of whom are without speaking parts or names and many of whom are simply referred to in the stage directions as "others."

Lovel (Lord Lovel):

He is a courtier and a supporter of Richard. He is present at the council meeting in III.iv when Lord Hastings is accused of treason. Along with Sir Richard Ratcliffe and on orders from Richard, he escorts Lord Hastings to his execution.

Margaret (Queen Margaret):

Margaret is the widow of Henry VI (a Lancastrian king who was murdered by Richard in *Henry VI, Part Three*). During the play, she accurately forecasts vengeance for herself and destruction for her enemies.

Shakespeare's Margaret remains in England where the play takes place rather than sailing home to France as she did according to history. Onstage, she becomes a choric figure: offering her opinion on the play's action, and prophesying doom and misery on Richard and his supporters. (In drama, an individual choric figure or a chorus is sometimes used to describe events which occur before the beginning of the play or to comment on the action of the play as it unfolds.)

Although she appears in just two scenes, her influence is evident throughout the play. She first enters in I.iii, speaking—as she often does—in asides. (An aside occurs when a character talks to the audience and is not overheard by the other characters onstage.) In this instance, Margaret comments to the audience on the bickering between her Yorkist enemies—Elizabeth and her followers on one side, and Richard and his on the other. When Margaret at last speaks directly to these characters (''Hear me, you wrangling pirates, that fall out / In sharing that which you have pill'd from me!'' [I.iii.157-58]), she curses them, and in doing so, she affects the play's action.

Margaret prays for the death of King Edward as well as his heirs and for a life of misery for Queen Elizabeth. She curses Lord Hastings and Earl Rivers with early death, and Richard with sleepless nights and ruin. She finishes by predicting that Buckingham will be betrayed by Richard: ''O Buckingham, take heed of yonder dog! / Look when he fawns he bites; and when he bites, / His venom tooth will rankle to the death'' (I.iii.288-90).

By the time she appears again (IV.iv) most of her prophecies have come to pass. She exults in her revenge and shows Elizabeth and the duchess of York how to curse Richard, who has become, as Margaret had predicted, an enemy to all of them.

When *Richard III* is produced onstage, Margaret's role is often omitted on grounds that the language in her scenes is too formal and repetitive to sound relevant to a modern audience. Yet, Margaret provides useful background information on Richard's grim quest for power. Her predictions and ghostlike presence (''Here in these confines slily have I lurk'd, / To watch the waning of mine enemies'' [IV.iv.3-4]) reinforce the theme of divine retribution in the play, as do the characters' recollections of her prophecies when they are led to their executions. In III.iv.92-93, for example, Lord Hastings laments, ''O Margaret, Margaret, now thy heavy curse / Is lighted on poor Hastings' wretched head!'' Likewise Buckingham in V.i.25 cries ''Thus Margaret's curse falls heavy on my neck.''

Finally, her presence in the play provides a connection between the events within the play and those which have affected the characters before the play begins.

Mayor (Lord Mayor of London):

He is the leader of the citizens of London, so it is important to Richard that the mayor is on his side. Thus in III.v, Richard and Buckingham carefully stage a scene to convince the mayor that they are justified in having executed Hastings for treachery. Later, in III.vii, they stage another elaborate scene to dupe the Lord Mayor into believing that Richard deserves to become king.

Messengers:

There are messengers scattered throughout this play of royal intrigue and civil war. In II.iv, a messenger arrives to tell Queen Elizabeth that her brother, Earl Rivers; her son Lord Grey; and her ally Sir Thomas Vaughan have been imprisoned by Richard of Gloucester and Buckingham, thus precipitating her flight to sanctuary with her youngest son, the duke of York. In III.ii, a messenger brings warning to Lord Hastings from Lord Stanley that Richard means them both harm and that both should escape while they still can. Imprudently, Lord Hastings chooses to ignore this warning. In IV.iv, four different messengers arrive to give King Richard updates on the progress of the noblemen who are raising armies against him. Finally, in V.iii, a messenger appears on the battlefield to inform King Richard that Lord Stanley will not fight on his side. This last message means that Richard will lose the war.

Morton (John Morton, Bishop of Ely):

He is a member of the council which has been convened to decide on the date for the prince's coronation, and is part of the famous strawberries episode (III.iv.31-34) during which Richard lulls the council (and in particular, Lord Hastings) into a false sense of security before angrily accusing Hastings of treason.

Murderers:

In I.iii, Richard hires two murderers to kill his brother, the duke of Clarence, who is imprisoned in the Tower. In I.iv, The first murderer kills Clarence and stuffs his body in a cask of wine; the second murderer has a change of heart and refuses to participate in the crime, and in fact at the last moment tries to warn Clarence that he is going to be stabbed. In spite of their violent intentions, the two murderers are meant to be somewhat comical, and their discussion of conscience in I.iv.117-53—before Clarence is murdered—is intended to be humorous.

Norfolk (Duke of Norfolk):

He is a nobleman of King Edward's court and, later, a supporter of King Richard. He is present at the council which is called ostensibly to set the date for Prince Edward's coronation but which results in the execution of Lord Hastings. He is listed among the dead after the battle on Bosworth Field (V.v.13).

Oxford (Earl of Oxford):

He is a nobleman and a supporter of Henry of Richmond. He first appears in V.ii as the two opposing armies are making their way toward the battlefield.

Page:

After Buckingham balks at murdering the two young princes, Richard turns to a young, "unrespective" or thoughtless page for advice on whom to hire to do his dirty work (IV.ii.29); the page suggests James Tyrrel.

Plantagenet (Edward Plantagenet, Earl of Warwick, referred to as "Boy"):

He is the young son of George, duke of Clarence. He is referred to as "Boy" in the stage directions of II.ii. In II.ii, he tells his grandmother, the duchess of York, that according to Richard, Clarence was executed by King Edward IV. This incident demonstrates that to achieve his ambitions, Richard will even lie to a child. In IV.iii, King Richard tells us that he has imprisoned this "son of Clarence," presumably to make his own shaky claim to the throne more secure (IV.iii.36).

Plantagenet (Margaret Plantagenet, Countess of Salisbury, referred to as "Girl"):

She is the countess of Salisbury and a young daughter of George, duke of Clarence. She is re-

> **Margaret prays for the death of King Edward as well as his heirs and for a life of misery for Queen Elizabeth. She curses Lord Hastings and Earl Rivers with early death, and Richard with sleepless nights and ruin. She finishes by predicting that Buckingham will be betrayed by Richard: 'O Buckingham, take heed of yonder dog! / Look when he fawns he bites; and when he bites, / His venom tooth will rankle to the death' (I.iii.288-90)."**

ferred to as "Girl" in the stage directions in II.ii. In IV.iii, Richard tells us that he has married her off to a commoner, presumably to make his own dubious claim to the throne more secure (see IV.iii.37).

Priest:

He is called "Sir John" by Lord Hastings (III.ii.109), who thanks him for a sermon he had lately delivered and promises to reward him for it. This encounter underscores Lord Hastings' optimism and complete ignorance to the danger he is in from Richard.

Ratcliffe (Sir Richard Ratcliffe):

He is one of Richard's most loyal supporters. His first appearance is in II.i as King Edward is trying to reconcile Richard's and Queen Elizabeth's factions. In III.iii, he escorts the queen's followers—Earl Rivers, Lord Grey, and Sir Thomas Vaughan—to their execution on orders from Richard. And in III.iv he and Lord Lovel escort Lord Hastings to his execution. In IV.iv, he warns King Richard that Richmond is on his way to England backed by a powerful navy and that Buckingham has joined him. Finally, he is with King Richard in V.iii on Bosworth Field on the day of battle, and

> When *Richard III* is produced onstage, Margaret's role is often omitted . . ."

offers reassurance after the king tells him of his bad dreams of the night before.

Richard (Richard, Duke of Gloucester, afterwards King Richard III of England):

Also known as Gloucester, Richard is the duke of Gloucester and later becomes King Richard III. He is the title character of the play and the scheming younger brother of King Edward IV and George, duke of Clarence.

The opening couplet in *Richard III* ("Now is the winter of our discontent / Made glorious summer by this son of York" [I.i.1-2]) and the final line of V.iv ("A horse, a horse! my kingdom for a horse!" [V.iv.13]) are probably the most famous lines in the play; appropriately, they are also the first and the last words that Richard speaks. Richard is the energizing force in the play. He is responsible for most of the play's dark comedy—which usually happens when he is mocking himself or ridiculing his victims. He has been called a Machiavel (one who views politics as amoral and that any means, however unscrupulous, can justifiably be used to achieve power) because of his ruthless drive for power. Almost as soon as he appears onstage he tells us that he is "determined to prove a villain" and mentions the traps he is laying against his own brothers (I.i.30-40). Richard describes himself as "deform'd, unfinish'd," and so unpleasant to look at that dogs bark at him, and he blames his wickedness on his looks (I.i.20-23).

A persistent thread of comedy runs through *Richard III*, a lot of it generated by Richard himself. Since the play is largely about treachery and vengeance, the comedy it contains is appropriately dark, consisting of dramatic irony as well as parody. Some of the humor comes from Richard's self-ridicule, but much of it comes when he mocks the confidence which others mistakenly place in him.

Dramatic irony occurs when the audience understands the real significance of a character's words or actions but the character or those around him or her do not. Richard's sympathetic comments to his brother Clarence as he is being led away to prison (I.i.42-116) result in dramatic irony because we know from the start that Richard is responsible for having Clarence jailed.

Another instance of dramatic irony occurs when Catesby suggests that Richard should be crowned king in place of the prince of Wales, and Lord Hastings states: "I'll have this crown of mine cut from my shoulders / Before I'll see the crown so foul misplac'd" (III.ii.43-44). We already know from Richard's conversation with Buckingham one scene earlier that Lord Hastings will indeed lose his head if he opposes Richard. Both of these incidents are meant to make us smile—although perhaps grimly—at Richard's trickery and his victims' naïveté.

Parody is the use of exaggerated imitation to ridicule someone or something that is meant to be taken seriously. Richard mocks both himself and Anne when he parodies a preening lover after Anne—against all odds—accepts his ring: "I'll be at charges for a looking-glass, / And entertain a score or two of tailors / To study fashions to adorn my body" (I.ii.255-57). Part of the humor in these lines comes from Richard's ability to make fun of himself.

Richard's most triumphant parody occurs in III.vii when he dupes the citizens of London into petitioning him to be their king. By imitating a holy man and appearing reluctant to accept the crown, Richard succeeds in getting the power he craves.

Richard does not announce his intention to become king until III.i, but his plots and murders lead in that direction, and by IV.ii, he is crowned. A focus of debate has been whether Richard controls events or whether he is simply a divine instrument meant to clear England of the corruption of civil war so that the country can begin anew. In either case, critics have pointed out that toward the end of the play Richard has lost his sense of humor and control. "I have not that alacrity of spirit / Nor cheer of mind that I was wont to have," he declares (V.iii.73-74). The night before battle, he is tormented by sleeplessness and haunted by the ghosts of those he has murdered. The following day he is himself killed in battle by Richmond.

While most critics agree that Richard is a Machiavellian villain and that he is witty—frequently poking fun at himself as well as at his victims—they are divided on the nature of Richard's wickedness.

A significant focus of controversy is the apparent contradiction between Richard's monstrous behavior and his continuing attractiveness to audiences. One argument suggests that he is not meant to be a realistic character but a melodramatic, comic villain whose extreme antics make us laugh. A somewhat different view is that Richard's witty dialogue and his ability to mock himself make him appealing.

It has also been argued that—with the exception of the two young princes—Richard's victims are not as innocent as they appear but are instead hypocrites who know they are being used and who try unsuccessfully to use Richard. According to this interpretation, Richard is simply more clever than is anyone else in the play at getting what he wants.

Richard (Richard, Duke of York):
See York

Richmond (Henry, Earl of Richmond, afterwards King Henry VII):

He is the earl of Richmond and later, King Henry VII, and is referred to as Richmond in the stage directions. He is also a Lancastrian who raises an army to defeat King Richard III and his reign of tyranny. Although Richmond succeeds Richard as king, his part in the play is small: essentially, his goodness is meant to contrast with Richard's wickedness. His oration to his soldiers in V.iii is inspirational and patriotic; Richard's oration in the same scene is grim and belligerent. After Richmond kills Richard on the battlefield in V.v, he closes the play by calling for a reconciliation between the Houses of York and Lancaster: ''We will unite the White Rose and the Red'' (V.v.19). He accomplishes this by pardoning Richard's soldiers, as well as by becoming king and making Yorkist King Edward's daughter Elizabeth his queen.

Rivers (Earl Rivers):

(In some editions of the play, Rivers is also identified as ''Anthony Woodvile'' in the *Dramatis Personae*). Rivers is Queen Elizabeth's brother and supports the succession of his young nephew, Edward, prince of Wales, to the throne; thus, he is a threat to Richard's ambitions to be king. Richard has him imprisoned and assassinated along with the

> **" Richard describes himself as 'deform'd, unfinish'd,' and so unpleasant to look at that dogs bark at him, and he blames his wickedness on his looks (I.i.20-23).''**

queen's brother, Lord Grey, and her ally Sir Thomas Vaughan.

Rotherham (Thomas Rotherham, Archbishop of York):

He is the archbishop of York. He is with the duchess, Queen Elizabeth, and her young son Richard, duke of York, when a messenger arrives in II.iv with news that the queen's brother, Earl Rivers, her son Lord Grey, and her ally Sir Thomas Vaughan have been imprisoned by Richard of Gloucester and Buckingham. He encourages the queen to seek sanctuary (refuge from Richard of Gloucester) with her young son York, and also promises to continue to be her ally.

Scrivener:

He appears in III.vi with a document which authorizes the execution of Hastings and which was composed long before Hastings is supposed to have committed his crime. The scrivener's observations demonstrate how corrupt life has become under Richard's influence.

Sheriff of Wiltshire:

He appears in V.i, leading the duke of Buckingham to his execution on orders from King Richard. His presence allows Buckingham an opportunity to voice his regrets for supporting Richard in his evil plots.

Soldiers:

Because this is a play about war and politics between royal and noble families, many of the scenes are peopled with noble or royal retainers such as attendants, councillors, gentleman, lords,

> **❝** **. . . toward the end of the play Richard has lost his sense of humor and control. 'I have not that alacrity of spirit / Nor cheer of mind that I was wont to have,' he declares (V.iii.73-74)."**

and soldiers, most of whom are without speaking parts or names and many of whom are simply referred to in the stage directions as "others."

Stanley (Lord Stanley, Earl of Derby):

Also called the earl of Derby, he is the earl of Richmond's stepfather, and as such is not trusted by Richard, who takes Stanley's son, George, as hostage, thereby trying to guarantee that Stanley won't dare to fight on Richmond's side. Richard's ploy, however, fails, because Stanley allies himself with Richmond in V.iii, and his refusal to fight for King Richard helps turn the battle in Richmond's favor.

Surrey (Earl of Surrey):

He is a nobleman and a supporter of King Richard. He first appears in V.iii as Richard's army arrives at Bosworth Field where the battle will take place.

Tressel:

Berekely and Tressel are two gentlemen attending on Lady Anne as she follows Henry VI's coffin in I.ii. Although Anne calls them by name at line 221, neither of them has a speaking part. They are named in the scene perhaps simply to emphasize how meager the funeral services are which have been allowed for the dead king.

Tyrrel (Sir James Tyrrel):

He is recruited by Richard to carry out the murders of the two young heirs of Edward IV after Richard's co-conspirator, Buckingham, balks at arranging the murders himself. He is described as "a discontented gentleman, / Whose humble means match not his haughty spirit" (IV.ii.36-37), and

who would be willing to do "any thing" for money (IV.ii.36-37, 39).

Urswick (Christopher Urswick):

He is a priest attending Henry, the earl of Richmond. Christopher Urswick is sent by Lord Stanley to tell Richmond, among other things, that Queen Elizabeth has offered her daughter's hand in marriage to Richmond rather than to Richard.

Vaughan (Sir Thomas Vaughan):

He is a supporter of Queen Elizabeth and an impediment to Richard's plans, so Richard and Buckingham order Ratcliffe to have Vaughan executed along with Earl Rivers and Lord Grey, the queen's relatives.

Woodvile (Anthony Woodvile, Earl Rivers):

See Rivers

York (Duchess of York):

She is the mother of King Edward IV; George, duke of Clarence; and Richard, duke of Gloucester. She grieves for the death of King Edward and the murder of Clarence as well as for the murder of her two grandsons. Ultimately, she curses Richard for his wickedness.

During most of the play, the duchess behaves as a relatively powerless member of the royal family—she reacts to rather than causes the events going on around her. On her first appearance, for example, she mourns the duke of Clarence's death and acknowledges Richard's responsibility for his murder, but the most she can accomplish is to reproach her son in the form of a blessing and hope that he might change his ways: "God bless thee," she says to Richard, "and put meekness in thy breast, / Love, charity, obedience, and true duty!" (II.ii.107-08).

Again, in II.iv and IV.i, as the duchess witnesses further indications of Richard's wickedness, she can only bewail her misfortunes and curse her own womb for having produced Richard (IV.i.53).

By IV.iv, however, Richard has murdered her two grandsons, and the duchess has had enough. Before leaving her son Richard forever, the duchess of York delivers to him her "most grievous curse" (IV.iv.188), and one that foreshadows his destruction in battle and the victory of Richmond's forces. "Bloody thou art, bloody will be thy end" she predicts, "Shame serves thy life and doth thy death attend" (IV.iv.195-96).

York (Richard, Duke of York):

The younger son of King Edward IV and thus second in line to the throne when the king dies. He is imprisoned with his brother Prince Edward in the Tower by his ambitious uncle Richard, duke of Gloucester, who later has the two of them murdered.

Further Reading

Bevington, David. " 'Why Should Calamity Be Full of Words?': The Efficacy of Cursing in *Richard III*." *Iowa State Journal of Research* 56, no. 1 (August 1981): 9-21.

Bevington analyzes the power of curses in the play—in particular, the effectiveness of self-cursing—and concludes that in the world of *Richard III*, people's words become instruments of divine justice that can turn against them.

Dillon, Janette. " 'I am myself alone': *Richard III*." In *Shakespeare and the Solitary Man*, 49-60. Totowa, N.J.: Rowman and Littlefield, 1981.

Dillon examines Richard's isolation and concludes that Richard is alone by choice because he is egotistical, ambitious, and ruthless, but that he is also forced into isolation through a "physical deformity which sets him apart from others."

Fergusson, Francis. "Richard III." In *Shakespeare: The Pattern in His Carpet*, 51-6. New York: Delacorte Press, 1970.

Fergusson asserts that Richard himself is the source of the play's energy and that Shakespeare drew upon history as well as upon classical and medieval drama to portray Richard as a heartless and comical villain.

Hamilton, A. C. "The Resolution of the Early Period: *Richard III*." In *The Early Shakespeare*, 186-202. San Marino, Calif.: The Huntington Library, 1967.

Hamilton discusses the fact that *Richard III* "combines the genres of history play and tragedy," remarking that if we look at the play's action from Richard's point of view, we see the history of his political progress; on the other hand, Margaret turns the play into a tragedy as each of her curses against Richard is fulfilled. Hamilton also makes some useful observations about the duchess of York's function in the play.

Miner, Madonne M. " 'Neither mother, wife, nor England's queen': The Roles of Women in *Richard III*." In *The Woman's Part: Feminist Criticism of Shakespeare*, edited by Carolyn Ruth Swift Lenz, Gayle Greene, and Carol Thomas Neely, 35-55. Chicago: University of Illinois Press, 1980.

Miner discusses the hatred of women that occurs in the play and how it affects Margaret, Anne, the duchess of York, and Queen Elizabeth, pointing out that the women are often used as "scapegoats."

Muir, Kenneth. "Image and Symbol in Shakespeare's Histories." *Bulletin of the John Rylands Library* 50 (1967-1968): 103-23.

Muir provides a useful discussion of the animal imagery which occurs in the play, as well as the numerous images taken from drama and Richard's own delight in playing roles.

Ritchey, David. "Queen Margaret (*Richard III*): A Production Note." *North Carolina Journal of Speech and Drama* 7, no. 2 (1973): 37-41.

Ritchey describes three different interpretations of Margaret's role in the play and explains the difficulties they cause for productions of *Richard III*.

Sheriff, William E. "The Grotesque Comedy of *Richard III*." *Studies in the Literary Imagination* 5, no. 1 (April 1972): 51-64.

This essay is useful for students who wonder about the humorous moments in such a grim play. Sheriff examines Richard's wittiness and his comedic use of dramatic irony and inversion—or saying one thing and meaning its opposite—and suggests that such humor is there to lighten what would otherwise be dry history already well-known to its Elizabethan audience.

Smith, Denzell S. "The Credibility of the Wooing of Anne in *Richard III*." *Papers on Language and Literature* 7, no. 2 (Spring 1971): 199-202.

Smith demonstrates how Richard succeeds against all odds in wooing Anne by matching his own words and actions to her changing emotions and thus skillfully manipulating her feelings about him.

Tanner, Stephen L. "Richard III versus Elizabeth: An Interpretation." *Shakespeare Quarterly* 24, no. 4 (Autumn 1973): 468-72.

Tanner assesses the verbal battle which occurs between Richard and Queen Elizabeth in Act IV over whether he will marry her daughter and concludes that contrary to what Richard and some critics believe, Elizabeth emerges the winner.

Tillyard, E. M. W. "Richard III." In *Shakespeare's History Plays*, 198-214. New York: The MacMillan Company, 1946.

In this overview, argues that divine retribution and the deliverance of England through God's grace is the theme of *Richard III*, and that fighting against Richard's "vast" evil is the cause that ultimately unites England through Richmond.

Weber, Karl. "Shakespeare's *Richard III*, I.iv.24-33." *Explicator* 38, no. 3 (Spring 1980): 24-6.

Weber presents a useful discussion of Clarence's vivid "undersea" nightmare in Act I, arguing that it "foreshadow[s] the rest of the play," as each image in the dream represents "the fate of England under Richard's rule."

Wilson, John Dover. Introduction to *Richard III*, by William Shakespeare, edited by John Dover Wilson, vii-xlv. Cambridge: Cambridge University Press, 1954.

Wilson provides an overview of *Richard III*, including analyses of the play's composition, date, sources, and style.

The Tragedy of Romeo and Juliet

circa 1595

Act I:

The play is set in Verona, a city in northern Italy. Two leading families, the Capulets and the Montagues, are involved in a long-standing and on-going feud. When the play opens, even the servants of the opposing households are trying to fight. More prominent members try to become involved, when Prince Escalus arrives and decrees that anyone involved in future disputes will be executed. The Montagues are concerned about their son Romeo, who has been behaving strangely. His friend Benvolio learns that Romeo is lovesick; he is hopelessly in love with a Capulet named Rosaline. Lord and Lady Capulet are giving a party, with one possible outcome being that their daughter Juliet will meet and like a young man named Paris who is interested in marrying her. Romeo learns of the party when he helps an illiterate Capulet servant read the list of invited guests. Benvolio advises him to go to the party to overcome his lovesickness. At the party, Romeo meets Juliet and they fall in love.

Act II:

Romeo's friends look for him after the party but finally give up and go home. They cannot find Romeo because he is hiding beneath Juliet's balcony. From his place of concealment, Romeo overhears Juliet talking to herself on her balcony about her feelings for him. He emerges from the darkness of

night, and they declare their love for each other. They agree that Romeo will send word to Juliet the next day about his plans for them. The next day, Romeo's friends mention that Juliet's cousin, Tybalt, has sent a challenge to a duel to Romeo's house because of Romeo's uninvited attendance at the party. Romeo tells Juliet's messenger, the nurse, to have Juliet go to Friar Lawrence's cell that afternoon, where they will be married. Juliet is excited and happy. They meet at Friar Lawrence's cell, and are married offstage after this act.

Act III:

That afternoon, Mercutio and Benvolio are in the Verona marketplace. The day is hot, and tempers are short. Tybalt approaches the two, attempting to instigate a fight. When Romeo arrives, he is challenged by Tybalt, but tries to avoid trouble. This angers his Mercutio, who fights Tybalt when Romeo refuses to accept Tybalt's challenge. Romeo tries to separate Mercutio and Tybalt, but Mercutio is stabbed under Romeo's arm and dies. Romeo, enraged by his friend's death, fights Tybalt and kills him. Romeo runs away before the prince and townspeople arrive. The prince banishes Romeo from Verona. Romeo flees to Friar Lawrence's cell and is discovered hiding there by the nurse, who has come with a message from Juliet. Friar Lawrence suggests a plan to have Romeo go and visit Juliet and then leave for Mantua, a nearby town, until everything can be worked out with the feuding families and the prince. Romeo agrees to the plan. He visits Juliet, and they part reluctantly. In the meantime, Juliet's parents have been planning their daughter's marriage to Paris and inform Juliet that she will marry him that Thursday. Observing her daughter's sorrow, Lady Capulet initially believes that Juliet is deeply mourning Tybalt. But when Juliet states her opposition to the wedding, Capulet threatens to throw her out and let her die if she refuses to marry Paris. The nurse advises Juliet to marry Paris, after which Juliet states her intention to go to Friar Lawrence for confession. Secretly, however, she is thinking of taking her life.

Act IV:

Juliet visits Friar Lawrence and announces her plan to commit suicide if she cannot escape marriage to Paris. To dissuade Juliet from this course of action, Friar Lawrence conceives of an alternate plan and gives Juliet a potion that will make her appear dead for forty-two hours. He directs her to drink the potion the night before she is supposed to

marry Paris. After she is laid in the Capulet tomb, the friar informs Juliet, Romeo will come and take her away to Mantua. Juliet agrees to the plan. She returns home and apologizes to her father. Pleased, he changes the wedding day from Thursday to Wednesday, forcing Juliet to take the potion a day earlier than planned. Even though she has fears about whether the plan will really work, she swallows the potion. The next morning, the wedding party is turned into a funeral.

Act V:

In Mantua, Romeo is unaware of Friar Lawrence's plan because he has failed to receive the message sent from Friar Lawrence via Friar John. Romeo hears of Juliet's "death" from the servant Balthasar, who witnessed Juliet's funeral. Romeo plans to return to Verona to die in the tomb where Juliet's body is, and he buys an illegal poison from an apothecary to carry out his intentions. Back in Verona, Friar Lawrence realizes that his letter never got through to Romeo. When Paris arrives at the tomb to lay flowers for Juliet, Romeo appears. The two men fight, and Romeo kills Paris, then brings the body inside the tomb. He sees Juliet and takes the quick-acting poison. Friar Lawrence arrives and quickly assesses the situation. When Juliet wakes up, the friar tries to convince her to leave, but she sees Romeo dead and refuses to go. They hear a noise, and Friar Lawrence runs away. Juliet then stabs herself with Romeo's knife. When the watchmen discover the bodies, they call the prince, the Capulets, and the Montagues. One of the watchmen also catches Friar Lawrence, who explains his knowledge of what has transpired. After Capulet and Montague agree to lay aside their murderous feud, the prince observes that everyone has been punished by this hatred, and that the morning has brought with it "a glooming peace" (V.iii.304).

Modern Connections

One of the most prominent features of *Romeo and Juliet* is the love the two title characters have for one another. In a number of ways the lovers' passion for each other demonstrates the practice of "courtly love." Identifying some of the aspects of courtly love can also highlight the similarities between the relationship between Romeo and Juliet and modern youthful romantic relationships. Courtly love flourished during the Middle Ages and influenced Renaissance literature. Traditionally, the system of courtly love defined a code of behavior for lovers. Under this system, love is seen as illicit, sensual, and marked by emotional suffering and anguish. Typically, the lover falls in love at first sight and remains in agony until he is sure his love is returned. Then, he is inspired to perform great deeds to demonstrate the depth of his love. Additionally, the lovers vow their faithfulness to each other and promise to keep their love a secret. The love between Romeo and Juliet follows this pattern. The two fall in love at first sight, they meet secretly and promise to conceal their relationship, and they vow their everlasting faithfulness to each other. Modern teenagers in love similarly may feel the need to meet secretly, to hide their relationships from their parents, and may often feel that their parents do not or would not understand the depth of their feelings toward their girlfriends or boyfriends.

An additional hurdle faced by lovers in Shakespeare's time was the fact that many marriages were arranged by parents who had economic and social considerations in mind. Romance and personal choice in the matter were often ignored and could cause conflict between parents and young people. Juliet's parents initially hope that Juliet will express interest in marrying Paris. When she does not, they become angered and verbally abusive. For modern readers who are unfamiliar with the concept of arranged marriages, knowing that such arrangements were common in Shakespeare's time may help students to better understand the actions of Romeo, Juliet, and their parents. However, for many modern students, the idea of arranged marriages is not an unfamiliar one, as the concept is a part of many religions.

Another prominent feature of the play is its presentation of the destructiveness of endless feuding between groups of people forced to live near each other. In such self-perpetuating feuds, new insults are always being made and old ones always being avenged. The score never seems to be settled, unless perhaps something catastrophic occurs that forces the feuding people to look seriously at themselves and their responsibility toward their families and each other. Tybalt, for example, grows enraged at the sound of Romeo's voice at the Capulet party and wants to fight him immediately. Although Lord Capulet restrains Tybalt at the party, he does not stop his wife's screams for revenge after Tybalt's death. Only after suffering the heavy, irreparable losses of their children do Capulet and Montague

join hands at the end of the play. Such tensions are also common in modern times and have been dramatically presented by film makers. For example, the 1961 film, *West Side Story*, is loosely based on *Romeo and Juliet*. In the film, the animosity that Shakespeare depicted between the Capulets and Montagues, referred to by the Chorus as an ''ancient grudge'' (Prologue, l.3), is represented as gang rivalry and ethnic hatred between the family and friends of the two main characters, Tony and Maria. Although Tony and Maria attempt to overcome these obstacles, they meet the same tragic fate as Romeo and Juliet. Baz Luhrmann's 1996 version of the story is perhaps more familar to modern readers than is *West Side Story*. The 1996 film, *William Shakespeare's Romeo and Juliet*, is set in present-day urban California, but uses Shakespeare's original language.

Characters

Abram:

He is a servant of the Montagues. Abram appears in the first scene of the play and quarrels with the Capulet servants, Sampson and Gregory.

Anthony:

In some editions of the play, Anthony and Potpan are named as servants of the Capulet household.

Apothecary:

The apothecary is a druggist in Mantua. He only speaks a few lines, but Romeo offers an insightful description of his poor shop and of his appearance. The apothecary is thin and wears ragged clothes. His shop has a few strange things spread throughout, perhaps to make it look like more than it is: a tortoise, a stuffed alligator, skins of strange fish, green pots, seeds, rose petals pressed into cakes for perfume. He is so poor that he sells Romeo a deadly, fast-acting poison even though it is against the law in Mantua to do so.

Attendants:

As the ruler of Verona, Escalus is accompanied by attendants. The attendants are described as the prince's Train in I.i, and simply as attendants in the final scene of the play.

Balthasar:

He is a servant to Romeo. Balthasar appears with Abram in the first scene of Act I, but does not participate in the quarrel with the Capulet servants. He is loyal to Romeo and tries to help him. After Juliet's funeral, he rushes to Mantua to bring the news of Juliet's "death" to Romeo. He shows his concern for Romeo and asks him to remain patient, to not act hastily. Balthasar returns with Romeo to Verona and accompanies him to the tomb, although Romeo tells him not to interfere. At the end of the play, Balthasar provides Prince Escalus with the letter which Romeo has written to his father. The letter supports Friar Lawrence's account of what has happened.

Benvolio:

He is a nephew to Montague and a cousin and friend to Romeo. His name means well-wisher, which reflects to some degree Benvolio's role in the play as a loyal friend and a peace-maker. Benvolio attempts to stop the fight between the servants at the beginning of the play. Early in the play, Benvolio wishes to help Romeo's parents by learning from Romeo why he has been acting so strangely and trying to avoid everyone. When he questions Romeo gently and learns that his problem is love-sickness, he counsels Romeo to look at other beauties and forget about anyone who is not interested in him. Benvolio suggests that Romeo go to the Capulet party and see other pretty young women.

Throughout the play, Benvolio demonstrates his common sense and his loyalty to his friends. Benvolio tries to serve as a restraining influence on Mercutio, who seems to constantly be talking himself into trouble. Also, when Benvolio and Mercutio discuss the challenge from Tybalt to Romeo, he shows confidence in Romeo by stating that Romeo will answer the challenge.

In the marketplace scene in which the stabbings of Mercutio and Tybalt occur, Benvolio senses that tempers are flaring, and that the hot weather will lead to trouble. When Tybalt enters and he and Mercutio exchange words, Benvolio advises that they should go somewhere private, or talk calmly in the marketplace, or just leave. This advice, of course, has no effect.

After the fight, Benvolio emphatically urges Romeo to run away before he is caught and put to death. Then, when the prince arrives, Benvolio attempts to provide a fair account of what has happened, maintaining that Romeo behaved proper-

> " Benvolio tries to serve as a restraining influence on Mercutio, who seems to constantly be talking himself into trouble."

ly, but that both Tybalt and Mercutio were hot-tempered and looking for a quarrel. He also points out how everything happened so quickly that he could not draw his sword in time to stop Tybalt and Romeo from fighting.

Capulet (Lady Capulet):

Lady Capulet is Lord Capulet's wife and Juliet's mother. Juliet's mother has two important conversations with her daughter during the play. The first one occurs in Act I. In it, Lady Capulet directs Juliet to think about marriage. She informs Juliet that Paris is interested in marrying her, and reminds Juliet that she herself became a mother when she was about Juliet's age. The second conversation takes place in III.v, just after Romeo's departure for Mantua. Lady Capulet informs Juliet that the marriage between her and Paris will take place and that preparations have begun. She at first misunderstands Juliet's sorrow as stemming from mourning for Tybalt. She becomes angry that Juliet refuses to marry Paris. She refers to Juliet as a fool and says she wishes Juliet were dead. Though she tries somewhat to check her husband's similarly angry words, after a long decisive speech from him to Juliet, Lady Capulet refuses to speak to her daughter. Though Juliet's mother shows some tenderness and concern for her in Act IV prior to the wedding morning, her larger, practical concern appears to be the wedding preparations, not Juliet's feelings. She seems genuinely sorrowful at the discovery of Juliet's body on the wedding morning and once again at the Capulet monument. She even suggests it may cause her to die.

Capulet (Lord Capulet):

A leading citizen of Verona and head of one of the two feuding families. His attitudes seem to display a mixture of qualities rather than conveying a sense of consistency of action. When the audience first sees him, he is calling for a sword to join in the fighting of the servants and young men in the opposing households. He acts this way even though he is an older man and a more dignified behavior would most likely be more appropriate for his age. However, he is concerned with maintaining order in his own house, especially after the prince's promise to execute any disturbers of the peace. Thus, he takes pains to prevent Tybalt from starting a brawl in his house at the party. Capulet is also motivated by his desire to appear as a good host. He jokes with the guests, compliments the dancers, orders the servants to regulate the heat in the room better by subduing the fire, and takes a peaceful attitude towards Romeo's uninvited presence at the feast.

His attitude towards Juliet shows this mixture of traits also. When Paris asks for her hand in marriage, he says she is too young and that Paris should let two more years pass. He also seems to say that his agreement is only a part of such an arrangement and that Juliet must agree also. Yet as negotiations with Paris continue in Act III, Capulet assumes that Juliet will do exactly as he wishes. In his conversation with Paris, he also shows more concern about his image than about his daughter's feelings. He thinks she is extremely grieved by Tybalt's death, not at all suspecting the real cause of her grief, Romeo's banishment. He appears to be more concerned about how the scheduling of the marriage will affect townspeople's attitudes towards the seriousness or casualness of his grieving for Tybalt. As Juliet and her parents discuss the arranged marriage to Paris and Juliet's unwillingess to participate in the wedding is revealed, Capulet threatens to throw Juliet out and let her die in the streets. Even after this confrontation with Juliet, Capulet continues with wedding preparations, indicating his complete disregard for Juliet's hopes for her future. When Juliet pretends that she has just returned from confession to Friar Lawrence and is sorry for her stubbornness, Capulet is so pleased he changes the wedding date, demonstrating again how out of touch he is with his daughter's true feelings.

After Juliet's death, sorrow is Capulet's dominant response. Yet his sadness appears to be tinged with the knowledge that he will die without heirs and that the wedding feast is spoiled. Only when he sees Juliet in the tomb bleeding and dead does his sorrow over her loss and over his role in the feud seem complete. Finally, Capulet extends his hand in forgiveness and reconciliation to Montague.

Catling (Simon Catling):

See Musicians

Chorus:

The Chorus speaks twice in the play, before the beginning of Act I and before Act II. The Chorus functions as a commentator on the action and basic meaning of the play. It sets the scene in Verona, a city in northern Italy, and, in a sonnet, summarizes the action. The play will be about two feuding households of equal rank, a pair of lovers from these houses whose misadventures lead them to take their lives, and whose parents thereby finally end their ancient grudges. At the beginning of Act II, the Chorus speaks about young love, "the charm of looks," and the power passion gives to people to overcome obstacles.

Citizens of Verona:

The citizens are unnamed townspeople who appear in public street scenes. Early in the play they attempt to stop the fighting between the two feuding households. They appear in Act III inquiring about Mercutio's murderer and they detain Benvolio so that the prince may question him. The citizens are described as running through the streets toward the Capulet monument in the final scene of the play.

Clown:

The clown is a servant to Capulet. The clown is given the responsibility of delivering Capulet's party invitation to certain people in Verona, but he cannot read. After running into Romeo on the street, he asks Romeo to help him read the list of names. The clown invites Romeo to attend the party. In some editions of the play, this role is identified as "servant" rather than "clown."

Escalus (Prince Escalus):

The ruler of Verona. Fourteenth- century Italy consisted of kingdoms, papal states, and local lordships. Verona under Prince Escalus was in the third category. The prince is physically present in three scenes (I.i, III.i, and V.iii), yet his presence is felt throughout the play for he makes the laws and the decisions in Verona.

In his first appearance, Escalus speaks very sternly about the fighting between the servants and the young men in the opposing households. He directs the fighting parties to throw their weapons to the ground, stating that they have started civil wars three times just by words alone. He threatens any disturber of the peace with death. This speech is effective in stopping the current fighting, and the prince effectively separates the angry Capulets and Montagues. Yet, the prince's approach does not put a permanent stop to the fighting, as the marketplace incident later shows.

In his second appearance, the prince must investigate the cause of the deaths of Mercutio and Tybalt. He shows lenience rather than exacting the letter of the law he pronounced earlier, making his rule seem inconsistent at best: he banishes Romeo rather than executing him, although he warns that Romeo's return would incur the death penalty. Furthermore, he appears to have based this decision on his personal interests, stating that the Capulet/Montague feud has caused the death of his kinsman, Mercutio.

Both Juliet and Romeo, as well as Friar Lawrence, seem to respect the prince's banishment of Romeo as a firm and definite ruling. Friar Lawrence devises two plans to comply with it, but hopes that the prince can be persuaded to relent.

In his final appearance, the prince is forced to investigate more deaths: those of Romeo and Juliet. He collects eye-witness testimony and corroboration of this evidence. In his grief, his words are brief to Capulet and Montague. From the point of view of the whole community, the prince pronounces insightful commentary of the actions which have occurred, commenting that through the feud, ''all are punish'd'' (V.iii.295). In other words, all have suffered and lost. Prince Escalus's words accurately describe the tone at the end of the play: ''a glooming peace this morning with it brings'' (V.iii.304-5). Peace has finally been achieved, but at a cost.

Friar John:
See John

Friar Lawrence:
See Lawrence

Gentlemen of both houses:
These gentlemen appear in public scenes involving the feuding households. Men from both houses are present in the marketplace scene. They assemble when the prince pronounces the sentence of banishment on Romeo and go to the Capulet monument at the end of the play.

Gentlewomen of both houses:
Gentlewomen from the Capulet household appear at Lord Capulet's party. Gentlewomen from both houses assemble when the prince pronounces

> **As Juliet and her parents discuss the arranged marriage to Paris and Juliet's unwillingess to participate in the wedding is revealed, Capulet threatens to throw Juliet out and let her die in the streets.''**

the sentence of banishment on Romeo and go to the Capulet monument at the end of the play.

Gregory:
As another a servant of the Capulets, he accompanies Sampson, and jokes and puns with his friend. Gregory tries to avoid being led into a fight with the Montague servants by Sampson.

Guards:
They have no speaking part and are not listed separately in stage directions. Some editions of the play refer to the watch as the guards.

John (Friar John):
Friar John is a Franciscan friar who has been asked by Friar Lawrence to carry an important letter to Romeo in Mantua. Before he can deliver the letter, he is quarantined in Verona because of the plague. As soon as he is able, he gives word to Friar Lawrence.

Juliet:
Juliet is the daughter of Lord and Lady Capulet and one of the two title characters. When the play begins, Juliet is about two weeks shy of her fourteenth birthday, we learn from the nurse's remarks. In Juliet's first meeting with her mother and the nurse, Juliet shows herself to be a docile, dutiful child. She comes when she is called, responding respectfully to her mother: ''Madam, I am here, / What is your will?'' (I.iii.5-6). When her mother discusses the topic of Paris's interest in her, Juliet consents to go to the party and meet Paris. She adds that she will only allow her looks to go as far as her mother gives her permission. Juliet's youthfulness

> "Prince Escalus's words accurately describe the tone at the end of the play: 'a glooming peace this morning with it brings' (V.iii.304-5). Peace has finally been achieved, but at a cost."

is echoed in comments by her father, who has hesitated over Paris's interest in marrying her.

The first meeting between Romeo and Juliet is a defining moment in Juliet's life. Romeo describes her as lovely and rich in beauty. Juliet speaks this way to him as well. Their words to each other complete a sonnet, in which Juliet, a heretofore inexperienced child, suddenly speaks with great naturalness, insight, and understanding about love. Equally suddenly, Juliet becomes resourceful, and not yet ready to share with the nurse her newfound discovery. Instead of asking the nurse Romeo's name directly, she asks the nurse about the identities of various young men leaving the party, Romeo among them. She realizes in a moment of illumination that she is in love with an enemy to her family.

When Juliet speaks to the night her love for Romeo, she speaks of his true perfection of self. Unlike the older generation in the play, she is able to look beyond names and feuds. She utters one of the most quoted lines in all of Shakespeare's works, when she says "That which we call a rose / by any other word would smell as sweet" (II.ii.43-4). She admits her complete love for Romeo, and it is at this moment that he reveals himself to her standing on the ground beneath her balcony. Although Juliet speaks of the "maiden blush" (II.ii.86) on her face and wonders if she has said too much, she bluntly asks Romeo "Dost thou love me?" (II.ii.80).

In addition to Juliet's ability to honestly expresses herself, some commentators have noted that she is quite practical, in contrast to Romeo. She is concerned about Romeo's safety, warning him about her kinsmen and wondering how he was able to get over the high orchard walls. Additionally, it is Juliet, not Romeo, who sets into motion the practical details of the wedding, instructing Romeo to send her word about where and when the event will take place (II.ii.144-46).

From this point on, Juliet shows herself to be focused on her husband and her love for him and willing to do whatever it takes for the two of them to be together. Her passion shows in her impatience for her wedding night. She can hardly wait and compares her feelings to those of a child with a new outfit to wear but having to wait overnight until the special holiday to do so. When the nurse brings a confused account of the death of Tybalt, making it sound as if Romeo has died, Juliet is devastated. Even when the account is made plain, Juliet threatens to take her life if she and Romeo cannot be together.

Juliet is willing to take risks and look for opportunities to allow herself and Romeo to be together. When Romeo and Juliet have one night of love together, it is in Juliet's own room. Juliet lets him go, reluctantly. When Juliet's parents come in to talk to her about Paris, she refuses to accept their proposal. The nurse advises her to accept, resulting in Juliet's decision not to confide in the nurse any longer. Juliet mentions her threat of suicide to Friar Lawrence, and states her willingness to do whatever he advises. Before Juliet takes the friar's potion, she thinks of everything that could go wrong with it. She considers the possibility that Friar Lawrence may have given her real poison to protect himself from discovery. She also considers the possibility of poor timing, which would mean that she would wake up in the tomb alone. However, all of these possible mischances are set aside for the chance for her and Romeo to be together. At the end of the play, she has the choice of leaving the tomb with the friar or staying with Romeo and joining him in death. She chooses death rather than living in a world without Romeo.

Lady Capulet:
See Capulet

Lady Montague:
See Montague

Lawrence (Friar Lawrence [in some editions, Laurence]):

Friar Lawrence is a Franciscan monk. He lives in modest quarters suitable to someone who is a follower of St. Francis. He is a priest who is able to conduct religious ceremonies such as marriage and burial. He is also able to hear confessions and forgive sins. He serves as an adviser to Romeo and later to Juliet, and he develops several plans for the young lovers to follow. Also, he comments on the action at key points. Many of his speeches have a philosophical content to them.

When the friar first appears on stage (II.iii), he is gathering weeds and flowers in the early morning while the dew is still fresh and before the day gets hot. He makes medicines and various preparations from the plants he gathers in his willow basket. He comments that there is something powerful and potentially good in each thing on the earth but that everything must be used in a good way to preserve its good qualities.

Friar Lawrence, a friend to Romeo, knows about Romeo's infatuation with Rosaline. When Romeo comes to him early in the morning, he jokes that maybe Romeo has been out with Rosaline and did not get home to rest. He thinks that Romeo's shift in affection from Rosaline to Juliet is sudden and hasty, but he agrees to marry them because he thinks that it may help to end the hatred between the feuding households. Just before the marriage, Friar Lawrence counsels the lovers on the benefits of moderation. He will not allow them to stay alone together until they are married.

To the young lovers in the play, Friar Lawrence seems trustworthy and wise, when many other adults in Verona seem to be full of rejection, ridicule, bad advice, and bad example. Romeo trusts Friar Lawrence so much that he goes to the priest's residence to hide before leaving town. Romeo is frustrated and upset and even threatens to stab himself. Friar Lawrence counsels Romeo against this course of action. He suggests that Romeo should develop a philosophic outlook, an idea heartily rejected by Romeo. When nothing else will work, the friar not only points out to Romeo all the worst things which could have happened but did not, but instructs Romeo to visit Juliet and then to leave town until everything can be worked out with the families and the prince.

Juliet trusts the friar when she has given up on the nurse. She goes to see the friar when her parents are insisting on her marriage to Paris. When Friar Lawrence sees how desperate and frantic Juliet is, he suggests the potion to her. This represents a change of plan from the one discussed with Romeo. This new plan does not make any reference to gaining the approval of the families, yet it attempts to preserve the happiness of the lovers.

> **When the play begins, Juliet is about two weeks shy of her fourteenth birthday, we learn from the nurse's remarks."**

The friar's plan fails, mostly due to accidents of mistiming. Romeo receives word of Juliet's "death" through his servant. The friar's news that Juliet is not actually dead has been prevented from getting through to Romeo. Lord Capulet changes the date of the wedding. Romeo arrives just before Juliet wakes up, and then kills himself. Still, Juliet could have been saved. The friar does get to the tomb in time to save her. When she wakes up, he tries to persuade her to leave. Yet, when he hears a noise, he runs out, afraid of discovery.

After the bodies of Romeo and Juliet are discovered, the friar offers the prince a summary of what has happened. Having confirmed the story with Romeo's letter to his father (delivered by Balthasar) the prince absolves the friar of wrongdoing, calling him a "holy man" (V.iii.270), and blames the feuding families for the deaths of Romeo and Juliet.

Maskers:

Five or six people wearing masks accompany Romeo and his friends to the Capulet party. Maskers going to a party at one time would have introduced themselves by a speech. Romeo wrote a speech, as a courteous interloper, but is told by Benvolio that such speeches are out of style now. Perhaps symbolically the maskers could be seen as representing love in hiding or a forbidden love. As a dramatic issue, the masks are necessary to get Romeo and his friends into a party to which they have not been invited.

Mercutio:

Mercutio is a kinsman to the prince and friend to Romeo. Mercutio is often interpreted as a comic foil to Romeo. (A foil is a character who by strong contract, underscores or enhances the distinctive qualities of another character.) Mercutio's bawdy discussions of sex, for example, and his witty and light-hearted use of language contrast sharply with Romeo's romantic view of love and his gloomy

> **Although Juliet speaks of the 'maiden blush' (II.ii.86) on her face and wonders if she has said too much, she bluntly asks Romeo 'Dost thou love me?' (II.ii.80).''**

lovesickness. It will be helpful in understanding Mercutio to look at some words related to his name: mercurial, an adjective meaning changeable; Mercury, the Roman messenger god and god of eloquence; and mercury, the poisonous element.

Mercutio's eloquence is displayed throughout the play. In scenes in which he appears and speaks, he tends to become the center of attention. He dominates his companions with his teasing and quick wit. When Romeo and his group of friends are walking to the Capulet party, Romeo is moping about Rosaline. The witty Mercutio tries to get Romeo's mind on something else. He also describes imagination in a powerful, memorable way in his "Queen Mab" speech (I.iii.52-94). The speech, a dramatic demonstration of Mercutio's eloquence, describes dreams as coming from a fairy creature. When Mercutio's cleverness threatens to run away with him, Romeo asks him to be quiet. When Mercutio and Benvolio look for Romeo after the Capulet party, Mercutio makes various obscene jokes at Romeo's expense, but Romeo will not reveal his hiding place. His wit and his bawdy humor are also displayed in his conversation with the nurse, who arrives looking for Romeo.

Mercutio's changeable nature shows in the fatal marketplace scene. At one moment he is joking with Benvolio about quarreling, and the next moment he is quarreling in deadly earnest himself. He had hoped to see Romeo answer Tybalt's challenge to a duel, and is disappointed by what he sees as Romeo's cowardice or submission. He suddenly jumps in and accepts Tybalt's challenge himself. He fights well, but is fatally injured when Tybalt takes unfair advantage of Romeo's well-meant interference.

Mercutio's bitterness—or poisonous attitude—is shown in his wishing a plague on both the Montagues and the Capulets. Despite his usually easy-going manner, when confronted by a member of the Capulet household Mercutio is eager to fight.

He becomes angered by Tybalt's taunts and Romeo's refusal to fight. When he is mortally wounded, curses the houses of Montague and Capulet. The extent of his feelings is revealed by the fact that this acrimonious denouncement is repeated three times by Mercutio: in III.i.91, 99-100, and 106.

Montague (Lady Montague):

Lady Montague is Lord Montague's wife and Romeo's mother. She has very few lines in the play. She seems to be a person of reason and restraint, physically holding her husband back from fighting and tells him not to "stir one foot to seek a foe" (I.i.80). In the final scene of the play, the audience hears from Lord Montague that his wife has died of grief over Romeo's banishment.

Montague (Lord Montague):

Head of the Montague household and Romeo's father. He appears very little in the play, yet he seems to be closer to Romeo than Juliet's parents are to her. For example, he describes Romeo's mysterious behavior to his nephew, Benvolio. He indicates that both he and his friends have tried to learn from Romeo the cause of his behavior. He is pleased at Benvolio's offer to talk to Romeo. During the prince's investigation of the marketplace brawl which left Mercutio and Tybalt dead, Montague defends his son to the prince, saying that Romeo simply acted as the law itself would have in taking Tybalt's life. In the final scene of the play, he appears to be genuinely grieved at his son's untimely death. Recognizing finally that the feud must be laid aside, Montague takes Capulet's hand extended in a gesture of peace. Moreover, he offers to make a memorial statue of Juliet in gold.

Musicians:

Three musicians are present at the Capulet house to play for the marriage between Juliet and Paris. They do not play after Juliet's body is discovered. Peter cannot resist trying to boss them and pun with them. Peter addresses them as Simon Catling, Hugh Rebeck, and James Soundpost. These names are taken from musical instruments.

Nurse:

The nurse is a servant in the Capulet household. The nurse is often interpreted as a comic foil to Juliet. (A foil is a character, who through strong contrast, underscores or enhances the distinctive qualities of another character.) She seems to be in higher standing than the other servants, since she is a companion to Juliet, is present in private family conversations, and has her own servant, Peter. In Renaissance England, unmarried, widowed, or poor women might work for relatives in positions like the one in which the nurse finds herself. At any rate, she is trusted by the Capulets and informed about their intimate affairs.

The nurse's main role in the play is as a companion and advisor to Juliet. She feels affection for Juliet, whom she has cared for since Juliet was an infant. It is revealed that the nurse lost her own child, Susan, and perhaps she views Juliet as a daughter. The nurse's affection for Juliet remains constant throughout the play, even if her advice is of questionable value. Juliet trusts the nurse enough to send her to Romeo the morning after the balcony scene to learn what Romeo's intentions are. On this errand, the nurse takes it upon herself to make sure that Romeo's intentions are honorable, since Juliet is young and inexperienced. When Juliet learns of what has happened in the marketplace, the nurse tries to comfort her and decides to bring Romeo to Juliet. On the morning after the lovers' one night of married happiness together, the nurse warns them that Romeo needs to leave Juliet's bedroom because Lady Capulet is coming. When Lord Capulet scolds Juliet harshly, the nurse tells him he is wrong to do so. She does not back down, so that he even yells at her. When Juliet and the nurse are left alone after the angry scene with Juliet's parents, the nurse tries to comfort and console Juliet.

The nurse, with her bumbling mannerisms and her bawdy language, is often thought to be one of Shakespeare's great comic characters. She is a talkative woman, and tends to repeat herself and to free-associate in her conversations. When she and Lady Capulet and Juliet are about to discuss Paris's offer for the first time, she repeats a story about Juliet as a toddler several times. Lady Capulet has to ask her to stop. When she brings the message back to Juliet from Romeo, Juliet has to ask her to get to the point faster. Under pressure, she also talks in a confusing style that misleads her listener. When she tries to tell Juliet about what has happened in the Verona marketplace, Juliet at first thinks that Romeo is dead because of the way the nurse is garbling the details.

Another aspect of the nurse's conversation is that she does not mind making vulgar jokes. She even does so with Juliet, since the jokes pertain to Juliet's wedding night and the possibility of preg-

> **To the young lovers in the play, Friar Lawrence seems trustworthy and wise, when many other adults in Verona seem to be full of rejection, ridicule, bad advice, and bad example."**

nancy. The nurse also converses in this vulgar manner with Mercutio.

The nurse is depicted as a practical, down-to-earth character. She advises Juliet to marry Paris. Even though she knows Juliet is married to Romeo, she considers that Romeo's banishment makes him useless to Juliet. She sees no obstacle to a second marriage in Juliet's secret wedding vows pronounced to Romeo. She even helps in the kitchen the night before the planned wedding between Juliet and Paris. In this scene, she jokes with Lord Capulet and he calls her by her name, Angelica.

Old Man:

This older relative of the Capulet family attends the Capulet party. Lord Capulet talks to him briefly at the party. He functions dramatically to show Lord Capulet's age. Both he and Capulet are older men, past dancing. They like to reminisce about the passage of time.

Page to Paris:

Paris's page accompanies him to Juliet's tomb. He is instructed to stay alone in the churchyard and whistle a warning to Paris if anyone approaches. Even though he is afraid, he does as he is told. When he realizes that Paris and another man (Romeo) are fighting, he runs to get the watch. He testifies to the prince at the end of the play about his knowledge of the occurrences within the tomb.

Pages:

Pages are young male servants to people of higher social standing. They run errands, carry messages, and accompany their masters. Mercutio has a page with him in the marketplace; after being stabbed by Tybalt, Mercutio sends his page for a surgeon. Paris also has a page.

> Mercutio is often interpreted as a comic foil to Romeo. . . . Mercutio's bawdy discussions of sex, for example, and his witty and light-hearted use of language contrast sharply with Romeo's romantic view of love and his gloomy lovesickness."

Paris:

Paris is a young nobleman and kinsman to Prince Escalus. He is a conventional young lover who seeks Juliet's hand in marriage. He is said by Juliet's mother to be handsome in appearance, and the nurse describes Romeo as a dishcloth compared to Paris. Observing the standards of the time, he first approaches Juliet's father about the possibility of his marrying Juliet. In fact, he has more conversations with Lord Capulet than with Juliet throughout the whole course of the play. When Capulet seems to express reservations about a marriage between his child and Paris based on Juliet's youth, Paris tries to be persuasive. He takes Capulet's advice in going to the party to try to win Juliet's hand there. He does not appear to be aware of Juliet's feelings at all, because he goes to see Friar Lawrence to arrange the wedding without even recognizing that Juliet has no romantic feelings for him and is, in fact, already married. However, he seems to be a genuine and forthright person. He is sorrowful at Juliet's funeral, and, in the last act, he brings flowers to her grave. This suggests that he has true feelings for Juliet, as it is a private action, not a public one performed for the benefit of an audience, such as her family. Additionally, he refers to Juliet as his love. Even at this point, however, he does not seem to really understand Juliet; he thinks she died from grief over Tybalt.

Peter:

Peter is the nurse's servant. He carries the nurse's fan for her on her errand to Romeo from Juliet. He talks in the sexual double meanings popular among the Capulet servants. At the nurse's orders, he stands at the gate when they return to Juliet with Romeo's message. After Juliet's funeral, he asks the musicians to play music to comfort him. When they won't, he refuses to pay them. He appears to enjoy the opportunity to boss the musicians, probably since he himself is usually ordered about.

Petruchio:

Petruchio is described as a mute follower of Tybalt. He is with Tybalt in the marketplace brawl.

Potpan:

In some editions of the play, Potpan and Anthony are named as servants of the Capulet household.

Rebeck (Hugh Rebeck):
See Musicians

Romeo:

Romeo is the son to Lord and Lady Montague and one of the two title characters. Romeo's first love interest is not Juliet but a young woman named Rosaline, who, like Juliet, happens to be a Capulet. When characters first refer to Romeo, he is described as acting in a peculiar way. His friend and cousin, Benvolio, discovers why: the cause is hopeless, incurable lovesickness. Rosaline has vowed to live unwed and without a lover. (Rosaline, incidentally, never appears in the play.) Romeo's infatuation with Rosaline and her resoluteness to remain celibate inspire Romeo's behavior. He goes out walking near the woods before dawn. If anyone sees him, he runs away into the woods to avoid having company. When the sun comes up, he returns home, retreats into his bedroom, and won't come out. Benvolio advises Romeo that his feelings are infatuation, based on a lack of experience with women. After being encouraged to do so by Benvolio and Mercutio, Romeo attends the Capulet party and sees Juliet. When they meet, they fall in love immediately.

Romeo is surrounded by a group of young male friends. Like his friends, Romeo enjoys joking. However, Romeo's jokes, unlike Mercutio's in particular, usually do not have a sexual double meaning. He also tends to be more serious than his friends. In speaking about going to the Capulet party, Romeo says that he plans to stand at the side of the dance floor and watch the other dancers. He even wonders whether they should be going at all and worries about the effect of these actions on the rest of his life.

Many observers debate Romeo's development in the play. Some argue that he is overly emotional, hasty and immature and that he remains that way throughout the play. While some readers view Romeo as immature for falling out of love with Rosaline and in love with Juliet so quickly, others maintain that Romeo's infatuation with Rosaline early in the play in a sense prepares him to experience real love. Even though Romeo's speeches about love early in the play are wordy and somewhat awkward, they show that he has a sense of beauty and is trying hard to express what it is like to be in love. When he first sees Juliet, he shows that he is able to appreciate true beauty and express it in a powerful way. His speeches become more eloquent.

Romeo is also criticized by some for his apparent lack of moderation. While he demonstrates self-control in his rejection of Tybalt's challenge to a fight, after Mercutio steps in and is killed, Romeo abandons his self-restraint and fights and kills Tybalt. In his earnestness to avenge Mercutio, he fails to consider the consequences his actions will have on his relationship with Juliet. His words "O, I am fortune's fool" (III.i.136), some would argue, suggest that he does consider the consequences of his emotional actions, but only after it is too late. Many others would argue that Romeo's words demonstrate his attempting to evade responsibility for his actions completely by blaming what has happened on fate.

After he learns he is to be banished for killing Tybalt, Romeo throws himself to the ground and weeps. Friar Lawrence tells him that banishment is better than death, but Romeo responds that being without Juliet is torture. Romeo's desperate weeping is alternately viewed as unmasculine and unproductive or as demonstrative of the passionate depth of his commitment to Juliet. He says he can't accept Friar Lawrence's calm, philosophical advice because Friar Lawrence, as a man who is celibate, is not in a position to understand Romeo's feelings: Juliet is his heaven, and hell is being in exile without her. Romeo only accepts Friar Lawrence's counsel when it includes a visit to Juliet.

Some readers believe that Romeo achieves greater maturity toward the plays end. When Romeo's servant brings word of Juliet's funeral, Romeo decides immediately what he will do and takes action, rather than weeping as he did when he was banished. He thinks quickly of the poison he knows he can buy in Mantua. When he rushes back to Verona, he does not take time to see who Paris is

> " The nurse, with her bumbling mannerisms and her bawdy language, is often thought to be one of Shakespeare's great comic characters."

before killing him and joining Juliet, but he does grant Paris's wish to be placed in the tomb near Juliet.

Sampson:

He is a servant of the Capulets. Sampson quarrels with Montague servants and bites his thumb at Montague servants as a gesture of defiance in order to provoke a fight. Additionally, he represents some fairly typical Renaissance attitudes towards women. He uses a biblical phrase about women being the "weaker vessels" (I.i.16), and his comments about women indicate that he thinks of them as sexual objects.

Servants:

The servants in the play are employed by the Capulet and Montague households. Servants announce the arrival of guests, set out napkins, silverware, and trenchers of food, and serve meals. They also are directed to clear furniture from the hall floor for dancing, tend to the fire and carry logs, and invite guests to various functions.

Soundpost (James Soundpost):
See Musicians

Torch-Bearers:

Torch-bearers carry light to the Capulet party in I.iv. Romeo expresses his wish to carry a torch so as to avoid dancing.

Tybalt:

He is a nephew to Lord Capulet and a cousin to Juliet. He does not speak many lines, but he influences the entire course of the play to a degree that exceeds his seemingly minor role in it. Throughout the play, he demonstrates his angry, resentful, and

> **Romeo's first love interest is not Juliet but a young woman named Rosaline, who, like Juliet, happens to be a Capulet."**

stubborn nature. When Tybalt first appears, Benvolio is attempting to stop the servants of the Capulet and Montague households from fighting. By contrast, Tybalt urges on the fight and succeeds in drawing Benvolio in to fighting with him. At the Capulet party, Tybalt recognizes Romeo's voice and within ten words is calling for his sword. He also refers to Romeo as a "slave" (I.v.55). Tybalt says he does not consider it a sin to strike Romeo dead.

Tybalt shows his stubbornness at the Capulet party. Lord Capulet urges Tybalt to control himself, telling him that he is acting like a boy trying to be a man. Although Tybalt has to give in to his uncle, he vows to get revenge on Romeo for coming to the Capulet party uninvited. The next day, Tybalt sends a letter to Romeo's house challenging him to a duel.

Tybalt's actions in Act III influence the remaining events of the play. He quarrels with Mercutio and challenges Romeo to a sword fight. Tybalt insults Romeo, and he insists that Romeo draw his sword and fight with him. Romeo refuses to fight and Mercutio instead takes up the challenge. Tybalt is a skilled fighter, according to Mercutio, who comments that Tybalt has studied dueling. Thus, when Mercutio taunts him and calls for a fencing move, Tybalt is able to display it. In addition to his being belligerent and stubborn, Tybalt also has no qualms about fighting unfairly. When Romeo steps between the fighters, Tybalt stabs Mercutio under Romeo's arm. After Mercutio is killed, Tybalt declares that Romeo will accompany Mercutio in death. Instead, Tybalt is slain.

Watchmen:

Three watchmen patrol at night to protect the town and to make sure that the prince's rulings are carried out. For example, Friar Lawrence warns Romeo that he must leave Juliet before the watch is set. Paris's page calls the watch when he realizes his master is in a fight at the Capulet tomb. The watchmen catch Balthasar and the Friar, gather prelimi-

nary evidence on what has happened, and report on their findings to the prince.

Further Reading

Andrews, John F., ed. Romeo and Juliet: *Critical Essays.* New York: Garland, 1993.
> Students will find accessible, brief character studies of Juliet by Dame Peggy Ashcroft and Julie Harris, actresses who have played the part, and of the nurse by Brenda Bruce, who has played her. Stanley Wells's essay is a lengthier study of the nurse's role. James C. Bryant's essay analyzes the Friar. Both Coppelia Kahn and Marianne Novy use feminist perspectives in their essays to analyze plot, character, and theme.

Brownfoot, Andrew. *High Fashion in Shakespeare's Time.* Stradbroke, England: Tarquin Publications, 1992.
> Students who want to visualize items of clothing mentioned in the play, including smock, rapier (the sword of a gentleman), and Elizabethan shoes, would find this book helpful.

Cole, Douglas, ed. *Twentieth Century Interpretations Of* Romeo and Juliet. Englewood Cliffs: Prentice-Hall, 1970.
> Cole's own essay and one by Granville-Barker discuss the plot of the play. Stoll's essay discusses character.

Evans, G. Blakemore. Introduction to *Romeo and Juliet*, by William Shakespeare. Cambridge: Cambridge University Press, 1984.
> Evans's introduction includes plot analysis. In his section on the characters, he discusses Mercutio, Friar Lawrence, the nurse, Romeo, and Juliet.

Evans, Robert O. "Mercutio's Apostrophe To Queen Mab." In *The Osier Cage: Rhetorical Devices in* Romeo and Juliet, 68-86. Lexington: University of Kentucky Press, 1966.
> Provides a close stylistic analysis of Mercutio's Queen Mab speech. Evans concludes that the speech contains statements of the main subjects of the play, and, for the alert members of the audience, suggestions about the course the action will take. Evans also discusses Mercutio as the most important character in the play after the title characters.

Hankins, John E. Introduction to *Romeo and Juliet*, by William Shakespeare. In *William Shakespeare: The Complete Works*, edited by Alfred Harbage, 855-58. Baltimore: Pelican, 1969.
> In addition to the discussion of the play's source and date, Hankins's introduction contains brief but helpful comments on the characters. His introduction helps clarify ironies in the plot and the themes of the play.

Holdridge, Barbara, ed. *Under the Greenwood Tree.* Owings Mills, Maryland: Stemmer House, 1986.
> Robin and Pat DeWitt's illustrations in this collection are especially well done for two excerpts from *Romeo and Juliet.* Their drawings suggest the rich lyricism of the first two acts of the play.

Kermode, Frank. Introduction to *Romeo and Juliet*, by William Shakespeare. In *The Riverside Shakespeare*, edited by G. Blakemore Evans, 1055-57. Houghton Mifflin: Chicago, 1974.

Kermode's introduction discusses sources, date, plot, and tragic theme. Kermode makes comments on plotting similarities and differences between *Romeo and Juliet* and *A Midsummer Night's Dream*.

Levenson, Jill L. *Shakespeare in Performance. Romeo and Juliet*. Manchester: Manchester University Press, 1987.

Levenson's study describes selected performances of the play, beginning with the Elizabethan version and ending with the Zeffirelli version. Illustrations are included.

Limon, Jerzy. ''Rehabilitating Tybalt: A New Interpretation of the Duel Scene.'' In *Shakespeare's* Romeo and Juliet, edited by Jay L. Halio, 97-106. Newark: University of Delaware Press, 1995.

Limon attempts to analyze Tybalt as a Renaissance gentleman concerned with family honor.

Mack, Maynard. ''The Ambiguities of *Romeo and Juliet*.'' In *Everybody's Shakespeare*, 69-90. Lincoln: University of Nebraska Press, 1993.

Mack discusses characters in the play in terms of their individualization and also their familiarity as types.

He explains how the plot blends comedy with tragedy. His comments on the opposite world views of Mercutio and the lovers would help students to see two distinctly different outlooks on experience, and why Shakespeare included both views in his love tragedy.

McDonald, Russ. ''Men and Women: Gender, Family, Society.'' *The Bedford Companion to Shakespeare: An Introduction With Documents*, 251-96. Boston: St. Martin's Press, 1996.

McDonald's later sections on Marriage and Money (pp. 262-65) as well as on Family Life (pp. 265-70) would help both teachers and students in understanding differences in outlook between the twentieth century and the early modern age on marriage and family relationships. Words such as ''jointure'' and ''dowry'' are explained. Also, the use of nurses by well-to-do houses is explained.

Watts, Cedric. *Twayne's New Critical Introductions to Shakespeare*: Romeo and Juliet. Boston: Twayne Publishers, 1991.

Watts discusses plot in Chapter 3, including such matters as the double time-scheme in the play and its use of ironic patterning. Watts discusses four characters in Chapter 4: Romeo, Juliet, the nurse, and Lord Capulet.

The Taming of the Shrew

circa 1593-94

Induction:

The beggar Christopher Sly, a tinker by trade, falls asleep outside of an alehouse on the heath after arguing with the hostess and having drunk too much. When a lord returns from hunting and discovers the sleeping Sly, he decides to play an elaborate trick on him. The tinker Sly is carried to the lord's bedroom and dressed in fine clothes, the lord instructing his servants to treat Sly like the lord of the manor when he wakes. A young page is directed to dress in the fashion of his mistress and pretend that he is Sly's wife. As the lord and his servants are waiting to begin fooling Sly, a group of travelling actors arrives. The lord enlists them in the prank, instructing them not to laugh at the behavior of his honor (Sly) since he has never seen a play before. When Sly wakes, he at first insists on his identity as Christopher Sly, the tinker. The servants and the page tell him that he suffers from a strange psychological malady and has been in and out of consciousness for years. Since the circumstances Sly finds himself in are far better than those of the life he remembers, he ceases to protest and agrees to watch a play. The events of the Induction have been a framing device for presenting what is called the inset play. Sly makes some brief comments about the inset play, but by the time the first act is over, he nods off, neither he nor the other characters in the Induction appearing again.

Act I:

Lucentio and his servant Tranio arrive in Padua on their way from Pisa to Lombardy, and Lucentio decides to stay a while in Padua and pursue his intellectual studies there. As they are discussing which course of study would be the most interesting for Lucentio, the two witness a scene which attracts their attention. Baptista is reminding Hortensio and Gremio, two suitors vying for the hand of Baptista's daughter Bianca in marriage, that he will not allow Bianca to wed until her older sister Katherina, or Kate, marries. But Kate is a terrible shrew unlikely to find a husband, and the two suitors leave, pessimistic about the chances that either one of them might wed Bianca soon. As they leave, Baptista suggests to Hortensio and Gremio that Bianca will enhance her education while she waits for Kate to marry and they should recommend any schoolmasters with whom they are familiar. While this action has taken place, Lucentio has been watching, and he, too, falls in love with Bianca. He plots with Tranio to install himself as Bianca's teacher, and they exchange clothes so that Tranio might maintain a presence in Padua as Lucentio. Biondello, a younger servant to Lucentio, is instructed to go along with the plan and treat Tranio like his master. Petruchio arrives at the house of his friend Hortensio, who jokingly tells Petruchio that he knows a marriageable but horribly shrewish woman with money if Petruchio is interested. Petruchio is, in fact, interested and insists on meeting Kate right away, confident he can tame her. Hortensio is pleased, and, disguising himself in an academic robe, he asks that Petruchio present him to Baptista as a music teacher. On the way to Baptista's house, they meet Gremio, who has arranged to present the disguised Lucentio to Baptista as a scholar of Latin. In turn, Lucentio has promised to advance Gremio's suit. Tranio encounters this group and asks them where Bianca lives. Pretending to be Lucentio, he informs them that he will compete with them for Bianca's hand in marriage.

Act II:

Bianca expresses her anger at Kate for being so contrary and for preventing her from being courted by Gremio and Hortensio. The two quarrel and Kate strikes Bianca. When Baptista scolds Kate for doing so, Kate objects that Baptista seems to be favoring his younger daughter. The group of suitors and disguised schoolmasters arrive, and Petruchio ex-presses to Baptista his interest in Kate while assuring him that he is of excellent lineage. Baptista directs a servant to escort the men to where his daughters are, but Petruchio says he is not in a position to woo Kate over a long period of time. Baptista then grants him permission to be alone with Kate and propose marriage. When Petruchio reveals his intentions to Kate, she thinks he is crazy. He ignores her insults and continues to praise her, his plan to tame her based on the persuasive power of insistent flattery. When Baptista and the others come into the room, Petruchio announces that he and Kate have agreed to marry on the next Sunday. He overcomes Kate's protests by saying that he and Kate have agreed that she should continue to act shrewish and contrary in public. Tranio announces his interest in Bianca, and, secretly on Lucentio's behalf, outdoes the wealthy Gremio in extolling the wealth he will bestow on Bianca in the form of a dowry for Baptista.

Act III:

Both Hortensio and Lucentio, disguised as Litio and Cambio respectively, try to monopolize Bianca's time with their lessons. When Sunday arrives, all are assembled outside of Baptista's house in antici-pation of Kate's wedding to Petruchio. But Petruchio is late, and a humiliated Kate leaves. Biondello appears and announces that Petruchio has been seen heading toward Baptista's house, dressed in out-landishly mismatched clothes and riding an old, diseased horse. When Petruchio arrives and asks for Kate, Baptista implores him to change into appro-priate clothes. Petruchio argues that Kate is marry-ing him, not his wardrobe. Petruchio goes off to look for Kate, neglecting to tell Baptista that his outlandish attire is a calculated attempt to teach Kate humility, a prerequisite to the curing of Kate's shrewishness. The actual wedding of Kate and Petruchio is reported to Tranio, and thus the audi-ence, by Gremio, who thinks it the wildest affair he has ever attended, Petruchio speaking too loudly and treating the priest brashly, overly defensive of Kate's reputation. At the wedding reception, Petruchio encourages the guests to stay and enjoy the banquet prepared for them, but he and Kate must go. Kate protests but Petruchio insists that she is his property now. He and his servant Grumio draw their swords, pretending that they are saving Kate from those who would detain her, although no one actually intends to do so. Kate and Petruchio depart, the witnesses to the preceding events commenting on the strange behavior of the couple.

Act IV:

Petruchio sends Grumio ahead to prepare the household for the newlyweds' arrival. Grumio describes to the other servants the events that have transpired on the journey from Baptista's, behavior in which Petruchio has acted more shrewish than the shrew. When Kate and Petruchio arrive, Petruchio is dissatisfied with all the food and drink his servants offer, complaining that none of it is good enough for his bride. At Baptista's house, Hortensio positions Tranio so that the latter might observe how Bianca kisses and courts her tutor Cambio. Hortensio thinks that Cambio, who is really Lucentio in disguise, is a lowly schoolteacher and not a fit match for Bianca. He has resigned himself to the fact that he will never win Bianca and announces his intention to marry, within three days, the wealthy widow who has been in love with him for quite some time. Tranio, who has nothing to lose by doing so, says that he will give up his interest in Bianca as well. Because he has promised Baptista that Lucentio's father, Vincentio, will guarantee the dowry that he, pretending to be Lucentio, has promised for Bianca, Tranio has set Biondello to watch for someone who might convincingly impersonate Vincentio. Biondello reports that he has found a suitable candidate in a pedant, a schoolteacher constrained by petty scholarship, who bears himself like a father. Tranio convinces the pedant that he is not safe in Padua and suggests that the pedant assume the identity of Vincentio in order to protect himself. Back at Petruchio's, Kate complains to Grumio that Petruchio is starving her to death, but Grumio, too, sends the food away as he goes along with his master's plan to make Kate more submissive. Even when Petruchio finally allows that a certain dish is suitable for Kate, the newly arrived Hortensio devours much of it before she can satisfy her hunger. A haberdasher and a tailor, in turn, bring in their wears for Kate's approval, but Petruchio, who has previously commissioned these wears, denounces the goods as inferior and not suitable for Kate. He tells Kate that they will forego the finery and visit her father in the humble clothes they already have. In Padua, Tranio presents the pedant to Baptista as Vincentio, and the three agree to meet later at Tranio's lodgings and work out the exact terms of the dowry. Lucentio has been present at this initial meeting of Baptista and the disguised pedant, but, later, Biondello is sent to translate the secret winks and nods Tranio has apparently been unsuccessful in communicating to Lucentio. Lucentio is to bring Bianca to Tranio's quarters for the later meeting, but first he should stop at the church and get married. If Lucentio and Bianca are already married, no one will be able to back out of the dowry arrangements. On the way to Baptista's, Petruchio makes Kate agree with all of his nonsensical assertions, threatening to turn back if she does not. They meet the real Vincentio on the way, Petruchio insisting that Vincentio is a young maid and Kate agreeing with that observation. Although Vincentio thinks they are mad, he accepts their offer to lead him to his son Lucentio's dwelling in Padua, a dwelling really occupied by Tranio pretending to be Lucentio.

Act V:

Vincentio knocks on the door of what he thinks is his son's lodging. The pedant is inside and claims to be Vincentio, charging the real Vincentio to be an impostor. Vincentio recognizes both Biondello and Tranio as his son's servants, but they deny knowing him, hoping to outface him and get safely away, Tranio even calling to have Vincentio arrested. Lucentio arrives and explains everything to his father, begging that he forgive the behavior of Tranio and Biondello since they have only gone along with a plan agreed to by Lucentio. Baptista is upset that he has been deceived, but Vincentio assures Baptista that he will be well compensated. After witnessing these proceedings, Petruchio demands a kiss of Kate on the public street, and she agrees, the couple seeming quite affectionate toward one another by this time. Sometime later, the three couples—Petruchio and Kate; Lucentio and Bianca; and Hortensio and the widow—meet at Lucentio's home. Petruchio proposes a test to see whose wife is most dutiful, and Hortensio and Lucentio, acquainted with Kate's reputation as a shrew, wager that their wives will win, and even Baptista offers to bet against Kate. Biondello is sent to request each wife, in turn, to present herself to her husband who desires her presence. Both Bianca and the widow refuse the request, saying they are too busy; only Kate comes when she is called. The play ends with Kate lecturing Bianca and the widow on the properly subservient role women should assume in the presence of their husbands. The men celebrate Kate's new attitude, congratulating Petruchio for having tamed her.

Modern Connections

Modern audiences are typically troubled by two problems in *The Taming of the Shrew*. The first is the problem of Christopher Sly's disappearance.

Shakespeare sets up an elaborate frame story for presenting *The Taming of the Shrew*, but, then, seems to abandon the frame story, that of Christopher Sly, at the end. As part of the trick the lord and his servants are playing on Sly, the latter is positioned to watch the inset play (*The Taming of the Shrew*). Sly watches for a while but then becomes disinterested and is not heard from again. The audience fully expects that the joke on Sly will be revealed to him when he is forced to assume, once again, his real identity. When Shakespeare's play fails to supply this closure, the audience is somewhat disappointed.

A play contemporary with Shakespeare's, *The Taming of a Shrew*, does provide this closure, Sly critically commenting on the action of the inset play throughout and resuming his normal life at the end. *The Taming of a Shrew* is thought, alternatively, to be a source for or an imitation of Shakespeare's play. It is also conjectured that *The Taming of a Shrew* might be a bad quarto version of Shakespeare's play or a play relying on the same source as *The Taming of the Shrew*. Regardless of the exact relationship of the two plays, the overriding questions are these: might Shakespeare have written Sly into the ending of the play, that ending becoming lost somehow in the printing process, or does Shakespeare intentionally eliminate Sly before the ending for some other purpose? Since Shakespeare's Christopher Sly, unlike his counterpart in *The Taming of a Shrew*, never expresses much interest in the play, it is likely that Shakespeare never intended to resolve the Sly frame story. The transformation of Sly back to himself is left to the imagination of the audience, and, in doing so, the audience might well imagine the transformation of the one character in the inset play who is not returned to her "true" self. That character is, of course, Kate.

Perhaps more troublesome to modern audiences is the question of Kate's true identity. As we might imagine, many who read *The Taming of the Shrew* are disturbed by Petruchio's harsh treatment of Kate. Although Petruchio usually seems less harsh on stage than he does in the stark black and white of print—on stage the actors playing Kate and Petruchio often convey an affection that many believe exists between the two characters—he still humiliates and starves her, forcing her to agree with whatever nonsense he chooses to utter. It is somewhat unsettling to see Kate, a feisty and outspoken woman, reduced to a shell of her former self at the play's end, a kind of puppet whose only intent is to please her husband. But why should we imagine that Kate has changed completely and irreversibly when all the other characters give up the disguises for which they are ill-suited and resume their real identities?

Lucentio adopts the disguise of Cambio, a schoolmaster, and Bianca falls in love with him, prompting Hortensio to give up his own disguise as the music teacher, Litio. Hortensio expresses his disgust with Bianca for being attracted to such a base fellow, scorning her that "leaves a gentleman, / And makes a god of such a cullion" (IV.ii.19-20). Lucentio must abandon that disguise and display the true worth of his birth in order to be accepted by Bianca's father, Baptista. In V.ii.65-70, Vincentio calls attention to Tranio's affected style of dress, absurd in that Vincentio knows him to be a servant of his son. The pedant, one who by definition is a stickler for petty detail, is patently inappropriate to play Vincentio, a father who should display love and concern for his son, emotions completely opposite to a pedant's passionless existence. Even Petruchio gives up his role of shrew tamer and resumes what the audience presumes to be his real identity of the witty, game-playing courtier. Yet, while each of these characters has only temporarily stepped outside of his natural and proper self, it seems as though by outward appearances that Kate changes completely, her outspoken, self-assertive nature lost and unrecoverable.

Modern interpretations of the play which argue against Kate's complete transformation do so believing that Elizabethan audiences would have applauded Petruchio's taming of Kate and his making of her something she is not by nature. Although it is true that Elizabethan audiences would have found the topic of silencing women in public more humorous than we tend to do nowadays, both Elizabethan and modern audiences might be expected to imagine a life after the play for both Sly and Kate. Perhaps Kate has not been tamed anymore than Sly has become a lord, Lucentio a schoolmaster, Tranio his master, or the pedant Lucentio's father, Vincentio. After all, if the men believe Petruchio when he overcomes Kate's early protests by saying "'Tis bargain'd 'twixt us twain, being alone, / That she shall still be curst in company" (II.i.304-05), why should the audience believe those same men when they celebrate Kate's display of the "properly" (by Elizabethan standards) subservient attitude at the end of the play? Kate might be deceiving them in the same way Petruchio has done.

The Taming of the Shrew may inspire modern readers to recall times when they, like many of the characters in the play, have taken on roles themselves, hiding their true identities, in order to achieve certain goals (romantic or otherwise). How often do people pretend to be something they aren't in order to get something they want, or think they want?

Characters

Baptista:

Baptista is a wealthy landowner in Padua. He has two daughters, Bianca and Katherina/Kate. The younger daughter, Bianca, is much sought after, but Baptista has resolved that she should not marry until her older sister, Kate, is married. He is firm with Bianca's suitors, Hortensio and Gremio, on this point and insists that Bianca devote her time to study until he finds a suitable husband for Kate. Kate accuses Baptista of favoring Bianca over her, but, actually, Baptista demonstrates that he wants the best for both his daughters. He spends much of his time in the play haggling over his daughters' dowries, trying to insure that both Bianca and Kate are provided with material comforts. He even conducts a kind of bidding war between Gremio and Tranio, who is pretending to be Lucentio, for Bianca's hand in marriage. He also insists that his daughters' husbands have appropriate pedigrees. He is extremely upset when Petruchio shows up for the wedding dressed in wild attire, but since he knows Kate to be a terrible shrew, one for whom it will be difficult to find a match, his desire to see Kate married overrides his fear of public ridicule. His opinion of Kate does not change after she is married; at the end of the play, he even bets that Kate will lose the contest to see which wife is the most dutiful to her husband. It is true that Baptista does not consider his daughters' affections for the men with whom he arranges their marriages, but he has determined that the best marriages are those with a secure financial future, reflecting the beliefs of the time period during which the play was written.

Bianca:

Bianca is Baptista's daughter and the younger sister of Kate. Apparently she is quite attractive. Both Hortensio and Gremio are actively courting her, and Lucentio falls in love with her at first sight. Lucentio calls Bianca a "young modest girl" (I.i.156)

and tells Tranio, "Sacred and sweet was all I saw in her" (I.i.176). Part of Bianca's attractiveness must be that she is a gem of modesty set against the foil of Kate's outspoken and grating disposition. Bianca takes full advantage of the contrast which her suitors perceive between herself and Kate. When Baptista pronounces that she must avoid the company of men and devote her time to academic pursuits, Bianca is the model of feminine modesty and duty. She tells her father, "Sir, to your pleasure humbly I subscribe" (I.i.810). But Bianca also has a selfish streak. Just before her submissive response to her father, she has told Kate, "Sister, content you in my discontent" (I.i.80). Bianca resents that Kate's willful behavior prevents her from enjoying the attention her suitors wish to shower upon her. That resentment comes fully into the open when Kate strikes Bianca for suggesting that Kate is envious of her.

We get a somewhat different picture of Bianca at the end of the play. Petruchio proposes that Bianca, Kate, and the widow be called by their husbands to see which of the three responds most readily. Biondello is sent to fetch Bianca for Lucentio and reports back that Bianca has claimed to be too busy to respond to her husband's desire. Only Kate responds promptly, and Lucentio loses his wager. When he tells Bianca that she has cost him the wager, she says, "The more fool you for laying on my duty" (V.ii.129). Apparently, different sets of rules exist in marriage and courtship. Once Bianca has landed Lucentio, she no longer needs to make him the center of her attention as she did in the secret confines of her cloistered cell. As a married woman, she is free to indulge her own desires.

Biondello:

Biondello is Lucentio's servant. Since the stage directions refer to him as a boy, it can be assumed that he is younger than Tranio. When Lucentio takes on the disguise of Cambio and pretends to be a schoolmaster so that he can get close to Bianca, Lucentio tells Biondello that he has killed a man in a quarrel and Tranio has disguised himself as Lucentio to save Lucentio's life. Biondello must now treat Tranio as Lucentio and serve him. Biondello never really believes the story Lucentio has made up, and he quickly learns the plan that is actually afoot. When the need arises, he is given the task of finding a person who might convincingly impersonate Vincentio, Lucentio's father, and he selects the pedant, "In gait and countenance surely like a father" (IV.ii.65). He serves as a messenger for

Tranio and is so involved in the intrigue set in motion by Lucentio and Tranio that he even denies knowing Vincentio when the latter recognizes him outside of Tranio's lodging. At the end of the play, Biondello is sent to fetch Kate, Bianca, and the widow for their husbands.

Cambio:

See Lucentio

Christopher Sly:

See Sly

Curtis:

Curtis is a servant at Petruchio's country house. He tries to get information from Grumio, another of Petruchio's servants, when the latter arrives in advance of the newly wedded Kate and Petruchio with the order to make the house ready. When Grumio finally gets around to telling Curtis how Petruchio and Kate have been acting on their journey from Baptista's home, Curtis summarizes Petruchio's behavior. He says, "By this reck'ning he is more shrew than she" (IV.i.85). Curtis calls Petruchio's other servants—Nathaniel, Philip, Gregory, Nicholas, and Joshua—together and sees that they are ready for the arrival of their master and new mistress. Later, Curtis informs Grumio that Petruchio is in Kate's chamber, lecturing her about the need to abstain from sexual activity, while poor Kate does not quite know what to make of the lecture.

Gremio:

Gremio is a wealthy suitor to Bianca, competing with Hortensio for her hand in marriage. When Baptista refuses to allow either of them to court Bianca until Kate is married, the two are quite amicable about the competition, both realizing that neither can succeed with Bianca until Kate is married, and they openly agree to work together toward that end, if possible. Secretly, both plot a way to stay close to Bianca in the interim. Gremio, following Baptista's suggestion, recommends Cambio as a schoolmaster to Bianca, unaware that Cambio is Lucentio in disguise. In return for the recommendation, Gremio expects that Lucentio will act as a go-between and advance Gremio's suit for Bianca, which, of course, Lucentio does not do since he is advancing his own suit. After Kate and Petruchio are married and the competition for Bianca opens once again, Gremio feels he should be allowed to

> **Lucentio calls Bianca a 'young modest girl' (I.i.156) and tells Tranio, 'Sacred and sweet was all I saw in her' (I.i.176)."**

marry Bianca because, as he tells Baptista, "I am your neighbor, and was suitor first" (II.i.334). Baptista does, in fact, tend to favor Gremio because of his greater material wealth, but, to be fair, Baptista opens the bidding, Bianca going to whomever offers the largest dowry. Tranio, disguised as Lucentio and presumably acting on his behalf, accuses Gremio of being too old for Bianca, while Gremio counters with the charge that Bianca could never be attracted to one so young and immature as Tranio. Tranio exaggerates Lucentio's wealth and outbids Gremio, who resigns himself to the fact that he will never have Bianca. At the end of the play, Gremio, with no hope of finding a mate in the group assembled at Lucentio's house, joins the party only to enjoy his share of the feast.

Grumio:

Grumio is Petruchio's main servant, accompanying Petruchio on his trips back and forth between his country house and the town of Padua. Grumio is a clown and a jokester who seems to enjoy being obstinate and acting thick headed. Language is always a problem with Grumio because he always plays on vagaries and claims not to understand what is being said unless it is spoken in the clearest and most direct terms. For example, when Petruchio first arrives in Padua to visit his old friend Hortensio, he asks Grumio to knock on Hortensio's door. Grumio pretends to understand that Petruchio wants him to knock either Petruchio or someone who has offended him. It is only when Petruchio refers specifically to knocking on the gate (I.ii.37) that Grumio understands fully what Petruchio has requested. Again, when Grumio answers the question posed to him by Curtis concerning the attitudes of Petruchio and his new bride on their trip home from Padua, Grumio is purposefully evasive. He grows annoyed with Curtis and strikes him, claiming that had not Curtis annoyed him he would have heard the details in full. Grumio then goes on to relate the details in full, contradicting what he has just said.

> **" Gremio feels he should be allowed to marry Bianca because, as he tells Baptista, 'I am your neighbor, and was suitor first' (II.i.334)."**

Grumio mimics his master, dressing outlandishly for Petruchio's wedding and going along with Petruchio's scheme to delude and humiliate Kate.

Haberdasher:

The haberdasher shows Kate a hat he has been commissioned by Petruchio to make for her. In front of Kate, however, Petruchio pretends that he is very displeased with the hat, calling it too small and too unfashionable for Kate. Even though Kate likes the hat and insists that she will have that one or none at all, Petruchio has refused it for her, and the haberdasher exits.

Hortensio:

Hortensio is a friend to Petruchio and is engaged in a somewhat good-natured rivalry with Gremio to win Bianca for a bride. When Baptista cuts Bianca off from her suitors until Kate is married, Hortensio guardedly mentions to Petruchio that he knows an eligible woman with money; the only problem is that she is an intolerable shrew. To Hortensio's surprise and in answer to his prayers, Petruchio is interested and wants to go propose to Kate immediately. Hortensio, then, goes along with Petruchio and disguises himself as Litio, a music teacher, so that he might get a head start on Gremio in wooing Bianca. But Hortensio soon becomes engaged in a contest with another suitor. Cambio, who is really Lucentio, vies with Hortensio for Bianca's time. It soon becomes clear to Hortensio that Bianca prefers Cambio to himself. He wants to share his new misery with other company. He brings Tranio, whom he believes to be Lucentio, to observe that Bianca is enamored of her tutor Cambio. Hortensio is upset that Bianca favors one whom he believes is of a lower class than himself that he swears to quit pursuing the love of Bianca. He accepts the consolation prize and vows to wed the widow he has known for only a brief time: During the gathering at Lucentio's house at the end of the play, Hortensio, along with Lucentio and Baptista, loses money when he wagers that Kate will be the least dutiful of all three wives, the widow included.

Hostess:

The hostess appears briefly at the beginning of the Induction. She scolds Christopher Sly and asks whether or not he intends to pay for the glasses he has broken while getting drunk. When he informs her that he, indeed, does not intend to pay, she leaves to get the sheriff, intending to have Sly arrested.

Huntsmen:

The huntsmen appear in the Induction. They return from hunting with the lord, discussing the attributes of several of the hunting dogs. When that lord discovers Sly asleep outside the tavern, the huntsmen carry Sly up to the lord's chambers and agree to join in the trick the lord intends to play on Sly.

Katherina:

Katherina, or Kate as she is called throughout the play, is Baptista's daughter and Bianca's older sister. Baptista has forbidden Bianca to marry until Kate is married, but marrying Kate off is a problem for Baptista because she is outspoken and willful; in short, she is a shrew. At least, that is the reputation she has throughout Padua. Kate has a mind of her own and does not like to be told what to do. After Baptista sends Bianca into the house and away from her suitors, he tells Kate she can stay while he goes to speak more with her younger sister. Kate says, "Why, and I trust I may go too, may I not? / What, shall I be appointed hours, / as though, (belike), I knew not what to take, / and what to leave?" (I.i.102-04). Kate wants nothing more than to be heard on matters that concern her. Instead of allowing this, Baptista arranges to wed Kate to Petruchio, a man she initially describes as ". . . one half lunatic, / A madcap ruffian and a swearing Jack" (II.i.287-88). When Petruchio is late for his wedding to Kate, she further expresses to Baptista her dissatisfaction with the match, complaining that her father has seen her betrothed to a wild and crazy man who never had any intention of marrying her. We can feel sympathy with Kate in her situation and hear a good deal of disappointment in her rebuke of Baptista and Petruchio.

Kate's relationship with her sister also suffers as the result of her reputation for being shrewish. Bianca resents Kate because she thinks her older sister is preventing her from getting married. Kate feels Bianca's resentment in every recriminating glance. After the two sisters quarrel, Kate striking Bianca and Baptista intervening between them, Kate can no longer tolerate those looks from her younger sister. She attacks her, saying, "Her silence flouts me, and I'll be reveng'd" (II.i.29). Kate also accuses her father of favoring Bianca, suggesting that he cares not about the feelings of his elder daughter. Petruchio, however, treats Kate differently than do Baptista and Bianca. Although he involves her in situations that are humiliating, he, at least, makes her the center of his attention. When he deprives her of food, refuses to buy her finery, and makes her mimic his ludicrous assertions, he does so with protests of love and devotion. Kate seems to be attracted to Petruchio because he shows interest in her, and perhaps she attempts to please him because doing so pleases her.

In the last scene of the play, Petruchio bets that Kate will answer his summons when the wives of Lucentio and Hortensio will not. He wins the bet. Kate then delivers a speech to Bianca and the widow, a speech that stresses the importance of wives' submission to their husbands. "Such duty as the subject owes the prince, / Even such a woman oweth to her husband" (V.ii.155-56). Kate mouthing such sentiments, it seems that Petruchio has reduced her to an automaton, a mere shell of her former independence. But perhaps she has learned to play Petruchio's game and is now the master of that game. She learns that she has power in a limited sphere, and that power is the ability to please Petruchio. He is her audience, an audience she has never had before. In the last line of the play, Lucentio says to Petruchio, "'Tis a wonder, by your leave, she will be tamed so" (V.ii.189). Lucentio, perhaps, has assessed the situation correctly: Kate has willed the taming, not Petruchio. She has allowed herself to change outwardly, but we might suspect that inwardly she is the same spirited, willful and opinionated Kate.

Litio:
See Hortensio

Lord:
This lord appears in the Induction. He stumbles over Sly's prostrate body and is at first upset that such a drunkard has passed out near his estate. He then decides, for his own amusement, to delude Sly into thinking that he is a proper lord when he awakes.

" Baptista arranges to wed Kate to Petruchio, a man she initially describes as '. . . one half lunatic, / A madcap ruffian and a swearing Jack' (II.i.287-88)."

Lucentio:
Lucentio is Vincentio's son. With Vincentio's permission, Lucentio is travelling abroad in order to expand his horizons and pursue his education. He has stopped in Padua on his way from Pisa to Lombardy and decides to remain in Padua for a while, exploring what that town has to offer. He must feel that Padua offers more cultural depth than Pisa because he says,

> . . . I have Pisa left
> And am to Padua come, as he that leaves
> A shallow plash to plunge him in the deep
> And with society seeks to quench his thirst.
>
> (I.i.21-24)

The comparison he makes between Pisa and Padua is, perhaps, like the comparison between a small town and a big city. He will "quench his thirst" for knowledge in the rich center of learning that is Padua. He is no great and intense scholar though. When Tranio says, "Let's be no Stoics, nor no stocks" (I.i.31), Lucentio readily agrees. He will pursue only those forms of education which offer entertainment, nothing tedious or demanding. But before Lucentio can embark on this quest for higher learning, he sees Bianca and falls in love with her at first sight. Her father, Baptista, has removed her from the company of men, with the exception of her male teachers. The only way Lucentio can get close is by adopting the disguise of Cambio, a schoolmaster. It is not clear why Lucentio insists that Tranio wear his clothes and impersonate him. He has already told Tranio that they should "take a lodging fit to entertain / Such friends as time in Padua shall beget" (I.i.44-45). Since he does not already have friends in Padua, there is apparently no need for Tranio to maintain Lucentio's presence and make it known that Lucentio is there.

This desire to develop or maintain his reputation bespeaks a certain arrogance in Lucentio. He leads a life full of class privilege, and things come

> In the last line of the play, Lucentio says to Petruchio, "'Tis a wonder, by your leave, she will be tamed so' (V.ii.189). Lucentio, perhaps, has assessed the situation correctly: Kate has willed the taming, not Petruchio."

easily for him. He has seen Bianca with her two suitors, Hortensio and Gremio, yet he believes he can impose himself between their suits and win Bianca for himself. She must see some inherent virtues through his disguise as Cambio, a lowly schoolmaster, for he does, in fact, win her rather easily. Lucentio deceives Baptista by marrying Bianca without his knowledge, and he places his own father in some humiliating circumstances. Yet he easily wins the blessing of both men when he pleads for mercy and asks their forgiveness. He does not offer any legitimate excuses; he only presents himself as one with a nature deserving of forgiveness. The only thing that Lucentio does not win is the contest at the end of the play. When Bianca does not come at his beck and call, he loses his wager. Lucentio can only congratulate Petruchio for having so thoroughly tamed his shrewish wife.

Page:

The page appears in the Induction. His name is Bartholomew, and he is a page to the lord who is setting Sly up as an unwitting actor in some amusing entertainment. The page is directed to clothe himself in the fashion he has seen his mistress and other ladies of noble station adopt. He is to pretend that he is Sly's wife. When Sly informs the page that the servants have told him he has been in and out of consciousness for fifteen years, the page says, "Ay, and the time seems thirty unto me, / Being all this time abandon'd from your bed" (Induction.ii.114-15). This is precisely the wrong thing to say to Sly, who wants to be intimate with his wife right away. The page has to think quickly. He asks that he might abstain from Sly's bed yet awhile because the doctors have cautioned that sex might return Sly to his former illness.

Pedant:

The pedant is chosen by Biondello to impersonate Vincentio, Lucentio's father, because, according to Biondello who has been sent to find a likely candidate for the role, he bears himself like a father would. When Tranio asks Biondello about his choice, Biondello says he is either "a mercantant, or a pedant, / I know not what . . ." (IV.iii.63-64). Tranio tells the pedant, who is from the town of Mantua, that the Duke of Padua has determined that any merchant from Mantua apprehended in Padua should be put to death, a proclamation stemming from a recent quarrel between the two towns. Tranio suggests that, to insure his safety, the pedant disguise himself as Vincentio. Pedants were often the objects of ridicule in Elizabethan drama because of their narrow mindedness and lack of creativity. True to that Elizabethan stereotype, the pedant in this play throws himself into the role of Vincentio and does it "by the numbers." Although he conducts the negotiations with Baptista convincingly enough, when confronted with the real Vincentio, he does not have the presence of mind to abandon his persona in precarious circumstances. He proclaims that he is, indeed, Vincentio and forces Tranio and Biondello to deny Lucentio's real father to his face.

Petruchio:

Petruchio arrives in Padua to visit his friend Hortensio. His father, Antonio, has died, and Petruchio has been forced to seek his fortune "farther than at home" (I.ii.51). His father has left him with a home, its goods, and some money, but Petruchio wants to see the world. But mainly, Petruchio wants to marry a rich woman and assure himself of a solid financial future. Moreover, he does not care if that woman is old or ugly, so long as she has money. Hortensio tells Petruchio about Kate, informing him that she is well off financially but horribly shrewish in her demeanor. But Kate is neither old nor ugly; she is, according to Hortensio, "young and beauteous, / Brought up as best becomes a gentlewoman" (I.ii.86-87). Petruchio wants to see her right away. He wants to marry Kate for her money, assuring Hortensio that he will be able to cure Kate of her shrewishness. When Petruchio tells Baptista that he does not have time to engage in an extended courtship with Kate, Baptista grants him an immediate audience with her. Petruchio proposes marriage to Kate and steamrolls over her objections to marriage and her ridicule of him. To everyone's surprise, he announces that the wedding day will be the following Sunday. No one, perhaps, is more surprised than Kate herself. Petruchio takes his leave, but when he next appears, he engages in a series of bizarre behaviors designed to cure Kate of her ill humor.

He shows up for the wedding dressed preposterously, believing that humiliating Kate will make her relinquish some of the pride he feels is responsible for her intolerance of others. He acts strangely during the wedding ceremony and carries her away from the wedding reception, insisting that she is now his sole property. At his country house, he is nasty and short tempered with the servants, demonstrating, for her benefit, how uncomfortable that kind of behavior makes others feel. He refuses all the food brought to her, claiming it is unfit, slowly starving her to make her more manageable. Again working on her pride, he refuses to buy the hat offered by the haberdasher and the dress offered by the tailor, even though she much admires and desires them. On their way to visit Baptista, Petruchio forces Kate to agree with every wild and illogical statement he makes. If she does not, he threatens to return home and forego the visit to her father.

At first glance, Petruchio's treatment of Kate seems somewhat harsh, but we might imagine (and Petruchio is usually portayed this way on stage) that he does all he does with a smile on his face. Whatever he does, he insists that he loves Kate and has her best interests at heart. More importantly, we might imagine that Kate allows him to do what he does. Knowing her reputation as we do, it is hard to imagine that Kate could not get out of this situation if she so chose. She protests, but not too loudly, possibly because, despite his original intentions, he is the first man to show a sustained interest in her. Kate and Petruchio seem to have genuine affection for one another. This affection is especially evident when Petruchio insists that Kate kiss him in public. At first, she resists but then says, ''Nay, I will give thee a kiss; now pray thee, love, stay'' (V.i.148). And when Kate wins for Petruchio the wager placed on the wife proving most manageable, Petruchio again says, ''Come on, and kiss me Kate'' (V.ii.180).

Players:

The players appear in the Induction. They arrive at the lord's house as he is planning the elaborate hoax on Christopher Sly. The players are enlisted in that hoax and are instructed by the lord to perform for Sly, providing a fit entertainment for the sophisticate Sly is supposed to be. The lord cautions the players to restrain themselves in front of Sly because he has never seen a play before.

" . . . Petruchio has been forced to seek his fortune 'farther than at home' (I.ii.51). His father has left him with a home, its goods, and some money, but Petruchio wants to see the world. But mainly, Petruchio wants to marry a rich woman and assure himself of a solid financial future.''

What he really means is that they are not to make fun of Sly when they see what a rustic clown he is. The players comprise the cast of characters in the inset play.

Servants:

There are several groups of servants in *The Taming of the Shrew*. In the Induction, the servants to the lord participate in the ruse foisted on Sly. They call him by exaggerated titles when he wakes and lead him to believe that he is a nobleman suffering from a delusional malady that makes him lose consciousness for long periods of time. In addition to Grumio, Petruchio has several servants at his country house. (See Curtis.) They bring food and drink to Kate, all of which is dashed from their hands and proclaimed unfit for Kate by Petruchio. Apparently they, with the exception of Grumio, are not aware of Petruchio's tactics for taming Kate. They marvel at their master's odd behavior. Baptista also has servants at his home. One of those servants is directed to escort Hortensio and Lucentio, in their disguises of schoolmasters, into the presence of their pupil Bianca.

Sly (Christopher Sly):

Christopher Sly is the main character in the Induction, or frame story. He falls asleep outside an Inn after drinking too much and arguing with the hostess there. A passing lord discovers Sly's drunken form and decides to make Sly believe that he is rich. That lord has his huntsmen carry Sly up to a richly appointed bedroom, dress him in fine clothes, and pretend that he is the sophisticated lord of the

> **" . . . Petruchio insists that Kate kiss him in public. At first, she resists but then says, 'Nay, I will give thee a kiss; now pray thee, love, stay' (V.i.148). And when Kate wins for Petruchio the wager placed on the wife proving most manageable, Petruchio again says, 'Come on, and kiss me Kate' (V.ii.180)."**

manor when he wakes. The essence of the joke is that no one could be less sophisticated than Sly. When he wakes up, the first thing he calls for is "a pot of small ale" (Induction.ii.1). He is offered a glass of sack but denies having ever drunk that in his life, the distinction between the two drinks probably like that between beer and champagne. When the servants address him with "your lordship" and "your honor," Sly tries to maintain his identity and describes who he really is: "Am not I Christopher Sly, old Sly's son of Burton-heath, by birth a pedlar, by education a card-maker, by transmutation a bear-herd, and now by present profession a tinker?" (Induction.ii.17-21). Sly does not seem to be convinced totally by the servants' story that he has been suffering from delusions for years. True to his nature, Sly only becomes interested in assuming the role of the lord of the manor when he is told that he has a wife, the lord's young page disguised. He wishes immediately to gratify his sexual desire, but the Page puts him off with the excuse that the doctors have prohibited such activity because it will only make Sly's condition worse. When it is proposed that Sly watch a play put on specifically for his amusement, he further shows his lack of sophistication. He asks whether the play "Is not a comonty a Christmas gambold or tumbling trick?" (Induction.ii.137-38), the forms of dramatic entertainment with which he is most familiar. The Page tells Sly "It is a kind of history" (Induction.ii.141), and Sly agrees to see the play. But at the end of the first scene, Sly is already nodding off. He is not heard or seen again, and the elaborate frame story is never resolved even though the audience expects to see

Sly acquainted with the joke and returned to his former self at the end of the play.

Tailor:

The tailor has been commissioned, like the haberdasher, to make a dress for Kate. When he shows that dress to her, a displeased Petruchio mocks both the style of the dress and the tailor himself. The tailor protests that he has made the dress according to Petruchio's exact specifications. Petruchio has the tailor read the list of those specifications, but when he reads "'The sleeves curiously cut'" (IV.iii.143), Petruchio says, "Ay, there's the villainy" (IV.iii.144). The direction for cutting the sleeves of the dress is just ambiguous enough for Petruchio to object that he will not purchase it for Kate. Petruchio is only trying to teach Kate a lesson, not punish the tailor: he has Hortensio take the tailor aside and promise to pay him for his goods.

Tranio:

Tranio is Lucentio's servant. He and Lucentio witness the scene of Baptista cloistering Bianca, cutting her off from her suitors. Tranio and Lucentio also overhear Baptista's remark that Bianca will only be allowed the male company of her schoolmasters, and they simultaneously conceive the same plan: Lucentio will disguise himself as one of those schoolmasters in order to court the woman with whom he has instantaneously fallen in love. Tranio will wear Lucentio's clothes, which bear the distinction of a higher class than those usually worn by Tranio, and will maintain Lucentio's presence in Padua. Tranio adjusts to his new role quite readily. It is hard to determine which of the subsequent intrigues are suggested by Lucentio and which are orchestrated by Tranio on his own initiative. He introduces himself to Baptista and the company of Bianca's suitors as Lucentio and proclaims his desire to court Baptista's younger daughter. He engages in an outrageous bidding contest for Bianca, pledging a dowry of greater wealth than that promised by Gremio. He enlists the pedant to impersonate Vincentio and guarantee the preposterous material possessions Tranio has claimed to have. He conducts the marriage negotiations with Baptista, and even directs Lucentio to stop at the church and marry Bianca before bringing her to those negotiations. Tranio is so good at playing his role that it almost seems as if Tranio has become Lucentio and Lucentio become the servant. Tranio's fall from that higher social position, though, is sudden. Vincentio exposes him as Lucentio's servant, a reality of class distinction Vincentio knows well, having raised Tranio since he was three years old.

Vincentio:

We learn from Lucentio at the beginning of the play that his father, Vincentio, is "A merchant of great traffic through the world" (I.i.12). He has taken up residence in Pisa and has encouraged Lucentio to travel and pursue his education away from that town. On their way to Padua to visit Kate's father, Petruchio and Kate encounter Vincentio, who tells them, "And bound I am to Padua, there to visit / A son of mine, which long I have not seen" (IV.v.56-57). The play is vague about how much time has elapsed since Lucentio and Tranio arrived in Padua, but, apparently, Lucentio has been away from home long enough for Vincentio to miss him. Vincentio thinks the behavior of Petruchio and Kate is odd. Petruchio describes Vincentio to Kate as a young maid, and Kate agrees with that assessment; then, Petruchio asserts that Vincentio is a grisled old man, and Kate agrees again. Despite this bizarre episode, Vincentio accepts their offer to lead him to Lucentio's house in Padua. Once there, Vincentio is confronted by the pedant who claims to be Lucentio's father. At first, Vincentio is only confused, but when he recognizes Tranio and Biondello and they deny knowing him, he becomes outraged, especially when Tranio calls out to have Vincentio arrested. He is used to being treated with respect and deference by Lucentio's servants. When they do not do so, he wants desperately to exercise his power and punish them. He says, "I'll slit the villain's nose, that would have sent me to jail" (V.i.131-32). He is still upset, even after Lucentio has arrived to explain the whole affair and has asked Vincentio to pardon Tranio. In the end, Vincentio displays his generous and gracious nature, assuring Baptista that he will be fully compensated for Lucentio's deception in secretly marrying Bianca.

Widow:

After Hortensio realizes that Bianca is lost to him, he resolves that, within three days, he will marry the widow who has loved him as long as he has loved Bianca. In the final scene, Petruchio suggests to the widow that Hortensio is afraid of her. She tells Kate, "Your husband, being troubled with a shrew, / Measures my husband's sorrow by his woe" (V.ii.28-29). She means that Petruchio assumes all wives are shrews because his own wife is one. But, ultimately, the widow proves to be a less

> "Tranio is so good at playing his role that it almost seems as if Tranio has become Lucentio and Lucentio become the servant."

manageable wife than Kate is. The widow fails the test; she does not come when she is called.

Further Reading

Barton, Anne. Introduction to *The Taming of the Shrew*, by William Shakespeare. In *The Riverside Shakespeare*, edited by G. Blakemore Evans, 106-09. Boston: Houghton Mifflin, 1974.

> Barton compares the disappearance of Christopher Sly in Shakespeare's play to the continued presence of Sly throughout *The Taming of a Shrew*, arguing that Shakespeare's excision of the Sly character might have been intentional. She also claims that when Shakespeare's play is staged, rather than read, the brutality of Petruchio's treatment of Kate is softened, the actors portraying those characters able to convey a real sense of affection and humor between the two.

Craig, Terry Ann. "Petruchio as an Exorcist: Shakespeare and Elizabethan Demonology." *Selected Papers from the West Virginia Shakespeare and Renaissance Association* 2, no. 3 (1978): 1-7.

> Craig suggests that in Kate's shrewishness and Petruchio's ridding her of that shrewishness, Shakespeare is parodying Elizabethan ideas about possession and exorcism.

Heilman, Robert B. "The *Taming* Untamed, or, The Return of the Shrew." *Modern Language Quarterly* 27, no. 2 (1966): 147-61.

> Heilman objects to readings of the play which supply Kate with modern sensibilities and suggest that she controls Petruchio by giving him what he wants. Heilman maintains that the comedy of Shakespeare's play depends on the audience's automatic response to the stereotypes of Kate as a brazen shrew and Petruchio as shrew tamer.

Huston, J. Dennis. " 'To Make a Puppet': Play and Play-Making in *The Taming of the Shrew*." *Shakespeare Studies* 9 (1976): 73-87.

> Huston examines the extent of role-playing in *The Taming of the Shrew*, arguing that several of the

characters learn to avoid the fixed identity society would impose upon them.

Jayne, Sears. "The Dreaming of *The Shrew*." *Shakespeare Quarterly* 17, no. 1 (1966): 41-56.

Jayne addresses the problem of Sly's disappearance in Shakespeare's play, suggesting that the inset play should be treated as if it were the dream of Christopher Sly.

Kahn, Coppelia. "*The Taming of the Shrew*: Shakespeare's Mirror of Marriage." *Modern Language Studies* 5, no. 1 (1975): 88-102.

Kahn argues that Kate wins the game she plays with Petruchio, making his determination to change her seem childish against her good-humored acceptance of reality, the play, ultimately, making fun of the Elizabethan male's fantasy of what a woman should be.

Kaufman, Michael W. "Spare Ribs: The Conception of Woman in the Middle Ages and the Renaissance." *Soundings* 56, no. 2 (1973): 554-65.

Kaufman proposes that the male characters' attitude toward Kate in *The Taming of the Shrew* accurately reflects the Medieval and Renaissance attitude toward shrewish women. Women who were too vocal or rebellious were thought to threaten patriarchal order, an order imposed by men and thought to be normal.

Muir, Kenneth. "Much Ado About the Shrew." *Trivium* 7 (1972): 1-4.

Muir reacts to readings of the play which see Petruchio's treatment of Kate as brutal. He argues that the two are obviously in love with one another, a kind of equality resulting from the fact that both get what they want in the end.

Perret, Marion. " 'A Hair of the Shrew'." *Hartford Studies in Literature* 11, no. 1 (1979): 36-40.

Perret demonstrates that Petruchio's taming of Kate is based on Shakespeare's knowledge of contemporary folk prescriptions for the curing of shrewishness. Kate's shrewish behavior results from an imbalance of bodily humors, which needs to be adjusted by Petruchio.

Ranald, Margaret Loftus. "The Manning of the Haggard; or *The Taming of the Shrew*." *Essays in Literature* 1: 2 (1974): 149-65.

Ranald argues that the view of marriage Shakespeare presents in *The Taming of the Shrew* is not typical. Shakespeare's audience would have viewed the marriage of Kate and Petruchio as one characterized by love, equality, and trust, not as a farce that celebrated wife beating.

Seligman, Kevin L. "Shakespeare's Use of Elizabethan Dress as a Comedic Device in *The Taming of the Shrew*: 'Something Mechanical Encrusted on the Living'." *Quarterly Journal of Speech* 60, no. 1 (1974): 39-44.

Seligman details how much of the humor in *The Taming of the Shrew* depends on the Elizabethan audience's understanding of the significance of different forms of dress, a significance that often escapes modern audiences. He discusses the wild wedding attire of Petruchio and Grumio, the garments worn by Tranio in disguise, and the scene with the haberdasher and tailor.

Thorne, W. B. "Folk Elements in *The Taming of the Shrew*." *Queen's Quarterly* 75, no. 3 (1968): 482-96.

Thorne identifies the folk motif of misrule, a temporary suspension of regulations and authority, in *The Taming of the Shrew*. This folk custom of misrule is important for maintaining a smoothly functioning society, especially when the young overcome the old.

West, Michael. "The Folk Background of Petruchio's Wooing Dance: Male Superiority in *The Taming of the Shrew*." *Shakespeare Studies* 7 (1974): 65-73.

West argues that the scenes of Petruchio's wooing of Kate are loaded with sexual imagery. Kate's concessions to Petruchio result from her discovery of physical pleasure, not from her desire to best him in an intellectual contest.

The Tempest

Plot Summary

Act I:

During a violent storm at sea, King Alonso of Naples is shipwrecked on an island along with his brother, Sebastian; his son, Ferdinand; his counselor, Gonzalo; and Antonio, duke of Milan. The storm and shipwreck are witnessed with distress by Miranda, who lives alone on the island with her father (the magician Prospero) and their servant, Caliban. Realizing that her father is responsible for the storm, Miranda begs him to calm the seas and save the passengers. Prospero reassures her that all are safe, and then tells her the story of their own exile on the island, explaining that he was usurped as duke of Milan twelve years earlier by his brother, Antonio, who, with the help of King Alonso, abandoned Prospero and his young daughter at sea in a leaky boat. Thanks to the kind-hearted Gonzalo—who supplied them with provisions as well as with books from Prospero's library—father and daughter survived and landed on this island, where they encountered Caliban (the ''savage and deformed'' son of the long-dead witch, Sycorax) and also Ariel (a spirit of the air whom they found imprisoned in a tree by Sycorax). They educated Caliban, taught him language and tried to civilize him, but when Caliban attempted to rape Miranda, Prospero made him a slave. As for Ariel, Prospero freed him from the tree and has since made use of the spirit's powers over the sea and air. Hoping one day to

achieve total freedom, Ariel serves his master faithfully; at Prospero's bidding, he created the tempest at sea and brought all of those aboard ship safely onto the island. Per Prospero's instructions, Ariel split the castaways into groups, leaving each group to believe that the others are dead. Ferdinand is separated from the rest and lured by Ariel's song to Prospero's cave, where he and Miranda meet and—in keeping with Prospero's plan—immediately fall in love. Prospero feigns disapproval, and asserting that Ferdinand's worth must be tested, he uses his magic to enslave the youth.

Act II:

Alone with his courtiers, Alonso mourns the disappearance and apparent death of his son, Ferdinand. Gonzalo tries to distract him with a discussion of the ideal commonwealth. Ariel arrives and charms all but Sebastian and Antonio to sleep with music. The two of them plot to kill Alonso so that Sebastian can succeed him as king of Naples, but Ariel foils their plan by wakening Gonzalo. Elsewhere on the island, first the jester Trinculo and afterward the tipsy butler Stephano discover Caliban. The three of them drink wine which Stephano has salvaged from the shipwreck, and Caliban drunkenly swears allegiance to Stephano, who drunkenly declares himself ruler of the island.

Act III:

Still enslaved by Prospero, Ferdinand gathers wood, cheerful at the thought that he is also serving Miranda. As Miranda and Ferdinand fall more and more deeply in love with one another, they vow to become husband and wife—much to Prospero's approval, who has been observing them in secret. Meanwhile, Ariel overhears Caliban persuading the drunken Stephano to kill Prospero and become king of the island with Miranda as his queen. Ariel dutifully declares that he will warn his master, and leads away the three drunken conspirators (Caliban, Stephano, and Trinculo) with his music. Elsewhere, King Alonso and his courtiers wander wearily about the island, while Antonio and Alonso's brother, Sebastian, continue to plot against the king. Prospero enters, and rendered invisible by his magic, he tempts the king's group with an imaginary banquet. Ariel appears as a harpy, calls Alonso, Antonio, and Sebastian "three men of sin," for their crimes twelve years ago against Prospero, and causes the

banquet to vanish before their eyes. Guilt-stricken, Alonso rushes off, hoping to find the body of his son, Ferdinand, and die alongside him. Sebastian and Antonio also leave, vowing to fight the evil spirits which inhabit the island, and Gonzalo, worried that all three of them have been driven mad by their guilt, follows them.

Act IV:

Pleased with Ferdinand's hard work and devotion to Miranda, Prospero releases the youth from servitude and gives his blessing to the young couple's engagement. In honor of their betrothal, Prospero calls upon Ariel and his fellow spirits to perform a celebratory masque. (A masque is a colorful, elaborate performance consisting of actors dressed in splendid costumes, usually depicting mythological characters involved in music and dance.) Prospero suddenly remembers Caliban's treacherous plot against him, and abruptly calls the masque to a halt, ordering Ariel to entrap and punish Caliban and his his co-conspirators, Trinculo and Stephano.

Act V:

Prospero's undertaking against all those who have betrayed him is nearly over. He summons Ariel to bring Alonso and his courtiers before him so that he can release them from their spell of madness and confusion, declaring that once he has returned everything to normal, he'll break his magic staff, dispose of his magic books, and free Ariel as he has promised. Prospero restores Alonso, Sebastian, and Antonio to their senses, then rebukes them for their treachery and demands the return of his dukedom. He praises Gonzalo as an honorable man, and reveals to the repentant Alonso his son Ferdinand—alive and well and playing chess with his fiancee, Miranda. Ariel appears with the ship's master and the boatswain, who announce that the ship is intact and ready to set sail for Italy. Ariel disappears once more and returns with Stephano, Trinculo, and Caliban, who are still drunk, and covered with bruises. Ultimately, Prospero forgives all of those assembled who have betrayed him, and resolves to return to Milan as duke, asking Ariel to give them "calm seas" and "auspicious gales" for their journey home, and then finally granting the airy spirit his freedom. As the play closes, Prospero—no longer a magician—turns to the audience and humbly requests the magic of their applause.

Modern Connections

The Tempest is filled with music, magic, and supernatural spirits, much of which appears during the betrothal masque conjured up by Prospero for Ferdinand and Miranda in IV.i. A masque is an elaborate theatrical production with little or no plot, usually featuring characters from mythology and consisting of music, dance, and splendid costumes. Masques were a popular form of courtly entertainment in Shakespeare's time, particularly during the reign of King James I. At their height, they were showcases for special effects: trapdoors and ropes on pulleys were used to raise and lower actors and props; scenery was painted on panels that would shift to reveal different locations or convey a sense of animation. Mountains were constructed onstage that would open up to reveal caves. Smoke was used to conceal stage machinery, and multicolored lighting was devised for illumination and dramatic effect. Renaissance audiences watching the betrothal masque in *The Tempest* would have been treated to goddesses dressed in gorgeous costumes and Juno ''magically'' descending in a ''car,'' or chariot. Today, audiences continue to be fascinated with the magic of special effects. It can be argued, for example, that films such as *Total Recall* (1990), *Jurassic Park* (1993), *Twister* (1996), and *Independence Day* (1996) have been more popular for their spectacular illusions and computer imaging than for their storylines.

Shakespeare wrote *The Tempest* at a time when Europeans were voyaging to and colonizing the Americas, or the New World. Critics have pointed out that colonial attitudes toward the original inhabitants of the New World were extreme and contradictory. On the one hand, natives were described as pure and noble dwellers in paradise; on the other, they were called vicious savages who needed to be civilized for their own good as well as for the safety of the colonists. It has been suggested that the character of Caliban reveals these distorted views at least in part, and that his presence also demonstrates the Renaissance fascination with the New World inhabitants as novelties or sideshows rather than as people. Trinculo underlines this point on his first encounter with Prospero's slave in II.ii.31-33, when he observes that a ''strange beast'' like Caliban would be worth a fortune in England, where ''they will not give a doit to relieve a lame beggar, [but] they will lay out ten to see a dead Indian.'' Thus Shakespeare reflects the advent of an issue which continues to be problematical today, as indigenous people work to preserve their heritage and to educate others about their culture.

Finally, the fact that Alonso and his courtiers at first believe themselves to be shipwrecked far from home on an uninhabited island results in Gonzalo's cheerful description in II.i.148-57, 160-65 of what, under the circumstances, could be an ideal commonwealth:

> I' th' commonwealth I would, by contraries,
> Execute all things; for no kind of traffic
> Would I admit; no name of magistrate;
> Letters should not be known; riches, poverty,
> And use of service, none; contract, succession,
> Bourn, bound of land, tilth, vineyard, none;
> No use of metal, corn, or wine, or oil;
> No occupation, all men idle, all;
> And women too, but innocent and pure;
> No sovereignty—
>
> . . .
>
> All things in common nature should produce
> Without sweat of endeavor: treason, felony,
> Sword, pike, knife, gun, or need of any engine,
> Would I not have; but nature should bring forth,
> Of it own kind, all foison, all abundance,
> To feed my innocent people.

Gonzalo's depiction of a community without commerce, laws, money, work, or literacy sounds extreme to his fellow castaways as well as to modern audiences; all the same, this exercise in reinventing society is relevant today in light of people's discontentment with taxes and ''big government,'' and in the wake of recent experiments in overhauling health care, welfare, and education.

Characters

Adrian:

He is a lord attending King Alonso of Naples, and a minor character in the play. After the tempest, Adrian is washed ashore in company with Alonso and several other members of the king's court. His and Gonzalo's efforts to cheer up the dejected king in II.i are ridiculed by Antonio and the king's brother, Sebastian. Thus Adrian's optimism serves as a foil to Sebastian and Antonio's mean-spirited cynicism. (A foil is a person or thing that highlights another character's traits through contrast.) When Alonso, Sebastian, and Antonio are temporarily driven crazy by Prospero's spells, Adrian sorrowfully watches over them, along with Gonzalo and Francisco (III.iii.104-09; V.i.7-13).

Alonso:

He is the king of Naples and the father of Ferdinand. King Alonso, his son, and his courtiers get caught in the tempest on their way home from the marriage of his daughter to the king of Tunis (II.i.69-72). In I.ii.121-32, we learn that as Prospero's "inveterate" enemy, Alonso contributed to his overthrow by sending troops to Milan "i' th' dead of darkness" to support Antonio's takeover and to banish Prospero and his daughter. In return for this support, Alonso was awarded an annual tribute from the usurping Duke Antonio's coffers, as well as the subjection of Milan to Naples. Thus, twelve years later, when Prospero discovers that Alonso and his follwers are nearby aboard a ship, he creates the tempest to wash them ashore and exact a long-overdue revenge.

Alonso's first appearance in the play occurs in I.i, while he is on board the ship during the storm, trying to exert his authority over the toiling crew. Faced with the fury of the tempest, the master of the ship, his boatswain, and his crew ignore the king's commands and order him below deck.

Alonso next appears in II.i, grieving over his missing son, Ferdinand, whom he believes to have been drowned, and refusing to be consoled even by his faithful counselor, Gonzalo. At the close of II.i, Alonso is saved by Ariel and Gonzalo from being assassinated in his sleep by his own brother, Sebastian, and Antonio.

By the time he appears again, in III.iii, Alonso is exhausted from wandering around the island with his courtiers, and announces his despair to Gonzalo: "Even here will I put off my hope, and keep it / No longer as my flatterer" (III.iii.7-8). At this point, Prospero exacts his final revenge by driving Alonso mad with an illusory banquet and with Ariel's appearance as a harpy.

At the close of the play in V.i, Prospero takes pity on his old enemy Alonso, releases him and his courtiers from madness, and shows him that his son and heir is not only alive, but engaged to Prospero's daughter, Miranda.

Even before he learns that his son is still alive, the remorseful Alonso repents of his crimes against Prospero and restores his dukedom, at the same time asking for Prospero's pardon (V.i.118-19). The subsequent union between Alonso's son and Prospero's daughter is seen as the ultimate reconciliation between the two men as they look foward to the future through their children. Indeed, when Alonso calls himself Miranda's "second father" and begs her for forgiveness of prior wrongs, Prospero sounds once more the note of reconciliation by urging Alonso to forget the past: "Let us not burthen our remembrances with / A heaviness that's gone" (V.i.199-200).

Antonio:

He is the current duke of Milan and the treacherous brother of Prospero, the former duke of Milan. At the beginning of the play, Prospero tells Miranda how as duke he retreated to his studies after entrusting Antonio, "whom next thyself / Of all the world I lov'd," with the practical side of governing Milan (I.ii.66-78). Greedy for total power, Antonio usurped his brother with the help of King Alonso of Naples, and set Prospero and the infant Miranda adrift in a rotten boat. As the play opens, Antonio is traveling nearby on the ship carrying King Alonso and his courtiers home from Tunis—thus providing Prospero with the opportunity to bring his enemies to justice.

Critics have noted that Antonio displays his villainous nature virtually from the moment he appears in the play. As the ship is being battered by the storm, Prospero's "perfidious" brother swears at the hard-working boatswain, calling him a "whoreson, insolent noisemaker"; shortly afterward, he accuses the crew members of being "drunkards" and blames them for any deaths that may occur as a result of the tempest (I.i.43-44, 56). Later, when he lands on the island with Alonso and his followers, Antonio ridicules Gonzalo for his optimism, mocking the old counselor's effort to cheer up the king and laughing at his description of the ideal commonwealth (II.i.1-190). Once Alonso is charmed asleep by Ariel, Antonio persuades Sebastian (Alonso's brother), to try to murder the king and succeed him on the throne of Naples—even though, as critics have observed, there is little point in being king now that everyone is shipwrecked on an island far away from home (II.i.202-96).

Antonio is one of the "three men of sin" (Alonso and Sebastian being the other two) who in III.iii are driven to madness by Ariel as punishment for their crimes against Prospero. Prospero restores his "unnatural" brother to health in V.i and forgives him for his crimes, along with Alonso and Sebastian. Antonio says very little for the rest of the play, and it has been argued that he, alone, remains unrepentant.

Ariel:

He is a spirit of the air. In I.ii.250-93, we learn that Ariel was once the servant of Sycorax, a wicked sorceress who had imprisoned the spirit in a "cloven pine" for refusing to fulfill her "earthy and abhorr'd commands" (I.ii.277, 273). Ariel remained trapped inside the tree for twelve years, crying out in pain, until Prospero arrived on the island, released him, and bound the airy spirit to his service. Thus at Prospero's command, Ariel stirs up the tempest which strands Alonso and his followers on the island (I.i). Again acting on his master's instructions, he beguiles Alonso's son, Ferdinand, with music—convincing the prince that his father is dead ("Full fadom five thy father lies") and leading him to the admiring and "admir'd" Miranda (I.ii.375-412; III.i.37). Ariel also saves Alonso and Gonzalo from assassination by Sebastian and Antonio (II.i.300-5), and warns Prospero of plots being formed against him by the drunken Stephano, Trinculo, and Caliban.

In III.iii, Ariel helps his master create an illusory banquet for Alonso, Sebastian, and Antonio, only to torment these "three men of sin" by whisking their feast away and then chastising them for their crimes against Prospero. In IV.i.57-138, the airy spirit presides over a betrothal masque in honor of Ferdinand and Miranda's engagement. In IV.i.255-66, he helps Prospero punish Caliban and his co-conspirators with cramps, pinches, and "dry convulsions."

As the play nears its conclusion, Ariel rounds up all the transgressors so that Prospero can judge and forgive them. The spirit's final task is to provide "calm seas [and] auspicious gales" for the journey back to Naples, after which Prospero regretfully sets him free (V.i.315-19).

Early in the play, Ariel expresses his impatience with servitude, receiving a threatening rebuke when he reminds Prospero in I.ii.242-50 of his promise to liberate the airy spirit. Nevertheless, Ariel fulfills Prospero's commands assiduously and with skill. In I.ii.195-205, he describes how he has accomplished "every article" of his master's instructions for the tempest:

> I boarded the King's ship; now on the beak,
> Now in the waist, the deck, in every cabin,
> I flam'd amazement. Sometime I'ld divide,
> And burn in many places; on the topmast,
> The yards and boresprit, would I flame distinctly,
> Then meet and join. Jove's lightning, the
>   precursors
> O' th' dreadful thunder-claps, more momentary
> And sight-outrunning were not; the fire and cracks

> **Alonso is saved by Ariel and Gonzalo from being assassinated in his sleep by his own brother, Sebastian, and Antonio."**

> Of sulphurous roaring the most mighty Neptune
> Seem to besiege, and make his bold waves
>   tremble,
> Yea, his dread trident shake.

Ariel carries out most of his duties while invisible, but he is capable of transforming himself into a variety of shapes—from several flames burning in "many places," to a harpy sufficiently formidable to dispose of a banquet with the clap of its wings. He is also comfortable in a variety of environments, being able to "fly, / To swim, to dive into the fire, to ride / On the curl'd clouds" (I.ii.190-92). In V.i.88-94, Ariel suggests that he is small enough to rest inside a flower or to ride on the back of a bat. Prospero, who relies upon him throughout the play, fondly calls him "delicate" and "dainty," referring to him as "my bird" (IV.i.49,184; V.i.95).

Finally, Ariel has been called morally neutral, being neither a demon nor an angel. It has also been observed that he shows both a detachment from and a connection to humanity when, at the close of the play, he declares that, were he human, he would feel pity for the punishment endured by Alonso and his followers (V.i.17-21).

Boatswain:

He is an officer on the ship bearing Alonso and his courtiers home to Naples from Tunis where they had celebrated the marriage of Alonso's daughter to the king of Tunis. As the play opens, the voyagers are caught in a violent tempest conjured up by Prospero, and the boatswain is struggling unsuccessfully to keep the ship from going aground. His blunt treatment of the royal passengers (who are superior to him in social rank) as they repeatedly come on deck to question him is an indication of the severity of the storm. As the boatswain himself puts it, "What cares these roarers [tempestuous waves] for the name of king?" (I.i.16-17). Throughout I.i, the king's counselor Gonzalo doggedly insists that the boatswain is destined to die by hanging on land rather than by drowning at sea, thus foreshadowing

> **Antonio is one of the 'three men of sin' (Alonso and Sebastian being the other two) who in III.iii are driven to madness by Ariel as punishment for their crimes against Prospero.''**

the ship's safe arrival. The boatswain's next and final appearance occurs at the close of the play, when he delivers the astounding news that the crew is safe and that the ship "Is tight and yare, and bravely rigg'd as when / We first put out to sea'' only three hours earlier (V.i.224-25).

Caliban:

Described in the character list as "a savage and deformed slave,'' Caliban is the son of Sycorax, an evil witch who has since died but who once held sway over the island now ruled by Prospero. Regarding him as a "beast'' and a "poisonous slave, got by the devil himself'' upon Sycorax, Prospero has forced Caliban into servitude (IV.i.140; I.ii.319). By contrast, Caliban considers himself mistreated and overworked. He bitterly accuses Prospero of befriending him in order to take advantage of his gratitude and rob him of the island which he considers his birthright:

> This island's mine by Sycorax my mother,
> Which thou tak'st from me. When thou cam'st first,
> Thou strok'st me and made much of me, wouldst give me
> Water with berries in't, and teach me how
> To name the bigger light, and how the less,
> That burn by day and night; and then I lov'd thee
> And show'd thee all the qualities o' th' isle,
> The fresh springs, brine-pits, barren place and fertile.
> Curs'd be I that did so!
> . . .
> For I am all the subjects that you have,
> Which first was mine own king;
> (I.ii.331-39, 341-42)

Calling him a liar, Prospero reminds Caliban that he was treated well until he tried to rape Miranda: "I have used thee / (Filth as thou art) with human care, and lodg'd thee / In mine own cell, till thou didst seek to violate / The honor of my child''

(I.ii.345-48). Caliban readily admits the attempted rape, retorting, "would't had been done! / Thou didst prevent me; I had peopled else / This isle with Calibans'' (I.ii.349-51).

This exchange sets the stage for Caliban's behavior during the rest of the play. On his own gathering wood in II.ii, Caliban continues to curse his master; then hearing a noise which he thinks must be Prospero's spirits coming to punish him, he throws himself onto the ground in an attempt to hide. The noise turns out to be the jester Trinculo, followed shortly afterward by the drunken butler Stephano. Stephano plies the frightened Caliban with liquor, and in drunken gratitude, Caliban swears his obedience to the butler, promising to serve him and to show him the best places on the island, and giddily celebrating his new-found "freedom'' (II.ii.125-86). Later in III.ii, Caliban persuades Stephano and Trinculo to try to murder Prospero, but the plot is foiled by Ariel in IV.i, and the three conspirators are punished with cramps, pinches, and convulsions.

At the close of the play, Caliban repents his plot against Prospero, and regrets his foolish admiration for Stephano: "I'll be wise hereafter,'' he declares, "And seek for grace. What a thrice-double ass / Was I to take this drunkard for a god, / And worship this dull fool!'' (V.i.295-98).

Critics are divided on what to make of Caliban. Those who view him negatively point out that he is a potential rapist who plots to commit murder. They observe that he foolishly trades one master (Prospero) for another (Stephano), and that his so-called wish for freedom turns out instead to be a desire for the self-indulgence he obtains through Stephano's wine. Those who regard Caliban with sympathy argue that Prospero and Miranda are intruders on the island, and that by choosing to serve Stephano rather than accept Prospero's "civilizing'' education and enslavement, Caliban practices a measure of self-determination.

It has been noted that while Caliban is brutal, he is also sensitively appreciative of beauty. In III.ii.135-43, he offers a lyrical description of the music that can be heard all over the island, referring to "sweet airs, that give delight and hurt not.'' In this context, Caliban has been regarded as an example of the distorted Renaissance view of the New World inhabitants, who on the one hand, were believed to be vicious savages and on the other, pure children of nature.

Alternatively, it has been argued that Caliban's blunt and savage "naturalness" acts as a foil to the concept of civilization demonstrated by the graceful and cultured Miranda, as well as to the perniciousness of civilization shown by the Machiavellian Antonio.

Ceres:

She is a character in the betrothal masque created by Prospero to honor and educate the newly engaged Miranda and Ferdinand; the masque is performed by Ariel along with a group of "meaner," or lesser, spirits (IV.i.35-138). (A masque is an elaborate production consisting of song, dance, and music and usually featuring ornate costumes and scenery as well as characters from mythology. In the Renaissance, masques were a popular form of courtly entertainment, particularly during the reign of James I.) Ceres is the Roman goddess of agriculture, or mother earth. At the beginning of the masque, she is called upon by Iris on behalf of Juno to celebrate "a contract of true love" between Ferdinand and Miranda (IV.i.84). Ceres introduces the lesson of chastity by warning Iris that she will not stay if Venus and her son, Cupid, have been invited. Ceres resents Venus and Cupid for helping "Dis" (Pluto) to abduct her daughter, Proserpine, to be his queen in the underworld. Eventually, Ceres joins Juno in singing a "marriage-blessing" to the young couple (IV.i.106).

Ferdinand:

He is the son and heir of King Alonso of Naples. Ferdinand is the first to leap overboard during the tempest, and in keeping with Prospero's plan, he lands on the island alone, separated from his father's group. Ariel uses song to convince the youth that his father is dead and that the island is enchanted, as well as to lure him into the presence of Miranda:

Full fadom five thy father lies,
Of his bones are coral made:
Those are pearls that were his eyes:
Nothing of him that doth fade,
But doth suffer a sea-change
Into something rich and strange.
(I.ii.397-402)

When he first encounters Prospero's daughter, Ferdinand is struck by her beauty. In fact, his first reaction to Miranda resembles her intial reaction to him: she believes that he is a spirit rather than a man, and he wonders whether she is goddess of the island (I.ii.410-28). The two of them quickly fall in love with one another, but Prospero, who has foreseen the match and secretly approves of it, decides to test

> "... at Prospero's command, Ariel stirs up the tempest which strands Alonso and his followers on the island (I.i)."

Ferdinand's love, "lest too light winning / Make the prize light," and forces the youth into servitude on the pretense that he is a spy (I.ii.452-53). Ferdinand replies that the loss of his father, and his own imprisonment and hard labor "are but light" to him as long as he is near Miranda (I.ii.486-94).

Ferdinand appears again in III.i, bearing firewood for Prospero and remaining steady in his love for Miranda. Prospero frees him from servitude in IV.i, blessing his engagement to Miranda with a betrothal masque. At the close of the play, Ferdinand is reunited with his father, who also gives his blessing to the marriage.

Miranda's love for Ferdinand is influenced to some extent by her innocence and inexperience. Up to this point she has seen only two other men: her father and Caliban. By contrast, Ferdinand bases his love for Miranda on all the women he has seen and known at his father's court, and concludes that while they all possessed at least one defect of some sort, she on the other hand is "perfect" and "peerless" (III.i.47).

The union of Ferdinand and Miranda has been said to symbolize the play's theme of reconciliation, bringing together as it does their parents, Alonso and Prospero, who were once bitter enemies.

Francisco:

He is a lord attending King Alonso of Naples, and a minor character in the play. After the tempest, Francisco is washed ashore in company with Alonso and several other members of the king's court. In II.i.114-23, he tries unsuccessfully to reassure the downhearted Alonso that his son, Ferdinand, survived the shipwreck (in some editions of the play, these lines are spoken by Gonzalo). Francisco's efforts to instill optimism in the king are undermined by Sebastian's assertion that Alonso himself is to blame for Ferdinand's fate. Francisco speaks once more in III.iii.40, when he briefly comments

> **"... Caliban considers himself mistreated and overworked. He bitterly accuses Prospero of befriending him in order to take advantage of his gratitude and rob him of the island which he considers his birthright ... (I.ii.331-39, 341-42)."**

on the strange spirits who deliver the illusory banquet conjured up by Prospero to torment the king.

Gonzalo:

He is an honest and trusted advisor to King Alonso of Naples. In I.ii.160-68, we learn that twelve years ago, when Prospero was usurped and he and his daughter, Miranda, were set adrift at sea, Gonzalo took pity on the two of them, supplying them not only with the food and water necessary to survive, but also with those things that make life easier:

> Some food we had, and some fresh water, that
> A noble Neapolitan, Gonzalo,
> Out of his charity, who being then appointed
> Master of this design, did give us, with
> Rich garments, linens, stuffs, and necessaries,
> Which since have steaded much; so of his
>   gentleness,
> Knowing I lov'd my books, he furnish'd me
> From mine own library with volumes that
> I prize above my dukedom.

Among these books are Prospero's volumes of magic, which enable him to control the spirits of the island and, as it happens, to create the tempest that brings Alonso and his court ashore.

Gonzalo is unusual among Alonso's stranded courtiers for his integrity and optimism. After the tempest washes them ashore in II.i.1-9, he tries to comfort his king by remarking on the "miracle" of their survival. When Alonso refuses consolation, Gonzalo tries to distract him with his own definition of the ideal comonwealth (II.i.148-57; 160-65). It is revealing that Prospero's treacherous brother, Antonio, and Alonso's equally untrustworthy brother,

Sebastian, systematically react with sarcasm to Gonzalo's cheerful efforts.

In II.i.300-05, Ariel wakes Gonzalo from his enchanted sleep just in time to save Alonso from being murdered by Sebastian and Antonio. Prospero spares "'the good old Lord Gonzalo'" from the madness which he subsequently inflicts on the others (V.i.8-19). At the close of the play, Prospero embraces Gonzalo as a "noble friend, / . . . whose honor cannot / Be measur'd or confin'd" (V.i.120-22).

Noting that Prospero's illusions are seen differently by each of the castaways, critics have observed that, significantly, Gonzalo is the only one of the king's followers to notice that their clothes are clean and dry in spite of the tempest; furthermore, apart from Adrian's comment in II.i.47 that the air is sweet, Gonzalo is alone in his assessment of the island as green and filled with "every thing advantageous to life" (II.i.50).

Iris:

She is a character in the betrothal masque created by Prospero to honor and educate the newly engaged Miranda and Ferdinand; the masque is performed by Ariel along with a group of "meaner," or lesser, spirits (IV.i.35-138). Iris is the "many-colored" goddess of the rainbow (IV.i.76), and as Juno's messenger she is the first to appear in the masque, summoning Ceres to wait upon her queen. Iris reinforces the betrothal masque's theme of prenuptial chastity when she reassures Ceres that the scandalous Venus and Cupid have not been invited to the celebration. She also mentions that Venus and her son had hoped to bewitch Miranda and Ferdinand into sleeping with one another before marriage, but were disappointed when the virtuous couple could not be tempted to break their vow of chastity (IV.i.92-100).

Juno:

She is a character in the betrothal masque created by Prospero to honor and educate the newly engaged Miranda and Ferdinand; the masque is performed by Ariel along with a group of "meaner," or lesser, spirits (IV.i.35-138). In Roman mythology, Juno is the queen of heaven, goddess of marriage and women, and wife of Jupiter. She appears in the masque along with Ceres to bless the young couple with a prosperous life together and fine children, but also to remind them not to have sex before marriage.

Mariners:

They are the crew on board the ship bearing Alonso to and from Tunis. When the ship gets caught in Prospero's tempest, the mariners are ordered by the master and boatswain to keep it from going aground, but in I.i.51, they announce that "all [is] lost" and that shipwreck is imminent (I.i.51). In I.ii.226-37, we learn that Ariel has in fact steered the ship safely into harbor and has charmed the mariners to sleep below deck while Prospero carries out his plans against Alonso and his courtiers.

Master (of a ship):

He is the commander of the ship bearing Alonso and members of his court from Tunis back to Naples when it is run aground by Prospero's storm. The master appears briefly in I.i.1, 3-4, to give orders to the boatswain during the tempest. This marks his only appearance during the storm, despite Alonso's insistence on speaking to him rather than merely to the boatswain. The master's next and final appearance in the play (this time without dialogue) occurs in V.i, when he and the boatswain are led onstage by Ariel. The boatswain, rather than the master, describes the remarkable preservation of the ship.

Miranda:

She is the daughter of Prospero, the usurped duke of Milan. Miranda, who is approximately fifteen years old, makes her first appearance in the play at I.ii.1-13, where she vividly reveals to us Prospero's powers as a magician while at the same time showing her compassion and empathy by begging her father to stop the tempest that he has created:

> If by your art, my dearest father, you have
> Put the wild waters in this roar, allay them.
> The sky it seems would pour down stinking pitch,
> But that the sea, mounting to th' welkin's cheek,
> Dashes the fire out. O! I have suffered
> With those that I saw suffer. A brave vessel
> (Who had, no doubt, some noble creature in her)
> Dash'd all to pieces! O, the cry did knock
> Against my very heart.

After reassuring her that all on board the ship are safe, Prospero acquaints his daughter with the story of her past—information which he has concealed from her until now, when he deems that both she and circumstances are ready. Miranda's name is derived from the word "admire," or wonder, and in fact, she listens with wonder and rapt attention to her father's description of his former life as duke of Milan and of their arrival on the island, calling it a tale which "would cure deafness" (I.ii.106).

> **At the close of the play, Prospero embraces Gonzalo as a 'noble friend, / . . . whose honor cannot / Be measur'd or confin'd' (V.i.120-22)."**

Miranda's capacity for wonder is a result of her innocence. She has lived on the island for twelve years with no one else around her but Prospero, the spirit Ariel, and Caliban (who tried to rape her, and who is regarded by her as more of a beast than a man). All that she remembers of her former life are the women who tended her (I.ii.47), and in keeping with the fanciful atmosphere of the play, this memory comes to her "rather like a dream than an assurance" (I.ii.45).

Prospero has been his daughter's only teacher. Remarking that her education with him has been more thorough and profitable than that of other girls who "have more time / For vainer hours, and tutors not so careful" (I.ii.172-74), he prepares her for her introduction to the world, explaining to her that among the people who have washed ashore are his enemies, Alonso and Antonio.

Nothing, however, prepares Miranda for her first view of Alonso's son, Ferdinand. She shows her inexperience by mistaking him for a spirit, and in response to her father's reassurance that he is a man, she remarks: "I might call him / A thing divine, for nothing natural / I ever saw so noble" (I.ii.418-20). She promptly falls in love with Ferdinand, despite her father's pretended disapproval. When Prospero tests Ferdinand's affections by calling him a spy and sentencing him to servitude, Miranda rushes to the youth's defense, asserting that "There's nothing ill can dwell in such a temple" (I.ii.458).

Miranda's next appearance is in III.i, where she expresses her compassion for Ferdinand as he wearily collects wood for her father, and where the two of them vow to marry each other.

Prospero drops his pretense of disapproval in IV.i, honoring the couple with a magical betrothal masque. In keeping with his role as Miranda's teacher, Prospero has the masquers remind the

> **Nothing . . . prepares Miranda for her first view of Alonso's son, Ferdinand. She shows her inexperience by mistaking him for a spirit, and in response to her father's reassurance that he is a man, she remarks: 'I might call him / A thing divine, for nothing natural / I ever saw so noble' (I.ii.418-20)."**

inexperienced Miranda about the importance of prenuptial chastity (IV.i.91-101).

Miranda appears once more in V.i. where she is presented for the first time to her future father-in-law, the newly repentant Alonso. Her reaction to Alonso and his courtiers again demonstrates her capacity for innocent wonder when she exclaims, in an often-quoted passage, "How many goodly creatures are there here! / How beauteous mankind is! O brave new world / That has such people in't!" (V.i.182-84).

Critics have remarked that since Miranda and Ferdinand were not involved in their fathers' conflict, their engagement represents a better future for Prospero and Alonso by marking an end to the discord between them.

Nymphs:

They are characters in the betrothal masque created by Prospero to honor and educate the newly engaged Miranda and Ferdinand; the masque is performed by Ariel along with a group of "meaner," or lesser, spirits (IV.i.35-138). These water nymphs, or "Naiades, of the windring brooks" are summoned by Juno and Ceres via Iris to "celebrate / A contract of true love" by dancing with the reapers (IV.i.128, 132-33). Appropriate to the theme of the betrothal masque, the nymphs are "temperate," or chaste (IV.i.132). Their dance with the reapers is abruptly broken off and the masque ended when Prospero suddenly remembers that he must thwart

Caliban's "foul conspiracy" against him (IV.i.139-40).

Prospero:

He is the usurped duke of Milan and the father of Miranda, as well as a powerful magician. Prospero is responsible for the tempest which casts Alonso and his courtiers upon the island where he and his daughter live. Faced with his daughter's distress at the storm and the foundering ship, Prospero concedes that he has caused the tempest, but assures her that no harm has come to any of the passengers. Declaring that "I have done nothing, but in care of thee" (I.ii.16), he doffs his magic robes and tells Miranda the story of their past. Twelve years ago, he explains, he was not merely the "master of a full poor cell," but the rightful duke of Milan and therefore a "prince of power" (I.ii.20, 55). As duke, he was more interested in his books and "secret studies" than in ruling his city-state, so he unwisely entrusted the running of his government to his brother, Antonio (I.ii.74-77). Unfortunately, this newly received power "awake'd an evil nature" in Antonio, who conspired with King Alonso of Naples, to unseat Prospero and take his title (I.ii.93). The duke, however, was so popular with his people that Antonio and Alonso didn't dare to assassinate him; instead they cast him adrift on the ocean with his infant daughter, eventually to land on the island.

Prospero concludes his narrative by observing that his luck has since changed for the better: his enemies Alonso and Antonio were aboard the ship caught in the tempest, and they are now on the island—at the mercy of the duke whom they usurped.

During the three to four hours following the storm, Prospero controls the action of the play and is thus the only character, apart from Ariel, who is aware of all that occurs. He involves himself directly in the courtship between Ferdinand and Miranda, first enslaving Ferdinand in order to test his constancy and afterward lecturing them both on the virtue of chastity, reinforcing his lesson with the betrothal masque (I.ii.451-53; IV.i.35-138). For the most part, however, Prospero remains aloof from those he is punishing. He relies on Ariel to awaken Gonzalo in time to prevent Antonio and Sebastian from murdering Alonso (II.i.297-305). Likewise, it is Ariel and not Prospero who appears directly before Antonio, Sebastian, and Alonso to whisk away the false banquet, condemn the three of them as "men of sin," and punish them temporarily with insanity (III.iii.53-58). It is also Ariel rather than Prospero who participates most actively in the punishment of Stephano, Trinculo, and Caliban, luring them with music into the ''filthy-mantled pool,'' tempting them with ''glistering apparel,'' and, at Prospero's command, sending goblins to plague them with cramps and pinches (IV.i.182, 193, 258-60).

At the close of the play Prospero confronts all of his enemies directly and rebukes them for their ill-treatment of him and his daughter. At the same time, he introduces the theme of reconciliation, making peace with Alonso through the marriage of their children, Miranda and Ferdinand, and even forgiving his treacherous brother, Antonio (V.i.185-200, 75-79).

Prospero has been described as godlike in his detachment, doling out punishment and regulating the other characters' perceptions of reality. He has also been compared to Christ for his redemption of the sinful Alonso and his followers.

Alternatively, Prospero has been called domineering and exploitative for the manner in which he manipulates his own daughter and Ferdinand. Further, he has been condemned as cruel with regard to his harsh rejection of Ariel's impatience for freedom (''If thou more murmur'st,'' he warns the airy spirit in I.ii.294-96, ''I will rend an oak / And peg thee in his knotty entrails till / Thou hast howl'd away twelve winters''). It has also been argued that his takeover of the island and his enslavement of Caliban smack of colonialism. According to these viewpoints, Prospero is as much in need of self-knowledge and redemption as are his enemies, and while he starts out patriarchal, colonial, and vengeful in his attitude, by the close of the play he has recognized his limitations and has also learned forgiveness. What's more, it has been suggested that Prospero must learn to control his anger with reason, and to temper his sometimes arcane studies with the practical art of government before he is ready to return to Milan as duke, and that once he accomplishes this, he resembles the ideal Renaissance Man.

Some critics have asserted that Prospero—who manipulates scenes and events in the play, stages masques, and directs the actions of other characters—represents Shakespeare's craft as playwright. Noting that *The Tempest* is likely to have been the last play which Shakespeare wrote completely on his own, these critics argue further that the play serves in part as Shakespeare's farewell to the

> **During the three to four hours following the storm, Prospero controls the action of the play and is thus the only character, apart from Ariel, who is aware of all that occurs.''**

theater, particularly when toward the end of the play, Prospero reviews his career as magician and declares his intention to retire: ''I'll break my staff, / Bury it certain fadoms in the earth, / And deeper than did ever plummet sound / I'll drown my book'' (V.i.54-57). These critics also refer to the elegiac tone of some of Prospero's lines—in particular, his famous observation to Miranda and Ferdinand that ''We are such stuff / As dreams are made on; and our little life / Is rounded with a sleep'' (IV.i.156-58).

Reapers:

They are characters in the betrothal masque created by Prospero to honor and educate the newly engaged Miranda and Ferdinand; the masque is performed by Ariel along with a group of ''meaner,'' or lesser, spirits (IV.i.35-138). Iris summons the reapers to join the nymphs in celebrating Miranda and Ferdinand's ''contract of true love'' (IV.i.133). Their dance with the nymphs is abruptly broken off and the masque ended when Prospero suddenly remembers that he must thwart Caliban's ''foul conspiracy'' against him (IV.i.139-40).

Sebastian:

He is the traitorous brother of King Alonso of Naples. Sebastian reveals his villainous temperament as early as I.i.40-41, when he calls the boatswain—who is struggling to keep their ship afloat during the tempest—a ''bawling, blasphemous, incharitable dog.'' Once ashore in II.i, he joins Antonio in making sarcastic remarks against Gonzalo each time the old counselor tries to cheer up the despairing Alonso. In II.i.124-36, Sebastian blames his brother for the shipwreck and for the apparent drowning of Ferdinand, arguing that if Alonso had agreed to let his daughter marry a

European rather than the king of Tunis, then the trip to Africa would have been unnecessary and the tempest would have been avoided. In II.i.202-96, Sebastian consents to Antonio's plot to assassinate Alonso; the two men are stopped in their attempt in the nick of time by Ariel and Gonzalo (II.i.297-307). Along with Alonso and Antonio, Sebastian is driven mad by Ariel for his sins (III.iii.53-60). Prospero forgives Sebastian in V.i, and restores him to health with his brother and Antonio. Later, when Prospero shows the three of them that Ferdinand has survived the tempest and is playing chess with Miranda, the reformed Sebastian describes the event as "A most high miracle!" (V.i.177).

Ship-Master:

See Master

Spirits:

They are the "strange shapes" and "meaner fellows," or less powerful spirits, who help Ariel perform illusions such as the false banquet in III.iii, the betrothal masque in IV.i, and the hounds which hunt Stephano, Trinculo, and Caliban in IV.i. Their appearance enhances the magical quality of the play and emphasizes the powers of Prospero, who can summon and dismiss them at will.

Stephano:

He is Alonso's butler and also a drunk. Along with Trinculo and Caliban, Stephano participates in the play's comic subplot. He escapes the tempest-tossed ship and makes it to the island by floating on "a butt of sack [Spanish wine] which the sailors heav'd overboard" (II.ii.121-22). He first appears in II.ii, where he inadvertently frightens Caliban (who initially thinks that Stephano and Trinculo are a couple of Prospero's spirits sent to punish him), afterward winning Caliban's adoration by plying him with wine. The drunken Caliban vows to worship Stephano, offering to gather wood for the butler and to show him the best food and water supplies on the island—just as he once did for Prospero. In III.ii Stephano enters into a conspiracy with Caliban and Trinculo to assassinate Prospero and become ruler of the island. Their plot is stymied by Ariel, who uses his music to lure the three drunks into a "filthy-mantled pool" (IV.i.182), distracts Stephano and Trinculo with fine clothing (IV.i.194-254), and finally chases and torments all three of them with spirits shaped like hunting dogs (IV.i.255-

66). Aching with cramps and bruises, Stephano repents of having wanted to be "king o' the isle" (V.i.288-89). Thus the comic subplot in which Stephano participates mirrors the more threatening conspiracy of Sebastian and Antonio against Alonso.

Trinculo:

He is Alonso's jester and a participant with Stephano and Caliban in the play's comic subplot. After the tempest, Trinculo is washed up on the island alone. In II.ii, he runs into Caliban, who has thrown himself on the ground to hide from what he thinks are Prospero's avenging spirits but what is in fact the arrival of Trinculo. Trinculo crawls under Caliban's cloak for shelter against another rainstorm, and shortly afterward Stephano appears, drunkenly mistaking the two of them for a four-legged, two-voiced monster. Trinculo takes part in Caliban and Stephano's drunken plot to assassinate Prospero, and like them, he receives a punishment of pinches, cramps, and bruises from Prospero's spirits once the plot is discovered.

When he first finds Caliban, Trinculo observes that this "strange fish" could be worth a lot of money in England, where "they will not give a doit to relieve a lame beggar, [but] they will lay out ten to see a dead Indian" (II.i.27, 31-33). Thus the jester articulates what has been identified as the play's focus on the New World and England's subsequent fascination with any discoveries from the Americas.

Further Reading

Berger, Harry, Jr. "Miraculous Harp: A Reading of Shakespeare's *Tempest*." *Shakespeare Studies* 5 (1969): 253-83.
    Berger contends that a preoccupation with Prospero's renunciation of his magic as well as with the theme of forgiveness is overly sentimental, and that Prospero is in fact more concerned with his final dramatic performance. To support his views, Berger closely analyzes Prospero's interactions with Caliban and Ariel.

Bevington, David. Introduction to *The Tempest,* by William Shakespeare. In *The Complete Works of Shakespeare,* edited by David Bevington, 1526-29. Updated 4th ed. New York: Longman, 1997.
    Bevington argues that *The Tempest* presents a magical world of the art and the imagination which is at the same time "no escape from reality," and that its principal character, Prospero, undergoes a learning

experience. Bevington also discusses Caliban as a sympathetic character.

Cantor, Paul A. "Prospero's Republic: The Politics of Shakespeare's *The Tempest.*" In *Shakespeare as Political Thinker,* edited by John Alvis and Thomas G. West, 239-55. Durham: Carolina Academic Press, 1981.

Cantor asserts that Prospero ultimately becomes a capable governor when he discovers how to combine his understanding of human nature with his power to rule.

Kermode, Frank. Introduction and Appendices to *The Tempest,* by William Shakespeare, edited by Frank Kermode, xi-xciii, 135-65. The Arden Edition of the Works of William Shakespeare. London: Methuen and Co., Ltd., 1964.

In his overview of *The Tempest,* Kermode looks at the play's publication and performance dates, and discusses the play's theme of art or culture versus nature. He also examines the play's connection to the Renaissance fascination with exploration and the New World.

Lindley, David. "Music, Masque, and Meaning in *The Tempest.*" In *The Court Masque,* edited by David Lindley, 47-59. Manchester: Manchester University Press, 1984.

Lindley discusses the importance of music and the Jacobean dramatic form known as the masque to the themes in *The Tempest,* and examines how Prospero uses masques and music to manipulate characters and events.

Marx, Leo. "Shakespeare's American Fable." *Massachusetts Review* 2 (Autumn 1960): 40-71.

Marx examines the Renaissance's conflicting attitudes to the New World as either a paradise or a brutal wilderness, and argues that *The Tempest* encompasses both of these perspectives.

Murry, John Middleton. "Shakespeare's Dream," in *Shakespeare,* 380-412. London: Jonathan Cape, 1936.

Murry examines Prospero's role in shaping reality and emphasizes the significance of education and self-knowledge in the transformation of the characters in the play.

Orgel, Stephen. Introduction to *The Tempest,* by William Shakespeare, edited by Stephen Orgel, 1-56. Oxford: Oxford University Press, 1987.

Orgel provides an overview of the play, including a discussion of themes and characters, as well as a presentation of the major critical interpretations.

Robinson, James E. "Time and *The Tempest.*" *Journal of English and Germanic Philology* 63 (1964): 255-67.

Robinson focuses on the significance of time in the play—real versus magic time, and also the three-hour time span of the play's action.

Seiden, Melvin. "Utopianism in *The Tempest.*" *Modern Language Quarterly* 31 (1970): 3-21.

Seiden contrasts Gonzalo's conception of the ideal commonwealth with Prospero's grim assessment of reality and argues that these two views together provide us with a better understanding of human nature and its potential.

Smith, Hallett. Introduction to *The Tempest,* by William Shakespeare. In *The Riverside Shakespeare,* edited by G. Blakemore Evans, 1606-10. Boston: Houghton-Mifflin Co., 1974.

Smith points out that the play is highly theatrical, with its emphasis on special effects, shows, and music. He focuses on the importance of time in the play, and examines the play's characters, contrasting, for example, Ariel with Caliban.

Spurgeon, Caroline, F. E. "Leading Motives in the Romances." In *Shakespeare's Imagery and What It Tells Us,* 291-308. Cambridge: Cambridge University Press, 1971.

Spurgeon focuses on Shakespeare's use of sound and particularly ocean imagery in the play, arguing that through this imagery, the playwright is demonstrating his awareness of "the common flow of life through all things."

Summers, Joseph H. "The Anger of Prospero: *The Tempest.*" In *Dreams of Love and Power: On Shakespeare's Plays,* 137-58. Oxford: Clarendon Press, 1984.

Summers argues that Prospero's anger humanizes him, and that he is freed of it during the course of the play, thanks to the opportunity for a new life as represented through Miranda and Ferdinand.

Wilson, J. Dover. *The Meaning of* The Tempest. Newcastle upon Tyne: The Literary Society of Newcastle upon Tyne, 1936.

Wilson sees *The Tempest* as a "summary" of Shakespeare's spiritual development as well as his "farewell to the theatre."

The Tragedy of Timon of Athens

circa 1607-08

Plot Summary

Act I:

Timon of Athens is set in ancient Greece. The first act takes place in Timon's palatial home. A poet, a painter, a jeweller, and a merchant enter a formal reception room in the house. Each of them has brought something they hope Timon will admire and want to purchase. Timon comes into the room, with several people crowding around him seeking his support or patronage. One of these is a messenger from Timon's friend Ventidius. When Timon hears that Ventidius has been thrown in jail because he can't repay a creditor, Timon quickly offers to pay the debt. An old man arrives, complaining that Timon's servant Lucilius is courting his daughter; Timon offers to put up as much money on behalf of Lucilius as the man means to bestow on his daughter, and the old Athenian agrees to the match. In the great banquet hall, Timon hosts a magnificent feast for his guests. During the course of the evening, they are entertained by a masque in which women dressed as mythical Amazons dance to the accompaniment of lutes. At the close of this lavish occasion, Timon gives one friend a precious jewel, another a valuable horse, as both his steward and his friend Apemantus try in vain to persuade him of the folly of his generosity.

Act II:

On the following day, a money-lender notes how much Timon owes him and other usurers; he

instructs his servant Caphis to go to Timon and demand repayment immediately. When Caphis arrives at Timon's house, he encounters Isidore and Varro—the servants of two other usurers. Timon appears, and the three servants insist that he pay off his debts to their masters. Timon draws the steward aside and asks for an explanation of his financial situation; the steward tells Timon that he has tried to inform him about his increasing indebtedness on many occasions, but Timon wouldn't listen. As the steward lays out in grim detail the extent of his master's financial ruin, Timon assures him there's nothing to worry about, for the friends to whom he's been so generous will undoubtedly come to his assistance. Timon sends the steward and three of his servants to seek money from these friends.

Act III:

Timon's servants appeal to three of his friends—Lucullus, Lucius, and Sempronius—but each of them declines to help. A crowd of servants sent by various Athenian usurers gathers at Timon's house. When Timon tries to pass through, they block his way and thrust their masters' bills at him, but they soon realize there's little hope of recovering payment and so they depart. Timon instructs his steward to invite all the friends who've turned him down to come to his house for another feast. The scene changes to a site where three senators are discussing a murder trial currently in progress. Alcibiades joins them and begs them to show mercy toward the defendant, an old and dear friend of his, but they refuse. When he reminds them of the debt of gratitude they owe him for his service in their wars, the senators banish him from Athens. In the final scene of Act III, the friends whom Timon has invited to dine with him arrive at his house. Servants carry in covered dishes and set them at each man's place. When the dishes are uncovered, it's revealed that they contain nothing but warm water—which Timon hurls in their faces, along with curses and insults.

Act IV:

Outside the walls of Athens, Timon delivers a scathing curse on the city and its inhabitants, and turns his back on it forever. At the place he selects for his exile—a cave near some woods and a barren seashore—Timon invokes nature to destroy mankind. As he digs for roots to eat, he discovers a hoard of gold. Alcibiades, accompanied by two prostitutes, unexpectedly encounters Timon. Learning that Alcibiades intends to make war on Athens, Timon urges him to destroy the city and wreak havoc on even its most innocent inhabitants. He offers his old friend gold to help pay the soldiers, and when the women see it, they beg him to give them gold, too. After Alcibiades and the women have left, Apemantus appears. He urges Timon to return to the city. Timon's response is a flood of verbal abuse. Some bandits, having heard rumors of Timon's new-found treasure, arrive to rob him—but Timon confounds them by giving them more than they could ever hope to steal. Timon's next visitor is his steward, whose faithfulness demonstrates that the world holds at least one honest man. Timon drives him away.

Act V:

The poet and painter seek out Timon. He sends them off with insults. The steward reappears, this time with two Athenian senators, who apologize profusely for their earlier treatment of Timon. They plead with him to persuade Alcibiades not to attack the city. Timon, however, says he doesn't care if every man, woman, and child in Athens is slaughtered. The senators are dejected, and they depart with the steward. One of Alcibiades's soldiers, sent in search of Timon, discovers his grave instead. Using wax to lift the inscription carved into Timon's tombstone, the soldier hurries back to Alcibiades. Outside the walls of Athens, Alcibiades listens to two senators plead with him to spare the city. Alcibiades yields to their entreaties, promising to punish Timon's enemies and his own, but leave other citizens unharmed. The soldier arrives and announces that Timon is dead. Alcibiades reads aloud the epitaph the soldier has copied. Then he enters Athens, vowing to temper justice with mercy.

Modern Connections

The historical characters in *Timon of Athens* lived nearly 2,500 years ago. Almost four hundred years have passed since the play was written. Yet the issues it raises are timeless—applicable to every period in history when materialism and corruption overwhelm humane social values. In 1973, at a small theater in Paris, a production of *Timon* crossed cultural, historical, and racial boundaries. Timon was played as a golden-haired, northern European youth; at the first banquet, entertainers performed a Middle Eastern-inspired dance to Arabian music;

Apemantus was played by a black actor, costumed in a way to suggest that he was a native of northern Africa. This production, directed by Peter Brook, underscored the universality of the play.

Timon of Athens depicts a society corrupted by greed. Many of its citizens are in debt to money-lenders. Conspicuous consumption—to use a twentieth-century term—leads Timon to bankruptcy. His natural inclination to entertain lavishly and dispense freely what he thinks is a limitless fortune leaves him at the mercy of his creditors. In the late twentieth century, personal indebtedness is at an all-time high. Persuaded by advertisers that happiness means new cars, new technologies, fashionable clothes, etcetera, many people charge purchases on credit cards and trust that they'll be able to pay for these things sometime in the future. As a result, an increasing number of people find themselves in bankruptcy court.

In modern society, materialism is criticized on several fronts, and basic values are asserted. But which values are impermanent and which ones endure? Timon imagines a society in which each person treats his assets as if they belonged to his friends as well as himself. This seems unrealistic. But what are the alternatives? When confronted with the truth, an idealist such as Timon may respond with bitterness and disillusion. On the other hand, a pragmatic approach to life may lead to Apemantus's attitude of empty cynicism. One can withdraw from society, rejecting its values, as Timon does; attempt to force it to conform to one's own views, as Alcibiades does; or take on the role of perpetual critic, like Apemantus.

When cynics such as Apemantus speak out, how do people generally respond? In the history of human society, truth-tellers have seldom been listened to. Their messages are unappealing. It's difficult to admit that we may be at fault—or that what we value has no intrinsic worth. Timon's refusal to listen to Apemantus and his steward is not so hard to understand.

Timon's generosity is problematical. On the one hand, he seems motivated by genuine open-handedness, a willingness to share his good fortune with everyone else—his servants as well as his friends. But his generosity is publicized; he demonstrates it in front of others, who cannot help but be aware of his gifts. If the highest level of charity is to give anonymously, to an unknown recipient, Timon falls short of the ideal. Is his generosity—even to his servant Lucilus—true charity?

Timon expects a return of some kind for his bounty, and he is devastated when he doesn't receive it. To give without wanting or expecting something in return requires an extraordinary degree of unselfishness. What is our response when we give time, or money, or something else of value to others—perhaps some charitable institution—and the result isn't what we had hoped it would be? What happens if the gift is used in ways we hadn't anticipated?

Finally, the play raises the question of how to respond when we are mistreated. Timon curses everyone who betrays him—and every other human being as well. There is no evidence that he understands human frailties, or that he forgives the people who have wronged him. This rigidity alienates him from his fellow human beings and leaves him physically and emotionally separated from society. But is the biblical injunction to turn the other cheek appropriate when friends betray us? Timon appears to have no doubts about how to respond. The rest of us may not be so sure.

Characters

Alcibiades:

An Athenian general and statesman, he lived in the fifth century B.C. During the Peloponnesian War (431-404 B.C.) between Athens and Sparta, Alcibiades served as a commander of the Athenian army; later he switched his allegiance and led Spartan forces against Athens.

In *Timon of Athens*, Alcibiades is portrayed as a man of action. He is a rationalist, fully convinced of the coexistence of good and evil in the world. He is also pragmatic; his tactics are both efficient and effective. Furthermore, he is depicted as an honorable man who remains loyal to his friends. Finally, Alcibiades is a survivor, and he is responsible for restoring order to Athens at the close of the play.

Alcibiades is present at Timon's first banquet. When Timon suggests that Alcibiades would rather "be at a breakfast of enemies than a dinner of friends" (I.ii.76-77), Alcibiades says this would be true only if all the enemies were freshly slaughtered and their corpses still bleeding. Alcibiades's fiery nature is most evident in III.v, when he pleads with some senators to spare the life of a dear friend of his. He acknowledges that the man is technically guilty of murder; but he argues that the deed was committed at the height of passion and that the man was provoked to it by an insult to his honor. Passion and anger are qualities highly regarded in a soldier, Alcibiades continues, and, at some time in their lives, all men experience these emotions. He urges the senators to temper justice with mercy, but they refuse. Frustrated by their obstinacy, Alcibiades reminds them of the long years of military service he has given Athens. Stung by his remarks, the senators banish him forever. He accuses them of corrupting the Senate with their money-lending and their senile minds, and after they leave he explodes in rage. Gaining control of his emotions, he vows to turn his "spleen and fury" (III.v.112) into calculated vengeance against Athens and its leaders.

In the course of raising a private army to attack Athens, Alcibiades unexpectedly encounters Timon in the wilderness. Timon's appearance has changed so much that Alcibiades fails to recognize him at first. Moved by the pitiable condition of his old friend, he offers Timon sympathy and consolation. Timon rejects these, but when he learns that Alcibiades means to attack Athens, he says there *is* some service he can do: show no mercy and slay every man, woman, and child in the city. Alcibiades accepts some of Timon's gold so he can pay his soldiers, but he declines to take his advice.

In the play's final scene, Alcibiades and his army approach Athens' city walls. Several senators plead with him to spare the city, offering to come to terms with him in his quest for vengeance. Alcibiades accepts the offer, swearing that the only Athenians who will be killed are those who personally wronged either him or Timon. A soldier whom Alcibiades had sent to seek out Timon arrives with a copy of the epitaph engraved on Timon's tomb. Alcibiades reads it aloud and then eulogizes his old friend, forgiving Timon's faults and emphasizing his nobility.

Alcibiades introduces the theme of mercy in III.v and raises it again at the conclusion of the play. He will avenge Timon and himself, but he means to spare those who took no part in betraying them. Despite Alcibiades's intentions to turn swords into plowshares and heal the wounds of political strife, it's questionable whether he will be able to reform Athens and rid it of corruption. Some commentators

> **When Timon suggests that Alcibiades would rather 'be at a breakfast of enemies than a dinner of friends' (I.ii.76-77), Alcibiades says this would be true only if all the enemies were freshly slaughtered and their corpses still bleeding."**

have noted ambiguities in his character, pointing to his sensuality and his eagerness to take up arms against his own country when his honor is offended.

Apemantus:

A deeply cynical man, he observes his fellow citizens with acute insight and never hesitates to speak the truth. On the other hand, he expounds his views rudely, with no attempt at grace or civility. His judgments of people—for example, the poet, the painter, and the Athenian lords—are all proven to be accurate. He tries to teach Timon that the Athenian lords are shallow, but his advice falls on deaf ears. Apemantus is depicted as vulgar, surly, and boorish; indeed, he is listed in the cast of characters as a *churlish* philosopher. Yet he holds a mirror up to others that faithfully reflects their natures.

In his first appearance, Apemantus declares that all men in Athens are scoundrels. This is the viewpoint Timon will adopt for himself after his friends have betrayed him. During the play's opening scene, Apemantus insults, in turn, the poet, the painter, and two Athenian lords. He takes particular aim at their deceitful flattery of Timon. Apemantus grudgingly joins the other guests at the banquet, complaining to Timon that they are all parasites. Before the meal begins, he offers a prayer to the gods, thanking them for making him a man who trusts no one. Throughout the dinner, he makes coarse and unflattering remarks, and he uses the masque as an opportunity to attack the thin veneer of manners that covers up rampant corruption. At the close of the banquet, when all the other guests have left, Apemantus warns Timon he is spending money on his false friends so lavishly that he'll soon be bankrupt. Timon dismisses his advice and refuses to listen to him.

Apemantus visits Timon in the wilderness and urges him to adopt another strategy than self-exile. He points out that while Timon is abasing himself in his cave, those who betrayed him are living in ease back in Athens. Apemantus recommends that Timon return to the city and take on the role of flatterer himself. He charges Timon with self-indulgence, saying that he has chosen exile out of vanity and false pride. He accuses him of excessive emotionalism, noting that Timon has swung from boundless generosity to contempt of all mankind. Their exchanges gradually descend from rational, well-articulated justifications of their respective positions to mere epithets: ''Beast!'' ''Slave!'' ''Toad!'' ''Rogue, rogue, rogue!'' (IV.iii.371-74).

Some commentators hold that Apemantus offers Timon a kind of redemption—a dispassionate, disinterested knowledge of the world. Others think he only makes Timon's situation more unendurable. Perhaps Apemantus's cynicism is not formed on the basis of a lifetime's experience, but is rather an expression of his inherent crankiness. He is not a nobleman, and thus his criticism of people who are financially more successful than he is may be a case of sour grapes. Many commentators regard him as vain and egotistical, willfully proud of his ability to speak the truth in a way that offends all who hear him.

Bandits:

Having heard about Timon's discovery of a cache of gold, they connive to steal it. They present themselves to Timon as destitute soldiers, but he isn't fooled. Thrusting gold into their hands, Timon urges them to continue their life of crime—a suitable occupation in a world where ''All that you meet are thieves'' (IV.iii.446).

Caphis:

A servant who belongs to a money-lending senator, he is sent by his master to demand that Timon pay back the money he owes. Together with other usurers' servants, Caphis confronts Timon in II.ii. With this encounter, Timon begins to understand how deeply in debt he is. Caphis and the other usurers' servants also trade jokes with Apemantus and the Fool; their crude humor focuses on vice and corruption in Athens.

Cupid:

Representing the god of love, he introduces the masque—an entertainment comprising instrumental music and dancing—during the banquet in I.ii.

Flaminius:

One of Timon's servants, he is sent to appeal to Lucullus on behalf of his master. Lucullus declines to help Timon and offers Flaminius a bribe if he will tell Timon he never saw Lucullus. Flaminius flings the coins in the man's face and unleashes a blistering denunciation of this treacherous friend.

Flavius:

See Steward. (The steward is almost always referred to by his title. Timon calls him Flavius only once, at I.ii.157.)

Fool:

He is a jester whose employer is unnamed, though the Fool seems to imply that she (the Fool's employer) operates a house of prostitution. He appears in II.ii, in the company of Apemantus. They swap insults with a group of money-lenders' servants, and the Fool makes jokes about usurers, fools, and whoremasters.

Hortensius:

A usurer's servant, he appears at Timon's door in III.iv to demand repayment of a loan. Hortensius admits that he's ashamed to be doing this, because in the past his master benefitted from Timon's generosity.

Hostilius:

See Strangers

Isidore's Servant:

He appears in II.ii on behalf of his master, a money-lender, demanding that Timon pay back the money he has borrowed. With other usurers' servants, he insults Apemantus and the Fool when they arrive on the scene.

Jeweller:

In the play's first scene, he brings Timon a gemstone, in hopes that he'll buy it. The jeweller flatters Timon, telling him that the jewel's worth and beauty will be magnified if it's purchased and worn by such an eminent person.

Lords:

Several unnamed Athenian noblemen are guests at Timon's banquets. They are generally depicted as self-seeking parasites who fawn upon Timon, extol his virtues, and receive extravagant gifts from him. At the first banquet, several lords flatter Timon and remark on his lavish generosity. When Timon presents one lord with an expensive jewel and another with a fine horse, they fervently express their gratitude, swearing they will always hold him in the highest esteem. However, none of the lords comes to Timon's aid when he needs their help. At the second banquet, they apologize profusely for not sending Timon money when he asked for it, but their excuses ring hollow. Timon's prayer before the meal (III.vi.70-84) perplexes them. Even when he dumps basins of warm water over their heads and into their laps, they still seem bemused. Timon must be out of his mind, they say, for nothing else would explain his abrupt change of behavior. They appear to be wholly unaware of—or perhaps they're unwilling to acknowledge—the effect of their violations of the bonds of friendship.

Lucilius:

One of Timon's servants, he provides an example of Timon's generous nature. An old Athenian comes to Timon's house in I.i, complaining that Lucilius has been courting his daughter. When Timon offers to give his servant a handsome sum of money, the old man quickly withdraws his objections to the marriage of the two young people. Lucilius is properly grateful, promising Timon he will never forget the debt he owes him.

Lucius:

He is one of the noblemen who refuse to aid Timon when he appeals for their help. Lucius makes his first appearance in III.ii, talking with three other men who tell him they've heard that Timon is destitute. Lucius is skeptical of the rumors. When one of them says that Lucullus has denied Timon any assistance, Lucius appears shocked. Lucius acknowledges that he has been the recipient of Timon's generosity on several occasions, but he downplays the worth of the gifts: "money, plate, jewels, and such like trifles" (III.ii.21-22). Lucius declares that had Timon appealed to him rather than Lucullus, he would have found a true friend eager to serve him. At that moment, Servilius appears and offers him the chance to prove his words. Lucius lies, telling Servilius that while he'd like nothing better than to be able to come to the aid of his dear

> **Perhaps Apemantus's cynicism is not formed on the basis of a lifetime's experience, but is rather an expression of his inherent crankiness. He is not a nobleman, and thus his criticism of people who are financially more successful than he is may be a case of sour grapes."**

friend, all his money is tied up in investments and he has nothing left to give Timon. He sends Servilius off with false assurances of eternal good wishes for his noble and honorable friend Timon. Later, Lucius sends his own servant to the beleaguered Timon, demanding repayment of an old debt. Lucius may be one of the lords who attend Timon's first banquet, but he is not specified in that scene. At III.iv.111, Timon instructs his steward that Lucius is to be invited to the second, mock banquet.

Lucius's Servant:

He is sent by his master, allegedly one of Timon's closest friends, to recover money that Lucius has lent Timon. Lucius's servant's remarks at III.iv.21-13 indicate the mad spiral of debt Timon has accrued through generous gifts to his friends.

Lucullus:

He is one of Timon's false friends, a flatterer and an ungrateful recipient of Timon's generosity. When Timon's servant Flaminius arrives at his house, Lucullus's first thought is that he's bringing yet another gift from Timon. When Flaminius tells him why he's come, Lucullus pretends to treat him as an equal, a man of the world like himself. "This is no time to lend money," says Lucullus (III.i.41-42), particularly when the potential borrower cannot provide as a pledge of repayment anything of greater value than friendship. Lucullus tries to bribe Flaminius, offering him money if he'll report to Timon that he wasn't able to locate Lucullus. Flaminius throws the coins back in his face. Lucullus is one of the guests at the first banquet (I.ii). Timon gives instructions that he be invited to the second one, in Act III, so Lucullus may be one of the unnamed lords present on that occasion.

Masquers:

These are women who, costumed as mythical warriors, dance and play on lutes for the entertainment of Timon's guests at the banquet in I.ii.

Merchant:

He is one of four men, known only by their occupations, who appear at Timon's house in the play's opening scene. Unlike his companions, he never indicates what he has brought for Timon to purchase from him. In the few remarks allotted to him, the merchant flatters Timon and responds genially to the taunts of Apemantus.

Messengers:

There are three anonymous messengers in the play. One appears in I.i, informing Timon that Ventidius is imprisoned and needs financial assistance. Another messenger appears briefly (I.i.241-22) to announce the arrival of his master Alcibiades at Timon's house. In V.ii, a third messenger informs some senators that Alcibiades has gathered an impressive army to march on Athens; he also tells them that Alcibiades is appealing to Timon to come and witness his attack against the city.

Old Athenian:

An example of the avarice that has corrupted Athens, he complains to Timon that Lucilius—one of Timon's servants—has been courting his daughter. She is his sole heir, the old man says, and far above Lucilius in both virtue and fortune. Unimpressed by Lucilius's honesty and love for his daughter, he threatens to disinherit her if she marries without his consent. When Timon says he's willing to provide Lucilius with a sum equal to the daughter's inheritance, the old man quickly accepts the offer.

Page:

A young servant to an unnamed master, he appears briefly in II.ii. He carries letters addressed to Timon and Alcibiades, but since he is illiterate he asks Apemantus to read the inscriptions so he will know which letter to deliver to which man.

Painter:

With the poet, the jeweller, and the merchant, he appears at Timon's house seeking his patronage. The painter has completed a portrait of Timon that, in the opinion of the poet, is a flattering and vivid representation. In their discussion of esthetics in I.i, the poet and painter reveal a decidedly mercenary view of art. In V.i, their obsession with money leads them to the place where Timon has gone into exile. Timon overhears them scheming about how to convince him to give them some of his gold. He promises to reward them handsomely if they rid him of some villainous men, and they quickly agree—not understanding that he means themselves. Hurling a stone at the retreating painter's back and challenging him to change it into gold, Timon drives them both away.

Philotus:

As the servant of an Athenian money-lender, he joins others of his kind in hounding Timon for repayment of money loaned by their masters (III.iv).

Phrynia:

She and Timandra are Alcibiades' mistresses; they are with him when he encounters Timon in exile. At first Phrynia responds to Timon's insults with spirit: "Thy lips rot off" (IV.iii.64). But when Timon offers gold to Alcibiades, the two women eagerly beg him to give them some, too. Though he calls them whores and sluts, and treats them contemptuously, they seem oblivious to his abuse, holding out their hands and swearing they'll "do anything for gold" (IV.iii.150).

Poet:

The poem he brings to Timon in I.i foreshadows the action of the play and functions almost as a prologue. The poet describes it as an allegory showing the uncertainty of man's fate, through the tale of a once rich man who is deserted by his false friends when he loses all his money. The poet and his fellow artists criticize Timon's friends as mercenary and hypocritical, yet their own behavior is equally dishonorable. The poet and his friends put a price tag on everything that is beautiful and noble, literally setting the stage for the conduct of the Athenian lords and senators later in the play. In V.i, the poet and painter seek out Timon in the wilderness, having heard about his hoard of gold and hoping to get their hands on some of it. However, when he accuses them of coming to see him for that purpose, they stoutly deny it, saying their only intention was to do any service he might require of them. Timon rails at their hypocrisy and drives them away.

Sempronius:

He is one of the lords who refuses to help Timon. In III.iii, he complains to Timon's servant that he feels insulted to be the first friend Timon has appealed to. When the servant declares that three other men have already been asked and have refused to assist Timon, Sempronius abruptly reverses his argument, saying it was a mark of disrespect for Timon to leave him to the last. Sempronius points out that he was ''the first man'' (III.iii.16) ever to receive a gift from Timon and thus he should have been the first one Timon turned to. He claims that if Timon had done so, he would have given three times what was needed. It's likely—but not definitely stated—that Sempronius is one of the guests at the first banquet in I.ii. Timon specifically instructs that he be invited to the second one, and thus he may be one of the unnamed lords who attend that mock feast.

Senators:

Several unnamed Athenian senators appear throughout the play. They are portrayed as self-centered men, untrustworthy and hypocritical. Some of them lend money at exorbitant rates of interest, such as the senator who, in II.i, sends his servant Caphis to demand that Timon repay a loan. This senator knows the extent of Timon's debts, and he hopes to get his money back before other usurers strip Timon of his remaining assets.

In III.v, Alcibiades appeals to three senators, asking for mercy in the case of a friend of his who has been charged with murder and is being tried by the Athenian Senate. His appeals are declined. The senators insist on upholding the letter of the law rather than its spirit. When Alcibiades reminds them of his many years of loyal service leading Athens' armies against her enemies, the senators banish him from Athens forever.

When Alcibiades gathers a force against them, some senators seek out Timon in the wilderness, beginning him to return to Athens and lead the defense of the city. They entreat Timon to forgive the mistreatment he suffered at their hands, and they offer him ''heaps and sums of love and wealth'' (V.i.152) to cover up, and make him forget, the wrongs inflicted on him. At first Timon pretends to be moved by their plight, then he says he doesn't care whether the city is sacked and destroyed. The senators' spirits rise, however, when Timon seems to change his mind. He promises to do some kindness for them, then he describes the nature of this ''kindness'': he says he'll delay cutting down a nearby tree until every Athenian who cares to come and hang himself on that tree has a chance to do so.

In the play's final scene, a group of senators appears on the city walls. They plead with Alcibiades to show mercy toward Athens and its citizens. They tell him that the senators who earlier treated him so harshly are no longer alive. They reportedly died of humiliation, ashamed that they weren't clever or deceitful enough to have prevented Alcibiades from mounting an attack on the city. One senator invites Alcibiades to enter the city with his troops and kill one-tenth of its population, if that will satisfy his anger against Athens. Another proposes that he kill only those who have personally offended him. Alcibiades agrees to enter peacefully and take his revenge only on those who have wronged him or Timon.

Servants:

Several unnamed servants appear throughout the play. Some are in the service of various unspecified noblemen and senators; their usual function is to announce someone's arrival. Others are usurers' servants; specified servants in this category include Caphis, Hortensius, Philotus, Titus, Isidore's Servant, Lucius's Servant, and Varro's Servants. Timon has three unnamed servants who gather with the steward in IV.ii, lamenting the downfall of their master and expressing their contempt of his false friends. Timon's Third Servant also appears in III.iii, appealing to Sempronius on behalf of Timon; when Sempronius turns him down, the Third Servant comments heatedly on the wickedness of Timon's false friends. See also Flaminius, Lucilius, and Servilius—other servants of Timon.

Servilius:

One of Timon's servants, he is sent to ask Lucius if he will lend Timon some money.

When Lucius declines to help, Servilius goes away meekly. Later, in III.iv, Servilius tries to persuade the usurers' servants to leave and come back later, for Timon is presently too agitated to listen to their demands.

Soldier:

Sent by Alcibiades to solicit Timon's presence when the army attacks Athens, he stumbles upon Timon's grave. Part of the tombstone epitaph is written in a language the soldier doesn't understand, so he makes an imprint of the epitaph with hot wax and carries it back to Alcibiades.

Steward:

The steward is depicted as a model of honesty and loyalty. He manages Timon's household, supervises the other servants, and keeps track of Timon's finances. The steward provides a unique perspective on the play's central character through his expressed belief in Timon's capacity for goodness and nobility of spirit. Despite his best efforts, he is unable to prevent Timon's downfall.

In I.ii, the steward tries to stop Timon from showering gifts on his friends. When Timon is besieged by his creditors' servants in II.ii, he accuses the steward of not keeping him informed about the state of his finances. The steward tells him that he's tried to do so on many occasions but Timon wouldn't listen to him. Timon is astounded to learn that he is virtually bankrupt, all his vast estate either sold or forfeited to pay off debts. This is the result of extravagant generosity, the steward reminds Timon—who begs him to cease his sermonizing. When Timon orders the steward to go and ask the senators to lend him more money, the steward replies that he's already appealed to them, but they were unwilling to help. Urging the steward not to be downhearted, Timon sends him to Ventidius instead.

When Timon's friends have all deserted him and he leaves Athens in a rage, the steward remains loyal and compassionate. In IV.ii, he generously distributes the last of his own money among Timon's servants and offers a sympathetic view of what has happened: "Poor honest lord, brought low by his own heart, / Undone by goodness" (IV.ii.37-38). The steward visits Timon in the wilderness, offering him understanding and kindness. Timon is moved to declare him the world's only honest man, but then he becomes suspicious that the steward—like the visitors who have come before him—is offering his services because he expects to be richly rewarded. The steward says that he is motivated only by love and his sense of duty. Timon gives him some gold, commanding him to leave and henceforth despise all men. The steward begs to be allowed to "stay and comfort" his master (IV.iii.534), but when Timon insists, he goes away. The steward's final appearance in the play is in V.i, when he leads two Athenian senators to Timon's cave so they can attempt to persuade him to return to the city. It's

clear to the steward that Timon's hatred cannot be changed, and he begs the senators to "Trouble him no further" (V.i.213).

Faithful and understanding to the end, the steward is incorruptible. He acts solely in Timon's interest, never his own. When Timon wrongly accuses him of mismanagement, even when he curses him, the steward remains stoical. He provides evidence of Timon's noble nature and helps demonstrate that his master was far more fortunate in his servants than in his friends.

On one occasion, Timon addresses his steward as Flavius (I.ii.157). Although the First Folio text uses the speech-prefix "Stew(ard)" throughout, some modern editions insert "Flavius" instead.

Strangers:

These are three men—one of them designated as Hostilius—who do not know Timon personally but are interested in him as an eminent public figure. They pass on rumors of Timon's financial ruin to Lucius in III.ii and observe his response to Timon's servant Servilius. After Lucius and the servant have left, they comment on Lucius's hypocrisy and the treachery he has displayed toward his generous benefactor. One stranger remarks on Timon's "noble mind" and "illustrious virtue" (III.ii.80); such praise from a man with no personal stake in Timon's fate is an indication of the reputation Timon enjoyed in Athens before his downfall.

Timandra:

She and Phrynia are Alcibiades' mistresses; they are with him when he unexpectedly meets Timon in the wilderness. When Timon tells Timandra he hopes she will continue her career as a prostitute—and thus continue infecting young men with venereal diseases—she tells him to go hang himself. However, when she and Phrynia realize that Timon has a hoard of gold, they grovel and abase themselves, saying they'll gladly hear more of his advice as long as it's accompanied by more money.

Timon:

Historically, Timon the Misanthrope lived in the fifth century B.C. According to Greek historians, he withdrew from the world and lived in solitude after he discovered his friends were deceitful. In classical literature, he is the standard symbol for misanthropy—hatred or distrust of all mankind.

In *Timon of Athens*, the principal character's background is a mystery. Of all Shakespeare's tragic heroes, Timon is the most alone. He has no wife or child, parents or siblings. In the first half of the play he appears to be a private citizen, yet there are suggestions later—in V.i, when the senators appeal to him to lead the defense of Athens against Alcibiades—that Timon may be a military commander or political statesman. It's not clear if he is a young man or middle-aged. There is no explanation of the source of his wealth, whether it was earned or inherited.

Timon seems to be the most extravagant man in Athens. The poet, the painter, the jeweller, and the merchant all attest to his generous patronage; not only has he purchased their poems, paintings, and gems, it would appear that he has bought them at prices far beyond their real value. When Timon learns that his friend Ventidius is in debtors' prison, he immediately offers to "pay the debt, and free him" (I.i.104). Timon endows his servant Lucullus with money to make him eligible for marriage and bestows lavish gifts on his friends, while entertaining them luxuriously. When Ventidius, released from prison, offers to pay back the money, Timon refuses. He insists that he "gave it freely" (I.ii.10) and expects nothing in return. Later, during the banquet scene, Timon says that it gives him great pleasure to share his wealth with his friends, for "We are born to do benefits; and what better or properer can we call our own than the riches of our friends?" (I.ii.101-3). Timon weeps for joy as he describes a circle of friends who regard each other as brothers and believe that whatever one individual possesses is the joint property of all.

Timon's idealistic vision and his seemingly boundless generosity can be looked at in several ways. Perhaps they are evidence of a noble, high-minded nature. They may also be signs of innocence or naiveté. Some commentators see stubbornness and pride in Timon's refusal to listen to the warnings of his steward and Apemantus. Others think he is reckless; they emphasize Timon's irresponsible use of his fortune. Most agree that he is foolish to believe his friends' declarations of love and esteem.

Timon is shocked when he learns that he has spent all his fortune. He sends appeals to various friends, serenely confident that they'll help him out of his financial straits. He is stunned when they refuse. His astonishment may be an indication of his unworldliness, or it may suggest that he lacks basic

"The steward provides a unique perspective on the play's central character through his expressed belief in Timon's capacity for goodness and nobility of spirit. Despite his best efforts, he is unable to prevent Timon's downfall."

common sense. Timon's disillusionment brings a complete reversal in his attitude: from pursuing his role as the most benevolent man in Athens, he becomes a misanthrope.

The first sign of his excessive hatred occurs in the prayer he offers up before the mock banquet. He begins with a plea for the reformation of society, moves to despair when he contemplates the idea that men are capable of reform, and closes with a wish for the destruction of humanity. Instead of the lavish feast Timon's guests expected, they find nothing but warm water when the dishes in front of them are uncovered. Timon hurls a flood of abuse at their heads—"detested parasites . . . wolves . . . fools of fortune" (III.vi.94-96)—along with the water in the basins. From this moment until his death, only the dark side of Timon's soul is evident.

In self-imposed exile, his bitterness and desolation are apparent. He repeatedly curses mankind in general and each of the persons, in particular, who present themselves to him near his cave in the wilderness. While digging for roots to eat, he discovers a hoard of gold, which he uses to humiliate his visitors. He expresses a wish to see Alcibiades damned—but only after he has carried out the destruction of Athens. He taunts Alcibiades's mistresses and plays on their greed. He calls Apemantus a slave and a dog, saying that he isn't "clean enough to spit upon" (IV.iii.359). Timon throws a stone at Apemantus's head, vowing that he values the stone more than Apemantus's life. He makes fools of the bandits who try to trick him, sending them off to "rob one another" and "cut throats" (IV.iii.445). When his faithful steward appears and offers to stay with him, Timon scorns the offer, refusing to be

> **Of all Shakespeare's tragic heroes, Timon is the most alone. He has no wife or child, parents or siblings."**

comforted or consoled. He seems unwilling to admit that there is "one honest man" in the world (IV.iii.497), but eventually he does so. Timon offers the senators who appeal to him for help a nearby olive tree on which, he says, Athenians are welcome to come and hang themselves.

Timon's own death is unexplained. He is never seen again after he is visited by the Athenian senators in V.i. During that encounter, he says he has been composing his epitaph—which somehow becomes etched into his gravestone and is discovered by one of Alcibiades's soldiers. Some commentators have suggested that Timon kills himself, but others deny there is any evidence to support the idea of suicide. On at least one occasion Timon expresses a longing for the emptiness of death and nothingness: he alludes to his body resting in a grave that is daily washed over by the sea (V.i.215-18). Perhaps his sojourn in the wilderness leads to healing and redemption. Or it may be that he dies with his heart still full of hatred.

It's debatable whether Timon's hatred is justified. Certainly he was terribly wronged by people he trusted and on whose friendship he relied. But to hate and denounce everyone because some men have proved false generally indicates a lack of judgment or discrimination. Perhaps his compassion for others—as attested to by the steward, Timon's servants, and Alcibiades—makes him too vulnerable, unable to react to disappointment in any other way. He seems to have no ability to endure misfortune or modify his perspective on life on the basis of his experiences. He can only swing wildly from one extreme—an idealistic vision of human fellowship—to the other—contempt for all mankind.

Titus:

A usurer's servant, he is one of several men in III.iv who crowd around the door of Timon's house, waiting in vain to receive the money Timon owes their masters.

Varro's Servants:

They are sent by their master, an Athenian money-lender, to demand that Timon repay a loan. In II.ii, one of Varro's servants appears on his behalf; in III.iv, two of Varro's servants hound Timon.

Ventidius:

One of Timon's friends and a recipient of his generosity, Ventidius turns his back on Timon when he has an opportunity to return the favor. In the beginning of the play, Ventidius is imprisoned because he cannot pay a debt, and he sends a messenger to Timon asking for help. Timon immediately declares his willingness to "pay the debt, and free him" (I.i.103). Ventidius comes to the banquet at Timon's house in I.ii, bringing news that his father has died, and thus he has come into his inheritance. He thanks Timon for getting him out of prison and offers to repay the money Timon put up for him; Timon refuses, assuring Ventidius that it was a gift, not a loan. When Timon realizes the extent of his own debts, he sends his steward to Ventidius, confident that the man who gained his freedom through Timon's generosity will aid him now. However, it is reported in III.iii that Ventidius has been as false as Timon's other friends. Ventidius may be one of the unnamed lords who attend Timon's second banquet.

Further Reading

Charney, Maurice. "*Timon of Athens.*" In *All of Shakespeare*, 309-18. New York: Columbia University Press, 1993.

> From a book written specifically for students, this chapter on *Timon* covers several aspects of the play and emphasizes its satiric elements. In addition to an extended evaluation of Timon as a less than tragic figure, Charney comments on the character of the steward and discusses at length the dramatic function of the poet and the painter, whom he regards as satirical figures.

Farley-Hills, David. "Anger's Privilege: *Timon of Athens and King Lear.*" In *Shakespeare and the Rival Playwrights, 1600-1606*, 166-206. London: Routledge, 1990.

> Farley-Hills views *Timon of Athens* as a satire on mankind's obsession with wealth and materialism. In this kind of drama, he asserts, each character has a symbolic role rather than an individual personality. It is Farley-Hills's opinion that "Of all Shakespeare's tragic heroes, Timon is the least open to psychological interpretation."

Handelman, Susan. "*Timon of Athens*: The Rage of Disillusion." *American Imago* 36, no. 1 (Spring 1979): 45-68.

Handelman considers various implications of the limited role of women in *Timon of Athens*. "There is no feminine representative of goodness and constancy" as in other Shakespearean tragedies, she points out; the only women in the play are the prostitutes who accompany Alcibiades and the performers in the masque. Handelman also evaluates Timon, describing him as self-absorbed and psychologically incapable of accepting loss.

Knights, L. C. "*Timon of Athens*." In *The Morality of Art*, edited by D. W. Jefferson, 1-17. London: Routledge and Kegan Paul, 1969.

Knights focuses on Timon as a man with no genuine means of upholding the egotistical, idealized view he has of himself. Timon has set himself above others through lavish generosity, Knights asserts, and when the artificial props or supports of his self-esteem are rudely withdrawn, Timon is left with nothing. Knights concludes that not only does Timon fail to gain self-knowledge, he never considers the possibility that he contributed to his downfall.

Mellamphy, Ninian. "Wormwood in the Wood Outside Athens: *Timon* and the Problem for the Audience." In *"Bad" Shakespeare: Revaluations of the Shakespeare Canon*, edited by Maurice Charney, 166-75. Rutherford, N.J.: Fairleigh Dickinson University Press, 1988.

Mellamphy focuses on audience response to a 1983 Canadian production of *Timon*. The Timon in this production was a naive idealist, brought down by his own stubbornness and pride. Alcibiades was played as a pragmatist who is able to compromise, as Timon cannot.

Nuttall, A.D. "Timon Says Grace: The Parodic Eucharist." In *Timon of Athens*, 113-35. Boston: Twayne, 1989.

Nuttall looks closely at the nature of Timon's generosity. He asserts that while Timon gives freely and expects nothing in return, his shock when he realizes his friends have taken him at his word represents an innocence that "is indeed a kind of stupidity." Additionally, Nuttall provides an extended comparison between the prayers before meals made by Apemantus (I.ii.62-71) and Timon (III.vi.70-84).

Oliver, H. J. Introduction to *Timon of Athens*, by William Shakespeare, xiii-lii. London: Methuen, 1959.

Oliver provides lengthy discussions of Timon, Apemantus, Alcibiades, and the steward. In his view, Timon is an essentially noble man, but prone to misjudgments and exaggerated emotions, and lacking the "depth or profundity" that would qualify him as a great tragic hero. Oliver also offers extended commentary on whether another dramatist collaborated with Shakespeare in writing *Timon of Athens* and whether the play was left unfinished.

Pasco, Richard. "Timon of Athens." In *Players of Shakespeare*, edited by Philip Brockbank, 129-38. Cambridge: Cambridge University Press, 1985.

A British actor with wide experience in Shakespearean roles, Pasco treats the character of Timon from his perspective of playing the part in a 1980 Royal Shakespeare Company production. Among the problems Pasco encountered were how to justify the ferocity of Timon's hatred of mankind and how to prevent Act IV, scene iii from degenerating into "one long shouting match between Timon and his visitors." Pasco insists that Timon grows and matures as a character and that he passes beyond misanthropy to a quiet acceptance of death.

Walker, Lewis. "*Timon of Athens* and the Morality Tradition." *Shakespeare Studies* XII (1979): 159-77.

Walker looks at *Timon of Athens* in terms of medieval English morality plays, which featured allegorical rather than naturalistic characters. From Walker's perspective, Timon and Apemantus bear a strong resemblance to symbolic figures in these earlier plays. Timon's progress through a sinful world to eventual repentance, Walker asserts, reflects similar journeys by such allegorical figures as Mankind and Everyman.

The Tragedy of Titus Andronicus

circa 1590-92

Act I:

The play is set in Rome at an unspecified time, perhaps the fourth or fifth century A.D. In a public place near the Senate House, a struggle for political power is underway between Saturninus and Bassianus, sons of the recently deceased emperor. Addressing the assembled senators and tribunes, Saturninus points out that he should succeed to the throne because he is the late emperor's first-born son. Bassianus argues that he should be the next emperor because his merits are greater than his brother's. Their debate is interrupted by the arrival of a nobleman, Marcus Andronicus, who declares that "the people of Rome" (I.i.20) have chosen his brother Titus to be the new emperor. A military procession enters with a flourish. Its most prominent figure is Titus Andronicus, whose Roman army has recently won a decisive victory over the Goths. He is accompanied by four of his sons (Martius, Mutius, Lucius, and Quintus) as well as his captives: Tamora, Queen of the Goths, her three sons (Alarbus, Demetrius, and Chiron), and her lover Aaron, a black-skinned Moor. When Lucius demands that one of Tamora's sons be sacrificed to avenge his brothers who were killed in battle against the Goths, Titus designates Alarbus. Tamora begs Titus to spare her eldest son, but he refuses, and his sons take Alarbus away. They return shortly and report that he has been hacked to pieces and disem-

bowelled. Marcus tells Titus that a group of Romans has selected him to be the new emperor, but Titus declines the office. Instead he gives his support to Saturninus, who proposes to show his gratitude by making Titus's daughter Lavinia his wife. Titus says he is agreeable to the marriage, and Lavinia voices no protest. Bassianus, however, objects, pointing out that he and Lavinia are betrothed; he and Marcus take Lavinia away. Lucius, Quintus, and Martius follow, demonstrating their support for Bassianus, and Mutius blocks the angry Titus from going after them. In the brawl that develops, Titus kills his son Mutius.

Now scornful of Lavinia, Saturninus asks Tamora if she will marry him, and she agrees. They depart for the wedding ceremony, and everyone but Titus goes with them. When Marcus and Titus's three sons return, Titus accuses them of dishonoring him. Saturninus and Tamora return from the ceremony. Bassianus and Lavinia also reappear, and Saturninus and Bassianus argue fiercely. Tamora urges her new husband to grant pardons to everyone, assuring him in a whispered aside that before long they will have their revenge on Bassianus and the Andronici. Saturninus publicly forgives those who have opposed him, and everyone departs, making plans to hunt in the forest together the following morning.

Act II:

Aaron enters after the others have left. He talks aloud to himself about how he means to manipulate Tamora's love for him and use her new power as Saturninus's wife to his own advantage. Demetrius and Chiron suddenly appear, arguing heatedly about Lavinia, whom they both desire. Aaron stops them when they draw their swords against each other. He proposes that they seize the opportunity of the hunting party, when the women of the court will be walking alone in the forest, to abduct and rape Lavinia. Demetrius and Chiron agree to the scheme.

Near the emperor's palace, the sounds of horns and baying dogs signal the start of the hunt, and members of the hunting party gather. Deep within a nearby forest, Aaron conceals a bag of gold beneath an elder tree. Tamora appears, and Aaron gives her a letter he's forged, telling her to make sure that Saturninus sees it. Noticing Bassianus and Lavinia approaching, Aaron tells Tamora to provoke Bassianus into a quarrel, then he leaves to find Tamora's sons. When Demetrius and Chiron arrive, Tamora tells them that Bassianus and Lavinia lured her to that spot, intending to tie her to a tree and leave her to die

or go mad. Demetrius and Chiron stab Bassianus to death and throw his body into a deep pit. Then they drag Lavinia away. Tamora goes off in search of Aaron, who appears from another direction with Martius and Quintus. Martius stumbles and falls into the pit containing Bassianus's corpse. Aaron leaves to find Saturninus, intending to frame Martius and Quintus for the murder of Bassianus. Quintus tries to pull his brother out of the hole, but instead he's drawn down into it by Martius's weight. Aaron returns with Saturninus, and Martius—trapped at the bottom of the pit—informs the emperor that Bassianus has been killed. Tamora, Titus, and Lucius arrive, and Tamora gives Saturninus the forged letter—allegedly a note from Martius and Quintus to an accomplice, informing him where to find his reward for murdering Bassianus. Aaron retrieves the sack of gold he had hidden earlier and shows it to Saturninus. The emperor orders that Martius and Quintus be imprisoned. Everyone returns to Rome, with Martius and Quintus under guard. Lavinia enters the clearing, bleeding from her mouth and wrists. To keep her from revealing that they raped her, Demetrius and Chiron have cut off her hands and cut out her tongue. They taunt her and make cruel jokes, then leave her alone in the forest. Her uncle Marcus comes upon her and is shocked and horrified at the specter of his mutilated niece. He tenderly escorts her back to Rome.

Act III:

On a street in Rome, Quintus and Martius are led in chains by judges, tribunes and senators taking them to be executed. Titus begs them to spare his son's lives, but they pass on with their prisoners. Lucius arrives and reports that because he drew his sword and tried to rescue his brothers, he has been banished from Rome. Marcus and Lavinia appear. Lucius is horror-struck by the sight of his sister, and Titus almost goes mad with grief and pity. Aaron arrives and says that if one of them will chop off a hand and send it to Saturninus, Quintus and Martius will not be executed. Titus tells Lucius and Marcus to decide between themselves which one will make this sacrifice, and the two of them go off to find an axe. As soon as they are gone, however, Titus turns to Aaron and asks him to chop off one of his hands. Aaron carries out the deed before Lucius and Marcus return. As he leaves, Aaron reveals in an aside to the audience that this has all been a deception: Quintus and Martius will be executed. Within moments a messenger appears, bearing back Titus's hand—along with the heads of his two sons. Titus responds with mad laughter. He vows that he will not rest until he has avenged his slain sons and ravished daughter. He takes up one head, asks Marcus to bring the other, and tells Lavinia to carry away his severed hand between her teeth. After they leave, Lucius declares his intention to go to the Goths and recruit an army to attack Rome and Saturninus.

Act IV:

In Titus's house, Lavinia has been following young Lucius everywhere. Marcus and Titus realize that she wants one of the books the boy carries about with him: Ovid's *Metamorphoses*. When they give it to her, she turns the pages furiously until she comes to the story of Philomela, who was raped and had her tongue cut out by her brother-in-law Tereus. Marcus guides her to a place where sand is strewn on the floor and shows her how to write in the sand with a stick. Grasping the stick in her mouth and guiding it with her stumps, Lavinia is able to name her attackers by writing ''*Stuprum* [rape]. Chiron. Demetrius'' (IV.i.78).

Titus begins to plan his vengeance. He sends young Lucius to the palace with a veiled message: weapons inscribed with verses. When the boy delivers these to Demetrius and Chiron, they fail to grasp the significance of Titus's gifts. Aaron, however, realizes this means that Titus has discovered who raped his daughter. The sound of trumpets is heard, heralding the birth of a child to Tamora. A nurse enters the room carrying a dark-skinned infant who is clearly the son of Aaron, not Saturninus. The nurse tells Aaron that Tamora wants him to kill the baby. Demetrius and Chiron say they'll gladly do it, but Aaron sweeps the child into his arms and draws his sword, swearing that no one will harm his son. Demetrius and Chiron ask Aaron what should be done. His first response is to stab the nurse to death so she cannot tell anyone else about the baby. He then sends Demetrius and Chiron to bribe a couple into giving up their newborn son, a fair-skinned child, as a substitute for Aaron's. The Moor leaves Rome, taking his infant son with him.

In a public place in the city, Titus distributes arrows, with notes attached to them, to Marcus, young Lucius, and several others of his kinsmen. He explains that the notes are petitions to the gods, seeking justice. Believing that he's out of his mind, Titus's relatives nevertheless draw their bows and send the arrows aloft. A half-witted countryman passes by on his way to the palace, with two pigeons in a basket under his arm. Titus inserts into the basket a knife wrapped in a piece of paper on which he's written a speech accusing Saturninus of murder. Titus instructs the man to give the basket directly to the emperor.

Within the palace, an enraged Saturninus shows Tamora and her sons the arrows and petitions for justice that have landed inside the palace walls. The countryman enters with his basket and presents it to Saturninus, who reads the speech and orders that the man be taken away and killed. A nobleman named Aemilius arrives with news that an army of Goths, led by Lucius, is marching on Rome. Tamora says she has a scheme for persuading Titus to help avert the attack.

Act V:

On an open field near Rome, Lucius tells his new allies, the Goths, that the Romans are on the verge of rebelling against Saturninus. Another Goth enters, bringing Aaron and the baby, who have been discovered near the encampment. To prevent Lucius from hanging him and his child, Aaron reveals everything he's done. Aemilius arrives with a message from Saturninus, proposing a peace talk, and Lucius agrees to the proposal.

In the courtyard of Titus's house, Tamora and her sons appear in disguise. She tells Titus that she is Revenge, come to help him destroy his enemies. Titus remarks that the two men with her appear to be Rape and Murder. Tamora asks Titus to invite Lucius to his house, where the emperor and empress will admit their wrongs and beg for mercy, and Titus agrees to do so. As Tamora is about to leave, Titus insists that the figures dressed as Rape and Murder remain with him—remarking in an aside to the audience that he's aware of their true identities. After Tamora has gone, Titus calls to his kinsmen and tells them to tie up Demetrius and Chiron. He then leads in Lavinia, and while he cuts the throats of the men who raped her, she catches their blood in a basin held in her mouth.

Sometime later, Lucius, Marcus, and the Goths arrive at Titus's house with Aaron, who is bound in chains and taken away. Saturninus, Tamora, Aemilius, and several tribunes arrive shortly thereafter, and Marcus invites them all to be seated. Titus enters and places in front of Tamora and Saturninus a meat pie he has prepared for them. They do not know that the pastry contains the blood and ground-up bones of Demetrius and Chiron. Titus then asks Saturninus whether he thinks a father would be justified in killing his daughter if she were raped. Saturninus says that would be the only way for a father to erase his daughter's shame and ease his own sorrow. At once, Titus stabs Lavinia. He reveals that she was raped by Demetrius and Chiron, and when Saturninus demands that they be brought before him, Titus replies: "Why, there they are, both baked in this pie; / Whereof their mother daintily hath fed" (V.i.ii.60-61). In rapid succession, Titus kills Tamora, Saturninus kills Titus, and Lucius kills Saturninus. Marcus and Lucius address the tribunes who have witnessed the bloodbath, detailing the crimes against the Andronicus family and urging the tribunes to reunite Rome. Aemilius proclaims his support for Lucius as the next emperor, and the other tribunes add their voices to his in hailing Lucius as Rome's new leader. An unrepentant Aaron is brought in, and Lucius orders that he be buried in the ground up to his chest and left to die. He further commands that Tamora's body be set out in the open for birds and beasts to devour.

Modern Connections

Titus Andronicus is frequently linked to a kind of drama known as "revenge tragedy." In this genre, once a person vows to avenge a wrong done to him or someone in his family, there is no turning back. The cycle of revenge, filled with violent and bloody incidents, is not complete until everyone who committed the wrong or was associated with it in any way has been punished. Forgiveness is an alien concept in revenge tragedy.

Cycles of revenge continue throughout the world in the late twentieth century. One faction or ethnic group within a nation oppresses or harms another. The oppressed group strikes back or waits until it reaches a position of power, then avenges the wrongs done to its members years ago. In some countries, people are presently fighting to avenge crimes that were committed against their ancestors decades or even centuries ago.

Group solidarity, an admirable trait in itself, is one ingredient in maintaining these cycles. Family solidarity is also, in itself, a virtue. The Andronici stand shoulder to shoulder against the world. They adhere to the Roman tradition that an attack on one member of the family is an attack on everyone related to them. They have intense disputes among themselves, but once an Andronici is threatened or harmed by someone outside the family, they close ranks. Their enemies behave similarly. Tamora allows, even encourages, her sons to rape Lavinia.

This is partly because Titus has, in her view, wrongly allowed the killing of Alarbus, and she knows that his daughter's rape will devastate him. It is also because she sees Lavinia not as an individual woman, but as an Andronici.

Modern societies all over the world encourage family loyalty. When one member succeeds, it's expected that his or her family will benefit as well. Siblings fight among themselves, yet if a younger brother or sister is threatened by a neighborhood bully, an older sibling is traditionally expected to intervene and protect them. This concept of family loyalty also exists in groups of non-related people, such as gangs, in which members in a sense "adopt" one another as family.

The Andronici share with their enemy Saturninus and with other Romans of this period the view that rape is a disgrace to the family. Through no fault of her own, Lavinia is personally disgraced and brings shame on her family. Traces of this attitude linger in modern societies. Rape victims frequently hesitate to report—to the police or even their own families—what has happened to them. The families of rape victims often do not feel free to talk openly about the crime, as they perhaps would if a relative had been robbed or their house had been broken into. Some progress has been made over the past few decades in removing the social stigma of rape.

Titus Andronicus demonstrates another, even more widespread social phenomenon that continues to this day: racism. The characterization of Aaron takes advantage of cultural prejudices against people whose physical aspect is markedly different from that of the dominant population. Racism existed in sixteenth-century England, and it has endured throughout the twentieth, in cultures all over the world. Moreover, the play raises disturbing questions about the traditional association of the color black with evil.

Aaron is described by literary critics as the most dynamic, fully developed character in the play. He's seen as the model—and a very strong one—for villains in Shakespeare's later plays, especially Richard III, Iago in *Othello*, and Edmund in *King Lear*. But those villains are all white men in white worlds. In *Titus Andronicus*, Aaron is thoroughly alienated from the society around him. Though Tamora, too, is "different"—a foreigner from another, despised culture—she's given an opportunity to become part of Rome when she marries Saturninus and becomes empress. By contrast, "her raven-colored love" (II.iii.83) is forever an outcast. The play does not explicitly connect Aaron's deliberate exclusion from Roman society with his malevolent attitude. But modern readers, aware of the effects of racism and prejudice, may see a linkage there.

Characters

Aaron:

Often referred to as the Moor, he is a dark-skinned adventurer and mercenary soldier who fought with the Goths against Rome. He is Tamora's lover, and one of the captives Titus leads into Rome in I.i. Aaron is also the chief villain of the play. As a dramatic character, he has a richly complex and ambiguous appeal.

On the one hand, he is the embodiment of evil. At II.iii.39, he tells Tamora, "Blood and revenge are hammering in my head." Yet we are not shown or told of any specific injury or injustice that he has suffered from the Andronici—except, in the course of war, to be defeated and captured. He seems inclined to villainy by his very nature: he *is* evil, and he *does* evil. He shows no pity or remorse. He proudly acknowledges that he has done "a thousand dreadful things" and regrets that he "cannot do ten thousand more" (V.i.124, 144). Deeply cynical, he scorns honest men. He has no moral code, and he mocks those who do.

On the other hand, he is a very engaging figure. His self-confidence is expressed nonchalantly, so that the audience is attracted rather than put off by his self-assurance. He is generally cheerful and open in his soliloquies and when he addresses the audience directly. It is as if he were coaxing us into sharing his sardonic perspective on events. His playfulness and sheer vitality sometimes put the audience at risk of forgetting the horrors he has brought about.

Aaron keeps the audience informed of his schemes and their implications, either through dialogue with Tamora and her sons or by direct address. He orchestrates nearly all the events that occur in Act II: Bassianus's murder, Lavinia's rape, the planting of "evidence," and the entrapment— literally and figuratively—of Quintus and Marcus. He sees to it that various characters get to the clearing in the forest at just the right time to advance his schemes. A master of strategy and manipulation,

Aaron is also capable of on-the-spot decision making. Clearly as surprised as anyone when Tamora's baby turns out to be his son rather than Saturninus's, he acts quickly to save the infant's life and protect Tamora. He stabs the nurse, lays out a detailed plan for substituting another baby for his own, tells Demetrius and Chiron where to dispose of the nurse's body, instructs them to send the midwife to him so he can kill her, too, and then charts a future life for his son and himself. All this happens within the space of a few moments.

Ingenious as he is, Aaron isn't entirely self-sufficient. From time to time, he requires the assistance or cooperation of Tamora and her sons to carry out his schemes. He boasts of his sexual power over her, and she appears to be as desirous of him as he claims she is. However, though they are lovers, there is no indication that he is in love with her.

Yet Aaron does have the capacity to care for another human being. His devotion to his son is clear. He willingly casts aside his role as Tamora's lover, with all the privileges that gives him, to leave Rome and seek safety for his child. When he tells Lucius in V.i that he's prepared to reveal all the wrongs committed against the Andronici, he makes this offer in exchange for his son's life, not his own. His commitment to the survival of the infant unexpectedly shows his humanity. He soothes the child, at IV.ii.176-81, with a kind of fierce tenderness.

The comparison between Aaron as the devoted father and Aaron the man who derives malicious joy from inflicting pain on others could hardly be more startling. As he catalogues his sins to Lucius in V.i, he takes pleasure in dwelling on his success in deceiving Titus into cutting off a hand in exchange for the lives of Quintus and Martius. "And when I had done it," Aaron says, "[I] drew myself apart, / And almost broke my heart with extreme laughter" (V.i.112-13). Upon witnessing Titus's reaction to the sight of Quintus and Martius's heads, the Moor continues, he laughed so hard he cried—and then he went to Tamora and shared the joke with her.

Aaron is defiant to the end. In the play's final scenes, far from showing remorse, he says that he regrets nothing. Even at the prospect of being set "breast-deep in earth" (V.iii.179) and left to starve to death, Aaron is as contemptuous of other people's opinions as ever, and he refuses to show any self-pity. Aaron's final words represent a stark challenge to traditional morality: "If one good deed in all my life I did, / I do repent it from my very soul" (V.iii.188-89).

Aemilius:

He is a nobleman and tribune who acts first as a messenger for Saturninus and then as a supporter of Lucius in the play's final scene. In IV.iv, Aemilius reports to the emperor that the Goths, under the leadership of Lucius, are marching on Rome. Saturninus asks him to take a message to Lucius proposing a peaceful meeting at Titus's house. He does so in V.i. Aemilius arrives for the feast at Titus's house in the company of Saturninus and Tamora, but at the close of the play, with Saturninus dead, he proposes that Lucius be the next emperor, noting that Lucius appears to be the choice of Rome's citizens.

Alarbus:

He is a Goth, the oldest of Tamora's three sons. In I.i, Titus orders that Alarbus be sacrificed so that the spirits of Titus's sons who were killed in the war against the Goths will rest in peace and honor. Tamora pleads with Titus to spare her son's life, but Alarbus is killed. Thereafter Tamora is obsessed with avenging his death.

Andronicus (Marcus Andronicus):

Unlike his brother Titus, he is a tribune, not a soldier. He represents the voice of the Roman people, or at least some faction of the populace, when he nominates his brother for emperor early in Act I. Overall, he is presented as a reasonable, unheroic man, who frequently attempts to persuade his more strong-willed brother to moderate his behavior. Marcus is, however, as committed to family honor as Titus. He often takes on the role of explaining or defending the conduct of the Andronici. But there is some question about whether, in his extended speeches to the other tribunes at the close of the tragedy (V.iii.67-95, 119-36), he may be trying to shift the blame from his family onto others.

As many commentators have noted, Marcus is often long-winded. His lengthy speech when he comes upon the raped and mutilated Lavinia in the forest has been the subject of a great deal of debate and commentary. Full of classical allusions and in a mood that can be described as aloof or emotionless, this speech is difficult for modern readers or audiences, who might think Marcus ought to be searching for a physician to bind up Lavinia's wounds instead of delivering a nostalgic oration. It has been suggested that Marcus uses elevated, formal language here to create an aura of tragedy around his disfigured niece. He is, in effect, memorializing her, emphasizing who she was rather than what she has

> "... [Aaron] is the embodiment of evil. At II.iii.39, he tells Tamora, 'Blood and revenge are hammering in my head.' ... He seems inclined to villainy by his very nature ... He shows no pity or remorse."

become. He clearly regards her with pity and compassion, and continues to treat her gently throughout the remainder of the play.

Marcus demonstrates a similar compassion for his grief-stricken brother, humoring his fantasies and assisting his schemes for revenge. In the so-called "fly scene" (III.ii), Marcus recognizes that his brother Titus is on the brink of madness. When Titus becomes enraged and calls him a murderer because he swatted a fly, Marcus says he did it because the fly resembled Aaron; Titus calms down and praises Marcus for the deed. Together they help Lavinia find a way to reveal the identities of the men who raped her. And, with sorrow, Marcus indulges his brother's delusion of sending aloft petitions for divine justice wrapped around arrows.

Marcus is not present when Demetrius and Chiron are killed. It isn't clear whether he knows what Titus has in store for the guests at the banquet. After the multiple murders, Marcus defends his family before the assembled tribunes, sharing the role of interpreter of events with his nephew Lucius. Titus endured more than "any living man could bear" (V.iii.127), Marcus argues, and the crimes committed against the Andronicis were unspeakable. If the tribunes judge that what the Andronici have done is wrong, Marcus says, he and Lucius will kill themselves. The tribunes respond by naming Lucius emperor.

Andronicus (Titus Andronicus):

A proud veteran of forty years' of military campaigns against the enemies of Rome, he is a popular hero. At the beginning of Act I, he is the people's choice to be their next emperor. But Titus is a highly contradictory figure. By the close of that act, he has betrayed his integrity through false pride,

> **Aaron's final words represent a stark challenge to traditional morality: 'If one good deed in all my life I did, / I do repent it from my very soul'** (V.iii.188-89)."

harsh inflexibility, and faulty judgment. On the other hand, by the end of Act III, he has suffered more unspeakable wrongs than "any living man could bear" (V.iii.127). Pursuing his revenge against those who have violated his daughter, murdered his son-in-law, and executed his sons, Titus becomes steeped in blood. It's questionable, however, whether he ever reflects on his own role in turning Rome into "a wilderness of tigers" (III.i.54).

Titus's first error is to agree to the ritual murder of Alarbus. He stubbornly refuses to be persuaded by either the logic or the emotionalism of Tamora's appeal on behalf of her son. He chooses rigid adherence to Roman tradition—a sacrifice to appease the spirits of dead warriors—rather than the nobler virtue of mercy. Next he rejects the opportunity to become emperor. Titus decribes himself as an old man, weary and exhausted. He predicts that if he were to assume office one day, he might have to resign it the next. He throws his political support behind the candidacy of Saturninus, failing to recognize how disastrous this choice will be for Rome. Without consulting his daughter Lavinia, he agrees to Saturninus's suggestion that she be his wife. Having given his word on this, Titus is astounded when his brother and sons do not accept his decision. Disregarding Lavinia's legal betrothal to Bassianus, and seeming not at all concerned with her personal wishes, Titus is only focused on what he sees as a challenge to his authority in the family. He emphasizes the integrity of his promise to Saturninus over the lawful oath sworn between Bassianus and Lavinia. Enraged by what he regards as treachery, Titus kills his son Mutius for daring to block his pursuit of the young couple and their defenders. When Marcus and Lucius point out how wrong he was to slay his son, Titus angrily says that no true son would ever dishonor his father as Mutius did. Titus is so furious that he bars his brother and

sons from burying Mutius in the family tomb, and only grudgingly relents when they fall on their knees and beg him to change his mind. By the end of Act I, Titus has committed offenses against his family, the laws of Rome, and divine principles of justice and mercy.

In the course of Act II, Titus's son-in-law Bassianus is murdered, Lavinia is raped and mutilated, and Titus's sons Martius and Quintus have been falsely charged with murder. Saturninus rejects Titus's appeal to delay passing judgment on them, and at the beginning of Act III, Quintus and Martius are being led to their execution. Titus desperately reminds the officials taking them away of his many years of service to Rome. He prostrates himself on the pavement, weeping helplessly, but his prayers for justice go unanswered. The next blow comes shortly after this one. Marcus appears with the wretched and disfigured Lavinia. Titus is distraught. In a passionate and moving speech beginning "For now I stand as one upon a rock / Environ'd with a wilderness of sea" (III.i.93-94), he contemplates the tide of suffering that threatens to overwhelm him. He is inconsolable, despite Lucius and Marcus's efforts to stop his weeping. He takes heart when Aaron appears and, deceptively, offers him a way to save Quintus and Martius. But after Aaron departs with his prize of Titus's hand, Titus renews his laments, despite Marcus's urging that he should rein in his grief. At this point, a messenger appears from Saturninus, with Titus's futilely sacrificed hand and the heads of his two sons. "Now is a time to storm," says Marcus (III.i.263), but Titus is through with tears. He assumes command of the remnants of his family and sets out on a course of revenge.

Many commentators on the play believe that Titus becomes morally corrupted as he carries out his schemes for revenge. It's debatable whether he is also driven mad, by his sufferings or by his obsession with vengeance. In III.ii, he goes into a frenzy when Marcus swats a fly. Nearly hysterical, he calls his brother a murderer. In IV.iii, he urges his kinsmen to scour the seas and "pierce the inmost center of the earth" (IV.iii.12) in search of the goddess Justice, who has fled the world. When his nephew Publius, humoring Titus, tells him that he's heard from the god Pluto that Justice is with "Jove in heaven, or somewhere else" (IV.iii.40), Titus wraps arrows with petitions to the gods and directs his kinsmen to send them skyward. Sometimes his lunacy is feigned, as in V.ii, when Tamora and her sons come to his house in disguise. He toys with them and turns Tamora's intention to use *him* into the crowning moment of his own revenge against *her*.

He carries out the final stages of his vengeance with a mixture of playfulness, guile, and cold-bloodedness. He orders Lavinia to hold a basin in her teeth to catch the blood of Tamora's sons when he slits their throats. Before he kills them, he vividly describes to Chiron and Demetrius what he means to do with their bodies. He greets his banquet guests dressed ''like a cook'' (V.iii.25), for he has indeed prepared the meal himself. When Tamora has eaten some of the pastry, Titus takes grim pleasure in telling her what she's just consumed. And then he kills her.

Modern readers and audiences may see the death of Lavinia as cruel or unnecessary. Titus's motives for stabbing her appear to be grounded in the tradition of his time and his country. With his reference to the tale of Virginius, he both justifies and foreshadows what he is about to do. Whether he does it tenderly, in effect delivering her from further suffering, or in obedience to what he thinks is appropriate to Roman tradition, is up to the reader—or to the performer who enacts the extraordinary role of Titus—to decide.

Bassianus:

He and Saturninus are the sons of the late emperor of Rome, and the play opens with Bassianus challenging his older brother's right to succeed to the throne. Later in the first scene he challenges Titus's decision to disregard Bassianus's betrothal to Lavinia. Yet he is more gracious than defiant in both of these instances. And, unlike most of the other characters in this play, he bears no grudge against the person who wronged him. Indeed, he defends Titus and speaks on his behalf when Titus falls into disfavor with Saturninus. Bassianus's graciousness deserts him, however, when he is provoked by Tamora into a verbal brawl in II.iii. She uses their heated exchange as the basis for convincing her sons that Bassianus and Lavinia are tormenting her. Though Bassianus is not responsible for what happens to him and his wife, his naiveté makes it easy for Aaron and Tamora to manipulate him.

Boy (young Lucius):

He is the son of Lucius and the grandson of Titus Andronicus. In III.ii, he is a witness to Titus's demented response when Marcus kills a fly. In IV.i, he reports that his aunt Lavinia follows him every-

In the so-called 'fly scene' (III.ii), Marcus recognizes that his brother Titus is on the brink of madness. When Titus becomes enraged and calls him a murderer because he swatted a fly, Marcus says he did it because the fly resembled Aaron; Titus calms down and praises Marcus for the deed.''

where and that her behavior frightens him. When Titus and Marcus calm him down, he says he knows his aunt loves him, and he apologizes to her. After Lavinia manages to communicate the names of her attackers, young Lucius vows that if he ''were a man'' he would drive a ''dagger in their bosoms'' (IV.i.107, 118). Titus gives him a role in revenging Lavinia, and he carries it out well. He delivers the weapons with cryptic messages written on them to Chiron and Demetrius, concealing his true feelings toward the men under a façade of good manners. With other males in his family, young Lucius helps Titus launch petitions for divine justice, earning his grandfather's praise.

Caius:

A kinsman of Titus, he's among the men who shoot arrows and messages in the direction of the emperor's palace in IV.iii. Caius is also one of the Andronici who help tie up Chiron and Demetrius in V.ii. He does not speak on either occasion.

Captain:

A Roman military officer, he announces the triumphant return of Titus Andronicus, ''Rome's best champion'' (I.i.65).

Child:

He is the infant son of Tamora, who orders him killed, and Aaron, who saves his life. Aaron leaves Rome with the baby, intending to raise him among the Goths, but they are both captured and returned to Rome. Near the close of the play, the child appears in Titus's house in the arms of an attendant. Though

> By the end of Act I, Titus has committed offenses against his family, the laws of Rome, and divine principles of justice and mercy. . . . In the course of Act II, Titus's son-in-law Bassianus is murdered, [his daughter] Lavinia is raped and mutilated, and Titus's sons Martius and Quintus have been falsely charged with murder . . . and at the beginning of Act III, Quintus and Martius are being led to their execution."

Aaron is condemned to death, nothing is said about the fate of his son.

Chiron:

He and Demetrius are Tamora's sons. Like his brother, Chiron is selfish and cruel, guilty of unspeakable crimes and utterly without remorse. After they rape and mutilate Lavinia, they humiliate her further by mocking the very wounds they inflicted on her. Chiron seems to have had some formal education, for he recognizes that the verses Titus sends with the weapons in IV.ii are from a poem by Horace. However, he doesn't realize the significance of the words: Titus now knows who raped Lavinia. Because of their limited intelligence, as well as their inclination toward evil, Chiron and Demetrius are easily duped by Aaron and Tamora, who have no qualms about using them to carry out their own schemes. Chiron and his brother accompany Tamora to Titus's house in V.ii and willingly remain there, as Titus requests, when she leaves. Smug in the belief that Titus is a demented old man, none of them suspects the fate that awaits the brothers at Titus's hands.

Clown:

An illiterate and dim-witted peasant, he is on his way to the palace with two pigeons in a basket when he is intercepted by Titus. He's confused when Titus asks him if he's a messenger from Jupiter, sent in response to Titus's petitions for divine justice. Slipping a knife wrapped in a written accusation of murder into the man's basket, Titus tells the clown to give the basket to Saturninus and "then look for your reward" (IV.iii.112). The unsuspecting clown follows Titus's instructions, and he is hanged.

Demetrius:

He and Chiron are Tamora's sons. Like his brother, Demetrius is brutal and vicious, capable of unbelievable savagery yet insensible to the enormity of his crimes. Far from showing any remorse over the rape and mutilation of Lavinia, they make cruel jokes at her expense before leaving her alone in the forest. No brighter than his brother, Demetrius is easily persuaded by Tamora that she has been threatened by Bassianus, and he kills Bassianus without hesitation. His disposition toward violent, unthinking action is evident again in IV.ii, when he sees Tamora's newborn son. Demetrius calls Aaron a villain and a foul fiend for disgracing Tamora, and he is ready in a moment to murder the infant. Instead, he and Chiron follow the Moor's advice and carry out his instructions about substituting another baby. Demetrius and Chiron's fate—to spend the last moments of their lives bound and gagged, forced to listen to Titus as he describes how he will transform their blood and brains and ground-up bones into the contents of a pastry and serve it to their mother—evokes horror, but little if any pity for them.

Goths:

Rome's defeated enemies at the beginning of the play, they later accept Lucius as their military commander and prepare to attack Rome with him at the head of their army. When Lucius attends the banquet at Titus's house in V.iii, several Goths accompany him. Historically, the Goths were a northern European people who attacked and overran Rome in 410 A.D.

Judges:

In III.i, they are part of a procession of Roman officials leading Quintus and Martius to the place where the brothers are to be executed. Titus tries to interrupt their progress, begging for pity on his sons. He reminds the officials of the service he has given to Rome, but they are not moved by his appeal.

Lavinia:

The only daughter of Titus Andronicus, she becomes a victim of the cycle of revenge that engulfs virtually everyone in Rome, the innocent as well as the guilty. Lavinia is generally a submissive figure. She is willing to marry Saturninus if that is what her father wants, even though she's betrothed to Bassianus. Aside from a formal speech welcoming her father back to Rome (I.i.157-64), she is rarely heard from in Act I. But at her husband's side in II.iii, Lavinia speaks boldly and haughtily to Tamora. The empress makes Lavinia pay for those words, rejecting her subsequent appeals for ''a woman's pity'' (II.iii.147) or at least a merciful death rather than rape. Lavinia's last words, as Chiron and Demetrius drag her off to rape her and cut off her tongue and hands, condemn Tamora as a traitor to women.

From that time forward, she cannot speak. Yet her very appearance is a powerful symbol of the viciousness that has swept Rome. The first sight of her mutilated body almost causes her brother Lucius to faint. She is a constant reminder to her father and her other relatives of the necessity for revenge. Her rape represents a violation of family honor. In effect, it is a political act, for it is a symbol of a disordered society as well as grisly testimony to the fact that Rome has become a place of chaotic violence. Titus and Saturninus adhere to their cultural tradition and apparently share the conventional interpretation of the story of Virginius—an ancient Roman who killed his daughter after she was raped. For these men, rape disgraces the victim and dishonors her family.

Before Titus kills Lavinia, he makes her a party to his revenge. He instructs her to hold the basin between her teeth and catch the blood which flows from the slit throats of Demetrius and Chiron. She enters the banquet room alongside Titus and observes Tamora eating the pastry containing the minced remains of Tamora's sons, Lavinia's rapists. Most commentators believe she's aware that her father means to kill her when their revenge is complete. But it requires an actor on stage, representing Lavinia, to interpret her feelings about this. No witnesses report her response as her father approaches her with his knife drawn, and she cannot say for herself with what emotions she anticipates death.

Lucius:

One of Titus's twenty-five sons, he is the only one who outlives his father. His survival may be

> ❝ . . . at her husband's side in II.iii, Lavinia speaks boldly and haughtily to Tamora. The empress makes Lavinia pay for those words, rejecting Lavinia's subsequent appeals for 'a woman's pity' (II.iii.147) or at least a merciful death rather than rape [by Tamora's sons]. Lavinia's last words . . . condemn Tamora as a traitor to women.❞

viewed as the result of chance or fortunate circumstances. It may also be seen as the result of Lucius's own ambitions and his carefully planned strategies. A forceful figure, Lucius frequently takes the initiative in preserving his family's honor. He is the one who asks Titus to yield up ''the proudest prisoner of the Goths'' (I.i.96) to appease the spirits of his brothers who were killed in the war. Lucius is also the first of Lavinia's brothers to defend Bassianus's lawful betrothal to her and the first to accuse Titus of being unjust when he kills Mutius. Lucius is not a disobedient son, however. When he stands up against his father, it's for the purpose of defending Roman ideals and principles—in these instances and again when he objects to Titus's order that Mutius's body not be given a proper burial in the family tomb. He demonstrates pity and compassion for Lavinia and for his grief-stricken father, both when Titus is confronted by the specter of his mutilated daughter and when Titus's efforts to save the lives of Quintus and Martius prove futile. Lucius himself tries to rescue his brothers from execution, and for this act he is banished from Rome. However, he takes advantage of his forced exile to revenge his family, gathering an army of Goths and leading them against Rome.

Lucius's desire for vengeance is evident in V.i, when Aaron and his infant son are captured near the Goths' encampment. At the sight of the man who tricked Titus into cutting off his hand, Lucius goes into a rage. He orders the soldiers to hang the infant before his father's eyes so that the Moor will suffer doubly before he himself is hanged. To save the child, Aaron promises he'll reveal all the wrongs that he and Tamora and her sons committed against the Andronici, if Lucius will let the child live. "Even by my god I swear to thee I will," replies Lucius (V.i.86). The baby is still alive when Marcus uses it—in the presence of the tribunes at V.iii.119—as evidence of Tamora's adulterous relationship with Aaron. But some commentators question whether Lucius truly intends to keep the vow he swore to its father. Some of this skepticism arises from Lucius's extended speech to the tribunes (V.iii.96-118), where he mixes indictments of Chiron and Demetrius with an account of himself as Rome's most ardent defender. He denies that he is calling undue attention to himself and declares that when no one else speaks for them, men are inclined to praise themselves. Shortly after that, Aemilius nominates Lucius to be the next emperor, and the assembled tribunes endorse him as well. It's debatable whether Lucius's reign will usher in a new Rome or whether the state will remain "a wilderness of tigers" (III.i.54).

Marcus Andronicus:

See Andronicus

Martius:

One of Titus's sons, his bravery and family loyalty are no match for Aaron's craftiness. With his brothers, Martius comes to the aid of Lavinia and Bassianus in I.i, thus earning his father's fury. When Titus refuses to allow the body of Mutius, another of his sons, to be buried in the family tomb, Martius boldly confronts his father and says he's willing to die to defend Mutius's honor. But Martius is duped by Aaron, who leads him and Quintus into the forest, places them in a compromising position, and implicates them in the murder of Bassianus. Saturninus orders that they be executed, and a messenger delivers their heads to Titus in III.i.

Messenger:

He appears in III.i, bringing Titus the severed heads of Quintus and Martius, together with the hand Titus had cut off in the belief that the lives of his two sons would thereby be spared. The messenger expresses pity for Titus and contempt for those who have mocked him.

Mutius:

One of Titus's sons, he defends Bassianus's right to marry Lavinia. This infuriates Titus, who had agreed she would marry Saturninus. When Lavinia and Bassianus flee the court in I.i, Mutius prevents Titus from going after them. In the brawl that follows, Titus kills Mutius.

Nurse:

She attends the delivery of Tamora's son and brings him to Aaron with instructions that the empress wants the child to be killed. Aaron kills the nurse instead, to prevent her from telling anyone else that the child is his, not Saturninus's.

Publius:

The son of Marcus Andronicus, he appears in IV.iii and V.ii. When his father laments that Titus's scheme to send petitions for justice to the gods is a sign of madness, Publius responds that Titus should be treated with kindness and indulgence. He is the spokesman for the various Andronici who appear when Titus calls for help in tying up Demetrius and Chiron before they are killed.

Quintus:

One of Titus's sons, he survives the war against the Goths, but not the cruelty of Aaron. In I.i, he defends Bassianus's right to marry Lavinia and thereby incurs his father's wrath. Saturninus later pardons Quintus and the other Adronici for helping Bassianus and Lavinia, and Quintus is a member of the hunting party that leaves Rome for a nearby forest in II.ii. During the hunt, Aaron leads Quintus and his brother Martius to the pit where Bassianus's corpse lies. Aaron runs off when Martius tumbles into the pit, and Quintus falls into the hole while trying to pull his brother out. Through a forged letter and a sack of gold he has planted as supposed evidence of their crime, Aaron frames Quintus and Martius for the murder of Bassianus. They are executed, and their heads are brought to Timon in III.i.

Saturninus:

He and Bassianus are the sons of the late emperor of Rome. With Titus's support, Saturninus succeeds to his father's throne. Saturninus is vain, quick-tempered, and headstrong. He often acts rashly and frequently shows poor judgment. His weaknesses are exploited by Tamora and Aaron, and their influence over him grows during the course of the play. He seems unaware that they are lovers and continues to rely on Tamora's advice about matters of state. Saturninus may be as much a victim of Aaron's trickery as are Titus and his sons.

Saturninus's hatred of the Andronici makes it easier for Aaron to convince him that Quintus and Marcius are guilty of Bassianus's murder. However, the execution of Titus's sons is clearly a perversion of justice. Most commentators do not regard Saturninus as a figure of unqualified evil like Aaron and Tamora. But through a combination of their manipulation and his own weakness, Saturninus contributes significantly to the political and moral degeneration of Rome.

Sempronius:

A kinsman of Titus, he joins other members of the Andronicus family in shooting message-laden arrows in the direction of the emperor's palace. Titus addresses him at IV.iii.10, so it's evident that Sempronius is present, but he does not speak.

Senators:

In I.i, several senators gather to hear Saturninus and Bassianus argue their competing claims to be Rome's next emperor. The senators have no part in choosing a new ruler, for Titus ensures Saturninus's succession by giving him his support. In III.i, some senators are part of a group of Roman officials who lead Quintus and Martius to their executions. Like the other officials, these senators are deaf to Titus's appeal for mercy.

Tamora:

As queen of the Goths, a people who have been at war with Rome for many years, she is an enemy of Rome. As a captive led through the streets of the capital, she suffers public humiliation. Tamora hates Titus and his sons even before her own son Alarbus is brutally killed as a sacrifice to the dead Andronici. Alarbus's death does, however, set in motion her schemes for revenge. It may also be seen as some justification for what she does. But she doesn't limit her vengefulness to Titus and his sons. She allows her own sons Demetrius and Chiron to rape Lavinia, refusing to be swayed by Lavinia's appeals to her womanly feelings. Tamora says she can be as pitiless as Titus when he remained unmoved by her tears and pleas on behalf of Alarbus.

Tamora's appeal to Titus in I.i is heartfelt and poignant. She speaks to him as one loving parent to another. She reminds him that Alarbus and his brothers fought valiantly "in their country's cause" just as Titus's sons did, and to be "slaughtered in the streets" is a fate no soldier deserves (I.i.113, 112). This speech, which concludes by pointing out that mercy is the truest sign of a noble nature, demonstrates a different Tamora than is usually evident. Or perhaps she is being manipulative here. Another speech (II.iii.10-29) provides a glimpse of her sensitivity to the natural world. Tamora seems at home in the forest, attuned to the cheerful and soothing sounds of Nature. She is, of course, suggesting in this speech that she and Aaron should use this opportunity of being alone in the woods to make love. The lyrical tone in which she couches her suggestion conveys a sense of Tamora at ease with the world and relishing its natural pleasures.

Such expressions of humanity are rare in Tamora. Elevated to empress of Rome when she marries Saturninus, she will seemingly do anything to hold onto her powerful position. Confined to her bed after childbirth, she sends Aaron instructions to kill the child so that she will not be disgraced—or killed—when Saturninus sees it and realizes it's not his child. The motherly feelings she expressed so eloquently on behalf of Alabarbus are nowhere in evidence now. She enjoys wielding power through her husband, and she's adept at manipulating him. She urges caution when he would do something rash and recommends delayed revenge when he wants immediate punishment of an enemy. Saturninus generally follows her counsel, recognizing her superior judgment and experience as a ruler (the play represents her as several years older than he is). On one fateful occasion, Demetrius and Chiron, who are generally led by her, disregard her advice; they fail to kill Lavinia after they have raped her. Lavinia survives and, as Tamora had warned, eventually incriminates her attackers.

Tamora's judgment about people isn't infallible, however. In V.ii, when she costumes herself as Revenge in order to enlist Titus's help in preventing Lucius and the Goths from advancing against Rome, she miscalculates. She regards Titus as a harmless lunatic, and she agrees to leave her sons with him. When Tamora and Saturninus return to Titus's house for the banquet, she anticipates the occasion will lead to a peace settlement with Lucius. Like a gracious guest, she eats some of the pastry her host sets before her. She has only a moment to react between the time Titus reveals that she's just consumed her sons who have been ground up and baked in a pie, and the instant he kills her. If her thoughts at that moment were expressible, there is nothing in the text to suggest what they might be.

> **When Tamora and Saturninus return to Titus's house for the banquet, she anticipates the occasion will lead to a peace settlement with Lucius. Like a gracious guest, she eats some of the pastry her host sets before her. She has only a moment to react between the time Titus reveals that she's just consumed her sons who have been ground up and baked in a pie, and the instant he kills her.**

Titus Andronicus:

See Andronicus

Tribunes:

These are Roman officials whose traditional function was to protect the rights of ordinary citizens when they were threatened by unjust rulers. In *Titus Andronicus*, the tribunes are part of the audience of officials who listen to the competing claims of Saturninus and Bassianus in I.i. Some tribunes are in the group of officials in III.i who lead Quintus and Martius to their executions. None of them responds to Titus's impassioned attempt to save the lives of his sons. Several tribunes attend Titus's banquet in V.iii; after all the killings, and after Marcus and Lucius defend the actions of the Andronici, the tribunes salute Lucius as Rome's new emperor.

Valentine:

A kinsman of Titus, he is one of the men who responds to Titus's call for help in tying up Demetrius and Chiron in IV.ii. He assists Titus and witnesses the deaths of Lavinia's rapists, but he does not speak.

Young Lucius:

See Boy

Further Reading

Broude, Ronald. "Four Forms of Vengeance in *Titus Andronicus*." *Journal of English and Germanic Philology* LXXVIII, no. 4 (October 1979): 494-507.

Broude sees four kinds of revenge in the play: human sacrifice to pacify the spirits of dead warriors, family vendettas, human justice, and divine vengeance. He regards Titus as the man chosen by the gods to carry out their revenge and help restore human justice in Rome.

Brower, Reuben A. "*Titus Andronicus*: Villainy and Tragedy." In *Shakespeare: The Tragedies*, edited by Robert B. Heilman, 28-36. Englewood Cliffs, N.J.: Prentice-Hall, 1984.

Brower focuses on Timon as an undeveloped tragic hero. He suggests that Timon represents a noble man subjected to unspeakable suffering, whose cries for justice remain unanswered. A principal failure of the play, Brower contends, is that it offers Timon only a grim set of possible responses: he can go mad, increase his suffering by rigidly adhering to "the very qualities that made him a hero," or become indistinguishable from the evil people who have tormented him.

Charney, Maurice. "*Titus Andronicus*." In *All of Shakespeare*, 211-18. New York: Columbia University Press, 1993.

In this chapter from a book written for students, Charney discusses the play's chief characters and principal themes. He argues that Lavinia still has a crucial role even after her tongue is cut out and she can no longer speak; that while the audience sees the worst side of Titus in Act I, he regains his tragic stature through suffering; and that Marcus is a voice of reason and moderation. Charney describes Aaron as "the most brilliant and fully developed character in *Titus Andronicus*," the one who sets the pattern for all of Shakespeare's later villains.

Cutts, John. "*Titus Andronicus*." In *The Shattered Glass: A Dramatic Pattern in Shakespeare's Early Plays*, 59-75. Detroit: Wayne State University Press, 1968.

Cutts devotes this chapter to the character of Titus, whom he regards as a deeply flawed man, incapable of seeing and acknowledging his own weaknesses. In Cutt's estimation, Timon is personally ambitious but unwilling to admit this to himself; he is willing to exploit or sacrifice members of his own family in pursuit of his selfish goals; and he tries to make himself appear less guilty by blaming everyone else for the disastrous cycle of revenge.

Dessen, Alan C. "The Sense of an Ending." In *Titus Andronicus*, 90-110, Manchester: Manchester University Press, 1989.

Dessen analyzes the distinctive ways nearly a dozen twentieth-century productions of *Titus Andronicus*—in England, Canada, and the United States—have presented the play's final scene. He demonstrates how an audience's response to the characters is shaped by the interpretations of actors and directors: for example, Lavinia has sometimes been portrayed as submissive, almost zombie-like in her final appearances and sometimes as an enthusiastic participant in her father's revenge; in some productions Lucius is depicted as Rome's savior at the close of the play, while in others he represents a continuation of violence and savagery. Dessen also describes different treatments of "the fate of Aaron's child."

Hughes, Alan. Introduction to *Titus Andronicus,* by William Shakespeare, 1-47. Cambridge: Cambridge University Press, 1994.

> Hughes emphasizes that *Titus Andronicus* was "written for the theater," and he notes that it succeeds on stage when its emotions and characterizations are treated with sincerity by actors and directors. He also declares that Titus's tragedy is complete by the close of Act I—after he repeatedly violates family bonds as well as "the laws of society, the state and heaven"—and that Aaron is the most theatrically effective character in the play. Hughes's introduction includes discussion of such issues as the play's date of composition, its sources, and stage history.

Kendall, Gillian Murray. " 'Lend me thy hand': Metaphor and Mayhem in *Titus Andronicus.'' Shakespeare Quarterly* 40, no. 3 (Fall 1989): 299-316.

> Kendall declares that in *Titus Andronicus,* "language reflects and promotes the violence of Shakespeare's most grotesquely violent play." She describes the multiple ways in which ordinary figures of speech—particularly those related to human body parts—take on new and deeply sinister meanings in this play.

Miola, Robert S. "*Titus Andronicus* and the Mythos of Shakespeare's Rome." *Shakespeare Studies* XIV (1981): 85-98.

> Miola looks closely at how Shakespeare used classical writers such as Ovid and Virgil to enhance the dignity and sadness of characters and events in *Titus Andronicus.* He focuses on the theme of rape as a violation of family honor as well as on the theme of civil strife in an essentially lawless society.

Scuro, Daniel. "*Titus Andronicus*: A Crimson-Flushed Stage!'' *Ohio State University Theatre Collection Bulletin* 17 (1970): 40-48.

> Scuro provides a survey of critical reaction to the most universally acclaimed production of *Titus Andronicus* in the twentieth century: the 1955 staging directed by Peter Brook and featuring Laurence Olivier as Titus. Scuro evokes the haunting intensity and brooding melancholy of Brook's formal, highly stylized presentation of the play.

Waith, Eugene M. Introduction to *Titus Andronicus,* by William Shakespeare, 1-69. Oxford: Oxford University Press, 1984.

> Waith discusses the ambiguous characterizations of Titus and Aaron, and argues that the violence in *Titus Andronicus* is "an integral part" of Shakespeare's dramatic technique. He also comments on the significance of the various ceremonies and spectacles in the play, contending that they enhance thematic issues—such as the necessity for political order—and serve as structural devices to link dramatic events. In addition, Waith provides a detailed history of the play in performance and an extended discussion of Shakespeare's use and manipulation of literary sources.

Willis, Susan. "*Titus Andronicus* in the Studio: Winter 1985." In her *The BBC Shakespeare Plays*, 292-313. Chapel Hill: University of North Carolina Press, 1991.

> Willis provides a lively account of the BBC-TV videotaping of *Titus Andronicus*. Among other intriguing details about this production, we learn that the makeup for the scene with Tamora and her sons as Revenge, Murder, and Rape (V.ii) was based on the rock group Kiss, and that the stumps fitted onto the hands of the actor playing Lavinia featured "real bones from a butcher shop."

The History of Troilus and Cressida

circa 1601-02

Act I:

The play opens within the walled city of Troy, which is besieged by Greek armies intent on recovering Helen. Helen has been abducted from Menelaus, her elderly Greek husband, by the younger Paris, son of Priam and brother of the renowned Trojan warrior Hector. In the opening scene, Troilus, the younger brother of Paris and Hector, debates whether or not to arm himself for the daily skirmish over Helen between the Trojan and Greek soldiers when he is engaged in his own romantic siege of Cressida's affections (Cressida is the daughter of the Trojan priest Calchas, who has taken sides with the Greeks). Troilus is finally convinced to arm himself that day by Aeneas, another famous Trojan warrior. Pandarus, Cressida's uncle, has been acting as a go-between for the two young Trojan lovers, and he advises Troilus to be patient. In an effort to convince Cressida that Troilus is mature and noble beyond his years, Pandarus tells Cressida that Helen loves Troilus even more than she loves Paris. Paris then situates Cressida so that she may see the Trojan warriors as they pass over the stage, returning from battle. Not only is this scene a clever theatrical device for acquainting the audience with some of the major characters but it also provides Pandarus with an opportunity to extol Troilus's virtues as Troilus is favorably compared to each returning warrior. Cressida is consistently resistant to and

dismissive of Pandarus's praise of Troilus, but when her uncle leaves, she admits that she is in love with Troilus and has been acting coy so that she might remain in control of the situation. In the Greek camp outside of Troy, the Greek princes are confused by their failure to topple Troy after seven long years of siege. Agamemnon, the Greek general, proposes that the Greek cause is being tested by the gods, and Nestor, his venerable old advisor agrees. Ulysses asks leave to speak and suggests that the Greek army has failed because the hierarchy of command is no longer honored within it. He cites Achilles, the greatest Greek warrior, as an example: Achilles rests on his laurels and makes fun of Agamemnon, who cannot compel him to fight the Trojans. Aeneas enters the Greek camp under truce and announces Hector's challenge to engage in a contest of strength with any Greek warrior who desires to fight for his mistress' honor. Ulysses proposes to Nestor that Hector's challenge provides them with the opportunity to deflate Achilles's pride and restore respect for authority by advancing Ajax, the Greek's second-best fighter, as their champion against Hector.

Act II:

Ajax quarrels with Thersites, his fool, and strikes him. Achilles, who has learned that Ajax will fight Hector in his place, visits Ajax and appropriates his fool—even though Thersites is too cynical and contrary to belong rightfully to either one. Inside the walls of Troy, Priam and his sons consider the latest ultimatum from the Greek armies to deliver Helen. Hector proposes that Helen is not worth the lives that have been sacrificed on her behalf; Helenus, a priest and another son of Priam, agrees with him. Troilus reminds the Trojan royal family that all had supported Paris in his abduction of Helen. Priam's daughter, the prophetess Cassandra, enters and warns the assemblage of the dire consequences of their continued defense of Helen. Paris, of course, argues that the defense of Helen should continue but is admonished by Priam for being less than impartial in the matter. Troilus finally convinces Hector—and thus the rest—that Helen gives Troy "a theme of honor and renown, / A spur to valiant and magnanimous deeds" (II.ii.199-200). Meanwhile, in the Greek camp, Achilles will not grant Agamemnon audience when the latter comes to his tent. When Achilles refuses to speak to him a second time, Agamemnon sends Ajax with a third request, but Ulysses intervenes, arguing deliberately that such a mission would be beneath the dignity of one as great as Ajax. Ulysses is sent instead;

when he returns, again with a negative reply, he, Agamemnon, and Nestor stand outside Achilles's tent and volubly praise Ajax.

Act III:

As he makes arrangements to bring Troilus and Cressida together, Pandarus asks Paris to tell Priam later, at dinner, that Troilus is absent because he is sick. Paris and Helen are in a frivolous mood, contrasting sharply with the condition of war they have precipitated all around them, and Helen insists that Pandarus sing for her. Pandarus humors her. Pandarus then brings Cressida to Troilus, and the latter is at first tongue-tied but soon confesses his love for Cressida, who does likewise, but in a seemingly more calculated attempt to enthrall Troilus completely. Pandarus conducts them to a chamber with a bed in the home of Calchas, his brother and Cressida's father. In the Greek camp, meanwhile, Calchas, who has gone over to aid the Greek army after having a prophetic vision that Troy would be ruined, asks the Greek princes to exchange his daughter for Antenor, an important Trojan lately taken prisoner. He has been of service to the Greek cause, so his request is granted. Ulysses sees another opportunity to prick the pride of Achilles and arranges for the Greek troops to either ignore Achilles completely or acknowledge him disdainfully as they pass by his tent. Achilles is upset at being so treated and sends word to Ajax, asking that Ajax invite Hector to Achilles's tent after the contest so Achilles might view the great Trojan warrior unarmed.

Act IV:

Early in the morning, the Trojan Aeneas accompanies the Greek Diomedes to Calchas's house so that Diomedes might conduct Cressida to her father in the Greek camp. Pandarus wakes Troilus and Cressida and jovially teases them in their embarrassment. After being informed of Cressida's situation by Aeneas, Pandarus informs her of her fate. Troilus and Cressida briefly exchange vows of fidelity and Troilus gives her his sleeve as a pledge of his love, promising to risk the dangers of the Greek camp and visit her there. Troilus accompanies Cressida to the gates of Troy and charges Diomedes to treat her well. Diomedes tells Troilus that he will treat Cressida according to her merit; he does not recognize any authority in Troilus to admonish him to do so. Both Troilus and Diomedes vow to fight aggressively when they encounter one another on the field of battle. When Cressida arrives in the Greek camp, she responds warmly to the flattery of the assembled Greek nobles, obliging each with a welcoming kiss when she is requested. Ulysses notes a deliberate coyness in her demeanor. Along with a Trojan contingent, Hector arrives to fight with Ajax. Aeneas asks Agamemnon whether the chivalric contest will be one to the death or one that might be halted by any spectator. Agamemnon defers to Hector's desire for the latter. The two combatants enter the lists and battle until Aeneas and Diomedes simultaneously call a halt to the action. When Ajax protests that he is just warming up, the decision is again left up to Hector, who ceases because he does not want to kill Ajax, his father's sister's son. Hector is cordially greeted by the Greek nobles and is invited to Agamemnon's quarters for feasting. Achilles surveys Hector and wonders aloud in which limb he will mortally wound the Trojan hero. Hector warns Achilles not to take him so lightly. Ajax reminds Achilles that the latter might engage Hector in battle whenever he has the nerve. Ulysses agrees to guide Troilus to Calchas's tent so that the young Trojan might see Cressida.

Act V:

Agamemnon takes his leave, and Hector is escorted to Achilles's tent. Achilles has earlier informed his aide Patroclus and the fool Thersites that though he will entertain Hector that night, he intends to kill him the next day. Ulysses positions Troilus outside of Calchas's tent that he might see Cressida. Thersites has followed them out of curiosity, and he takes up a position away from them to witness what will happen. Diomedes approaches, and Cressida emerges from her father's tent to meet him. She is familiar with Diomedes but, at first, resists his advances. When he starts to leave, she calls him back and agrees to meet him later, giving him Troilus's sleeve as a pledge of that promise. When she refuses to inform Diomedes whose sleeve it is, he determines to wear it on his helmet in the field of battle and see who it entices to quarrel. Troilus is devastated by Cressida's infidelity and must be restrained by Ulysses; he initially refuses to believe it is his Cressida who has so quickly become unfaithful. He vows to avenge his disgrace on Diomedes's head. All the while, Thersites has been cynically commenting on the folly of these proceedings. Aeneas arrives and informs Troilus that they must leave and arm themselves for battle as Hector is probably doing at that very moment. In Priam's palace, Andromache, Hector's wife, begs her husband not to fight this day; she has had a vivid dream

that Hector will be killed in battle. Cassandra has had a similar vision, and when Hector will not be swayed by their premonitions, Andromache and Cassandra enlist Priam to dissuade Hector from his intention to fight. Hector, having promised the Greeks to meet them on the field, is deferential to his father and asks his permission to do what is noble; Priam consents. Hector has been influenced enough by his wife's fear that he tries to dissuade Troilus from fighting, but the young lover is incensed. Pandarus brings a letter from Cressida to Troilus, who tears it up and throws it to the wind. A series of alarums and excursions, brief glimpses of the larger battle that rages between the Greeks and Trojans, follows: Troilus engages Diomedes and the two fight; the life of Thersites is spared by Hector; Diomedes appears and orders his servant to deliver Troilus's horse to Cressida; Agamemnon appears and bemoans a list of Greek warriors who have been killed; Nestor has the dead body of Patroclus sent to Achilles and sends word to Ajax to hurry to arms since Hector is unstoppable; Ajax appears calling for a fight with Troilus; Troilus appears to Diomedes and the two exit fighting; Hector and Achilles fight, and when Hector chivalrously allows Achilles time to catch his breath, the Greek hero runs off; Hector uncharacteristically pursues a fleeing Greek soldier so that he might possess his beautiful armor; Achilles plots with his followers, the Myrmidons, to ambush Hector; Hector is surprised by Achilles and shot by the Myrmidon archers as he rests without his armor; the cry goes out that Hector is dead; Agamemnon respects Hector's courage and silences the triumphant cries; Troilus informs Aeneas that Hector is dead and that his body has been dragged through the field while tied to the tail of Achilles horse. Troilus vows to fight determinedly to the end, but the outcome of this battle is never revealed. Pandarus approaches Troilus and is rebuked and struck by him. In a somewhat strange and disconcerting moment, Pandarus is left on stage to make a final appeal to the pimps ("traders in the flesh" [V.x.46]) in the audience.

Modern Connections

Elizabethan audiences would probably have been intimately familiar with the details and nuances of the Trojan War from both medieval and classical accounts. The Elizabethan age glamorized and romanticized the myths and accounts of antiquity. Shakespeare's *Troilus and Cressida* disappoints that romanticism by presenting a picture of the Trojan War, in which all its participants fall short of their mythological proportions and become all too human and frail. But Shakespeare's intention, perhaps, is not to present a pessimistic world both inside and outside the walls of Ilium in order to induce a similar pessimism and cynicism in his contemporary audiences; rather, he reduces the mythological figures of the antique world to human proportions in order to debunk the notion that the antique world embodied a nobility and virtue against which the Elizabethan world could not compare. It is worth noting that the practice of idealizing the past is not limited to the Elizabethan's idealization of antiquity. Many societies look back on past times and wistfully recall values that the present time may lack.

Many of the characters in Shakespeare's *Troilus and Cressida* border on the despicable, and none of the characters are consistently noble and virtuous. Thersites is a character so vicious, unsavory, and ungovernable that the Greeks, in not only tolerating his presence but finding him amusing, condemn their own virtue. Pandarus, by his own admission, is a bawd pure and simple. Helen, renowned throughout the ages for her beauty and command of men, is pictured as a trifling and superficial woman. At the beginning of the play, it is related that she has found great amusement in flirting with the young Troilus as she counts the hairs in his fledgling beard. Later, we see her at play, singing and dancing while the brutalities she has instigated are safely distanced from her by the walls of Troy. Paris is as his father, Priam, accurately describes him when he says to him,

Paris, you speak
Like one besotted on your sweet delights.
You have the honey still, but these the gall;
So to be valiant is no praise at all.

(II.ii.143-46)

Shakespeare's Cressida is no better than Helen; she is, most critics agree, a coquettish whore. Achilles, the great and powerful Greek warrior, is so self-indulgent and proud that he will not leave his tent to fight and maintain the reputation that has evoked the praise to which he has been accustomed. And his furtive and cowardly killing of Hector hardly allows us to understand why he has been so highly praised throughout the play. Even Hector, the Trojan pillar, is not consistent. He withdraws his objection that Helen is not worth the lives her defense has exacted when Troilus appeals to Hector's pride and alludes

to the opportunity the war has provided for glorious deeds in battle. In the final battle, Hector follows and kills a Greek soldier who is trying to run away so that he might have that soldier's attractive armor.

Shakespeare systematically denies audiences any opportunity to continue in their idealizations of the antique world. The Trojan War, fought over the idealization of Helen's worth, becomes a metaphor for the danger of disguising the "real" with the "ideal," illustrated at two moments in Shakespeare's play. Near the beginning, Ulysses offers that the Greek army has failed because the hierarchy of authority is no longer recognized, and he justifies that hierarchy in the Great Chain of Being, a conception of the universe often advanced as the conservative norm in Elizabethan England. But in building Ajax up as an ideal figure, Ulysses only succeeds in creating a substitute for Achilles who, in leading by example, is a distraction from and subversion to divinely sanctioned authority. Near the end of the play, Troilus strikes Pandarus and exclaims, "Hence, broker, lackey! Ignominy, shame / Pursue thy life, and live aye with thy name!" (V.x.33-34) But Pandarus gets the last words in the play and wonders aloud why he is so mistreated for that which he was asked to do. He has given Troilus just what the young Trojan wanted. If Troilus has idealized the relationship had with Cressida and suffers as a consequence, that is his fault, not Pandarus's.

When Troilus finds out that Hector has died, he becomes stronger and articulates his new resolution to stay the field and do what must be done. When he proclaims that Hector is dead, Aeneas says, "My lord, you do discomfort all the host" (V.x.10). Troilus explains that it is not his purpose to do so; he wants only to announce his conviction, the discovery, finally, of who he is. Similarly, perhaps Shakespeare's purpose is not to evoke pessimism in his audience, but to suggest that his own age can find its own identity, its own literary and cultural legacy by turning from an idealization of the past just as Troilus does in the absence of his dominant brother. The same concept can be applied in modern times. Often, in today's society, some people argue that life in the present day compares unfavorably to the past in a number of areas including values, political policies, and art. In the United States, for example, political leaders and time periods long or even recently past are often held up as models that current leaders and times do not measure up to. Yet, what is often forgotten or overlooked is the fact that these people, these past times were plagued with their own vices and problems. Just as in Shakespeare's time, the danger in idealizing the past is that the value of the present is not fully realized.

Characters

Achilles:

In most accounts of the Trojan battles, Achilles is the most prominent Greek warrior. In Shakespeare's account, Achilles has that reputation but performs no noteworthy deeds. He spends most of his time in his tent being amused by the impersonations of his aide Patroclus and accepting the adulation of the common soldiers for deeds he has performed in the past. In the minds of his military commanders, Achilles sets a dangerous precedent for the other soldiers who imitate him and take their ease, refusing to fight the Trojans. Achilles's arrogance has grown to such a degree that he refuses to answer even a summons from the Greek general Agamemnon. It is implied that the Trojan war drags on as a consequence of his inactivity.

When Hector issues his challenge to fight any Greek willing to do so, Achilles is the natural choice. But Ulysses, Nestor, Agamemnon, and others have hatched an elaborate plot to bring Achilles down a peg by advocating Ajax as the Greek champion. In another calculated effort to puncture Achilles's pride, a Greek contingent passes Achilles's tent and treats him with less respect than that to which he has been accustomed. Achilles questions Ulysses, who is the last person in this entourage, and Ulysses advises him of what today we might call the "old gunslinger syndrome": The reputation that is not constantly renewed against every ambitious newcomer becomes tarnished and fades. Shakespeare downplays the fact that Achilles refuses to fight the Trojans because he has made a pledge to Polyxena, Hector's sister, not to do so. When he first sees Hector after the Trojan hero's tournament with Ajax, Achilles taunts him by conjecturing in which limb he will fatally wound him. In the next scene, however, he receives a letter from Polyxena reminding him of his pledge, which Achilles immediately renews. He is finally galvanized to action when the slain body of Patroclus is sent to him during the play's last battle. He kills Hector in a treacherous ambush with the help of his Myrmidon archers after Hector has treated him chivalrously in an earlier encounter.

Aeneas:

We learn from other accounts that Aeneas is the son of the goddess Venus and the Trojan Anchises. It is Aeneas who, in Virgil's *Aeneid*, survives the destruction of Troy and is the connecting link between the two great civilizations of Greece and Rome. In Shakespeare's play, he is not much more than a messenger, announcing Hector's arrival to the tournament and negotiating the conditions of that fight, and, later, informing Troilus that he must leave his position outside of Calchas's tent in the Greek camp to arm for impending battle. Shakespeare is sometimes criticized for not fully developing Aeneas as a character. Other critics argue that there is no way Shakespeare could have presented in *Troilus and Cressida* all the information that circulated about mythological Trojan and Greek heroes. As the Prologue suggests, the play "Leaps o'er the vaunt and firstlings of those broils / Beginning in the middle" (Pro. 27-28). The action is reduced "To what may be digested in a play" (Pro. 29).

Agamemnon:

Agamemnon is the supreme general of the Greek forces outside the walls of Ilium. He has staged the siege of Troy to assuage the honor of his brother, Menelaus, whose wife Helen has been kidnapped by Paris. After seven long years of siege, Agamemnon still believes in the Greek cause and suspects that its failures are the consequence of a trial imposed by the god Zeus. Agamemnon is a fair-minded leader who respects the valiant heroism of his enemy, Hector. When he is informed that Hector has been killed by Achilles, he says, "If it be so, yet bragless let it be, / Great Hector was as good a man as he" (V.ix.5-6). But apparently, Agamemnon does not have an imposing physical presence, for Aeneas has no idea that the person to whom he talking is the great Greek leader.

Ajax:

Ajax has Greek and Trojan blood and is related to Hector; he is the son of Hector's aunt. He is selected by the Greek commanders to answer Hector's general challenge to individual combat. He is strong, being perhaps the Greeks' second-best warrior. Alexander, Cressida's servant, satirically describes Ajax in the following manner: "he is as valiant as the lion, churlish as the bear, slow as the elephant; a man into whom nature hath so crowded humors that his valor is crush'd into folly, his folly sauc'd with discretion" (I.ii.21-23). Ajax is somewhat dull-witted, unaware that he has been picked to fight Hector in order to make Achilles jealous. He believes that all the praise heaped upon him is sincere and quite quickly becomes arrogant. When his engagement with Hector is halted, Ajax expresses his desire to fight on, having only just warmed to his task, but accepts Hector's decision to cease fighting and embraces the Trojan defender.

Alexander:

Alexander is a servant to Cressida. Early in the play, when Cressida inquires, he identifies Helen and Queen Hecuba, Priam's wife, and informs her of their intent to witness the battle from a vantage point on the eastern tower. He relates how Hector has gone early to battle eager to avenge his embarrassment at being knocked down the previous day by Ajax.

Andromache:

Andromache is Hector's wife. She has a dream that Hector will be killed and begs him to forego the final battle of the play. Hector discounts her premonition and dismisses her. We get some sense of their relationship when Hector says, "Andromache, I am offended with you, / Upon the love you bear me, get you in" (V.iii.78-79). Andromache dutifully departs.

Antenor:

Antenor is an important Trojan military commander. He is captured by the Greeks and exchanged for Cressida at the request of her father Calchas who has left her behind in defecting to the Greek side in the Trojan War. According to Calchas, Antenor is crucial to the Trojan side in plotting the stratagems of war.

Attendants:

These are the attendants in Priam's palace, waiting upon the Trojan royals. They attend Helen and Paris in the scene in which Helen entices Pandarus to sing. Attendants enter with the Trojan contingent which accompanies Hector to the tournament in the Greek camp.

Calchas:

Calchas is Cressida's father. He has the gift of prophecy and has had a vision of Troy's destruction, prompting him to abandon the walled city and join

"Achilles's arrogance has grown to such a degree that he refuses to answer even a summons from the Greek general Agamemnon."

the Greeks outside. When he requests that Antenor be exchanged for Cressida, he suggests that he is owed that much, having endured the reputation of a traitor and the separation from his daughter in doing the Greek side some unstipulated service.

Cassandra:

Cassandra is Priam's daughter and is sister to Hector, Paris, and Troilus. She has the gift of prophecy but has been cursed by the gods to never have her prophetic voice believed. As the Trojan royal family discusses whether or not to continue their resistance to the Greek siege, Cassandra enters raving and proclaims, "Troy must not be, nor goodly Ilion stand. / Our fire-brand brother Paris burns us all" (II.ii.109-10). She later supports Andromache, pleading with Hector not to arm for the final battle.

Cressida:

Cressida is the daughter of Calchas and the niece of Pandarus. She is united with Troilus through the efforts of her uncle, Pandarus, who has to work at convincing her that Troilus is a worthy match. He situates her so that she might see a parade of noble Trojan warriors as they pass. Pandarus devalues each of these warriors in order to inflate the value of Troilus in Cressida's eyes. But Cressida resists her uncle's efforts. When he leaves, she says, "But more in Troilus thousandfold I see / Than in the glass of Pandar's praise may be" (I.ii.284-85). She again plays the coquette when she is conducted into the Greek camp after being exchanged for Antenor. Cressida kisses all of the Greek commanders with barely subdued enthusiasm, prompting Ulysses to remark that everything about her can be set down "For sluttish spoils of opportunity, / And daughters of the game" (IV.v.62-63); he considers her a prostitute. Diomedes's assessment of her is no more noble. He is interested only in her physical beauty, and he refuses to play her trifling games of love-

> **Alexander, Cressida's servant, satirically describes Ajax in the following manner: 'he is as valiant as the lion, churlish as the bear, slow as the elephant; a man into whom nature hath so crowded humors that his valor is crush'd into folly, his folly sauc'd with discretion' (I.ii.21-23)."**

making. When she plays hard to get and refuses his early advances, he walks away, and she is forced to go after him, losing the advantage which she seems to find so enjoyable in her relationships with men.

Cressida perhaps knows what men want of her, and she attempts to maintain a sense of dignity in what she seems to perceive as the only way available to her. In her soliloquy after Pandarus attempts to convice her of Troilus's worth, Cressida says, "Men prize the thing ungain'd more than it is" (I.ii.289), realizing that "Achievement is command; ungain'd beseech" (I.ii.293). Even when she admits to Troilus that she loves him, she is in control, pretending embarrassment at having revealed too much when her real intention is to inflame his passion all the more and gain firmer control. Cressida is unfaithful, and typically viewed as a whore, but it is arguable that she follows the only path that yields the results she seems to be seeking.

Deiphobus:

Deiphobus is another of Priam's sons, a brother to Hector, Paris, and Troilus. He is part of the procession of returning Trojan warriors upon which Pandarus and Cressida comment near the beginning of the play. He, along with Aeneas, accompanies Diomedes to Cressida as Diomedes escorts her from Troy to the Greek camp. He appears in the last scene of the play without speaking.

Diomedes:

Diomedes is the Greek chosen to escort Cressida to the Greek camp after she has been exchanged for Antenor, a prisoner of war. Diomedes is a no-

nonsense man, a slave neither to courtesy nor to courtly convention. When Troilus commands him to treat Cressida well, Diomedes replies that he will do as he pleases; he will not be dictated to by the young Trojan. When Cressida acts coy with him after inviting him to visit her at her father's tent, he walks away uninterested in her games of love. Cressida calls him back and he says, "No, no, good night, I'll be your fool no more" (V.ii.32). She gives him Troilus's sleeve as a pledge that she will meet him later, and Diomedes announces his callous intention to wear that sleeve in battle the next day in order to find out who initially gave it to Cressida, adding insult to Troilus's injury. Diomedes and Troilus engage one another several times in the final battle without a decisive outcome.

Hector:

He is the son of Priam and brother to Paris and Troilus. Hector is the embodiment of the idealism and romance associated with Troy, and his death precipitates the fall of that legendary city. He is strong, brave, and unselfish and commands the respect of his enemies. He has the reputation, among Trojans and Greeks alike, of fighting only those soldiers who oppose him in offensive positions, sparing those who are defenseless or fleeing. He is kind and deferential to his father even though Priam, like everyone else, yields to Hector's wishes. Informed of Andromache's dream and fear for his life, he is as concerned with Troilus's safety as he is unconcerned with his own. In his encounters with the two most renowned Greek fighters Achilles and Ajax, he treats both according to the code of chivalry.

But there are chinks in Hector's armor. The first appears when he retreats from his position that Helen is not worth all the suffering undergone on her behalf. He succumbs to Troilus's argument that Helen provides Troy with a theme for enacting noble deeds, a direct appeal to the heroic nature of Hector, but one that reveals a streak of selfish pride in the noble Trojan. The second chink appears when Hector, contrary to his reputation for doing otherwise, pursues the fleeing Greek soldier, intent on acquiring that soldier's ornate armor. When he says, "Most putrefied core, so fair without, / Thy goodly armor thus hath cost thy life" (V.viii.1-2), it is a metaphor, in Shakespeare's play, for both the Trojan War itself and Hector's outdated chivalry.

Helen:

Helen is depicted as a woman of great outer beauty but little inner substance. On the few occasions in the play when we hear of or see her activities, she seems to be occupied with petty diversions and courtly entertainments, seemingly unmindful of her pivotal role in affairs of state. She provides the theme for the Trojan War, a theme as empty of substance as she is and as fragile and false as Cressida's love turns out to be.

Helenus:

Helenus is another of Priam's sons, brother to Hector, Paris, and Troilus. He is also a priest. When Hector provides reasons that the defense of Helen should not be prolonged, Troilus objects that such petty reasons diminish great Priam's power and sway. Helenus sides with Hector and accuses Troilus of being incapable of reasoning. Troilus responds, ''You are for dreams and slumbers, brother priest, / You fur your gloves with reason'' (II.ii.37-38), implying that Helenus, by reason of his vocation, is cowardly and passionless.

Margarelon:

Margarelon is the bastard son of Priam. He appears briefly in the final act and challenges Thersites, who, before he runs away, protests that he is a bastard too and bastards should not fight one another since they share the same shameful stigma.

Menelaus:

Menelaus is the brother of Agamemnon and the rightful husband of Helen. He is the ruler of Sparta, the Greek city from which Paris has abducted Helen. Menelaus is history's most famous cuckold, a name derived from the cuckoo bird, which had a reputation for taking over the nests of other birds, just as Paris now occupies the nest that rightfully belongs to Menelaus. Cuckolds were assigned symbolic horns, representative of the frustrated masculine virility invoked by the absence of the cuckold's wife in her diversion to pleasures elsewhere. Menelaus and his symbolic horns are the object of much ridicule in the play. Even the courteous and respectful Hector cannot resist poking fun at Menelaus. Upon meeting Menelaus, Hector says of Helen, ''She's well, but bade me not commend her to you'' (IV.v.180). Agamemnon has agreed to the siege of Troy so that he might help his brother regain his wife and his honor. If the Trojan excuse for war—the defense of the superficial and frivolous Helen—is flimsy and unjustifiable, the Greek cause—to regain for Menelaus an adulterous wife who no longer wants him—is equally so.

> **" Cressida kisses all of the Greek commanders with barely subdued enthusiasm, prompting Ulysses to remark that everything about her can be set down 'For sluttish spoils of opportunity, / And daughters of the game' (IV.v.62-63); he considers her a prostitute."**

Nestor:

Nestor is a Greek commander, an advisor to Agamemnon. He is a sage old man well-respected for his age and knowledge. His enthusiasm for war is greater than his physical ability to actively engage in fighting. He says that he will answer Hector's challenge to individual combat if no other Greek soldier has the courage to do so. When he meets Hector before his tournament of single arms with Ajax, he tells the Trojan hero that in his own day he would have been more than a match for Hector. Despite his reputation for wisdom, it is Ulysses who proposes the most plausible answer for the failure of the Greek armies to topple Troy after seven years' siege. And it is Ulysses who conceives of the stratagem to induce Achilles to action, proposing that idea to Nestor first only because the venerable old man has the ear and respect of Agamemnon.

Pandarus:

Pandarus is Calchas's brother and Cressida's uncle. His function in the play is to bring Troilus and Cressida together. He treats both young lovers as commodities, inflating Troilus's worth in the mind of Cressida and perversely displaying a great sense of pride in Cressida's beauty, a beauty that is said to rival that of Helen. When Troilus and Cressida foreshadow the association their names will have with ''true'' and ''false'' love, Pandarus adds, ''Let all constant men be Troiluses, all false women Cressids, and all brokers-between Pandars'' (III.ii.202-04). In fact, Pandarus predicts accurately; ''panderers,'' ''bawds,'' ''pimps'' all are synonymous. In the last speech of the play, after he has been rejected by Troilus, Pandarus asks the bawds in the audience to

> **Hector is the embodiment of the idealism and romance associated with Troy, and his death precipitates the fall of that legendary city."**

"weep out at Pandar's fall" (V.x.48), as if the entire play has been about Pandarus's tragic circumstances. In a sense, Pandarus is right. By giving him the last lines in the play, Shakespeare reduces the epic love story of Troilus and Cressida to the tawdry spectacle of prostitution, beauty as a commodity and pretext for war.

Paris:

Paris is Priam's son and brother to Hector and Troilus. With the full consent of Priam and the rest of the Trojan royal family, he has inflicted damage on their Greek enemies by abducting Helen from her husband, Menelaus, in Sparta, an action that sparked Greek retaliation and precipitated the Trojan War. Paris really is a fire brand, a description of him stemming from the fact that his mother, Hecuba, had dreamed she was touched by fire when she gave birth to him. He is lusty and passionate, delighting in his possession of Helen. His fierce defense of her is admittedly selfish, and he is the first to agree with Troilus when the latter reframes the defense of Helen as the defense of the honor and integrity of Troy.

Patroclus:

Patroclus is an aide to Achilles. Apparently, he has the gift of mimicry. According to Ulysses, Patroclus endlessly entertains Achilles with impersonations of a pompous, self-important Agamemnon and a feeble, old, shuffling Nestor. Later, when Thersites impersonates Ajax, Patroclus takes the part of a questioning Thersites. After the soldiers parade by Achilles's tent, Ulysses informs Achilles that the latter has been treated unceremoniously because his warlike reputation has faded. Patroclus apologizes to Achilles for making him "an effeminate man / In time of action" (III.iii.218-19). In a later scene, Thersites refers to Patroclus's reputation as a "male varlot" (V.i.16), Achilles's "masculine whore" (V.i.17).

Priam:

Priam is the King of Troy, the husband of Hecuba, and the father of Hector, Paris, Deiphobus, Helenus, Cassandra, and Troilus. He conducts the Trojan synod which will determine whether or not Troy continues to harbor Helen. In a later scene, he is recruited by Andromache and Cassandra to exercise his authority over Hector and make his son refrain from what Andromache and Cassandra feel will be the fateful battle. Although he is appealed to as a source of great strength and authority, on both occasions Priam defers to the judgment of Hector. Priam's castle is called Ilium, a name from which is derived *The Iliad*, Homer's epic account of the Trojan War.

Servant (to Diomedes):

Diomedes's servant appears briefly in the last act as he is directed by Diomedes, who has apparently gained a momentary advantage over Troilus, to take Troilus's horse to Cressida.

Servant (to Paris):

Paris's servant engages in a humorous exchange with Pandarus when he comes to see Paris and ask him to make excuse for Troilus's absence from dinner.

Servant (to Troilus):

In I.ii, a servant to Troilus informs Pandarus that Troilus wants to speak with him. Both the stage direction and speech prefix designate this servant as "Boy." In III.ii, a servant to Troilus informs Pandarus that Troilus is waiting to be conducted to Cressida. Both the stage direction and speech prefix designate this servant as "Man." They might be the same person, but, more probably, they are different characters.

Soldiers:

These are common foot soldiers. They appear at the end of the procession that is returning from battle, filing past the vantage point of Pandarus and Cressida.

Thersites:

Thersites is Ajax's fool at the beginning of the play, but Achilles finds Thersite amusing and, in effect, takes him away from Ajax. Thersites comments cynically on Cressida's fall to the lusty Greek Diomedes, but he is not sympathetic to Troilus; he seems to hate everyone. His language is filled with base and graphic imagery. Thersites's cynicism is almost certainly meant to illustrate the extreme of human depravity. Although cynicism pervades the play, that cynicism is probably meant as a way of stripping away the idealization of the Trojan War and its participants, and is fundamentally different from the hopeless pessimism embodied by Thersites.

Troilus:

Troilus is the son of Priam and the brother of Hector and Paris. He is young and idealistic. He appeals to Pandarus to woo Cressida for him, believing that she is a beautiful and worthy maid. When he argues with Hector over the desirability of continuing to protect Helen, he may have in mind his idealized conception of Cressida. He envisions Cressida as having the kind of beauty that Helen is thought to have, a beauty that sets men at war against one another. He is unaware that neither of the women is what she seems. When Pandarus brings the two lovers together, Troilus is passionate and vows his faithfulness and seems to view the arranged tryst (Pandarus has prepared a chamber for them complete with a bed and a guaranteed privacy) as a lasting love affair.

Later, when Troilus watches Cressida caress Diomedes and show him affection, his pain is almost palpable to the audience. Troilus cannot believe his eyes, preferring to think that there are two Cressidas than to think that she has so soon betrayed his love. His reason and passion struggle against one another. He knows by reason that Cressida cannot be in two places at once, but his emotion desperately wants to make it so. He does not mature, however, in this moment of witnessing Cressida's infidelity. He still clings to a romanticized version of their relationship, vowing to avenge the loss of that romance on the head of Diomedes. Troilus, as Cressida comments in V.ii.111-12, is full of turpitude, a disquiet that will not go away until he abandons his idealized conception of Cressida. But at the end of the play he says, "Hope of revenge shall hide our inward woe" (V.x.31), a statement that applies as much to his disappointment in Cressida as it does to the circumstances of Hector's death.

Ulysses:

Ulysses is a Greek commander. He issues two great speeches in the play. In the first (I.iii.75-137), he explains that the Greek army has failed in achiev-

> **If the Trojan excuse for war—the defense of the superficial and frivolous Helen—is flimsy and unjustifiable, the Greek cause—to regain for Menelaus an adulterous wife who no longer wants him—is equally so."**

ing its goal because "degree" is no longer respected. He goes on to describe the Great Chain of Being: The heavens themselves are ordered, each planet observing the superiority of the sun. This order should be paralleled on earth in the affairs of men, the gods sanctioning kings and generals to rule over other men in degree of diminishing succession. Order is only maintained when each man observes the degree and rank of his superiors. In the second (III.iii.112-41), Ulysses tells Achilles that one only knows one's value when it is reflected in the attitudes of others. The eye of the observer is the only weather vane of worth. Although Ulysses has a large presence throughout the play, like Aeneas, he is not fully rendered to Elizabethan audiences who would have been thoroughly acquainted with his stature and his past deeds through Homer's *The Odyssey*, a works that details Ulysses's perilous journey home to his wife Penelope after the conclusion of the Trojan War.

Further Reading

Barton, Anne. Introduction to *Troilus and Cressida*, by William Shakespeare. In *The Riverside Shakespeare*, edited by G. Blakemore Evans, 443-47. Boston: Houghton Mifflin, 1974.

> Barton discusses the textual history and presents a general reading of the play. She argues that no character in *Troilus and Cressida* is consistent or representative of truth or nobility. The only thing that saves the audience from the characters' destructive nihilism, Barton maintains, is the integrity and artistry of the play shaped by Shakespeare.

> **When Troilus and Cressida foreshadow the association their names will have with 'true' and 'false' love, Pandarus adds, 'Let all constant men be Troiluses, all false women Cressids, and all brokers-between Pandars' (III.ii.202-04). In fact, Pandarus predicts accurately; 'panderers,' 'bawds,' 'pimps' all are synonymous."**

Cole, Douglas. "Myth and Anti-Myth: The Case of *Troilus and Cressida*." *Shakespeare Quarterly* 31, no. 1 (1980): 76-84.

Cole argues that Shakespeare's treatment of the myth of Troy undermines the way societies create myth as a way to connect with specific histories and define their values.

Dusinberre, Juliet. "*Troilus and Cressida* and the Definition of Beauty." *Shakespeare Survey* 36 (1983): 85-95.

Dusinberre examines how concepts of beauty function in the play. She argues that Helen and Cressida are valued only for their physical beauty and not their spiritual or moral beauty.

Fly, Richard D. "Cassandra and the Language of Prophecy in *Troilus and Cressida*." *Shakespeare Quarterly* 26, no. 2 (1975): 157-71.

Fly examines the prophecy that abounds in *Troilus and Cressida* and argues that from the prophecies of Cassandra and Calchas to the Elizabethan audience's knowledge of the fate of Troy, the play is pervaded by a sense of doom.

Foakes, R. A. "*Troilus and Cressida* Reconsidered." *University of Toronto Quarterly* 32, no. 2 (1963): 142-54.

Addressing the confused question of *Troilus and Cressida*'s genre, Foakes argues that the first three acts are comedy and the last two lead to an unresolved ending that is both comic and tragic.

Franson, J. Karl. "An Antenor—Aeneas Conspiracy in Shakespeare's *Troilus and Cressida*." *Studies in the Humanities* 7, no. 1 (1978): 43-47.

Franson demonstrates that Shakespeare takes from Chaucer's account of Troilus and Cressida the idea that Antenor was the one who betrayed Troy. He argues that in the exchange of Antenor for Cressida

the obviously greater value of Antenor is ignored by the Greeks, implying a conspiracy, involving Aeneas, to get Antenor back into the walled city of Troy.

Greene, Gayle. "Language and Value in Shakespeare's *Troilus and Cressida*." *Studies in English Literature* 21, no. 2 (1981): 271-85.

Greene argues that in the sixteenth century, the ability of language to communicate meaning completely and effectively was being questioned. The characters' failure to communicate in *Troilus and Cressida* defeats the hierarchical social order described by Ulysses.

Hunter, G. K. "*Troilus and Cressida*: A Tragic Satire." *Shakespeare Studies* 13 (1974-75): 1-23.

Hunter discounts the notion that Shakespeare relied heavily or exclusively upon medieval sources for the story of Troilus and Cressida, arguing that Shakespeare's play adopts the tone and themes of Homer.

Kaula, David. " 'Mad Idolatry' in Shakespeare's *Troilus and Cressida*." *Texas Studies in Literature and Language* 15, no. 1 (1973): 25-38.

Kaula points out the biblical allusions in *Troilus and Cressida* and argues that there is an implied Christian reading of the play opposed to the idolatry of the Greeks and Trojans.

Kimbrough, Robert. "The Troilus Log: Shakespeare and 'Box-Office'." *Shakespeare Quarterly* 15, no. 3 (1964): 201-09.

Kimbrough argues that, in *Troilus and Cressida*, Shakespeare was trying to please a sophisticated, courtly audience that was extremely cynical and desired keen satire in the dramatic entertainment offered to them.

Powell, Neil. "Hero and Human: The Problem of Achilles." *Critical Quarterly* 21, no. 2 (1979): 17-28.

Powell defends Achilles as the only consistent character in *Troilus and Cressida*.

Rabkin, Norman. "*Troilus and Cressida*: The Uses of the Double Plot." *Shakespeare Studies* 1 (1965): 265-82.

Rabkin discusses the ways in which *Troilus and Cressida* poses the value of both love interests and political ends as a struggle between reason and emotion.

Rowland, Beryl. "A Cake-Making Image in *Troilus and Cressida*." *Shakespeare Quarterly* 21, no. 2 (1970): 191-94.

By examining the sexual implications of cake baking in Pandarus's insistence that Troilus be patient in his realization of union with Cressida, Rowland argues that Troilus's attraction to her is physical only.

Roy, Emil. "War and Manliness in Shakespeare's *Troilus and Cressida*." *Comparative Drama* 7, no. 2 (1973): 107-120.

Roy argues that both the Greek and Trojan warriors manifest an Oedipal struggle in their repeated warlike activities.

Stockholder, Katherine. "Power and Pleasure in *Troilus and Cressida*, or Rhetoric and Structure of the Anti-Tragic." *College English* 30, no. 7 (1969): 539-54.

Stockholder analyzes Cressida, Hector, Helen, Troilus, and Ulysses and proposes that Shakespeare undoes the tragic import of his play by offering characters who are only concerned with their transitory images and who do not fulfill the expectations of audiences familiar with the characters' historical significance.

Thompson, Karl F. "*Troilus and Cressida*: The Incomplete Achilles." *College English* 27, no. 7 (1966): 532-36.
   Thompson argues that Shakespeare's play is full of inconsistencies, most notably in Shakespeare's failure to develop fully the characters of Ulysses and Achilles and to account for the latter's pledge to Hector's sister, Polyxena, that he would not fight the Trojans.

Twelfth Night, or What You Will

circa 1601-02

Plot Summary

Act I:

Duke Orsino of Illyria is lovesick for Olivia, a rich countess who refuses to see him and remains shut up in her house, mourning for her dead brother. Close by, the gentlewoman Viola has landed on Illyria's coast after being shipwrecked while traveling with her twin brother, Sebastian, whom she fears has been drowned at sea. Uncertain about her future, Viola disguises herself in men's clothing, calls herself Cesario, and goes to find employment with the duke. Meanwhile, Olivia's drunken and free-loading uncle, Sir Toby Belch, keeps trying unsuccessfully to arrange a marriage between his niece and his foolish but rich friend Sir Andrew Aguecheek. Duke Orsino sends his new and trusted page Cesario (Viola in disguise) to deliver words of love to the countess. Olivia tells her self-important steward, Malvolio, to send the page away, but Viola, who has herself fallen in love with Orsino, loyally insists upon delivering the duke's message. Olivia finally agrees to listen to the page, but as usual rejects the duke's message of love. Unexpectedly, however, she falls in love with the disguised Viola.

Act II:

Viola's twin brother, Sebastian, appears in Illyria after having been saved from drowning by the sea captain Antonio. Convinced that his sister is dead and that his own luck is bad, Sebastian sets off alone to seek his fortune. Olivia sends a ring to Viola/Cesario, pretending that she is returning one that the page had delivered to her, but in fact hoping that Viola/Cesario will visit her again. When she realizes that her "outside," (her disguise as Cesario) has "charm'd" the countess, Viola feels pity, but concludes that time "must untangle this, not I, / It is too hard a knot for me t'untie" (II.ii.18, 40-41). Malvolio scolds Sir Toby, Sir Andrew Aguecheek, and Feste (Olivia's hired clown, or fool) for drinking and singing until well after midnight. When Sir Toby vows revenge against the puritanical steward, Olivia's serving-lady Maria offers to write a letter that will fool Malvolio into thinking that the countess loves him, and will thus "make him an ass" (II.iii.168-69). The next day, Sir Toby and his friends watch in hiding as Malvolio reads Maria's phony love letter and convinces himself that Olivia adores him. Per the letter's instructions, Malvolio plans to smile all the time and to wear yellow stockings "cross-garter'd"—actions which are in fact guaranteed to irritate the countess (II.v.200).

Act III:

Viola/Cesario continues to court Olivia on Orsino's behalf. Sir Andrew Aguecheek angrily notices that the countess is in love with the page and threatens to leave, so Sir Toby—reluctant to lose the rich Sir Andrew as a source of ready cash—suggests that his friend challenge Viola/Cesario to a duel. Meanwhile, Antonio lends Sebastian a purseful of money but plans to steer clear of the duke's palace, where he would be arrested for crimes he once committed against Orsino and the state. When Malvolio appears smiling and cross-gartered before Olivia, she concludes that he is insane and puts him into Maria's custody. Egged on by Sir Toby, Sir Andrew and Viola/Cesario unwillingly duel with each other. Antonio intervenes to protect Viola/Cesario, whom he mistakes for her brother, Sebastian. Officers arrive to stop the duel, and, recognizing Antonio, they arrest him for his earlier offenses against Illyria. Before he is taken away, Antonio confuses Viola/Cesario by calling her Sebastian and asking for her help.

Act IV:

Realizing that Viola/Cesario is fearful, the equally timid Sir Andrew now feels secure enough to finish the duel, but meets and mistakenly challenges Sebastian instead. Olivia intervenes, takes the amazed Sebastian to her home, and marries him, all the while thinking that he is Orsino's page. Meanwhile, after imprisoning Malvolio in a darkened room in Olivia's house, Sir Toby, Maria, and Feste take their revenge on the steward by tormenting him and treating him as though he were crazy.

Act V:

Viola/Cesario speaks in Antonio's defense when he is brought before the duke, but angers Antonio (who still thinks she is her brother, Sebastian) by claiming not to know him. Olivia arrives and feels betrayed when Viola/Cesario denies having been married to her. Sir Andrew and Sir Toby appear and accuse the astonished page of having injured them. When Sebastian appears, looking exactly like Viola/Cesario, everyone is amazed, but the confusion and accusations are at last cleared up. Olivia is happy to be married to Sebastian, and Orsino proposes marriage to Viola, who happily accepts. Feste delivers a letter from Malvolio to Olivia, in which the steward complains of having been badly treated by the countess and her uncle, Sir Toby. Olivia orders that Malvolio be released and brought to her. On his arrival, Malvolio once more bitterly complains of his mistreatment, and the practical joke against him is revealed, including the fact that Sir Toby has married Maria in gratitude for the phony love letter which she wrote. Olivia tries to calm Malvolio, promising him justice, but the steward leaves, swearing that he will be "reveng'd on the whole pack" of them (V.i.378). The play closes with a song sung by Feste.

Modern Connections

Twelfth Night is a holiday that occurs on January 6, which is the festival of Epiphany and the last day of the twelve days of Christmas. During Shakespeare's time, Twelfth Night marked the end of a period of seasonal festivities when dances, parties, and banquets were held and plays were performed, and the traditional social order was temporarily overturned—ideally to allow any tensions that had built up over the year to be safely released. A king or lord of misrule was crowned, and traditional social roles (master/servant, bishop/choirboy, king/fool) were reversed. Today, Halloween, New Year's Eve, and Mardi Gras perform a similar function: on these holidays, many people eat and drink whatever they want, go to parties until early in the morning, and temporarily lose their cares and sometimes their inhibitions by wearing costumes or masks, pretending for a short time to be someone else.

Although Shakespeare never makes it clear whether or not the play's action occurs during the Christmas season, *Twelfth Night* has been described as carnivalesque in plot and tone, and indeed, Sir Toby Belch, for example, seems to be perpetually drinking and partying until late at night with his friend Sir Andrew Aguecheek. There are also plenty of role reversals in the play, including a fool speaking words of wisdom (Feste), a humorless steward made to look like a fool (Malvolio), and a woman (Viola) pretending to be a man.

Women were not employed in acting troupes during Shakespeare's time, so female roles—such as Juliet in *Romeo and Juliet* or Ophelia in *Hamlet*—had to be performed by boys whose voices had not yet deepened. This fact added an extra bit of humor to the action in *Twelfth Night*: Renaissance audiences knew that the part of Viola was played by a boy, and would find it amusing when Viola disguised herself as Cesario, thereby in reality becoming a boy playing a woman playing a young man.

Today, the part of Viola is customarily performed by a woman, which allows modern audiences to focus more on her heart-to-heart discussions with Duke Orsino regarding the differences between the sexes—an issue that continues to interest us today. In II.iv.29-41, for example, Orsino supports his remark that women should marry men who are older than themselves by arguing that men's "fancies are more giddy and unfirm, / More longing, wavering, sooner lost and worn, / Than women's are." Today, those who say that men behave badly, or that they are just like little boys, are voicing arguments similar to the duke's. Orsino then asserts that men need to marry younger women because female beauty does not last very long: "women," he declares, "are as roses, whose fair flow'r / Being once display'd, doth fall that very hour." This sounds very much like the still current attitude of some people that men grow distinguished but women grow old.

Viola, however, strongly disagrees with Orsino's claim in II.iv.93-103 that women cannot love as passionately and profoundly as men can. Still disguised as the male page Cesario, Viola asserts that men are all talk and no commitment when it comes to love: "We men may say more, swear more, but indeed / Our shows are more than will; for still we prove / Much in our vows, but little in our love"

(II.iv.116-18). The debate over the intensity of a man's love versus a woman's persists today, and men are often stereotyped as being afraid of commitment.

Finally, *Twelfth Night* focuses not only on the roles of the sexes, but on those of the different social classes as well. As a countess, Olivia is a member of the nobility; on the other hand, her steward, Malvolio, is a commoner and is expected to recognize and remain in his place as Olivia's inferior. All the same, Malvolio has hopes. Just before he falls victim to Sir Toby and Maria's practical joke, the steward is heard fantasizing about marrying the countess, telling himself that weddings between commoners and the nobility have happened before. "There is example for't," he says, "the Lady of the Strachy married the yeoman of the wardrobe" (II.v.39-40). In the United States, there isn't a formal class system like the one that plagues Malvolio, but there are divisions between the rich, the middle class, and the poor. There are no rules which prevent marriages between members of different financial classes; nevertheless someone who is poor or middle class usually cannot afford to travel in the same circles as someone who is fabulously wealthy. Like Malvolio, some Americans may dream about marrying someone rich and famous, but that doesn't mean it is likely to happen.

Characters

Aguecheek (Sir Andrew Aguecheek):

He is a friend of Sir Toby Belch, a suitor to Sir Toby's rich niece, Olivia, and a participant in the play's subplot. (A subplot is a secondary or subordinate plot which often reflects on or complicates the major plot in a work of fiction such as a play.) In I.iii.20, Toby praises Sir Andrew Aguecheek for being gallant, or "as tall a man as any's in Illyria." He defends his friend as cultured and talented, claiming that Sir Andrew knows how to play a musical instrument and can speak "three or four languages word for word" (I.iii.25-28). Maria, on the other hand, calls Sir Andrew a "fool and a prodigal," a "great quarreller" and a "coward," who spends his nights getting drunk with Toby (I.iii.24, 30, 31, 36-37). What Sir Toby in fact values about his friend is his money, for Sir Andrew has a comfortable income of "three thousand ducats a year," and he spends it generously (I.iii.22).

Aguecheek—whose name suggests that he has a thin or pinched face as though he had a chill, or an ague—makes his first appearance in I.iii.44-139, where he shows himself to be indeed foolish. When, for example, Toby introduces him to Maria with the admonishment to ''accost'' or greet her, Sir Andrew mistakenly thinks that Maria's last name is ''Accost'' (I.iii.49, 52). In response to a question in French, Sir Andrew proves that, contrary to Toby's claim, he has little knowledge of foreign languages, revealing instead his other, less academic interests: ''What is '*pourquoi*'? Do, or not do? I would I had bestowed that time in the tongues that I have in fencing, dancing, and bear-baiting'' (I.iii.91-93).

Sir Andrew's principal grievance in the play is that he is wasting his time and money courting Olivia when she clearly has no interest in him but is in fact more attentive to Duke Orsino's page, Viola/Cesario. Off and on during the play, he threatens to abandon his suit and go home, but Sir Toby flatters him, exploiting his love of ''masques and revels'' to convince Aguecheek to stay longer and spend more money (I.iii.113-14). In III.ii he even persuades the cowardly Sir Andrew to challenge Viola/Cesario to a duel. At the close of the play (V.i.173-208), Aguecheek's money has been used up, and his head has been bloodied in a sword fight with Sebastian (whom he had mistaken for Viola/Cesario). Sir Toby, who has also been injured, takes the opportunity to tell Sir Andrew what he really thinks of him, and calls the knight ''an ass-head and a coxcomb and a knave, a thin fac'd knave, a gull!'' (V.i.206-07).

Critics note that Sir Andrew Aguecheek's drunken revels with Sir Toby contribute to the festive, holiday atmosphere of the play. Further, because of his foolishness, his phony gallantry, and his lack of skill in wooing (in III.i.86-91, he memorizes flowery words that he hears Viola/Cesario using on Olivia, hoping to try them out later, himself), Sir Andrew has been described as a parody of a courtly lover. As such, he is also a parody of Duke Orsino— Sir Andrew's rival for Olivia's affections. (To parody means to imitate something or someone for the purposes of comic effect or ridicule.)

Critics have also remarked that sometimes Aguecheek is a poignant character, as for example, when he admits in I.iii.82-86 that he is not as witty or clever as he would like to be; and again in II.iii.181, when in response to Toby's comment that he is adored by Maria, Sir Andrew wistfully replies, ''I was ador'd once too.'' All the same, critics

> **❝** **Sir Andrew's principal grievance in the play is that he is wasting his time and money courting Olivia when she clearly has no interest in him but is in fact more attentive to Duke Orsino's page, Viola/Cesario.''**

conclude that while these moments reveal Shakespeare's skill at creating complex characters, Sir Andrew Aguecheek remains a ridiculous figure.

Andrew (Sir Andrew Aguecheek):
See Aguecheek

Antonio:
He is a sea captain who becomes Sebastian's devoted friend after rescuing him from a shipwreck. Antonio's discussion with his new friend in II.i introduces the fact that Sebastian and his sister, Viola, are twins who were ''born [with] in an hour'' of one another (II.i.19). Antonio's affection for Sebastian is so strong that he decides to follow the young man to Orsino's household, even though Antonio has ''many enemies in Orsino's court,'' and would face danger if he went there (II.i.45-48).

When he catches up with Sebastian in III.iii, Antonio explains that he was once in a sea battle against the count's galleys and is wanted in Illyria for piracy. Antonio's status as an outlaw is significant to the action of *Twelfth Night* because it means that he must often leave Sebastian and not ''walk too open'' or he might be arrested (III.iii.37). Inevitably, during one of these separations he encounters Viola/Cesario and thinks that she is her brother Sebastian, adding to the chaos in this play of shifting identities and miscommunication.

Scholars have remarked that during the Renaissance, friendship was considered more important than was sexual love, and that friendship is in fact one of the themes in *Twelfth Night*. Antonio repeatedly expresses his affection for Sebastian. In III.iii, he worries about Sebastian's safety in a foreign land, and helps him out by securing him room and board at a local inn; he even lends Sebastian a

> **Antonio's affection for Sebastian is so strong that he decides to follow the young man to Orsino's household, even though Antonio has 'many enemies in Orsino's court,' and would face danger if he went there (II.i.45-48)."**

purseful of money for buying souvenirs (III.iii.38-46). Thus Antonio feels deeply hurt when, mistaking her for Sebastian, he defends Viola/Cesario against Sir Andrew Aguecheek, only to be recognized and arrested by Orsino's men, and to have the astonished Viola/Cesario declare that she's never seen him before (III.iv.312-57). Feeling betrayed, the unhappy Antonio rethinks his definition of friendship. He concludes that he had been misled by Sebastian's good looks into thinking that he was a worthy companion, but now realizes that an honorable mind is more important when it comes to friendship than a pleasing exterior: "In nature there's no blemish but the mind; / None can be call'd deform'd but the unkind" (III.iv.367-68).

When he is delivered over to the duke in V.i, Antonio again reproaches Viola/Cesario for her apparent betrayal. Shortly afterward, it is his turn to be astonished when the real Sebastian appears, prompting Antonio to exclaim as he looks wonderingly at Viola and her brother, "How have you made division of yourself? / An apple, cleft in two, is not more twin / Than these two creatures. Which is Sebastian?" (V.i.222-24).

Attendants:

These are unnamed characters with no speaking parts. Attendants accompany the duke and Olivia throughout the play.

Belch (Sir Toby Belch):

He is Olivia's uncle and a co-director of the play's subplots involving Aguecheek and Malvolio. (A subplot is a secondary or subordinate plot which often reflects on or complicates the major plot in a work of fiction such as a play.) He is also a free-loader who lives off his niece and takes money from his friend, Sir Andrew Aguecheek. Sir Toby Belch is annoyed with Olivia, who has "abjur'd the company / And sight of men" and has chosen instead to spend seven years of her young life hidden and in mourning for her dead brother (I.ii.40-41). Believing that "care's an enemy to life," Toby indulges in food, drink, and song, and hopes to do so as long as there is "drink in Illyria" (I.iii.2-3, 40). His last name is appropriate to his dissipated manner of living, and his dissipation is in keeping with the play's festive title.

While characters like Viola and Feste comment on the passing of time and the decay of youthfulness, and while Olivia spends her hours keeping her brother's memory alive with her tears, Sir Toby alters time to suit his own purpose. During a long night of partying, for example, he announces to Sir Andrew that "Not to be a-bed after midnight is to be up betimes"—or that staying up late is the same as getting up early. He then cites a Latin quote which claims that being up before dawn is good for one's health (II.iii.1-3). Shortly afterward, when Olivia's steward, Malvolio, chastises him for being unconcerned about where he is or how late it has gotten ("Is there no respect of place, persons, nor time in you?"), Sir Toby retorts that he has indeed been keeping time—in the "catches," or round-songs which he and his friends have been singing by turns (II.iii.91-92, 93).

Critics note that Sir Toby's drunken carelessness stands in direct opposition to Malvolio's strictness and self-importance. "Art any more than a steward?"—Sir Toby sneers at the scolding Malvolio, who is in fact simply another of Olivia's servants, and thus lower in rank than both her and her uncle (II.iii.114). "Dost thou think because thou art virtuous there shall be no more cakes and ale?"—Sir Toby adds, annoyed with the steward for being a killjoy (II.iii.114-16).

Thanks to Maria, Toby gets his revenge against the officious steward when Malvolio is fooled into believing that Olivia wants to marry him. The "gulling" of Malvolio begins as a joke shared with the audience, who listens in with Toby, Fabian, and Sir Andrew Aguecheek as Malvolio reads aloud a phony love-letter and succeeds at convincing himself that the letter is both genuine and meant for him (II.v). It ends with Malvolio's imprisonment in a dark room for his apparent insanity. By that time, the joke has gotten old even for Sir Toby, who is already in serious trouble with his niece for his dissolute behavior and cannot afford to add this practical joke to his list of misdemeanors (IV.ii.66-71).

Critics remark that thanks to his drunken jokes and festive, topsy-turvy approach to life, Sir Toby Belch is an appealing character; at the same time, he is a sponger with a mean streak. To hang on to his lucrative source of income, Sir Toby spends much of his time persuading the well-off but foolish Sir Andrew that he has a chance at marrying Olivia. He even arranges a comically timid duel between Aguecheek and Viola/Cesario to prevent Sir Andrew's departure. But at the close of the play, Sir Andrew is out of money and both he and Sir Toby have been soundly beaten by Sebastian. Now, Sir Toby scorns his former meal-ticket, calling him ''an ass-head and a coxcomb and a knave, a thin-fac'd knave, a gull!'' (V.i.206-07).

Captain (Sea Captain):

His first and only appearance occurs in I.ii when he comes ashore with Viola after having rescued her from a shipwreck. The captain's role in the play is brief but useful since he provides us with important introductory information. For example, he tells Viola the name of the country where the play is set (Illyria), as well as the name of its ruler (Duke Orsino). He also informs her that he saw her brother Sebastian still alive and clinging to a mast after their ship sank, thus preparing the way for Sebastian's entrance in II.i. Finally, the captain is the character to whom Viola confides her plan to disguise herself as the youth, Cesario, and seek employment with Orsino. At the close of the play, Viola mentions that she left her ''maiden weeds,'' or female clothing, in the captain's safekeeping while she masqueraded as Cesario, and that he can ''confirm'' that she is in fact Viola (V.i.249-56). The last we hear of the captain is that he has been imprisoned on charges brought against him by Malvolio; thus the captain's function at this point is to shift our attention away from the lovers and toward the steward, who, as Olivia now remembers, has himself been taken into custody for madness (V.i.274-83).

Cesario (Viola/Cesario):

See Viola

Clown:

See Feste

> **Believing that 'care's an enemy to life,' Toby indulges in food, drink, and song, and hopes to do so as long as there is 'drink in Illyria' (I.iii.2-3, 40).''**

Countess:

See Olivia

Curio:

Curio is one of two gentlemen who serve Duke Orsino (the other is Valentine). In I.i.16 he invites Orsino deer hunting, thus giving the lovesick duke the opportunity to use the word ''hart'' (a term for a male deer) as a pun on the word ''heart'' and also providing Orsino with the chance to make an allusion to the Roman myth about the hunter Actaeon, who was transformed into a stag by the goddess Diana after seeing her bathing, and subsequently killed by his own hunting dogs. (A pun is a play on words which depends for its humor on the similarity of the sound of the words—for example, ''heart'' and ''hart,'' ''son'' and ''sun,'' ''dear'' and ''deer.'' An allusion is a brief or implied reference to something or someone in, for example, literature or history.) Orsino's ability to play word games even while he is pining for Olivia suggests that he is enamored with the idea of love rather than genuinely in love with the countess. Curio speaks again, in II.iv, when he seeks out Olivia's jester, Feste, to sing for the duke.

Duke (Duke Orsino):

See Orsino

Fabian:

He is one of Olivia's servants as well as a character in the play's subplot. (A subplot is a secondary or subordinate plot which often reflects on or complicates the major plot in a work of fiction such as a play.) In II.v, Fabian is invited by Sir Toby Belch to join him in spying on Malvolio when he finds and reads the phony love-note forged by Maria to look as though it were written to the steward by Olivia. Like Maria and Sir Toby, Fabian resents Malvolio for bringing him ''out o' favor'' with the countess, and thus looks forward to Malvolio's humiliation (II.v.7-8). Fabian's main function during the phony-letter scene is to restrain Sir Toby's outrage as Malvolio's fantasies about Olivia become increasingly arrogant. ''Nay, patience,'' Fabian counsels Sir Toby, ''or we break the sinews of our plot'' and spoil the practical joke (II.v.75-76).

In III.ii and iv, Fabian helps Toby direct the various elements of the subplot. In III.ii, for example, he joins in persuading Sir Andrew Aguecheek to challenge his ''rival,'' Viola/Cesario, to a duel. In III.iv.84-141, he participates once more in the practical joke against Malvolio. Shortly afterward, he sees ''More matter for a May morning'' (in other words, additional subject matter for a comedy) when Sir Andrew Aguecheek arrives with his timidly written challenge to Viola/Cesario (III.iv.142). Fabian's final moment of stage directing comes when he helps Toby to convince Viola/Cesario that Sir Andrew is a skilled and ferocious opponent (III.iv.257-72). His final appearance in the play occurs in V.i, when his employer, Olivia, puts an end to the comic subplot by ordering Fabian to release the ''notoriously abus'd'' Malvolio (V.i.315, 379). At this point, the confusion among the lovers has been resolved and each pair has been united (Orsino and Viola; Olivia and Sebastian). Hoping to forestall any ''quarrel'' or ''brawl'' that would spoil the wonder of the moment and the lovers' happiness, Fabian voluntarily confesses to the role that he played, along with Sir Toby and Maria, in the humiliation of Malvolio (V.i.355-68).

Feste (Feste, the Clown):

Feste, also referred to as ''clown,'' is Olivia's professional jester, or fool. During the Renaissance, monarchs and sometimes members of the nobility retained fools in their households as a source of entertainment—to sing, make witty observations, and to engage in practical jokes. The traditional costume of a fool consisted of motley, or particolored cloth. Thus in I.v.57, when Feste declares, ''I wear not motley in my brain,'' he means that although his body is clothed in the official garb of the jester, his mind is not ''naturally'' foolish—unlike, for example, the genuinely foolish mind of Sir Andrew Aguecheek.

To a certain extent—and true to his profession—Feste contributes to the holiday tone of *Twelfth Night*. His very name makes up part of the word, ''festival,'' and he is frequently called upon during the play to sing or to make jokes. Critics have

compared him to the Lord of Misrule who according to tradition is crowned, then placed in charge of Twelfth-night festivities and high jinks. Indeed in II.iii, Feste joins the drunken revels of Sir Toby Belch and Sir Andrew Aguecheek, singing lovesongs at their request, participating in round-songs, and remarking that the raucous Sir Toby is in ''admirable fooling'' (II.iii.80). Additionally, in IV.ii, Feste observes the time-honored, Twelfth-Night practice of role-reversal when he disguises himself as the wise priest Sir Topas and treats the steward Malvolio like a madman or fool.

Feste has also been referred to as the only character in *Twelfth Night* who remains detached from the play's conflicts, thus being able to comment objectively on the other characters' actions and shortcomings. In I.v.57-72, for example, he argues that his employer Olivia is a fool when he points out that she mourns for her dead brother even though his soul lies safely in heaven. After singing for the duke in II.iv, Feste asks the god of melancholy to protect Orsino, and also asserts that the duke's mind is as changeable as the colors in an opal, thereby implying that his love-sickness is pure self-indulgence and likely to change its focus—as it does in V.i when Orsino readily settles for Viola in lieu of Olivia. None of this behavior surprises Feste because, as he observes in III.i.38-39, all sorts of people all over the world do silly things: ''Foolery . . . does walk about the orb like the sun, it shines every where.'' In III.i, Viola sums up Feste's conventional function as commentator and wise fool when she declares that to be successful, a jester must pay close attention to the variety of social mores and human attitudes which occur around him:

> This fellow is wise enough to play the fool,
> And to do that well craves a kind of wit.
> He must observe their mood on whom he jests,
> The quality of persons, and the time;
> And like the haggard, check at every feather
> That comes before his eye. This is a practice
> As full of labor as a wise man's art;
> For folly that he wisely shows is fit,
> But wise men, folly-fall'n, quite taint their wit.
> (III.i.60-68)

Characters such as Olivia, Orsino, and Viola are not insulted by Feste's sharp observations because fools are expected to make entertaining comments and are exempt from the rules of tact which apply to the rest of society. It is significant, then, that the self-important Malvolio is the only person in the play who considers Feste's witticisms offensive (I.v.83-89).

Critics have acknowledged Feste's role in communicating the play's more wistful theme of the shortness of life and the decay of youth. In I.v.52, Feste reminds Olivia that "beauty's a flower," or that it fades quickly. Elsewhere, he comments on the weakness of the body and the ravages of time by asserting that self-indulgence or "pleasure will be paid, one time or another." (II.iv.70-71).

Finally, *Twelfth Night* is filled with songs, many of which are sung by Feste, and most of which warn the listener of the harsh effects of time on love, beauty, and youth. In II.iii.47-52, he sings a verse which stresses the urgency of enjoying love and youth for the short time that it lasts. Feste closes the play with a song that documents the stages in a person's life—beginning with carefree childhood and including the grimmer aspects of adulthood, aging, and overindulgence.

Gentlewoman:

A gentlewoman is mentioned in the stage directions of III.i as accompanying Olivia.

Lords:

These are unnamed minor characters with no lines to speak. They appear with Orsino in the opening scene of the play.

Malvolio:

He is Olivia's steward. Malvolio's name means "ill will." He wears dark clothing and has no sense of humor, both of which are appropriate to Olivia's observance of mourning. The countess values Malvolio as a servant because he "is sad [serious] and civil" (III.iv.5). However, she also chides him for being "sick of self-love," and—in a remark which looks ahead to Malvolio's gulling and his subsequent bitterness—Olivia adds that "To be generous, guiltless, and of free disposition, is to take those things for bird-bolts that you deem cannon-bullets"—something Malvolio is unable to do (I.v.90, 91-93).

Olivia's servant Fabian dislikes Malvolio for bringing him "out o' favor" with the countess (II.v.7-8). Sir Toby Belch feels particularly antagonistic toward the steward because he condemns Toby's drunkenness, sabotages fun, and has ideas above his social station in life. Feste and Malvolio are complete opposites—in names and professions as well as their personalities. The steward has nothing but contempt for Feste's word games and riddles: "I marvel your ladyship takes delight in

> **"** ... Feste observes the time-honored, Twelfth-Night practice of role-reversal when he disguises himself as the wise priest Sir Topas and treats the steward Malvolio like a madman or fool."

such a barren rascal," Malvolio tells the countess (I.v.83-84).

Thus the stage is set for the "gulling," or fooling, of Malvolio in II.v and all that it entails: his smiles, yellow stockings, and crossed garters which astound Olivia in III.iv; and his imprisonment for apparent madness by Toby and Maria in IV.ii. Both the festival of Twelfth Night and Shakespeare's play of the same name are about the inversion of social and personal expectations. Malvolio had hoped to rise above his social status and become a count; instead, he falls so low that by IV.ii, he has been locked in a dark room and is being badgered by a fool dressed in a fake beard and priestly robes. Seeking to be released from the dark room, Malvolio finds himself in the humiliating and ironic situation of having to "convince" Feste that he is not insane. "I am as well in my wits, fool, as thou art," he tells the jester, to which Feste replies, "Then you are mad indeed, if you be no better in your wits than a fool" (IV.ii.88,89-90).

Critics are divided over the justness of Malvolio's treatment, especially with regard to his incarceration in the dark room. Some have argued that he is a scapegoat who is humiliated simply for the sake of a few laughs. Others contend that the practical joke is genuinely funny and that it stays within the limits of good taste up until the moment that Malvolio is imprisoned and tormented by "Sir Topas." Alternatively, some critics point out that Malvolio would not have been fooled by Maria's nonsensical letter if he had not already harbored delusions of grandeur. Even before he catches sight of the letter, the steward can be heard fantasizing about marriage with Olivia, calling himself "Count Malvolio," and imagining his nemesis Sir Toby curtseying before him (II.v.23-80). In any case, the steward's angry threat in V.i.378—"I'll be reveng'd on the whole pack of you"—sounds an ominous note in the wake

> **"** *Twelfth Night* **is filled with songs, many of which are sung by Feste, and most of which warn the listener of the harsh effects of time on love, beauty, and youth. In II.iii.47-52, he sings a verse which stresses the urgency of enjoying love and youth for the short time that it lasts."**

of Twelfth Night festivities and in anticipation of the joyful multiple marriages which await the close of this romantic comedy.

Ultimately most people agree that there is a difference between reading about the gulling of Malvolio and actually seeing it performed onstage. When they are caught up in the momentum of the actors' performances, and once they are able to see the grinning Malvolio in his cross-gartered yellow stockings, many audience members applaud Maria and Toby's revenge from start to finish. On the other hand, while experiencing the joke as it slowly unfolds in print, the reader has time to feel sympathy for the steward.

Maria:

She is Olivia's lady-in-waiting. In I.iii, Maria draws our attention to Sir Toby Belch's habitual late nights and drunkenness when she warns him that his niece, Countess Olivia, has lost patience with his dissolute behavior. She also prepares us for the entrance shortly afterward of Sir Andrew Aguecheek by referring to him as ''a foolish knight'' whom Sir Toby ''brought in one night here to be [Olivia's] wooer'' (I.iii.15-17). In I.v.1-31, she introduces us to the clown, Feste, when she scolds him on behalf of his employer, Olivia, for having been absent when Olivia wanted entertainment.

Maria's reproofs frequently give way to jokes and lively wordplay. She teases Sir Andrew Aguecheek for his foolishness in I.iii.66-79 and outdoes Feste at punning in I.v.1-31. Her cleverness inspires admiration in Sir Toby Belch, whose affection for her is apparent in the nicknames he gives her—

names which also happen to indicate her small size. In II.iii.179, for example, Toby refers to her affectionately as ''a beagle true-bred.'' Elsewhere he fondly describes her as a ''little villain'' and as his ''metal [gold] of India'' (II.v.13, 14). In III.ii.66, he calls her ''the youngest wren of nine'' (in other words, the smallest in a nest of wrens—a type of bird which is very small even after it is full-grown).

In II.iii, Maria tries without success to quiet Sir Toby and his friends in their noisy revels, only to be chastised soon afterward by Malvolio, who suspects her of encouraging Toby's drunkenness. In revenge, she invents the practical joke which humiliates Malvolio and forms part of the play's subplot. Calling the steward a puritanical ''time-pleaser,'' or flatterer, who is conceited enough to believe ''that all that look on him love him,'' Maria devises a trick meant to exploit ''that vice in him'' (II.iii.148, 152-53). She mimics Olivia's handwriting while composing ''some obscure epistles of love'' and drops them where Malvolio is certain to find them (II.iii.155-56). Maria is confident that the steward thinks so highly of himself that he will believe it possible for the countess to fall in love with him, and sure enough, Malvolio convinces himself that the epistle, or letter, was written by Olivia to him. Maria helps things along by telling Malvolio that Olivia ''affects'' (is fond of) him (II.v.23-24), and by warning the countess that Malvolio is crazy, or ''tainted in 's wits'' (III.iv.13). Her practical joke is so successful that the delighted Sir Toby marries her ''in recompense'' (V.i.364).

Musicians:

The musicians play for Orsino in the opening scene of the play. Although they are not mentioned specifically in the stage directions of II.iv (perhaps the are included in the ''others'' that accompany the duke), Orsino asks for music, and the stage directions indicate that music is played at this point in the scene.

Officers:

The officers (1. Officer, 2. Officer) appear in III.iv when they arrest Antonio, and speak a couple of lines during the course of this action. The officers appear agin in V.i when they present Antonio to Orsino. Only the first officer speaks in this scene.

Olivia:

She is a rich countess who is loved by Orsino even though she does not feel the same way about him. In I.i.23-31, we learn that Olivia plans to spend seven years mourning for her dead brother, during which time she will hide her face with a veil, reject any declarations of love, and weep daily to keep her brother's memory alive. Orsino considers the countess beautiful but cruel (II.iv.80-86). Viola's friend the captain describes Olivia as "a virtuous maid" (I.ii.36). Viola/Cesario calls her beautiful but "too proud," and scolds her for refusing to marry and for thus failing to "leave the world [a] copy" of her beauty by having children (I.v.243, 250-51). Olivia's uncle, Sir Toby Belch, is impatient with her: "What a plague means my niece to take the death of her brother thus?" he wonders in I.iii.1-2. Feste, who is Olivia's professional clown, or fool, argues that she is in fact the real fool since she wastes her youth and beauty in seclusion while weeping for a brother whose "soul is in heaven" (I.v.69-72).

When Viola/Cesario arrives with messages of love from the duke, Olivia is prepared to reject them as calmly as she has always done, and indeed she announces yet again that she "cannot love" Orsino, and that "He might [or should] have took his answer long ago," since she has consistently sent him the same negative reply (I.v.263-64). Olivia is not prepared, however, for her own infatuation with the duke's page (that is, the young gentlewoman, Viola, disguised as the youth, Cesario). "How now?" Olivia asks herself, "Even so quickly may one catch the plague? / Methinks I feel this youth's perfections / With an invisible and subtle stealth / To creep in at mine eyes" (I.v.294-98). Critics have pointed out that like several other characters in the play (Sebastian and Viola, for example), Olivia quickly accepts what happens to her as part of her fate. "Well, let it be," she concludes; "Fate, show thy force: ourselves we do not owe; / What is decreed must be; and be this so" (I.v.298, 310-11).

By the time she sees Viola/Cesario again, Olivia is passionately in love and determined to win the page's affections, even at the cost of her own pride. Orsino earlier described Olivia as cruel, and she in her turn accuses Viola/Cesario of being scornful and proud (III.i.144-51). Viola/Cesario pities the countess for her mistake, and for the "thriftless sighs" which Olivia's unrequited love will wring from her (II.ii.39). *Twelfth Night* is, however, a comedy: Renaissance comedies are meant to end in marriages and happiness. Thus when Olivia encounters Sebastian in IV.i, she mistakes him for Viola/Cesario, takes him home, and in IV.iii, she marries him. At the close of the play, her new husband, Sebastian, suggests that by falling in

> " Maria, Olivia's lady-in-waiting, shares this negative view of the steward, declaring that 'he is a kind of puritan,' and then defining that term with the explanation that Malvolio is self-righteous and conceited, and 'so cramm'd (as he thinks) with excellencies, that it is his grounds of faith that all that look on him love him' (II.iii.140, 150-52)."

love with his disguised twin sister, Olivia was merely proving that nature meant for her all along to love someone like Sebastian (V.i.259-63).

Critics have argued that Olivia's prolonged period of mourning is as artificial as Orsino's courtly love, and that like the duke, the countess needs to be awakened from her dream world by Viola and her brother.

Orsino (Duke Orsino, also known as the Count):

He is the duke of Illyria. Although he appears less often than most of the other major characters, his speeches are important to the play's assessment of love and human nature. When the play begins, Orsino is so preoccupied with unrequited love for Olivia that he feels unable to do anything but listen to music. "If music be the food of love, play on," he tells his musicians, "Give me excess of it; that surfeiting, / The appetite may sicken, and so die" (I.i.1-3). He hopes to kill his feelings for Olivia by letting them gorge themselves to death on music— which has been described as the "food of love." Unfortunately, his feelings tire of the music before they can be sickened by it, and so his love for Olivia survives. Several lines afterward, the duke compares his love-sick heart to a "hart" (deer) which has been attacked by "cruel" hunting dogs (I.i.17-22). Later, when he hears that Olivia is in mourning for her dead brother and refuses to care for anyone else for the next seven years, Orsino is impressed by

> In II.iii, Maria tries without success to quiet Sir Toby and his friends in their noisy revels, only to be chastised soon afterward by Malvolio, who suspects her of encouraging Toby's drunkenness. In revenge, she invents the practical joke which humiliates Malvolio and forms part of the play's subplot."

Orsino does not in fact appear in any scenes with his adored Olivia until the final one (V.i), when he gives up on her and at last falls in love with his former page, Viola. Although Olivia had never once been in love with him (according to Sir Toby, she refuses to marry anyone who is older than she is, or whose income or social rank is higher than hers [I.iii.109-11]), she acknowledges that Orsino is noble, good-looking, well-educated, brave, and admired by his people (I.v.258-62). As for Orsino's own affections, critics have observed that the duke is more devoted to love than he ever is to Olivia, and that his feelings are sterile and lack self-awareness. Thus as the play closes, he is able to shift instantly from idolizing Olivia to loving Viola, especially since in the meantime, through her sensible conversations and her fidelity, Viola has taught Orsino the enduring connection between love and friendship.

her ability "To pay this debt of love" to someone who is simply a brother, and his mind boggles when he thinks about how great Olivia's devotion will be when she someday receives a wound from Cupid's "rich golden shaft," or the gold-tipped arrow of romantic love (I.i.32-38). As the scene closes, the duke decides to indulge rather than kill his love by surrounding himself with the heady fragrance of flowers (I.i.39-40).

Orsino's use of elaborate, poetic language to identify his feelings indicates that he is experiencing courtly love—a system of romantic love which flourished during the Middle Ages. According to this system, a man falls deeply in love—usually at first sight and, initially at least, without his affection being returned. The woman who is the object of this love is extraordinarily beautiful, but also extremely cruel for her refusal to reciprocate. The spurned lover feels ill and loses sleep; he alternately burns and freezes from the intensity of his passion. He is, as Orsino explains to Viola/Cesario, "Unstaid and skittish" in all of his thoughts and emotions "Save in the constant image of the creature / That is belov'd" (II.iv.18, 19-20). In conformity with tradition, the heartsick courtly lover often prefers to be alone, contemplating his unhappiness. As Duke Orsino puts it, "I myself am best / When least in company" (I.iv.37-38). When the afflicted lover finds himself with other people, he spends much of his time debating the nature of love. So for example in II.iv.29-41 and 89-109, the duke discusses with Viola/Cesario the differences between male and female affections and fidelity.

Priest:

He is brought in by Olivia in IV.iii.22 to perform the marriage ceremony between her and the amazed but willing Sebastian, whom Olivia has mistaken for Viola/Cesario. Olivia sends for the priest once more in V.i.142, so that he can testify that she and Viola/Cesario are married. Like everyone else in the play, the priest is unable to tell any difference between Sebastian and Viola/Cesario, so he does indeed verify Olivia's claim, which results in Viola's astonished denial and Orsino's jealous rage (V.i.156-170).

Sailors:

These are unamed characters who appear with the captain and Viola in I.ii. They have no speaking parts.

Sea Captain:

See Captain

Sebastian:

He is Viola's twin brother. The two of them were victims of a shipwreck, and each believes the other has been drowned at sea. Unlike his sister, Sebastian makes only a few, short appearances in the play. He first enters in II.i, accompanied by his devoted rescuer, Antonio. Mourning the apparent death of Viola and feeling aimless in the foreign country of Illyria, Sebastian initially decides to head for Duke Orsino's court, but then in III.iii, opts instead for touring the local sights.

Sebastian has been called a passive character. His argument for setting off on his own in II.i is that he has been the victim of bad luck and does not want the ''malignancy'' of his own fate to influence Antonio's luck. In IV.i.24-43, he fights with Sir Toby and Sir Andrew, but only because they attack him first after mistaking him for Viola/Cesario. When Olivia offers to take him to her home afterward, he is amazed but goes along without questioning her—agreeing to be ''rul'd'' by her request, and concluding that ''If it be thus to dream, still let me sleep!'' (IV.i.64, 63). His reaction to Olivia's proposal of marriage in IV.iii is the same: even though he is astonished by her behavior, he submits to a hasty wedding. In IV.iii.1-21, Sebastian describes his state of mind: sometimes he thinks he is the victim of a misunderstanding, while at other times he wonders whether he or the citizens of Illyria are insane. In any case, Sebastian wishes that Antonio were with him, and observes that ''His counsel now might do me golden service'' (IV.iii.8).

It is made clear in the play that Sebastian is a very young man. Antonio refers to him as a ''young gentleman'' and a ''boy'' (III.iv.312; V.i.77), and he affectionately lends Sebastian a purseful of money with which to buy souvenirs (III.iii.44-45). Once the confusion regarding Viola and her brother has been solved in V.i.263, Sebastian himself refers to his youthfulness, telling Olivia that she has married ''a maid,'' or virgin, as well as a man. This reference to a maid highlights his resemblance to (and hence confusion with) his sister, Viola, but it also emphasizes Sebastian's youthfulness.

Critics point out that at first, Sebastian's arrival throws the unsuspecting members of Olivia's and Orsino's households into confusion (since they mistake him for Viola/Cesario), but that ultimately, Sebastian's presence on the stage with his sister is necessary to the happy resolution of the play. Both he and Olivia are contented with their marriage to one another, and Viola is free to stop being Cesario and to marry her beloved Orsino.

Servant:
A servant appears in III.iv and addresses Olivia.

Toby (Sir Toby Belch):
See Belch

Valentine:
He is one of two gentlemen who serve Duke Orsino (the other is Curio). Valentine has a couple

> **Orsino considers the countess beautiful but cruel (II.iv.80-86). Viola's friend the captain describes Olivia as 'a virtuous maid' (I.ii.36). Viola/ Cesario calls her beautiful but 'too proud,' and scolds her for refusing to marry and for thus failing to 'leave the world [a] copy' of her beauty by having children (I.v.243, 250-51).''**

of brief speeches which present information important to action of the play. The first one occurs in I.i.23-31 when, after trying unsuccessfully to deliver a message from Orsino to Olivia, he informs the lovesick duke that the countess is observing seven years of mourning for her dead brother, during which time she will remain cloistered at home with her face veiled. Then in I.iv.1-8, Valentine remarks to Viola (newly disguised as Cesario) that within only three short days, she has won the duke's favor as a page. Shortly afterward, Orsino uses his favorite new page ''Cesario'' to court Olivia, thereby inadvertently initiating a love triangle between himself, Viola/Cesario, and the countess.

Viola (Cesario; Viola/Cesario):
She is a gentlewoman from a country called Messaline, and also the twin sister of Sebastian. Viola first appears on the coast of Illyria in I.ii, accompanied by the captain who saved her from drowning in a shipwreck, and concerned about the fate of her missing brother, who had been traveling with her. ''And what should I do in Illyria?''—she wonders—''My brother he is in Elysium [heaven]'' (I.ii.3-4). Once the captain gives her reason to hope that her brother is still alive, Viola sets about the business of fending for herself in a foreign country. At the close of I.ii, Viola has decided to disguise herself and seek employment with Duke Orsino; I.ii is the first and last time that Viola appears in women's clothing. For the rest of the play she wears

> **Orsino does not in fact appear in any scenes with his adored Olivia until the final one (V.i), when he gives up on her and at last falls in love with his former page, Viola.''**

men's clothing appropriate to her disguise as Orsino's page, Cesario.

By her next appearance in the play and after only three days, Viola/Cesario has become the duke's favorite attendant. Orsino sends her to court Olivia for him, with strict instructions to ''stand at her doors'' and insist upon admittance (I.iv.16). In an aside, Viola/Cesario confesses that she has herself fallen secretly in love with the duke: ''Yet a barful strife! / Whoe'er I woo, myself would be his wife (I.iv.42). (An aside occurs when a character speaks to the audience without being overheard by the other characters onstage. Asides are used to reveal the character's inner thoughts.) In spite of her own feelings, Viola/Cesario loyally persists until she is allowed to deliver her message to Olivia, leading Malvolio to complain that Orsino's page is ''fortified against any denial'' (I.v.145). Olivia promptly rejects the duke's lovesick message, but she is intrigued with his messenger's boldness; by the end of the interview, the countess has fallen in love with Viola/Cesario, with chaotic results.

In II.i, Sebastian offers a brief but affectionate description of his twin, Viola, whom he thinks has drowned at sea:

> A lady, sir, though it was said she much
> resembled me, was yet of many accounted
>   beautiful;
> but though I could not with such estimable wonder
> overfar believe that, yet thus far I will boldly
>   publish
> her: she bore a mind that envy could not but call
>   fair.
>
> (II.i.25-29)

All other assessments of Viola occur after she has disguised herself as Cesario; therefore, they focus not on her womanly beauty but on her apparent boyishness, and more on the boldness of her mind than on its ''fairness,'' or virtue. Malvolio, for example, grumpily asserts that Viola/Cesario is ''Not yet old enough for a man, nor young enough for a boy; as a squash is before 'tis a peascod, or a codling when 'tis almost an apple. 'Tis with him in standing water, between boy and man. He is very well-favor'd, and he speaks very shrewishly. One would think his mother's milk were scarce out of him'' (I.v.156-62). The steward's difficulty in settling on an accurate description of Viola/Cesario results in dramatic irony. Dramatic irony happens when the audience understands the real significance of a character's words or actions, but the character or those around him or her do not. In this case, both Viola and the audience know that she is a woman, but everyone else is struggling to decide whether she is a boy or an extremely young-looking man. Another example of dramatic irony is the duke's remark to his page that ''they shall yet belie thy happy years, / That say thou art a man''; this produces a comical moment because we know that no matter how many years pass, Viola/Cesario will never become a man (I.iv.30-31); Orsino's observation shortly afterward that Viola/Cesario's ''small pipe'' (vocal chords), is as high and clear as a ''maiden's'' is also amusing for its dramatic irony, since we know and Viola/Cesario knows that she is indeed a maiden and that her ''shrill and sound'' voice will never break (I.iv.32-33). (See also Feste's arch but good-natured blessing that Viola/Cesario may someday grow a beard, and her wistfully comic aside in response [III.i.44-48]). These moments of dramatic irony contribute to a sympathetic portrait of Viola by giving us something in common with her—we as the audience share information with Viola which for the moment she feels she must withhold from the other characters.

Viola has been called a central character because of her influence over other characters in the play. Some critics suggest that her disguise as Cesario allows her and the audience to see through the pretenses of characters like Olivia and Orsino. For example, Olivia's reclusive and elaborate period of mourning for her brother stands in contrast to Viola's optimistic and active engagement with the world of Illyria in spite of her own brother's apparent death. Additionally, Viola's patient and self-sacrificing love for Orsino helps the duke to reassess his own artificial and self-indulgent love of love.

Viola's observations about the destructive influence of time and melancholy on youth and beauty have been compared to similar remarks made by Feste. In I.v.241-43, for example, she upbraids

Olivia for wasting her beauty by leading it to the grave rather than marrying and transmitting her beauty to her children. In II.iv.110-15, thinking of her own hidden love for Orsino, Viola paints a vivid picture of the effects of time and unrequited, unproclaimed love on the "damask cheek" of a maiden who "sate like Patience on a monument, / Smiling at grief."

It has also been pointed out that Viola can be fatalistic in her attitude to time. When she discovers that Olivia has fallen in love with her, Viola/Cesario pities the countess, but concludes that time "must untangle this, not I / It is too hard a knot for me t'untie" (II.ii.40-41).

Interestingly, unlike other Shakespearean female characters who adopt disguises, Viola does not remove her men's clothing at the end of the play, and the rest of the characters, including Duke Orsino, are left to take her true identity on faith.

Viola/Cesario:

See Viola

Further Reading

Barton, Anne. Introduction to *Twelfth Night,* by William Shakespeare. In *The Riverside Shakespeare*, edited by G. Blakemore Evans, 403-07. Boston: Houghton Mifflin Co., 1974.
> Barton discusses the meaning of the play's subtitle— *What You Will*. She also explains the importance of the Twelfth Night, or Epiphany, celebrations of misrule to Elizabethan society and to the play. Finally, she contends that Illyria is a timeless fairy-tale world suitable only to the lovers—Orsino and Viola, Olivia and Sebastian—and that the rest of us are brought back to real life through Feste's closing song.

Berry, Ralph. "The Season of *Twelfth Night*." *New York Literary Forum* 1 (1978): 139-49.
> Focusing on Maria and Sir Toby in II.iii, Berry defends the view that *Twelfth Night* is ultimately more dark and wistful than festive and romantic.

———. "*Twelfth Night*: The Experience of the Audience." *Shakespeare Survey* 34 (1981): 111-19.
> Berry argues that the play's audience participates in the practical joke that is perpetrated on Malvolio and is thus also implicated in the guilt when the joke goes

> **"** At the close of I.ii, Viola has decided to disguise herself and seek employment with Duke Orsino; I.ii is the first and last time that Viola appears in women's clothing."

on too long and turns bad. He concludes that the "ultimate effect of *Twelfth Night* is to make the audience ashamed of itself."

Bevington, David. Introduction to *Twelfth Night; or, What You Will*, by William Shakespeare. In *The Complete Works of Shakespeare*, edited by David Bevington, 326-29. Updated 4th ed. New York: Longman, 1997.
> Bevington discusses the play in light of the Elizabethan festival of misrule known as Twelfth Night, and looks at the interaction between the play's major characters with regard to love and the Elizabethan notion of friendship. He also contends that "Malvolio's comeuppance is richly deserved."

Charney, Maurice. "Comic Premises of *Twelfth Night*." *New York Literary Forum* 1 (1978): 151-65.
> Charney supports the argument that *Twelfth Night* is a festive play that celebrates the holiday spirit of misrule and self-indulgence.

Downer, Alan S. "1592: Feste's Night." *College English* 22 (November 1960): 117-23.
> Downer argues that the character Feste is central to the play because he presents truth and exposes the other characters' foibles.

Forbes, Lydia. "What You Will?" *Shakespeare Quarterly* 13 (Autumn 1962): 475-85.
> Forbes examines the themes of deception and self-knowledge in *Twelfth Night*, focusing in particular on how these themes might be treated by someone directing the play.

Langman, F. H. "Comedy and Saturnalia: The Case of *Twelfth Night*." *Southern Review* (Australia) 7 (July 1974): 102-22.
> Langman regards Viola as the force of moderation and unsentimentality in the play, and asserts that *Twelfth Night* is a significant comedy about self-knowledge and the limits of extravagance rather than merely a light and festive entertainment.

Munday, Mildred Brand. " 'For Saying So There's Gold': A Note on Price and Value in *Twelfth Night*." *CEA Critic* (College English Association) 23 (March 1961): 105-14.
> Munday contends that the play's characters reveal their own false emotions whenever they try to reward faithfulness and cleverness with money.

Prouty, Charles T. Introduction to *Twelfth Night, or What You Will*, by William Shakespeare, edited by Charles T. Prouty, 14-23. The Pelican Shakespeare. Rev. ed. Baltimore: Penguin Books, 1972.

> Prouty discusses the formalized, Renaissance conventions of courtly love and how they apply to each of the lovers in the play.

Schwartz, Elias. *''Twelfth Night* and the Meaning of Shakespearean Comedy.'' *College English* 28 (April 1967): 508-19.

> Schwartz asserts that *Twelfth Night* depicts life as joyful and good even with all its limitations, and that the play's acceptance of human foolishness and the briefness of human life gives it a wistful tone.

Seiden, Melvin. ''Malvolio Reconsidered.'' *University of Kansas City Review* 28 (December 1961): 105-114.

> Seiden contends that the practical joke played on Malvolio is meant to shift our laughter toward the steward and away from Orsino, Viola, Olivia, and Sebastian, whose love would seem ridiculous if we looked at it too closely. Seiden further asserts that although we are not meant to sympathize with Malvolio, we can still see him as someone who is proud of his work rather than merely vain.

Taylor, Michael. ''*Twelfth Night* and *What You Will*.'' *Critical Quarterly* 16 (Spring 1974): 71-80.

> Taylor argues that Viola and Sebastian represent the ''what you will'' aspect of the play, and that their determination, decisiveness, and self-sufficiency invigorate the indolent and self-indulgent world of ''twelfth night'' as represented by Sir Toby and Malvolio.

Yearling, Elizabeth. ''Language, Theme, and Character in *Twelfth Night*.'' *Shakespeare Survey* 35 (1982): 79-86.

> In her examination of the power of language in *Twelfth Night* and its ability to reveal or hide the truth, Yearling looks at the major characters in the play, but gives particular scrutiny to the roles of Sir Toby and Viola.

The Two Gentlemen of Verona

Act I:

The historical period in which the dramatic action occurs is not specified—it may be the fifteenth or sixteenth century. The first act takes place in the Italian city of Verona. As the play begins, two young men—close friends since childhood—are bidding each other farewell. One of them, Valentine, is about to leave for Milan, to learn the sophisticated ways of courtly society. He says he regrets that his friend Proteus will not be going with him, though he understands that love keeps him in Verona. The setting shifts to a garden outside a villa, where Julia, the object of Proteus's love, is talking with her maid Lucetta. When Lucetta tries to give her mistress a letter from Proteus, Julia pretends to be outraged by her maid's boldness and sends Lucetta away. Immediately regretting this, she calls her back. When Lucetta gives her the letter, Julia takes one look at it, then tears it into pieces and sends Lucetta away again. Julia picks up some of the pieces from the ground where she has thrown them and reads the words written on the fragments, treating each scrap with passionate tenderness. The scene shifts once again, this time to an unspecified location, where Proteus's father Antonio and Antonio's servant Panthino are deep in conversation. In the course of their talk, Antonio decides that Proteus ought to be travelling or studying at a university instead of remaining at home, and he

resolves to send Proteus to Milan the very next day. Proteus enters, reading a letter from Julia. He pretends to his father that it's from Valentine, urging him to come to Milan. Antonio tells Proteus that's precisely what he wants him to do and that he should prepare to leave immediately.

Act II:

At the duke of Milan's palace, Valentine's young page Speed makes fun of his master, telling him that he shows all the signs of being madly in love with Silvia—the duke's daughter. Silvia joins them presently, and Valentine gives her a love letter she has commissioned him to write, on her behalf, to someone she loves but will not name. Silvia hands the letter back to Valentine, telling him the words ''are for you'' (II.i.127). He fails to understand, but when Silvia leaves, Speed explains to him that Silvia was expressing her love indirectly by having Valentine write a letter to himself. Back in Verona, Proteus and Julia meet briefly as he is about to set off for Milan. They exchange rings in token of the constancy of their love for each other. On a street in Verona, Proteus's servant Launce appears, weeping and leading his large dog Crab. Launce describes to himself the heart-rending scene that took place when he parted from his family; everyone was grief-stricken except Crab, who, to Launce's disgust, shed not one tear. Panthino appears and drags Launce away to the ship that will take him and his master to Milan. Sometime later, at his palace in Milan, the duke announces to Valentine, Silvia, and Sir Thurio—one of Silvia's suitors—that Proteus has arrived. Valentine introduces Proteus to Silvia, who welcomes him to her father's house. When they are alone, Valentine tells Proteus that he's in love with Silvia and that they're engaged to be married. Unfortunately, explains Valentine, her father wants her to marry Thurio, so the young couple has made plans to elope. When Valentine leaves, Proteus reveals in a soliloquy that he is now in love with Silvia himself. On the day that has been fixed for the elopement, Proteus speaks in another soliloquy of his intention to warn the duke about Valentine and Silvia's plans. Back in Verona, Julia tells Lucetta that she intends to travel to Milan to be with Proteus. She asks her maid to help her put together a masculine disguise to wear on the journey.

Act III:

In Milan, Proteus tells the duke about the elopement, including the fact that Valentine will use a cord ladder to carry Silvia away from her chamber in a tower. Valentine enters, and Proteus leaves. The duke, a widower, invents a story about a woman he loves and wants to marry. He leads the unsuspecting Valentine to give him advice about how to court her and gain admittance to her room, which, he says, is high above the ground. The duke removes Valentine's cloak and finds a letter to Silvia and the cord ladder Valentine means to use for the elopement. The duke rages at Valentine and orders him to leave Milan at once. Proteus and Launce come upon the grieving Valentine. Proteus tells him that Silvia has heard of his banishment and pleaded with her father to change his mind. The duke is so angry with her, Proteus reports, that he has made her a virtual prisoner in her chamber. Proteus offers to accompany Valentine to the north gate of the city, and they depart, ordering Launce to find Speed and tell him where they're headed so he can meet them there. However, when Speed appears, Launce draws him into an extended conversation about a woman he is thinking of marrying. When he finally gives Speed the message from Valentine, the boy races off. Back at the palace, the duke assures Thurio that now, with Valentine banished, Silvia will bestow her affections on him. Proteus joins them, and the duke asks him to assist Thurio in courting Silvia. Proteus advises Thurio to gather a consort of musicians together and serenade Silvia outside her chamber window. Thurio regards this as excellent advice. He says he has already written a sonnet that will serve the purpose, and he and Proteus go off to find musicians to provide an accompaniment for it.

Act IV:

In a forest somewhere between Milan and Mantua, Valentine and Speed encounter a band of outlaws, who threaten to rob them. Valentine explains that he has no money with him. He tells them he was banished from Milan for killing a man. Impressed by Valentine's appearance, and by his claim to be able to speak foreign languages, the outlaws ask him to be their leader. Given the choice between accepting the offer or being killed if he doesn't, Valentine agrees. Back in Milan, Julia, disguised as a page, has found lodging at an inn. She asks the innkeeper to take her to Proteus, and he leads her to the place outside the ducal palace where Thurio's serenade to Silvia is about to begin. During the song—which is usually sung by the actor playing Proteus, though the text does not specify who the singer should be—Julia learns from the innkeeper that Proteus is reported to be in love with Silvia. The serenade over, Thurio and the musicians depart. As Julia stands hidden nearby, Proteus woos Silvia, but she rejects his suit and calls him a traitor to love. Proteus admits that he did once love another woman, but, he lies, she is dead. When Silvia reminds him that he's betraying his friendship with Valentine by courting her, Proteus says he's also heard that Valentine is dead. He begs her for a picture of herself, and she agrees, telling him to send a servant for it the next morning.

Early the following day, a courtier named Sir Eglamour arrives beneath Silvia's window, as she has asked him to do. She tells him that she means to follow Valentine into banishment and asks Eglamour if he will accompany her for protection. He agrees, and they arrange to meet that evening at the cell of a cleric, Friar Patrick. Sometime after Eglamour leaves, Launce appears, relating his disastrous attempt to deliver Crab as a present from Proteus to Silvia. He reports that the dog stole a chicken leg from Silvia's plate, farted under the table, and urinated on Silvia's dress. Proteus enters with Julia, still disguised as a page; she has introduced herself to Proteus as Sebastian, a young man seeking employment. Proteus is outraged to learn that Launce has lost the dog he bought for Silvia—a small, elegant one—and tried to replace it with the hulking Crab. He dismisses Launce and employs Julia in his place. He tells Julia to fetch the picture Silvia has promised him. Pulling from his finger the ring she gave him when he left Verona, Proteus instructs Sebastian/Julia to present it to Silvia. Proteus leaves, and Silvia enters. Silvia is unaware that the messenger from Proteus is Julia, but she will have neither the ring nor the letter he has sent along with it. Together, the two young women lament Proteus's inconstancy and Julia's unhappy fate.

Act V:

At sunset, Eglamour meets Silvia at Friar Patrick's cell near the city walls, and together they leave the city. Back at the duke's palace, Proteus and Sebastian/Julia are jesting with Thurio when they are joined by the duke. He reports that a cleric, Friar Laurence, has encountered Silvia and Eglamour in the forest. Realizing that Silvia is on her way to find Valentine, the duke asks them to help him recover his daughter. In the forest, Silvia is captured by the outlaws, who report that her companion ran away so fast they were unable to catch him. In another part of the forest, Valentine hears people approaching and steps aside so they won't see him. Proteus appears, with Silvia and Sebastian/Julia. As Valentine listens, Proteus—who has rescued Silvia from the outlaws—renews his courtship of Silvia, but she continues to rebuff him. Proteus declares he will force her to love him and moves toward her menacingly, as if he means to rape her. Valentine intervenes and denounces Proteus as a traitorous friend. Proteus says he is overwhelmed by shame and guilt. Valentine forgives him and, as a sign that he regards Proteus as truly penitent, he offers to give Silvia to him. Julia faints. As they revive her, she shows them a ring. Proteus recognizes that it's the one he gave Julia when he left Verona, and the supposed page reveals her true identity. Declaring that man's greatest fault is inconstancy, Proteus turns to Julia, and they join hands. The outlaws suddenly appear, with the duke and Thurio as their prisoners. Seeing Silvia, Thurio asserts his claim to her, but quickly withdraws it when Valentine threatens to kill him. The duke declares that he's content to have Valentine as a son-in-law, and he revokes the banishment. Valentine calls for one more act of forgiveness: the outlaws, he says, are reformed and ready to return to society. The duke pardons every one of them, and the entire party sets off for Milan, where, Valentine predicts, they will celebrate two marriages and the prospect of mutual happiness.

Modern Connections

In *The Two Gentlemen of Verona*, the principal characters—and some of the secondary ones as well—feel compelled to act and speak in certain ways when they fall in love. The conventions of courtly love (a practice which flourished during the Middle Ages and influenced Renaissance literature) required such things as serenades, the frequent exchange of letters, and extravagant praise of one's beloved. Are young people today free to express love according to their individual natures, or is there a standard they have to follow? In the past, young women in love have had to act coy, as Julia does in I.ii, and mask their feelings. Additionally, society has not always encouraged young women to speak openly of their love; rather, they have had to indicate their feelings indirectly, as Silvia does in II.i with her comments on the letter Valentine has written for her. Do some of these conventions affect the way modern young people in love conduct themselves? Has the experience of romantic love changed significantly since Shakespeare's time?

Most commentators believe that *The Two Gentlemen of Verona* places a higher value on friendship than on romantic love. They believe the play depicts Proteus's betrayal of Valentine as a worse sin than his betrayal of Julia. What would happen today if two young men—or two young women—who have been the closest of friends fell in love with the same person? Would one of them have to step aside, sacrificing love so that the friendship could continue? Or would the friendship come to an end?

The play also addresses the issue of constancy or faithfulness in love. Julia and Silvia—and Launce, too, in his own way—represent constancy. Proteus, on the other hand, seems to fall in and out of love with very little justification. He's attracted to Silvia at least as much because of Valentine's praise of her as for her merits alone. He appears to believe that all men are vulnerable to beauty and that they are helpless to resist its power. Is it human nature, as Proteus claims, to be attracted to others even when one is already committed to an individual? Is it hopelessly idealistic to expect that one's partner will be faithful forever?

Another issue raised in the play is the relation between older and younger generations. When Antonio decides that the time has come for his son to leave home, his decision is final, and Proteus accepts this—perhaps in part because he's not altogether unhappy at the prospect. But what happens when parents' choices for their children are not the ones the children would choose for themselves? The duke insists that his daughter marry Thurio, though he knows she detests him. Such tyrannical fathers are less common today. However, even in the late twentieth century, parents continue to attempt to influence the direction of their children's lives. Are young people today more inclined to defy their parents, as Silvia does? Does the tension between parental authority and their children's desire for independence necessarily lead to antagonism? Though the world has changed in countless ways since the sixteenth century, perhaps the conflict between generations is timeless.

Characters

Antonio:

A nobleman of Verona, he is Proteus's father. Antonio is easily manipulated by his servant Panthino and follows his advice; yet he is a tyrant toward his son Proteus. In I.iii, when Panthino suggests that

Proteus ought to be out in the world, gaining knowledge and experience, Antonio quickly agrees. He says he's been thinking the very same thing over the past month—though there's some doubt about whether he's telling the truth here. He asks Panthino where he thinks Proteus ought to be sent, and he takes his servant's advice: Proteus should go to Milan the next day. When Antonio tells his son that he's to leave for Milan almost immediately, he appears brusque and decisive: "what I will, I will, and there's an end" (I.iii.65). He appoints Panthino to see to it that Proteus is on his way to Milan the following day.

Crab:

Crab is Launce's dog. He appears with his master in Act II, and Launce reveals how hurt he is that Crab didn't shed a tear as Launce prepared to leave for Milan. In Act IV, Launce describes how he tried to pass Crab off as a gift to Silvia from Proteus, but Crab misbehaved badly. The dog was supposed to be punished for his behavior, but Launce takes the whipping for Crab.

Duke of Milan:

See Milan

Eglamour:

A courtier whose name suggests constancy in love, he accompanies Silvia when she flees Milan. When he appears below her chamber window in IV.iii, she says she's chosen him as her escort because she knows he's devoted to the memory of his own true love—a woman who died, and on whose grave he has sworn perpetual chastity. Eglamour pities Silvia's circumstances and agrees to help her. In V.i, they meet at Friar Patrick's cell and set out for Mantua. Their journey takes them through a forest where, we learn in V.iii, they are attacked by outlaws. According to the report of one of the outlaws, Sir Eglamour took to his heels when he saw them, abandoning the woman he'd promised to protect. Earlier in the play, when Julia and Lucetta are reviewing a list of Julia's suitors, one name they mention is that of "the fair Sir Eglamour" (I.ii.9), a knight of Verona; this is not the same Sir Eglamour who provides dubious assistance to Silvia.

Host:

An innkeeper in Milan, he escorts Julia—who is disguised as a young boy—to the place where

Silvia is being serenaded. He and Julia conceal themselves from the serenaders. After the song, Julia responds to the host's direct comments on the music with veiled allusions to Proteus's unfaithfulness. The host tells her that, according to Launce, Proteus is madly in love with Silvia. During the exchange between Proteus and Silvia that follows the serenade, the host falls asleep. Julia wakes him when Proteus leaves, and the host accompanies her back to the inn, where, he assures her, Proteus is staying.

Julia:

A young woman of Verona, she loves Proteus and remains constant, even when he betrays her. Julia is alternately resourceful and vulnerable, charming and petulant, courageous and foolish. Commentators generally regard her as the most authentic, true to life character in the play. Several of them have noted an interesting paradox: Julia disguises herself and assumes a male role as the page Sebastian, yet she remains true to herself through the period of her transformation.

Julia seems younger and less self-assured than Silvia, her unwilling rival for Proteus's love. Her mood swings, playfulness, and emotional outbursts betray her immaturity. In I.ii, as she finds herself falling in love with Proteus, she seems astonished by her feelings and unable to control them. At first she pretends to be indifferent when Lucetta includes Proteus's name in a catalogue of Julia's suitors: "he of all the rest hath never moved me" (I.ii.27). She throws a tantrum when Lucetta produces a letter from Proteus. Yet only moments before she had said she wished she knew what he thought of her, and the letter is a likely source of such information. In the course of her soliloquy at I.ii.50-65, she goes back and forth between self-criticism and condemnation of Lucetta, before concluding on a note of humility. Then, in an outburst of petulance, she tears up the letter, unread. In another mood altogether, she retrieves the scraps, treating each one as if it had individual significance. Finding one that bears her name, she throws it to the ground and stamps on it. One that has Proteus's name inscribed on it is tucked into the bodice of her dress. And when she finds a third that has both their names, she folds it so that "Proteus" and "Julia" are pressed against each other.

Her naiveté is reflected in her idealization of Proteus. As she prepares to follow Proteus to Milan, Julia insists that Lucetta is wrong to question his

> **Silvia's own feelings on the question of marriage are of no importance to [her father], the duke. He locks her in her room when she refuses to transfer her affection from Valentine to Thurio."**

faithfulness: "His words are bonds, his oaths are oracles, / His love sincere, his thoughts immaculate" (II.vii.75-76). She has a rude awakening, however, when she reaches the city and observes the serenade to Silvia. With only an anonymous innkeeper to support her, she suffers heartbreak and disillusion. She stands helplessly by while she hears Proteus woo Silvia and claim that the girl he loved in Verona has died.

Yet Julia is resilient. Shortly after receiving this devastating blow, she conceives a plan that will allow her to stay in Milan until, she hopes, Proteus comes to his senses. However, as Proteus's page, she is given an assignment that increases her suffering: to woo Silvia on Proteus's behalf. "How many women would do such a message?" (IV.iv.90), she asks herself. She pities Proteus, she says, because she loves him. And because she loves him, she's willing to suffer and be humiliated. Her interview with Silvia is poignant. When Silvia asks her to describe the woman in Verona whom Proteus has betrayed, Julia responds with a veiled description of herself and of a festival in which she played Ariadne, a legendary figure who was deserted by her lover. Julia weeps, and Silvia is moved to tears as well. Yet when Silvia leaves, Julia recovers some degree of self-assurance—and displays a streak of envy as well. Looking at the portrait of Silvia that she is supposed to carry back to Proteus, Julia remarks uncharitably that "the painter flatter'd her a little" (IV.iv.187). She declares that if she were dressed as well as the woman in the picture, she would look just as beautiful as she does. Neither of them has a perfect forehead, Julia notes, and their eyes are the same color. The only difference she can find is that Silvia's hair is auburn, while hers is blond—and a wig would easily mask that difference. With renewed self-confidence, Julia returns to Proteus.

❝❝ As she prepares to follow Proteus to Milan, Julia insists that Lucetta is wrong to question his faithfulness: 'His words are bonds, his oaths are oracles, / His love sincere, his thoughts immaculate' (II.vii.75-76)."

But she faces further shame and humiliation. Julia is with Proteus when he rescues Silvia. She remains silent while Proteus speaks once again of his love for Silvia, and she says nothing when he attacks her. Julia's swoon when she hears Valentine offer Silvia to Proteus has been variously interpreted. Some commentators think that she only pretends to faint. Most think her swoon is genuine—a natural response to the shock she has received. She has just heard Proteus apologize for his behavior toward his friend, and perhaps this gives her renewed hope. If so, Valentine's offer now dashes that hope. Yet when she is revived, Julia recovers her poise. She calls attention to the ring Proteus gave her before he left Verona, and, when he recognizes it, she reveals her true identity. She chides him for his unfaithfulness and for the shame he has brought upon her. Her anger fades, however, when Proteus apologizes and Valentine joins their hands together. Julia's conception of love is generous. It includes forgiveness, as well as pity and constancy. As many commentators have pointed out, Julia's view of love is the most noble one in the play.

Launce:

He is Proteus's servant. Launce's natural wit and native intelligence are concealed beneath the façade of a rustic buffoon. Launce's realistic appraisals of love and friendship provide insights into the principal themes and characters in the play. Sometimes his commentary is direct. For example, when he observes Proteus hypocritically offering to help Valentine—after he has repeatedly betrayed him—Launce remarks, "my master is a kind of knave" (III.i.264). More often his commentary is indirect or implicit. Through descriptions of events that apparently focus on himself and through exchanges with Valentine's servant Speed, Launce provides a parody of romantic love, idealized concepts of friendship, and Proteus's faithlessness to Julia.

Launce's description of how he and his family part follows directly after the scene in which Julia and Proteus bid farewell to each other. The copious weeping of Launce and his family may be compared to the "tide of tears" that overwhelms Julia and prevents her from speaking (II.ii.14). Proteus believes that some lovers become literally speechless when they must say goodbye. Launce, on the other hand, complains in II.iii that his dog Crab was mute as well as dry-eyed at the prospect of leaving his family. In that same scene, Launce has great difficulty in sorting out the props he uses—shoes, hat, walking stick—to tell his sad story. His predicament sheds a different light on issues that recur throughout the play: the confusion of identities and the difficulty of recognizing another person's true nature.

Launce in love is an implicit mockery of Proteus and Valentine in love. His hard-headed, practical approach parodies their fantasies and romantic raptures. In III.i, Launce indicates that he has given some thought to marrying a milkmaid—a woman with "more qualities than a water-spaniel" (III.i.272-73)—and that he has received a written report about her. He charitably regards the vices listed there as virtues, recognizing that a person's strengths and weaknesses are often reverse sides of the same coin. When he hears that she has "more faults than hairs" on her head (III.i.364), he's momentarily downcast. But he cheers up when he learns that she has "more wealth than faults" (III.i.367). In his concern with the mercenary aspects of marriage, Launce is not unlike the duke of Milan, who is happy to see his daughter marry a fool, so long as he is a rich fool. Incidentally, the written report on the milkmaid's qualities is also a burlesque of the flurry of love letters the principal characters are constantly writing to each other.

Launce's relationship with Speed represents an ironic treatment of the theme of friendship in the play. Since Proteus and Valentine are such close friends, it might be expected their servants would be, too. But Speed's airs and affectations offend Launce. Further, he doesn't trust Speed with secrets. Whereas Valentine foolishly tells Proteus all the details of his planned elopement with Silvia, Launce remains tight-lipped when Speed tries to interrogate him about how matters stand between Proteus and Julia. Speed thinks that Launce is too thick-headed to understand the meaning of clever words and phrases, but he's mistaken. Launce's ability to manipulate words is as deft as Speed's, but in a different vein. He exploits Speed's arrogance in III.i, when he pretends he's illiterate and gets Speed to read out the items on the report about the milk-maid. Launce keeps him at this task long enough to insure that the page will receive a whipping from his master for keeping him waiting.

In addition to serving as a kind of ironic chorus to the main action, Launce is truly comic himself. For example, the business with the shoes in II.ii—"This shoe is my father. No, this left shoe is my father; no, no, this left shoe is my mother" (II.ii.14-16)—invariably evokes gales of laughter from theater audiences. Launce's affection for Crab is both funny and touching. In IV.iv, Launce scolds Crab for having forgotten all that he's taught him about how to act properly. In the duke's dining room, Launce points out, in the company of the ruling family and their courtiers, Crab has behaved like a common cur. His misconduct would have earned him a whipping, except that Launce stepped forward and took the blame—and the whipping—for him.

Commentators have frequently noted that Launce's willingness to suffer for love is comparable to Julia's. When Julia is sent to Silvia to plead for Proteus, she muses to herself, "How many women would do such a message?" (IV.iv.90). Only moments before, while reminding Crab that he's covered up for him on many occasions, Launce remarks to his dog, "How many masters would do this for his servant?" (IV.v.29-30). After Proteus sends Launce away and tells him not to return again unless he can find the small dog that was stolen from him, the rustic clown never reappears. His place as Proteus's servant is taken by Julia, the woman with whom he shares a similar notion of the kind of devotion that love requires.

Lucetta:

She is Julia's confidante as well as her maid. Lucetta's lively wit and facility with words, as well as her affection for Julia, are evident in the two scenes in which she appears. In I.ii, she gives Julia a letter from Proteus that she has accepted on her behalf. Julia acts offended and says that Lucetta had no right to do this. Though Julia sends Lucetta away—with instructions to return the letter to its sender—she's not really angry with her. When Julia calls her back, Lucetta makes a show of dropping the letter, then picking it up again. Recognizing that

> **Looking at the portrait of Silvia that she is supposed to carry back to Proteus, Julia remarks uncharitably that 'the painter flatter'd her a little' (IV.iv.187)."**

Julia is eager to read it, Lucetta teases her and holds it back for awhile. When she finally gives it to her mistress, Julia tears it up and orders Lucetta to leave the pieces lying on the ground. Lucetta departs, understanding Julia's true feelings about the letter and Proteus. In II.vii, Julia turns to Lucetta for advice about how she "may undertake / A journey to [her] loving Proteus" (II.vii.6-7). Lucetta's response is eminently practical; she recommends that Julia cool her ardor until Proteus returns to Verona. When Julia insists she will go to Milan, disguised as a boy, Lucetta offers sound advice mixed with a bawdy joke. She will make Julia a pair of men's breeches, says Lucetta, but they must have a codpiece (used to conceal an opening in the front of men's breeches): though Julia doesn't really need one, it will serve as a handy pincushion. Lucetta also tries to warn Julia about what she may discover when she gets to Milan. Men can be deceitful, she points out, and Julia should be prepared to find her lover unfaithful. Julia denies that Proteus is like other men, and she sets off on her journey, heedless of her maid's sound advice.

Milan:

The ruler of Milan, he is also Silvia's father. The duke makes no secret of the fact that he wants his daughter to marry Sir Thurio, a man of great wealth but with little else to recommend him. Silvia's own feelings on the question of marriage are of no importance to the duke. He locks her in her room when she refuses to transfer her affection from Valentine to Thurio. The duke's principal objection to Valentine as a potential son-in-law seems to be the young man's inferior status. Though Valentine is a gentleman, he has neither wealth nor a noble title. The duke regards Valentine as an upstart who is trying to marry above his station in life.

The duke is sometimes cunning or sly. In order to trick Valentine into talking about his plans to

> **Julia's conception of love is generous. It includes forgiveness, as well as pity and constancy."**

elope with Silvia, the duke invents a tale about a woman he's in love with and solicits Valentine's advice in conducting the affair. But since the duke conceives this plan after he has learned all the details of the elopement from Proteus, the only point of the duke's game seems to be to humiliate Valentine. The duke is not so clever when it comes to Proteus. He trusts Proteus alone with Silvia because he believes in Proteus's reputation as a young man who is constant in love; the duke mistakenly thinks that faithfulness to Julia will keep Proteus from courting Silvia.

In V.iv, the duke rapidly changes his mind about Valentine. The young man's spirited assertion of his claim to Silvia at V.iv.126-31 impresses the duke. Whereas earlier he described Valentine as a "base intruder, [an] overweening slave" (III.i.157), he now calls Thurio "degenerate and base" (V.iv.136) and praises Valentine as "worthy of an empress" (V.iv.141). The duke forgives Valentine's past offenses against authority and welcomes him as a son-in-law. At Valentine's urging, he pardons the outlaws as well, and orders that suitable employment be found for each of them.

Musicians:

They accompany the serenade to Silvia in IV.ii.

Outlaws:

They are a band of robbers who live in the forest between Milan and Mantua. Though they have a reputation as menacing figures, they seem more absurd than threatening. Some of them are gentlemen by birth—a fact of which they're very proud. Each of them has been banished from society for one crime or another, such as abducting a lady or stabbing a gentleman. But, the outlaws are careful to point out, these crimes were committed while they were under the influence of youthful, uncontrollable emotions. The outlaws are impressed by Valentine's beauty, his poise, and his professed ability to speak several languages. They offer to make him their leader, adding that if he doesn't accept the office they'll kill him. Valentine accepts, but only if they will promise to "do no outrages / On silly women or poor passengers" (IV.i.69-70). The outlaws have no difficulty going along with this; indeed, they assert that they "detest such vile practices" (IV.i.71). In V.iv, Valentine swears to the duke that the outlaws are endowed with many worthy qualities. The duke accepts Valentine's description of them as "full of good, / And fit for great employment" (V.iv.156-57). He pardons them all and admits them back into society.

Panthino:

He is a servant to Antonio, Proteus's father. In I.iii, Panthino has little trouble persuading Antonio that Proteus ought to be seeking his fortune in other lands or devoting himself to studies at a university, rather than living idly at home in Verona. He reminds Antonio that Proteus's friend Valentine is in Milan and recommends that Proteus should be sent there. He points out that a group of gentlemen are leaving for Milan the next day, and that Proteus could travel in their company. By the time he's finished, he has led his master to adopt his own point of view of what should be done, how it should be done, and when it should be done. Panthino also has an exchange with Launce in II.iii. In this scene, Panthino has no patience with Launce's grief over leaving Verona; he brusquely hurries him along to the ship where Proteus and the others are waiting.

Proteus:

A young gentlemen of Verona, his father sends him to Milan to gain worldly experience and knowledge of life at court. Proteus has the same name as a sea god in Greek and Roman mythology who could alter his shape and assume various forms whenever he wanted. The adjective "protean" is derived from the name of this sea god; it means a changing, variable, or inconstant person. In the play, Proteus is as changeable and unfaithful as his name suggests. He abruptly switches his affections from Julia to Silvia soon after arriving in Milan. In V.iv, only moments after he was about to rape Silvia, he declares that he is overwhelmed by "shame and guilt" (V.iv.73) and begs Valentine to forgive him. He quickly sets aside his ardent devotion to Silvia after his page Sebastian is revealed as Julia and Valentine urges that they be reconciled. At the prospect of marriage to Julia, Proteus swears that now he has his "wish for ever" (V.iv.119).

Commentators disagree sharply about the character of Proteus. Many describe him as treacherous, egotistical, predatory, or contemptible. Others view him sympathetically, defending him as an immature, confused young man; in their judgment, he doesn't really mean to hurt anyone. They see him as motivated not by malice, but by the irresistible power of romantic love. Readers who share this point of view contend that from the moment he first considers abandoning his love for Julia and pursuing Silvia instead, Proteus agonizes over his betrayal of Valentine's friendship. Both those who defend Proteus and those who condemn him cite his soliloquies at II.iv.192-214 and II.vi.1-43 to reinforce their respective claims. These passages have been variously read as evidence that he's torn apart by guilt, that he's giving thoughtful consideration to what he's about to do, that he's chiefly motivated by self-gratification but pretending not to be, and that he's simply a scoundrel. Commentators with widely varying opinions of Proteus frequently agree on one thing: Proteus seems to take his deception of Valentine more seriously than his betrayal of Julia.

Proteus's concept of love appears to be more heavily influenced by romantic conventions than by genuine emotion. Like Valentine, he tries to pattern his behavior on the model of courtly love. Throughout the play he shows greater familiarity with the outward signs of being in love—exchanging letters and rings, serenading his mistress, and so on—than a true understanding of the nature of love itself. Proteus has only a superficial appreciation of what love requires. This shallow perspective is reflected in Valentine's description of him as a man who is "a votary of fond desire" (I.i.52); Proteus is more devoted to erotic love than to Julia. In the play's first scene, when Proteus is alone, he complains that loving Julia has changed his very shape and form, causing him to desert his friends and lose his identity. Whether he's truly lost his sense of self at this stage of the dramatic action is debatable. But when desire for Silvia leads him to be unfaithful to Julia and betray Valentine, he does become untrue to himself. In II.vi, he admits that the course he has chosen will inevitably lead to a terrible compromise of the image he previously held of himself. However, he's uncertain now about his essential integrity and how to be faithful to it: "I cannot now prove constant to myself / Without some treachery us'd to Valentine" (II.vi.31-32). That Proteus is more focused on the superficial aspects of love than on its substance may be seen in the episode where he begs Silvia to give him a portrait of herself. If he cannot have the real woman to love, he says, he will speak and "sigh and weep" (IV.ii.122) to an image of her.

> **❝❞ Launce's realistic appraisals of love and friendship provide insights into the principal themes and characters in the play."**

Indeed, he says, this would be appropriate, for as long as she remains devoted to another man, he is "but a shadow," so to her shadow he will "make true love" (IV.ii.124, 125).

The onset of Proteus's obsession with Silvia provides important clues to an understanding of his character. In the opinion of many modern commentators, Proteus is not entirely to blame for his obsession. In II.iv, shortly after Proteus arrives in Milan, Valentine praises Silvia extravagantly and urges Proteus to join him in regarding her as the most beautiful, desirable woman on earth. When Proteus asks if he may not prefer his own love, Valentine says no—though he does grant that Julia is worthy enough to hold up the hem of Silvia's gown so that it doesn't touch "the base earth" (II.iv.159). When Valentine leaves—after telling him about the plans for eloping with Silvia—Proteus appears amazed that his affections have shifted from Julia to Silvia so quickly. He says he doesn't know whether it was the evidence of his own eyes or Valentine's praise of her that caused this. Recognizing that if he loves Silvia he'll be false to both Valentine and Julia, Proteus says he will try to do the ethical thing; but if he can't stop himself from falling in love with Silvia, he adds, he'll use all his skills to obtain her. His skills apparently include telling Silvia's father about the elopement, falsely reporting to Silvia that Julia is dead, hoodwinking the duke and Sir Thurio, and continuing to play the role of true friend to Valentine. He even tries to rape Silvia when, as he thinks, they are alone in the forest.

Proteus is, of course, startled when Valentine suddenly appears and prevents the attack. The depth of his repentance is not so clear. His apology comes quickly, and is just as quickly accepted. Whether Proteus is genuinely repentant is not a question that usually arises in discussions of *The Two Gentlemen of Verona*. As commentators have noted, Proteus's redemption is required to assure that the comedy has a happy ending.

> **In addition to serving as a kind of ironic chorus to the main action, Launce is truly comic himself.**"

Silvia:

The duke's daughter, she has spent her life at court and is thus familiar with the rules and conventions that govern daily life there. She acts as a referee in the ''fine volley of words'' (II.iv.33) between Valentine and Thurio, and coyly reveals her feelings to Valentine by having him write a love letter on her behalf. But Silvia is more than a young woman with courtly accomplishments and fine manners. She defies her father and leaves the security of Milan to seek out her beloved Valentine when he is banished. And she demonstrates poise and self-control at critical moments—for example, when she's captured by the outlaws in V.iii.

Silvia's loyalty to Valentine cannot be shaken. She is a model of constancy and seems never to doubt his love for her. Her innate sensitivity is evident in her many compassionate expressions of sympathy for Julia, particularly in IV.iv, when Julian/Sebastian attempts to woo Silvia on Proteus's behalf. Silvia's sensitivity is also evident in her reaction to Proteus's courtship: she is repulsed by him and almost feels ashamed that he is attracted to her. Normally even-tempered and moderate in her choice of words, Silvia repeatedly and bluntly rebukes Proteus. Silvia calls Proteus treacherous and cunning, a ''perjured, false, disloyal man'' (IV.ii.95). She tells him she despises him, and, when he rescues her from the outlaws, she says she would rather have been ''seized by a hungry lion'' (V.iv.33) than saved by Proteus.

From one perspective, Silvia seems enviable. She has physical beauty, inner strengths and virtues, an eminent position in society, and—according to the song—all the young men adore her. Yet in the world of the play she is often treated as a commodity. Her father has the right to pick and choose who she will marry. Thurio regards her as a prize he's entitled to because of his wealth. Proteus swears that he worships her—but he threatens to rape her when she continues to resist him. Even Valentine,

who appears to love Silvia deeply and sincerely, seems to think he has the right to offer her as a token of his friendship for Proteus.

Silvia's silence during this last episode has troubled many readers and commentators. Some have suggested that her complete faith in Valentine gives her confidence that he wouldn't really hand her over to the man who, only moments before, was on the verge of attacking her. Others have suggested that she accepts the notion that masculine friendship is a higher ideal than romantic love, and therefore she modestly raises no objections to Valentine's offer. It's also possible that as a woman, Silvia has no role to play in working out the happy ending of the comedy.

Speed:

Employed as a page to Valentine, he is frequently referred to as ''boy,'' which emphasizes his youthfulness. Speed has a quick wit, and he is more clever at manipulating words than his master. Like Launce and Lucetta, he provides an ironic commentary on romantic love. In II.i, he pokes fun at what he sees as Valentine's love-sickness. Speed believes that beauty has no objective reality. He tells Valentine that his perception of Silvia's beauty is biased by his love for her. But this is understandable, Speed adds, for ''Love is blind'' (II.i.70). The page's superior insight is evident in II.i, when Valentine presents Silvia with the love letter she has asked him to write. Speed immediately perceives what Silvia intended to accomplish with this ploy. Valentine doesn't understand until, after she has left, Speed explains it to him.

Speed seems to revel in his facility with words, and he delights in argumentation. At I.i.72-150, while Proteus waits to hear a report on Julia's reaction to the letter he entrusted Speed to deliver to her, the page indulges in an extended development of strained metaphors and puns on the words ship, sheep, and shepherd. But Speed meets his match in the seemingly slow-witted Launce. Launce regards Speed as ''an unmannerly slave, that will thrust himself into secrets'' (III.i.383-84). In II.v, when Speed tries to find out from Launce how the affair between Julia and Proteus is progressing, Launce responds deviously. The frustrated Speed is forced to admit that he cannot understand. In III.i, Launce pretends that he is unable to read, and he asks Speed to help him with a written report about the woman Launce contemplates marrying. Speed's function in this episode is limited to a mechanical recital of the list of items describing the woman's virtues and vices, while Launce gets to make all the jokes. Only when the entire list has ben reviewed does Launce tell Speed that Valentine is waiting for him at the north gate of the city. So much time has elapsed that Speed faces a beating for being late, and he hurries off. Speed's final appearance is in IV.i, when he and Valentine are captured by the outlaws. He speaks only briefly there, and then he disappears from the play.

Thurio:

A nobleman at the duke's court in Milan, he wants to marry Silvia. Silvia's father favors Sir Thurio above all her other suitors. According to Valentine, this is because Thurio is wealthy. Silvia is generally polite to Thurio, but she refuses to marry him. Thurio tries to adhere to the rules of courtly love, yet his attachment to Silvia seems conventional rather than sincere. As Valentine points out, Sir Thurio knows all the right words and phrases, but he uses them mechanically or unimaginatively; Valentine easily defeats him in a competition of wit and word-play at II.iv.9-46. Thurio is easily fooled by Proteus, who promises to help him woo Silvia. He stands by helplessly while Proteus assumes the featured role in the serenade. Admittedly, Thurio is not a devoted lover. He agrees to help the duke pursue Silvia and Eglamour into the forest, but he does so, as he says, "to be revenged on Eglamour" (V.ii.51-52), not for love of Silvia. He gives up his claim to her in V.iv with more sense than sensibility, declaring that a man is a fool to endanger his life for a girl who doesn't love him.

Valentine:

A young gentleman of Verona, he goes to Milan to broaden his education and become familiar with courtly customs. Valentine is the name of two Italian saints, one of whom is the patron saint of lovers. In *The Two Gentlemen of Verona*, Valentine tries to follow the rules traditionally set forth for young men who are head over heels in love. In several scenes, he demonstrates his familiarity with the language of love, though it's questionable how much he understands about love itself. Valentine has drawn a variety of responses from readers of the play. Some commentators emphasize his immaturity and misplaced idealism, while others see him as a selfish egotist. A considerable number of readers have called him a fool or a simpleton. Most agree, however, that he generally means well and that he's a faithful friend to Proteus.

> **Proteus seems to take his deception of Valentine more seriously than his betrayal of Julia."**

Valentine may not be a fool, but he is easily manipulated by others, and his ability to comprehend what's happening around him sometimes seems severely limited. In II.i, he fails to grasp what Silvia is trying to say to him when she returns the letter he's written for her to an unknown lover. Speed remarks that her intentions are as clear "as a nose on a man's face, or a weathercock on a steeple!" (II.i.136). But not to Valentine, who requires a lengthy explanation of the jest from Speed. When the duke invents a story about a woman he loves who is promised to another man and whose bedchamber is "aloft, far from the ground" (III.i.114), Valentine fails to see that the duke's description matches Silvia's situation exactly. He stands helplessly while his cloak is removed to reveal a cord ladder and a letter from Silvia. Even then, Valentine doesn't understand that he's been deliberately placed in a compromising situation, that the duke knew about the elopement, and that the only one who could have told him was Proteus. In terms of its consequences, Valentine's most serious misjudgment occurs in II.iv, when he overpraises Silvia and refers to Julia disdainfully. His bragging words about his own love and his contemptuous attitude toward Julia are more than rude or arrogant. They help persuade Proteus that there is only one woman in the world worth loving, and her name is Silvia.

Generations of readers have sought an explanation for Valentine's sudden forgiveness of Proteus in the final scene and his startling offer: "All that was mine in Silvia I give thee" (V.iv.83). Some see this behavior as irrational or foolish. Several commentators regard it as Valentine's acknowledgment that he is partly to blame for Proteus's treachery. Either consciously or unconsciously, they argue, Valentine is admitting that his excessive praise of Silvia was arrogant and that it inspired envy in Proteus. Several other commentators assert that Valentine's behavior here reflects the play's emphasis on friendship as a higher ideal than romantic love. Seen from this perspective, Valentine's ac-

> **"When Valentine leaves— after telling him about the plans for eloping with Silvia—Proteus appears amazed that his affections have shifted from Julia to Silvia so quickly."**

tions represent an endorsement of the superior claim of friendship. According to some scholars, an Elizabethan audience would share this point of view and thus would have seen Valentine's behavior as a suitable climax to the dramatic action.

Other commentators have argued that such forgiveness reflects the true spirit of generosity embodied in Julia, Silvia, and Launce. To be able to ignore or forgive the offenses of others represents the highest standards of ethical conduct. Another way of looking at Valentine's behavior here is to see it as his recognition that reconciliation necessarily involves compromise. If a peaceful resolution of the conflict is to be achieved, giving up Silvia may be the only way to attain this. Some readers find Valentine charitable and generous by nature, a young man so full of warmth and kindness that he will sacrifice Silvia so that Proteus may have her. A few have suggested that Valentine is testing Proteus's repentance and renewed vows of friendship: he hopes that Proteus will refuse the offer, but he's willing to risk losing Silvia in order to find out whether his friend is truly penitent. Finally, some commentators, noting that *The Two Gentlemen of Verona* is among Shakespeare's earliest plays, view Valentine's abrupt forgiveness of Proteus and his offer of Silvia as evidence of a dramatist who has not yet mastered his craft and who could find no other, more rational, means of reconciling the characters and achieving a happy ending for the comedy.

Further Reading

Arthos, John. "*The Two Gentlemen of Verona*." In *Shakespeare: The Early Writings*, 104-73. Totowa, N.J.: Rowman and Littlefield, 1972.

Arthos sees significant philosophical issues woven into the romantic comedy of this play, including

questions about the nature of faithfulness, what suffering can teach us about friendship and love, and what constitutes perfection. He views Silvia as an illustration of what perfection may be: holy, wise, and fair. Proteus, by contrast, shows us that love without reason leads to loss of integrity and the betrayal of truth.

Berry, Ralph. "Love and Friendship." In *Shakespeare's Comedies: Explorations in Form*, 40-53. Princeton: Princeton University Press, 1972.

Berry regards Valentine as a self-absorbed young man who affects the pose of a conventional romantic lover and adapts his behavior in keeping with what he sees as the rules of that convention. Berry perceives Proteus as a self-conscious role-player, too, and he compares the play's final scene to a major theatrical production staged—for their own benefit—by "the two egotists of Verona."

Carroll, William C. "'Forget to Be a Woman.'" In *The Metamorphoses of Shakespearean Comedy*, 103-37. Princeton: Princeton University Press, 1985.

In a section (pp. 107-17) of this chapter, Carroll discusses the implications of Julia's adoption of the role of Sebastian. Ironically, he points out, her willingness to change, to be flexible, demonstrates her constancy in love. Carroll argues that Julia and Silvia are portrayed as steadfast—though not rigid—in a world where men swear vows and quickly betray them.

Charney, Maurice. "*The Two Gentlemen of Verona*." In *All of Shakespeare*, 11-17. New York: Columbia University Press, 1993.

Charney asserts that the play's characters are not fully developed figures; their actions are not explainable in terms of ordinary human motives, he contends, because all of them—but most particularly Proteus— are driven by the whims of love. Charney further maintains that the play establishes friendship as a higher ideal than romantic love and that Valentine's offer to give up Silvia ought to be viewed in this light.

Ewbank, Inga-Stina. "'Were man but constant, he were perfect': Constancy and Consistency in *The Two Gentlemen of Verona*." In *Shakespearian Comedy*, Stratford-upon-Avon Studies 14, 31-57. London: Edward Arnold, 1972.

Ewbank shows how, on the one hand, the play uses the conventional language of courtly love to express real feelings and, on the other hand, exposes that language as lifeless. She believes that a central problem with the play is its emphasis on "what characters say"— that is, their attitudes—rather than on who they are as individuals.

Girard, René. "Love Delights in Praises: A Reading of *The Two Gentlemen of Verona*." *Philosophy and Literature* 13, no. 2 (October 1989): 231-47.

Girard contends that Proteus desires Silvia not because she is more beautiful than Julia, but because his long friendship with Valentine has conditioned him to want whatever Valentine wants. In addition, Girard declares that Valentine unconsciously makes Julia seem pathetic when he overpraises Silvia in II.iv; in order to justify his own choice, Valentine must insinuate that Proteus's preference for Julia is irrational. In Girard's view, Valentine eventually realizes he's partly to blame for what happened, and his offer of Silvia to Proteus is an effort to atone for his error.

MacCary, W. Thomas. "*The Two Gentlemen of Verona.*" In *Friends and Lovers*, 91-109. New York: Columbia University Press, 1985.

MacCary focuses on how Proteus and Valentine learn to let go of their idealized notion of love—a fantasy that prevents them from distinguishing between illusion and reality. In MacCary's judgment, the play dramatizes a universal truth: all lovers unconsciously use their objects of desire to provide a frame of reference for their own self-images; thus Valentine and Proteus must learn to love actual women, not an ideal of one, before they can determine their true selves.

Ornstein, Robert. "*Two Gentlemen of Verona.*" In *Shakespeare's Comedies*, 48-62. Newark: University of Delaware Press, 1986.

Ornstein traces the development, scene by scene, of Shakespeare's portrait of "male rivalry and romantic egotism" in *The Two Gentlemen of Verona*. In extended analyses of the central characters, Ornstein declares that Valentine's arrogant and egotistical boasting about Silvia (II.iv) implicates him in Proteus's unfaithfulness to Julia; that Proteus's infidelity is motivated not by passion for Silvia but by the thrill of competition with his friend; and that Julia's courage and self-composure show her to be "stronger than the man who betrays her."

Schlueter, Kurt. Introduction to *The Two Gentlemen of Verona,* by William Shakespeare, 1-49. Cambridge: Cambridge University Press, 1990.

Schlueter's introduction includes an extended overview of the play's stage history from 1762 to the present, as well as an analysis of its structure and literary sources. Schlueter argues that the dramatic action is linked to a "test-of-friendship" motif. He sees Valentine as well-intentioned but foolish, an essentially passive figure who "walks blindly into the trap Silvia's father has set for him" in III.i.

Slights, Camille Wells. "Common Courtesy in *The Two Gentlemen of Verona.*" In *Shakespeare's Comic Commonwealths*, 57-73. Toronto: University of Toronto Press, 1993.

Slights maintains that the play upholds the value of courtly manners and style, though it also demonstrates that this value can be perverted. In her view, the comedy shows Valentine and Proteus learning that the superficial elegance of a courtier—for example, fine manners and verbal dexterity—is more easily attained than are the true qualities of what it means to be a gentleman: honesty, sensitivity, and social responsibility.

The Two Noble Kinsmen

1613

Act I:

A Prologue precedes the start of the dramatic action. It praises the literary source of *The Two Noble Kinsmen*: Chaucer's "The Knight's Tale," a narrative poem set in legendary Greece. The play itself begins with an elaborate procession accompanying Theseus, duke of Athens, and Hippolyta, the Amazon queen, to their wedding. The ritual is interrupted by the sudden appearance of three queens, dressed in mourning clothes, who fall on their knees and beg Theseus to help them. They report that their husbands were slain in battle by Creon, king of Thebes, and that Creon has refused to allow their bodies to be buried. The queens ask Theseus to delay his marriage to Hippolyta and go to war against Creon at once. As Theseus considers whether to proceed with the wedding or postpone it, the queens appeal to Hippolyta and her younger sister Emilia to intercede on their behalf. Hippolyta urges Theseus to put off the ceremony in deference to avenging the slain kings, and Emilia endorses her sister's petition. Theseus agrees to set out with his army for Thebes as soon as possible. The setting shifts from Athens to Thebes, where Palamon and Arcite, Creon's nephews, are discussing his vicious rulership. They resolve to leave Thebes but change their minds when they learn that Theseus has declared war on the city and its sovereign. In Athens, Hippolyta and Emilia converse with each other

about friendship, love, and marriage. The scene shifts back to Thebes, and the triumph of Theseus over Creon. Theseus tells the three queens they are now free to retrieve the bones of their dead husbands and honor them appropriately. A herald tells Theseus that Palamon and Arcite have been captured, and the duke orders that they be treated well. In the final scene of Act I, the three queens perform funeral rites for their husbands' remains.

Act II:

In a jail near Theseus's palace in Athens, the jailer talks with the young man who is wooing his daughter. The daughter enters and speaks excitedly about the new prisoners—Palamon and Arcite—who have been placed in the jail. The cousins, in shackles, appear in a room above and talk together about their imprisonment and their friendship for each other. Emilia walks into a garden below their cell. Palamon sees her and decides immediately that he is in love with her. A moment later, Arcite does the same. Friendship turns into rivalry, as the young men dispute who is more worthy of Emilia and who has the greater claim to her. The jailer interrupts their dispute and takes Arcite away to meet with Theseus. When the jailer returns, he tells Palamon that Arcite has been banished from Athens. However, in some woods outside the city, Arcite vows not to leave the kingdom. Hearing about the sports competitions being held as part of the celebration of the spring festival in Athens, Arcite decides to disguise himself and enter the contest. Somewhere near the prison, the jailer's daughter soliloquizes about her love for Palamon, acknowledging the hopelessness of her passion. Arcite triumphs at the ceremonial games and Theseus, not realizing who he is, praises his accomplishments. Arcite is given a position as Emilia's attendant. In the closing scene of Act II, which takes place in some woods near the prison, the jailer's daughter searches for Palamon, whom she has released from his jail cell.

Act III:

Drawing apart from the May Day celebrations, Arcite retires to a secluded place and happily contemplates his role as Emilia's attendant. Palamon bursts from behind a bush and accuses Arcite of treachery. Arcite says he will bring him some nourishment and tools to cut through his prison irons—and then they can fight a duel to determine who will have Emilia. When Arcite returns, the cousins reminisce about their earlier romantic encounters with young women. Meanwhile, the jailer's daughter

appears alone in the woods twice. On the first occasion, she relates that she hasn't eaten or slept for two days. The second time, she appears to be on the edge of madness. She stumbles onto a group of countrymen and women who are preparing a traditional morris dance as part of the May festivities, and they persuade her to join them in the dance. Theseus, Pirithous, Hippolyta, Emilia, and Arcite arrive on the scene and are entertained by the performance.

When they have all returned to the city, Arcite and Palamon meet and prepare for their duel. Their swordfight is interrupted by the arrival of Theseus, Hippolyta, Emilia, and Pirithous. Theseus angrily charges them with breaking the law of Athens and orders that they be killed. Palamon reveals his own and Arcite's identities, and explains that Emilia is the object of their dispute. Hippolyta, Emilia, and Pirithous beg Theseus to show mercy toward the young men. The duke asks Emilia to choose one of them for her husband, but she declines to do so. Theseus then orders Palamon and Arcite to go back to Thebes. Each of them must find three knights willing to assist them and then return to Athens for a trial-by-combat. Under the terms established by Theseus, the victorious cousin will wed Emilia and the defeated one—together with his three knights—will be executed.

Act IV:

The jailer, anxious to learn whether he'll be punished because his daughter has released Palamon from prison, is assured by his friends that Theseus has pardoned him. The young man who has been courting the jailer's daughter reports that, in his judgment, she has lost her wits. The jailer's daughter appears, and her conduct supports this assessment. The jailer, his brother, and his friends marvel at her deranged mind and treat her compassionately. In the duke's palace, Emilia contemplates pictures of Palamon and Arcite, describing to herself each man's virtues. When Theseus, Hippolyta, and Pirithous intrude upon her solitude, she maintains that she cannot choose between the two kinsmen— even though she is overcome by the thought that one of them must lose the tournament and die. Act IV closes with a scene in which a doctor interviews the jailer's daughter and then recommends that the only way to cure her madness is to trick her into believing that the wooer is Palamon.

Act V:

Outside Athens, the two cousins and their six knights prepare for the tournament. Arcite and Palamon embrace and bid each other farewell. Arcite and his knights withdraw to an altar dedicated to Mars, the god of war. Arcite prays for victory, and the response to his prayer is a clamor of banging armor and the sounds of battle. Palamon and his knights kneel at an altar dedicated to Venus, the goddess of love. He praises her powers and asks her to be on his side in the contest; music is heard and doves flutter from behind the altar. The final prayer is Emilia's. She appeals to Diana, the goddess who protects virgins, to ensure that the man who loves her best will gain the victory. A rose tree with a single bloom rises from the altar.

In the Athenian prison, the young man who loves the jailer's daughter reports to the doctor that he has almost persuaded her that he is Palamon. The doctor recommends a further step: the wooer should sleep with her. The jailer expresses grave doubts about this, but the doctor insists it's the most effective way to cure her insanity. The jailer's daughter, still in a state of madness, joins them. When the doctor and the jailer leave to attend the tournament, the wooer and the jailer's daughter slip away together.

The combat between Palamon and Arcite begins, but Emilia refuses to witness it. Still unable to decide which man she prefers, she sends a servant to find out how the contest is unfolding. For a time, Palamon appears to be winning, but Arcite is ultimately the victor. Theseus brings Arcite to Emilia and places their hands together as a sign of their betrothal. Soon after this, the jailer joins Palamon and his knights as they await their execution. When Palamon inquires about the jailer's daughter, the jailer reports that her health is restored and she will soon be married. Just as Palamon lays his head on the executioner's block, Pirithous bursts in with startling news: Arcite's horse has reared up and fallen backward, crushing Arcite's body beneath him. Mortally injured, Arcite is carried in by attendants, accompanied by Theseus, Hippolyta, and Emilia. Arcite urges Palamon to "Take Emilia, and with her all the world's joy" (V.iv.90-91). Arcite and Emilia kiss, and then he dies. As Arcite's body is borne away, Theseus marvels at the turn of events and acknowledges that mankind has little choice but to accept the dictates of the gods. He gives instructions for Arcite's funeral rites and for the wedding of Palamon and Emilia that will follow it. The play closes with an epilogue, in which the speaker ex-

presses uncertainty as to how the play will be received by the audience.

Note on the Authorship

For more than three centuries, critics and commentators debated whether *The Two Noble Kinsmen* was the work of an individual author or the result of a collaboration between two or more dramatists. Most scholars now believe that the play was written by William Shakespeare and John Fletcher. It is impossible to determine precisely which scenes were written by which playwright, but several late twentieth-century scholars attribute to Shakespeare all of Act I as well as II.i, III.i-ii, IV.iii, V.i, and V.iii-iv. The remaining scenes—II.ii-vi, III.iii-vi, IV.i-ii, and V.ii—are attributed to Fletcher. Thus Shakespeare is credited with the basic design; with the introduction of all the central characters; several scenes in the middle of the play; and all of Act V except the scene in which the jailer's daughter makes her final appearance.

Modern Connections

The conflict between love and friendship dramatized in *The Two Noble Kinsmen* is not an issue limited to one period of human history or to one culture. Friendships—particularly those that begin in childhood or adolescence—have always been among the most meaningful relationships in a person's life. But what happens if two friends love the same person? Today such friends would probably stop short of trying to kill each other, but it's likely that anger and resentment would threaten their relationship. When a young man or woman becomes involved in a love affair, he or she will usually have less time to spend with old friends. Thus love may put a strain on friendship or limit its expression. On the other hand, the loved one may be jealous of the lover's old friends. The friendship between Theseus and Pirithous continues even after Theseus marries Hippolyta, and it seems apparent that she is not always confident that she is the most important person in her husband's life. Even when a couple is as rational as they are, doubts may arise about conflicting loyalties. Sometimes a friendship ends tragically, as with Emilia and Flavina (Emilia's childhood friend who died when the girls were eleven). How might this affect the surviving friend's outlook on life and love? Persons who die young are likely to be idealized, and those who survive may have difficulty establishing new friendships, because no one can ever measure up to the romantic images that live in our memories.

Emilia's nostalgic remembrance of Flavina (in I.iii) may indicate an unwillingness to let go of youthful innocence. As a person matures, the uncomplicated delights of childhood are replaced by concerns that burden our lives, or at least make them more problematic. Reluctance to let go of carefree days and take on the responsibilities of adulthood is a natural emotion. Yet movement from one stage of life to another is an inevitable consequence of human existence. Hippolyta seems to understand and accept this. Emilia does not, but it's hard for us to blame her. Maturity brings opportunities and experiences that are denied to children and adolescents. If one is fortunate, it also brings satisfaction or contentment. Some people may question whether these are acceptable substitutes for the uninhibited joy of childhood. But maturity is part of nature's design, and most people, like Hippolyta, accept it. That doesn't mean, however, that we will always face it without the same hesitation demonstrated by Emilia.

It's also hard to accept the idea that we have less control over our lives than we like to think we have. *The Two Noble Kinsmen* portrays a world in which human destiny is manipulated by impersonal or superhuman forces. Arcite seems to be a young man who knows what he wants and pursues it aggressively; he seizes opportunities and makes the most of them. He wins the tournament and gains Emilia, and then, because of some stroke of fate or intervention by the gods, he loses his life. The unpredictability of events and our inability to know what courses our lives will take can be frightening to contemplate. Theseus accepts, with sadness, whatever outcome the gods—or fate or chance—decree, and he urges others to do so, too. Many people think that this is easier said than done. We'd like to believe that if life isn't predictable, at least it isn't arbitrary or unfair. Some readers see the death of Arcite as unjust. It may be that Palamon and Emilia were predestined to end up together. If we're unable to locate a pattern in human events, or in our own lives, does that mean there isn't one? Or does it perhaps mean that such patterns are hidden from human sight?

The play also seems to suggest that we are at the mercy of love unless we learn to channel our natural desires in ways that promote our personal well-being and benefit society. It's possible to look at the jailer's daughter as a pathetic example of what happens when love and sex rule our lives. Her obsession with Palamon leads her to endanger her father's job, run away from home, neglect her health, and even consider whether life is worth living without the man she loves. By contrast, Palamon and Arcite become bitter rivals and try to destroy each other because they are so overcome by Emilia's beauty. Hippolyta gives up her life as a warrior and subdues that part of her personality in order to marry Theseus. However, she appears content with the choices she has made. The lusty desires of the jailer's daughter are tamed and redirected, and she appears headed for marriage with her devoted wooer; but we don't see for ourselves how satisfied *she* is with her new role. By the end of the play, is Emilia content? If she had been given the choice of continuing to resist heterosexual love, would she have taken it rather than marrying one of the cousins? In the world of the play, she has no such choice, for society requires that she marry. Is there a wider range of possibilities for young men and women today than the ones available to the characters in *The Two Noble Kinsmen*?

Characters

Arcite:

One of the play's title characters, he is the nephew of Creon, king of Thebes, and the cousin of Palamon. Arcite is the victor in the trial-by-combat to determine who will marry Emilia, but he is mortally wounded when his horse rears up and falls backward on him. With his dying breath, he bestows his right to Emilia on Palamon: his kinsmen, dearest friend, and rival. Arcite and Palamon resemble each other in many ways. Born into the same distinguished family, each of them has won many honors in competitions and on the battlefield. They have hunted wild animals fearlessly and pursued women with youthful warmth and enthusiasm. Each of them is determined to have Emilia for himself. Yet despite the many similarities between them, it is possible to find some differences as well.

Arcite seems more conscientious and practical than Palamon. When the two of them are discussing the impact of Creon's corrupt rule in Thebes, Palamon complains that veteran soldiers are being mistreat-

> Arcite is the victor in the trial-by-combat to determine who will marry Emilia, but he is mortally wounded when his horse rears up and falls backward on him."

ed. Arcite reminds him that the entire community is affected and that there are "decays of many kind" (I.ii.29). In the Athenian prison, when Palamon laments that their future is bleak, he focuses on the loss of further honors. By contrast, Arcite mourns the fact that he will never have a wife and children. He points out to Palamon that at least they will find comfort in each other's company and that making the best of their situation is better than self-pity. When Arcite is released from prison, he disguises himself and enters an athletic contest sponsored by Theseus. He distinguishes himself there and is rewarded by being given a place in Emilia's household.

At the opening of Act III, thinking he is alone in the woods outside Athens, he soliloquizes about his good fortune and expresses some guilt that while he now has the opportunity to be in Emilia's presence every day, Palamon still languishes in jail. His cousin has, however, been freed and, hidden behind a bush, he overhears Arcite. He rushes out at Arcite and calls him a traitor. Arcite repeatedly tries to calm him down, addressing him as "Dear cousin Palamon," "kinsman," and "Sweet Palamon" (III.i.43, 69, 92), but he is unsuccessful. Despite Palamon's continued resentment, Arcite thoughtfully supplies him with food and wine for nourishment, clean shirts and perfumes, files to remove his prison irons, and a sword and a suit of armor so he will be well equipped for their duel. His repeated courtesies are generally met with only grudging thanks from Palamon. When their duel is interrupted by the sounds of hunting horns, signalling the approach of Theseus and his party, Arcite urges that Palamon hide himself. They can take up their swords against each other on another occasion, he counsels; for now they should be discreet. Palamon rejects his cousin's advice, and by the end of their encounter with Theseus the kinsmen are bound to the terms of a contest that will lead to the death of one of them.

Before the trial-by-combat begins, Arcite prays to Mars, the god of war and soldiers. This is a blunt, impersonal prayer, and it reflects Arcite's conviction that wars decide human destiny. He asks the god to guide him in the contest and help him to gain the victory. Whether through the intercession of Mars or because of his own skill, Arcite wins the tournament and Emilia. Other fates intervene, however, and, for no apparent reason except that he seems suddenly terrified by the sound of his own hooves on the pavement, the horse Arcite is riding tries to unseat him. According to Pirithous's description of the event (V.iv.48-84), Arcite's efforts to stay in the saddle and bring the horse under control are superlative. But then the horse stands upright "on his hind hooves" (V.iv.76) and pitches backward, crushing Arcite beneath him. As the fatally injured Arcite bids farewell to Palamon, he says that he "was false, / Yet never treacherous" (V.iv.92-93)—apparently conceding that he did not have the first claim to Emilia but denying that he was ever dishonorable. Arcite asks for his cousin's forgiveness and one kiss from Emilia, and then he dies.

Some modern commentators believe that the love between Arcite and Palamon is more than friendship. Calling attention to the intensity of their relationship and to the erotic language the young men use in the prison episode (II.ii) and in the scene where they arm each other before their duel in the woods (III.vi), these critics assert that there is at least a latent homosexual attraction between the kinsmen. Other commentators, however, find no evidence for this. They see Arcite and Palamon as devoted friends and comrades in arms, young men whose commitment to each other is an example of friendship in its noblest form.

Artesius:

An Athenian soldier, Artesius is one of the attendants in the bridal procession in I.i and an observer of the three queens' appeal to Theseus. When Theseus decides to go to war against Thebes, he instructs Artesius to gather the Athenian forces and meet him at the port of Aulis.

Boy:

Wearing a white robe to emphasize his innocence, the Boy is part of Theseus and Hippolyta's wedding procession in I.i. He strews flowers as he sings a song calling on Nature to bless the marriage.

Countrymen:

Rustics from a village outside Athens, they perform a folk dance for the entertainment of Theseus and his court in connection with the festival of spring. In II.iii, four of the countrymen talk excitedly—and lewdly—about preparations for the performance, to be directed by the local schoolmaster. In high spirits, they speak of the honor the dance will reflect on their village and of how they will outshine all the dancers in Athens. In III.v, six countrymen meet in a clearing in the forest, costumed for the dance: one is dressed as the Lord of May, another as a servingman, a third as the host of an inn, a fourth as a shepherd, and a fifth as a fool or jester. The sixth—the Bavian or Babion—is dressed as a baboon. When it becomes apparent that the countrywoman who was to dance the part of the female fool has failed to show up, the men fear the performance will have to be cancelled. But the jailer's daughter suddenly appears and is drafted into their troupe as a replacement.

In the course of hunting down a stag, Theseus, Hippolyta, Pirithous, Emilia, Arcite, and their attendants enter the clearing. At the schoolmaster's invitation, they interrupt the hunt to witness the morris dance, performed to the accompaniment of a small drum called a tabor and to the sound of the tinkling bells some of the dancers wear on their costumes. In *The Two Noble Kinsmen*, the morris dance serves as a comic contrast to the elaborate rituals and ceremonies that take place in Athens and Thebes.

Countrywomen:

They are women from a village near Athens who take part in the morris dance performed for Theseus and his court in III.v. Five countrywomen show up for the performance as they

had promised. Wearing costumes and ribbons, they take the roles traditionally called for in a morris dance: the Lady of May, a chambermaid, the wife of an inn owner, a country wench or shepherdess, and a female baboon. Cecily, the sixth countrywoman, reneges on her promise to join the dance. Her part, that of the female fool, is taken by the jailer's daughter. For more on the performance of the morris dance, see Countrymen.

Doctor:

He is called in to evaluate and heal the deranged mind of the jailer's daughter. In IV.iii, he expresses pity for her condition and says there is nothing he can do himself to cure her obsession with Palamon.

> **❝❝ As the fatally injured Arcite bids farewell to Palamon, he says that he 'was false, / Yet never treacherous' (V.iv.92-93)— apparently conceding that he did not have the first claim to Emilia but denying that he was ever dishonorable. Arcite asks for his cousin's forgiveness and one kiss from Emilia, and then he dies.❞**

He suggests that the man whom she apparently loved before should take on the role of Palamon and make her fall in love with him all over again. He remarks that she is suffering from a delusion, and this must be replaced by another delusion. In V.ii, the he suggests an additional remedy: the wooer should take her to bed. The jailer objects that this is going too far, but the doctor says that preserving her chastity is much less important than curing her madness. When the jailer leaves, the doctor refers to him as a fool and expresses some doubt about whether the girl is still a virgin. It doesn't really matter whether she is or not, he says to the wooer, "'tis nothing to our purpose" (V.ii.32). In lewd terms, he says that if the jailer's daughter indicates any willingness for a sexual encounter, the wooer should seize the opportunity. At the close of V.ii, the girl proposes to the wooer that they sleep together, and the couple slips away.

Some commentators are repulsed by the doctor's obscene language in the latter scene and appalled by his attitude toward the jailer's daughter. Others have argued that he is doing no more than fighting fire with fire—diverting her sexual appetite from one man to another and channeling her lust in a direction approved by society.

Emilia:

Like her sister Hippolyta, she belongs to a race of female warriors, yet by nature she is gentle and passive. Some commentators regard her as an ideal figure rather than a real woman. They see her as cold and aloof, unwilling to choose between Palamon and Arcite because she lacks passion or sexual desire. Others treat her as an ambiguous figure, incapable of discerning the differences between the two men who love her and reluctant to move from maidenhood to maturity. It may be that her failure to choose between the cousins is no more than a reflection of dramatic necessity. Her betrothal to Arcite when he wins the tournament, and then to Palamon when Arcite is killed, would seem less justifiable if she had ever expressed a preference for one over the other. In the end, she must take whichever man the fates decree.

At times Emilia's love for Palamon and Arcite appears to be so unsubstantial that it hardly seems to matter which one becomes her husband. Though she has several opportunities to choose between them, she refuses to do so. Sometimes she appears to love the young men equally. For example, in IV.ii, she talks aloud to herself as she gazes at small portraits of them that she holds in her hands. "Good heaven, / What a sweet face has Arcite!" she remarks, "Here love himself sits smiling" (IV.ii.6-7, 14). Yet only a moment later she exclaims "Palamon, thou art alone / And only beautiful" (IV.ii.37-38). Even during their trial-by-combat in V.iii, she continues to weigh their comparative merits. Apparently, she is not instinctively drawn to either one of them—as she was to her childhood friend Flavina.

Emilia's nostalgic reminiscence of Flavina, a girl who died when she and Emilia were only eleven, is often regarded as central to the issues of love and friendship in the play. With its emphasis on innocence and spontaneity, this speech (I.iii.55-82) evokes a time before questions of judgment and experience intrude on human relationships. Whatever song, whatever flower was the favorite of one girl, it immediately became the favorite of the other as well. If Flavina disapproved of something, then so did Emilia. Such innocent, unpremeditated love, says Emila, is not possible between a man and a woman.

Emilia's prayer to Diana, the goddess who protects virgins, seems to equate chastity with the suppression or inhibition of desire. The images she associates with the goddess—"shadowy, cold, and constant . . . / . . . solitary, white as chaste, and pure / As wind-fanned snow" (V.i.37-40)—suggest a wish to withdraw from the world and remain a virgin. Emilia describes herself in this prayer as dressed in the robes and flowers of a bride, but still a maiden at heart.

She faces a change in her life from which there will be no return. In her soliloquies, she sometimes shows anxiety and resentment of this fact. And, on occasion, she also displays something approaching self-pity. For instance, when Theseus sets the terms of the contest between Palamon and Arcite—the loser will be executed—Emilia begs him to change his mind. Otherwise, she says, her good name will be stained forever, and she will be "the scorn of women" (III.vi.250). When the cousins and their knights arrive in Athens for the tournament, she laments that her "unspotted youth must now be soiled / With blood of princes" (IV.ii.59-60) and her chastity will become the altar upon which her "unhappy beauty" (IV.ii.64) will be sacrificed. At the end of the play, she seems resigned to her fate, but there is no evidence that she welcomes the new role that society and the fates impose on her.

Executioner:
In V.iv, he is ready to carry out the execution of Palamon and his knights. But when Arcite is killed and Palamon becomes betrothed to Emilia, the executioner's services are no longer required.

Gentleman:
In IV.ii, Theseus sends him to Emilia to tell her that Palamon and Arcite have returned from Thebes.

Gerrold:
See Schoolmaster

Guard:
He keeps watch over Palamon and his knights as they await their execution in V.iv.

Herald:
He appears in I.iv, bringing Palamon and Arcite to Theseus. He tells the duke they are Creon's nephews and that they were wounded defending Thebes against the Athenians.

Hippolyta:
An Amazon queen, she becomes the wife of Theseus, duke of Athens. In Greek mythology, Amazons were a nation of female warriors. Armed conflicts between Greeks and Amazons were frequent, and the legendary Greek hero Theseus married Hippolyta after defeating her in battle.

In *The Two Noble Kinsmen*, Hippolyta's former status as a fearless warrior and her new role as Theseus's wife are emphasized early in the play by the second Theban queen. She points out to Hippolyta that the duke "shrunk thee into / The bound thou wast o'erflowing" (I.i.83-84), that is, removed her from the ranks of males and placed her in a position appropriate to women. The Theban queen notes that when Theseus subdued Hippolyta in battle, he also captured her affections. Hippolyta speaks frequently of her love for Theseus and gives many indications that she is content with her role as his wife. Though at I.iii.44-47, she remarks to Emilia that she isn't sure whether Theseus loves her more than he does his friend Pirithous, she doesn't appear to be truly anxious about this. Many commentators on the play view Hippolyta as a representative of mature, conjugal love. They see her as moving gracefully and willingly from one stage of her life to the next.

In the opening scene, Hippolyta is the focus of the spectacular bridal procession, but as the play progresses her prominence shrinks, and she assumes a subsidiary role. In I.i, she is a bold and well-spoken advocate for the Theban queens. She frequently speaks on behalf of others—for example, when she pleads with Theseus (at III.vi.195ff.) to show mercy toward Palamon and Arcite. Both in her response to people seeking her assistance and in conversations with her sister, Hippolyta demonstrates sensitivity and compassion. She also shows a sensible nature and an inclination to do what is expected of her. More than once, she urges Emilia to choose Palamon or Arcite and embrace the idea of married love. However, she fails to persuade her sister to adopt her own perspective on the proper role of women.

Hymen:

Representing the god of marriage, he is at the head of the procession leading Theseus and Hippolyta to their wedding in V.i.

Jailer:

The principal officer of a prison in Athens, he shows kindness and compassion toward the men placed in his custody as well as toward the daughter he evidently cares for very much. He is protective toward her, indulges her mad delusions, and looks out for her best interests. His concern for his daughter is evident from the beginning, when he tells her suitor, in II.i, that he will agree to a marriage only if she consents to it.

Palamon's escape from prison, arranged by the jailer's daughter, distracts the jailer from noticing that her health is deteriorating and leads him to view

> " At times Emilia's love for Palamon and Arcite appears to be so unsubstantial that it hardly seems to matter which one becomes her husband."

her erratic behavior as obstinacy rather than insanity. But when the wooer accurately names her condition—"she is mad" (IV.i.46)—and the jailer's Brother advises him to "take it patiently" (IV.i.114), he responds as a loving father. He joins the others in helping her act out her delusion that they are aboard a ship, with a fresh wind filling the sails. The jailer engages a physician to minister to his daughter. He goes along with the doctor's advice that her madness will be cured if she can be persuaded that her wooer is actually Palamon. But he strongly objects to the idea that her chastity must be violated before the cure can be complete.

Since it will be the jailer's duty to take into custody the men who lose the tournament, he leaves his daughter to the care of the wooer and goes off to witness the contest. When Palamon and his knights are defeated, the jailer escorts them to prison and stays with them while they wait to be executed. In answer to Palamon's inquiry about his daughter's health, the jailer reports that she is well again and will be married before long. He gratefully accepts on her behalf the money that Palamon and his knights give him, and he prays that the gods will look kindly on them.

Jailer's Brother:

In IV.i, he joins the jailer and the jailer's friends as they observe the jailer's daughter's erratic behavior. Showing pity and compassion for her distracted state, he indulges her fantasies and counsels the others to treat her gently.

Jailer's Daughter:

Her father is in charge of the prison where Palamon and Arcite are held after their capture in I.iv. She falls in love with Palamon, even though she realizes that he is far above her in social status. Her love becomes an obsession, and she loses her sanity. By the close of the play, she is reportedly restored to

❝ **Hippolyta speaks frequently of her love for Theseus and gives many indications that she is content with her role as his wife. Though at I.iii.44-47, she remarks to Emilia that she isn't sure whether Theseus loves her more than he does his friend Pirithous, she doesn't appear to be truly anxious about this.❞**

health and about to marry the man with whom she was in love before Palamon entered her life.

The jailer's daughter has a series of soliloquies which trace the course of her infatuation and gradual descent into madness. In II.iv, she recollects that when she first saw Palamon she thought he was a very attractive young man. Before long, she began to pity him, regretting that he was shut up in prison. ''Then,'' she says, ''I loved him, / Extremely loved him, infinitely loved him'' (II.iv.14-15). She wonders how she can make her feelings clear, for she would gladly be his lover. She resolves to free him from prison, though she admits that by doing this she'll be breaking the law and endangering her father's position. In III.ii, after she has released Palamon, he disappears into the woods and she cannot find him. As she searches through the night, listening to the howling of wolves and other strange noises, she admits that she has lost all fear for herself; her only concern is Palamon's safety. She remarks that she's becoming bewildered and light-headed: she hasn't slept or eaten for two days. She fears she may be slipping into a frame of mind that will lead to suicide—''let not my sense unsettle, / Lest I should drown, or stab, or hang myself'' (III.ii.29-30). This expressive prelude to madness is followed by another soliloquy which demonstrates her state of mind. Still wandering in the forest, she imagines she's by the sea. She thinks she spies a ship foundering on the rocks and sinking beneath the water, all its crewmen lost. She wishes she had a seashell, so she might transform it into a ship and voyage to exotic lands. She ends this soliloquy with

a plaintive song about searching through the world for her lover.

The character of the jailer's daughter is a blend of pathos and comedy. Some of her delusions develop into exuberant games, in which her family and friends sympathetically take part. She joins the countrymen and women in their morris dance, ironically taking the part of the female fool. Many of the remarks she makes to others in her mad scenes satirize love and poke fun at people. Her speeches are often interwoven with ribald humor and sexual allusions. A lusty young woman, the jailer's daughter is frank and open in expressing her desires—both when she has her wits about her and after her has lost them. In her open pursuit of Palamon, she provides a sharp contrast to Emilia's hesitancy about love and sex. But in a way, she has no more freedom of choice than Emilia does. The jailer's daughter is led to accept a substitute lover and husband—the wooer—in place of Palamon.

Readers and audiences have demonstrated a wide range of responses to the jailer's daughter. Some find her charming, a breath of fresh air blowing through the formal, highly structured world of Athens. They admire her uninhibited attitude toward sexuality. Others wonder if perhaps she is infatuated with the idea of love itself, rather than with a particular individual; thus one object of desire serves as well as another. It has been suggested that her obsession with Palamon is self-destructive. And some late twentieth-century commentators assert that her open eroticism represents a threat to a well-ordered, male dominated society—a force that must be controlled and modified by marriage.

Jailer's Friends:

Two men who support and console the jailer, they appear in IV.i. They bring the jailer word that Theseus will not punish him for Palamon's escape from prison. They listen compassionately as the wooer and the jailer describe the jailer's daughter's mad delusions. When she joins them and acts irrationally, they follow the jailer's brother's lead and respond sympathetically, playing along with her fantasy that they are all aboard a sailing vessel.

Knights:

These are six Thebans who come to Athens for the tournament in Act V—three of them to fight alongside Palamon and three alongside Arcite. According to the terms dictated by Theseus for the contest, the cousin who is defeated will be executed, as will the knights who have supported him.

In IV.ii, as the Thebans approach Athens, Pirithous and a messenger describe to Theseus and the court their fierce and noble bearing. The messenger represents Arcite's principal fellow-in-arms as ''hardy, fearless, proud of dangers,'' with broad shoulders and long, black hair ''shining / Like ravens' wings'' (IV.ii.80, 83-84). Pirithous counters with a description of Palamon's principal knight: a similarly fearless-looking man, with blond, curly hair, a beardless face, and a voice like a trumpet. The messenger raves about a third knight, this one with brawny arms whose sinews swell like women in the early months of pregnancy. Several modern commentators have remarked on the erotic nature of the verbal portraits drawn by Pirithous and the messenger.

When Arcite and Palamon pray before the altars of their patron god and goddess, the knights kneel with them. During the battle, Emilia's servant reports that at one point Palamon nearly had victory within his grasp, but Arcite's knights came to their leader's rescue. When Arcite wins the contest, his knights attend him as Theseus links Arcite's hands with Emilia's. By contrast, Palamon's knights accompany their leader to prison. They face execution with patient fortitude, and when Palamon mounts the scaffold, they indicate they will cheerfully follow him there. Their sacrifice becomes unnecessary, however, when Arcite dies and Palamon is betrothed to Emilia.

Messengers:

Messengers appear on three occasions during the play. In IV.ii, a messenger brings Theseus the news that Palamon and Arcite, accompanied by six Theban knights, are approaching Athens. He describes several of the knights in great detail. In V.ii, a messenger brings word to the jailer and the doctor that the tournament between Palamon and Arcite is about to begin. In V.iv, a messenger arrives just as Palamon mounts the scaffold and lays his head on the executioner's block. The messenger brings the proceedings to a halt and is immediately followed by Pirithous, who relates the death of Arcite.

Nymphs:

A group of young maidens representing demi-goddesses, they form part of Theseus and Hippolyta's elaborate wedding procession in I.i.

> **A lusty young woman, the jailer's daughter is frank and open in expressing her desires—both when she has her wits about her and after her has lost them.''**

Palamon:

One of the title characters, he is the nephew of Creon, king of Thebes, and the cousin of Arcite. Palamon is the first to see Emilia and declare that he's in love. As the one who survives at the close of the play, he is the last to claim her as his bride. The young men's passion for Emilia turns their close attachment to each other into heated rivalry. The relationship between Palamon and Arcite becomes the focus of one of the play's principal issues: the conflict between love and friendship. Some commentators find little basis for distinguishing one cousin from another. Both young men are nobly born, competitive by nature, brave in battle, deeply concerned with personal honor and reputation, and relentless in asserting what they see as their right to Emilia. Much of what can be said about Palamon applies equally to Arcite, but some differences can be found between them.

Palamon sometimes seems more impetuous, less thoughtful than Arcite. On the basis of one glimpse of Emilia, he links his honor and his life to winning her. When Arcite admits that he is in love with her, too, Palamon accuses him of treachery and threatens to use his prison shackles to knock his cousin's brains out. In III.vi, the kinsmen have a chance to avoid being recaptured by the duke, but Palamon scorns to take it, viewing it as the coward's way out. He boldly tells Theseus who they are— and reveals that all the time Arcite has been in Emilia's service, he has been in love with her.

Palamon also has a strain of melancholy or sullenness. Facing the prospect of a lifetime in prison, he fears the cousins will die unknown, their former triumphs forgotten by those who will outlive them. It falls to Arcite to raise his spirits by reminding him that at least they are in this together. Palamon refuses Arcite's overtures of renewed friendship in III.i and has to be coaxed into eating the food and drinking the wine that his cousin brings him in

❝ The relationship between Palamon and Arcite becomes the focus of one of the play's principal issues: the conflict between love and friendship.❞

III.iii. When Arcite appears with armor and swords in III.vi, Palamon greets him ill-naturedly, and Arcite accuses him of pouting like a schoolboy. Emilia alludes to Palamon's inclination toward melancholy at V.iii.49-55, remarking that his ''dark humors'' make him more attractive.

Palamon's most famous speech, his prayer to Venus in V.i, is strangely morbid. It's appropriate that he chooses Venus to intercede on his behalf, for he is about to enter a contest that will determine whether he wins the woman he loves. Yet as commentators have pointed out, Palamon's prayer does not show love in a favorable light. His petition is filled with images of decay. Describing the power of love to transform people, Palamon gives as an example an eighty-year-old man—his body cramped and twisted, his eyes cloudy and swollen—who took a bride of fourteen and fathered a son. Increasingly grotesque as it develops, Palamon's prayer seems to regard love as a means of forcing people into absurd situations and behavior.

There is some suggestion, toward the end of the play, that Palamon is favored over Arcite. Emilia notes, at V.iii.74-76, that she carries Palamon's picture near her heart, while Arcite's is on the right side of her body; but she says this is not intentional—''chance would have it so'' (V.iii.75). After Emilia is formally betrothed to Arcite, Theseus says he rather expected Palamon to win the tournament, since he is ''as brave a knight as e'er / Did spur a noble steed'' (V.iii.115-16). Palamon's noble nature is clearly apparent in V.iv. He faces execution with graceful acceptance of his fate, apologizes to his knights for leading them to this end, and spares a few moments—and his purse—to the matter of the jailer's daughter. And he assures the fatally injured Arcite that he is ''Palamon, / One that yet loves thee dying'' (V.iv.89-90).

Some commentators have called attention to what they see as suggestions of homosexuality in the relationship between Palamon and Arcite. Others have disputed this, while agreeing that several of the exchanges between the cousins, particularly their conversations in prison (II.ii) and when they help each other put on their armor before their duel in the woods (III.vi), employ homoerotic language. Still others deny there is any sexual component at all. In their judgment, Palamon and Arcite's expressions of devotion and commitment to each other represent no more than the highest form of friendship.

Pirithous:

An Athenian general, he is Theseus's closest friend. According to Hippolyta (at I.iii.35-47), Pirithous and Theseus have fought side by side in countless battles and faced death together on many occasions. Hippolyta confesses to Emilia that she wonders who Theseus loves more: Pirithous or herself.

Theseus consistently relies on Pirithous for personal services, and at times he stands in for the duke. For example, Pirithous escorts Hippolyta in the wedding procession that opens the play, and at I.i.221-25, Theseus instructs him to stay in Athens and supervise the rest of the marriage festivities until after he returns from Thebes. In II.v, when Arcite distinguishes himself in the athletic contests held as part of the May festival, Theseus tells Pirithous to find a place for Arcite in the royal household. Pirithous installs Arcite in the service of Emilia—unaware of the young man's passion for her. Pirithous also draws out Theseus's fair-mindedness when the duke is inclined toward harshness. In III.vi, Theseus orders that Palamon and Arcite be killed because they have violated the Athenian law against private duels. Pirithous kneels to his friend and sovereign, and appeals to him to show mercy.

On two occasions in the play, Pirithous serves as a vivid narrator. In IV.ii.91-116, he describes, with what some have considered unusual warmth of detail, one of the Theban knights who will fight on Palamon's side in the tournament. And in V.iv.48-84, Pirithous paints a stunning verbal picture of the catastrophe that leaves Arcite fatally injured.

Queens:

Three royal widows, they look to Theseus to avenge the wrongs done to them and their dead husbands. In I.i, they intrude on the wedding procession and recite their sad tale. Their husbands revolted against Creon's rule in Thebes and were killed. Creon would not permit their bodies to be cremated and buried according to religious customs, and thus their corpses lie rotting on the battlefield where they fell. The women implore Theseus to punish Creon for this violation of sanctity. When he says he will do so, but not until after his marriage to Hippolyta, they tell him he should not put his personal happiness above the duty he owes them and their dead husbands. They successfully appeal to Hippolyta and Emilia to intercede for them, and Theseus agrees to delay the wedding. After Theseus and the Athenian forces have attacked and defeated Creon, the queens recover their husbands' bodies and, in I.v, bury them with appropriate honor and solemnity.

Schoolmaster:

A pedantic man who delights in showing off his learning, he serves as the choreographer, stage manager, and master of ceremonies for the morris dance in III.v. Unaware that he is a figure of fun, he laces his instructions to the dancers with Latin phrases and uses made-up or pretentious words to impress the countrymen and women with his intellectual accomplishments. The failure of one of the dancers to show up for the performance devastates him, though he reacts to the prospect of having to cancel the dance with his usual, high-flown diction: ''Our business is become a nullity, / Yea, a woeful and a piteous nullity'' (III.v.54-55). The jailer's daughter saves the day by suddenly appearing in their midst. Everyone urges her to take the place of the absent countrywoman. Before she agrees, she playfully skewers the schoolmaster's pompousness, calling him a fool, a mender of broken utensils, and a conjurer.

When Theseus, his royal household, and his courtiers enter the clearing in the forest where the villagers have gathered, the schoolmaster invites them to stay and watch the dance. He prefaces the performance with a long-winded introduction (V.iii.102-34), full of self-conscious wordplay, in which he describes various characters in the dance. He closes the performance with an epilogue in which he promises they will repeat the dance at next year's spring festival. As Theseus and his party return to the hunt, the schoolmaster sends them off with ceremonious wishes for success and bestows generous praises—partly in Latin—on the performers.

At III.v.22, one of the villagers addresses the schoolmaster as Gerrold.

Servant:

During the combat between Palamon and Arcite in V.iii, he tells Emilia about the progress of the contest. Initially he reports that Palamon and his knights are winning, then he brings her word that Arcite is the victor.

Taborer:

A drummer who accompanies the morris dancers, he appears in III.v, when the countrymen and women entertain Theseus and his courtiers.

Theseus:

One of the greatest of the legendary Greek heroes, he was celebrated as an incomparable warrior. His numerous exploits included the destruction of the Minotaur in the labyrinth on the island of Crete. The mythology that developed around the figure of Theseus included his friendship with Pirithous and his marriage to Hippolyta, the Amazon queen.

In *The Two Noble Kinsmen*, Theseus represents justice and a well-ordered community. He defends virtue and avenges violations of the rules of a civil society. A serious-minded man, he faithfully adheres to the standard of behavior imposed on him by others and accepts—with some degree of sadness—the notion that the fates are unpredictable and sometimes unjust. He embodies many of the principles of the ideal knight of medieval chivalry, yet on occasion he finds himself torn between conflicting demands of love and duty.

His sensitivity is evident in the first scene of the play, when the Theban queens disrupt the celebration of his marriage to Hippolyta. He recalls the beauty of the first queen on her own wedding day, when she was as young and beautiful as Hippolyta is now. The ravages of time and grief have transformed the queen, and Theseus is stricken by this recognition. When the Theban queens beg him to delay his marriage until after he has attacked Thebes and made Creon pay for his abusive treatment of their husbands' corpses, Theseus hesitates. The conflict he feels between love and duty is resolved when his bride, her sister Emilia, and his friend Pirithous add their voices to the queens', urging him to place his responsibility to order and justice above his personal desires.

Theseus's love for Hippolyta seems beyond question. Yet she herself wonders if his devotion to Pirithous is stronger than his commitment to her. The two men have been inseparable comrades for many years, and perhaps the bond between them is stronger than that between husband and wife. Theseus's struggle between love and friendship, however, is less evident than Palamon and Arcite's. Sometimes, as when he decrees that Palamon and Arcite must die because they have violated the prohibition against private duels (III.vi.136), Theseus demonstrates a harsh side of his nature. On these occasions, his wife and his best friend join together to persuade him to take a more merciful course.

Perhaps Theseus's most prominent characteristic is his acceptance of the role of the gods in human destiny. He attributes to them (V.iii.107-8) the outcome of Palamon and Arcite's trial-by-combat. And at the close of the play, he acknowledges that there is little that mankind can do but submit to the ungovernable turns of fate. It is useless for us to question reality, he concludes, so let us instead be grateful for it.

Valerius:

A Theban, he brings word to Palamon and Arcite in I.ii that Creon demands to see them. Valerius warns the two young men that the king is enraged because Theseus has declared war on Thebes.

Waiting-woman:

One of Emilia's attendants, she appears with her mistress in II.ii. They walk in the garden near Palamon and Arcite's prison cell, and the waiting-woman respectfully answers Emilia's teasing remarks about love. Toward the end of their conversation, Emilia turns the waiting-woman's innocent remarks into material for mildly bawdy jokes.

Wooer:

Known only by this designation, he is in love with the jailer's daughter. He remains faithful to her despite her obsession with Palamon and patiently devotes himself to curing her madness. His first appearance is in II.i, when he and her father discuss the possibility of a wedding. The jailer says that he's willing to settle all that he has on his daughter if she has given her consent to the marriage. The wooer assures her father that she has agreed to be his bride.

However, the jailer's daughter becomes infatuated with Palamon. In IV.i, the wooer reports to the jailer that he believes she has gone mad. He relates that he observed her by a lake, her hair unbound, singing to herself, and sighing ''Palamon, fair Palamon'' (IV.i.81). When he approached her, he says, she plunged into the water, and he had to rescue her. At this point in the wooer's narrative, the jailer's daughter enters, and her madness is apparent to everyone.

The doctor called in by the jailer recommends that the wooer present himself to the jailer's daughter as Palamon and court her again, this time under the guise of the man with whom she's obsessed. The wooer follows the doctor's advice and reports, in IV.ii, that she is half persuaded that he is Palamon. The doctor tells the wooer to sleep with the young woman if she asks him to. ''Please her appetite,'' he says (IV.ii.36), and the cure will be complete. The wooer regards this as sound advice and, at the end of the scene, when she proposes that they go off to bed, he readily agrees. When she asks him if he will be gentle with her, he assures her that he will. In the final scene of the play, the jailer reports to Palamon that his daughter is restored to health and will ''be married shortly'' (V.iv.28).

Further Reading

Bawcutt, N. W. Introduction to *The Two Noble Kinsmen,* by William Shakespeare and John Fletcher, 7-46. Harmondsworth: Penguin Books, 1977.

> Bawcutt provides a lengthy discussion of the ways in which *The Two Noble Kinsmen* shows that human lives are manipulated by impersonal or superhuman powers. In Bawcutt's judgment, the play demonstrates that although ''we may not understand the ultimate order that governs life,'' we should not question or condemn that order. He points to Thesus as the character most committed to playing out the role life has assigned him.

Berggren, Paula S. '' 'For What We Lack, We Laugh': Incompletion and *The Two Noble Kinsmen.*'' *Modern Language Studies* XIV, no. 4 (Fall 1984): 3-17.

> Berggren believes that the play demonstrates the difficulty of moving gracefully and naturally from innocence to experience. An important part of her discussion of interrupted or disconnected action in *The Two Noble Kinsmen* centers on Arcite's death, which she views as undeserved and lacking justice.

Brownlow, F. W. *"The Two Noble Kinsmen."* In *Two Shakespearean Sequences: "Henry VI" to "Richard II" and "Pericles" to "Timon of Athens,"* 202-15. Pittsburgh: University of Pittsburgh Press, 1977.

Brownlow regards the play as a dramatization of the conflict between lust and violence on the one hand, and reason and order on the other. He sees Theseus as the spokesman for "a state of law, justice and reason," and the jailer's daughter as the representative of the maxim that sex brings an end to innocence.

Charney, Maurice. *"The Two Noble Kinsmen."* In *All of Shakespeare*, 361-69. New York: Columbia University Press, 1993.

Charney focuses on the sharp contrasts between different kinds of love in the play: the jailer's daughter's frank and open passion, Palamon and Arcite as friends as well as rivals, and Emilia's indifference to the issue of which man will be her husband. In this context, Charney explores the theme of adult love as destructive of childhood innocence. Charney's book is written for the student audience.

Edwards, Philip. "On the Design of *The Two Noble Kinsmen.*" *Review of English Literature* 5, no. 4 (October 1964): 89-105.

Edwards views the play as a bleak treatment of the progression from innocent love to mature passion—a sequence in which people have less control over their lives than they believe, for we all must do "what chance and circumstance and our own sexuality" impel us to do. Edwards also maintains that the characters in *The Two Noble Kinsmen* show no real individuality, growth, or development.

Richmond, Hugh. "Performance as Criticism: *The Two Noble Kinsmen.*" In *Shakespeare, Fletcher, and "The Two Noble Kinsmen,"* edited by Charles H. Frey, 163-85. Columbia: University of Missouri Press, 1989.

Richmond offers an in-depth analysis of twentieth-century productions of the play, pointing out that the majority of these productions emphasized elements of music, dance and ritual, and that many of them treated the play as a kind of sequel to Shakespeare's *A Midsummer Night's Dream*—especially with regard to ritual elements and the conflict between love and friendship. He also notes that modern audiences have generally shown strong, positive responses to the jailer's daughter, who is "more humorous, more dynamic, and more significant" in performance "than can easily be perceived on the printed page."

Roberts, Jeanne Addison. "Crises of Male Self-Definition in *The Two Noble Kinsmen.*" In *Shakespeare, Fletcher, and "The Two Noble Kinsmen,"* edited by Charles H. Frey, 133-44. Columbia: University of Missouri Press, 1989.

Roberts explores the ways in which female characters in the play challenge conventional notions of patriarchal societies and male dominance. She calls attention to Hippolyta's and Emilia's status as Amazons, that is, female warriors who are independent of men and compete with them as equals. By the end of the play, Roberts observes, two threats to patriarchal order—Emilia's steadfast commitment to virginity and the jailer's daughter's unbridled eroticism—have been subdued by matrimony.

Waith, Eugene M. "Shakespeare and the Ceremonies of Romance." In *Shakespeare's Craft: Eight Lectures*, edited by Philip H. Highfill, Jr., 113-37. Carbondale: Southern Illinois University Press, 1982.

Waith proposes that *The Two Noble Kinsmen* should be read in the context of spectacle and theatrical pageantry, extremely popular modes of drama when the play was written. He calls attention to the relation between the stylized formality of the play and its thematic concern with chivalry and honor.

————. Introduction to *The Two Noble Kinsmen,* by William Shakespeare and John Fletcher, 1-66. Oxford: Oxford University Press, 1989.

In the interpretive section of his introduction to the play, Waith focuses on the conflict between love and friendship. He also provides an extended description of the ideals of chivalry that are part of the play's literary background: bravery, duty, nobility and generosity of spirit, protection of the weak and powerless, compassion, loyalty to one's friends, and—in terms of courtly romance—love at first sight. In other sections of his introduction, Waith reviews the issues of authorship, sources, and structure as well as the play's stage history from 1613 to 1986.

Weller, Barry. *"The Two Noble Kinsmen*, the Friendship Tradition, and the Flight from Eros." In *Shakespeare, Fletcher, and "The Two Noble Kinsmen,"* edited by Charles H. Frey, 93-108. Columbia: University of Missouri Press, 1989.

Weller maintains that the play centers on the conflict between marriage and friendship. In his view, *The Two Noble Kinsmen* dramatizes the idea that intense friendship—that is, when one's friend is virtually an "other self"—is a threat to society and its continuance.

The Winter's Tale

circa 1610-11

Act I:

The play opens in Sicilia. King Polixenes of Bohemia is visiting King Leontes of Sicilia. The two men have been close friends since childhood, and Leontes asks Polixenes to extend his visit. Polixenes objects that he has pressing business and concerns at home and must leave. Leontes, then, asks his wife, Hermione, to prevail upon Polixenes with the same request. Hermione is eloquently insistent, and Polixenes agrees to stay. At this point, Leontes reveals his jealousy. He is convinced that Hermione and Polixenes are secretly having an intimate affair. To corroborate what he feels is known by all, Leontes questions Camillo, a Sicilian lord and trusted advisor, about the affair. When Camillo objects that he does not believe Polixenes and Hermione are intimate, Leontes appeals to Camillo's loyalty, after which Camillo agrees to poison Polixenes. Later, however, Camillo cannot bring himself to kill the Bohemian king and informs Polixenes of Leontes's plot against his life. Polixenes assures Camillo the same status and favor in Bohemia which he now enjoys in Sicilia, and Camillo guides Polixenes and his followers safely from the now hostile palace of Leontes.

Act II:

Leontes receives report of Polixenes's flight and Camillo's betrayal of Leontes in helping

Polixenes, the report only further confirming Leontes's deluded but intense jealousy. Leontes confronts Hermione, accusing her of having been intimate with Polixenes. He takes from her their young son, Mamillius, who has been sharing a close moment with his mother and her waiting women. Hermione is pregnant, and Leontes insists that the child belongs to Polixenes. Henceforth, Hermione will only have the comfort of that bastard child; no longer will she be permitted to see Mamillius. Although Hermione protests that she has always been faithful, Leontes has her taken away to prison. Antigonus, a Sicilian lord, voices his objections to Leontes's harsh treatment of Hermione but is dismissed by Leontes, who announces that he has sent Cleomines and Dion (both Sicilian lords) to consult the oracle at Apollo's temple at Delphos. The two messengers will bring back the oracle's proclamation of the truth regarding Hermione's fidelity, Leontes indicating that he will abide by the truth contained therein. Some short time passes, and Hermione gives birth to a baby girl in prison. Paulina, the wife of Antigonus, takes the baby girl to Leontes, hoping to soften his resistance to Hermione's appeals to the truth. But when Leontes sees the child, he calls it a bastard and demands that it be removed from his sight. He refuses to listen to Paulina and calls Antigonus henpecked for allowing his wife to address the king so boldly, threatening Antigonus with a charge of treason if he does not command Paulina to leave immediately. When Paulina finally exits, she leaves the baby with Leontes, and he commands Antigonus to take the child to some remote place and leave it to thrive or perish according to destiny.

Act III:

A trial is arranged for Hermione, and she is brought forth to answer the charge against her. She claims that a sentence of death would be welcome in place of the great shame and misery she now experiences in being falsely accused and separated from friends and family. Cleomines and Dion enter with the judgment of Apollo's oracle, a judgment sealed by Apollo's high priest and brought with great haste to Sicilia. An officer reads the oracle's proclamation: " 'Hermione is chaste, Polixenes blameless, Camillo a true subject, Leontes a jealous tyrant, his innocent babe truly begotten, and the king shall live without an heir, if that which is lost be not found' " (III.i.132-36). Leontes, however, is so convinced that he is right that he pronounces the oracle false. Immediately a servant enters and announces that Mamillius has died. As Hermione is escorted away, Leontes asks that she be tenderly

ministered to. He asks forgiveness of Apollo and announces that he will make amends to Polixenes and take Camillo back into his service. Paulina then announces that Hermione, too, has died of grief.

The scene shifts to a remote part of Bohemia where Antigonus abandons the baby girl as instructed by Leontes. Hermione has appeared to Antigonus in a dream the night before, instructing him to name the child Perdita, and informing him that he will never see Paulina again because of his involvement in such a cruel business. He leaves a bundle with the child, a bundle containing money and documents that will attest to her aristocracy. In a raging storm, he exits "pursued by a bear" (III.iii.58). An old shepherd discovers the baby girl and takes care of her. His son, a rustic clown, reports that he has seen the storm sink a ship off the coast and a bear tear a man to pieces. The man is Antigonus, and the ship is that which has carried him to Bohemia.

Act IV:

Time, the Chorus, informs the audience that sixteen years have passed since the end of Act III. Leontes has suffered for the losses incurred by his rash behavior, and Perdita has grown up believing the old shepherd to be her father and the clown her brother. In the Bohemian palace of Polixenes, Camillo expresses his desire to visit Leontes. Polixenes convinces Camillo to stay in Bohemia and help Polixenes discover why his son, Florizel, so frequently absents himself from home and spends his time in the home of the shepherd presumed to be Perdita's father. The two eventually make their way to that shepherd's home and participate in a sheep-shearing festival being held there, themselves disguised as shepherds. Autolycus, a rogue and a thief, tricks the clown thought to be Perdita's brother and picks his pocket of the money with which the clown was intending to buy supplies for the sheep-shearing festival. When Autolycus learns of the festival, he determines to steal more money from the revelers there.

At the shepherd's home, Perdita is dressed like the mock queen of the sheep-shearing festival. Florizel is there dressed like a common swain, and the audience soon learns that the two are deeply in love. Perdita worries that Florizel's father will disapprove of her because of her low birth, but Florizel assures her that Polixenes will never find out. Just then, Polixenes and Camillo enter in disguise. As the hostess for the day's festivities, Perdita greets them and gives them flowers, and Polixenes engages her in a debate on art versus nature. There then ensues a series of dances. Autolycus appears singing his wares. He pickpockets the guests who have just purchased his trinkets. Polixenes, feeling the moment right to expose his son, approaches Florizel and asks whether or not he has informed his father of his love interest. Florizel, unaware that he is speaking to Polixenes, answers that, for reasons which cannot be revealed at the present moment, he might not do so. Polixenes then casts off his disguise and scolds Florizel for deceiving him and consorting with one so base born. He stalks off angrily, vowing to mar Perdita's beauty and punish her shepherd father for trying to cheat his way to nobility.

Florizel stubbornly maintains that he will not abandon Perdita and proposes that they run away, trusting their future to fate. Camillo, seeing in these circumstances an opportunity to visit his old master, advises Florizel to sail to Sicilia and present himself to Leontes as Polixenes's son, naming Perdita his princess, with the hope that, after some time, Florizel and Polixenes might be reconciled. Seeing Autolycus in his peddlar's attire, Camillo has Florizel exchange clothes with him in order that Florizel might make his escape from Bohemia undiscovered. Autolycus encounters the old shepherd and the clown on their way to Polixenes. They have determined that their best course of action for avoiding the promised punishment is to tell Polixenes that they were not engaged in blatant social climbing, since Perdita is not a blood relative; she is a foundling child discovered years before by the shepherd. They bring with them the documents that prove what they say is true. Autolycus, wearing Florizel's clothes and pretending to be a courtier—Shakespeare has apparently forgotten that Florizel was attired like a swain at the sheep-shearing festival—offers to be their advocate, and the old shepherd and his son accept the offer. Autolycus sends them ahead, secretly intending to be the first to inform Prince Florizel of the existence of the bundle found beside the infant Perdita, for what he might gain in doing so.

Act V:

The play now shifts back to Sicilia. Leontes is being encouraged by his advisors to marry again and produce an heir. Paulina reminds Leontes of the oracle's prediction that he would be heirless until his lost daughter was found. She then chastises him for forsaking Hermione's memory. He agrees not to marry until Paulina finds him a suitable mate. A servant enters and announces the arrival of Florizel and Perdita. Leontes much admires the beauty and royal bearing of the couple, remarking on Florizel's great resemblance to Polixenes, and remembering his own son Mamillius. A lord then enters and announces that Polixenes has just arrived in Sicilia and demands that Florizel and his impostor princess be arrested. Perdita's father and brother, who fled Bohemia with Florizel and Perdita at Autolycus's instigation, are now held captive by Polixenes. When Florizel exclaims that Camillo has betrayed him, the lord informs him that Camillo is also now in Sicilia, to the surprise and delight of Leontes. Florizel asks Leontes to be his advocate and appeal to Polixenes to grace the union of Florizel and Perdita. Many of the play's complexities are now unravelled in the reports delivered by several gentlemen in response to the questioning of Autolycus, who has also sailed to Sicilia. It is reported that the old shepherd and his son have explained to Polixenes the circumstances of Perdita's discovery when she was a baby and have given him the bundle found next to the infant. In that bundle, Polixenes and Camillo have found the letters written by Antigonus, understanding that Perdita is really the long-lost daughter of Leontes. The clown also tells the story of Antigonus's terrible fate in the jaws of the bear. It is also reported that Perdita has been reunited with her father, a touching reunion that moved tears in many of those who witnessed it. Polixenes and Leontes have been reconciled, both kings sanctioning the union of Florizel and Perdita. For their part in loving and caring for Perdita, the old shepherd and his son are promoted to the status of gentlemen. They encounter Autolycus and treat him generously, despite the wrongs he has done them.

Perdita has expressed a desire to see the statue of her mother, which has been crafted by a renowned Italian sculptor and is now in the possession of Paulina. When Paulina presents the statue, all are impressed with how lifelike it is. Leontes is especially moved and thinks the statue breathes. He embraces the statue and it is warm. Hermione is still alive. Paulina directs Hermione to her long-lost daughter, Perdita, and proclaims that the oracle has been fulfilled. Leontes, then, insists that Paulina allow him to find her a suitable husband, as he has allowed her to find him a perfectly suitable wife. He selects Camillo and directs him to take Paulina by the hand. All exit to discuss the events of the lost years at more length.

Modern Connections

The Winter's Tale touches on issues which are as relevant to modern audiences as they were to those of Shakespeare's time. The first issue, the relationship between art and nature, serves as an introduction to a more serious issue, that of the relationship between people who perceive themselves to be of different social classes. The terms of that relationship between art and nature are laid out in the debate between Perdita and Polixenes at the sheep-shearing festival held at the home of the old shepherd. Perdita, who is acting as the hostess of that festival, greets Polixenes and Camillo and gives them flowers. She mentions that the "streak'd gillyvors / (Which some call Nature's bastards)" (IV.iv.82-83) are more appropriate to the season than the flowers she gives them, but she does not plant those gillyvors in her garden, because she feels their variegated colors result from the art of hybridization practiced by human planters, not from nature. Polixenes replies,

> Yet Nature is made better by no mean
> But Nature makes that mean; so over that art
> Which you say adds to Nature, is an art
> That Nature makes.
>
> (IV.iv.89-92)

Polixenes's argument is that if the nests birds make and the hives bees create are considered natural because nature provides the birds and bees with the instinct to create those nests and hives, why, then, are the things man creates sometimes considered artificial? By Polixenes's reasoning, the human need to create what we call "art" is an instinctive impulse, and the human artifacts that result from that impulse are natural rather than artificial. There can be, then, no distinction made between art and nature. The final scene of the play, in which the statue of Hermione crafted by the renowned Italian artist Julio Romano comes to life, demonstrates that it is difficult, if not impossible, to distinguish between art and nature. We can understand the attraction this notion would have for Shakespeare, an artist reaching the culmination of his creative career in the writing of the romances.

In today's world, just as in the world of *The Winter's Tale* and in Shakespeare's England, the boundaries of art are hotly debated and similarly blurry. The discussion of what constitutes art today may focus on literature, music, film, architecture, and a variety of other forms of creative expression. What some people consider to be meaningful music or powerful literature, for example, others might consider to be irritating noise or the pretentious scribbling of a hack. There are many views on what artistic expression is or should be.

We need, however, to look at the discussion between Polixenes and Perdita in a different light because their dispute serves as a metaphor that reveals a concern with class distinctions. Polixenes tells Perdita,

> You see, sweet maid, we marry
> A gentler scion to the wildest stock,
> And make conceive a bark of baser kind
> By bud of nobler race.
>
> (IV.iv.92-95)

Polixenes is willing to concede that something good might come of wedding base and noble kinds of plant life, but, later, he reacts vehemently against the idea of his noble Florizel marrying Perdita, whom he takes to be only the daughter of a base and lowly shepherd. Perdita, on the other hand, argues that different kinds of flowers should remain as they occur in nature and should not be mixed. Yet, as the lowly shepherd girl she believes herself to be, she should be making the botanical argument Polixenes makes, since she hopes to marry her "wildest stock" to the "gentler scion" of Prince Florizel. Concerning humankind, Polixenes seems to embrace the notion that the stock of gentility and nobility should remain pure, but the notion that nobility expresses its inward goodness in its actions is contradicted by several of the characters in the play itself.

These characters, who are of the nobility and from whom we would expect that nobility to show itself in generosity and understanding, engage in actions that are either self-serving or destructive. Antigonus, a Sicilian lord who voices some hesitant resistance to Leontes's harsh treatment of Hermione and his baby girl, nonetheless abandons that baby to the elements and the possibility of death, placing his own safety with the king above the infant's life. Camillo, a Sicilian lord held up as the ideal of service and allegiance, deceives Florizel in order to fulfill his wish to visit Leontes. Leontes exhibits a jealousy and tyrannous willfulness so destructive that it causes the death of his own son and the banishment of his wife and daughter. And Polixenes, in his passionate outburst at discovering Florizel's intention to marry Perdita, appears vicious and vindictive. He threatens to hang the old shepherd thought to be Perdita's father and exclaims to Perdita, "I'll have thy beauty scratch'd with briers and made / More homely than thy state" (IV.iv.425-46).

To complicate matters, when *The Winter's Tale* is read from the vantage point of an allegedly ''classless'' society, our readings often produce unexpected or ambiguous sympathies. Perdita's shepherd father and brother are promoted to the gentility as reward for having looked after Perdita from her infancy. Their new status does not change them; they are generous with Autolycus, refusing to ''lord it'' over him. Yet, the new title of ''gentlemen'' seems somewhat ill-fitting since we have been conditioned to see them as lower-class shepherds. When Polixenes prohibits Florizel from marrying a shepherd's daughter, we may argue against him and assert that Florizel loves her for her inner qualities and not for her title. At least intellectually we might do this. Secretly, we perhaps eagerly anticipate the revelation that Perdita is a king's daughter to prove Polixenes wrong.

Characters

Antigonus:

Antigonus is a Sicilian lord married to Paulina. He opposes the brutal way Leontes treats Hermione and the baby girl to which Hermione has just given birth. He protests that Hermione has been faithful to Leontes and says, ''If it prove / She's otherwise, I'll keep my stables where / I lodge my wife'' (II.i.133-35), suggesting that if one as ideally gracious as Hermione has given in to lustful desires, all women are suspect, their sexual drive differing not at all from the notoriously lusty horses in the stables. When Paulina openly accuses the Sicilian king of being ignorant and obstinate, Leontes charges Antigonus to silence his wife. Antigonus, however, either cannot or does not immediately silence her, and Leontes says, ''Thou dotard, thou art woman-tir'd; unroosted / By the Dame Partlet here'' (II.iii.75-76). Leontes is suggesting that Antigonus is henpecked and unable to control his wife, eventually threatening Antigonus with a charge of treason if the latter does not do what Leontes commands. Antigonus swears his allegiance to Leontes and agrees to take the baby girl to some remote place and abandon it to live or die.

Antigonus next appears in the wilderness of Bohemia. Hermione has appeared to him in a dream, instructing him to name the baby Perdita, and informing him that he will never see Paulina again for his part in the cruelty done Perdita. He lays Perdita down and places a bundle next to her. The bundle contains gold, letters written by Antigonus explaining Perdita's birthright, and tokens of Hermione verifying that Perdita is of the nobility. He leaves the infant, heading off in the storm toward the ship that waits for him off the fantastical Bohemian coast. Antigonus's departure is followed by the much cited stage direction—''Exit pursued by a bear'' (III.iii.58). We immediately learn from the clown that the bear has torn Antigonus to pieces and the storm has sunk the ship and drowned the mariners who waited for him.

Archidamus:

Archidamus is a Bohemian lord, part of Polixenes's entourage visiting the palace of Leontes in Sicilia. He appears in the first scene of the play telling Camillo that Bohemia will not be able to match the magnificence of Sicilia's offerings to their guests if their roles are ever reversed. He and Camillo also speak about the great bond between Leontes and Polixenes, and Archidamus praises the young Prince Mamillius.

Autolycus:

Autolycus is a rogue and a thief. He encounters the clown (Perdita's adoptive brother), who is on his way to buy goods for the sheep-shearing festival to be held at the clown's father's home. Autolycus pretends to have been robbed, evoking the clown's sympathy. Autolycus then proceeds to pick the clown's pocket. When Autolycus finds out about the planned rustic festivities, he determines to attend and steal even more money. He is a huge success at the festival, selling his wares and picking the pockets of the guests there. The old shepherd and his clown son are just too gullible for Autolycus to leave them alone. As they make their way to Polixenes, intending to inform the Bohemian king of the secret surrounding Perdita's origin, Autolycus pretends to be a courtier and offers to be their advocate with the king. He misdirects them to the ship which is about to carry Perdita and Florizel to Sicilia, hoping that he can gain favor with the prince by revealing the existence of the mysterious bundle found by the infant Perdita's side. The prince, however, is concerned with Perdita's seasickness and pays little attention to Autolycus. When the contents of that bundle later confirm Perdita's royalty, benefitting the old shepherd and the clown in the process, Autolycus is chagrined to learn that he has done some good despite his selfish and dishonest intentions.

Autolycus contrasts sharply with the other characters in the play struggling to demonstrate their nobility. He knows exactly who he is and claims to be nothing more. At his first appearance in the play, Autolycus reveals that he has served Prince Florizel and says, "My father nam'd me Autolycus, who being, as I am, litter'd under Mercury, was likewise a snapper-up of unconsider'd trifles" (IV.iii.24-26). In short, he carries on his father's tradition of thievery. Referring to the revelations offered by Perdita's bundle near the end of the play, Autolycus says, "had I been the finder-out of this secret, it would not have relish'd among my other discredits" (V.ii.121-23). He realistically admits that even if the prince had opened the bundle when Autolycus first suggested he do so, the praise and thanks Autolycus would have received would not have made up for his numerous villainies. As others around him are elevated to new and greater social status, Autolycus knows that he is a thief by nature, not likely to change for the better even though he promises the old shepherd and his son that he will change his ways if they commend him to Prince Florizel.

Camillo:

Camillo is a Sicilian lord and trusted advisor to Leontes. He agrees to poison Polixenes when Leontes insists that he do so. But Camillo cannot bring himself to carry out the task when the time comes. He informs Polixenes of Leontes's plot to kill him and agrees to guide Polixenes from Sicilia to safety, Polixenes assuring him that he will compensate the favor by awarding Camillo the same social status and financial security in Bohemia as he now enjoys in Sicilia. Leontes accuses Camillo, in his absence, of being a traitor, but Apollo's oracle absolves Camillo of those charges. When the play shifts to Bohemia, we find Camillo some sixteen years later pining for the friendship of Leontes. He feels sorry for Leontes, who has been grieving for his deceased wife and son and regretting his harsh treatment of his infant daughter. Camillo wants to visit Leontes, but Polixenes convinces him to put that visit off, enlisting Camillo in an effort to discover why Florizel spends so much time at the home of the old shepherd. He and Polixenes discover that Florizel is in love with Perdita, one whom they believe is a lowly shepherd girl, and Polixenes strenuously objects to the marriage and event threatens Perdita and her adoptive family. Camillo then counsels Florizel to take Perdita and sail to Sicilia. In his effort to find a way to visit Leontes, he knowingly puts Florizel

> **❝** Antigonus's departure is followed by the much cited stage direction—'Exit pursued by a bear' (III.iii.58). We immediately learn from the clown that the bear has torn Antigonus to pieces . . .**❞**

and Perdita in danger of being found by Polixenes; Camillo hopes that once Polixenes discovers where his son and Perdita have fled to, Polixenes will follow them, and will take Camillo with him.

At the end of the play, Leontes selects Camillo to be Paulina's husband, referring to Camillo as one "whose worth and honesty / Is richly noted" (V.iii.144-45). Leontes's description of Camillo is somewhat ironic considering that Camillo has so recently and openly deceived the young Prince Florizel. Although Camillo's counsel actually benefits the young couple, Camillo does not know that when he proposes they flee the wrath of Polixenes. He is motivated by his own desires to return to his home and his friends in Sicilia. Camillo acts nobly in refusing to poison Polixenes, but his deception of Florizel somewhat offsets that noble action.

Cleomines:

Cleomines is a Sicilian lord. He, along with Dion, is sent to Apollo's temple at Delphos with directions to bring back, to Leonte's palace in Sicilia, the oracle, the god Apollo's revelation of what was determined to be the truth concerning the accusation against Hermione. He and Dion make the trip to Delphos and back quite quickly. On their way back, in III.i, they discuss how impressed they were with the awe-inspiring proceedings at Apollo's temple. They also acknowledge that the contents of the oracle have been sealed by Apollo's high priest; they are ignorant of the decision of the oracle. When they arrive in Sicilia, the trial of Hermione is already in progress, and they deliver the oracle to an officer who reads it publicly. At the beginning of the last act of the play, Cleomines is one of several lords assembled to encourage Leontes to marry again. Cleomines comforts Leontes and tells him that he has done penance enough for the

> **At his first appearance in the play, Autolycus reveals that he has served Prince Florizel and says, 'My father nam'd me Autolycus, who being, as I am, litter'd under Mercury, was likewise a snapper-up of unconsider'd trifles' (IV.iii.24-26). In short, he carries on his father's tradition of thievery."**

wrongs he committed so many years before. When Paulina reminds Leontes of the oracle's prediction and saddens him with the memory of Hermione, Cleomines says she is being too harsh on the repentant king. When the servant announces to Leontes that Florizel and Perdita have arrived, Cleomines is sent by the king to bring the young couple into the royal presence.

Clown:

The clown is the old shepherd's son and is thought, in Bohemia, to be Perdita's brother. He first appears reciting to the old shepherd the story of Antigonus's desperate encounter with the bear and the sinking of the ship in the storm, a story he will later tell to corroborate further the revelation of Perdita's noble birth. The clown is a down-to-earth, gullible character, easy prey for the likes of Autolycus. Even though the rogue Autolycus thrice deceives him, the clown is not bitter or vindictive; he agrees, at the end of the play, to appeal to Prince Florizel on Autolycus's behalf. Polixenes believes the clown and his father are fortune hunters, advancing Perdita as a worthy match for Florizel in hopes that they might improve their social status. Since nothing could be farther from the truth, the clown proposes that his father immediately tell Polixenes that Perdita is a foundling and no blood relation to the two of them. Even though attaining the status of gentleman was never the clown's intention, he is delighted when that happens. He is also extremely pleased that he becomes a gentleman before his father, even if only moments before.

Dion:

Dion is a Sicilian lord. He is sent by Leontes to Delphos with another lord, Cleomines. Dion and Cleomines make the trip to Delphos and back quite quickly. On their way back, in III.i, they discuss how impressed they were with the awe-inspiring proceedings at Apollo's temple. They also acknowledge that the contents of the oracle have been sealed by Apollo's high priest; they are ignorant of the decision of the oracle. When they arrive in Sicilia, the trial of Hermione is already in progress, and they deliver the oracle to an officer who reads it publicly. At the beginning of the last act of the play, Dion counsels Leontes to marry again. He suggests that Leontes would be selfish not to do so, since his refusing to produce an heir would be a risky business, exposing the Sicilian state to many uncertain perils.

Dorcas:

Dorcas is a shepherdess in the pastoral world of Bohemia. She participates in the dancing at the sheep-shearing festival held at the home of Perdita's shepherd father. She is also one of the throng eager to buy Autolycus's ribbons and sing the ballads purchased from him.

Emilia:

Emilia is a lady of the Sicilian court waiting on Hermione. While Hermione is in prison, Emilia is with her. Emilia is called from Hermione's side to meet Paulina who has been refused a visit to Hermione. Emilia tells Paulina that Hermione has given birth to a baby girl and is doing as well as can be expected under the circumstances. When Paulina proposes that the infant be taken to Leontes in hopes that he will soften at the sight of her, Emilia agrees that the plan is a good one and Paulina perfect for the task. Emilia leaves to inform Hermione of the proposition, one which the prisoner and her waiting women had already conceived, and brings the infant girl back to Paulina.

Florizel:

Florizel is the prince of Bohemia, the son of Polixenes. He falls in love with Perdita, believing her to be only a shepherd's daughter, and spends a lot of time at her home, a fact that causes his father great concern. At the sheep-shearing festival, Florizel dresses like a country swain and goes by the name of Doricles. Unaware that he is speaking to his disguised father, Florizel admits his love for Perdita and announces his intention to marry her. At this, Polixenes is enraged, calling Florizel ''base'' (IV.iv.418), threatening to hang the old shepherd and scar Perdita's face. Florizel takes Camillo's advice and sails to Sicilia, presenting Perdita as his princess to Leontes there. In a remarkable series of revelations, the problem with Perdita's presumed low birth is removed, making Florizel's marriage to her perfectly permissible.

Florizel is remarkably consistent in his love for Perdita. When Perdita suggests that Florizel will have to abandon her when his father finds out about the relationship, Florizel says, ''Or I'll be thine, my fair, / Or not my father's'' (IV.iv.42-43). Despite his father's angry outburst on learning of their love, Florizel maintains that he will carry out his intention to marry Perdita. He says, ''I am but sorry, not afeard; delay'd, / But nothing alt'red'' (IV.iv.463-64). Florizel's consistency in love is admirable, given such widespread opposition to its success. Even Leontes, to whom Florizel appeals for help in persuading his father to accept the marriage, says he is sorry ''[Florizel's] choice is not so rich in worth as beauty'' (V.i.213-14). To his credit, Florizel sees the worth in Perdita, finding in her a grace and beauty independent of her social position.

Gentlemen:

There are several gentlemen in the play. In II.ii, a gentleman accompanies Paulina to the prison where she intends to visit Hermione. On Paulina's command, he fetches the jailer for her. In V.ii, a gentleman tells Autolycus that he has overheard the old shepherd tell Polixenes that he found Perdita in the Bohemian wilderness many years before. This gentleman also informs Autolycus that when the bundle found next to the infant Perdita was opened by Polixenes and Camillo, both men were speechless and had wondrous expressions on their faces. A second gentleman enters and declares, ''The oracle is fulfill'd; the King's daughter is found'' (V.ii.22-23). A third gentleman enters and apprises Autolycus and the other two gentlemen fully of what has transpired at Leontes's palace. He tells them of the tearful and moving reunion between Perdita and Leontes, relates how the clown has testified to seeing Antigonus ravaged by a bear, and informs them that the two kings and their children have gone to view Hermione's statue in a place kept by Paulina. At this time, the second gentleman remembers having observed that Paulina has visited that place two or three times a day since Hermione's death.

> At the end of the play, Leontes selects Camillo to be Paulina's husband, referring to Camillo as one 'whose worth and honesty / Is richly noted' (V.iii.144-45).''

Hermione:

Hermione is the queen of Sicilia, Leontes's wife. Leontes asks her to try and convince Polixenes to extend his visit in Sicilia a bit longer, and Hermione does it a little too well. She, at least in Leontes's view, is a little too convincing as the gracious and flattering wife, engaging in an exchange of praises with Polixenes. Like the others around her, Hermione is amazed at Leontes's sudden and unstoppable hatred of her. He imprisons her, takes away her newborn infant, and causes his son to die of grief for his mother. At her trial, Hermione appears to be a beaten and fragile woman. She feels her pleas of innocence will fall on deaf ears and thinks it unfair that she is summoned to answer ridiculous charges against her when she is still weak from childbirth. She entrusts her fate to the decision of the oracle, which proclaims her innocent, an innocence Leontes continues to refute. But after it is announced that Mamillius has died, Hermione swoons and is taken away. Paulina reenters and says Hermione, too, has died. Hermione is not seen again until the end of the play when a statue of her allegedly comes to life. Even then, she is hesitant to be too friendly with Polixenes for fear that Leontes might be upset. But Leontes encourages Polixenes and Hermione to embrace; he has learned his lesson.

Hermione is glorified and placed on a pedestal, both figuratively and literally, after her presumed death. In life, she appears, like many people, to be desirous of praise and pleased to be the center of attention. When Leontes tells her that she has spoken to good purpose on two occasions, she knows one of those occasions to be her persuasion of Polixenes to stay, and she will not rest until she is further flattered. She says, ''I prithee tell me; cram's with praise, and make's / As fat as tame things'' (I.ii.91-92).

> **Despite his father's angry outburst on learning of their love, Florizel maintains that he will carry out his intention to marry Perdita. He says, 'I am but sorry, not afeard; delay'd, / But nothing alt'red' (IV.iv.463-64)."**

The hoax she perpetuates at Leontes's expense—letting him believe for so many years that she is dead—has received mixed reations from audiences and critics. While some people believe Hermione's actions should be condemned, others feel that Leontes's actions—his cruel treatment of her, which results in the death of their son, and the banishment of a helpless infant—make Hermione's actions somewhat justifiable, if a little unusual.

Jailer:

The jailer has custody of Hermione after she has been sent to prison by Leontes. He has orders that no one is to see Hermione while she is there. The jailer refuses to conduct Paulina to Hermione, but he does allow Paulina to confer with Emilia. When Paulina proposes to take Hermione's infant out of the prison, the jailer objects that he does not have the authority to allow her to do so. He finally agrees to the proposal when Paulina says she will take responsibility for the deed.

Ladies:

These are the ladies attending Hermione. In II.i, they entertain the young Mamillius to keep him out of his mother's way. The young prince engages in good-natured banter with one of these ladies, pointing out that she wears too much makeup. A second lady tells Mamillius he will soon have competition for Hermione's affection since his mother will shortly give birth to another child. These ladies are present when Leontes enters and accuses Hermione of adultery, and they go off to prison with her. They appear again without speaking when they accompany Hermione to her trial.

Leontes:

Leontes is the king of Sicilia. His jealousy of Hermione and Polixenes precipitates the tragedy of the first part of the play. He acts irrationally against the evidence that shows Hermione to have been completely faithful to him. He plots to poison Polixenes, he imprisons Hermione, and he sends his defenseless infant child to a remote area of Bohemia to live or die as fate would have it. At the trial of his wife, Leontes denounces the truth of the oracle that proclaims Hermione innocent of adultery. Immediately following Leontes's rash speech, young Prince Mamillius dies, and it is announced that Hermione dies as well. For nearly twenty years, Leontes presumes his wife to be dead, and he seems to suffer great remorse for what he has done to both her and his children. At the end of the play, he is miraculously reunited with his daughter, Perdita, and a statue of Hermione comes to life and embraces him; she is not dead after all.

In his extreme jealousy, Leontes is like Shakespeare's Othello. But unlike Othello's jealousy, which results from the external manipulations of the evil Iago, Leontes's jealousy seems to stem wholly from within himself. In the end, though, the distinction does not hold, for both men are in the powerful grip of the same human emotion.

We can almost feel that emotion when Leontes describes his reaction to Hermione placing her hand in the hand of Polixenes. He says in an aside,

> Too hot, too hot!
> To mingle friendship far is mingling bloods.
> I have *tremor cordis* on me; my heart dances,
> But not for joy; not joy.
>
> (I.ii.108-11)

His pounding heart makes the rush of blood stop his ears to any rational explanation of his wife's behavior with his best friend. Leontes identifies so completely with his boyhood friend that he, perhaps, becomes confused and projects his own great affection for Polixenes onto Hermione. Perhaps Polixenes and Leontes are so alike in Leontes's mind that if Hermione loves the latter, she cannot help but feel the same way about the former.

It is reported that Leontes and Polixenes were very much alike as youngsters, and they are also alike as adults. Polixenes reacts emotionally to Florizel's desire to marry Perdita and will not be stopped in his efforts to prevent their marriage. He misreads the truth of the situation in the same way that Leontes misreads Hermione's behavior. Neither man will listen to reason; both follow the dictates of the truth they perceive emotionally. The different consequences of each man's actions is dictated only by genre. Leontes acts in the domain of tragedy, the consequences of his actions only partially compensated in the play's comic ending— Mamillius is still dead. Polixenes operates in the domain of comedy, the destructive potential of his actions completely allayed by the comic ending of the play, in which a happy marriage brings union, harmony, and a dissolution of all problems.

Lords:

These are the Sicilian lords of Leontes's kingly court. In II.i, a lord reports to Leontes that he has seen Polixenes and his men make their way to waiting ships as they escaped from the city. When Leontes questions how Polixenes was able to pass the guards of the city so easily, the lord reminds him that Polixenes had been given authority nearly equal to that of Leontes. Later, when Leontes rashly accuses Hermione of adultery and sends her to prison, this same lord urges Leontes to call her back. He protests that Hermione is innocent and faithful, but Leontes says he is not compelled to listen to counsel on this matter. In II.iii, several lords try to prevent Paulina from confronting Leontes with his infant child. One of these lords tells Paulina she must not enter into Leontes's presence. At Hermione's trial, a lord calls for Apollo's oracle to be read after Hermione consigns her fate to the findings of the oracle. In V.i, a lord announces that Polixenes and Camillo have arrived in Sicilia, Polixenes calling for the arrest of Florizel and Perdita, who are at that moment in the company of Leontes. The lord is himself somewhat amazed at the contents of the message he is delivering. He also describes how Perdita's shepherd father and brother quake in fear at Polixenes's threats of punishment. An assemblage of lords appears in the last scene of the play without speaking.

Mamillius:

Mamillius is the young son of Hermione and Leontes. He is an unfortunate victim of Leontes's harsh treatment of Hermonia. Leontes sees Mamillius as a carbon copy of himself and considers Mamillius to be the center of his world. Hermione, pregnant with another child, is sometimes intolerant of Mamillius's demands, passing him off to her ladies-in-waiting. But mother and son share an intimate moment when Hermione asks him to tell her a tale. As if anticipating what is about to happen to them,

> **Like the others around her, Hermione is amazed at Leontes's sudden and unstoppable hatred of her. He imprisons her, takes away her newborn infant, and causes his son to die of grief for his mother.**

Mamillius says, "A sad tale's best for winter" (II.i.25) and begins his tale of "sprites and goblins" (II.i.26). But before he can finish, Leontes bursts in and makes his rash and cruel accusations against Hermione. Leontes uses Mamillius as a pawn against his mother. He commands that Mamillius be removed from his mother's influence, knowing that the two are close. Mamillius begins to sicken when his mother is confined to prison, concerned for her welfare. When Leontes claims that the oracle, which exonerates Hermione, is false, it is immediately announced that Mamillius has died of grief for his mother.

Mariner:

The mariner transports Antigonus to Bohemia and accompanies Antigonus ashore. A storm is brewing, and the mariner is uneasy about abetting Antigonus in the latter's unwelcome task of abandoning the infant Perdita in the wilderness. He begs Antigonus to be quick about the business, cautioning him not to go too far inland. The mariner is drowned in the storm that sinks his ship.

Mopsa:

Mopsa is a shepherdess. She is the sweetheart of the clown, Perdita's presumed brother. She dances with him at the sheep-shearing festival, and he buys her ribbons from the peddlar Autolycus. She appreciates his gift even though he had promised to buy the ribbons for her before the festival. The clown buys sheet music from Autolycus, and Mopsa and Dorcas sing, with Autolycus, a ballad arranged for three parts.

Officers:

These officers are present at the trial of Hermione. An officer reads the indictment against Hermione, in which Leontes accuses her of committing adul-

In his extreme jealousy, Leontes is like Shakespeare's Othello. But unlike Othello's jealousy, which results from the external manipulations of the evil Iago, Leontes's jealousy seems to stem wholly from within himself."

tery with Polixenes. Later, another officer reads the oracle delivered by Cleomines and Dion, the oracle clearing Hermione's name and accusing Leontes of tyranny.

Old Shepherd:

The old shepherd finds Perdita after Antigonus abandons her in the wilds of Bohemia. After his son recounts the misfortunes of Antigonus and the mariners who wait for him on the sea, the old shepherd says, "thou met'st with things dying, I with things new-born" (III.iii.113-14). His statement signals the play's change from tragedy to comedy, a change from Leontes's miseries to Perdita's hopes. He and his son take the gold found in the farthel left beside the infant Perdita and spend a good deal of it building their estate. But the old shepherd is not answerable to Polixenes's charge that he is a social climber intent on improving his status. His main concern seems to have been caring for and loving the girl he considers his own. When he is made a gentleman and encounters Autolycus who has practiced to deceive him on several occasions, the old shepherd tells his son they must treat Autolycus kindly "for we must be gentle, now we are gentlemen" (V.ii.152-53). The truth is he has always conducted himself as a gentleman, especially in his great desire to see Perdita do well. He makes her the queen of the sheep-shearing festival and encourages to be as competent in that role as his wife, who he remembers fondly as a whirlwind of welcome, had so often been. When Perdita hears that Polixenes has the old shepherd quaking in fear for his life, she cries, "O my poor father!" (V.i.202) in the presence of her biological father, Leontes. Leontes has given her life, but the old shepherd, we would assume, has her love, respect, and gratitude.

Paulina:

Paulina is the wife of Antigonus. When she learns that Leontes has imprisoned Hermione on charges of adultery, Paulina goes to the prison to visit the queen. Learning that Hermione has just delivered a baby girl, Paulina takes the child to Leontes, hoping to evoke pity and a change of attitude from him. Leontes declares the child a bastard, and Paulina becomes incensed. Leontes has chosen the wrong woman to make angry; Paulina is relentless in her opposition to his rash and illogical behavior. After Hermione is declared dead, Paulina hounds Leontes with her memory for sixteen years, functioning as his conscience, keeping him constantly remorseful and contrite. In the last act, several of Leontes's counselors urge him to marry and produce an heir to his kingdom. Paulina objects, reminding him of the oracle's pronouncement that he would remain without an heir until what was lost had been found. She encourages Leontes to choose an heir as the great Alexander did, on merit. Leontes agrees with her and dutifully admits that had he listened to her years ago Hermione would still be alive. In his preface to this admission, he refers to Antigonus's wife as "Good Paulina / Who hast the memory of Hermione . . ." (V.i.49-50). This description is exactly correct. Paulina is the keeper of Hermione, both her memory and her living person. It is Paulina who announces that Hermione has died, and it is Paulina who keeps the statue of Hermione, a statue which, according to the gentleman at V.ii.104-08, Paulina has visited two or three times a day since Hermione supposedly died. What Paulina has done is unmistakable: she has kept, either on her own or in collusion with Hermione, the knowledge of Hermione's continued existence a secret from Leontes. At the play's end Leontes selects Camillo to be Paulina's new husband.

Perdita:

Perdita is the daughter of Hermione and Leontes, born while her mother was held in prison at the direction of Perdita's father, who thought Hermione an adulteress and Perdita a bastard. Her name means "the lost one," a name given to her by Antigonus, after Hermione had appeared to him in a dream, instructing him to do so. Antigonus, on the orders of Leontes, left Perdita in the barren wilds of Bohemia where she was discovered and raised by an old shepherd. Perdita displays a beauty and grace that belies her homely origins. When Polixenes complains that his son, Florizel, spends too much time at the home of the old shepherd thought to be Perdita's father, Camillo says, "I have heard, sir, of such a man, who hath a daughter of most rare note. The report of her is extended more than can be thought to begin from such a cottage" (IV.ii.41-44). Perdita has gained a reputation for qualities far surpassing her social class. Even the old shepherd cannot refrain from praising her. When Polixenes says that she dances well, the old shepherd says, "So she does any thing, though I report it / That should be silent" (IV.iv.177-78).

The ultimate endorsement of her grace and beauty is the fact that Prince Florizel falls in love with her. He steadfastly persists in that love for her, despite Polixenes's efforts to keep them apart. Perdita loves Florizel with equal intensity. The old shepherd says, "I think there is not half a kiss to choose / Who loves another best" (IV.iv.175-76). But Perdita believes herself to be the daughter of a shepherd and is uneasy that Polixenes will not approve of her as a wife to his noble son. She is correct. Polixenes is extremely angry when he discovers the affair between Perdita and Florizel. He cannot, however, prevent the inevitable. Perdita's origins are discovered and she is reunited with Leontes. She is now a suitable match for the Bohemian prince. At the end of the play, after being reunited with her mother, Perdita is strangely silent, but she has performed her function in the play, fulfilling the oracle and providing comic resolution to the entanglements and problems presented in the play.

Polixenes:

Polixenes is the king of Bohemia. At the beginning of the play he is visiting Leontes, the king of Sicilia. The two kings have been friends since childhood, Polixenes fondly remembering that childhood as one of carefree innocence as yet untempered by the realities of the world. The two were, then, indistinguishable in their innocence and energy. Polixenes reminds Leontes, "We were as twinn'd lambs that did frisk i' th' sun / And bleat the one at th' other" (I.i.66-67). Polixenes announces that he must return home, and Leontes insists that he stay longer. Polixenes, however stubbornly refuses to give in to Leontes's request; he misses his own young son and must attend to affairs of state in Bohemia. Polixenes, though, relents when Hermione implores him to stay. Leontes interprets Hermione's ability to influence Polixenes as proof that the two are intimately involved. When Camillo informs Polixenes of Leontes's plan to kill him, Polixenes

> As if anticipating what is about to happen to them, Mamillius says, 'A sad tale's best for winter' (II.i.25) and begins his tale of 'sprites and goblins' (II.i.26)."

cannot understand what has happened to the friend who has ever been close to him and so much like himself. He flees to Bohemia.

Polixenes is more like Leontes than he would, perhaps, like to think. The world has hardened the two men in similar ways. Both are made self-indulgent by the power they wield. When Polixenes discovers that his son, Florizel, means to marry Perdita, one whom Polixenes believes is a low-class shepherd girl, he breaks out in a burst of passion. He threatens both Perdita and her shepherd relatives and expresses disgust with his son's deception. Polixenes is motivated by a passion which is, arguably, every bit as irrational and destructive as Leontes's earlier jealousy. He follows Perdita and Florizel to Sicilia, calls for their arrest, and makes life miserable for the old shepherd and the clown, threatening them with torture. A tragedy similar to that produced by Leontes's purely emotional responses—the death of Mamillius and Leontes's twenty-year separation from his wife and daughter—is avoided only by the comic elements of the second part of the play that reveal Perdita to be of royal blood.

Servants:

In II.iii, one of Leontes's servants reports that Mamillius has rested well the previous night and expresses his hope that the young prince is on the mend. When Paulina storms in, this same servant tells her that the king has not slept and has commanded that no one be conducted into his presence. Later in the same scene, a servant announces that Cleomines and Dion have landed in Sicilia and are on their way to the court. In III.ii, just after Leontes has denied the truth of the oracle, another of Leontes's servants has the unenviable task of informing Leontes that Mamillius has died. At the beginning of the last

"Leontes uses Mamillius as a pawn against his mother. He commands that Mamillius be removed from his mother's influence, knowing that the two are close."

act, one of Leontes's servants announces that Florizel and Perdita have arrived in Sicilia and request an audience with the king.

The old shepherd presumed to be Perdita's father has servants as well. During the sheep-shearing festival, one of these servants is greatly impressed with the novelty of Autolycus. He recommends that the old shepherd allow Autolycus to come in and entertain the guests as he peddles his wares. Another servant ushers in a group of animal herders and carters dressed like wild men to perform "a dance of twelve Satyrs" (IV.iv.342).

Shepherdesses:
See Shepherds

Shepherds:
All of the speech prefixes of "shepherd" in the play refer to the old shepherd who finds the infant Perdita and raises her as his own daughter. At the sheep-shearing festival in IV.iv, a group of shepherds and shepherdesses perform a rustic dance.

Time:
A Chorus appears at the beginning of Act IV as a personification of Time, informing the audience that sixteen years have passed since the last scene. He tells of Leontes's long years of contrition and reveals that Perdita is now a beautiful adult woman. Curiously, Time says "I mentioned a son o' th' King's, which Florizel / I now name to you" (IV.i.22-23), suggesting that he has been narrating all the events of the play, which, of course, he has not. Time, in the role of Chorus, bridges the gap between the tragedy of the first part of the play and the comedy of the last part.

Further Reading

Bateson, F. W. "How Old Was Leontes?" *Essays and Studies*, 2nd Series, 31 (1978): 65-74.
From the many clues in the text, Bateson calculates that Leontes is in his late twenties at the beginning of the play, and in his mid forties at the end. He also argues that the play is concerned with aging and the development that comes with it.

Bonjour, Adrien. "Polixenes and the Winter of His Discontent." *English Studies* 50, no. 2 (1969): 206-12.
Bonjour compares Polixenes's emotional outburst at finding Florizel to be in love with a shepherd's daughter to Leontes' jealousy early in the play.

Erickson, Peter B. "Patriarchal Structures in *The Winter's Tale*." *PMLA* 97, no. 5 (1982): 819-29.
Erickson discusses Hermione, Paulina, and Perdita, arguing that, although the power of women is still contained by the power of men, the relationships between men and women are not as destructive in *The Winter's Tale* as those same relationships are in Shakespeare's tragedies.

Estrin, Barbara L. "The Foundling Plot: Stories in *The Winter's Tale*." *Modern Language Studies* 7, no. 1 (1977): 27-38.
As in many foundling stories, *The Winter's Tale* presents Perdita as a genuine princess thought to be something else, paralleling the theme of nature versus art which runs throughout the play.

Gokak, V. K. "The Structure of Daffodils in *The Winter's Tale*." *Literary Criterion* 6, no. 1 (1963): 137-52.
Gokak examines the references to flowers in *The Winter's Tale* and discusses how those flowers function symbolically in the play.

Gourlay, Patricia Southard. " 'O My Most Sacred Lady': Female Metaphor in *The Winter's Tale*." *English Literary Renaissance* 5, no. 3 (1975): 375-95.
Gourlay discusses the three women in *The Winter's Tale*, Hermione, Paulina, and Perdita, in light of the Renaissance conception of women as either temptress or idealized madonna figure.

Gurr, Andrew. "The Bear, the Statue, and Hysteria in *The Winter's Tale*." *Shakespeare Quarterly* 34, no. 4 (1983): 420-25.
Gurr proposes that the scene of the bear chasing Antigonus concludes the tragedy of the first part of the play, and the scene of Hermione's statue coming to life concludes the comedy of the latter half. Both scenes, Gurr notes, are startling and memorable theatrical devices that punctuate the different genres and allude to the art and nature debate.

Kaula, David. "Autolycus' Trumpery." *Studies in English Literature* 16, no. 2 (1976): 287-303.
Kaula reads *The Winter's Tale* as a religious allegory. In this allegory, Kaula maintains, Autolycus's use of material trinkets to distract his gulls as he robs them is

associated with Elizabethan attitudes toward Catholicism. Kaula goes on to argue that Perdita, on the other hand, represents Protestantism, her true and noble nature evident even when unadorned with outward pomp and title. Hermione's statue coming to life signals a switch from the idolatry of Catholicism to the true worship of Protestantism.

Livingston, Mary L. "The Natural Art of *The Winter's Tale*." *Modern Language Quarterly* 30, no. 3 (1969): 340-55.

Livingston discusses the art against nature debate evident throughout the play. She discusses Autolycus as a distributor of ballads and the scene of Hermione's statue coming to life. She argues that Shakespeare's play is a finely crafted work of art that ultimately proclaims art superior to nature.

Mowat, Barbara Adams. "A Tale of Sprights and Goblins." *Shakespeare Quarterly* 20, no. 1 (1969): 37-46.

Mowat compares the jealousy of Leontes to the jealousy of Othello, concluding that the tragedy of *The Winter's Tale* is not the high tragedy of *Othello*, the action of the former play being less noble and less ideal.

Nathan, Norman. "Leontes' Provocation." *Shakespeare Quarterly* 19, no. 1 (1968): 19-24.

In contrast to what the play suggests and most critics believe, Nathan offers that Hermione, in her open and friendly manner with Polixenes, gives Leontes sufficient cause for jealousy.

Smith, Hallett. Introduction to *The Winter's Tale*, by William Shakespeare. In *The Riverside Shakespeare*, edited by G. Blakemore Evans, 1564-68. Boston: Houghton Mifflin, 1974.

Smith discusses *The Winter's Tale* in relation to Shakespeare's other tragicomic romances. He compares Shakespeare's play to its source, Robert Greene's *Pandosto*, noting the changes Shakespeare has made. He also discusses the play's theme of art versus nature and analyzes several of the play's characters.

Smith, Jonathan. "The Language of Leontes." *Shakespeare Quarterly* 19, no. 4 (1968): 317-27.

Smith argues that the particular words and phrases Leontes uses at different moments in play give some indication of his varying moods.

Studing, Richard. " 'That Rare Italian Master': Shakespeare's Julio Romano." *Humanities Association Bulletin* 22, no. 3 (1971): 22-26.

Studing argues that Julio Romano was famous enough that Shakespeare would have known about him. Although he was not known as a sculptor, Shakespeare would have chosen him for the naturalism associated with his paintings.

Wells, Evelyn K. "A Gallimaufry of Gambols." *Country Dancer* (Summer 1964): 4-8.

Wells discusses the folk ballads and dances Shakespeare uses to enliven the sheep-shearing festival in Act IV of *The Winter's Tale*.

Character/Topic Index

Brother:
Two Noble Kinsmen: See **Jailer's Brother**

Brutus (Decius Brutus):
Julius Caesar: 198

Brutus (Junius Brutus):
Coriolanus: See **Tribunes**

Brutus (Marcus Brutus):
Julius Caesar: 198

Buckingham (Duke of Buckingham):*
Henry VI, Part Two: 156
Richard III: 372

Buckingham (Duke of Buckingham):
Henry VIII: 182

Bullcalf:
Henry IV, Part Two: 115

Bullen (Anne Bullen, afterwards Marchioness of Pembroke, afterwards Queen Anne):
Henry VIII: 183

Bullingbrook (Henry Bullingbrook [Bolingbroke], Duke of Herford, afterwards King Henry IV of England):*
Henry IV, Part One: See **Henry**
Henry IV, Part Two: See **Henry**
Richard II: 358

Burgundy (Duke of Burgundy):
Henry V: 130
Henry VI, Part One: 144
King Lear: 227

Bushy (Sir John Bushy):
Richard II: 359

Butts (Doctor Butts):
Henry VIII: 183

C

Cade (Jack Cade, also known as John Cade):
Henry VI, Part Two: 156

Cadwal:
Cymbeline: See **Arviragus**

Caesar (Julius Caesar):
Julius Caesar: 199

Caesar (Octavius Caesar):*
Antony and Cleopatra: 18
Julius Caesar: 201

Caius:
Titus Andronicus: 441

Caius (Doctor Caius):
Merry Wives of Windsor: 289

Caius Ligarius:
Julius Caesar: See **Ligarius**

Caius Lucius:
Cymbeline: See **Lucius**

Caius Martius:
Coriolanus: See **Coriolanus**

Calchas:
Troilus and Cressida: 453

Caliban:
Tempest: 414

Calphurnia (also Calpurnia):
Julius Caesar: 201

Cambio:
Taming of the Shrew: See **Lucentio**

Cambridge (Earl of Cambridge):
Henry V: 130

Camillo:
Winter's Tale: 507

Campeius (Cardinal Campeius):
Henry VIII: 183

Canidius:
Antony and Cleopatra: 18

Canterbury (Archbishop of Canterbury):
Henry V: 130

Caphis:
Timon of Athens: 426

Captain:
Antony and Cleopatra: 19
King Lear: 227
Richard II: 360
Titus Andronicus: 441

Captain (Sea Captain):
Twelfth Night: 465

Captains:
Henry VI, Part One: 144

Capuchius:
Henry VIII: 183

Capulet (Lady Capulet):
Romeo and Juliet: 385

Capulet (Lord Capulet):
Romeo and Juliet: 385

Cardinal Beauford (Cardinal Beauford, Bishop of Winchester):
Henry VI, Part One: See **Beauford**
Henry VI, Part Two: See **Beauford**

Cardinal Bourchier (Cardinal Bourchier, Archbishop of Canterbury):
Richard III: See **Bourchier**

Cardinal Campeius:
Henry VIII: See **Campeius**

Cardinal of Winchester (Henry Beauford, Bishop of Winchester, afterwards Cardinal Beauford):
Henry VI, Part One: See **Beauford**
Henry VI, Part Two: See **Beauford**

Cardinal Pandulph:
King John: See **Pandulph**

Cardinal Wolsey, Archbishop of York:
Henry VIII: See **Wolsey**

Carlisle (Bishop of Carlisle):
Richard II: 360

Carpenter:
Julius Caesar: See **Commoners**

Carriers:
Henry IV, Part One: 102

Casca:
Julius Caesar: 201

Cassandra:
Troilus and Cressida: 453

Cassio:
Othello: 334

Cassius:
Julius Caesar: 201

Catesby (Sir William Catesby):
Richard III: 373

Cathness (in some editions, Caithness):
Macbeth: 254

Catling (Simon Catling):
Romeo and Juliet: See **Musicians**

Cato (Young Cato):
Julius Caesar: 203

Celia:
As You Like It: 35

Ceres:
Tempest: 415

Cerimon:
Pericles: 347

Cesario (Viola/Cesario):
Twelfth Night: See **Viola**

Chamberlain:
Henry IV, Part One: 103

Chamberlain (Lord Chamberlain):
Henry VIII: 184

Chancellor (Lord Chancellor):
Henry VIII: 184